NEW!

for *Invitation to the Life Span*, Fifth Edition

Engaging Every Student. Supporting Every Instructor. Setting the New Standard for Teaching and Learning.

Achieve for *Invitation to the Life Span*, Fifth Edition, sets a whole new standard for engaging and appraising your students' progress with ease, by way of **assessments**, **activities**, and **analytics**. It also brings together all of the features that instructors and students loved about our previous platform, LaunchPad—interactive e-book, LearningCurve adaptive quizzing and other assessments, interactive learning activities, extensive instructor resources—in a powerful new platform that offers:

- A cleaner, more intuitive, **mobile-friendly** interface.
- Powerful analytics.
- Self-regulated learning with goal-setting surveys.
- A fully integrated iClicker classroom response system, with questions available for each unit or the option to integrate your own.
- An **expansive Video Collection for Developmental Psychology!**

Our resources were **co-designed with instructors and students**, on a foundation of *years* of **learning research**, and rigorous testing over multiple semesters. The result is superior content, organization, and functionality. Achieve's pre-built assignments engage students both *inside and outside of class*. And Achieve is effective for students at *all levels* of motivation and preparedness, whether they are high achievers or need extra support.

Macmillan Learning offers **deep platform integration** of Achieve with all LMS providers, including Blackboard, Brightspace, Canvas, and Moodle. With integration, students can access course content and their grades through one sign-in. And you can pair Achieve with course tools from your LMS, such as discussion boards and chat and Gradebook functionality. LMS integration is also available with Inclusive Access. For more information, visit MacmillanLearning.com/College/US/Solutions/LMS-Integration or talk to your local sales representative.

Achieve was built with **accessibility** in mind. Macmillan Learning strives to create products that are usable by all learners and meet universally applied accessibility standards. In addition to addressing product compatibility with assistive technologies such as screen reader software, alternative keyboard devices, and voice recognition products, we are working to ensure that the content and platforms we provide are fully accessible. For more information, visit MacmillanLearning.com/College/US/Our-Story/Accessibility

Achieve for *Invitation to the Life Span*: Setting the New Standard for Teaching and Learning

LearningCurve Adaptive Quizzing

Based on extensive learning and memory research, and proven effective for hundreds of thousands of students, LearningCurve focuses on the core concepts in every chapter, providing individualized question sets and feedback for correct and incorrect responses. The system adapts to each student's level of understanding, with follow-up quizzes targeting areas where the student needs improvement. Each question is tied to a learning objective and linked to the appropriate section of the e-book to encourage students to discover the right answer for themselves. LearningCurve has consistently been rated the #1 resource by instructors and students alike.

- LearningCurve's game-like quizzing promotes retrieval practice through its unique delivery of questions and its point system.
- Students with a firm grasp on the material get plenty of practice but proceed through the activity relatively quickly.
- Unprepared students are given more questions, therefore requiring that they do what they should be doing anyway if they're unprepared—practice some more.

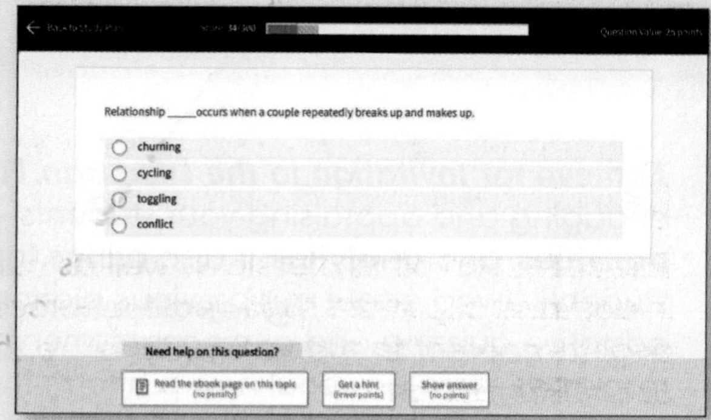

- Instructors can monitor results for each student and the class as a whole, to identify areas that may need more coverage in lectures and assignments.

E-book

Macmillan Learning's e-book is an interactive version of the textbook that offers highlighting, bookmarking, and note-taking. Built-in, low-stakes self-assessments allow students to test their level of understanding along the way, and learn even more in the process thanks to the *testing effect*. Students can download the e-book to read offline, or to have it read aloud to them. Achieve allows instructors to assign chapter sections as homework.

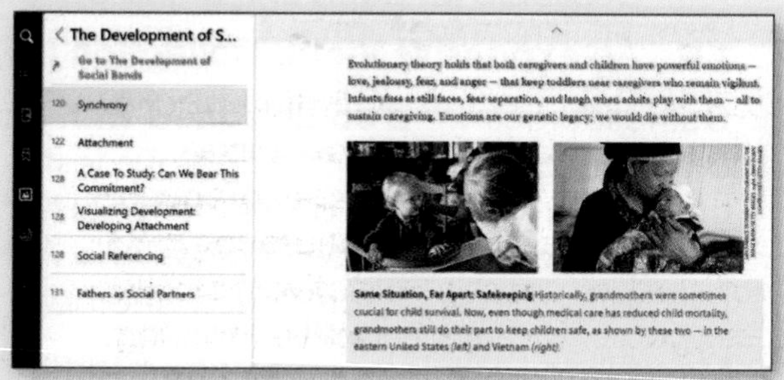

Test Bank

The Test Bank for *Invitation to the Life Span*, Fifth Edition, offers thousands of questions, all meticulously reviewed. Instructors can assign out-of-the-box exams or create their own by:

- Choosing from thousands of questions in our database.
- Filtering questions by type, topic, difficulty, and Bloom's level.
- Customizing multiple-choice questions.
- Integrating their own questions into the exam.

Exam/Quiz results report to a Gradebook that lets instructors monitor student progress individually and classwide.

Practice Quizzes

Practice Quizzes mirror the experience of a quiz or test, with questions that are similar but distinct from those in the test bank. Instructors can use the quizzes as is or create their own, selecting questions by question type, topic, difficulty, and Bloom's level.

Achieve for *Invitation to the Life Span*: Engaging Every Student

Achieve is designed to support and encourage active learning by connecting familiar activities and practices out of class with some of the most effective and approachable in-class activities, curated from a variety of active learning sources.

Expansive Video Collection for Developmental Psychology

This collection offers classic as well as current, in-demand clips from high-quality sources, with original content to support *Invitation to the Life Span*, Fifth Edition.

Accompanying assessment makes these videos assignable, with results reporting to the Achieve Gradebook. Our faculty and student consultants were instrumental in helping us create this diverse and engaging set of clips. All videos are closed-captioned and found only in **Achieve**.

Data Connections

Data Connections activities require interpretation of data on many important topics, from prevalence of risk-taking to rates of neurocognitive disorders. These interactive activities engage students in active learning, promoting a deeper understanding of the science of development. Instructors can assign these activities and accompanying assessment in the online courseware that accompanies this book.

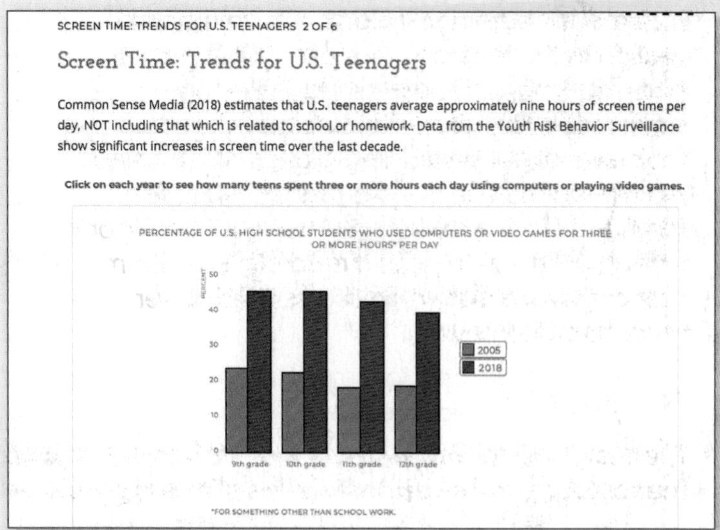

Instructor Activity Guides

Instructor Activity Guides provide instructors with a structured plan for using Achieve's active learning opportunities in both face-to-face and remote learning courses. Each guide offers step-by-step instructions—from pre-class reflection to in-class engagement to post-class follow-up. The guides include suggestions for discussion questions, group work, presentations, and simulations, with estimated class time, implementation effort, and Bloom's taxonomy level for each activity.

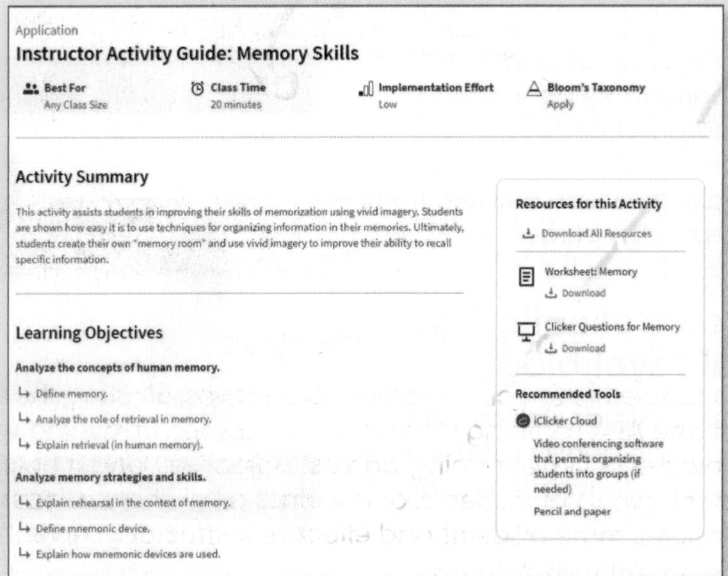

iClicker Classroom Response System

Achieve seamlessly integrates iClicker, Macmillan Learning's highly acclaimed classroom response system. iClicker can help make any classroom—in-person or virtual—more lively, engaging, and productive.

- iClicker's attendance feature helps make sure students are actually attending in-person classes.
- Instructors can choose from flexible polling and quizzing options to engage students, check their understanding, and get their feedback in real time.
- iClicker allows students to participate using laptops, mobile devices, or in-class remotes.
- iClicker easily integrates instructors' existing slides and polling questions—there is no need to re-enter them.
- Instructors can take advantage of the questions in our Instructor Activity Guides and our book-specific questions within Achieve to improve the opportunities for all students to be active in class.

Achieve for *Invitation to the Life Span*: Supporting Every Instructor

Learning Objectives, Reports, and Insights

Content in Achieve is tagged to specific Learning Objectives, aligning the coursework with the textbook and with the APA Learning Goals and Outcomes. Reporting within Achieve helps students see how they are performing against objectives, and it helps instructors determine if any student, group of students, or the class as a whole needs extra help in specific areas. This enables more efficient and effective instructor interventions.

Achieve provides reports on student activities, assignments, and assessments at the course level, unit level, subunit level, and individual student level, so instructors can identify trouble spots and adjust their efforts accordingly. Within Reports, the Insights section offers snapshots with high-level data on student performance and behavior, to answer such questions as:

- What are the top Learning Objectives to review in this unit?
- What are the top assignments to review?
- What's the range of performance on a particular assignment?
- How many students aren't logging in?

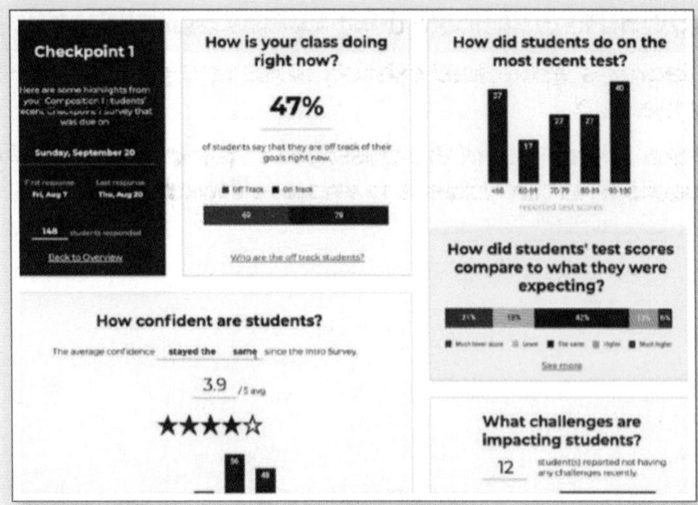

Achieve's **Innovation Lab** offers surveys that help students self-direct, and develop confidence in, their own learning:

- The **Intro Survey** asks students to consider their goals for the class and how they plan to manage their time and learning strategies.
- **Checkpoint surveys** ask students to reflect on what's been working and where they need to make changes.
- **Each completed survey generates a report** that reveals how each student is doing, beyond the course grade.

These tools help instructors engage their students in a discussion on soft skills, such as metacognition, effective learning and time management strategies, and other non-cognitive skills that impact student success.

Additional Instructor Resources in Achieve: All Within One Place

Image Slides and Tables

Presentation slides feature chapter illustrations and tables and can be used as is or customized to fit an instructor's needs. Alt text for images is available upon request via WebAccessibility@Macmillan.com

Instructor's Resource Manuals

Downloadable PDF manuals include a range of resources, such as chapter summaries, teaching tips, discussion starters, and classroom and student activities.

Lecture Slides

Accessible, downloadable presentation slides provide support for key concepts and themes from the text, and can be used as is or customized to fit an instructor's needs.

Customer Support

Our Achieve Client Success Team—dedicated platform experts—provides collaboration, software expertise, and consulting to tailor each course to fit your instructional goals and student needs. Start with a demo at a time that works for you to learn more about how to set up your customized course. Talk to your sales representative or visit www.MacmillanLearning.com/College/US/Contact-Us/Training-and-Demos for more information.

Pricing and bundling options are available at the Macmillan Student Store: Store.MacmillanLearning.com

Invitation to the Life Span

FIFTH EDITION

Kathleen Stassen Berger

Bronx Community College
City University of New York

worth publishers
Macmillan Learning
New York

Senior Vice President, Content Strategy: Charles Linsmeier

Program Director, Social Sciences: Shani Fisher

Senior Executive Program Manager: Christine Cardone

Senior Development Editor: Andrea Musick Page

Assistant Editor: Dorothy Tomasini

Executive Marketing Manager: Katherine Nurre

Marketing Assistant: Steven Huang

Executive Media Editor: Laura Burden

Director of Media Editorial, Social Sciences: Noel Hohnstine

Assistant Media Editor: Conner White

Director, Content Management Enhancement: Tracey Kuehn

Senior Managing Editor: Lisa Kinne

Senior Content Project Manager: Peter Jacoby

Lead Media Project Manager: Joseph Tomasso

Senior Workflow Supervisor: Susan Wein

Senior Photo Editor: Sheena Goldstein

Photo Researcher: Krystyna Borgen, Lumina Datamatics, Inc.

Director of Design, Content Management: Diana Blume

Senior Design Services Manager: Natasha A. S. Wolfe

Cover Designer: John Callahan

Interior Design: Heather Marshall, Studio Montage, and Lumina Datamatics, Inc.

Design credits: Pavlenko Volodymyr/Shutterstock, Katrina Lee/Shutterstock, Andrii Arkhipov/Shutterstock, simpleicon/Shutterstock, GoperVector/Shutterstock, a Sk/Shutterstock

Art Manager: Matthew McAdams

Illustrations: Lumina Datamatics, Inc., Charles Yuen, Matthew McAdams

Composition: Lumina Datamatics, Inc.

Printing and Binding: LSC Communications

Library of Congress Control Number: 2021941606

ISBN-13: 978-1319-33198-6

ISBN-10: 1-319-33198-X

International Edition ISBN-13: 978-1-319-43755-8

International Edition ISBN-10: 1-319-43755-9

Printed in the United States of America

2 3 4 5 6 26 25 24 23

Worth Publishers
120 Broadway
New York, NY 10271
www.macmillanlearning.com

ABOUT THE AUTHOR

© 2016 MACMILLAN

Kathleen Stassen Berger received her undergraduate degree at Stanford University and Radcliffe College, and then she earned an M.A.T. from Harvard University and an M.S. and Ph.D. from Yeshiva University. Her broad experience as an educator includes directing a preschool, serving as chair of philosophy at the United Nations International School, and teaching child and adolescent development to graduate students at Fordham University in New York and undergraduates at Montclair State University in New Jersey and Quinnipiac University in Connecticut. She also taught social psychology to inmates at Sing Sing Prison who were earning paralegal degrees.

Berger is a professor at Bronx Community College of the City University of New York, as she has been for most of her professional career. She began there as an adjunct in English and for the past decades has been a full professor in the Social Sciences Department, which includes psychology, sociology, economics, anthropology, political science, and human services. She has taught Introduction to Psychology, Child and Adolescent Development, Adulthood and Aging, Social Psychology, Abnormal Psychology, and Human Motivation. Her students—from diverse ethnic, economic, and educational backgrounds, of many ages, ambitions, and interests—honor her with the highest teaching evaluations.

Berger is also the author of *The Developing Person Through Childhood and Adolescence*, *The Developing Person Through the Life Span*, and *A Topical Approach to the Developing Person Through the Life Span*. She is also the author of *Grandmothering: Building Strong Ties with Every Generation* (2019).

Berger developmental texts are used at more than 700 colleges and universities worldwide and are published in Spanish, French, Italian, and Portuguese as well as English. Her research interests include adolescent identity, immigration, bullying, and grandparents, and she has published articles on developmental topics in the *Wiley Encyclopedia of Psychology*, *Developmental Review*, and in publications of the American Association for Higher Education and the National Education Association for Higher Education. She continues teaching and learning from her students as well as from her four daughters and three grandsons.

Brief Contents

GLOBALSTOCK/E+/GETTY IMAGES
ALEXSAVA/E+/GETTY IMAGES

BAONA/ISTOCK/GETTY IMAGES

EDZBARZHYVETSKY/DEPOSIT PHOTOS

PIXEL-SHOT/SHUTTERSTOCK.COM

IKO/SHUTTERSTOCK

MASKOT/GETTY IMAGES

Contents

LEREN LU/DIGITALVISION/ GETTY IMAGES

Part One: The Beginnings 1

PAUL THOMAS/EYEEM/GETTY IMAGES

Part Two: The First Two Years 72

LIGHTFIELD STUDIOS/SHUTTERSTOCK.COM

MARC ROMANELLI/BLEND IMAGES/GETTY IMAGES

RICHARD BAILEY/CORBIS/GETTY IMAGES

TEMPURA/E+/GETTY IMAGES

MOMO PRODUCTIONS/DIGITALVISION/GETTY IMAGES

PREFACE

"Fresh brains."

That is what a child told me when I asked why she might understand something that I did not.

"Children have fresh brains," she repeated. She implied that my brain had been around for a long time, so it might no longer be able to think very well.

I disagree, of course. I believe that my years of teaching, thinking, studying, and writing have led to some important knowledge that is far beyond what any child knows. But that child reminded me of one of the discoveries of child development: Children raise adults while adults raise them. As a professor, author, and mother, I recognize that each new generation changes society, culture, and every adult who listens to them.

Older generations have accumulated important knowledge about child development, which I explain in this textbook. Some of what we know is lifesaving: The child death rate has plummeted over the past century, in part because more is known about infection, education, attachment, and more. As you will learn, in every nation, child health, intelligence, and probably happiness have increased over the past decades.

But at the same time, careful listening and attention to fresh brains is needed. This edition of this textbook, I hope, will help you with both.

When I first began to teach child development, I realized that this topic is not only fascinating but also that scholars have discovered important information for everyone. I searched for a textbook that would respect my students and the science. I could not find it, so I wrote it. I continue to believe that a text can convey critical insights about child development without ignoring the joy of actual children.

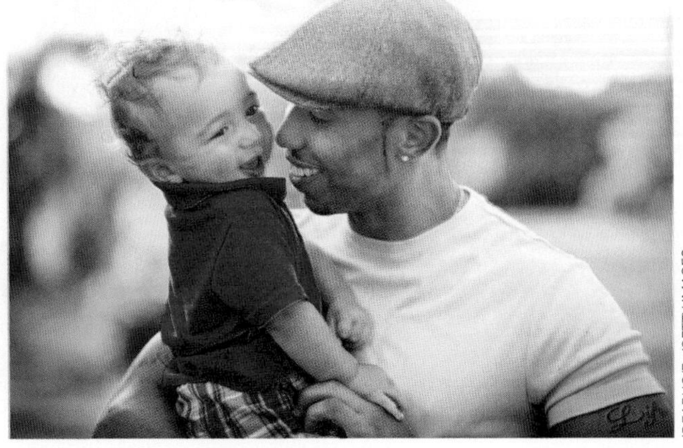
IDEABUG/E+/GETTY IMAGES

Our old brains must protect, admire, and appreciate the fresh brains of the two billion or so children alive today. Accordingly, this edition recognizes problems and possibilities not imagined in earlier editions. This is my contribution to that goal.

New Topics and Research

Every year, scientists discover and explain new concepts and research. The best of these are integrated into the text, including hundreds of new references on many topics such as epigenetics, prenatal nutrition, the microbiome, early-childhood education, autism spectrum disorder, vaping, high-stakes testing, gender-nonbinary children, the COVID-19 pandemic's impact on emerging adults, and diversity of all kinds—ethnic, economic, and cultural.

FATIHHOCA/ISTOCK/GETTY IMAGES

Cognizant that the science of human development is interdisciplinary, I include recent research in biology, sociology, neuroscience, education, anthropology, political science, and more—as well as my home discipline, psychology. A list highlighting this material is available at macmillanlearning.com.

NEW and Updated Coverage of Neuroscience

Of course, neuroscience continues in the text as well. In addition to Inside the Brain features, cutting-edge research on the brain appears in virtually every chapter, often with charts, figures, and photos. A list highlighting this material is available at macmillanlearning.com.

NEW! Career Alerts

In several chapters, students will read about career options for various applied settings related to development through childhood and adolescence. These Career Alerts are informed by the Bureau of Labor Statistics' Occupational Outlook Handbook, which describes duties, education and training, pay, and outlook for hundreds of occupations.

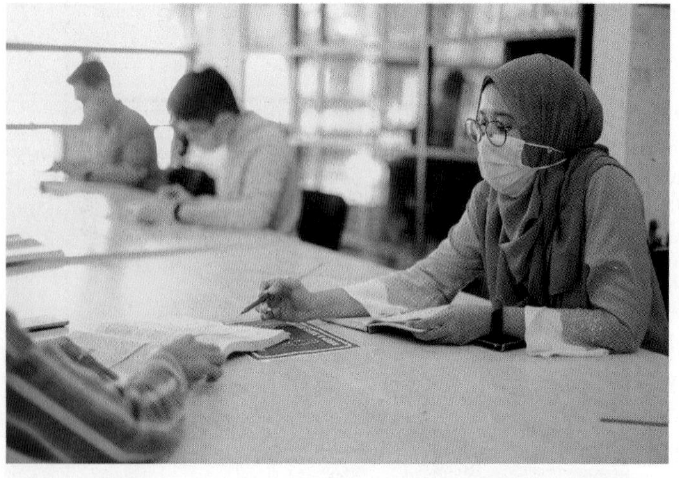
CHEE GIN TAN/E+/GETTY IMAGES

NEW! Chapter Apps

Free Chapter Apps that students can download to their smartphones have been added, offering a real-life application of the science of life-span development. Callouts to the Chapter Apps (one per chapter) appear in the margins, along with brief descriptions and links to their iTunes and/or Google Play downloads.

Renewed Emphasis on Critical Thinking in the Pedagogical Program

Critical thinking is essential for all of us lifelong, as we try to distinguish opinion from science, fake news from facts. Virtually every page of this book presents not only facts but also questions with divergent interpretations, sometimes with references to my own need to reconsider my assumptions. Think Critically questions encourage students to examine the implications of what they read.

Every chapter is organized around learning objectives. Much of what I hope students will always remember from this course is a matter of attitude, approach, and perspective—all hard to quantify. The What Will You Know? questions at the beginning of each chapter indicate important ideas or provocative concepts—one for each major section of the chapter.

In addition, after every major section, What Have You Learned? questions help students review what they have just read. Some of these questions are straight forward, requiring only close attention to the chapter. Others are more complex, seeking comparisons, implications, or evaluations. Cognitive psychology and research on pedagogy show that vocabulary, specific knowledge, and critical thinking are all part of learning. These features are designed to foster all three; I hope students and professors will add their own questions and answers, following this scaffolding.

Updated Features: Opposing Perspectives, A View from Science, A Case to Study, and Inside the Brain

In this edition of *Invitation to the Life Span*, I've included four unique features. Opposing Perspectives focuses on controversial topics—from prenatal sex selection to e-cigarettes. I have tried to present information and opinions on both sides of each topic so that students will weigh evidence, assess arguments, and recognize their biases while reaching their own conclusions.

A View from Science, which explains research, and A Case to Study, which illustrates development via specific individuals, have been extensively updated. Since new discoveries in neuroscience abound, Inside the Brain features explore topics such as the intricacies of prenatal and infant brain development, brain specialization and speech development, and brain maturation and emotional development.

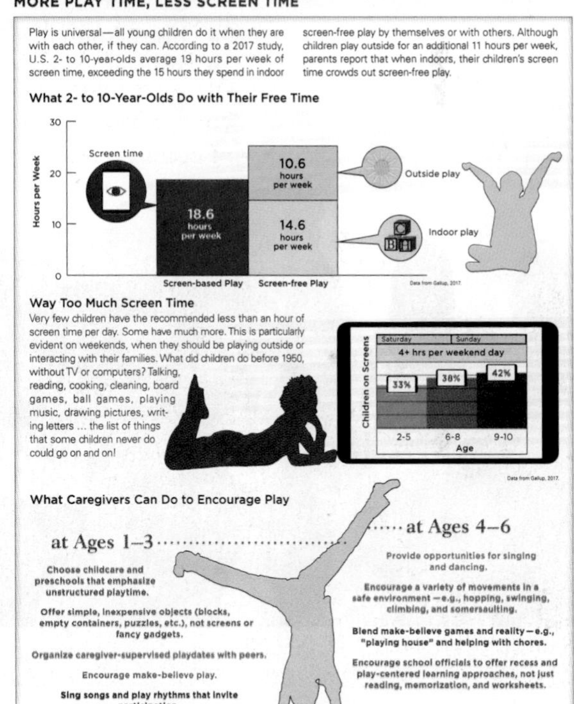

NEW and Updated Visualizing Development Infographics

Data are often best understood visually and graphically. Every chapter of this edition includes a full-page illustration of a key topic that combines statistics, maps, charts, and photographs. These infographics focus on key issues such as immunization trends, media use, caregiving, and more. My editors and I worked closely with noted designer and 2018 Guggenheim Fellow Charles Yuen to develop these Visualizing Development infographics.

NEW! ACHIEVE for *Invitation to the Life Span*, Fifth Edition

Achie/e

Achieve for *Invitation to the Life Span* integrates assessments, activities, and analytics into your teaching. Featuring an interactive e-book, LearningCurve adaptive quizzing and other assessments, Data Connections activities, and extensive instructor resources, Achieve for *Invitation to the Life Span*, Fifth Edition, includes updated video resources, and new Instructor Activity Guides, revised and updated Instructor's Resources, new iClicker questions. See the very front of the text for more information about these engaging digital resources.

In addition, Macmillan Learning offers **deep platform integration** of Achieve with all LMS providers. With integration, students can access course content and their grades through one sign-in. And you can pair Achieve with course tools from your LMS, such as discussion boards and chat and Gradebook functionality. For more information, visit www.macmillanlearning.com/College/US/Solutions/LMS-Integration or talk to your local sales representative.

ADDITIONAL INSTRUCTOR RESOURCES IN ACHIEVE: ALL IN ONE PLACE

- Image slides and tables
- Presentation slides feature illustrations and tables and can be used as is or customized to fit an instructor's needs. Alt text for images is available upon request via WebAccessibility@Macmillan.com.

Also Available: Achieve Read & Practice

Achieve Read & Practice is the marriage of our LearningCurve adaptive quizzing and our mobile, accessible e-book in one easy-to-use and affordable product. The benefits of Read & Practice include:

- It is easy to get started.
- Students come to class having read the materials and are more prepared for discussion.
- Instructors are able to use analytics to help students as needed.
- Student course performance improves.

ALEX WONG/GETTY IMAGES

Ongoing Features

Many characteristics of this book have been acclaimed since the first edition.

Writing That Communicates the Excitement and Challenge of the Field

An overview of the science of human development should be lively, just as people are. To that end, each sentence conveys tone as well as content. Chapter-opening vignettes describe real (not hypothetical) situations to illustrate the immediacy of development. Examples and explanations abound, helping students make the connections between theory, research, and their own experiences.

Coverage of Diversity

Cross-cultural, international, intersectional, multiethnic, sexual orientation, socioeconomic status, age, gender identity—all of these words and ideas are vital to appreciating how people develop. Research uncovers surprising similarities and notable differences: We have much in common, yet each human is unique. From the emphasis on contexts in Chapter 1 to the coverage of death and dying in the Epilogue, each chapter highlights variations.

New research on family structures, immigrants, bilingualism, and ethnic differences are among the many topics that illustrate human diversity. Respect for human diversity is evident throughout. Examples and research findings from many parts of the world are included, not as add-ons but as integral parts of each age.

Up-to-Date Coverage

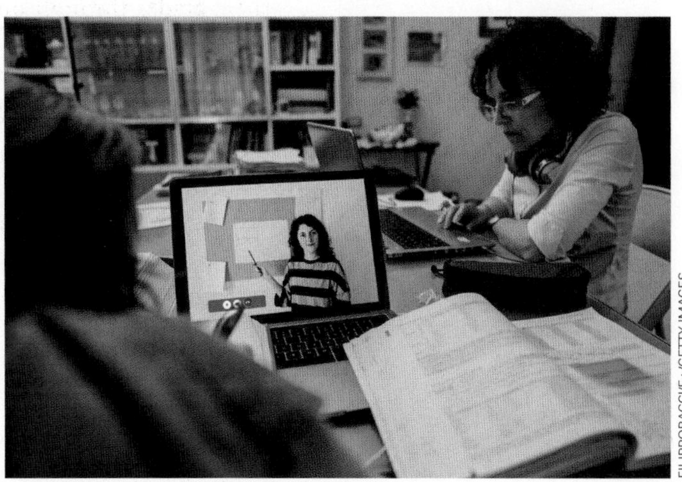
FILIPPOBACCI/E+/GETTY IMAGES

My mentors welcomed curiosity, creativity, and skepticism; as a result, I read and analyze thousands of articles and books on everything from how biology predisposes infants to autism spectrum disorder to the many ways the COVID-19 pandemic has affected emerging adults. The recent explosion of research in neuroscience and genetics has challenged me once again, first to understand and then to explain many complex findings and speculative leaps. My students ask nuanced questions and share current experiences, always adding perspective.

Topical Organization Within a Chronological Framework

Two chapters begin the book with discussions of definitions, theories, genetics, and prenatal development. These chapters provide a foundation for a life-span perspective on plasticity, nature and nurture, multicultural awareness, risk analysis, gains and losses, family bonding, and many other basic concepts.

The other six parts correspond to the major periods of development and proceed from biology to cognition to emotions to social interaction because human growth usually follows that path. Puberty begins adolescence, for instance. The ages of such events vary among people, but 0–2, 2–6, 6–11, 11–18, 18–25, 25–65, and 65+ are the approximate and traditional ages of the various parts.

In some texts, emerging adulthood (Chapter 11) is subsumed in a stage called early adulthood (ages 20 to 40), which is followed by middle adulthood (ages 40 to 65). I decided against that for two reasons. First, there is no event that starts middle age, especially since the evidence for a "midlife crisis" has crumbled. Second, as these chapters explain, current young adults merit their own part because they are distinct from both adolescents and adults.

I know, as you do, that life is not chunked—each passing day makes us older, each aspect of development affects every other aspect, and each social context affects us in a multitude of ways. However, we learn in sequence, with each thought building on the previous one. Thus, a topical organization within a chronological framework scaffolds comprehension of the interplay between age and domain.

Photographs, Tables, and Graphs That Are Integral to the Text

Students learn a great deal from this book's illustrations because Worth Publishers encourages their authors to choose the photographs, tables, and graphs and to write captions that extend the content. Observation Quizzes accompany some of them, directing readers to look more closely at what they see. The online Data Connections further this process by presenting numerous charts and tables that contain detailed data for further study.

Integration with Achieve

Callouts to accompanying online materials are in the margins throughout the book. These point to special videos and activities that reinforce what students are learning in the text.

Child Development and Nursing Career Correlation Guides

Many students taking this course hope to become nurses or early-childhood educators. This book and accompanying test bank are correlated to the NAEYC (National Association for the Education of Young Children) career preparation goals and the NCLEX (nursing) licensure exam. These two supplements are available in Achieve.

Thanks

I would like to thank the academic reviewers who have read this book in every edition and who have provided suggestions, criticisms, references, and encouragement. They have all made this a better book. I want to mention especially those who have reviewed this book:

Ty Abernathy, *Mississippi State University*
Natalie M. Alizaga, *Canada College*
James Alverson, *Northern Kentucky University*
Renee Babcock, *Central Michigan University*
Karen Beck, *Rio Hondo College*
Kazuko Y. Behrens, *SUNY Polytechnic Institute*
Malasri Chaudhery-Malgeri, *Schoolcraft College*
Katie E. Cherry, *Louisiana State University and Agricultural & Mechanical College*
Cynthia R. Deutsch, *Central Virginia Community College*
Debbie DeWitt, *Blue Ridge Community College*
Monique Johnson Dixon, *St. Phillip's College*
Crystal Dunlevy, *The Ohio State University—Columbus*
Andrea Fillip, *College of the Mainland*
Tiffany Marie Green, *The University of Alabama*
Nicole Hamilton, *St. Phillip's College*
Sara Harris, *Illinois State University*
Carmon Weaver Hicks, *Ivy Tech Community College Central Indiana*
Ronald James Jorgensen, *Pima County Community College—Downtown Campus*
Sonya Kitsko, *Robert Morris University*
Dorothy Marsil, *Kennesaw State University*
Daniel S. McConnell, *University of Central Florida*
Kelly Munly, *Penn State Altoona*
Valerie Neeley, *University of Texas—Rio Grande Valley*
Alexis Nicholson, *St. Phillip's College*
Laura Ochoa, *Bergen Community College*
Sujata Ponappa, *The Ohio State University—Columbus*
Lori Puterbaugh, *St. Petersburg College*
Maria Romero-Ramirez, *The University of Texas—Rio Grande Valley*
Lisa Rosen, *Texas Women's University*
Kevin Sumrall, *Lone Star College—Montgomery*
Christine Ziemer, *Missouri Western State University*
Ginny Zhan, *Kennesaw State University*

Kathleen Stassen Berger

New York, May 2021

PART I

CHAPTER 1 CHAPTER 2

The Beginnings

The science of human development has many beginnings. Chapter 1 introduces the science and some old and new theories, strategies, and methods that help us understand how people grow and change. Chapter 2 traces early development, from the genes at conception to the first reactions at birth.

Throughout these two chapters, the interaction of nature (heredity) and nurture (the environment) is illustrated. Genes influence everything, from when we are born to how we die. Nurture affects everything, too, beginning with the mother's health and the father's attitude at conception. Understanding the interplay of biology and culture is the foundation that allows us to reach *the goal of our study: a happy, productive and meaningful life for the almost 8 billion people on Earth, of all ages, cultures, and aspirations.*

LEREN LU/DIGITALVISION/GETTY IMAGES

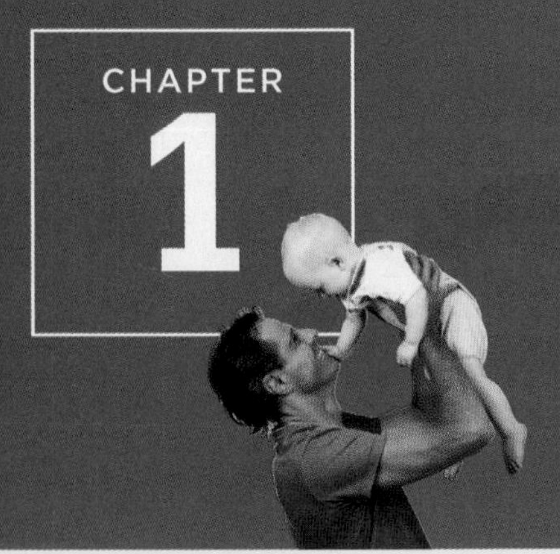

CHAPTER 1

THE BEGINNINGS

The Science of Human Development

what will you know?

- What makes the study of human development a science?
- Are changes with maturation the same for everyone, or is each life unique?
- Do the major theories agree that development stops at about age 20?
- Can scientists do experiments with people?
- Has science discovered what we need to know about development?

In midsummer, I felt out of place in my new apartment, surrounded by over a hundred sealed boxes. I could not find some things I needed—scissors, clean sheets, an alarm clock, a dog dish—and opened unlabeled boxes that held what I did not want—cords to electronic devices that were long gone, light bulbs for fixtures I no longer own, three heating pads, more than a thousand paper clips, and about 200 dried-out markers.

The worst part was not boxes, but memories and loneliness. I thought about the life span, not in generalities, but very personally. I found my parents' marriage photo, old letters from people who professed their love for me but whose names I did not recognize, hundreds of blurry photos and fading school reports of my young children, now grown. I unpacked dozens of unread books, and found sympathy cards sent when my husband died.

Scientists are trained to be objective, proceeding step-by-step to plan, collect data, evaluate alternatives, draw conclusions. So, to cope with my swirling emotions, I made lists: 36 boxes in the children's room, 44 boxes in the guest bedroom, 16 boxes in my home office. To be found: a nearby vet, plumber, grocery store, post office, and compost site. The lists helped: I made a plan (five boxes a day) and kept track of my progress.

Developmentalists know that people need other people. I asked others about vets, plumbers, mail, and so on. I also invited my friends for dinner and spoke to my neighbors. I offered emergency child care to a family down the hall with a 6-month-old baby; I praised an older woman who exercises by walking back and forth

PHOTO CREDIT: GLOBALSTOCK/E+/GETTY IMAGES

in the hall; I offered to buy groceries for my neighbors. No takers, but many smiles.

One couple did not smile. They frowned; their huge Doberman barks behind their double-locked door when I walk by with my mutt. My knowledge of human development kept me from feeling rejected: I know that some people are suspicious of newcomers. Their problem; not mine.

Now, in mid-fall, all the boxes are finally empty, and my thoughts return to the present. I see the sunrise and the river from my windows; I greet people of many colors, ages, and backgrounds on the street; I bought, and filled, four big bookcases as well as gave away dozens of books I will never read. I finally feel at home, where I should be, as a scientist, a developmentalist, and an author.

My personal transition benefits from my life-span perspective: People of all ages move on with their lives, experiencing frustration and joy, with unique circumstances and universal patterns. I hope this chapter, and the book as a whole, helps you appreciate that everyone has past memories and unlabeled boxes.

We all, eventually, can find what we need. This chapter begins that process, describing the perspectives, theories, and methods that provide a foundation for learning about the life span.

Understanding How and Why

The **science of human development** *seeks to understand how and why people—all kinds of people, everywhere, of every age—change over time.* The goal is a happy, productive, and meaningful life for everyone, of all ages, cultures, and aspirations.

science of human development
The science that seeks to understand how and why people of all ages and circumstances change or remain the same over time.

scientific method
A way to answer questions using empirical research and data-based conclusions.

The Scientific Method

Development over the life span is *multi-directional, multi-contextual, multi-cultural*, and *plastic*—four terms that will be explained soon. First, we emphasize that developmental study is a *science*. It depends on theories, data, analysis, critical thinking, and sound methodology, like every other science. Scientists ask questions to ascertain "how and why."

Science is especially useful when we study people because lives depend on it. Should birth take place at home or in hospitals? How should children be punished, when, and for what? Should schools encourage independence or obedience, be optional or required, begin at age 2 or 6, end at age 13, or 30, or never? Do adults need a job, a partner, a child? Does the thinking of older people grow shallow or deep?

Questions abound; opinions are strong; answers matter. That is why we need science.

STEP BY STEP

As you surely realize, facts may be twisted, opinions lead people astray, and false assumptions distort data. To counter prejudices and narrow observations, scientists follow the five steps of the **scientific method** (see Figure 1.1):

1. *Begin with curiosity.* Ask questions: Consider theory, study research, and gather observations, all of which suggest topics to be studied.

GREGORY COSTANZO/ GETTY IMAGES

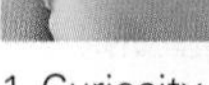
1. Curiosity

GEOSTOCK/STOCKBYTE/PHOTODISC
2. Hypothesis

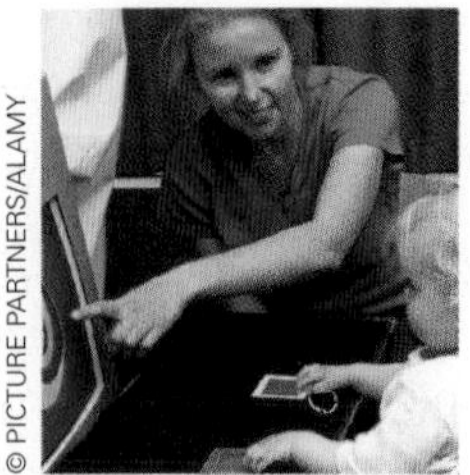
© PICTURE PARTNERS/ALAMY
3. Test

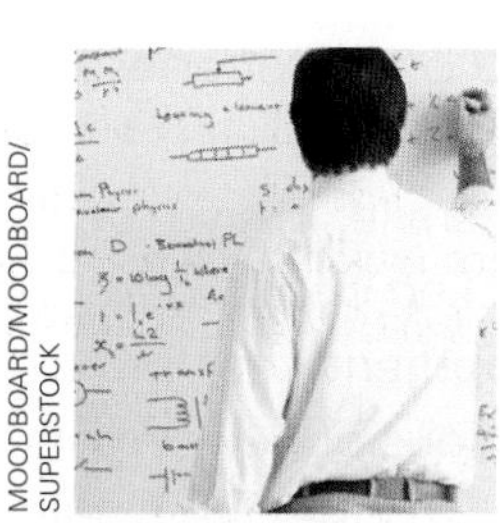
MOODBOARD/MOODBOARD/ SUPERSTOCK
4. Analyze data and draw conclusions

© BLAKE KENT/DESIGN PICS/DESIGN PICS/CORBIS
5. Report the results

FIGURE 1.1 Process, Not Proof Built into the scientific method—in questions, hypotheses, tests, and replication—is a passion for possibilities, especially unexpected ones.

hypothesis
A specific prediction that can be tested, and proven or disproved.

replication
Repeating a study, usually using different participants, perhaps of another age, SES, or culture.

2. *Develop* a ***hypothesis***, a prediction that can be verified.
3. *Test the hypothesis.* Design a study and conduct research to gather empirical evidence.
4. *Draw conclusions.* Use evidence (Step 3) to support or refute the hypothesis (Step 2). Consider alternate interpretations, unexpected results, and possible biases.
5. *Report the results.* Share data, conclusions, and limitations. Suggest further research to explore new questions and to corroborate conclusions (back to Step 1).

Thus, developmental scientists begin with curiosity and then collect data, drawing conclusions only after analyzing the evidence.

REPLICATION

Repeating a study's procedures and methods with different participants is **replication**. Scientists study the reports of other scientists (Step 5), sometimes trying to duplicate a previous study. Conclusions are revised, refined, rejected, or confirmed after replication, with many scientists describing exactly how replication should occur (e.g., Locey, 2020; Fabrigar et al., 2020; Willer & Emanuelson, 2020). Inside the Brain shows this process in more detail.

INSIDE THE BRAIN

Music and the Brain

The scientific method at work is illustrated in developmental research on music. Does music make people smarter? That question (Step 1) arose from a study 30 years ago: College students who listened to Mozart scored higher on tests of spatial intelligence than students who did not hear Mozart (Rauscher et al., 1993).

That study involved less than 100 participants and did not replicate with people of other ages or even with other college students, but the popular press did not wait. Nor did some politicians and businessmen.

The governor of Georgia in the mid-1990s proposed a budget item of $105,000 to give every Georgia newborn a free CD of classical music. (The legislature voted it down.) Someone patented *The Mozart Effect* and recorded an opera (Mozart's Don Giovanni) that he claimed would develop the fetal brain: Hundreds of pregnant women bought that CD, despite strong criticism from many scientists (Dowd, 2008).

Although the original study was flawed in many ways, the topic was intriguing (Step 1). Dozens of researchers tested some version of the general idea that music aids cognitive development (Step 2) (Perlovsky et al., 2013).

A hypothesis must be quite specific. Among hundreds of tested hypotheses were: Brains react differently to Mozart versus Bach (Verrusio et al., 2015); fetal brain waves reflect what music is played (González et al., 2017); rats are smarter if they hear Mozart (Sampaio et al., 2017). None of these hypotheses was confirmed, but science is designed to explore possibilities.

Sometime a hypothesis that is not proven is as noteworthy as one that is confirmed. When further research found that

Mozart was not necessarily better than other composers, or that European classical music was not necessarily better than contemporary, non-Western music, many researchers thought more broadly about the relationship of music and brain development.

Another hypothesis emerged, that the brain is affected by sound. Hundreds of studies tested that idea, gathering evidence (Step 3) that led to a conclusion (Step 4) that noises affect the newborn brain. That research was published (Step 5), with practical results. Many hospitals now play soothing music in NICUs (neonatal intensive care units), reduce loud alarms, and keep voices low (Lordier et al., 2019).

Other scientists have studied the effect of music on regions of the brain. Decades of research has found that merely listening to music does not aid the mind, but that playing a musical instrument might (Herholz & Zatorre, 2012; Rose et al., 2019).

Neurological studies of expert musicians show many brain differences from nonmusicians, not only in auditory areas (which might be expected) but also in the inferior frontal regions (Bermudez et al., 2009). That led to two possibilities: Either those musicians were born with unusual neurological gifts, or hours and years of practice sculpted their brains.

A new hypothesis (Step 2) arose. Might learning to play a musical instrument in childhood itself affect the brain, advancing emotional control, creativity, and memory? Some research says that is a wishful fantasy (Hogan et al., 2019); other research suggests that extensive music instruction over the years leads to special connections and activity in brain (Kraus & White-Schwoch, 2020; Sammler & Elmer, 2020).

Consider one study in detail. Three groups of 6-year-olds, all from similar low-income families, were compared (Habibi et al., 2018a, 2018b). At baseline, their brains were scanned, and the neurological activity of children in all three groups was similar.

Then, for two years, one group spent six to seven hours each week learning to play an instrument (usually the violin), one group spent three to four hours in a special sports program (soccer or swimming), and a third group had no afterschool programming.

After two years, the researchers found (Step 4) that children in the music group improved on several measures of brain development and cognition in auditory areas, but they showed no differences from the other groups in most brain regions. (Several aspects of a brain region called the *cingulate cortex* were studied: You do not need to know the term, only that they looked closely at many specific brain regions.)

The scientists wondered if a longer period of music training would have led to more changes. The researchers explain:

> Because we are investigating brains of young children during a period of intense change related to typical development, the short time of intervention about 2 years (23–25 months), and the limited intensity of the intervention possibly explain the lack of more widespread differences. The fact that we detected discriminating changes in the auditory regions and in the corpus callosum seems to indicate that there was an effect on regions directly stimulated by the intervention and suggests that, differences in functionally related regions may well appear at a later stage.
>
> *[Habibi et al., 2018b, p. 4345]*

They conclude that "music training is a powerful intervention that may facilitate regional brain maturation during childhood" (Habibi et al., 2018b, p. 4346).

Many other researchers continue to explore the relationship between music and the brain. Science sometimes unearths unanticipated findings that are intriguing. That happened in this case. On some measures, the sports group improved more than the children with no special lessons. The researchers suggested that:

> participation in activities other than music may in fact be associated with . . . [cognitive skills] . . . provided that the activities are socially interactive and comparably motivating and engaging.
>
> *[Habibi et al., 2018a, p. 79]*

This entire body of research demonstrates a basic lesson of science: Do not leap to conclusions. Any one study—even one that fails to replicate—can raise new questions. Questions, data, replication, surprises, and alternate explanations are the basis of science.

The Nature-Nurture Debate

An example of the need for science concerns a great puzzle of life, the *nature–nurture debate*. **Nature** refers to the influence of the genes that people inherit. **Nurture** refers to environmental influences, beginning with the health, diet, and stress of the future person's mother at conception, and continuing lifelong, including experiences in the family, school, community, and nation.

The nature–nurture debate has many manifestations, among them *heredity–environment*, *maturation–learning*, and *sex–gender*. Under whatever name, the basic question is, "How much of any characteristic, behavior, or emotion is the result of

nature
In development, nature refers to genes. Thus, traits, capacities, and limitations inherited at conception are nature.

nurture
In development, nurture includes all environmental influences that occur after conception, from the mother's nutrition while pregnant to the culture of the nation.

JANEK SKARZYNSKI/AFP/GETTY IMAGES

Chopin's First Concert
Frederick Chopin, at age 8, played his first public concert in 1818, before photographs. But this photo shows Piotr Pawlak, a contemporary prodigy playing Chopin's music in the same Polish Palace where that famous composer played as a boy. How much of talent is genetic and how much is cultural? This is a nature–nurture question that applies to both boys, 200 years apart.

THINK CRITICALLY: Why not assign a percent to nature and a percent to nurture so that they add up to 100 percent?

differential susceptibility
The idea that people vary in how sensitive (for better or worse) they are to particular experiences, either because of their genes or because of their past experiences. (Also called *differential sensitivity*.)

genes and chromosomes, set at conception, and how much is the result of experiences, including those that affect biology (such as food) and those that affect attitudes (such as family relationships)?"

BORN THAT WAY?

Some people believe that most traits are inborn, that children are innately good ("an innocent child") or bad ("beat the devil out of them"). Others stress nurture, crediting or blaming parents, or neighborhoods, or drugs, or peers, or additives in the food, and much more when someone is good or bad, a hero or a villain.

Neither belief is accurate. As one group of scholars explain, human characteristics are neither inborn nor made (Hambrick et al., 2018). Genes and the environment *both* affect every characteristic: Nature always affects nurture, and then nurture affects nature.

Any attempt to determine precisely how much of a trait is genetic and how much is environmental is bound to fail, because genetic and environmental influences continuously interact, amplifying or muting each other. The question is: Which genes interacting with which environmental influences affect whom, when, and why? The answer is "it depends."

DIFFERENTIAL SUSCEPTIBILITY

The impact of any good or bad experience might be magnified or inconsequential, depending on genes or experiences. For example, a beating, or a beer, or a blessing might be a turning point for one person but have no impact on another. That is called **differential susceptibility** (Ellis et al., 2011a). People vary in how sensitive they are to particular words, or drugs, or events, either because of their genes or their past.

Asthma is an example. Because of heredity, some people begin wheezing when they are near a cat, but others do not. Yet because of past experience, (primarily the reactions of adults), some children are terrified at the first signs of an asthma attack: Fear makes their throats tighten. Others are nonchalant. Both the genes and the reaction are examples of differential susceptibility.

Dogs and neighborhood have an effect, too (Krzych-Fałta et al., 2018). If a child lives in a rural area, fur-bearing pets reduce the rate of asthma, but in urban areas, such animals increase the incidence. Differential susceptibility again.

Developmentalists use a floral metaphor to capture this idea. Some people are like *dandelions*—hardy, growing and thriving in good soil or bad, with or without ample sun and rain. They are not susceptible to the environment. Other people are like *orchids*—quite wonderful, but only under ideal conditions (Ellis & Boyce, 2008; Laurent, 2014).

A person who seems unfazed by poverty, or abuse, or prejudice is a dandelion; someone who suffers with those circumstances but blossoms when family and community are supportive is an orchid.

The same idea helps describe the varied levels of sensitivity to environmental stimuli. Research on over a thousand college students found that about a third are strongly influenced by the moods of other people (the orchids), about a third not (the dandelions), and about a third are in the middle, dubbed *tulips* (Lionetti et al., 2018).

Understanding differential susceptibility is useful for educators. Children who are orchids may be prodigious learners when they have great teachers, but may resist education when their teachers are hostile. Other children learn no matter who their teacher is.

This metaphor was used in a research study that assessed children after a preschool intervention, called Ready to Learn, a series of videos and computer games funded by the U.S. Department of Education to teach math and literacy. The short-term

benefits were notable: Children who watched them were a few months ahead in school achievement in first grade than other children (Hurwitz, 2020).

But would those effects endure? Six years later, some children showed no effects (dandelions), but some (orchids) were changed by their preschool experience (Hurwitz & Schmitt, 2020).

Knowing the reading readiness of the children at age 5 helped predict this differential susceptibility. Those 5-year-olds whose literacy scores were average (perhaps they knew letters, but not words) were still average six years later (they could read at grade level), no matter whether they had Ready to Learn or not.

However, the videos produced long-term benefits for two groups: those whose preschool abilities were above average and those whose abilities were low (Hurwitz & Schmitt, 2020). The researchers hypothesize that children who were ahead of their peers were already motivated, so they enjoyed the special curriculum. Over the next six years, Ready to Learn gave them an additional boost.

Meanwhile, those who, as preschoolers, were struggling with reading needed the extra help that the intervention provided; they also benefited from special instruction (Hurwitz & Schmitt, 2020).

what have you learned?

1. What are the five steps of the scientific method?
2. Why is replication important?
3. What basic question is at the heart of the nature–nurture controversy?
4. What is the difference between a dandelion and an orchid?
5. How might differential susceptibility apply to adults?

The Life-Span Perspective

The **life-span perspective** (Baltes et al., 2006; Fingerman et al., 2011; Raz & Lindenberger, 2013) takes into account all phases of life and all aspects of development. This perspective is multi-disciplinary, with insights from psychology, biology, history, and sociology.

life-span perspective
An approach to the study of human development that includes all phases, from birth to death.

Since 2000, new methods to study the brain have added to our understanding of how people "change over time." A recent collection of 20 articles written by 44 experts used "a life-span perspective" to "bring together the latest knowledge on the development of educational neuroscience" (Thomas et al., 2020). By including the entirety of life (see Table 1.1) this perspective has led to four insights: Human development is multi-directional, multi-contextual, multi-cultural, and plastic.

TABLE 1.1 Age Ranges for Different Developmental Stages

Infancy	0 to 2 years
Early childhood	2 to 6 years
Middle childhood	6 to 11 years
Adolescence	11 to 18 years
Emerging adulthood	18 to 25 years
Adulthood	25 to 65 years
Late adulthood	65 years and older

As you will learn, developmentalists are reluctant to specify chronological ages for any period of development, because time is only one of many variables that affect each person. However, age is a crucial variable, and development can be segmented into periods of study. Approximate ages for each period are given here.

Development Is Multi-Directional

Multiple changes, in every direction, characterize the life span, making development *multi-directional*. If all human traits were charted from birth to death, some traits would appear, others disappear, with increases, decreases, spirals, and zigzags (see Figure 1.2). The traditional idea—that development advances linearly until about age 18, steadies, and then declines—has been refuted by life-span research.

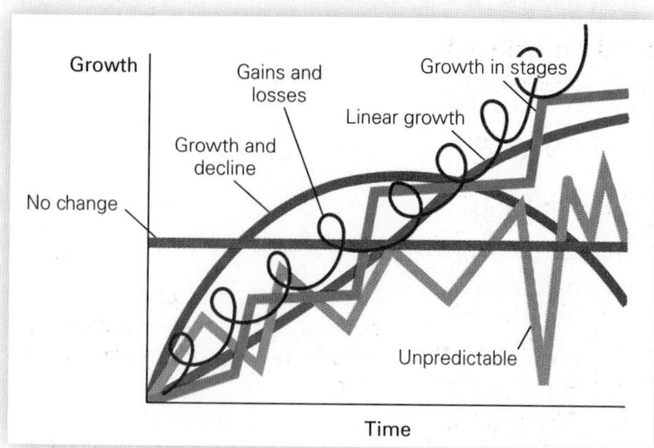

FIGURE 1.2 Patterns of Developmental Growth
Many patterns of developmental growth have been discovered by careful research. Although linear progress seems most common, scientists now find that almost no aspect of human change follows the linear pattern exactly.

MORE VARIATIONS

The pace of change varies as well. Sometimes *discontinuity* is evident: Change can occur rapidly and dramatically, as when caterpillars become butterflies. Sometimes *continuity* is found: Growth can be gradual, as when redwoods grow taller over hundreds of years.

Sometimes no change occurs. For instance, chromosomal sex is lifelong. The 23rd pair of chromosomes is usually XY or XX (male or female), and rarely, some other combination, such as XXY or XYY. That does not change.

Obviously, the power and meaning of those chromosomes change: being female, for instance, was not the same for our great-grandmothers as it is for current young women. Further, prenatal and postnatal hormones affect gender, as do many nonbiological experiences, so XX and XY are just the beginning. Gender traits show discontinuity, continuity, *and* stability.

Although sex/gender traits are varied and change in complex ways (Hyde et al., 2019) the chromosomes themselves stay the same lifelong. When scientists unearth a bone fragment of someone who died 100,000 years ago, DNA analysis tells them if the person was male or female.

Given the multi-directional paths of human development, theorists see *gains and losses* throughout life, often at the same time (Lang et al., 2011; Villar, 2012). Growth, transformation, improvement, and decline are apparent in each person's life.

Gains and losses are also apparent historically and generationally. Are young adults today better or worse off than their parents? Both. One author (herself a millennial) contrasts the views of middle-aged adults with those of young adults (Filipovic, 2020).

According to her, boomers think that Millennials "want to move up the ladder too quickly; we job-hop with no sense of loyalty; we're overly-sensitive to criticism and under-receptive to feedback." But, she says "the reality is essentially the opposite; we are working very hard just to tread water (Filipovic, 2020, p. 17).

This is just one example. Generations often have opposite perceptions. No matter what your age, personality, or politics, you can see both progress and regression in civic values, economic status, and human health. Science and technology continually change human life, for better and worse, and often for both. Everyone gains and loses lifelong.

CRITICAL PERIODS

critical period
Time when a particular development must occur. If it does not, as when something toxic prevents that growth, then it cannot develop later.

Some changes are sudden and profound because of a **critical period**, a time when something *must* occur for normal development, or the only time when an abnormality might arise. For instance, the critical period for humans to grow arms and legs, hands and feet, fingers and toes, is between 28 and 54 days after conception.

After day 54, that critical period is over. Unlike some insects, humans never grow replacement limbs or digits. Scientists are able to pinpoint the critical period for limb formation because of a tragedy. Between 1957 and 1961, thousands of newly pregnant women in 30 nations took *thalidomide*, an antinausea drug. This change in nurture (in the mother's blood reaching the embryo by the umbilical cord) disrupted nature (the genetic program directing limb formation).

If an expectant woman took thalidomide between day 28 and day 54, her newborn's arms or legs were malformed or absent (Moore & Persaud, 2007). Whether

all four limbs, or just arms, or just forearms were missing depended on timing. If thalidomide was ingested only after day 54, the newborn had normal body structures.

SENSITIVE PERIODS

Scientist studying the life span find that humans have few critical periods. Often, however, a particular development occurs more easily—not exclusively—at a certain time. Such a time is called a **sensitive period**.

An example is language. If children do not communicate in their first language between ages 1 and 3, they might do so later (hence, not critical), but their grammar is often impaired (hence, sensitive). Similarly, childhood is a sensitive period for learning to pronounce a second or third language. A new language can be learned later, but strangers might detect an accent and ask, "Where are you from?"

Some adults maintain language learning ability, but exceptions are rare. A study of native Dutch speakers who become fluent in English found only 5 percent had truly mastered English (Schmid et al., 2014). People learning a new language in adulthood almost always stumble with idioms, articles, and accents.

sensitive period
A time when a particular developmental growth is most likely to occur, although it may still happen later.

ecological-systems approach
A perspective on human development that considers all of the influences from the various contexts of development. (Later renamed *bioecological theory.*)

Development Is Multi-Contextual

As one scholar explained, "human development is fundamentally contextual" (Pluess, 2015, p. 138). That means that everyone is profoundly affected by their surroundings; to understand people, a *multi-contextual* perspective is needed. This provides insight that might reduce the political polarization evident in many nations: People with opposite views are not evil or ignorant; their context affected them.

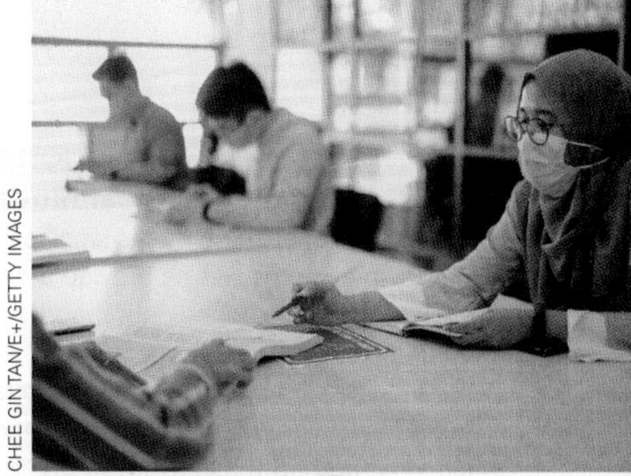

CHEE GINTAN/E+/GETTY IMAGES

Universal or Cultural? When and where? Socially distanced, masked college students in a library could be anywhere but not any time – this photo was taken in Malaysia in the spring of 2020. One benefit of a cross-cultural perspective is that it helps us recognize what is true everywhere, and what is not.

THE SOCIAL CONTEXT

Especially crucial is the social context, which includes everyone who influences each developing person, immediately and over time, directly and indirectly.

For example, a college student may be persuaded by other students in their social network to come to a party. The people at the party provide the immediate social context. That affects whether the student will leave soon after arriving, or stay till 3 A.M., eating and drinking. Next morning, the social context of that party will indirectly affect that student in their early-morning classes, which are another social context, this one created by the professor and the classmates.

The broader social context also affects that student, such as the risk of COVID-19, and how the state's political leaders and the college administration respond. Whether or not a school allows in-person classes, forbids social gatherings, or mandates masks is not a simple decision, but one influenced by the social context of the people making the decision, whose own history affects their evaluation of consequences (Spitzer, 2020).

ECOLOGICAL SYSTEMS

A leading developmentalist, Urie Bronfenbrenner (1917–2005), emphasized the power of contexts. Just as a naturalist studying an organism examines *ecology* (the multifaceted relationship between the organism and its environment), Bronfenbrenner believed that each person is affected by many social contexts and interpersonal interactions. Therefore, he recommended that developmentalists take an **ecological-systems approach** (Bronfenbrenner & Morris, 2006). This approach recognized three nested levels (see Figure 1.3).

- Most obvious is the *microsystem*—each person's immediate social contexts, such as family and peer group.

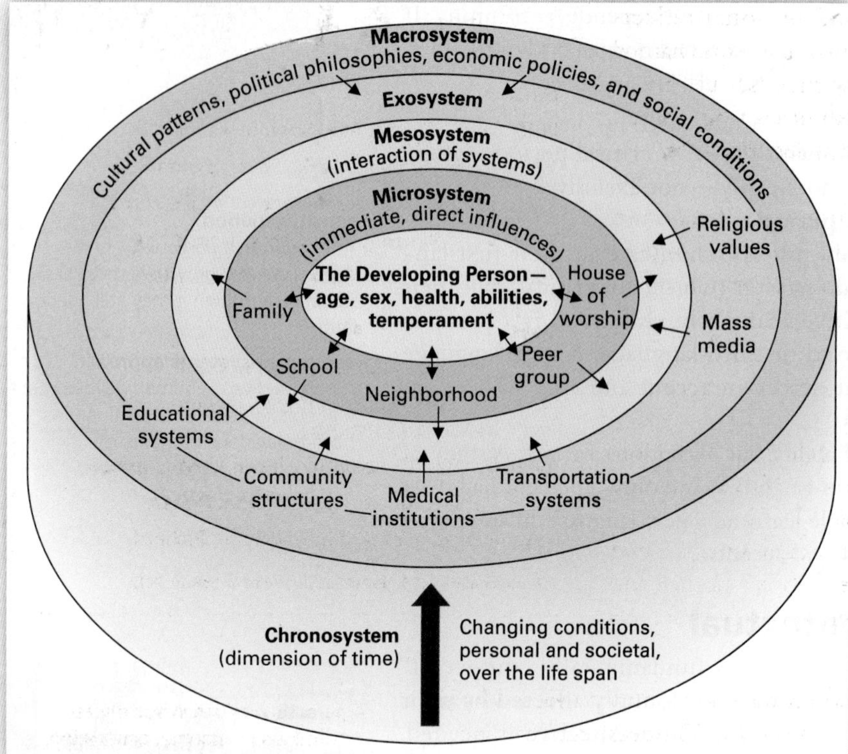

FIGURE 1.3 The Ecological Model According to developmental researcher Urie Bronfenbrenner, each person is significantly affected by interactions among a number of overlapping systems, which provide the context of development. Microsystems—family, peer group, classroom, neighborhood, house of worship—intimately and immediately shape human development. Surrounding and supporting the microsystems are the exosystems, which include all the external networks (such as community structures and local educational, medical, employment, and communications systems) that affect the microsystems. Influencing both of these systems is the macrosystem, which includes cultural patterns, political philosophies, economic policies, and social conditions. Mesosystems refer to interactions among systems, as when parents and teachers coordinate to educate a child. Bronfenbrenner eventually added a fifth system, the chronosystem, to emphasize the importance of historical time.

- Also important is the *exosystem* (local institutions such as school and church).
- Beyond that is the *macrosystem* (the larger setting, including cultural values, economic policies, and political processes).

Two more systems affect these three.

- One is the *mesosystem*, consisting of the connections among the other systems.
- The other is the *chronosystem* (literally, "time system"), which is the historical context.

Before he died, Bronfenbrenner added a sixth system, the *bioecological system*, which is the internal biology of the person. All developmentalists now recognize biological systems, because signals from the stomach, lungs, heart, hormones, and neurotransmitters affect all the other systems. Further, all the microbes within each person (the *microbiome*) are also part of each person (more on microbiome later).

In the student-at-party example above, the students' immediate social circle is the microsystem, the college culture (is it a "party school?") is the exosystem, and the national emphasis on higher education is part of the macrosystem. The party itself is a mesosystem, in that it connects the microsystem and the exosystem.

Every gathering also reflects the chronosystem. Food and drink vary with each decade, and even the fact of a college party reflects history: Few 20-year-olds a century ago were in college, and college students themselves spent most of their time studying, not partying. In 2020 and 2021, COVID-19 was part of the chronosystem, making the college experience unlike how it was in 2019. Further, the snacks and beverages, the air temperature and oxygen, and perhaps the smells and smoke, affect the biosystem.

THE HISTORICAL CONTEXT

The recent pandemic is an immediate example, but historical events have always affected development. Imagine if you were born before contraception, or cell phones, or social media. Your life would not be what it is.

All persons born within a few years of one another are called a **cohort**, a group defined by its members' shared birth age, such as Millennials, Generation X, Boomers, and so on. Cohorts travel through life together, experiencing particular values, events, and technologies at about the same age. For example, the pandemic affected everyone differently depending on how old they were in 2020. Examples are child education, adolescent social life, adult employment, older adults' death of friends.

cohort
People born within the same historical period who therefore move through life together, experiencing the same events, new technologies, and cultural shifts at the same ages.

Even something that seems private and personal reflects cohort. Consider a person's name. If you know someone named Liam, he is probably quite young: Liam is the most popular name for boys born between 2017–2019 but was not even in the top 200 until the twenty-first century (U.S. Social Security Administration, 2019). (See Table 1.2.)

These rankings are from the United States overall. Variation in popular names is found by nation, by culture, and by region. For example, in 2019 Oliver was the most popular boy's name in Maine, but was fourteenth in Texas.

TABLE 1.2 Popular First Names

Girls:	
2019:	Olivia, Emma, Ava, Sophia, Isabella
1999:	Emily, Hannah, Alexis, Sarah, Samantha
1979:	Jennifer, Melissa, Amanda, Jessica, Amy
1959:	Mary, Susan, Linda, Karen, Donna
1939:	Mary, Barbara, Patricia, Betty, Shirley
Boys:	
2019:	Liam, Noah, Oliver, William, Elijah
1999:	Jacob, Michael, Matthew, Joshua, Nicholas, Christopher
1979:	Michael, Christopher, Jason, David, James
1959:	Michael, David, James, John, Robert
1939:	Robert, James, John, William, Richard

Information from U.S. Social Security Administration, 2019.

THE SOCIOECONOMIC CONTEXT

Some scholars believe that **socioeconomic status**, abbreviated **SES**, underlies every other system. SES reflects income, education, occupation, and neighborhood. The combination affects development much more than money alone.

To emphasize that SES is not just about money, imagine two U.S. families comprised of an infant, an unemployed mother, and a father who earns less than the 2019 federal poverty line for a family of three ($21,330).

- One family depends on the father's minimum wage job which provides $16,965 annual income ($7.25 per hour, 45 hours a week, for 52 weeks), with neither parent a high school graduate, living in an underserved neighborhood. Their SES would be low.
- The other father is a student who is earning his Ph.D. His only income is a $20,000 annual grant; he lives in campus housing with his college-graduate wife, who temporarily left her job to care for the baby. Their SES is middle class.

socioeconomic status (SES) A person's position in society as determined by income, occupation, education, and place of residence. (Sometimes called *social class*.)

As you see, when measuring SES in order to understand the impact on human development, education may be more influential than income. Nonetheless, income may be pivotal, both as a result and a cause of all the other indicators of SES.

This is especially true for low-SES children in the United States. Even more than in other developed nations, income inequality is increasing in the United States, and children born into low-SES families are likely to become low-SES adults. The main reason is that low family income reduces access to good education (Hoffmann et al., 2020).

CHAPTER APP 1

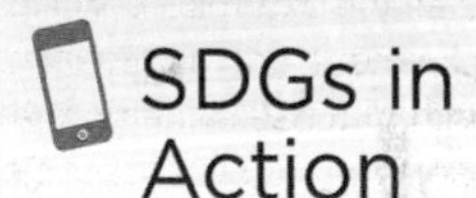

SDGs in Action

iOS:
https://tinyurl.com/u6hpjwl

ANDROID:
https://tinyurl.com/uo4vaqp

RELEVANT TOPIC:
Income inequality and social justice

Organized around the United Nations' Sustainable Development Goals (a global to-do list for tackling poverty, inequality, and climate change), this app educates users about challenges in the world today and motivates them to take action.

From a life-span perspective, age and cohort are entangled with SES. In past cohorts, people older than 65 were often poor. Currently, however, pensions and health policies (e.g., Social Security and Medicare in the United States), as well as senior discounts in housing, groceries, transportation, and more, flipped the connection between age and poverty. Now young children have higher rates of poverty, and they are most often harmed by it (Cantillon et al., 2017).

For many reasons, low SES is particularly damaging for the young. If early education is not funded publicly, then quality of preschools depends on parents' income. Another problem is stressed and inattentive parents. Of course, some low-SES parents read and talk with their children for hours a day, and some relatives or neighbors provide what parents or government do not. But on average, the poorest Americans are the youngest, and the poorest adults are those with young children.

In this example, it is apparent that deprivation begins with money, the *capital* referred to in capitalism. However, *social capital* (the support from people, including relatives, neighbors, religious institutions, and the larger society) creates the context, which includes the other two aspects of SES, neighborhood and education (Lin, 2017).

SOVFOTO/UNIVERSAL IMAGES GROUP VIA GETTY IMAGES

The Impact of Culture
Vygotsky lived in Russia from 1896 to 1934, when war, starvation, and revolution led to the deaths of millions. Throughout this turmoil, Vygotsky focused on learning.

OBSERVATION QUIZ
What suggests that this photo was taken a century ago? (see answer, page 35) ↑

DATA CONNECTIONS: Economic Equality and Human Development explores various nations' Gini indices, which measure economic equality in a particular society.  Achieve

Development Is Multi-Cultural

In order to learn about "all kinds of people, everywhere, at every age" (as in the definition of our study), we need to recognize development as *multi-cultural.* **Culture** is defined broadly, to include "shared beliefs, conventions, norms, behaviors, expectations" (Bornstein et al., 2011, p. 30).

The crucial importance of a multi-cultural perspective was stressed by one of the leading proponents of development, Lev Vygotsky (1896–1934). He noted that people do not develop in isolation but rather in relationship to the culture of their community, transmitted by the words, objects, and actions of other people (Vygotsky, 2012). (Vygotsky's ideas are explained in Chapter 5.)

SOCIAL CONSTRUCTIONS

Thus, culture is far more than food or clothes; it is a set of ideas, beliefs, and patterns. Culture is a powerful **social construction**, that is, a concept created, or *constructed*, by a society. Social constructions affect how people think and act—what they value, ignore, and punish (see A Case to Study).

A CASE TO STUDY

A Very Rude Child?

Each group has a culture: There are ethnic cultures, national cultures, family cultures, college cultures, and so on. This makes everyone multi-cultural, which can lead to an internal cultural clash, as well as a clash when someone from one family or ethnic culture is also part of another school or national culture.

Such conflicts are particularly evident in moral issues. Someone from one culture may criticize someone else for not understanding "common courtesy" or "human decency" or "basic respect," unaware that rudeness, indecency, or disrespect in one place may be acceptable in another.

Even worse may be when a person has internalized the standards of two cultures and behaves according to one when within another. That can make someone feel ashamed and guilty, or unable to sleep, because they did not act as their family wished. That happened to one of my students.

She wrote:

> My mom was outside on the porch talking to my aunt. I decided to go outside; I guess I was being nosey. While they were talking I jumped into their conversation which was very rude. When I realized what I did it was too late. My mother slapped me in my face so hard that it took a couple of seconds to feel my face again.
>
> *[C., personal communication]*

This mother and aunt came to the United States as adults, and they continued the culture of their childhood. My student grew up in a U.S. city, attending public school. She nonetheless reflected her parents' homeland. That is why she labeled her own behavior "nosey" and "very rude." She later wrote that she expects children to be "seen but not heard" and that her own son makes her "very angry" when he interrupts.

However, she also reflected her school culture, because in her school, children were encouraged to speak. In many classrooms, children who do not express their thoughts are downgraded. This particular student had adjusted well to the U.S. academic culture. She was on the college Dean's list, she joined in class discussions, and she wrote thoughtful papers in her weekly college assignments in my class.

Do you think she was a rude child, or, on the contrary, that her mother should not have slapped her? Your answer reflects your culture.

DIFFERENCE OR DEFICIT

Quiet children and talkative children may each be appropriate in their respective cultures. Neither norm is bad; both depend on the context. Everyone needs to learn when to talk and when to listen.

If you understand that, you have avoided the **difference-equals-deficit error**, which is the mistaken idea that unusual "beliefs, conventions, norms, behaviors, expectations" are not as good as conventional ones. The difference-equals-deficit error leads people to believe that people from other cultures are to be pitied, feared, criticized, and changed.

The belief that one's own culture is best has benefits: Generally, people who appreciate their communities' beliefs, norms, and conventions are happier, prouder, and more willing to help strangers. However, that becomes destructive if it limits a person's ability to function in other cultures, and if it reduces respect for people from other groups. Too quickly and thoughtlessly, differences are considered problems (Akhtar & Jaswal, 2013).

The difference-equals-deficit error is one reason that a careful multicultural approach is necessary. Cultural differences are not always wrong and inferior, nor the opposite, right and superior. For example, one immigrant child, on her first day in a U.S. school, was teased about the food she brought for lunch. The next day, she dumped the contents of her lunchbox in the garbage as soon as she arrived at school.

This example illustrates the problem of difference equals deficit. A child's lunch in another culture might, or might not, be more nutritious than conventional peanut butter and jelly sandwiches. In this example, her classmates noticed difference and misjudged it as a deficit. That bounced back to harm that girl (hungry children learn less).

culture
A system of shared beliefs, norms, behaviors, and expectations that persist over time and prescribe social behavior and assumptions.

social construction
An idea that is built on shared perceptions, not on objective reality.

difference-equals-deficit error
The mistaken belief that a deviation from some norm is necessarily inferior.

THINK CRITICALLY: How does the difference-equals-deficit error apply to attitudes of native-born citizens about immigrants, and vice versa?

ethnic group
People whose ancestors were born in the same region. Usually they share a language, culture, and/or religion.

race
The concept that some people are distinct from others because of physical appearance, typically skin color. Social scientists think race is a misleading idea, although race can be a powerful sociological idea, not based in biology.

ETHNIC AND RACIAL GROUPS

Cultural variations fuel wars and violence when differences are seen as deficits. To prevent that, we need to understand *ethnicity* and *race*. Members of an **ethnic group** almost always have the same ancestors, and often have the similar national origins, religion, and language. Ethnicity is a social construction, not a biological one.

Ethnic groups do not always share a culture. There are "multiple intersecting and interacting dimensions" to ethnic identity (Sanchez & Vargas, 2016, p. 161). Because of past histories, people may be the same ethnically but not culturally (e.g., people of Irish descent in Ireland, Australia, and North America). The opposite is also true: People of one culture may come from several ethnic groups (consider British culture).

Race is even more affected by history than ethnicity is. Historically, most North Americans thought that race was an inborn genetic characteristic that differentiated one group from another. Now biologists recognize race as a social construction, not a genetic one. One team writes:

> We believe the use of biological concepts of race in human genetic research—so disputed and so mired in confusion—is problematic at best and harmful at worst. It is time for biologists to find a better way.
>
> [*Yudell et al., 2016, p. 564*]

Consequently, this book refers to ethnicity and to genes when they are relevant, more often than to race. Racial terms such as White, Black, and so forth are used only when the data are presented that way, or when race is used to lump people together.

MYRTO PAPADOPOULOS FOR THE WASHINGTON POST VIA GETTY IMAGES

Difference, But Not Deficit This Syrian refugee living in a refugee camp in Greece is quite different from the aid workers who assist there, as evident in her head covering (hijab) and the cross on her tent. But the infant, with a pacifier in her mouth and a mother who tries to protect her, illustrates why developmentalists focus on similarities rather than on differences.

Actual skin color varies much more than color words suggest. Africa "far exceeds pigmentary diversity [than] anywhere else on the planet" (Tang & Barsh, 2017), an amazing conclusion when the term "White" excludes people of Asian descent, some of whom have skin that is lighter than anyone of European descent, and when people still use the pejorative term "Red," a color that no one has.

The fact that race and ethnicity are social constructions does not make them insignificant. They can be very powerful, a matter of life and death. But since they are created by societies, they can be changed by societies. In the United States, the concept of race was invented to justify slavery (Wilkerson, 2020). Then, a century ago, an influx of immigrants created a dilemma. At first, Americans of Irish, Italian, and Greek ethnicity were *not* considered White (Gordon, 2017). Now they are: The social construction changed, not the biology.

Similar issues arise for people in the United States whose ancestors lived in Latin American nations (Telles, 2018). Are they Hispanic, Chicano, Latino, or Latinx? The U.S. Census did not give them any way to identify themselves until 1980, and since then has said they "can be of any race." On the census form, some check "White," some "Black," some "Other"; some leave the question blank, and some check "American Indian." Often, the same person checks a different category in one census than they did ten years earlier.

Because everyone in the United States is affected by "shared beliefs, conventions, norms, behaviors, expectations" of U.S. culture, everyone notices color, sometimes reacting in destructive ways, sometimes not. It is obvious that race has been destructive of human potential, but it is not obvious that racial identity can be constructive.

THINK CRITICALLY: To fight racism, must race be named and recognized?

Yet the data show that African American (an ethnic group) adolescents who are proud of being Black (a racial category), and Mexican Americans (an ethnic group) who identify as Brown (a racial category) tend to achieve academically, avoid drug addiction, and are proud of themselves (Huguley et al., 2019; Perry et al., 2019; Yu et al., 2019).

INTERSECTIONALITY

intersectionality
The idea that the various identities need to be combined. This is especially important in determining if discrimination occurs.

Intersectionality begins with the idea that we each are pushed and pulled—sometimes strongly, sometimes weakly, sometimes by ourselves, sometimes by others—by gender, religion, generation, nation, age, culture, and ethnicity. Our many identities interact with, and influence, each other (see Figure 1.4).

Intersectionality brings special attention to people who are simultaneously in several marginalized groups. For example, when Crenshaw (1989) first introduced the term *intersectionality*, she recognized that the courts allowed discrimination against African American women because the double jeopardy of racism and sexism was ignored.

Intersectionality recognizes that each identity—race, gender, religion, age, or citizenship—can divide rather than unite people, such as Latinx versus African American, or men versus women. It also can gloss over the discrimination experienced by people who are in multiple marginalized groups.

That was emphasized by a public health leader, who says the phrase "We are all in this together" implies that all Americans are equally vulnerable to COVID-19, ignoring the unequal risks of the virus. She wrote:

> Intersectionality highlights how power and inequality are structured differently for groups, particularly historically oppressed groups, based on their varied interlocking demographics (e.g., race, ethnicity, gender, class).
> *[Bowleg, 2020, p. 917]*

FIGURE 1.4 Identities Interacting We all are in the middle, with many identities. Our total selves are affected by them all, with variation by culture and context as to which are more salient.

More generally, like interlocking gears, systems of social categorization and group power intersect to influence everyone, every day. Our

study highlights age as a category. For instance, a person is more likely to experience ageism if they are also a person of color who has a disability.

THINK CRITICALLY: How would your life be different if you were of another gender, ethnicity, family background, sexual orientation, health status, ability, and so on?

Development Is Plastic

The term ***plasticity*** denotes two complementary aspects of development: People can be molded (as plastic can be), yet people maintain a certain durability (as plastic does). This provides both hope and realism—hope because change is possible and realism because development builds on what has come before.

plasticity
The idea that abilities, personality, and other human characteristics are moldable, and thus can change.

dynamic-systems approach
A view of human development as an ongoing, ever-changing interaction between the physical, cognitive, and psychosocial influences.

Both brain and behavior are far more moldable than once was thought. Plasticity is basic to the life-span perspective because it simultaneously incorporates two facts:

1. People can change over time.
2. New behavior is affected by what has already happened.

This is evident in the **dynamic-systems approach**, a framework that many contemporary developmentalists use. The idea is that human development is an ongoing, ever-changing interaction between the individual and all the systems, domains, and cultures.

Note the word *dynamic*: Physical contexts, emotional influences, the passage of time, each person, and every aspect of the ecosystem are always interacting, always in flux, always in motion. Also note the word "systems." Every part of a system affects every other part, an idea already explained in the ecological-systems framework.

The most surprising example of plasticity in recent years involves the brain. Expansion of neurological structures, networks of communication between one cell and another, and even creation of neurons (brain cells) occurs in adulthood. This neurological plasticity is evident in hundreds of studies mentioned later in this text.

Plasticity is especially useful when anticipating growth of a particular person: Everyone is constrained by past circumstances, but no one is confined by them.

AN EXAMPLE: DAVID

I have seen plasticity in myself, in my children, and in everyone I have known for decades. Consider my nephew David.

My sister-in-law, Dot, contracted rubella (also called German measles) early in her third pregnancy. The disease was not diagnosed until David was born, blind and dying. Heart surgery two days after birth saved his life, but eye surgery at 6 months to remove a cataract activated the virus and destroyed that eye. Malformations of his thumbs, ankles, teeth, feet, spine, and brain became evident. David did not walk, talk, or even chew for years.

Yet dire early predictions—from me as well as many others—have proven false. David is now a productive adult, and happy. When I questioned him about his life he said, "I try to stay in a positive mood. . . . And I usually succeed" (personal communication, 2020). Plasticity has been evident in David's life again and again.

His family loved and nurtured him (consulting the Kentucky School for the Blind when he was a few months old). Educators taught him: He attended three preschools, each with a specialty (for children with cerebral palsy, intellectual disability, and blindness), and then public kindergarten at age 6.

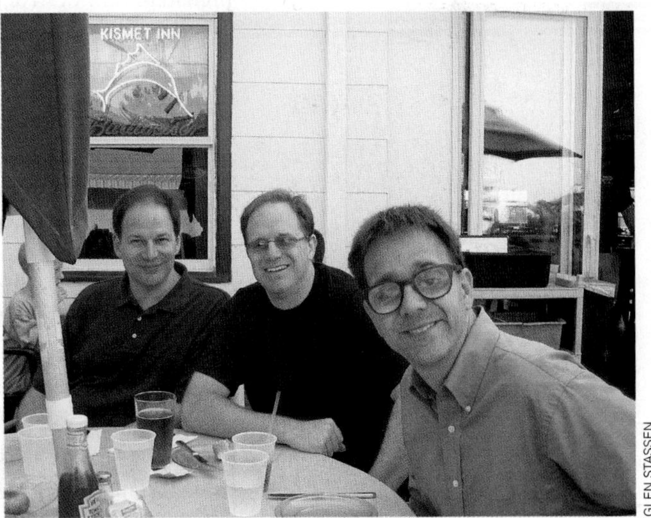

GLEN STASSEN

My Brother's Children Michael, Bill, and David (left to right) are adults now, with quite different personalities, abilities, numbers of offspring (4, 2, and none), and contexts (in Massachusetts, Pennsylvania, and California). Yet despite genes, prenatal life, and contexts, I see the shared influence of Glen and Dot, my brother and sister-in-law—evident here in their similar, friendly smiles.

TABLE 1.3 Four Characteristics of Development

Characteristic	Application in David's Story
Multi-directional. Change occurs in every direction, not always in a straight line. Gains and losses, predictable growth, and unexpected transformations are evident.	David's development seemed static (or even regressive, as when early surgery destroyed one eye), but then it accelerated each time he entered a new school or college.
Multi-contextual. Human lives are embedded in many contexts, including historical conditions, economic constraints, and family patterns.	The high SES of David's family made it possible for him to receive daily medical and educational care. His two older brothers protected him.
Multi-cultural. Many cultures — not just between nations but also within them — affect how people develop.	In Appalachian regions, like the one in which David lived, the culture is more collectivistic and therefore supportive of all members of the community.
Plastic. Every individual, and every trait within each individual, can be altered at any point in the life span. Change is ongoing, although it is neither random nor easy.	David's measured IQ changed from about 40 (severely intellectually disabled) to about 130 (far above average), and his physical disabilities became less crippling as he matured.

David's innate challenges and strengths were molded by his family and teachers, evidence of plasticity. By age 10, David had skipped a year of school and was a fifth-grader, reading at the eleventh-grade level with a magnifying glass. For David as well as many other people with visual problems, plasticity allows hearing to advance (Battal et al., 2020). David learned a second and a third language and joined the church choir.

Now, in adulthood, David's listening skills continue to be impressive. He once told me:

> I am generally quite happy, but secretly a little happier lately, especially since November, because I have been consistently getting a pretty good vibrato when I am singing, not only by myself but also in congregational hymns in church. [*I asked, what is vibrato? David answered*] When a note bounces up and down within a quartertone either way of concert pitch, optimally between 5.5 and 8.2 times per second.

Plasticity does not undo a person's genes, childhood, or permanent damage. The prenatal brain destruction remains, and David, age 53, still lives with his mother. But his temperament, past learning, and current abilities continue to keep him functioning and happy. When his father died in 2014, David comforted the rest of us (he said, "Dad is in a better place").

I have witnessed David develop strengths, as well as cope with lifelong impairment. All four of the characteristics of the life-span perspective are evident in David's life, as summarized in Table 1.3. All four are probably evident in every life.

what have you learned?

1. What aspects of development show continuity?
2. What is the difference between a critical period and a sensitive period?
3. Why is it useful to know when sensitive periods occur?
4. What did Bronfenbrenner emphasize in his ecological-systems approach?
5. What are some of the social contexts of life?
6. How does cohort differ from age group?
7. What factors comprise a person's SES?
8. How are culture, race, and ethnicity distinct from each other?
9. How is human development plastic?

Theories of Human Development

As you read earlier in this chapter, the scientific method begins with observations, questions, and theories (Step 1). That leads to hypotheses that can be tested (Step 2). A *theory* is a comprehensive and organized explanation of many phenomena; a *hypothesis* is more limited and may be proven false. Theories are general, and they are useful as a starting point; hypotheses are specific, a step in the scientific method.

Theories sharpen perceptions and organize the thousands of behaviors we observe every day. Each **developmental theory** is a systematic statement of principles and generalizations, providing a framework for understanding how and why people change over the life span.

developmental theory A group of ideas, assumptions, and generalizations about human growth. A developmental theory provides a framework to interpret growth and change.

psychoanalytic theory A theory of human development that contends that irrational, unconscious drives and motives underlie human behavior.

Imagine building a house from a heap of lumber, nails, and other materials. Without a plan and workers, the heap cannot become a home. Likewise, observations of human development are raw materials, but theories put them together. As Kurt Lewin (1945) once quipped, "Nothing is as practical as a good theory."

Dozens of theories appear throughout this text. Here we introduce four groups of theories that are useful regarding development over the life span.

Psychoanalytic and Psychodynamic Theories

Hundreds of theories of human development are called *psychodynamic*, which stress the power of a person's past experiences and emotions to shape their current thoughts and actions. The first cluster of psychodynamic theories are called *psychoanalytic*.

FREUD

Inner drives and motives are the foundation of **psychoanalytic theory**, as developed by Sigmund Freud (1856–1939). According to Freud, development in the first six years affects personality, impulses, and emotions lifelong.

That early development occurs in three stages, each characterized by sexual pleasure centered on a particular part of the body. Infants experience the *oral stage* because their erotic body part is the mouth, followed by the *anal stage* in early childhood, with the focus on the anus. In the preschool years (the *phallic stage*), the penis becomes a source of pride and fear for boys and a reason for sadness and envy for girls.

Then, in middle childhood comes *latency*, a quiet period that ends with a fourth stage, the *genital stage*, at puberty. Freud thought that the genital stage continued throughout adulthood, which makes him the most famous theorist who thought that development stopped after puberty (see Table 1.4).

Freud maintained that at each stage, sensual satisfaction (from the mouth, anus, or genitals) is linked to developmental needs, challenges, and conflicts. How people experience and resolve these conflicts — especially those related to weaning (oral), toilet training (anal), male roles (phallic), and sexual pleasure (genital) — determines personality because "the early stages provide the foundation for adult behavior" (Salkind, 2004, p. 125).

AKG/PHOTO RESEARCHERS

Freud at Work In addition to being the world's first psychoanalyst, Sigmund Freud was a prolific writer. His many papers and case histories, primarily descriptions of his patients' symptoms and sexual urges, helped make the psychoanalytic perspective a dominant force for much of the twentieth century.

Some of Freud's ideas are now accepted by most psychologists, among them that people use repression and rationalization to avoid thoughts they do not want to reach conscious awareness. Some of his ideas (erotic stages of childhood, mothers as the first love object) are controversial. But some are considered wrong. For example, developmentalists now know that adults change lifelong.

TABLE 1.4 Comparison of Freud's Psychoanalytic and Erikson's Psychosocial Stages

Approximate Age	Freud (psychosexual)	Erikson (psychosocial)
Birth to 1 year	*Oral Stage* The lips, tongue, and gums are the focus of pleasurable sensations in the baby's body, and sucking and feeding are the most stimulating activities.	*Trust vs. Mistrust* Babies either trust that others will satisfy their basic needs, including nourishment, warmth, cleanliness, and physical contact, **or** develop mistrust about the care of others.
1–3 years	*Anal Stage* The anus is the focus of pleasurable sensations in the baby's body, and toilet training is the most important activity.	*Autonomy vs. Shame and Doubt* Children either become self-sufficient in many activities, including toileting, feeding, walking, exploring, and talking, **or** doubt their own abilities.
3–6 years	*Phallic Stage* The phallus (the Latin word for "penis") is the most important body part, and pleasure is derived from genital stimulation. Boys are proud of their penises; girls wonder why they don't have them.	*Initiative vs. Guilt* Children either try to undertake many adultlike activities **or** internalize the limits and prohibitions set by parents. They feel either adventurous **or** guilty.
6–11 years	*Latency* Not really a stage, latency is an interlude. Sexual needs are quiet; psychic energy flows into sports, schoolwork, and friendship.	*Industry vs. Inferiority* Children busily practice and then master new skills **or** feel inferior, unable to do anything well.
Adolescence	*Genital Stage* The genitals are the focus of pleasurable sensations, and the young person seeks sexual stimulation and satisfaction in heterosexual relationships.	*Identity vs. Role Confusion* Adolescents ask themselves "Who am I?" They establish sexual, political, religious, and vocational identities **or** are confused about their roles.
Adulthood	Freud believed that the genital stage lasts throughout adulthood. He also said that the goal of a healthy life is "to love and to work."	*Intimacy vs. Isolation* Young adults seek companionship and love **or** become isolated from others, fearing rejection. *Generativity vs. Stagnation* Middle-aged adults contribute to future generations through work, creative activities, and parenthood **or** they stagnate. *Integrity vs. Despair* Older adults try to make sense of their lives, either seeing life as a meaningful whole **or** despairing at goals never reached.

TED STRESHINSKY/THE LIFE IMAGES COLLECTION/GETTY IMAGES

A Legendary Couple In his first 30 years, Erikson never fit into a particular local community, since he frequently changed nations, schools, and professions. Then he met Joan. In their first five decades of marriage, they raised a family and wrote several books. If Erikson had published his theory at age 73 (when this photograph was taken) instead of in his 40s, would he still have described life as a series of crises?

ERIKSON'S THEORY

Many of Freud's followers developed theories themselves. Theories that emphasize the power of unconscious emotional conflicts to influence adult behavior (a basic psychoanalytic idea) are called *psychodynamic* (Kealy & Ogrodniczuk, 2019). The most influential in human development was Erik Erikson (1902–1994), who described eight psychosocial stages, each characterized by a challenging crisis (summarized in Table 1.4).

Although Erikson's first five stages build on Freud's theory, he added three adult stages, perhaps because of his own experience. He was a wandering artist in Italy, a teacher in Austria, and a Harvard professor in the United States.

Erikson named two polarities at each stage (which is why the word *versus* is used in each), but he recognized that many outcomes between these opposites are possible (Erikson, 1993a). For most people, development at each stage leads to neither extreme.

For instance, the generativity-versus-stagnation stage of adulthood rarely involves a person who is totally stagnant—no children, no work, no creativity. Instead, most adults are somewhat stagnant and somewhat generative. As the dynamic-systems concept describes it, the balance between stuck and productive may shift year by year.

Erikson, like Freud, believed that adult problems echo childhood conflicts. For example, an adult who cannot form a secure, close relationship (intimacy versus isolation) may not have resolved the crisis of infancy (trust versus mistrust).

However, Erikson's stages differ significantly from Freud's in that they emphasize family and culture, not sexual urges. He called his theory *psychosocial*, partly to stress the power of the social environment.

◆◆ Especially for Teachers Your kindergartners are talkative and always moving. They almost never sit quietly and listen to you. What would Erik Erikson recommend? (see response, page 35)

Behaviorism

The second influential theory, **behaviorism**, "began with a healthy skepticism about introspection" in direct opposition to the psychoanalytic emphasis on unconscious, hidden urges (differences are described in Table 1.5) (Staddon, 2014). Behaviorists emphasize nurture, including the social context and culture but especially the immediate responses from other people to whatever a person does.

behaviorism A theory of human development that studies observable actions. Behaviorism is also called *learning theory* because it describes how people learn to do what they do.

Behaviorists believe that people at every age, from newborn to centenarian, learn how to think and act, influenced by the responses of other people, and the constraints of the body and the environment. Every behavior—from reading a book to robbing a bank, from saying "Good morning" to a stranger to saying "I love you" to a spouse—follows laws of behavior, according to this theory. Every action is learned, step-by-step.

CLASSICAL CONDITIONING

More than a century ago, Ivan Pavlov (1849–1936), a Russian medical doctor born in poverty who had won a Nobel Prize for his work on digestion, noticed something in his experimental dogs that awakened his curiosity (Step 1 of the scientific method) (Todes, 2014). The dogs drooled not only when they saw and smelled food, but also when they heard the footsteps of the attendants who brought the food.

This observation led Pavlov to hypotheses and experiments in which he conditioned dogs to salivate when they heard a specific noise (Steps 2 and 3). Pavlov began by sounding a tone just before presenting food. After a number of repetitions of the tone-then-food sequence, dogs began salivating at the sound, even when there was no food.

This simple experiment demonstrated *classical conditioning*, when a living creature learns to associate a neutral stimulus (the sound) with a meaningful stimulus (the food), gradually reacting to the neutral stimulus in the same way as to the meaningful one (Step 4). The fact that Pavlov published (Step 5) in Russian is one reason his conclusions took decades to reach the United States (Todes, 2014).

A Contemporary of Freud Ivan Pavlov was a physiologist who received the Nobel Prize in 1904 for his research on digestive processes. It was this line of study that led to his discovery of classical conditioning, when his research on dog saliva led to insight about learning.

◆◆ OBSERVATION QUIZ How is Pavlov similar to Freud in appearance, and how do both look different from the other theorists pictured? (see answer, page 35) ↑

TABLE 1.5 Three Types of Learning

Behaviorism is also called *learning theory* because it emphasizes the learning process, as shown here.

Type of Learning	Learning Process	Result
Classical Conditioning	Learning occurs through association.	Neutral stimulus becomes conditioned response.
Operant Conditioning	Learning occurs through reinforcement and punishment.	Weak or rare responses become strong and frequent — or, with punishment, unwanted responses become extinct.
Social Learning	Learning occurs through modeling what others do.	Observed behaviors become copied behaviors.

AP PHOTO

Rats, Pigeons, and People
B. F. Skinner is best known for his experiments with rats and pigeons, but he also applied his knowledge to human behavior. For his daughter, he designed a glass-enclosed crib in which temperature, humidity, and perceptual stimulation could be controlled to make her time in the crib enjoyable and educational. He encouraged her first attempts to talk by smiling and responding with words, affection, or other positive reinforcement.

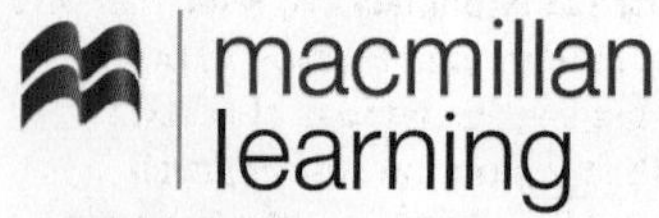

VIDEO ACTIVITY: Modeling: Learning by Observation features the original footage of Albert Bandura's famous experiment.

operant conditioning
The learning process that reinforces or punishes behavior. (Also called *instrumental conditioning.*)

reinforcement
In behaviorism, the positive experience that follows a behavior, making it likely that the behavior will occur again.

social learning theory
A theory that emphasizes the influence of other people. Even without reinforcement, people learn via role models. (Also called *observational learning.*)

THINK CRITICALLY: Is your speech, hairstyle, or choice of shoes similar to those of your peers, or someone famous? Why?

OPERANT CONDITIONING

The most influential North American behaviorist, B. F. Skinner (1904–1990), was inspired by Pavlov (Skinner, 1953). Skinner agreed that classical conditioning explains some behavior. Then he went further, experimenting to demonstrate another type of conditioning.

In **operant conditioning** (also called *instrumental conditioning*), animals (including humans) perform some action and then a response occurs. If the response is useful or pleasurable, the animal is likely to repeat the action; if the response is painful or discouraging, then repetition is unlikely. In both cases, the animal has been conditioned. Thus, responses are crucial; that is how learning occurs.

Pleasant consequences are sometimes called *rewards*, and unpleasant consequences are sometimes called *punishments*. Behaviorists hesitate to use those words, however, because what people think of as punishment can actually be a reward, and vice versa.

For example, how should a parent punish a child? Withholding dessert? Spanking? Not letting the child play? Speaking harshly? If a child hates that dessert, being deprived of it is actually a reward, not a punishment. Another child might not mind a spanking, especially if he or she craves parental attention. For that child, the intended punishment (spanking) is actually a reward (attention).

Any consequence that follows a behavior and makes the person (or animal) likely to repeat that behavior is called a **reinforcement**, *not* a reward. Once a behavior has been conditioned, humans and other creatures will repeat it even if reinforcement occurs only occasionally.

Almost all daily behavior, from combing your hair to joking with friends, is a result of past operant conditioning, according to behaviorists. Likewise, things people fear, from giving a speech to eating raw fish, are avoided because of past unpleasant consequences.

Not only do parents reinforce certain ideas; cultures do, too. Japanese parents threaten to punish their children by refusing to let them come home; American parents threaten the opposite, grounding, which is to make the children stay home (Bornstein, 2017). These strategies depend on past learning that made opposite experiences reinforcing: Most Japanese youth want to be with the parents; most U.S. youth prefer to be with friends. (Of course, a multi-cultural view reminds us that there are many exceptions to this.)

According to behaviorism, people are never too old to learn. If an adult fears public speaking (a common phobia), then repeated reinforcement for talking (as a professor praising a student's question) could lead to speeches before an audience.

SOCIAL LEARNING

A major extension of behaviorism is **social learning theory**, first described by Albert Bandura (b. 1925). This theory notes that because humans are social beings, they learn from observing others, even without personal reinforcement (Bandura, 1986, 1997).

For example, children who witness domestic violence are influenced by it, even when they personally do not experience it. As differential susceptibility and multi-contextualism would predict, the particular lesson learned depends on each individual's genes and experiences. If the father of three boys often hits their mother, one son might admire the abuser, another might try to protect the victim, and the third might disappear when fighting begins.

As adults, past social learning leads the first man to slap his wife, the second to be especially kind, and the third to be more like a dandelion than an orchid, forgetting the past. If you know a family with many grown siblings, do they all agree on the kind of child rearing they experienced? Probably not. According to social learning, each has a particular view of their parents, and that affects them.

cognitive theory
A theory of human development that focuses on how people think. According to this theory, our thoughts shape our attitudes, beliefs, and behaviors.

Cognitive Theory

In **cognitive theory**, each person's ideas and beliefs are crucial. This theory has dominated psychology since about 1980 and has branched into many versions. The word *cognitive* refers not just to thinking but also to attitudes, beliefs, and assumptions. The way that people think, as well as the thoughts they keep in their minds, has a major influence on their emotions and actions.

PIAGET'S STAGES

The most famous cognitive theorist was Jean Piaget (1896–1980), who began by observing his own three infants and later studied thousands of older children (Inhelder & Piaget, 1958/2013b). Unlike other scientists of the early twentieth century, Piaget realized that babies are curious and thoughtful, trying to understand their experiences.

From this work, Piaget developed his central thesis: How people think (not just what they know) changes with maturation and experience, and then their thinking influences not only how they think but also what they do.

Piaget maintained that cognitive development occurs in four major age-related periods, or stages: *sensorimotor, preoperational, concrete operational*, and *formal operational* (see Table 1.6). Each period is characterized by particular mental processes: Infants think via their senses; preschoolers have language but not logic; school-age children have simple logic; adolescents and adults can use formal, abstract logic (Inhelder & Piaget, 1958/2013b; Piaget, 1952/2011).

Intellectual advancement occurs because humans seek *cognitive equilibrium*, that is, a state of mental balance. An easy way to achieve this balance (called *assimilation*) is to interpret new experiences through the lens of preexisting ideas.

© FARRELL GREHAN/CORBIS

Would You Talk to This Man?
Children loved talking to Jean Piaget, and he learned by listening carefully—especially to their incorrect explanations, which no one had paid much attention to before. All his life, Piaget was absorbed with studying the way children think. He called himself a "genetic epistemologist"—one who studies how children gain knowledge about the world as they grow.

TABLE 1.6 Piaget's Periods of Cognitive Development

	Name of Period	Characteristics of the Period	Major Gains During the Period
Birth to 2 years	Sensorimotor	Infants use senses and motor abilities to understand the world. Learning is active, without reflection.	Infants learn that objects still exist when out of sight (*object permanence*) and begin to think through mental actions. (The sensorimotor period is discussed further in Chapter 3.)
2–6 years	Preoperational	Children think symbolically, with language, yet children are *egocentric*, perceiving from their own perspective.	The imagination flourishes, and language becomes a significant means of self-expression and social influence. (The preoperational period is discussed further in Chapter 5.)
6–11 years	Concrete operational	Children understand and apply logic. Thinking is limited by direct experience.	By applying logic, children grasp concepts of conservation, number, classification, and many other scientific ideas. (The concrete-operational period is discussed further in Chapter 7.)
12 years through adulthood	Formal operational	Adolescents and adults use abstract and hypothetical concepts. They can use analysis, not only emotion.	Ethics, politics, and social and moral issues become fascinating as adolescents and adults use abstract, theoretical reasoning. (The formal-operational period is discussed further in Chapter 9.)

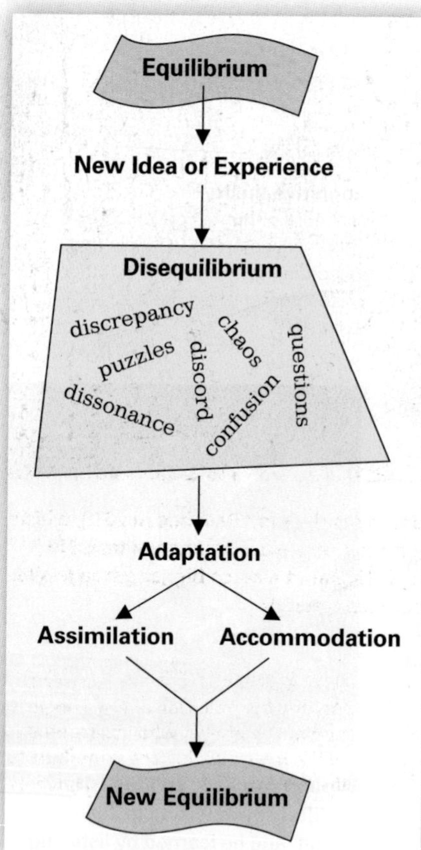

FIGURE 1.5 Challenge Me Most of us, most of the time, prefer the comfort of our conventional conclusions. According to Piaget, however, when new ideas disturb our thinking, we have an opportunity to expand our cognition with a broader and deeper understanding.

evolutionary theory
When used in human development, the idea that many current human emotions and impulses are a legacy from thousands of years ago.

For example, infants discover that new objects can be grasped in the same way as familiar ones; adolescents explain the day's headlines as evidence that supports their existing worldviews; older adults speak fondly of the good old days as embodying values that should endure.

Sometimes, however, a new experience is jarring and incomprehensible. That causes disequilibrium. As Figure 1.5 illustrates, disequilibrium leads to cognitive growth because it forces people to reassess their old concepts (called *accommodation*) to include the new information. Learning occurs when new information requires more analysis (Brown et al., 2014).

Like Freud, Piaget thought that the adolescent stage continued lifelong. That is no longer what experts think: A *postformal* stage might occur, as you will read in Chapter 11. The experiences of adulthood, especially dramatic ones such as becoming a parent or surviving a serious illness, might change the way a person thinks.

INFORMATION PROCESSING

Another influential cognitive theory, called *information processing*, is not a stage theory but rather provides a detailed description of the steps of cognition, focusing on what happens in the brain to cause intellectual growth.

Many researchers, not just those influenced by information-processing theory, now think that some of Piaget's conclusions were mistaken. However, every developmentalist appreciates his basic insight: Thoughts influence emotions and actions. This is sometimes called a *constructive* view of human cognition, because people of all ages build (construct) their understanding of themselves and their world, combining their experiences and their interpretations.

Evolutionary Theory

Charles Darwin's basic ideas were first published over 150 years ago (Darwin, 1859), but serious research on human development inspired by **evolutionary theory** is quite recent. According to evolution, every species strives to survive and reproduce. That is true for humans, too. Consequently, many human impulses, needs, and behaviors evolved to help people live and thrive over the past 200,000 years (Konner, 2010).

To understand contemporary human development, this theory contends, we must consider what humans needed long ago. The fears, impulses, and aspirations that protected the human species were encoded into human genes, and thus are in our genes today.

For example, why are many people afraid when they see a snake, but almost no one is frightened when they see a parked car? Snakes cause less than one U.S. death in a million, but cars cause more than one death in a hundred, so we should fear cars much more than snakes. Evolutionary theory has an answer: Our fear instinct evolved to protect life millennia ago.

Thus, fears have not caught up to modern life: The latest, fastest automobile is coveted by many, even though it may be a death trap. If everyone always drove slowly (under 30 miles an hour), thousands of lives would be saved. But I, and many other drivers, exceed speed limits, watch for police cars, and prefer not to visit the snakes at the zoo.

◆◆ Especially for Teachers and Counselors of Teenagers
Teen pregnancy is disruptive to adolescent education, family life, and sometimes even health. According to evolutionary theory, what can be done about this? (see response, page 35)

Evolutionary theory notes that, although humans inherited irrational fears (snakes, blood, thunder), humans also inherited wonderful impulses, such as

cooperation, spirituality, and compassion. People survived because they cared for one another (Rand & Nowak, 2016). Humanity benefited from protective parental instincts that allow mother and fathers to care for children for decades and allow the human brain to grow much more than the brains of other primates (Konner, 2010).

Evolutionary theory in developmental psychology has intriguing explanations for many phenomena: women's nausea in pregnancy, 1-year-olds' attachment to their parents, adolescent rebellion, male–female differences in emerging adults' sexual behavior, parents' investment in their children, and the diseases of late adulthood.

All of these interpretations are controversial. Evolutionary explanations for male–female differences are particularly hotly disputed (Ellemers, 2018). Nonetheless, this theory provides many hypotheses to be explored.

SANJAY KANOJIA/AFP/GETTY IMAGES

A Sacred River? This is the Ganges river at Allahabad in 2013, which the Indian government is working to clean — a monumental task. No nation is working to rid the Pacific Ocean of a much bigger garbage site. What would evolutionary theory recommend?

◆◆ OBSERVATION QUIZ
Beyond the pollution of the Ganges by humans' garbage, what characteristics of the river, visible here, contribute to the pollution? (see answer, page 35) ↑

what have you learned?

1. What is the role of the unconscious in psychoanalytic theory?
2. How do Erikson's stages differ from Freud's?
3. How is behaviorism a reaction to psychoanalytic theory?
4. How do classical and operant conditioning differ?
5. What is the basic idea of cognitive theory?
6. What are the criticisms of Piaget's theory?
7. What is the emphasis of information processing?
8. How does evolutionary theory apply to human development?

Doing Science

As you already read, the study of human development is a science. Developmentalists are astonished when anyone says they do not "believe" in science, because "science is not a belief system; it is, instead, a very special way of learning about the true nature of the observable world" (Alberts, 2017, p. 1353).

That "special way" requires evidence, with three basic research designs and three strategies to study change over time. Each of these six can provide insight, and each has limitations. Knowing the strengths and weaknesses of each gets us closer to the goal expressed on page 3, "to understand how and why people—all kinds of people, everywhere, of every age—change over time."

Three Methods of Science

Every scientist follows the scientific method, moving from curiosity (Step 1) to conclusions (Step 4). But those steps in between are the pivot. With all the social sciences, three basic methods are used to understand people.

HISTORICAL HIGHLIGHTS OF DEVELOPMENTAL SCIENCE

As evident throughout this textbook, much more research and appreciation of the brain, social context, and the non-Western world has expanded our understanding of human development in the 21st century. This timeline lists a few highlights of the past.

200,000–50,000 BCE With their large brains, long period of child development, and extensive social and family support, early humans were able to sustain life and raise children more effectively than other primates.

c. 400 BCE In ancient Greece, ideas about children from philosophers like Plato (c. 428–348 BCE) and Aristotle (384–322 BCE) influenced further thoughts about children. Plato believed children were born with knowledge. Aristotle believed children learn from experience.

1650–1800 European philosophers like John Locke (1632–1704) and Jean Jacques Rousseau (1712–1778) debate whether children are born as "blank slates" and how much control parents should take in raising them.

1797 First European vaccination: Edward Jenner (1749–1823) publicizes smallpox inoculation, building on vaccination against smallpox in Asia, the Middle East, and Africa.

1750–1850 Beginning of Western laws regulating child labor and protecting the rights of children.

1879 First experimental psychology laboratory established in Leipzig, Germany.

1885 Sigmund Freud (1856–1939) publishes *Studies on Hysteria*, one of the first works establishing the importance of the subconscious and marking the beginning of the theories of psychoanalytic theory.

1895 Ivan Pavlov (1849–1936) begins research on dogs' salivation response.

1905 Max Weber (1864–1920), the founder of sociology, writes *The Protestant Ethic and the Spirit of Capitalism*, about human values and adult work.

1905 Alfred Binet's (1857–1911) intelligence test published.

1907 Maria Montessori (1870–1952) opens her first school in Rome.

1913 John B. Watson (1878–1958) publishes *Psychology As the Behaviorist Views It.*

50,000 BCE — 400 BCE — 0 — 500 — 1000 — 1500 — 1650 — 1700 — 1750

140 BCE In China, imperial examinations are one of the first times cognitive testing is used on young people.

500–1500 During the Middle Ages in Europe, many adults believed that children were miniature adults.

1100–1200 First universities founded in Europe. Young people pay to be educated together.

1837 First kindergarten opens in Germany, part of a movement to teach young children before they entered the primary school system.

1859 Charles Darwin (1809–1882) publishes *On the Origin of Species*, sparking debates about what is genetic and what is environmental.

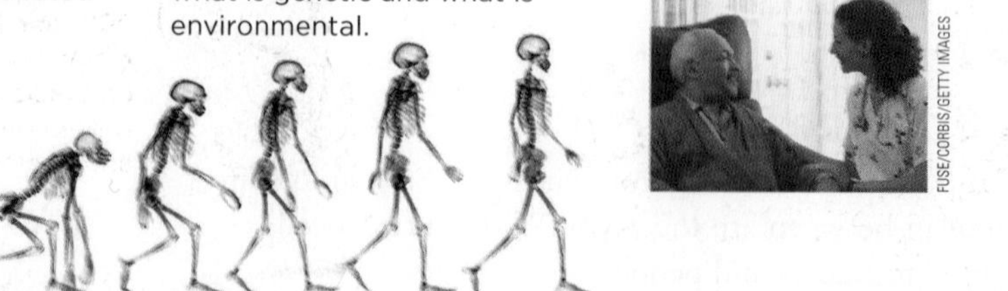

1900 Compulsory schooling for children is established for most children in the United States and Europe.

1903 The term "gerontology," the branch of developmental science devoted to studying aging, first coined.

1920 Lev Vygotsky (1896–1934) develops sociocultural theory in the former Soviet Union.

1923 Jean Piaget (1896–1980) publishes *The Language and Thought of the Child.*

1933 Society for Research on Child Development, the preeminent organization for research on child development, founded.

1939 Mamie (1917–1983) and Kenneth Clark (1914–2005) receive their research grants to study race in early childhood.

1943 Abraham Maslow (1908–1970) publishes *A Theory of Human Motivation*, establishing the hierarchy of needs.

1950 Erik Erikson (1902–1994) expands on Freud's theory to include social aspects of personality development with the publication of *Childhood and Society*.

1951 John Bowlby (1907–1990) publishes *Maternal Care and Mental Health*, one of his first works on the importance of parent-child attachment.

1953 Publication of the first papers describing DNA, our genetic blueprint.

1959 Harry Harlow (1905–1981) publishes *Love in Infant Monkeys*, describing his research on attachment in rhesus monkeys.

1961 The morning sickness drug thalidomide is banned after children are born with serious birth defects, calling attention to the problem of teratogens during pregnancy.

1961 Alfred Bandura (b. 1925) conducts the Bobo Doll experiments, leading to the development of social learning theory.

1979 Urie Bronfenbrenner (1917–2005) publishes his work on ecological systems theory.

1986 John Gottman (b. 1942) founded the "Love Lab" at the University of Washington to study what makes relationships work.

1987 Carolyn Rovee-Collier (1942–2014) shows that even young infants can remember in her classic mobile experiments.

1990–Present New brain imaging technology allows pinpointing of brain areas involved in everything from executive function to Alzheimer's disease.

1994 Steven Pinker (b. 1954) publishes *The Language Instinct*, focusing attention on the interaction between neuroscience and behavior.

1996 Giacomo Rizzolatti publishes his discovery of mirror neurons.

2000 Jeffrey Arnett conceptualizes emerging adulthood.

2003 Mapping of the human genome is completed.

2013 DSM-5, which emphasizes the role of context in understanding mental health problems, is published.

1800 | 1850 | 1900 | 1950 | 2000

1953 B.F. Skinner (1904–1990) conducts experiments on rats and establishes operant conditioning.

1955 Emmy Werner (1929–2017) begins her Kauai study, which focuses on the power of resilience.

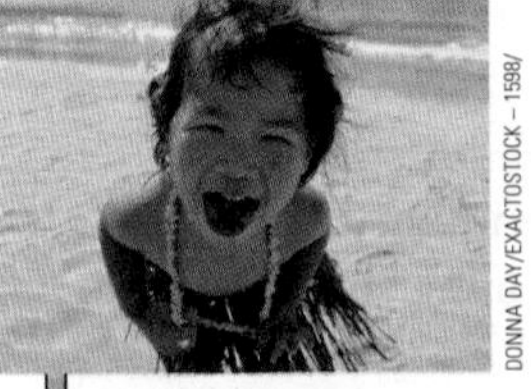

1956 K. Warner Schaie's (b. 1928) Seattle Longitudinal Study of Adult Intelligence begins.

1965 Head Start, an early childhood education program, launched in the United States.

1965 Mary Ainsworth (1913–1999) starts using the "Strange Situation" to measure attachment.

1966 Diana Baumrind (1927–2018) publishes her first work on parenting styles.

1972 Beginning of the Dunedin, New Zealand, study—one of the first longitudinal studies to include genetic markers.

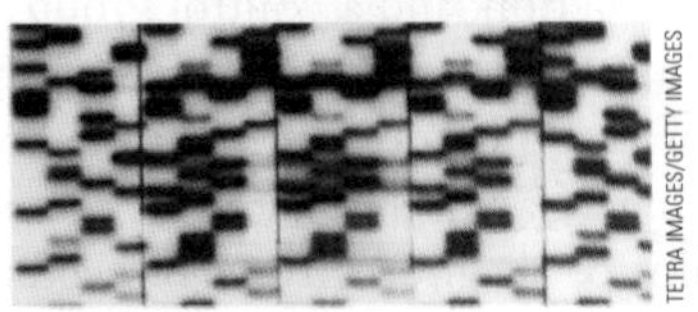

1990 Barbara Rogoff (b. 1950) publishes *Apprenticeship in Thinking*, making developmentalists more aware of the significance of culture and context. Rogoff provided new insights and appreciation of child-rearing in Latin America.

1993 Howard Gardner (b. 1943) publishes *Multiple Intelligences*, a major new understanding of the diversity of human intellectual abilities. Gardner has since revised and expanded his ideas in many ways.

2013 U.S. President Barack Obama announces his administration's Brain Research through Advancing Innovative Neurotechnologies (BRAIN) Initiative.

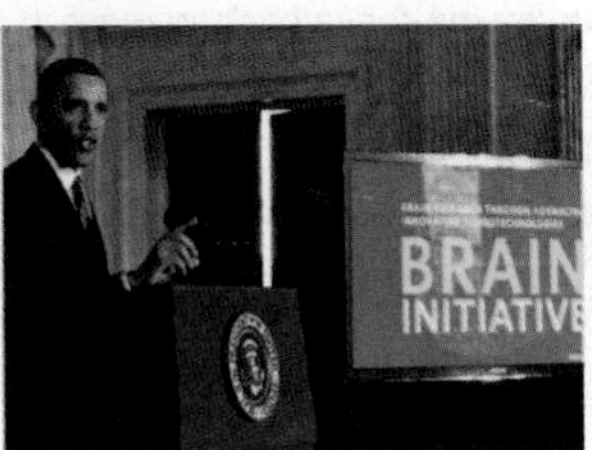

2017 Several U.S. cities expand public funding for early-childhood education (universal pre-K).

2021 and beyond Onward. Many more discoveries are chronicled in this book, as researchers continue to test and explore.

OBSERVATION

scientific observation
Watching and recording participants' behavior in a systematic and objective manner—in a natural setting, in a laboratory, or in searches of archival data.

Scientific observation requires researchers to record behavior systematically and objectively. Observations can occur in a naturalistic setting such as a home, or in a laboratory, where scientists observe what people do.

Observation can also use data that reflect what people have already done, such as the frequency of words used by all the people on Twitter, or the locations of all the people using cell phones, or the official birth statistics for a particular place. All three kinds of observation—in natural settings, in laboratories, and in official statistics—evoke hypotheses, providing questions to be studied further.

VIDEO: Natural Experiments in Psychology explores a longitudinal study in which researchers observed a social phenomenon as it was occurring among the Eastern Band of Cherokee Indians in western North Carolina.

For example, some researchers investigated the connection between belonging to a religious group and spending money on groceries (Kurt et al., 2018). They considered, county by county, what proportion of the people who lived in that place belonged to a religious group and then what the sales were per grocery store within each county. They found that counties with more religious people had lower grocery store sales.

Observations are intriguing, but they raise more questions than answers. Do religious people really spend less money on groceries? Since people who are older and poorer also tend to be more religious, did age or SES influence grocery shopping?

The researchers thought of this, and controlled for the average age and income in the counties, but that still doesn't prove that being religious *causes* less grocery spending. Maybe religious people tend to live in places with more, but smaller, grocery stores, so the underlying variable is population density, not religion.

EXPERIMENTS

experiment
A research method in which the researcher adds one variable (called the independent variable) and then observes the effect on another variable (called the dependent variable) in order to learn if the independent variable causes change in the dependent variable.

independent variable
In an experiment, the variable that is added by the researcher to see if it affects the dependent variable.

dependent variable
In an experiment, the variable that may change as a result of the independent variable (whatever new condition the experimenter adds). In other words, the dependent variable depends on the independent variable.

An **experiment** aims to establish causality. In the social sciences, experimenters typically impose a particular treatment on a group of participants or expose them to a specific condition and then note how they respond.

In technical terms, the experimenters manipulate an **independent variable**, which is the extra treatment or special condition (also called the *experimental variable*; a *variable* is anything that can vary). They note whether this independent variable affects whatever they are studying, called the **dependent variable** (which *depends* on the independent variable).

Thus, the independent variable is the new, special treatment; any change in the dependent variable is the result. The purpose of an experiment is to find out what causes what, that is, whether an independent variable affects the dependent variable.

A typical experiment (as diagrammed in Figure 1.6), has two groups of participants. One group, the *experimental group*, experiences the particular treatment or condition (the independent variable); the other group, the *comparison group* (also called the *control group*), does not.

Past studies have found that sometimes when people know that they are in an experiment that knowledge changes their behavior. For that reason, part of the research design may be to have another group experience something as well.

In the first pages of this chapter you already read an experiment that had an experimental group of kindergartners who had extensive music instruction, another group who had sports instruction, and a control group who had no special instruction. You can see why three groups were needed. If only the intensive music group was tested, it might seem as if the music affected the brain, but it could be that the maturation alone, or having an afterschool activity, caused advances in cognition.

In that study, the brains of all three groups showed the effects of maturation, as the 5-year-olds became 7-year-olds with more advanced neurological processing. In addition, both afterschool activities advanced cognition more than in children who were the control group. Though the music curriculum was best at affecting the brain, that experiment showed that other programs could help, too.

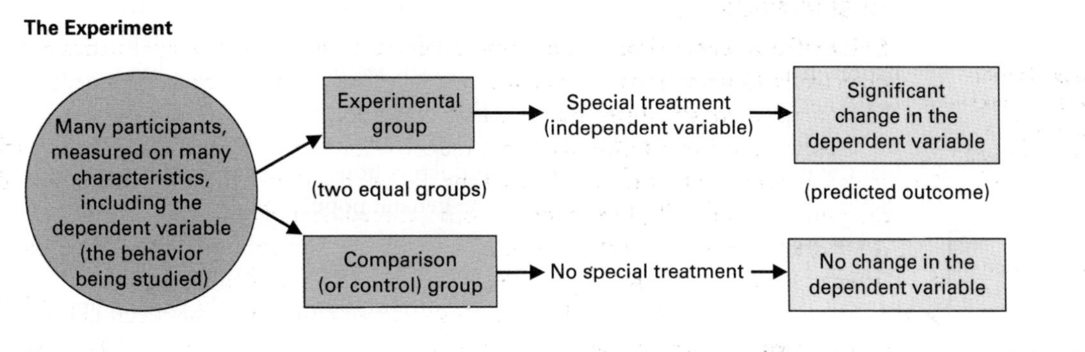

Procedure:

1. Divide participants into two groups that are matched on important characteristics, especially the behavior that is the dependent variable on which this study is focused.
2. Give special treatment, or intervention (the independent variable), to one group (the experimental group).
3. Compare the groups on the dependent variable. If they now differ, the cause of the difference was probably the independent variable.
4. Publish the results.

FIGURE 1.6 **How to Conduct an Experiment** The basic sequence diagrammed here applies to all experiments. Many additional features, especially the statistical measures listed in Table App.1 in the Appendix and various ways of reducing experimenter bias, affect whether publication occurs. (Scientific journals reject reports of experiments that were not rigorous in method and analysis.)

Likewise, you just read about an observational study that suggested that religion and grocery purchases were correlated. The researchers wondered if religious thoughts, not some other variable, caused the connection. Accordingly, they did an experiment (Kurt et al., 2018).

They divided 502 people who identified as religious (about a third each: Protestant, Catholic, other) into two groups. Both groups were asked to analyze the body language of a speaker of a video, but half saw a video designed to increase their religious thoughts, and half saw a neutral video. To be specific, the experimental group watched a speaker discussing God's presence, and the control group saw a speaker presenting tips on oil painting.

Then all 502 completed an imaginary grocery shopping trip. After making their selections, they were asked to imagine that, as they were about to pay, they saw a special issue of their favorite magazine. How much would they pay for it? Some in both groups said they wouldn't pay anything.

However, religious thoughts mattered. Those who had seen the oil painting video were willing to pay more than those who were reminded about the presence of God. The researchers concluded that religion really does restrain spending (Kurt et al., 2018).

As you remember from the scientific method, no single experiment is considered proof. Other interpretations are possible; replication is needed. But you can see that experiments provide more information about causes than observations can.

What Can You Learn? Scientists first establish what is, and then they try to change it. In one recent experiment, Deb Kelemen (shown here) established that few children under age 12 understand a central concept of evolution (natural selection). Then she showed an experimental group a picture book illustrating the idea. Success! The independent variable (the book) affected the dependent variable (the children's ideas), which confirmed Kelemen's hypothesis: Children can understand natural selection if instruction is tailored to their ability.

THE SURVEY

A third research method is the **survey**, in which information is collected from a large number of people by interview, questionnaire, or some other means. This is a quick, direct way to obtain data. Surveys keep people from assuming that everyone is like people we know. However, survey results can be misleading.

survey
A research method in which information is collected from a large number of people by interviews, written questionnaires, or some other means.

For example, a survey asked people's opinion of designated sites at which people can take drugs they have purchased elsewhere (Davis et al., 2018). Many European nations have such places: Medical professionals are nearby to save a life if someone overdoses, and counselors are available if people want to quit.

Such sites are illegal in most of the United States, because local authorities believe that the public is opposed. Public health doctors hope those authorities were wrong; that is why they presented a survey to the general population.

THINK CRITICALLY: What other titles would increase or decrease approval?

The survey described data on overdose deaths, and asked if life-saving sites should be legal. For half of the surveys, the title was "Overdose Prevention." Approval was 45 percent. The other half were titled "Safe Consumption." Only 29 percent approved (Davis et al., 2018).

For the public health advocates, these are encouraging results, in that they suggest that people do not have hardened positions. But this also illustrates a problem with every survey: As political pollsters know, how questions are asked influences the result.

Studying Development over the Life Span

In addition to conducting observations, experiments, and surveys, developmentalists must measure how people "change or remain the same over time." To capture that, scientists design cross-sectional, longitudinal, or cross-sequential studies.

"It's a one-year timer. It gives an added sense of urgency to my research grant."

AARON BACALL/CARTOON COLLECTIONS/CARTOONSTOCK

Not Long Enough For understanding the human life span, scientists wish for grants that are renewed for decades.

CROSS-SECTIONAL RESEARCH

The quickest and least expensive way to study developmental change is with **cross-sectional research**, which compares people of one age with similar people of another age. For example, when reading ability is compared between children who are 5, 8, and 11 years old, it seems that until third grade children are "learning to read," and then from age 8 onward they are "reading to learn."

Cross-sectional design seems simple. However, the people being compared may differ in several ways, not just age. One recent issue is the result of remote learning. Is it fair to compare reading in third-graders who lost a year of in-class instruction because of the COVID-19 pandemic with sixth-graders who had daily, in-person school until age 10? Age is not the only difference between these two populations.

cross-sectional research
A research design that compares people who differ in age but not in other important characteristics.

longitudinal research
A research design that follows the same individuals over time.

LONGITUDINAL RESEARCH

To help discover when age itself causes a developmental change, scientists undertake **longitudinal research**. They collect data repeatedly on the same individuals over time.

For example, very few children from low-SES families graduate from college. Why? Many people blame high school guidance counselors, or college admission practices, or university faculty, for this result.

Indeed, a longitudinal study of 790 infants born in Baltimore to low-income parents found that only 4 percent of them had graduated from college by age 28 (Alexander et al., 2014). It was fortunate that this study was longitudinal, because high schools and colleges did not need to shoulder the blame between them.

Instead, comparing the lives longitudinally of those 28-year-olds found that experiences before age 5 predicted who would graduate from college. Preschool education and friendly neighbors were more influential than high school! This has practical implications: If the goal is more low-income college graduates, then good preschools, free for every child, may be the best investment.

Unfortunately, longitudinal research has a major problem. The historical context sometimes changes rapidly. Because technology, culture, and politics alter life

experiences, data collected decades ago may be accurate for those individuals but not for the next generations.

For example, many recent substances might be harmful or beneficial, among them *phthalates* and *bisphenol A* (BPA) (chemicals used in manufacturing plastic containers), *hydrofracking* (a process used to get gas for fuel from rocks), *e-waste* (from old computers and cell phones), *chlorpyrifos* (an insecticide), and *electronic cigarettes* (vaping). Some nations and states ban or regulate each of these; others do not.

Longitudinal data that reveal which specific innovations might harm people years later are not yet possible. The more useful longitudinal studies trace experiences and conditions that continue to impact development in every generation, such as SES, family structure, or social networks (see A View from Science).

A VIEW FROM SCIENCE

Do You Need Friends?

Every research design has strengths as well as weaknesses. No single study is conclusive.

Accordingly, many scholars turn to *meta-analysis*, which combines the results of many studies. This avoids drawing conclusions from any one study, which might have too few participants, or some unknown bias.

Meta-analysis is especially useful in longitudinal research, because it is particularly difficult to follow a large number of people over many years. Thus, a meta-analysis can reveal significant trends when dozens of studies reveal something that no one study could prove alone. A meta-analysis "has become "widely" accepted as a standardized, less biased way to weigh the evidence" (de Vrieze, 2018, p. 1186).

In the best meta-analyses, the researchers explain exactly how they chose studies that are the grist for their analysis. Care is taken to find all relevant studies, published and unpublished, on a particular topic. Only those that are scientifically rigorous are included.

For instance, a meta-analysis on the effects of loneliness on heart and stroke deaths began with searching 16 electronic databases. Then the researchers asked experts if they knew any studies that had not been published (Valtorta et al., 2016).

They found thousands to look at more closely. They then eliminated the duplicates and those without careful design, control groups, and detailed data, and found 23 with reliable longitudinal results. The conclusion: lack of social connections increased heart disease by 29 percent and stroke by 31 percent (Valtorta et al., 2016). Thus, science tells us, not only to avoid high blood pressure and stop smoking, but to spend time with friends.

CROSS-SEQUENTIAL RESEARCH

Scientists have discovered a third strategy, combining cross-sectional and longitudinal research. This combination is called **cross-sequential research** (also referred to as *cohort-sequential* or *time-sequential research*). With this design, researchers study several groups of people of different ages (a cross-sectional approach), follow them over the years (a longitudinal approach), and then combine the results.

cross-sequential research
A hybrid research design that includes cross-sectional and longitudinal research. (Also called *cohort-sequential research* or *time-sequential research*.)

A cross-sequential design lets researchers compare, say, 16-year-olds with the same individuals at age 1, as well as with data for people who were 16 long ago, who are now ages 31, 46, and 61 (see Figure 1.7). Cross-sequential research is complicated, in recruitment and analysis, but it allows scientists to disentangle age and history.

The first well-known cross-sequential study (the *Seattle Longitudinal Study*) found that some intellectual abilities (vocabulary) increase even after age 60, whereas others (how quickly a person can process information and answer) start to decline at age 30 (Schaie, 2005/2013). This study also discovered that declines in adult math ability are more closely related to education than to age, something neither cross-sectional nor longitudinal research could reveal.

Especially for Future Researchers
What is the best method for collecting data? (see response, page 35)

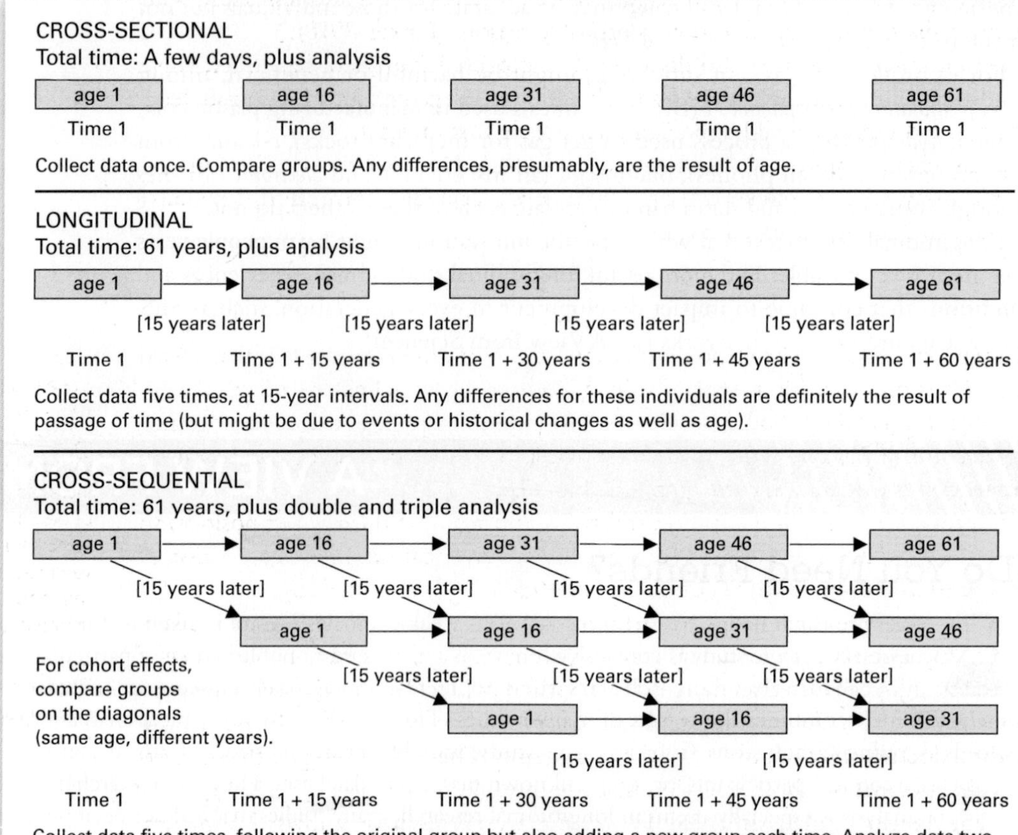

FIGURE 1.7 **Which Approach Is Best?** Cross-sequential research is the most time-consuming and complex, but it yields the best information. One reason that hundreds of scientists conduct research on the same topics, replicating one another's work, is to gain some advantages of cohort-sequential research without waiting for decades.

what have you learned?

1. Why does observation not prove "what causes what"?
2. Why do experimenters need a control (or comparison) group?
3. What are the strengths and weaknesses of the survey method?
4. Why would a scientist conduct a cross-sectional study?
5. Why would a scientist conduct a longitudinal study?
6. Why isn't all research cross-sequential?
7. When is a meta-analysis useful?

Cautions and Challenges from Science

The scientific method illustrates and illuminates human development as nothing else does. Facts, consequences, and possibilities have benefited people of all ages.

For example, thanks to science, infectious diseases in children, illiteracy in adolescents, and sexism and racism at every age are much less prevalent today than a

century ago. Early death—from accidents, war, or disease—is also less likely, with scientific discoveries and education as probable reasons (Pinker, 2018).

Developmentalists have also discovered unexpected sources of harm. Excessive weight gain in pregnancy, fuzzy baby blankets, video games, hospitalization, lead, asbestos, and vaping are all less benign than people first thought.

Thus, science improves lives and discovers hazards. However, science also can lead people astray. We now discuss three problems: misinterpreting correlation, depending on numbers, and ignoring ethics.

Correlation and Causation

Many people confuse correlation with causation. A **correlation** exists between two variables if one variable is more (or less) likely to occur when the other does. A correlation is *positive* if both variables tend to increase together or decrease together, *negative* if one variable tends to increase while the other decreases, and *zero* if no connection is evident. (Try the quiz in Table 1.7.)

correlation
Usually a number between +1.0 and −1.0 that indicates whether and how much two variables are related. Correlation indicates whether an increase in one variable will increase or decrease another variable. Correlation indicates only that two variables are somehow related, not that one variable causes the other to increase or decrease.

quantitative research
Research that provides data expressed with numbers, such as ranks or scales.

Expressed in numerical terms, correlations vary from +1.0 (the most positive) to −1.0 (the most negative). Correlations are almost never that extreme; a correlation of +0.3 or −0.3 is noteworthy; a correlation of +0.8 or −0.8 is astonishing.

Many correlations are unexpected; for instance, first-born children are more likely to develop asthma than are later-born children; teenage girls have higher rates of mental health problems than do teenage boys; and counties in the United States with more dentists have fewer obese adults. That last study controlled for the number of medical doctors and the poverty of the community. The authors suggest that dentists provide information about nutrition that improves health (Holzer et al., 2014).

That dentist explanation may be wrong. Every scientist knows the mantra: *Correlation is not causation*. Just because two variables are correlated does not mean that one causes the other—even if it seems logical that it does.

Correlations reveal *only* that the variables are connected somehow. Either one could cause the other (might dentists prefer to work where fewer people are obese?), or a third variable may cause the correlation (might dentists choose to live in regions that have safe hiking paths, lakes with lifeguards, and inexpensive and well-equipped gyms?).

TABLE 1.7 Quiz on Correlation

Two Variables	Positive, Negative, or Zero Correlation?	Why? (Third Variable)
1. Ice cream sales and murder rate	________	________
2. Reading ability and number of baby teeth	________	________
3. Sex of adult and their average number of offspring	________	________

For each of these three pairs of variables, indicate whether the correlation between them is positive, negative, or nonexistent. Then try to think of a third variable that might determine the direction of the correlation. The correct answers are on page 34.

Quantity and Quality

A second caution concerns how much scientists should rely on numerical data, which results in **quantitative research** (from the word *quantity*). Since quantities can be easily summarized, compared, charted, and replicated, many scientists prefer quantitative research. Quantitative data are easier to replicate, easier to compare across cultures, and less open to bias. A principal of a school might brag that the children learn math, but the test scores might disprove that boast.

qualitative research Research that considers individual qualities instead of quantities (numbers).

However, with numerical data, nuances and individuality are lost. Many developmental researchers thus turn to **qualitative research** (from the word *quality*)—asking open-ended questions, reporting answers in narrative (not numerical) form.

Qualitative researchers are "interested in understanding how people interpret their experiences, how they construct their worlds" (Merriam, 2009, p. 5). Qualitative research reflects cultural and contextual diversity. (See Opposing Perspectives.)

OPPOSING PERSPECTIVES

Measuring Education and Health

Those who want to assess education and health often have opposite opinions about how best to indicate development. On the one hand, students take many tests to indicate their mastery of material. The idea is that schools with low test scores should be closed or changed, and that students who do not meet certain standards should not move to the next grade (a practice derisively called *social promotion*) or earn a high school diploma. State and national governments favor test scores as an objective measure of learning.

The opposite perspective is that relying on test scores make educators focus only on facts, not values, attitudes, or creativity—all of which schools should develop. Indeed, some argue that a focus on numbers reduces true learning and undercut what is important about the human spirit (Muller, 2018).

The same problem is apparent in health. If doctors focus only on measurable phenomena, they may ignore the purpose of life. For example, is a person kept alive on a ventilator, unable to think or talk to people, really living? Data on heart rate, oxygen, and so on say yes, but, as the Epilogue discusses, this may be too narrow a definition of "living."

Some studies now use quantitative and qualitative measures, which provide richer, but also more verifiable, details (Morgan, 2018). For example, one study compared very old (over age 90) people and their children (age 51–75) (Scelzo et al., 2018). Quantitative research reported scores on various measures of physical health. Generally, the very old were in poorer physical shape but better psychological health than the merely old.

This study also reported qualitative data. For example, one man over age 90 said:

> I lost my beloved wife only a month ago and I am very sad for this. We were married for 70 years. I was close to her during all her illness and I have felt very empty after her loss. But thanks to my sons I am now recovering and feeling much better. I have 4 children, 10 grandchildren, and 9 great-grandchildren. I have fought all my life and I am always ready for changes. I think changes bring life and give chances to grow. I have had a heart condition for which I have undergone surgery but I am now okay. I have also had two very serious car accidents and I have risked losing my life. But I am still here!! I am always thinking for the best. There is always a solution in life. This is what my father had taught me: to always face difficulties and hope for the best. I am always active. I do not know what stress is. Life is what it is and must be faced. . . . I feel younger now than when I was young!
>
> *[Scelzo et al., 2018, p. 33]*

Ideally, qualitative research illustrates quantitative research, as was true in this study. This man is in poor physical health (heart condition) but good psychological health (much hope, no stress). As you see, any one study, with any one method, benefits from other studies and methods. The opposing perspectives ask, "Which data are more important?"

Ethics

The most important challenge for all scientists is to follow ethical standards. Each professional society involved in research of human development has a *code of ethics* (a set of moral principles). Most colleges and hospitals have an *Institutional Review Board (IRB)*, a group that requires research to follow guidelines set by the federal government.

◆◆ Especially for Future Researchers and Science Writers Do any ethical guidelines apply when an author writes about the experiences of family members, friends, or research participants? (see response, page 35)

Although they often slow down research, some studies conducted before IRBs were established were unethical, especially when the participants were children, members of minority groups, incarcerated individuals, or animals. Crucial is that

individuals consent freely to participation and are not harmed by their involvement.

AP IMAGES/JOHN BOMPENGO/ASSOCIATED PRESS

Risky Shot? Most vaccines undergo years of testing before they are used on people, but vaccines protecting against Ebola were not ready until the 2014 West African epidemic finally waned after 11,000 deaths. Thus, the effectiveness of Ebola vaccines is unknown. However, when deadly Ebola surfaced again in the Democratic Republic of Congo in 2018, public health doctors did not wait for longitudinal data. Here Dr. Mwamba, a representative of Congo's Expanded Program on Immunization, receives the vaccine. He hopes that it will protect him and thousands of other Congolese citizens. Scientists should know in 2021 if the vaccine halted a new epidemic.

EBOLA AND THE COVID-19 PANDEMIC

Many ethical dilemmas arose in the 2014–2015 West African Ebola epidemic (Gillon, 2015; Rothstein, 2015; Sabeti & Sabeti, 2018). Those problems have reemerged in the more recent Ebola crisis (Gostin et al., 2019) and in the COVID-19 pandemic (Wang et al., 2020). Among them:

- Should vaccines be given before their safety is demonstrated with large control and experimental groups?
- When should each nation, or each state or county in the United States, develop their own rules, and when should other regions or nations help?
- Should quarantine or other public health measures restrict individuals?

These issues have led to some international efforts, including funding secure, biocontainment laboratories in many nations, in order to quickly recognize deadly diseases (Le Duc & Yuan, 2018). However, public health doctors note that much more needs to be done, because the political and economic cooperation necessary for world health is missing.

The problem is that individuals and cultures have strong opinions that they expect research to confirm. Scientists might try (sometimes without noticing it) to achieve the results they want while maintaining their national and cultural values. Even when the science is clear, individuals may not accept the results.

Obviously, collaboration, replication, and transparency are essential. Hundreds of questions regarding human development need answers, and researchers need to follow ethical standards to reach conclusions, even when the conclusions are not what they, or their culture, wants. That leads to the most crucial ethical mandate. Developmental science needs to find answers to issues that will help everyone. For instance:

- Do we know enough about prenatal drugs to protect every fetus?
- Do we know enough about education so that every child is ready for the future?
- Do we know enough about poverty to enable everyone to be healthy?
- Do we know enough about transgender children, or contraception, or romance to ensure that every child is loved?
- Do we know enough about single parenthood, or divorce, or same-sex marriage to ensure optimal family life?

The answers to these questions are *NO*, *NO*, *NO*, *NO*, and *NO*.

Scientists and funders tend to avoid questions that might produce unwanted answers. People have strong opinions about drugs, schools, economics, sexuality, and families (the five questions above) that may conflict with conclusions from science. Religion, politics, and customs shape scientific research, sometimes stopping investigation before it begins.

Indeed, there are unanswered questions about almost every aspect of human development, and opinions may precede or distort research. Human thinking is limited by culture and context.

The next cohort of developmental scientists will build on what is known, mindful of what needs to be explored, raising questions that no one has asked before. Remember that the goal is to help everyone fulfill their potential. The next 14 chapters are a beginning.

VIDEO ACTIVITY: Eugenics and the "Feebleminded": A Shameful History demonstrates what can happen when scientists fail to follow a code of ethics.

THINK CRITICALLY: Can you think of an additional question that researchers should answer?

Answers to Table 1.7 (p. 31):

1. Positive; third variable: heat
2. Negative; third variable: age
3. Zero; each child must have a parent of each sex; no third variable

what have you learned?

1. Why does correlation not prove causation?
2. What are the advantages and disadvantages of quantitative research?
3. What are the advantages and disadvantages of qualitative research?
4. What is the role of the IRB?
5. Why might a political leader avoid funding developmental research?
6. What questions about human development remain to be answered?

SUMMARY

Understanding How and Why

1. The study of human development is a science that seeks to understand how people change or remain the same over time. As a science, it begins with questions and hypotheses and then gathers empirical data. Replication confirms, modifies, or refutes conclusions.

2. Nature (genes) and nurture (environment) always interact, and each human characteristic is affected by that interaction. In differential susceptibility, both genes and experiences can make some people change when others remain unaffected.

The Life-Span Perspective

3. Development is multi-directional, with losses and gains at every point. Both continuity (sameness) and discontinuity (sudden shifts), and critical and sensitive periods are evident in the processes of human development.

4. Urie Bronfenbrenner's ecological-systems approach stresses the contexts of life, that each individual is situated within family, school, community, and cultural systems. Changes in the context affect all other aspects of the system. This is evident in SES and in history, with cohort and poverty affecting every life.

5. Culture includes beliefs and patterns; ethnicity refers to ancestral heritage. Race is a social construction, not a biological one. Differences are not deficits; they are alternate ways to think or act which may be attuned to particular cultures, as Vygotsky explained.

6. Development is plastic, which means that change is ongoing, even as some things do not change. A dynamic-systems approach is needed to understand development.

Theories of Human Development

7. Psychoanalytic theory (Freud) and psychodynamic theories emphasize that adult actions and thoughts originate from unconscious impulses and childhood experiences. Erikson described eight successive stages of development, including three in adulthood, each reflecting the social context.

8. Behaviorism emphasizes conditioning—a lifelong learning process in which an association between one stimulus and another (classical conditioning) or the consequences of reinforcement and punishment (operant conditioning) guide behavior. Social learning theory recognizes that people learn by observing others.

9. Cognitive theorists believe that thoughts and beliefs powerfully affect attitudes, actions, and perceptions, and those affect behavior. Piaget proposed four age-related periods of cognition. Information processing looks more closely at the relationship between brain activity and thought.

10. Evolutionary theory contends that contemporary humans inherit genetic tendencies that have fostered survival and reproduction of the human species for tens of thousands of years. The fears, impulses, and reactions that were useful 100,000 years ago continue to this day.

Doing Science

11. Commonly used research methods are scientific observation, the experiment, and the survey. Each can provide insight and discoveries, yet each is limited.

12. Developmentalists study change over time, often with cross-sectional and longitudinal research. Ideally, results from both methods are combined in cross-sequential analysis.

Cautions and Challenges from Science

13. A correlation shows that increases and decreases in variables are related, not that one causes the other.

14. Quantitative research provides numerical data, useful for comparing contexts and cultures via verified statistics. By contrast, more nuanced data come from qualitative research, which reports on individual lives.

15. Ethical behavior is crucial in all of the sciences. The scientific method requires that results are objectively gathered, reported, and interpreted. Participants must understand and consent to their involvement. Scientists continue to study, report, discuss, and disagree—asking questions and eventually reach conclusions that aid all humankind.

KEY TERMS

science of human development (p. 3)
scientific method (p. 3)
hypothesis (p. 4)
replication (p. 4)
nature (p. 5)
nurture (p. 5)
differential susceptibility (p. 6)
life-span perspective (p. 7)
critical period (p. 8)
sensitive period (p. 9)
ecological-systems approach (p. 9)
cohort (p. 10)
socioeconomic status (SES) (p. 11)
culture (p. 12)
social construction (p. 12)
difference-equals-deficit error (p. 13)
ethnic group (p. 13)
race (p. 13)
intersectionality (p. 14)
plasticity (p. 15)
dynamic-systems approach (p. 15)
developmental theory (p. 17)
psychoanalytic theory (p. 17)
behaviorism (p. 19)
operant conditioning (p. 20)
reinforcement (p. 20)
social learning theory (p. 20)
cognitive theory (p. 21)
evolutionary theory (p. 22)
scientific observation (p. 26)
experiment (p. 26)
independent variable (p. 26)
dependent variable (p. 26)
survey (p. 27)
cross-sectional research (p. 28)
longitudinal research (p. 28)
cross-sequential research (p. 29)
correlation (p. 31)
quantitative research (p. 31)
qualitative research (p. 32)

APPLICATIONS

1. It is said that culture is pervasive but that people are unaware of it. List 30 things you did today that you might have done differently in another culture. Begin with how and where you woke up.

2. Cognitive theory suggests the power of thoughts. Find someone who disagrees with you about some basic issue (e.g., abortion, immigration, socialism) and listen carefully to the ideas and reasons. Then analyze how cognition and experience shaped the other person's ideas and your own.

3. Design an experiment to answer a question that you have about human development. Specify the question and the hypothesis and then describe the experiment. How would you prevent your conclusions from being biased and subjective?

4. A longitudinal case study can be insightful but also limited in application to other people. Describe the life of one of your older relatives, explaining what aspects of their development are unique, and what aspects might be relevant for everyone.

ESPECIALLY FOR ANSWERS

Response for Teachers (from p. 19) Erikson would note that the behavior of 5-year-olds is affected by their developmental stage and by their culture. Therefore, you might design your curriculum to accommodate active, noisy children.

Response for Teachers and Counselors of Teenagers (from p. 22) Evolutionary theory stresses the basic human drive for reproduction, which gives teenagers a powerful sex drive. Thus, merely informing teenagers of the difficulty of caring for a newborn (some high school sex-education programs simply give teenagers a chicken egg to nurture) is not likely to work. A better method would be to structure teenagers' lives so that pregnancy is impossible—for instance, through education or readily available contraception.

Response for Future Researchers (from p. 29) There is no best method for collecting data. The method used depends on many factors, such as the age of participants (infants can't complete questionnaires), the question being researched, and the time frame.

Response for Future Researchers and Science Writers (from p. 32) Yes. Anyone you write about must give consent and be fully informed about your intentions. They can be identified by name only if they give permission. For example, family members gave permission before anecdotes about them were included in this text. My nephew David read the first draft of his story (see pages 15–16) and is proud to have his experiences used to teach others.

OBSERVATION QUIZ ANSWERS

Answer to Observation Quiz (from p. 12) Vygotsky's facial expression. In photos, men were not supposed to smile! Also, the photo is not in color: This is a formal portrait.

Answer to Observation Quiz (from p. 19) Both are balding, with white beards. Note also that none of the other theorists in this chapter has a beard—a cohort difference, not an ideological one.

Answer to Observation Quiz (from p. 23) The river is slow-moving (see the boat) and shallow (see the man standing). A fast-moving, deep river is able to flush out contaminants more quickly. In addition, waste from the dog adds to the pollution.

CHAPTER 2

THE BEGINNINGS

From Conception to Birth

what will you know?

- Genetically, are some newborns more like their mother and others more like their father?
- When can a fetus born early survive?
- How can serious birth disorders be avoided?
- Are Caesarian births better than vaginal births?

I did not tell her, but I worried about my eldest daughter's pregnancy. I knew that she was eating well, that she was taking prenatal vitamins with folic acid, that she avoided cigarettes and alcohol, and that she had excellent medical care. But she had had a miscarriage, and so had I. Might that be genetic?

I kept quiet (pregnant women worry enough on their own), but I welcomed every reassuring report: The embryo survived the critical period, measurements of the fetal neck precluded Down syndrome, blood tests confirmed a healthy pregnancy, a sonogram at three months revealed a typically developing boy, another sonogram at eight months indicated that he weighed more than 2,500 grams ($5^1/_2$ pounds), so he would not be low-birthweight. That last fact freed me to worry about the birth itself.

Several other factors assured me that he would not be preterm. Every aspect of life is influenced by genes, and his mother was born three weeks late. Another factor was age. Teenagers have more early babies than older women, and Bethany was in her late 30s. A third was nutrition. Bethany was not too thin. A fourth was birth order. First births are more often late than early.

But my expectant-grandmother self overcame my rational-scientist self. Although the due date was weeks after the end of the semester, I recruited one of my colleagues to proctor my final exams if the birth happened early; I warned my students that I might not be in my office after the last class; I packed my bags, waiting for a call that labor had started.

Weeks later, exams were over, grades were calculated, due date came and went. No call. Waiting. Impatience. So, I drove to my daughter's home, to be ready. For several days I cooked, read, took the dog

to the vet, picked blueberries. Someone told my daughter to drink a certain tea. She did. No contractions. Someone else said walking might start labor; we hiked up a small mountain. No contractions.

One night a thunderstorm awakened me; the future mother slept through it. The next day, we went to another prenatal checkup. The midwife listened to the fetal heartbeat (fine), measured the maternal blood pressure (fine), felt the birth position (head down, fine), and sonogrammed again to check the amniotic fluid. Not fine! Too low.

Induction was recommended. We checked into the hospital. Another midwife examined her, and announced a surprise: Labor had started hours earlier. That's why the fluid was low. The nurse said the thunderstorm did it; something about the air.

The actual birth also held surprises, detailed later in this chapter. Spoiler alert: Mother and babe were fine. Grandmother was not.

As evident in the preceding paragraphs and in every chapter of this book, each moment of life reflects genes (post-term birth), health (good nutrition), unusual experiences (climbing that mountain, two midwives), and universal forces (grandmother worry, thunderstorm). Another universal is chromosomes and hormones. How did we know that this fetus was a boy?

In the Beginning

As you know, as members of the same species, all living humans are remarkably alike, which is not true of reptiles, or birds, or even our closest mammalian relatives, the chimpanzee (two species). As you also know, each human is amazingly distinct, unlike anyone else. How universality combines with uniqueness requires explanation, the first major topic of this chapter.

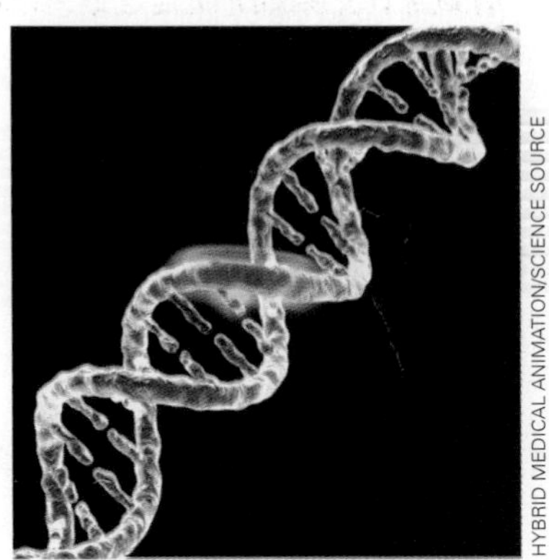

HYBRID MEDICAL ANIMATION/SCIENCE SOURCE

Twelve of 3 Billion Pairs This is a computer illustration of a small segment of one gene. Even a small difference in one gene can cause major changes in a person's phenotype.

From Chromosomes and Genes

Humans have about 21,000 genes, located on designated spots on 46 chromosomes*, arranged in pairs. Twenty-two of the chromosome pairs (44 in all, called autosomes) are closely matched.

THE 23RD PAIR

The chromosomes at the 23rd pair, unlike the matched pairs of the other 22, can be either a match (XX), or not (XY). The Y chromosome is much smaller than the X, and contains fewer genes. However, it contains a special gene, called SRY, which, at about eight weeks after conception, activates hormones that direct the fetus to grow a penis. By 12 weeks, the penis is visible on a high-resolution sonogram. (The midwife saw that, and told my daughter she was carrying a boy.)

The Y comes from the father. This is how it happens. Conception requires two reproductive cells, a *sperm* from a man and an *ovum* from a woman. Each reproductive cell is called a **gamete**, and when those two gametes combine they create one new cell, called a **zygote**, which could become a person. (Every human was once a zygote!)

gamete
A reproductive cell. In humans it is a sperm or an ovum.

zygote
The single cell formed from the union of two gametes, a sperm and an ovum.

*[Rarely the number of chromosomes is not 46, explained later.]

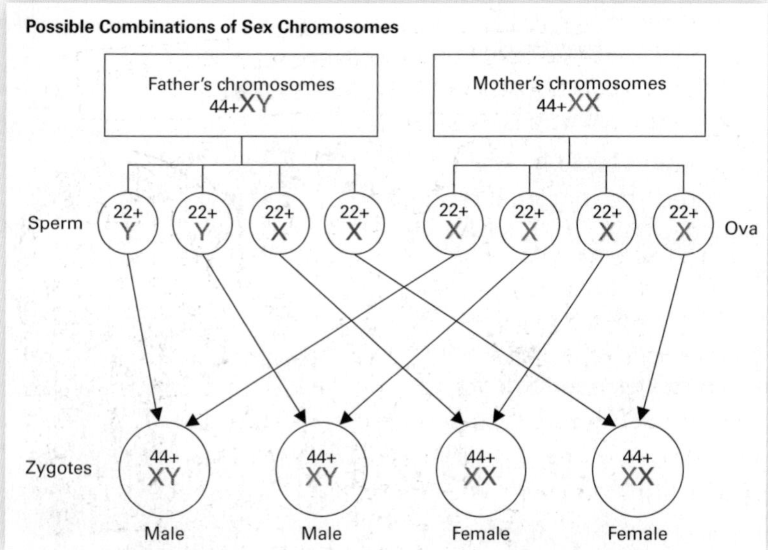

FIGURE 2.1 Determining a Zygote's Sex Any given couple can produce four possible combinations of sex chromosomes; two lead to female children and two, to male. In terms of the future person's sex, it does not matter which of the mother's Xs the zygote inherited. All that matters is whether the father's Y sperm or X sperm fertilized the ovum. However, for X-linked conditions it matters a great deal because typically one, but not both, of the mother's Xs carries the trait.

Zygotes duplicate and multiply: Adult bodies contain over 30 trillion cells, each a copy of the original zygote, with all 46 chromosomes and 21,000 genes. That is why archeologists with a fragment of an ancient bone can know the sex and genetic heritage of someone who died thousands of years ago, and why analyzing a drop of blood detects if someone is, or is not, related to someone else.

Only one type of cell of the human body does *not* contain all of that person's chromosomes. That cell is the gamete. Each sperm or ovum contains only half of each pair of chromosomes, only 23 instead of 46. That is essential, since gametes need to combine to make a new person with 46 chromosomes.

Whether a particular gamete contains the first or second half of each pair of chromosomes is random, and varies from one pair to another (see Figure 2.1). That means that each man or woman can produce 2^{23} different gametes—more than 8 million versions of their 46 chromosomes (actually 8,388,608). Each of those 8 million possible sperm from the father interacts with the 8 million possible ova from the mother.

Your parents could have given you an astronomical number of full siblings, each unique, each with half of the same genes and chromosomes that you have. Your brothers all inherited your father's Y; your sisters all inherited his X. Each of them, genetically, is only half like you.

genome
The full set of genes that are the instructions to make an individual member of a certain species.

allele
A variation that makes a gene different in some way from other genes for the same characteristics. Many genes never vary; others have several possible alleles.

ALL THE SAME GENOME

The entire packet of instructions to make a living organism is called the **genome**. There is a genome for every species and variety of plant and animal—even for every bacterium and virus.

Members of the same species are similar genetically—more than 99 percent of any human's genes are identical to those of any other person because, although they differ in tiny details, all human chromosomes contain the same basic genes.

That confirms our universal genetic bonds. Not only do all humans have similar bodies (two eyes, hands, and feet; the same organs, blood, and bones), but also we all use words, we all love and hate, we all hope and fear, for ourselves and for our descendants, friends, and strangers.

TINY GENETIC DIFFERENCES

Yet none of us is exactly like anyone else, and our uniqueness also starts with genes. Any variation, such as a difference in the precise sequence of chemicals within a gene, is called an **allele**. Genes are strings of four basic chemicals, connecting in pairs on each gene, with a total of about 3 billion pairs in the human genome.

Most alleles cause insignificant differences (such as the shape of an eyebrow) in a basic trait (everyone has eyebrows). These insignificant differences are how we recognize each other. When you search for a well-known friend among a crowd of thousands, you do not mistakenly greet someone who superficially looks like them. Tiny variations distinguish each face and each body—inside and out.

By contrast, a few alleles are crucial. For example, some alleles make it more likely that someone will have a heart attack in midlife, or survive to 100. More on genes, both the universal and unique, will be described soon, but first we must acknowledge other material that affect those 21,000 coding genes.

Epigenetics

Some people assume that *genetic* means that a trait is unchangeable. That is false. It is now known that nutrients, toxins, and experiences affect prenatal and postnatal development in the brain as well as in every body activity. Plasticity is lifelong.

Epigenetics refers to the many aspects of the science of how the environment affects genetic expression. This begins at conception and continues until death.

Not All Genetic Every child becomes their own person—not what their parents fantasize.

GENOTYPE AND PHENOTYPE

A distinction is made between the *genotype* and *phenotype*. **Genotype** is all the genetic material that the 46 chromosomes carry. Genotype is inherited, passed down by the gametes when they create the next generation. Genotype can be detected with advanced technology, but genotype is not necessarily apparent when looking at someone.

Phenotype is the actual appearance and manifest behavior of a person: how a person looks, functions, and acts. The phenotype reflects the genotype, but it is not identical to it. Humans are designed, by genes, to be profoundly shaped by their environment. In other words, every genotype can produce many phenotypes.

This distinction could be physical. For example, a person might inherit genes for being 6 feet tall, but be severely malnourished in childhood and grow only to 5 feet. In that case the genotype was for tall stature, but the phenotype is short stature.

Psychological traits can also be on the genotype but not the phenotype. For example, some people inherit a tendency to be shy. That is in their genotype, and that trait could be passed on to their children.

Some shy people avoid human contact as much as possible, but others have many close friends and acquaintances. For the latter, because of their genotype, they might take a few deep breaths before they walk into a room of strangers, but their phenotype is a friendly, outgoing person.

epigenetics
The study of how environmental factors affect genes and genetic expression—enhancing, halting, shaping, or altering the expression of genes.

genotype
An organism's entire genetic inheritance, or genetic potential.

phenotype
The observable characteristics of a person, including appearance, personality, intelligence, and all other traits.

METHYLATION

The Greek root *epi-* means "around, above, below." Early research on *epi*genetics focused on biological elements that were literally around, above, and below the genes at conception. Those factors direct how genes are expressed without changing the basic genetic code.

The first major epigenetic influence on the genes is with *methylation*, when a chemical called methyl surrounding each gene enhances, transcribes, connects, empowers, silences, and alters genetic instructions. Methylation continues throughout life, from conception until death. Some people have the genetic tendency for a particular trait, disease, or behavior, but that tendency might never appear because it was never turned on. Think of a light switch: A lamp might have a new bulb and be plugged into power, but the room stays dark unless the switch is flipped.

Scientists continually discover new functions—for good or ill—of methyl and other noncoding material that surrounds the genes (Iorio & Palmieri, 2019; Larsen, 2018). Applications are many—treating and controlling diseases, modifying crops to resist pathogens, developing vaccines.

microbiome
All the microbes (bacteria, viruses, and so on) with all their genes in a community; here the millions of microbes of the human body.

THE MICROBIOME

Another profound biological effect on each person genes is the **microbiome**, which refers to all of the microbes (bacteria, viruses, fungi, archaea, yeasts) that live within every part of the body. The microbiome includes "germs," the target of disinfectants and antibiotics. Nonetheless, most microbes are helpful, enhancing life, not harming it.

Microbes have their own DNA, influencing immunity, weight, diseases, moods, and much more (Dominguez-Bello, 2019; Dugas et al., 2016). Particularly crucial is how the microbiome affects nutrition, since gut bacteria break down food for nourishment.

◆◆ Especially for Medical Doctors
Can you look at a person and then write a prescription that will personalize medicine to their particular genetic susceptibility? (see response, page 71)

In one telling study, researchers in Malawi studied twins when one was malnourished and the other was not, even though both lived together and were fed the same food at the same time. Did a greedy twin grab food from his brother? No! When scientists analyzed each twin's microbiome, they found crucial differences. That is why only one suffered (Smith et al., 2014).

SOCIAL EXPERIENCES

Other factors that silence or amplify the 21,000 human genes begin with social experiences, such as chronic loneliness, that can change how genes direct the functioning of the brain (Cacioppo et al., 2014). This occurs lifelong, but here is an example from early life.

If a baby is born preterm, protective factors (being held and comforted by the mother, skin-to-skin) and stressful factors (painful intubations, punctures) affect the genes of the tiny person, with epigenetic changes evident years later (Provenzi et al., 2020). Thanks to research on epigenetics, such harm has been reduced: Lights are dimmed, noises quieted, and parental touch encouraged in the neonatal intensive care unit (NICU) (Griffiths et al., 2019).

More generally, even when a particular person inherits genes for a serious disease, epigenetic factors matter. As one review explains, "there are, indeed, individuals whose genetics indicate exceptionally high risk of disease, yet they never show any signs of the disorder" (Friend & Schadt, 2014, p. 970). Why? Epigenetics.

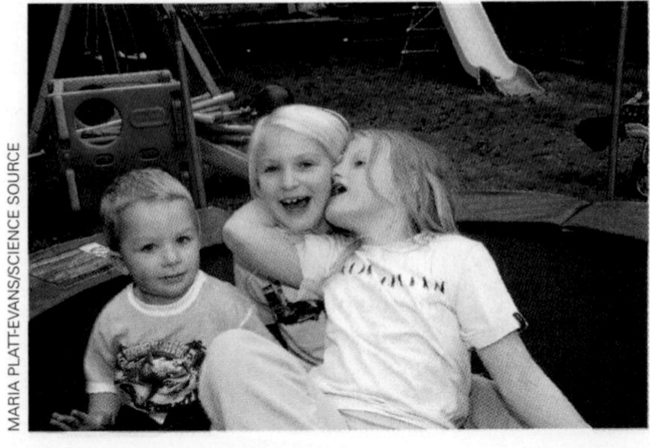
MARIA PLATT-EVANS/SCIENCE SOURCE

She Laughs Too Much No, not the smiling sister, but the 10-year-old on the right, who has Angelman syndrome. She inherited it from her mother's chromosome 15. Her two siblings inherited the mother's other chromosome 15 and do not have the condition. If she had inherited the identical deletion on her father's chromosome 15, she would have developed Prader-Willi syndrome, which would cause her to be overweight as well as always hungry and often angry. With Angelman syndrome, however, laughing, even at someone's pain, is a symptom.

Genetic Interactions

It might seem as if each child is half mother and half father, since each child has 23 chromosomes from each parent. But that is not true, because the genes and alleles on each chromosome interact with those on the other one at that site (genes on chromosome 1 from the father with genes on chromosome 1 from the mother, 2 with 2, and so on), and that interaction produces a zygote unlike either parent. Thus, each new person is a product of two parents but is unlike either one.

COPY NUMBER VARIATIONS

One early element of genetic interaction is mutations that occur before, during, and after conception, often triggered by other genes or by epigenetic elements. Attention has focused on *copy number variations,* which are genes with repeats or deletions (from one to hundreds) of base pairs. Copy number variations are at least five times as common as variations in single genes (Saitou & Gokcumen, 2020), and those variations correlate with heart disease, intellectual disability, mental illness, and many cancers.

Usually, the interactions and duplications that create genetic diversity help the species, because creativity, prosperity, and survival are enhanced when one person

is unlike another. Two economists suggest that there is an optimal balance between diversity and similarity: Human societies prosper when they are close to that ideal (Ashraf & Galor, 2013).

Not everyone agrees that contemporary human societies are close to the perfect balance, but most scholars agree that some diversity is beneficial (Spolaore & Wacziarg, 2018). If immediate relatives have children together, and if that occurs generation after generation, diversity is reduced and genetic problems appear.

ADDITIVE HEREDITY

Interactions among genes and alleles are often called *additive* because their effects *add up* to influence the phenotype. The phenotype then reflects the contributions of every additive gene. Height, hair curliness, and skin color, for instance, are usually the result of additive genes. Indeed, height is probably influenced by 700 genes, each contributing a very small amount (Marouli et al., 2017).

Most Americans have ancestors of varied height, hair curliness, skin color, and so on, with background variations much more nuanced than any simple idea of "Black" or "White." A child's phenotype may not mirror the parents' phenotypes (although the phenotype always reflects the genotype), in part because of the interactions of their unique set of genes.

You can probably see this in your family; I can see it in mine. Our daughter Rachel is of average height, shorter than her parents but taller than either of our mothers. She apparently inherited some of her grandmothers' height genes via our gametes. And none of my daughters has exactly my shape or coloring—apparent when we borrow clothes from each other and notice that a dress that is flattering to one is ugly on another.

Genetic variations are particularly apparent among African Americans in the United States. Historically, the continent of Africa was, genetically, the most diverse (Choudhury et al., 2018). Added to that, current North Americans who identify as Black carry genes from many regions of Europe and from many tribes of indigenous Americans. Similarly, Americans who identify as White are notably diverse. As Chapter 1 explained, race is a social construction, not a genetic one.

DOMINANT-RECESSIVE HEREDITY

Not all genes are additive. In one nonadditive form, some alleles are dominant (more influential) and others recessive (hidden). That leads to some intriguing genetic interactions. If a person inherits a dominant gene from one parent and a recessive gene for exactly that trait from the other, the dominant gene overpowers the recessive gene.

A person is called a **carrier** of the recessive gene when it is on the genotype but not the phenotype. In other words, people might carry a hidden gene in their DNA, which they will transmit to half of their gametes. Only if someone inherits the same recessive gene from each parent, which makes two recessive genes but no dominant gene for that particular trait, does the trait appear on the phenotype.

carrier
A person whose genotype includes a gene that is not expressed in the phenotype. The carried gene occurs in half of the carrier's gametes and thus is passed on to half of the carrier's children. If such a gene is inherited from both parents, the characteristic appears in the phenotype.

Most recessive genes are harmless. One example is eye color. Brown eyes are dominant. Everyone with brown eyes has at least one dominant brown-eye gene.

Blue eyes are recessive. If both parents have blue eyes, then every eye-color gene on every one of their gametes will have one or the other of their blue-eye genes. In that case, all their children will have blue eyes. If a child has one blue-eyed parent (who always has two recessive blue-eye genes) and one brown-eyed parent, that child will usually have brown eyes.

Usually, not always. Brown-eyed parents all have one brown-eye gene (otherwise they would not have brown eyes), but they might carry a blue-eye gene.

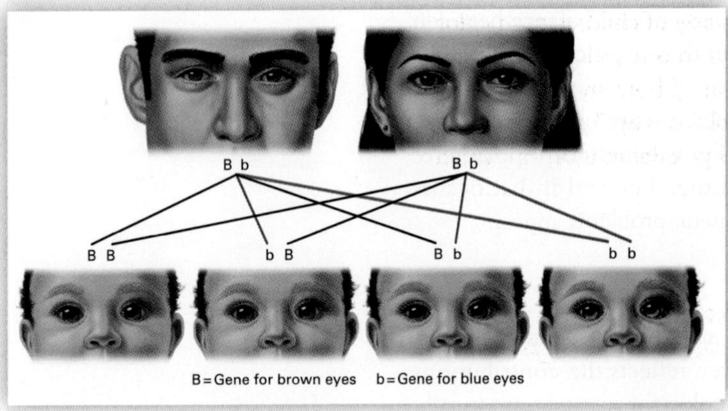

FIGURE 2.2 Changeling? No. If two brown-eyed parents both carry the blue-eye gene, they have one chance in four of having a blue-eyed child. Other recessive genes include the genes for red hair, Rh negative blood, and many genetic diseases.

◆◆ OBSERVATION QUIZ
Why do these four offspring look identical except for eye color? (see answer, page 71) ↑

X-linked
A gene carried on the X chromosome. If a male inherits an X-linked recessive trait from his mother, he expresses that trait because the Y from his father has no counteracting gene. Females are more likely to be carriers of X-linked traits but are less likely to express them.

If they do, if one parent has blue eyes and the other brown eyes, every one of their children will have at least one blue-eye gene (from the blue-eyed parent), and half of the children will have another blue-eye recessive gene (from the carrier parent).

Those children will have blue eyes, because they have no dominant brown-eye gene. The other half will have a brown-eye gene. Their eyes will be brown, but they will be carriers of the blue-eye gene, just like their brown-eyed parent. Sometimes both parents are carriers. If each brown-eyed parent carries the blue-eye recessive gene, the chances are one child in four will inherit a blue-eye recessive gene on both gametes, and hence have blue eyes (see Figure 2.2).

This eye color example presumes that only one pair of genes determines eye color. However, as with almost every trait, eye color is *polygenic* (many genes), so other genes affect eye color, making eyes various shades of blue and brown, greenish or greyish.

MOTHER TO SON

A special case of the dominant–recessive pattern occurs with genes that are **X-linked** (located on the X chromosome). If an X-linked gene is recessive—as are the genes for red–green color blindness, several allergies, a few diseases, and some learning disorders—the fact that it is on the X chromosome is significant (see Table 2.1).

Remember that the Y chromosome is much smaller than the X, containing far fewer genes. Consequently, the X has many genes that are unmatched on the Y. If one of those X genes is recessive, there is no dominant gene on the Y to keep it hidden.

Thus, if a boy (XY) inherits a recessive gene on his X from his mother, he will have no corresponding dominant gene on his Y from his father to overpower it, so his phenotype will be affected. Girls, however, need to inherit a double recessive (one from each parent) before that trait will appear in their phenotype.

TABLE 2.1 The 23rd Pair and X-Linked Color Blindness

23rd Pair	Phenotype	Genotype	Next Generation
1. XX	Non-color-blind woman	Not a carrier	No color blindness
2. XY	Non-color-blind man	Typical X from mother	No color blindness
3. ⓍX	Non-color-blind woman	Carrier from father	Half her children will inherit her Ⓧ. The girls with her Ⓧ will be carriers; the boys with her Ⓧ will have color blindness.
4. XⓍ	Non-color-blind woman	Carrier from mother	Half her children will inherit her Ⓧ. The girls with her Ⓧ will be carriers; the boys with her Ⓧ will have color blindness.
5. ⓍY	Color-blind man	Inherited from mother	All his daughters will have his Ⓧ. None of his sons will have his Ⓧ. All his children will have typical vision, unless their mother also had an Ⓧ for color blindness.
6. ⓍⓍ	Color-blind woman (rare)	Inherited from both parents	Every child will have one Ⓧ from her. Therefore, every son will have color blindness. Daughters will be only carriers, unless they also inherit an Ⓧ from the father, as their mother did.

Ⓧ = X that carries recessive gene for color blindness

That is why males are more likely to be color blind. A study of children with color blindness in northern India found a sex ratio of nine boys to one girl. In that study, marriages were almost always within a small group of neighbors and relatives, so specific genes tended to stay within each group. That explains why 7 percent of the children in one village were color blind, compared to only 3 percent in another (Fareed et al., 2015).

Twins

You read that each human is genetically unique, that even full brother and sisters share only half of their genes. However, there is one major exception: Although every zygote is genetically unique, not every newborn is.

MONOZYGOTIC MULTIPLES

About once in 300 human conceptions, one zygote not only duplicates but also splits to become two separate zygotes, or even four or eight. One separation can create **monozygotic (MZ) twins**, so called because they came from one (*mono-*) zygote (also called *identical twins*). (Rarely, an incomplete split creates *conjoined twins*, once called Siamese twins.)

monozygotic (MZ) twins
Twins who originate from one zygote that splits apart very early in development. (Also called *identical twins*.) Other monozygotic multiple births (such as triplets and quadruplets) can occur as well.

Separations at the four- or eight-cell stage create monozygotic quadruplets or octuplets. Because monozygotic multiples originate from one zygote, they have identical genetic instructions.

Remember, however, that epigenetics begins as soon as conception occurs: Monozygotic multiples look and act very much alike, but their environment is not identical. That is why, in one set of monozygotic triplets, two developed Alzheimer's disease (which is genetic) at ages 73 and 76, but the third, at age 85, had "no cognitive complaints or deficits" (Zhang et al., 2019, p. 3375).

VIDEO ACTIVITY: Identical Twins: Growing Up Apart shows how genes play a significant role in physical, social, and cognitive development.

Diverse experiences of monozygotic multiples begin prenatally. For example, the particular spot in the uterus where each twin implants may allow one fetus to get more nourishment from the placenta than the other: If early malnutrition is severe, that will impair the body and brain lifelong.

Experiences after birth can also differ markedly. That was evident in monozygotic triplets who were adopted by three different families, as shown in the documentary film *Three Identical Strangers*. Depression (and many other psychopathologies) is partly genetic, but one of those monozygotic triplets became so depressed as an adult that he died by suicide, to the surprise of the other two.

Monozygotic multiples are fortunate in several ways. They can donate a kidney or other organ to each other with no organ rejection. They can befuddle their parents and teachers, who may need visible ways (such as different earrings or haircuts) to tell them apart.

Usually, monozygotic twins establish their own identities. For instance, both might inherit athletic ability, but one might choose to play basketball and the other, soccer.

As one monozygotic twin wrote:

> Twins put into high relief *the* central challenge for all of us: self-definition. How do we each plant our stake in the ground, decide how sensitive, callous, ambitious, conciliatory, or cautious we want to be every day? . . . Twins come with a built-in constant comparison, but defining oneself against one's twin is just an amped-up version of every person's life-long challenge: to individuate—to create a distinctive persona in the world.
>
> [*Pogrebin, 2010, p. 9*]

That woman and her twin sister married and had a son and then a daughter within months of each other. Coincidence? Genetic? Sister pressure?

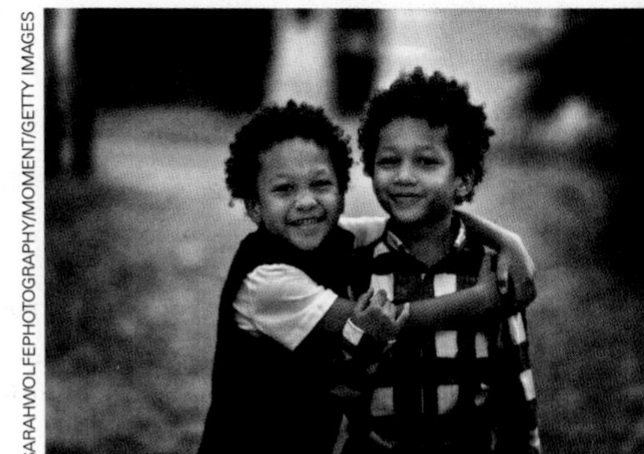

SARAHWOLFEPHOTOGRAPHY/MOMENT/GETTY IMAGES

Not Exactly Alike These two 4-year-old boys in South Carolina are identical twins, which means they originated from one zygote. But one was born first and heavier, and, as you see here, one might be more affectionate to his brother.

dizygotic (DZ) twins
Twins who are formed when two separate ova are fertilized by two separate sperm at roughly the same time. (Also called *fraternal* twins.)

DIZYGOTIC TWINS

About once in 60 natural* conceptions, **dizygotic (DZ) twins** are conceived. They begin life when two ova are fertilized by two sperm at about the same time. Usually, women release only one ovum per month, so most human newborns are singletons.

However, women might inherit a gene that increases the frequency of multiple ovulation. That gene is more frequent in some ethnic groups than others (common in West Africa and rare in East Asia). (See Figure 2.3.) In addition, older women are more likely to have some cycles with two ova and some cycles with none, so their rate of twinning increases. Diet may also matter (Smits & Monden, 2011).

Dizygotic twins are sometimes called *fraternal twins*, although because *fraternal* means "brotherly" (as in *fraternity*), that name is inaccurate. Of course, MZ twins are always the same sex (their 23rd chromosomes are either XX or XY), but for DZ twins (as with any two siblings) some are brothers, some are sisters, and some are brother and sister.

Like all children from the same parents, dizygotic twins have about half of their genes in common. They can differ markedly in appearance, or they can look so much alike that only genetic tests determine whether they are MZ or DZ. In the rare incidence that a woman releases two ova at once *and* has sex with two men over a short period, twins can have different fathers. Then they share only one-fourth of their genes.

People say that twinning "skips a generation," but actually it skips fathers, not mothers. Since dizygotic twinning requires multiple ovulation, the likelihood of a woman ovulating two ova and thus conceiving twins depends on her genes from her parents. Her husband's genes do not affect her ovulation. However, half of a man's genes are from his mother. If he is a fraternal twin, there is a 50-percent chance that his genes include the multiple ovulating X. All his daughters will inherit his X, so they may have twins because their paternal grandmother did.

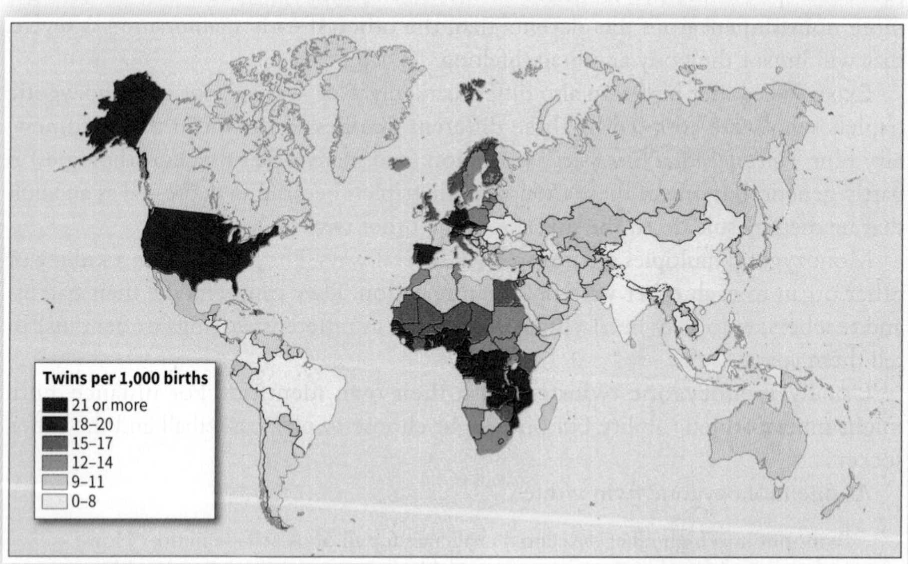

FIGURE 2.3 **More Is Not Always Better** Twinning is more common in Africa, and less common in East Asia. That has been true historically and continues to be the case in the twenty-first century, as this map shows. In medically advanced nations such as the United States, fertility drugs and IVF doubled the number of twins in the early twenty-first century, reaching a peak of 33.9 per 1,000 births in 2014. Recently, U.S. rates have fallen slightly as the challenges of low-birthweight newborns become more apparent.

*The rate is much higher with fertility treatments, as discussed in Chapter 12.

ONE BABY OR MORE?

Humans usually have one baby at a time, but sometimes twins are born. Most often they are from two ova fertilized by two sperm (*lower left*), resulting in dizygotic twins. Sometimes, however, one zygote splits in two (*lower right*), resulting in monozygotic twins; if each of these zygotes splits again, the result is monozygotic quadruplets.

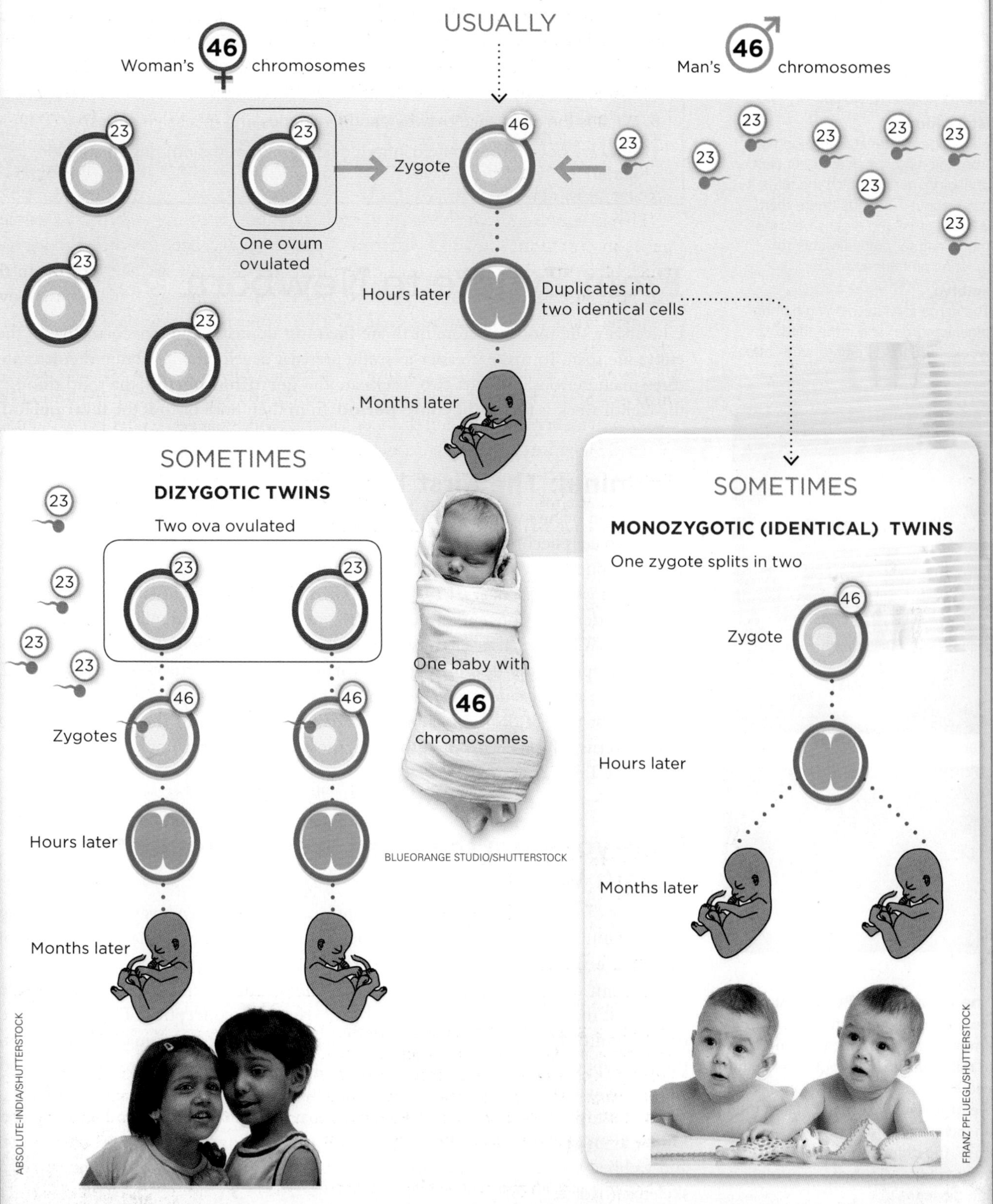

BLUEORANGE STUDIO/SHUTTERSTOCK

ABSOLUTE-INDIA/SHUTTERSTOCK

FRANZ PFLUEGL/SHUTTERSTOCK

germinal period
The first two weeks of prenatal development after conception, characterized by rapid cell division and the beginning of cell differentiation.

embryonic period
The stage of prenatal development from approximately the third week through the eighth week after conception, during which the basic forms of all body structures, including internal organs, develop.

fetal period
The stage of prenatal development from the ninth week after conception until birth, during which the fetus gains about 7 pounds (more than 3,000 grams) and organs become more mature, gradually able to function on their own.

embryo
The name for a developing human organism from about the third week through the eighth week after conception.

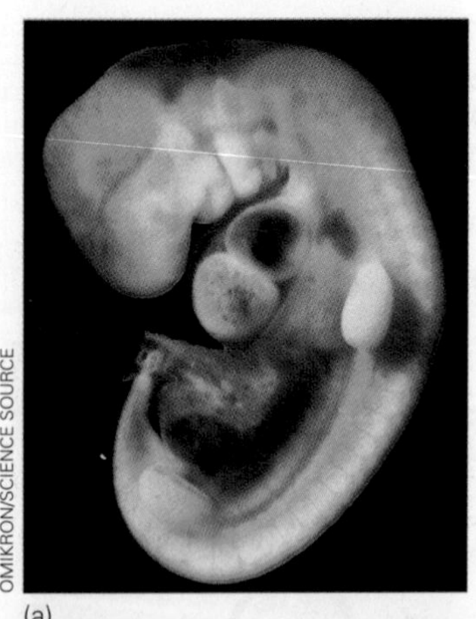

OMIKRON/SCIENCE SOURCE

(a)

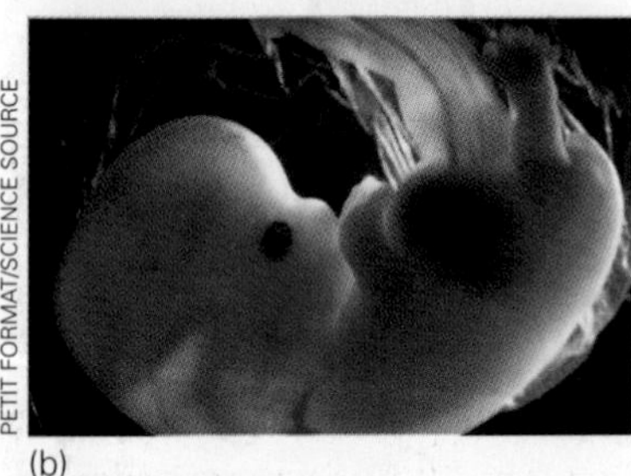

PETIT FORMAT/SCIENCE SOURCE

(b)

The Embryonic Period At 4 weeks past conception *(a)*, the embryo is only about 1/8 inch (3 millimeters) long, but already the head has taken shape. By 7 weeks *(b)*, the organism is somewhat less than an inch (2 centimeters) long. Eyes, nose, the digestive system, and even the first stage of toe formation can be seen.

what have you learned?

1. How is the sex of a zygote determined?
2. What is the influence of methylation on genes?
3. What is the influence of the microbiome?
4. How do monozygotic twins, dizygotic twins, and single-born siblings differ genetically?
5. How could a child inherit a disease neither parent has?
6. What is the difference between additive genes and recessive genes?
7. How are boys more likely to inherit disorders from their mother than their father?

From Zygote to Newborn

Universally, the months before birth are the most dramatic and transformative of the entire life span. To make it easier to study, prenatal development is often divided into three main periods. The first two weeks are the **germinal period**; the third through the eighth week is the **embryonic period**; from then until birth is the **fetal period**.

Germinal: The First 14 Days

Conception occurs when a sperm and an ovum join to form a zygote, the only time when two cells become one. This usually occurs in one of the woman's fallopian tubes, which connects the ovary to the uterus, but it can also occur in a laboratory dish, through in *vitro fertilization (IVF)*. [**Life-Span Link:** IVF is discussed in Chapter 12.]

No matter how conception occurs, the one-celled zygote duplicates, divides, and multiplies. When it has copied itself about five times, it differentiates. About a week after conception, the developing mass forms two distinct parts—a shell that will become the *placenta* and a nucleus that will become the *embryo*.

The first task of the shell is *implantation*, embedding into the nurturing lining of the uterus. This is far from automatic; most zygotes never implant (Kim & Kim, 2017) (see Table 2.2).

Embryo: From the Third Week Through the Eighth Week

The start of the third week after conception initiates the *embryonic period*, during which the mass of inner cells takes shape—not recognizably human but worthy of the name **embryo**. (Here, *embryo* refers to day 14 to day 56.)

At about day 14, a thin line called the *primitive streak* appears down the middle of the cell mass; it forms the neural tube 22 days after conception. The neural tube develops into the central nervous system, that is, the brain and spinal column. Soon the head appears, as eyes, ears, nose, and mouth start to form and a minuscule blood vessel that will become the heart begins to pulsate.

By the fifth week after conception, buds that will become arms and legs emerge. Upper arms and then forearms, palms, and webbed fingers grow. Legs, knees, feet, and webbed toes, in that order, appear a few days later, each with the beginning of a skeleton (Sadler, 2015).

At the end of the eighth week after conception (56 days), the embryo weighs just one-thirtieth of an ounce (1 gram) and is about 1 inch (2½ centimeters) long. It moves frequently, about 150 times per hour, imperceptible to the woman.

Random arm and leg movements are more frequent early in pregnancy than later on (Rakic et al., 2016). All the body parts and organs are present in primitive form, including a tiny intersex gonad, which will become the sexual reproductive system.

As you see, the head forms first and the extremities last, part of a developmental sequence called *cephalocaudal* (literally, "head-to-tail") and *proximodistal* (literally, "near-to-far"). This directional pattern continues until puberty, when it reverses. (Feet first, brain last, in adolescence!)

TABLE 2.2 Vulnerability During Prenatal Development

The Germinal Period
An estimated 65 percent of all zygotes do not grow or implant properly and thus do not survive the germinal period.

The Embryonic Period
About 20 percent of all embryos are aborted spontaneously. This is usually called an early *miscarriage*, a term that implies something wrong with the woman when in fact the most common reason for a spontaneous abortion is a chromosomal abnormality.

The Fetal Period
About 5 percent of all fetuses are aborted spontaneously before viability at 22 weeks or are *stillborn*, defined as born dead after 22 weeks. This is much more common in poor nations.

Birth
Because of all these factors, only about 27 percent of all zygotes grow and survive to become living newborn babies.

Information from Cunningham et al., 2014; Kim & Kim, 2017.

Fetus: From the Ninth Week Until Birth

The organism is called a **fetus** from the beginning of the ninth week after conception until birth. The fetal period encompasses dramatic change, the transformation of a tiny, sexless creature smaller than the final joint of your thumb to a newborn boy or girl about 20 inches (51 centimeters) long.

fetus
The name for a developing human organism from the start of the ninth week after conception until birth.

At the end of the embryonic period, the 23rd pair of chromosomes usually produce hormones that cause the reproductive organs to develop inside (ovaries) or outside (testicles and penis) the body (Zhao et al., 2017). Those same hormones affect development of the brain and the body.

INSIDE THE BRAIN

Male and Female

One hormone, *testosterone*, may be particularly significant. An expert states, "To describe the organizational effects of testosterone as profound is to rather understate the case" (Hardy, 2019, p. 108). Testosterone is much more prevalent in the male fetus than the female one, affecting brain and skeleton.

Because of hormones, parts of the hippocampus are larger in the female fetus; parts of the amygdala are larger in males. The way the hip bones connect to the legs, the length of the second and fourth fingers (called the 2D and 4D ratio), and the weight of the fetus show, on average, tiny male/female differences that are related to hormones.

No one now doubts that sex differences occur in the fetal brain. However, the significance is controversial. According to one scholar, neuroscientists are susceptible to *neurosexism*, seeing and explaining gender differences "in the absence of data" (Fine, 2014, p. 915). The question is: How much does the relatively minor dimorphism in male and female brains or bodies influence behavior?

To make it more complicated, although sex differences in brains appear when the *average* male is compared to the *average* female, overlap is common, with some males having neurological characteristics typical for females, and vice versa. Very few adults (less than 10 percent) are typical for their sex in every one of a dozen traits that distinguish male and female brains (Joel et al., 2015). Most brains are a male/female mosaic.

That reality helps explain gender differences. Traditionally, testosterone and other hormones shaped the body and brain of the fetus into male or female forms. However, some people are sure that they are not the sex their birth certificate says they are. Instead, they may be *transgender*, having a gender identity and/or expression that does not match their physical or sexual characteristics, or their sex assigned at birth. Or they may be *intersex*, born with sex chromosomes, external genitalia, or an internal reproductive system not considered standard for males or females.

These will be discussed in Chapter 9, since puberty is the traditional time when sex differences become significant, but here we need to recognize that early hormonal differences do not always direct the fetus to be distinctly male or female.

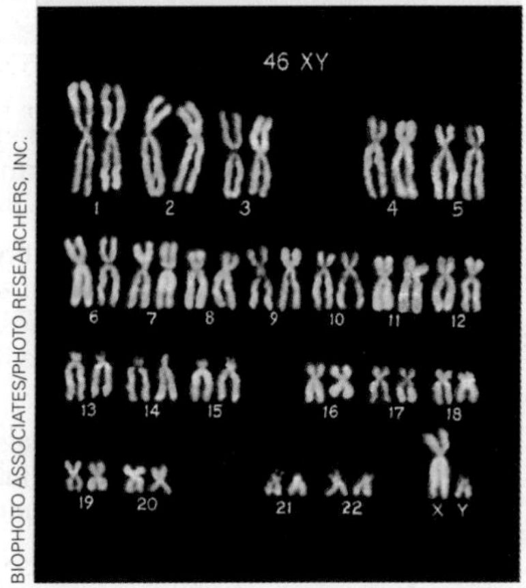

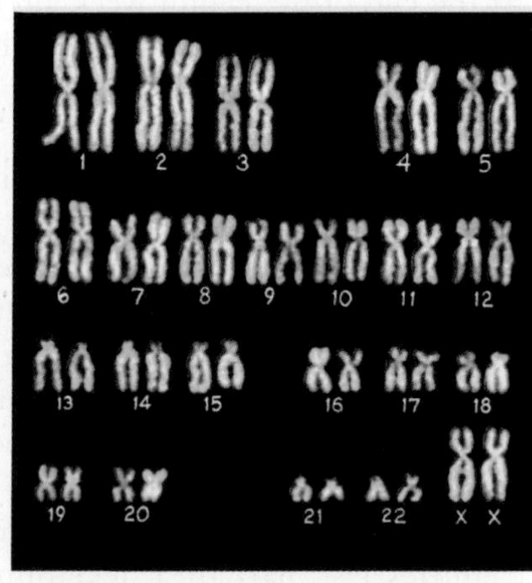

BIOPHOTO ASSOCIATES/PHOTO RESEARCHERS, INC.

Uncertain Sex Every now and then, a baby is born with "ambiguous genitals," meaning that the child's sex is not abundantly clear. When this happens, a quick analysis of the chromosomes is needed, to make sure there are exactly 46 and to see whether the 23rd pair is XY or XX. The karyotypes shown here indicate a typical baby boy *(left)* and girl *(right)*.

age of viability
The age (about 22 weeks after conception) at which a fetus might survive outside the mother's uterus if specialized medical care is available.

Early growth is rapid. By three months, the fetus weighs about 3 ounces (87 grams) and is about 3 inches (7.5 centimeters) long. Those numbers—3 months, 3 ounces, 3 inches—are approximate. (Metric measures—100 days, 100 grams, 100 millimeters—are similarly imprecise, but useful as a memory guide.)

THE MIDDLE THREE MONTHS

The 3- to 6-month-old fetus is very active, with "large body movements—whole body flexion and extension, stretching and writhing, and vigorous leg kicks that somersault the fetus through the amniotic fluid" (Adolph & Franchak, 2017). The heartbeat becomes stronger and faster when the fetus is awake and moving. Digestion and elimination develop. Fingernails, toenails, and buds for teeth form, and hair grows, including eyelashes!

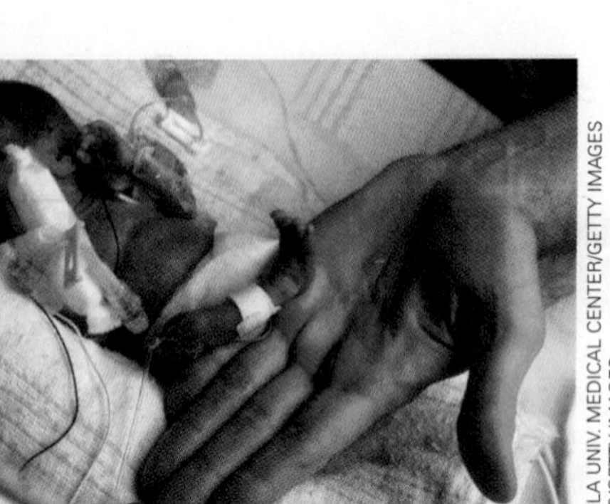

LOYOLA UNIV. MEDICAL CENTER/GETTY IMAGES NEWS/GETTY IMAGES

One of the Tiniest Rumaisa Rahman was born at 26 weeks and 6 days, weighing only 8.6 ounces (244 grams). Nevertheless, now age 17, she is living a full, normal life. Rumaisa gained 5 pounds (2,270 grams) in the hospital and then, six months after her birth, went home. Her twin sister, Hiba, who weighed 1.3 pounds (590 grams) at birth, had gone home two months earlier. At their 1-year birthday, the twins seemed typical, with Rumaisa weighing 15 pounds (6,800 grams) and Hiba 17 pounds (7,711 grams) (Nanji, 2005).

Those developments inspire awe, but the crucial mid-pregnancy development is that the central nervous system becomes active, regulating heart rate, breathing, and sucking. This brain maturation allows the fetus to reach the **age of viability**, when a fetus born far too early might survive.

Every day of prenatal life within the uterus increases viability. If birth occurs before 22 weeks, death is certain, because advanced technology cannot maintain life without some brain response. (Reports of survivors born before 22 weeks are unreliable, because the date of conception is unknown.)

After the age of viability, at the end of the middle trimester, life is still fragile. Currently, if birth occurs in an advanced neonatal unit, some very preterm babies survive, and some of those reach age 2 without major impairments. Rates vary by nation, by sex (girls fare better), and by medical advances.

Among the best survival rates are those of Japan and France. In Japan, about half of 22-week-old newborns born alive survive the first week of life, and about half of those survivors escape major cognitive disabilities (Kono et al., 2018). In France, when membranes are ruptured prematurely because continued pregnancy might be fatal to the woman, only 11 percent of 22-week fetuses survive to age 2 (most die at birth or soon thereafter), but 66 percent do so if they were born 25 weeks past conception (Lorthe et al., 2018).

THE FINAL THREE MONTHS

Each day of the final three months benefits the fetal brain and body. Many aspects of prenatal life are awe inspiring; the fact that any ordinary woman provides a far better home for a viable fetus than the most advanced medical technology is one of them.

In the final three prenatal months, the neurological, respiratory, and cardiovascular systems all develop. The lungs expand and contract, and breathing muscles strengthen as the fetus swallows and spits out amniotic fluid. The valves of the heart go through a final maturation, as do the arteries and veins throughout the body; the testicles of the male fetus descend.

The various lobes and areas of the brain are also established, and pathways between one area and another are forged. For instance, sound and sight become coordinated. This enables newborns to quickly connect voices heard during pregnancy with faces of people who talk to them in the hours after birth. That may be why they recognize their mother after seeing her only once or twice, assuming she talks to the baby soon after birth and her face is close enough for the baby to see.

That phenomenal accomplishment (recognizing Mother) occurs within a day or two after birth. Neurological plasticity allows the fetus to respond to voices of familiar people by the sixth month after conception (Webb et al., 2015). If a baby is born prematurely, impairments are more common in movement, intelligence, and/or vision than in hearing (Kono et al., 2018).

By full term, human brain growth is so extensive that the cortex has become folded and wrinkled (see Figure 2.4). Although some huge mammals (whales, for instance) have bigger brains than humans, no other creature needs as many folds, because, relative to body size, the human brain is much larger.

Beyond brain growth, with an estimated 86 billion neurons at birth, another process occurs in the final months of pregnancy—cell death, called *apoptosis*. Research

CHAPTER APP 2

What to Expect Pregnancy and Baby Tracker

iOS:
https://tinyurl.com/y6esrn5a

ANDROID:
https://tinyurl.com/nufnyqg

RELEVANT TOPIC:
Prenatal health and development, birth, and the new family

This app, based on the tried and true *What to Expect When You're Expecting*, guides users through pregnancy day by day and week by week, based on their due date. Users receive personalized updates, tips, and articles on their development, and are joined with a virtual community of parents-to-be with similar due dates.

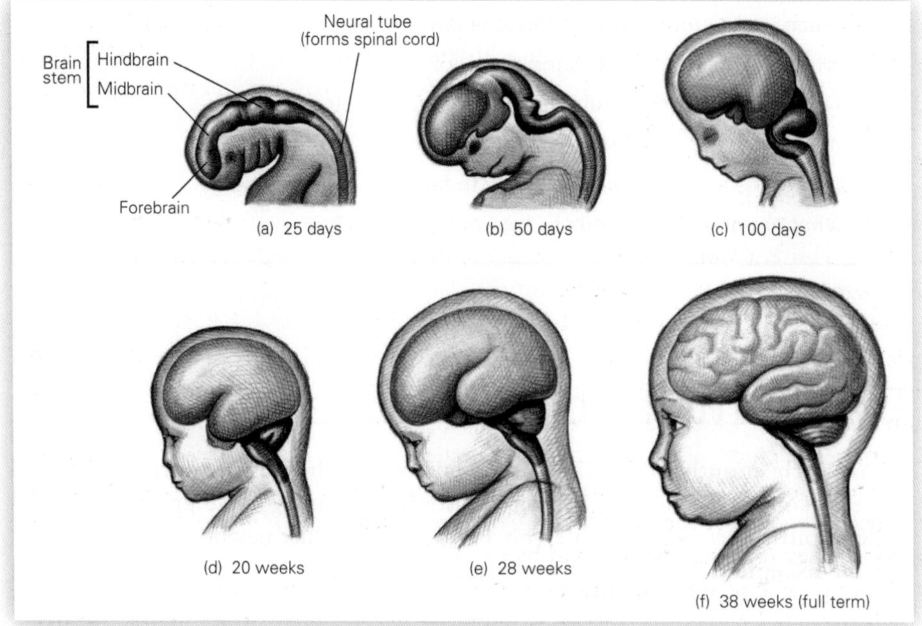

FIGURE 2.4 **Prenatal Growth of the Brain** Just 25 days after conception *(a)*, the central nervous system is already evident. The brain looks distinctly human by day 100 *(c)*. By the 28th week of gestation *(e)*, at the very time brain activity begins, the various sections of the brain are recognizable. When the fetus is full term *(f)*, all parts of the brain, including the cortex (the outer layers), are formed, folding over one another and becoming more convoluted, or wrinkled, as the number of brain cells increases.

on apoptosis has primarily centered on nonhuman creatures. Programmed cell death is widespread in prenatal development, and the effects may be transmitted from one generation to the next (Hamada & Matthews, 2019).

Some apoptosis is easy to understand: Abnormal and immature neurons, such as those with missing or extra chromosomes, are lost. So are neurons if the woman takes toxic drugs. Sometimes, however, seemingly normal neurons die: One estimate finds that almost half of all brain cells are gone before birth (Underwood, 2013). Why?

Perhaps death of any neuron that is not fully functioning creates space in the brain for the remaining neurons to coordinate thinking, remembering, and responding. Surviving preterm babies often have intellectual and emotional deficits, with gestational age the chief predictor (Heitzer et al., 2020). Among the many hypotheses for this correlation is less prenatal apoptosis.

That is speculation. However, there is no doubt that, in the final months of pregnancy, the membranes and bones of the skull become thicker so they protect the brain. This helps prevent "brain bleeds," a hazard of preterm birth if paper-thin blood vessels in the cortex collapse.

Another development pertains to the *fontanels*, which are areas on the top of newborn head where the skull bones have not yet fused. Fontanels enable the fetal head to become narrower as it moves through the vagina during birth. During the first weeks of life, the fontanels gradually close so the skull protects the entire brain. Preterm babies have larger fontanels, making them vulnerable to brain damage (Frémondière et al., 2019).

what have you learned?

1. **What must happen before the developing organism is called an embryo?**
2. **When is the embryo about 3 inches long?**
3. **When and how do sex organs develop?**
4. **What brain growth occurs during prenatal development?**
5. **What must happen before a fetus is viable?**
6. **Why is the age of viability unlikely to fall below 22 weeks?**
7. **What happens to the fetus in the final trimester?**

Problems and Solutions

Those early months place the future person on the path toward health and success—or not. Sometimes inherited disorders, or unfavorable prenatal life, or a difficult birth, affect a person lifelong. Fortunately, healthy newborns are the norm, not the exception. However, if something is amiss, it may be part of a cascade of problems (Rossignol et al., 2014).

VIDEO: Genetic Disorders offers an overview of various genetic disorders.

Chromosomal and Genetic Problems

The first set of problems is caused by chromosomes or genes. If all notable anomalies and disorders are included, 92 percent of people do not develop a serious inherited condition by early adulthood—but that means 8 percent do (Chong et al., 2015).

NOT EXACTLY 46

As you know, most humans have 46 chromosomes, created by two gametes, each with 23 chromosomes. However, the 46 chromosomes on the parents' cell do not always split exactly in half to make sperm or ova.

About half of all zygotes have more than or fewer than 46 chromosomes (Milunsky & Milunsky, 2016). Most of them fail to duplicate, divide, differentiate, and implant. They stop growing before anyone knew that conception occurred. Those who survive that germinal period usually are *spontaneously aborted* (miscarried) during the embryonic period. Ninety-nine percent of newborns have the usual 46 (Benn, 2016).

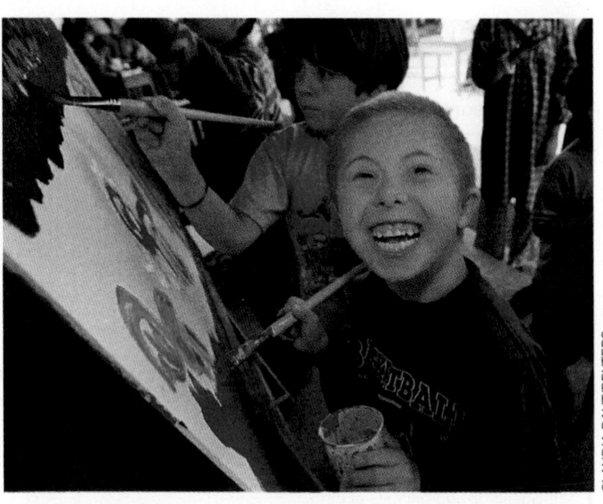
CLAUDIA DAUT/REUTERS

Universal Happiness All young children delight in painting brightly colored pictures on a big canvas, but this scene is unusual for two reasons: Daniel has trisomy-21, and at the time this photograph was taken, this was the only school in Chile where children with and without disabilities shared classrooms.

TRISOMIES

If an entire chromosome is added, that leads to a recognizable *syndrome*, a cluster of distinct characteristics that tend to occur together. Usually the cause is three chromosomes at a particular location instead of the typical two (a condition called a *trisomy*). One in 10,000 newborns has three chromosomes at the 13th site (called *Patau syndrome*), and 1 in 5,000 has three at the 18th (called *Edwards syndrome*). For those trisomies, if a fetus survives prenatal life, death usually occurs soon after birth (Acharya et al., 2017).

A much more common trisomy is at the 21st site, which occurs about once in 700 births (Parker et al., 2010). Trisomy-21 is called **Down syndrome**. No individual with Down syndrome is just like another, but this trisomy usually produces telltale characteristics—a thick tongue, round face, and slanted eyes, as well as distinctive hands, feet, and fingerprints. The hippocampus (important for memory) is usually smaller.

Down syndrome
A condition in which a person has 47 chromosomes instead of the usual 46, with 3 rather than 2 chromosomes at the 21st site. People with Down syndrome typically have distinctive characteristics, including unusual facial features, heart abnormalities, and language difficulties. (Also called *trisomy-21*.)

Many people with Down syndrome also have hearing problems, heart abnormalities, muscle weakness, and short stature. They are slow to develop intellectually, especially in language, with a notable deficit in the ability to rhyme (Næss, 2016).

By middle age, they are at risk of *Alzheimer's disease (AD)*, because one gene on chromosome 21 increases amyloid plaque—a sign of AD. Since everyone with Down syndrome has an extra chromosome 21, many also have too much amyloid. Research on adults with Down syndrome may help all adults avoid *major neurocognitive disorder* (formerly called *dementia*) (Hamlett et al., 2018).

◆◆ Especially for Teachers
Suppose you know that one of your students has a sibling who has Down syndrome. What special actions should you take? (see response, page 71)

PROBLEMS OF THE 23RD PAIR

Every human has at least 44 autosomes and one X chromosome; an embryo cannot develop without those 45. However, about one in every 300 infants is born with only one sex chromosome (no Y) or with three or more (not just two) (Benn, 2016).

Each particular combination of sex chromosomes results in a specific syndrome (see Table 2.3), but all affect cognition, fertility, and sexual maturation (Hong & Reiss, 2014). One problem at the 23rd site, called *Turner syndrome*, occurs when only one sex chromosome is present. Girls with Turner syndrome have wide necks and low hairlines, evident in early life. By contrast, children with an extra sex chromosome (XXY, for instance) may seem typical until adolescence or adulthood, when sexual maturation and fertility are impaired.

GENE DISORDERS

Many of the 7,000 *known* single-gene disorders are dominant (Milunsky & Milunsky, 2016). Most are relatively mild because severe dominant disorders usually are fatal, and thus cause death before the person is old enough to pass that gene to another generation.

TABLE 2.3 **Common Abnormalities Involving the Sex Chromosomes**

Chromosomal Pattern	Physical Appearance	Psychological Characteristics	Incidence*
XXY (Klinefelter Syndrome)	Males. Usual male characteristics at puberty do not develop—penis does not grow, voice does not deepen. Usually sterile. Breasts may develop.	Can have some learning disabilities, especially in language skills.	1 in 700 males
XYY (Jacob's syndrome)	Males. Typically tall.	Risk of intellectual impairment, especially in language skills.	1 in 1,000 males
XXX (Triple X syndrome)	Females. Normal appearance.	Impaired in most intellectual skills.	1 in 1,000 females
XO (only one sex chromosome) (Turner syndrome)	Females. Short, often "webbed" neck. Secondary sex characteristics (breasts, menstruation) do not develop.	Some learning disabilities, especially related to math and spatial understanding; difficulty recognizing facial expressions of emotion.	1 in 6,000 females

*Incidence is approximate at birth.
Information from Aksglaede et al., 2013; Benn, 2016; Hamerton & Evans, 2005; Powell, 2013; Stochholm et al., 2013.

fragile X syndrome
A genetic disorder in which part of the X chromosome seems to be attached to the rest of it by a very thin string of molecules. The cause is a single gene that has more than 200 repetitions of one triplet.

However, a few dominant disorders are not evident in the phenotype until adulthood, including early-onset Alzheimer's disease, one form of *muscular dystrophy*, *Marfan syndrome*, and *Huntington's chorea*. Tragically, the Oklahoma-born folk singer, Woody Guthrie, who wrote "This Land Is Your Land," died of Huntington's, as did two of his daughters. His son, Arlo, inherited his talent but not his disorder.

Recessive diseases are more numerous than dominant ones because they are passed down by carriers who are unaware of their recessive genes. There are thousands of recessive diseases; advance carrier detection is now possible for several hundred.

A few recessive conditions are X-linked, including *hemophilia*, *Duchenne muscular dystrophy*, and **fragile X syndrome**, which is caused by more than 200 repetitions on one stretch of one gene (Plomin et al., 2013). (Some repetitions are normal, but not this many.) The deficits caused by fragile X syndrome are the most common form of *inherited* intellectual disability. (Many other forms, such as trisomy-21, begin with gametes, not genes.)

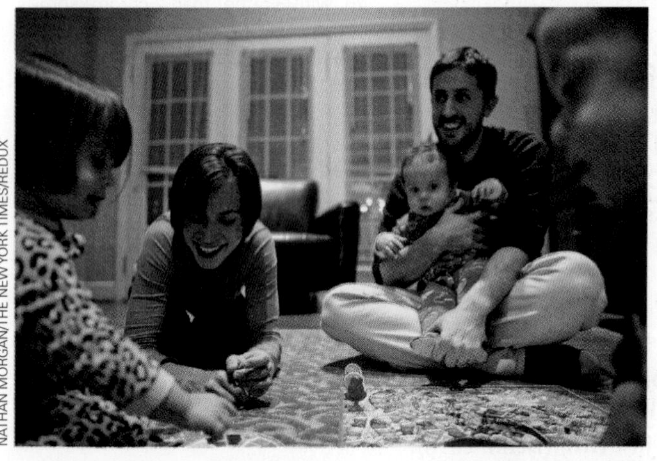

NATHAN MORGAN/THE NEW YORK TIMES/REDUX

Who Has the Fatal Dominant Disease? The mother, but not the children. Unless a cure is found, Amanda Kalinsky will grow weak and experience significant cognitive decline, dying before age 60. She and her husband, Bradley, wanted children without Amanda's dominant gene for a rare disorder, Gerstmann-Straussler-Scheinker disease. Accordingly, they used IVF and pre-implantation testing. Only zygotes without the dominant gene were implanted. This photo shows the happy result.

COMMON GENETIC DISORDERS

About 1 in 10 North American adults carries an allele on their autosomes for *cystic fibrosis*, *thalassemia*, or *sickle-cell disease*. Why so common? Because carriers benefited from the gene, which makes the gene frequent in the population.

Consider the most studied example: sickle-cell disease. Carriers of the sickle-cell gene die less often from malaria, which is prevalent and lethal in parts of Africa. Indeed, four distinct alleles cause sickle-cell disease, each originating in a malaria-prone region, each recessive.

The gene protected more people (the carriers) than it harmed. If a carrier had children with a noncarrier, half of the children would be carriers and half not, and none of the children would have the disease. Those who were carriers would be more likely to survive malaria and become parents themselves, so the next generation would have more carriers.

What if *both* parents were carriers? If they had four children, odds were that only one would inherit the double recessive and die young. The other three would

not have the disease, and two of them would be carriers, protected against an early malaria death, while the third was more likely to die of malaria. Consequently, each generation included more carriers, and thus the gene became widespread.

This connection between genes and local diseases is common. Almost every lethal disease is more frequent in one place than in another (Weiss & Koepsell, 2014). If a particular allele is protective, it becomes more common in that population.

About 8 percent of Americans with African ancestors have the recessive gene for sickle-cell disease—they are protected against malaria. Cystic fibrosis is more common among people with ancestors from northern Europe, because carriers may have been protected from cholera.

Additive genes can also be beneficial. Dark skin is protective against skin cancer if a person is often exposed to direct sun. Light skin allows more vitamin D to be absorbed from the sun, if a person lives where sunlight is scarce. Being relatively short is beneficial in cold climates, or when food is scarce.

MULTIPLE GENES

Most important human traits (for health, intelligence, emotions, and so on) are the result of several genes, not a single one. Those many genes came from ancestors who lived in many places.

Indeed, modern Europeans inherited between 1 and 4 percent of their genes from Neanderthals, who became extinct about 30,000 years ago. Neanderthal genes protect contemporary humans against some skin conditions and other diseases but may also make them vulnerable to allergies and depression—depending on which bits of Neanderthal genes they happen to inherit (Saey, 2016).

Some genes are simultaneously beneficial and harmful, making the interaction among the genes crucial. Anxiety, for instance, causes people to anticipate problems. Communities benefit if that genetic risk leads to better preparation for hurricanes, earthquakes, wars, and epidemics, especially if anxiety genes are accompanied by genes that enable the person to communicate well with others.

Even schizophrenia may have a benefit. The renowned singer, songwriter, and musician Bruce Springsteen described his father as an angry, emotionally abusive man, who probably had schizophrenia (Springsteen, 2017). Did that help his son become a creative, musical genius? Indeed, many great artists and writers apparently suffered from serious mental illness, from Van Gogh to Virginia Woolf, from Anthony Bourdain to Andrew Solomon—you can think of many more. Is there any connection here?

Every person has genetic tendencies, such as for moods, imagination, and empathy, that are both beneficial and harmful. For most traits, the combination of many genes and experiences makes a given person wonderful or troubled, a genius or a fool. From a life-span perspective, that fool may become a genius, if circumstances change.

DATA CONNECTIONS: Common Genetic Diseases and Conditions describes several different types of gene disorders. Achieve

CAREER ALERT

The Genetic Counselor

An understanding of life-span development is useful for every career. As students contemplate their future work, they should consult career counselors and check the *Occupational Outlook Handbook* of the U.S. Bureau of Labor Statistics, which lists prospects, salary, and qualifications.

Beyond those basics, however, this text contains Career Alerts, to raise questions and issues that arise from a

developmental perspective, issues that might not be found in a standard description of the career. You will see some of these issues in this discussion of genetic counseling.

There is far greater demand for genetic counselors than there are people trained in this area, so job prospects are good. Salary is good, too: The median in 2019 was $81,880. Training requires a master's degree and then passing an exam to be certified (not required in every state). Although demand is high, the need is much higher: One estimate is that only 10 percent of all women who are diagnosed with breast cancer have genetic testing, which could help them with preventive care and could alert their female relatives that testing is needed (Pal et al., 2020).

For all those reasons, many students who read this book should consider becoming genetic counselors. However, the work is much more challenging than it might seem. The first challenge is to understand and communicate complex biological and statistical material, so that clients understand the implications of whatever genes they have.

This is difficult: Not only are new discoveries made every day, but every disorder is polygenic and multifactorial, and methylation and the microbiome are relevant. Testing often reveals possibilities; clients want certainties. Further, when the reason for the consultation is a future child, more complications arise, because any prospective child will inherit only half of each parent's genes, making predictions complex.

Facts, medical treatments, and quality of life for a future, not-yet-conceived child are difficult to explain, but genetic counselors must consider much more than that. Each adult has emotions, assumptions, and values that differ between the future parents, and between the couple and the counselor. Answers are usually in possibilities, not absolutes. Counselors must draw charts, rephrase results, and repeat basic facts.

Thus, counselors must not only understand biology, know recent discoveries, and explain odds and consequences, but they must also reflect "hopes, dreams, fears, choices, actions, suffering, reactions, strengths, . . . weaknesses . . . cognitive understanding" (Biesecker et al., 2019).

Even when the facts are clear, people disagree. For example, 152 pregnant women in Wisconsin learned that their embryo had trisomy-13 or trisomy-18. Slightly more than half of the women decided to abort; most of the rest decided to continue the pregnancy but provide only comfort care for the newborn. But, three chose full medical intervention to preserve life (their three babies died within the first weeks) (Winn et al., 2018).

In another study, pregnant women learned that their fetus had an extra sex chromosome, a trisomy at the 23rd site. Half the women aborted; half did not (Suzumori et al., 2015). Unfortunately, no matter what the decision, outsiders tell parents they made the wrong choice—something genetic counselors never do.

Before deciding on this profession, ask yourself what you would do in the following situations, each of which has occurred:

- Parents of a child with a disease caused by a recessive gene from both parents ask whether another baby will suffer the same condition. Usually the odds are one in four, and in vitro conception and testing can detect the harmful gene before implantation. However, tests may reveal that the husband is not a carrier. Should the counselor tell the parents that their next child won't have this disease because the husband is not the father of the first child?
- A woman learns that she is at high risk for breast cancer because she carries one of several alleles (BRCA1, BRCA2, PALB2, TP53, PTEN, CDH1, CHEK2, and/or ATM). She wants to have her breasts removed, but she decides to keep it secret from her four sisters, who also may be at risk and may want to have genetic testing if they knew.
- A pregnant couple are both "little people," with genes for short stature. They want to know whether their embryo will have typical height. They plan to abort such a fetus.
- A person is tested for a genetic disease that runs in the family. The results are good (not a carrier) and bad (the person carries another serious condition). Should the counselor reveal a risk that the client did not ask about?

This fourth issue is new: Even a few years ago, the cost of testing precluded unrequested results. But now *genome-wide association study (GWAS)* is routine, capturing the entire genome, so counselors learn about thousands of unsuspected conditions. Generally, counselors ask in advance under what circumstances the client wants to know about other conditions that might be found.

People generally say they want to know about other conditions, but GWAS includes many uncertainties and genes "of unknown significance." How and when should this be communicated (Clift et al., 2020)?

Professionals explain probabilities; people decide based on their values, not those of the counselor. Can you live with that?

THINK CRITICALLY: Instead of genetic counseling, should we advocate health counseling?

Harmful Substances During Pregnancy

As just described, genetic factors begin at conception, but for most babies, nurture is even more significant than nature. This begins with the prenatal environment.

Monthly, even weekly, scientists discover another **teratogen**, which is anything—drugs, viruses, pollutants, malnutrition, stress, and more—that increases the risk of prenatal abnormalities and birth complications. People once thought that the placenta protected the fetus against every insult. Then, about six decades ago, it became apparent that teratogens caused visible birth defects—such as blindness from rubella or missing limbs from thalidomide.

teratogen
An agent or condition, including viruses, drugs, and chemicals, that can impair prenatal development and result in birth defects or even death.

That was just the beginning. Now it is apparent that invisible problems in the brain, resulting in a child's hyperactivity, aggression, or intellectual disability, are also caused by teratogens. Fathers and other relatives have an impact, too, in that they add stress or joy depending on their attitudes.

A CASE TO STUDY

He Cannot Get the Right Words Out

Many children have difficulties in thinking and behavior that *could* be connected to teratogens. One of my students wrote:

> I was nine years old when my mother announced she was pregnant. I was the one who was most excited. . . . My mother was a heavy smoker, Colt 45 beer drinker and a strong caffeine coffee drinker.
>
> One day my mother was sitting at the dining room table smoking cigarettes one after the other. I asked "Isn't smoking bad for the baby?" She made a face and said "Yes, so what?"
>
> I said "So why are you doing it?"
>
> She said, "I don't know." . . .
>
> During this time I was in the fifth grade and we saw a film about birth defects. My biggest fear was that my mother was going to give birth to a fetal alcohol syndrome (FAS) infant. . . . My baby brother was born right on schedule. The doctors claimed a healthy newborn. . . . Once I heard healthy, I thought everything was going to be fine. I was wrong, then again I was just a child. . . .
>
> My baby brother never showed any interest in toys . . . he just cannot get the right words out of his mouth . . . he has no common sense . . .
>
> Why hurt those who cannot defend themselves?
>
> [*J., personal communication*]

As you remember from Chapter 1, one case is not proof. J. blames her mother, but genetic risks, inadequate prenatal care, and troubling postnatal experiences may be part of her brother's sorry cascade. Moreover, her mother was of low SES (itself a correlate of harm), and she was poorly nourished. Boys and later-born children are more vulnerable, which may help explain why J. was a good student, unlike her brother.

It is not unusual for a newborn to seem to have escaped a teratogen, yet the brain is damaged. That is a major concern for the fetus when the mother contracts COVID-19. Of particular concern is her inability to breathe sufficient oxygen, which may reduce oxygen to the fetal brain (Dashraath et al., 2020). For my student, for her mother, and for everyone who was pregnant during the pandemic, there is much more we need to understand and do to protect every fetus.

DATA CONNECTIONS: Teratogens examines the effects of various teratogens and the preventive measures that reduce their risk to a developing fetus. Achieve

THE CRITICAL TIME

Timing is crucial. Some teratogens cause damage only during a *critical period*, which may occur before a woman knows she is pregnant (see Figure 2.5). [**Life-Span Link:** Critical and sensitive periods are described in Chapter 1.] Consequently, women need to avoid drugs, supplement a balanced diet with folic acid and iron, update their immunizations, and gain or lose weight if needed *before* pregnancy

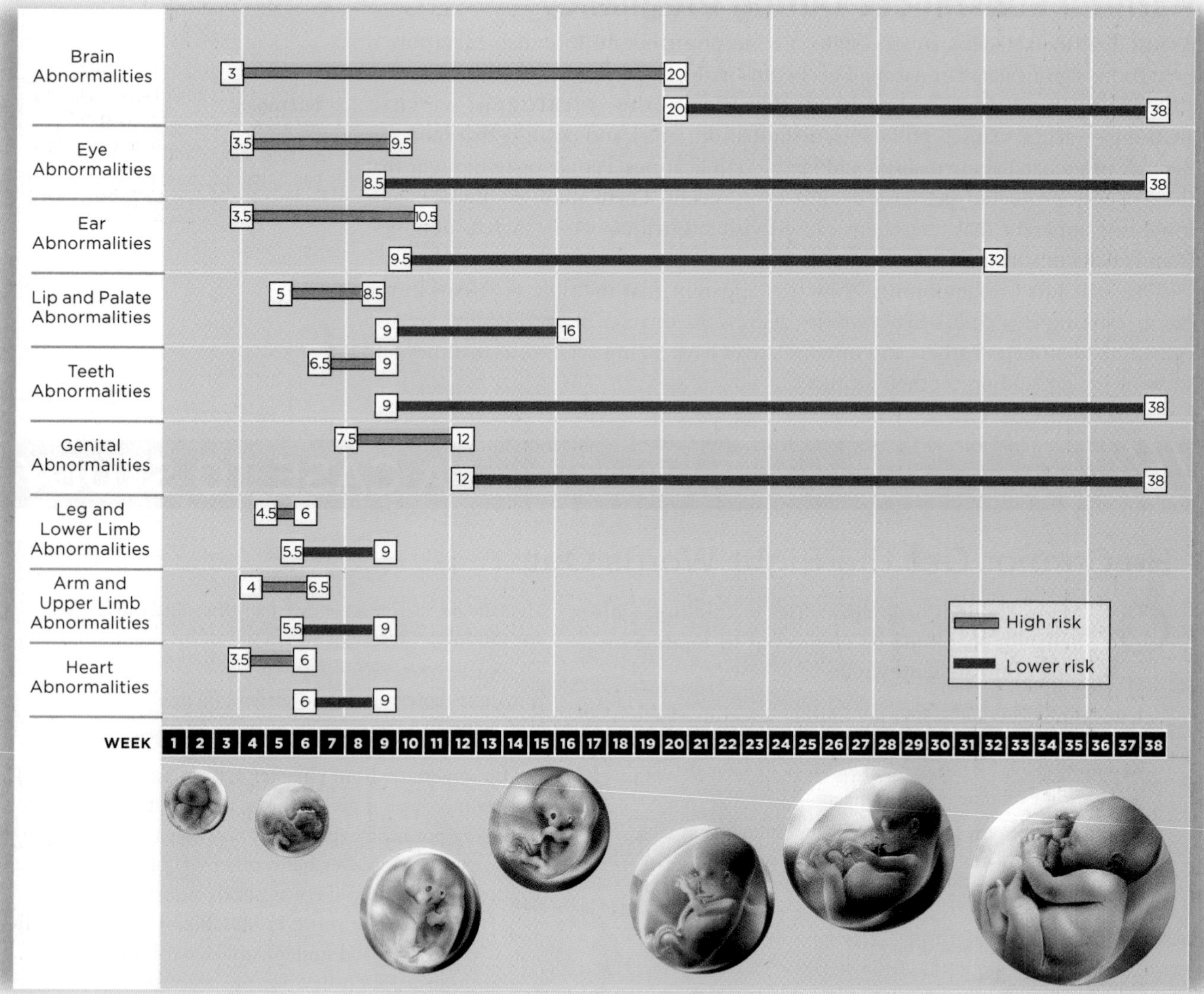

FIGURE 2.5 One More Reason to Plan a Pregnancy The embryonic period, before a woman knows she is pregnant, is the most sensitive time for causing structural birth defects. However, at no time during pregnancy is the fetus completely safe from harm. Individual differences in susceptibility to teratogens may be caused by a fetus's genetic makeup or peculiarities of the mother, including the effectiveness of her placenta or her overall health. The dose and timing of the exposure are also important.

occurs. Here, fathers may be particularly influential. Always people are affected by the health habits and emotional support of the other people closest to them.

Pregnancy overall is a critical period, not only the crucial first eight weeks. Of course, the first days and weeks after conception (the germinal and embryonic periods) are critical for body formation, but teratogens can affect the fetal brain at any time. For example, a longitudinal study of 7-year-olds found that, although alcohol affects body structures early in pregnancy, it is the second half of pregnancy when binge drinking is an especially potent behavioral teratogen (Niclasen et al., 2014).

HOW MUCH IS TOO MUCH?

Beyond time, a second factor influencing harm from teratogens is the amount and/or frequency of exposure. Many teratogens have a *threshold effect*; they are virtually harmless until exposure reaches a certain level, and then they "cross the threshold" to damage the fetus.

Is there a safe dose or timing for psychoactive drugs? Research has focused on alcohol, a drug ingested by most young women in many nations. Early in pregnancy, a woman's heavy drinking can cause **fetal alcohol syndrome (FAS)**, which distorts the facial features of a child (especially the eyes, ears, and upper lip). Later in pregnancy, behavior can be affected; *fetal alcohol effects (FAE)* occur, not FAS (Hoyme et al., 2016).

fetal alcohol syndrome (FAS) A cluster of birth defects, including abnormal facial characteristics, slow physical growth, and reduced intellectual ability, that may occur in the fetus of a woman who drinks alcohol while pregnant.

Currently, pregnant women are advised to avoid all alcohol, but many women in France (between 12 and 63 percent, depending on specifics of the research) do not heed that message (Dumas et al., 2014). Most of their babies seem fine. Should all women who *might* become pregnant refuse a legal substance that most men use routinely? Wise? Probably. Necessary? Maybe not.

INNATE VULNERABILITY

Genes also matter. When a woman carrying dizygotic twins drinks alcohol, for example, the twins' blood alcohol levels are equal, yet one twin may be more severely affected because of different alleles for the enzyme that metabolizes alcohol (Hemingway et al., 2019). Similar differential susceptibility occurs for many teratogens (McCarthy & Eberhart, 2014).

Although the links from genes to teratogens to damage are sometimes difficult to verify, two examples of genetic susceptibility are proven. First, male fetuses are more often spontaneously aborted, stillborn, or harmed by teratogens than are female fetuses. The male–female hazard rate differs from one teratogen to another (Lewis & Kestler, 2012).

Second, one maternal allele reduces folic acid, and that deficit can produce *neural-tube defects*—either *spina bifida*, in which the tail of the spine is not enclosed properly (enclosure normally occurs at about week 7), or *anencephaly*, when part of the brain is missing. Neural-tube defects are more common in certain ethnic groups (e.g., Irish, English, and Egyptian), but even those with the gene usually have healthy babies.

In one study (Smithells et al., 2011), about half of a group of 550 mothers who were genetically at risk, in that they already had a child with a neural-tube disorder, were given extra folic acid. The other half ate normally. The rate of newborns with neural-tube defects was 1 in 250 among the supplemented mothers and 13 in 300 in the nonsupplemented ones, proof that folic acid helps. But, note that almost 96 percent of the women who were at genetic risk and did *not* take supplements had healthy babies.

Also, one supplemented woman bore a second child with a neural-tube defect. Why? Was the dose too low, or did she skip taking the pills, or was some other genetic risk the problem?

OPPOSING PERSPECTIVES

Pesticides

With many possible teratogens, observers reach opposite conclusions. To illustrate the problem, consider pesticides, which are chemicals that eliminate something (such as insects) that harms growing crops. No biologist doubts that pesticides can impair development in frogs, fish, and bees, but the pesticide industry insists that careful use (e.g., spraying plants, not workers) benefits people by providing fresh, low-cost food and does not harm the developing brain.

Many developmentalists, however, find that the babies of pregnant women who breathe or ingest these toxins will have brain damage (Heyer & Meredith, 2017). One scientist said, "Pesticides were designed to be neurotoxic. Why should we be surprised if they cause neurotoxicity?" (Lanphear, quoted in Mascarelli, 2013, p. 741).

The problem is that research can be interpreted in many ways (Gingrich et al., 2020). In 2000, the United States removed one pesticide, *chlorpyrifos*, from household use (it had been used to kill roaches and ants), and banned it from agriculture in 2016, in the last month of the Obama administration. However, it was reinstated in the first year of the Trump administration. Is that a developmental issue, an economic issue, or a political issue? Chlorpyrifos is widely used in other nations, and is very profitable.

Analysis of umbilical cord blood finds that fetuses exposed to chlorpyrifos become children with lower IQs and more behavior problems than other children (Horton et al., 2012). Analysis of mother's urine immediately after birth suggests that the chemicals increase the rate of attention deficit disorder (Dalsager et al., 2019). However, the research can be interpreted in many ways. As a team of scientists explains:

> For the commonly used pesticide chlorpyrifos, an industry-funded toxicity study concludes that no selective effects on neurodevelopment occur even at high exposures. In contrast, the evidence from independent studies points to adverse effects of current exposures on cognitive development in children.
>
> *[Mie et al., 2018]*

The companies that sell chlorpyrifos argue that parents who harvest sprayed crops are often migrants who move from place to place and fear deportation. Moving, and fear, disrupts children's schooling. That, rather than exposure to pesticides, could explain the correlation between pregnant women exposed to pesticides and children's behavior.

Further, even if chlorpyrifos is a teratogen, does that outweigh the economic benefits for farmers, chemical companies, and parents who need to buy fruits and vegetables? Developmentalists believe the fetal brain needs to be protected no matter what the cost, and suggest there are better ways to make sure good food is available. Not everyone agrees.

TAYLOR JONES/ZUMA PRESS/FLORIDA CITY/FL/USA/NEWSCOM

No More Pesticides Carlos Candelario, shown here at age 9 months, was born without limbs, a birth defect that occurred when his mother (Francisca, show here) and father (Abraham) worked in the Florida fields. Since his birth in 2004, laws prohibit spraying pesticides while people pick fruit and vegetables, but developmentalists worry about the effect of the residue on developing brains.

Low Birthweight: Causes and Consequences

We have considered genes at conception and teratogens during prenatal development. Soon we consider birth itself. Before that, however, we explore a problem that is caused by factors at conception, during pregnancy, and at birth. Specifically, we need to understand why some babies are born too small. This is the main cause of early infant death, as well as a factor that affects a person lifelong.

low birthweight (LBW)
A body weight at birth of less than 2,500 grams (5½ pounds).

very low birthweight (VLBW)
A body weight at birth of less than 1,500 grams (3 pounds, 5 ounces).

extremely low birthweight (ELBW)
A body weight at birth of less than 1,000 grams (2 pounds, 3 ounces).

The World Health Organization defines **low birthweight (LBW)** as under 2,500 grams (5½ pounds). LBW babies are further grouped into **very low birthweight (VLBW)**, under 1,500 grams (3 pounds, 5 ounces), and **extremely low birthweight (ELBW)**, under 1,000 grams (2 pounds, 3 ounces).

About 8 percent of babies born in the United States are low birthweight, a rate similar to Brazil, Greece, and Lebanon. About 50 nations have fewer low-birthweight newborns than the United States, with the lowest rate of all in Sweden (less than 4 percent). About 100 nations are worse than the United States, with several (including Bangladesh, Nepal, and Mozambique) having rates of 20 percent or more (Blencowe et al., 2019).

It would be better for everyone—mother, father, baby, and society—if all newborns were in the womb for at least 36 weeks and weighed more than 2,500 grams

(5½ pounds).* Being underweight at birth has lifelong consequences, including heart disease, less education, and more obesity.

TOO SOON OR TOO SMALL

Babies born **preterm** (two or more weeks early; no longer called *premature*) are often LBW, because fetal weight normally doubles in the last trimester of pregnancy, with 900 grams (about 2 pounds) of that gain occurring in the final three weeks. As already mentioned, every week past week 22 adds weight and maturation (see At About This Time).

preterm
A birth that occurs two or more weeks before the full 38 weeks of the typical pregnancy—that is, at 36 or fewer weeks after conception.

At About This Time: Average Prenatal Weights*

Period of Development	Weeks Past Conception	Average Weight (nonmetric)	Average Weight (metric)	Notes
End of embryonic period	8	1/30 oz	1 g	Most common time for spontaneous abortion (miscarriage).
End of first trimester	13	3 oz	85 g	
At viability (50/50 chance of survival)	22–25	20–32 oz	565–900 g	A birthweight of less than 2 lb, 3 oz (1,000 g) is extremely low birthweight (ELBW).
End of second trimester	26–28	2–3 lb	900–1,400 g	Less than 3 lb, 5 oz (1,500 g) is very low birthweight (VLBW).
End of preterm period	35	5½ lb	2,500 g	Less than 5½ lb (2,500 g) is low birthweight (LBW).
Full term	38	7½ lb	3,400 g	Between 5½ lb and 9 lb (2,500–4,000 g) is considered normal weight.

*To make them easier to remember, the weights are rounded off (hence the imprecise correspondence between metric and nonmetric). Actual weights vary. For instance, full-term infants sometimes weigh more than 9 pounds; viable newborns, especially twins or triplets, may weigh less 5½.

Other LBW babies have gained weight slowly throughout pregnancy and are *small-for-dates*, or **small for gestational age (SGA)**. A full-term baby weighing only 2,600 grams and a 30-week-old fetus weighing only 1,000 grams are both SGA, even though the first is not technically low birthweight. Low birthweight varies dramatically from nation to nation, and, within the United States, from county to county as both a cause and a predictor of lifelong poverty (Robertson & O'Brien, 2018) (see Figure 2.6).

small for gestational age (SGA)
A term for a baby whose birthweight is significantly lower than expected, given the time since conception. For example, a 5-pound (2,265-gram) newborn is considered SGA if born on time but not SGA if born two months early. (Also called *small-for-dates.*)

In most nations, malnutrition is the most common reason for low birthweight. Women who begin pregnancy underweight, who eat poorly during pregnancy, or who gain less than 3 pounds (1.3 kilograms) per month in the last six months often have underweight infants.

Hungry women are common in some nations of Africa and South Asia, but undernutrition is also possible in developed nations. In the United States, poor nutrition is thought to be a major reason that less income correlates with more underweight

*Usually, this text gives pounds before grams. But hospitals worldwide report birthweight using the metric system, so grams precede pounds and ounces here.

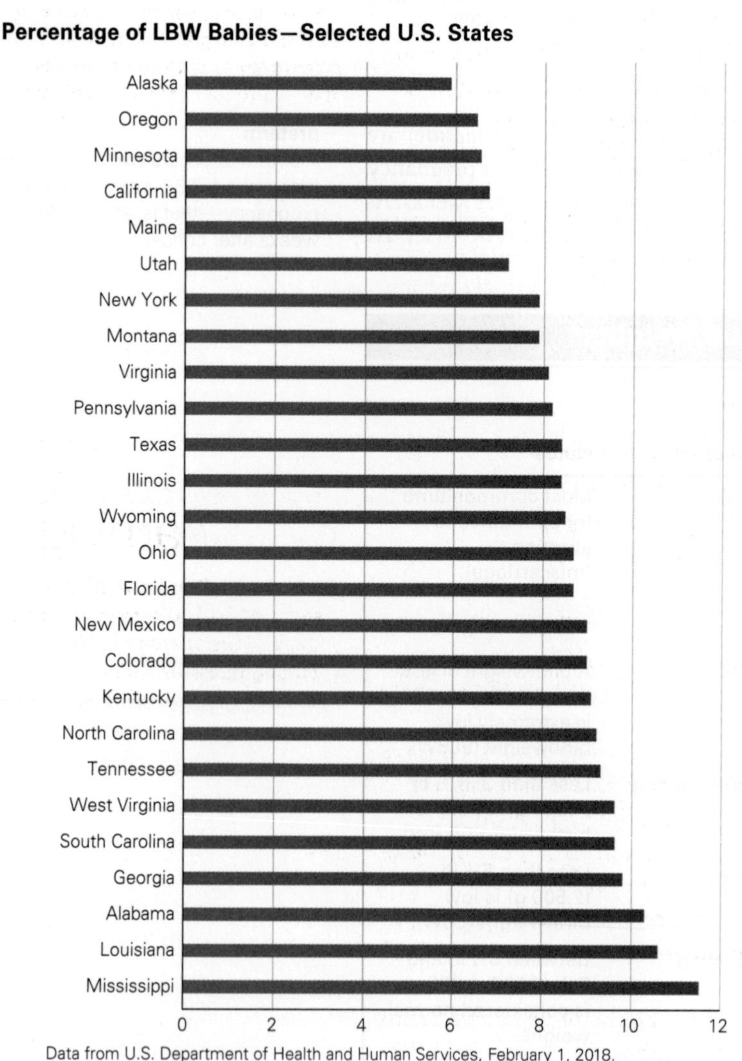

FIGURE 2.6 Where Were You Born? Rates of low birthweight vary by nation, from about 4 to 20 percent, and, as you see here, within nations. Why? Poverty is a correlate—is it also a cause?

newborns, although stress, medical care, and pollution are also factors (Clayborne et al., 2017; Lamichhane et al., 2020).

The second most common reason for low birthweight, particularly in developed nations, is drug use. Almost every psychoactive drug—including legal ones such as cigarettes and alcohol—reduces nutrition and birthweight.

A third reason is multiple births. Twins gain weight more slowly in pregnancy and are born, on average, three weeks early. Triplets and quadruplets are even earlier and smaller.

CONSEQUENCES OF LOW BIRTHWEIGHT

Every developmental milestone—smiling, holding a bottle, walking, talking—is delayed in low-birthweight infants, and rates of cognitive, visual, and hearing impairments increase. As toddlers, LBW children may cry often, pay attention less, and disobey more (Pascal et al., 2018; Ross et al., 2020).

Problems continue, especially if birthweight was very low. Children who were extremely SGA or preterm tend to have neurological problems for decades, including smaller brain volume, lower IQ, and behavioral difficulties (Beauregard et al., 2018; Linsell et al., 2018; Stålnacke et al., 2019).

In adulthood, risks persist, with higher rates of diabetes, obesity, heart disease, and depression. Social problems are evident also. A meta-analysis found that an adult who was underweight at birth was less likely to have a romantic partner or children (Mendonça et al., 2019).

However, remember plasticity. By age 4, even some extremely low birthweight infants exhibit typical brain development, especially if they had no medical complications and their mother was well educated.

In adulthood, early birth may no longer matter. Some adults function well and have full lives, even when they weighed under 3 pounds at birth (Xu et al., 2018). Two paragraphs ago you read that many low-birthweight adults had no romantic partnerships, but the same study also found that when partnerships were formed, they were as satisfying and enduring as partnerships of adults who were not small at birth (Mendonça et al., 2019).

Plasticity is lifelong. Humans can overcome many hazards as they grow older. However, it is better to prevent low birthweight in the first place. How can this be done? Eating well and avoiding drugs is an obvious first step.

Beyond that, the macrosystem and microsystem of the pregnant women is important. For this, data on immigrants to the United States provide insight. As already mentioned, low SES correlates with low birthweight (Martinson & Reichman, 2016), and, for many reasons, immigrants tend to be poor. Thus, it might be expected that they would have more low-birthweight newborns.

But they do not. In what is called the **immigrant paradox**, the newborns of immigrant women tend to be heavier and healthier than those born to native-born women of the same SES and ethnicity (Fuentes-Afflick et al., 2014; Marks et al., 2014). This paradox was once called the *Hispanic paradox* when birthweight data from women born in Mexico and other Latin American countries surprised demographers. Now the data on immigrants from the Caribbean, Africa, eastern Europe, and Asia also show paradoxical SES effects.

immigrant paradox
The surprising, paradoxical fact that low-SES immigrant women tend to have fewer birth complications than native-born peers with higher incomes.

Why? One hypothesis is that immigrant fathers and communities cherish pregnant women, keeping them drug-free and well-fed, buffering the stress of poverty. The women themselves may welcome motherhood more than nonimmigrant women (Fleuriet & Sunil, 2018; Luecken et al., 2013). Ironically, after several generations of U.S. life, prenatal as well as postnatal health suffers (Fox et al., 2018).

RISING AND FALLING RATES OF LBW

Low birthweight is less common in most nations than it was. Because they were not SGA, a billion adults alive who would have died a century ago. Fewer pregnant women are severely malnourished, so their fetuses weigh more, and that increases survival. In 1990, the worldwide death rate in the first month of life was 36 per thousand; in 2017 it was 19 per thousand (World Bank, 2018).

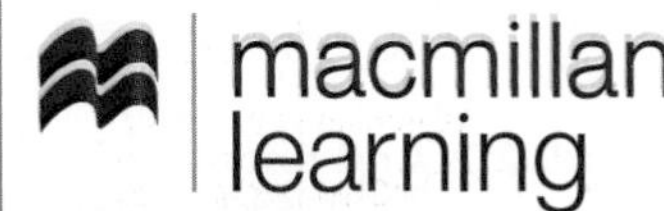

Watch **VIDEO: Low Birthweight in India** to learn about the various causes of LBW among babies in India.

Success is particularly evident in China, Cuba, and Chile, where low birthweight has plummeted since 2000. In those nations, prenatal care has become a national priority, a conclusion of a study provocatively titled *Low birth weight outcomes: Why better in Cuba than Alabama?* (Neggers & Crowe, 2013).

Although most nations have reduced low birthweight, in some nations, rates are rising. Many of those nations are in sub-Saharan Africa, where global warming, HIV/AIDS, food shortages, and civil wars all reduce nutrition for the poorest women.

In other rising nations, the increase in LBW is unexpected. One puzzle comes from the United States. The rate of low birthweight fell steadily until 1990, when it was 7.0, comparable with most other developed nations. But it continued to fall in most nations, down to 4 per 1,000 births, but in the United States it rose to 8.28 percent in 2018 (Martin et al., November 27, 2019).

Added to the puzzle is that several changes in maternal ethnicity, age, and health since 1990 should have *decreased* LBW. For instance, although the rate of LBW among African Americans is higher than the national average (14 percent compared with 8 percent), and although teenagers have smaller babies than do women in their 20s, the birth rate among both groups was much lower in 2018 than in 1990.

Similarly, unintended pregnancies (more often LBW) are less common (Finer & Zolna, 2016), and two conditions that produce heavier babies (maternal obesity and diabetes) have increased since 1990. What could the explanation be?

One hypothesis is that fertility measures have produced more multiple births: twins and triplets are much more often born small. That could be part of the explanation, but LBW rates are rising for naturally conceived singletons in every ethnic group (Womack et al., 2018). In the past decade, reproductive technology and expertise recommends against multiple births, and fewer in vitro twins have been born. But the LBW rate continues to increase (Martin et al., November 27, 2019).

Perhaps the problem is nutrition. The U.S. Department of Agriculture (Coleman-Jensen et al., 2015) reported an increase in the rate of *food insecurity* (measured by skipped meals, use of food stamps, and outright hunger) between the first seven years of the twenty-first century and the next seven, from about 11 percent to about 15 percent (see Figure 2.7).

THINK CRITICALLY: Food scarcity, drug use, and single parenthood have all been suggested as reasons for the LBW rate in the United States. Which is it—or are there other factors?

The group most likely to be food insecure are young mothers. Some undereat so that their children have food—unaware that they are harming a future child. Maternal hunger adds stress to their children, who become stressed in return, affecting

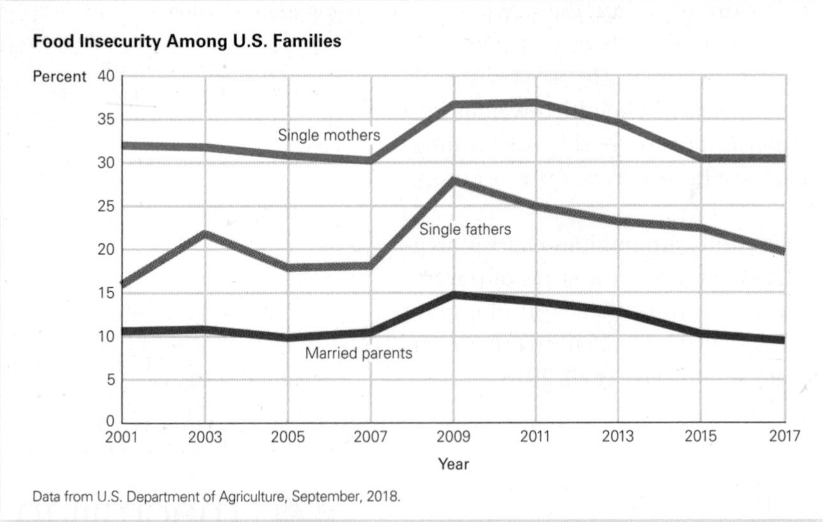

FIGURE 2.7 And Recovery? As you can see, all family types were affected by the Great Recession that began in 2007—especially single fathers, who were most likely to lose their jobs and not know how to get food stamps. But why are children of single mothers hungry more often than children of single fathers and three times as often as children of married parents? The data show correlation; researchers do not agree about causes.

OBSERVATION QUIZ
Is the gap between single mothers and single fathers increasing or decreasing? (see answer, page 71) ↑

their mothers and their future siblings (King, 2018).

A related possibility is lack of health care among the poorest Americans, especially young adults. Since untreated infections and chronic illness correlate with LBW, health care may be an explanation.

Another hypothesis is drug use, more common among young women in the United States than in most other nations (Natarajan, 2017). In the United States, the birth rate is highest among 20- to 24-year-olds, and so is drug use—in that age group, one in every nine women smoke cigarettes during pregnancy (Drake et al., 2018). In the past few years, cigarette smoking has decreased in every age group, but vaping (e-cigarette use) is increasing, particularly among young women. Research on lower animals finds that vaping reduces birthweight (Cardenas et al., 2019).

Looking beyond the United States, some trends are ominous. In recent years, low birthweight has decreased markedly in Asia, but that may be reversed as smoking and drinking among young Asian women are increasing. That seems to be happening in Japan, where low birthweight was slightly more than 6 percent in 2000 but almost 10 percent in 2015. Smoking and drinking are among the possible culprits, but so is undereating during pregnancy (Tamura et al., 2018). In Japan as well as in the United States, young women are particularly likely to want to be thinner than is healthy.

In every hypothesis, we must distinguish correlation from causation. Since low birthweight varies from nation to nation and year to year, the social context matters. For developing nations, the first steps are obvious—less hunger and better prenatal care. But for developed nations, many hypotheses need to be explored.

what have you learned?

1. What chromosomal miscounts might result in a surviving child?
2. What is the cause and consequence of Down syndrome?
3. How likely are you to be a carrier of a recessive condition?
4. Why is sickle-cell disease very common in some parts of Africa?
5. What is the role of the genetic counselor?
6. What are the main causes of low birthweight?
7. Are there important differences in low birthweight from one nation to another?

Birth

About 38 weeks (266 days) after conception, the fetal brain signals massive increases in the hormone *oxytocin* to start labor. Birth occurs after 12 hours of active labor for first births and 7 hours for subsequent ones. These are averages: Labor may take

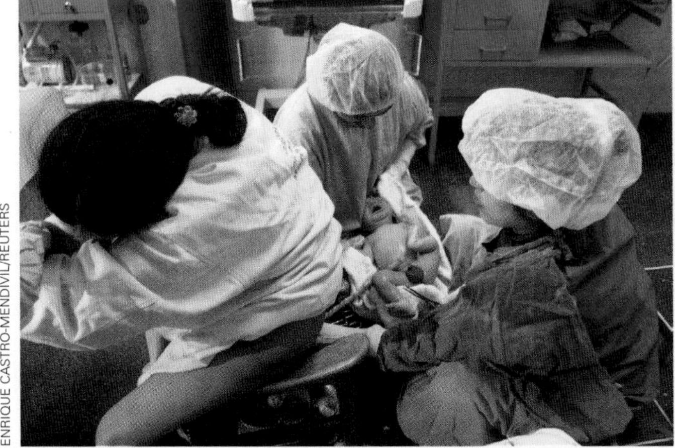

ENRIQUE CASTRO-MENDIVIL/REUTERS

FRANK HERHOLDT/THE IMAGE BANK/GETTY IMAGES

Choice, Culture, or Cohort? Why do it that way? Both of these women (in Peru, on the *left*, in England, on the *right*) chose methods of labor that are unusual in the United States, where birth stools and birthing pools are uncommon. However, in all three nations, most births occur in hospitals—a rare choice a century ago.

twice or half as long. Some women believe they are in active labor for days, and others say 10 minutes.

The other average is the due date. Only about 1 baby in 20 is born exactly on their due date. Birth is still *full term* two weeks before or after that date. You just read about babies born preterm, as occurs in about 10 percent of U.S. births, some already 2,500 grams even though early. In developed nations, post-term births are rare (less than 1 percent) because usually labor is induced after a week past due.

Variations in How and Where

Birth is universal, but specifics vary tremendously. Even such a simple fact as birth position is not standard. In some nations, women labor standing, squatting, or sitting, and give birth upright.

In most hospital births, women give birth lying on their backs, a position that makes it easier for a doctor or midwife to assist the fetal head emerging from the vagina. This raises another possible variation—where should birth occur?

HOSPITAL OR HOME

Traditionally in every nation, birth occurred at home. That is still the case in about half of the world. If a nation has few doctors, and if hospitals are distant and poorly equipped, birth happens at home, ideally with a trained attendant (Lane & Garrod, 2016). That is quicker and safer than a hospital birth.

In developed nations, births are almost always in hospitals. Some European nations have a relatively high percentage (more than 10 percent) of home births, with the highest proportion (about a third) in the Netherlands. In that country, home births are integrated into the national health care system, and are "at least as safe" as hospital births (Walker, 2017).

In what is termed "the cross-Atlantic divide," less than 1 percent of U.S. births are home births. Rates vary markedly from state to state, higher in the West, with Montana having about 3 percent of home births, and lower in the South, with Alabama having less than half a percent (MacDorman & Declercq, 2019).

Although home births, overall, are less expensive than hospital births, in most U.S. states they are not covered by public or private insurance. That is part of the reason home births are more common among White, relatively educated women

◆◆ Especially for Conservatives and Liberals
Do people's attitudes about medical intervention at birth reflect their attitudes about medicine at other points in their life span, in such areas as assisted reproductive technology (ART), immunization, and life support? (see response, page 71)

than among women of color or of low SES, especially those who are under age 20 (MacDorman & Declercq, 2019).

RISKS AND BENEFITS

Unlike in Europe, in the United States, although it is rare for a viable fetus to die at birth, the risk is higher for home births. As you already read, very preterm or severely deformed babies might die at birth, but overall about 1 in 10,000 home births result in the death of a newborn, a rate about four times the rate in hospitals births (Grünebaum et al., 2020). The reason is that a sudden emergency might require immediate intervention that is possible only in a hospital, such as surgery.

Given that, why would any woman plan a home birth? The reasons include exactly such intervention: Home births are far less likely to involve surgery (such as a *cesarean section* or *episiotomy*) and other methods to speed labor. Home births involve less drugs and less intervention of any kind. If surgery seems necessary, a woman can be taken to a hospital.

Home births may also be less stressful for the woman, in part because more familiar people—partners, parents, friends—can be part of the process. Many women choosing a home birth have already had a baby in a hospital, and were not happy with the experience (MacDorman & Declercq, 2019).

A third option is increasingly available: either a self-standing birthing center, or a hospital that allows midwives to deliver babies, and that encourages fathers to be present at birth unless surgery is needed. Midwife births, whether at home, in a birthing center, or in a hospital, have lower rates of various complications and interventions than physician births, in part because midwives emphasize breathing, massage, and social support (Bodner-Adler et al., 2017; Raipuria et al., 2018; Renfrew et al., 2014).

An innovation that makes birth easier in hospitals or homes is a **doula**, a person trained to support the laboring woman. Doulas time contractions, use massage, provide encouragement, and do whatever else is helpful. Often they come to the woman's home during early labor and return after birth to encourage breast-feeding. Doulas are chosen by many women, but they have proven to be particularly helpful for immigrant, low-income, or unpartnered women who may feel intimidated by doctors (Kang, 2014; Saxbe, 2017).

ELIOT ELISOFON/THE LIFE PICTURE COLLECTION/GETTY IMAGES

They Called It "Catching" the Baby Midwife Mahala Couch shows her strong hands that "caught" thousands of newborns in the back woods of Southern Appalachia. Midwife births became illegal in about 1920, but many women preferred home birth with Mahala over hospital birth with a doctor. Currently, midwives are trained, certified, and legal in most states and nations.

doula
A woman who helps with the birth process. In Latin America, traditionally a doula was the only professional who attended childbirth. Now doulas are likely to arrive at the woman's home during early labor and later work alongside a hospital's staff.

cesarean section (c-section)
A surgical birth in which incisions through the mother's abdomen and uterus allow the fetus to be removed quickly instead of being delivered through the vagina.

THE CESAREAN

The most common intervention occurs only in hospitals, only with physicians, never at home, and never by midwives. A **cesarean section** (or **c-section**) is a surgical procedure in which the fetus is removed though incisions in the abdomen and uterus, instead of being pushed by contractions through the vagina.

C-sections were once rare, a last-ditch effort to save a new life when the mother was dying and vaginal birth was impossible. Now, with better anesthesia and fetal monitoring, more than one birth in five worldwide (21 percent in 2015, compared to 12 percent in 2000) is a c-section (Boerma et al., 2018).

Cesareans are medically indicated for about 10 percent of births. Multiple births (twins or more), breech births (fetus is not positioned head down), prior c-section, long active labor (more than 24 hours), a narrow pelvis, a large fetus, and advanced maternal age are all conditions that suggest surgery. However, none of these *requires* a c-section.

For instance, a large study of all births (78,880) in the state of Washington focused on the relationship between age and various complications. Sixty percent of new mothers aged 50 or older delivered via c-section; 40 percent delivered vaginally (Richards et al., 2016).

Public health experts are troubled by increases in c-sections in the past decade and by international disparities. Too few (4 percent) cesareans are performed in central Africa, including about 1 percent in South Sudan, where childbirth is still a leading cause of death. Too many occur in the Caribbean and Latin America (44 percent), with the highest of all in the Dominican Republic (58 percent) (Boerma et al., 2018).

Nations with very low cesarean rates also have high levels of childbirth deaths, but nations with high cesarean rates are not necessarily healthier. In the United States, the cesarean rate was 32 percent in 2018 (Martin et al., November 27, 2019).

Cesareans have immediate advantages for hospitals (easier to schedule, quicker, and more expensive than vaginal deliveries) and for women (advance planning, quick birth). Disadvantages appear later. After a c-section, breast-feeding is harder and medical complications more likely. Babies born via c-section are more likely to develop asthma or become obese as children (Chu et al., 2017; Mueller et al., 2017). One reason: Vaginal deliveries provide a beneficial microbiome (Wallis, 2014).

The New Family

Birth is the most dramatic transformation of the entire life span. This is evident in changes to the terminology: A fetus becomes a baby, a woman or man becomes a mother or father, an older person becomes a grandparent, an adult sister or brother becomes an aunt or uncle, and, if this baby is not the first-born and thus all those name changes have already occurred, an older child may become a sister or brother.

All those people are profoundly affected by birth. Here we focus only on three of them: baby, mother, and father.

THE BABY

Newborns usually breathe and cry on their own. The first breaths of air bring oxygen to the lungs and blood, and the infant's color changes from bluish to reddish. ("Reddish" refers to blood color, visible beneath the skin, and applies to newborns of all skin tones.) Eyes open wide; tiny fingers grab; even tinier toes stretch and retract. Usually full-term babies are instantly, zestfully, ready for life.

Newborn health is often measured by the **Apgar scale**, first developed by Dr. Virginia Apgar. When she earned her M.D. in 1933, Apgar wanted to work in a hospital but was told that only men did surgery. She became an anesthesiologist, present at many births but never the doctor in charge.

Apgar scale
A quick assessment of a newborn's health, from 0 to 10. Below 5 is an emergency—a neonatal pediatrician is summoned immediately. Most babies are at 7, 8, or 9—almost never a perfect 10.

Apgar saw that "delivery room doctors focused on mothers and paid little attention to babies. Those who were small and struggling were often left to die" (Beck, 2009, p. D1). To save young lives, Apgar developed a simple rating scale of five vital signs—color, heart rate, cry, muscle tone, and breathing. Nurses used the scale and summoned help if the score was below 7. Many new lives were saved.

Newborns respond to people, even in the first hours of life (Zeifman, 2013). They listen, stare, cry, stop crying, and cuddle. In the first day or two, a professional might administer the **Brazelton Neonatal Behavioral Assessment Scale (NBAS)**, which records 46 behaviors, including 20 reflexes. Many of them are listed in Table 2.4. One way health professionals improve parental bonding to newborns is by demonstrating the newborn's abilities on the NBAS (Barlow et al., 2018).

Brazelton Neonatal Behavioral Assessment Scale (NBAS)
A test that is often administered to newborns, which measures responsiveness and records 46 behaviors, including 20 reflexes.

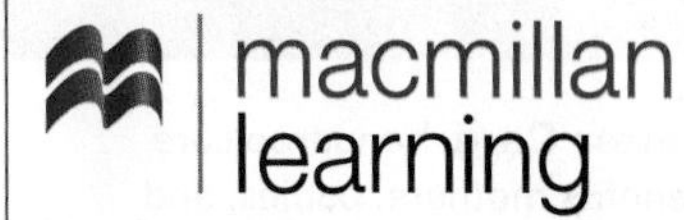

VIDEO: Newborn Reflexes shows several infants displaying the reflexes discussed in this section.

NEW MOTHERS

Birth is, of course, a physical and psychological stress on the mother. She may be euphoric, so happy that she has her own baby that she finds it hard to relax. Or she may be in pain and disappointed with some aspect of the birth process, which almost never occurs exactly as mothers hope.

TABLE 2.4 Newborn Reflexes

Technically, a reflex is an involuntary response to a particular stimulus. The strength of reflexes varies, depending on genes, drugs, and health. Three sets of reflexes aid survival:

Reflexes that maintain oxygen supply

- The *breathing reflex* begins even before the umbilical cord, with its supply of oxygen, is cut.
- Additional reflexes that maintain oxygen are reflexive *hiccups* and *sneezes*, as well as *thrashing* (moving the arms and legs about) to escape something that covers the face.

Reflexes that maintain constant body temperature

- When infants are cold, they *cry, shiver*, and *tuck their legs* close to their bodies. When they are hot, they try to *push away* blankets and then stay still.

Reflexes that manage feeding

- The *sucking reflex* causes newborns to suck whatever touches their lips—fingers, toes, blankets, and rattles, as well as nipples of various textures and shapes.
- In the *rooting reflex*, babies turn their mouths toward anything brushing against their cheeks—a reflexive search for a nipple—and start to suck.
- *Swallowing* also aids feeding, as does *crying* when the stomach is empty and *spitting up* when too much is swallowed quickly.

Other reflexes promoted survival of the species in ancient times but now they signify healthy brain development. Among them:

- *Babinski reflex.* When a newborn's feet are stroked, the toes fan upward.
- *Stepping reflex.* When newborns are held upright, feet touching a flat surface, they move their legs as if to walk.
- *Swimming reflex.* When held horizontally on their stomachs, newborns stretch out their arms and legs.
- *Palmar grasping reflex.* When something touches newborns' palms, they grip it tightly.
- *Moro reflex.* When someone bangs on the table they are lying on, they fling their arms out and then bring them together on their chests, crying with wide-open eyes.

kangaroo care
A form of newborn care in which mothers (and sometimes fathers) rest their babies on their naked chests, like kangaroo mothers that carry their immature newborns in a pouch on their abdomen.

Some mothers are immediately given their newborns to hold and breast-feed. This may aid early development of the *mother–infant bond*, a strong, loving connection that mothers have for their baby. Some have claimed that people are like sheep and goats, who nurture their newborns if, and only if, they smell and nuzzle them immediately after birth (Klaus & Kennell, 1976).

However, the hypothesis that early skin-to-skin contact is *essential* for human nurturance is false (Eyer, 1992; Lamb, 1982). Substantial research on monkeys began with *cross-fostering*, when newborns are removed from their biological mothers in the first days of life and raised by another monkey, female or male. A strong and beneficial relationship between infant and foster parent may develop (Suomi, 2002).

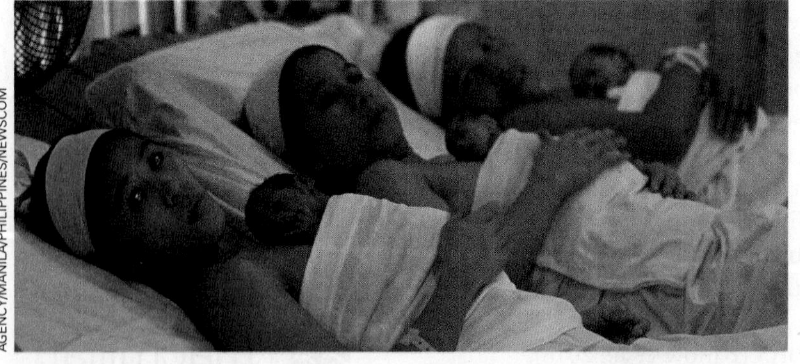

Better Care Kangaroo care benefits mothers, babies, and hospitals, saving space and medical costs in this ward in Manila. Kangaroo care is one reason Filipino infant mortality in 2010 was only one-fifth of what it was in 1950.

For people, bonding can begin before birth, or it may not be established until days later. The benefits of early contact are evident with **kangaroo care**, in which the newborn lies between the mother's breasts, skin-to-skin, listening to her heartbeat and feeling her body heat. A review of 124 studies confirms that kangaroo-care newborns sleep more deeply, gain weight more quickly, and spend more time alert

than do infants with standard care, as well as being healthier overall (Boundy et al., 2016).

When birth hormones decrease, many new mothers are less enraptured with their infants. In the first weeks after birth, about one new mother in eight experiences **postpartum depression**, called *baby blues* in the mild version and *postpartum psychosis* in the most severe form.

postpartum depression
A new mother's feelings of inadequacy and sadness in the days and weeks after giving birth.

The first sign that something is amiss may be euphoria after birth. A new mother may be unable to sleep, stop talking, or eat normally. After that initial high, severe depression may set in, with long-term impact on the child. Postpartum depression may not be evident right away; anxiety and depression symptoms are stronger two or three months after birth (Kozhimannil & Kim, 2014).

Postpartum depression is caused not only by hormonal changes and the body stresses of the birth, but also by circumstances of family support and the reality of the baby. One single mother who experienced postpartum depression thought:

> My only problem in life was that I didn't have a baby. On the day I had a baby, I discovered that no, I had other problems. I hadn't any money, I was in debt, the family was fighting about the debt, it was partly my fault . . . and I started to see I wasn't such a good mother as I had thought I would be. I used to think what could be difficult? It's enough for you to love the baby and everything will be fine. This didn't happen because the baby didn't respond. I'm affectionate, I'd come and take her, hug her and the baby didn't like this. She didn't like to be hugged, she didn't like affection.
>
> *[O'Dougherty, 2013, p. 190]*

With postpartum depression, the mother feels sad and inadequate, and baby care (feeding, diapering, bathing, breast-feeding) feels very burdensome. The newborn cry may trigger anger, a terrifying reaction that makes some women overprotective, insisting that no one else care for the baby. This signifies a fearful mother, not a healthy one.

Fortunately, postpartum depression can be prevented, diagnosed, and treated (O'Hara & McCabe, 2013). To help with diagnosis, consider the questions of the Edinburgh Postnatal Depression scale (see Table 2.5).

A mother who experiences postpartum depression feels terrible ("the worst time of my life," one said). She usually recovers by the time the baby is 6 months old. Unfortunately, her baby may not experience the joyful interaction and frequent talking that infants need to thrive. Family support, for both the mother and the baby, may be crucial.

TABLE 2.5 The Edinburgh Postnatal Depression Scale

The Edinburgh Postnatal Depression Scale asks women how they felt *in the past week.*

1. *I have been able to laugh and see the funny side of things.*
   0-As much as I always could | 1-Not quite so much now
   2-Definitely not so much now | 3-Not at all

2. *I have looked forward with enjoyment to things.*
   0-As much as I ever did | 1-Rather less than I used to
   2-Definitely less than I used to | 3-Hardly at all

3. *I have blamed myself unnecessarily when things went wrong.*
   3-Yes, most of the time | 2-Yes, some of the time
   1-Not very often | 0-No, never

4. *I have been anxious or worried for no good reason.*
   0-No, not at all | 1-Hardly ever
   2-Yes, sometimes | 3-Yes, very often

5. *I have felt scared or panicky for no very good reason.*
   3-Yes, quite a lot | 2-Yes, sometimes
   1-No, not much | 0-No, not at all

6. *Things have been getting on top of me.*
   3-Yes, most of the time I haven't been able to cope at all
   2-Yes, sometimes I haven't been coping as well as usual
   1-No, most of the time I have coped quite well
   0-No, I have been coping as well as ever

7. *I have been so unhappy that I have had difficulty sleeping.*
   3-Yes, most of the time | 2-Yes, sometimes
   1-Not very often | 0-No, not at all

8. *I have felt sad or miserable.*
   3-Yes, most of the time | 2-Yes, quite often
   1-Not very often | 0-No, not at all

9. *I have been so unhappy that I have been crying.*
   3-Yes, most of the time | 2-Yes, quite often
   1-Only occasionally | 0-No, never

10. *The thought of harming myself has occurred to me.*
   3-Yes, quite often | 2-Sometimes
   1-Hardly ever | 0-Never

The total score ranges from 0 to 30. Below 9 indicates no problem; 9–12 suggests normal "baby blues"; above 12 indicates depression. High scores indicate that more intense screening is needed by a trained clinician, to discern if the new mother is truly depressed, anxious, or suicidal. (A 2 or 3 on question 10 is alarming, even if the rest are 0 or 1.)

Fathers and Others

The newborn's appearance (big hairless head, tiny feet, and so on) stirs the human heart, a genetic response that has aided survival of our species. Hormones triggered by the birth process affect both parents, who often are enraptured by their scraggly newborns as well as appreciative of each other. As one father, himself a nurse, wrote:

> Throughout most of this pregnancy I was able to form intelligent thoughts and remained relatively coherent, but as soon as we were admitted to the labor and delivery unit I felt my IQ plummet and all that I have learned as a nurse escaped me. . . . In my wife's own words, the whole ordeal was hot, sweaty, messy and a "crime scene of body fluids". . . . even when she felt "hot, sweaty and disgusting" I was in complete awe of her and couldn't have been prouder of her. She was as beautiful to me in those moments as she was on our wedding day and I will never forget it.
>
> *[cjcsoon2bnp, February 13, 2017]*

Especially for Nurses in Obstetrics
Can the father be of any practical help in the birth process? (see response, page 71)

Not every depressed mother reduces her baby's development. The research finds that if she manages to respond sensitively to her baby's needs, within a well-functioning, supportive family (with good emotional management, communication, and clear roles and routines) the baby may develop well (Parade et al., 2018).

Some new mothers have other family members—the father, a same-sex partner, a grandparent, a sibling—who provide essential emotional and practical support. Fathers themselves may need support after birth. Some experience pregnancy and birth biologically, not just psychologically, with weight gain and indigestion during pregnancy, pain during labor, and depression after birth (Gutierrez-Galve et al., 2015; Leavitt, 2009).

couvade
Symptoms of pregnancy and birth experienced by fathers.

Paternal experiences of pregnancy and birth are called **couvade**, expected in some cultures, a normal variation in many, and considered pathological in others (Piechowski-Jozwiak & Bogousslavsky, 2018). Fathers in many nations have been studied, with at least one-quarter of all first-time fathers in India, Poland, Australia, and England experiencing couvade (Brennan, 2010; Ganapathy, 2014).

A detailed study in Jordan found quite high rates. In that study, 59 percent of first-time fathers experienced couvade, with 8 or more of 26 possible symptoms in the final three months of pregnancy (Mrayan et al., 2019). More than half of the prospective fathers had heartburn, leg cramps, mood swings, and digestive problems, all symptoms that are common in pregnant women.

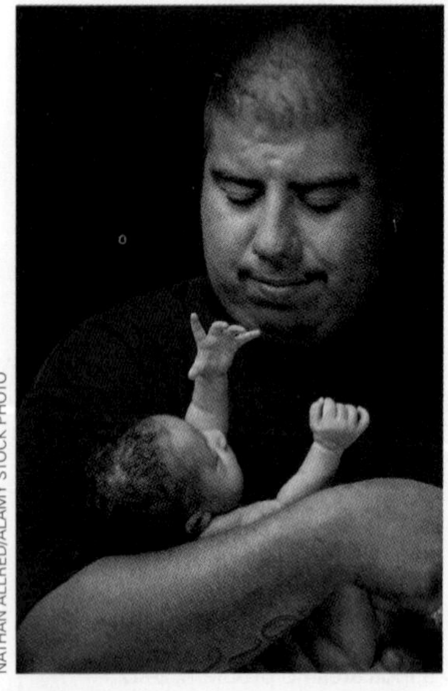
NATHAN ALLRED/ALAMY STOCK PHOTO

Mutual Joy For thousands of years hormones and instincts have propelled fathers and babies to reach out to each other, developing lifelong connections.

Many new fathers hesitate to talk about their emotions. The data show that many prospective and new fathers do not sleep well, and have irrational fears about serious illness or deaths, of their partners or newborns. One did not want to complain because, he said, "I'm always conscious that [partner]'s got it a lot worse." Another said at the birth, "I felt a bit more like a spare part . . . I just felt in the way" (quoted in Darwin et al., 2017).

Father emotions continue after birth. One said:

> When I hear my boy cry I become a stupid and clueless mess. . . . I know logically that as long as he is clean/dry, warm, and fed that he is not suffering and just needs to be held and settled but that doesn't stop me from going into crisis mode.
>
> *[cjcsoon2bnp, February 13, 2017]*

Some men find relief at work, where they put the stress of pregnancy and fatherhood behind them. If they work with other new fathers, they might talk about their feelings. An engineer said, "We probably spend half the day talking about babies and kids and that sort of thing. . . . I know that there's guys there that have had similar experiences and they know what it's like. They know how I'm feeling if I say Oh, we've had a rough night. . . . Some people have had worse experiences so you think, what we're going through is normal" (quoted in Darwin et al., 2017).

ONE GRANDMOTHER'S EXPERIENCE

The birth experience may affect other family members. As you already read, they may provide critical support for mothers, fathers, and infants. Time to tell more about the birth first mentioned in the beginning of this chapter.

> I held a bent right leg in place with all my strength, fighting against strong muscles to move it. A nurse strained as she held the left. The midwife commanded "push . . . push . . . push." Bethany's arm muscles bulged as she pulled a sheet tied to a metal stanchion above her. A circle of fetal skull visible, then larger, then crowning. Tissues tore, Bethany pushed once more.
>
> "Yes! Yes! Yes!" the midwife shouted. A head emerged, quickly followed by all 4139 grams of Caleb. Apgar was a stellar 9, every other number was good.
>
> Bethany, smiling, began to nurse. Four professionals looked on, relaxed now. This is grandmother bliss. Decades of praying, studying, teaching, and mothering led me to a miracle, 6:11 a.m., my first-born with her firstborn. Celestial music rang in my ears.
>
> The ringing grew louder, a buzzing, roaring crescendo. Bethany shimmered, overhead lights became stars, flashing bright and then dark. I was flat on the floor, looking up at four faces staring down. I had fainted. . . .
>
> I know about birth, personally and professionally. I interpret numbers and jargon; I analyze monitors and body language; I judge doctors and nurses; I evaluate hospitals, notice stray paper on floors, hear sharp voices in corridors, see faded pictures on walls. Nothing here amiss; this hospital was excellent.
>
> I also know my daughter: strong, healthy, drug-free. I expected Caleb to be well-formed and Bethany okay. I was relieved and happy—not surprised—when my almost perfect daughter began nursing my quite perfect grandson. Then why did I faint when all the drama was over? Indeed, why faint at all?
>
> *[Berger, 2019]*

When I analyzed it, I realized that the hormones and evolutionary forces that foster bonding between parents and newborns, as well as depression in parents, affect grandmothers as well. I was not a dispassionate observer: We all are emotionally entangled in our own lives and in those of people we love.

As described in later chapters, the experiences and relationships of each person continues to death, and maybe beyond. Conception is one moment, birth is another: They begin a long journey.

what have you learned?

1. What is the typical birth process?
2. Who was Virginia Apgar and what did she do?
3. What are the immediate and long-term results of a cesarean birth?
4. Why do cesarean rates vary internationally?
5. What are the advantages and disadvantages of a hospital birth versus a home birth?
6. How are newborns socially interactive?
7. What causes postpartum depression?
8. How are fathers affected by birth?
9. Why is kangaroo care beneficial?
10. When does the parent–infant bond form?

SUMMARY

In the Beginning

1. Genes are the foundation for all development. Human conception occurs when two gametes (an ovum and a sperm, each with 23 chromosomes) combine to form a zygote. Those 46 chromosomes contain the genes, about 21,000 in all.

2. Sex is determined by the 23rd pair of chromosomes, with a Y sperm creating an XY (male) zygote and an X sperm creating an XX (female) zygote. If one zygote splits, that creates monozygotic twins; if two ova are fertilized at the same time, that creates dizygotic twins.

3. Genes may interact additively, or they can follow a dominant–recessive pattern. The genotype may not be expressed in the phenotype, which is the actual characteristics of the person.

From Zygote to Newborn

4. In the germinal period (first two weeks after conception), cells duplicate and differentiate, and the developing organism implants itself in the lining of the uterus. In the embryonic period (third through eighth week), organs and body structures are formed, except the sex organs.

5. In the fetal period (ninth week until birth), the fetus grows and all the organs begin to function. Crucial for viability is brain development at 22 weeks, when a fetus born that early might survive. Every week after that increases weight and odds of survival.

Problems and Solutions

6. If a zygote has more or fewer than 46 chromosomes, it usually does not implant. However, if an extra chromosome is at the 21st site (Down syndrome) or at the 23rd site, that person has lifelong disabilities but may have a good life.

7. Everyone is a carrier for genetic abnormalities. Usually these conditions are recessive, and no fetus is affected unless both parents carry the same disorder. Genetic testing and counseling can help many couples avoid having a baby with serious chromosomal or genetic problems.

8. Thousands of teratogens, especially drugs and alcohol, have the potential to harm the embryo or fetus. Actual harm occurs because of a cascade: Genes, critical periods, dose, and frequency all have an impact.

9. Low birthweight (less than 5½ pounds, or 2,500 grams) may result from multiple fetuses, placental problems, maternal illness, genes, malnutrition, smoking, drinking, and drug use. Underweight babies may experience physical and intellectual problems lifelong. Newborns that are small for gestational age (SGA) are especially vulnerable.

10. Maternal behavior increases the risk of problems, including low birthweight. Fathers, other relatives, and the society also can affect the incidence of disabilities.

Birth

11. Ideally, infants are born full term, weighing 7 pounds, with an Apgar of at least 8. Medical assistance speeds contractions, dulls pain, and saves lives, but some interventions may be unnecessary, including about half of the cesareans performed in the United States.

12. Newborns are primed for social interaction, and fathers and mothers are often emotionally connected to their baby and to each other. Paternal support correlates with shorter labor and fewer complications.

13. About one women in seven experiences postpartum depression, feeling unhappy, incompetent, or unwell after giving birth. The most vulnerable time is when the baby is several weeks old, with social support crucial for mother, father, and infant.

KEY TERMS

gamete (p. 37)
zygote (p. 37)
genome (p. 38)
allele (p. 38)
epigenetics (p. 39)
genotype (p. 39)
phenotype (p. 39)
microbiome (p. 40)
carrier (p. 41)
X-linked (p. 42)
monozygotic (MZ) twins (p. 43)
dizygotic (DZ) twins (p. 44)
germinal period (p. 46)
embryonic period (p. 46)
fetal period (p. 46)
embryo (p. 46)
fetus (p. 47)
age of viability (p. 48)
Down syndrome (p. 51)
fragile X syndrome (p. 52)
teratogen (p. 55)
fetal alcohol syndrome (FAS) (p. 57)
low birthweight (LBW) (p. 58)
very low birthweight (VLBW) (p. 58)
extremely low birthweight (ELBW) (p. 58)
preterm (p. 59)
small for gestational age (SGA) (p. 59)
immigrant paradox (p. 61)
doula (p. 64)
cesarean section (c-section) (p. 64)
Apgar scale (p. 65)
Brazelton Neonatal Behavioral Assessment Scale (NBAS) (p. 65)
kangaroo care (p. 66)
postpartum depression (p. 67)
couvade (p. 68)

APPLICATIONS

1. Pick one of your traits and explain the influences that both nature *and* nurture have on it. For example, if you have a short temper, explain its origins in your genetics, your culture, and your childhood experiences.

2. Go to a nearby greeting-card store and analyze the cards about pregnancy and birth. Do you see any cultural attitudes (e.g., variations depending on the sex of the newborn or of the parent)? If possible, compare those cards with cards from a store that caters to another economic or ethnic group.

3. Draw a genetic chart of your biological relatives, going back as many generations as you can, listing all serious illnesses and causes of death. Include ancestors who died in infancy. Do you see any genetic susceptibility? If so, how can you overcome it?

4. Interview three mothers of varied backgrounds about their birth experiences. Make your interviews open-ended—let the mothers choose what to tell you, as long as they give at least a 10-minute description. Then compare and contrast the three accounts, noting especially any influences of culture, personality, circumstances, and cohort.

ESPECIALLY FOR ANSWERS

Response for Medical Doctors (from p. 40): No. Personalized medicine is the hope of many physicians, but appearance (the phenotype) does not indicate alleles, recessive genes, copy number variations, and other genetic factors that affect drug reactions. Many medical researchers seek to personalize chemotherapy for cancer, but although this is urgently needed, success is still experimental, even when the genotype is known.

Response for Teachers (from p. 51): Your first step would be to make sure you know about Down syndrome, by reading material about it. You would learn, among other things, that it is not usually inherited (your student need not worry about their progeny) and that some children with Down syndrome need extra medical and educational attention. This might mean you need to pay special attention to your student, whose parents might focus on the sibling.

Response for Conservatives and Liberals (from p. 63): Yes, some people are much more likely to want nature to take its course. However, personal experience often trumps political attitudes about birth and death; several of those who advocate hospital births are also in favor of spending one's final days at home.

Response for Nurses in Obstetrics (from p. 68): Usually not, unless they are experienced, well taught, or have expert guidance. But their presence provides emotional support for the woman, which makes the birth process easier and healthier for mother and baby.

OBSERVATION QUIZ ANSWERS

Answer to Observation Quiz (from p. 42): This is a figure drawn to illustrate the recessive inheritance of blue eyes, and thus eyes are the only difference shown. If this were a real family, each child would have a distinct appearance.

Answer to Observation Quiz (from p. 62): Decreasing. The reason may be related to greater gender equity. Note, however, that the recession impacted fathers dramatically, as many wage-earners lost their jobs and did not immediately know how to get public or private help in feeding their families.

PART II

CHAPTER 3 CHAPTER 4

The First Two Years

Adults don't change much in a year or two. They might have longer, grayer, or thinner hair; they might gain or lose weight; they might learn something new. But if you saw friends you hadn't seen for several years, you'd recognize them immediately.

Imagine caring for your sister's newborn every day for two months. You would learn everything about that baby—how to dress, when to play, what to feed, where to sleep. Toward the end of the two months, the baby would recognize you, smiling broadly, nestling comfortably in your arms, responding with happy noises when you spoke.

Then imagine you left to live abroad for two years. When you returned, your sister might ask you to pick up the toddler at the day-care center.

You would need to ask the teacher which child to take, because several of them might be the child you once knew so well. In those two years, weight quadruples, height increases by a foot, hair grows. Emotions change, too—fewer tears, more fears—including fear of you, a stranger.

Two years are less than 3 percent of the average human life. However, in those 24 months, people reach half their adult height, learn to run, climb and talk in sentences, and express every emotion—not just joy and fear but also love, jealousy, and shame. Invisible growth of the brain enables all these changes and more. The next two chapters describe this transformation.

PAUL THOMAS/EYEEM/GETTY IMAGES

THE FIRST TWO YEARS

Body and Mind

what will you know?

- What infant body part grows most in the first two years?
- What does it signify if an infant doesn't look for an object that disappears?
- Why do people talk to babies too young to talk back?
- How long should a baby be breast fed?

A neuroscientist learned about a Korean fortune-telling ritual for 1-year-olds:

> The unsuspecting baby is placed in front of an assortment of objects and is encouraged to pick one. . . . If the baby picks up a banana, she will never go hungry; choosing a book means she is destined for academia; a silver coin foretells wealth, or a paintbrush, creativity.
>
> I was intrigued. The very same evening I placed Olivia [her infant daughter] in front of a collection of items.
>
> A stethoscope: would she be a doctor? A stuffed dog: a vet? A plant: a Green Peace activist? A piece of pastry: a chef? And a colorful model of the brain; a neuroscientist?
>
> Olivia inspected the objects closely, took her time, and then went straight for the iPhone I had happened to leave at the corner of the table.
>
> I shouldn't have been surprised. The little girl was obsessed with this piece of machinery. She would skillfully roll herself from one side of the room to the other to grab hold of it. . . . When she finally grabbed hold of the phone she would quickly insert it into her mouth and attempt to chew. . . . Although she was only a few months old and could not even say a word she was able to infer that these metal rectangles must be extremely valuable. Little Livia's fondness for iPhones tells us something important about how our brains work.
>
> *[Sharot, 2017, pp. 152–153]*

This incident introduces the chapter for three reasons.

First, humans hope that the next generation will not only continue our values and choices, but also surpass them. Did you notice that the mother thought a stethoscope meant doctor (not nurse), a stuffed dog meant vet (not dog walker), that a plant signified Greenpeace (not farmer), and that one choice offered by a neuroscientist was a brain?

PHOTO CREDIT: ALEXSAVA/E+/GETTY IMAGES

Second, Livia employed every available sense and skill. Livia "inspected the object closely," and she "skillfully" rolled, grabbed, and mouthed the cell phone.

Third, all caregivers, every object, and each culture shape the infant body and mind, as did Korean tradition and the twenty-first-century cell phone. As you will read in this chapter on physical and cognitive development, the social context fosters every skill. Thus, babies hear, pronounce, and finally speak their home language, not any of the 600 other languages that infants elsewhere learn.

All three—parental hopes, infant curiosity, and cultural patterns are evident in every aspect of the infant body and mind. Now the details.

Body Changes

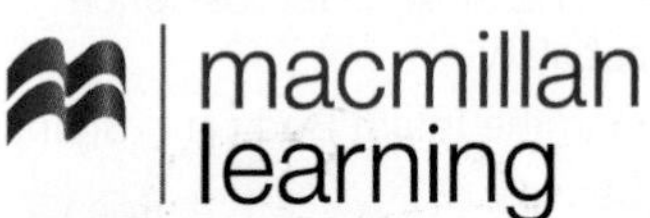

VIDEO: Physical Development in Infancy and Toddlerhood offers a quick review of the physical changes that occur during a child's first two years.

In infancy, slow growth is a sign of serious problems, so gains are closely monitored. Measurement of height, weight, and head circumference reveal whether an infant is progressing as expected—or not.

Body Size

Birthweight doubles by 4 months and triples by a year; the average 7-pound newborn might be 21 pounds on their first birthday (9,525 grams, up from 3,175 grams). Almost an inch is added every month, from about 20 inches (51 centimeters) at birth to about 30 inches (76 centimeters) at 12 months.

Growth then slows, but not by much. Most 24-month-olds weigh about 28 pounds (13 kilograms) and have added another 4 inches (10 centimeters) in the previous year. Typically, 2-year-olds are half their adult height and about one-fifth their adult weight (see Figure 3.1).

Each of these numbers is a **norm**, which is a standard for a particular population. The "particular population" for the norms just mentioned are North American infants. Remember, however, genetic diversity. Some perfectly healthy, well-fed babies are smaller or larger than the norm.

norm
An average, or standard, calculated from many individuals within a specific group or population.

percentile
A point on a ranking scale of 0 to 100. The 50th percentile is the midpoint; half of the people in the population being studied rank higher and half rank lower.

COMPARED TO THEMSELVES

Growth is often expressed in a **percentile**, ranking people on a scale from 0 to 100, so that someone who is exactly average would be at 50. Percentile ranks

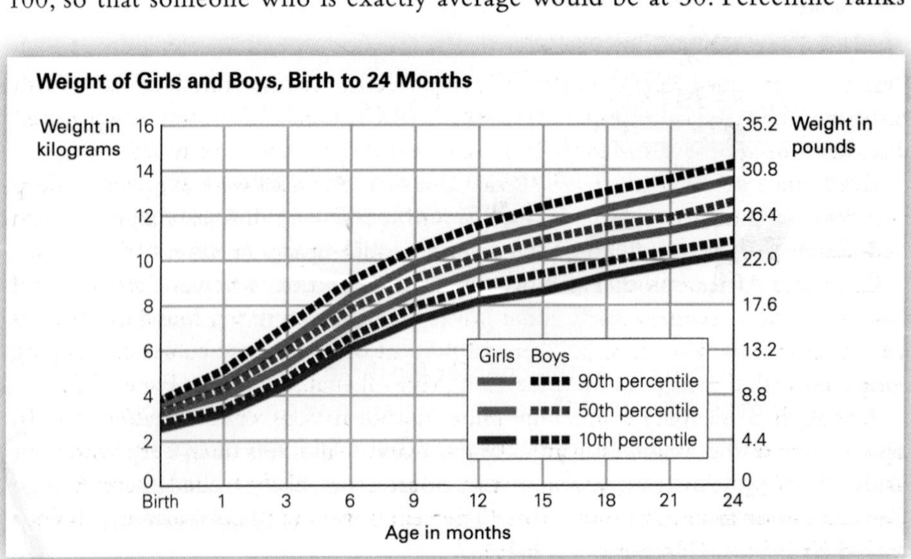

FIGURE 3.1 **Averages and Individuals** Norms and percentiles are useful—most 1-month-old girls who weigh 10 pounds should be at least 25 pounds by age 2. But although females weigh less than males on average lifelong, it is obvious that individuals do not always follow the averages.

could apply to any measurement, but for infants, percentiles are often used for growth.

For example, a 12-month-old's weight at the 30th percentile means that 29 percent of 12-month-olds weigh less and 70 percent weigh more. Healthy children vary in size, so any percentile between 10 and 90 is okay, as long as the percentile is close to the previous one for that individual.

If the percentile moves markedly up or down, that could signify trouble. A notable drop in weight, say from the 50th to the 20th percentile, suggests poor nutrition. A sudden increase, perhaps from 30th to 60th signifies overfeeding, especially if height remains at the 30th percentile.

If an infant's percentile rank falls too low, that is *failure to thrive*. The cause could be organic, such as allergies, the microbiome, and liver problems, perhaps combined with the context, such as specifics of the diet and caregiving (Lazzara et al., 2019).

Sleep

Throughout life, health and growth correlate with regular and ample sleep (El-Sheikh & Kelly, 2017). As with many health habits, sleep patterns begin in the first year.

Newborns sleep about 15 to 17 hours a day. Every week brings a few more waking minutes. By 12 months, the norm is 12 to 13 hours a day. These are averages; individuals vary. Parents report that, among every 20 young infants in the United States, one sleeps nine hours or fewer per day and one sleeps 19 hours or more (Sadeh et al., 2009).

ADEY BRYANT/CARTOONSTOCK

Danger Here Not with the infant (although those pillows should be removed), but for the family. It is hard to maintain a happy marriage if the parents are exhausted.

Sleep varies not only because of biology (maturation and genes), but also because of caregiving. Infants who drink cow's milk and eat solid foods sleep more soundly—easier for parents but not necessarily good for the baby (Dalrymple, 2019).

Culture matters, too. In the United States, one study found that Latinx infants wake more often during the night and sleep an hour less than European American infants, with Asian American and African American infants between those two groups (Ash et al., 2019). Why? Diet? Caregiver attention? Household noise? Something else? We do not know.

It is known that pain keeps infants (and their parents) awake. Colicky babies and hungry babies sleep less. But no infant follows an adult sleep pattern. One observer said, "parents are rarely well-prepared for the degree of sleep disruption a newborn infant engenders, and many have unrealistic expectations about the first few postnatal months" (C. Russell et al., 2013, p. 68).

WHERE SHOULD BABIES SLEEP?

One expectation is where the baby will sleep. Traditionally, most middle-class North American infants were expected to sleep in cribs in their own rooms; it was feared that they would be traumatized if their parents had sex in the same room.

By contrast, most infants in Asia, Africa, and Latin America were expected to sleep near their mothers, a practice called **co-sleeping**, often in their parents' bed, called **bed-sharing**. In those cultures, nighttime parent–child separation was considered cruel.

co-sleeping
A custom in which parents and their children (usually infants) sleep together in the same room.

bed-sharing
When two or more people sleep in the same bed.

Asian and African mothers still worry about separation, whereas European and North American mothers worry about privacy. A 19-nation survey found that parents act on these fears: The extremes were 82 percent of Vietnamese babies co-sleeping compared with 6 percent in New Zealand (Mindell et al., 2010) (see Figure 3.2).

Although co-sleeping is more common in poor nations, culture matters, too: In Japan—one of the wealthiest nations of the world—mothers often sleep with their babies. In North America, younger women are more likely to bed-share: A large Canadian study found that more than 40 percent of new mothers under age 25 sleep with their infants (Gilmour et al., 2019).

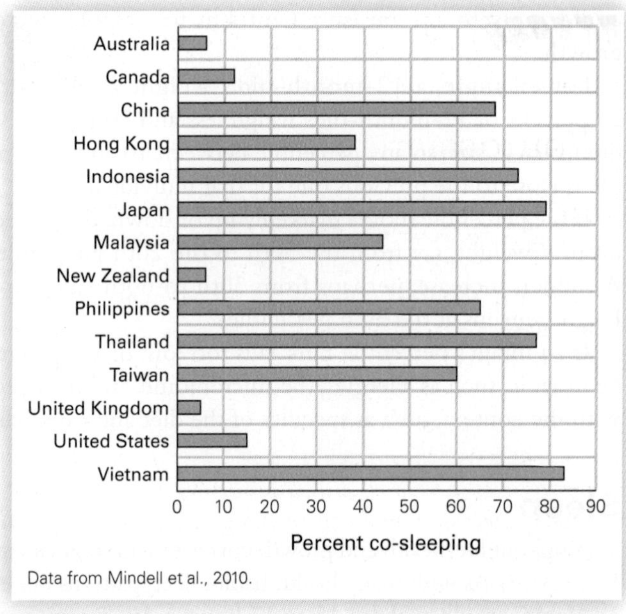

FIGURE 3.2 Awake at Night
Why the disparity between Asian and non-Asian rates of co-sleeping? It may be that Western parents use a variety of gadgets and objects—monitors, night-lights, pacifiers, cuddle cloths, sound machines—to accomplish some of what Asian parents do by having their infant next to them.

sudden infant death syndrome (SIDS)
A situation in which a seemingly healthy infant, usually between 2 and 6 months old, suddenly stops breathing and dies unexpectedly while asleep.

The argument for co-sleeping is that the parents can quickly respond to a hungry or frightened baby. However, bed-sharing increases the risk of **sudden infant death syndrome (SIDS)** (described at the end of this chapter). A detailed study in Texas found that about half of all infants who died suddenly and unexpectedly were bed-sharing at the time (Drake et al., 2019).

For that reason, some pediatricians advise against co-sleeping, advice that tired mothers may ignore. Canadian mothers are told not to share a bed with their infant, but two-thirds of Canadian women with Asian or Caribbean heritage do so, following the practice of their own mothers (Gilmour et al., 2019).

Especially for New Parents
You are aware of cultural differences in sleeping practices, which raises a very practical issue: Should your newborn sleep in bed with you? (see response, page 110)

Many experts now realize the benefits of co-sleeping and seek ways to safeguard the practice (Ball & Volpe, 2013). They tell parents *never* to sleep beside an infant if they have been drinking or using drugs, and *never* to use a comforter, pillow, or soft mattress near a sleeping infant. In nations where bed-sharing is the norm, the "bed" is often a hard pallet (Drake et al., 2019).

Developmentalists remind parents that babies learn from experience. If they become accustomed to bed-sharing, they may crawl into their parents' bed long past infancy. The entire social context matters, which explains why some studies find benefits from co-sleeping, and other studies find danger (Baddock et al., 2019).

Brain Development

Throughout fetal and infant development, the brain grows more rapidly than any other organ, from about 25 percent of adult weight at birth to 75 percent at age 2 (Vannucci & Vannucci, 2019). Infant genes propel and protect this brain growth: If teething or a stuffed-up nose temporarily slows eating, body weight is affected before brain weight, a phenomenon called **head-sparing**. That term expresses well what nature does—safeguard the brain.

head-sparing
A biological mechanism that protects the brain when malnutrition disrupts body growth. The brain is the last part of the body to be damaged by malnutrition.

Many other terms in neuroscience are not as self-explanatory, but they are useful to understand the brain. They are explained in Inside the Brain.

EXUBERANCE AND PRUNING

An estimated fivefold increase in dendrites occurs in the first two years, with about 100 trillion synapses present at age 2. No other mammal has such extensive post-natal brain growth. Human anatomy necessitates extensive postnatal brain growth.

INSIDE THE BRAIN

Neuroscience Vocabulary

Communication within the *central nervous system (CNS)*—the brain and spinal cord—begins with nerve cells, called **neurons**. At birth, the human brain has about 86 billion neurons. Neurogenesis, (the creation of new neurons) is rapid in the first days of life, although most neurogenesis occurs before birth and some occurs in adulthood (Kostović et al., 2019).

Within and between areas of the central nervous system, neurons connect to other neurons by intricate networks of nerve fibers called **axons** and **dendrites**. Each neuron has a single axon and numerous dendrites, which spread out like the branches of a tree. Most of the brain growth in infancy is new dendrites.

The axon of one neuron meets the dendrites of other neurons at intersections called **synapses**, which are critical communication links within the brain. Neurons communicate by *firing*, or sending electrochemical impulses through their axons to synapses to be picked up by the dendrites of other neurons. The dendrites bring the message to the cell bodies of their neurons, which, in turn, may fire, conveying messages via their axons to the dendrites of other neurons.

Axons and dendrites do not touch at synapses. Instead, the electrical impulses in axons typically cause the release of **neurotransmitters**, which stimulate other neurons. There are about a hundred types of neurotransmitters.

Neurotransmitters carry information from the axon of the sending neuron, across a pathway called the *synaptic gap*, to the dendrites of the receiving neuron, a process speeded up by *myelin*, a coating on the outside of the axon.

In humans most neurons (about 70 percent) are in the **cortex** (see Figure 3.3), the brain's six outer layers (sometimes called the *neocortex*). Most thinking, feeling, and sensing occur in the cortex (Johnson & de Haan, 2015; Kolb et al., 2019).

The brain has two halves and four lobes, which are general regions, each containing many parts. No important human activity is exclusively left- or right-brain, or in one lobe or another. Although each lobe and hemisphere has specialized functions, thousands of connections transmit information among the parts.

Specialization in the brain is the result of various constraints and experiences, and is not foreordained by genes (Johnson & de Haan, 2015). Indeed, one genetic attribute of the brain is plasticity; human brains are designed to be adaptable.

The back of the brain is the *occipital lobe*, where vision is located; the sides of the brain are the *temporal lobes*, for hearing; the top is the *parietal lobe*, which includes smell, touch, and spatial understanding, and the front is the *frontal lobe*, which enables people to plan, imagine, coordinate, decide, and create. Humans have a much larger frontal cortex relative to body size than any other animal. The very front of the frontal lobe is called the **prefrontal cortex**, crucial lifelong, as you will read in later chapters.

Pleasure and pain arise from the **limbic system**, a cluster deep inside the brain, which include areas that are heavily involved in emotions and motivation. Two crucial parts of the limbic system are the amygdala and the hippocampus.

The **amygdala** is a tiny structure, about the same shape and size as an almond. It registers strong emotions, both positive and negative, especially fear. The amygdala is present in infancy, but growth depends partly on early experience. Increased amygdala activity may cause terrifying nightmares or sudden terrors.

Another structure in the emotional network is the **hippocampus**, located next to the amygdala. A central

neuron
One of billions of nerve cells in the central nervous system, especially in the brain.

axon
A fiber that extends from a neuron and transmits electrochemical impulses from that neuron to the dendrites of other neurons.

dendrite
A fiber that extends from a neuron and receives electrochemical impulses transmitted from other neurons via their axons.

synapse
The intersection between the axon of one neuron and the dendrites of other neurons.

neurotransmitter
A brain chemical that carries information from the axon of a sending neuron to the dendrites of a receiving neuron.

cortex
The outer layers of the brain in humans and other mammals. Most thinking, feeling, and sensing involves the cortex.

prefrontal cortex
The area of the cortex at the very front of the brain that specializes in anticipation, planning, and impulse control.

limbic system
The parts of the brain that interact to produce emotions, including the amygdala, the hypothalamus, and the hippocampus. Many other parts of the brain also are involved with emotions.

amygdala
A tiny brain structure that registers emotions, particularly fear and anxiety.

hippocampus
A brain structure that is a central processor of memory, especially memory for locations.

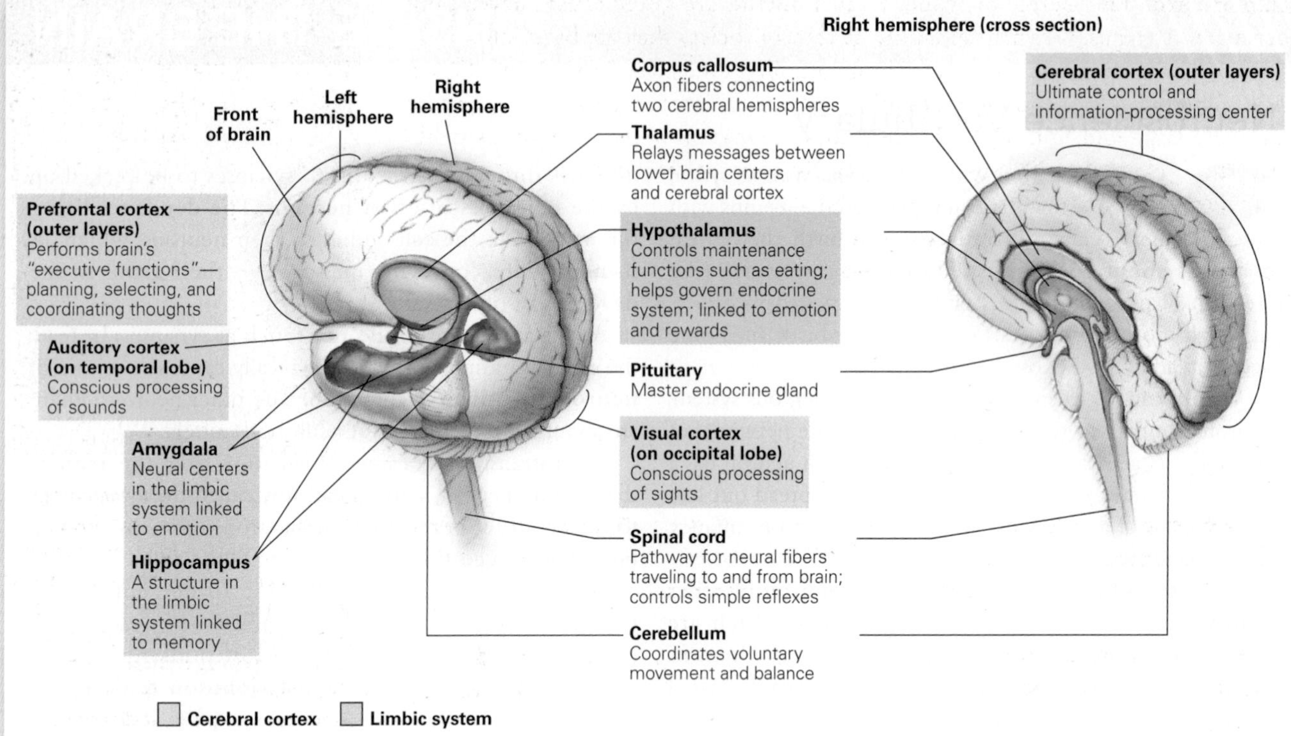

FIGURE 3.3 Connections A few of the hundreds of named parts of the brain are shown here. Although each area has particular functions, the entire brain is interconnected. The processing of emotions, for example, occurs primarily in the limbic system, where many brain areas are involved, including the amygdala, hippocampus, and hypothalamus.

hypothalamus
A brain area that responds to the amygdala and the hippocampus to produce hormones that activate other parts of the brain and body.

cortisol
The primary stress hormone; fluctuations in the body's cortisol level affect human emotions.

pituitary
A gland in the brain that responds to a signal from the hypothalamus by producing many hormones, including those that regulate growth and that control other glands, among them the adrenal and sex glands.

processor of memory, especially memory for locations, the hippocampus responds to the amygdala by summoning memory. Some places feel comforting (perhaps a childhood room) and others evoke fear (perhaps a doctor's office), even when the experiences that originated those emotions are long gone.

Sometimes considered part of the limbic system is the **hypothalamus**, which responds to signals from the amygdala and to memories from the hippocampus by producing hormones, especially **cortisol**, a hormone that increases with stress. Another nearby brain structure, the **pituitary**, responds to the hypothalamus by sending out hormones to various body parts.

The descriptions here are only a beginning. From a developmental perspective, the important finding is that all thoughts and actions originate in the complexity of the brain. Thus, understanding the brain helps us understand how humans live their lives.

Birth would be impossible if the fetal head were large enough to contain the brain networks humans need.

transient exuberance
The great but temporary increase in the number of dendrites that develop in an infant's brain during the first two years of life.

Early dendrite growth is called **transient exuberance**: *exuberant* because it is so rapid and *transient* because some of it is temporary. Just as a gardener might prune a rose bush by cutting away some growth to enable more, or more beautiful, roses to bloom, unused brain connections atrophy and die (Gao et al., 2017).

As one expert explains it, there is an "exuberant overproduction of cells and connections followed by a several yearlong sculpting of pathways by massive elimination" (Insel, 2014, p. 1727). Notice the word *sculpting*, as if a gifted artist created an intricate sculpture from raw marble or wood. Human infants are gifted artists, developing their brains to adjust to whatever family, culture, or society they are born into.

Many neurological diseases result from "pruning gone awry" early in life (Sakai, 2020). The brains of children with autism spectrum disorder, for instance, may be unusually large and full, which hinders communication between neurons while overloading the senses (Lewis et al., 2013). By contrast, schizophrenia may sometimes be the result of overpruning (Sakai, 2020).

Ideally, extending and eliminating dendrites is attuned to experience, as the appropriate links in the brain are established, protected, and strengthened (Gao et al., 2017). As with the rose bush, pruning needs to be done carefully, allowing further growth.

FRANCOIS PAQUET-DURAND/SCIENCE SOURCE

Connecting The color staining on this photo makes it obvious that the two cell bodies of neurons (stained chartreuse) grow axons and dendrites to each other's neurons. This tangle is repeated thousands of times in every human brain. Throughout life, those fragile dendrites will grow or disappear as the person continues thinking.

NECESSARY AND POSSIBLE EXPERIENCES

A scientist named William Greenough identified two experience-related aspects of brain development (Greenough et al., 1987).

- **Experience-expectant growth.** Some basic experiences are needed for the brain to grow, just as a tree requires water. Those experiences are part of almost every infant's life. Brains *expect* such experiences; development suffers without them.
- **Experience-dependent growth.** Human brains also have built-in plasticity, as explained in Chapter 1. Neurological connections await experiences that vary by culture.

The basic, expected experiences *must* happen for normal brain maturation to occur, and they almost always do. For example, in the Amazon and in the Arctic, on isolated farms and in crowded cities, almost all babies have things to see, objects to manipulate, and people to love.

experience-expectant Brain functions that require certain basic common experiences (which an infant can be expected to have) in order to develop normally.

experience-dependent Brain functions that depend on particular, variable experiences and therefore may or may not develop in a particular infant.

In contrast, dependent experiences *might* happen; because of them, one brain differs from another. Experiences vary, such as the language heard, the faces seen, the emotions expressed, and, as you just read, the place for sleep. *Depending* on those particulars, some dendrites grow, and some neurons die. The newborn brain is ready for anything and then becomes a "narrower nervous system . . . tuned exactly" to the particulars of the person (Lichtman, quoted in Sakai, 2020, p. 16096).

Harming the Infant Body and Brain

Thus far, we have focused on the expected and the dependent. Every family tries to ensure that their children survive in good health, and thrive within their culture. Most infants do. However, some infant brains lack basic, expected experiences.

NECESSARY STIMULATION

To begin with, infants need stimulation. Some adults imagine that babies need quiet, perhaps in a room painted a neutral color. No. Babies need sights and sounds, emotional expressions, and social interactions that encourage movement (arm waving, crawling, grabbing, and walking).

Severe lack of stimulation stunts the brain. As one review explains, "enrichment and deprivation studies provide powerful evidence of . . . widespread

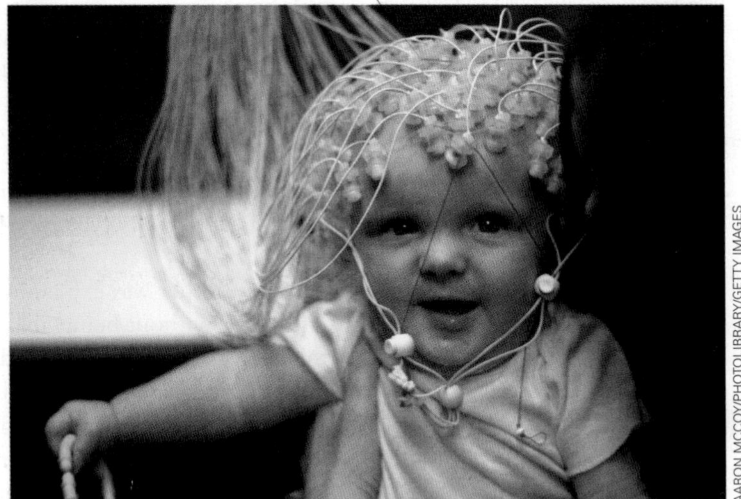

AARON MCCOY/PHOTOLIBRARY/GETTY IMAGES

Face Lit Up, Brain Too Thanks to scientists at the University of Washington, this young boy enjoys the EEG of his brain activity. Such research has found that babies respond to language long before they speak. Experiences of all sorts connect neurons and grow dendrites.

CHAPTER APP 3

Sprout Baby

IOS:
http://tinyurl.com/y33575ce

RELEVANT TOPIC:
Physical development and well-being during infancy

This app enables parents of infants to log growth spurts, illnesses, and medications, as well as sleeping routines, diaper changes, and feeding times. Informed by CDC and WHO data, the app also helps parents compare their baby's progress against that of the general population and provides several other "extras."

effects of experience on the complexity and function of the developing system" of the brain (Stiles & Jernigan, 2010, p. 345).

Proof came first from rodents! Some "deprived" rats (raised alone in small, barren cages) were compared with "enriched" rats (raised in large cages with toys and other rats). At autopsy, brains of the enriched rats were larger, with more dendrites (Diamond, 1988; Greenough & Volkmar, 1973). Subsequent research with other mammals confirms that isolation and sensory deprivation stunt development, which is now sadly evident in longitudinal studies of human orphans from Romania, described later.

STRESS AND THE BRAIN

Some infants experience the opposite problem, too much of the wrong kind of stimulation (Bick & Nelson, 2016). If the infant brain reacts to stress by producing too much cortisol, that derails the connections in the brain, causing odd responses later on. Years later, that person may be hypervigilant (always on the alert) or emotionally flat (never happy or sad).

Note that the brain is responding to fear, not to physical pain. Of course, infants should never be hit, and occasional stress—routine inoculations, temporary hunger, an unwanted diaper change—is part of normal infant life. If caregivers communicate comfort, infants can handle some discomfort.

However, intense and frequent stress floods the brain with cortisol, causing damage. For example, if infants witness a violent fight between their parents, they may suffer lasting harm, evident in brain and behavior (Mueller & Tronick, 2019).

◆◆ Especially for Parents of Grown Children
Suppose you realize that you seldom talked to your children until they talked to you and that you often put them in cribs and playpens. Did you limit their brain growth and their sensory capacity? (see response, page 110)

This distinction is important for caregivers to know. All babies cry. Because the prefrontal cortex has not yet developed, telling infants to stop crying is pointless because they cannot *decide* to stop crying.

Some adults yell at crying babies (which may terrify the baby) or even worse, shake them. That makes blood vessels in the brain rupture and neural connections break, causing **shaken baby syndrome**, an example of *abusive head trauma* (Christian & Block, 2009). Death is the worst consequence; lifelong intellectual impairment is the more likely one.

shaken baby syndrome
A life-threatening injury that occurs when an infant is forcefully shaken back and forth, a motion that ruptures blood vessels in the brain and breaks neural connections.

Not every infant who has symptoms of head trauma is the victim of abuse: Legal experts worry about false accusations (Byard, 2014). Nonetheless, infants are vulnerable, so the response to a screaming, frustrating baby should be to comfort, or, if the caregiver is also frustrated, to place in a crib and walk away, never to shake, yell, or hit.

Lest you cannot imagine the frustration that some parents feel when their baby keeps crying, consider what one mother said about her colicky baby.

> There were moments when, both me and my husband . . . when she was apoplectic and howling so much that I almost got this thought, 'now I'll take a pillow and put over her face just until she quietens down, until the screaming stops.'
>
> *[quoted in Landgren et al., 2012, p. 55]*

That mother was explaining how hard it was to hear her colicky infant cry hour after hour without being able to provide comfort. You will be pleased to know that this baby became a much-loved 4-year-old, and this mother was among the many who said that parents should not be blamed if they cannot always soothe their crying infants.

The Senses

The senses all function at birth. Newborns have open eyes, sensitive ears, and responsive noses, tongues, and skin. Indeed, very young babies use all their senses to attend to everything. For instance, in the first days of life, they stare at everyone and suck almost anything in their mouths.

Genetic selection over more than 100,000 years affects all the senses. Humans cannot hear what mice hear, or see what bats see, or smell what puppies smell, because humans do not need to. However, survival requires babies to respond to people, and newborns do so with every sense, as you will now see in detail.

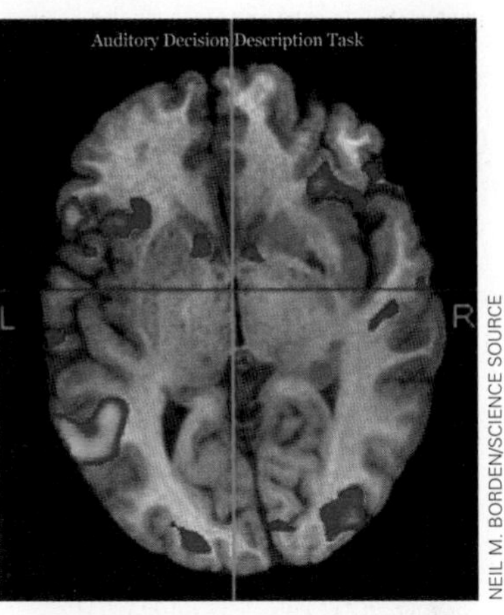

NEIL M. BORDEN/SCIENCE SOURCE

Listen, Imagine, Think, and Tap A person has just heard "banana" and "round, red fruit," and is told to tap if the two do not match. An MRI reveals that 14 areas of the brain are activated. As you see, this simple matching task requires hearing (the large region on the temporal lobe), imagined seeing (the visual cortex in the occipital lobe at the bottom), motor action (the parietal lobe), and analysis (the prefrontal cortex at the top). Imagine how much more brain activation is required for the challenges of daily life.

HEARING

Hearing develops during the last trimester of pregnancy, as the fetus hears the mother's heartbeat, digestion, and voice. Loud noises—a car backfire, a slammed door—are heard, too, and can cause a fetus to startle.

After birth, familiar sounds are soothing: One reason kangaroo care reduces newborn stress is that the infant's ear rests on the mother's chest, making the heartbeat audible. Soon, infants turn their heads to see the source of a voice—an ability that requires instant calculation of the difference between when the sound reaches the left and right ears.

Hospitals in the United States test newborns for 35 disorders. Many are genetic problems (some mentioned in Chapter 2), but the most common inborn problem is a hearing disorder (Sontag et al., 2020). That alerts the parents, because infants need to hear voices (expectant) to learn whatever language their parents speak (dependent).

Hearing infants respond to pitch, cadence, shouts, whispers. They like rhythms, not only the familiar heartbeat but also the steady rhythm of music. They particularly prefer speech sounds over mechanical ones, especially voices combined with sight and touch (Ramírez-Esparza et al., 2017).

For deaf infants, if early implants or hearing aids are not possible, the parents must communicate with dramatic gestures and facial expressions, and learn sign language. Professional follow-up is needed if tests reveal deafness, for both baby and family (Zehnhoff-Dinnesen et al., 2020).

SEEING

By contrast, vision is immature at birth, because the fetus has had nothing much to see. Indeed, one scientist writes that newborns seem "apparently blind" (Brodsky, 2016). Newborns focus only on things between 4 and 30 inches (10 and 75 centimeters) away, and even that is blurry.

Almost immediately, experience combines with maturation of the visual cortex to improve the ability to see shapes and notice details. Movement captures attention, as does contrast. One result is that by 6 weeks, vision is sufficiently developed that, when babies see a person, they focus on the eyes—those colorful dots on a plain surface.

As experience builds, dendrites grow and scanning improves. Thus, 1-month-olds might stare at the hairline, but 3-month-olds look closely at the eyes and mouth, smiling more at happy faces than at angry or expressionless ones.

Very young infants pay attention to patterns, colors, and motion—the mobile above the crib, for instance. They smile more broadly at people they know. Each month they are better able to *track* (follow with their eyes) a moving object, allowing researchers to know what interests them (Stone & Bosworth, 2019).

Because **binocular vision** (coordinating both eyes to see one image) is impossible in the womb (nothing is far enough away), many newborns seem to use their two eyes independently, momentarily appearing wall-eyed or cross-eyed. Usually, experience allows both eyes to focus on one thing between 2 and 4 months (Seemiller et al., 2018).

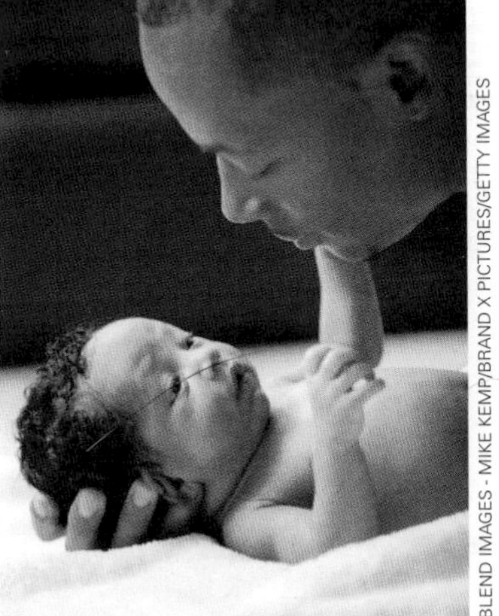
BLEND IMAGES - MIKE KEMP/BRAND X PICTURES/GETTY IMAGES

Who's This? Newborns look intensely at faces. Repeated sensations become perceptions, so in about six weeks this baby will smile at Dad, Mom, and every other face. If this father in Utah responds like typical fathers everywhere, by 6 months cognition will be apparent: The baby will chortle with joy at seeing him but become wary of unfamiliar faces.

TASTING AND SMELLING

As with hearing and vision, taste and smell rapidly adapt to the social context. Babies appreciate what their mothers eat, prenatally through amniotic fluid, then through breast milk, and finally through smells and spoonfuls of the family dinner.

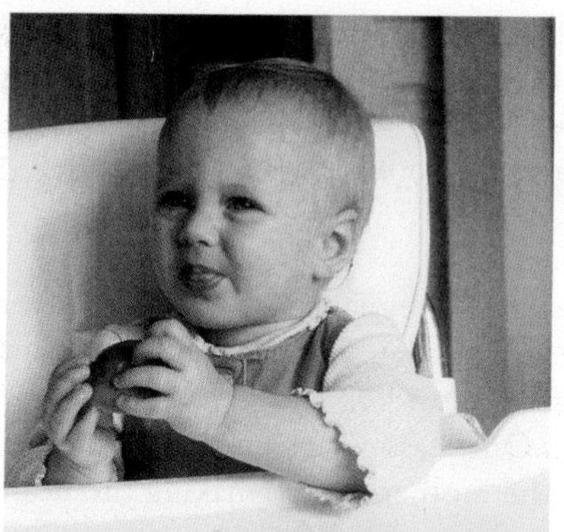
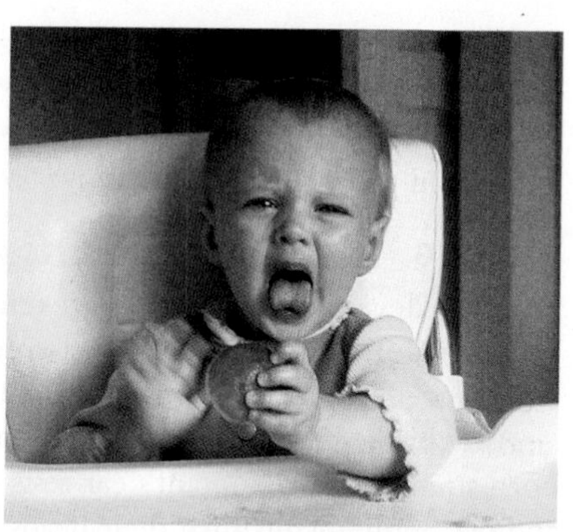

Learning About a Lime As with most infants, Jacqueline's curiosity leads to taste and then to a slow reaction, from puzzlement to tongue-out disgust. Jacqueline's responses demonstrate that the sense of taste is acute in infancy and that quick brain perceptions are still to come.

binocular vision
The ability to focus the two eyes in a coordinated manner in order to see one image.

Preferences for mother's diet may aid survival, as each culture prioritizes foods that were consumed by past generations who lived in that place. For example, bitter foods provide some defense against malaria, hot spices help preserve food, other spices slow cancer, high-fat foods reduce starvation, and so on (Aggarwal & Yost, 2011; Kuete, 2017; Prasad et al., 2012). Thus, for infants, preferring family tastes may not only aid bonding, it may save their lives.

Families maintain cultural tastes, despite immigration or changing historical circumstances. Foods that were protective may no longer be so. Indeed, when starvation was a threat, humans developed a taste for high-fat foods; now their descendants enjoy French fries, whipped cream, and bacon, jeopardizing their health.

Adaptation also occurs for the sense of smell. When breast-feeding mothers used a chamomile balm to ease cracked nipples during the first days of their babies' lives, those babies preferred that smell almost two years later, compared with babies whose mothers used an odorless ointment (Delaunay-El Allam et al., 2010).

As babies learn to recognize each person's scent, they prefer to sleep next to their caregivers, and they nuzzle into their caregivers' chests—especially when the adults are shirtless. One way to help infants who are frightened of the bath (some love bathing, some hate it) is for the parent to join the baby in the tub. The smells of the adult's body mixed with the smell of soap, and the pleasant touch, sight, and voice of the caregiver, make the warm water comforting.

TOUCH AND PAIN

The sense of touch is acute in infants. Wrapping, rubbing, massaging, and cradling soothe many newborns. Even when their eyes are closed, some infants stop crying and visibly relax when held securely by their caregivers.

Gentle touch can comfort an infant only a few weeks old (Tuulari et al., 2019). The infant heartbeat becomes slow and rhythmic, not rapid and erratic (as with stress), when stroked gently and rhythmically on the arm (Fairhurst et al., 2014).

Pain and temperature are not among the traditional five senses, but they are often connected to touch. Some babies cry when being changed, distressed at the sudden coldness on their skin. Some touches are unpleasant—a poke, pinch, or pat—although this varies from one baby to another. An infant's facial expression, heart rate, and body movement suggest that pain can be felt, but less so than later on when the axons of the brain are better connected.

Physiological measures, including hormones, heartbeat, and rapid brain waves, are studied to assess infant pain, but infant brains are immature: Their responses to pain are both similar and dissimilar to that of adults (Moultrie et al., 2016). However, the past assumption that newborns feel no pain has been replaced by the idea that infant pain is probably less intense than adult pain but not absent altogether (Koress et al., 2019; Maxwell et al., 2019).

THINK CRITICALLY: What political controversy makes objective research on newborn pain difficult?

For many newborn medical procedures, from a pin-prick to minor surgery, a taste of sugar right before the event is an anesthetic. Breast-feeding also relieves pain (Gad et al., 2019). There are two possible reasons for that: (1) Distraction reduces pain (the brain processes one sensation at a time), and (2) breast milk is a mild anesthetic.

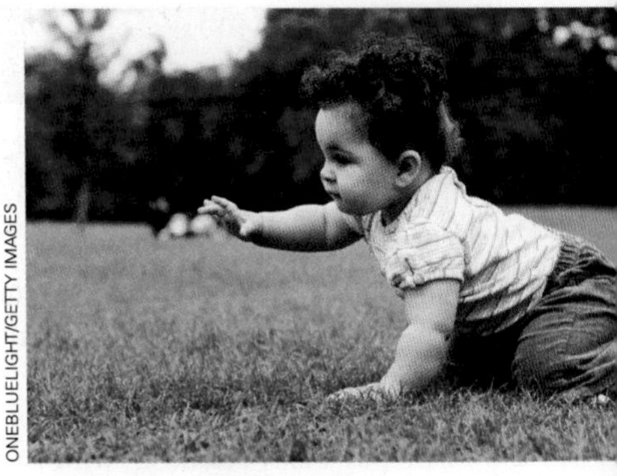

ONEBLUELIGHT/GETTY IMAGES

Advancing and Advanced At 8 months, she is already an adept crawler, alternating hands and knees, intent on progress. She will probably be walking before a year.

Motor Skills

A **motor skill** is any skilled movement of the body, from the newborn's head-lifting to the toddler's stair-climbing and, later, from handwriting to dance moves. Every motor skill begins with basic maturation and then depends on motivation and practice.

GROSS MOTOR SKILLS

Deliberate actions that coordinate many parts of the body, producing large movements, are called **gross motor skills**. These skills emerge directly from reflexes and proceed as prenatal development did, in a *cephalocaudal* (head-down) and *proximodistal* (center-out) direction. Infants first control their heads, lifting them up to look around. Then they control their upper bodies, their arms, and finally their legs and feet. (See At About This Time.)

Sitting requires muscles to steady the torso, which is no simple feat. By 3 months, most babies can sit propped up in a lap. By 6 months, they can usually sit unsupported, but "novice sitting and standing infants lose balance just from turning their heads or lifting their arms" (Adolph & Franchak, 2017).

Crawling is another example of the head-down and center-out direction of skill mastery. As they gain muscle strength, infants wiggle, attempting to move forward by pushing their arms, shoulders, and upper bodies against whatever surface they are lying on. Motivation is crucial: Babies want to move forward to explore objects just out of reach (as Livia did with the cell phone in the opening anecdote).

motor skill
The learned abilities to move some part of the body, in actions ranging from a large leap to a flicker of the eyelid. (The word *motor* here refers to movement of muscles.)

gross motor skills
Physical abilities involving large body movements, such as walking and jumping. (The word *gross* here means "big.")

OBSERVATION QUIZ
Which of these skills has the greatest variation in age of acquisition? Why? (see answer, page 111) ←

At About This Time: Age Norms (in Months) for Gross Motor Skills

	When 50% of All Babies Master the Skill	When 90% of All Babies Master the Skill
Sits unsupported	6	7.5
Stands holding on	7.4	9.4
Crawls (creeps)	8	10
Stands not holding	10.8	13.4
Walks well	12.0	14.4
Walks backward	15	17
Runs	18	20
Jumps up	26	29

Note: As the text explains, age norms are affected by culture and cohort. The first five norms are based on babies from five continents [Brazil, Ghana, Norway, United States, Oman, and India] (World Health Organization, 2006). The next three are from a U.S.-only source [Coovadia & Wittenberg, 2004; based on Denver II (Frankenburg et al., 1992)]. Mastering skills a few weeks earlier or later does not indicate health or intelligence. Being very late, however, is a cause for concern.

Usually by 5 months, infants add their legs to this effort, inching forward (or backward) on their bellies. By 10 months, most infants can lift their midsections and move. As soon as they are able, babies walk (falling frequently but getting up undaunted and trying again). Walking is quicker than crawling, and it has another advantage—free hands (Adolph et al., 2012). That illustrates the drive that underlies

OPPOSING PERSPECTIVES

My Late Walkers

Our first child, Bethany, was born when I was in graduate school. At 14 months, she was growing well and talking but had not yet taken her first step. I told my husband that genes are more influential than anything we did. My emphasis on genes was a perspective shared by many scientists, who had been impressed by early reports of Minnesota twins reared apart (Bouchard et al., 1990). I had read that babies in Paris are late to walk, and my grandmother was French.

To my relief, Bethany soon took her first step. Eight years later, we had two more children, Rachel and Elissa, also slow to walk. I was not worried, because by then Bethany was the fastest runner in her school. My students with Guatemalan and Ghanaian ancestors bragged about their infants who walked before a year; those from China and France had later walkers. Genetic, I thought.

Fourteen years after Bethany, Sarah was born. I could finally afford a full-time caregiver, Mrs. Todd, from Jamaica. She thought Sarah was the most advanced baby she had ever known, except for her own daughter, Gillian.

"She'll be walking by a year," Mrs. Todd told me. "Gillian walked at 10 months."

"We'll see," I graciously replied.

I underestimated Mrs. Todd. She bounced my delighted baby on her lap, day after day, and spent hours giving her "walking practice." Sarah took her first step at 12 months—late for a Todd, early for a Berger, and a humbling lesson for me.

As a scientist, I know that a single case proves nothing. My genetic explanation might be valid, especially since Sarah shares only half her genes with Bethany and since my daughters are only one-eighth French, a fraction I had conveniently ignored when I sought reassurance about my late-walking first-born.

However, I am not the only scientist who recognizes the validity of a perspective opposite to the one I had 40 years ago. I now recognize the power of practice and culture.

RADIUS IMAGES/ALAMY STOCK PHOTO

No Stopping Him Something compels infants to roll over, sit, stand, and walk as soon as their bodies allow it. This boy will fall often, despite his balancing arms, but he will get up and try again. Soon he will run and climb. What will his cautious mother (behind him) do then?

every motor skill: Babies are powerfully motivated to do whatever they can as soon as they can.

Practice of every motor skill advances development, not only of the skill but overall (Leonard & Hill, 2014). When U.S. infants are grouped by ethnicity, generally African American babies walk earlier than Latinx babies, who are ahead of those of European descent. Is this culture or genes? I once thought it was genetic, but I may be wrong (see Opposing Perspectives).

In every culture that allows it, once toddlers are able to walk by themselves, they practice obsessively, barefoot or not, at home or in stores, on sidewalks or streets, on lawns or in mud: "In 1 hour of free play, the average toddler takes about 2,400 steps, travels the length of about 8 U.S. football fields, and falls 17 times" (Adolph & Franchak, 2017).

In some cultures, babies are massaged and stretched from birth onward and are encouraged to walk as soon as possible. They do so, long before a year (Adolph & Franchak, 2017). The latest walkers (15 months) may be in rural China, where infants are bundled up against the cold (Adolph & Robinson, 2013).

Some cultures discourage walking because danger lurks (poisonous snakes, open fires, speeding cars), and toddlers are safer if they cannot wander. By contrast, some cultures encourage running over long distances: Their children can run marathons (Adolph & Franchak, 2017).

FINE MOTOR SKILLS

fine motor skills
Physical abilities involving small body movements, especially of the hands and fingers, such as drawing and picking up a coin. (The word *fine* here means "small.")

Small body movements are called **fine motor skills**. The most valued fine motor skills are finger movements, enabling humans to write, draw, type, tie, and so on. Movements of the tongue, jaw, lips, and toes are fine motor movements, too. Fine motor skills develop slowly over the early years: In cephalocaudal direction, mouth skills precede finger skills, which precede toe skills.

Once again, practice matters. Drawing, for instance, begins with marks on paper. Over the next years, some children practice drawing and writing, with distinctive signatures by adolescence. But infants are far from that, even picking up a small object is difficult.

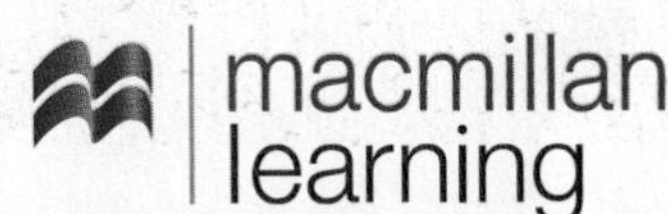

VIDEO: Fine Motor Skills in Infancy and Toddlerhood shows the sequence in which babies and toddlers acquire fine motor skills.

At About This Time: Age Norms (in Months) for Fine Motor Skills

	When 50% of All Babies Master the Skill	When 90% of All Babies Master the Skill
Grasps rattle when placed in hand	3	4
Reaches to hold an object	4.5	6
Thumb and finger grasp	8	10
Stacks two blocks	15	21
Imitates vertical line (drawing)	30	39

Data from World Health Organization, 2006.

Instead, in the first year, "infants flap their arms, rotate their hands, and wiggle their fingers, and exhibit bouts of rhythmical waving, rubbing, and banging while holding objects" (Adolph & Franchak, 2017). Toward the end of that year and throughout the second, finger skills improve as babies master the pincer movement (using thumb and forefinger to pick up objects) and self-feeding, first with hands, then fingers, then, at age 2, with utensils. Again, practice matters: Some Chinese 2-year-olds master chopsticks, a skill beyond many adults from other families). (See At About This Time.)

what have you learned?

1. When is, and isn't, an infant's low height or weight percentile a problem?
2. How do sleep patterns change over the first 18 months?
3. What are the reasons for and against bed-sharing?
4. How does the brain change from birth to age 2?
5. How can pruning increase brain potential?
6. What is the difference between experience-expectant and experience-dependent growth?
7. How does vision change over the first year?
8. When and why is it important to understand how well an infant hears?
9. How are taste, smell, and pain affected by the social context?
10. Why and when do babies crawl and walk?
11. Which fine motor skills develop in infancy?

The Eager Mind

You have just read that, as soon as maturation allows, infants use every sense and skill to connect with other people and to explore their world. The same inner drive occurs with cognition.

KLAUS VEDFELT/GETTY IMAGES

No Fear Like all infants, this 11-month-old girl is eager to explore through sight and touch. Praise to all three — this mother for encouraging learning, this baby for reaching out, and this dog for gently licking her hand. Most dogs recognize babies, tolerating actions they would not accept from adults of any species.

One team wrote that infants are "scientist[s] in the crib" (Gopnik et al., 1999), a suggestion that was "frequently met with incredulity" (Halberda, 2018, p. 1215). However, "the field of developmental neuroscience has burgeoned over the last 20 years with advances in technology and methods that are well suited for measuring the human brain in vivo in infants" (Guyer et al., 2018, p. 687). Incredulity faded as evidence accumulated.

As scientists have discovered more about the infant brain, they have documented an inborn readiness to learn. As one team wrote: "from early on in development, infants display perception biases and attentional patterns that strongly suggest a motive to acquire information" (Lucca & Wilbourn, 2018, p. 942).

Gaze-Following

One example is seeing. Very young babies look at whatever is likely to advance their understanding. They wisely follow their caregivers' gaze, instinctively knowing that caregivers look at things that might tell them something important.

For example, following adults' lead, they scan the faces of people, ignoring the ceiling, the floor, or the person's feet. Have they learned that adults look at faces because expressions are informative, or is gaze-following natural for infants?

Both. It was thought that gaze-following occurred only as a response to adults, who might say, "Javier, look, here comes Daddy," or "Sophia, see your teddy bear." Adults naturally try to direct the baby's vision, calling their name, pointing at an object, and so on. Very young babies respond by looking at whatever the adult shows.

But we now know that infants follow an adult's gaze even without caregiver cues (Gredebäck et al., 2018). If adults tilt their heads or move their pupils, babies look at what adults look at.

Early Logic

Nature and nurture may allow some infant understanding of math and science. In one study, a toy dinosaur was removed from a display where it had been next to a flower. A screen then covered the display. A moment later, the screen was lifted, either to show the flower again or to reveal the dinosaur instead of the flower (Cesana-Arlotti et al., 2018).

Cameras and computers measured how long the babies looked at these displays. Infants stared longer when the flower was surreptitiously replaced with the dinosaur than when the flower was still there. This indicated that they knew how things should be and were surprised when their basic understanding was wrong.

Many other events (such as a ball suspended in the air rather than falling, or a toy becoming two toys) that are contrary to the basic laws of how things work elicit the same surprise. From such research, many developmentalists believe that infants have some innate logic. Scientific reasoning may not be a "hard-won accomplishment mastered later in life," but rather an "inherent attribute of the mind" (Halberda, 2018, p. 1214).

Infant Memory

Is infant intellect impressive, or markedly immature? Both. To further understand this, consider memory, which "is crucial for the acquisition of the tremendous amount of knowledge and skills infant[s] and children acquire in the first years of life" (Vöhringer et al., 2018, p. 370).

WITH WORDS OR NOT

implicit memory
Memory that is not verbal, often unconscious. Many motor and emotional memories are implicit.

An insight regarding infant memory begins with the distinction between *implicit* and *explicit* memory. **Implicit memory** is not verbal; it is memory for movement,

Selective Amnesia As we grow older, we forget about spitting up, nursing, crying, and almost everything else from our early years. However, strong emotions (love, fear, mistrust) may leave lifelong traces.

emotions, or thoughts that are not put into words. Implicit memory is evident by 3 months, begins to stabilize by 9 months, and continues to affect a person's reactions lifelong. It comes from old parts of this brain that develop first, including the cerebellum and the amygdala (Vöhringer et al., 2018).

Explicit memory takes longer to emerge, as it depends on language. It arises mainly from the cortex. Explicit memory improves dramatically throughout childhood (Hayne et al., 2015). Verbal memory, especially vocabulary, continues to increase in adolescence and adulthood. If you tell a child not to do some forbidden activity, do not be surprised if the child does it and tells you "I forgot." That might be true at age 3, it is less likely to be true a decade later.

explicit memory
Memory that can be recalled in the conscious mind, usually factual memories that are expressed with words.

REMIND ME!

The most dramatic proof of implicit memory comes from a series of innovative experiments in which 3-month-olds learned to move a mobile by kicking their legs (Rovee-Collier, 1987, 1990). Infants lay on their backs connected to a mobile by means of a ribbon tied to one foot.

Virtually all babies realized that kicking made the mobile move. They then kicked more vigorously and frequently, sometimes laughing at their accomplishment. So far, this is no surprise—observing the effects of self-activated movement is highly reinforcing to infants. Would they remember that kicking produced movement of the mobile?

One week later, some 3-month-olds were placed in the same cribs, with the same mobile-and-ribbon apparatus tied to their foot. Most started to kick immediately; they remembered! Other 3-month-old infants who had experienced the initial event were retested two weeks later. They kicked randomly, taking time to realize the fun they could have. Was two weeks too long for the fragile infant memory to endure?

But then, the lead researcher, Carolyn Rovee-Collier, allowed still other 3-month-old infants who had initially learned to kick, a "reminder session" two weeks later. They could watch the mobile move when they were not connected to it. The next day, when a ribbon again tied their leg to the mobile, they kicked almost immediately.

Apparently, watching the mobile the previous day reminded them about what they had previously experienced. Other research similarly finds that, with infant implicit memories, certain experiences can evoke a buried memory. If Daddy, who routinely plays with a 3-month-old, goes on a long trip, and the mother shows Daddy's picture and says

He Remembers! Infants are fascinated by moving objects within a few feet of their eyes—that's why parents buy mobiles for cribs and why Rovee-Collier tied a string to a mobile and a baby's leg to test memory. Babies not in her experiment, like this one, sometimes flail their limbs to make their cribs shake and thus make their mobiles move. Piaget's stage of "making interesting sights last" is evident to every careful observer.

OBSERVATION QUIZ
Do you see anything here that is less than ideal? (see answer, page 111)

IAN BODDY/SPL/SCIENCE SOURCE

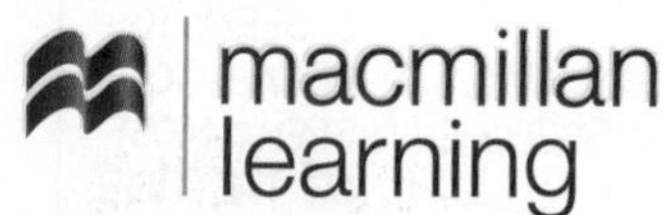

VIDEO: Contingency Learning in Young Infants shows Carolyn Rovee-Collier's procedure for studying instrumental learning during infancy.

his name on the day before his return, the baby might grin broadly when he reappears.

Without reminders, Daddy (or Grandma, or a friendly dog) might seem to be forgotten. Early implicit memories may seem to be lost, but later experiences might evoke them. Even as an adult, certain people or places might trigger a sense of pleasure, or dread, because of seemingly forgotten early experiences.

How to Learn

One other aspect of the eager mind of infants merits mention—babies learn how to learn. As you remember from Chapter 2, infants are born with reflexes. Some fade and others build, depending on experience. By the second year of life, toddlers are eager to explore and investigate, but some toddlers seem hesitant. Why the difference? Have some learned to be cautious, not curious?

In one experiment, 15-month-olds observed adults trying to get a toy from a container (Leonard et al., 2017). The adult said, "How can I get this toy out of here?" and then worked to do so. Half the infants saw the toy come out quickly, and the other half watched the adult working hard for half a minute to release the toy (see Figure 3.4).

Then the infants were shown another toy. The experimenter pushed a button to demonstrate that the toy played music. The 15-month-olds were intrigued, happy that the experimenter handed them the musical toy. However, the experimenter had turned off the switch before handing it to them, so the toy did not play. Every baby tried to make the toy play music.

VIDEO: Event-Related Potential (ERP) Research shows a procedure in which the electrical activity of an infant's brain is recorded to see whether the brain responds differently to familiar versus unfamiliar words.

But some tried much harder than others. One baby quickly threw the toy to the floor in frustration, and another tried for more than two minutes. If babies had seen the adult keep trying to get the toy, they pushed the button an average of 22.5 times. However, if they had seen the adult succeed quickly, they pushed, on average, only 12 times (Leonard et al., 2017).

The idea that hard work pays off is a learning strategy that helps throughout a person's education—and it may begin in infancy. Similar implicit learning strategies are learned early on: Some babies are persistent, active, talkative, and others much more quiet and passive.

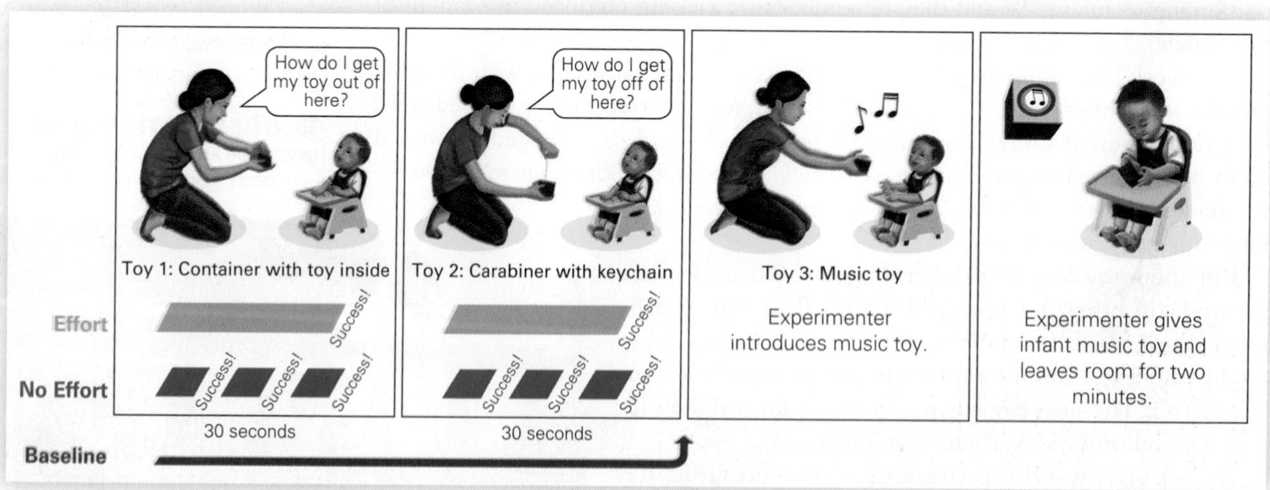

FIGURE 3.4 **If At First You Don't Succeed . . . Quit?** Two times, with two toys, babies watched an adult try to get toys from a container. One group saw the toys quickly released, and another group saw them released only after some effort. A third control group (the baseline) saw no demonstration; they were just given the toy. Then the babies were shown another toy. This third toy played music when the adult turned it on, but then (unbeknownst to the babies) the music-playing was deactivated. When babies were handed the quiet toy, how long did they try to turn on the music? (Answer is in the text.) If you don't take time to read the text, what does that suggest about your childhood?

Piaget's Sensorimotor Intelligence

Now we turn to Jean Piaget, the groundbreaking theorist who studied infant cognition a century ago. Piaget lacked the technological advances that undergird our current research on infant cognition, but his insights were revolutionary. Our current appreciation of the infant mind builds on what Piaget discovered.

Piaget recognized that the senses and motor skills are the raw materials for infant cognition. That is why he called cognition in the first two years **sensorimotor intelligence** (see Table 3.1). Piaget described the interplay of sensation, perception, action, and cognition in six stages, in three *circular reactions*. He emphasized that, as in a circle, there is no beginning and no end to learning. Each experience leads to the next, which loops back (see Figure 3.5).

VIDEO: Sensorimotor Intelligence in Infancy and Toddlerhood shows how senses and motor skills fuel infant cognition.

sensorimotor intelligence
Piaget's term for the way infants think—by using their senses and motor skills—during the first period of cognitive development.

primary circular reaction
The first of three types of feedback loops in sensorimotor intelligence, this one involving the infant's own body. The infant senses motion, sucking, noise, and other stimuli and tries to understand them.

secondary circular reaction
The first of three types of feedback loops in sensorimotor intelligence, involving the infant and an object or another person, as with shaking a rattle or playing peek-a-boo.

STAGES ONE AND TWO: PRIMARY CIRCULAR REACTIONS

In **primary circular reactions**, the circle is within the infant's body, as one movement or sense brings a reaction in another.

Stage one, called the *stage of reflexes*, lasts only a month. As you remember from Chapter 2, newborns have many reflexes. Piaget thought that these reflexes soon become attuned to experience: Sucking brings milk, swallowing relieves hunger, and so on.

Stage two, called *first acquired adaptations* (also called *stage of first habits*), begins as the mind of the infant adjusts to whatever responses the reflexes elicit. Adaptation is cognitive; it includes repeating old patterns (assimilation) and developing new ones (accommodation). [**Life-Span Link**: Assimilation and accommodation were mentioned in Chapter 1.] Sucking adjusts to swallowing, for instance.

STAGES THREE AND FOUR: SECONDARY CIRCULAR REACTIONS

In stages three and four, development advances from primary to **secondary circular reactions**. These reactions extend beyond the infant's body; this circular reaction is between the baby and something else.

During stage three (4 to 8 months), infants attempt to produce exciting experiences, a stage called *making interesting sights last*. Realizing that rattles make noise, for

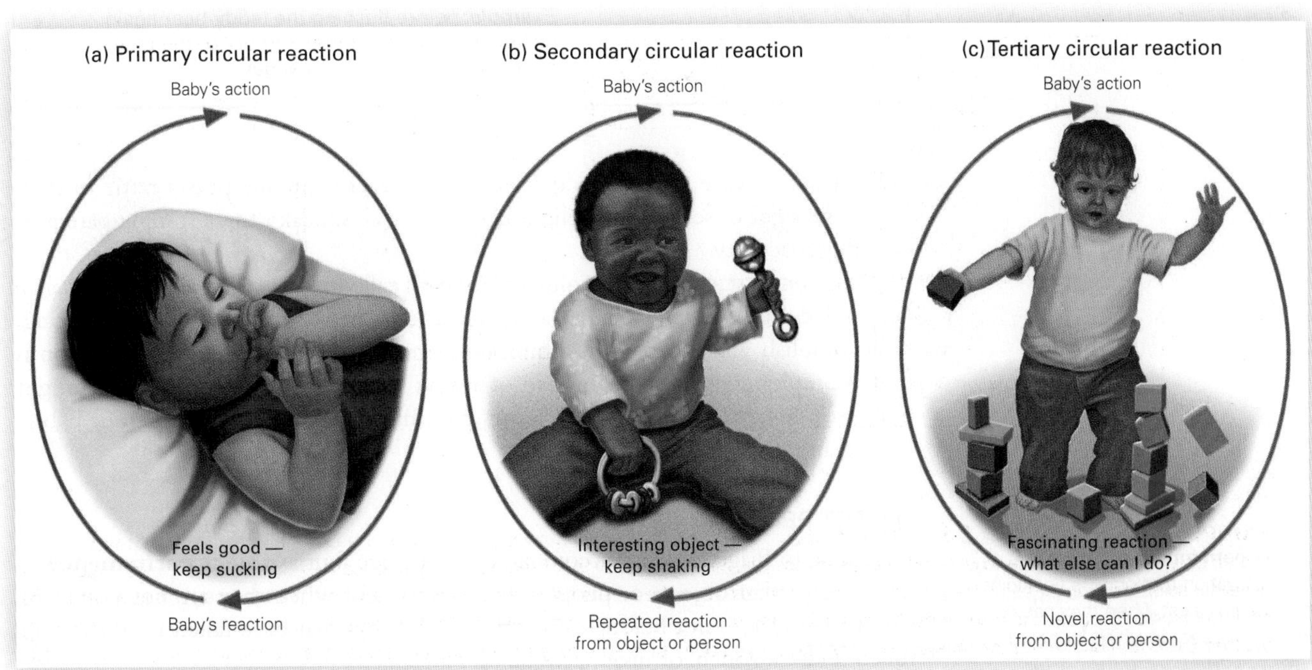

FIGURE 3.5 Never Ending
Circular reactions keep going because each action produces pleasure that encourages more action.

TABLE 3.1 The Six Stages of Sensorimotor Intelligence

For an overview of the stages of sensorimotor thought, it helps to group the six stages into pairs.

Primary Circular Reactions	
The first two stages involve the infant's responses to its own body.	
Stage One (birth to 1 month)	*Reflexes:* sucking, grasping, staring, listening *Example:* sucking anything that touches the lips or cheek
Stage Two (1–4 months)	*The first acquired adaptations:* accommodation and coordination of reflexes *Examples:* sucking a pacifier differently from a nipple; attempting to hold a bottle to suck it
Secondary Circular Reactions	
The next two stages involve the infant's responses to objects and people.	
Stage Three (4–8 months)	*Making interesting sights last:* responding to people and objects *Example:* clapping hands when mother says "patty-cake"
Stage Four (8–12 months)	*New adaptation and anticipation:* becoming more deliberate and purposeful in responding to people and objects *Example:* putting mother's hands together in order to make her start playing patty-cake
Tertiary Circular Reactions	
The last two stages are the most creative, first with action and then with ideas.	
Stage Five (12–18 months)	*New means through active experimentation:* experimentation and creativity in the actions of the "little scientist" *Example:* putting a teddy bear in the toilet and flushing it
Stage Six (18–24 months)	*New means through mental combinations:* thinking before doing, new ways of achieving a goal without resorting to trial and error *Example:* before flushing the teddy bear again, hesitating because of the memory of the toilet overflowing and mother's anger

example, they wave their arms and laugh whenever someone puts a rattle in their hand. The sight of something delightful—a favorite squeaky toy, a smiling parent—can trigger activity.

Next comes stage four (8 months to 1 year), called *new adaptation and anticipation* (also called the *means to the end*). Babies may ask for help (fussing, pointing, gesturing) to accomplish what they want. Thinking is more innovative because adaptation is more complex. For instance, instead of always smiling at Grandpa, an infant might first assess his mood. Stage-three babies continue an experience; stage-four babies initiate and anticipate.

OBJECT PERMANENCE

object permanence
The realization that objects (including people) still exist when they can no longer be seen, touched, or heard.

According to Piaget, a major accomplishment of stage four is **object permanence**—the concept that objects or people continue to exist when they are not visible. At about 8 months—not before—infants look for toys that have fallen from the crib, rolled under a couch, or disappeared under a blanket.

As another scholar explains:

> Many parents in our typical American middle-class households have tried out Piaget's experiment in situ: Take an adorable, drooling 7-month-old baby, show her a toy she loves to play with, then cover it with a piece of cloth right in front of her eyes. What do you observe next? The baby does not know what to do to get the toy! She looks around, oblivious to the object's continuing existence under the cloth cover, and turns her attention to something else interesting in her environment. A few months later, the same baby will readily reach out and yank away the cloth cover to retrieve the highly desirable toy. This experiment has been done thousands of times and the phenomenon remains one of the most compelling in all of developmental psychology.
>
> *[Xu, 2013, p. 167]*

Piaget developed many experiments in object permanence. He found that:

- Infants younger than 8 months do not search for an attractive object momentarily covered by a cloth. They do not have the concept of object permanence.
- At about 8 months, infants remove the cloth immediately after an object is covered but not if they have to wait a few seconds. Peek-a-boo brings laughter.
- At 18 months, infants search after a wait. However, if they have seen the object put first in one place (A) and then moved to another (B), they search in A but not B.
- By 2 years, children fully grasp object permanence, progressing through several stages, including A and B displacements (Piaget, 1954/2013a). Hide-and-seek becomes fun.

Thousands of scientists have explored aspects of object permanence. Many believe that infants understand object permanence before they are able to "yank away the cloth cover" (Baillargeon & DeVos, 1991; Spelke, 1993). Brain waves, heartbeats, and gaze tracking suggests that the infant mind develops before infant behavior. Piaget may have been wrong to equate motor immaturity with intellectual inability.

This is controversial. Does infant gaze indicate comprehension? (Dunn & Bremner, 2019). If a 6-month-old looks surprised when a disappearing object reappears, does that infant understand object permanence? Experts dispute methods of measuring infant cognition, particularly what gaze reveals (Dunn & Bremner, 2017). But no one doubts Piaget's basic insight: Infants are thinking long before they are talking.

We will soon describe language development, which also begins long before the first words. But first we need to describe what Piaget noticed after age 1.

STAGES FIVE AND SIX: TERTIARY CIRCULAR REACTIONS

In their second year, infants start experimenting in thought and deed—or, rather, in the opposite sequence, deed and thought. They act first (stage five) and think later (stage six).

Tertiary circular reactions begin when 1-year-olds take independent actions to discover the properties of other people, animals, and things. Infants no longer respond only to their own bodies (primary reactions) or merely react to other people or objects (secondary reactions). Instead they are more creative.

Piaget's stage five (12 to 18 months), called *new means through active experimentation*, builds on the accomplishments of stage four. Goal-directed and purposeful activities become more expansive.

Toddlers delight in squeezing all the toothpaste out of the tube, drawing on the wall, or uncovering an anthill—activities they have never observed. Piaget referred to the stage-five toddler as a **"little scientist"** who "experiments in order to see." As you read, a scientific approach may appear earlier, but in the beginning of the

tertiary circular reaction
Piaget's description of the cognitive processes of the 1-year-old, who gathers information from experiences with the wider world and then acts on it. The response to those actions leads to further understanding, which makes this circular.

little scientist
Piaget's term for toddlers' insatiable curiosity and active experimentation as they engage in various actions to understand their world.

Especially for Parents
One parent wants to put all breakable or dangerous objects away because the toddler is able to move around independently. The other parent says that the baby should learn not to touch certain things. Who is right? (see response, page 110)

second year, "flexible and productive hypothesis testing" begins "with a vengeance" (Cesana-Arlotti et al., 2018, p. 1263).

At the sixth stage (18 to 24 months), toddlers add *mental combinations*, intellectual experimentation via imagination, to supplement or supersede the active experimentation of stage five. Because they combine ideas, stage-six toddlers can pretend as well as think about consequences, hesitating a moment before yanking the cat's tail or dropping a raw egg on the floor.

what have you learned?

1. What suggests that infants develop strategies for learning by watching adults?
2. What kinds of memory do infants have, and not have?
3. Why did Piaget call cognition in the first two years "sensorimotor intelligence"?
4. What is the controversy about object permanence?
5. In sensorimotor intelligence, what is the difference between stages three and four?
6. What does the active experimentation of the 1-year-old suggest for caregivers?

Language: What Develops in the First Two Years?

Infant linguistic learning far surpasses that of full-grown adults from every other species. Language begins when newborns cry, and by age 2, they produce sentences.

At About This Time: The Development of Language in the First Two Years

Age*	Means of Communication
Newborn	Reflexive communication — cries, movements, facial expressions.
2 months	A range of meaningful noises — cooing, fussing, crying, laughing.
3–6 months	New sounds, including squeals, growls, croons, trills, vowel sounds.
6–10 months	Babbling, including both consonant and vowel sounds repeated in syllables.
10–12 months	Comprehension of simple words; speechlike intonations; specific vocalizations that have meaning to those who know the infant well. Deaf babies express their first signs; hearing babies also use specific gestures (e.g., pointing) to communicate.
12 months	First spoken words that are recognizably part of the native language.
13–18 months	Slow growth of vocabulary, up to about 50 words.
18 months	Naming explosion — three or more words learned per day. Much variation: Some toddlers do not yet speak.
21 months	First two-word sentence.
24 months	Multiword sentences. Half of the toddler's utterances are two or more words long.

*The ages in this table reflect norms. Many healthy, intelligent children attain each linguistic accomplishment earlier or later than indicated here.

The Universal Sequence

Infants worldwide follow the same sequence of language development. As you will see, language development begins at birth. As one scholar explains, "infants are acquiring much of their native language before they utter their first word" (Aslin, 2012, p. 191).

ARIEL SKELLEY/GETTY IMAGES

Who Is Babbling? Probably both the 6-month-old and the 27-year-old. During every day of infancy, mothers and babies communicate with noises, movements, and expressions.

LISTENING AND RESPONDING

In the first weeks of life, infants prefer to hear voices over other noises: They are naturally attuned to speech. They like alliteration, rhymes, repetition, melody, rhythm, and varied pitch. Sing your favorite lullaby (itself an alliterative word) to yourself. You can hear what babies like, sounds over content and singing over talking (Tsang et al., 2017). These early listening abilities and preferences arise from the brain, part of what makes us human.

For their part, adults—including those with no formal education at all—know how to talk to babies. In every spoken language, caregivers use higher pitch, simpler words, repetition, varied speed, and exaggerated emotional tone when addressing infants. Researchers who study such talk describe it as a distinct dialect, called *child-directed speech*, nicknamed *motherese*. Babies respond with attention and emotion, listening intently.

BABBLING

At first, babies simply cry and "coo" (happy sounds, like a dove). By 7 months, they begin to recognize words that sound distinctive: *Bottle*, *doggie*, and *mama*, for instance, might be differentiated, (not *baby*, *Bobbie*, and *Barbie*). They begin to repeat certain syllables (*ma-ma-ma*, *da-da-da*, *ba-ba-ba*), a vocalization called **babbling** because of the way it sounds. Babbling is universal; even deaf babies babble.

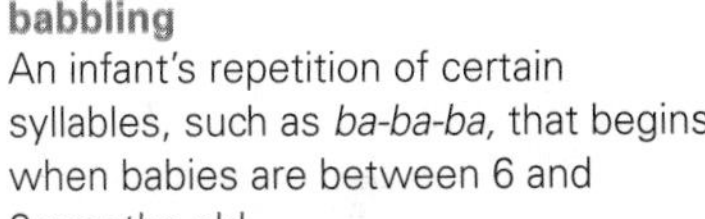

babbling
An infant's repetition of certain syllables, such as *ba-ba-ba*, that begins when babies are between 6 and 9 months old.

Caregivers usually encourage those noises, and it is wise that they do so. Babbling predicts later vocabulary, even more than the other major influence—the education of the mother (McGillion et al., 2017).

Before uttering their first word, infants notice patterns of speech, such as which sounds are commonly spoken together. A baby who often hears that something is "pretty" expects the sound of *prit* to be followed by *tee* (MacWhinney, 2015) and is startled if someone says "prit-if."

Infants also learn the relationship between mouth movements and sound. In one study, 8-month-olds watched a film of someone speaking, with the audio a fraction of a second ahead of the video. Even when the actor spoke an unknown language, babies noticed the mistiming (Pons & Lewkowicz, 2014).

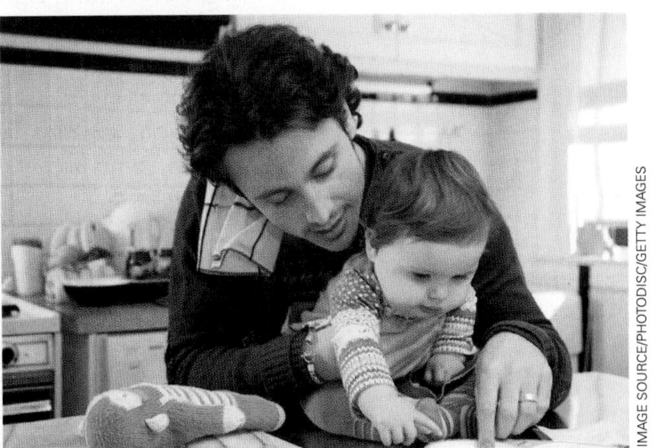

IMAGE SOURCE/PHOTODISC/GETTY IMAGES

Show Me Where Pointing is one of the earliest forms of communication, emerging at about 10 months. As you see here, pointing is useful lifelong for humans.

GESTURES

Some caregivers, recognizing the power of gestures, teach "baby signs" to their 6- to 12-month-olds, who communicate with hand signs months before they move their tongues, lips, and jaws to make words. There is no evidence that baby signing accelerates talking (as had been claimed), but it may make parents more responsive, which itself is positive (Kirk et al., 2013).

For deaf babies, sign language is crucial in the first year: It not only predicts later ability to communicate with signs but also advances crucial cognitive development (Hall et al., 2017). Remember how important gaze-following was for infant

learning? Deaf infants are even better at gaze-following than hearing infants, because they rely on visual signs from their caregivers (Brooks et al., 2019).

Even for hearing babies and without adult signing, gestures are a powerful means of communication (Goldin-Meadow, 2015). One early gesture is pointing and responding to pointing from someone else. The latter requires something quite sophisticated—understanding another person's perspective.

Most animals cannot interpret pointing, but most infants look toward wherever someone else points and already point with their tiny index fingers. Pointing is well developed by 12 months, especially when the person who is pointing also speaks (e.g., "look at that") (Daum et al., 2013).

Infants younger than a year old who are adept at pointing tend to be those who will soon begin talking. That is one reason adults need to respond to pointing as if it is intended to communicate—which it is (Bohn & Köymen, 2018).

FIRST WORDS

Finally, at about a year, the average baby utters a few words, understood by caregivers if not by strangers. Those words often coincide with the age of the first attempts to walk. Perhaps a certain amount of brain maturation is needed for both, or perhaps caregivers need to talk more to walkers, warning, guiding, and encouraging them (Walle & Campos, 2014).

At first, vocabulary increases gradually (perhaps one new word a week). Adults need to talk often to 1-year-olds because understood vocabulary is thought to be about 10 times the size of spoken vocabulary. The first words are the names of familiar things (*mama* and *dada* are common). Soon each becomes a **holophrase**, a single word that expresses an entire thought, via gestures, facial expressions, tone, loudness, and cadence. Imagine "Dada," "Dada?" and "Dada!" Each is a holophrase.

holophrase
A single word that is used to express a complete, meaningful thought.

CULTURAL DIFFERENCES

Early communication transcends linguistic boundaries. In one study, 102 adults listened to 40 recorded infant sounds. They were asked which of five possibilities (pointing, giving, protesting, action request, food request) was the reason for each cry, grunt, or whatever. About half of the sounds and the adults, were from Scotland and the other half from Uganda (Kersken et al., 2017).

Adults in both cultures scored significantly better than chance (although no one got everything right). The number correct was similar whether the sounds came from Scottish or Ugandan infants, and whether the adults were parents or not. Apparently, human baby noises are understood no matter what a listener's language or experience.

Cultures and families vary in how much child-directed speech children hear. Some parents read to their infants, teach them signs, and respond to every burp or fart as if it were an attempt to talk. Other parents are much less verbal. They use gestures and touch; they say "hush" and "no" instead of expanding vocabulary.

Traditionally, in small farm communities, the goal was for everyone to be "strong and silent." If adults talked too much, they might be called blabbermouths or gossips; a good worker did not waste time in conversation.

In certain rural areas of the world, that notion remains. One such place is in Senegal, where some mothers traditionally feared talking to their babies lest that encourage evil spirits to take over the child (Zeitlin, 2011). As with most customs, originally nontalking was adaptive: Quiet adults did not waste time in "idle conversation."

However, communication is crucial in the twenty-first-century global economy, conversation is no longer considered idle but is the lubricant that "greases the wheels

A CASE TO STUDY

Early Speech

As you read, sensitive caregiving is crucial for early cognition, as babies innately look at and listen to their caregivers in order to learn. For their part, caregivers are sensitive and responsive to the infant's attempts to understand words. This is evident in early language: Parents may understand what an infant is trying to say long before other people do.

Consider 13-month-old Kyle, who was advanced in language development. He knew standard words such as *mama*, but he also knew *da, ba, tam, opma*, and *daes*, which his parents knew to be, respectively, "downstairs," "bottle," "tummy," "oatmeal," and "starfish." He also had a special sound to call squirrels (Lewis et al., 1999).

When acquaintances came to visit, they were often mystified by Kyle's attempts to speak. Who would know that *daes* meant "starfish," or how a person might call squirrels? Only Kyle and his very astute parents.

Even a devoted grandmother might not interpret correctly. I know this personally. I was caring for my 16-month-old grandson when he said, "Mama, mama." He looked directly at me, and he didn't seem wistful.

"Mommy's not here," I told him. That didn't stop him; he repeated "mama, mama," more as a command than a complaint. I tried several things. I know that some languages use "ma" for milk. I offered some in his sippy cup. He said, "No, no."

When his father appeared, Isaac repeated "mama." Then his dad lifted him, and Isaac cuddled in his arms. I asked Oscar what "mama" means. His reply: "Pick me up."

Aha. I understood Isaac's logic: When he saw his mother, he said "mama," and she picked him up. So, he thought *mama* meant "pick me up."

Now Isaac is 5 years old, a proficient talker, explaining about bird families (pigeons are the parents, because they are bigger), about why he should get a seat on the subway (he says plaintively to other riders, "I need to sit down," and to my embarrassment, they usually let him sit), and about what his brother has done wrong (told to his parents, who listen sympathetically but almost never punish the older boy).

I also listen to Isaac's current chatter, repeating some of his phrases and saying "uh-huh," knowing that early responses continue to affect later talking. Isaac is well on his way to becoming a highly verbal adult. Kyle already is.

of progress," as Texas statesman John Boren (1972) said. Governments, teachers, and most parents recognize this: A child's first words may be celebrated as much or more than a child's first steps. But some parents do not realize that responding to babbling promotes speech later on.

In one study in Senegal, professionals from the local community (fluent in *Wolof*, a language spoken there) taught new mothers in some villages about infant development, including language (A. Weber et al., 2017). A year later, their toddlers were compared to toddlers in similar villages where the educational intervention had not been offered.

The newly educated mothers talked more to their babies, and the babies, in turn, talked more, with 20 more utterances in 5 minutes than the control group The researchers did not challenge traditional notions directly; instead they taught generalities about early language development and infant cognition. The mothers applied what they learned, and the babies responded.

The Naming Explosion

Spoken vocabulary builds rapidly once the first 50 words are mastered, with 21-month-olds typically saying twice as many words as 18-month-olds (Adamson & Bakeman, 2006). This language spurt is called the **naming explosion**, because many early words are nouns, that is, names of persons, places, or things.

naming explosion
A sudden increase in an infant's vocabulary, especially in the number of nouns, that begins at about 1[illegible]s of age.

Infants learn what to call each caregiver (often *dada, mama, nana, papa, baba, tata*), sibling, and pet. Other common early words refer to favorite foods (*nana* can mean "banana" as well as "grandma") and to elimination (*pee-pee, wee-wee, poo-poo, ka-ka, doo-doo*).

Notice that all of these words have two identical syllables, a consonant followed by a vowel. Many early words follow that pattern—not just *baba* but also *bobo, bebe, bubu, bibi*. Some of the first words are only slightly more complicated—*ma-me, ama*, and so on. Meanings vary by language, but every baby says such words, and every culture assigns them meaning.

Words that are hard to say are simplified: Rabbits are "bunnies," stomachs are "tummies," and no man waits until his child calls him father; he is Daddy or Papa instead.

PUTTING WORDS TOGETHER

grammar
All of the methods—word order, verb forms, and so on—that languages use to communicate meaning, apart from the words themselves.

mean length of utterance (MLU)
The average number of words in a typical sentence (called utterance because children may not talk in complete sentences). MLU is often used to measure language development.

Grammar includes all of the methods that languages use to communicate meaning. There are many ways to add sounds to words and to put words together—that is grammar.

Word order, prefixes, suffixes, intonation, verb forms, pronouns and negations, prepositions and articles—all of these are aspects of grammar. Grammar can be discerned in holophrases because one word can be spoken differently to convey different meanings. In tonal languages (such as Chinese) grammar as well as vocabulary determines whether the voice is raised at the beginning or the end of the word.

In every language, grammar is essential when two words are combined, an advance that typically occurs between 18 and 24 months. For example, "Baby cry" and "More juice" follow grammatical word order. Children do not usually say "Juice more," and even toddlers know that "Cry baby" is not the same as "Baby cry."

By age 2, children combine three words. English grammar uses subject–verb–object order; the grammar of other languages use other sequences and their toddlers do likewise. Thus, toddlers say, "Mommy read book" rather than any of the other five possible sequences of those three words. Adults might say the same three-word sentence with a few grammatical changes, "Mom reads books," not "books read Mom." As you see, grammar changes meanings markedly.

Children's proficiency in grammar correlates with sentence length, and the use of prefixes and suffixes to add meaning. That is why **mean length of utterance (MLU)** is used to measure a child's language progress at age 1 and continuing throughout childhood. Each word is an utterance, and if the word has a suffix or prefix, that makes it two utterances. Thus, "ground" is one, "grounding" or "foreground" or "groundless" are each two.

For example, a program designed to increase the spoken language of 3- and 4-year-olds used MLU as a way to measure success of the intervention (Lake & Evangelou, 2019). The child who says, "The baby boy is crying" [6 MLU] is more advanced than the child who says, "Boy is crying" [4 MLU] or simply, "Baby cry!" [2 MLU].

Theories of Language Learning

Worldwide, people who are not yet 2 years old verbalize hopes, fears, and memories—sometimes in more than one language. By adolescence, people communicate with nuanced words and gestures, some writing poems and lyrics that move thousands of their co-linguists. How is language learned so easily and so well?

Answers come from at least three schools of thought. The first theory says that infants are directly taught, the second that social impulses propel infants to communicate, and the third that infants understand language because of genetic brain structures that arose 200,000 years ago.

THEORY ONE: INFANTS NEED TO BE TAUGHT

One set of hypotheses arose from behaviorism. The essential idea is that learning is acquired, step by step, through association and reinforcement.

B. F. Skinner (1957) noticed that spontaneous babbling is usually reinforced. Often, when a baby says "ma-ma-ma-ma," a grinning mother appears, repeating the sound and showering the baby with attention, praise, and perhaps food.

Positive responses to early vocalization are especially likely if the baby is the firstborn, which may explain why children born later, on average, have smaller vocabularies than the oldest child in a family. Norms indicate many differences in language acquisition among young children, such as that boys are slower to talk than girls or that bilingual children may mix languages.

Those averages reflect patterns of reinforcement, according to behaviorists. For instance, the earlier language development of girls may occur because mothers talk more to their daughters than their sons (K. Johnson et al., 2014). Of course, such generalities should not be used to ignore language delays (Feldman, 2019).

Thus, behaviorists believe that repetition and reinforcement strengthen the association between object and word, so infants learn language faster if parents speak to them often, saying "time for your bath, the water is warm, let's wash your legs," rather than silently bathing the 6-month-old. Few parents know this theory, but many use behaviorist techniques by praising and responding to the toddler's simple, mispronounced speech, thus teaching language.

Behaviorists note that some 3-year-olds converse in elaborate sentences; others just barely put one simple word before another. Such variations correlate with the amount of language each child has heard.

Indeed, to some extent infants are "statistical learners" of language, deciding the meanings and boundaries of words based on how often those sounds are heard (Saffran & Kirkham, 2018). Parents of the most verbal children teach language throughout infancy—singing, explaining, listening, responding, and reading to their babies every day, giving their children a rich trove of verbal data, long before the infant utters a first spoken word (see Figure 3.6).

THEORY TWO: SOCIAL IMPULSES FOSTER INFANT LANGUAGE

The second theory arises from the sociocultural reason for language: communication. According to this perspective, infants communicate because humans are social beings, dependent on one another for survival and joy.

All human infants (and no chimpanzees) seek to master words and grammar in order to join the social world. In a series of studies on language learning in bonobos, Michael Tomasello (2017) confirmed that nonhuman primates could learn language via reinforcement, but he focused on language learning that is unique to humans.

Tomasello found that other primates, even with reinforcement, could not learn the perspective-taking and cooperative aspects of language. Only humans are innately motivated to do so. That social function of speech, not the words, undergirds early language learning, according to this theory.

This theory challenges child-directed videos, CDs, and downloads named to appeal to parents (*Baby Einstein*, *Brainy Baby*, and *Mozart for Mommies and Daddies—Jumpstart your Newborn's I.Q.*). Commercial apps for tablets and smartphones, such as *Shapes Game HD* and *VocabuLarry*, have joined the market. Parents who allow infants to watch such

FIGURE 3.6 Maternal Responsiveness and Infants' Language Acquisition Learning the first 50 words is a milestone in early language acquisition, as it predicts the arrival of the naming explosion and the multiword sentence a few weeks later. Researchers found that half of the infants of highly responsive mothers (top 10 percent) reached this milestone at 15 months. The infants of less responsive mothers (bottom 10 percent) lagged significantly behind, with half of them at the 50-word level at 21 months.

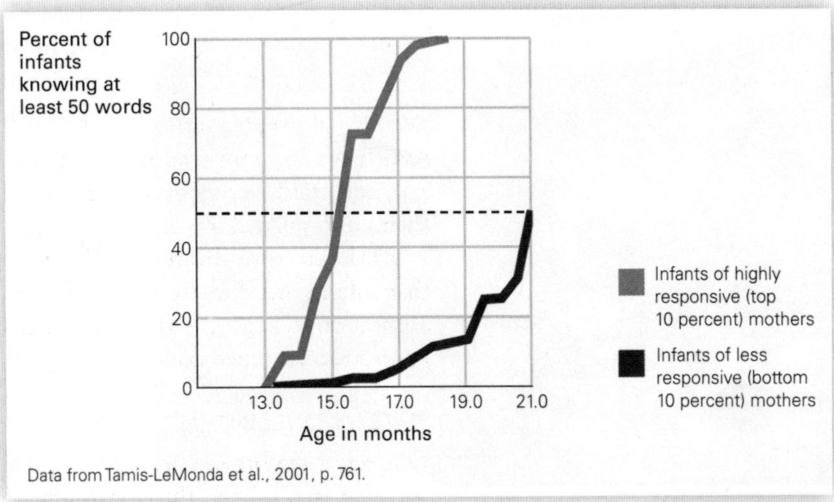

Data from Tamis-LeMonda et al., 2001, p. 761.

programs might believe that rapid language learning is aided by video, although the naming explosion is universal, so video watching that correlates with the naming explosion is coincidence, not cause.

Developmentalists who are influenced by this second theory worry that screen time during infancy may be harmful, because it reduces the social interaction that is essential for learning to communicate. One recent study found that toddlers could learn a word from either a book or a video but that only book learning, not video learning, enabled children to use the new word in another context (Strouse & Ganea, 2017).

Another study focused particularly on teaching "baby signs," 18 hand gestures that refer to particular objects (Dayanim & Namy, 2015). The babies in this study were 15 months old, an age at which all babies use gestures and are poised to learn object names. The 18 signs referred to common early words (such as *baby, ball, banana, bird, cat,* and *dog*), with all 18 signs taught by an attractive video.

In this experiment, the toddlers were divided into four groups: video only, video with parent watching and reinforcing, book instruction of the 18 signs with parent reading and reinforcing, and a control group with no instruction. Not surprisingly, the no-instruction group learned words (as every normal toddler does) but not signs, and the children in the other three groups learned some signs. The two groups with parent instruction learned most, with the book-reading group remembering signs better than either video group. Why?

The crucial factor seemed to be parent interaction. When parents watch a video with their infants, they talk less than when they read a book or play with toys (Anderson & Hanson, 2016). Since adult input is essential for language learning, cognitive development is reduced by video time. Infants best understand and apply what they have learned when they learn directly from another person (Barr, 2013).

Screen time cannot "substitute for *responsive*, loving face-to-face relationships" (Lemish & Kolucki, 2013, p. 335). Direct social interaction is pivotal for language, according to theory two.

THEORY THREE: INFANTS TEACH THEMSELVES

A third theory holds that language learning is genetically programmed. Adults need not teach it (theory one), nor is it a by-product of social interaction (theory two). Instead, it arises from a particular gene (FOXP2), brain maturation, and the overall human impulse to imitate.

This theory points out that humans are genetically programmed to imitate for survival, but until a few millennia ago, no one needed to learn a language other than their own. Thus, human genes allow experience-dependent language learning in infancy, with the brain pruning whatever connections that experience-dependent language does not need. In adulthood brains cannot resurrect neurons and dendrites that have been lost.

The prime spokesman for this perspective was Noam Chomsky (1968, 1980). Although behaviorists focus on variations among children in vocabulary size, Chomsky focused on similarities in language acquisition—the evolutionary universals, not the differences. Chomsky's perspective continues to influence current linguists, especially those with an evolutionary perspective (Berwick & Chomsky, 2016).

Noting that all young children master basic grammar according to a schedule, with the MLU a universal measure of language acquisition, Chomsky hypothesized that children are born with a brain

Family Values Every family encourages the values and abilities that their children need to be successful adults. For this family in Ecuador, that means strong legs and lungs to climb the Andes, respecting their parents, and keeping quiet unless spoken to. A "man of few words" is admired. By contrast, many North American parents babble in response to infant babble, celebrate the first spoken word, and stop their conversation to listen to an interrupting child. If a student never talks in class, or another student blurts out irrelevant questions, perhaps the professor should consider cultural influences.

structure he called a **language acquisition device (LAD)**, which allows children to derive the rules of grammar quickly and effectively from the speech they hear every day.

language acquisition device (LAD) Chomsky's term for a hypothesized mental structure that enables humans to learn language, including the basic aspects of grammar, vocabulary, and intonation.

For example, universally, a raised tone indicates a question, and infants prefer questions to declarative statements. This suggests that infants are wired to learn language, and caregivers ask them questions long before they can answer back.

According to theory three, language is experience-expectant, as the developing brain quickly and efficiently connects neurons to support whichever language the infant hears. The deep structures of language are universal, while the specifics are merely the surface structure. Because of this experience-expectancy, the various languages of the world are all logical, coherent, and systematic. Then surface learning occurs as each brain adjusts to a particular language.

The LAD works for deaf infants as well. All 6-month-olds, hearing or not, prefer to look at sign language over nonlinguistic pantomime. For hearing infants, this preference disappears by 10 months, but deaf infants begin signing at that time, which is their particular expression of the universal LAD.

Consider one example from English of the deep and surface structure of language. The English articles (*the, an, a*) signal that the next word will be the name of an object. According to theory three, since babies have "an innate base" that primes them to learn, the deep structure of language alerts them that nouns need to be learned first. In their early brain exuberance, articles facilitate that learning so they attend to them (Shi, 2014).

This explains why articles are a useful clue for infants learning English but are bewildering for adults who want to learn English. The genetic timing of brain exuberance and pruning (as explained earlier in this chapter) means that an adult may be highly intelligent and motivated, but their language-learning genes are past the sensitive learning time. To avoid errors, they may omit "the" and "a."

ALL TRUE?

A master linguist explains that "the human mind is a hybrid system," perhaps using different parts of the brain for each kind of learning (Pinker, 1999, p. 279). Another writes of

> a constellation of factors that are unique to human development—infants' prolonged period of dependency, exquisite sensitivity to experience, and powerful learning strategies—collectively spark a cascade of developmental change whose ultimate result is the acquisition of language and its unparalleled interface with cognition.
>
> *[Perszyk & Waxman, 2018, p. 246]*

The idea that every theory is partially correct, with a "cascade" of factors, may seem naive. However, many scientists who study language acquisition have arrived at this conclusion. They contend that language learning is neither the exclusive product of repeated input (behaviorism) nor the result of social motivation, nor of a specific human neurological capacity (LAD). Instead, "different elements of the language apparatus may have evolved in different ways," and thus, a "piecemeal and empirical" approach is needed (Marcus & Rabagliati, 2009, p. 281).

Neuroscience is the most recent method to investigate the development of language. It was once thought that language was located in two specific regions of the brain (Wernicke's area and Broca's area). But now neuroscientists believe that language arises from other regions as well. Some genes and regions are crucial, but hundreds of genes and areas contribute.

Neuroscientists describing language development write about "connections," "networks," "circuits," and "hubs" to capture the idea that language is interrelated and complex (Dehaene-Lambertz, 2017; Pulvermüller, 2018). Even with a narrow

focus, on verbal expression, a neuroscientist notes that "speech is encoded at multiple levels in different parallel pathways" (Dehaene-Lambertz, 2017, p. 52).

That neuroscientist began her detailed description of the infant brain and language with the same amazement that traditional linguists have expressed for decades:

> For thousands of years and across numerous cultures, human infants are able to perfectly master oral or signed language in only a few years. No other machine, be it silicon or carbon based, is able to reach the same level of expertise.
>
> *[Dehaene-Lambertz, 2017, p. 48]*

what have you learned?

1. What aspects of language develop in the first year?
2. When does vocabulary develop slowly and when does it develop quickly?
3. What is typical of the first words that infants speak?
4. What indicates that toddlers use some grammar?
5. According to behaviorism, how do adults teach infants to talk?
6. According to sociocultural theory, why do infants try to communicate?
7. Do people really have a language acquisition device?
8. Why do developmentalists accept several theories of language development?

Surviving and Thriving

The main goal of scientists who studied infants a century ago was to discover how to keep babies alive. Even in 1950, worldwide, one newborn in seven died in their first year.

Now, however, 96 percent of all newborns survive, usually to live to old age (United Nations, 2020). Variation is dramatic: In some nations (Iceland, Hong Kong) only 1 baby in 1,000 dies before age one, and in others (Chad, Central African Republic) 1 in 12 does.

These data suggest the need to:

- understand the dramatic improvements in survival; and
- prevent the deaths that still occur.

Sometimes one mode of infant care is much better than another, a fact not recognized before international comparisons of public health. We consider three examples: sudden infant death, immunization, and nutrition. Each of these has dramatically improved rates of infant survival, and each varies markedly from one region to another.

Sudden Infant Death Syndrome

Every year until the mid-1990s, tens of thousands of infants died of SIDS, called *crib death* in North America and *cot death* in England. Tiny infants smiled at their caregivers, waved their arms at rattles that their small fingers could not yet grasp, went to sleep, and never woke up.

Scientists tested hypotheses (the cat? the quilt? natural honey? homicide? spoiled milk?) to no avail. Grief-ridden parents were sometimes falsely accused. Finally, a major risk factor—sleeping on the stomach—was discovered, thanks to the work of one scientist.

Susan Beal, a 35-year-old mother of five young children, began to study SIDS deaths in South Australia. She responded to phone calls, often at 5 or 6 A.M. that another baby had died. Her husband supported her work, often becoming the sole child-care provider so she could leave home at a moment's notice.

Sometimes she was the first professional to arrive, before the police or the coroner, and initially she was embarrassed to question the grief-stricken parents. But soon she learned that parents were grateful to talk, in part because they tended to blame themselves, and they needed to express that emotion to someone who was not likely to accuse them. Beal reassured them that scientists shared their bewilderment.

She was more than a sympathetic listener. She was a scientist, doing research using observation. (See Chapter 1.) Accordingly, she took meticulous notes on dozens of circumstances at each of more than 500 deaths, including sketches of the baby's position at the death and open-ended questions of the parents. She disproved some hypotheses (birth order did not matter) and confirmed others (parental smoking increased the risk).

A breakthrough came when Beal noticed an ethnic variation: She saw far more SIDS victims of European descent than of Chinese descent than would be expected, given the population in that part of Australia. Genetic? Most experts thought so.

But Beal was trained as a scientist, and thus examined alternate hypotheses for her data. Her notes revealed that almost all SIDS babies died while sleeping on their stomachs, contrary to the Chinese custom of placing infants on their backs to sleep. She developed a new hypothesis: Sleeping position mattered.

To test her hypothesis, Beal did an experiment. She convinced a large group of non-Chinese parents to put their newborns to sleep on their backs. Almost none of them died suddenly.

After several years of gathering data, she drew a surprising conclusion: Back-sleeping reduced SIDS. Her published report (Beal, 1988) caught the attention of doctors in the Netherlands, where pediatricians had always told parents to put their babies to sleep on their stomachs. Two Dutch scientists (Engelberts & de Jonge, 1990) recommended back-sleeping; thousands of parents took heed. SIDS was reduced in Holland by 40 percent in one year — a stunning replication.

In the United States, Benjamin Spock's *Baby and Child Care*, first published in 1946, sold more copies than any other book than the Bible. He advised stomach-sleeping, and millions of parents followed that advice. In 1984, SIDS killed 5,245 babies in the United States.

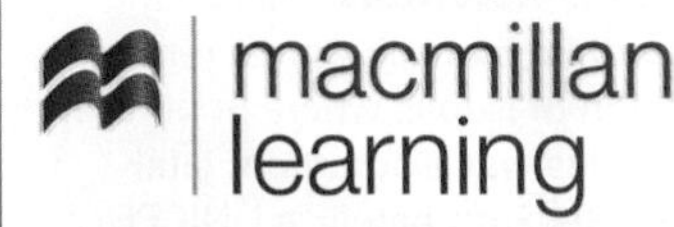

VIDEO: Interview with Susan Beal provides more information about her research. http://www.youtube.com/watch?v=ZIPt5q2QJ9I

But Beal's 1988 article, and the Dutch 1990 data, spread to the United States. By 1994, a "Back to Sleep" campaign cut the SIDS rate dramatically (Kinney & Thach, 2009; Mitchell, 2009). By 1996, the U.S. SIDS rate was half of what it had been. By 2018, the U.S. Centers for Disease Control and Prevention reported 1,300 SIDS deaths, less than one-quarter of the previous number, even though the population of infants had increased over the past decades (see Figure 3.7). Consequently, in the United States alone, about 120,000 people are alive who would be dead if they had been born before 1990.

Stomach-sleeping is a proven, replicated risk, but it is not the only one. Other risks include low birthweight, winter, being male, exposure to cigarettes, soft blankets or pillows, bed-sharing, and physical abnormalities (in the brain stem, heart, mitochondria, and microbiome) (Neary & Breckenridge, 2013; Ostfeld et al., 2010). Most SIDS victims experience several risks, a cascade of biological and social circumstances.

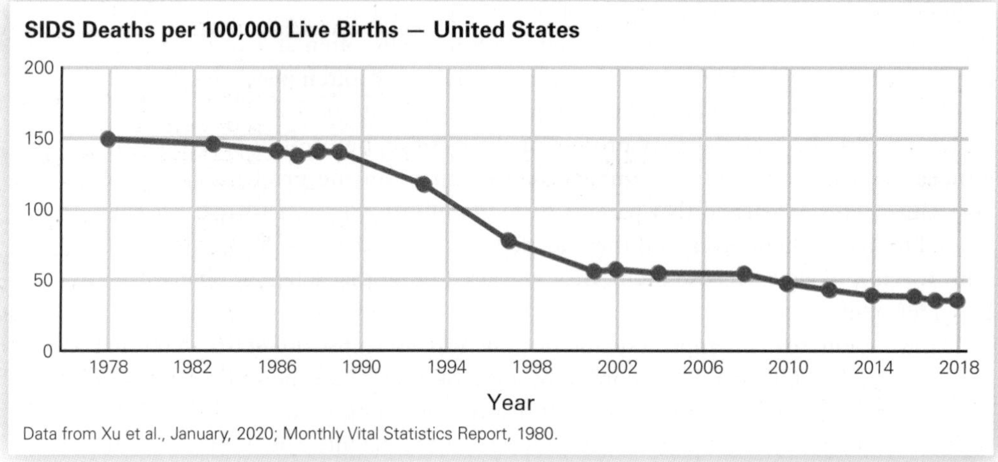

FIGURE 3.7 Alive Today As more parents learn that a baby should be on his or her "back to sleep," the SIDS rate continues to decrease. Other factors are also responsible for the decline—fewer parents smoke cigarettes in the baby's room.

Immunization

A century ago, millions of infants and young children died every year of deadly diseases, including measles, chicken pox, polio, mumps, rotavirus, and whooping cough. Even in developed nations, in the first half of the twentieth century, almost every child had at least one of these diseases. Usually they recovered, and then they were immune.

Indeed, some parents took their toddlers to play with a child who was sick, hoping their child would catch the disease. That protected that child later in life, since many diseases are more deadly in adulthood than childhood.

We now know that **immunization** can occur in two ways: recovery from the illness, or with vaccination. That usually involves giving the person a small dose of the live virus, or a small dose of the deactivated virus, to triggers the body's natural immune system. For COVID-19, another way to create a vaccine is to deactivate the molecular elements that allow the virus to spread. Ideally, vaccination provides total protection without any side effects.

immunization
A process that stimulates the body's immune system by causing production of antibodies to defend against attack by a particular contagious disease. Creation of antibodies may be accomplished either naturally (by having the disease), by injection, by drops that are swallowed, or by a nasal spray.

This is complex, because immunization reduces but does not eliminate the disease, and careful testing is required to ensure no severe side effects. Nonetheless, currently vaccines are recommended for 14 serious childhood diseases and are "estimated to prevent 2–3 million deaths annually" (Hill et al., 2020).

Stunning successes in immunization include the following:

- Smallpox, the deadliest disease for children in the past, was eradicated worldwide as of 1980. Vaccination against smallpox is no longer needed.
- Polio, a crippling and sometimes fatal disease, has been virtually eliminated in the Americas. Only 784 cases were reported anywhere in the world in 2003. However, wars and false rumors halted immunization in Northern Nigeria in 2005 and in rural Pakistan and Afghanistan in 2019. Rates of polio worldwide are now higher than they were a decade ago (Roberts, 2020).
- Before the varicella (chicken pox) vaccine, more than 100 people in the United States died each year from that disease, and 1 million were itchy and feverish for a week. Now, far fewer people get chicken pox, and almost no one dies of varicella.
- Measles (rubeola, not rubella) is disappearing, thanks to a vaccine developed in 1963. Prior to that time, 3 to 4 million cases occurred each year in the United States alone (Centers for Disease Control and Prevention, May 15, 2015). In 2012 in the United States, only 55 people had measles, although globally about 20 million measles cases occurred that year. (See Figure 3.8.)

True Dedication This young Buddhist monk lives in a remote region of Nepal, where until recently measles was a common, fatal disease. Fortunately, a UNICEF porter carried the vaccine over mountain trails for two days so that this boy — and his whole community — could be immunized.

SCOTT EELLS/REDUX

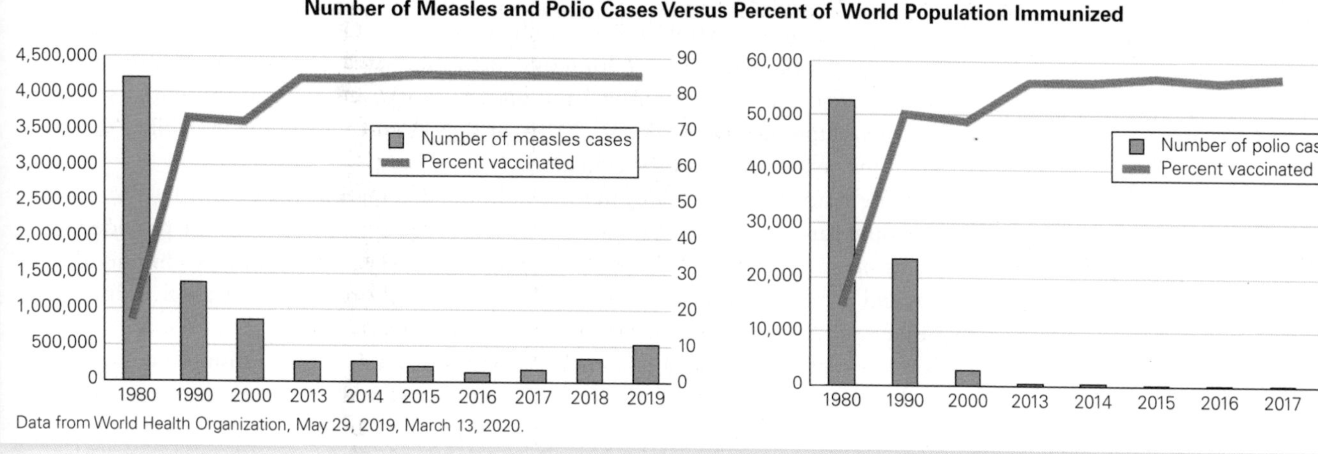

FIGURE 3.8 Ask Grandma Neither polio nor measles is completely eradicated, because some parents do not realize the danger. They may never have seen the serious complications of these diseases.

OBSERVATION QUIZ
Which regions have the most and least improvement since 1990? (see answer, page 111) ↑

Many other diseases are now preventable with vaccines, including diphtheria, pertussis, tetanus, mumps, dengue, tuberculosis, and rotavirus. The most recent vaccines are those that prevent COVID-19. We do not yet know long-term effects, but immunization is far better than contracting the virus (Paltiel et al., 2021).

HERD IMMUNITY

Widespread vaccination not only reduces a person's risk for disease, but also protects those who cannot be safely vaccinated, such as very young infants and people with impaired immune systems (immune deficient, HIV-positive, or undergoing chemotherapy). The reason is that each vaccinated person stops transmission, a phenomenon called *herd immunity*.

Usually, if almost all the people in a community (a herd) are immunized, no one dies of that disease. The specific percentage that needs to be immunized varies by disease. Measles, for instance, is highly contagious, so public health experts believe herd immunity requires successful vaccination of about 95 percent of the population.

Because of herd immunity, although no vaccine is 100-percent effective, the disease disappears if all children are required to be fully immunized before enrolling in schools or day-care centers. The other way to achieve herd immunity is for almost everyone to contract the disease. That is what happened with the so-called Black Death in the fourteenth century, which killed an estimated one-third of the entire world population (Kelly, 2005). Every nation and family suffered, but eventually, the disease disappeared.

That may also be occurring with the Zika virus now (Pattnaik et al., 2020). Five years ago, an epidemic of Zika caused thousands of birth defects, first in Brazil and then elsewhere. The need for a vaccine was urgent, but by the time clinical trials were ready, the epidemic had subsided and funds for the vaccine were hard to find. From a scientist's perspective this is ironic: The time to develop a vaccine and prepare for mitigation is before an epidemic, not after!

If herd immunity is low, an outbreak can occur. That happened in the United States in 2019. At least 1,249 people had measles (including a newborn who caught it from the mother)—the highest rate since 1994 (Patel et al., 2019). In the tiny islands of Samoa, the immunization rate fell to 31 percent and a measles epidemic killed 83 people, and sickened thousands, mostly children (Thornton, 2020).

ANTI-VAX SENTIMENTS

The success of immunization has, ironically, led to the anti-vax movement (Berman, 2020). Few people today know someone who died or was disabled because of a childhood disease. Consequently, some parents worry more about potential side effects of vaccines (DeStefano et al., 2019), or they want to avoid the irritability that children may experience after vaccination.

Income matters as well. Although childhood vaccination is free in the United States, some parents cannot afford regular pediatric visits where vaccines are provided. Rates of no vaccination at all (even against polio, that once caused many childhood deaths and paralyzed millions, including President Franklin Roosevelt) are five times higher among those with no health insurance (Hill et al., 2020).

Some parents have heard the rumor that immunization causes autism. Thousands of studies in many nations refute this (only one discredited, fraudulent study backed it). Some of the best data come from Denmark, where detailed medical records for every resident have been analyzed. Between 1999 and 2010, Danish births totaled 657,461. Those infants who were fully vaccinated were slightly *less* likely to be among the 6,517 who were diagnosed with autism before age 10 (Hviid et al., 2019).

Especially for Nurses and Pediatricians A mother refuses to have her baby immunized because she wants to prevent side effects. She wants your signature for a religious exemption, which in some jurisdictions allows the mother to refuse vaccination. What should you do? (see response, page 111)

Public health professionals are troubled that 15 U.S. states allow parents to refuse vaccination because of "personal belief," and 45 states allow religious exemptions. That policy reduces herd immunity. After a measles outbreak in 2015 at Disneyland, California no longer allows refusal for personal beliefs, but religious exemptions are still permitted. Some Californians joined religions that opposed vaccination, and thus had clergy who signed their refusal.

Recent data alarm many pediatricians. In 14 U.S. states in 2019, the measles, mumps, and rubella (MMR) vaccination rate was below 90 percent, which is below herd immunity. Further, almost half of all infants were not immunized against influenza, which can be fatal for them. These data predate the COVID-19 pandemic, which kept many parents away from routine health care, so many more infants are now at risk (Hill et al., 2020).

If only a few parents refuse immunization, their children may still be protected, because most others are immunized and thus the virus never reaches the unvaccinated child. But if too many parents consider only their own child, that harms public health. If herd immunity is reduced, some children will become sick, and a few will become seriously ill and die (Giubilini & Savulescu, 2019).

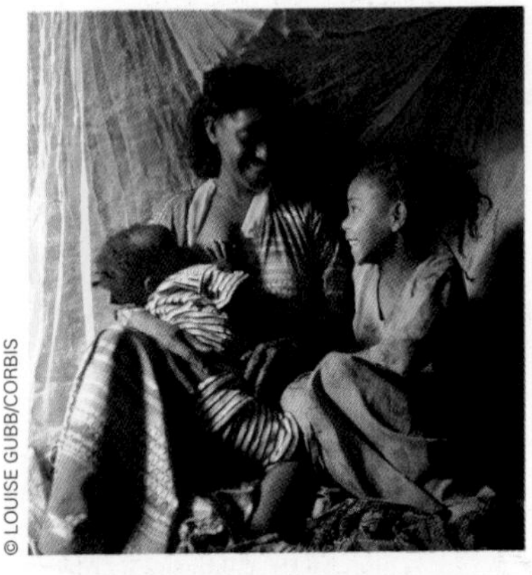

© LOUISE GUBB/CORBIS

Well Protected Disease and early death are common in Ethiopia (where this photo was taken), but neither is likely for 2-year-old Salem. He is protected not only by the nutrition and antibodies in his mother's milk but also by the large blue net that surrounds them. Treated bed nets, like this one provided by the Carter Center and the Ethiopian Health Ministry, are often large enough for families to eat, read, and sleep in together, without fear of malaria-infected mosquitoes.

DATA CONNECTIONS: Saving Lives: Immunization in the United States details the rates at which infants and children receive the vaccines that are recommended for them. Achieve

Nutrition

As already explained, infant mortality worldwide has plummeted in recent years for several reasons: advances in prenatal and newborn care, fewer sudden infant deaths, and, as you just read, immunization. One additional measure is making a huge difference: better nourishment.

BREAST IS BEST

Ideally, nutrition starts with *colostrum*, a thick, high-calorie fluid secreted by the mother's breasts at birth. This benefit is not understood in some cultures, where the mother does not breast-feed until her milk "comes in" two or three days after birth. (Sometimes other women nurse the newborn; sometimes herbal tea is given.) Worldwide research confirmed that colostrum saves infant lives, especially if the infant is preterm (Andreas et al., 2015; Moles et al., 2015).

IMMUNIZATION

Before the measles vaccine was introduced in 1963, 30 million people globally contracted measles each year. About 2 million of them died, usually because they were both malnourished and sick (World Health Organization, April 28, 2017). Thankfully, worldwide vaccination efforts now mean that no child need die of measles.

Measles is highly infectious, so 95 percent of the population must be immunized in order for herd immunity to protect the entire community. The United States achieved that: A decade ago, measles incidence was close to zero. Experts thought it would soon be eliminated in all developed countries, so public health workers focused on the very poorest nations.

ESTIMATED MEASLES VACCINE COVERAGE — SELECTED NATIONS

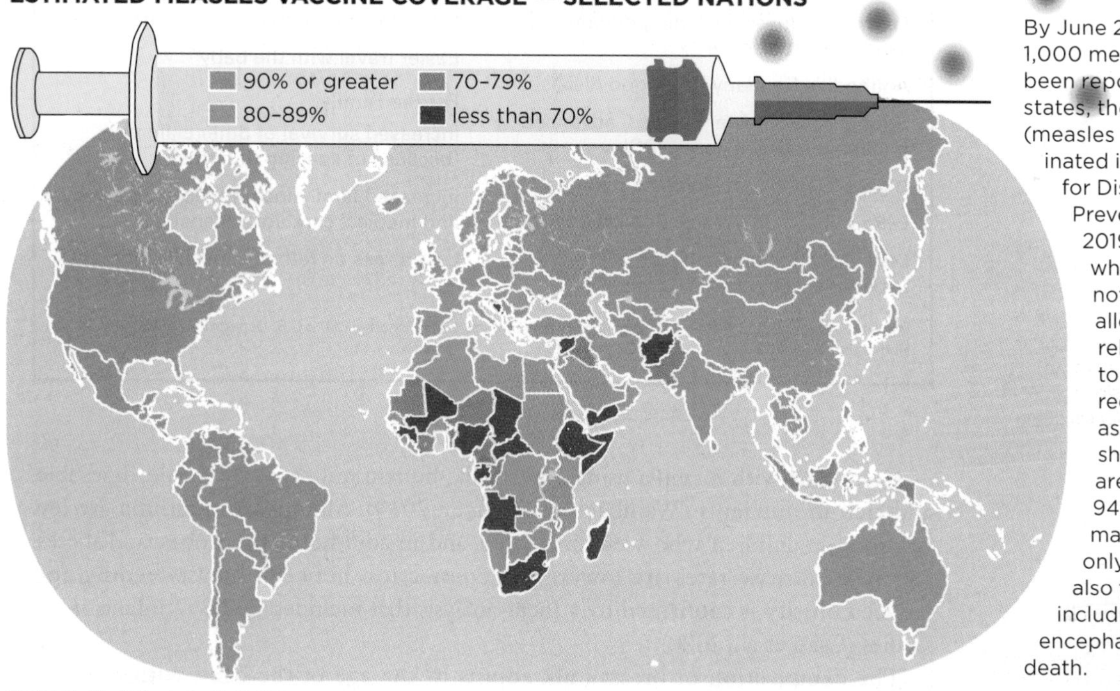

By June 2019, more than 1,000 measles cases had been reported in 28 U.S. states, the most since 1992 (measles was declared eliminated in 2000) (Centers for Disease Control and Prevention, June 17, 2019). To understand what went wrong, note that many states allow personal or religious exemptions to immunization requirements. Thus, as the U.S. map below shows, several states are not at that safe 94 percent — leaving many vulnerable, not only to discomfort but also to complications, including pneumonia, encephalitis, and even death.

Data from World Health Organization, May 29, 2019.

VACCINE EXEMPTION AND HERD IMMUNITY — UNITED STATES

MMR vaccination rate >94%

Nonmedical exemption rate above U.S. median (2%)

WA OR ID MT ND MN WI MI NY VT NH ME MA RI CT NJ DE MD DC PA VA OH IN IL IA NV CA UT CO KS MO KY TN AR OK NM AZ TX AL GA SC FL AK HI

Data from Mellerson et al., 2018.

TABLE 3.2 The Benefits of Breast-Feeding

For the Baby	For the Mother
Balance of nutrition (fat, protein, etc.) adjusts to age of baby	Easier bonding with baby
Micronutrients not found in formula	Reduced risk of breast cancer and osteoporosis
Less infant illness, including allergies, ear infections, stomach upset	Natural contraception (with exclusive breast-feeding, for several months)
Less childhood asthma	Pleasure of breast stimulation
Better childhood vision	Satisfaction of meeting infant's basic need
Less adult illness, including diabetes, cancer, heart disease	No formula to prepare; no sterilization
Antibodies for many childhood diseases	Easier travel with the baby
Stronger jaws, fewer cavities, advanced breathing reflexes (less SIDS)	**For the Family**
Higher IQ, better academic outcomes	Increased survival of other children (because of spacing of births)
Later puberty, fewer teenage pregnancies	Increased family income (because formula and medical care are expensive)
Less likely to become obese or hypertensive by age 12	Less stress on father, especially at night

Information from Beilin & Huang, 2008; Riordan & Wambach, 2009; Schanler, 2011; U.S. Department of Health and Human Services, 2011.

Compared with formula using cow's milk, human milk is more sterile, digestible, and rich in nutrients (Wambach & Spencer, 2019). Allergies and asthma are less common in children who were breast-fed, and in adulthood, their obesity, diabetes, and heart disease rates are lower. The connection between breast-feeding and reduced obesity is confirmed by a meta-analysis that included 332,297 infants in 26 studies (Qiao et al., 2020).

The composition of breast milk adjusts to the age of the baby, with milk for premature babies distinct from that for older infants. Quantity increases to meet demand: Twins and even triplets can be exclusively breast-fed for months. Of course, adequate maternal nutrition is required.

Formula is advised for medical reasons only in unusual cases, such as when the mother uses toxic drugs or is HIV-positive. Even with HIV, however, breast milk without supplementation is advised by the World Health Organization. In some nations, the infants' risk of catching HIV from their mothers is lower than the risk of dying from infections, diarrhea, or malnutrition as a result of bottle-feeding (A. Williams et al., 2016).

Doctors worldwide recommend breast-feeding with no other foods—not even juice—for the first months of life. (Table 3.2 lists some of the benefits of breast-feeding.) Some pediatricians suggest adding foods at 4 months; others advise waiting until 6 months (Fewtrell et al., 2011).

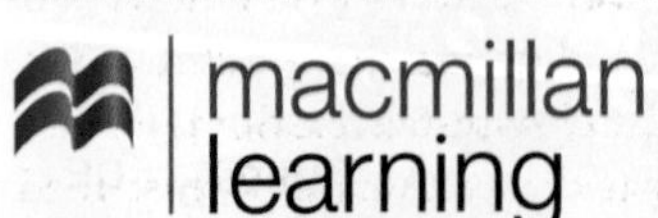

VIDEO: Nutritional Needs of Infants and Children: Breast-Feeding Promotion shows UNICEF's efforts to educate women on the benefits of breast-feeding.

THE SOCIAL CONTEXT

Breast-feeding was once universal, but by the mid-twentieth century, many mothers thought formula was better. That has changed again. In 2016 in the United States, most (84 percent) newborns were breast-fed, as were more than half (57 percent) of all 6-month-olds and more than a third (36 percent) of all 1-year-olds (Centers for Disease Control and Prevention, 2019).

Encouragement of breast-feeding from family members, especially fathers, is crucial. In addition, ideally nurses visit new mothers weekly at home; such visits (routine in some nations, rare in others) increase the likelihood that breast-feeding will continue. Although every expert agrees that breast milk is beneficial, given the complex needs of human families, sometimes formula-feeding is the better choice.

Indeed, some critics fear that breast-feeding has reached cult status, shaming those who do not do it (Jung, 2015). No single behavior, even those seemingly recommended in this book (breast-feeding, co-sleeping, handwashing, exercising, family planning, immunization) defines good motherhood (see Opposing Perspectives).

OPPOSING PERSPECIVES

Breast-Feeding in My Family

A hundred years ago, my grandmother, an immigrant who spoke accented English, breast-fed her 16 children. If women of her generation could not provide adequate breast milk (for instance, if they were very sick), the alternatives were milk from another woman (called a wet nurse), from a cow, or from a goat. Those alternatives increased the risk of infant malnutrition and death.

Grandma did not use any of these options. Four of her babies died in infancy.

By the middle of the twentieth century, scientists had analyzed breast milk and created *formula*, designed to be far better than cow's milk. Formula solved the problems of breast-feeding, such as insufficient milk and the exhaustion that breast-feeding mothers often experienced. Bottle-fed babies gained more weight than breast-fed ones; in many nations by 1950, only poor or immigrant women breast-fed.

That is why my mother formula-fed me. She explained that she wanted me to have the best that modern medicine could provide.

She recounted an incident meant to convey that my father was less conscientious than she was. He had volunteered to give me my 2 A.M. feeding (babies were fed on a rigid four-hour schedule). But the next morning, she noticed the full bottle in the refrigerator. She queried him. He said I was sound asleep, so he decided I was "fat enough already." She told me this story to indicate that men are not good caregivers. I never told her that my perspective was opposed to hers; I think Dad was right, since overfeeding infants is likely to result in overweight adults.

When I had my children, I read that companies that sold formula promoted it in Africa and Latin America by paying local women to dress as nurses and to give new mothers free formula that lasted a week. When the free formula ran out, breast milk had dried up. So mothers in those nations used their little money to buy more formula—diluting it to make it last, not always sterilizing properly (fuel was expensive), and supplementing the formula with herbal tea.

Public health workers reported statistics: Formula-fed babies had more diarrhea (a leading killer of children in poor nations) and a higher death rate. The World Health Organization (WHO) recommended a return to breast-feeding and curbed promotion of formula.

In sympathy for those dying babies, I was among the thousands of North Americans who boycotted products from the offending manufacturers, and I breast-fed my children. But the recommended four-hour schedule had them hungry and me stressed: I gladly took my pediatrician's advice to feed my 2-month-olds occasional bottles of formula (carefully sterilized), juice, water, and spoons of baby cereal and bananas.

International research continues, producing another cohort change. Currently, most (about 80 percent) U.S. mothers breast-feed in the beginning (unlike my mother), and 19 percent breast-feed exclusively until 6 months (unlike me). My grandchildren were nourished exclusively on breast milk for six months.

As of 2015, about 200 hospitals in the United States and hundreds more worldwide are "Baby-Friendly," a UNICEF designation that includes breast-feeding every newborn within half an hour of birth and giving them nothing but breast milk except in unusual circumstances. Some critics fear the other extreme—that the pressure to breast-feed punishes women who are unable to stay with their babies for six months (Jung, 2015).

Each generation has a perspective on infant care that opposes some practices of their elders. What will happen when my grandchildren become parents?

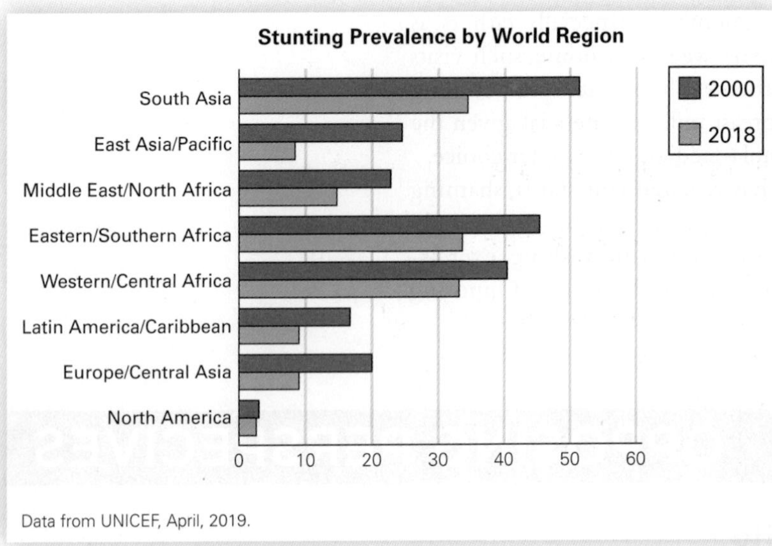

FIGURE 3.9 Evidence Matters Genes were thought to explain height differences among Asians and Scandinavians, until data on hunger and malnutrition proved otherwise. The result: Starvation is down and height is up almost everywhere—especially in Asia. Despite increased world population, far fewer young children are stunted (255 million in 1970; 156 million in 2015). Evidence now finds additional problems: Civil war, climate change, and limited access to contraception have increased stunting in East and Central Africa in the past decade.

protein-calorie malnutrition
A condition in which a person does not consume sufficient food of any kind. This deprivation can result in several illnesses, severe weight loss, and even death.

stunting
The failure of children to grow to a normal height for their age due to severe and chronic malnutrition.

wasting
The tendency for children to be severely underweight for their age as a result of malnutrition.

MALNUTRITION

Protein-calorie malnutrition occurs when a person does not consume enough food to sustain normal growth. A child may suffer from **stunting**, being short for their age because chronic malnutrition kept them from growing, or **wasting**, being severely underweight for their age and height (2 or more standard deviations below average). Many nations, especially in East Asia, Latin America, and central Europe, have seen improvement in child nutrition in the past decades, with an accompanying decrease in wasting and stunting (see Figure 3.9).

In other nations, however, primarily in Africa, wasting has increased. A third of all the infants worldwide who suffer from malnutrition are in African nations south of the Sahara Desert (Akombi et al., 2017). Explanations include lack of contraception, high birth rate, maternal AIDS deaths, reduced farming because of climate change, and civil wars that disrupt food distribution.

Chronically malnourished infants and children suffer in three ways:

- **Learning suffers.** If malnutrition continues long enough to affect height, it also affects the brain. If hunger reduces energy and curiosity, children learn less.
- **Malnutrition causes disease.** Both *marasmus* during the first year (when body tissues waste away), and *kwashiorkor* after age 1 (when growth slows down, hair becomes thin, skin becomes splotchy, and the face, legs, and abdomen swell with fluid [edema]), are directly caused by poor diet.
- **Other diseases are more deadly.** A detailed study in India of deaths before age 5 found that malnutrition was a risk factor for 68 percent of them (India State-Level Disease Burden Initiative Malnutrition Collaborators, 2019). If malnourished children experience malaria, or pneumonia, or measles, they are much more likely to die than if the same disease occurred in a well-nourished child.

Prevention, more than treatment, is needed because if a malnourished child reaches a hospital, special feeding can restore weight, but the risk of later disease and death is high. For example, one follow-up of 400 children who were treated for malnutrition, gained weight, and returned to their homes found that 20 years later, half of them had died, most often from malaria and kwashiorkor (Mwene-Batu et al., 2020). Ideally, prenatal nutrition, then breast-feeding, and then supplemental iron and vitamin A stop malnutrition before it starts.

Breast milk from a well-nourished mother is the best protection against severe malnutrition. However, wasting and stunting in Africa correlates with breast-feeding that continues after a year, especially if the mother herself is malnourished. Thus, public health recommendations need to reflect the family and community: Infants survive best if breast-fed, but after 6 months, ample, digestible food is also needed (Akombi et al., 2017).

Developmentalists now believe that the best way to prevent childhood deaths is to educate and support the mothers. Fathers and national policies are crucial as well (Karlsson et al., 2019), but worldwide it seems that maternal education is the strongest correlate of healthy infants (Sabates & Di Cesare, 2019; Vikram & Vanneman, 2020).

This is another example of the theme expressed at the beginning of this chapter. The entire social context of infancy shapes the body and mind of each baby, and the actions of immediate caregivers are especially important. The next chapter focuses on the infant's social world.

what have you learned?

1. What are the risk factors for SIDS?
2. Why do public health doctors wish that all infants worldwide would get immunized?
3. Why would a parent blame immunization for autism spectrum disorder?
4. How does a community reach herd immunity?
5. What are the reasons for exclusive breast-feeding for the first six months?
6. What is the relationship between malnutrition and disease?
7. What diseases are caused directly by malnutrition?
8. What is the difference between stunting and wasting?
9. In what ways does malnutrition affect cognition?

SUMMARY

Body Changes

1. In the first two years of life, infants grow taller, gain weight, and increase in head circumference—all indicative of development. On average, birthweight doubles by 4 months, triples by 1 year, and quadruples by 2 years, when toddlers weigh about 30 pounds.

2. Sleep gradually decreases over the first two years. As with all areas of development, variations are caused by both nature and nurture. Bed-sharing is the norm in many developing nations, and co-sleeping is increasingly common in developed ones.

3. Brain size increases dramatically, from about 25 percent to 75 percent of adult weight between birth and age 2. Complexity increases as well, with proliferating dendrites and synapses. Both growth and pruning aid cognition. Experience is vital for brain development.

4. At birth, the senses already respond to stimuli. Prenatal experience makes hearing the most mature sense. Vision is the least mature sense at birth, but it improves quickly. Infants use all of their senses to strengthen their early social interactions.

5. Infants gradually improve their motor skills as they grow and their brains develop. Gross motor skills are practiced as soon as they are possible. Babies gradually develop the fine motor skills to grab, aim, and manipulate almost anything within reach. Experience, time, and motivation allow infants to advance in all of their motor skills.

The Eager Mind

6. Infants learn so quickly that developmentalists now suggest that some basic understanding is programmed into the brain—no experience necessary. Infants follow the gaze of adults to learn what merits their attention.

7. Infant memory is fragile but not completely absent. Reminder sessions help trigger memories, and young brains learn motor sequences and respond to repeated emotions (their own and those of other people) long before explicit memory, using words.

8. Piaget realized that very young infants are active learners who seek to understand their complex observations and experiences. The six stages of sensorimotor intelligence begin with reflexes and end with mental combinations. The six stages occur in pairs, with each pair characterized by a circular reaction.

9. Infants first react to their own bodies (primary), then respond to other people and things (secondary), and finally, in the stage of tertiary circular reactions, infants become more goal-oriented, creative, and experimental as "little scientists."

Language: What Develops in the First Two Years?

10. Eager attempts to communicate are apparent in the first weeks and months. Infants babble at about 6 months, understand words and gestures by 10 months, and speak their first words at about 1 year.

11. Vocabulary builds slowly until the infant knows approximately 50 words. Then the naming explosion begins. Grammar is evident in the first holophrases, and combining words together in proper sequence is further evidence that babies learn grammar as well as vocabulary.

12. Various theories explain how infants learn language. Each major theory emphasizes different aspects of learning: that infants must be taught, that their social impulses foster language learning, and that their brains are genetically attuned to language. Neuroscientists find that many parts of the brain, and many strategies for learning, are involved in early language accomplishments.

Surviving and Thriving

13. A global, cross-cultural understanding of infant development has benefited babies worldwide. One example is the

discovery that "back to sleep" would prevent three-fourths of all sudden infant deaths.

14. Another major discovery is immunization, which has eradicated smallpox and virtually eliminated polio and measles. Public health workers worry that too many parents avoid immunization, decreasing herd immunity.

15. Breast milk helps infants resist disease and promotes growth of every kind. Most babies are breast-fed at birth, but rates over the first year vary depending on family and culture. Pediatricians now recommend breast milk as the only nourishment for the first months.

16. Severe malnutrition stunts growth and can cause death, both directly and indirectly through vulnerability if a child becomes sick. Stunting and wasting are both signs of malnutrition, which has become less common worldwide except in some nations of sub-Saharan Africa.

KEY TERMS

norm (p. 74)
percentile (p. 74)
co-sleeping (p. 75)
bed-sharing (p. 75)
sudden infant death syndrome (SIDS) (p. 76)
head-sparing (p. 76)
neuron (p. 77)
axon (p. 77)
dendrite (p. 77)
synapse (p. 77)
neurotransmitter (p. 77)
cortex (p. 77)
prefrontal cortex (p. 77)
limbic system (p. 77)
amygdala (p. 77)
hippocampus (p. 77)
hypothalamus (p. 78)
cortisol (p. 78)
pituitary (p. 78)
transient exuberance (p. 78)
experience-expectant (p. 79)
experience-dependent (p. 79)
shaken baby syndrome (p. 80)
binocular vision (p. 81)
motor skill (p. 83)
gross motor skills (p. 83)
fine motor skills (p. 84)
implicit memory (p. 86)
explicit memory (p. 87)
sensorimotor intelligence (p. 89)
primary circular reactions (p. 89)
secondary circular reactions (p. 89)
object permanence (p. 90)
tertiary circular reactions (p. 91)
little scientist (p. 91)
babbling (p. 93)
holophrase (p. 94)
naming explosion (p. 95)
grammar (p. 96)
mean length of utterance (MLU) (p. 96)
language acquisition device (LAD) (p. 99)
immunization (p. 102)
protein-calorie malnutrition (p. 108)
stunting (p. 108)
wasting (p. 108)

APPLICATIONS

1. Observe three infants (whom you do not know) in a public place such as a store, playground, or bus. Look closely at body size and motor skills, especially how much control each baby has over their legs and hands. From that, estimate the baby's age in months, and then ask the caregiver how old the infant is.

2. Elicit vocalizations from an infant—babbling if the baby is under age 1, using words if the baby is older. Write down all of the baby's communication for 10 minutes. Then ask the primary caregiver to elicit vocalizations for 10 minutes, and write these down. What differences are apparent between the baby's two attempts at communication? Compare your findings with the norms described in the chapter.

3. Immunization regulations and practices vary, partly for social and political reasons. Ask at least two faculty or administrative staff members what immunizations the students at your college must have and why. If you hear "It's a law," ask why.

4. *This project can be done alone, but it is more informative if several students pool responses.* Ask 3 to 10 adults whether they were bottle-fed or breast-fed and, if breast-fed, for how long. If someone does not know, or expresses embarrassment, that itself is worth noting. Do you see any correlation between adult body size and infant feeding?

ESPECIALLY FOR ANSWERS

Response for New Parents (from p. 76): From the psychological and cultural perspectives, babies can sleep anywhere as long as the parents can hear them if they cry. The main consideration is safety: Infants should not sleep on a mattress that is too soft, nor beside an adult who is drunk or on drugs. Otherwise, families should decide for themselves.

Response for Parents of Grown Children (from p. 80): Probably not. Brain development is programmed to occur for all infants, requiring only the stimulation that virtually all families provide—warmth, reassuring touch, overheard conversation, facial expressions, movement. Extras such as baby talk, music, exercise, mobiles, and massage may be beneficial but are not essential.

Response for Parents (from p. 92): It is easier and safer to babyproof the house because toddlers, being "little scientists," want to explore. However, it is important for both parents to encourage

and guide the baby. If having untouchable items prevents a major conflict between the adults, that might be the best choice.

Response for Nurses and Pediatricians (from p. 104): It is difficult to convince people that their method of child rearing is wrong, although you should try. In this case, listen respectfully and then describe specific instances of serious illness or death from a childhood disease. Suggest that the mother ask her grandparents whether they knew anyone who had polio, tuberculosis, or tetanus (they probably did). If you cannot convince this mother, do not despair: Vaccination of 95 percent of toddlers helps protect the other 5 percent. If the mother has genuine religious reasons, talk to her clergy adviser.

OBSERVATION QUIZ ANSWERS

Answer to Observation Quiz (from p. 83): Jumping up, with a three-month age range for acquisition. The reason is that the older an infant is, the more impact both nature and nurture have.

Answer to Observation Quiz (from p. 87): The mobile is a good addition—colorful and too high for the baby to reach. (Let's hope it is securely fastened and those strings are strong and tight!) But there are two things that are not what a developmentalist would recommend. First, the crib and the wall are both plain white, limiting what the baby can focus on, and second, the crib bumper is a SIDS risk.

Answer to Observation Quiz (from p. 103): Most is East Asia, primarily because China has prioritized public health. Least is western and central Africa, primarily because of civil wars. In some nations, high birth rates have dramatically increased the numbers of stunted children, even though rates in the region are lower.

CHAPTER 4

THE FIRST TWO YEARS
The Social World

what will you know?

- Does a difficult newborn become a difficult child?
- What do infants do if they are securely attached to their caregivers?
- Is one theory of infant/parent interaction more valid than another?
- What is the best care for infants and toddlers, and who provides it?

Bone-tired after a day of teaching, I was grateful to find a seat on the crowded downtown train. At the next stop, more people boarded, including a woman who stood in front of me. In one arm she held a baby, about 18 months old, and she wrapped her other arm around a pole while holding several heavy bags. For an instant I thought I might offer my seat, but I was too tired. But at least I could hold her bags on my lap.

"Can I help you?" I asked, offering a hand. Wordlessly she handed me . . . the baby, who sat quietly and listened as I expressed admiration for her socks, pointed out the red and blue stripes, and then sang a lullaby. I could feel her body relax. Her eyes stayed on her mother.

I should not have been surprised. Mothers everywhere need help with infant care, and strangers everywhere attend to infant cries, bring gifts to newborns, and read books, consult experts, and volunteer time to become caregivers, teachers, helpers.

Other passengers watched me to make sure all was well. We all — mother, strangers, and I — were doing what our culture expects. And the baby did what healthy babies do. She responded to my off-key singing, reassured by the proximity of her mother.

This example opens this chapter because it illustrates infant emotions and caregiver responses. You will read about psychosocial changes over the first two years, from synchrony to attachment to social referencing, quite evident in this baby.

At the end of the chapter, we explore a controversy: Who should care for infants? Only mothers, or also fathers, grandmothers, day-care teachers, and strangers? Would you have handed me your baby? Individuals and cultures answer this question in opposite ways.

Fortunately, as this chapter explains, despite diversity of temperament and caregiving, most infants develop well if their emotional needs are met. This baby seemed fine.

Emotional Development

Psychosocial development during infancy can be seen as two interwoven strands—nature/nurture, universal/particular, or experience-expectant/experience-dependent. To portray these strands with words, one after the other, we must pull them apart, so this chapter zigzags, from universal to particular and back, again and again.

Early Emotions

We begin with universal: In their first two years, all infants progress from reactive pain and pleasure to complex patterns of socio-emotional awareness, a movement from basic instincts to learned responses (see At About This Time).

One way to describe this process is to categorize emotions as primary or secondary. *Primary emotions* are called "natural kinds," which means they are innate and universal. Four emotions are primary: happiness, sadness, fear, and anger. Some scholars include two more: surprise and disgust. Primary emotions are evident in very young babies, even blind ones (Valente et al., 2018).

Thus, because of internal signals, newborns are happy and relaxed when fed and drifting off to sleep. Discomfort is also part of daily life: Newborns cry when they are hurt or hungry, tired or frightened (as by a loud noise or a sudden loss of support).

By the second week and increasing to 6 weeks, some infants have bouts of uncontrollable crying, called *colic*, perhaps the result of immature digestion or the infant version of a migraine headache (Gelfand, 2018). Others have *reflux*, probably the result of immature swallowing. About 10 to 20 percent of babies cry "excessively," defined as more than three hours a day, more than three days a week, for more than three weeks.

Fortunately, early emotions do not necessarily predict later life. A longitudinal study of 291 infants found that, by age 2, infants with colic were no more likely to have behavioral problems than those without (Bell et al., 2018). As you will later read, newborn temperament is shaped by caregiver response.

At About This Time: Developing Emotions

Newborn	Distress; contentment
6 weeks	Social smile
3 months	Laughter; curiosity
4 months	Full, responsive smiles
4–8 months	Anger surprise
9–14 months	Fear of social events (strangers, separation from caregiver)
12 months	Fear of unexpected sights and sounds
18 months	Self-awareness; pride; shame; embarrassment

As always, culture and experience influence the norms of development. This is especially true for emotional development after the first 8 months.

SMILING AND LAUGHING

Soon, crying decreases and additional emotions become recognizable. Colic usually subsides by 3 months. Beginning at about 6 weeks, happiness is expressed by a fleeting **social smile**, evoked by a human face.

social smile
A smile evoked by a human face, normally first evident in infants about 6 weeks after birth.

The social smile is universal; all babies do it when they are old enough, evidence of the maturation of the human social impulse. Preterm babies smile later, because the social smile is affected by age since conception, not age since birth (White-Traut et al., 2018).

Laughter builds over the first months, often in tandem with curiosity: A typical 6-month-old chortles upon discovering new things, particularly social experiences that balance familiarity and surprise, such as Daddy making a funny face. That is just what Piaget would expect, "making interesting experiences last." Very young infants

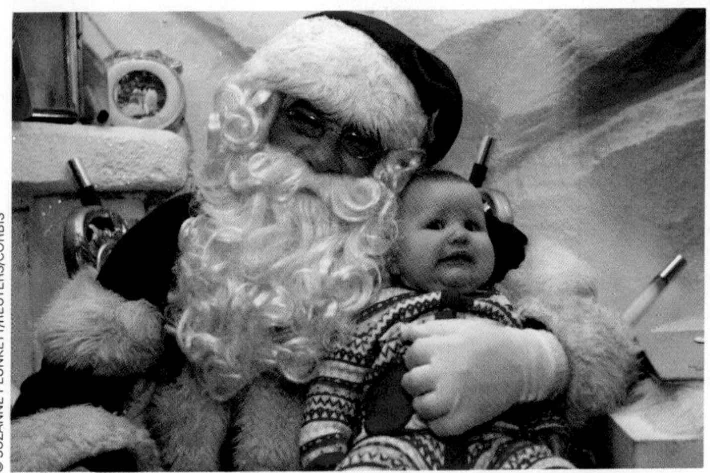

Developmentally Correct Both Santa's smile and Olivia's grimace are appropriate reactions for people of their age. Adults playing Santa must smile no matter what, and if Olivia smiled, that would be troubling to anyone who knows about 7-month-olds. Yet every Christmas, thousands of parents wait in line to put their infants on the laps of oddly dressed, bearded strangers.

prefer seeing happy faces more than sad ones, even if the happy faces are not looking at them (Kim & Johnson, 2013).

Soon happiness becomes more discriminating. In one study, infants first enjoyed a video of dancing to music as it normally occurs, on the beat. Then some watched a video in which the soundtrack was mismatched with dancing. Eight- to-12-month-old babies, compared to younger ones, were quite curious — but less delighted — about offbeat dancing. The researchers concluded "babies know bad dancing when they see it" (Hannon et al., 2017).

ANGER AND FEAR

The primary emotions of fear and anger are soon evident in response to external events. By 6 months, anger is usually triggered by frustration, especially if babies cannot grab or move as they wish. Infants hate to be strapped in, caged in, closed in, or just held in place when they want to explore.

In infancy, anger is a healthy response to frustration, unlike sadness, which also may appear in the early months (Thiam et al., 2017). Sadness indicates withdrawal instead of a bid for help, and it is accompanied by a greater increase in the body's production of cortisol. For that reason, developmentalists are troubled if a very young baby is sad.

FEAR

Fear is also a primary emotion, evident in a newborn's fear of falling or of loud noises. Soon, however, that primary emotion is either soothed with comfort or, instead, spreads because circumstances are frightening. Fear is affected by three factors: awareness of discrepancy, temperament, and social context. Two kinds of social fear are typical, increasing from the middle of the first year and then decreasing:

separation anxiety
An infant's distress when a familiar caregiver leaves; most obvious between 9 and 14 months.

stranger wariness
An infant's expression of concern—a quiet stare while clinging to a familiar person, or a look of fear—when a stranger appears.

- **Separation anxiety**—clinging and crying when a comforting caregiver is about to leave. Some separation anxiety is typical at age 1, intensifies by age 2, and then usually subsides.
- **Stranger wariness**—fear of unfamiliar people, especially when they quickly move close. Knowing that, in the subway incident that opened this chapter, I first distracted the baby by talking about her socks, and then sang quietly to her, keeping some distance between her face and mine.

If separation anxiety and stranger fear remain intense after age 3, impairing a child's ability to leave home, to go to school, or to play with other children, they may become a disorder (American Psychiatric Association, 2013). In adulthood, they may become generalized anxiety disorder or social phobia (Rudaz et al., 2017). But in 1-year-olds, both reactions are typical.

These early emotions are experience-expectant and then experience-dependent, responsive to context (LoBue & Adolph, 2019). [**Life-Span Link:** Experience-expectant and experience-dependent brain function are described

in Chapter 3.] Infants at home with Mother when a stranger comes to visit are likely to smile in welcome. But if a stranger yells, approaching quickly to a few inches of the babies face, almost any 1-year-old will cry and try to move away.

Many 1-year-olds are wary of anything unexpected, from the flush of the toilet to the pop of a jack-in-the-box, from closing elevator doors to the tail-wagging approach of a dog. With repeated experience and reassurance, older infants might enjoy flushing the toilet (again and again) or calling the dog (crying if the dog does *not* come).

Note the transition from instinct to learning to thought, from the amygdala to the cortex. Context is crucial for fear (LoBue & Adolph, 2019).

Especially for Nurses and Pediatricians
Parents come to you concerned that their 1-year-old hides her face and holds onto them tightly whenever a stranger appears. What do you tell them? (see response, page 142)

Toddlers' Emotions

Primary emotions take on new strength during toddlerhood, as both memory and mobility advance and secondary emotions arise. Throughout the second year and beyond, emotions become less frequent but more focused, targeted toward infuriating, terrifying, or exhilarating experiences. Both laughing and crying are louder and more discriminating.

TEMPER TANTRUMS

The new strength of emotions is apparent in tantrums. Toddlers are famous for fury. When something angers them, they might yell, scream, cry, hit, and throw themselves on the floor. Logic is beyond them: If adults tease or get angry, that makes it worse. Parental insistence on obedience exacerbates the tantrum (Cierpka & Cierpka, 2016).

One child said, "I don't want my feet. Take my feet off. I don't want my feet." Her mother tried logic, which didn't work, and then offered to get scissors and cut off the offending feet. A new wail erupted, with a loud shriek "Nooooo!" (Katrina, quoted in Vedantam, 2011).

With temper tantrums, soon sadness comes to the fore. Then comfort—not punishment—is helpful (Green et al., 2011). Outbursts of anger are typical at age 1 and 2, but if they persist and become destructive, that signifies trouble, in parent or child (Cierpka & Cierpka, 2016).

JOSEPH FARRIS/CARTOONSTOCK

Empathy Wins Crying babies whose caregivers sympathize often become confident, accomplished, and caring children. Sleep deprivation makes anyone unhappy, but this man's response is much better for both of them than anger or neglect.

SELF AND OTHERS

Secondary emotions emerge in toddlerhood, including pride, shame, jealousy, embarrassment, and guilt. These emotions involve awareness of other people, which typically arises from family responses: Emotions are expressed, controlled, and guided in infancy and throughout childhood (Hajal & Paley, 2020).

Positive as well as negative emotions show social awareness and learning (Aktar et al., 2018; Ogren et al., 2018). Many toddlers try to help a stranger who has dropped something or who is searching for a hidden object, and some express sympathy for someone who is hurt (Aitken et al., 2020).

Over time, children learn when and whom to help by watching adults. Some adults donate to beggars, others look away, and still others complain to the police. Attitudes about ethnicity, or immigration, or clothing, begin with the infant's preference for the familiar and interest in novelty. Then upbringing adds appreciation or rejection.

Another emotion that reflects the social context is jealousy. Some adults seem pathologically jealous, perhaps demanding to know the whereabouts of their partner at every moment. Other adults are trusting, confident that their partner is loving and loyal. This difference might begin in infancy (see A View from Science).

A VIEW FROM SCIENCE

Jealousy

With all emotions, scientists wonder how and why they develop. To illustrate the science behind this quest, consider *jealousy*, a secondary emotion. Jealousy arises when people feel they have a special bond with someone that might be broken by a third person.

Although the word *jealousy* is sometimes used regarding things, that is considered *envy*, not jealousy. Here we focus on jealousy when it refers to a person's distress that arises when they are not the focus of another person's attention.

Newborns do not know enough to be jealous, but infants do (Hart, 2018). In a series of studies, when mothers ignored their 9-month-olds and showered attention on another baby, the infants looked more at their mothers, touching them and moving closer. An electroencephalogram (EEG) showed activity in the same part of the infant brain that was known to be associated with jealousy in adults (Mize et al., 2014; Mize & Jones, 2012).

In general, emotions exist for good reasons, yet their excesses are destructive. Consider the primary emotions: Happiness makes life satisfying, but the search for happiness can lead to drug addiction; sadness prompts us to repair problems but can lead to depression; fear keeps us safe but can become a phobia; anger results in needed political and private reforms but can lead to violence.

But how can jealousy be beneficial? As one team wrote, "the grip of the 'green-eyed monster' has been known to cause misery and produce some drastic coping behaviors ranging from paranoid stalking to violent aggression" (Yong & Li, 2018, p. 121). Jealousy triggers domestic abuse and homicidal rage. Yet all humans develop it at about age 1; why?

Some research suggests that the strength of infant jealousy is more affected by the relationship with the caregiver than by temperament (Hart, 2018). Children who are securely attached are less jealous when their caregiver attends to another child (Murphy et al., 2020).

An interesting speculation has emerged: Might jealousy appear at about age 1 because, at that age, our fertile foremothers sometimes had a new baby? In ancient times, toddlers with younger siblings needed to assert their need for attention and breast milk or risk death (Hart, 2018).

Within a few years, jealousy could subside if children were secure in maternal love. Then siblings could be buddies, not rivals. Thus, if adults are still irrationally jealous, perhaps they had insecure and hostile family relationships.

Of course, infant survival no longer requires jealousy, and jealousy in adults is often harmful. However, as is evident in love, lust, hate, disgust, and many other primary and secondary feelings, human emotions are not always rational responses to current reality, but they may reflect infant experiences.

THINK CRITICALLY: Are any of your emotions more destructive than helpful? Are you jealous? Does that emotion serve you well?

RECOGNIZING THE SELF

self-awareness
A person's realization that he or she is a distinct individual whose body, mind, and actions are separate from those of other people.

In addition to social awareness, another foundation for emotional growth is **self-awareness**, the realization that one's body, mind, and activities are distinct from those of other people. Closely following the new mobility that results from walking is an emerging sense of individuality.

In a classic experiment (Lewis & Brooks, 1978), 9- to 24-month-olds looked into a mirror after a dot of rouge had been surreptitiously put on their noses. If they reacted by touching the red dot on their noses, that meant they knew the

BSIP/UIG VIA GETTY IMAGES

BARTOSZ HADYNIAK/PHOTODISC/GETTY IMAGES

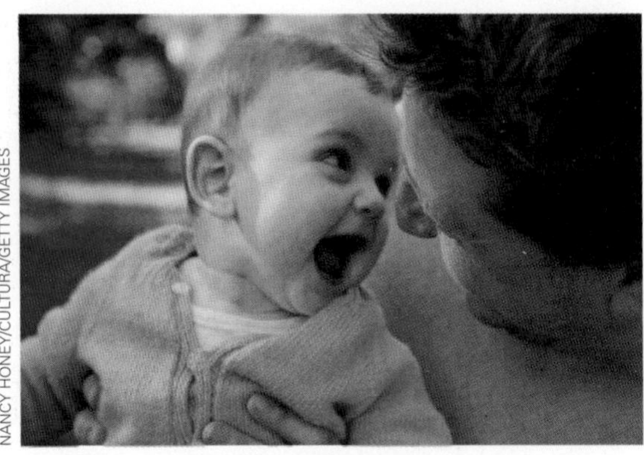

NANCY HONEY/CULTURA/GETTY IMAGES

Open Wide Synchrony is evident worldwide. Everywhere, babies watch their parents carefully, hoping for exactly what these three parents express, and responding with such delight that adults relish these moments.

move closer with smiling eyes and pursed lips, letting that waving arm touch a face or, even better, grab hair. The mutual synchrony is part of early adaptation and then "making interesting experiences last," Piaget's stages 2 and 3 of sensorimotor development (described in Chapter 3).

Synchronizing adults open their eyes wide, raise their eyebrows, smack their lips, and emit nonsense sounds. Hair-grabbing might make adults bob their heads back and forth, in a playful attempt to shake off the grab, to the infants' joy. Over the early months, an adult and an infant might develop a routine of hair-grabbing with cue and response, producing laughter in both parties.

Another adult and infant might develop a different routine, perhaps with hand-clapping, or lip-smacking, or head-turning. Synchrony becomes a mutual dance, with both knowing the steps. Often mothers and infants engage in *social games*, which are routines passed down from adult to infant in that culture. Social games soon become synchronized, with the infant anticipating and reacting to each move (Markova, 2018).

Detailed research, originally with two cameras, one focused on the infant and one on the caregiver, has examined the timing of every millisecond of arched eyebrows, widening eyes, pursed lips, and so on. The video of that interaction, with time stamps to indicate when every move occurs, reveals a tight relationship between adult and infant.

Physiological measures, such as heart rate, brain waves, and breathing, have recently been added to the video measures of synchrony (Bell, 2020; McFarland et al., 2020). Babies pick up on the mother's body rhythms and vice versa. In every interaction, infants read emotions and develop social skills, while coordinating their body and brain, and adults react in ways influenced by culture and their own innate bonding.

This may be most obvious when someone who is ordinarily stern interacts with an infant. Imagine a stone-faced grandfather suddenly animated when holding an infant grandchild.

OBSERVATION QUIZ

The universality of synchrony is evident here, not only in the babies but also in the parents, each of whom began at birth with a quite different relationship to the baby. Can you guess what those differences are? (see answer, page 142) ↑

CHAPTER APP 4

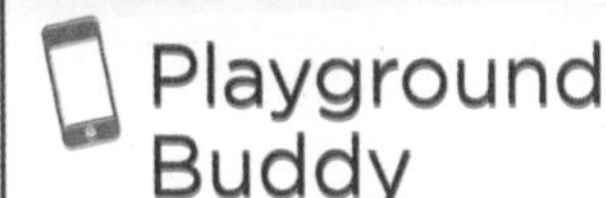

Playground Buddy

iOS:
https://tinyurl.com/waplr56

ANDROID:
https://tinyurl.com/r9jykb7

RELEVANT TOPIC:
Psychosocial development during infancy

With a worldwide database of over 200,000, this app shows caregivers the location and street views of nearby playgrounds. Users can also send the details to others, even those who do not have the app.

THE STILL FACE

Caregiver responsiveness to infant actions aids psychosocial and biological development, evident in heart rate, weight gain, and brain maturation. Experiments involving the **still-face technique** suggest that synchrony is experience-expectant (needed for normal brain growth) (Hari, 2017; Tronick, 1989; Tronick & Weinberg, 1997).

still-face technique
An experimental practice in which an adult keeps his or her face unmoving and expressionless in face-to-face interaction with an infant.

In still-face studies, at first an infant is propped in front of an adult who responds normally. Then, on cue, the adult stops all expression, staring quietly with a "still face" for a minute or two. Sometimes by 2 months, and clearly by 6 months, infants

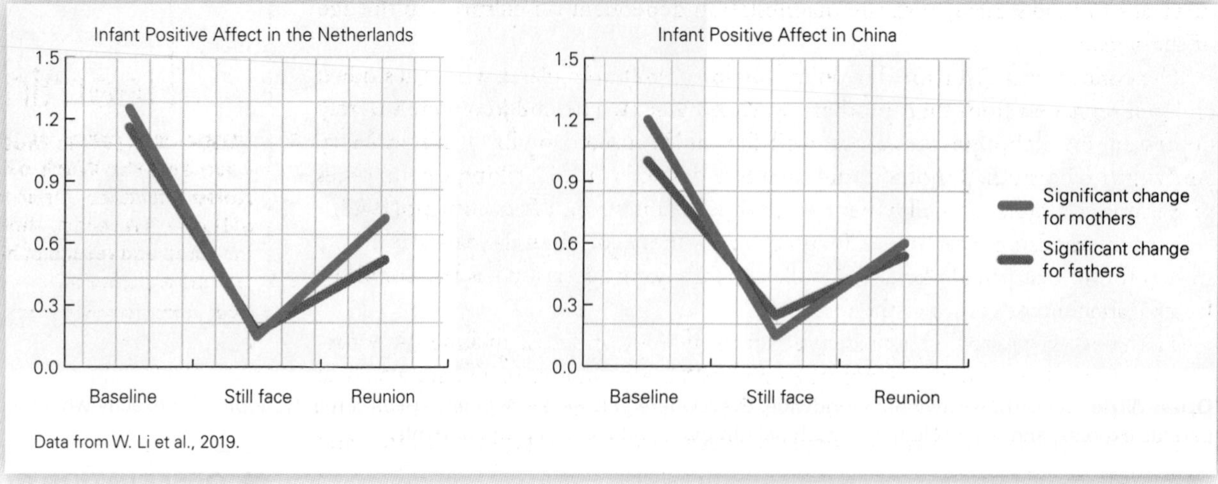

FIGURE 4.2 **Dramatic, and Tiny, Differences** As you see, the drop in positive affect (infants smiling, making happy noises, and so on) is almost identical with mothers and fathers, in Chinese and Dutch infants, when parents are suddenly nonresponsive.

◆◆ OBSERVATION QUIZ
What small differences do you see in these two charts? (see answer, page 142) ↑

enjoy the full attention and mutual interaction in the first moments and then are upset when their caregivers are unresponsive.

Babies smile and laugh when their parents interact with them, and frown, fuss, drool, look away, kick, cry, or suck their fingers when the still face occurs. By 5 months, they also vocalize, as if to say, "React to me!" This research has been done with fathers as well as mothers, in various nations (W. Li et al., 2019). Some differences appear, but everywhere babies enjoy social interaction and, when the still face begins, their happiness ends (see Figure 4.2).

Although reactions to the still face are universal, it is also true that infants are influenced by their past experiences. This was shown in one study that examined 4-month-olds and their mothers before, during, and after a still-face episode (Montirosso et al., 2015).

When the mothers were still-faced, some infants (33 percent) remained active, looking around at other things, apparently expecting that the caregivers would soon resume connection. When the still-face episode was over, they quickly reengaged. The researchers called those infants "socially engaged."

THINK CRITICALLY: What will happen if no one plays with an infant?

By contrast, a larger group (60 percent) were "disengaged." During the still face, they became passive, looking sad. When the still face was over and their mothers were active again, they took several minutes to return to positive responses.

Finally, a small group (7 percent) were "negatively engaged." During the still face they cried and were angry. They kept crying, even when the still face was over.

The mothers of each type differed in how they played with their infants. The socially engaged mothers matched the infants' actions (bobbing heads, opening mouths, and so on), but the negatively engaged mothers almost never matched and sometimes expressed anger—not sympathy—when the baby cried (Montirosso et al., 2015). That absent synchrony is a troubling sign for future emotional and brain development.

Attachment

attachment
According to Ainsworth, "an affectional tie" that an infant forms with a caregiver—a tie that binds them together in space and endures over time.

Attachment—the connection between one person and another, measured by how they respond to each other—is a lifelong process. The original research on attachment began by recognizing the infant's innate need to bond with a caregiver.

That early research led to the investigation of mutual attachment in many dyads and circumstances, with studies of adult attachment to an infant and then adults to each other. Developmentalists are convinced that attachment is basic to the

survival of *Homo sapiens*, with the manifestation dependent on culture and the age of the person.

The concept was first named by John Bowlby (1982) in England, who had studied children separated from their mothers by World War II. The children were severely depressed, even though they were well fed and housed. Bowlby inspired Mary Ainsworth who studied mothers and infants in Uganda (1967), taking careful notes on varieties of interaction. She then wrote about many forms of attachment (1982).

Early research on attachment focused on mothers and their 1-year-olds. Many studies found that once infants can walk, synchrony, just described, is less common. Instead, attachment comes to the fore.

The concept of attachment has spread from infancy, and now includes how parents attach to their children—even before birth, how children of all ages attach to their parents, and how romantic partners attach to each other (see At About This Time). Studies have occurred in virtually every nation, with typical children and those with disabilities.

Two signs universally indicate attachment: *contact-maintaining* and *proximity-seeking*. Both take many forms.

macmillan learning

VIDEO ACTIVITY: Mother Love and the Work of Harry Harlow features classic footage of Harlow's research, showing the setup and results of his famous experiment.

At About This Time: Stages of Attachment

Birth to 6 weeks	*Preattachment.* Newborns signal, via crying and body movements, that they need others. When people respond positively, the newborn is comforted and learns to seek more interaction. Newborns are also primed by brain patterns to recognize familiar voices and faces.
6 weeks to 8 months	*Attachment in the making.* Infants respond preferentially to familiar people by smiling, laughing, babbling. Their caregivers' voices, touch, expressions, and gestures are comforting, often overriding the infant's impulse to cry. Trust (Erikson) develops.
8 months to 2 years	*Classic secure attachment.* Infants greet the primary caregiver, play happily when the caregiver is present, show separation anxiety when the caregiver leaves. Both infant and caregiver seek to be close to each other (proximity) and frequently look at each other (contact). In many caregiver–infant pairs, physical touch (patting, holding, caressing) is frequent.
2 to 6 years	*Attachment as launching pad.* Young children seek their caregiver's praise and reassurance as their social world expands. Interactive conversations and games (hide-and-seek, object play, reading, pretending) are common. Children expect caregivers to comfort and entertain.
6 to 12 years	*Mutual attachment.* Children seek to make their caregivers proud by learning whatever adults want them to learn, and adults reciprocate. In concrete operational thought (Piaget), specific accomplishments are valued by adults and children.
12 to 18 years	*New attachment figures.* Teenagers explore and make friendships independent from parents, using their working models of earlier attachments as a base. With formal operational thinking (Piaget), shared ideals and goals become influential.
18 years on	*Attachment revisited.* Adults develop relationships with others, especially relationships with romantic partners and their own children, influenced by earlier attachment patterns. Past insecure attachments from childhood can be repaired rather than repeated, although this does not always happen.

Information from Grobman, 2008.

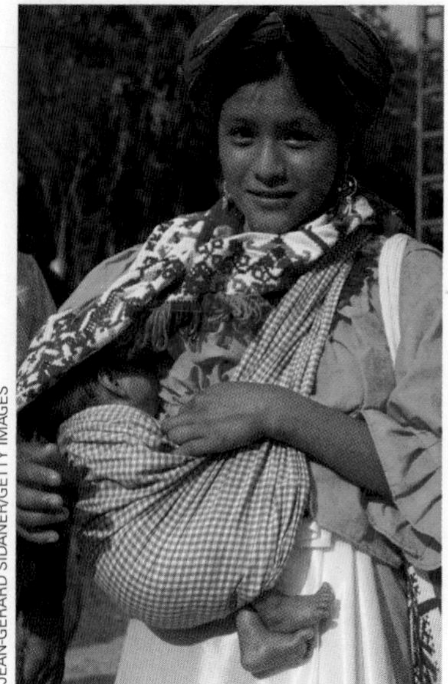
JEAN-GERARD SIDANER/GETTY IMAGES

Same or Different? A theme of this chapter is that babies and mothers are the same worldwide, yet dramatically different in each culture. Do you see similarities between the Huastec mother in Mexico and mothers in the United States?

For instance, Ugandan mothers never kiss their infants, but they often massage them. Hugs, handshakes, smiles, and words vary by culture and relationship. Contact can be frequent—some adults phone or text their distant mothers every day—and others connect only on holidays. Some attached family members all sit, together but at a distance, in the same room of a large house, each reading quietly. Others stay physically close, leaning on each other, slapping hands, nodding together. All are cultural differences; all signify attachment.

SECURE AND INSECURE ATTACHMENT

Attachment is classified into four types: A, B, C, and D. Infants with **secure attachment** (type B) feel comfortable and confident. The caregiver is a *base for exploration*, providing assurance and enabling discovery.

A securely attached toddler might, for example, scramble down from the caregiver's lap to play with an intriguing toy but periodically look back and vocalize (contact-maintaining) or bring the toy to the caregiver for inspection (proximity-seeking). Some mothers, while talking with another adult, absent-mindedly stroke their child's hair, or keep their eyes on the child, not the conversation partner.

The caregiver's presence gives the child courage to explore; departure causes distress; return elicits positive contact (such as smiling or hugging) and then more playing. This balanced reaction—the child concerned but not overwhelmed by comings and goings—indicates security. Similarly, the caregiver is watchful but not worried.

By contrast, insecure attachment (types A and C) is characterized by fear, anxiety, anger, or indifference. Some insecure children play independently without seeking contact; this is **insecure-avoidant attachment** (type A). A type A infant might ignore the parent, not looking at them. The opposite reaction is **insecure-resistant/ambivalent attachment** (type C). Children with type C attachment cling to their caregivers and are angry at being left.

Infants may be securely or insecurely attached to mothers, fathers, or other caregivers—sometimes just to one person, sometimes to several. Every baby seeks attachment: Temperament may affect the expression, but not the need (Groh et al., 2017).

Ainsworth's original schema differentiated only types A, B, and C. Later researchers discovered a fourth category (type D), **disorganized attachment** (Main & Solomon, 1990). Type D infants may suddenly switch from hitting to kissing their mothers, from staring blankly to crying hysterically, from pinching themselves to freezing in place.

Among the general population, almost two-thirds of infants are secure (type B). About one-third are insecure, either indifferent (type A) or unduly anxious (type C), and about 5 to 10 percent are disorganized (type D).

Children with type D attachment are especially worrisome to developmentalists, because those infants have no consistent strategy for social interaction, not even avoidance or resistance. Without intervention to improve early attachment, type D toddlers are at risk for later psychopathology, including severe aggression and major depression (Cicchetti, 2016; Groh et al., 2012). Of course, much more information about family life is needed before type D attachment is considered evidence that a particular child needs to be in foster care (White et al., 2019).

secure attachment
A relationship in which an infant obtains both comfort and confidence from the presence of his or her caregiver.

insecure-avoidant attachment
A pattern of attachment in which an infant avoids connection with the caregiver, as when the infant seems not to care about the caregiver's presence, departure, or return.

insecure-resistant/ambivalent attachment
A pattern of attachment in which an infant's anxiety and uncertainty are evident, as when the infant becomes very upset at separation from the caregiver and both resists and seeks contact on reunion.

disorganized attachment
A type of attachment that is marked by an infant's inconsistent reactions to the caregiver's departure and return.

ATTACHMENT PARENTING

Some people advocate *attachment parenting*, which prioritizes the mother–infant relationship during the first three years of life far more than Ainsworth or Bowlby did (Komisar, 2017; Sears & Sears, 2001). Attachment parenting mandates that mothers should always be near their infants (co-sleeping, "wearing" the baby in a wrap or

sling, breast-feeding on demand). Some experts suggest that attachment parenting is too distant from the research concept and evidence (Ennis, 2015).

Another potential problem with attachment parenting is that it requires intensive maternal devotion to the infant, which may clash with the mother's wish to share caregiving responsibilities with the father and others (Sánchez-Mira & Saura, 2020) and the father's wish to be intimately connected to mother and babe (Faircloth, 2020). It also precludes other activities of the mother, so she feels guilty for caring for other children, or for working.

Attachment parenting may be an extreme. However, the consensus of many researchers is not only that attachment is important for infant development but also that mothers can learn to strengthen the mother–infant bond.

Consequently, the U.S. government has supported more than a thousand programs of *home visiting*, when nurses or other professionals visit new mothers in their homes, teaching them how to care for their infants. The hope is that home visiting reduces the incidence of maltreatment later on (Berlin et al., 2018).

That hope is only sometimes realized. Apparently, it is crucial that the visitors are culturally sensitive, since expression of attachment varies. This is stressed in New Zealand, where every mother is visited.

Universal visiting means that mothers do not feel singled out for being insufficiently maternal, as may happen in the United States. Visiting nurses in New Zealand are taught to individualize their work, sometimes focusing on medical needs, sometimes on education, sometimes on emotions (de Haan & Connolly, 2019).

MEASURING ATTACHMENT

Scientists take great care to measure what they purport to measure. This is especially important when they want to measure emotions. They develop an *operational definition*, which is an observable behavior that indicates the construct, so that other scientists know what is measured and can replicate the study.

For instance, if you wanted to study love between romantic partners, what would your empirical measurement be? Ask each partner how much they loved each other? Ask other questions, such as whether they had, in the past year, thought of ending the relationship or sacrificed something for their partner?

As you remember from Chapter 1, the interview method of research may be inaccurate. You could instead, do an observational study, perhaps video their interaction,

Excited, Troubled, Comforted This sequence is repeated daily for 1-year-olds, which is why the same sequence is replicated to measure attachment. As you see, toys are no substitute for mother's comfort if the infant or toddler is secure, as this one seems to be. Some, however, cry inconsolably or throw toys angrily when left alone.

and count how often they made eye contact, or expressed agreement, or moved closer together? Or you could tally details of cohabitation, marriage, physical affection, shared finances? None of these is exactly what people call "love," but all might indicate some aspect of love, and all could be measured.

Measuring the bond between caregiver and infant is likewise complicated. For that reason, Mary Ainsworth (1973) developed an experiment, a laboratory procedure called the **Strange Situation** to measure attachment. The Strange Situation measures details on 1-year-olds' reactions to stress, with and without the caregiver.

Strange Situation
A laboratory procedure for measuring attachment by evoking infants' reactions to the stress of various adults' comings and goings in an unfamiliar playroom.

The specifics of the Strange Situation are as follows: In a well-equipped playroom, an infant is observed for eight episodes, each lasting no more than three minutes. First, the child and caregiver are together. Next, according to a set sequence, the caregiver and a stranger enter and leave the room. Infants' responses indicate A, B, C, or D attachment.

Researchers focus on the following:

> *Exploration of the toys.* A secure toddler plays happily.
>
> *Reaction to the caregiver's departure.* A secure toddler notices when the caregiver leaves and shows some sign of missing them. A pause in playing, a plaintive sound, a worried expression are all significant signs of attachment.
>
> *Reaction to the caregiver's return.* A secure toddler welcomes the caregiver's reappearance, seeking contact, and then plays again. Typically, toddlers run to their caregiver for a hug, and then resume investigation of the toys.

Scientists are carefully trained to measure attachment in the Strange Situation, via watching videos, calibrating ratings, and studying manuals. Researchers are certified only when they reach a high standard of accuracy. They learn which common behaviors signify insecurity, contrary to what untrained observers might think. For instance, clinging to the caregiver may be type C; being too friendly to the stranger suggests type A.

Many scientists who study attachment in older children and adults have developed other measures. Detailed questionnaires and interviews are calibrated to signify secure or insecure attachment.

THINK CRITICALLY: Is the Strange Situation a valid way to measure attachment in every culture, or is it biased toward the Western idea of the ideal mother–child relationship?

For example, the *Adult Attachment Interview (AAI)* asks adults about their relationship with their mothers. Ideally, the adults describe their parents as caring but not perfect (Booth-LaForce & Roisman, 2014). That indicates secure attachment, type B, called *autonomous.*

The AAI reveals past insecure attachment if the adult expresses rejection of their mother ("I never want to see her again"—type A *dismissing*) or sanctification of her ("she was a saint"—type C *preoccupied*). It is especially troubling if an adult is confused and incoherent (type D, *unresolved*), with few details about their awful, or perfect, childhood.

The measurement of attachment has made longitudinal studies possible, assessing the later development of infants who are types A, B, C, or D. We now know that infant–caregiver attachment affects brain development and the immune system (Bernard et al., 2019). Childhood circumstances, such as domestic violence or divorce, can weaken the links between childhood attachment and adult relationships (Fearon & Roisman, 2017).

ORPHANAGES IN ROMANIA

No scholar now doubts that the lack of attachment in infancy predicts lifelong problems. Unfortunately, thousands of children born in Romania have verified that conclusion.

When Romanian dictator Nicolae Ceausesçu forbade birth control and abortions in the 1980s, illegal abortions became the leading cause of death for Romanian women aged 15 to 45 (Verona, 2003).

To avoid that risk, many parents abandoned their infants. Crowded, state-run orphanages 170,000 unwanted children (Marshall, 2014). The children experienced no synchrony or attachment.

In the two years after Ceausesçu was ousted and killed in 1989, thousands of those children were adopted by North American, western European, and Australian families. Infants under 6 months of age fared best; the adoptive parents established synchrony and attachment. Slightly older adopted infants usually did well.

For those adopted after age 1, early signs were encouraging: Skinny toddlers gained weight, started walking, and grew quickly, developing motor skills they had lacked (H. Park et al., 2011). However, if social deprivation had lasted more than a year, emotions and cognition suffered.

Many of the late adoptees were overly friendly to strangers, a sign of insecure attachment. By age 11, their average IQ was only 85, which is 15 points lower than the statistical norm. The older they had been at adoption, the worse they fared (Nelson et al., 2014). Some became impulsive, angry teenagers. Apparently, the stresses of adolescence and emerging adulthood exacerbated their cognitive and social deficits. (See Table 4.1.)

When these children grew up, many developed serious emotional or conduct problems (Golm et al., 2020; Sonuga-Barke et al., 2017). Some overly friendly 4-year-olds, as adolescents, developed *disinhibited social engagement disorder* (Guyon-Harris et al., 2018). That disorder leads to vulnerability in adulthood, because victims tend to follow people who will harm them.

None of this is inevitable. Other research on children adopted nationally and internationally finds that many develop well (see Figure 4.3). However, every stress—such as parental maltreatment, institutional life, cultural loss, and the adoption process—makes it more difficult for children to become happy, well-functioning adolescents and adults (Barroso et al., 2019; Grotevant & McDermott, 2014).

Romania no longer permits international adoption, even though some infants are still institutionalized. Research confirms that early emotional deprivation, not genes

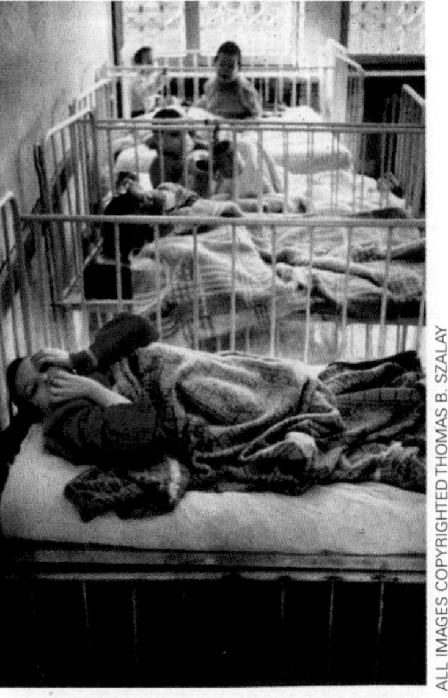

Hands on Head These children in Romania, here older than age 2, probably spent most of their infancy in their cribs, never with the varied stimulation that infant brains need. The sad results are evident here — that boy is fingering his own face, because the feel of his own touch is most likely one of the few sensations he knows. The girl sitting up in the back is a teenager. This photo was taken in 1982, before Romania ended such harsh child-care practices.

TABLE 4.1 Predictors of Attachment Type

Secure attachment (type B) is more likely if:

- The parent is usually sensitive and responsive to the infant's needs.
- The infant–parent relationship is high in synchrony.
- The infant's temperament is "easy."
- The parents are not stressed about income, other children, or their marriage.
- The parents have a working model of secure attachment to their own parents.

Insecure attachment is more likely if:

- The parent mistreats the child. (Neglect increases type A; abuse increases types C and D.)
- The mother is mentally ill. (Paranoia increases type D; depression increases type C.)
- The parents are highly stressed about income, other children, or their marriage. (Parental stress increases types A and D.)
- The parents are intrusive and controlling. (Parental domination increases type A.)
- The parents have alcohol use disorder. (Father with alcoholism increases type A; mother with alcoholism increases type D.)
- The child's temperament is "difficult." (Difficult children tend to be type C.)
- The child's temperament is "slow-to-warm-up." (This correlates with type A.)

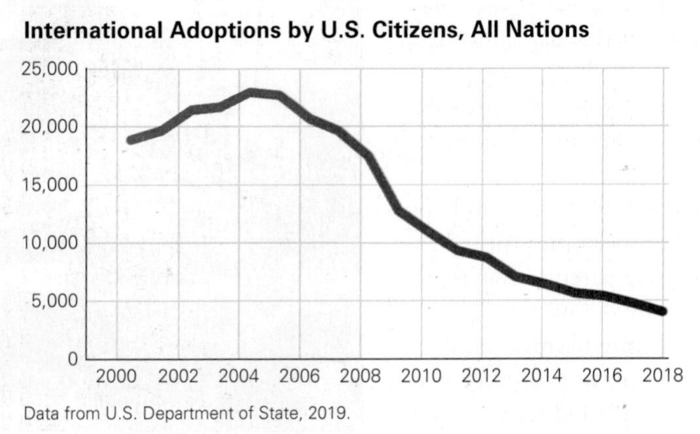

FIGURE 4.3 **Declining Need?** No. More couples seek to adopt internationally, and millions of children in dozens of nations have no families. This chart does not reflect changing needs of families; it reflects increasing nationalism within and beyond the United States. Sadly, babies have become weapons in national politics.

or nutrition, is their greatest problem. Infants develop best in their own families, second best in foster families, and worst in institutions (Nelson et al., 2014).

This is true for infants everywhere: Families usually nurture their babies better than strangers who provide good physical care but not emotional attachment. The longer children live in hospitals and orphanages, the more social and intellectual harm occur (Julian, 2013).

Developmentalists of every political stripe who understand attachment are horrified that thousands of children of immigrants were separated from their parents at the border between Mexico and the United States (Roth et al., 2018). Attachment research confirms that children need dedicated caregivers, and that disrupting that relationship causes lifelong harm.

Fortunately, most institutions have improved or closed, although many (estimated 2.7 million) children worldwide are living without their parents, about half of them in institutions (W. Li et al., 2019). If children are adopted early on, or if their early life was with devoted foster parents, they are much less impaired than those Romanian orphans (Grotevant & McDermott, 2014).

Many adoptive families are as strongly attached as any biological family, and their children become happy and successful. I know this personally (see A Case to Study).

A CASE TO STUDY

Can We Bear This Commitment?

Parents and children capture my attention, wherever they are. Recently I spotted one mother ignoring her stroller-bound toddler on a crowded subway (I resisted my impulse to tell her to talk to her child), I overheard another mother unfairly berating her 8-year-old (I did intervene, but other witnesses criticized me as the mother walked away, commanding her son to come with her), and I smiled at a third mother breast-feeding a 7-month-old in a public park (that was illegal three decades ago).

I notice signs of secure or insecure attachment—the contact-maintaining and proximity-seeking moves that parents do, seemingly unaware that they are responding to primordial depths of human love. I particularly observe families I know. I am struck by the powerful bond between parent and child, as strong (or stronger) in adoptive families as in genetic ones.

One adoptive couple is Macky and Nick. They echo my own responses to my biological children. Two examples:

- When Alice was a few days old, I overheard Nick phone another parent, asking which detergent is best for washing baby clothes. That reminded me that I also switched detergents for my newborn.
- Years later, when Macky was engrossed in conversation, Nick interrupted to say they needed to stop talking because the girls needed to get home for their naps. Parents at social occasions everywhere do that, with one parent telling the other it's time to leave, as my husband sometimes told me.

My appreciation of that family's attachment was cemented by a third incident. In Macky's words:

> I'll never forget the Fourth of July at the spacious home of my mother-in-law's best friend. It was a perfect celebration on a perfect day. Kids frolicked in the pool. Parents socialized nearby, on the sun-drenched lawn or inside the cool house. Many guests had published books on parenting; we imagined they admired our happy, thriving family.
>
> My husband and I have two daughters, Alice who was then 7 and Penelope who was 4. They learned to swim early and are always the first to jump in the pool and the last to leave. Great children, and doesn't that mean great parents?
>
> After hours of swimming, the four of us scrambled up to dry land. I went inside to the library to talk with my

father, while most people enjoyed hot dogs, relish, mustard, and juicy watermelon.

Suddenly we heard a heart-chilling wail. Panicked, I raced to the pool's edge to see the motionless body of a small child who had gone unnoticed underwater for too long. His blue-face was still. Someone was giving CPR. His mother kept wailing, panicked, pleading, destroyed. I had a shameful thought—thank God that is not my child.

He lived. He regained his breath and was whisked away by ambulance. The party came to a quick close. We four, skin tingling from the summer sun, hearts beating from the near-death of a child who was my kids' playmate an hour before, drove away.

Turning to Nick, I asked, "Can we bear this commitment we have made? Can we raise our children in the face of all hazards—some we try to prevent, others beyond our control?"

That was five years ago. Our children are flourishing. Our confidence is strong and so are our emotions. But it takes only a moment to recognize just how entwined our well-being is with our children and how fragile life is. We are deeply grateful.

VICTOR J. BLUE/THE NEW YORK TIMES/REDUX

A Grateful Family This family photo shows (from *left* to *right*) Nick, Penelope, Macky, and Alice. When they adopted Alice as a newborn, the parents said, "This is a miracle we feared would never happen."

Social Referencing

The third social connection that developmentalists look for during infancy, after synchrony and attachment, is **social referencing**. Much as a student might consult a dictionary or other reference work, social referencing means seeking emotional information from other people. A reassuring glance, a string of cautionary words, a facial expression of alarm, pleasure, or dismay—those are social references.

social referencing
Seeking information about how to react to an unfamiliar or ambiguous object or event by observing someone else's expressions and reactions. That other person becomes a social reference.

As you read in Chapter 3, gaze-following begins in the first months of life, as part of cognition. After age 1, when infants can walk and are "little scientists," their need to consult others becomes urgent—for emotional evaluation, not merely cognition.

Toddlers search for clues in gazes, faces, and body position. They heed their familiar caregivers, but they also use relatives, other children, and even strangers to help them assess objects and events.

From early infancy to late adolescence, children are selective, noticing that some strangers are reliable references and others are not. For instance, infants as young as 14 months are less likely to accept social referencing from a stranger whose reactions seemed odd (e.g., they smiled happily at opening an empty box) (Crivello & Poulin-Dubois, 2019).

Social referencing has many practical applications. Consider mealtime. Caregivers the world over pretend to taste and say "yum-yum," encouraging toddlers to eat beets, liver, or spinach. Toddlers read expressions, insisting on the foods that the adults *really* like.

If the mother enjoys eating it, and then gives some to the toddler, then they eat it—otherwise not. Some tastes (spicy, bitter, sour) are rejected by very young infants, but if they see their caregivers relish it, they learn to like it (Forestel & Mennella, 2017).

Through this process, some children develop a taste for raw fish or curried goat or smelly cheese—foods that children in other cultures refuse. Similarly, toddlers use social cues to understand the difference between real and pretend eating, as well as to learn which objects, emotions, and activities are forbidden.

DEVELOPING ATTACHMENT

Attachment begins at birth and continues lifelong. Much depends not only on the ways in which parents and babies bond, but also on the quality and consistency of caregiving, the safety and security of the home environment, and individual and family experience. While the patterns set in infancy may echo in later life, they are not determinative.

How Many Children Are Securely Attached?

The specific percentages of children who are secure and insecure vary by culture, parent responsiveness, context, and specific temperament and needs of both the child and the caregiver. Generally, about a third of all 1-year-olds seem insecure.

50–70%	10–20%	10–20%	5–10%
Secure Attachment (Type B)	Avoidant Attachment (Type A)	Ambivalent Attachment (Type C)	Disorganized Attachment (Type D)

Attachment in the Strange Situation May Influence Relationships Through the Life Span

Attachment patterns formed in infancy affect adults lifelong, but later experiences of love and rejection may change early patterns. Researchers measure attachment by examining children's behaviors in the Strange Situation where they are separated from their parent and play in a room with an unfamiliar caregiver. These early patterns can influence later adult relationships. As life goes on, people become more or less secure, avoidant, or disorganized.

Securely Attached [Type B]
In the Strange Situation, children are able to separate from caregiver but prefer caregiver to strangers.
› Later in life, they tend to have supportive relationships and positive self-concept.

Insecure-Avoidant [Type A]
In the Strange Situation, children avoid caregiver.
› Later in life, they tend to be aloof in personal relationships, loners who are lonely.

Insecure-Resistant/Ambivalent [Type C]
In the Strange Situation, children appear upset and worried when separated from caregiver; they may hit or cling.
› Later in life, their relationships may be angry, stormy, unpredictable. They have few long-term friendships.

Disorganized [Type D]
In the Strange Situation, children appear angry, confused, erratic, or fearful.
› Later in life, they can demonstrate odd behavior—including sudden emotions. They are at risk for serious psychological disorders.

The Continuum of Attachment

Avoidance and anxiety occur along a continuum. Neither genes nor cultural variations were understood when the Strange Situation was first developed (in 1965). Some contemporary researchers believe the link between childhood attachment and adult personality is less straightforward than this table suggests.

Fathers as Social Partners

Synchrony, attachment, and social referencing are evident with fathers as well as with mothers. Indeed, fathers may elicit more smiles and laughter from their infants than mothers do. They tend to play more exciting games, swinging and chasing, while mothers do more caregiving and comforting (Fletcher et al., 2013).

This gender division—women as caregivers and men as playmates—is apparent in every nation. But children develop well when the roles are reversed, or when both parents are male or both parents are female. Each couple coordinates; children thrive (Shwalb et al., 2013).

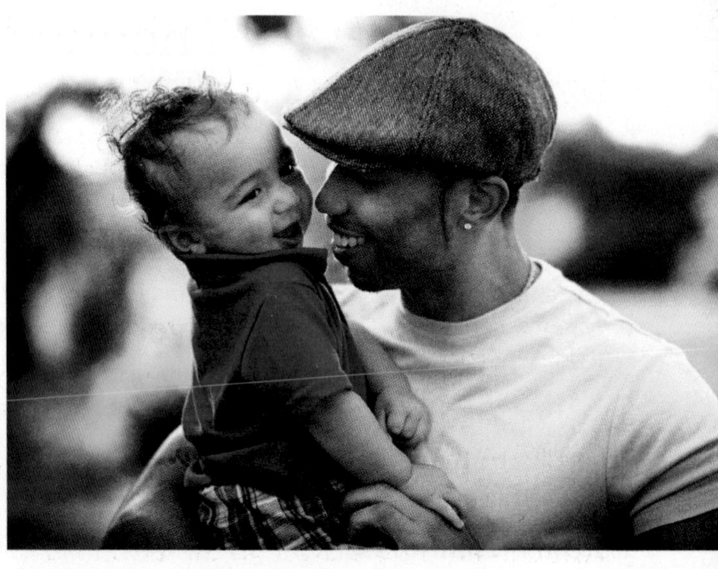

JIM HOLMES/CORBIS

Not Manly? Where did that idea come from? Fathers worldwide provide excellent care for their toddlers and enjoy it, evident in the United States and in every other nation.

Further, too much can be made of gender differences, because similarities are also evident. One researcher reports that "fathers and mothers showed patterns of striking similarity: they touched, looked, vocalized, rocked, and kissed their newborns equally" (Parke, 2013, p. 121). He found only one gender difference: Women did more smiling.

Gender differences in child rearing vary more by nation, by income, by cohort, and by ideology than by natal sex or by ethnic background. Variation is dramatic, from fathers who have nothing to do with infants to fathers who are intensely involved. The latter is common in the United States in the twenty-first century, unlike in former times (Abraham & Feldman, 2018).

THINK CRITICALLY: Why are mothers less stressed by infant crying if fathers help? Do passive fathers blame mothers? Do mothers blame themselves?

Contemporary fathers worldwide tend to be more involved with their children than their own fathers were (Sriram, 2019). The effects are evident not only in infants but in fathers themselves. As one man in India said, "my child transformed me" (Kaur, 2019).

For every parent, stress decreases child involvement. That brings up another difference between mothers and fathers. When money is scarce and stress is high, some fathers opt out. That choice is less possible for mothers (Qin & Chang, 2013; Roopnarine & Hossain, 2013).

The reactions of both men and women to infants are also affected by their temperament, genes, and early-childhood experiences (Senese et al., 2019). This is another reason why infant boys and girls need responsive caregiving: The effects will endure decades later when they have children of their own.

what have you learned?

1. Why does synchrony affect early emotional development?
2. How are proximity-seeking and contact-maintaining attachment expressed by infants and caregivers?
3. How does infant behavior differ in each of the four types of attachment?
4. How might each of the four types of attachment be expressed in adulthood?
5. What has been learned from the research on Romanian orphans?
6. How is social referencing important in toddlerhood?
7. What are the differences and similarities between mothers and fathers in infancy?

Theories of Infant Psychosocial Development

That infants are emotional and social creatures is one of those universal truths, recognized by everyone who studies babies. However, each of the theories discussed in Chapter 1 has a distinct perspective on this universal reality, as you will now see.

Psychoanalytic Theory

Psychoanalytic theory connects biosocial and psychosocial development. Sigmund Freud and Erik Erikson each described two distinct stages of early development, one in the first year and one beginning in the second year.

Especially for Nursing Mothers
You have heard that if you wean your child too early, he or she will overeat or develop alcohol use disorder. Is it true? (see response, page 142)

FREUD: ORAL AND ANAL STAGES

According to Freud (1935/1989, 2001), the first year of life is the *oral stage*, so named because the mouth is the young infant's primary source of gratification. In the second year, with the *anal stage*, pleasure comes from the anus—particularly from the sensual satisfaction of bowel movements and, eventually, the psychological pleasure of controlling them.

Freud believed that the oral and anal stages are fraught with potential conflicts. If a mother frustrates her infant's urge to suck—weaning too early, for example, or preventing the baby from sucking a thumb or a pacifier—that may later lead to an *oral fixation*. Adults with an oral fixation are stuck (fixated) at the oral stage, and therefore they eat, drink, chew, bite, or talk excessively, still seeking the mouth-related pleasures of infancy.

Similarly, if toilet training is overly strict or if it begins before maturation allows sufficient control, that causes a clash between the toddler's refusal—or inability—to comply and the wishes of the adult, who denies the infant normal anal pleasures. That may lead to an *anal personality*—an adult who seeks self-control, with a strong need for regularity and cleanliness in all aspects of life.

REUTERS/JOSE MIGUEL GOMEZ/NEWSCOM

All Together Now Toddlers in an employees' day-care program at a flower farm in Colombia learn to use the potty on a schedule. Will this experience lead to later personality problems? Probably not.

ERIKSON: TRUST AND AUTONOMY

According to Erikson, the first crisis of life is **trust versus mistrust**, when infants learn whether or not the world can be trusted to satisfy basic needs. Babies feel secure when food and comfort are provided with "consistency, continuity, and sameness of experience" (Erikson, 1993a, p. 247). If social interaction inspires trust, the child (later the adult) confidently explores the social world.

The second crisis is **autonomy versus shame and doubt**, beginning at about 18 months, when self-awareness emerges. Toddlers want autonomy (self-rule) over their own actions and bodies. Without it, they feel ashamed and doubtful. Like Freud, Erikson believed that problems in early infancy could last a lifetime, creating adults who are suspicious and pessimistic (mistrusting) or easily shamed (lacking autonomy).

trust versus mistrust
Erikson's first crisis of psychosocial development. Infants learn basic trust if the world is a secure place where their basic needs (for food, comfort, attention, and so on) are met.

autonomy versus shame and doubt
Erikson's second crisis of psychosocial development. Toddlers either succeed or fail in gaining a sense of self-rule over their actions and their bodies.

Behaviorism

From the perspective of behaviorism, emotions and personality are molded as adults reinforce or punish children. Behaviorists believe that parents who respond joyously to every glimmer of a grin will have children with a sunny disposition. The opposite is also true:

> Failure to bring up a happy child, a well-adjusted child—assuming bodily health—falls squarely upon the parents' shoulders. [By the time the child is 3] parents have already determined . . . [whether the child] is to grow into a happy

> person, wholesome and good-natured, whether he is to be a whining, complaining neurotic, an anger-driven, vindictive, over-bearing slave driver, or one whose every move in life is definitely controlled by fear.
>
> *[Watson, 1928/1972, pp. 7, 45]*

SOCIAL LEARNING

Behaviorists recognize that behavior reflects social learning: Babies observe other people carefully, as explained in social referencing. Toddlers express emotions in various ways—from giggling to cursing—just as their parents or older siblings do.

For example, a boy might develop a hot temper if his father's outbursts seem to win his mother's respect; a girl might be coy, or passive-aggressive, if that is what she has seen at home. These examples are deliberately sexist: Gender roles, in particular, are learned, according to social learning.

Especially for Pediatricians A mother complains that her toddler refuses to stay in the car seat, spits out disliked foods, and almost never does what she says. How should you respond? (see response, page 142)

KEEPING BABY CLOSE

Parents often unwittingly encourage certain traits in their children. Should they explore, or learn that danger lurks if they wander off? Should babies have many toys, or will that make them greedy? When babies cry, caregivers must decide: Pick them up, feed them, give a pacifier, shut the door? Should an infant be breast-fed until age 2, switch to a bottle, or sip from a cup?

These questions highlight the distinction between **proximal parenting** (being physically close to a baby, often holding and touching) and **distal parenting** (keeping some distance—providing toys, encouraging self-feeding, talking face-to-face instead of communicating by touch). Caregivers tend to behave in proximal or distal ways very early, when infants are only 2 months old (Kärtner et al., 2010). Each pattern reinforces some behavior.

proximal parenting Caregiving practices that involve being physically close to the baby, with frequent holding and touching.

distal parenting Caregiving practices that involve remaining distant from the baby, providing toys, food, and face-to-face communication with minimal holding and touching.

working model In cognitive theory, a set of assumptions that the individual uses to organize perceptions and experiences. For example, a person might assume that other people are trustworthy and be surprised by an incident in which this working model of human behavior is erroneous.

For instance, toddlers who, as infants, were often held, patted, and soothed (proximal) became toddlers who are more obedient but less likely to recognize themselves in a mirror. This finding has been replicated in Greece, Cameroon, Italy, Israel, Zambia, Scotland, and Turkey: Distal child-rearing correlates with cultures that value individual independence, whereas proximal care correlates with cultures that value collective action and family interdependence (Carra et al., 2013; Keller et al., 2010; Ross et al., 2017; Scharf, 2014).

Indeed, international variations of parenting practices, including not only proximal and distal parenting but also in frequency of synchrony, secure attachment, and social referencing, suggest that children are taught to respond in a particular way because of how their parents treat them (Foo, 2019). That is exactly what behaviorists believe.

Cognitive Theory

Cognitive theory holds that thoughts determine a person's perspective. Early experiences are important because beliefs, perceptions, and memories make them so, not because they are buried in the unconscious (psychoanalytic theory) or burned into the brain's patterns (behaviorism).

From this perspective, cognitive processes, including language and information, affect attachment, as children and caregivers develop a mutual understanding. Together they build (co-construct) a **working model**, which is a set of assumptions that becomes a frame of reference for later life (Posada & Waters, 2018). It is a "model" because early relationships form a prototype, or blueprint; it is "working" because it is a work in progress, not fixed or final; it is cognitive because the child's understanding and interpretation is crucial.

Ideally, infants develop "a working model of the self as lovable and competent," because the parents are "emotionally available, loving, and supportive of their mastery

"Which one generates the most synapses?"

Brainy Baby Fortunately, infant brains are designed to respond to stimulation of many kinds. As long as the baby has moving objects to see (an animated caregiver is better than any mobile), the synapses proliferate.

efforts" (Harter, 2012, p. 12). However, reality does not always conform to this ideal.

A 1-year-old girl might develop a model, based on her parents' erratic actions, that people are unpredictable. She will continue to apply that model to everyone: Her childhood friendships will be insecure, and her adult relationships will be guarded.

The crucial idea, according to cognitive theory, is that an infant's early experiences are less influential than the interpretation of those experiences (Olson & Dweck, 2009). Children may misinterpret their experiences, or parents may offer inaccurate explanations, thus forming ideas that affect later thinking and behavior.

In this way, working models formed in childhood echo lifelong. A hopeful message from cognitive theory is that people can rethink and reorganize their thoughts, developing new models. That mistrustful girl in the example above might marry someone who is faithful and loving, so she may gradually develop a new working model.

Evolutionary Theory

Remember that evolutionary theory stresses two needs: survival and reproduction. Human brains are extraordinarily plastic, a necessity that evolved to enable people to survive in a vast range of local conditions, as *Homo sapiens* left the savannas of East Africa for the colder regions of Europe.

Human brains allow adjustment to climate and culture, but that means that each infant must be nourished, protected, and taught for two decades, much longer than the offspring of any other species. Since survival depends on this lengthy protection, it is part of our DNA.

EMOTIONS FOR SURVIVAL

Infant emotions are part of this evolutionary mandate. All of the reactions described in the first part of this chapter—from the hunger cry to the temper tantrum—can be seen from this perspective (Konner, 2010, 2016).

For example, newborns are extraordinarily dependent, unable to walk or talk or even sit up and feed themselves for months after birth. They must attract adult devotion—and they do. That first smile, the sound of infant laughter, and their role in synchrony are all powerfully attractive to adults—especially to parents.

Adults call their hairless, chinless, round-faced, big-stomached, small-limbed offspring "cute," "handsome," "beautiful," "adorable," yet each of these characteristics is often considered ugly in adults. Parents willingly devote hours to carrying, feeding, changing, and cleaning their infants, who never express gratitude.

The love of a parent for a child is part of evolution: For hundreds of thousands of years, humans have needed that love to survive. If humans were motivated solely by money or power, no one would do so. Yet evolution has created adults who find parenting worth every sacrifice.

Evolutionary theory holds that both caregivers and children have powerful emotions—love, jealousy, fear, and anger—that keep toddlers near caregivers who remain vigilant. Infants fuss at still faces, fear separation, and laugh when adults play with them—all to sustain caregiving. Emotions are our genetic legacy; we would die without them.

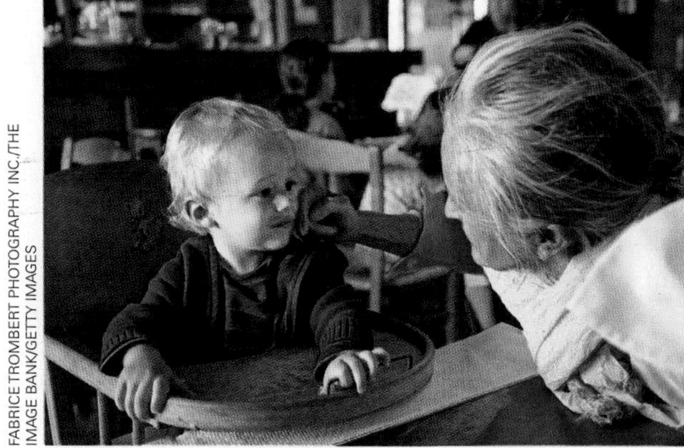

FABRICE TROMBERT PHOTOGRAPHY INC./THE IMAGE BANK/GETTY IMAGES

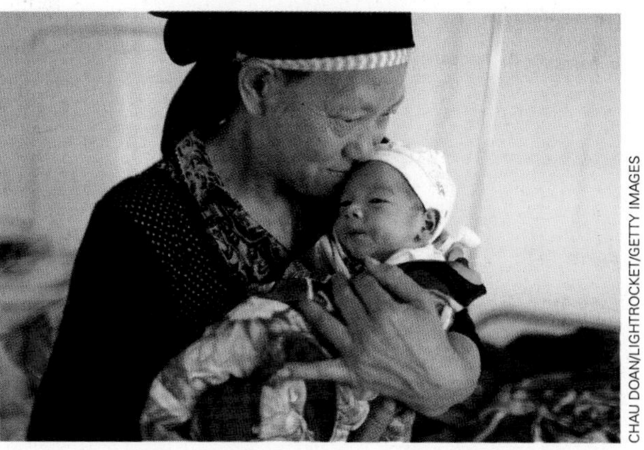

CHAU DOAN/LIGHTROCKET/GETTY IMAGES

Same Situation, Far Apart: Safekeeping Historically, grandmothers were sometimes crucial for child survival. Now, even though medical care has reduced child mortality, grandmothers still do their part to keep children safe, as shown by these two — in the eastern United States *(left)* and Vietnam *(right).*

ALLOCARE

Evolutionary social scientists note that if mothers were the exclusive caregivers of each child until children were adults, a given woman could rear only one or two offspring—not enough for the species to survive. Instead, before the introduction of reliable birth control, the average interval between births for humans was two to four years.

Humans birth children at relatively short intervals because of **allocare**—the care of children by *alloparents*, caregivers who are not the mother. Allocare is essential for *Homo sapiens'* survival. Compared with many other species (mother chimpanzees space births by four or five years and never let another chimp hold their babies), human mothers have evolved to let other people help with child care.

allocare
Literally, "other-care"; the care of children by people other than the biological parents.

The impulse for allocare comes not only from mothers. Evolution has programmed the human brain so that fathers and grandmothers want to help, and want others to help (Abraham & Feldman, 2018). That explains why, as described in the opener of this chapter, a woman on the subway handed her baby to a stranger, and why I was happy that she did.

Allocare is universal for our species—but each community has distinct values and preferences for who should care for children and when (Konner, 2018). Indeed, cultures and theories differ in every aspect of infant care, as you have read regarding breast-feeding, co-sleeping, language, and much else. Now we consider mother care versus other care.

what have you learned?

1. According to Freud, what might happen if a baby's oral needs are not met?
2. How might Erikson's crisis of "trust versus mistrust" affect later life?
3. How do behaviorists explain the development of emotions and personality?
4. What does the term *working model* mean within cognitive theory?
5. What is the difference between proximal and distal parenting?
6. How does evolution explain the parent–child bond?
7. Why is allocare necessary for survival of the human species?

Who Should Care for Babies?

Summarizing the research on infant care is difficult, because humans are inclined to believe that the practices of their own family or culture are best. They may be right: Each community tries to care for their infants in such a way that those babies will function well within their culture. However, believing one's own culture is best universally risks the difference-equals-deficit error. Science is needed!

Some cultures assume that infants need exclusive maternal care; others believe that early group care is better. Some cultures expect fathers to avoid infant care. In those places, if a man tries to care for his child, the mother becomes a "gatekeeper" who criticizes how he holds, feeds, or plays with his child. Some mothers also discourage grandparents, especially their husband's mother (hence the mother-in-law jokes).

By contrast, other mothers expect relatives to provide extensive care, and some nations consider child care a public good. They pay professionals to care for young children, just as they pay firefighters or the police. These variations affect how adults perceive the world.

Beyond national differences, opinions are affected by personal experience (adults who experienced nonparental care are likely to approve of it), by gender (males are more often critical of day-care centers), and by education (higher education increases support for nonparental care) (Galasso et al., 2017; Rose et al., 2018; Shpancer & Schweitzer, 2018).

In the United States

In the United States, norms do not mandate exclusive mother care. Only 20 percent of infants are cared for solely by their mothers (i.e., no other relatives or babysitters) (Babchishin et al., 2013). The U.S. Bureau of Labor Statistics reports that, in 2018, 60 percent of the mothers of infants under 1 year were in the labor force.

TED RICHARDSON/RALEIGH NEWS & OBSERVER/MCT/GETTY IMAGES

Contrast This with That Three infants again, but this infant day-care center provides excellent care, as can be seen by comparing this scene with what is depicted in the photo on page 127.

OBSERVATION QUIZ
What three things do you see that suggest good care? (see answer, page 142) ↑

One reason why most mothers of young children work for pay is that they need the money. The United States is the only developed nation that does not mandate that employers pay for mothers to stay home to care for their newborns (see Figure 4.4). Professional infant day care, either in a center or at home, is privately paid, and thus too expensive for many families.

Consequently, many mothers who need to work enlist family members (especially fathers and grandmothers) to care for babies. Of all the "stay-at-home" parents in 2016, 17 percent were fathers and 83 percent were mothers. More often, both parents are employed, sharing child care (Livingston & Parker, 2019).

In the United States, in 1993, the U.S. Congress passed a law requiring companies with 50 employees or more to offer *unpaid* maternity leave for 12 weeks. Some states and employers go beyond that, offering more time or some pay. Paternal leave is almost never paid in the United States, with one exception: As of 2018, the U.S. military allows 21 days of paid leave for new fathers who are secondary caregivers, and up to six weeks for mothers or fathers in the military who are primary caregivers.

PROBLEMS WITH NONMATERNAL CARE

Beyond the cost (either the cost of foregone employment or the cost of paid care), is there any problem with allocare? Certainly, quality matters: Some relatives and

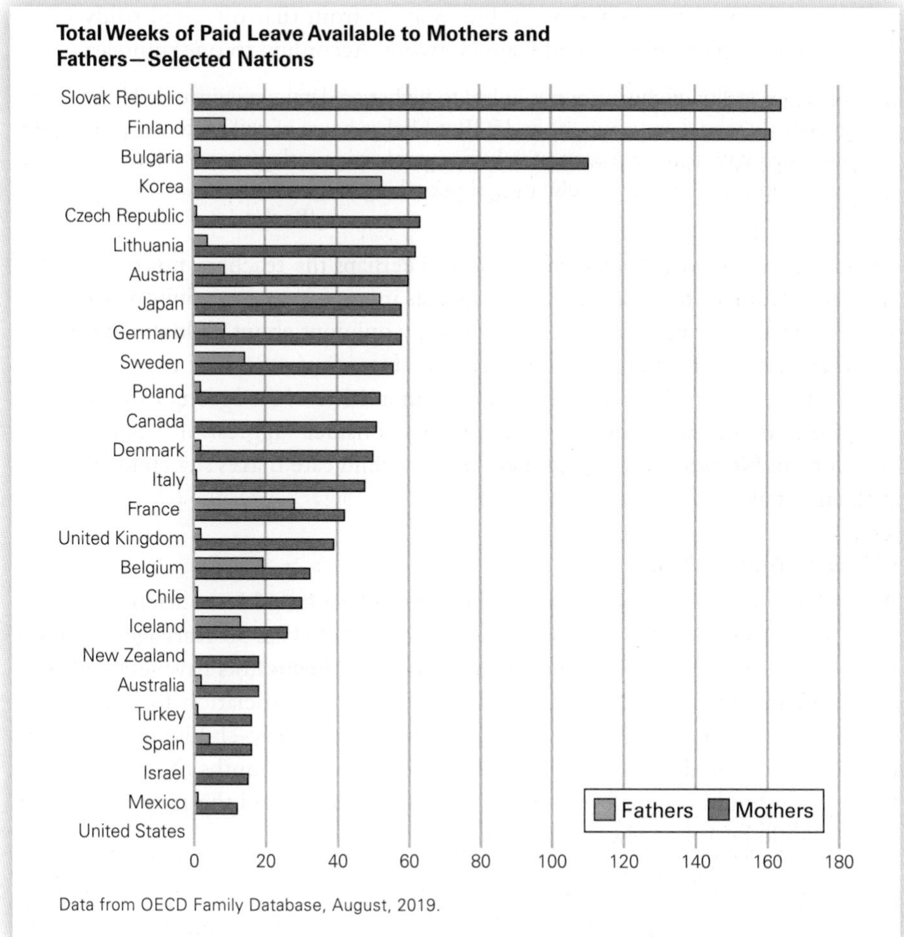

FIGURE 4.4 Out of Date? Laws requiring paid maternity leave are changing every year. For some of these nations, these numbers will soon need updating. Change may occur in the United States, because more women are in the 117th Congress. Current U.S. laws are more reflective of the 1950s, when most new mothers were married and expected to quit employment when their babies were born.

some day-care centers may not provide the personal interaction that infants need. But even with good care, some believe that allocare during infancy leads to insecure attachment or emotional problems.

The first worry has been disproven. Secure mother–infant attachment (as measured by the Strange Situation) is as common with regular father care, grandparent care, or professional day care, as it is with exclusive maternal care.

The most often-cited longitudinal research on this comes from the Early Child Care Network of the National Institute of Child Health and Human Development (NICHD), which followed over 1,300 children born in 1991 from birth through adolescence. Like other, smaller studies, the NICHD research confirmed that the mother–child relationship was pivotal, and that responsive mothers, employed or not, had securely attached infants.

In retrospect, this makes sense. Every week, if someone else cares for a baby 40 hours, mothers still spend over 100 hours with their babies. Indeed, infants may benefit from mother's employment because father–infant attachment is more likely.

Regarding the second concern, behavioral problems, the evidence is mixed. A mega-analysis of eight large, high-quality studies on infant caregiving (Dearing & Zachrisson, 2017) reported that half of the studies of group care found that the children had more externalizing problems (such as aggression, particularly in boys) later on. The other half of the studies did not find this. Indeed, one reported better emotional adjustment for children who experience day care before age 3.

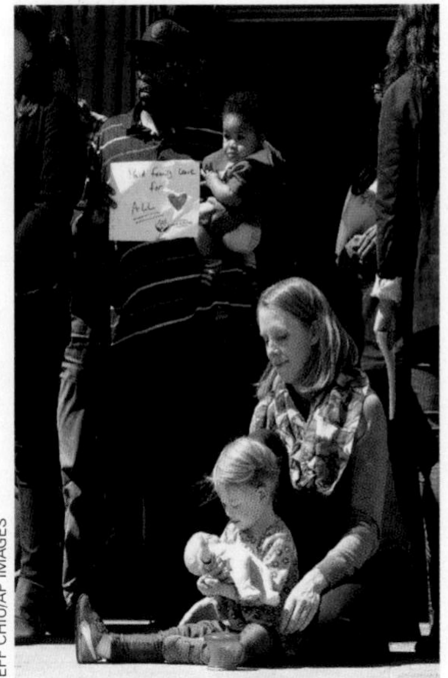

JEFF CHIU/AP IMAGES

Double Winner Baby and victory in the same month! These women are advocating for six weeks of paid maternity leave. The San Francisco Board of Supervisors voted yes, making this the first jurisdiction in the United States to mandate fully paid leave. The law went into effect in 2017 — too late for this woman now. Perhaps her next baby?

The concern about behavior problems arose from that oft-cited study of the 1,300 children in the Early Child Care Network. According to one summary:

> [H]igher quality of child care was linked to higher academic-cognitive skills in primary school and again at age 15. [But h]igher hours of child care were associated with teacher reports of behavior problems in early primary school and youth reports of greater impulsivity and risk taking at age 15.
>
> *[Burchinal et al., 2014, p. 542]*

Notice who reports "behavior problems." Perhaps the teachers, not the children, are the deciding factor. If a 15-year-old reports more risk-taking, adults may be worried, but peers may be admiring. As with many opinions about children, we need to consider who, what, and why a particular assessment is given.

This is evident in Norway, where no detrimental results of group care from ages 1 to 5 are found. Behavior that U.S. teachers consider "aggression" may be "self-assertion" in Norway. Norwegians believe early child care makes shy children bolder (Solheim et al., 2013).

HISTORICAL CHANGES

Another factor is relevant in analyzing the effects of allocare. Most currently reported longitudinal studies began with children who were in day care 30 years ago. Infant day care has improved since then, as many governments and educators have set standards.

For example, within the past decade, the National Association for the Education of Young Children (NAEYC, the organization for early-childhood educators) updated its standards for care of babies from birth to 15 months (NAEYC, 2014). Group size should be small (no more than eight infants), and the ratio of adults to babies should be 1:4 or fewer (see Table 4.2).

Each infant should receive personal attention, with a curriculum that fosters emotional and intellectual growth. Teachers are told to "engage infants in frequent face-to-face social interactions"—including talking, singing, smiling, and touching (NAEYC, 2014, p. 4). Every staff member must respect cultural differences and try to follow the mother's wishes. Maternal involvement is encouraged, including breast-feeding (bottles of pumped milk are stored for each baby), a practice that was absent in infant day care 20 years ago.

TABLE 4.2 High-Quality Day Care

High-quality day care during infancy has five essential characteristics:

1. *Adequate attention to each infant*
   A small group of infants (no more than eight) needs two reliable, familiar, loving caregivers. Continuity of care is crucial.
2. *Encouragement of language and sensorimotor development*
   Infants need language — songs, conversations, and positive talk — and easily manipulated toys.
3. *Attention to health and safety*
   Cleanliness routines (e.g., handwashing), accident prevention (e.g., no small objects), and safe areas to explore are essential.
4. *Professional caregivers*
   Caregivers should have experience and degrees/certificates in early-childhood education. Turnover should be low, morale high, and enthusiasm evident.
5. *Warm and responsive caregivers*
   Providers should engage the children in active play and guide them in problem solving. Quiet, obedient children may indicate unresponsive care.

In Other Nations

Outside the United States, nations disagree about allocare, for cultural, ideological, and economic reasons. Publicly paid infant care is rare in most nations of South Asia, sub-Saharan Africa, and South America, where many adults believe it is harmful. Those nations also have laws that require paid maternal leave, and sometimes paid paternal leave, evidence of the belief that mothers should stay home to care for infants.

By contrast, people in some nations believe that subsidized infant care is a public right. Government-sponsored, paid, regulated child care is prevalent in Australia, Chile, China, Denmark, Finland, France, Germany, Iceland, Israel, the Netherlands, Norway, and Sweden.

Sometimes the data find that early day care benefits the children. In the Netherlands, children who attended day care were slightly less likely to develop emotional problems than other children (Broekhuizen et al., 2018). That seems true in other nations, too. In northern Europe, legislators believe that the first years are crucial for later life, so quality of infant care is high (Garvis et al., 2019). Teachers are well trained and paid at rates comparable for teachers of older children, and children thrive.

That is less true in Germany and Australia, because a prime reason those nations chose to pay for day care was to increase the birth rate (Harrison et al., 2014). In France, subsidized care can begin at 12 weeks, but only about 10 percent of all infants receive it. The waiting list is long, parents pay part of the cost, and the adult–infant ratio is 1:5 under age 1 and 1:8 from age 1 until 3, when it increases again.

When infants do not have individualized care, quality suffers. In France, "ensuring high quality provision seems at odds with affordability and availability of places for under-threes." The government emphasizes expansion so more mothers can work, rather than emphasizing quality of care (Fagnani, 2013).

Norway takes the opposite course (see Figure 4.5). Norwegians believe that the youngest babies are best cared for by their mothers, so they pay employed women their full salary to stay home with their babies for 47 weeks after birth, with some

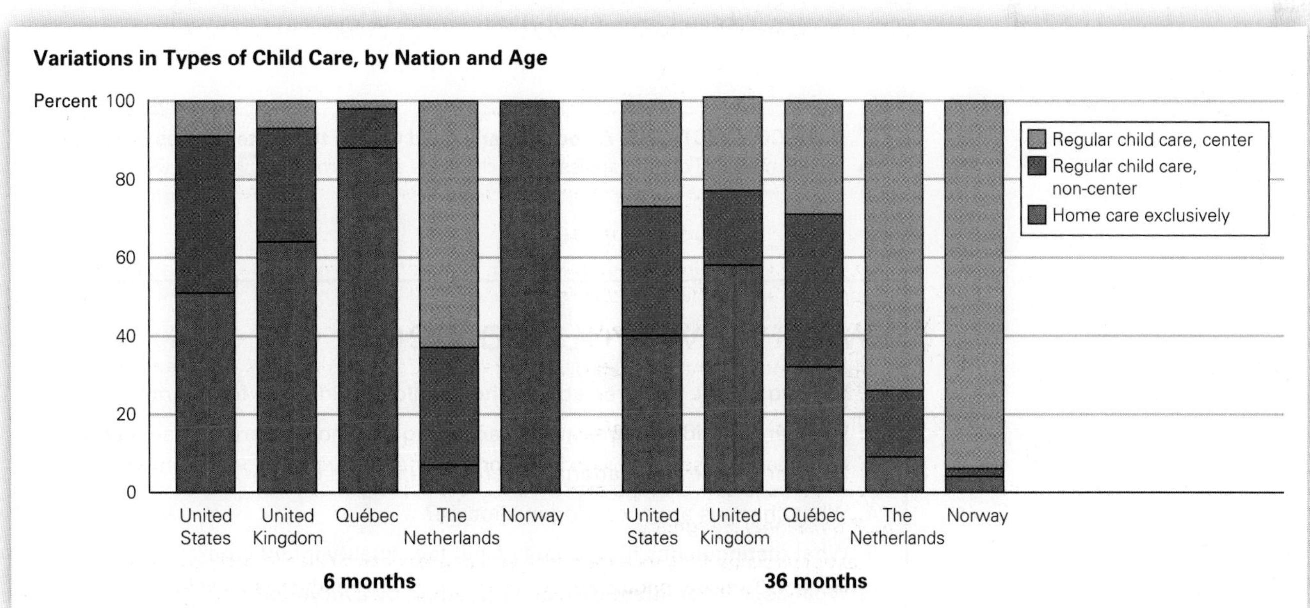

FIGURE 4.5 Who Cares for the Baby? Infants are the same everywhere, but cultures and governments differ dramatically. Does a 6-month-old need their mother more than a 3-year-old? Norway and Quebec say yes; the United States, United Kingdom, and the Netherlands say no.

OBSERVATION QUIZ
Which nation has the most extreme shift at age 1? (see answer, page 142) ↑

Especially for Day-Care Providers
A mother who brings her child to you for day care says that she knows she is harming her baby, but economic necessity compels her to work. What do you say? (see response, page 142)

paid leave for fathers as well. Then, at age 1, center day care is available for everyone, with a low adult:child ratio.

In sparsely populated Norwegian areas, one teacher may have only two students, although a 1:4 ratio is more common. In 2016, most Norwegian 1-year-olds (72 percent) were in center care, as were almost all 2-year-olds (92 percent) and 3-year-olds (96 percent) (Statistics Norway, 2018).

Conclusions from the Science

A strength of the scientific method is evident in this discussion of what babies need and what cultures provide. When differences are evident, no one study, or no one's past experience, expresses a universal truth. Instead, family structures, cultural values, and economic patterns affect every aspect of infant care. That gets us back to the beginning of this chapter. Babies have universal needs, for attention, attachment, and exploration, but conclusions from one study may differ from another.

The science agrees on three universals:

1. Synchrony and mutual attachments are beneficial.
2. Quality of consistent care matters.
3. Babies need loving and responsive caregivers.

The research also finds many particulars:

1. Cultures and families vary in what emotions are encouraged and how they are expressed.
2. Who provides care also varies.
3. Infants can thrive with mothers, fathers, or other people.

As is true of many topics in child development, questions remain. But one fact is without question: Each infant needs personal responsiveness. Someone should serve as a partner in the synchrony duet, a base for secure attachment, and a social reference who encourages exploration. Then, infant emotions and experiences—cries and laughter, fears and joys—will ensure that development goes well.

DATA CONNECTIONS: A Look at Early Child Care in the United States explores how various maternal demographics affect child-care arrangements. Achieve

what have you learned?

1. Why do people disagree about who should provide care for infants?
2. What are the advantages and disadvantages of nonmaternal infant care?
3. What are some international differences in infant care?
4. What changes are occurring in allocare?
5. What distinguishes high-quality from low-quality infant care?
6. What aspects of infant care are agreed on by everyone?

SUMMARY

Emotional Development

1. Two primary emotions, contentment and distress, appear in newborns. Smiles and laughter are soon evident. Between 4 and 8 months of age, anger emerges in reaction to restriction and frustration, and it becomes stronger by age 1.

2. Reflexive fear is apparent in very young infants. Fear of something specific depends on the context. Typically some fear of strangers and of separation is strong by age 1, and continues until age 2. After that, these fears subside or may become disorders.

3. Self-recognition (measured by the mirror/rouge test) emerges at about 18 months. Social awareness and self-awareness produce more selective and intense emotions. Secondary emotions, including jealousy, pride, and shame, emerge.

4. Temperament is inborn, but the expression of temperament is influenced by the context, with evident plasticity. Some children outgrow their fear and shyness, depending on their early experiences.

The Development of Social Bonds

5. Often by 2 months, and clearly by 6 months, infants become more responsive and social: Synchrony is evident. Caregivers and infants engage in reciprocal interactions, with split-second timing.

6. Attachment was first described 50 years ago, when Bowlby and Ainsworth described how infants relate to their mothers. Attachment is measured in infancy by a baby's reaction to the caregiver's presence, departure, and return in the Strange Situation.

7. Secure attachment provides encouragement for infant exploration, and its influence is lifelong. Adults are attached as well, evident not only as parents but also as romantic partners.

8. As they become more mobile and engage with their environment, infants use social referencing (looking to other people's facial expressions and body language) to detect what is safe, frightening, or fun.

9. Infants frequently use fathers as partners in synchrony, as attachment figures, and as social references, developing emotions and exploring their world. Contemporary fathers often play with their infants.

Theories of Infant Psychosocial Development

10. According to all major theories, caregivers are especially influential in the first two years. Freud stressed the mother's impact on oral and anal pleasure; Erikson emphasized trust and autonomy. Both believed that the impact of these is lifelong.

11. Behaviorists focus on learning. They note that parents teach their babies many things, including when to be fearful or joyful, and how much physical and social distance (proximal or distal parenting) is best.

12. Cognitive theory holds that infants develop working models based on their experiences. Interpretation is crucial, and that can change with maturation.

13. Evolutionary theorists recognize that both infants and caregivers have impulses and emotions that have developed over millennia to foster the survival of each new member of the human species. Attachment is one example.

Who Should Care for Babies?

14. Research confirms that every infant needs responsive caregiving, secure attachment, and cognitive stimulation. These three can occur at home or in a good day-care center. Quality matters, as does consistency of care.

15. Some people believe that infant day care benefits babies and that governments should subsidize high-quality infant care. Other cultures believe the opposite—that infant care is best done by the mothers, who are solely responsible for providing it.

16. National and international research finds much variation in policies and opinions regarding infant day care. Some nations provide extensive day care for young children, and virtually all nations (except the United States) mandate paid maternal leave for employed women who have a baby.

17. Allocare in infancy can benefit cognition, and does not necessarily reduce secure attachment. In some nations, behavior problems may increase with infant allocare, but this does not seem to be true in Norway or the Netherlands.

KEY TERMS

social smile (p. 113)
separation anxiety (p. 114)
stranger wariness (p. 114)
self-awareness (p. 116)
temperament (p. 117)
synchrony (p. 120)
still-face technique (p. 121)
attachment (p. 122)
secure attachment (p. 124)
insecure-avoidant attachment (p. 124)
insecure-resistant/ambivalent attachment (p. 124)
disorganized attachment (p. 124)
Strange Situation (p. 126)
social referencing (p. 129)
trust versus mistrust (p. 132)
autonomy versus shame and doubt (p. 132)
proximal parenting (p. 133)
distal parenting (p. 133)
working model (p. 133)
allocare (p. 135)

APPLICATIONS

1. One cultural factor that influences infant development is how infants are carried from place to place. Ask four mothers whose infants were born in each of the past four decades how they transported them—front or back carriers, facing out or in, strollers or carriages, in car seats or on mother's laps, and so on. Why did they choose the mode(s) they chose? What are their opinions and yours on how such cultural practices might affect infants' development?

2. Record video of synchrony for three minutes. Ideally, ask the parent of an infant under 8 months of age to play with the infant. If no infant is available, observe a pair of lovers as they converse. Note the sequence and timing of every facial expression, sound, and gesture of both partners.

3. Contact several day-care centers to try to assess the quality of care they provide. Ask about factors such as adult/child ratio, group size, and training for caregivers of children of various ages. Is there a minimum age? Why or why not? Analyze the answers, using Table 4.2 as a guide.

ESPECIALLY FOR ANSWERS

Response for Nurses and Pediatricians (from p. 115): Stranger wariness is normal up to about 14 months. This baby's behavior actually might indicate secure attachment.

Response for Nurses (from p. 119): It's too soon to tell. Temperament is not truly "fixed" but variable, especially in the first few months. Many "difficult" infants become happy, successful adolescents and adults, if their parents are responsive.

Response for Nursing Mothers (from p. 132): Freud thought so, but there is no experimental evidence that weaning, even when ill-timed, has such dire long-term effects.

Response for Pediatricians (from p. 133): Consider the origins of the misbehavior—probably a combination of the child's inborn temperament and the mother's distal parenting. Acceptance and consistent responses (e.g., avoiding disliked foods but always using the car seat) is more warranted than anger. Perhaps this mother is expressing hostility toward the child—a sign that intervention may be needed. Find out.

Response for Day-Care Providers (from p. 140): Reassure the mother that you will keep her baby safe and will help to develop the baby's mind and social skills by fostering synchrony and attachment. Also tell her that the quality of mother–infant interaction at home is more important than anything else for psychosocial development; mothers who are employed full time usually have wonderful, secure relationships with their infants. If the mother wishes, you can discuss ways to be a responsive mother.

OBSERVATION QUIZ ANSWERS

Answer to Observation Quiz (from p. 118): Watch the facial expressions.

Answer to Observation Quiz (from p. 121): The first baby is adopted, the second was probably born at home, and the third parent is the father, not the mother. Synchrony is universal! Although not evident here, it is also true that each is in a different nation: United States, Ethiopia, and England.

Answer to Observation Quiz (from p. 122): Mothers elicit slightly more positive emotions than fathers do, and Dutch infants express slightly more positive emotions than Chinese infants.

Answer to Observation Quiz (from p. 136): Remontia Green is holding the feeding baby in just the right position as she rocks back and forth—no propped-up bottle here. The two observing babies are at an angle and distance that makes them part of the social interaction, and they are strapped in. Finally, look at the cribs—no paint, close slats, and positioned so the babies can see each other.

Answer to Observation Quiz (from p. 139): Norway. Almost every mother stays home with her infant for the first year (she is paid her salary to do so), and almost every mother enrolls her 1-year-old in public day care.

PART III

CHAPTER 5 CHAPTER 6

Early Childhood

From ages 2 to 6, children spend most of their waking hours discovering, creating, laughing, and imagining — all the while acquiring the skills they need. They chase each other and attempt new challenges (developing their bodies); they play with sounds, words, and ideas (developing their minds); they invent games and dramatize fantasies (learning social skills and morals).

These were once called the *preschool years* because school started in first grade. But first grade is no longer first; most children begin school long before age 6. Instead, these years are called *early childhood*; those who were once called *preschoolers* are now *young children*. By whatever name, this is a time of extraordinary growth, impressive learning, and spontaneous play, joyful not only for young children but also for anyone who knows them.

LIGHTFIELD STUDIOS/SHUTTERSTOCK.COM

CHAPTER 5

EARLY CHILDHOOD
Body and Mind

what will you know?

- Why are some young children overweight?
- How should adults answer when children ask, "Why?"
- Does it confuse young children if they hear two or more languages?
- Does preschool have any effect on later life?

Many children, including my grandsons, go to the playground after school. The 4- and 5-year-olds are always in motion, running and chasing; they are not ready for the games organized by the older children.

I am struck not only by the younger children's joy in motion, but also by the immaturity of their thoughts and language.

Once my grandson came to me, crying. "I bumped my head," he told me.

I thought of the animism of preoperational thought and said, "Tell me what pole you bumped it on, and I will tell that pole never to bump my grandson again."

"I bumped it on another head," he said as he ran back to play. Of course! Without a firm idea of what his words would mean to me, what he needed was sympathy. Young children need to be listened to, that is how they learn.

I am not surprised that two young heads bumped each other. Nature makes young children active and social. This chapter describes growth during these years — in body, brain, and motor skills.

My role is to protect my grandson when his immaturity might harm him. I hold his wrist when we cross the street, I remind him to wear his coat, I carry Band-Aids in my bag because covering a scrape makes pain disappear. I wish every young child was as easy to comfort.

Growth of the Body

In early childhood, as in infancy, the body and mind develop according to powerful epigenetic forces. This means that nature and nurture continually interact: Growth is biologically driven and socially guided, experience-expectant and experience-dependent.

Growth Patterns

Compare the body of an unsteady 24-month-old with that of a cartwheeling 6-year-old. Height and weight increases are obvious. However, those are not the most radical changes; shape and proportions are. The lower body lengthens and fat gives way to muscle.

The average body mass index (BMI, a ratio of weight to height) is lower at ages 5 and 6 than at any other time of life. Gone are the infant's protruding belly, round face, short limbs, and large head. The center of gravity moves from the breast to the belly, enabling cartwheels, somersaults, rhythmic dancing, and pumping legs on a swing.

During each year of early childhood, well-nourished children grow about 3 inches (about 7½ centimeters) and gain almost 4½ pounds (2 kilograms). By age 6, the average child in a developed nation:

- is at least 3½ feet tall (more than 110 centimeters);
- weighs between 40 and 50 pounds (between 18 and 23 kilograms);
- looks lean, not chubby; and
- has adultlike body proportions (with legs constituting about half the total height).

Young children enjoy developing their motor skills as brain maturation allows advances. Adults need to provide space, playmates, and freedom; children will do the rest. Most North American 6-year-olds can climb a tree and jump over a puddle as well as throw, catch, and kick a ball; many can ride bicycles, swim in a pool, print their names. In other continents, some 6-year-olds can climb cliffs, swim in the ocean, embroider clothes.

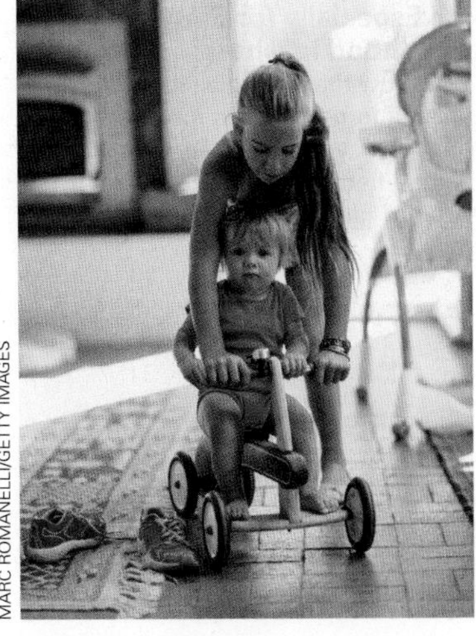

MARC ROMANELLI/GETTY IMAGES

Short and Chubby Limbs No Longer Siblings in New Mexico, ages 7 and almost 1, illustrate the transformation of body shape and skills during early childhood. Head size is almost the same, but arms are twice as long, evidence of proximodistal growth.

◆◆ OBSERVATION QUIZ

Can this toddler pedal the tricycle? (see answer, page 171) ↑

Nutrition

Although they rarely starve, young children may be malnourished, even in nations with abundant food. Small appetites are often satiated by unhealthy snacks, crowding out needed vitamins. That provides a clue for caregivers. If no salty, fried, or sugary snacks are available, children will eat what they see adults enjoying: the fruits, vegetables, and whole grains that we know are best for humans of all ages.

OBESITY AMONG YOUNG CHILDREN

Older adults often encourage children to eat, protecting them against famine that was common a century ago. Unfortunately, that may be destructive. As family income decreases, obesity increases—a sign of poor nutrition, reducing immunity and increasing illness (Rook et al., 2014).

Children who grow up in food-insecure households learn to eat whenever food is available, becoming less aware of hunger and satiety signals in their bodies. Consequently, as adults, they overeat, risking obesity, diabetes, and strokes (Hill et al., 2016).

This is a problem in many nations: "Childhood obesity is one of the most serious public health challenges of the 21st century. The problem is global and is steadily affecting many low- and middle-income countries, particularly in urban settings" (Sahoo et al., 2015, pp. 187–188).

One Chinese father complained:

> I told my boy his diet needs some improvement . . . my mum said she is happy with his diet . . . [that he] eats enough meat and enough oil is used in cooking. . . . In their time, meat and oil were treasures so now they feel the more the better. . . . I decided to move out with my wife and son . . . his grandparents were a big problem . . . we couldn't change anything when we lived together.
>
> [*Li et al., 2015*]

DAVE CARPENTER/CARTOONSTOCK

Who Is Fooling Whom? He doesn't believe her, but maybe she shouldn't believe what the label says, either. For example, "low fat" might also mean high sugar.

◆◆ Especially for Early-Childhood Teachers
You know that young children are upset if forced to eat a food they hate, but you have eight 3-year-olds with eight different preferences. What do you do? (see response, page 171)

There is some good news in the United States. Rates of obesity among young children fell when many day-care centers increased exercise and improved snacks: carrot sticks and apple slices, not cookies and chocolate milk (Sisson et al., 2016). Rates rose again in 2016, to 13.9 percent, which is still far lower than the rates for older children and adults (Hales et al., 2017). That shows something hopeful: Parents and communities can make a difference if they choose to.

ORAL HEALTH

Not surprisingly, tooth decay correlates with obesity; both result from too much sugar and too little fiber (Hayden et al., 2013). Sweet drinks are the usual problem.

"Baby" teeth are replaced naturally from ages 6 to 10. The schedule is genetic, with girls a few months ahead of boys. However, tooth brushing and dentist visits should become habitual years before adult teeth erupt. Poor oral health in early childhood harms those permanent teeth (forming below the first teeth) and can cause jaw malformation, chewing difficulties, and speech problems.

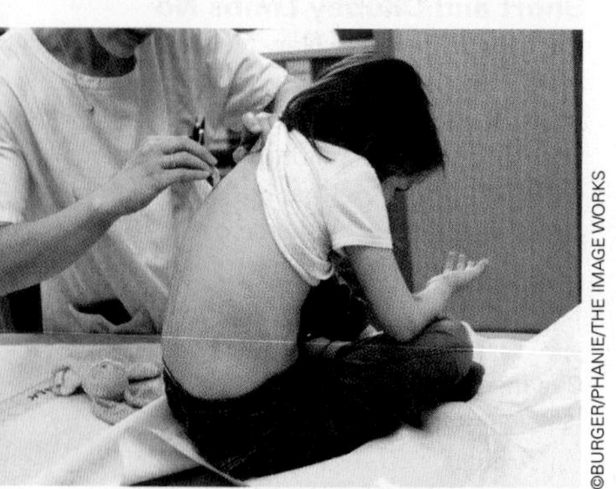
©BURGER/PHANIE/THE IMAGE WORKS

Not Allergic Anymore? Many food allergies are outgrown, so young children are more likely to have them than older ones. This skin prick will insert a tiny amount of a suspected allergen. If a red welt develops in the next half hour, the girl is still allergic. Hopefully, no reaction will occur; but if her breathing is affected, an EpiPen is within reach.

FOOD ALLERGIES

An estimated 10 percent of children are allergic to a specific food, almost always a common, healthy one: Cow's milk, eggs, peanuts, tree nuts (such as almonds and walnuts), soy, wheat, fish, and shellfish are the usual culprits (Licari et al., 2019). Such allergies are increasing, with one reason being increasing rates of cesarean births, which triples the risk of food allergies (Adeyeye et al., 2019).

For some foods, an allergic reaction is a rash or an upset stomach, but for other foods—especially peanuts or shellfish—the reaction is sudden shock and shortness of breath that could be fatal (Dyer et al., 2015). When a child has a severe allergic reaction, someone should immediately inject epinephrine to stop the reaction. In 2012, all Chicago schools had EpiPens, which were used in dozens of emergencies (DeSantiago-Cardenas et al., 2015).

Some experts advocate total avoidance of the offending food—there are peanut-free schools, where no one is allowed to bring a peanut-butter sandwich for lunch lest an allergic child unwittingly come in contact with it. However, feeding allergic children a tiny bit of peanut powder (under medical supervision) often decreases that allergic reaction (Vickery et al., 2017).

The Growing Brain

By age 2, most neurons have connected to other neurons and substantial pruning has occurred, and the brain already weighs 75 percent of what it will weigh in adulthood.

Growth continues during childhood and adolescence, reaching 90 percent at age 6. That 15 percent is crucial, as it includes dendrites, myelination, and the prefrontal cortex, all of which are crucial.

MYELINATION

myelin
The fatty substance coating axons that speeds the transmission of nerve impulses from neuron to neuron.

corpus callosum
A long, thick band of nerve fibers that connects the left and right hemispheres of the brain and allows communication between them.

Myelin is a fatty coating on the axons that protects and speeds signals between neurons. (Myelin is sometimes called the *white matter* of the brain; the *gray matter* is the neurons—although neuroscientists know that the white/gray, or myelin/neuron, dichotomy makes brains seem simpler than is the case.)

Myelin is far more than mere insulation. It speeds the connections between neurons that are far from each other. "Myelin organizes the very structure of network connectivity . . . and regulates the timing of information flow through individual circuits" (Fields, 2014, p. 266).

The network connections are crucial because the brain is divided into two halves called *hemispheres*. Those two are connected by the **corpus callosum**, a long, thick

band of axons that myelinates and grows particularly rapidly in early childhood (Ansado et al., 2015). For that reason, compared to toddlers, 5-year-olds become much better at coordinating the two sides of their brains and, hence, both sides of their bodies. They can hop, skip, and gallop.

Both sides of the brain are usually involved in every skill, not only gross motor skills such as skipping but also fine motor skills such as eating with utensils or buttoning one's coat. Intellectual skills also use many parts of the brain, as do social responses to other people.

Each hemisphere is sometimes thought to specialize in particular intellectual abilities, with logic and language primarily on the left side of the brain and creativity and emotions on the right. But recent research finds that this left–right distinction has been exaggerated. No one is exclusively left-brained or right-brained, except individuals with severe brain injury in childhood. In that case, all of the necessary thinking is located in the intact hemisphere.

Compensating for brain destruction in adulthood, as with a stroke, is much more difficult because childhood is when neurological plasticity is strongest. The brains of children develop the dendrites to do what the family and culture encourages: balancing on one foot, calculating long division, thrilling at a concerto. Adult brains have become more specialized.

Left-handed people tend to have thicker, better myelinated corpus callosa, because they must often switch between the two sides of their bodies. When they can choose which hand to use, they prefer their left (e.g., brushing their teeth), but the culture often requires using the right hand (e.g., shaking hands). Therefore, the corpus callosum must be well developed.

Indeed, the brain is the source of all types of **lateralization** (literally, *sidedness*). The entire human body is lateralized, apparent not only in right- or left-handedness but also in the feet, the eyes, the ears, and the brain itself. Genes, prenatal hormones, and early experiences all affect which side does what, and then the corpus callosum puts it all together.

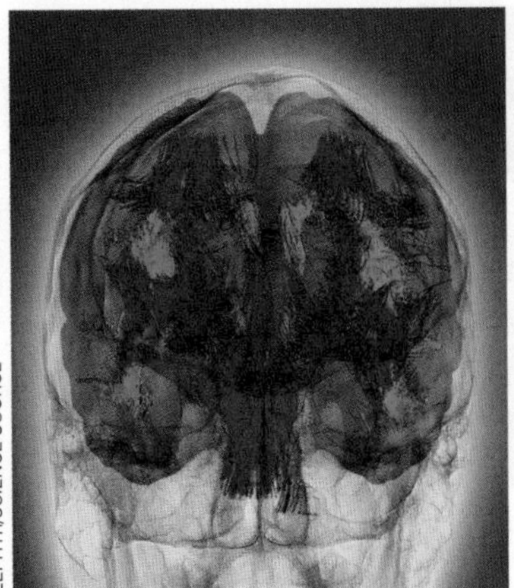

ZEPHYR/SCIENCE SOURCE

Mental Coordination? This brain scan of a 38-year-old depicts areas of myelination (the various colors) within the brain. As you see, the two hemispheres are quite similar, but not identical. For most important skills and concepts, both halves of the brain are activated.

lateralization
Literally, "sidedness," referring to the specialization in certain functions by each side of the brain, with one side dominant for each activity. The left side of the brain controls the right side of the body, and vice versa.

BRAIN MATURATION

The brain continues to develop for many years after early childhood. Nonetheless, neurological control advances significantly between ages 2 and 6, evident in several ways:

- Sleep becomes more regular.
- Emotions become more nuanced and responsive.
- Temper tantrums subside.
- Uncontrollable laughter and tears are less common.

One example is overwhelming fear. Because the amygdala is not well connected to more reflective and rational parts of the brain, many young children become suddenly overcome with terror, even of something that exists only in their imagination. Common phobias in young children are of the dark, of the ocean, of dogs, of strangers.

Since the emotional parts of the brain are immature, not yet controlled by reason, comfort and reassurance are needed, not logic. Then the fear will diminish. If a phobia persists past early childhood, psychotherapists can often reduce it in a single session, which is evidence that early phobias are not deep rooted (Davis et al., 2018).

FATIHHOCA/ISTOCK/GETTY IMAGES

Open Your Arms! But four children keep their arms closed because Simon didn't say to do so. You can almost see their prefrontal cortices (above the eyes) hard at work.

INHIBITION AND FLEXIBILITY

Neurons have only two kinds of impulses: on–off or, in neuroscience terms, *activate–inhibit*. Each is signaled by biochemical messages from dendrites to axons to neurons.

GRANT DIFFORD/GREATSTOCK/ALAMY

The Joy of Rivalry Look closely at this sister and brother in Johannesburg, South Africa. Just as 1-year-olds run as soon as they are able, siblings everywhere quarrel, fight, and compromise, ideally testing their physical and intellectual skills, which, as seems to be the case here, is fun.

◆◆ Especially for Early-Childhood Teachers
You know you should be patient, but frustration rises when your young charges dawdle on the walk to the playground a block away. What should you do? (see response, page 171)

A balance of activation and inhibition (on/off) is needed lifelong; people should neither leap too quickly nor freeze in fear. But many young children are unbalanced neurologically. They are impulsive, flitting from one activity to another, or they get stuck in one thought or action, a trait called perseveration. Young children may repeat a phrase or question again and again, or they may not be able to stop laughing, crying, or even running once they start.

Both impulsivity and perseveration are linked to brain maturation. No young child is perfect at regulating attention, because immaturity of the prefrontal cortex makes controlling the limbic system almost impossible. Caregivers need to be patient as well as provide guidance. The comforting truth is that brains mature.

The relationship between stress and brain activity depends partly on the age of the person and partly on the amount of stress. Both too much and too little stress reduce learning.

In an experiment, brain scans and hormone measurements were taken of 4- to 6-year-olds immediately after a fire alarm (Teoh & Lamb, 2013). As measured by their cortisol levels, some children were upset and some were not. Two weeks later, they were questioned about the event. Those with higher cortisol reactions to the alarm remembered more details.

For some of them, adults asked questions sternly, demanding immediate yes/no answers. Then memories were less accurate. There are evolutionary reasons for both the better and the worse memories: People need to remember experiences that arouse emotions in order to avoid, or adjust to, similar experiences in the future. At the same time, brains need to shut down to protect from excess stress.

what have you learned?

1. How are growth rates, body proportions, and motor skills related during early childhood?
2. What is changing in rates of early-childhood obesity and why?
3. How is childhood obesity affected by family income?
4. How does myelination advance skill development?
5. How is the corpus callosum crucial for learning?
6. What do impulse control and perseveration have in common?

Thinking During Early Childhood

Young children express charming ideas: clouds are alive, parents know all the answers, their own culture is right and much more that makes adults smile. All wrong, all wonderful. But another aspect of the thinking of young children is more impressive than charming: 2- to 6-year-olds are remarkable learners, with many new thoughts and discoveries.

Piaget: Preoperational Thought

preoperational intelligence
Piaget's term for cognitive development between the ages of about 2 and 6; it includes language and imagination (which involve symbolic thought), but logical, operational thinking is not yet possible at this stage.

symbolic thought
A major accomplishment of preoperational intelligence that allows a child to think symbolically, including understanding that words can refer to things not seen and that an item, such as a flag, can symbolize something else (in this case, a country).

Early childhood is the time of **preoperational intelligence**, the second of Piaget's four periods of cognitive development (described in Table 1.6 on p. 21). Preoperational children are no longer limited by their senses and motor abilities.

Children now think in symbols, not just via senses and motor skills. In **symbolic thought**, an object or a word can stand for something else, including something out of sight or imagined. The rapid acquisition of vocabulary is a dramatic example of

symbolic thought. Children do not yet understand logical operations, (which is why this is *pre*- operational thought, unlike the next two stages that allow logical operations), but thinking in symbols frees their minds to think many new thoughts.

ANIMISM

Symbolic thought without logic helps explain **animism,** the belief that natural objects (such the sun and clouds) are alive and that nonhuman animals have the same characteristics as the child. Children's stories often include animals or objects that talk and listen (Aesop's fables; *Winnie-the-Pooh*; *Good Night, Gorilla*; *The Day the Crayons Quit*). Preoperational thought can reach new heights, making such stories compelling because it is symbolic and magical, not logical and realistic.

Many preindustrial peoples believed in animism, praying to the sky and to rivers, for instance. One way to depict human history is to notice that societies advanced in cognitive development (e.g., Oesterdiekhoff, 2014). When *homo sapiens* developed language, for instance, they were no longer stuck in sensorimotor thought.

Other scholars think that the child's "enchanted animism"—that is, their appreciation of trees, clouds and so on—is a much-needed corrective to "progress" that includes global warming, pollution, and deforestation (Merewether, 2018).

animism
The belief that natural objects and phenomena are alive, moving around, and having sensations and abilities that are humanlike.

centration
A characteristic of preoperational thought in which a young child focuses (centers) on one idea, excluding all others.

egocentrism
Piaget's term for children's tendency to think about the world entirely from their own personal perspective.

focus on appearance
A characteristic of preoperational thought in which a young child ignores all attributes that are not apparent.

static reasoning
A characteristic of preoperational thought in which a young child thinks that nothing changes. Whatever is now has always been and always will be.

irreversibility
A characteristic of preoperational thought in which a young child thinks that nothing can be undone. A thing cannot be restored to the way it was before a change occurred.

conservation
The principle that the amount of a substance remains the same (i.e., is conserved) even when its appearance changes.

OBSTACLES TO LOGIC

Piaget noted four limitations that make logic difficult for young children: *centration*, *focus on appearance*, *static reasoning*, and *irreversibility*.

Centration is the tendency to focus on one aspect of a situation to the exclusion of all others. For example, young children may insist that Daddy is a father, not a brother, because they center on the role that he fills for them. This illustrates a particular type of centration that Piaget called **egocentrism**—literally, "self-centeredness." Egocentric children contemplate the world exclusively from their personal perspective.

Egocentrism is *not* selfishness. One 3-year-old chose to buy a model car as a birthday present for his mother: His "behavior was not selfish or greedy; he carefully wrapped the present and gave it to his mother with an expression that clearly showed that he expected her to love it" (Crain, 2011, p. 133).

A second characteristic of preoperational thought is a **focus on appearance**, to the exclusion of other attributes. For instance, a girl given a short haircut might worry that she has turned into a boy. In preoperational thought, a thing is what it appears to be—evident when young children joyously don the shoes of grown-ups, clomping noisily and unsteadily around the house.

Third, preoperational children use **static reasoning**. They believe that the world is stable, unchanging, always in the state in which they currently encounter it. Many children cannot imagine that their own parents were once children. If they are told that Grandma is their mother's mother, they still do not understand how people change with maturation. One child asked his grandmother to tell his mother not to spank him because "she has to do what her mother says."

The fourth characteristic of preoperational thought is **irreversibility**. Preoperational thinkers fail to recognize that reversing a process might restore whatever existed before. A young girl might cry because her mother put lettuce on her sandwich and still reject the food when the lettuce is removed, because she thinks what is done cannot be undone.

CONSERVATION AND LOGIC

Piaget reported many ways in which preoperational intelligence disregards logic. A famous series of experiments involved **conservation**, the notion that the amount of something remains the same (is conserved) despite changes in its appearance.

Tests of Various Types of Conservation

Type of Conservation	Initial Presentation	Transformation	Question	Preoperational Child's Answer
Volume	Two equal glasses of pink lemonade.	Pour one into a taller, narrower glass.	Which glass contains more?	The taller one.
Number	Two equal lines of candy.	Increase spacing of candy in one line.	Which line has more candy?	The longer one.
Matter	Two equal balls of cookie dough.	Squeeze one ball into a long, thin shape.	Which piece has more dough?	The long one.
Length	Two pencils of equal length.	Move one pencil.	Which pencil is longer?	The one that is farther to the right.

FIGURE 5.1 Conservation, Please According to Piaget, until children grasp the concept of conservation at (he believed) about age 6 or 7, they cannot understand that the transformations shown here do not change the total amount of liquid, candies, cookie dough, and pencils.

Suppose two identical glasses contain the same amount of lemonade, and the liquid from one glass is poured into a taller, narrower glass. Then ask a young child whether one glass contains more or, alternatively, if both glasses contain the same amount. Before age 6, most children say that the narrower glass (with the higher level) has more. (See Figure 5.1 for other examples.)

Easy Question; Obvious Answer *(left)* Sadie, age 5, carefully makes sure both glasses contain the same amount. When one glass of pink lemonade is poured into a wide jar, she triumphantly points to the tall glass as having more *(right)*. Sadie is like all 5-year-olds; only a developmental psychologist or a 7-year-old child knows better.

All four characteristics of preoperational thought are evident in this mistake. Young children fail to understand conservation because they focus (*center*) on what they see (*appearance*), noticing only the immediate (*static*) condition. They do not realize that they could pour the lemonade back into the wider glass and re-create the level of a moment earlier (*irreversibility*).

Piaget's original tests of conservation required children to respond verbally to an adult's questions. Contemporary researchers have made tests of logic simple and playful, and then young children sometimes succeed. Moreover, before age 6, children indicate via eye movements or gestures that they understand conservation, although they cannot yet put their understanding into words (Goldin-Meadow & Alibali, 2013).

As with sensorimotor intelligence in infancy, Piaget underestimated preoperational children. Piaget was right about his basic idea, however: Young children are not very logical (Lane & Harris, 2014). Their cognitive limits make smart 3-year-olds sometimes foolish, as Caleb was.

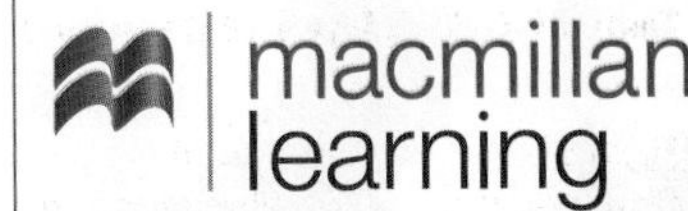

VIDEO ACTIVITY: Achieving Conservation focuses on the cognitive changes that enable older children to pass Piaget's conservation-of-liquid task.

A CASE TO STUDY

Stones in the Belly

As we were reading about dinosaurs, my 3-year-old grandson, Caleb, told me that some dinosaurs (*sauropods*) have stones in their bellies. It helps them digest their food and then poop and pee.

"I didn't know that dinosaurs ate stones," I said.

"They don't eat them."

"Then how do they get the stones in their bellies? They must swallow them."

"They don't eat them."

"Then how do they get in their bellies?"

"They are just there."

"How did they get there?"

"They don't eat them," Caleb repeated. "Stones are dirty. We don't eat them."

I changed the subject, as I knew that his mother had told him not to eat pebbles, or sand, or anything else he found on the ground.

At dinner he asked my daughter, "Do dinosaurs eat stones?"

"Yes, they eat stones so they can grind their food," she answered.

At that, Caleb was quiet.

Preoperational cognition was evident. Caleb is highly verbal; he can name several kinds of dinosaurs, as can many young children. But logic eludes him.

It was obvious to me that the dinosaurs must have swallowed the stones. However, in his static thinking, Caleb said the stones "are just there." He rejected the thought that dinosaurs ate stones because he has been told that stones are too dirty to eat.

Caleb is egocentric, reasoning from his own experience, and animistic, in that he thinks other creatures act as he does. A dinosaur would not do something he would not do. He trusts his mother, who told him never to eat stones. Static thinking was also evident, preventing him from considering my authority as his mother's mother.

Nonetheless, Caleb is curious, another hallmark of preoperational thought. That is why he checked with his authority, my daughter.

Should I have expected him to tell me that I was right when his mother agreed with me? No. That would have required far more understanding of reversibility and far less egocentrism than most young children can muster.

Vygotsky: Social Learning

For decades, Piaget's description of the magical, illogical, and self-centered aspects of cognition dominated our conception of early-childhood thought. Then Vygotsky emphasized another side of early cognition—that each person's thinking is shaped by other people. His focus on the sociocultural context contrasts with Piaget's emphasis on the individual.

DIGITALVISION/HERO IMAGES/GETTY IMAGES

Learning to Button Most shirts for 4-year-olds are wide-necked and without buttons, so preschoolers can put them on themselves. But the skill of buttoning is best learned from a mentor, who knows how to increase motivation.

mentor
Someone who teaches a person. Mentors teach by example and encouragement, as well as directly. Anyone can be a mentor: peers, relatives, neighbors, strangers, or teachers.

zone of proximal development (ZPD)
Vygotsky's term for the skills—cognitive as well as physical—that a person can exercise only with assistance, not yet independently.

scaffolding
Temporary support that is tailored to a learner's needs and abilities and aimed at helping the learner master the next task in a given learning process.

MENTORS

Vygotsky believed that cognitive development is embedded in the social context at every age (Vygotsky, 1987). He stressed that children are curious, observing and thinking about everything they see.

Young children are famous for their exasperating penchant to ask "why," "how," "where," and "why" again. They want to know how machines work, why weather changes, where the sky ends. They seek answers from a **mentor**, who might be a parent, teacher, peer, or a stranger.

The answers they get are affected by the mentor's perceptions and assumptions, which they themselves have learned in childhood. Thus, according to Vygotsky, culture is transmitted from one generation to the next.

According to Vygotsky, children learn because mentors:

- Present challenges.
- Offer assistance (without taking over).
- Provide information.
- Encourage motivation.

Learning from mentors indicates intelligence, according to Vygotsky: "What children can do with the assistance of others might be in some sense even more indicative of their mental development than what they can do alone" (1980, p. 85).

SCAFFOLDING

Vygotsky believed that all individuals learn within their **zone of proximal development (ZPD)**, an intellectual arena in which new ideas and skills can be mastered. *Proximal* means "near," so the ZPD includes the ideas and skills that children are close to mastering but cannot yet demonstrate independently.

Learning depends, in part, on the wisdom and willingness of mentors to provide **scaffolding**, a sensitive support for new ideas and skills, much like a scaffolding constructed on a building so workers can stand on it as they wash the windows, or construct the next level, or finish the walls. A metaphorical scaffold, says Vygotsky, helps children take the next step within their developmental zone (Mermelshtine, 2017).

Good mentors provide plenty of scaffolding, encouraging children to look both ways before crossing the street (pointing out speeding trucks, cars, and buses while holding the child's hand) or letting them stir the cake batter (perhaps covering the child's hand on the spoon handle, in what Vygotsky called *guided participation*), Thus:

> When providing scaffolding, a teacher or a peer tutor does not make the task easier but instead makes the learner's job easier by giving the child maximum support in the beginning stages and then gradually withdrawing this support as the child's mastery of a new skill increases.
>
> *[Bodrova & Leong, 2018, p. 226]*

Adults guide learning in culturally specific ways (Hoyne & Egan, 2019). Book-reading may be time for teaching vocabulary, or morals, or quiet listening. A study of 27 preschool classes found that some teachers never asked questions, and others asked one every 10 seconds. Questions led to increased vocabulary and reasoning (Hindman et al., 2019). That is exactly what Vygotsky would expect.

◆ **OBSERVATION QUIZ**
Is the girl below right-handed or left-handed? (see answer, page 171) ↓

TIM HALL/GETTY IMAGES

Count by Tens A large, attractive abacus could be a scaffold. However, in this toy store the position of the balls suggests that no mentor is nearby. Children are unlikely to grasp the number system without a motivating guide.

A VIEW FROM SCIENCE

Don't Do What I Do

Adults might wish that children would not use them as role models, but children watch closely and try to follow the example of their parents. Ideally, adults are good mentors, but young children curse, kick, or worse because someone showed them how.

Researchers are struck by how salient mentors are. In **overimitation,** children learn rituals, tool use, grammar, emotional expression. Overimitation is a "flexible and . . . highly functional phenomenon" (Hoehl et al., 2019, p. 90).

Overimitation was demonstrated in a series of experiments with 3- to 6-year-olds, 64 of them from San communities (once pejoratively called "Bushmen") in South Africa and Botswana, 64 from cities in Australia, and 19 from aboriginal communities within Australia.

The goal of the research was to reveal variations in imitation: Australian middle-class adults often scaffold with words and actions, but San adults rarely do. The researchers expected the Australian children but not the San children to follow adult demonstrations (Nielsen et al., 2014).

overimitation
When a person imitates an action that is not a relevant part of the behavior to be learned. Overimitation is common among 2- to 6-year-olds when they imitate adult actions that are irrelevant and inefficient.

In part of the study, some children watched an adult open a box, which could easily and efficiently be opened by pulling down a knob by hand. Instead, the adult waved a red stick above the box three times and used that stick to push down the knob. Then each child (individually, so they did not see what the others did) was given the stick and asked to open the box.

The researchers' hypothesis was *disproven*. No matter what their culture, the children did what the adult did, waving the stick three times, not touching the knob with their hands.

Other San and Australian children did not see the demonstration. When they were given the stick and asked to open the box, they simply pulled the knob.

Then they observed an adult do the stick-waving opening—and they copied those inefficient actions, even though they already knew the easy way. Children everywhere learn from others not only through explicit guidance, but also through observation.

Overimitation is universal: Children are naturally "socially motivated," which is one reason they learn so much.

Fortunately, adults enjoy transmitting knowledge, and children like imitating, as long as copying is within the zone of possibility. Children naturally imitate adults who seem to know something, even when the adults are unaware that they are modeling (Hoehl et al., 2019; Tomasello, 2016a, 2016b).

That is how culture is transmitted, according to Vygotsky.

LANGUAGE AS A TOOL

Although all of the elements of a culture guide children, Vygotsky thought language is pivotal in two ways: private speech and social mediation.

First, talking to oneself, called **private speech**, is evident when young children talk aloud to review, decide, and explain events to themselves (and, incidentally, to anyone else within earshot). Almost all young children sometimes talk to themselves; about a third sing to themselves as well (Thibodeaux et al., 2019).

With time, children become more circumspect, sometimes whispering. Many adults use private speech when no one can hear them, and many write down ideas to help them think.

Second, language advances thinking by facilitating social interaction (Vygotsky, 2012). This **social mediation** function of speech occurs as mentors guide mentees in their zone of proximal development, learning numbers, recalling memories, and following routines. Adults sometimes are explicit ("do it this way") but often merely encourage ("good job").

private speech
The internal dialogue that occurs when people talk to themselves (either silently or out loud).

social mediation
Human interaction that expands and advances understanding, often through words that one person uses to explain something to another.

Combining Piaget and Vygotsky

Developmentalists respect both Piaget and Vygotsky. The two can be seen as contrasting, in that Piaget emphasized the immaturity of the child's mind, and Vygotsky stressed the power of the social context. But considering them as opposites misses the point: Both appreciated the active curiosity of young children, and both valued

Especially for Driving Instructors
Sometimes your students cry, curse, or quit. How would Vygotsky advise you to proceed? (see response, page 171)

the extraordinary language development of young children. This is evident in two examples: STEM education and theory of mind.

MICHELLE DEL GUERCIO/SCIENCE SOURCE/GETTY IMAGES

Future Engineers in the Bronx Playing with Legos helps children learn about connecting shapes, which makes math and geometry easier to learn in school and makes STEM careers more likely. Once, Legos were only marketed to boys, but no longer — there now are kits designed to appeal to girls.

STEM LEARNING

Many adults are concerned that too few college students choose a STEM (science, technology, engineering, math) career. Why?

As you might expect (since this topic is in this chapter), developmentalists believe that STEM education begins in early childhood, when children's curiosity (Piaget) and their social learning (Vygotsky) might include learning about numbers and science. For some young children, knowledge of math and physics develops month by month. They learn to:

- Count objects, with one number per item (called *one-to-one correspondence*).
- Remember times and ages (bedtime at 8 P.M.; a child is 4 years old).
- Understand sequence (first child wins, last child loses; bath after dinner).
- Know which numbers are greater than others (four bites are more than two).
- Understand how to make things move (toy cars, balls, game pieces).
- Appreciate temperature, from ice to steam, or from mittens to swimsuits.

How do they learn this? Piaget stressed discovery: Children need to explore and figure out ideas. This is evident, for instance, in specifics of conservation. Children with more experience pouring water are quicker to understand of the conservation of liquids. Vygotsky stressed that "scaffolding and elaboration from parents and teachers provide crucial input to spatial development" (Verdine et al., 2017, p. 25).

Both theorists thought words are pivotal, as part of symbolic thought (Piaget) or mediation (Vygotsky). Some 2-year-olds hear sentences such as "One, two, three, takeoff," "Here are two cookies," or "Dinner in five minutes" several times a day. They are encouraged to touch an interesting bit of moss, or are alerted to the phases of the moon outside their window, or hear about the relationship between pace and slope as they climb a hill.

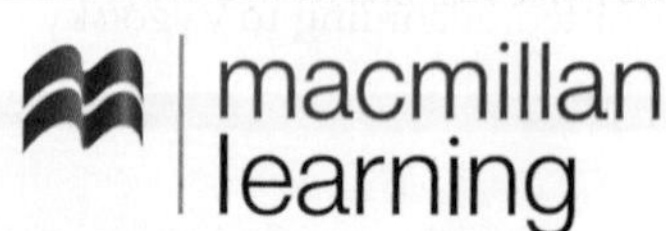

VIDEO: Learning Cause and Effect presents a research study that demonstrates how the way parents interact with their children affects how they learn about the world around them.

Some early-childhood programs include science. For instance, one teacher read *The Three Little Pigs* and then put straw, sticks, and bricks on a table. The children took turns trying to move the material by blowing (Brenneman et al., 2019). Measuring how far the straw could be blown, or testing other materials (Pebbles? Sand?) could help the children think like scientists.

Other children never hear about STEM in everyday experiences—and they have a harder time with math in first grade, with science in the third grade, and with physics in high school. If, as Vygotsky believed, words mediate between brain potential and comprehension, STEM education begins long before college.

THEORY OF MIND

theory of mind
A person's theory of what other people might be thinking. In order to have a theory of mind, children must realize that other people are not necessarily thinking the same thoughts that they themselves are. That realization seldom occurs before age 4.

To know what goes on in another's mind, people develop a *folk psychology*, which includes ideas about other people's thinking, called **theory of mind**. Theory of mind is an emergent ability, slow to develop but evident in most children by age 4 or 5 (S. Carlson et al., 2013).

Some aspects of theory of mind are manifest sooner than others. Longitudinal research finds that typical 2-year-olds do not know that other people think differently than they do, but 6-year-olds have a well-developed theory of mind (Wellman et al., 2011).

The development of theory of mind can be seen when young children try to escape punishment by not telling the truth when questioned. Their faces often betray them: worried or shifting eyes, pursed lips, and so on. Parents sometimes say, "I know when you are lying," and, to the consternation of most 3-year-olds, parents are usually right.

Four-year-olds can usually tell the difference between lies and the truth, but until they are a little older, children do not have sufficient theory of mind to realize that

prosocial lies ("That is a pretty dress") were less wrong than lies to escape punishment ("I didn't break the vase") (Vendetti et al., 2019).

In one experiment, 247 children, aged 3 to 5, were left alone at a table that had an upside-down cup covering dozens of candies (Evans et al., 2011). The children were told *not* to peek, and the experimenter left the room.

For most children (57 percent), curiosity overcame obedience. They lifted up the cup. The candies spilled onto the table, and it was impossible for the children to put them back under the cup. The examiner returned, asking how the candies got on the table. Only one-fourth of the participants (more often the younger ones) told the truth (see Figure 5.2).

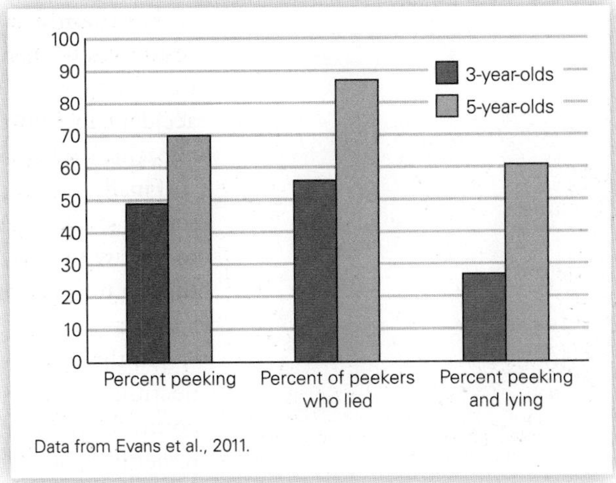

FIGURE 5.2 Better with Age? Could an obedient and honest 3-year-old become a disobedient and lying 5-year- old? Apparently yes, as the proportion of peekers and liars in this study more than doubled over those two years. Does maturation make children more able to think for themselves or less trustworthy?

The rest lied. Skill at lying increased with age. The 3-year-olds typically told hopeless lies (e.g., "The candies got out by themselves"); the 4-year-olds told unlikely lies (e.g., "Other children came in and knocked over the cup"). Some of the 5-year-olds, however, told plausible lies (e.g., "My elbow knocked over the cup accidentally").

How does this relate to Piaget and Vygotsky? First, maturation is evident, as Piaget would expect. The 3-year-olds were not yet logical, but some of the 5-year-olds were. In other research with this group, those who told better lies showed other signs of brain maturation as Piaget would expect. (Stage theories, such as Piaget's, predict that all aspects of thinking advance together, so a child who could tell plausible lies would be expected to be better at theory of mind.)

Second, theory of mind depends not only on maturation but also on social experience, as Vygotsky would contend. Children who are more likely to tell the truth have less experience with being punished for lying (Mojdehi et al., 2020; Talwar et al., 2017).

Another example is with siblings (Hou et al., 2020; McAlister & Peterson, 2013). One researcher who was among the first to study theory of mind quipped, "Two older siblings are worth about a year of chronological age" (Perner, 2000, p. 383). Practice in discerning another's point of view helps in teasing, trickery, and cooperation.

Especially for Social Scientists Can you think of any connection between Piaget's theory of preoperational thought and 3-year-olds' errors in this theory-of-mind task? (see response, page 171)

Executive Function

Scientists who specialize in the development of cognition now go beyond how children think (Piaget) and learn (Vygotsky). Many are interested in **executive function**, a cognitive ability that is nascent at age 2 and that continues to improve throughout life. Even more than parental SES or tested intelligence, a child's executive function predicts later academic achievement.

executive function The cognitive ability to organize and prioritize the many thoughts that arise from the various parts of the brain, allowing the person to anticipate, strategize, and plan behavior.

Executive function also protects adolescents from destructive emotional outbursts (Poon, 2018), promotes coping skills in adulthood (Nieto et al., 2019), and forestalls death in old age (Reimann et al., 2018). Thus, executive function, which "dramatically improves in early childhood" (Doebel, 2020, p. 943), is a key cognitive ability.

THE THREE ASPECTS

Executive function combines three cognitive abilities: (1) *memory*, (2) *inhibition*, and (3) *flexibility*. (These three may be called *updating*, *emotional control*, and *shifting*.) Together, these enable people to use their minds effectively (Miyake et al., 2000).

Memory in executive function is *working memory*, which is remembering what was seen a minute ago or yesterday, or what can easily be brought to mind, not for what happened years ago. Young children who are proficient in this aspect of cognition remember what they had for lunch, where they put their mittens, what they saw at the museum.

Inhibition is the second crucial cognitive skill. This is the ability to control responses, to stop and think for a moment before acting or talking. Children with this ability are able to restrain themselves from hitting or crying when someone else accidentally bumps them, and to raise their hands without blurting out an answer to a teacher's question.

Finally, *flexibility* is the ability to see things from another perspective rather than staying stuck in one idea. One example from early childhood is when children want to play with a toy that another child has. Executive function enables the child with the toy to share, and it allows the onlookers to switch to another activity or wait for a turn.

All three relate to brain development, as described earlier in this chapter. Connections between one region of the brain and another allows better memory, and controlling impulsivity and perseverance allows inhibition and flexibility. As you remember, brain maturation is needed for all three: Executive function is woefully absent at age 2, and then begins to build during early childhood.

The result, as a leading expert explains, is that young children gain "core skills critical for cognitive, social, and psychological development" that allow "playing with ideas, giving a considered response rather than an impulsive one, and being able to change course or perspectives as needed, resist temptations, and stay focused" (Diamond, 2016).

Developmentalists have many creative ways to measure executive function in young children. To measure memory, for instance, 3- to 5-year-olds are shown a series of barnyard animals and asked to remember them in order. For inhibition, they are asked to push a button when they see a fish but not a shark. For flexibility, they are asked to alternate stamping on a picture of a dog and one of a bone (both are presented together, again and again). Scores on all of these improve with age during early childhood (Espy, 2016).

Advances in executive functioning can occur during early childhood, if the curriculum of a preschool encourages it. This can benefit all children, including those with emotional problems from their family life (Sasser et al., 2017; Zelazo, 2020).

INSIDE THE BRAIN

The Role of Experience

Why do executive control, concrete operational thought, social interaction, and even lying improve with age? There are many factors, of course, but developmentalists increasingly recognize the crucial maturation of the prefrontal cortex. With modern neuroscience, this can be traced quite precisely: A notable advance in all of these abilities occurs between ages 4 and 5, probably because the prefrontal cortex matures markedly at this point (Devine & Hughes, 2014).

Children who are slow in language development are also slow in theory of mind, a finding that makes developmentalists suggest that underlying deficits—genetic or neurological—may be crucial for both. Remember the plasticity of the brain: The early years may be particularly important for neurological control.

In studies of adults as well, many brain regions are involved in theory of mind and much depends on past history and context (Preckel et al., 2018). Developmentalists suggest that when a young child is slow in language learning, in addition to targeted work on vocabulary, articulation, and so on, therapists and teachers need to advance executive function (Nilsson & de López, 2016).

Social interactions with other children promote brain development, advancing both theory of mind and executive function, just as Vygotsky would have predicted. Detailed studies find that theory of mind activates several brain regions (Koster-Hale & Saxe, 2013).

This makes sense, as all aspects of executive function interact, and are not likely to reside in just one neurological region. Brain research finds that, although each cognitive

ability arises from a distinct part of the brain, experience during childhood advances neurological coordination.

Remember plasticity: Experience strengthens neuronal connections. This is true not only within each neuron and the dendrites reaching another neuron, but also in regions of the brain. Thus, while theory of mind promotes empathy in one brain region, and while each type of memory arises from a particular part of the brain, the prefrontal cortex is able to coordinate all the aspects of executive function (Feola et al., 2020; Wade et al., 2018).

That is why a correlation is found between theory of mind and executive function. As a child advances in one, that child also advances in the other. Repeated coordination in the brain allows the child, for instance, to comfort a sad friend in exactly the way that sad friend is best comforted.

what have you learned?

1. How does preoperational thought differ from sensorimotor intelligence and from concrete operational thought?
2. What barriers to logic are evident in preoperational children?
3. According to Vygotsky, what should parents and other caregivers do to encourage children's learning?
4. How does scaffolding relate to a child's zone of proximal development?
5. How can adults increase STEM education?
6. How does the development of theory of mind relate to Piaget and Vygotsky?
7. What are the three aspects of executive function?
8. What is the relationship between executive function and learning in school?

Language Learning

The four years of early childhood are the most explosive, impressive, and astonishing period of language learning of the entire life span. Two-year-olds use short, telegraphic sentences ("Want cookie," "Where Daddy go?"), omitting adjectives, adverbs, and articles. By contrast, 6-year-olds seem to be able to say almost anything (see At About This Time), using every part of speech, with vocabulary 20 or 30 times as large as the toddler. Some preschoolers are fluent in two or three languages, a contrast to adults who struggle for years to learn a new language.

The Sensitive Time

Brain maturation, myelination, scaffolding, and overimitation make early childhood ideal for this accomplishment. As Chapter 1 explained, scientists once thought that early childhood was a *critical period* for language learning—the *only* time when a first language could be mastered. Not so. If a person knows one language well, that can be a scaffold for learning a second language, even in adulthood (Mayberry & Kluender, 2018).

However, language learning is more difficult after age 10 or so. Early childhood is a *sensitive period* for mastering vocabulary, grammar, and pronunciation. Young children are called "language sponges"; they soak up every verbal drop they encounter, although that is obviously an exaggeration (Enever & Lindgren, 2017).

One of the valuable (and sometimes frustrating) traits of young children is that they may talk nonstop to adults, to each other, to themselves, to their toys—unfazed

VIDEO ACTIVITY: Language Acquisition in Young Children presents a new sign language created by deaf Nicaraguan children and provides insights into how language evolves.

At About This Time: Language in Early Childhood

Approximate Age	Characteristic or Achievement in First Language
2 years	Vocabulary: 100–2,000 words Sentence length: 2–6 words Grammar: Plurals, pronouns, many nouns, verbs, adjectives Questions: Many "What's that?" questions
3 years	Vocabulary: 1,000–5,000 words Sentence length: 3–8 words Grammar: Conjunctions, adverbs, articles Questions: Many "Why?" questions
4 years	Vocabulary: 3,000–10,000 words Sentence length: 5–20 words Grammar: Dependent clauses, tags at sentence end (". . . didn't I?" ". . . won't you?") Questions: Peak of "Why?" questions; many "How?" and "When?" questions
6 years and up	Vocabulary: 5,000–30,000 words Sentence length: Some seem unending (". . . and . . . who . . . and . . . that . . . and . . .") Grammar: Complex, depending on what the child has heard, with some children correctly using the passive voice ("Man bitten by dog") and subjunctive ("If I were . . .") Questions: Some about social differences (male–female, old–young, rich–poor) and many other issues

by misuse, mispronunciation, ignorance, stuttering, and so on (Marazita & Merriman, 2010). Language comes easily, partly because preoperational children are not self-critical. Egocentrism has advantages; this is one of them.

The Vocabulary Explosion

The average child knows about 500 words at age 2 and more than 10,000 at age 6 (Herschensohn, 2007). That's more than six new words a day.

As with many averages, the range is vast: The number of root words (e.g., *run*, not *running* or *runner*, is a root word) that 5-year-olds know ranges from 2,000 to 6,000 (Biemiller, 2009). That vast range of vocabulary size occurs because counting a child's words is difficult, although building vocabulary is crucial (Treffers-Daller & Milton, 2013).

To understand why vocabulary is difficult to measure, consider the following: Children listened to a story about a raccoon that saw its reflection in the water. The children were asked what *reflection* means. Five of the answers:

1. "It means that your reflection is yourself. It means that there is another person that looks just like you."
2. "Means if you see yourself in stuff and you see your reflection."
3. "Is like when you look in something, like water, you can see yourself."
4. "It mean your face go in the water."
5. "That means if you the same skin as him, you blend in."

[*Hoffman et al., 2014, pp. 471–472*]

Which of the five children knew *reflection*? None? All? Two, three, or four?

In another example, a story included "a chill ran down his spine." Children were asked what *chill* meant. One answer: "When you want to lay down and watch TV—and eat nachos" (Hoffman et al., 2014, p. 473). That child got no credit for "chill"; is that fair?

FAST-MAPPING

Children develop interconnected categories for words, a kind of grid or mental map that aids speedy vocabulary acquisition. Learning a word after one exposure is called **fast-mapping** (Woodward & Markman, 1998), because, rather than figuring out the exact definition after hearing a word used in several contexts, children hear a word once and quickly stick it into a category in their mental language grid.

fast-mapping
The speedy and sometimes imprecise way in which children learn new words by tentatively placing them in mental categories according to their perceived meaning.

Picture books offer many opportunities to advance vocabulary through scaffolding and fast-mapping. A mentor might encourage the next steps in the child's zone of proximal development, such as that tigers have stripes and leopards spots, or, for an older child, that calico cats are almost always female and that lions with manes are always male.

This process explains children's learning of colors. Generally, 2-year-olds fast-map color names (K. Wagner et al., 2013). For instance, "blue" is used for some greens or grays.

This mistake does not mean that children cannot see the hues. Instead, they apply words they know to broad categories and have not yet learned the boundaries that adults use, or specifics such as chartreuse, turquoise, olive, navy, slate grey. As one team of scientists explains, adults' color words are the result of slow-mapping (K. Wagner et al., 2013), not what young children do.

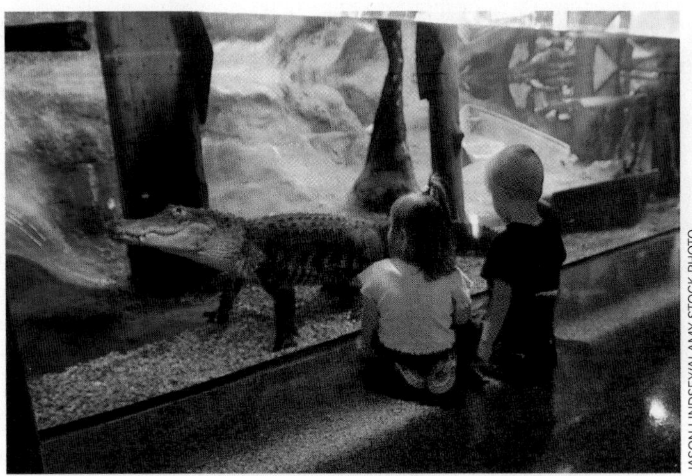

JASON LINDSEY/ALAMY STOCK PHOTO

What Is It? These two children at the Mississippi River Museum in Iowa might call this a crocodile, but really it is an alligator. Fast-mapping allows that mistake, and egocentrism might make them angry if someone tells them they chose the wrong name.

WORDS AND THE LIMITS OF LOGIC

Closely related to fast-mapping is a phenomenon called *logical extension*: After learning a word, children use it to describe other objects in the same category.

One child told her father that she had seen some "Dalmatian cows" on a school trip to a farm. Instead of telling her there are no such cows, he remembered the Dalmatian dog she had petted the weekend before. He realized that she saw Holstein cows, not Jersey ones.

Bilingual children who don't know a particular word in the language they are speaking often insert a word from the other language, *code-switching* in the middle of a sentence. That mid-sentence switch may be considered wrong, but it is actually evidence of the child's drive to communicate. By age 5, children realize who understands which language, and they avoid substitutions when speaking to a monolingual person. That illustrates theory of mind.

Some words are particularly difficult for every child, such as, in English, *who/whom, have been/had been, here/there, yesterday/tomorrow*. More than one child has awakened on Christmas morning and asked, "Is it tomorrow yet?" A child told to "stay there" or "come here" may not follow instructions because the terms are confusing. It might be better to say, "Stay there on that bench," or "Come here to hold my hand."

All languages make verbal distinctions that are difficult to grasp; children everywhere learn those distinctions. Abstractions are particularly difficult for preoperational children; actions are easier to understand. A hole is to dig; love is hugging; hearts beat.

CHAPTER APP 5

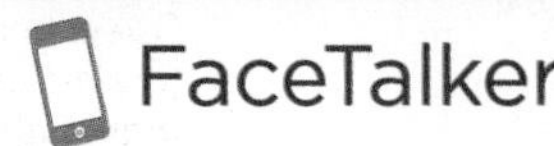

iOS:
https://tinyurl.com/y5xycx6p

RELEVANT TOPIC:
Language learning in early childhood

FaceTalker is a fun way for teachers to demonstrate the sounds animals make, introduce literature or poetry, and enliven lessons on basic arithmetic, ancient Egypt, music, art, and more.

Acquiring Grammar

Remember from Chapter 3 that *grammar* includes structures, techniques, and rules that communicate meaning. Grammar is essential in speech, reading, and writing. A large vocabulary is useless unless a person knows how to put words together. Each language has particular grammar rules, some of which make no logical sense. No wonder toddlers' first sentences contain only one word.

Children apply rules of grammar as soon as they figure them out, using their own theories about how language works (Meltzoff & Gopnik, 2013). For example, English-speaking children learn to add an *s* to form the plural: Two-years-olds follow that rule, asking for cookies or blocks.

They add an *s* to make the plural of words they have never heard before, even nonsense words. If preschoolers are shown a drawing of an abstract shape, told it is called a *wug*, and then shown two of these shapes, they say there are two *wugs* (Berko, 1958).

Children may apply grammar rules when they should not. This error is called **overregularization**. By age 4, many children overregularize that final *s*, talking about *foots, tooths*, and *mouses*. This signifies knowledge, not lack of it: Many children first say words correctly (*feet, teeth, mice*), repeating what they have heard. When

overregularization
The application of rules of grammar even when exceptions occur, making the language seem more "regular" than it actually is.

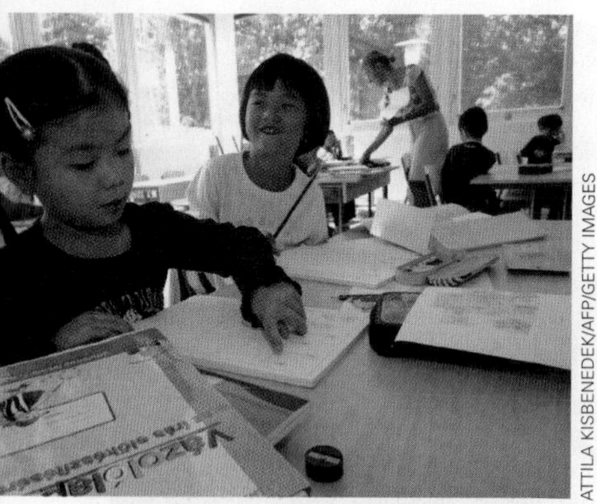

ATTILA KISBENEDEK/AFP/GETTY IMAGES

Bilingual Learners These are Chinese children learning a second language. Could this be in the United States? No, this is a class in the first Chinese-Hungarian school in Budapest. There are three clues: the spacious classroom, the letters on the book, and the large windows and many trees outside.

pragmatics
The practical use of language that includes the ability to adjust language communication according to audience and context.

they learn grammar, they overregularize, following the rules as they know them (Ramscar & Dye, 2011). The child who says "I goed to the store" needs to hear "Oh, you went to the store?," not criticism.

More difficult to learn is an aspect of language called **pragmatics**—knowing which words, tones, and grammatical forms to use with whom (Siegal & Surian, 2012). In some languages, words differ when talking to someone older, or not a close friend. In some cultures, there is a distinct term for referring to maternal grandparents and another to paternal ones.

English does not make those distinctions, but young children nonetheless learn pragmatics, changing their vocabulary and tone depending on the context and audience. For instance, 4-year-olds might pretend to be a doctor, a teacher, or a parent. Each role requires different speech.

There is much they still must learn about proper use of language. Young children may blurt out "Why is that lady so fat?" or "Grandpa's breath smells." The pragmatics of polite speech require more social understanding than many young children possess.

Learning Two Languages

Language-minority people (those who speak a language that is not their nation's dominant one) suffer if they are not fluent in the majority language. In the United States, non–English speakers are impaired in school achievement, self-esteem, and employment (Han, 2012; Miranda & Zhu, 2013; O'Neal, 2018). That is a correlation, not a reason for blame.

Some of the problem is prejudice from English speakers, who think difference means deficit, but some is directly connected to language. Fluency in English erases some liabilities; fluency in another language then becomes an asset.

Early childhood is the best time to learn a second language, for neurological reasons as well as practical ones (Klein et al., 2014). If a child learns two languages, that activates the brain lifelong, because executive function is required to inhibit one language in order to speak the other one (Cargnelutti et al., 2019). Indeed, the bilingual brain may even provide some resistance to Alzheimer's disease in old age (Costa & Sebastián-Gallés, 2014).

LANGUAGE LOSS AND GAINS

Language-minority parents want their children to master the majority language, but they fear a *language shift*, when a child becomes fluent in the majority language and loses their heritage language. Some language-minority children in Mexico shift to Spanish; some children of Canada's First Nations shift to French; some children in the United States shift to English. In China, some children shift from Mandarin, Cantonese, or other Chinese dialect, troubling their parents.

To prevent this, adults need to remember that young children are preoperational: They center on the immediate status of their language (not on future usefulness or past glory), on appearance more than substance.

Since language is integral to culture, if a child is to become fluently bilingual, everyone who speaks with the child should respect both cultures, in songs, books, and daily conversation. Children learn from listening and talking, so they need to hear twice as much talk to become fluent in two languages.

The same practices make a child fluently trilingual, as some 5-year-olds are. Young children who are immersed in three languages may speak all three with no accent—except the accent of their mother, father, and friends. This was evident in one 6-year-old in the United States who spoke Korean and Farsi with his two parents and English at school, each language with whomever understood it, translating and code-switching as needed (Choi, 2019).

◆◆ Especially for Immigrant Parents
You want your children to be fluent in the language of your family's new country, even though you do not speak that language well. Should you speak to your children in your native tongue or in the new language? (see response, page 171)

Sadly, most young children who are bilingual or trilingual are deficient in both, or all three, languages. Crucial is exposure "to both languages in ways that do not diminish the amount of exposure to each" (Hoff, 2018, p. 84).

LISTENING, TALKING, AND READING

Because understanding the printed word is crucial in the twenty-first century, a meta-analysis of about 300 studies analyzed which activities in early childhood aided reading later on. Both vocabulary and phonics (precise awareness of spoken sounds) predicted literacy (Shanahan & Lonigan, 2010). Five specific strategies and experiences were particularly effective for children of all income levels, languages, and ethnicities.

VIDEO: Beyond the 30 Million Word Gap explores how exposure to language may influence brain function in children.

1. *Code-focused teaching.* In order for children to read, they must "break the code" from spoken to written words. One step is to connect letters and sounds (e.g., "*A*, alligators all around" or "*B* is for baby").
2. *Book-reading.* Vocabulary and print-awareness develop when adults read to children.
3. *Parent education.* When parents know how to encourage cognition (listening and talking), children become better readers. Adult vocabulary expands children's vocabulary.
4. *Language enhancement.* Within each child's zone of proximal development, adults help children expand vocabulary. That requires mentors who know each child's zone and individualize conversation.
5. *Early-education programs.* Children learn from teachers, songs, excursions, and other children. (We discuss variations of early education next, but every study finds that preschools advance language acquisition.)

what have you learned?

1. What is the evidence that early childhood is a sensitive time for learning language?
2. How does fast-mapping aid the language explosion?
3. How can overregularization signify a cognitive advance?
4. When should children learn grammar?
5. What aspects of language seem difficult for young children?
6. Why is early childhood the best time to learn a second (or third) language?
7. What are three ways that adults can encourage language development?

Early-Childhood Schooling

Today, virtually every nation provides some early-childhood education, sometimes financed by the government, sometimes private, sometimes for a privileged few, and sometimes for every child. In some nations, as much public money is invested in early education as in primary or secondary school. In other nations, no money at all is allocated for education before age 6 (Blossfeld et al., 2017).

Among developed nations, the United States invests relatively little money, and educates comparatively few children. In 2018 in the United States, 44 percent of 4-year-olds and 16 percent of 3-year-olds were in publicly funded preschools (Friedman-Krauss et al., 2019).

By contrast, in Northern Europe, more than 95 percent of all 3- to 5-year-olds are enrolled in government-funded schools. In some other places (mostly Africa and South Asia), no government funds support early education. The reasons for the international variations are historical, economic, and political, not developmental. The evidence reviewed in the previous pages is not disputed: Young children are amazingly capable and eager to learn.

Homes and Schools

The theories explained in this chapter do not translate directly into specific practices in early education, so no program can legitimately claim to follow Piaget or Vygotsky exactly (Hatch, 2012).

Unfortunately, quality is notoriously difficult to judge (Votruba-Drzal & Dearing, 2017; Elicker & Ruprecht, 2019). "[B]ecause quality is hard for parents to observe, competition seems to be dominated by price" (Gambaro et al., 2014, p. 22). The easiest way to reduce costs is to hire fewer teachers. That reduces individualized learning. Without major support from other sources, low cost may be low quality.

The converse is not true: High cost does not mean high quality. As you have learned, children are active learners. They need social interaction with other children and with adults who guide them. However, one aspect—child–teacher interaction—correlates with learning. A bad sign is a teacher who sits and watches; effective teachers talk, laugh, guide, and play with happy, talkative children.

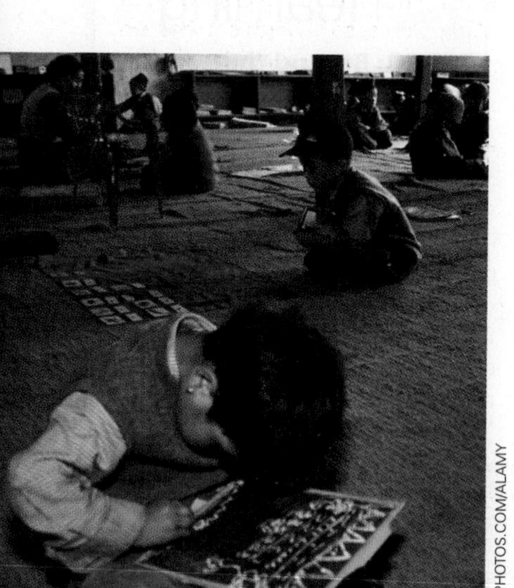

Tibet, China, India, and . . . Italy? Over the past half-century, as China increased its control of Tibet, thousands of refugees fled to northern India. Tibet traditionally had no preschools, but young children adapt quickly, as in this preschool program in Ladakh, India. This Tibetan boy is working a classic Montessori board.

Quality cannot be judged by the name of a program or by its sponsorship. Educational institutions for 3- to 5-year-olds are called preschools, nursery schools, day-care centers, pre-primary programs, pre-K classes, and kindergartens. Sponsors can be public (federal, state, or city), private, religious, or corporate.

In order to sort through this variety, we review some distinctions among types of programs. One broad distinction concerns the program goals. Is the goal to encourage each child's creative individuality (*child-centered*) or to prepare the child for formal education (*teacher-directed*), or is it to prepare low-SES children for first grade (*intervention*)?

Child-Centered Programs

Many programs are called *child-centered*, or *developmental*, because they stress each child's development and growth. They emphasize "teaching the whole child," which means individualized social and emotional learning, not academics (Hyson & Douglass, 2019). Teachers in such programs believe children need to follow their own interests rather than adult directions.

For example, they agree that "children should be allowed to select many of their own activities from a variety of learning areas that the teacher has prepared" (Lara-Cinisomo et al., 2011). The physical space and the materials (such as dress-up clothes, art supplies, puzzles, blocks, and other toys) are arranged to allow exploration.

Most child-centered programs encourage artistic expression, including music and drama (Bassok et al., 2016). Some educators believe that young children see the world more imaginatively than older people do. According to advocates of child-centered programs, this peak of creative vision should be encouraged; children need to tell stories, draw pictures, dance, and make music.

Child-centered programs are often influenced by Piaget, who emphasized that each child discovers new ideas if given a chance, or by Vygotsky, who thought that children learn from playing, especially with other children. Neither wanted children to be rushed to adulthood.

MONTESSORI SCHOOLS

One type of child-centered school began in 1907, when Maria Montessori opened a nursery school in a poor neighborhood in Rome, Italy (Standing, 1998). She believed that children needed structured, individualized projects to give them a sense of accomplishment. Her students completed puzzles, used sponges and water to clean tables, traced shapes, and so on.

Contemporary **Montessori schools** still emphasize individual pride and achievement, presenting many literacy-related tasks (e.g., outlining letters and looking at books) to young children. Specific materials differ from those that Maria Montessori developed, but the underlying philosophy is the same. Children seek out learning tasks; they do not sit quietly in groups while a teacher instructs them. That makes Montessori programs child-centered (Lillard, 2013).

Montessori schools encourage children to help other children (Lillard & Taggart, 2019). That is something Vygotsky valued as well. Children from Montessori schools seem to enjoy learning together throughout childhood, just as Vygotsky would expect.

Montessori schools
Schools that offer early-childhood education based on the philosophy of Maria Montessori, which emphasizes careful work and tasks that each young child can do.

Reggio Emilia
A program of early-childhood education that originated in the town of Reggio Emilia, Italy, and that encourages each child's creativity in a carefully designed setting.

Waldorf
An early-childhood education program than emphasizes creativity, social understanding, and emotional growth. It originated in Germany with Rudolf Steiner, and now is used in thousands of schools throughout the world.

REGGIO EMILIA

Another form of early-childhood education is **Reggio Emilia**, named after the town in Italy where it began. In Reggio Emilia, children are encouraged to master skills that are not usually taught in North American schools until age 7 or so, such as writing. Although many educators admire the Reggio philosophy and practice, it is expensive to duplicate in other nations—there are few dedicated Reggio Emilia schools in the United States.

Reggio schools do not provide large-group instruction, with lessons in, say, forming letters or cutting paper. Instead, hands-on activities are chosen by individual children. Drawing, cooking, and gardening are stressed. This program begins with the idea that democracy and freedom of personal expression belong in the classroom (McNally & Slutsky, 2017).

Measurement of achievement, such as standardized testing to see whether children recognize the 26 letters of the alphabet, is antithetical to the Reggio conviction that each child should explore and learn in their own way. Learning is documented via scrapbooks, photos, and daily notes, not to measure progress but to make each child and parent proud of accomplishments. (This also enhances memory, a crucial part of executive function.)

ELIZABETH FLORES KRT/NEWSCOM

Child-Centered Pride How could Rachel Koepke, a 3-year-old from a Wisconsin town called Pleasant Prairie, seem so pleased that her hands (and cuffs) are blue? The answer arises from northern Italy – Rachel attended a Reggio Emilia preschool that encourages creative expression.

WALDORF

A third type of child-centered program is called **Waldorf**, first developed by Rudolf Steiner in Germany in 1919. The emphasis again is on creativity and individuality—with no homework, no tests, no worksheets. As much as possible, children play outdoors; appreciation of nature is basic to Waldorf education. Children of various ages learn together, because older children serve as mentors for younger ones, and the curriculum follows the interests of the child, not the age of the child.

There is a set schedule—usually circle time in the beginning and certain activities on certain days (always baking on Tuesdays, for instance)—but children are not expected to master specific knowledge at certain ages. All child-centered schools emphasize creativity; in Waldorf schools, imagination is particularly prized (Kirkham & Kidd, 2017).

Teacher-Directed Programs

Teacher-directed preschools stress academics, often taught by one adult to the entire group. The curriculum includes learning the names of letters, numbers, shapes, and colors according to a set timetable; every child naps, snacks, and goes to the bathroom on schedule as well. Children learn to sit quietly and listen to the teacher. Praise and other reinforcements are given for good behavior, and time-outs (brief separation from activities) are imposed to punish misbehavior.

The goal of teacher-directed programs is to make all children "ready to learn" when they enter elementary school. For that reason, basic skills are stressed, including precursors to reading, writing, and arithmetic, perhaps through teachers asking questions that children answer together in unison. Behavior is also taught, as children learn to respect adults, to follow schedules, to hold hands when they go on outings, and so on.

Children practice forming letters, sounding out words, counting objects, and writing their names. If a 4-year-old learns to read, that is success. (In a child-centered program, this might arouse suspicion that there was too little time for play or socializing.)

Many teacher-directed programs were inspired by behaviorism, which emphasizes step-by-step learning and repetition, with reinforcement (praise, gold stars, prizes) for accomplishment. Another inspiration for these programs comes from information processing, which notes that children who have not learned basic vocabulary and listening skills by kindergarten often fall behind in primary school. To avoid that problem, teacher-directed programs stress the precursors for school success, as discovered in information processing.

OPPOSING PERSPECTIVES

Child-Centered Versus Teacher-Directed Preschools

Most developmentalists advocate child-centered programs. They believe that from ages 3 to 6 young children learn best when they can interact in their own way with materials and ideas (Sim & Xu, 2017). On the other hand, many parents and legislators want proof that early education will improve later school achievement.

The critics of teacher-directed education fear "trad[ing] emotional grounding and strong language skills known to support learning for assembly-line schooling that teaches children isolated factoids" (Hirsh-Pasek & Golinkoff, 2016, p. 1158).

As Penelope Leach wrote, "Goals come from the outside. . . . It is important that people see early learning as coming from inside children because that's what makes clear its interconnectedness with play, and therefore the inappropriateness of many 'learning goals'" (Leach, 2011, p. 17). Another developmentalist asks, "Why should we settle for unimaginative goals . . . like being able to identify triangles and squares, or recalling the names of colors and seasons" (Christakis, 2016).

However, children who enter kindergarten without knowing names and sounds of letters may become first-graders who cannot read (Ozernov-Palchik et al., 2017). Understanding how written symbols relate to sounds is crucial, and children are unlikely to learn literacy skills in creative play (Gellert & Elbro, 2017).

Early familiarity with numbers and shapes predicts school achievement later on. As you will soon read, federally funded programs have shifted over the past decades to be more teacher-directed, largely because national policy directives from the government have advocated that change—to the distress of many childhood educators (Walter & Lippard, 2017).

Many developmentalists argue that social skills, emotional development, and creative play are essential but difficult to measure with standardized tests (Hyson & Douglass, 2019). A truly brilliant child is characterized by all the complex skills of executive function, not the easy-to-measure skills of letter recognition (Golinkoff & Hirsh-Pasek, 2016).

However, the divide between child-centered and teacher-directed programs goes deeper than that. It is possible that the emphasis on individual exploration is contrary to the wishes and needs of families who want their children to do as they are told, listen to adults, and master the learning tools of their culture. In other words, child-centered education may be based on the narrow values of middle class, Western, European American teachers (Trawick-Smith, 2019).

Finding the right balance between formal and informal assessment, between creativity and skills, between child-centered and teacher-directed learning, is a worthy the goal. Achieving it is the challenge. (See Figure 5.3.)

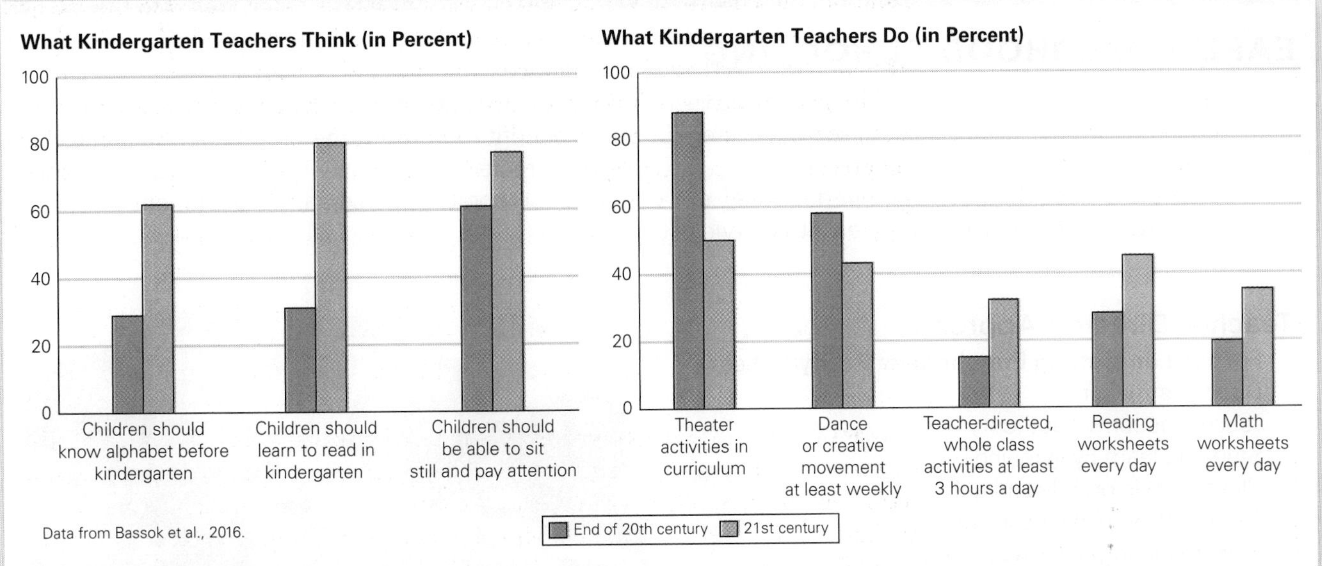

FIGURE 5.3 Less Play, More Work These data come from a large survey of more than 5,000 public-school teachers throughout the United States. In 1998 and 2010, kindergarten teachers were asked identical questions but gave different answers. Smaller, more recent surveys suggest that these trends continue, and they now involve preschool teachers. Some use worksheets for 3-year-olds.

Intervention Programs

Several programs designed for children from low-SES families were established in the United States decades ago. Some solid research on the results of these programs is now available.

HEAD START

In the early 1960s, millions of young children in the United States were thought to need a "head start" on their formal education because they entered first grade lagging behind other children. Consequently, since 1965, the federal government has funded a massive program for 4-year-olds called **Head Start**.

Head Start
A federally funded early-childhood intervention program for low-income children of preschool age.

The goals for Head Start have changed over the decades, from lifting families out of poverty to promoting literacy, from providing dental care and immunizations to teaching Standard English, from focusing on 4-year-olds to including 2- and 3-year-olds.

Nonetheless, the data on success of the program have meant that the program has continued for 55 years. In 2018, more than 9 billion dollars in federal funds were allocated to Head Start, which enrolled almost 1 million children.

The United States has about 8 million 3- and 4-year-olds, so only about 12 percent of U.S. children that age attend Head Start. Many of the other children are in private programs. According to official U.S. statistics in *The Condition of Education 2018* report, about twice as many 3- to 5-year-olds from high-SES families were in preschools compared to children from low-SES families. This is ironic, because early education is most likely to benefit children who are least likely to get it (Cebolla-Boado et al., 2017).

Whether or not a child receives government-funded preschool largely depends on where that child lives. Some U.S. states provide early education for all 4-year-olds (Oklahoma, Florida, and Vermont), some provide none (Idaho, Indiana, Utah, South Dakota, and Wyoming), and only three (Alabama, Michigan, and Rhode Island) reach 10 quality goals set by professionals (Friedman-Krauss et al., 2019).

EARLY-CHILDHOOD SCHOOLING

Preschool can be an academic and social benefit to children. Around the world, increasing numbers of children are enrolled in early-childhood education.

Programs are described as "teacher-directed" or "child-centered," but in reality, most teachers' styles reflect a combination of both approaches. Some students benefit more from the order and structure of a teacher-directed classroom, while others work better in a more collaborative and creative environment.

Teacher-Directed Approach

Focused on Getting Preschoolers Ready to Learn

Direct instruction
Teacher as formal authority
Students learn by listening
Classroom is orderly and quiet
Teacher fully manages lessons
Rewards individual achievement
Encourages academics
Students learn from teacher

WORTH PUBLISHERS

Child-Centered Approach

Focused on Individual Development and Growth

Teacher as facilitator
Teacher as delegator
Students learn actively
Classroom is designed for collaborative work
Students influence content
Rewards collaboration among students
Encourages artistic expression
Students learn from each other

Different Students, Different Teachers

There is clearly no "one right way" to teach children. Each approach has potential benefits and pitfalls. A classroom full of creative, self-motivated students can thrive when a gifted teacher acts as a competent facilitator. But students who are distracted or annoyed by noise, or who are shy or intimidated by other children, can blossom under an engaging and encouraging teacher in a more traditional environment.

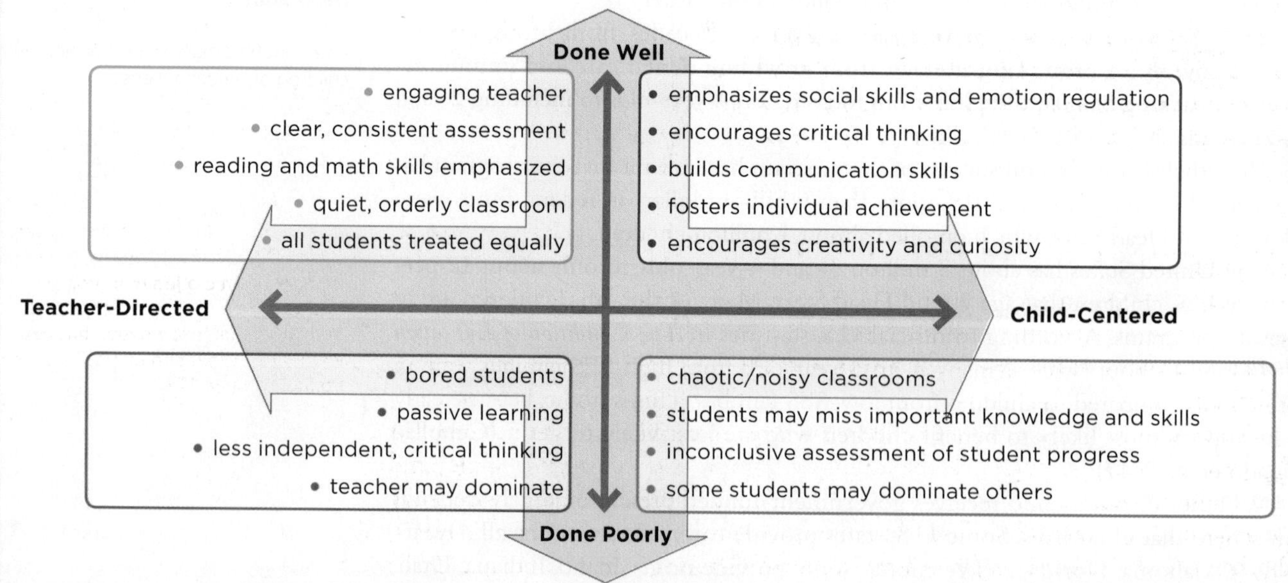

Those three are quite selective in who is allowed to enroll, but the children who do attend are well educated.

As you read in Opposing Perspectives, although most Head Start programs were child-centered initially, they have become increasingly teacher-directed as waves of legislators have approved and shaped them. In 2016, new requirements were put in place for Head Start, mandating that programs be open at least six hours a day and 180 days a year (initially, most programs were half-day) and prioritizing children who are homeless, or are disabled, or are learning English.

© OCTAVIO JONES/ZUMA PRESS/CORBIS

If You're Happy and You Know It Gabby Osborne (pink shirt) has her own way of showing happiness, not the hand-clapping that Lizalia Garcia tries to teach. The curriculum of this Head Start class in Florida includes learning about emotions, contrary to the wishes of some legislators, who want proof of academics.

Such changes were made partly because federal research found that Head Start is most beneficial for children in poverty, or in rural areas, or with disabilities (U.S. Department of Health and Human Services, 2010). Those children are least likely to find other sources of early education (Crosnoe et al., 2016).

The children *least* likely to be in such programs are Spanish-speaking, or from families with income slightly above poverty-level, or whose mothers are not employed. These are precisely the children for whom early education may be especially helpful, a conclusion found not only in Head Start but in other research as well. That makes early education an issue of educational justice (Morgan, 2019; Nxumalo & Adair, 2019).

Historical data show that most Head Start children of every background were advanced in language and social skills, but by elementary school non–Head Start children often caught up. However, there was one area in which the Head Start children maintained their superiority—vocabulary.

That finding also supports what you just learned about language development. Almost every preschool expands vocabulary. Children will fast-map those words, gaining a linguistic knowledge base that facilitates later learning.

DATA CONNECTIONS: A Look At Early-Childhood Education in the United States demonstrates changes in enrollment since the 1960s and examines some of the types of early-childhood-education programs. Achieve

Long-Term Gains from Intensive Programs

This discussion of philosophies, practices, and programs may give the impression that the research on early-childhood cognition is contradictory. That is not true. Specifics are debatable, but empirical evidence and longitudinal evaluation find that preschool education advances learning. Executive function—memory, emotional control, flexibility—is crucial for later learning, and it begins to develop before age 6.

Especially for Unemployed Early-Childhood Teachers You are offered a job in a program that has ten 3-year-olds for every adult. You know that is too many, but you want a job. What should you do? (see response, page 171)

The best longitudinal evidence comes from three intensive programs that enrolled children for years—sometimes beginning with home visits in infancy, sometimes continuing in after-school programs through first grade. One program, called *Perry* (or *High/Scope*), was spearheaded in Michigan (Schweinhart & Weikart, 1997); another, called *Abecedarian*, got its start in North Carolina (Campbell et al., 2001); a third, called *Child–Parent Centers*, began in Chicago (Reynolds, 2000). They all focused on children from low-SES families.

FRANK PORTER GRAHAM CHILD DEVELOPMENT INSTITUTE

Lifetime Achievement The baby in the framed photograph escaped the grip of poverty. The woman holding it proved that early education can transform children. She is Frances Campbell, who spearheaded the Abecedarian Project. The baby's accomplishments may be the more impressive of the two.

All three programs compared experimental groups of children with matched control groups, and all reached the same conclusion: Early education has substantial long-term benefits that become most apparent when children are in the third grade or later.

By age 10, children who had been enrolled in any one of these three programs scored higher on math and reading achievement tests than did other children from the same backgrounds, schools, and neighborhoods. They were less likely to be placed in classes for children with special needs, or to repeat a year of school, or to drop out of high school before graduation.

For all three programs, benefits continued.

- In adolescence, the children who had undergone intensive preschool education had higher aspirations, possessed a greater sense of achievement, and were less often abused.
- As young adults, they were more likely to attend college and less likely to go to jail.
- As middle-aged adults, they were more often employed, paying taxes, healthy, and not needing government subsidies (Campbell et al., 2014; Reynolds & Ou, 2011; Schweinhart et al., 2005).

All three research projects found that providing direct cognitive training, with specific instruction in various school-readiness skills, was useful. Each child's needs and talents were considered—a circumstance made possible because the child/adult ratio was low. This meant that the best of child-centered and teacher-directed education was combined, with all of the teachers working together on the same goals so that children were not confused. In all three, teachers involved parents, with strategies to enhance the home–school connection.

These programs were expensive (ranging from $7,500 to $23,000 annually per young child in 2020 dollars). From a developmental perspective, the decreased need for special education and other social services later on made early education a "wise investment" (Duncan & Magnuson, 2013, p. 128). Additional benefits to society over the child's lifetime, including increased employment and tax revenues, as well as reduced crime, are worth much more than the cost of the programs.

Many professionals try to steer away from political issues, but this one transcends partisanship. Any cuts to preschool education not only mean less child-centered learning (which is more expensive) but also less high-quality, teacher-directed learning. In most U.S. states, full-day kindergarten programs (always locally funded) are optional and sometimes unavailable.

Every child should be offered high-quality preschool education, but how should costs be paid? Should the government pay for every child, thus making education a public right like the police or fire protection, or should the government reduce taxes by requiring parents to pay all the costs? Scientists who know the research on early-childhood education are dismayed when the wishes of the adults (lower taxes) supersede the needs of the children.

Compared to a decade ago, much more is known about early cognition: 2- to 5-year-olds are capable of learning languages, concepts, math, theory of mind, and much more. What a child learns before age 6 is pivotal for later schooling and adult

life. The amazing potential of young children is also a theme of the next chapter, where we discuss other kinds of learning, such as in emotional regulation and social skills.

CAREER ALERT

The Preschool Teacher

Preschool teachers are increasingly in demand, as more and more families and communities understand how much young children can learn, and more and more mothers enter the job market. Added to that is the growing realization by public leaders that social skills and self-confidence developed in early childhood continue lifelong: A child who has good early education is likely to become an adult who is a competent and compassionate member of the community.

For developmentalists, important new insights come from neurological research, which helps preschool teachers understand what, how, and when young children learn. For example, since the auditory, visual, and motor cortexes are undergoing rapid myelination, children need to coordinate both hemispheres of brain and body by running, climbing, and balancing. But the immature motor cortex is not yet ready for writing, or tying shoelaces, or sitting quietly in one place.

Research on the developing brain finds that early childhood is the best time for learning language, so the curriculum should be language-rich—talking, listening, singing, hearing stories, making rhymes, engaging in verbal play. Young children can learn to recognize and name letters just as they learn to distinguish a baseball from a soccer ball.

Fostering control of gross motor skills may be particularly important for children who are at risk for attention-deficit/hyperactivity disorder (ADHD), the label given to active children who find it especially hard to concentrate, quietly, on one activity. Such children need to exercise their bodies, which helps their brains mature (Halperin & Healey, 2011; Hillman, 2014).

That is another reason for preschool education—children are most likely to develop their brains by playing with other children. Screen time, a common activity for children who are not in preschool, does not foster the brain regulation that children need.

Moreover, preschool teachers help children learn how to cooperate with other children, a valuable life lesson that is best learned in childhood. Thus, preschool teachers can be proud that they are nurturing compassionate, prosocial adults.

The joy and satisfaction of working with young children is crucial, because at the moment, salary and working conditions are not yet what they should be.

There is marked variation in state-by-state certification requirements and in neighborhood-by-neighborhood salary levels. However, on average, the U.S. Bureau of Labor Statistics reports that, compared to teachers overall, preschool teachers are most in demand and least well paid—the average annual salary is below $30,000 a year.

This is changing, but students should enter this field for emotional reasons, not financial ones. If you are interested in early-childhood education, you can find more details from a professional group called the National Association for the Education of Young Children (NAEYC).

what have you learned?

1. What are the long-term benefits of early-childhood education?
2. In child-centered programs, what do the teachers do?
3. Why are Montessori schools still functioning 100 years after the first such schools opened?
4. What are the advantages and disadvantages of teacher-directed preschools?
5. Who benefits most from Head Start?
6. Why do teachers, parents, professionals, and politicians disagree about early education?

SUMMARY

Growth of the Body

1. Children continue to gain weight and add height during early childhood. Motor skills develop; clumsy 2-year-olds become agile 6-year-olds who move their bodies well.

2. Many adults overfeed children, not realizing that young children are naturally quite thin. Many children eat too much of the wrong foods: They may consume too much sugar and too little fiber, resulting in obesity and poor oral health.

3. The brain continues to grow in early childhood, reaching 75 percent of its adult weight at age 2 and 90 percent by age 6. Myelination accounts for much of that weight, connecting the left and right brains, and the prefrontal cortex with the other regions. Impulsivity and perseveration decrease.

4. The two hemispheres of the brain work together, each controlling one side of the body. People are naturally left- or right-handed, as their brains dictate, with the corpus callosum connecting left and right.

Thinking During Early Childhood

5. Piaget stressed the egocentric and illogical aspects of thought during early childhood. He called this stage of thinking preoperational intelligence because young children do not yet use logical operations to think about their observations and experiences.

6. Vygotsky stressed the social aspects of childhood cognition, noting that children learn by participating in various experiences, guided by more knowledgeable adults or peers. Such guidance assists learning within the zone of proximal development, which encompasses the knowledge that children are close to understanding and the skills they can almost master.

7. Two examples of the developing cognition of young children are STEM education and theory of mind—an understanding of what others may be thinking. Culture and experiences influence these, as both Piaget and Vygotsky would agree.

8. An important part of developing cognition during early childhood is the emergence of executive function, or cognitive control, as children learn to regulate and control their sensory impulses in order to use their minds more effectively. Three components are usually included in executive function: memory, inhibition, and flexibility.

Language Learning

9. Language develops rapidly during early childhood, a sensitive period but not a critical one for language learning. Vocabulary increases dramatically, with thousands of words added between ages 2 and 6. In addition, basic grammar is mastered.

10. The child's ability to learn language is evident in fast-mapping (the quick use of new vocabulary words) and in overregularization (applying the rules of grammar even when they are not valid).

11. Many children learn to speak more than one language, gaining cognitive as well as social advantages. Early childhood is the best time to learn two languages. The benefits of bilingualism are lifelong.

Early-Childhood Schooling

12. Child-centered programs emphasize the individuality of each child and are suspicious of standardized tests. Montessori, Reggio Emilia, and Waldorf schools are examples.

13. Behaviorist principles led to many specific practices of teacher-directed programs. Children learn to listen to teachers and become ready for kindergarten. Teacher-directed programs are preferred by many parents and legislators.

14. Head Start is a U.S. federal government program primarily for low-income children. Longitudinal research finds that early-childhood education reduces the risk of later problems, such as needing special education. High-quality programs increase the likelihood that a child will become a law-abiding, gainfully employed adult.

15. Some nations provide early education for all 3- and 4-year-olds. Others do for none. In the United States this varies from state to state, but overall only about half of all 3- and 4-year-olds are in preschool.

KEY TERMS

myelin (p. 146)
corpus callosum (p. 146)
lateralization (p. 147)
preoperational intelligence (p. 148)
symbolic thought (p. 148)
animism (p. 149)
centration (p. 149)
egocentrism (p. 149)
focus on appearance (p. 149)
static reasoning (p. 149)
irreversibility (p. 149)
conservation (p. 149)
mentor (p. 152)
zone of proximal development (ZPD) (p. 152)
scaffolding (p. 152)
overimitation (p. 153)
private speech (p. 153)
social mediation (p. 153)
theory of mind (p. 154)
executive function (p. 155)
fast-mapping (p. 158)
overregularization (p. 159)
pragmatics (p. 160)
Montessori schools (p. 163)
Reggio Emilia (p. 163)
Waldorf (p. 163)
Head Start (p. 165)

APPLICATIONS

1. Keep a food diary for 24 hours, writing down what you eat, how much, when, how, and why. Then think about nutrition and eating habits in early childhood. Did your food habits originate in early childhood, in adolescence, or at some other time? Explain.

2. Go to a playground or other place where many young children play. Note the motor skills that the children demonstrate, including abilities and inabilities, and keep track of age and sex. What differences do you see among the children?

3. Replicate one of Piaget's conservation experiments. The easiest one is conservation of liquids (illustrated in Figure 5.1). Work with a child under age 5 who tells you that two identically shaped glasses contain the same amount of liquid. Then ask the child to carefully pour one glass of liquid into a taller, narrower glass. Ask the child which glass now contains more or if the glasses contain the same amount.

ESPECIALLY FOR ANSWERS

Response for Early-Childhood Teachers (from p. 146): Remember to keep food simple and familiar. Offer every child the same food, allowing refusal but no substitutes—unless for all eight. Children do not expect school and home routines to be identical; they eventually taste whatever other children enjoy.

Response for Early-Childhood Teachers (from p. 148): One solution is to remind yourself that the children's brains are not yet myelinated enough to enable them to quickly walk, talk, or even button their jackets. Maturation has a major effect, as you will observe if you can schedule excursions in September and again in November. Progress, while still slow, will be a few seconds faster.

Response for Driving Instructors (from p. 153): Use guided participation to scaffold the instruction so that your students are not overwhelmed. Be sure to provide lots of praise and days of practice. If emotion erupts, do not take it as an attack on you.

Response for Social Scientists (from p. 155): According to Piaget, preschool children focus on appearance and on static conditions (so they cannot mentally reverse a process). Furthermore, they are egocentric, believing that everyone shares their point of view. No wonder they believe that they had always known the puppy was in the blue box and that Max would know that, too.

Response for Immigrant Parents (from p. 160): Children learn by listening, so it is important to speak with them often. Depending on how comfortable you are with the new language, you might prefer to read to your children, sing to them, and converse with them primarily in your native language and find a good preschool where they will learn the new language. The worst thing you could do is to restrict speech in either tongue.

Response for Unemployed Early-Childhood Teachers (from p. 167): It would be best for you to wait for a job in a program in which children learn well, organized along the lines explained in this chapter. You would be happier, as well as learn more, in a workplace that is good for children. Realistically, though, you might feel compelled to take the job. If you do, change the child/adult ratio—find a helper, perhaps a college intern or a volunteer grandmother. But choose carefully—some adults are not helpful at all. Before you take the job, remember that children need continuity: You can't leave simply because you find something better.

OBSERVATION QUIZ ANSWERS

Answer to Observation Quiz (from p. 145): No. There are no pedals! Technically this is not a tricycle; it has four wheels. The ability to coordinate both legs follows corpus callosum development in the next few years, as explained on page 146.

Answer to Observation Quiz (from p. 152): Right-handed. Her dominant hand is engaged in something more comforting than exploring the abacus.

CHAPTER 6

EARLY CHILDHOOD
The Social World

what will you know?

- Why do 6-year-olds have fewer sudden tempers, tears, and terrors than 2-year-olds?
- When should adults stop children from chasing and grabbing each other?
- Is spanking harmful for children?
- Do maltreated children become abusive adults?

At age 4, my youngest grandson considers himself a "big kid." I can see why he thinks so. He is much taller, more verbal, and more socially aware than he was just a few years ago. He also knows how to interact with his older brother: Being a younger sibling may advance theory of mind. But he still has much to learn about the larger social world, the topic of this chapter.

When we wait for the bus, he begs his brother to play "the monster game." The older boy usually says no. As you will read, the impulse to play is strong in young children, as is some understanding of emotions.

Accordingly, the 4-year-old often cries, and the big brother stops the wailing by pretending to be a blind monster, clomping around with arms outstretched to catch the smaller boy, who laughs as he runs ahead, never caught. Should I intervene, telling one not to cry, telling the other not to reward the tears?

As he runs, the 4-year-old sometimes bumps into strangers who are also waiting for the bus. Some smile, some seem annoyed, but no one expresses anger. I would not mind if they did; I wish my grandson were wiser about other people.

One stranger asked the boy his name, which he readily gave, as well as his address.

"Don't tell strangers where you live," the man said.

My grandson repeated his address.

Young children love to play, and parents (or, in this case, grandmothers and siblings) need to keep them safe. Strangers have much to learn as well. That man thought he was protecting the boy from maltreatment. He did not know what you will learn in this chapter: The people who are most likely to abuse children already know their address.

Emotional Development

Remember that primary and secondary emotions are already evident by age 2, but much more needs to be learned. Especially important is the realization that some reactions should not be expressed (Pala & Lewis, 2020). People must learn to channel, postpone, or redirect emotions.

ALLEN BROWN/DBIMAGES/ALAMY STOCK PHOTO

Learning Emotional Regulation Like this girl in Hong Kong, all 2-year-olds burst into tears when something upsets them — a toy breaks, a pet refuses to play, or it's time to go home. Mothers who comfort young children and help them calm down are teaching them to regulate their emotions.

Controlling Emotions

Controlling the expression of feelings, called **emotional regulation**, is a lifelong endeavor, with ages 3 to 5 "of critical importance" in its development (Harrington et al., 2020).

Think of giving someone a gift. If the receiver is 3-years-old, you can immediately tell whether the child liked the present, because their emotions are visible (Galak et al., 2016). If the receiver is an adult, you may not be sure, because adults can disguise disappointment. Early childhood is when that learning begins.

Although some emotions still burst forth at age 6 (as they can in adulthood), by the time children enter first grade, most of them can feel angry, frightened, sad, or anxious, without the explosive outbursts of temper, or terror, or tears of 2-year-olds. Some emotions are easier to control for some children than for others, but even temperamentally angry or fearful children learn to regulate their emotions (Moran et al., 2013; Suurland et al., 2016; Tan et al., 2013).

Note that the goal is regulation, not removal. Emotionally healthy people acknowledge other people's emotions as well as their own, expressing them appropriately. Indeed, decades of research in *emotional intelligence* suggests that intrapersonal and interpersonal understanding are among the essential aspects of intelligence first described by Howard Gardner (1983) (explained in Chapter 7). Those aspects of intelligence begin during early childhood.

By adulthood, one aspect of emotional regulation, specifically postponement of gratification, is a sign of maturity: Students study now for an exam next week, lovers postpone marriage, adults save for retirement.

Of course, no one of any age is always able to resist impulses. But curbing the urge for immediate gratification is a useful trait that begins in early childhood, guided by family and culture (see A View from Science).

VIDEO ACTIVITY: Can Young Children Delay Gratification? illustrates how most young children are unable to overcome temptation even when promised an award.

A VIEW FROM SCIENCE

Waiting for the Marshmallow

You probably have heard of the famous marshmallow test (Mischel et al., 1972; Mischel, 2014). Young children sat in front of one marshmallow and were told they could eat it immediately or wait — sometimes as long as 15 minutes — while the researcher left the room. They were promised another marshmallow if they didn't eat the first one before the adult returned.

Those who waited used various tactics — they looked away, closed their eyes, or sang to themselves. Decades later, the researchers contacted the children. Those who delayed gobbling up one marshmallow in order to get two became more successful as teenagers, young adults, and even middle-aged adults — doing well in college, for instance, and having happy marriages.

This experiment has been replicated many times. The average child waits about six minutes. Relatively few 4-year-olds can sit in front of a marshmallow for 15 minutes without eating it, but those who wait are likely to become more successful years later (Shoda et al., 1990).

In a replication, children of the Nso people in Cameroon waited longer than the California children in Mischel's original experiment (Lamm et al., 2018). Another replication found that family background made a difference, with children from higher-SES families waiting longer (T. Watts et al., 2018).

Does national and family culture directly affect willingness to wait? Or are some African groups or high-SES families genetically more likely to be patient, and thus the relationship between them and children's waiting is a correlation but not a cause? An experiment set out to answer this question (Kidd et al., 2013).

Remember from Chapter 1 that to discover cause, scientists usually compare two groups. Thus, children were given paper to draw on and a sealed jar containing a few used crayons, but they were told to wait a moment, because the examiner was getting better crayons and art supplies.

Each of them waited alone, and after two minutes, the examiner returned to tell half of them, "I'm sorry, but I made a mistake. We don't have any other art supplies after all. But why don't you just use these instead?" He then opened the jar. The other half got new, multi-colored crayons and other supplies.

The deprived group experienced another disappointment. They were given one small sticker and promised better stickers, but the examiner returned to say there were no more stickers. The advantaged group were given several large, desirable stickers.

Then these children were given the marshmallow test, offering one marshmallow immediately or two after a 15-minute wait. The dependent variable was how long the children waited. Did the children's prior experience matter?

Children with a reliable adult waited, on average, 12 minutes, with 64 percent waiting the full 15 minutes. Those whose adult was unreliable waited an average of three minutes. Only 7 percent waited 15 minutes (Kidd et al., 2013).

The researchers' conclusion was that children make rational decisions based on their experience. If their parents and cultures teach patience and keep their promises, children learn to control impulses, becoming adults who plan and invest. Otherwise, children and adults wisely gobble up whatever they can grab.

THINK CRITICALLY: Does money "burn a hole in your pocket," so you spend it when you get it? Why?

Initiative Versus Guilt

emotional regulation
The ability to control when and how emotions are expressed.

initiative versus guilt
Erikson's third psychosocial crisis, in which young children undertake new skills and activities and feel guilty when they do not succeed at them.

Erikson's third developmental stage is **initiative versus guilt**. *Initiative* includes saying something new, beginning a project, expressing an idea. Depending on what happens next, children feel proud or guilty. Gradually, they learn to rein in boundless pride and avoid crushing guilt.

Pride is typical in early childhood. As one team expressed it:

> Compared to older children and adults, young children are the optimists of the world, believing they have greater physical abilities, better memories, are more skilled at imitating models, are smarter, know more about how things work, and rate themselves as stronger, tougher, and of higher social standing than is actually the case.
>
> *[Bjorklund & Ellis, 2014, p. 244]*

That *protective optimism* helps young children try new things. In that way, they learn. As Erikson predicted, an optimistic self-concept protects young children from guilt and shame and encourages initiative.

Young children often brag about what they have done. As long as the boast is not a lie, other young children like them for it. At about age 7, a developmental shift has built up in the brain (see Inside the Brain), and children begin to appreciate modesty more than boasting (Lockhart et al., 2018). By then, they have learned some emotional regulation; they can finally keep quiet about how wonderful they are.

CHAPTER APP 6

Peek-a-Zoo

IOS:
https://tinyurl.com/wdhttw6

RELEVANT TOPIC:
Emotional development in early childhood

This simple app prompts preschoolers to identify behaviors or emotions exhibited by different animals ("Who is surprised?"), helping them to learn social cues.

Motivation

Motivation is the impulse that propels someone to act. It comes either from a person's own desires or from the social context.

INSIDE THE BRAIN

Emotional Connections

The new initiative and then industry that Erikson described results from myelination in the limbic system, growth of the prefrontal cortex, and a longer attention span—all indicative of neurological maturation. Emotional regulation and cognitive maturation develop together, each advancing the other (Bridgett et al., 2015; Frydenberg, 2017).

The prefrontal cortex allows emotional regulation. For maturation of that part of the brain to continue during childhood, sufficient sleep is needed (McRae & Gross, 2020). Overtired children have emotional meltdowns, with overwhelming anger and sadness.

This is true day by day: A 3-year-old without a nap may be emotionally untethered. It also is true over the long term: 6-year-olds who rarely sleep long and deeply may be unable to regulate their emotions.

Another influence on neuronal connections is the emotions of other people in the child's life. The process is reciprocal and dynamic: Anger begets anger, which leads to more anger; joy begets joy, and so on. Brain development, specifically growth of the amygdala and hippocampus (which regulate emotions), is reduced if children are repeatedly stressed (as in four or more *adverse childhood experiences*, described at the end of this chapter) (Luby et al., 2019).

Evidence finds that, moment by moment, reciprocity between the emotions of parents and their children occurs in brains as well as in voices and faces. For instance, researchers studied brain waves in mothers and children as they did a difficult puzzle together. When the mothers' neurological scans revealed frustration, soon the children's scans did too, and vice versa. As the scientists explain, "mothers and children regulate or deregulate each other" (Atzaba-Poria et al., 2017, p. 551).

FROM WITHIN

Intrinsic motivation arises from within, when people do something for the joy of doing it: A musician might enjoy making music even if no one else hears it; the sound is intrinsically rewarding. Intrinsic motivation advances creativity, innovation, and emotional well-being (Weinstein & DeHaan, 2014).

intrinsic motivation
A drive, or reason to pursue a goal, that comes from inside a person, such as the joy of reading a good book.

extrinsic motivation
A drive, or reason to pursue a goal, that arises from the wish to have external rewards, perhaps by earning money or praise.

All of Erikson's psychosocial needs—including the young child's initiatives—are intrinsic: Children feel inwardly compelled to act.

The power of that internal impulse is evident when adults want children to do something and the children want to do something else. For example, suppose an adult is in a hurry to go somewhere with a child. The adult's "hurry, we are late," may clash with the child's wish to walk along a ledge, pick up a leaf, throw a snowball, or whatever.

◆◆ Especially for College Students
Is extrinsic or intrinsic motivation more influential in your study efforts? (see response, page 203)

FROM THE CULTURE

Extrinsic motivation comes from outside the person. External praise or some other reinforcement is the goal, such as when a musician plays for applause or money. Four-year-olds might brush their teeth because they are praised and rewarded with musical toothbrushes and tasty toothpaste.

If an extrinsic reward is removed, the behavior may stop unless it has become a habit. Young children might not brush their teeth if parents don't notice and praise them for doing so. For most of us, tooth-brushing was extrinsically rewarded at first, and that continued long enough for it to become habitual.

Then motivation becomes intrinsic: Tooth-brushing has become a comforting, internally motivated routine for many adults.

JOSE LUIS PELAEZ INC/BLEND IMAGES - KIDSTOCK/BRAND X PICTURES/GETTY IMAGES

Both Accomplished Note the joy and pride in this father and daughter in West New York, New Jersey. Who has achieved more?

SPONTANEOUS JOY

Intrinsic motivation is evident when children play, question, exercise, create, destroy, and explore for the sheer joy of it. That serves them well. For example, a longitudinal study found that 3-year-olds who were strong in intrinsic motivation were, two years later, advanced in early math and literacy (Mokrova et al., 2013). The probable reason: They enjoyed counting things and singing songs, when alone.

In contrast, exaggerated external praise ("Your drawing is amazingly wonderful!") undercuts motivation (Brummelman et al., 2017). If children believe the praise, they might be afraid to try again, fearing they won't do as well. If they suspect that the praise was inaccurate, they discount the entire activity.

IMAGINARY FRIENDS

An example of intrinsic motivation is apparent when children invent dialogues for their toys, concentrate on creating a work of art or architecture, or talk to imaginary friends. Invisible companions are rarely encouraged by adults (thus, no extrinsic motivation), but many 2- to 7-year-olds have them. Imaginary friends are considered a sign of creativity, not of pathology, in young children.

An international study of 3- to 8-year-olds found that about one child in five said that they had an invisible companion, with notable variation by culture: 38 percent of children in the Dominican Republic, but only 5 percent in Nepal, said they had such a friend (Wigger, 2018).

Another study, this one in the United States, found that about half the children remembered having imaginary friends, either completely invisible ones or inanimate toys, such as stuffed animals, upon which they bestowed independent opinions, speech, and action. Many of those children also imagined entire worlds (Taylor et al., 2020).

what have you learned?

1. How might protective optimism lead to new skills and competencies?
2. Why is postponement of gratification an example of emotional regulation?
3. What did Erikson think was characteristic of young children?
4. What is an example (not in the text) of intrinsic motivation?
5. What is an example (not in the text) of extrinsic motivation?
6. Why might a child have an imaginary friend?

Play

Play is timeless and universal—apparent in every part of the world over thousands of years. Some developmentalists believe that play is children's most productive, enjoyable activity. Indeed, some think that deprivation of play is likely to lead to emotional pathology. Many psychologists use play with children to repair a child's emotional damage as well as to understand what children think and feel (Jennings & Holmwood, 2020).

The Historical Context

As Chapter 5 explained, one dispute in early education is which is more important: child-centered creative play or teacher-directed learning. To further understand that debate, it helps to know how attitudes have changed over the past 100 years.

PARTEN'S STAGES OF PLAY

In 1932, American sociologist Mildred Parten thought play was valuable for children's development. She described five stages of social play, each more advanced than the previous one:

1. *Solitary:* A child plays alone, unaware of other children playing nearby.
2. *Onlooker:* A child watches other children play.
3. *Parallel:* Children play in similar ways but not together.
4. *Associative:* Children interact, sharing materials or activities, but not taking turns.
5. *Cooperative:* Children play together, creating dramas or taking turns.

Parten considered play intrinsic, with children from age 1 to 6 gradually advancing from solitary to cooperative play. This was apparent as toddlers were onlookers and then children gradually learned how to play together.

Research on contemporary children finds much more age variation than Parten did, in part because of experience. Those who stay home until formal education begins, might be onlookers (stage 2) in kindergarten; those who have been in interactive, child-centered programs might reach cooperative play (stage 6) by age 4.

THE CURRENT CONTROVERSY

Whether play is essential or merely fun is "a controversial topic of study" (Pellegrini, 2011, p. 3). Some legislators want less play so young children learn more reading and math; some educators predict emotional and academic problems if children are deprived of play (Golinkoff & Hirsh-Pasek, 2016; Nerren, 2020).

Developmental psychologists are impressed with the young child's ability to use play to process emotions. One source notes that play varies, with "twists and turns . . . abrupt changes in play patterns—between seriousness and frolic, earnestness and whimsy, reality and pretense, often leading to higher levels of play" (Johnson & Wu, 2019, p. 81). Higher levels of play leads to more mature social skills.

SCREEN TIME

The largest change in the twenty-first century is that there is less active play and more screen time, when children watch television or computer screens (see Figure 6.1). That troubles developmentalists. Pediatricians, psychologists, and teachers all

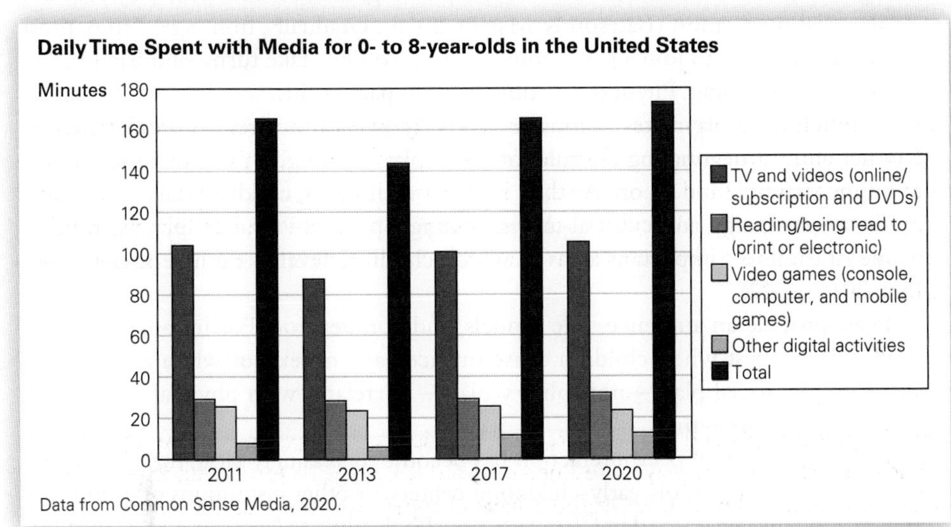

FIGURE 6.1 Learning by Playing Fifty years ago, the average child spent three hours a day in outdoor play. Screens have largely replaced that, with specifics changing over the years. Children seem safer if parents can keep an eye on them at home, but what are they learning?

find that screen time reduces conversation, imagination, and exercise (Downing et al., 2017).

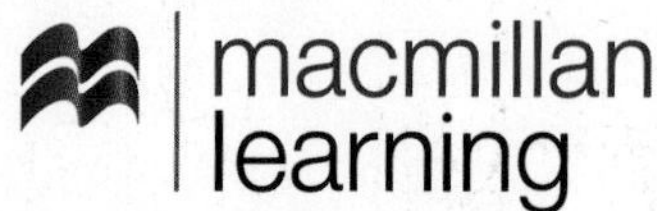

VIDEO: The Impact of Media on Early Childhood explores how screen time can affect young children's cognition.

A study in Canada of 2,441 children, followed longitudinally from before birth until age 5, found that the average 3-year-old watched screens more than two hours a day (Madigan et al., 2019). One result was to "disrupt interactions with caregivers"; another was to reduce cognitive and emotional development. Because this was a careful longitudinal study, the conclusions are causes, not merely correlations.

Similar results are found in other nations, with many young children using screens several hours each day. The consequences include obesity, emotional immaturity, and less intellectual growth. The American Academy of Pediatrics (2016) recommends no more than an hour a day of watching a screen for 2- to 6-year-olds (infants should watch less than that). They also urge parents not to let children watch programs or play games that include violence, sex, or racist, sexist stereotypes.

A recent concern with the COVID-19 pandemic is that many children were home all day, and some schools instituted remote learning—which meant that children watched screens far more than experts recommend. Since screens are inevitable, some pediatricians suggest how to reduce the harm (Vanderloo et al., 2020). One is that adults make watching interactive, by interpreting, conversing, and explaining.

Increased screen time is not the only problem seen as a result of reduced play during the pandemic. Less physical activity, less social development, and more parental stress also result from closed schools and playgrounds (Moore et al., 2020). Epidemiologists point out that children under age 10 were least likely to be infected with the virus, and yet schools were often the first institutions to be closed.

Social Play

A major concern with virtual schooling and social distancing is lack of peer interaction. Young children play best with *peers*, that is, people of about the same age and social status.

PLAYMATES

THINK CRITICALLY: Why were schools more likely to be closed than bars during the recent pandemic? [My nephew suggested a solution: classes in bars, with dismissal before "happy hour."]

The need for playmates is very evident during early childhood. Although infants are intrigued by other children, babies do not play together because peer play requires some social maturation (Bateson & Martin, 2013). Gradually, from age 2 to 6, most children learn how to join a peer group, manage conflict, take turns, find friends, and keep the action going. Physical touching is often part of this.

Children need playmates, because even the most playful parent is outmatched by another child at negotiating the rules of tag, at play-fighting, at pretending to be sick, at killing dragons, and so on. As they interact with peers, children learn emotional regulation, empathy, and cultural understanding. Specifics vary, but "play with peers is one of the most important areas in which children develop positive social skills" (Xu, 2010, p. 496).

Peers provide an audience, role models, and competition. For instance, running skills develop best when children chase or race each other, not when a child runs alone. Active social play—not solitary play—correlates with physical, emotional, and intellectual growth.

The importance of peer interaction has become increasingly clear, now that many children attend preschools, early-childhood centers, or other institutions of group care and learning. As you learned in Chapter 5, preschools advance language and science, but

in this chapter we highlight another part of early-childhood programs: Play with peers advances social understanding.

Beyond that, especially for low-SES families, schools reduce parental stress by providing food, health services, and adult interaction for children. That was all impeded when COVID-19 led to school lockdowns (Masonbrink & Hurley, 2020).

TECHNOLOGY

Adults once feared that technology would cause children to become socially isolated. A more nuanced view considers the social setting. When a child watches a video alone, interpersonal emotional understanding is reduced. However, if a child is with other children, digital play can advance development.

One detailed study of 3- to 5-year-olds in a Scotland preschool focused on digital technology. In that classroom, computers, smart boards, digital cameras, and so on were available during free play time, in the same way that puzzles, dress-up clothes, and dolls often are (Arnott, 2016).

Children used various digital tools as part of social interaction. Sometimes technology encouraged cooperation, as with this boy and girl, both aged 4:

> Grace begins to use the SMART board and Chris begins to use his finger to point at the screen to illustrate which selection she should choose as he verbally directs. Chris continues this process for each step of the way and Grace obeys. Then, when the game reaches a section where Grace does not need to make a selection and she needs to wait, he holds up his hand and says, "now wait."

EMILY FLAKE/THE NEW YORKER COLLECTION/THE CARTOON BANK

"Keep in mind, this all counts as screen time."

Caught in the Middle Parents try to limit screen time, but children are beguiled and bombarded from many sides.

Sometimes one child was the leader, with others merely watching. For example:

> Three boys have formed a cluster around the computer. Chris is controlling the computer by using the mouse. Harvey is sitting next to him in front of the computer and Steven is hovering close by. Harvey offers encouragement to Chris, "You got 10!" he shouts with an excited tone. Steven becomes more and more excited with this activity and begins to show it by bouncing up and down while he stands next to the computer. He begins to cheer. Suddenly, Harvey turns to Steven and sharply says "Shhh- Don't do that!". Steven is immediately silent and observes quietly.
>
> [*Arnott, 2016, p. 280*]

In this preschool, children's technology use was almost always a social activity. Sometimes they shared, sometimes they mentored each other, sometimes they merely watched, providing encouragement and later trying it themselves. The social context, including the physical space and the overall routines and rules, framed the interactions. It was unusual for the children to be hostile or to fight for control. (Rarely, the teachers intervened.)

ROUGH-AND-TUMBLE

One form of social play, often unappreciated as a source of emotional growth, is called **rough-and-tumble**, because it looks rough and children seem to tumble over one another. The term was coined by British scientists who studied animals in East Africa (Blurton-Jones, 1976). They noticed that young monkeys often chased, attacked, rolled over in the dirt, and wrestled quite roughly without injuring one another, all while seeming to smile (showing a *play face*).

rough-and-tumble play
Play that seems to be rough, as in play wrestling or chasing, but in which there is no intent to harm.

When the scientists who studied monkeys in Africa returned to London, they saw that puppies, kittens, and even their own children engaged in rough-and-tumble play. Children chase, wrestle, and grab each other, with established rules, facial expressions, and gestures to signify "just pretend."

THINK CRITICALLY: Some experts believe that play should be encouraged at all ages. Do adults play too often or not often enough?

Developmentalists now recognize that rough-and-tumble play happens everywhere, with every mammal species, and it has for thousands of years (Fry, 2014). It is more common among males than females, and it flourishes best in ample space with minimal supervision (Pellegrini, 2013).

Neurological benefits from such play are evident. The easiest example comes from watching rodents. Young rats try to bite the nape of another's neck. If a bite occurs, the two rats switch roles and the bitten tries to bite the other's nape.

This is all playful. If the rats wanted to hurt each other, they would try to bite organs, not napes. Rat rough-and-tumble play increases rat brain development (Pellis et al., 2018). Puppies, kittens, and human children in rough-and-tumble play are also careful not to hurt each other.

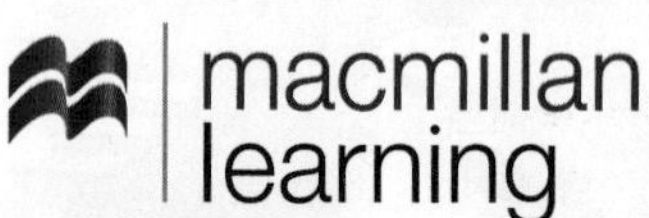

VIDEO: Pretend Play and Emotional Control describes a study that measured whether or not sociodramatic play helps young children develop emotional control.

Controlled experiments on humans, with some children allowed to play and a matched control group never playing, would be unethical. However, correlations suggest that the limbic system connects more strongly with the prefrontal cortex when children engage in rough-and-tumble play.

Indeed, longitudinal research on boys who played carefully but roughly with peers and parents (usually with fathers) finds that they become caring, compassionate men (Fry, 2014; Raeburn, 2014). Isolated loners are the ones to worry about.

SOCIODRAMATIC PLAY

sociodramatic play
Pretend play in which children act out various roles and themes in plots or roles that they create.

Another major type of social play is **sociodramatic**, when children act out various roles and plots. Through such acting, children:

- explore and rehearse social roles.
- learn to explain their ideas and persuade playmates.
- practice emotional regulation by pretending to be afraid, angry, brave, and so on.
- develop self-concept in a nonthreatening context.

As children combine their imagination with that of their friends, they advance in theory of mind, gaining emotional regulation as they do so (Goldstein & Lerner, 2018; Kavanaugh, 2011). Again, play and playmates are part of growing up emotionally as well as physically healthy.

what have you learned?

1. What are children thought to gain from play?
2. Why do pediatricians want to limit children's screen time?
3. How can technology enhance children's learning instead of inhibiting it?
4. Why does playing with peers increase physical development and emotional regulation?
5. What do children learn from rough-and-tumble play?
6. What do children learn from sociodramatic play?

MORE PLAY TIME, LESS SCREEN TIME

Play is universal—all young children do it when they are with each other, if they can. According to a 2017 study, U.S. 2- to 10-year-olds average 19 hours per week of screen time, exceeding the 15 hours they spend in indoor screen-free play by themselves or with others. Although children play outside for an additional 11 hours per week, parents report that when indoors, their children's screen time crowds out screen-free play.

What 2- to 10-Year-Olds Do with Their Free Time

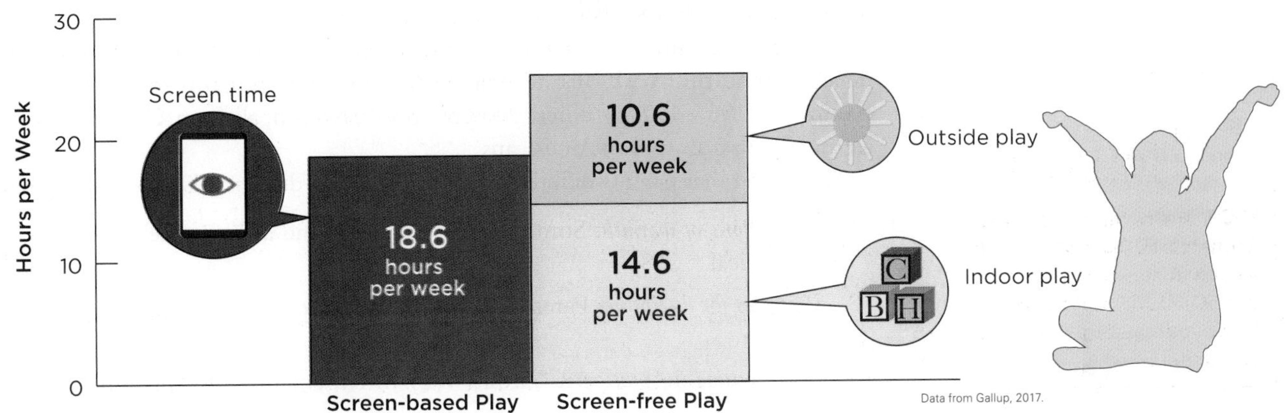

Data from Gallup, 2017.

Way Too Much Screen Time

Very few children have the recommended less than an hour of screen time per day. Some have much more. This is particularly evident on weekends, when they should be playing outside or interacting with their families. What did children do before 1950, without TV or computers? Talking, reading, cooking, cleaning, board games, ball games, playing music, drawing pictures, writing letters … the list of things that some children never do could go on and on!

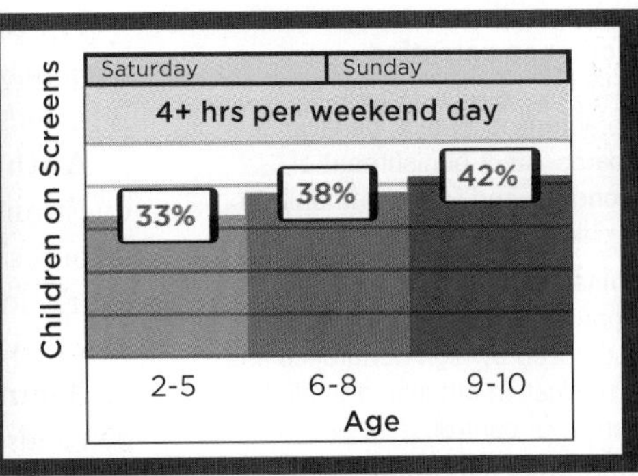

Data from Gallup, 2017.

What Caregivers Can Do to Encourage Play

at Ages 1–3

Choose childcare and preschools that emphasize unstructured playtime.

Offer simple, inexpensive objects (blocks, empty containers, puzzles, etc.), not screens or fancy gadgets.

Organize caregiver-supervised playdates with peers.

Encourage make-believe play.

Sing songs and play rhythms that invite participation.

at Ages 4–6

Provide opportunities for singing and dancing.

Encourage a variety of movements in a safe environment—e.g., hopping, swinging, climbing, and somersaulting.

Blend make-believe games and reality—e.g., "playing house" and helping with chores.

Encourage school officials to offer recess and play-centered learning approaches, not just reading, memorization, and worksheets.

Information from American Academy of Pediatrics, 2018.

Challenges for Caregivers

Caring for young children is difficult: They are energetic and curious but not wise, emotionally expressive but not controlled. How best to provide care is challenging.

Styles of Caregiving

Some parents are so strict that they seem abusive, and others are so lenient that they seem neglectful. Cultures, ethnic groups, neighbors disagree.

BAUMRIND'S CATEGORIES

Although thousands of researchers have traced the effects of parenting on child development, the work of one person, 60 years ago, remains influential. Diana Baumrind (1967, 1971) studied 100 preschool children, all from California, almost all middle-class European Americans.

She found that parents differed on four important dimensions:

1. *Expressions of warmth.* Some parents are warm and affectionate; others are cold and critical.
2. *Strategies for discipline.* Parents vary in how they explain, criticize, persuade, and punish.
3. *Expectations for maturity.* Parents vary in expectations for responsibility and self-control.
4. *Communication.* Some parents listen patiently; others demand silence.

authoritarian parenting
An approach to child rearing that is characterized by high behavioral standards, strict punishment of misconduct, and little communication from child to parent.

permissive parenting
An approach to child rearing that is characterized by high nurturance and communication but little discipline, guidance, or control.

authoritative parenting
An approach to child rearing in which the parents set limits and enforce rules but are flexible and listen to their children.

On the basis of these dimensions, Baumrind identified three parenting styles: *authoritarian*, *permissive*, and *authoritative* (summarized in Table 6.1). A fourth style, *neglectful*, not described by Baumrind, was suggested by other researchers.

Authoritarian parenting. The authoritarian parent's word is law, not to be questioned. Misconduct brings strict punishment, usually physical. Authoritarian parents set down clear rules and hold high standards. Discussion about emotions and expressions of affection are rare. One adult raised by authoritarian parents said that "How do you feel?" had only two possible answers: "Fine" and "Tired."

Permissive parenting. Permissive parents (also called *indulgent*) make few demands. Discipline is lax, partly because expectations are low. Permissive parents are nurturing and accepting, listening to whatever their offspring say, which may include "I hate you"—a remark that authoritarian parents would not tolerate.

Authoritative parenting. Authoritative parents set limits, but they are flexible. They consider themselves guides, not authorities (unlike authoritarian parents) and

TABLE 6.1 Characteristics of Parenting Styles Identified by Baumrind

				Communication	
Style	Warmth	Discipline	Expectations of Maturity	Parent to Child	Child to Parent
Authoritarian	Low	Strict, often physical	High	High	Low
Permissive	High	Rare	Low	Low	High
Authoritative	High	Moderate, with much discussion	Moderate	High	High

not friends (unlike permissive parents). The goal of punishment is for the child to understand what was wrong and what should have been done differently.

Neglectful/uninvolved parenting. Neglectful parents ignore their children's behavior; they seem not to notice. Their children do whatever they want. The child's behavior may be similar to those of the permissive parent, but the parents' attitude is quite different: Neglectful parents do not care, whereas permissive parents care very much.

neglectful/uninvolved parenting An approach to child rearing in which the parents seem indifferent toward their children, not knowing or caring about their children's lives.

corporal punishment Discipline techniques that hurt the body (*corpus*) of someone, from spanking to serious harm, including death.

Long-term effects of parenting styles have been reported in many nations. Cultural and regional differences are apparent, but everywhere authoritative parenting seems best (Pinquart & Kauser, 2018). The following trends have been found in many studies, although you will soon read that results are not as universal as the early research found.

- *Authoritarian* parents raise children who become conscientious, obedient, and quiet but not especially happy. Such children may feel guilty or depressed, internalizing their frustrations and blaming themselves when things don't go well. As adolescents, they sometimes rebel, striking out on their own. As adults, they are quick to blame and punish.
- *Permissive* parents raise children who lack self-control. Inadequate emotional regulation makes them immature and impedes friendships, so they are unhappy. They tend to continue to live at home, still dependent on their parents in adulthood.
- *Authoritative* parents raise children who are successful, articulate, happy with themselves, and generous with others. These children are usually liked by teachers and peers, especially in cultures that value individual initiative (e.g., the United States).
- *Neglectful/uninvolved* parents raise children who are immature, sad, lonely, and at risk of injury and abuse, not only in early childhood but also lifelong.

REUTERS/ERIK DE CASTRO

Protect Me from the Water Buffalo These two are at the Carabao Kneeling Festival. In rural Philippines, hundreds of these large but docile animals kneel on the steps of the church, part of a day of gratitude for the harvest.

OBSERVATION QUIZ
Is the father above authoritarian, authoritative, or permissive? (see answer, page 203) ↑

PROBLEMS WITH THE RESEARCH

Baumrind's categories have been criticized, not only because her sample was small and from only one community, but because a multi-cultural, multi-contextual approach, considering differential susceptibility, suggests that each child needs individualized discipline. For example, fearful children require reassurance, and impulsive ones need strong guidelines. Parents of such children may, to outsiders, seem permissive or authoritarian.

Punishment

The most strident disputes occur about punishment. Every child misbehaves, and every child needs guidance to keep them safe and strong. Parents must respond when their child does something forbidden, dangerous, or mean. But how?

PHYSICAL PUNISHMENT

Corporal punishment (so called because it involved the *corpus*, the Latin word for body) is illegal in some nations, the norm in others. A massive international study of low- and moderate-income nations found that 63 percent of 2- to 5-year-olds had been physically punished (slapped, spanked, hit with an object) in the past month but that some children had never experienced corporal punishment (Deater-Deckard & Lansford, 2016). Beyond individual differences, cultural differences were apparent.

When rates worldwide are considered, it is apparent that punishment methods are part of an overall culture, not an isolated event. Cultures that emphasize physical punishment also stress obedience and authority, often handing down severe prison

URBANZONE/ALAMY STOCK PHOTO

Smack Will the doll learn never to disobey her mother again?

THINK CRITICALLY: The varying rates of physical punishment in schools could be the result of prejudice, or they could be because some children misbehave more than others. Which is it?

sentences. Preventive medical care, guaranteed income, and women's rights are not part of daily life for most people in those nations (Lansford et al., 2020; Pate & Gould, 2012).

Within the United States, how children are disciplined depends more on region and ethnicity than on the child's misdeeds. Spanking is more frequent:

- in the southern United States than in New England;
- by mothers than by fathers;
- among conservative Christians than among nonreligious families;
- among African Americans than among European Americans;
- among European Americans than among Asian Americans;
- among U.S.-born Latinx than among immigrant Latinx; and
- in low-SES families than in high-SES families.

(Lee & Altschul, 2015; S. Lee et al., 2015; MacKenzie et al., 2011).

These are general trends, but exceptions abound: Some African American mothers in the South never spank, and some secular, European American, high-SES fathers in New England routinely do. Individual parents make their own decisions, despite what their neighbors do.

◆ Especially for Parents Suppose you agree that spanking is destructive, but you sometimes get so angry at your child's behavior that you hit him or her. Is your reaction appropriate? (see response, page 203)

Given a multi-cultural, multi-contextual perspective, it is not surprising that many spanked children become fine adults, who believe they were not harmed by spanking. Nonetheless, a positive correlation between spanking and aggression is found in all ethnic groups, in many nations (Lansford et al., 2014; Wang & Liu, 2018). Children who are *not* spanked are *more* likely to develop emotional regulation.

Although some adults believe that physical punishment will "teach a lesson," others argue that the lesson learned is that "might makes right." Children who were physically disciplined become more likely to use corporal punishment on others—first on their classmates, later on their partners, and then on their children (Thompson et al., 2017).

OPPOSING PERSPECTIVES

Spare the Rod?

Opinions about spanking are influenced by past experience and cultural norms. That makes it hard for opposing perspectives to be understood by people on the other side (Ferguson, 2013). Try to suspend your own assumptions as you read this.

What might be right with spanking? Over the centuries, billions of parents have done it, so it has stood the test of time. Spanking is less common in the twenty-first century than in the twentieth (Taillieu et al., 2014), but 85 percent of U.S. adolescents who were children at the end of the twentieth century recall being slapped or spanked by their mothers (Bender et al., 2007). In low- and middle-income nations, over a third of the mothers believe that physical punishment is essential to raise a child well (Deater-Deckard & Lansford, 2016).

As you read, spanking correlates with later depression, low achievement, aggression, crime, and so on, but proponents of spanking suggest that a third variable, not spanking itself, is the reason for that connection. One possible third variable is misbehavior: Perhaps disobedient children cause spanking, not vice versa.

Perhaps children become delinquent, depressed, and so on not *because* they were spanked but *in spite of* being spanked. Noting problems with correlational research, one team explains, "Quite simply, parents do not need to use corrective actions when there are no problems to correct" (Larzelere & Cox, 2013, p. 284).

An underlying variable may be low SES. Parents who spank their children often have less education and money than other parents, and low SES correlates with low academic achievement, aggression, and depression. Thus, to help children, it may be more effective to increase parents' SES, not to reduce spanking.

Some question exactly how the variables are defined in the research. If one variable is simply use of physical

punishment, yes or no, without separating severe from mild corporal punishment, then the correlation between physical punishment and psychological harm may reflect the consequences of abusive punishment, not the harm of occasional spanking (Larzelere et al., 2017).

Now the opposing perspective.

What might be wrong with spanking? One problem is adults' emotions: Angry spankers may become abusive. Children have been seriously injured and even killed by parents who use corporal punishment.

Another problem is the child's immature cognition. Parents assume that the transgression is obvious, but children may think that the parents' anger, not the child's actions, caused spanking (Harkness et al., 2011). Most parents tell their children why they are being spanked, but when they are hit, children are not likely to listen or understand, much less to learn.

Almost all of the research finds that children who are physically punished suffer overall (Grogan-Kaylo et al., 2018). Compared to children punished in other ways, they are more depressed, antisocial, and lonely. Many hate school and have few close friends.

Emotional and social problems are more common in adults who were spanked as children, and that seems true for relatively mild spanking as well as for more severe spanking.

One reason for these correlations is that spanked children more often have angry, depressed, unloving parents. However, even among children of warm and loving parents, spanked children tend to be more anxious, worried they will lose their parents' affection (Lansford et al., 2014).

So who is right? You can guess which perspective is mine. I agree with most developmentalists that alternatives to spanking are better for children and a safeguard against abuse. The same study that found spanking common in developing nations also reported that 17 percent of the children experienced severe violence that no developmentalist would condone (Bornstein et al., 2016). That alone is reason to stop.

But a developmental perspective requires recognition of cultural differences, and scientists must seek out research that is contrary to what they think. I found such a study (Ellison et al., 2011). This research confirmed that religiously conservative parents spank their children more often than other parents (no surprise), but that if spanking occurred *only* in early (not middle) childhood, their children were not more depressed or aggressive than other children (surprise).

The authors of that study suggested that, since spanking was the norm in that group, spanked children felt cared for. Moreover, religious leaders told the parents never to spank in anger. As a result, some children may "view mild-to-moderate corporal punishment as legitimate, appropriate, and even an indicator of parental involvement, commitment, and concern" (Ellison et al., 2011, p. 957).

With all research, we need to be careful not to stereotype, not to conclude that all members of a particular group are like the average member. Another study of conservative Christians found that many thought their faith condoned spanking (Perrin et al., 2017).

In that study, when they learned that "sparing the rod" (Proverbs 13:24) refers to the guiding rod that shepherds use, which was never used to punish, and that long-term harm can result from spanking, many changed their minds. Some concluded that physical punishment is contrary to "not throwing the first stone" (John 8:7), a belief in forgiveness.

A dynamic-systems, multi-cultural perspective reminds me that everyone is influenced by background, cognition, and context. Probably my opinions are too narrow about several developmental controversies that I explain in this text. I do not think this is one of them.

ALTERNATIVES TO SPANKING

If spanking is harmful but discipline is necessary, what is a parent to do? Some employ **psychological control**, using children's shame, guilt, and gratitude to control their behavior (Barber, 2002). For instance, a parent might say "if you loved me you would . . ." or "I have done so much for you, so you should be grateful."

psychological control
A disciplinary technique that involves threatening to withdraw love and support, using a child's feelings of guilt and gratitude to the parents.

time-out
A disciplinary technique in which a person is separated from other people and activities for a specified time.

Some researchers think that psychological control is no better, and may be worse than, corporal punishment (Scharf & Goldner, 2018). One team called psychological control "a covert form of aggression," which correlates with less empathy and poorer understanding of the child (Bi & Keller, 2019).

Another alternative is **time-out**, in which a misbehaving child is required to sit quietly, without toys or playmates, for a short time. Time-out is not to be done in anger, or for too long; it is recommended that parents use a calm voice and that the time-out last only one to five minutes (Morawska & Sanders, 2011). Time-out is punishment if the child enjoys "time-in," when the child is engaged with parents or with peers.

Time-out is favored by many experts. They advise that time-out is part of a close parent–child relationship, a way to punish a behavior that the child knows is wrong. The message is that the child needs to stop and think, and thus indicates the parent's connection to the child, not rejection (Dadds & Tully, 2019)

Often combined with the time-out is another alternative to physical punishment and psychological control—**induction**, in which the parents discuss the infraction with the child, so children themselves will come to understand why their behavior was wrong. Ideally, a strong and affectionate parent–child relationship allows children to express their emotions and parents to listen.

induction
A disciplinary technique in which the parent tries to get the child to understand why a certain behavior was wrong. Listening, not lecturing, is crucial.

sex differences
Physical differences between males and females, in organs, hormones, and body shape.

gender differences
Differences in male and female roles, behaviors, clothes, and so on that arise from society, not physiology.

Induction takes time and patience, and, like other discipline measures, it does not always succeed. Young children are especially likely to believe that they behaved properly, given the situation. Simple induction ("Why did he cry?") may help children recognize that they have hurt someone else, but even that is hard before a child develops theory of mind.

Nonetheless, induction pays off over time. Children whose parents used induction when they were 3-year-olds became children with fewer externalizing problems in elementary school (Choe et al., 2013b).

What do parents actually do? A survey of discipline in early childhood found that most parents use more than one method (Thompson et al., 2017). In the United States, time-out is the most common punishment, and about half of the parents sometimes spank. Many other methods—induction, counting, distraction, hand-smacking, removal of a toy or activity—were also used.

In general, specifics of parenting style and punishment seem less crucial than whether or not children know that they are loved, guided, and appreciated (Grusec et al., 2017). If some parents seem too strict or too lenient, remember that if their children consider discipline fair, and believe they are loved and valued, they are likely to develop well (Pinquart & Kauser, 2018).

Becoming Boys and Girls

Another challenge for caregivers is to promote a healthy understanding of sex and gender, so children can be proud of themselves and accepting of others.

SEX AND GENDER

Many researchers try to distinguish **sex differences**, which are innate, the result of XX or XY chromosomes and the hormones they produce, from **gender differences**, which are cultural. Some gender differences are obvious, such as in clothes and hair styles, and some are less apparent, such as differences in children's achievement scores on math tests or in who dominates a group conversation among adults.

In theory this distinction between sex and gender seems straightforward; in practice it is not. Culture and biology are not separate influences but are "interacting components of nature and nurture" (Eagly & Wood, 2013, p. 349). The interaction between sex and gender is such that some scholars propose one word, *sex/gender*, to denote both (Hyde et al., 2019).

Be that as it may, during early childhood most children develop distinct identities. By age 4, children believe that certain toys (such as dolls or trucks) and roles (Daddy, Mommy, nurse, teacher, police officer, soldier) are reserved for one sex or another, even when their experience is otherwise. As one expert explains:

> [F]our-year-olds say that girls will always be girls and will never become boys. . . . They are often more absolute about gender than adults are. Indeed, they'll tell their very own pants suited doctor mother that girls wear dresses and women are nurses.
>
> *[Gopnik, 2016, p. 140]*

By age 6, children are often quite rigid. Despite their parents' and teachers' wishes, children say, "girls are stupid" or "boys stink" or "no girls [or boys] allowed."

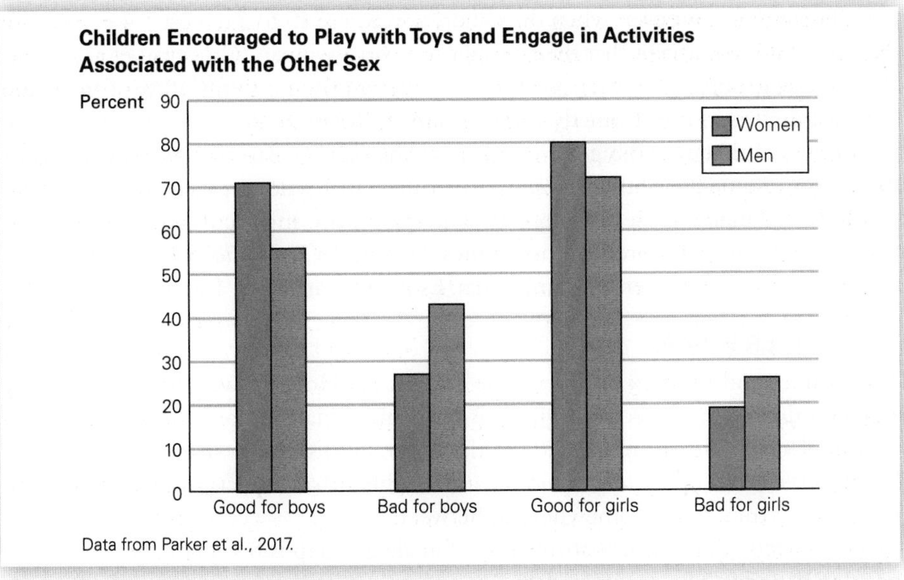

FIGURE 6.2 Similarities? What is more remarkable—that most people think girls should be encouraged to play with trucks and boys encouraged to play with dolls, or that some people do not? Your answer probably depends on whether you thought gender equality has been achieved or is still far away.

Many parents believe they treat their sons and daughters the same and want to free their children from gender stereotypes. Few adults today would forbid a boy from pushing a toy stroller with a doll strapped in it, or a girl from pushing around a truck.

A 2017 survey found that most adults went one step further. They thought parents should *encourage* their children to play with toys associated with the other sex (Parker et al., 2017). The most disagreement arose when men were asked about boys; 43 percent of the men thought boys should *not* be encouraged to do things usually stereotyped for girls, such as care for dolls or wear bracelets (see Figure 6.2). But notice that even they were in the minority.

transgender
A broad term for people whose gender identity and/or gender expression differ from what is typically expected of the sex they were assigned at birth. Some (but not all) transgender people take hormones or undergo surgery to make their bodies align with their gender identity.

Nonetheless, children may reject such encouragement. A meta-analysis of 75 studies found that young girls have strong preferences for girl toys, especially dolls, and boys for boy toys, especially trucks (Davis & Hines, 2020).

TRANSGENDER CHILDREN

Sex and gender may be especially challenging when a child is **transgender**, identifying as being a gender other than the one assigned at birth (Rahilly, 2015). Most parents have no problem if a daughter plays with trucks or a son plays with dolls, but it may be harder to accept that a child has quite distinct ideas about what gender they are, when that gender is not the one on their birth certificate. One mother said:

> Since he was two, all he can say is that he wants to be a girl, or that he is a girl. He knows that he is not, but there is no way to change his mind. He is 6 now, and he still asks me every day "Mom, can I be a girl when I grow up?"
>
> *[quoted in Malpas, 2011, p. 453]*

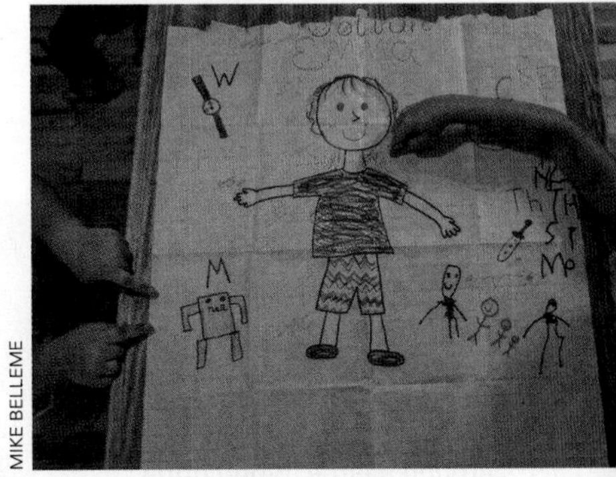

MIKE BELLEME

Not Emma In a North Carolina kindergarten, each child had an "All About Me" day in which the teacher would draw a picture of the child for all of the other children to copy. Emma was given a boy's name at birth but identifies as a girl. On her day, she proudly wore a light-pink shirt with a heart, pink glittery shoes, and long hair—and she came home bawling because the teacher drew this picture with her boy name (barely visible here). Her parents consoled her, had her edit her name and draw longer hair, with some other additions. Shouldn't children be allowed to be who they are?

Unlike in that family, some parents during early childhood accept their child's insistence that they are transgender. A study of 36 transgender children, whose parents accepted their transition to the other sex before age 6, compared them with their siblings and with cisgender children who were the same age. (The term *cisgender* refers to those whose gender identity matches their birth sex.)

The researchers found that all the children had definite preferences for clothes, toys, and activities. The transgender children chose whatever conformed to their new gender, just as the cisgender children did (Fast & Olson, 2018).

Parental acceptance is far from guaranteed, however. One study of 129 transgender adolescents found that only a third of the mothers and a fourth of the fathers responded positively when their children first said they were transgender. As time went on, some parents became more accepting, more often when the natal sex was female than male. But even when the children were age 15 to 21, most (64 percent) of the fathers did not accept that their former son was a woman (Grossman et al., 2019).

Another group of children who may challenge their parents' idea of male and female are *intersex*, not distinctly male or female (Ernst et al., 2018). They are born with genitalia that are ambiguous, with genitalia that appear male or female, unlike their chromosomes, or with a chromosome pattern that is not typically male or female.

There are many causes of intersex conditions, the most common of which is an allele that impedes prenatal hormones, leading to *congenital adrenal hyperplasia (CAH)*. Incidence of intersex is unknown: Estimates vary from 1 in 50 to 1 in 2,000.

THE GENDER BINARY

Transgender and intersex children raise a question: How do we define masculinity and femininity? Some people argue that male and female are on a *continuum*, which is a line that stretches from one side to the other, in this case from extremely masculine at one end to extremely feminine at the other. Most aspects of most people are not at the extremes, but somewhere in between.

This rejects the notion that male and female are opposites, a concept called the **gender binary**. (The prefix *bi-* means "two," as in *bicycle, bifurcate, bisexual*). According to the nonbinary perspective, every aspect of human brains, behavior, and bodies is somewhere along that continuum. For example, some men are shorter than the average woman, and some women are more gifted in math than the average man.

gender binary
The idea that gender comes in two—and only two—forms, male and female.

THINK CRITICALLY: Should children be encouraged to combine both male and female characteristics, or is learning male and female roles crucial for becoming a happy man or woman?

That gender traits are not opposites, but instead overlap between males and females, is now understood by most adults. We expect men to sometimes cry; we cheer the U.S. women's soccer team who won the World Cup, even if women generally cry more often than men do or if most professional athletes are male. The nonbinary perspective is prominent in studies of the human brain. Although male and female brains are alike on most measures, one study found a dozen neurological characteristics that differed notably between the *average* male and female brain (Joel et al., 2015).

However, that study found that many men had neurological characteristics typical for women, and vice versa. Fewer than 10 percent of the people in this study had brains that were typical for their sex in all of the dozen traits that distinguish male and female brains (Joel et al., 2015). From studies such as this one, a team of researchers

REUTERS/AKHTAR SOOMRO

ILYAS DEAN/THE IMAGE WORKS

Same Situation, Far Apart: Are Children the Same Everywhere? These boys are refugees from Afghanistan, and the Muslim girl is in Pakistan. Is it jarring to see them mock fighting, or carrying a large, blond bride doll? Cultures differ; gender roles do not.

conclude that most human brains and behaviors are a male/female mosaic (Hyde et al., 2019).

Another team found that transgender and intersex people often have brains that are not like most people of their natal sex (Ristori et al., 2020). That study also concludes that in order "to provide reliable conclusions, more data is needed." As best we know, transgender individuals are similar to other individuals in most ways, with any differences caused by social reactions, not qualities inherent to them.

The research raises an issue for developmentalists. Why are male and female distinctions recognized by most 2-year-olds, significant to most 4-year-olds, and accepted as natural by 6-year-olds, despite the reality that most brain differences between the average male and female are "really small" and plastic (Ristori et al., 2020)?

Gender differences are important for many people, even before birth as "gender reveal" parties signify. All of the major theories "devote considerable attention to gender differences. . . . the primary difference among the theories resides in the causal mechanism responsible" (Bornstein et al., 2016, pp. 10, 11). Consider the four comprehensive theories first mentioned in Chapter 2 (see Table 6.2).

Some recent research suggests a *gender similarities hypothesis*, the idea that our human emphasis on sex differences blinds us to the reality that the sexes have far more in common than traditional theories recognize (Hyde, 2016). Perhaps instead of looking for sex differences, we should notice gender similarities. According to some researchers, similarities far outweigh differences in the brain, body, and behavior (Roseberry & Roos, 2016; Xiong et al., 2018).

TABLE 6.2 How the Major Theories Explain Gender Differences

Theory	Essential Idea
Psychoanalytic	During the *phallic stage* (age 3–5), children notice whether or not they have a penis (*phallus* is the Greek word for penis). Boys experience *castration anxiety* and girls, *penis envy*. Both sexes masturbate and adore the parent of the other sex, named the *Oedipus* or *Electra complex*, after the characters in ancient Greek dramas.
Behaviorism	Children are conditioned to follow gender roles because they are reinforced or punished. For example, boys are called "handsome," girls called "pretty," and they are told "Boys don't cry" or "Girls don't fight." Peers reinforce gender-typical behavior: If a boy brings his doll to school, his classmates will punish him, not physically, but with words and laughter. He quickly learns. In social learning theory, an extension of behaviorism, children model themselves after their parents. Generally, mothers become more domestic when they have young children, and fathers tend to work longer hours. Children follow the examples they see, unaware that their very existence caused gender divergence.
Cognitive theory	Young children's immature cognition leads them to think in simple, egocentric categories, when appearance trumps logic. This is apparent in all children, including those who are transgender: Children want their hair and clothes to register their gender.
Evolutionary theory	Evolutionary theory holds that sexual passion is a basic human drive, because all creatures must reproduce. Males and females follow that evolutionary mandate by seeking to attract the other sex — walking, talking, and laughing in traditional feminine or masculine ways. This evolutionary drive is born into our species, with genes, chromosomes, and hormones dictating the boy/girl differences apparent in children.

Teaching Right and Wrong

A final challenge for parents is to teach morality. Young children are ready to learn right and wrong, an outgrowth of attachment and social awareness. Moral values are essential for our species; we depend on each other for protection, cooperation, and care.

EMPATHY

empathy
The ability to understand the emotions and concerns of another person, especially when they differ from one's own.

prosocial behavior
Actions that are helpful and kind but that are of no obvious benefit to the person doing them.

antipathy
Feelings of dislike or even hatred for another person.

With the cognitive advances of early childhood, and increased interaction with peers, these innate moral impulses are strengthened. Children develop **empathy**, an understanding of other people's feelings and concerns. Empathy depends on both experiences and brain maturation (Levy et al., 2019; Stern et al., 2019).

Empathy leads to compassion and **prosocial behavior**—"voluntary behavior meant to help another" (Padilla-Walker & Carlo, 2014, p. 6). Expressing concern, offering to share, and including a shy child in a game are examples of children's prosocial behavior. Prosocial behavior seems to result more from emotion than from intellect, more from empathy than from theory.

The link between empathy and prosocial behavior was traced longitudinally in children from 18 months to 6 years. Empathetic 2-year-olds were more likely to share, help, and play with other children in the first grade (Z. Taylor et al., 2013).

Feeling distress at another's pain may also be a part of human nature. But this innate emotion must be shaped to lead to moral behavior. Children learn to care deeply for family members, for people of their ethnicity, for peers, for all of humanity, or for no one. The basic ethical value of compassion is evident in all children, but parents shape that into specific morals (Poelker & Gibbons, 2019).

LIZ BANFIELD/PHOTOLIBRARY/GETTY IMAGES

DAVID HANCOCK/ALAMY STOCK PHOTO

Pinch, Poke, or Pat Antisocial and prosocial responses are actually a sign of maturation: Babies do not recognize the impact of their actions. These children have much more to learn, but they already are quite social.

ANTIPATHY

Empathy appears early in life: Infants mirror the smiles of other people, and young children are happy when other children are happy. **Antipathy** develops a little later, influenced by experience and culture, as children learn to dislike some people.

Just as empathy can lead to prosocial behavior, antipathy can lead to antisocial actions. A 2-year-old might look at another child, scowl, and then kick hard without provocation. Generally, parents and teachers teach better behavior, and children become more prosocial and less antisocial with age.

At every age, antisocial behavior indicates less empathy. That may originate in the brain. An allele or gene may have gone awry. But at least for children, lack of empathy correlates with parents who neither discuss nor respond to emotions (Richards et al., 2014; Z. Taylor et al., 2013). Antisocial parents tend to have antisocial children, a correlation that is probably both genetic and environmental, and may be particularly strong in boys (Li et al., 2017).

AGGRESSION

Early childhood is prime time for both aggressive behavior and victimization: Almost every young child is both an aggressor and a victim at some point (Saracho,

2016). Not surprisingly, given their moral sensibilities, young children judge whether another child's actions are fair or not.

The focus at first is on effects, not motives: A child who accidentally spilled water on another's painting may be the target of that child's anger. As young children gain in social understanding, particularly theory of mind, they gradually become better at understanding intentions, and that makes them more likely to forgive an accident (Choe et al., 2013a). Again, parents and teachers guide antisocial actions.

The distinction between impulse and intention is critical in deciding when and how adults need to stop a child's aggression. Researchers recognize four general types of aggression, each of which is evident in early childhood (see Table 6.3).

Instrumental aggression is common among 2-year-olds, who often want something and try to get it. This is called *instrumental* because it is a tool, or instrument, for getting something that is desired. The harm in grabbing a toy, and hitting if someone resists, is not understood until the child is old enough to have a better understanding of harm and possessions.

Because instrumental aggression occurs, **reactive aggression** also is common among young children. Almost every child reacts when hurt, whether or not the hurt was deliberate. The reaction may be aggressive—a child might punch in response to an unwelcome remark. As the prefrontal cortex matures and emotional regulation is possible, the impulse to strike back becomes controlled. Both instrumental aggression and reactive aggression are reduced with maturity (Olson et al., 2011).

Relational aggression (usually verbal) destroys self-esteem and disrupts social networks. A child might tell another, "You can't be my friend" or "You are fat," hurting another's feelings. Worse, a child might spread rumors, or tell others not to play with so-and-so.

These are examples of relational aggression, which becomes more hurtful and sometimes more common as social understanding advances. One study found that about one in every five preschool children commonly uses relational aggression (Swit & McMaugh, 2012). Before high school, almost every child has experienced some exclusion from a social group.

instrumental aggression
Hurtful behavior that is intended to get something that another person has.

reactive aggression
An impulsive retaliation for another person's intentional or accidental hurtful action.

relational aggression
Nonphysical acts, such as insults or social rejection, aimed at harming the social connection between the victim and other people.

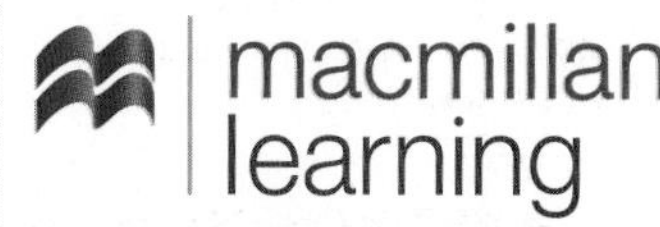

VIDEO: Interview with Lawrence Walker discusses what parents can do to encourage their children's moral development.

TABLE 6.3 The Four Forms of Aggression

Type of Aggression	Definition	Comments
Instrumental aggression	Hurtful behavior that is aimed at gaining something (such as a toy, a place in line, or a turn on the swing) that someone else has	Apparent from age 2 to 6; involves objects more than people; quite normal; more egocentric than antisocial.
Reactive aggression	An impulsive retaliation for a hurt (intentional or accidental) that can be verbal or physical	Indicates a lack of emotional regulation, characteristic of 2-year-olds. A 5-year-old can usually stop and think before reacting.
Relational aggression	Nonphysical acts, such as insults or social rejection, aimed at harming the social connections between the victim and others	Involves a personal attack and thus is directly antisocial; can be very hurtful; more common as children become socially aware.
Bullying aggression	Unprovoked, repeated physical or verbal attack, especially on victims who are unlikely to defend themselves	In both bullies and victims, a sign of poor emotional regulation; adults should intervene before the school years. (Bullying is discussed in Chapter 8.)

bullying aggression
Unprovoked, repeated physical or verbal attack, especially on victims who are unlikely to defend themselves.

The fourth and most ominous type is **bullying aggression**, done to dominate. Bullying aggression occurs among young children but should be stopped before kindergarten, when it becomes more destructive. Not only does it destroy the self-esteem of victims, it also impairs the later development of the bullies, who learn destructive habits that harm them lifelong.

A 3-year-old bully needs to learn the effects of their actions; a 10-year-old bully may be feared and admired; a 50-year-old bully may be hated and lonely. (An in-depth discussion of bullying appears in Chapter 8.)

Most types of aggression become less common from ages 2 to 6, because the brain matures, emotional regulation increases, and empathy builds. Prosocial actions increase, and antisocial ones decrease. Parental influence, again, is influential (Jambon et al., 2019b).

Teachers matter. One study found that close teacher–student relationships in preschool decrease aggression and victimization later on. The probable reason—children want to please the teachers, who guide them toward prosocial behavior (Runions & Shaw, 2013).

In addition, when children understand the social context, they are more selective in aggression, which decreases victimization (Ostrov et al., 2014). Each type of aggression is influenced by genes as well as by age (Lubke et al., 2018). Thus, some 3-year-olds are innately more aggressive than other children, and they are more likely to become antisocial children and adolescents. That should alert parents and teachers: Those children, particularly, need to develop empathy and emotional regulation.

what have you learned?

1. What are the four main styles of parenting?
2. What are the consequences of each style of parenting?
3. Why is discipline part of being a parent?
4. What are the arguments for and against corporal punishment?
5. How is psychological control similar to, and different from, corporal punishment?
6. When is time-out effective and when is it not?
7. What are the arguments for and against induction?
8. When do children recognize male and female differences?
9. What are the arguments for and against the idea that gender identity is innate?
10. What are the similarities and differences of the four kinds of aggression?
11. Are prosocial and antisocial behaviors inborn or learned?

Harm to Children

Adults worry about deadly childhood diseases. Is that fever a sign of meningitis? Could that headache signify a brain tumor? The reality, however, is that children are twice as likely to die accidentally than from illness.

Avoidable Injury

The high rate of accidental death is evident worldwide. Even in the poorest nations, children are more likely to die accidentally than to die of malnutrition or malaria.

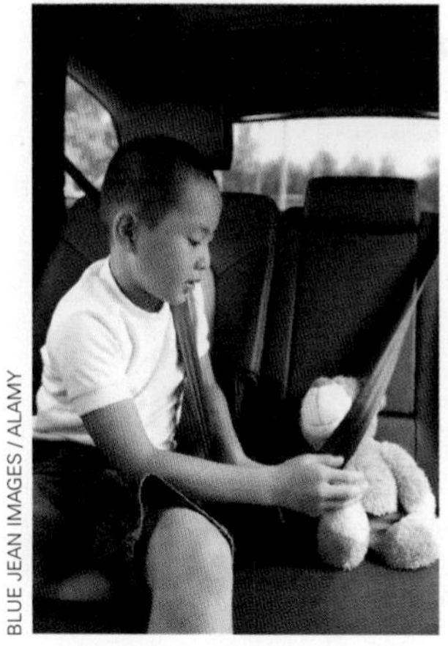

BLUE JEAN IMAGES / ALAMY

© DAVID R. FRAZIER/DANITADELIMONT.COM

Same Situation, Far Apart: Keeping Everyone Safe
Preventing child accidents requires action by both adults and children. In the United States *(left)*, adults passed laws and taught children to use seat belts — including this boy who buckles his stuffed companion. In France *(right)*, teachers stop cars while children hold hands to cross the street — each child keeping his or her partner moving ahead.

◆◆ OBSERVATION QUIZ
Should we worry that the boy is buckling his stuffed animal and not himself? (see answer, page 203) ↑

In developed nations (including the United States) accidents kill more children than all other causes combined. Everywhere, motor vehicles cause most accidental deaths, either with children as pedestrians, in poor nations, or as passengers, in rich nations.

INJURY CONTROL

Instead of using the term *accident prevention*, public health experts prefer **harm reduction** or **injury control**. Consider the implications. *Accident* implies that an injury is random, unpredictable; if anyone is at fault, it's a careless parent or an accident-prone child. Instead, *injury control* suggests that the impact of an injury can be limited, and *harm reduction*, that harm can be minimal.

Reducing serious harm requires attention to three levels of prevention.

- **Primary prevention** considers the overall conditions that affect the likelihood of injury. Laws and customs reduce risk for everyone, of every age and circumstance.
- **Secondary prevention** is more targeted, averting harm in high-risk situations or for vulnerable individuals.
- **Tertiary prevention** begins after an injury has already occurred, limiting damage.

harm reduction/injury control Reducing the potential negative consequences of behavior, such as safety surfaces replacing cement at a playground.

primary prevention Actions that change overall background conditions to prevent some unwanted event or circumstance.

secondary prevention Actions that avert harm in a high-risk situation, such as using seat belts in cars.

tertiary prevention Actions, such as immediate and effective medical treatment, after an adverse event (such as illness or injury).

An example comes from data on motor-vehicle deaths. As compared with 50 years ago, far more cars are on the road, but the rate of children killed by cars in the United States is only one-fourth of what it was (Centers for Disease Control, July 3, 2018) (see Figure 6.3). How has each level of prevention bought this about?

Primary prevention includes sidewalks, stop lights, pedestrian overpasses, streetlights, and traffic circles. Cars have been redesigned (e.g., better headlights, windows, and brakes), and drivers' competence has improved (e.g., stronger penalties for drunk driving). Reduction of traffic via improved mass transit provides additional primary prevention. Everyone benefits.

Secondary prevention includes crossing guards, flashing lights on school buses, salt on icy roads, warning signs before blind curves, speed bumps, reflective vests, toddlers belted into strollers, and automatic air bags.

Some jurisdictions have taken secondary prevention to include free, infant car seats, professionally installed before newborns are taken home from hospitals. That is one reason that, in 2017 in the entire United States, only 81 infant passengers died in motor-vehicle accidents, about one-sixth the number 15 years earlier.

Finally, *tertiary prevention* includes speedy ambulances, efficient emergency room procedures, effective follow-up care, and laws against hit-and-run drivers. All these have improved over decades ago.

◆◆ Especially for Urban Planners
Describe a neighborhood park that would benefit 2- to 5-year-olds (see response, page 203)

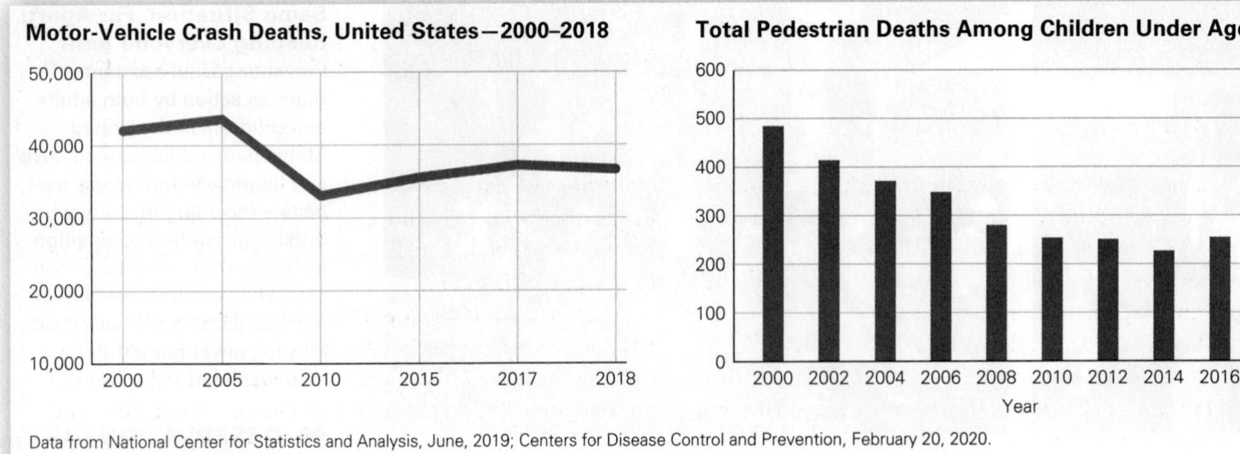

FIGURE 6.3 No Matter What Statistic Motor-vehicle fatalities of pedestrians, passengers, and drivers, from cars, trucks, and motorcycles, for people of all ages, were all lower in 2018 than in 2000, a dramatic difference since the population had increased by a third and the number of cars increased as well. Proof could be shown in a dozen charts, but here is one of the most telling: deaths of child pedestrians. All three levels of prevention—in roads, cars, drivers, police, caregivers, and the children themselves—contributed to this shift.

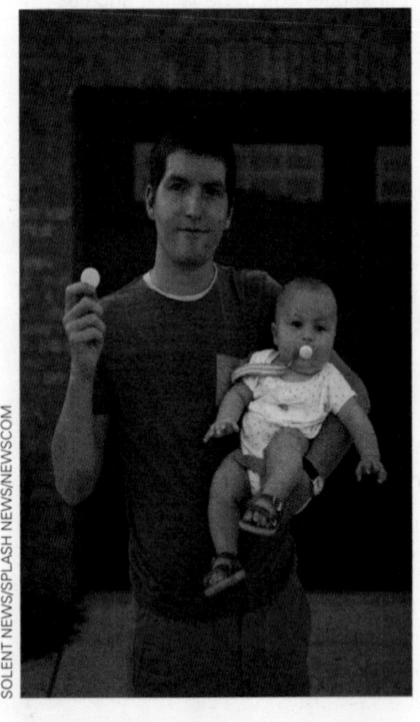

SOLENT NEWS/SPLASH NEWS/NEWSCOM

Forget Baby Henry? Infants left in parked cars on hot days can die from the heat. Henry's father invented a disc to be placed under the baby that buzzes his cell phone if he is more than 20 feet away from the disc. He hopes that all parents will buy one.

Medical personnel speak of the *golden hour*, the hour following an accident in which a victim should be treated. Of course, there is nothing magical about 60 minutes in contrast to 61 minutes, but the sooner a victim reaches a trauma center, the better chance of recovery (Schroeder et al., 2019).

EARLY-CHILDHOOD DANGERS

People of all ages need to be protected from accidents, but this topic is in this chapter because the youngest children (age 2 to 6) are more likely to be seriously hurt than slightly older children. Why? There are three sets of factors: in the child, in the microsystem, and in the macrosystem.

First, unlike infants, young children's motor skills allow them to run, leap, scramble, and grab in a flash, yet their immature prefrontal cortex makes them impulsive; they plunge into danger. Their curiosity is boundless; their impulses uninhibited; their analysis limited.

Other reasons are in the microsystem. Families overestimate what children understand. Parents think that they know their children, yet "young children routinely do unpredictable things that lead to injuries" (Morrongiello, 2018, p. 218).

A child who has never seemed interested in, for instance, the kitchen knife rack might one day carve, cut, or stab, never having learned how dangerous knives can be. Children run away and get lost, swallow pills and don't tell anyone that they feel sick, or start a fire and run away when they cannot put it out.

Finally, research finds that changes in the macrosystem are the most important of all, because they are primary and secondary prevention, controlling injury so tertiary prevention is not needed. Although accidents used to be blamed solely on foolish children and neglectful parents, the data now show that community policies have a notable effect.

Serious injury is unlikely if a child falls on a safety surface instead of on concrete, if a car seat and airbags protect the body in a crash, if a bicycle helmet cracks instead of a skull, or if swallowed pills come from a tiny bottle. Reducing harm should not assume that parents always do the right thing. I did not (see A Case to Study).

A CASE TO STUDY

"My Baby Swallowed Poison"

Our daughter Bethany, at age 2, climbed onto the kitchen counter to find, open, and swallow most of a bottle of baby aspirin. Where was her inattentive mother? I was 15 feet away, nursing our second child and watching television. I did not notice what Bethany was doing until I checked on her during a commercial.

Bethany is alive and well today, protected by all three levels of prevention. Primary prevention included laws limiting the number of baby aspirin per container; secondary prevention included my pediatrician's written instruction of me when Bethany was a week old to buy syrup of ipecac; tertiary prevention was my phone call to Poison Control.

I told the helpful stranger who answered the phone, "My baby swallowed poison." He calmly asked me a few questions and then advised me to give Bethany ipecac to make her throw up. I did, and she did. [Ipecac is no longer recommended in such cases, but calling Poison Control (800-222-1222) still is.]

That ipecac had been purchased two years before, when I was a brand-new mother and followed every word of my pediatrician's advice. If the doctor had waited to tell me about poisons until Bethany was able to climb, I might have not have followed his advice, because by then I was more confident in my ability to prevent harm.

I still blame myself, but remembering all the mistakes I made in parenting (only a few mentioned in this book), I am grateful for every level of prevention.

In all this discussion of harm, although changes in the macrosystem are most effective, they are also slowest: It takes decades from the time research discovers a problem to the passage of laws to protect children. Fences around pools, safety locks on guns, seat belts in cars were all advocated by developmentalists long before laws required them. The slow public process is evident in the history of lead poisoning (see A View from Science).

A VIEW FROM SCIENCE

Lead in the Environment

Lead was recognized as a poison a century ago (Hamilton, 1914). The symptoms of *plumbism*, as lead poisoning is called, were obvious—intellectual disability, hyperactivity, and even death if the level reached 70 micrograms per deciliter of blood.

The lead industry defended the heavy metal. Correlation is not causation, they argued. Low-income children (who often had high blood levels) had lower IQs because of third variables, such as malnutrition, inadequate schools, and parents who let their children eat flaking chips of lead paint (which tastes sweet). This made sense to some developmental psychologists (Scarr, 1985) and, I confess, in the first textbook I wrote (Berger, 1980).

Lead remained a major ingredient in paint (it speeds drying) and in gasoline (it raises octane) for most of the twentieth century. Gradually, chemical analyses of blood and teeth, with careful longitudinal and replicated research, proved that lead, not only in paint but also in dust and air, was poisoning children (Needleman et al., 1990; Needleman & Gatsonis, 1990).

Studies found that blood lead levels predict attention deficits, school suspensions, and aggression (Amato et al., 2013; Goodlad et al., 2013; Nkomo et al., 2018). Lead is especially destructive of the brains of fetuses, infants, and young children (Hanna-Attisha et al., 2016), with long-term effects. Children who have high blood lead levels have higher rates of psychopathology in adulthood, including severe depression and anxiety (Reuben et al., 2019).

Many parents now wipe window ledges clean, avoid exposing their children to construction dust, test drinking water, and discard lead-based medicines and crockery (available in some other nations). They make sure their babies consume sufficient calcium (in dairy products and certain vegetables) because calcium helps the body eliminate lead (Kordas et al., 2018).

Remember, however, that public health advocates find that primary prevention, with changes in regulations that affect everyone, are more effective than relying on individual

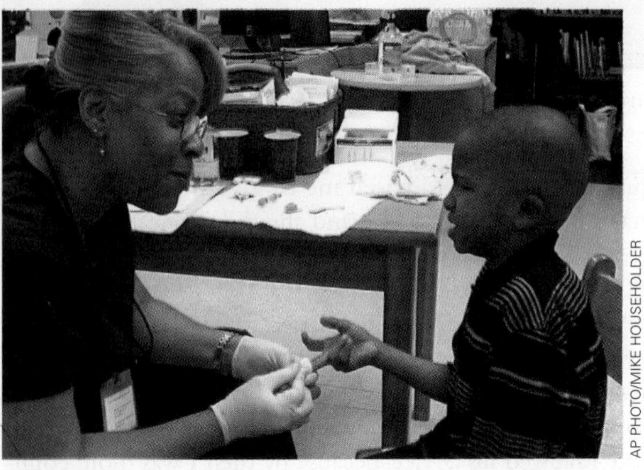

Not His Choice His parents want to know his blood lead level, but this nurse volunteered to test the children of Flint, Michigan. Earlier choices were made by people distant from this scene, who sought to save money instead of health.

parents. They fear that blaming parents distracts from the role of industry, laws, and public officials.

Despite complaints from industry, the United States banned lead in paint (in 1978) and automobile fuel (in 1996). The blood level that caused plumbism was set at 40 micrograms per deciliter, then 20, and then 10. Danger is now thought to begin at 5 micrograms, but no level has been proven to be risk-free (MMWR, April 5, 2013).

Regulation has had two dramatic effects. First was in the lead in children's bodies. The percentage of U.S. 1- to 5-year-olds with more than 5 micrograms of lead per deciliter of blood was 8.6 percent in 1999–2001, 4.1 percent in 2003–2006, 2.6 percent in 2007–2010, and less than 1 percent in 2010–2014 (Raymond et al., January 20, 2017) (see Figure 6.4).

The second was in adolescent crime. Three times as many teenagers were arrested in the United States in 1994 compared to 2018. Teenage crime reduction may reflect the difference between teenagers who had high lead levels in their brains as babies (born before 1978) and teenagers with very low levels (born after 1996). Research in Canada, Germany, Italy, Australia, New Zealand, France, Finland, as well as the United States finds that teenage crime plummeted about 20 years after laws reduced lead in the environment. Nations that were first to reduce lead were also first to see reductions in adolescent crime.

Not surprisingly, companies that use lead in manufacturing think that other factors, such as fewer unwanted births, improved law enforcement, and better education, are the main reasons for the historic low of teenage arrests. But scientists in Sweden have undertaken meticulous longitudinal research, controlling for all the other factors, and concluded that reduced lead levels in children directly reduced crimes by 7 to 14 percent (Grönqvist et al., 2014).

That finding makes the example of Flint, Michigan, all the more tragic. In April 2014, cost-saving officials (appointed by the state to take over the city when the tax base shrunk as the auto industry left) changed the municipal drinking water from Lake Huron to the Flint River. That river contained chemicals from industrial waste that increased lead leaching from old pipes, contaminating tap water used for drinking and mixing infant formula.

The percentage of young children in Flint with blood lead levels above 5 micrograms per deciliter doubled when the water source changed, from 2.4 to 4.9 percent, and more than tripled in one neighborhood, from 4.6 to 15.7 percent (Hanna-Attisha et al., 2016). The action of that state official was an "abject failure to protect public health" (Bellinger, 2016, p. 1101).

The consequences may harm these children lifelong, not only in their education but also in their activity level (hyperactivity is more common in lead-poisoned children). Some of those children will be in prison because of the water they drank as babies.

Developmentalists have known about the dangers of lead for a century, and about the specific harm to infant brains for decades. Why didn't the Michigan administrator know or care?

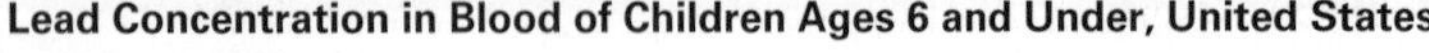

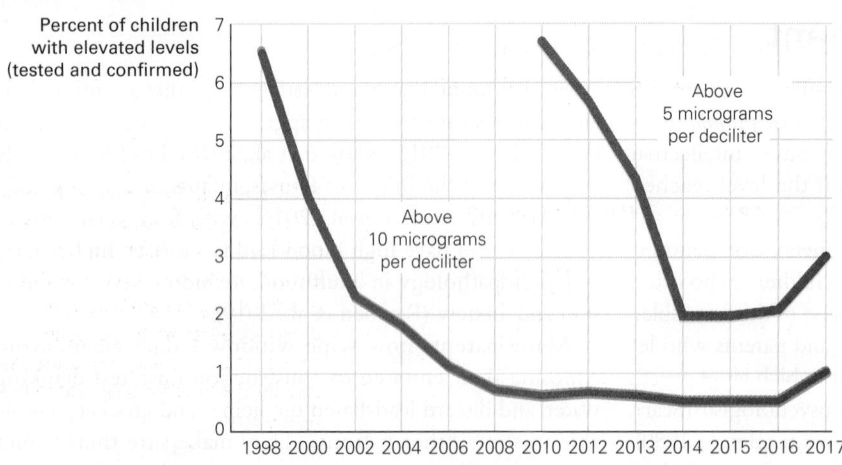

FIGURE 6.4 **Dramatic Improvement in a Decade** Once researchers established the perils of high lead levels in children's blood, the percentage of children suffering from plumbism fell by more than 300 percent. Levels are higher in states that once had heavy manufacturing and lower in mountain and Pacific states.

Abuse and Neglect

The research on child accidents has revealed another problem. **Child maltreatment** includes all intentional harm to, or avoidable endangerment of, anyone under 18 years of age. Thus, child maltreatment can be *abuse*, which is deliberate action that harms a child's physical, emotional, or sexual well-being, or *neglect*, which is failure to meet essential needs, such as for food, medical care, or learning.

child maltreatment
Intentional harm to or avoidable endangerment of anyone under 18 years of age.

reported maltreatment
Harm or endangerment about which someone has notified the authorities.

substantiated maltreatment
Harm or endangerment that has been reported, investigated, and verified.

FROM RARE TO COMMON

Until about 1960, people thought child abuse was a rare and sudden attack by a disturbed stranger, usually a man. Today we know better.

A Boston doctor treated children who injured themselves in accidents, according to their caregivers. But X-rays showed prior injuries, broken bones that healed without medical care, scalding that suggested forced holding in hot water, bruises on both sides of a child's face instead of on one side as would happen in a fall. That doctor began to describe a "battered child syndrome" (Kempe & Kempe, 1978).

We now know that maltreatment is neither rare nor sudden, and that 90 percent of perpetrators are one or both of the child's parents—more often the mother than the father (U.S. Department of Health and Human Services, 2019). That makes it worse: Ongoing maltreatment at home, with no protector, is much more damaging than a single outside incident. That also reveals the path for prevention: Help stressed, angry parents before they harm their children.

How often does maltreatment occur? No one knows. Not all instances are noticed, not all that are noticed are reported, and not all reports are substantiated. Part of the problem is in distinguishing harsh discipline from abuse, and a momentary lapse from ongoing neglect. If the standard were perfect parenting all day and all night from birth to age 18, as judged by neighbors and professionals, then every child is mistreated at least once. Only severe or chronic cases are tallied.

Reported maltreatment (technically a referral) means simply that the authorities have been informed. Since 1993, the number of children referred to authorities in the United States has ranged from about 2.7 million to 4.1 million per year, with 3.6 million in 2018 (U.S. Department of Health and Human Services, 2019).

Substantiated maltreatment means that a case has been reported, investigated, and verified (see Figure 6.5). In 2018, 677,529 U.S. children suffered substantiated maltreatment. Every year in the United States, substantiated maltreatment harms more than 1 in every 100 children aged 2 to 5 years old.

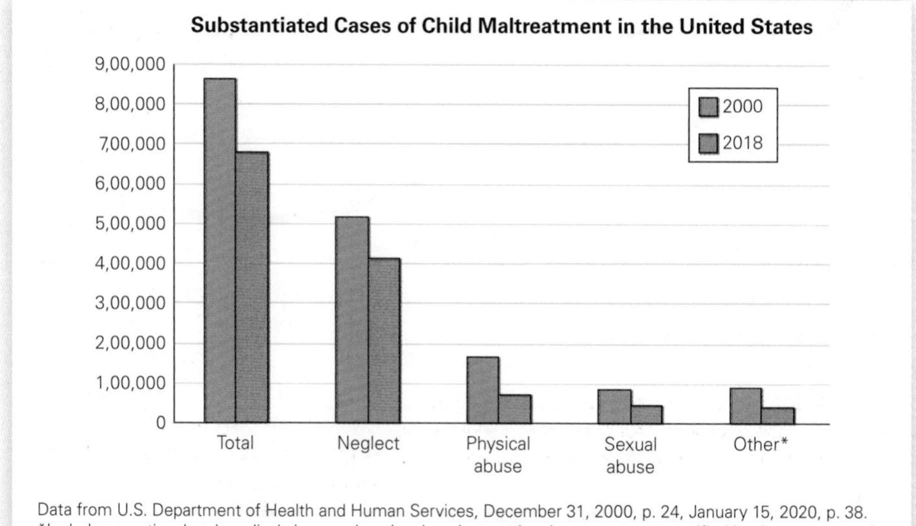

Data from U.S. Department of Health and Human Services, December 31, 2000, p. 24, January 15, 2020, p. 38.
*Includes emotional and medical abuse, educational neglect, and maltreatment not specified by the state records.

FIGURE 6.5 **Not Good News** It might seem to be good news that physical and sexual abuse are increasingly uncommon. But, the effects of neglect are particularly ominous, because crucial brain development depends on nutritional, cognitive, and emotional care in the early years.

The 5-to-1 ratio of reported versus substantiated cases occurs because:

- Each child is counted only once, so five reports about a single child result in one substantiated case.
- Substantiation requires proof. Most investigations do not find unmistakable harm or a witness.
- About two-thirds of all reports come from professionals, who are *mandated reporters*, required to report any signs of *possible* maltreatment. Investigation usually finds no harm.
- About one-third of all reports are "screened out," either because the victim is not a child or because the case belongs to another jurisdiction, such as the military or a Native American tribe.
- A report may be false or deliberately misleading (though few are) (Sedlak & Ellis, 2014).

Data on substantiated maltreatment in the United States in 2018 indicate that 62 percent of cases were neglect, 11 percent physical abuse, 7 percent sexual abuse, 16 percent multiple forms of abuse, and 6 percent other (psychological, medical, educational, and so on).

Ironically, neglect is often ignored by the public, who are "stuck in an overwhelming and debilitating" concept that maltreatment always causes immediate bodily harm (Kendall-Taylor et al., 2014, p. 810). Neglect is "the most common and most frequently fatal form of child maltreatment" (Proctor & Dubowitz, 2014, p. 27).

HOPEFUL SIGNS

If we rely on official U.S. statistics, positive trends are apparent. Substantiated child maltreatment increased from about 1960 to 1990 but decreased from 1990 to 2010. Other sources also report declines, particularly in sexual abuse.

However, trends since 2010 suggest that rates may be increasing again (see Figure 6.6). There are many possible explanations. The growing gap between rich and poor families is the most plausible, since poverty correlates with neglect. One troubling finding is that COVID-19 produced fewer reports. Authorities worry that, with more children required to stay inside homes with stressed or absent caregivers, abuse and neglect are undetected.

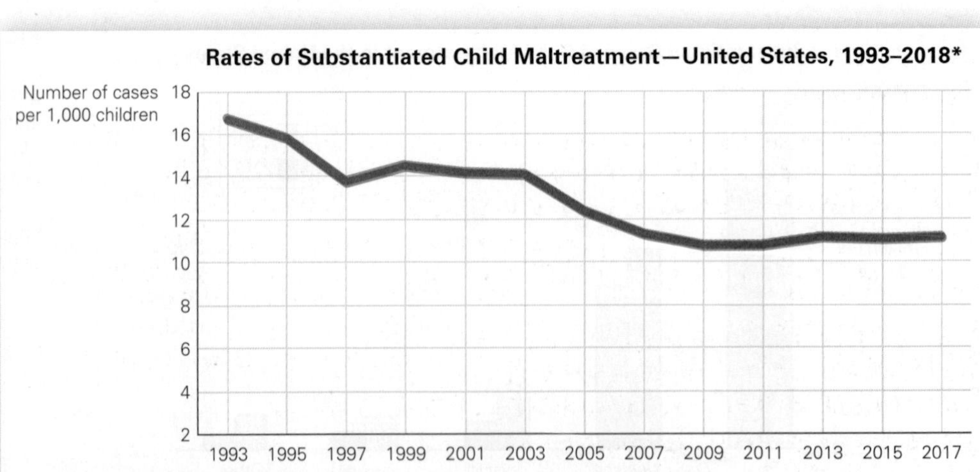

FIGURE 6.6 **Getting Better? Still Far Too Many** The number of substantiated cases of maltreatment of children under age 18 in the United States is too high, but there is some good news: The rate has declined significantly from its peak (15.3 per 1,000) in 1993.

State-by-state reports also raise doubts about the data. The 2016 rate of child victimization was seven times higher in Massachusetts than in Virginia, 23.3 versus 3.2 per 1,000 children. But no one thinks children are seven times safer in Virginia.

Maybe people in Massachusetts are quicker to report harm? Maybe people in Virginia accept severe punishment more readily than people in Massachusetts?

Certain customs (such as circumcision, pierced ears, and spanking) are considered abusive among some groups but not in others; their effects vary accordingly. Willingness to report also varies. The United States has become more culturally diverse, and people have become more suspicious of government but also of each other. Does that reduce reporting or increase it?

CONSEQUENCES OF MALTREATMENT

Hate is corrosive; love is healing. A warm and enduring friendship can repair some damage, but mistreated children typically regard other people as hostile. That keeps them from making the social connections that might help. Instead they become friendless, aggressive, and isolated.

Not always, fortunately. When others love them, some recover. That love sometimes comes from the formerly abusive parent who expresses regret for past behavior (Schafer et al., 2014). More often, recovery comes from a loving and patient spouse or from a close relationship with a child. Unfortunately, insecure attachments can echo in the next generation, but abused children do not necessarily become abusive parents (Widom et al., 2015a). Some avoid the mistakes of their parents, especially if friends or partners show them a better way.

In the chilling memoir *Educated*, Tara Westover (2018) describes the mistreatment she and her six siblings endured as children. For her, abuse came primarily from her brother, neglect primarily from her father. However, with the help of many outsiders, including students and professors at Brigham Young University and then at Cambridge, she recovered as an adult. Three of her siblings did not.

Even for those who recover, however, the consequences of maltreatment may last for decades (Toth & Manly, 2019). Immediate impairment is obvious, when a child is bruised, broken, afraid to talk, or failing in school. More crippling effects endure lifelong, in social skills and self-esteem. Westover, despite great success as an adult, experienced an episode of crippling depression.

◆◆ Especially for Nurses
While weighing a 4-year-old, you notice several bruises on the child's legs. When you ask about them, the child says nothing, and the parent says that the child bumps into things. What should you do? (see response, page 203)

Even if maltreatment stops at age 5, emotional problems (externalizing for the boys and internalizing for the girls) linger (Godinet et al., 2014). Adult drug abuse, social isolation, and poor health result from maltreatment decades earlier.

Finding and keeping a job is a critical aspect of adult well-being, yet adults who were maltreated suffer in this way as well. One study carefully matched 807 children who had experienced substantiated abuse with other children of the same sex, ethnicity, and family SES.

About 35 years later, when maltreatment was a distant memory, those who had been mistreated were 14 percent less likely to be employed. The researchers concluded: "[A]bused and neglected children experience large and enduring economic consequences" (Currie & Widom, 2010, p. 111).

In this study, women had more difficulty finding and keeping a job than men. It may be that self-esteem, emotional stability, and social skills are even more important for female employees than for male ones. This study is just one of hundreds of longitudinal studies, all of which find that maltreatment affects people decades after broken bones have healed or skinny bodies have filled out.

ADVERSE CHILDHOOD EXPERIENCES

As already explained, maltreatment is much more devastating when it arises from the child's home, rather than from an isolated incident with a disturbed stranger. We now have evidence that shows how true this is.

adverse childhood experiences (ACEs)
A range of potentially traumatic childhood stresses, including abuse, neglect, family disruption and dysfunction, and parental incarceration, that can have lasting, negative effects on health and well-being.

permanency planning
An effort by child-welfare authorities to find a long-term living situation that will provide stability and support for a maltreated child. A goal is to avoid repeated caregiver or school changes, which are particularly harmful.

foster care
When a person (usually a child) is cared for by someone other than the parents.

kinship care
A form of foster care in which a relative, usually a grandmother, becomes the approved caregiver.

Thousands of researchers have demonstrated that an accumulation of harmful events in childhood is devastating in adulthood. Nine possible **adverse childhood experiences (ACEs)** are almost always included in this research:

- Abuse of the child (physical, sexual, verbal);
- Problems of someone else in the household (mental illness, addiction, prison); and
- Parental conflict (separation, divorce, domestic violence).

Other ACEs that are often included are poverty, frequent change of residence, and neighborhood conditions (Hughes et al., 2017).

Adverse experiences in childhood affect people decades later, even if the person has left them behind. ACEs are common (60 percent of U.S. adults have experienced at least one), but the lifelong damage is most evident when a child experiences four or more. That is the case for about 15 percent of adults (Merrick et al., 2019). Four ACEs double the rate of deadly adult diseases (cancer, heart disease, and so on) and increase sixfold the rate of adult sexual abuse, mental illness, substance abuse, and self-inflicted harm (Hughes et al., 2017).

We have known for decades that childhood abuse may have long-term effects, but the research on ACEs has added three new discoveries:

- A multiplier effect: Accumulated ACEs magnify the impact more than simply adding them together.
- Psychosocial impact exceeds biological impact. The increased risk of suicide, for instance, is greater than the increased risk of cancer. Devastation to self-esteem is profound, reducing later education, employment, and relationships.
- Problems should not be blamed on ethnic, immigrant, or racial status. Although prejudice and poverty increase the incidence of ACEs, background factors are not the cause. Instead, actual childhood experiences are. Thus, many children from low-SES, immigrant, Black, or Latinx families escape ACEs, and some middle-class, native-born, White children experience four or more.

The research on ACEs comprises a mandate for pediatricians, parents, and political leaders: Avoid stereotypes and protect every child from the direct conditions that increase harm (Jones et al., 2020; McEwen & Gregerson, 2019; Rasmussen et al., 2020).

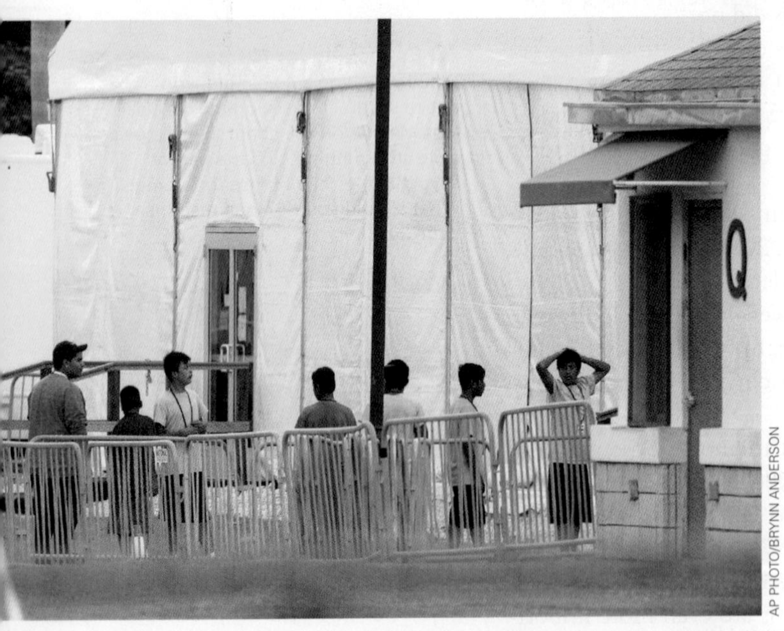

AP PHOTO/BRYNN ANDERSON

Line Up, Single File These children were separated from their parents at the border between Mexico and the United States. Here, on June 22, 2018, they are in McCallen, Texas, hoping to see their parents again soon. We do not know what happened next.

PLANNING FOR THE FUTURE

To avoid those long-term effects, social workers now advocate **permanency planning**, which is planning how to nurture the child until adulthood (Scott et al., 2013). Uncertainty, a string of temporary placements, return and then removal again from parents, frequent changes in schools and neighborhoods, are all destructive. They make four or more ACEs more likely.

Sometimes the best plan is for long-term **foster care**, in which another adult is the caregiver for years instead of the abusive parents. If the other adult is a relative, the arrangement is called **kinship care**.

Every year for the past decade in the United States, almost half a million children have been officially in foster care. At least another million are unofficially in kinship care, because relatives realize that the parents are unable or unwilling to provide good care.

Most foster children are from low-income families and are people of color—a statistic that reveals problems in primary prevention. In the United States, most foster children have physical, intellectual, and emotional problems that arose in their original families. Obviously, foster parents need much more than financial subsidies to provide good care for such children.

The best permanency plan is adoption by another family, who will provide care lifelong. However, adoption is difficult, for many reasons:

- Judges and biological parents are reluctant to release children for adoption.
- Most adoptive parents prefer infants, but many biological parents do not release their children until they have tried, and failed, to provide good care. Even then, they may hope to do better, and thus refuse to allow adoption.
- Some agencies screen out families not headed by married, heterosexual couples.

DATA CONNECTIONS: Children Are the Poorest Americans examines U.S. poverty rates by state and age group. Achieve

JESSICA ANTOLA/CONTOUR/GETTY IMAGES

She Recovered and Sang Maya Angelou was abused as a child, but she was also loved and protected by her brother and other family members. The result was extraordinary insight into the human condition, as she learned "why the cage bird sings."

Three Levels of Prevention, Again

Remember the goal of our study is to help every person to achieve full potential. Primary prevention follows naturally from learning about development. For example, one factor that predicts maltreatment is insecure attachment: Efforts to improve parent–child relationships can prevent serious abuse (Toth & Manly, 2019). That is primary prevention.

Noticing and reporting is secondary prevention. Warning signs need to be spotted and intervention needs to begin early, so a risky situation does not worsen. Relationship problems should be repaired before they become harmful (Toth & Manly, 2019). Table 6.4 lists signs of child maltreatment, both neglect and abuse. None of these signs *proves* maltreatment, but investigation is needed whenever they occur.

Tertiary prevention limits harm after injury has occurred. Some readers of this book will become the doctors and nurses who treat injured children, some will help the parents by treating addiction, assigning a housekeeper, locating family helpers, securing better living quarters. If this is your plan, we commend you.

TABLE 6.4 **Signs of Maltreatment in Children Aged 2 to 10**
Injuries that do not fit an "accidental" explanation, such as bruises on both sides of the face or body; burns with a clear line between burned and unburned skin; "falls" that result in cuts, not scrapes
Repeated injuries, especially broken bones not properly tended (visible on X-ray)
Fantasy play, with dominant themes of violence or sexual knowledge
Slow physical growth, especially with unusual appetite or lack of appetite
Ongoing physical complaints, such as stomachaches, headaches, genital pain, sleepiness
Reluctance to talk, to play, or to move, especially if development is slow
No close friendships; hostility toward others; bullying of smaller children
Hypervigilance, with quick, impulsive reactions, such as cringing, startling, or hitting
Frequent absence from school
Frequent changes of address
Turnover in caregivers who pick up child, or caregiver who comes late, seems high
Expressions of fear rather than joy on seeing the caregiver
Child is fearful, easily startled by noise, defensive, and quick to attack
Confusion between fantasy and reality

what have you learned?

1. What can be concluded from the data on rates of childhood injury?
2. How do injury deaths compare in developed and developing nations?
3. What is the difference between primary, secondary, and tertiary prevention?
4. Why have the rates of child accidental death declined?
5. Why is reported maltreatment five times higher than substantiated maltreatment?
6. Why is neglect considered worse than abuse?
7. What are the long-term consequences of childhood maltreatment?
8. When is adoption part of permanency planning?
9. Why does permanency planning rarely result in adoption?

SUMMARY

Emotional Development

1. Emotional regulation is crucial during early childhood. It occurs in Erikson's third developmental stage, initiative versus guilt. Children normally feel pride when they demonstrate initiative, but sometimes they feel guilt or even shame at an unsatisfactory outcome.

2. Intrinsic motivation is particularly strong in early childhood, when a child concentrates on a drawing or engages in a conversation with an imaginary friend.

Play

3. All young children enjoy playing—preferably with peers who teach them lessons in social interaction that their parents do not. Screen time may slow down social learning.

4. Active play takes many forms, with rough-and-tumble play fostering social skills and sociodramatic play developing emotional regulation.

Challenges for Caregivers

5. Three classic styles of parenting are authoritarian, permissive, and authoritative. Generally, children are happier and more successful when their parents express warmth and set guidelines. A fourth style of parenting, neglectful/uninvolved, is always harmful.

6. Punishment can have long-term consequences, with both corporal punishment and psychological control teaching lessons that few parents want their children to learn. Other methods include time-out and induction.

7. Young children notice gender differences in clothes, toys, playmates, and future careers. By age 6, most believe that males and females are opposites, a false gender binary. A nonbinary perspective is helpful, not only to understand transgender and intersex children, but also to recognize substantial overlap in traits of cisgendered people.

8. Young children's sense of self, attachment to caregivers, and social awareness become the foundation for morality. Compassion is innate, but children need to be taught who to care for, and what behaviors are appropriate.

9. Prosocial emotions lead to caring for others; antisocial behavior includes instrumental, reactive, relational, and bullying aggression. The first two usually become less common as children become more aware of the difference between deliberate and accidental harm.

Harm to Children

10. Accidents cause more child deaths in the United States than all diseases combined. Close supervision and public safeguards can protect young children from their own eager, impulsive curiosity.

11. Harm reduction occurs on many levels, including long before and immediately after each harmful incident. Primary prevention protects everyone, secondary prevention focuses on high-risk conditions and people, and tertiary prevention occurs after harm as occurred.

12. Substantiated maltreatment is less common than it was a few decades ago, but it still occurs for about 700,000 children in the United States each year. The effects of child maltreatment may endure in adulthood, even when abuse ended years earlier.

13. Sometimes foster care is needed, with kinship care—formal or not—a common practice. Adoption is much less available now for many reasons.

KEY TERMS

emotional regulation (p. 173)
initiative versus guilt (p. 174)
intrinsic motivation (p. 175)
extrinsic motivation (p. 175)
rough-and-tumble play (p. 179)
sociodramatic play (p. 180)
authoritarian parenting (p. 182)
permissive parenting (p. 182)
authoritative parenting (p. 182)
neglectful/uninvolved parenting (p. 183)
corporal punishment (p. 183)
psychological control (p. 185)
time-out (p. 185)
induction (p. 186)
sex differences (p. 186)
gender differences (p. 186)
transgender (p. 187)
gender binary (p. 188)
empathy (p. 190)
prosocial behavior (p. 190)
antipathy (p. 190)
instrumental aggression (p. 191)
reactive aggression (p. 191)
relational aggression (p. 191)
bullying aggression (p. 192)
harm reduction/injury control (p. 193)
primary prevention (p. 193)
secondary prevention (p. 193)
tertiary prevention (p. 193)
child maltreatment (p. 197)
reported maltreatment (p. 197)
substantiated maltreatment (p. 197)
adverse childhood experiences (ACEs) (p. 200)
permanency planning (p. 200)
foster care (p. 200)
kinship care (p. 200)

APPLICATIONS

1. Children's television programming is rife with stereotypes about ethnicity, gender, and morality. Watch an hour of children's TV, especially on a Saturday morning, and describe the content of both the programs and the commercials. Draw conclusions about stereotyping, citing specific evidence, not generalities.

2. Gender indicators often go unnoticed. Go to a public place (park, restaurant, busy street) and spend at least 10 minutes recording examples of gender differentiation, such as articles of clothing, mannerisms, interaction patterns, and activities. Quantify what you see, such as baseball hats on eight males and two females. Or (better, but more difficult) describe four male–female conversations, indicating gender differences in length and frequency of talking, interruptions, vocabulary, and so on.

3. Ask three parents about punishment, including their preferred type, at what age, for what misdeeds, and by whom. Ask your three informants how they were punished as children and how that affected them. If your sources all agree, find a parent (or a classmate) who has a different view.

ESPECIALLY FOR ANSWERS

Response for College Students (from p. 175): Both are important. Extrinsic motivation includes parental pressure and the need to get a good job after graduation. Intrinsic motivation includes the joy of learning, especially if you can express that learning in ways others recognize. Have you ever taken a course that was not required and was said to be difficult? That was intrinsic motivation.

Response for Parents (from p. 184): No. The worst time to spank a child is when you are angry. You might seriously hurt the child, and the child will associate anger with violence. You would do better to learn to control your anger and develop other strategies for discipline and for prevention of misbehavior.

Response for Urban Planners (from p. 193): Remember that young children like to move and are unaware of many dangers. So, the park would have many places to encourage running and developing movement skills—climbing and swinging equipment—with safety surfaces, open spaces, and fences, so children cannot wander off. You would want adults to be aware of what is happening, but not interfering much, so benches with a good view of active children should be included.

Response for Nurses (from p. 199): Most children have bruises and scrapes from ordinary play, and yet most maltreated children are not spotted until the abuse becomes dramatic. As a nurse, you are a mandated reporter, and even if not, you would need to make sure the child and the parent have the help they need. If you are afraid of making a problem worse, don't let that fear stop you. Instead, it can lead you to follow up to ensure a caring and preventive response to your report.

OBSERVATION QUIZ ANSWERS

Answer to Observation Quiz (from p. 183): It is impossible to be certain based on one moment, but the best guess is authoritative. He seems patient and protective, providing comfort and guidance, neither forcing (authoritarian) nor letting the child do whatever he wants (permissive).

Answer to Observation Quiz (from p. 193): No. This is the stage when imaginary friends are common, a sign of intelligence. His understanding of the need for seat belts is likely to extend to himself once he is satisfied that his companion is secure.

PART IV

CHAPTER 7 CHAPTER 8

Middle Childhood

Every year has joys and sorrows, gains and losses. But if you were pushed to choose one best period, you might select middle childhood. The years from 6 to 11 are usually a time of health and growth. Children master new skills, learn thousands of words, and enter a wider social world. They are safe and happy; the dangers of adolescence (drugs, early sex, violence) are distant.

But not always. For some children, these years are the worst, not the best. They hate school or fear home; they live with asthma or disability; they are bullied or lonely.

Nor are these years straightforward for every adult who cares for these children. Instead, controversies abound. Should reading and math crowd out music, or handwriting, or physical activity? Does single parenthood, divorce, cohabitation, or poverty harm children? The next two chapters explore the joys and complications of middle childhood.

MARC ROMANELLI/BLEND IMAGES/GETTY IMAGES

CHAPTER

7

MIDDLE CHILDHOOD

Body and Mind

what will you know?

- Who is accountable when a child is obese?
- Why are some math concepts difficult at age 4 but easier at age 8?
- Are schools in the United States better than schools in other nations?
- Should disabled or gifted children be in regular classes?

After school I sit on a bench, watching two of my grandchildren and hundreds of other children play. Many parents, grandparents, and babysitters are on other benches, sometimes talking to each other, sometimes reading.

I admire the few parents who are more active: One father pretends to chase the younger children, including his daughter, to their shrieks of joy. Another father plays soccer with the older children, encouraging both the novices ("Nice kick!") and his own skilled son. One mother stays near her blind daughter, who nonetheless climbs up the ladder to go down the slide.

But most adults, like me, sit and watch. In middle childhood, children enjoy being together; no adults needed except when a child is temporarily hurt or wants a snack (I bring fruit; other adults bring cookies, or dried seaweed, or chips).

What do we see? Much running, chasing, and climbing: Children seem compelled to develop their motor skills. They hang onto metal rings, swinging their legs, grabbing for another metal ring; they run across a bridge designed to be unsteady.

They are compelled to use their minds: They organize games—four square, touch football, kickball. They follow rules that they set together, considering age and skill to form equal teams. At this age they are logical, beyond the egocentrism of younger children.

I admire their energy, their cognitive awareness, and their social impulses. When they disagree about rules and boundaries, they settle the argument quickly. As this chapter describes, adults do not agree so easily about how best to keep children in middle childhood safe, healthy, and learning.

PHOTO CREDIT: EDZBARZHYVETSKY/DEPOSIT PHOTOS

A Healthy Time

Unlike the first five years or the next 10, growth in middle childhood (usually defined as ages 6 to 11) is slow and steady. Bodies are more skilled each year, and health is good.

In middle childhood, unless puberty starts early, children gain about 2 inches and 5 pounds a year (5 centimeters and 2 kilograms). The death rate is by far the lowest of any age group, about 1 per 10,000, which is about half the rate of younger or older children, and 1/70th the overall rate (National Center for Health Statistics, 2019). (See Figure 7.1.)

Children maintain health if they regularly see doctors and dentists and if adults teach good practices (wash hands, brush teeth, eat vegetables). Health habits need to be solidified, because children whose medical care was poor before age 10 suffer in adulthood, even if their later care and habits are excellent (Juster et al., 2016; McEwen & McEwen, 2017).

DATA CONNECTIONS: Death at an Early Age? Almost Never! shows how middle childhood is typically the healthiest period of the entire life span. Achieve

Physical Activity

One crucial habit is being active. The benefits of physical activity—especially games with rules, which children now can follow—last a lifetime. Exercise advances physical, emotional, and mental health, as well as school achievement. This includes organized sports as well as free play (like the running around I saw in the playground).

Team sports teach cooperation, self-control, and emotional regulation—all essential lessons. Many parents consider sports a way to connect with their children.

One father said:

> It's about being acknowledged sort of. To be praised and to be able to talk about [the game] later. . . . And to share experiences. For instance when [our son] played football [soccer] when he was eight and we could see him score a goal . . . yes. I played football all through my childhood and youth, but my parents did not attend one match. Not one.
>
> *[quoted in Stefansen et al., 2018, p. 166]*

MIND AND BODY

Some cultures believe that exercise improves the brain; other cultures assume that strong muscles indicate low intelligence. That false stereotype affects school

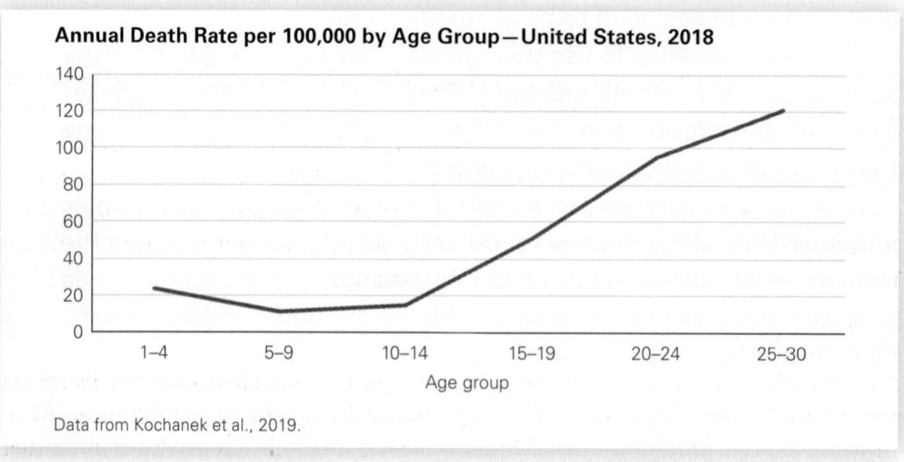

FIGURE 7.1 Death at an Early Age? Almost Never! Rates continue to rise with age, up to 13,574 for those aged 85 and older, so this figure cannot portray the entire life span. Details are remarkable as well. Not only are fatal diseases rare, thanks to immunization, but accidents and homicides also dip during middle childhood—and rise rapidly thereafter.

VLADIMIR GRIGOREV/ALAMY STOCK PHOTO

MILATAS/ISTOCK/GETTY IMAGES

Same Situation, Far Apart Given the contrast between the Russian children in front of their rural school (*left*) and the Japanese girls beside their urban school (*right*), you might see the differences here. But child psychologists notice that children everywhere chase and catch, kick and throw, and as in these photos, jump rope while chanting rhymes.

curriculum and, later, how athletes in college view themselves and are viewed by others (Stone et al., 2012).

This later view was notable in the United States historically. For example, Dizzy Dean, a star Major League pitcher in the 1930s, said, "The Good Lord was good to me, He gave me a strong right arm, a good body, and a weak mind" (Gregory, 1993).

The opposite assumption was evident in ancient Greece and is now evident in Japan, where physical activity is thought to promote learning and character (Webster & Suzuki, 2014). Many Japanese public schools have swimming pools, indoor gyms, and outdoor yards with structures for climbing, swinging, and so on. Children have an hour of recess (in several segments) in a long school day, and scheduled gym class. Despite or because of this emphasis on physical activity, Japanese children score high on international tests of achievement.

Unfortunately, some schools in the United States have cut sports, recess, and gym in order to focus on reading and math. A study of all elementary schools in Illinois found that schools with lowest reading scores also had the least time for physical activity (Kern et al., 2018), in part because some adults thought that poor readers needed more reading instruction. But the correlation might be reversed: Less physical activity might cause less learning.

Many studies have found that children's brains benefit from exercise (Voelcker-Rehage et al., 2018). Children find it much easier to sit in class if they have time to run around outside.

FINE MOTOR SKILLS AND SCHOOL

Fine motor skills mature every year of middle childhood, which aids school achievement. For example, writing requires finger control; reading print requires eye control. Education in the arts is a way to develop motor skills that lead to better education overall.

Selective attention, concentrating on some stimuli while ignoring others, improves markedly with music, the visual arts, and drama. All these promote executive function as well, which is a better predictor of school achievement than intelligence as measured by IQ tests (explained later in this chapter).

THINK CRITICALLY: How is a person "ready" for school? Are you "ready" for your current education?

MUSIC, ART, AND DRAMA

For example, as you remember from Chapter 1, some researchers provided hands-on instruction in visual arts or in playing a musical instrument. Children enrolled in those special programs scored higher, overall, than children who had neither

SHAWN PATRICK OUELLETTE/PORTLAND PRESS HERALD VIA GETTY IMAGES

Buddhism in Maine? Yes. These schoolchildren are performing a play called *Buddha Walks* on St. Patrick's Day (March 17) in 2017. There are many ways to teach children about other cultures: Drama is one of the best, as in this Lebanon, Maine, elementary school.

curriculum. One study that provided extra music training was reviewed in Chapter 1. The conclusions from that study were echoed by a study in the Netherlands (Jaschke et al., 2018).

The children in the visual arts curriculum became better at drawing and at fine motor skills, which was expected. They also became better at seeing shapes and objects and remembering what they had seen, an ability called *visual-spatial memory*. Other cognitive abilities were on par with the control group.

The effects of the music curriculum were more far-reaching. The children became better at various executive control skills, include planning ahead and inhibiting unwanted responses (Jaschke et al., 2018). The authors suggest that a narrow focus on academics that excludes the arts is short-sighted.

The children improved in all three aspects of executive function.

- For memory, children had to reproduce the configuration of dots (on a 4-by-4 matrix) they had just seen.
- For inhibition, a Go/No Go task required pushing a button to indicate whether a plane on the screen went to the left or the right, but not pushing if an X appeared after a few seconds on the screen. Those with poor inhibition pushed too soon.
- For flexibility, children were given a modified "Tower of London" task. They had to plan ahead to move colored balls, one at a time according to specific rules, from one stick to another to match a display. Several displays were presented; the children had to change tactics to match them all.

Similarly, theater productions require brain maturation in order to execute needed motor skills: walking across the stage at the appropriate moment, making the required facial expression, gesturing in the right direction, remembering the words and sequence.

How could body movement improve intellectual functioning? A review suggests direct benefits on cerebral blood flow and neurotransmitters, and indirect results from better moods (Singh et al., 2012). The connection may go beyond that. *Embodied cognition* is the idea that our sensorimotor actions are closely linked to our thinking.

Much more needs to be understood: One of the most prolific areas of research currently concerns the link between body movements, the senses, and cognition (e.g., Hirai et al., 2020; Thompson & Goldstein, 2019). However, many studies of learning in children begin with the arts or with sports. The child who doodles while taking notes, or who sings to themselves to learn spelling words, or who practices putting the ball in the basket, may be a child who is developing the mind as well as the body.

Health Problems in Middle Childhood

Some chronic health conditions, including Tourette syndrome, stuttering, and allergies, get worse during middle childhood. Even minor anomalies—wearing glasses, repeatedly coughing or blowing one's nose, or having a visible birthmark—can affect children's self-esteem. We will now look at two more obvious examples of physical conditions that affect how children feel about themselves.

childhood obesity
In a child, having a BMI above the 95th percentile, according to the U.S. Centers for Disease Control and Prevention's 1980 standards for children of a given age.

CHILDHOOD OBESITY

Childhood obesity is defined as a BMI above the 95th percentile for children of a particular age. That percentile is based on children in the United States, as measured

50 years ago. Now far more than 5 percent of children are in the obese category. For example, in 2016, 18 percent of U.S. 6- to 11-year-olds were obese (Hales et al., 2017). (See Figure 7.2.)

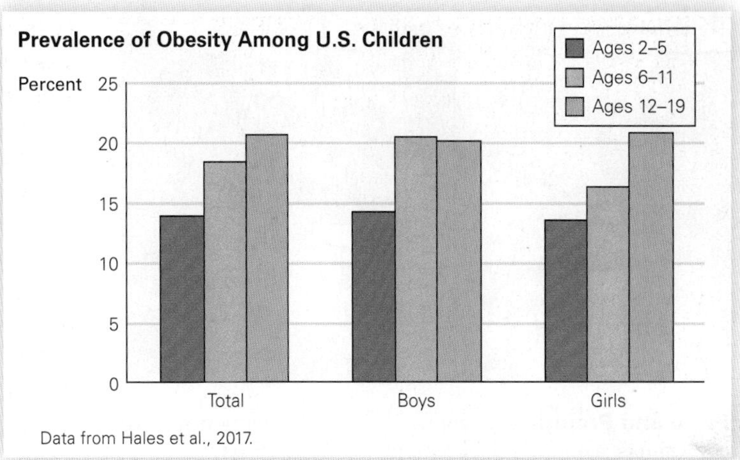

FIGURE 7.2 So Many Reasons You can probably think of many explanations—some related to environment, some to genetics, and some to socioeconomic status—for childhood obesity. One is that many rural areas and low-income neighborhoods are "food deserts," without nearby stores that offer fresh fruits and vegetables and other healthy foods.

The immediate effects are psychological: Obese children tend to be more depressed, and, either as a cause or correlate, have fewer friends. The long-term effects are worse: Obesity is an underlying cause of many of the most serious diseases of adulthood (J. Smith et al., 2020).

What affects children's weight? Once genes were thought to determine weight. Soon other internal factors (especially the microbiome) were suspected. Now many environmental factors are recognized as well (Albataineh et al., 2019).

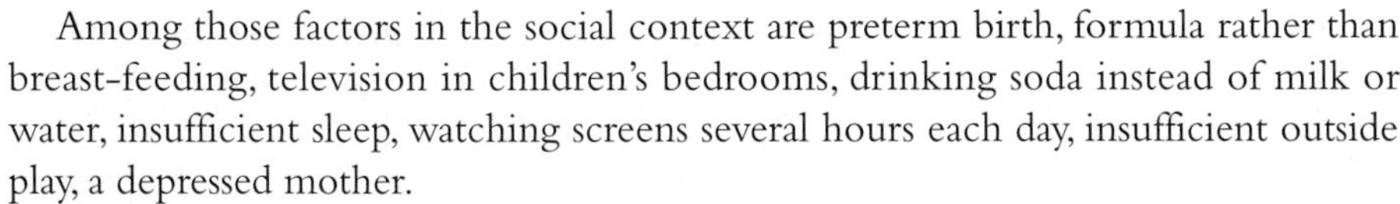

Among those factors in the social context are preterm birth, formula rather than breast-feeding, television in children's bedrooms, drinking soda instead of milk or water, insufficient sleep, watching screens several hours each day, insufficient outside play, a depressed mother.

Children themselves have *pester power*—the ability to get adults to do what they want (Powell et al., 2011), which includes pestering their parents to buy calorie-dense snacks that are advertised on television or that other children eat. Parents need to say no, which is easier if they always buy and eat healthy foods.

The best strategy is to be proactive, before a child is overweight. Rather than targeting parents *or* children, educating parents and their children together may improve weight and health, not just immediately but also over the long term (Yackobovitch-Gavan et al., 2018).

A dynamic-systems approach that considers individual differences, parenting practices, school lunches, fast-food restaurants, advertising, and community norms is needed. Prevention must be tailored to the particular child, family, and culture (Baranowski & Taveras, 2018; Harrison et al., 2011).

The need for a coordinated effort sometimes discourages individual efforts because each intervention, in isolation, has little impact (Bleich et al., 2013). Often the companies that produce high-calorie snacks, and the companies that depend on advertising revenue, resist accepting their role, and a school, a parent, or a child alone is unlikely to sustain a new eating practice. The microsystem, macrosystem, and exosystem all have an impact.

Further, cultural patterns matter. Every nation is worried about childhood obesity, but measures that work in one place may be rejected in another (Bagchi, 2019). For example, Mexico taxes sugar-sweetened beverages to reduce obesity; that has met stiff opposition in the United States (Paarlberg et al., 2018).

On the other hand, many U.S. efforts to increase exercise in school have succeeded, but using the school day for gym classes may be rejected in developing nations. Given the long-term effects of childhood obesity, solutions require a concerted effort of parents, communities, and nations.

ASTHMA

Another childhood condition that can affect learning is **asthma**, a chronic inflammatory disorder of the airways that makes breathing difficult. Sufferers have periodic attacks, sometimes requiring a rush to the hospital emergency room, a frightening experience for children who know that asthma might kill them (although it almost never does in childhood).

asthma
A chronic disease of the respiratory system in which inflammation narrows the airways from the nose and mouth to the lungs, causing difficulty in breathing. Signs and symptoms include wheezing, shortness of breath, chest tightness, and coughing.

If asthma continues in adulthood, which it does about half the time, it can be fatal (Banks & Andrews, 2015). But a child's most serious problem related to asthma

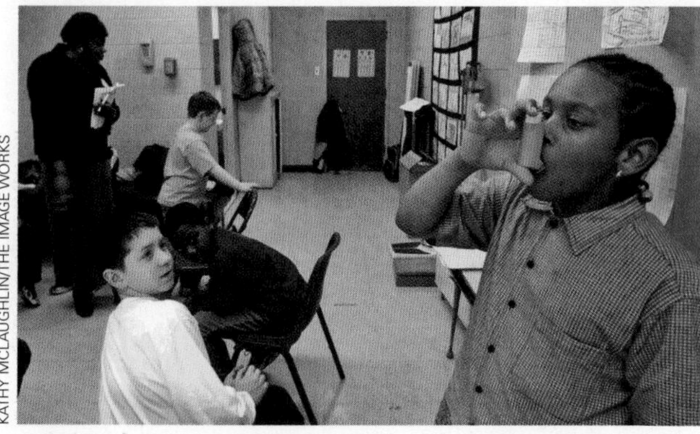

KATHY MCLAUGHLIN/THE IMAGE WORKS

Pride and Prejudice In some city schools, asthma is so common that using an inhaler is a sign of pride, as suggested by the facial expressions of these two boys. The "prejudice" is beyond the walls of this school nurse's room, in a society that allows high rates of childhood asthma.

is frequent absence from school. This impedes learning and friendships, which thrive between children who see each other every day.

In the United States, childhood asthma rates more than doubled from 1980 to 2000, increased more gradually from 2000 to 2010, and recently have decreased somewhat (probably because clean-air regulations have meant less smog) (Zahran et al., 2018).

Currently, about 1 in every 10 U.S. 5- to 11-year-olds has been diagnosed with asthma and still has the condition. For more than half of them, asthma has meant missing school and having an attack in the past year, with rates somewhat higher for boys, African Americans, and children of Puerto Rican descent (Zahran et al., 2018).

Rates increase as income falls. For children whose families are under the poverty threshold, 15 percent currently have asthma, as do only 9 percent of those whose annual family income is above $100,000 (Centers for Disease Control and Prevention, National Center for Health Statistics, July 3, 2018).

Researchers have found many causes. Some genetic alleles have been identified, as have many aspects of modern life—carpets, pollution, house pets, airtight windows, parental smoking, cockroaches, dust mites, less outdoor play. None acts in isolation. A combination of genetic sensitivity to allergies, early respiratory infections, and compromised lung functioning increases wheezing and shortness of breath (Mackenzie et al., 2014).

Some experts suggest a *hygiene hypothesis*: that "the immune system needs to tangle with microbes when we are young . . . despite what our mothers told us, cleanliness sometimes leads to sickness" (Leslie, 2012, p. 1428). Children may be overprotected from viruses and bacteria, especially in modern nations.

In their concern about hygiene, parents prevent exposure to minor infections, germs, and family pets that would strengthen their child's immunity, preventing many allergic reactions. This is true for asthma as well as many allergies (Liu, 2015).

The hygiene hypothesis is supported by data showing that

- first-born children develop asthma more often than latter-born ones;
- asthma and allergies are less common among farm-dwelling children; and
- children born by cesarean delivery (very sterile) have a greater incidence of asthma.

Remember the microbiome—those many bacteria within our bodies. Some microbes in the lungs affect asthma (Singanayagam et al., 2017). Accordingly, changing the microbiome—via diet, drugs, or exposure to animals—may treat asthma. However, asthma has multiple, varied causes and types; no single treatment will help everyone.

what have you learned?

1. How does growth during middle childhood compare with growth earlier or later?
2. Why is middle childhood considered a healthy time?
3. How does physical activity affect the child's development?
4. How do fine motor skills interact with academic skills?
5. What seems to be the effect of learning to play a musical instrument?
6. What are several reasons some children weigh more than the norm?
7. What are the short-term and long-term effects of childhood obesity?
8. Why is asthma more common now than it was 50 years ago?

Cognition

Learning is rapid during middle childhood. By age 11, some children beat their elders at chess, play music that adults pay to hear, publish poems, and win prizes for science projects or spelling bees. Others scavenge on the streets or kill in wars, mastering lessons that no child should know. How do they learn so quickly?

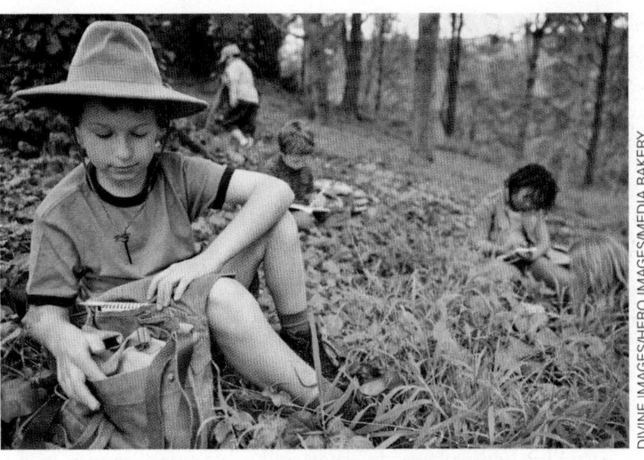

DIVINE IMAGES/HERO IMAGES/MEDIA BAKERY

Notebooks and Weeds "Write about it," said the teacher to the students on a field trip near San Diego, California. Will this boy describe the air, the plants, the trees — or will his canvas bag distract him? Concrete operational thought is not abstract: He probably won't write about Mother Earth, global warming, or God's kingdom.

OBSERVATION QUIZ
Why are these four children sitting far apart from each other? (see answer, page 239) ↑

Piaget and Concrete Thought

Piaget called middle childhood the time for **concrete operational thought**, characterized by new logical abilities. *Operational* comes from the Latin verb *operare*, meaning "to work; to produce." By calling this period operational, Piaget emphasized productive thinking.

One example is with *conservation* (explained in Chapter 5). Preoperational children focus on appearance, which prevents them from grasping conservation, but concrete operational children understand it. They soon can apply conservation not only to liquids but also to length, volume, and so on.

Another logical operation is **classification**, the organization of things into groups (or *categories* or *classes*) according to some characteristic that they share. For example, *family* includes parents, siblings, and cousins. Other common classes are animals, toys, and food. Each class includes some elements and excludes others; each is part of a hierarchy.

Food, for instance, is an overarching category, with the next-lower level of the hierarchy being meat, grains, fruits, and so on. Most subclasses can be further divided: Meat includes poultry, beef, and pork, each of which can be divided again.

Adults grasp that items at the bottom of a classification hierarchy belong to every higher level: Bacon is always pork, meat, and food. They also grasp that the higher categories include many other items—that most food, meat, and pork are not bacon.

This mental operation of moving up and down the hierarchy is beyond preoperational children but aids learning in school children. Some are so delighted to discover classification that they might include in their address "United States, North America, Earth, Solar System, Milky Way."

A third example is **seriation**, the knowledge that things can be arranged in a logical *series*. Seriation is crucial for using (not merely memorizing) the alphabet or the number sequence. By age 5, most children can count up to 100, but because they do not yet grasp seriation, they cannot correctly estimate where any particular two-digit number would be placed on a line that starts at 0 and ends at 100.

Concrete operational logic allows children to understand math. A study of 6- and 7-year-olds testing their understanding of conservation of liquids found that those who understood it were much better at adding and subtracting than children of the same age who did not understand (Wubbena, 2013).

Indeed, every logical concept helps with math. Concrete operational thinkers begin to understand that 15 is always 15 (conservation), that numbers from 20 to 29 are all in the 20s (classification), that 134 is less than 143 (seriation), and that because $5 \times 3 = 15$, it follows that $15 \div 5$ must equal 3 (reversibility). By age 11, children use mental categories and subcategories flexibly, inductively, and simultaneously, unlike at age 7.

Piaget recognized the limits of concrete logic: During these years, children have trouble grappling with emotional nuances or philosophical issues. They tend to be quite matter-of-fact, unlike the next stage, formal operational thought, when adolescents speculate, imagine, and consider abstractions. This was evident in Philip in A Case to Study.

concrete operational thought
Piaget's term for the ability to reason logically about direct experiences and perceptions.

classification
The logical principle that things can be organized into groups (or categories or classes) according to some characteristic that they have in common.

seriation
The concept that things can be arranged in a logical series, such as the number sequence or the alphabet.

TOBY MAUDSLEY/THE IMAGE BANK/GETTY IMAGES

Numbers and Sequence Their lockers are numbered, not named, as was true in preschool. Are these children (from Stockholm, Sweden) also aware that their lockers were assigned according to how many inches tall each child is?

A CASE TO STUDY

Is She Going to Die?

Philip is a delightful 7-year-old, with many intellectual skills. He speaks French to his mother and English to everyone else; he can already read fluently and calculate Pokemon trades; he does his schoolwork conscientiously.

He is my grandson's friend, but everyone else likes Philip, too. He knows how to cooperate when he plays soccer, to use "bathroom words" that make his peers laugh, and to use polite phrases that adults appreciate. Thus, his mind is developing just as it should, following the lead of mentors, as evident in his mother's French and his peers' jokes.

Last year, his mother, Dora, needed open-heart surgery. She and her husband, Craig, explained to Philip how long she would be away and who would take him to and from school, cook his dinner, and so on. Craig did the talking; Dora did not want to show her fear.

Philip responded to his parents' description by mirroring their attitude, quite factual, without emotions. He had few questions, mostly about exactly what the surgeon would cut.

A day later he told his parents that when he told his classmates that his mother was having an operation on her heart, one of them foolishly asked, "Is she going to die?" Philip reported this to illustrate his friend's stupidity; he was unaware that his friend's question, or his repeating it, was insensitive. His parents exchanged wide-eyed glances but listened without comment.

Later Craig asked Dora,

"What is wrong with him? Does he have no heart?"

The fact that children are concrete operational thinkers (Piaget) and their perceptions arise from the immediate social context (Vygotsky) is illustrated not only by Philip but by every child in middle childhood.

A child who is told that their parents are divorcing might ask "Where will I live?" instead of expressing sympathy, surprise, or anger. Aspects of cognition that adults take for granted—empathy, emotional sensitivity, hope and fears for the future—develop gradually.

Dora's surgery went well; no repeat surgery is anticipated. Someday Philip might blame his 7-year-old self for his nonchalance; Craig and Dora can reassure him that he reacted as a child. Adolescents have more than enough "heart"; they gain it during middle childhood.

ABC/PHOTOFEST

A Boy in Memphis Moziah Bridges (known as Mo Morris) created colorful bowties, which he first traded for rocks in elementary school. He then created his own company (Mo's Bows) at age 9, selling $300,000 worth of ties to major retailers by age 14. He is shown here with his mother, who encouraged his entrepreneurship.

Vygotsky and Mentors

Like Piaget, Vygotsky felt that educators should consider children's thought processes, not just the products. He also believed that middle childhood was a time for much learning, with the specifics dependent on the family, school, and culture.

Vygotsky appreciated children's curiosity and creativity. For that reason, he believed that an educational system based on rote memorization rendered the child "helpless in the face of any sensible attempt to apply any of this acquired knowledge" (Vygotsky, 1994a, pp. 356–357).

THE ROLE OF INSTRUCTION

Unlike Piaget, who thought children would discover most concepts themselves, Vygotsky stressed instruction from teachers and other mentors (Daniels, 2017). They provide the scaffold between potential and achievement by engaging each child in their zone of proximal development, as explained in Chapter 5.

Household chores, screen time, family dinner, neighborhood play—every experience, from birth on, teaches a child, according to Vygotsky. He stressed scaffolding and mentoring. Thus, children can be taught logic: They do not need to *discover* conservation, classification, seriation, and so on. Vygotsky emphasized that the lessons a child learns depend on parents, teachers, and the social context, not merely maturation.

Culture affects *how* children learn, not just what they learn. Many traditional Western schools expect children to learn directly, by listening to a teacher and demonstrating what they know on homework and tests: It is cheating to ask someone else for answers, or to look at a classmate's paper. By contrast, in some other cultures learning occurs socially and indirectly, by observation and joint activity (Rogoff, 2016).

ABACA PRESS/SIPA USA VIA AP IMAGES

Following Instructions In middle childhood, children become quite capable of following adults' instructions, as these children in Tallinn, Estonia are. Their teacher told them to put out their right hand, so that Pope Francis could greet each child quickly. The teacher must not have given the most important instruction about greeting a pope: Keep your eyes open.

MEMORY

Many scientists who study memory are impressed with 7- to-12-year-olds. The memory process, from input to storage to retrieval, is affected by both maturation (Piaget) and experience (Vygotsky). Advances are evident, year by year.

When sensations become perceptions, the brain selects the meaningful ones and transfers them to working memory for further analysis. It is in **working memory** that current, conscious mental activity occurs. Processing, not mere exposure, is essential for getting information into working memory.

working memory
Memory that is active at any given moment.

For this reason, working memory improves markedly in middle childhood, because children think about what they want to remember. That enables them to become better learners; they can organize material into chunks that help them remember bits of knowledge.

Working memory is particularly important for learning to read, because each letter, word, and sentence needs to be connected with the other letters, words, and sentences—all held in the memory for long enough to process what has been read. Children do some of this on their own as their brains mature, but good teachers help them connect ideas, allowing working memory to become a powerful tool (Cowan, 2014) (see Table 7.1).

Cultural differences are evident. For example, many Muslim children are taught to memorize all 80,000 words of the Quran; they learn strategies to remember long passages. These strategies are unknown to other children, but they help the Muslim children with other cognitive tasks (Hein et al., 2014).

A very different example is the ability to draw a face, an ability admired by U.S. children. They learn strategies to improve their drawing, such as knowing where to

TABLE 7.1 Advances in Memory from Infancy to Age 11

Child's Age	Memory Capabilities
Under 2 years	Infants remember actions and routines that involve them. Memory is implicit, triggered by sights and sounds (an interactive toy, a caregiver's voice).
2–5 years	Young children use words to encode and retrieve memories. Explicit memory begins, although children do not yet use memory strategies. Children remember things by rote (their phone number, nursery rhymes).
5–7 years	Children realize that they need to remember some things, and they try to do so, usually via rehearsal (repeating an item again and again). This is not the most efficient strategy, but repetition can lead to automatization.
7–9 years	Children can be taught new strategies, including visual clues (remembering how a particular spelling word looks) and auditory hints (rhymes, letters). Children benefit from organizing things to be remembered.
9–11 years	Memory becomes adaptive and strategic as children continue to learn various memory techniques from teachers and other children. They can organize material themselves, developing their own memory aids.

Especially for Teachers
How might Piaget's and Vygotsky's ideas help in teaching geography to a class of third-graders? (see response, page 239)

put the eyes, mouth, and chin. (Few spontaneously draw the eyes mid-face rather than at the top, but most learn to do so.)

Crucial to memory is not merely *storage* (how much material has been deposited) but also *retrieval* (how readily past learning can be brought into working memory). For everyone at every age, retrieval is easier for some memories (especially of vivid, emotional experiences) than for others. And for everyone, memory is imperfect: We all forget and distort memories and need strategies for accurate recall.

Some schools teach those strategies and allow children to practice them as they consolidate learning. That is what Vygotsky would hope.

For example, some children are taught to memorize the dialogues of Shakespeare, or the books of the Bible, or the entire Gettysburg Address. Other children are mentored differently: They learn how to look up those passages on their tablets rather than learn them by heart.

KNOWLEDGE BASE

knowledge base
A body of knowledge in a particular area that makes it easier to master new information in that area.

The more people already know, the better they can learn. Having an extensive **knowledge base**, or a broad body of knowledge in a particular subject, makes it easier to remember and understand new information. As children gain knowledge during the school years, they become better able to judge (1) accuracy, (2) what is worth remembering, and (3) what is insignificant (Woolley & Ghossainy, 2013).

Past experience, current opportunity, and personal motivation all facilitate increases in the knowledge base. Motivation and mentoring explain why a child's knowledge base may not be what parents or teachers prefer.

Some schoolchildren memorize lyrics and rhythms of hit songs, know plots and characters of television programs, or recite names and statistics of basketball (or soccer, baseball, or cricket) stars. Yet they do not know whether World War I was in the nineteenth or twentieth century or whether Pakistan is in Asia or Africa.

Concepts are learned best when connected to personal and emotional experiences. For example, children from South Asia, or who have classmates from there, more easily learn the boundaries of Pakistan—if their teachers take advantage of that diversity.

During middle childhood, children learn ways to remember, thus expanding the knowledge base. Familiar examples include spelling rules ("*i* before *e* except after *c*") and how to screw a light bulb ("lefty-loosey, righty-tighty"). Preschoolers ignore such mnemonics; 7-year-olds begin to use them; 9-year-olds can create and master more complicated rules.

Children also develop other ways to remember, such as saying information out loud, singing the material, connecting it with already known material, discussing it with other people. As the brain matures, and as mentors guide learning, 11-year-olds can remember much more than 5-year-olds (Hassevoort et al., 2018; Ngo et al., 2018; Q. Yu et al., 2018).

Language

As you remember, many aspects of language advance during early childhood. Young children have mastered the basic vocabulary and grammar of their first language. That increases their knowledge base, enabling more advanced learning and thinking.

During middle childhood, they make notable advances in vocabulary, comprehension, speaking ability, and grammar. Here are some specifics.

VOCABULARY

By age 6, children already use every part of speech—adjectives, adverbs, interjections, and conjunctions, as well as thousands of nouns and verbs—to form sentences that may go on and on. That enables them to build vocabulary, because concrete

operational children are logical; they can understand prefixes, suffixes, compound words, phrases, and metaphors, even if they have not heard them before.

For example, 2-year-olds know *egg*, but 10-year-olds also know *egg salad, egg-drop soup, egghead, a good egg*, and *last one in is a rotten egg*—a phrase from the nineteenth century still used in school playgrounds today.

In middle childhood, beyond basic vocabulary, some words become pivotal for understanding the curriculum, such as *negotiate, evolve, allegation, deficit, molecules*. Consequently, vocabulary is taught in every elementary school classroom, thus expanding the knowledge base so more learning can occur.

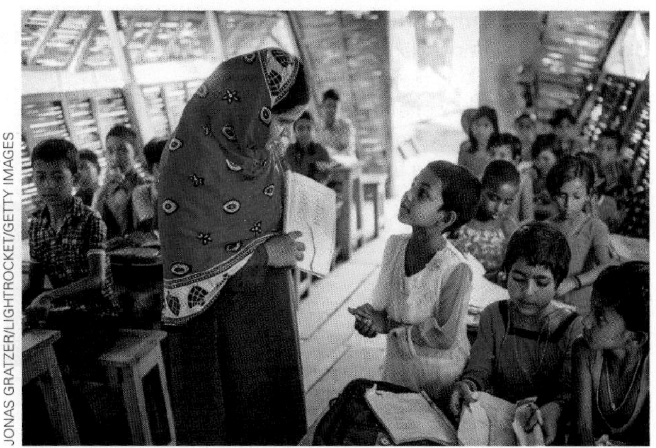

JONAS GRATZER/LIGHTROCKET/GETTY IMAGES

Go with the Flow This boat classroom in Bangladesh picks up students on shore and then uses solar energy to power computers linked to the internet as part of instruction. The educational context will teach skills and metaphors that peers of these students will not understand.

UNDERSTANDING METAPHORS

Metaphors, jokes, and puns are comprehended in middle childhood—and not earlier. Some jokes ("What is black and white and red all over?" and "Why did the chicken cross the road?") are funny only during middle childhood. Younger children don't get the jokes, and teenagers find them lame and stale.

The new cognition of 6- to 11-year-olds allows them to enjoy puns, unexpected answers to normal questions, as well as metaphors and similes. A lack of metaphorical understanding, or an inability to see the humor in a pun, indicates a cognitive problem (Thomas et al., 2010).

Metaphors are context specific, building on the knowledge base. An American who lives in China noted phrases that U.S. children understand but children in cultures without baseball do not, including "dropped the ball," "on the ball," "play ball," "throw a curve," "strike out" (Davis, 1999). If a teacher says "Keep your eyes on the ball," some immigrant children might not pay attention because they are looking for that ball.

ADJUSTING LANGUAGE TO THE CONTEXT

Another aspect of language that advances markedly in middle childhood is pragmatics, defined in Chapter 5. Pragmatics is evident when a child knows which words to use with teachers (never calling them a *rotten egg*) and informally with friends (who can be called rotten eggs or worse).

As children master pragmatics, they become more adept at making friends. Shy 6-year-olds cope far better with the social pressures of school if they use pragmatics well (Coplan & Weeks, 2009). By contrast, children with autism spectrum disorder are usually very poor at pragmatics (Klinger et al., 2014).

Mastery of pragmatics allows children to change styles of speech, or *linguistic codes*, depending on their audience. Each code includes many aspects of language—not just vocabulary but also tone, pronunciation, grammar, sentence length, idioms, and gestures.

Sometimes the switch is between *formal code* (used in academic contexts) and *informal code* (used with friends); sometimes it is between standard (or proper) speech and dialect or vernacular (used on the street). Code is used in texting—numbers (411), abbreviations (LOL), emoticons (:-D), and spelling (r u ok?), which some children do dozens of times a day.

THINK CRITICALLY: Do children from some backgrounds need to become especially adept at code-switching? Does this challenge advance cognitive development?

SPEAKING TWO LANGUAGES

Code is obvious when children speak one language at home and another at school. Every nation includes many such children; most of the world's 6,000 languages are not school languages. In the United States, about one school-age child in four has

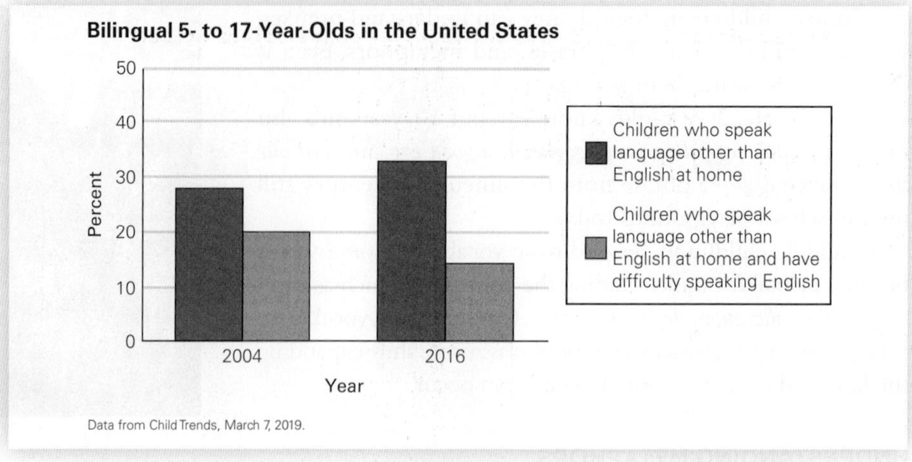

FIGURE 7.3 Home and Country Do you see good news? A dramatic increase in the number of bilingual children is a benefit for the nation, but the hundreds of thousands of children who still have trouble with English suggests that more education is needed.

a home language that is not English (see Figure 7.3); in other nations, almost every child's school language is unlike their home language.

If children learn two languages in the first three years of life, no brain differences are detectable between monolingual and bilingual children. However, from about age 4 through adolescence, the older children are when they learn a second language, the more likely their brains will change to accommodate the second language, with greater cortical thickness on the left side (the language side) and thinness on the right (Klein et al., 2014).

This neurological change reflects what we know about language learning: In infancy and early childhood, language is learned effortlessly; in middle childhood, some work (indicated by brain growth) is required.

This also explains an interesting finding: When bilingual individuals who have a home language and a school language are asked to reason about something in their second language, they tend to be more rational and less emotional. That usually (but not always) leads to better thought (Costa et al., 2017).

English Language Learners (ELLs)
Children in the United States whose proficiency in English is low—usually below a cutoff score on an oral or written test. Many children who speak a non-English language at home are also capable in English; they are *not* ELLs.

immersion
A strategy in which instruction in all school subjects occurs in the second (usually the majority) language that a child is learning.

bilingual education
A strategy in which school subjects are taught in both the learner's original language and the second (majority) language.

ESL (English as a Second Language)
A U.S. approach to teaching English that gathers all of the non-English speakers together and provides intense instruction in English. Students' first languages are never used; the goal is to prepare them for regular classes in English.

BILINGUAL EDUCATION

Educators and political leaders in the United States argue about how to teach English to **English Language Learners (ELLs)**, whose first language is not standard English. One strategy is called **immersion**, with instruction entirely in the new language. The opposite strategy is to teach children in their first language, adding instruction of the second language as a "foreign" tongue (a strategy rare in the United States but common elsewhere).

Between these extremes lies **bilingual education**, with instruction in two languages, and **ESL (English as a Second Language)**, with all non-English speakers taught English in one multilingual group, preparing them to join English-only classes. Every method for teaching a second language sometimes succeeds and sometimes fails.

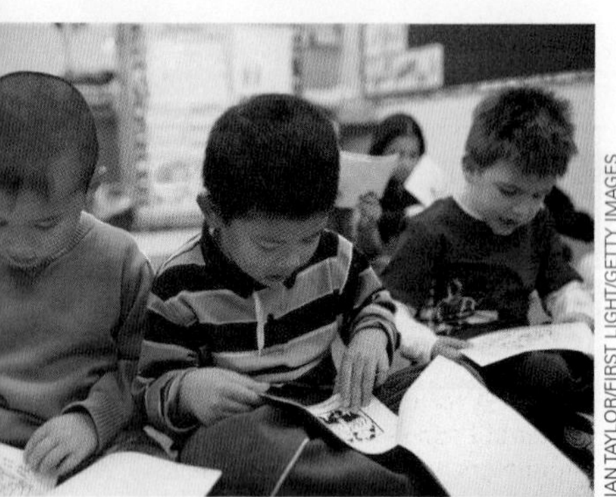
IAN TAYLOR/FIRST LIGHT/GETTY IMAGES

Months or Years? ESL classes, like this one in Canada, often use pictures and gestures to foster word learning. How soon will these children be ready to join the regular classes?

Language learning depends not only on the child but also on the literacy of the home environment (frequent reading, writing, and listening in any language helps); the warmth, training, and skill of the teacher; and the national context. If parents fear the possibility of deportation, that adds to stress and impairs learning, especially in middle childhood (Brabeck & Sibley, 2016; Dearing et al., 2016).

In the United States, specifics differ for each state, grade, family, and child, but the general trends are discouraging. Unless a child is already bilingual at age 5, ELLs tend to fall further behind their peers with each passing year, leaving school at higher rates than other students their age.

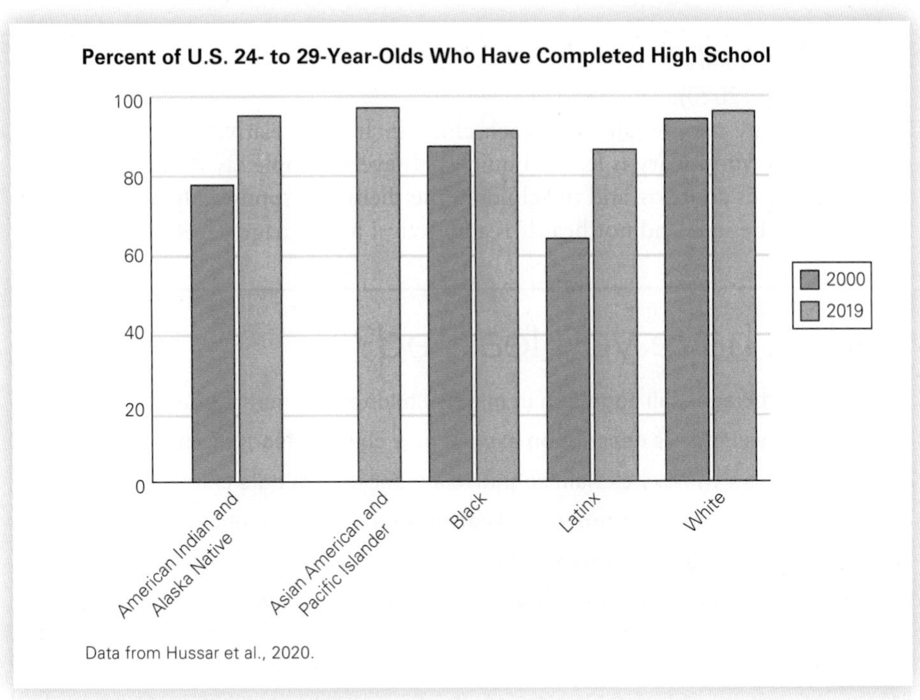

FIGURE 7.4 **Getting Better?** Apparently, every group is improving, with those lowest at the turn of the century improving more than the others. The ethnic disparities suggest that poverty and prejudice continue to reduce high school completion for Black Americans. However, the data also reveal that poverty alone does not explain the Latinx rates. Experts who delve deeply into the data are convinced that fluency in English matters.

*Data from this source are not available for Asian Americans in 2000, but other data suggest that they already were very high.

Children whose first language is Spanish are particularly impaired through school if they do not also speak English well. As a result, in the United States, some Latinx young adults do not graduate from high school. (See Figure 7.4.)

SOCIOECONOMIC STATUS

Decades of research have found a strong correlation between academic achievement and socioeconomic status. Language may be the crucial factor.

Not only do children from low-SES families usually have smaller vocabularies than those from higher-SES families, but also their grammar is simpler (fewer compound sentences, dependent clauses, and conditional verbs), and their sentences are shorter (Hart & Risley, 1995; Hoff, 2013). That slows down school learning.

Many researchers seek underlying causes. Possibilities include poor health, hunger, lead in the brain, crowded households, few books at home, lack of exercise, low maternal education, authoritarian child rearing, inexperienced teachers, air pollution, neighborhood violence, lack of role models . . . the list could go on and on (Pace et al., 2017; Rowe et al., 2016). All of these conditions correlate with low SES and less learning, but it is difficult to isolate the impact of each.

However, one factor is proven to be a cause, not just a correlate: language heard early on. Some caregivers use simpler vocabulary and talk much less to infants and young children than others do (Daneri et al., 2019). Some parents rarely read to their children or to themselves.

Remember that children are astute observers, even over-imitating. A leading developmental psychologist often saw her parents reading, so when they gave her Socrates at age 10, she plowed in and found it fascinating. Is it surprising that she wrote *The Philosophical Baby*? (Gopnik, 2009).

Especially for Parents You've had an exhausting day but are setting out to buy groceries. Your 7-year-old son wants to go with you. Should you explain that you are so tired that you want to make a quick solo trip to the supermarket this time? (see response, page 239)

Maternal education is crucial (Vernon-Feagans et al., 2020). Educated mothers and fathers are not only more likely to read to their children, they also are more likely to take their children to museums, zoos, and libraries. They naturally engage children in conversation about the interesting sights around them.

In some families, dinner is the time when everyone regularly eats together and discusses the day. Families in which the children eat separately from the parents, or in which everyone watches television as they eat, may need to rethink those customs. Family stability and routines are an important factor in child language and SES (Lecheile et al., 2020).

Ideally, many people talk with each child, including relatives, teachers, friends, and strangers. Vocabulary is learned quickly if several people say the same words in slightly different contexts, and the children use them in response. The idea that children should "be seen and not heard" is antithetical to language development.

what have you learned?

1. Why did Piaget call cognition in middle childhood concrete operational?
2. How does Piaget's description explain how children learn math?
3. How does Vygotsky explain cognitive advances in middle childhood?
4. Why does memory improve markedly during middle childhood?
5. How and why does the knowledge base increase in middle childhood?
6. What is characteristic of vocabulary development between the ages of 6 and 10?
7. How does a child's age affect the understanding of metaphors and jokes?
8. Why would a child's linguistic code be criticized by teachers but admired by friends?
9. What factors in a child's home and school affect language learning?
10. What methods are used to teach children a second language?
11. How and why does low SES affect language learning?

Teaching and Learning

As we have just described, school-age children are great learners, using logic, developing strategies, accumulating knowledge, and expanding language (see At About This Time). In every nation, new responsibilities and formal instruction begin at about age 6 because that is when the human body and brain are ready. Worldwide, 92 percent of the 6- to -11-year-olds are in school (91 percent of the girls, 93 percent of the boys) (UNESCO, 2019).

In middle childhood, anything can be learned. Children worldwide learn whatever adults in their culture teach.

The Curriculum

What should they learn? Every nation seeks to teach reading, writing, and arithmetic—the classic "three Rs." But beyond literacy and math, nations choose what to teach.

What subjects are most important? As already mentioned, the time spent on physical education, on the arts, and on other aspects of the curriculum varies from nation to nation. Variation abounds in the United States, not only from state to state but also from school district to school district, and school to school.

The reason is that, for the most part, U.S. primary education is controlled and funded by each state or district. That itself is controversial: Most nations have a national curriculum and policies, paid by national taxes.

AT ABOUT THIS TIME

Math

Age	Norms and Expectations
4–5 years	• Count to 20. • Understand one-to-one correspondence of objects and numbers. • Understand *more* and *less*. • Recognize and name shapes.
6 years	• Count to 100. • Understand *bigger* and *smaller*. • Add and subtract one-digit numbers.
8 years	• Add and subtract two-digit numbers. • Understand simple multiplication and division. • Understand word problems with two variables.
10 years	• Add, subtract, multiply, and divide multidigit numbers. • Understand simple fractions, percentages, area, and perimeter of shapes. • Understand word problems with three variables.
12 years	• Begin to use abstract concepts, such as formulas and algebra.

Math learning depends heavily on direct instruction and repeated practice, which means that some children advance more quickly than others. This list is only a rough guide meant to illustrate the importance of sequence.

AT ABOUT THIS TIME

Reading

Age	Norms and Expectations
4–5 years	• Understand basic book concepts. For instance, children learning English and many other languages understand that books are written from front to back, with print from left to right, and that letters make words that describe pictures. • Recognize letters — name the letters on sight. • Recognize and spell own name.
6–7 years	• Know the sounds of the consonants and vowels, including those that have two sounds (e.g., *c, g, o*). • Use sounds to figure out words. • Read simple words, such as *cat, sit, ball, jump*.
8 years	• Read simple sentences out loud, 50 words per minute, including words of two syllables. • Understand basic punctuation, consonant–vowel blends. • Comprehend what is read.
9–10 years	• Read and understand paragraphs and chapters, including advanced punctuation (e.g., the colon). • Answer comprehension questions about concepts as well as facts. • Read polysyllabic words (e.g., *vegetarian, population, multiplication*).
11–12 years	• Demonstrate rapid and fluent oral reading (more than 100 words per minute). • Vocabulary includes words that have specialized meaning in various fields. • For example, in civics, *liberties, federal, parliament,* and *environment* all have special meanings. • Comprehend paragraphs about unfamiliar topics. • Sound out new words, figuring out meaning using cognates and context. • Read for pleasure.
13+ years	• Continue to build vocabulary, with greater emphasis on comprehension than on speech. Understand textbooks.

Reading is a complex mix of skills, dependent on brain maturation, education, and culture. The sequence given here is approximate; it should not be taken as a standard to measure any particular child.

THE HIDDEN CURRICULUM

Differences between nations, and between schools in the United States, are especially stark in the **hidden curriculum**—all of the implicit values and assumptions of schools. Schedules, tracking, teacher characteristics, discipline, teaching methods, sports competitions, student government, and extracurricular activities are all part of the hidden curriculum. This teaches children far beyond the formal, published curriculum that lists what is taught in each grade.

hidden curriculum
The unofficial, unstated, or implicit patterns within a school that influence what children learn. For instance, teacher background, organization of the play space, and tracking are all part of the hidden curriculum—not formally prescribed, but instructive to the children.

An obvious example is the physical surroundings. Some schools have spacious classrooms, wide hallways, and large, grassy playgrounds; others have cramped, poorly equipped classrooms and cement play yards. In some nations, school is held outdoors, with no chairs, desks, or books; classes are canceled when it rains. What does that tell the students?

BRENDAN FITTERER/ZUMA PRESS/NEW PORT RICHEY/FLORIDA/U.S./NEWSCOM

ROMEO GACAD/AFP/GETTY IMAGES

Room to Learn? In the elementary school classroom in Florida (*left*), the teacher is guiding two students who are working to discover concepts in physics — a stark contrast to the Filipino classroom (*right*) in a former storeroom. Sometimes the hidden curriculum determines the overt curriculum, as shown here.

OBSERVATION QUIZ
How many children are in the classroom in the Philippines? (see answer, page 239) ↑

TEACHER ETHNICITY

Another aspect of the hidden curriculum is the gender, ethnicity, or economic background of the teachers. If these are unlike the students, children may conclude that education is irrelevant for them.

School organization is also significant. If the school has gifted classes, those in other classes may conclude that they are not capable of learning. If a school is all boys or all girls, what is the message? If the school is tracked by reading scores, how much do those in lower tracks expect to read?

The United States is experiencing major demographic shifts. Since 2010, half of the babies born are from Hispanic, Asian, Black, or Native American families, whereas more than two-thirds of adults identify as White/non-Hispanic. Partly because of the age and ethnic distribution of adults, and partly because of past gender and racial discrimination, many experienced teachers are older White women.

Few young children ever have a young male teacher of color. Many older White women are excellent teachers, but schools also need many excellent Black and Brown men. The hidden curriculum could teach that caring, intelligent educators come from many backgrounds. Does it?

CHAPTER APP 7

Khan Academy

iOS:
http://tinyurl.com/y34g8v4f

ANDROID:
http://tinyurl.com/ybrxqdh3

RELEVANT TOPIC:
Schooling and academic development in middle childhood

Appropriate for students of all ages, this app contains thousands of interactive exercises, videos, and articles pertaining to arithmetic and pre-algebra, science, grammar, history, and much more. Users can take practice exercises, quizzes, and tests, receiving instant feedback and step-by-step hints. Content can be bookmarked and downloaded for access even without an internet connection.

TEACHER EXPECTATIONS

Less visible, yet probably more influential, is the message about learning that comes from teacher attitudes. If a teacher expects a child to be disruptive, or unable to learn, that child is likely to confirm those expectations. Not surprisingly, teachers who are themselves Black or Latinx have more favorable attitudes about the learning potential of students from those backgrounds (Glock & Kleen, 2019).

Fortunately, teacher expectations are malleable: Learning increases and absences decrease when teachers believe all of their students are educable and they teach accordingly, encouraging every child (Sparks, 2016).

One cultural value is whether students should speak or be quiet. In the United States, adults are expected to voice opinions. Accordingly, teachers welcome student questions, call on children who do not speak up, ask children to work in pairs so that each child talks, grant points for participation.

Consequently, North American students learn to speak, even when they do not know the answers. Teachers say "good question" or "interesting idea" when students say something that the teacher considers wrong. Elsewhere, children are expected to be quiet.

This was dramatically apparent to me when I taught at the United Nations International School. Some of my students shouted out answers, some raised their hands, some never spoke except when I called on them. When I called on one quiet student from South Asia, he immediately stood up and answered—surprising me and his classmates. I hope our surprise did not undercut his learning: I fear it did.

SCHOOL CLIMATE

A crucial aspect of the hidden curriculum affecting motivation is whether the structures, administration, and teachers foster a culture of competition or cooperation. In some schools, children help each other, laugh together, and admire their teachers. In other schools, children compete for grades and try to gain teacher praise or avoid teacher blame. The tenor of the school relationships is the essential of *school climate* (Wang & Degol, 2016).

One aspect of climate is whether the students feel encouraged or criticized for being themselves. That is reflected in how safe they feel to explore ideas and form friendships. Another part is the attitude toward learning, either a growth mindset or fixed mindset (also called *incremental* or *entity*) (Dweck, 2016; Kearney et al., 2020).

- The *growth mindset* is that learning develops with effort, with one person's growth likely to advance another's. Mistakes are "learning opportunities"; sharing ideas and strategies does not diminish one's own education—quite the opposite.
- The *fixed mindset* is the belief that ability is determined early on, perhaps at conception, so failure is evidence of inborn inadequacy. People compete to prove they are smarter than the others.

With a fixed mindset, children who realize that they are not good at math, for instance, or that writing is hard, stop trying, because they believe they will never be good at math, writing, or whatever. They deflect attention from their failure ("school sucks"; "the teacher is unfair") rather than trying harder to master the material.

Teachers reciprocate with their own fixed mindset. They attribute poor student performance to low intelligence, or to innate temperament, or to a particular neighborhood or family. That gets them off the hook: No one could expect them to change the student's nature.

On the other hand, children with a growth mindset seek challenges. They work hard at learning, enjoy discussions with their classmates, change their opinions, and choose difficult courses. Teachers with a growth mindset believe that every child can succeed; they encourage effort, curiously, collaboration. A resistant student is a challenge (see A View from Science).

A VIEW FROM SCIENCE

Studying Teachers in Finland

As part of their work in graduate school, future teachers studied experienced teachers in Finland, using scientific observation and interviews (Ronkainen et al., 2019). They spent many days in classrooms, interviewing teachers, transcribing, and videotaping. They also consulted theory and research on growth mindset, discussing their observations with each other.

One researcher observed Anne, who taught 21 first-grade students, including three who spoke another language (Rissanen et al., 2019).

Growth mindset was apparent when Anne divided the children into groups. She did not put the most able in one group and the least able in another; she instead mixed them so that they could work together. She and her aide

(the student/teacher ratio in Finland is about 10:1) worked closely with each group, challenging them to learn from each other.

Her goals indicated a growth mindset: She sought to teach process, not facts. Anne said:

> I try to communicate that mistakes are ok and it's not very serious if you make them and somehow through that encourage them, like, let's just do this again and let's give it another try.

Anne herself sometimes deliberately made mistakes, so she could demonstrate that mistakes are an opportunity to learn. She encouraged students to try what was hard for them, after first appreciating what they had done so far. For example, she said to one child:

> Let's look back a bit, because you were absent when we worked with these . . . well, you can start. You already draw such beautiful numbers so there's no point in practicing them now, but you can start from here. Tell me, how many balloons are here?

In this interchange, if she had told that child he was a good artist, she would be praising him for a fixed quality. Instead, she praised him for practicing at drawing "such beautiful numbers." She then presented the new challenge in a way that allowed the child to blame his failure on an external reason ("You were absent") and pushed him to stop doing what was easy and to "start from here" to master the new task. She scaffolded education by beginning with counting balloons.

However, the observer wrote that sometimes Anne accepted a child's fixed mindset. One boy had his head down on his desk, and Anne asked him to sit up. He sat up but soon put his head down again. Anne said:

> He is the kind of student who is not very open to receiving any kind of support or help, and he has a strong conviction that he is very able and knows everything and, in reality, quite often he does not. So I have to be very sensitive with him, and, like now, this posture of his is one indication that he is not very willing to work.

Rather than being "very sensitive," should Anne have challenged him? The observer noted other times when Anne blamed lack of effort on innate personality. She said of a shy student, "I usually don't ask her anything unless I really see she is willing to answer," and she left another anxious student alone, deciding that she should be sensitive to his anxiety.

With every teacher/student interaction, many responses and interpretations are possible. This observer thought that teachers should push every student. Anne disagreed.

As you remember from Chapter 1, some scientists begin with direct observation, as this one did, to develop hypotheses to be tested. The team analyzed Anne's attitudes to determine when she used a growth mindset (Rissanen et al., 2019). Other researchers, also studying Finland, find that despite the official endorsement of a growth mindset, many teachers in Finland have a fixed mindset (Andere, 2020).

The next step might be a longitudinal experiment, to discover how first-graders fare under various teacher attitudes. Fortunately, as you see, teacher education in Finland encourages teachers to reflect on their practices, using evidence, not assumptions, as a guide.

Trends in Math and Science Study (TIMSS)
An international assessment of the math and science skills of fourth- and eighth-graders. Although the TIMSS is very useful, different countries' scores are not always comparable because sample selection, test administration, and content validity are hard to keep uniform.

Progress in International Reading Literacy Study (PIRLS)
Inaugurated in 2001, a planned five-year cycle of international trend studies in the reading ability of fourth-graders.

Programme for International Student Assessment (PISA)
An international test taken by 15-year-olds in 50 nations that is designed to measure problem solving and cognition in daily life.

International Testing

Every nation wants to improve education. Longitudinal data show that the national economy advances when school achievement rises (Hanushek & Woessmann, 2015). Better-educated children become healthier and more productive adults, which explains why many developing nations are building more schools and colleges.

Nations seek not only *more* education, but also *more effective* education. To measure that, almost 100 nations have participated in at least one massive international test of children's learning.

- **Trends in Math and Science Study (TIMSS)** assesses achievement in science and math.
- **Progress in International Reading Literacy Study (PIRLS)** tests reading.
- **Programme for International Student Assessment (PISA)**, measures application of learning to everyday issues.

East Asian nations always rank high, and scores for more than a dozen nations (some in Europe, most in Asia) surpass those for the United States (see Tables 7.2 and 7.3).

TABLE 7.2 TIMSS Ranking and Average Scores of Math Achievement for Fourth-Graders

	2015	2019
Singapore	618	625
Hong Kong	615	602
Korea	608	600
Chinese Taipei	597	599
Japan	593	593
Russian Federation	564	567
N. Ireland	570	566
England	546	556
United States	539	535
Belgium	546	532
Finland	545	532
Netherlands	540	532
Canada (Quebec)	533	532
Germany	528	521
Sweden	504	521
Australia	516	516
Italy	508	515
Canada (Ontario)	518	512
New Zealand	486	487
Iran	431	443
Kuwait	342	383

Information from Mullis et al., 2020.

TABLE 7.3 PIRLS Distribution of Reading Achievement for Fourth-Graders

	2011	2016
Russian Federation	568	581
Singapore	567	576
Hong Kong	571	569
Ireland	552	567
Finland	568	566
N. Ireland	558	565
Poland	526	565
Chinese Taipei	553	559
England	552	559
United States	556	549
Italy	541	548
Denmark	554	547
Australia	527	544
Canada	548	543
Germany	541	537
Israel	541	530
Spain	513	528
New Zealand	531	523
France	520	511
Iran	457	428

Information from Mullis et al., 2012b, 2017a.

One surprising example is that Finland's scores increased dramatically after a wholesale reform of its public education system (Sahlberg, 2011, 2015, 2021). In 1985 ability grouping was abolished, and in 1994 the curriculum began to encourage collaboration and active learning rather than competitive passive education. The advances of the children may be the result of these policies, or it may be the result of the quality and preparation of the teachers.

Only the top 3 percent of Finland's high school graduates are admitted to teachers' colleges. They study for five years at the university at no charge, earning a master's degree, studying both the theory and the practice of education.

Some teachers gain additional credits, including classroom experience, to become specialists for children with disabilities (Takala et al., 2019). They usually work with children who are within the regular class, although about 3 percent of Finnish students (usually older than age 9) are thought to have such pervasive learning difficulties that they are educated in separate classes (Sundqvist et al., 2019).

THINK CRITICALLY: Finland's success has been attributed to many factors, some mentioned here and some regarding the geography and population of the nation. What do you think is the most influential reason?

Finnish teachers are granted more autonomy than is typical in other nations. Since the 1990s, they have had more time and encouragement to work with colleagues. They are encouraged to respond to each child's temperament as well as the child's skills. This strategy has led to achievement, particularly in math (Viljaranta et al., 2015).

"Big deal, an A in math. That would be a D in any other country."

PROBLEMS WITH INTERNATIONAL COMPARISONS

Although many educators admire primary education in Finland, or Singapore, or other high-scoring nations, many also say that factors in the culture, demographics, or history affect learning more than specific practices in the schools (Andere, 2020). Some fear that teacher education may become "decontextualised, ahistorical" (Afdal, 2019).

Similar problems may be evident with international testing. Elaborate and extensive measures are in place to make the PIRLS, TIMSS, and PISA valid. Test items are designed to be fair and culture-free, and participating children represent the diversity (economic, ethnic, etc.) of each nation's child population. Thousands of experts work to ensure validity and reliability. Consequently, most social scientists respect the data gathered from these tests.

The tests are far from perfect, however. Creating questions that are equally valid for everyone is impossible.

For example, in math, should fourth-graders be expected to understand fractions, graphs, decimals, and simple geometry? Nations introduce these concepts at different ages, and some schools stress math more than others: Should every fourth-grader be expected to divide fractions?

After such general issues are decided, items are written. The following item tested math:

> Three thousand tickets for a basketball game are numbered 1 to 3,000. People with ticket numbers ending with 112 receive a prize. Write down all the prize-winning numbers.

VIDEO ACTIVITY: Educating the Girls of the World examines the situation of girls' education around the world while stressing the importance of education for all children.

Only 26 percent of fourth-graders worldwide got this one right (112; 1,112; 2,112—with no additional numbers). About half of the children in East Asian nations and 36 percent of the U.S. children were correct. Those national scores are not surprising; children in Singapore, Japan, and China have been close to the top on every international test for 30 years, and the United States has been above average but not by much.

Children from North Africa did especially poorly; only 2 percent of Moroccan fourth-graders were correct. Does that suggest inferior education, or is that item biased in favor of some cultures? Is basketball, or 3,000 tickets for one game, or a random prize, rare in North Africa?

Another math item gives ingredients—4 eggs, 8 cups of flour, ½ cup of milk—and asks:

> The above ingredients are used to make a recipe for 6 people. Sam wants to make this recipe for only 3 people. Complete the table below to show what Sam needs to make the recipe for 3 people. The number of eggs he needs is shown.

Eggs	2
Flour	?___
Milk	?___

The table lists 2 eggs, and the child needs to fill in amounts of flour and milk. Fourth-grade children in Ireland and England scored highest on this item (about half got it right), while those in Korea, China, and Japan scored lower (about 33 percent). The United States scored higher than East Asian nations but lower than England.

This is puzzling, since East Asians usually surpass others in math. Why not on this question? Are English and Irish children experienced with recipes that include eggs, flour, and milk, unlike Japanese children? Or are Asian children distracted by a question that assumes that a boy is cooking?

WHO TAKES THE TEST?

Beyond the need to write questions that are fair for everyone is the problem of student selection. Ideally, all children at a particular grade level take the test, but dropouts, absentees, and children with disabilities may be low achieving but not tested.

Some critics say this is especially problematic in China (Singer & Braun, 2018). For one thing, the Chinese children who take the test are in the major cities, not rural areas. In addition, the Chinese children are highly motivated to do well, but the U.S. children may not be. Thus, the tests may reflect culture, more than competence.

Schooling in the United States

For decades, the U.S. government has sponsored the **National Assessment of Educational Progress (NAEP)**, which is a group of tests designed to measure achievement in reading, math, and other subjects. The NAEP finds fewer children proficient than do state tests.

For example, New York's tests reported 62 percent proficient in math, but the NAEP found only 32 percent; 51 percent were proficient in reading on New York's state tests, but only 35 percent according to NAEP (Martin, 2014).

The NAEP also finds that Hispanic American and African American fourth-graders are about 11 percent lower than their European American peers in reading and 9 percent lower in math (McFarland et al., 2019). An even wider achievement gap is evident between high- and low-SES schools.

The TIMSS and the PIRLS report that the income and ethnic gaps are larger in the United States than in the other nations. Why? Other nations (e.g., Canada) have more ethnic groups and immigrants than the United States, but a smaller gap.

The reason may be economic. Schools are funded primarily by local taxes in the United States, and by national taxes in most other nations. As a result, U.S. children in high-SES neighborhoods attend well-funded public schools.

About 80 percent of all children in the United States attend their local public school, but those schools vary because local school districts and states determine many aspects of the hidden curriculum. Overall, many issues are not settled in U.S. education, as the following 10 items make clear.

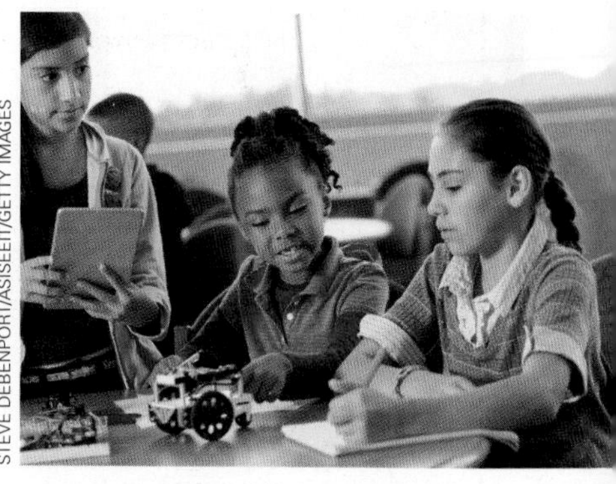

STEVE DEBENPORT/ASISEEIT/GETTY IMAGES

Future Engineers After-school clubs now encourage boys to learn cooking and girls to play chess, and everyone is active in every sport. The most recent push is for STEM (Science, Technology, Engineering, and Math) education — as in this after-school robotics club.

National Assessment of Educational Progress (NAEP)
An ongoing and nationally representative measure of U.S. children's achievement in reading, mathematics, and other subjects over time; nicknamed "the Nation's Report Card."

TEN QUESTIONS

1. *Private schools.* Should public schools be well-supported by public funds, or should smaller class sizes, special curricula, well-paid teachers, and expensive facilities (e.g., a stage, a pool, a garden) be available only in private schools, which depend on tuition from wealthy parents? About 11 percent of students in the United States attend private schools (see Figure 7.5). In some nations of Europe, the rate is close to 2 percent.

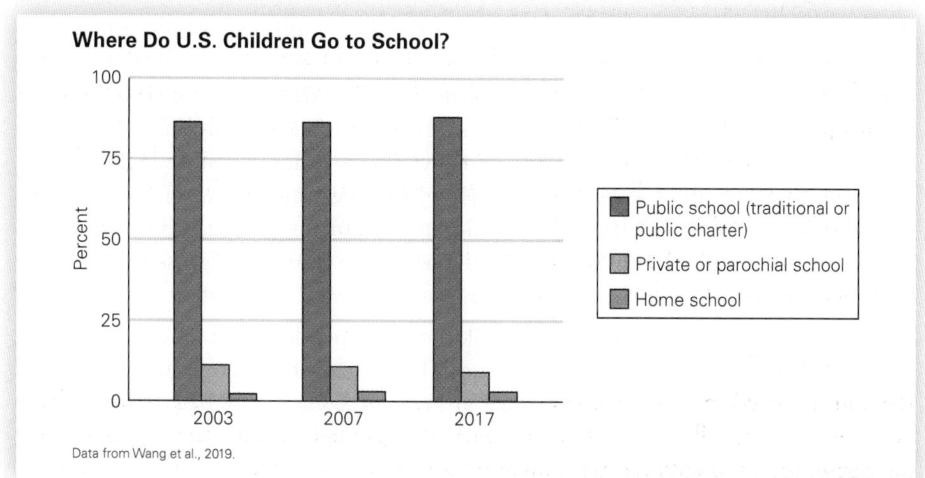

FIGURE 7.5 **Where'd You Go to School?** Note that although home schooling is still the least-chosen option, the number of home-schooled children may be increasing. Not shown is the percentage of children attending the nearest public school, which is decreasing slightly because of charter schools and magnet schools. More detailed data indicate that the average home-schooled child is a 7-year-old European American girl living in a rural area of the South with an employed father and a stay-at-home mother.

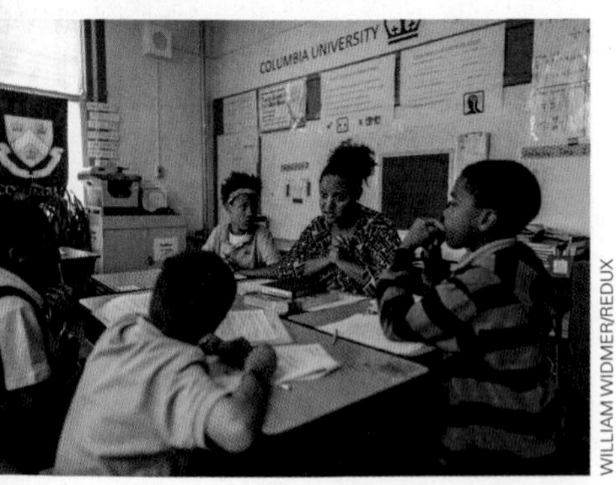
WILLIAM WIDMER/REDUX

Plagiarism, Piracy, and Public School Charter schools often have special support and unusual curricula, as shown here. These four children are learning about copyright law in a special summer school class at the ReNEW Cultural Arts Academy, a charter school in New Orleans.

Ten Questions
1. Private schools?
2. Charter schools?
3. Home schooling?
4. Religion?
5. The arts?
6. Computers?
7. Class size?
8. Soft skills?
9. Corporal punishment?
10. Suspensions?

2. *Charter schools.* Should more charter schools open or close? Charter schools are funded and licensed by states or local districts. Thus, they are public schools but are exempt from some regulations, especially those negotiated by teacher unions (hours, class size, etc.). Most charter schools have some control over admissions and expulsions, which makes them more segregated, with fewer children with disabilities (Stern et al., 2015). Quality varies. Some achievement scores are lower than other public schools and others are higher, with students more likely to go to college (Prothero, 2016).
3. *Home schooling.* In 35 of the 50 U.S. states, and in several other nations, parents can teach their children at home, never sending them to any school. In the United States, home-schooled children must learn certain subjects (reading, math, and so on), but each family decides schedules and discipline. About 3 percent of all U.S. children are home-schooled (Grady, 2017; Ray, 2013; Snyder & Dillow, 2013). The major disadvantage for home-schooled children is not academic (some have high test scores) but social: no classmates.
4. *Religion in school.* Should public education be free of religion to avoid bias toward one religion or another? In the United States, thousands of parochial schools were founded when Catholics perceived Protestant bias in public schools. In the past 20 years, many Catholic schools have closed, but schools teaching other religions—Judaism, Islam, evangelical Christianity—have opened.
5. *Language and the arts.* Should children learn a second language in primary school? In Canada and in most European nations, almost every child studies two languages by age 10. In the United States, less than 5 percent of children under age 11 do. Other elements of the curriculum—art, music, drama, dance—also vary by nation.
6. *Digital learning.* Can computers advance education? Some enthusiasts hope that connecting schools to the internet or, even better, giving every child a laptop (as some schools do) will advance learning. The results are not dramatic, however. Sometimes computers improve achievement, but not always (Lim et al., 2013).
7. *Class size.* Are too many students in each class? Do smaller classes mean more individualized education, or reduce ability to learn from peers? Mixed evidence comes from nations where children score high on international tests. Sometimes they have large student–teacher ratios (Korea's average is 28-to-1) and sometimes small (Finland's is 10-to-1).
8. *Learning to care.* Should teachers nurture empathy, cooperation, and caring, even though that cannot be tested by multiple-choice questions? Many scholars argue that "soft skills" are crucial for achievement and employment, as well as for a healthy society.
9. *Corporal punishment.* Should children be physically punished? In more than 100 nations, physical punishment is illegal in schools. However, in 19 of the 50 U.S. states (Alabama, Arkansas, Arizona, Colorado, Florida, Georgia, Idaho, Indiana, Kansas, Kentucky, Louisiana, Missouri, Mississippi, North Carolina, Oklahoma, South Carolina, Tennessee, Texas, and Wyoming) children can be legally "paddled," and only two (Iowa and New Jersey) ban corporal punishment in private schools. The hope is that obedient children will learn more, but children who are physically punished in primary school have lower grades in high school, are less likely to earn a diploma, and are more often depressed (Gershoff et al., 2019).
10. *Suspensions and exclusions.* Should children be suspended from school, or sent to special classrooms, for behavioral issues? That correlates more with policy than education. Between 2011 and 2019 in New York City, only half as many children were suspended, from 70,000 to 33,000 per year (about 1 in 16 to 1 in 36), but reading scores did not change much.

EDUCATION IN MIDDLE CHILDHOOD

Only 20 years ago, gender differences in education around the world were stark, with far fewer girls in school than boys. Now girls have almost caught up. However, many of today's children suffer from decades of past educational inequality: Recent data find that the best predictor of childhood health is an educated mother.

Worldwide Primary School Enrollment, 1978–2018

This graph shows net enrollment rate, which is the ratio of enrolled school-age children to the population of children who are the same school age. Progress toward universal education and gender equity is evident.

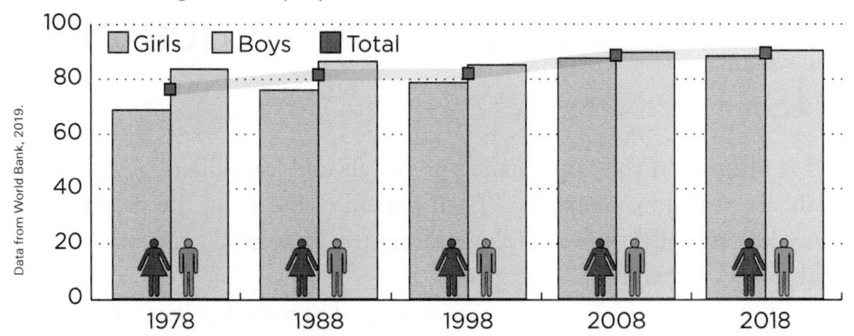

Data from World Bank, 2019.

Worldwide concerns now focus less on the existence of school and more on its quality. International tests usually find the United States is middling. Improvements are evident, but many other nations have improved even more!

Worldwide, Basic Elementary Education Leads To:

LESS –

- Child and maternal mortality
- Transmission of HIV
- Early marriage and childbirth
- War

MORE +

- Better paying jobs
- Agricultural productivity
- Use of medical care
- Voting

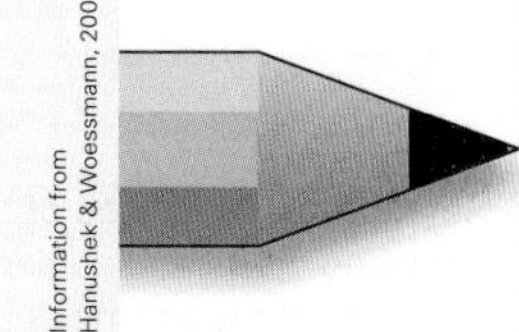

Information from Hanushek & Woessmann, 2007.

How U.S. Fourth-Graders ARE DOING

Primary school enrollment is high in the United States, but not every student is learning, as these percentages from the National Assessment of Educational Progress (NAEP) show. While numbers are improving, less than half of fourth-graders are proficient in math and reading.

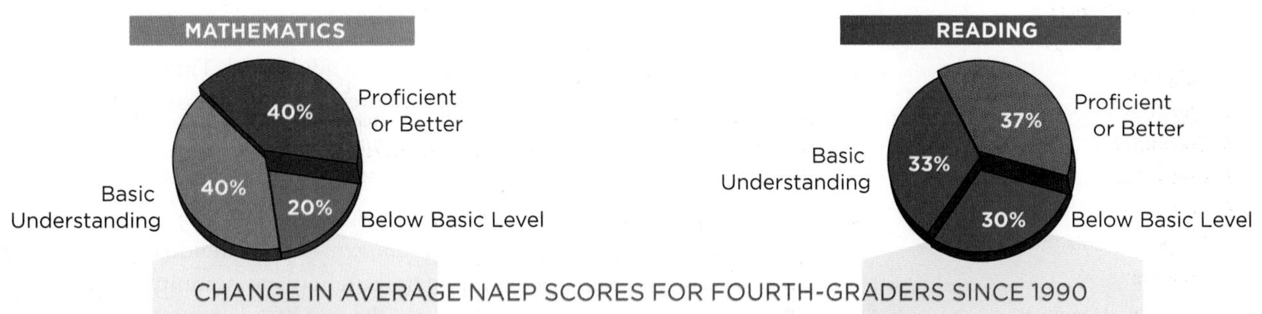

Data from National Center for Education Statistics, 2018

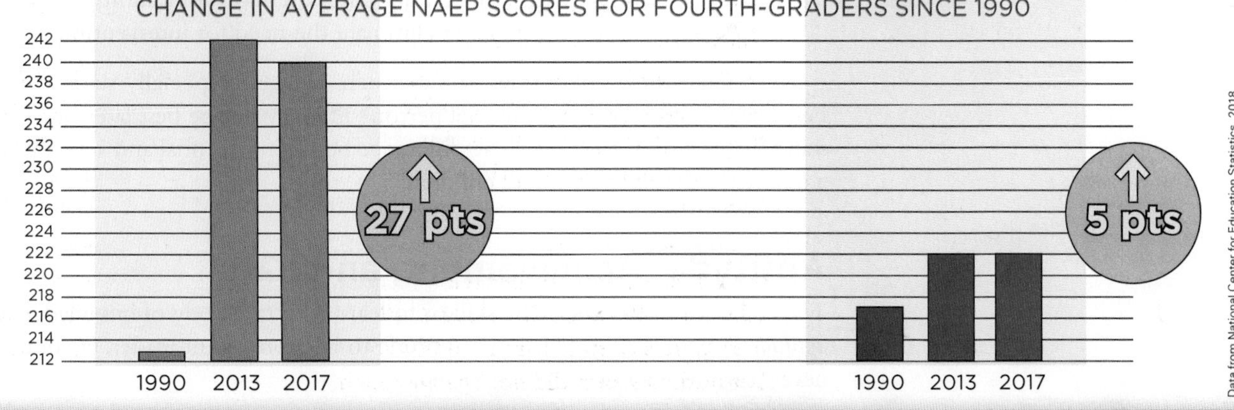

Data from National Center for Education Statistics, 2018

what have you learned?

1. How does the hidden curriculum differ from the official school curriculum?
2. What are the TIMSS, the PIRLS, and the PISA?
3. Which nations score highest on international tests?
4. What discipline methods work best in schools?
5. Why do nations differ in teaching religion, language, and cooperation?

Children with Distinct Educational Needs

Every child is unique, so this topic can apply to all children, lifelong. As an expert on differently abled children explains, "Each period of life, from the prenatal period through senescence, ushers in new biological and psychological challenges, strengths, and vulnerabilities" (Cicchetti, 2013b, p. 458).

Traditionally, however, some children have been designated as having characteristics that require particular educational strategies. Very few children (about 1 percent) have obvious physical disabilities, such as blindness. Another 10 to 20 percent are thought to need special education because of something unusual in their brains.

comorbid
Refers to the presence of two or more unrelated disease conditions at the same time in the same person.

Most disorders are **comorbid**, which means that more than one problem is evident in the same person. Comorbidity is now considered "the rule, rather than the exception" (Krueger & Eaton, 2015, p. 27).

Before focusing on that 20 percent, we need to reiterate that some of what follows applies to every child. Four general principles are evident.

1. *Abnormality is normal,* meaning that everyone has some aspects of behavior that are unusual. The opposite is also true: Everyone with a serious disorder is, in some ways, like everyone else. The cutoff between what is, and is not, a disorder is arbitrary (Clark et al., 2017).
2. *Disability changes year by year.* A severe disorder in childhood may become milder, but another problem may become disabling in adulthood. Thus, education must be adaptive, treating current problems and preventing future ones.
3. *Plasticity and compensation are part of human nature.* Many conditions, especially those that originate in the brain, respond to maturation and treatment (Livingston & Happe, 2017).
4. *Diagnosis and treatment reflect the social context.* Each individual interacts with the surrounding settings—including family, school, community, and culture—which modify, worsen, cause, or eliminate the need for intervention.

All four of these affect how best to teach children, especially since what seems best for education at one point in a person's life may not be best later on. To understand that, we need to explain the difference between potential and accomplishment, a difference that matters for all children.

Aptitude, Achievement, and IQ

The ability to master a specific skill or to learn a certain body of knowledge is called *aptitude.* A person might have the aptitude to be a proficient reader, for instance, but never learn to read or write.

Achievement is what is actually mastered. Thus, a person who is at a second-grade reading level might actually be in the second grade, but might be in the first or the third grade, or might even be an adult. If a second-grade reader is 9 years old, and therefore is in the fourth grade, then something is amiss—with aptitude, or with the home, or with the school.

To measure aptitude for education, intelligence tests were created. People assumed that one general aptitude (often referred to as *g*, or *general intelligence*) could be assessed by answers to a series of questions (vocabulary, memory, and so on). A child's number of correct answers was divided by the average for children that age to compute an *IQ* (*intelligence quotient*), thought to measure brain functioning.

The average IQ is 100; two-thirds of all children are between 85 and 115. If mental age is below 85, then the person is thought to be unable to learn as well as most people. (See Figure 7.6.)

"MY FATHER SAYS, THESE INTELLIGENCE TESTS ARE BIASED TOWARD THE INTELLIGENT."

Yes, But . . . Measuring anything is biased! The assumption is that whatever is measured is important.

There are dozens of tests that measure IQ. The traditional ones were developed by Alfred Binet (Stanford-Binet) and by Arnold Wechsler (WISC, WAIS, WIPPSI). A low aptitude could be caused by genes, or toxins (e.g., lead), or brain damage. People with psychological disorders (e.g., schizophrenia or major depression) tend to average lower IQ scores, because their brains do not process ideas as well as others (Abramovitch et al., 2018).

By contrast, if aptitude is average or higher, and achievement is low, that suggests that something in the environment slows down learning. Is something in the home or in the school holding back learning?

PLASTICITY AND INTELLIGENCE

Probably you have already spotted one problem with aptitude tests, especially when they are used to determine education. Intelligence is not fixed at birth, or at any age. Instead, the brain is quite plastic (Glenn et al., 2018; Patton et al., 2019).

Both genes and experiences produce many variations in how brains process information. Neuroscientists use the term **neurodiversity** to acknowledge, and celebrate, our differences. For example, some children find math easy, others are adept at languages, some are more attuned to nature, others to human emotions.

neurodiversity The idea that each person has neurological strengths and weaknesses that should be appreciated, in much the same way diverse cultures and ethnicities are welcomed. Neurodiversity seems particularly relevant for children with disorders on the autism spectrum.

Every human has a mix of aptitudes and abilities, and as the discussion of growth mindset makes clear, aptitude does not determine accomplishments: Someone with low aptitude for a particular achievement may, with effort and practice, achieve what was difficult.

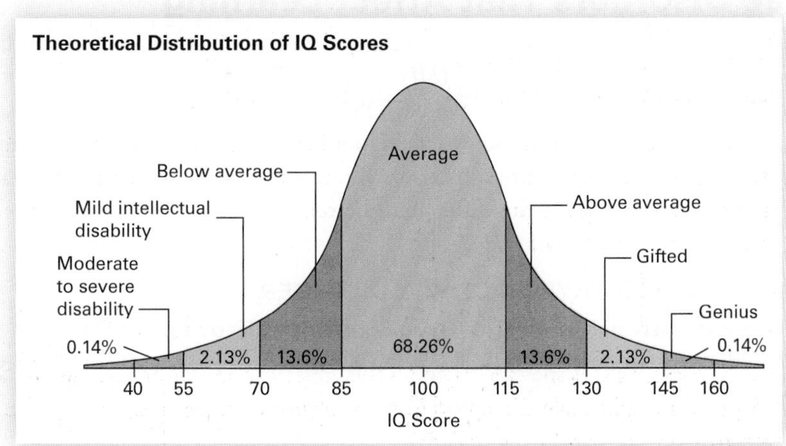

FIGURE 7.6 In Theory, Most People Are Average Almost 70 percent of IQ scores fall within the "average" range. Note, however, that this is a norm-referenced test. In fact, actual IQ scores have risen in many nations; 100 is no longer exactly the midpoint. Furthermore, in practice, scores below 50 are slightly more frequent than indicated by the normal curve (shown here) because severe disability is the result not of normal distribution but of genetic and prenatal factors.

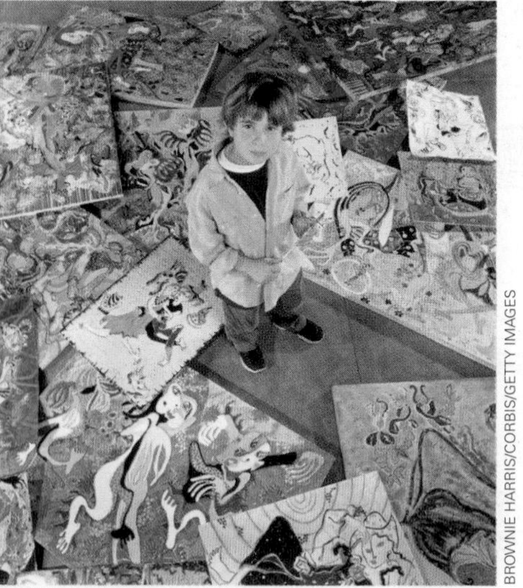
BROWNIE HARRIS/CORBIS/GETTY IMAGES

A Gifted Child Gardner believes every person is naturally better at some of his nine intelligences, and then the social context may or may not appreciate the talent. In the twenty-first century, verbal and mathematical intelligence are usually prized far more than artistic intelligence, but Georgie Pocheptsov was drawing before he learned to speak. The reason is tragic: His father suffered and died of brain cancer when Georgie was a toddler, and his mother bought paints and canvases to help her son cope with his loss. By middle childhood (shown here), Pocheptsov was already a world-famous artist. Now a young adult, his works sell for hundreds of thousands of dollars — often donated to brain tumor research.

TABLE 7.4 Gardner's Nine Multiple Intelligences

1. Linguistic (with words, talking, reading, and writing)
2. Logical-mathematical (with numbers, rules of math and logic)
3. Musical (singing, listening, playing, composing)
4. Spatial (understanding how objects fit or rotate, as with architects)
5. Bodily-kinesthetic (moving the body well, as in dancing, sports)
6. Interpersonal (understanding the emotions and needs of other people)
7. Intrapersonal (understanding the emotions and needs of oneself)
8. Naturalistic (understanding nature, as in biology, zoology, or farming)
9. Spiritual/existential (profound thinking, sometimes deeply religious)

Although everyone has some of all nine intelligences, Gardner believes each individual excels in particular ones. For example, someone might be gifted spatially but not linguistically (a visual artist who cannot describe her work), or might have interpersonal but not naturalistic intelligence (an astute clinical psychologist whose houseplants die).

MULTIPLE INTELLIGENCES

Two leading developmentalists (Robert Sternberg and Howard Gardner) are among those who believe that humans have multiple intelligences, not just one. Sternberg's are described in Chapter 12. Gardner's are described here, because they are particularly relevant to childhood education.

Gardner originally described seven intelligences, each associated with a particular brain region (Gardner, 1983). He subsequently added two more (Gardner, 1999, 2006) (see Table 7.4).

Schools, cultures, and families dampen or expand particular intelligences. If two children are born with kinesthetic aptitude, the child whose school values sports is more likely to develop that intelligence than the child whose school allows no active play. Gardner (2011) believes that schools often are too narrow, teaching only some aspects of intelligence and thus stunting children's learning.

This theory illustrates neurodiversity, in that brain research finds distinct regions that specialize in particular abilities, and those regions are roughly compatible with the nine intelligences that Gardner described (Shearer & Karanian, 2017). The innate differences among people are also affected by the social context, including the school curriculum, because intelligences are "constructed through the participation of individuals in culturally valued activities" (Cavas & Cavas, 2020, p. 405).

◆◆ Especially for Teachers
What are the advantages and disadvantages of using Gardner's nine intelligences to guide your classroom curriculum? (see response, page 239)

Three Disorders That Affect Learning

To illustrate the many complexities with disorders that affect education, we discuss *attention-deficit/hyperactivity disorder (ADHD)*, *specific learning disorder*, and *autism spectrum disorder (ASD)*. As a reference, we use DSM-5 (the fifth edition of the *Diagnostic and Statistical Manual of Mental Disorders*, published by the American Psychiatric Association in 2013). (Many other disorders and several other references merit attention, but there is not space or time for them here.)

attention-deficit/hyperactivity disorder (ADHD)
A condition characterized by a persistent pattern of inattention and/or by hyperactive or impulsive behaviors; ADHD interferes with a person's functioning or development.

ATTENTION-DEFICIT/HYPERACTIVITY DISORDER

Someone with **attention-deficit/hyperactivity disorder (ADHD)** is inattentive, active, and impulsive. In DSM-5, symptoms start before age 12 (in DSM-IV, age 7).

Partly because the definition now includes older children, the rate of children diagnosed with ADHD has increased worldwide (Polanczyk et al., 2014). In 1980, about 5 percent of all U.S. 4- to 17-year-olds were diagnosed with ADHD; more recent rates are 8 percent of 4- to 11-year-olds, and 14 percent of 12- to 17-year-olds (Xu et al., 2018).

Every young child is sometimes inattentive, impulsive, and active, gradually settling down with maturation. That is evident earlier in this chapter, as selective attention and executive function gradually allow more memory and learning.

However, those with ADHD "are so active and impulsive that they cannot sit still, are constantly fidgeting, talk when they should be listening, interrupt people all the time, can't stay on task, . . . accidentally injure themselves." All this makes them "difficult to parent or teach" (Nigg & Barkley, 2014, p. 75). Diagnosis can lead to helpful treatment, often involving medication.

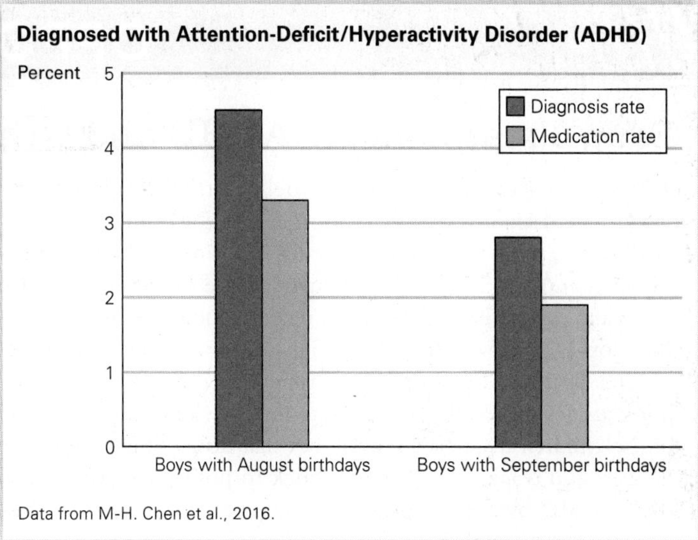

FIGURE 7.7 **One Month Is One Year** In the Taiwanese school system, the cutoff for kindergarten is September 1, so some boys enter school a year later because they were born a few days later. Those who are relatively young among their classmates are less able to sit still and listen. They are almost twice as likely to be given drugs to quiet them down.

OBSERVATION QUIZ
This chart also shows medication rate. Are those August birthdays more likely to be medicated than the September birthdays? (see answer, page 239) ↑

Because many adults are upset by children's moods and actions, and because any physician can write a prescription to quiet a child, thousands of U.S. children may be overmedicated. *But,* because many parents do not recognize that their child needs help, or they are suspicious of drugs and psychologists (Moldavsky & Sayal, 2013; Rose, 2008), thousands of children may suffer needlessly. This controversy is explored in Opposing Perspectives.

It is sometimes difficult to determine if a child's activity level is typical for their age or is a disorder that needs attention. This was evident in a study of 378,000 schoolchildren in Taiwan (M-H. Chen et al., 2016).

In that nation, boys who were born in August, and hence entered kindergarten when they had just turned 5, were diagnosed with ADHD at the rate of 4.5 percent, whereas boys born in September, starting kindergarten when they were almost 6, were diagnosed at the rate of 2.8 percent. Diagnosis typically occurred years after kindergarten, but August-birthday boys were at risk throughout their school years. (See Figure 7.7.) Obviously, maturation mattered.

This example highlights not only the need to consider the child's age but also the need to consider the child's gender. For ADHD diagnosis, "boys outnumber girls 3-to-1 in community samples and 9-to-1 in clinical samples" (Hasson & Fine, 2012, p. 190). Could typical male activity be the reason? Are boys overdiagnosed or girls underdiagnosed?

Recognizing this possibility, experts recently have been diagnosing more girls with ADHD than was true a decade ago. The most recent report finds the male/female ratio closer to 2:1, not 3:1 (Xu et al., 2018).

Often a girl's main symptom is inattentiveness, not hyperactivity, so she falls under a subcategory of ADHD previously known as attention deficit disorder (ADD). Again, the question of the cutoff appears: At what point does a distracted child merit a diagnosis? Who is the best judge of when a child has ADHD? Parent? Teacher? Doctor? Neuroscientist?

LEARNING DISORDERS

The DSM-5 diagnosis of **specific learning disorder** includes problems that cause low achievement in reading, math, or writing (including spelling) (Lewandowski & Lovett, 2014). Disabilities in these areas undercut academic achievement, destroy

specific learning disorder
A marked deficit in a particular area of learning that is not caused b[illegible] an apparent physical disa[illegible] an intellectual disab[illegible] unusually stre[illegible]

OPPOSING PERSPECTIVES

Drug Treatment for ADHD and Other Disorders

Many child psychologists believe that the public discounts the devastation and lost learning that occur when a serious disorder is not recognized or treated. On the other hand, many parents are suspicious of drugs and psychotherapy and avoid recommended treatment (Gordon-Hollingsworth et al., 2015).

This controversy continues among experts. A leading book argues that ADHD is accurate for only about a third of the children diagnosed with it, but that drug companies, doctors and teachers are far too quick to push pills, making "ADHD by far the most misdiagnosed condition in American medicine" (Schwartz, 2015).

A critical review of that book notes failure to mention the millions of people who "have experienced life-changing, positive results" from treatment—including medication (Zametkin & Solanto, 2017, p. 9).

In the United States, more than 2 million people younger than 18 take prescription drugs to regulate their emotions and behavior. The rates are about 14 percent for teenagers (Merikangas et al., 2013), about 10 percent for 6- to 11-year-olds, and less than 1 percent for 2- to 5-year-olds (Olfson et al., 2010). Most children in the United States who are diagnosed with ADHD are medicated; in England and Europe, less than half are (Polanczyk et al., 2014).

In China, psychoactive medication is rarely prescribed for children: A Chinese child with ADHD symptoms is thought to need correction, not medication (Yang et al., 2013). An inattentive, overactive Nigerian child is more likely to be beaten than sent to the doctor.

Most professionals believe that contextual interventions (instructing caregivers and schools on child management, changing the diet, eliminating screens) should be tried before drugs (Daley et al., 2009; Leventhal, 2013). Many parents and teachers wonder whether professionals understand how hard it is to manage an overactive, unmedicated child. Opposing perspectives!

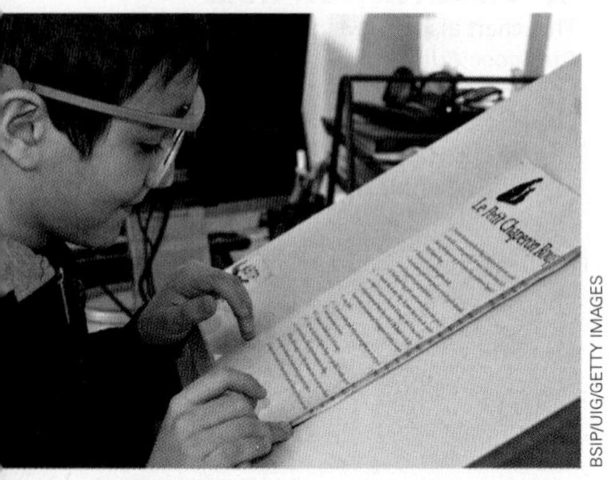

BSIP/UIG/GETTY IMAGES

Happy Reading Those large prism glasses keep the letters from jumping around on the page, a boon for this 8-year-old French boy. Unfortunately, each child with dyslexia needs individualized treatment: These glasses help some, but not most, children who find reading difficult.

dyslexia
Unusual difficulty with reading; thought to be the result of some neurological underdevelopment.

dyscalculia
Unusual difficulty with math, probably originating from a distinct part of the brain.

self-esteem, and qualify a child for special education (according to U.S. law) or formal diagnosis (according to DSM-5).

The most commonly diagnosed learning disorder is **dyslexia**—unusual difficulty with reading. Historically, some children with dyslexia figured out themselves how to cope—as did Hans Christian Andersen and Winston Churchill. Most children with dyslexia, however, endure years of shame and low achievement as well as punishment, because it was assumed that they were not working hard enough to learn. That made it worse. We now know that the origin is in the brain, not the personality (van den Bunt et al., 2018).

Another common learning disorder is **dyscalculia**, unusual difficulty with math. For example, when asked to estimate the height of a normal room, second-graders with dyscalculia might answer "200 feet," or, when shown cards of the 5 and 8 of hearts, and asked which is higher, they might use their fingers to count the hearts on each card (Butterworth et al., 2011).

Although learning disorders can appear in any skill, the DSM-5 recognizes only dyslexia, dyscalculia, and one more—*dysgraphia,* or difficulty in writing. Few children write neatly at age 5, but practice allows most children to write easily and legibly by age 10.

Because many disorders are comorbid, it is not unusual for a child with one learning disability to also have another, or to be unusually anxious, angry or depressed. The biological aspects of brain development affect the cognitive aspects of learning, which influence the emotions.

For every child with a learning disorder, targeted help from teachers and guidance for parents is needed (Crnic et al., 2017). Remember plasticity: Skills improve, not with general practice, such as doing more homework, but with specific practice, such as sounding out letters. The current thinking is that a *multisensory*

approach is needed, with hearing, vision, and motor skills all used to overcome the disability.

VIDEO: Current Research into Autism Spectrum Disorder explores why the causes of ASD are still largely unknown.

AUTISM SPECTRUM DISORDER

Of all the children with learning disabilities, those with **autism spectrum disorder (ASD)** are especially puzzling. Before school age, children with ASD have unusual patterns of language, of play, and of social interaction. Causes and treatments are hotly disputed and have changed dramatically in the past decades.

autism spectrum disorder (ASD) A developmental disorder marked by difficulty with social communication and interaction—including difficulty seeing things from another person's point of view—and restricted, repetitive patterns of behavior, interests, or activities.

Currently the defining symptom is still impaired social interaction, making children with autism less adept at conversation, at social play, and at understanding emotions. Other common symptoms include slow language development, repetitive play, and sensitivity to smells and sounds. Theory of mind (explained in Chapter 5) develops much later, even if executive function is typical (Jones et al., 2018).

Far more children and adults have signs of autism than once was suspected. Now, in the United States, among all 3- to 17-year-olds, parents say that 1 child in every 36 has been diagnosed as having ASD (G. Xu et al., 2019). Medical records of 8-year-olds find that 1 in 35 boys and 1 in 143 girls are on the spectrum (Maenner et al., 2020).

DSM-5 has changed the terminology relating to ASD. People "on the spectrum" may have a mild, moderate, or severe form. Prior to DSM-5, *Asperger's syndrome* (people who were highly verbal but socially inept) was considered a separate disorder; now Asperger's is part of that spectrum.

Why is autism so much more common that it once was? Two hypotheses were suggested that now are proven false. One is that unaffectionate or unavailable mothers (the so-called refrigerator mothers) caused children to withdraw so far from social interaction as to develop autism (Bettelheim, 1975). Before that idea was proven wrong, thousands of mothers were blamed.

The other disproven hypothesis was that infant vaccinations caused autism. Hundreds of studies in many nations refute this idea (only one discredited, fraudulent study backed it). Nonetheless, some parents still refuse to immunize their children.

The current quest of millions of health professionals is to figure out how to counter parents' irrational fears of childhood vaccines and, thus, to prevent epidemics of measles and mumps that can harm children lifelong. The key professionals in this battle are nurses: Because they are closest to the parents, they may be able to convince them to immunize their children to stop a "resurgence of childhood diseases" (Kubin, 2019).

Four new groups of hypotheses about increases of autism are suggested.

1. One cluster focuses on the environment, such as new chemicals in food, air, or water.
2. Another cluster considers prenatal influences: mothers who use drugs, eat foods with traces of pesticides or hormones, contract viruses such as some strains of influenza.
3. A third set of hypotheses is that ASD itself has not increased, but diagnosis has. In 2000 in the United States, education for children with ASD became publicly funded, so parents may be more willing to seek a diagnosis and doctors to provide one.
4. Finally, DSM-5 itself may be the reason. Since the definition has been expanded, more children fit the category and more doctors recognize the symptoms, so children who once were overlooked are now categorized as having ASD.

As more children are diagnosed, some people wonder whether ASD is a disorder needing a cure or whether, instead, schools need to adjust to neurodiversity.

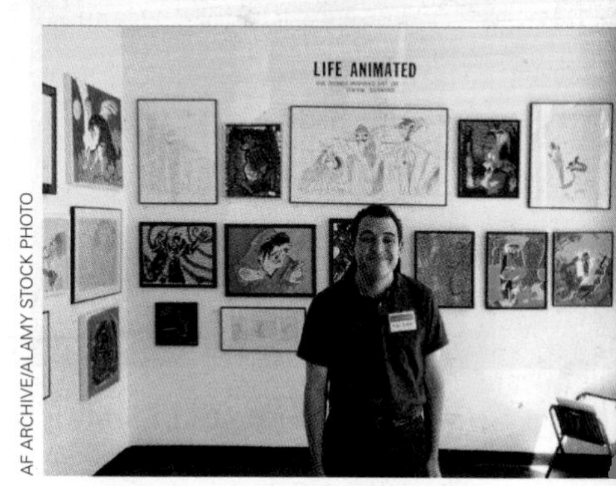

AF ARCHIVE/ALAMY STOCK PHOTO

Not a Cartoon At age 3, Owen Suskind was diagnosed with autism. He stopped talking and spent hour after hour watching Disney movies. His father said his little boy "vanished," as chronicled in the Oscar-nominated documentary *Life Animated.* Now, at age 23 (shown here), Owen still loves cartoons, and he still has many symptoms of autism spectrum disorder. However, he also has learned to speak and has written a movie that reveals his understanding of himself, *The Land of the Lost Sidekicks.*

Not every child is outgoing, flexible, and a fluent talker—the opposite of people with ASD.

Special Education

The overlap of the biosocial, cognitive, and psychosocial domains is evident to developmentalists, as is the need for parents, teachers, therapists, and researchers to work together to help each child. However, deciding if a child should be educated differently than the other children is not straightforward, nor is it closely related to individual needs. Parents, schools, and therapists often disagree.

PROBLEMS AND POSSIBILITIES

As you read, the distinction between typical and atypical is not clear-cut (Clark et al., 2017). Nor is the best educational setting obvious. In the United States, under the 1975 Education of All Handicapped Children Act, all children can learn, and all must be educated in the **least restrictive environment (LRE)**.

least restrictive environment (LRE) A legal requirement that children with special needs be assigned to the most general educational context in which they can be expected to learn.

response to intervention (RTI) An educational strategy intended to help children who demonstrate below-average achievement in early grades, using special intervention.

individual education plan (IEP) A document that specifies educational goals and plans for a child with special needs.

That means that differently abled children are usually educated with children who are not diagnosed with problems (a practice once called *mainstreaming*). Sometimes the strategy is now called *inclusion,* which means that all children are "included" in the general classroom, with "appropriate aids and services" (ideally from a trained teacher who works with the regular teacher). Often that teacher also assists other children who need special help but are not formally diagnosed.

A more recent strategy is called **response to intervention (RTI)** (Al Otaiba et al., 2015; Jimerson et al., 2016). First, all children are taught specific skills; for instance, learning the sounds that various letters make. Then the children are tested, and those who did not master the skill receive special "intervention"—practice and individualized teaching, within the regular class.

Then they are tested again, and, if need be, intervention occurs again. If children do not respond adequately to repeated, focused intervention, they are referred for special education. RTI requires repeated data analysis, which is essential for effective RTI, and for appropriate referral. School psychologists say that such analysis is often lacking (Silva et al., 2020).

KATHRYN SCOTT/THE DENVER POST/GETTY IMAGES

How It Should Be but Rarely Is In this well-equipped classroom in Centennial, Colorado, two teachers are attentively working with three young children, indicating that each child regularly receives individualized instruction. At this school, students with developmental disabilities learn alongside the entire group, so the earlier a child's education begins the better. Sadly, few nations have classrooms like this, and in the United States, few parents can find or afford special help for their children. Indeed, most children with learning disorders are not diagnosed until middle childhood.

When it is determined that a child needs special education, the school proposes an **individual education plan (IEP)**, designed for the particular child. Unfortunately, educators do not always know the best IEP, partly because research on remediation focuses on the less common problems. For example, in the United States, one source claims that "research funding in 2008–2009 for autistic spectrum disorder was 31 times greater than for dyslexia and 540 times greater than for dyscalculia" (Butterworth & Kovas, 2013, p. 304).

As Figure 7.8 shows, the proportion of children designated as needing individualized education in the United States rose from 10 percent in 1980 to 14 percent in 2018. The greatest rise was in children with learning disorders (National Center for Education Statistics, May, 2020). The U.S. school system deems more children as having special educational needs than does any other nation. Is this a reason for national pride or shame?

How many children really need special education? Some U.S. experts fear that neurodiversity, RTI, and inclusion may limit help for differently abled children. If "everyone is special," will that prevent help for children who desperately need it? (Kauffman et al., 2017). On the other hand, if "abnormality is normal," then RTI makes sense for all children.

Often, however, diagnosis and intervention occur too late, or not at all. The numbers of children in public schools who are designated as needing special education increase as children grow older. That is the opposite of what would occur if early intervention succeeded.

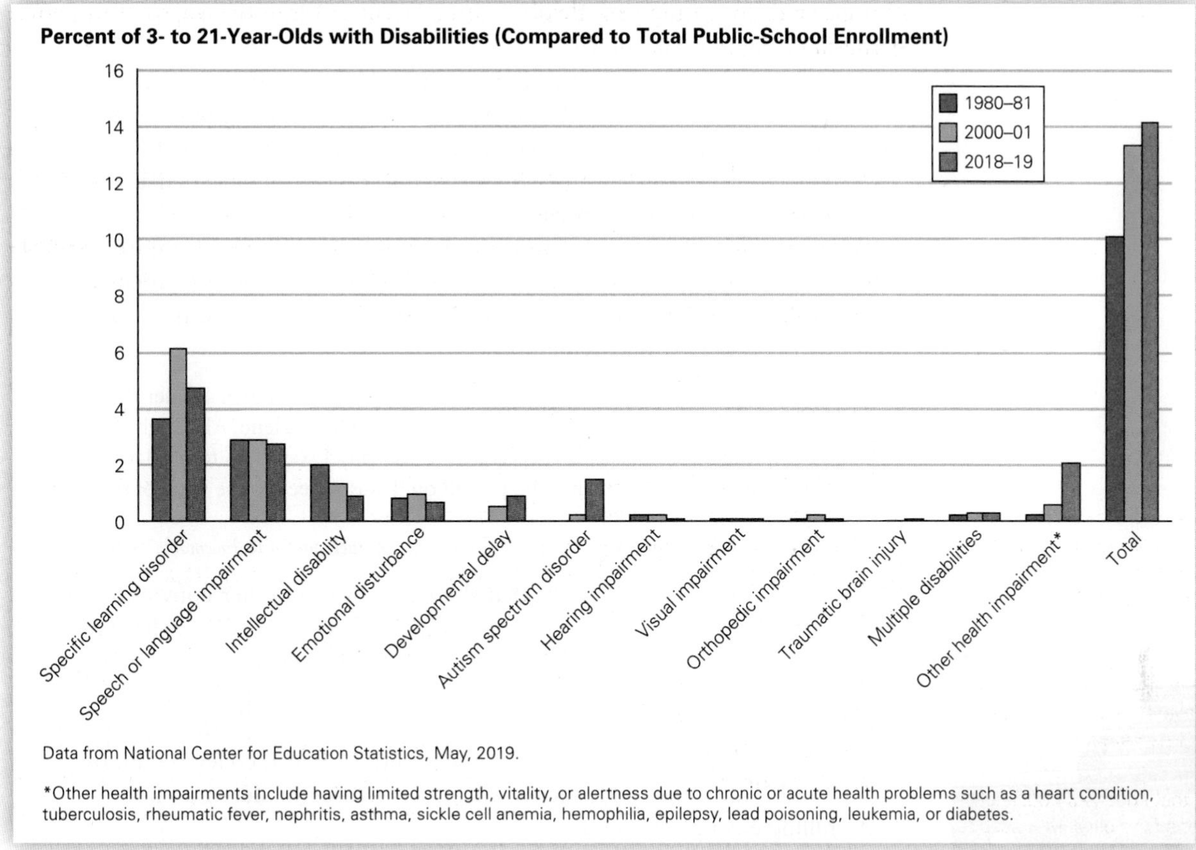

FIGURE 7.8 **Changing Labels** Note that while fewer children have intellectual disability, more have autism. Many experts think that is a change in name, not substance.

Sometimes the current approach is called "wait to fail," which means that ADHD and learning disorders are not diagnosed until a child has been struggling for years without help for sensory, familial, or cultural problems. As one expert says, "We need early identification, and . . . early intervention. If you wait until third grade, kids give up" (Shaywitz, quoted in Stern, 2015, p. 1466).

A similar problem occurs with autism spectrum disorder. Signs of autism appear by age 2, but children are not usually diagnosed until age 4, on average (MMWR, March 28, 2014), with many children not diagnosed until they are in primary school. This is years after the most effective intervention can begin.

GIFTED AND TALENTED

Children who are unusually gifted may also have special educational needs, again not recognized until a child is bored and even disruptive. Federal laws in the United States do not include gifted children as a special category. Instead, each U.S. state, and sometimes each school district, selects and educates such children in a particular way.

Controversies begin with how such children are designated. Some score very high on IQ tests, which qualifies them as gifted. Others are talented in other ways, perhaps in music or art. Should children who are unusually intelligent, talented, or creative be home-schooled, promoted, segregated, or enriched? Each of these has been tried and found lacking.

Historically, parents home-schooled gifted or talented children, either teaching their child themselves or hiring a special coach or tutor. For example, Mozart composed music at age 3 and Picasso created works of art at age 4. Both boys had fathers who recognized their talent. Mozart's father transcribed his earliest pieces and toured

Europe with his gifted son; Picasso's father removed him from school in second grade so he could create all day.

Although intense early education nourished their talent, neither Mozart nor Picasso had happy adult lives. Mozart had a poor understanding of math and money. He had six children, only two of whom survived infancy, and he died in debt at age 35. Picasso regretted never being taught to read or write. He married at age 17, and had four children by three women.

When school attendance became required, about a century ago, gifted children were allowed to skip early grades and join other children of the same mental age, not their chronological age. Many accelerated children never learned how to get along with others. As one woman remembers:

> Nine-year-old little girls are so cruel to younger girls. I was much smaller than them, of course, and would have done anything to have a friend. Although I could cope with the academic work very easily, emotionally I wasn't up to it. Maybe it was my fault and I was asking to be picked on. I was a weed at the edge of the playground.
>
> *[Rachel, quoted in Freeman, 2010, p. 27]*

Calling herself a weed suggests that she never overcame her conviction that she was less cherished than the other children. Her intellectual needs may have been met by skipping two grades, but her emotional and social needs were severely neglected.

My own father skipped three grades, graduating from high school at age 14. Because he attended a one-room school, and because he was the middle child of five, his emotional and social needs were met until he began college—almost failing because of his immaturity. He recovered, but some other children do not.

A chilling example comes from:

> Sufiah Yusof [who] started her maths degree at Oxford [the leading University in England] in 2000, at the age of 13. She too had been dominated and taught by her father. But she ran away the day after her final exam. She was found by police but refused to go home, demanding of her father in an email: "Has it ever crossed your mind that the reason I left home was because I've finally had enough of 15 years of physical and emotional abuse?" Her father claimed she'd been abducted and brainwashed. She refuses to communicate with him. She is now a very happy, high-class, high-earning prostitute.
>
> *[Freeman, 2010, p. 286]*

STEVE GRANITZ/WIREIMAGE/GETTY IMAGES

And Tomorrow? The education of gifted children is controversial, as is the future of Sunny Pawar, "just a normal boy" from the slums of Mumbai (shown here at age 8) and also a talented star in *Lion*, a 2016 Oscar-nominated film made in Australia. After a worldwide tour to promote the film, he returned to his one-room home and attends school, where he gets none of the perks of being a movie star. What next?

The fate of the creative child may be worse than the intellectually gifted child. If not given an education that suits them, they joke in class, resist drudgery, ignore homework, and bedevil their teachers. They may become innovators, inventors, and creative forces in the future, but they also may become drug addicts or dropouts, and never earn a degree or get a steady job, because they feel stifled by normal life.

Among the well-known creative geniuses who were not exemplary students were Bill Gates, Richard Branson, Steve Jobs, and hundreds of thousands of others, probably some of whom you know personally.

One such person was Charles Darwin, whose "school reports complained unendingly that he wasn't interested in studying, only shooting, riding, and beetle-collecting" (Freeman, 2010, p. 283). At the behest of his physician father, Darwin entered college to study medicine, but he hated it and left.

Without a college degree, Darwin began his famous five-year trip around South America at age 22, collecting specimens and developing the theory of evolution—which disputed conventional religious dogma as only a highly creative person could do.

Since both acceleration and home-schooling led to later social problems for gifted children, a third education strategy has become popular, at least in the United States. Such children are taught as a group in their own separate class. Ideally, such children

are neither bored nor lonely; each is challenged and appreciated by their classmates and teacher.

Some research supports the strategy of special education for children with exceptional music, math, or athletic gifts. Their brain structures develop in ways to support their talents (Moreno et al., 2015). Since plasticity means that children learn whatever their context teaches, perhaps some children need gifted and talented classes.

Such classes require unusual teachers, bright and creative, individualizing instruction. For example, a 7-year-old artist may need freedom, guidance, and inspiration for magnificent art but also need patient, step-by-step instruction in sounding out simple words. A classmate might read at the twelfth-grade level but have immature social skills. The teacher must be highly skilled, to help both of them learn from each other.

High-achieving students are especially likely to have great teachers if the hidden curriculum includes putting children with special needs together, sorting students by past achievement, allowing private or charter schools to select and expel students.

The argument against gifted and talented classes is that *every* child needs such teachers, no matter what the child's abilities or disabilities. If each school district (and sometimes each school principal) hires and assigns teachers, as occurs in the United States, then the best teachers may have the most able students, and the school districts with the most money (the most expensive homes) have the highest paid teachers. Should it be the opposite?

Mainstreaming, IEPs, and so on were developed when parents and educators saw that segregation of children with disabilities led to less learning and impaired adult lives. The same may happen if gifted and talented children are separated from the rest.

Some nations (China, Finland, Scotland, and many others) educate all children together, assuming that all children could become high achievers if they put in the effort, guided by effective teachers. Since every child is special, should every child have special education?

what have you learned?

1. Should traditional IQ tests be discarded? Why or why not?
2. What is the difference between ADHD and typical child behavior?
3. What do dyslexia, dyscalculia, and dysgraphia have in common?
4. What are the symptoms of autism spectrum disorder?
5. Why has ASD increased in the past decades?
6. How might the concept of neurodiversity affect education for special children?
7. What is the difference between mainstreaming and inclusion?
8. What are the arguments for and against special classes for gifted children?

SUMMARY

A Healthy Time

1. Middle childhood is the healthiest period of the entire life span. Death and disease rates are low, and typically good health habits protect every part of the body.

2. Both gross and fine motor skills increase during middle childhood. Physical activity aids health and joy in many ways, as well as benefits the mind. Art and music benefit fine motor skills, which may also improve learning.

3. Worldwide, rates of obesity and asthma are increasing. Family habits and national policies interact to increase or decrease the rate of these problems. In childhood, the main problem with obesity and asthma may be self-concept and friendship.

Cognition

4. According to Piaget, middle childhood is the time of concrete operational thought, when egocentrism diminishes and logical thinking begins. The concepts of classification and seriation help with thinking, especially in math.

5. Vygotsky stressed the social context of learning, including the specific lessons of school and learning from peers, adults, and culture.

6. Both the knowledge base and memory improve during middle childhood, influenced by maturation, and mentoring.

7. In middle childhood, logic and the eagerness for social experiences advance language, particularly expanded vocabulary and pragmatics. Children of low SES are usually lower in linguistic skills, primarily because they hear less language during the early years.

8. Learning the school language is crucial for academic success. In some nations all children learn a second language in middle childhood. Many methods are used in the United States to teach children whose home language is not English.

Teaching and Learning

9. The hidden curriculum may be more influential on children's learning than the formal curriculum. This includes the characteristics and expectations of the teachers.

10. International assessments are useful as comparisons. Reading is assessed with the PIRLS, math and science with the TIMSS, and practical intelligence with the PISA. Culture affects answers as well as learning: East Asian scores are high, Finland scores have improved, and U.S. scores are middling.

11. School climate affects how happy and motivated the students are. Crucial is that the students and teachers have a growth mindset, believing that effort makes more difference in education than inborn (fixed) characteristics.

12. In the United States, each state, each district, and sometimes each school retains significant control, hence variation in the hidden curriculum, in national assessments (NAEP), and in funding. Variations and controversies ensue. Most children attend their local public school, but some parents choose charter schools, others private schools, and still others opt for home schooling.

Children with Distinct Educational Needs

13. Every child has some special educational strengths and needs, which are reflected in aptitude as well as achievement. Intellectual aptitude is usually measured with IQ tests, with scores that can change over time. Achievement is what a person has actually learned, a product of aptitude, motivation, and opportunity.

14. Critics of IQ testing contend that intelligence is manifested in multiple ways, which makes *g* (general intelligence) too narrow and limited. Gardner describes nine distinct intelligences, each influenced by both brain and culture.

15. Children with attention-deficit/hyperactivity disorder (ADHD) have potential problems in three areas: inattention, impulsiveness, and activity. DSM-5 recognizes learning disorders, specifically dyslexia (reading), dyscalculia (math), and dysgraphia (penmanship).

16. Children on the autism spectrum typically have problems with social interaction and language. Neurodiversity suggests caution in treatment and analysis.

17. About 14 percent of all children in the United States receive special education services. These begin with an IEP (individual education plan) and assignment to the least restrictive environment (LRE), usually within the regular classroom.

18. Many strategies have been used to educate children who do not learn as the typical child does. Once they all were excluded from other children, but then mainstreaming and inclusion became the goal. Currently, response to remediation is a first step, before a child is formally adjudicated as needing an IEP.

19. Children who are gifted may also need to be educated separately. However, some argue that every child needs to learn with other children, while every teacher needs to target the particular needs of each child.

KEY TERMS

childhood obesity (p. 208)
asthma (p. 209)
concrete operational thought (p. 211)
classification (p. 211)
seriation (p. 211)
working memory (p. 213)
knowledge base (p. 214)
English Language Learners (ELLs) (p. 216)
immersion (p. 216)
bilingual education (p. 216)
ESL (English as a Second Language) (p. 216)
hidden curriculum (p. 219)
Trends in Math and Science Study (TIMSS) (p. 222)
Progress in International Reading Literacy Study (PIRLS) (p. 222)
Program for International Student Assessment (PISA) (p. 222)
National Assessment of Educational Progress (NAEP) (p. 225)
comorbid (p. 228)
neurodiversity (p. 229)
attention-deficit/hyperactivity disorder (ADHD) (p. 230)
specific learning disorder (p. 231)
dyslexia (p. 232)
dyscalculia (p. 232)
autism spectrum disorder (ASD) (p. 233)
least restrictive environment (LRE) (p. 234)
response to intervention (RTI) (p. 234)
individual education plan (IEP) (p. 234)

APPLICATIONS

1. Compare play spaces and school design for children in different neighborhoods—ideally, urban, suburban, and rural areas. Note size, safety, and use. How might this affect children's health and learning?

2. Visit a local elementary school and look for the hidden curriculum. For example, do the children line up? Why or why not, when, and how? Does gender, age, ability, or talent affect the grouping of children or the selection of staff? What is on the walls? For everything you observe, speculate about the underlying assumptions.

3. What do you remember about how you learned to read? Compare your memories with those of two other people, one at least 10 years older and the other at least 5 years younger than you are. Can you draw any conclusions about effective reading instruction? If so, what are they? If not, why not?

4. Parents of differently abled children often consult internet sources. Pick one disability and find 10 websites that describe causes and educational solutions. How valid, how accurate, and how objective is the information? What disagreements do you find? How might parents react to the information provided?

ESPECIALLY FOR ANSWERS

Response for Teachers (from p. 214): Here are two of the most obvious ways. (1) Use logic. Once children can grasp classification and class inclusion, they can understand cities within states, states within nations, and nations within continents. Organize your instruction to make logical categorization easier. (2) Make use of children's need for concrete and personal involvement. You might have the children learn first about their own location, then about the places where relatives and friends live, and finally about places beyond their personal experience (via books, photographs, videos, and guest speakers).

Response for Parents (from p. 217): Your son would understand your explanation, but you should take him along if you can do so without losing patience. You wouldn't ignore his need for food or medicine, so don't ignore his need for learning. While shopping, you can teach vocabulary (does he know pimientos, pepperoni, polenta?), categories (root vegetables, freshwater fish), and math (which size box of cereal is cheaper?). Explain in advance that you need him to help you find items and carry them and that he can choose only one item that you wouldn't normally buy. Seven-year-olds can understand rules, and they enjoy being helpful.

Response for Teachers (from p. 230): The advantages are that all of the children learn more aspects of human knowledge and that many children can develop their talents. Art, music, and sports should be an integral part of education, not just a break from academics. The disadvantage is that they take time and attention away from reading and math, which might lead to less proficiency in those subjects on standardized tests and thus to criticism from parents and supervisors.

OBSERVATION QUIZ ANSWERS

Answer to Observation Quiz (from p. 211): At this age children like to be near each other. That is your clue: An adult instructed them to sit apart. Their teacher is influenced by Piaget, who thought each person should discover cognitive principles on their own.

Answer to Observation Quiz (from p. 220): About 60 (six rows, ten in a row). Did trying to count make you realize that the children at the back cannot see or hear the teacher very well? None of them have glasses, so some of them cannot read the board.

Answer to Observation Quiz (from p. 231): Yes, not only overall but also in response to the diagnosis. When a September birthday boy is diagnosed with ADHD, he is less likely to be medicated than an August birthday boy—the opposite of what would be expected if only boys with real problems were diagnosed.

CHAPTER 8

MIDDLE CHILDHOOD
The Social World

Learning from Each Other
Middle childhood is prime time for social comparison. Swinging is done standing, or on the belly, or twisted, or head down (as shown here) if someone else does it.

what will you know?

- What helps children thrive in difficult family or neighborhood conditions?
- Should parents marry, risking divorce, or not marry, risking separation?
- Why would children lie to adults to protect a bully?

Ward Sutton is a professional cartoonist who won the prestigious Herblock Prize in 2018. In his acceptance speech, he thanked Kay Brown, a parent of his fifth-grade classmate. Kay noticed that Ward liked to draw, and suggested that he create a cartoon for the community newspaper. As Ward described it, "my first published editorial cartoon pulled no punches on the hard-hitting topic of . . . students leaning back in their chairs in class. Because, if you did that you might, you know, tip over. Hey, I had to start somewhere!"

Ward and Kay start this chapter because their story illustrates the nature of 10-year-olds and the importance of the community that supports them. His focus on the practical problems of fifth-graders (tipped chairs) is typical of concrete operational thought, as were his social concerns about his peers.

Later, bigger issues became salient: Ward praised his small Colorado town for upholding the freedom of speech, specifically for its willingness to copy and send his cartoons even though some were pointed political satire. But back to childhood: As a young boy, Ward was much more concerned with earning the respect of his peers. He was also beginning to understand the morals of his community. Both of these topics are discussed in this chapter.

You will read about Ward's encounter with friends, neighbors, parents, and the police at the end of this chapter. Middle childhood is the time when children become aware of the wider community, as occurred with Ward, when Kay channeled his doodles into something meaningful, or, as explained later in this chapter, when the police, his parents, and his neighbors taught Ward a lifelong lesson.

The Nature of the Child

Steady growth, brain maturation, and intellectual advances make children more independent (see At About This Time). Between ages 6 and 11, children learn to care for themselves, with notable advances.

Children who are in middle childhood, unlike their much-younger selves, not only hold their spoon but also make their lunch, not only zip their pants but also pack their suitcases, not only walk to school but also organize games with friends. No longer tightly supervised, older children venture outdoors alone.

At About This Time: Signs of Psychosocial Development from Age 6 to 11*

Children responsibly perform specific chores.

Children make decisions about a weekly allowance.

Children can tell time and have set times for various activities.

Children have homework, including some assignments over several days.

Children are punished less often than when they were younger.

Children try to conform to peers in clothes, language, and so on.

Children voice preferences about their after-school care, lessons, and activities.

Children are responsible for younger children, pets, and, in some places, work.

Children strive for independence from parents.

*Of course, culture is crucial. For example, giving a child an allowance is typical for middle-class children in developed nations since about 1960. It was rare, or completely absent, in earlier times and other places.

Industry and Inferiority

Throughout the centuries and in every culture, school-age children are industrious. They busily master whatever skills their culture values, as Ward did with his drawing. Physical maturation, described in the previous chapter, makes such activity possible.

In Erikson's fourth psychosocial crisis, **industry versus inferiority**, the child "must forget past hopes and wishes, while his exuberant imagination is tamed and harnessed to the laws of impersonal things," becoming "ready to apply himself to given skills and tasks" (Erikson, 1993a, pp. 258, 259). Simply trying new things, as in the previous stage (initiative versus guilt), is insufficient. Sustained activity that leads to accomplishments that make one proud is necessary.

industry versus inferiority The fourth of Erikson's eight psychosocial crises, during which children attempt to master many skills, developing a sense of themselves as either industrious or inferior, competent or incompetent.

Think of learning to read and learning to add, both of which are painstaking and tedious. For instance, slowly sounding out "Jane has a dog" or writing "3 + 4 = 7" for the hundredth time is not exciting. Yet school-age children busily practice reading and math: They are intrinsically motivated to read a page, finish a worksheet, memorize a spelling word, color a map, and so on. Similarly, they enjoy collecting, categorizing, and counting whatever they gather—perhaps stamps, stickers, stones, or seashells. That is industry.

Overall, children judge themselves as either *industrious* or *inferior*—deciding whether they are competent or incompetent, productive or useless, winners or losers. Self-pride depends not only on actual accomplishments but also on the perceptions of others, especially peers. Social rejection is both a cause and a consequence of feeling inferior (Rubin et al., 2013). A fixed mindset (described in Chapter 7) is depressing.

TAO IMAGES LIMITED/ALAMY IMAGES

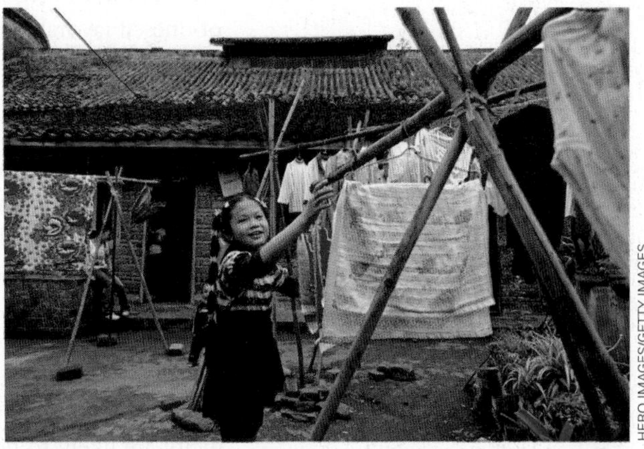

HERO IMAGES/GETTY IMAGES

Same Situation, Far Apart: Helping at Home Sichuan, in China *(right)*, and Virginia, in the United States *(left)*, provide vastly different contexts for child development. Children everywhere help their families with household chores, as these two do, but gender expectations vary a great deal.

Parental Reactions

Did you pause a moment ago when you read that 6- to 11-year-olds can "venture outdoors alone"? Cohort and context make a difference. Recently in the United States, many parents do not allow their children outside without an adult, even to walk to school, much less to go to town with money in their pocket. By contrast, in some eras and nations, 10-year-olds are sole caregivers for younger children outside the home, or they go alone to paid employment every day.

In every community, however, parents gradually grant more autonomy in middle childhood, which helps children feel happy and capable (Yan et al., 2017). Time spent with parents decreases while time alone, and with friends, increases.

One study of U.S. families found that 12-year-olds, on average, spent almost half an hour less each day with their mothers than 8-year-olds did (70 versus 95 minutes). Note that these are averages: This study found substantial variation by context and family structure, from almost no time to several hours each day (Lam et al., 2012).

Self-Concept

As children mature, they develop their *self-concept,* which is their idea about themselves, including about their intelligence, personality, abilities, gender, and ethnicity. The younger child's rosy self-concept is modified in middle childhood.

Opinions about oneself gradually become more specific and logical, the result of increases in cognitive development and social awareness. Mothers continue to be influential, but fathers, teachers, and peers gain influence, sometimes helping children feel proud but sometimes not (Verschueren, 2020).

Genes, brain maturation, and family experiences all affect the self-concept (Bick et al., 2019). One idea, called *adjustment-erosion model,* suggests that emotional problems at age 6 (the overly aggressive or pathologically shy first-grader) affect later academic difficulties more than vice versa (Deighton et al., 2018). Notice the developmental process: Emotional regulation and social skills developed in early childhood affect school success in middle childhood.

THINK CRITICALLY: When would a realistic, honest self-assessment be harmful?

COMPARED TO OTHERS

Crucial during middle childhood is **social comparison**—comparing oneself to others (Dweck, 2013; Lapan & Boseovski, 2017). Ideally, social comparison helps school-age children value themselves for who they are, abandoning the fantasy self-evaluation of preschoolers.

social comparison
The tendency to assess one's abilities, achievements, social status, and other attributes by measuring them against those of other people, especially one's peers.

Social comparison makes the self-concept more realistic, because children incorporate comparison to peers when they judge themselves. The human tendency to think of oneself favorably remains, but it now is grounded in reality (Thomaes et al., 2017).

Some children—especially those from some ethnic or religious groups—become aware of social prejudices that they need to overcome. Middle childhood is also the time when all children start to establish their ethnic attitudes (identifying as White or "of color"), which are consolidated in adolescence and adulthood (Hagerman, 2020).

During these years, children also become aware of gender discrimination, with girls complaining that they are not allowed to play certain sports and boys complaining that teachers favor girls. African American and Latinx children notice discrimination against their groups, not just against them as individuals as egocentric preschoolers do. Their school achievement is reduced because of it (Brown & Tam, 2019; Seaton, 2020).

Over the years of middle childhood, children who are proud of their gender and ethnicity are likely to develop healthy self-esteem (Corenblum, 2014). This is particularly crucial when the child becomes aware of prejudice in the society, a problem encountered by every transgender child and by most children who identify with a minority religious

or ethnic group. More on these important issues is presented in Chapter 10, on identity development in adolescence.

Parental acceptance and support are vital, but the parents themselves may experience stress if they are not affirmed by their community (Hidalgo & Chen, 2019). Especially when the outside world seems hostile, parents and schools who teach about successful people from many ethnicities, genders, or nationalities are likely to help children feel valued (Hernández et al., 2017). Self-acceptance and pride bolster self-confidence more than alerting children to prejudice (Reynolds & Gonzales-Backen, 2017).

PICTORIAL PRESS LTD/ALAMY

Black Panther Mythical superheroes, and the perpetual battle between good and evil, are especially attractive to boys in middle childhood but resonate with people of all ages, genders, and ethnic groups. *Black Panther* was first a comic-book hero in 1966 and then became a 2018 movie that broke records for attendance and impact. It features not only African American heroes but also an army of strong women — busting stereotypes and generating self-esteem for many children.

CULTURE AND SELF-ESTEEM

Academic as well as social competence are aided by realistic self-perception. That is beneficial, because unrealistically high self-esteem reduces effortful control, and without some control children are more aggressive and less conscientious than they might be.

The same consequences occur if self-esteem is too low. Obviously, the goal then is to find a middle ground. This is not easy: Children may be too self-critical or not self-critical enough. Their self-control interacts with the reactions of their parents and culture. Cultures differ on what that middle ground is.

High self-esteem is neither universally valued nor universally criticized, although criticism is more likely. Reflect on cultural sayings: Australians say that "tall poppies are cut down"; the Chinese say, "the nail that sticks up is hammered"; Americans say "pride goeth before a fall"; and the Japanese discourage social comparison aimed at making oneself feel superior.

The self-conscious emotions (pride, shame, guilt) first evident in early childhood develop during middle childhood. They guide social interaction, yet they can overcome a child's self-concept, leading to psychopathology (Muris & Meesters, 2014). Especially during middle childhood (less so in adolescence), school achievement and family status can be crucial in developing self-esteem, affecting self-concept lifelong. An adult can feel inferior to other adults because of self-concept in childhood.

In addition, the onset of concrete thinking in middle childhood leads children to notice material possessions. Objects that adults find superficial (name-brand sunglasses, sock patterns) become important.

Insecure 10-year-olds might desperately want the latest jackets, smartphones, and so on. Or they may want something else that makes them seem special, such as lessons in African dance, or a brilliant light for their bicycle, or—as one of my daughters pestered me to buy—a bread-maker (used often for several weeks, discarded after several years).

From a life-span perspective, a developmental trend appears. Children in many cultures develop aspects of self-esteem during middle childhood. That is refined in adolescence (perhaps with a dip at puberty), and increases again in emerging adulthood. Not until very late adulthood (after age 70 or beyond) does self-esteem, on average, decrease (Orth et al., 2018).

Resilience and Stress

In infancy and early childhood, children depend on their immediate families for food, learning, and life itself. In middle childhood, some children continue to benefit from supportive families, and others escape destructive families by finding their own niche in the larger world.

TABLE 8.1 Dominant Ideas About Resilience, 1965 to Present

Year	Idea
1965	All children have the same needs for healthy development.
1970	Some conditions or circumstances — such as "absent father," "teenage mother," "working mom," and "day care" — are harmful for every child.
1975	All children are *not* the same. Some children are resilient, coping easily with stressors that cause harm in other children.
1980	Nothing inevitably causes harm. Both maternal employment and preschool education, once thought to be risks, are often helpful.
1985	Factors beyond the family, both in the child (low birthweight, prenatal alcohol exposure, aggressive temperament) and in the community (poverty, violence), can be very risky for children.
1990	Risk–benefit analysis finds that some children are "invulnerable" to, or even benefit from, circumstances that destroy others.
1995	No child is invincible. Risks are always harmful — if not in education, then in emotions; if not immediately, then long term.
2000	Risk–benefit analysis involves the interplay among many biological, cognitive, and social factors, some within the child (genes, disability, temperament), the family (function as well as structure), and the community (including neighborhood, school, church, and culture).
2008	Focus on strengths, not risks. Assets in child (intelligence, personality), family (secure attachment, warmth), community (schools, after-school programs), and nation (income support, health care) must be nurtured.
2010	Strengths vary by culture and national values. Both universal ideals and local variations must be recognized and respected.
2012	Genes as well as cultural practices can be either strengths or weaknesses; differential susceptibility means that identical stressors can benefit one child and harm another.
2015	Communities are responsible for child resilience. Not every child needs help, but every community needs to encourage healthy child development.
2020	Resilience is seen more broadly as a characteristic of mothers and communities.

Surprisingly, some children seem unscathed by early experiences. They have been called "resilient" or even "invincible." Current thinking about resilience (see Table 8.1), with insights from dynamic-systems theory, emphasizes that no one is truly untouched by past history or current context, but some weather early storms and a few not only survive but become stronger because of it (Luthar, 2015; Masten, 2014; Rutter, 2012).

Many developmental scholars and mental health practitioners try to find the balance between protective factors and traumatic ones. They confirm that too many *adverse childhood experiences* (*ACEs*; see Chapter 6) make resilience difficult (Powell et al., 2020). They seek a "nuanced characterization of the developmental origins of risk and resilience pathways" to acknowledge the mix of brain and experience that enables stress to be overcome (Morris et al., 2020, p. 247).

DEFINING RESILIENCE

Resilience has been defined as "a dynamic process encompassing positive adaptation within the context of significant adversity" (Luthar et al., 2000, p. 543) and "the capacity of a dynamic system to adapt successfully to disturbances that threaten system function, viability, or development" (Masten, 2014, p. 30). Both researchers emphasize three parts of this definition:

- Resilience is *dynamic*, not a stable trait. That means a given person may be resilient at some periods but not others. The effects from one period reverberate as time goes on.
- Resilience is a *positive adaptation* to stress. For example, if parental rejection leads a child to a closer relationship with another adult, that is positive resilience, not passive endurance.
- Resilience is not a trait, but a reaction to significant adversity.

Watch **VIDEO: Mindfulness in Schools** to learn how children can better cope with stress and anxiety.

resilience
The capacity to adapt well to significant adversity and to overcome serious stress.

CUMULATIVE STRESS

An important discovery is that stress accumulates over time, including minor disturbances (called "daily hassles"). A long string of hassles, day after day, takes a greater toll than an isolated major stress. Almost every child can withstand one trauma, but "the likelihood of problems increased as the number of risk factors increased" (Masten, 2014, p. 14).

The social context, especially supportive adults who do not blame the child, is crucial. A chilling example comes from the "child soldiers" in the 1991–2002 civil war in Sierra Leone (Betancourt et al., 2013). Thousands of children witnessed and perpetrated murder, rape, and other traumas. When the war was over, 529 war-affected youth, then aged 10 to 17, were interviewed. Many were severely depressed, with crippling anxiety.

These war-damaged children were interviewed again two and six years later. Surprisingly, many had overcome their trauma and were functioning well. Recovery was more likely if:

- The war occurred when they were in middle childhood, not adolescence.
- At least one caregiver survived and was reunited with the child.
- Their communities did not reject them, no matter which side they had joined.
- Daily routines (school, family responsibilities) were restored.

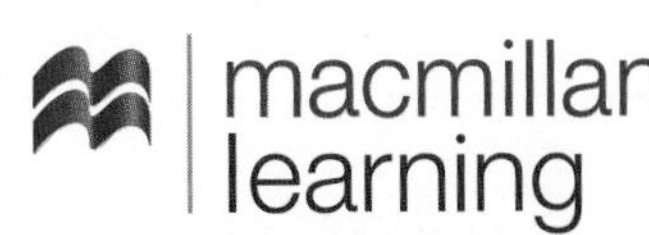

VIDEO ACTIVITY: Child Soldiers and Child Peacemakers examines the state of child soldiers in the world and then explores how adolescent cognition impacts the decisions of five teenage peace activists.

FAMILY AS A BUFFER

In England during World War II, many city children were sent to loving families in rural areas to escape the German bombs dropped every day. To the surprise of researchers, those children who stayed in London with their parents were more resilient, despite nights huddled in air-raid shelters, than those who were physically safe but without their parents (Freud & Burlingham, 1943).

Similar results were found in a longitudinal study of children exposed to a sudden, wide-ranging, terrifying wildfire in Australia. Almost all of the children suffered stress reactions at the time, but 20 years later, the crucial factor was not proximity to the fire but whether or not it separated them from their mothers (McFarlane & Van Hooff, 2009).

Whenever war, disasters, racism, or national policies separate parents and children, developmentalists predict lifelong problems for the children. This has long been evident in Holocaust survivors from the second World War, refugees of civil wars in African nations, and children in Vietnam. Recently, the same consequences have been found in immigrant children in the United States, who experience many health problems if their parents are not with them (Perreira & Pedroza, 2019).

For that reason, thousands of developmental scholars and dozens of professional societies have expressed their horror at the 2018–2020 U.S. policy of separating children from their parents at the United States–Mexico border. For example, the Society of Developmental and Behavioral Pediatrics fears that "a generation of children will experience lifelong repercussions" from being forcefully separated from their parents. Their statement reads:

> Children and parents belong together. Children who are separated from their primary caregivers may experience toxic stress and a disruption of attachment that can have severe emotional, behavioral and physical implications.
>
> *[Society for Developmental and Behavioral Pediatrics, 2018]*

BERND JONKMANNS/LAIF/REDUX

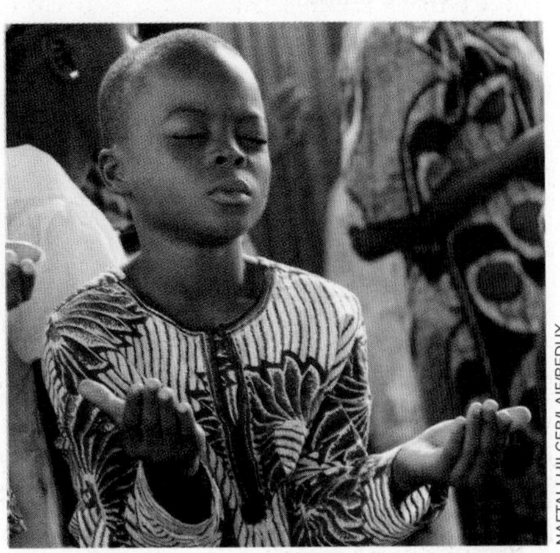

NAFTALI HILGER/LAIF/REDUX

Same Situation, Far Apart: Praying Hands Differences are obvious between the northern Indian girls entering their Hindu school *(left)* and the West African boy in a Christian church *(right)*, even in their clothes and hand positions. But underlying similarities are more important. In every culture, many 8-year-olds are more devout than their elders. That is especially true if their community is under stress. Faith aids resilience.

COGNITIVE COPING

Obviously, these examples are extreme, but the general finding is confirmed by many studies. Disasters take a toll, but resilience is possible. Factors in the child (especially problem-solving ability), in the family (consistency and care), and in the community (good schools and welcoming religious institutions) help children recover (Masten, 2014).

The child's interpretation is crucial (Lagattuta, 2014). Cortisol increases in low-income children *if* they interpret events connected to their family's status as a personal threat and *if* the family lacks order and routines (thus increasing daily hassles) (Coe et al., 2018). If low-SES children do not feel personally to blame, and if their family is not chaotic, they may be resilient.

In general, children's interpretations of family situations (poverty, divorce, and so on) determine how they are affected. Think of people you know: Some adults from low-SES families did not feel deprived. Only later did they realize that they were poor. President Jimmy Carter, for instance, had no shoes as a child: He thought his challenge was to avoid splinters from the floor of his classroom. For him and other children who did not feel deprived, poverty was less likely to cast a shadow over adult life.

Some children consider the family they were born into a temporary hardship; they look forward to the day when they can leave childhood behind. If they also have personal strengths, such as the cognitive abilities to imagine a better life, they may shine in adulthood—evident in the United States in thousands of success stories, from Abraham Lincoln to Oprah Winfrey.

parentification
When a child acts more like a parent than a child. Parentification may occur if the actual parents do not act as caregivers, making a child feel responsible for the family.

The opposite reaction is called **parentification**, when children feel responsible for the entire family, acting as caregivers of everyone, including their actual parents. Here again the child's interpretation is crucial. For instance, suppose a child witnesses domestic abuse. This is never good, but if the child feels responsible for the abuser or the abused, recovery is less likely (Fortin et al., 2011).

THINK CRITICALLY: Is there any harm in having the oldest child take care of the younger ones? Why or why not?

One final example: Many children of immigrants become translators for their parents, who know neither the language nor the culture. If those children feel burdened by their role as language brokers, that increases their depression. But, if they feel they are making a positive contribution to their family well-being, they themselves benefit (Weisskirch, 2017b).

what have you learned?

1. What is the difference between Erikson's stages for children in early and middle childhood?
2. Why is social comparison particularly powerful during middle childhood?
3. Why do cultures differ in how they value pride or modesty?
4. How do gender and ethnicity affect self-concept?
5. What is the difference between resilience and enduring difficult circumstances?
6. What is the role of mothers in coping with stress?
7. Why and when might minor stresses be more harmful than major stresses?
8. How might a child's interpretation of events help them cope with repeated stress?

Families During Middle Childhood

No one doubts that genes affect personality as well as ability, that peers are vital, and that schools and cultures influence what, and how much, children learn. Some have gone further, suggesting that genes, peers, and communities have so much influence that parents have little impact—unless they are grossly abusive (Harris, 1998, 2002; McLeod et al., 2007). This suggestion arose from studies about the impact of the environment on child development.

MONKEYBUSINESSIMAGES/ISTOCK/GETTY IMAGES

Shared Environment? All three children live in the same home in Brooklyn, New York, with loving, middle-class parents. But it is not hard to imagine that family life is quite different for the 9-year-old girl than for her sister, born a year later, or their little brother, age 3.

OBSERVATION QUIZ
Are significant gender differences evident here? (see answer, page 271) ↑

Shared and Nonshared Environments

Many studies have found that children are much less affected by *shared environment* (influences that arise from being in the same environment, such as for two siblings living in one home, raised by their parents) than by *nonshared environment* (e.g., the distinct experiences and surroundings of two people). Basic values and traits, and even sexual orientation, once thought to be heavily affected by parents, seem more influenced by genes and nonshared environment than by growing up in a particular home (Twito & Knafo-Noam, 2020; Y. Xu et al., 2020).

Since genes and nonshared environment are so powerful, might parents be insignificant? That hypothesis avoids "misplaced blame on parents for negative outcomes in their children . . . adding guilt to the grief parents are already feeling" (Sherlock & Zietsch, 2018, p. 155). But it also suggests that parents should not take credit for the accomplishments of their children.

Could it be that parents are merely caretakers, needed for basic care (food, shelter), harmful when severely neglectful or abusive, but inconsequential in typical household routines, prohibitions, and praise? If a child becomes a murderer or a hero, should parents be neither blamed nor credited?

That conclusion is too extreme: Parents are not the only influence, of course, but research affirms parent power. The analysis of shared and nonshared influences was correct, but the conclusion was based on a false assumption. Siblings raised together do *not* share the same environment.

For example, if relocation, divorce, unemployment, or a new job occurs in a family, the impact on each child differs depending on that child's age, genes, resilience, sex, and gender. Always, age and community matter:

- Moving to another town upsets schoolchildren more than infants;
- Divorce harms boys more than girls;
- Poverty may hurt preschoolers the most; and
- Low SES is more devastating for children in the United States and Latin America than in Northern Europe.

Differential susceptibility adds to the variation: One child might be more affected than another. When siblings are raised together, experiencing the same family conditions, the mix of genes, age, and gender may lead one to become antisocial, another to be pathologically anxious, and a third to be resilient, capable, and strong.

Not all characteristics are genetic. For example, one study of 7-year-old twins found that the child's ability to recognize emotions (whether a particular facial expression or voice indicated anger or happiness, for instance) was affected by the twins' family experiences but not by genes (Schapira et al., 2019). The authors acknowledge that later on, genes may become more influential, but this was not apparent for these 7-year-olds. Of course, if a parent rejects a child, that matters, as happened in a study of monozygotic twins (Caspi et al., 2004).

If you wonder how a mother could reject her own child, consider this woman's experience when her boys were born.

> He was in the hospital and everyone was all "poor Jeff, poor Jeff" and I started thinking, "Well, what about me? I'm the one's just had twins. I'm the one's going through this, he's a seven-week-old baby and doesn't know a thing about it" . . . I sort of detached and plowed my emotions into Mike [Jeff's twin brother].
>
> *[quoted in Caspi et al., 2004, p. 156]*

This mother later blamed Jeff for favoring his father: "Jeff would do anything for Don but he wouldn't for me, and no matter what I did for either of them [Don or Jeff], it wouldn't be right" (quoted in Caspi et al., 2004, p. 157). She said Mike was much more lovable.

In the same study, a mother of identical twin daughters said

> Susan can be very sweet. She loves babies . . . she can be insecure . . . she flutters and dances around. . . . There's not much between her ears. . . . She's exceptionally vain, more so than Ann. Ann loves any game involving a ball, very sporty, climbs trees, very much a tomboy. One is a serious tomboy and one's a serious girlie girl. Even when they were babies I always dressed one in blue stuff and one in pink stuff.
>
> *[quoted in Caspi et al., 2004, p. 156]*

Especially for Scientists How would you determine whether or not parents treat all of their children the same? (see response, page 271)

Since Susan and Ann were monozygotic, both might have been "sweet . . . vain . . . or a serious tomboy." The fact that parents sometimes treat each monozygotic twin differently confirms that genes alone do not determine development. This will surprise no one who has a brother or a sister. Children from the same family do not always experience that family in the same way.

Family Structures

Both the idea, expressed in a book about good marriages, that "marriage is the essential relationship of adulthood . . . [with] unique rewards" (Wallerstein & Blakeslee, 2006) and the contrasting idea, in a popular magazine article, that "Love is the marrow of life, and yet, so often people attempt to funnel it into the narrow channels prescribed by marriage and the nuclear family" (Catron, 2019) seem to miss the dilemma. Especially when children are involved, the connection between family structure and family function is convoluted.

family structure
The legal and genetic relationships among relatives living in the same home. Possible structures include nuclear family, extended family, stepfamily, single-parent family, and many others.

Standard North American Family (SNAF)
A family with a mother and a father and their biological children, which is no longer the norm in the United States.

Family structure refers to the genetic and legal connections among related people. Genetic connections may be quite direct, as from parent to child, between cousins, between siblings, between grandparents and grandchildren, or more distantly, such as from great aunts, second cousins, and long-dead ancestors. Legal ties may be through marriage or adoption.

Sometimes family structure is measured by who lives in the household. This is the way the U.S. Census does it, zeroing in on whether one or two parents live in the same home as the child. (See Table 8.2.)

A common structure is called the **Standard North American Family (SNAF)** (Smith, 1993), because it traditionally has been the U.S. norm. (There are more single-person households than any other type, but "family" typically signifies adults and children.)

The SNAF has two parents, at least one child, and no other relatives. Traditionally the children are biological progeny, from the father's sperm and the mother's ova. Other *two-parent family* structures are headed by adoptive parents, foster parents, stepparents, and same-sex couples.

About a third of 6- to 11-year-olds in the United States live in a *single-parent family*. Before 2000, this family structure was usually the result of divorce, with one parent (almost always the mother) becoming a custodial parent. Since 2000, divorce

TABLE 8.2 Family Structures (percent of U.S. 6- to 11-year-olds in each type)*

Two-Parent Families (69%)

1. **Nuclear family** (56%). Named after the nucleus (the tightly connected core particles of an atom), the nuclear family consists of a man and a woman and their biological offspring under 18 years of age. In middle childhood, about half of all children live in nuclear families. About 10% of such families also include a grandparent, and often an aunt or uncle, living under the same roof. Those are *extended* families.
2. **Stepparent family** (9%). Divorced fathers usually remarry; divorced mothers remarry about half the time. If the stepparent family includes children born to two or more couples (such as children from the spouses' previous marriages and/or children of the new couple), that is a *blended* family.
3. **Adoptive family** (2%). Although as many as one-third of infertile couples adopt children, they usually adopt only one or two. Thus, only 2% of children are adopted, although the overall percentage of adoptive families is higher than that.
4. **Grandparents alone** (1%). Grandparents take on parenting for some children when biological parents are absent (dead, imprisoned, sick, addicted, etc.). That is a *skipped-generation* family.
5. **Two same-sex parents** (1%). Some two-parent families are headed by a same-sex couple, whose legal status (married, step-, adoptive) varies.

Single-Parent Families (31%)

One-parent families are increasing, with about half of the newborns now born to unmarried mothers, but such families average fewer children than two-parent families, and many single mothers find partners by the time their children are school age.

1. **Single mother — never married** (14%). In 2010, 41% of all U.S. births were to unmarried mothers; but when children are school age, many such mothers have married or have entrusted their children to their parents' care. Thus, only about 14% of 6- to 11-year-olds, at any given moment, are in single-mother, never-married homes.
2. **Single mother — divorced, separated, or widowed** (12%). Although many marriages end in divorce (almost half in the United States, fewer in other nations), many divorcing couples have no children. Others remarry. Thus, only 12% of school-age children currently live with single, formerly married mothers.
3. **Single father** (4%). About 1 father in 25 has physical custody of his children and raises them without their mother or a new wife. This category increased at the start of the twenty-first century but has decreased since 2005.
4. **Grandparent alone** (1%). Sometimes a single grandparent (usually the grandmother) becomes the sole caregiving adult for a child.

More Than Two Adults (10%) [Also listed as two-parent or single-parent family]

1. **Extended family** (10%). Some children live with a grandparent or other relatives, as well as with one (5%) or both (10%) of their parents. This pattern is most common with infants (20%) but occurs in middle childhood as well.
2. **Polygamous family** (0%). In some nations (not the United States), men can legally have several wives. This family structure is more favored by adults than children. Everywhere, polyandry (one woman, several husbands) is rare.

*Less than 1% of children under age 12 live without any caregiving adult; they are not included in this table.

The percentages in this table are estimates, based on data in U.S. Bureau of the Census' Current Population Reports (2015) and *America's Families and Living Arrangements* (2011). The category "extended family" in this table is higher than most published statistics, since some families do not tell official authorities about relatives living with them.

rates are lower, but single parenthood is increasing, because many women raise children without living with a partner.

An **extended family** includes relatives in addition to parents and children who live in one household. Usually, the additional persons are grandparents or sometimes uncles, aunts, or cousins of the child. Occasionally, the parent generation is missing, and the grandparents are sole caregivers. That is called a *skipped family*, because the middle generation is skipped. Although many children spend short periods living with their grandparents, a skipped generation family that endures more than five years is rare, less than 1 percent of all U.S. households.

extended family
A family of relatives in addition to the nuclear family, usually three or more generations living in one household.

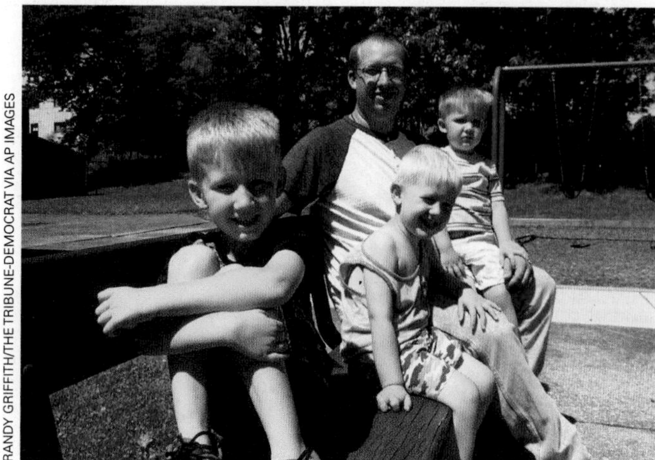

RANDY GRIFFITH/THE TRIBUNE-DEMOCRAT VIA AP IMAGES

Fortunate Boys This single father *(left)* in Pennsylvania takes his three sons to the playground almost every day, and this nuclear family *(right)* in Mali invests time and money in their only child's education. All four boys have loving fathers. Does family function make family structure irrelevant?

A fourth form, a *polygamous family*, occurs when one person has more than one marriage partner. That is increasingly unusual, estimated at 2 percent worldwide, and perhaps .03 percent in the United States. Polygamous families are most common in West Africa, but even those nations have more two-parent families than families with one man and two or more wives (Kramer, 2020).

In many ways, the distinction between family structures is not as simple in practice as it is on the census. Many parents of young children live near, but not with, the grandparents, who provide meals, emotional support, money, and child care. Many nonresident parents are still actively involved with their children who live in a single-parent family.

Function and Dysfunction

family function
The way a family works to meet the needs of its members. Children need families to provide basic material necessities, to encourage learning, to help them develop self-respect, to nurture friendships, and to foster harmony and stability.

Family function refers to how the people in a family actually care for each other. Some families function well; others are dysfunctional. The most important function of a family is to give every family member a sense of belonging, a connection that is expressed by caring for the other members of the family.

THE NEEDS OF CHILDREN

Beyond a sense of belonging, specific needs of each family member depend partly on the person's age. Families that function well for children aged 6–11 provide five things:

1. *Physical necessities.* In middle childhood, children can eat, dress, and wash themselves, but they need food, clothing, and shelter. Ideally, their families provide these things.
2. *Learning.* These are prime years for education. Families support, encourage, and guide schooling—connecting with teachers, checking homework, and so on.
3. *Self-respect.* During these years social comparison can deflate self-esteem, so families help each child excel at something—sports, the arts, or academics.
4. *Peer relationships.* Children need friends. Families choose schools and neighborhoods with friendly children and arrange play dates, group activities, overnights, and so on.
5. *Harmony and stability.* Families provide protective, predictable routines in a home that is a safe, peaceful haven. Family conflict and chaos is destructive.

VISUALIZING DEVELOPMENT

FAMILY STRUCTURES AROUND THE WORLD

Children usually fare best when two parents or caregivers actively care for them. This is most likely to occur if the parents are married, although there are many exceptions. Many developmentalists focus on the rate of single parenthood, shown on this map. Single parents can raise children well, especially with support from their families, friends, and communities.

RATES OF SINGLE PARENTHOOD

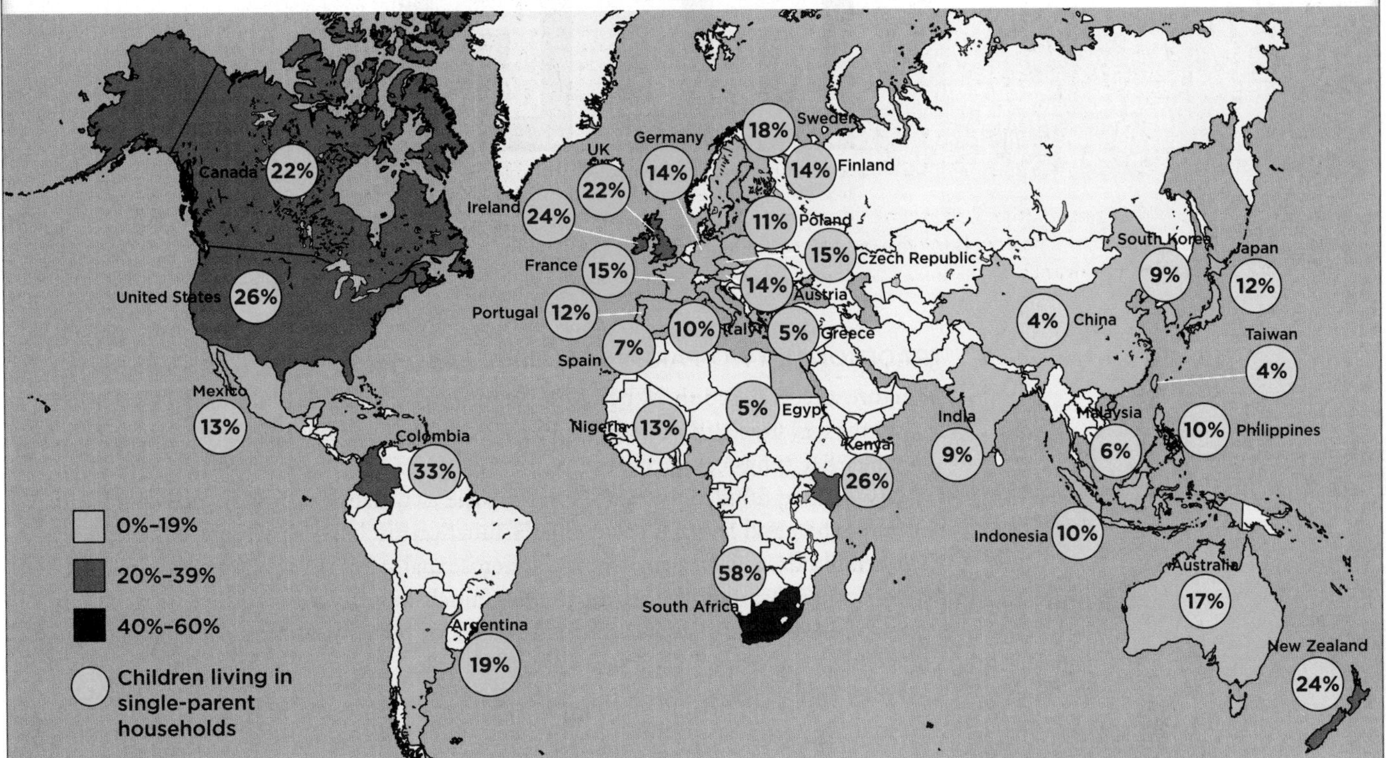

Data from Wilcox, 2011; OECD, 2011.

LIVING ARRANGEMENTS OF U.S. 0- TO 18-YEAR-OLDS

Note that, while fewer children live with their two married biological parents from birth to age 18, it is not that more children are living in stepfamilies but that more individuals have decided to raise children on their own. Another shift is evident: Single parents once were almost always mothers, but now some are single fathers.

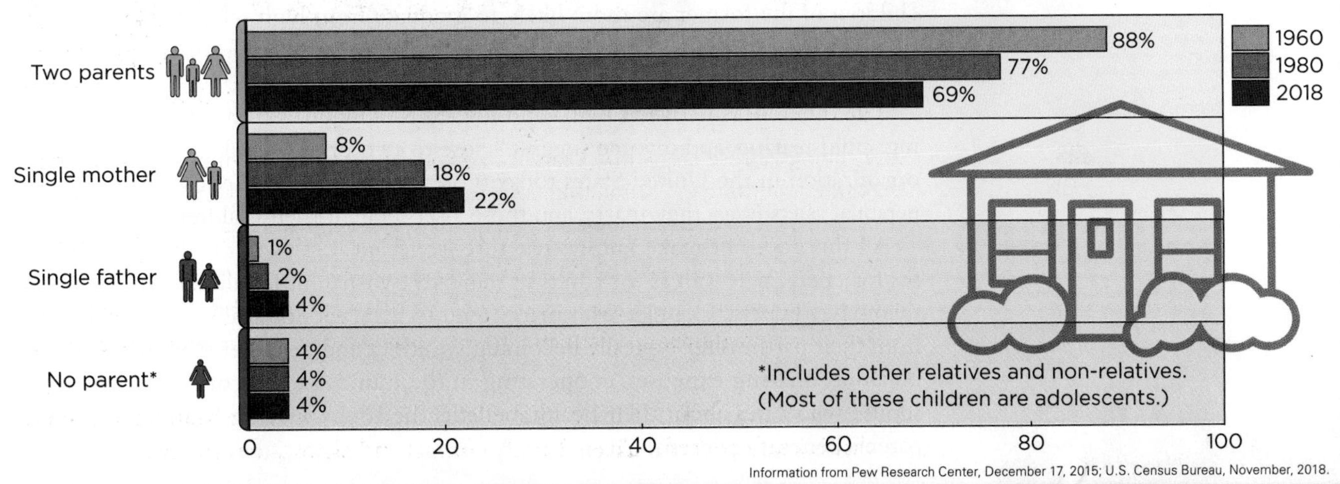

Information from Pew Research Center, December 17, 2015; U.S. Census Bureau, November, 2018.

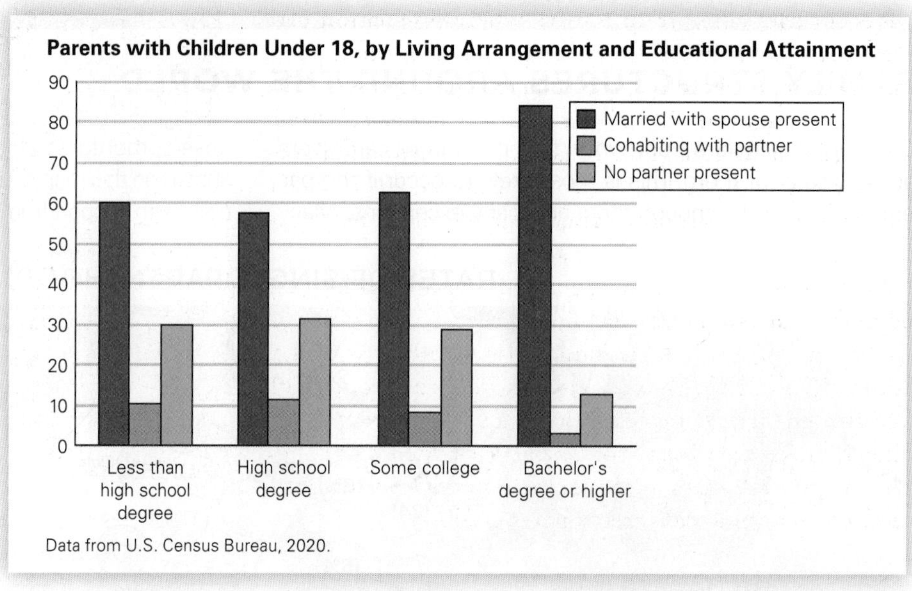

Data from U.S. Census Bureau, 2020.

FIGURE 8.1 Who Needs Help? Feeding, dressing, teaching, guiding, tending, bathing, healing, and tucking into bed, only to be awakened by a sick or frightened child—parenthood is exhausting. As the text makes clear, structure does not determine function, but raising children is more difficult as a single parent, especially when there are fewer available educational and economic resources.

TRADITIONAL TWO-PARENT FAMILIES

Structure affects function. When two parents live with their children and both care for family well-being, that makes it more likely that the five family functions mentioned earlier (physical necessities, learning, self-respect, friendship, and harmony/stability) will be fulfilled. Now we examine the two-parent structures listed above, to illustrate when and how function and dysfunction are likely. (See Figure 8.1.)

When children with two married, heterosexual parents are compared with children in other families, the former seems much better. The children's grades and school attendance are higher, and their rates of physical and emotional disorders (e.g., depression and oppositional defiance disorder) are lower.

But be careful interpreting that data. First, those are averages: Many SNAF families function poorly for children, and many non-SNAF families include children who are healthy, happy, high-achievers.

Second, do not confuse correlation and causation. Think about who the adults were before they married. A young adult's education, earning potential, and emotional maturity affect how likely they are to marry and to raise children in a stable, two-parent family.

For example, highly educated first-time mothers in the United States are usually (78 percent) married when they conceive their first child, but only 11 percent of those low in SES are married at conception (Gibson-Davis & Rackin, 2014). If the children of the former are more likely to graduate from high school, it is a mistake to attribute graduation to the parents' marital status at conception and not to the parent's income or education.

The differences between high- and low-SES individuals in marriage, childbearing, child rearing, and divorce suggest "close to two different subsystems" of family organization in the United States today (Cherlin, 2020, p. 69). Spouses tend to have personal assets *before* they marry, and those assets benefit their children.

All this does not make family structure irrelevant. Let us think about the benefits for children as well as for adults in standard two-parent families. First, the adults themselves benefit. Couples who marry tend to gain, economically and emotionally, from their partnership, typically becoming wealthier and healthier than either would be alone. Sharing expenses, cooperating in the mundane tasks of daily life, with a spouse who cares about their health, benefits the adults. Having healthy and happy parents benefits children.

Recent data come from Russia, where population data reveal that married men live years longer than single men, who are more likely to be drug addicted and depressed. The reason is thought to be that the husband/father role leads men to take better care of themselves and women to look out for their husband's health (Ashwin & Isupova, 2014). Then, of course, having a healthy, sober, resident father helps the children.

Simply living in the same household with offspring, day and night, tends to increase family bonding. As you will read in Chapters 10, 12, and 15, families sustain adults as well as children. The benefits are obvious in middle childhood: With two involved parents, it is likely that someone will read to the children, check their homework, invite their friends over, buy them clothes, take them to the doctor—in other words, do all the time-consuming tasks that children need.

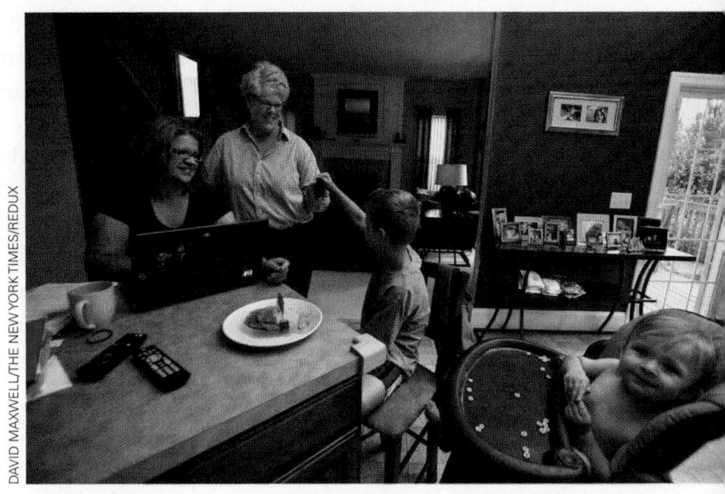

DAVID MAXWELL/THE NEW YORK TIMES/REDUX

Middle American Family This photo shows a typical breakfast in Brunswick, Ohio — Cheerios for 1-year-old Carson, pancakes that 7-year-old Carter does not finish eating, and family photos crowded on the far table.

OBSERVATION QUIZ
What do you notice about this family? (see answer, page 271) ↑

MARRIED SAME-SEX COUPLES

What about the children of married, same-sex couples? A large study comparing male–female and same-sex couples found that the major predictor of their children's well-being was not the parents' sexual orientation but their income and stability (Cenegy et al., 2018). Similar findings come from other two-adult families, such as adoptive parents, a couple raising grandchildren, and so on. A couple's mutual commitment, emotional health, and economic security benefit the children, no matter what their biological connections.

Community support also matters. Another study compared school achievement of 2 million children, in 2008 and again in 2015. In 2008, if children of same-sex couples lived where neighbors were hostile, they averaged lower grades in school than children of other-sex couples.

By 2015, no matter what the neighborhood, no differences by gender of the parents were found (Boertien & Bernardi, 2019). The culture had shifted, so the children of same-sex couples were more accepted within their communities.

STEPFAMILIES

The data suggest that remarriage benefits the adults more than the children. Not only is parental support, emotional as well as financial, diminished for stepchildren, but also the children's relationship with their parents may be problematic. Children may blame one or both biological parents for the separation, and may reject the stepparent, because of loyalty to their absent parent, anger at their remarried parent, or distrust of all parents.

Not surprisingly, many stepparents find it hard to bond with a child of their new partner's former lover, especially when the child is hostile. Added to that, parents often have opposite strategies for discipline and guidance. This occurs with biological parents as well, but a solid parental alliance is particularly elusive when it includes three adults—two of whom disliked each other so much that they divorced, and a third who does not know the history of the child.

Practical circumstances matter, too. When their parents remarry, many children find that their lives are disrupted again, including in such daily routines as where they sleep, what they eat, where they go to school. Remember that stability and harmony are coveted in middle childhood.

For all these reasons, stepchildren are more likely to be angry or sad, to fight with friends, to fail in school, to resist family rules, and to harm themselves (e.g., cutting, accidents, eating disorders). Disputes between half-siblings and stepsiblings are common. As both a cause and a correlate, adult stepchildren are less likely than biological children to live near their parents.

Sometimes remarried adults have a child together. That may strengthen the adults' relationship, but the children from former marriages may feel increasingly rejected.

The new, shared children have difficulty, too. Technically they are in a standard family, but "shared children scored lower than other groups of siblings on a variety of outcomes, such as educational attainment, antisocial behavior, and depressive symptoms" (Sanner et al., 2020, pp. 605–606).

In all this discussion of family types, remember that although structure *affects* function, structure does not *determine* function. Some stepparent families function well. As a review of research on stepfamilies concludes:

> The case that divorce and family instability reduce children's well-being is strong. At the same time, the magnitude of these consequences vary considerably across individuals and groups.
>
> *[Raley & Sweeney, 2020, p. 92]*

TOGETHER, BUT NOT MARRIED

cohabitation An arrangement in which a couple lives together in a committed romantic relationship but are not formally married.

What about parents who live together without marrying? **Cohabitation** has become the norm in the United States among young adults, as well as common among older adults who have new partners after divorce (Sassler & Lichter, 2020). This relationship has benefits for the adults, sexually, emotionally, and economically. Most (59 percent) of all U.S. adults under age 45 have cohabited (Graf, 2019).

Some cohabiting couples eventually marry, but many do not. If they stay together for years, they function like a married couple. If they have children together, the children sometimes—but not always—develop well.

Much depends on the culture (Lesthaeghe, 2020). In most European nations, children of cohabiting parents fare as well as those of married parents (Rijken & Liefbroer, 2016). In African and Latin American nations, cohabiting mothers average more education and income than married mothers. Their children are healthier and better educated, probably because of their mothers' SES (Pierce & Heaton, 2019).

However, in the United States, cohabitation benefits the adults but not necessarily the children (Sassler & Lichter, 2020). Adults gain easier sexual and emotional interaction and save on housing costs. But cohabiting parents are more likely to separate than married ones, and then their children's lives are disrupted. When fathers are absent, children achieve less in school (Cavanagh & Fomby, 2019).

MACMILLAN ARCHIVE/DANNY GOLDFIELD

Don't Assume We know this is a mother and her child, but structure and function could be wonderful or terrible. These two could be half of a nuclear family, or a single mother with one adoptive child, or part of four other family structures. That does not matter as much as family function: If this scene is typical, with both enjoying physical closeness in the great outdoors, this family functions well.

SINGLE-PARENT FAMILIES

On average, the single-parent structure functions less well for children, because single parents have less income, time, and stability. Most single parents fill many roles—including wage earner, daughter or son (single parents often depend on their own parents), and lover (many seek a new partner). Single parents of any sex often seek a new spouse, in part to help with parenthood. But as the research on stepparent families explained, new complications may appear (Booth & Dunn, 2014).

In general, single parents have less time and energy to provide emotional and academic support for their children. If they are depressed (and many are), that makes it worse. Neesha, in A Case to Study, is an example.

The focus has been on the single parent who lives with the children, but the other parent also matters, not only for financial support. Nonresidential fathers are typically less involved with their children every year that they are not living with them, although patterns set in infancy predict relationships later on (Fagan & Palkovitz, 2018). One interesting component is the mother's *gatekeeping*: That is, some mothers encourage father involvement and others limit it.

A CASE TO STUDY

How Hard Is It to Be a Kid?

Neesha's fourth-grade teacher referred her to the school guidance team because Neesha often fell asleep in class, was late 51 days, and was absent 15 days. Testing found Neesha at the seventh-grade level in reading and writing and at the fifth-grade level in math. Since achievement was not Neesha's problem, something psychosocial must be amiss.

The counselor spoke to Neesha's mother, Tanya, a single parent who was depressed and worried about paying the rent on a tiny apartment where she had moved when Neesha's father left three years earlier. He lived with his girlfriend, now with a new baby as well.

Tanya said she had no problems with Neesha, who was "more like a little mother than a kid," unlike her 15-year-old son, Tyrone, who suffered from fetal alcohol effects and whose behavior worsened when his father left.

Tyrone was recently beaten up badly as part of a gang initiation, a group he considered "like a family." He was currently in juvenile detention, after being arrested for stealing bicycle parts. Note the nonshared environment here: Although the siblings grew up together and their father left them both, 12-year-old Tyrone became rebellious whereas 7-year-old Neesha became *parentified*, "a little mother."

The school counselor also spoke with Neesha.

> Neesha volunteered that she worried a lot about things and that sometimes when she worries she has a hard time falling asleep. . . . she got in trouble for being late so many times, but it was hard to wake up. Her mom was sleeping late because she was working more nights cleaning offices. . . . Neesha said she got so far behind that she just gave up. She was also having problems with the other girls in the class, who were starting to tease her about sleeping in class and not doing her work. She said they called her names like "Sleepy" and "Dummy." She said that at first it made her very sad, and then it made her very mad. That's when she started to hit them to make them stop.
>
> *[Wilmshurst, 2011, pp. 152–153]*

Neesha was coping with poverty, a depressed mother, an absent father, a delinquent brother, and classmate bullying. She seemed resilient—her achievement scores are impressive—but shortly after Neesha was interviewed,

> The school principal received a call from Neesha's mother, who asked that her daughter not be sent home from school because she was going to kill herself. She was holding a loaded gun in her hand and she had to do it, because she was not going to make this month's rent. She could not take it any longer, but she did not want Neesha to come home and find her dead. . . . While the guidance counselor continued to keep the mother talking, the school contacted the police, who apprehended [the] mom while she was talking on her cell phone. . . . The loaded gun was on her lap. . . . The mother was taken to the local psychiatric facility.
>
> *[Wilmshurst, 2011, pp. 154–155]*

Whether Neesha's resilience would continue depended on her ability to find support beyond her family. Perhaps the school counselor helped:

> When asked if she would like to meet with the school psychologist once in a while, just to talk about her worries, Neesha said she would like that very much. After she left the office, she turned and thanked the psychologist for working with her, and added, "You know, sometimes it's hard being a kid."
>
> *[Wilmshurst, 2011, p. 154]*

Courts and social workers are increasingly recommending joint physical custody of children after a divorce. When both parents are directly involved in caregiving, children of divorce are healthier, physically and emotionally, than when only one parent has custody (Baude et al., 2016; Braver & Votruba, 2018).

When a father is the lone caregiver, he suffers the same problems as single mothers—too much to do and not enough money to do it. In all this, remember the correlation is not cause. Millions of successful adults in the United States are proof that single parents can be nurturing, encouraging caregivers.

EXTENDED FAMILIES

In general, extended families are idealized, but the reality is quite different. Of course, "relationships between grandparents and grandchildren can offer tremendous benefits to family members of each generation" (Margolis & Arpino, 2019, p. 23). But that does not require living together: Sharing a home with grandparents does not usually work out well (Berger, 2019).

Most extended families are a temporary solution to a serious problem. Although many grandchildren live with grandparents for vacations, it is unusual for an extended-family household to last five years or more. When that occurs, it is usually because of poverty or serious illness, either in the parent generation or the elder generation. As you already know, that family circumstance does not make life easier for children.

Sometimes it is thought that extended families are particularly beneficial in infancy. But even then, the data do not confirm benefits. For example, every pediatrician now agrees that the ideal nutrition for infants is breast milk. However, if young mothers are living with their own mothers, they are *less* likely to breast-feed their babies (Pilkauskas, 2014).

By middle childhood, children want some independence. They are more likely to resent than to appreciate living with several adult generations who have ideas about how they should dress, speak, and act.

Culture is always influential. In the slums of Mumbai, India, rates of psychological disorders among school-age children were *higher* in two-parent families than in extended families, presumably because grandparents, aunts, and uncles provided more care and stability in that city than two parents alone (Patil et al., 2013). The opposite is true for many families in the United States: Extended families are more chaotic, exactly what children do not need.

Often in North American extended families, grandparents, aunts, and uncles come and go, reducing the stability that 6- to 11-year-olds need. But, again, social context matters. One factor is immigration status. In the United States, extended families may function better for immigrant families than for the U.S.-born (Areba et al., 2018). With every family type, function matters more than structure.

See what the data say about family types in **DATA CONNECTIONS: Family Structure in the United States and Around the World.** Achieve

Family Trouble

However, while it is true that structure does not determine function, and that no structure is always good or harmful, three factors always make dysfunction more likely: frequent changes, poverty, and conflict.

STABILITY AND CHANGE

Children cherish safety and stability, not change. When children experience many changes in caregivers (e.g., mother, stepmother, aunt, father) and in locations (moving from one neighborhood, state, or nation), they are more likely to develop emotional difficulties.

Having a stable network of friends and teachers is an asset, and staying in one neighborhood makes that easier. Indeed, a leading expert on the effects of divorce on children suggested that the harm comes not directly from divorce, but from disruptions in the child's life (Cherlin, 2009).

Many studies find that family instability, and family chaos (such as no routines for sleeping, eating, or homework), increase children's internalizing and externalizing problems as well as adversely affect their health. That is thought to be the main reason that children who are homeless suffer physiologically as well as psychologically, evident in cortisol level, blood pressure, weight, and in likelihood of hospitalization (Cutuli et al., 2017).

A well-functioning family can soften the impact of change. If a child is living in a temporary shelter for homeless families, but with a mother who provides stability,

THINK CRITICALLY: Can you describe a situation in which having a single parent would be better for a child than having two parents?

affection, routines, and hope, resilience is possible (Masten, 2014). Of course, those who care about children should do whatever they can to provide a stable home for everyone, but even in dire circumstances, the quality of caregiving matters.

A telling example comes from children in military families. Enlisted parents have higher incomes, better health care, and more education than do civilians from the same backgrounds. But they have one major risk: instability.

For some children, parental deployment disrupts the child's routines and home life, causing depression and aggression (Fairbank et al., 2018; Williamson et al., 2018). Caregivers of such children are encouraged to avoid changes in the child's life during the deployment: no new homes, rules, or schools. Middle childhood is a particularly vulnerable time (Alfano et al., 2016).

JOSE LUIS PELAEZ INC/DIGITALVISION/GETTY IMAGES

Stay Home, Dad The rate of battle deaths for U.S. soldiers is lower for those deployed in Iraq and Afghanistan than for any previous conflict, thanks to modern medicine and armor. However, psychological harm from repeated returns and absences is increasing, especially for children.

Similar transitions occur when deployed parents come home: They are welcomed, of course, but the child's life might change again—and that causes more stress. Repeated shifts between one-parent and two-parent households are difficult for children.

On a broader level, children who are displaced because of hurricanes, fire, war, and so on may suffer psychologically, particularly if daily life becomes unpredictable. To comfort their parents, they may keep quiet about their distress, but the data on health and achievement show that moving from place to place is highly stressful (Masten, 2014). All children must cope with some disruption: Families and children need to find ways to maintain stability.

During the COVID-19 pandemic, every child was stressed. Erratic school schedules made the problem worse. Adults may not have realized how harmful this was, since children were less likely to be sick with the virus, but childhood depression and anxiety increased when parents were stressed, and nonhome supports (schools, neighbors, grandparents) disappeared.

From a developmental perspective, the psychosocial consequences of the pandemic for children were worse than the biological ones. Adults could institute routines (avoiding chaos), help children figure out something to do (e.g., washing hands, wearing masks), and exemplify stability (avoiding panic and anger) (Singh et al., 2020).

Routines are especially useful coping measures in middle childhood, as are parents who spend time listening to their children. Temperament and family circumstances affect how children react, but the psychosocial needs of children should not be ignored.

WEALTH AND POVERTY

Family income affects both function and structure. Marriage rates fall in times of economic recession, and divorce increases with unemployment. Low SES correlates with many other problems, and "risk factors pile up in the lives of some children, particularly among the most disadvantaged" (Masten, 2014, p. 95).

Several scholars have developed the *family-stress model*, which holds that any risk factor (such as poverty, divorce, single parenthood, unemployment) damages a family if, and only if, it increases stress on the parents, making them less patient and responsive to the children (Masarik & Conger, 2017).

This is not to minimize the effects of low income, especially if the parents and children are aware that other families have more money. Ongoing economic hardship almost always increases family stress (Duran et al., 2019). When parents worry about providing food and shelter for their children, that renders them tense and hostile. The parents' *reaction* to income may exacerbate or minimize stress (Evans & Kim, 2013; D. Lee et al., 2013; Mazza et al., 2017).

A curious correlation between income and child health is evident: Children in high-income families are more likely to have developmental problems than children

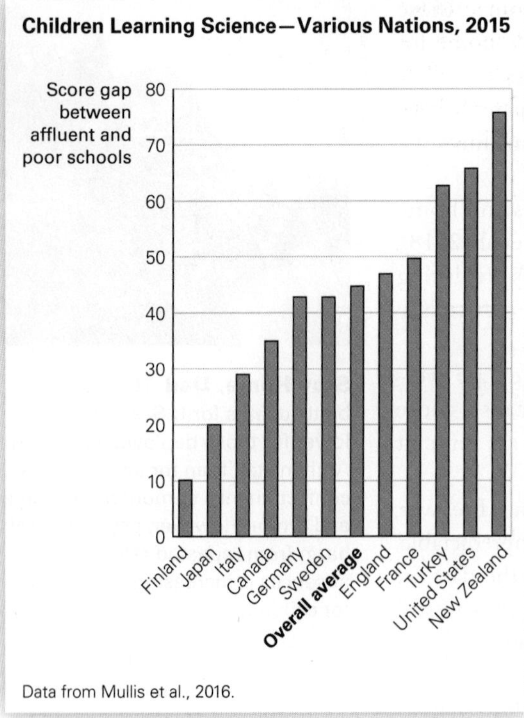

FIGURE 8.2 Families and Schools This graph shows the score gap in fourth-grade science on the 2015 TIMSS between children in schools where more than 25 percent of the children are from high-SES homes compared to children in schools where more than 25 percent are from low-SES homes. Generally, the nations with the largest gaps are also the nations with the most schools at one or the other end of the spectrum and the fewest in between. For example, only 23 percent of U.S. children were in schools where most children were from middle-income families, compared to 37 percent in Japan.

of middle-SES parents (Luthar et al., 2018). Stress may be the underlying reason: Some wealthy parents are anxious about maintaining their status, and their stress makes them pressure their children to excel. That may cause emotional problems for children and drug abuse, delinquency, and academic failure later on.

But do not conclude that children are better off poor than rich. Poverty always adds stress; high income sometimes does. The crucial question is whether economic pressures affect the parents' ability to provide the care and guidance that children need (Roubinov & Boyce, 2017). Back to family routines: If parents set clear guidelines for sleep, eating, and homework, children benefit. If parents are too caught up in their own financial concerns, children suffer.

National policies matter, too. In Norway, for instance, family poverty has minimal effect on children, because national health care, early education, and public schools provide a "buffering effect of the social safety net" (Bøe et al., 2018, p. 1). In the United States, parents must do that buffering themselves (see Figure 8.2).

CONFLICT

Every researcher agrees that family conflict harms children, especially when adults fight about child rearing. The children of fighting families are often more aggressive, angry, and demanding than other children. Such fights are more common in stepfamilies, divorced families, and extended families, but traditional two-parent families are not immune.

One of my students wrote about growing up with two married parents:

> My mother externalized her feelings with outbursts of rage, lashing out and breaking things, while my father internalized his feelings by withdrawing, being silent and looking the other way. One could say I was being raised by bipolar parents. Growing up, I would describe my mom as the Tasmanian devil and my father as the ostrich, with his head in the sand. . . . My mother disciplined with corporal punishment as well as with psychological control, while my father was permissive. What a pair. [C., 2013]

This student is now a single parent, having twice married, given birth, and divorced. She is one example of a general finding: The effects of childhood family conflict echo in adulthood, financially as well as psychologically.

Children suffer not only if they are abused, physically or emotionally, but also if they merely witness their parents' abuse of each other or of their other children. Fights between siblings can be harmful, too (Buehler, 2020).

This correlation raises a question. Might child aggression be caused by genes, not by witnessing family fights? If that were so, the correlation between family conflict and child problems is caused by a third variable, specifically genes passed down from parents to children.

This hypothesis was tested in a longitudinal study of 867 adult twins (388 monozygotic and 479 dizygotic), who had married and had an adolescent child (Schermerhorn et al., 2011). Both parents were asked independently about marital conflict. The teenagers' problems were compared to their cousin, who was the child of their parent's twin.

Thus, this study had data from 5,202 individuals—one-third of them adult twins, one-third of them spouses of twins, and one-third of them adolescents who were genetically linked to an adolescent cousin. If their parent was a monozygotic twin, they had one-fourth of their genes in common with their cousin; if their parent was a dizygotic twin, one-eighth of the same genes.

The researchers found that although genes had some effect, witnessing conflict itself had a powerful effect, increasing externalizing problems in the boys and internalizing problems in the girls. Quiet disagreements did little harm, but open conflict (e.g., yelling heard by the children) and divorce did (Schermerhorn et al., 2011). That leads to an obvious conclusion: Parents should not fight in front of their children.

what have you learned?

1. How might siblings raised together not share the same family environment?
2. What is the difference between family structure and family function?
3. Why is a harmonious, stable home particularly important during middle childhood?
4. What are the advantages for children in a two-parent family structure?
5. What are the benefits and problems of a stepparent family?
6. What determines whether a same-sex couple can function well for children?
7. Why does it matter for children if their family is headed by one or two parents?
8. What are the advantages and disadvantages of the extended family structure?
9. How are family structure and family function affected by culture?
10. Using the family-stress model, explain how family income affects family function.

The Peer Group

Peers become increasingly important in middle childhood. With their new awareness of reality (concrete operational thought), children become painfully aware of their classmates' opinions, judgments, and accomplishments.

The Culture of Children

Peer relationships, unlike adult–child relationships, involve partners who negotiate, compromise, share, and defend themselves as equals. Consequently, children learn social lessons from one another that grown-ups cannot teach (Rubin et al., 2013). Adults may follow a child's lead, but they are always much older and bigger, with their own values and experiences. They cannot substitute for a friend.

Child culture includes the customs, rules, and rituals that are passed down to younger children from slightly older ones, with no thought about the origins or implications. The child's goal is to join a culture and thus be part of the peer group. Jump-rope rhymes, insults, and superstitions are examples.

child culture
The idea that each group of children has games, sayings, clothing styles, and superstitions that are not common among adults, just as every culture has distinct values, behaviors, and beliefs.

For instance, "Ring around the rosy/Pocketful of posies/Ashes, ashes/We all fall down," may have originated as children coped with the Black Death, which killed half the population of Europe in the fourteenth century. (*Rosy* may refer to the skin rash or to the rosary, a set of beads used for prayer; *posies* refers to a flower thought to be protective.) Children are thought to have passed down that rhyme for centuries, laughing together with no thought of sudden death.

Remember that cultures are social constructions, so they can change. In the United States, rigid distinctions between boys' and girls' culture have eroded, and

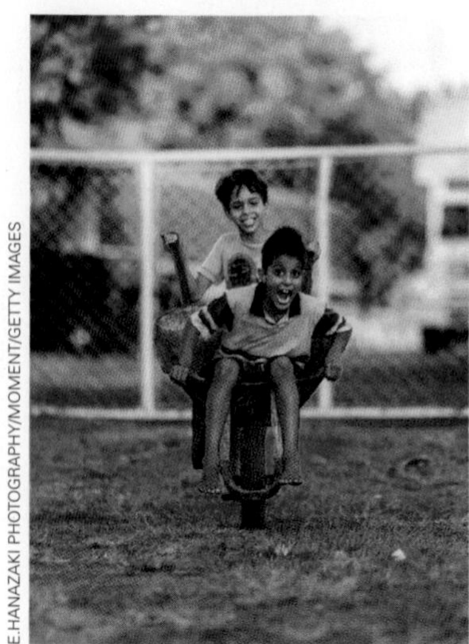

E.HANAZAKI PHOTOGRAPHY/MOMENT/GETTY IMAGES

No Toys Many boys in middle childhood are happiest playing outside with equipment designed for work. This wheelbarrow is perfect, especially because at any moment the pusher might tip it.

child culture reflects this. Participants in teams and games are more likely to include children of all genders, whereas boys' and girls' sports were once segregated. Boys played baseball, girls played jacks, and both played basketball but by different rules that kept girls less active. That "six-on-six" style was banned in the United States gradually from 1958–2015.

Throughout the world, child culture may clash with adult culture. Many children reject clothes that parents buy as too loose, too tight, too long, too short, or wrong in color, style, brand, decoration, or some other aspect that adults might not notice. If their schools are multiethnic, children may be more open than their parents to other races, religions, lifestyles.

Appearance and independence from adults are important to children. Classmates pity those (especially boys) whose parents kiss them ("mama's boy"), criticize those who betray children to adults ("tattletale," "grasser," "snitch," "rat"), and dislike children who please the teachers ("teacher's pet," "suck-up") (Trusz, 2017). Keeping secrets from parents and teachers is a moral mandate. Parental choices in hairstyle, clothes, and shoes may be rejected.

The culture of children is not always benign. For example, because communication with peers is vital, children learn whatever language or dialect the other children speak. Immigrant parents proudly note how well their children speak a second language, but all parents are distressed when their children spout their peers' curses, accents, and slang.

Because they value independence, children may gravitate toward friends who defy authority, sometimes harmlessly (passing a note in class), sometimes not (shoplifting, smoking). This is part of the nature of children, who often do what their parents do not want them to do; it is in the nature of parents to be upset when that happens. This is easier to criticize in other cultures and centuries, as in the following example.

In 1922, the magazine *Good Housekeeping* published an article titled "Aren't You Glad You Are Not Your Grandmother?" In it, a daughter quotes letters from her dead grandmother that she found in the attic. One letter describes an incident that occurred when that daughter's father—also long dead—was a boy and snuck out of his house to play with other boys:

> When the door was left unlocked for a moment, out he ran in his little velvet suit. We did not miss him for a while because we thought he was doing his Latin Prose, and then some wealthy ladies . . . saw him literally in the gutter, groping in the mud for a marble. . . . Horace's father was white with emotion when he heard of it. He went out, brought Horace in, gave him another whipping, and, saying that since he acted like a runaway dog he should be treated like one, he went out, bought a dog-collar and a chain, and chained Horace to the post of his little bed. He was there all the afternoon, crying so you could hear nothing else in all the house. . . . I went many times up to the hall before his door and knelt there stretching out my arms to my darling child, the tears flooding down my cheeks. But, of course, I could not open the door and go in to him, to interfere with his punishment.
>
> *[Fisher, 1922, p. 8]*

The author was grateful that mothers now (in 1922!) knew more than did nineteenth-century parents with their "ignorance of child-life" (Fisher, 1922, p. 15). It is not surprising that the boy wanted to play with other boys. However, this raises a question, what peer activities and norms should adults discourage or prevent? The children at my grandson's playground went behind a building to look at a cell phone. A parent stopped them.

Was that right? I think so, but what ignorance of child-life do parents have today? If I knew, that would not be ignorance, but a developmental perspective makes me humble.

Friendships

Teachers sometimes separate friends, but that may be a mistake. Developmentalists find that children help each other learn both academic and social skills (Bagwell & Schmidt, 2011). The loyalty of children to their friends may work for their benefit or harm (Rubin et al., 2013).

Both aspects of friendship are expressed by these two Mexican American children.

> *Yolanda:*
>
> There's one friend . . . she's always been with me, in bad or good . . . She's always telling me, "Keep on going and your dreams are gonna come true."
>
> *Paul:*
>
> I think right now about going Christian, right? Just going Christian, trying to do good, you know? Stay away from drugs, everything. And every time it seems like I think about that, I think about the homeboys. And it's a trip because a lot of the homeboys are my family, too, you know?
>
> [*quoted in Nieto, 2000, pp. 220, 249*]

Yolanda later went to college; Paul went to jail. This is echoed by other children. Many aspects of adult personality are influenced by childhood friends (Wrzus & Neyer, 2016).

Indeed, quite apart from a child's family, school, and IQ, a study found that the intelligence of a best friend in sixth grade affected a child's intelligence at age 15 (Meldrum et al., 2018). Again, this can work to benefit children or not. As one study concludes, if low-achievers "select[ed] similarly low-achieving students as friends, this may dampen their academic achievement over time" (Laninga-Wijnen et al., 2019, p. 347).

Friendships become more intense and intimate over the years of middle childhood, as social cognition and effortful control advance. Six-year-olds may befriend anyone of the same sex and age who will play with them. By age 10, children demand more. They choose carefully, share secrets, expect loyalty, change friends less often, are upset when they lose a friend, and find it harder to make new friends.

Older children tend to choose friends whose interests, values, and backgrounds are similar to their own. By the end of middle childhood, close friendships are usually between children of the same sex, age, ethnicity, and socioeconomic status (Rubin et al., 2013).

None of these preferences for like-minded friends precludes crossing traditional divides, as all children increasingly develop the skills of friendship, which differ from pair to pair. Traditionally, many girls become astute at sympathetic reassurance and many boys enjoy joint excitement. All children find friendship increasingly satisfying over the years of childhood, as they adjust to each other (Rose & Asher, 2017).

JOHNNY HAWKINS/CARTOONSTOCK

"Oh yeah? Well, my vocabulary is bigger than your vocabulary!"

Better Than Children of all genders, ethnic groups, religions, nations, and family structures think they are better than children of other groups. They can learn not to blurt out insults, but a deeper understanding of the diversity of human experience and abilities requires maturation.

THINK CRITICALLY: Do adults also choose friends who agree with them or whose background is similar to their own?

Popular and Unpopular Children

In the United States, two types of popular children and three types of unpopular children become apparent in middle childhood (Cillessen & Marks, 2011). At every age, children who are friendly and prosocial (likely to help with homework, say something complimentary) are well-liked.

In addition, over the years of middle childhood, status becomes increasingly important, and peer culture gains influence. In some classrooms and cultures, as puberty approaches, aggression is admired, as with a child who is able to utter a cutting remark. Some children are both popular and aggressive (Cillessen & Mayeux, 2004; Laninga-Wijnen et al., 2019; Shi & Xie, 2012).

As for the three types of unpopular children, some are *neglected*, not rejected; they are ignored, but not shunned. The other two types are actively rejected, either

aggressive-rejected
A type of childhood rejection, when other children do not want to be friends with a child because of that child's antagonistic, confrontational behavior.

withdrawn-rejected
A type of childhood rejection, when other children do not want to be friends with a child because of their timid, withdrawn, and anxious behavior.

bullying
Repeated, systematic efforts to inflict harm on other people through physical, verbal, or social attack on a weaker person.

aggressive-rejected, disliked because they are antagonistic and confrontational, or **withdrawn-rejected**, disliked because they are timid and anxious. Children as young as age 6 are aware if they are rejected and decide if they should try to be more accepted or should seek other friends (Nesdale et al., 2014).

Both aggressive-rejected and withdrawn-rejected children have three difficulties: They often (1) misinterpret social situations, (2) lack emotional regulation, and (3) experience mistreatment at home. All three problems not only cause rejection, but the rejection itself makes the other problems worse (Stenseng et al., 2015). If children do not learn when to be assertive and when to be quiet, they may become bullies or victims.

Whether a particular child is popular or not also depends on cultural norms, which change over time. As you read in Chapter 4, temperament is partly genetic: Some children are naturally more aggressive, or more outgoing, or more fearful than others. But culture affects whether those inborn traits are accepted, channeled, or curbed.

This is illustrated by research on shyness (Chen, 2019). A 1990 survey in Shanghai found that shy children were liked and respected (Chen et al., 1992), but 13 years later, when competition with the West became a national priority, shy children in the same Shanghai schools were less popular (Chen et al., 2005). Other research found that shyness is more accepted in rural China (Zhang & Eggum-Wilkens, 2018).

In general, several aspects of the social context and school culture, specifically academic achievement, friendships, and being in middle childhood (not adolescence) all affect whether or not shy Chinese children are accepted by their peers (X. Chen et al., 2013; X. Chen et al., 2019; Liu et al., 2015).

Within the United States, a similar shift from acceptance to rejection of a personality trait is evident in male aggression. Once that was acceptable ("Boys will be boys!"), but now teachers, women, and men themselves teach boys to restrain their impulse to lash out. This is most apparent in the new understanding of bullies, as now explained.

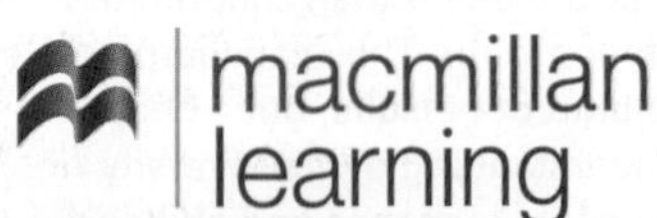

VIDEO ACTIVITY: Bullying: Interview with Nikki Crick explores the causes and repercussions of the different types of bullying.

Bullying

Bullying is defined as repeated, systematic attacks intended to harm those who are unable or unlikely to defend themselves. It occurs in every nation, in every community, in every kind of school (religious/secular, public/private, progressive/traditional, large/medium/small), and perhaps in every child.

Bullying is of four types:

- *Physical* (hitting, pinching, shoving, or kicking)
- *Verbal* (teasing, taunting, or name-calling)
- *Relational* (destroying peer acceptance)
- *Cyberbullying* (using electronic means to harm another)

The first three types begin in preschool and are common in primary and secondary school. Cyberbullying is more common later on and is discussed in Chapter 9.

CHAPTER APP 8

Go Speak Up

iOS:
https://tinyurl.com/y8zvb997

ANDROID:
https://tinyurl.com/mzkng83

RELEVANT TOPIC:
Bullying

This app enables students to quickly and anonymously report bullying or harassment to teachers or school administrators. It also allows students to report online incidents via a screengrab tool.

VICTIMS

Almost every child experiences an isolated attack or is called a derogatory name during middle childhood. Victims of bullying, however, endure shameful experiences again and again—pushed and kicked, called names, forced to do degrading things, and so on—with no defense.

Victims tend to be "cautious, sensitive, quiet . . . lonely and abandoned at school. As a rule, they do not have a single good friend in their class" (Olweus, 1999, p. 15).

Even having a friend who is also a victim helps. Such friends may not be able to provide physical protection, but they can and do provide psychological

defense—reassuring victims that their condition is not their fault and that the bully is mean, stupid, racist, or whatever (Schacter & Juvonen, 2019). That is a good antidote, because the worst harm is loss of self-respect.

Although it is often thought that victims are particularly unattractive or odd, this is not necessarily the case. Victims are chosen because of their emotional vulnerability and social isolation, not their appearance. Children who are new to a school, whose background and home culture are unlike that of their peers, who are gender nonconforming, who have disabilities, or whose clothes indicate poverty, are especially vulnerable.

THINK CRITICALLY: The text says that both former bullies and former victims suffer in adulthood. Which would you rather be, and why?

Bullies can find something (fat or thin, glasses or unruly hair, an odd accent or unusual shoes) in almost any child to mock. As social awareness increases in middle childhood, such comments are more likely to hit the mark, because children become more self-conscious and hence more vulnerable.

As one boy said,

> You can get bullied because you are weak or annoying or because you are different. Kids with big ears get bullied. Dorks get bullied. You can also get bullied because you think too much of yourself and try to show off. Teacher's pet gets bullied. If you say the right answer too many times in class you can get bullied. There are lots of popular groups who bully each other and other groups, but you can get bullied within your group too. If you do not want to get bullied, you have to stay under the radar, but then you might feel sad because no one pays attention to you.
>
> *[quoted in Guerra et al., 2011, p. 306]*

Remember the three types of unpopular children? *Neglected* children are not victimized; they are ignored, "under the radar." *Rejected* children fit into the bully network. Withdrawn-rejected children are likely victims; they are isolated, depressed, and friendless. Aggressive-rejected children may be **bully-victims** (or *provocative victims*), with neither friends nor sympathizers (Kochel et al., 2015). They suffer the most, because they strike back ineffectively, which increases the bullying.

bully-victim
Someone who attacks others and who is attacked as well. (Also called *provocative victims* because they do things that elicit bullying.)

BULLIES

Unlike bully-victims, most bullies are *not* rejected. Many are proud, pleased with themselves, with friends who admire them and classmates who fear them. Some are quite popular: Bullying is a form of social dominance and authority (Pellegrini et al., 2011).

The link between bullying and popularity has long been apparent during early adolescence (Pouwels et al., 2016), but bullies are already "quite popular in middle childhood." Adults, however, have become aware that bullying is destructive. As one comprehensive summary of the research explains, bullying "is now recognized as a major and preventable public health problem" (National Academies of Sciences, Engineering, and Medicine, 2016, p. 13).

Bullying begins during the preschool years, and teachers often recognize it and try to stop it. What changes from ages 6 to 12 is that bullies become skilled at avoiding adult awareness, at picking rejected and defenseless victims, and at using nonphysical methods—which avoid adult punishment (Pouwels et al., 2017). As children become better at hiding bullying from adults, the harm to victims increases (H. Nelson et al., 2019).

Boys are bullies more often than girls, typically attacking smaller, weaker boys. Boy bullies tend to be physically bigger than their victims. Girl bullies, by contrast, are more likely to use words to demean shyer, more soft-spoken girls. Especially in the final years of middle childhood, boys who are thought to be gay become targets, with suicide attempts one consequence (National Academies of Sciences, Engineering, and Medicine, 2016).

Especially for Parents of an Accused Bully
Another parent has told you that your child is a bully. Your child denies it and explains that the other child doesn't mind being teased. What should you do? (see response, page 271).

AP IMAGES/JACQUELINE LARMA

Power to Peers Bullying is a way some children gain respect. If, instead, the school gives training and special shirts to bystanders, they can gain status by befriending victims. That seems to work in this school in Bensalem, Pennsylvania.

CAUSES AND CONSEQUENCES OF BULLYING

Bullying may begin early in life. Many toddlers try to dominate other children (and perhaps their parents) at some point. When they hit, kick, and so on, usually someone teaches them better ways to interact. However, if home life is chaotic, if discipline is ineffectual, if siblings are hostile, or if attachment is insecure, children do not learn prosocial strategies. Instead, vulnerable young children develop externalizing and internalizing problems, becoming bullies or victims (Turner et al., 2012).

By middle childhood, bullying is not the outburst of a frustrated child but an attempt to gain status. That makes it a social action: Bullies rarely attack victims when the two of them are alone. Instead, a bully might engage in a schoolyard fight, with onlookers who are more likely to cheer than stop the fight; or a bully might utter an insult that provokes laughter in all except the target. By the end of middle childhood, bullies choose victims whom other children reject.

Siblings matter. Some brothers and sisters defend each other; children are protected if bullies fear that an older sibling will retaliate. On the other hand, if children are bullied by peers in school *and* siblings at home, they are four times more likely to develop serious psychological disorders by age 18 (Dantchev et al., 2018).

In schools with high rates of bullying, children are less likely to focus on academics and more likely to concentrate on the social dynamics of the classroom—hoping to avoid becoming the next victim. Bystanders as well as bullies and victims risk lower school achievement, with higher rates of mental illness in adulthood. Many victims become depressed; many bullies become increasingly cruel; as adults they have higher rates of prison and early death (Willoughby et al., 2014).

CAN BULLYING BE STOPPED?

Many victimized children find ways to halt ongoing bullying—by ignoring, retaliating, defusing, or avoiding. Friendships help.

We know what does *not* work: simply increasing students' awareness of bullying, instituting zero tolerance for fighting, or putting bullies together in a therapy group or a classroom. This last measure tends to make daily life easier for teachers, but it increases aggression.

Since one cause of bullying is poor parent–child interaction, alerting parents may "create even more problems for the child, for the parents, and for their relationship" (Rubin et al., 2013, p. 267). This does not mean that parents should be kept ignorant, but it does mean that parents need help in understanding how to break the bully-victim connection (Nocentini et al., 2019).

Adults sometimes recommend that children tell authorities when they see bullying. However, many children worry that the bully, or their peers, might turn on them. Remember the culture of childhood, which mandates not telling adults. Often parents themselves discourage their children from intervening (Grassetti et al., 2018).

An article about parental attitudes found that many parents were naive, some claiming that their child would not experience bullying because the school was small (Stives et al., 2019). Instead of recognizing that bullies occur in every school, gaining status by threats, mockery, and occasional physical attacks, one father said that, if his son told him he was bullied,

> I would explain to him that bullies usually are very unhappy people and have a tendency to have low self-esteem. Most bullies sometimes don't have a loving/caring home environment. I would tell him to be kind to any bullies. Be a friend whenever possible.
> *[quoted in Stives et al., 2019, p. 367]*

That response helps neither victim nor bully.

Decades of research has reached some conclusions. To decrease bullying, the entire school should be involved, with teachers, aides, children, and parents all taught to recognize bullying and how to reduce it (Juvonen & Graham, 2014).

A Spanish concept, *convivencia*, describes a culture of cooperation and positive relationships within a community. Convivencia has been applied specifically to schools. When teachers are supportive and protective of every child, and the school community encourages friendship, empathy, and cooperation among all students, bullying decreases (Zych et al., 2017).

However, programs that might seem good might be harmful, especially if they call attention to bullying but do nothing about it (National Academies of Sciences, Engineering, and Medicine, 2016).

Longitudinal research on whole-school efforts finds variations depending on the age of the children (younger is easier), on the indicators (peer report, teacher report, absence rate, direct observation), as well as on the tactics (encouraging friendship and decreasing adult hostility is more effective than punishing overt bullying).

Bystanders are crucial: If they do not intervene—or worse, if they watch and laugh—bullying flourishes. Some children who are neither bullies nor victims feel troubled but also feel fearful and powerless. However, if they empathize with victims, feel effective (high in effortful control), and refuse to admire bullies, aggression is reduced. The best way for teachers to help victims is sometimes to encourage bystanders but be aware that a culture of friendship and caring is crucial (Iotti et al., 2020).

Appreciation of human differences is not innate (remember, children seek friends who are similar to them), so adults need to encourage multicultural sensitivity. Then peers are more effective than teachers at halting bullying (Palmer & Abbott, 2018).

As they mature during middle childhood, children become more socially aware, which creates a conflict—they know how someone's actions might hurt a child but are also aware of the possible harm to themselves if they befriend a bullied child. This raises the final question related to peers in middle childhood—moral development.

Children's Morality

Some moral values seem inborn. Babies prefer a puppet who is helpful to other puppets over a mean puppet, and young children believe that desired objects (cookies, stickers, candy) should be shared equally. The ideas of fairness, kindness, and equality are present in the minds of children (Rizzo & Killen, 2016; Van de Vondervoort & Hamlin, 2016).

As children grow older, their thinking helps them understand and analyze moral issues, as famously explained by Lawrence Kohlberg (see A View from Science).

A VIEW FROM SCIENCE

Kohlberg's Theory

Remember that scientists build on the theories and conclusions of other scientists. Piaget explored how cognitive development affects moral development (1932/2013b). Piaget's idea that thinking about right and wrong leads to behavior was developed by Kohlberg (1963), whose description of moral reasoning (see Table 8.3), connects to Piaget's stages of cognition.

- **Preconventional moral reasoning** is similar to preoperational thought in that it is egocentric, with children most interested in their personal pleasure or avoiding punishment.
- **Conventional moral reasoning** parallels concrete operational thought in that it relates to current, observable practices: Children watch what their parents, teachers, and friends do and try to follow suit.
- **Postconventional moral reasoning** is similar to formal operational thought because it uses abstractions, going beyond what is concretely observed, being willing to question "what is" in order to decide "what should be."

According to Kohlberg, intellectual maturation advances moral thinking. During middle childhood, children's answers

TABLE 8.3 Kohlberg's Three Levels and Six Stages of Moral Reasoning

Level I: Preconventional Moral Reasoning

The goal is to get rewards and avoid punishments; this is a self-centered level.

- *Stage one: Might makes right* (a punishment-and-obedience orientation). The most important value is to maintain the appearance of obedience to authority, avoiding punishment while still advancing self-interest. Don't get caught!
- *Stage two: Look out for number one* (an instrumental and relativist orientation). Everyone prioritizes their own needs. The reason to be nice to other people is so that they will be nice to you.

Level II: Conventional Moral Reasoning

Emphasis is placed on social rules; this is a parent- and community-centered level.

- *Stage three: Good girl and nice boy.* The goal is to please other people. Social approval is more important than any specific reward.
- *Stage four: Law and order.* Everyone must be a dutiful and law-abiding citizen, even when no police are nearby.

Level III: Postconventional Moral Reasoning

Emphasis is placed on moral principles; this level is centered on ideals.

- *Stage five: Social contract.* Obey social rules because they benefit everyone and are established by mutual agreement. If the rules become destructive or if one party doesn't live up to the agreement, the contract is no longer binding. Under some circumstances, disobeying the law is moral.
- *Stage six: Universal ethical principles.* Universal principles, not individual situations (level I) or community practices (level II), determine right and wrong. Ethical values (such as "life is sacred") are established by individual reflection and religious ideas, which may contradict egocentric (level I) or social and community (level II) values.

preconventional moral reasoning
Kohlberg's first level of moral reasoning, emphasizing rewards and punishments.

conventional moral reasoning
Kohlberg's second level of moral reasoning, emphasizing social rules.

postconventional moral reasoning
Kohlberg's third level of moral reasoning, emphasizing moral principles.

shift from being primarily preconventional to being more conventional: Concrete thought, classroom discussions, and peer experiences help children advance their moral analysis. Schools are too focused on facts, ignoring moral issues, according to Kohlberg. That is why postconventional reasoning is not usually present until adolescence or adulthood, if then.

Kohlberg began his research by posing moral dilemmas to school-age boys (and eventually girls, teenagers, and adults). The most famous example of these dilemmas involves a poor man named Heinz, whose wife was dying. He could not pay for the only drug that could cure his wife, a drug that a local druggist sold for 10 times what it cost to make.

> Heinz went to everyone he knew to borrow the money, but he could only get together about half of what it cost. He told the druggist that his wife was dying and asked him to sell it cheaper or let him pay later. But the druggist said "no." The husband got desperate and broke into the man's store to steal the drug for his wife. Should the husband have done that? Why?
>
> *[Kohlberg, 1963, p. 19]*

Kohlberg's assessment of morality depends not on *what* a person answers but *why* they say what they do. For instance, suppose a child says that Heinz should steal the drug. That itself does not indicate the level of morality. The reason could be that Heinz needs his wife to care for him (preconventional), or that people will blame him if he lets his wife die (conventional), or that the value of a human life is greater than the law (postconventional).

Or suppose another child says Heinz should not steal. Again, the reason is crucial. If it is that he will go to jail, that is preconventional; if it is that business owners will blame him, that is conventional; if it is that no one should deprive anyone else of their livelihood, that is postconventional.

Kohlberg has been criticized for not appreciating cultural or gender differences. For example, loyalty to family overrides other values in some cultures, so some people might avoid postconventional actions that hurt their family. Also, Kohlberg's original participants were all boys, which may have led him to discount female values of nurturance and relationships (Gilligan, 1982).

Overall, Kohlberg seemed to value rational principles more than individual needs, unlike other scholars of moral development who consider emotions more influential than logic (Haidt, 2013). Regarding global warming, for instance, the facts about the world's temperature rising by a degree over a decade are less compelling for children in middle childhood than the image of the stranded polar bear cub on a melting ice flow.

Nonetheless, Kohlberg's research has become a starting point for many current studies of moral development, especially outside the United States, in China (Moheghi et al., 2020; Zhang, 2019). Remember from Chapter 1 that the strength of the scientific method is that later research builds on earlier research. Kohlberg's ideas have been criticized on many grounds, but they still echo (Gibbs, 2019).

Although Kohlberg's ideas can be criticized for relying too heavily on cognitive maturation, there is no doubt that middle childhood is prime time for moral development. These are:

> years of eager, lively searching on the part of children . . . as they try to understand things, to figure them out, but also to weigh the rights and wrongs. . . . This is the time for growth of the moral imagination, fueled constantly by the willingness, the eagerness of children to put themselves in the shoes of others.
>
> *[Coles, 1997, p. 99]*

Many lines of research have shown that children develop their own morality, guided by peers, parents, and culture (Killen & Smetana, 2014). Children's growing interest in moral issues is guided by three forces: (1) child culture, (2) empathy, and (3) education.

MORAL RULES OF CHILD CULTURE

As already explained, when child culture conflicts with adult morality, children often align with peers. A child might lie to protect a friend, for instance. Friendship itself has a hostile side: Many close friends (especially girls) resist other children who want to join their play (Rubin et al., 2013). Boys are particularly likely to protect a bully if he is a friend.

Three moral imperatives of child culture in middle childhood are:

- Defend your friends.
- Don't tell adults about children's misbehavior.
- Conform to peer standards of dress, talk, and behavior.

These three can explain both apparent boredom and overt defiance as well as standards of dress that mystify adults (such as jeans so loose that they fall off or so tight that they impede digestion—both styles worn by my children, who grew up in different cohorts). Given what is known about middle childhood, it is no surprise that children do not echo adult morality.

Part of child culture is that as children become more aware of their peers, they may reject other children who are outsiders as well as stay quiet about their own problems. When teachers ask, "Who threw that spitball?" or parents ask, "How did you get that bruise?" children may be mum.

A CASE TO STUDY

The Unthinkable Is Okay

The fact that children place prime value on being accepted by peers sometimes results in a conflict between the moral values of society and the actions of children. A child may do something that the parents think their child would never do. This is not the time to argue, or despair; it is the time to teach. This is illustrated by another memory that Ward Sutton (who opened this chapter) told at his acceptance speech for the 2018 Herblock award.

> In the summer of 1974, I was seven years old.
>
> There was a kid living in my neighborhood. [. . .]
>
> For some reason this kid had built up animosity towards a family down the block. He started telling my friend Steve and me that this family had done all sorts of bad things, like hiding razor blades in the apples they gave out to trick-or-treaters at Halloween.
>
> Fake news for seven year olds [. . .] target[s] people who had done absolutely nothing wrong.
>
> Steve became convinced of the conspiracy theory and fell in line, and then the two of them told me they were starting a club and I couldn't join unless I went along with them. [. . .]
>
> We snuck behind the family's house in the woods out back. We threw some rocks at the house and when there was no response we realized the family was not home. Then we escalated things, finding bricks, smashing windows, breaking in and vandalizing the home.
>
> I was a shy, introverted kid who never would have ever done anything like this on my own. But once I was swayed to join in, it was like a switch had been flipped and any sense of right or wrong was thrown by the wayside. Suddenly the unthinkable was okay. [. . .]

Then the family came home. We ran. Police arrived. Steve was caught. I lied. To my parents. To everyone. Said I didn't know anything about it. Steve confessed, and eventually I did, too. As terrible as it all was, the worst of it was the fact that I had lied. My mother wouldn't speak to me for what felt like an eternity. [. . .]

My father brought me back to the house to apologize to the family face-to-face. I begged him not to make me do it. [. . .] I expected them to be angry with me, but they weren't. They were gracious, and mostly puzzled at what could have possibly possessed me to do something like this. [. . .]

I couldn't even explain why I had done it.

As you might imagine, this episode was hugely formative for me. It awakened my moral compass and informed what I would create going forward. [. . .]

I've never spoken of it publicly until today. For the longest time, I wished I could live that day all over again, and that someone could have talked some sense into me: "Stop and think about what you're doing."

Sutton's cartoons are often ethical commentaries on world affairs. He says he draws them because he hopes people will smile, and then stop and think. Would that still have happened if his parents, his neighbors, and the police had acted differently?

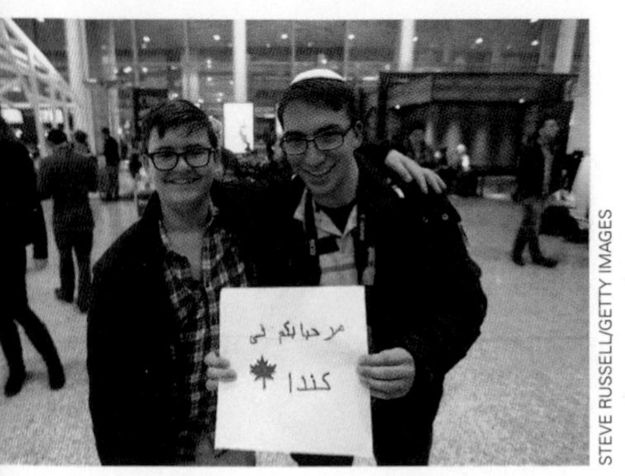

STEVE RUSSELL/GETTY IMAGES

Universal Morality Remarkable? Not really. By the end of middle childhood, many children are eager to express their moral convictions, especially with a friend. Chaim Ifrah and Shai Reef believe that welcoming refugees is part of being a patriotic Canadian and a devout Jewish person, so they brought a welcoming sign to the Toronto airport where Syrian refugees (mostly Muslim) will soon deplane.

EMPATHY

Empathy is thought to be the wellspring of morality. As middle childhood advances, children become more socially perceptive and more open to learning about other people (Weissberg et al., 2016). This does not always lead to increased morality as adults might define it. One example was just described: Bullies become adept at picking victims, and bystanders become better at noticing victims. Social awareness may make them either quicker to defend or hesitant to act (Pozzoli & Gini, 2013).

Here, diversity in schools and neighborhoods can be helpful. Empathy is not an abstract idea as much as a recognition of the humanity of other people. In order to achieve that, befriending a child from another group lets children understand. Teachers and parents can help with this, not only through direct contact but, once children can read on their own, by offering books about children in other lands, centuries, and cultures.

MATURATION AND MORALITY

Both maturation and culture matter. One study measured generosity by counting how many of 10 chosen stickers 5- to 12-year-olds from five nations (United States, Canada, China, Turkey, South Africa) were willing to donate to another unknown child. Generosity increased with age. The average 5-year-old gave away two and kept eight; the average 12-year-old gave away five and kept five (Cowell et al., 2017).

Beyond that, culture had an impact. Children from Toronto, Canada, were most generous, and children from Cape Town, South Africa, were least generous, a difference thought to reflect national wealth (Cowell et al., 2017). Those national differences paled when individual behavior was considered: Some children from each of the five nations kept all or almost all stickers to themselves, and some from each nation gave more than half away.

One significant advance in morality over the years of middle childhood is that children begin to understand the difference between intentions and actions (doing harm but intending to be helpful is forgiven) and between lying deliberately and saying something that is untrue by mistake (Rizzo et al., 2019). Ideally, they also recognize when they themselves inadvertently harmed someone else. They also learn to consider psychological as well as physical harm, trying not to hurt someone's feelings (Jambon & Smetana, 2014).

THINK CRITICALLY: If one of your moral values differs from that of your spouse, your parents, or your community, should you still try to teach it to your children? Why or why not?

ADVANCING MORALITY

Fortunately, children enjoy thinking about and discussing moral values, and then peers help one another advance in moral behavior. Children may be more ethical than adults (once they understand moral equity, they complain when adults are not

fair), and they are better at stopping a bully than adults are. Bullies are more likely to listen to other children than to adults.

We close this chapter with a study that examined the role of adults and peers on the development of morality. The researchers began with an update on one of Piaget's moral issues: whether punishment should seek *retribution* (hurting the transgressor) or *restitution* (restoring what was lost). Piaget found that children advance from retribution to restitution between ages 8 and 10 (Piaget, 1932/2013b), which many ethicists consider a moral advance (Claessen, 2017).

To learn how this occurs, researchers asked 133 9-year-olds:

> Late one afternoon there was a boy who was playing with a ball on his own in the garden. His dad saw him playing with it and asked him not to play with it so near the house because it might break a window. The boy didn't really listen to his dad, and carried on playing near the house. Then suddenly, the ball bounced up high and broke the window in the boy's room. His dad heard the noise and came to see what had happened. The father wonders what would be the fairest way to punish the boy. He thinks of two punishments. The first is to say: "Now, you didn't do as I asked. You will have to pay for the window to be mended, and I am going to take the money from your pocket money." The second is to say: "Now, you didn't do as I asked. As a punishment you have to go to your room and stay there for the rest of the evening." Which of these punishments do you think is the fairest?
>
> *[Leman & Björnberg, 2010, p. 962]*

The children's answers were split almost equally. Then, 24 pairs were formed of children who had opposite views. Each pair was asked to discuss the issue, trying to reach agreement. (The other children did not discuss it.) Six pairs were boy–boy, six were boy–girl with the boy favoring restitution, six were boy–girl with the girl favoring restitution, and six were girl–girl.

The conversations typically took only five minutes, and the retribution side was more often chosen. Piaget would consider that a moral backslide, since more restitution than retribution advocates switched.

However, several weeks later all of the children were queried again. Many changed their opinion toward the more advanced, restitution thinking (see Figure 8.3). This

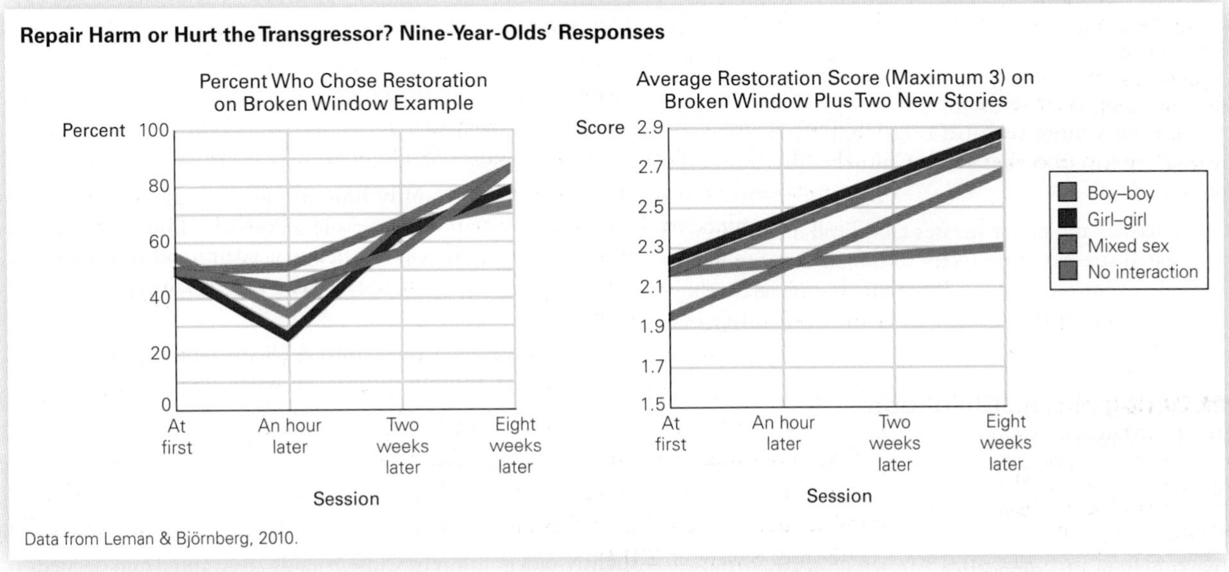

FIGURE 8.3 **Benefits of Time and Talking** The graph on the left shows that most children, immediately after their initial punitive response, became even more likely to seek punishment rather than to repair damage. However, after some time and reflection, they affirmed the response that Piaget would consider more mature. The graph on the right indicates that children who had talked about the broken-window example moved toward restorative justice even in examples that they had not heard before, which was not true for those who had not talked about the first story.

advance occurred even for the children who merely thought about the dilemma again, but children who had discussed it with another child were particularly likely to decide that restitution was better.

The main conclusion from this study was that "conversation on a topic may stimulate a process of individual reflection that triggers developmental advances" (Leman & Björnberg, 2010, p. 969). This provides a lesson for parents and teachers who seek to advance the thinking and actions of children in middle childhood. The tactic is to encourage children themselves to think about behavior, talking with their friends. Raising moral issues and letting children talk about them may advance morality—not immediately, but soon.

what have you learned?

1. How does the culture of children differ from the culture of adults?
2. What are the different kinds of popular and unpopular children?
3. What do victims and bullies have in common?
4. How might bullying be reduced?
5. What three forces affect moral development during middle childhood?
6. What are the main criticisms of Kohlberg's theory of moral development?
7. How does the age of a person affect their thinking about right and wrong?
8. What factors influence one child to have a more advanced moral development than another?

SUMMARY

The Nature of the Child

1. All theories of development acknowledge that school-age children become more independent and capable in many ways. Erikson emphasized industry, when children busily strive to master various tasks.

2. Children develop their self-concept during middle childhood, basing it on a more realistic assessment of their competence than they had in earlier years. Cultures differ in their evaluation of high self-esteem.

3. Both daily hassles and major stresses take a toll on children, with accumulated stresses more likely to impair development than any single event on its own. Resilience is aided by the child's interpretation of the situation and the availability of supportive adults, peers, and institutions.

Families During Middle Childhood

4. Families influence children in many ways, as do genes and peers. Although most siblings share a childhood home and parents, each sibling experiences different (nonshared) circumstances within the family.

5. The five functions of a supportive family are to satisfy children's physical needs; to encourage learning; to support friendships; to protect self-respect; and to provide a safe, stable, and harmonious home.

6. The most common family structure worldwide is the two-parent family, usually with other relatives nearby and supportive. Two-parent families include adoptive, same-sex, grandparent, and stepfamilies, each of which sometimes functions well for children. However, each of these also has vulnerabilities.

7. Single-parent families have higher rates of change—for example, in where they live and who belongs to the family. Instability is particularly hard during middle childhood, as are changing routines about homework, sleep, food, and so on.

8. Income affects family function for two-parent families as well as single-parent households. Poor children are at greater risk for emotional, behavioral, and academic problems because the stresses that often accompany poverty hinder effective parenting.

9. No matter what the family SES, instability and conflict are harmful. Children suffer even when the conflict does not involve them directly but their parents or siblings fight.

The Peer Group

10. Peers teach crucial social skills during middle childhood. Each cohort of children has a culture, passed down from slightly older children. Close friends are wanted and needed.

11. Popular children may be cooperative and easy to get along with or may be competitive and aggressive. Unpopular children may be neglected, aggressive, or withdrawn, sometimes becoming victims.

12. Bullying is common among school-age children. Both bullies and victims have difficulty with social cognition; their interpretation of the normal give-and-take of childhood is impaired.

13. Bullies themselves may be admired, which makes their behavior more difficult to stop. Overall, a multifaceted, long-term, whole-school approach—with parents, teachers, and bystanders working together—seems the best way to halt bullying.

14. School-age children seek to differentiate right from wrong as moral development increases over middle childhood. Peer values, cultural standards, empathy, and education all affect their personal morality.

15. When values conflict, children often choose loyalty to peers over adult standards of behavior. When children discuss moral issues with other children, they develop more thoughtful answers to moral questions.

KEY TERMS

industry versus inferiority (p. 241)
social comparison (p. 242)
resilience (p. 244)
parentification (p. 246)
family structure (p. 248)
Standard North American Family (SNAF) (p. 248)
extended family (p. 249)
family function (p. 250)
cohabitation (p. 254)
child culture (p. 259)
aggressive-rejected (p. 262)
withdrawn-rejected (p. 262)
bullying (p. 262)
bully-victim (p. 263)
preconventional moral reasoning (p. 265)
conventional moral reasoning (p. 265)
postconventional moral reasoning (p. 265)

APPLICATIONS

1. Go someplace where many school-age children congregate (such as a schoolyard, a park, or a community center) and use naturalistic observation for at least half an hour. Describe what popular, average, withdrawn, and rejected children do. Note at least one potential conflict. Describe the sequence and the outcome.

2. Focusing on verbal bullying, describe at least two times when someone said something hurtful to you and two times when you said something that might have been hurtful to someone else. What are the differences between the two types of situations?

3. How would your childhood have been different if your family structure had been different, such as if you had (or had not) lived with your grandparents, if your parents had (or had not) gotten divorced, if you had (or had not) been adopted, if you had lived with one parent (or two), if your parents were both the same sex (or not)? Avoid blanket statements: Appreciate that every structure has advantages and disadvantages.

ESPECIALLY FOR ANSWERS

Response for Scientists (from p. 248): Proof is very difficult when human interaction is the subject of investigation, since random assignment is impossible. Ideally, researchers would find identical twins being raised together and would then observe the parents' behavior over the years.

Response for Parents of an Accused Bully (from p. 263): The future is ominous if the charges are true. Your child's denial is a sign that there is a problem. (An innocent child would be worried about the misperception instead of categorically denying that any problem exists.) You might ask the teacher what the school is doing about bullying. Family counseling might help. Because bullies often have friends who egg them on, you may need to monitor your child's friendships and perhaps befriend the victim. Talk about the situation with your child. Ignoring the situation might lead to heartache later on.

OBSERVATION QUIZ ANSWERS

Answer to Observation Quiz (from p. 247): Did you notice that the two males are first, and that the father carries the boy? Everyone should notice gender, ethnic, and age differences, but interpretation of such differences is not straightforward. This scene may or may not reflect male–female roles.

Answer to Observation Quiz (from p. 253): Both parents are women. The evidence shows that families with same-sex parents are similar in many ways to families with other-sex parents, and children in such families develop well.

PART V

CHAPTER 9 CHAPTER 10

Adolescence

It is said that adolescence begins with biology and ends with culture. In the eighteenth century, the transition from biology to culture took only a few years. Puberty began at age 14 or so, and by age 17 many girls were married, and many boys found jobs. By age 20, most young people were adults: young women were mothers and young men were workers.

By contrast, now puberty begins earlier, at age 10 or 11, and adulthood begins later. Some U.S. scholars use age 25 as the end of adolescence (Curtis, 2015), in part because most grown children still depend on their parents' support.

In this text, we still begin with biology (Chapter 9) followed by culture (Chapter 10), and a new stage (*emerging adulthood*—Chapter 11) covers ages 18 to 25, followed by two chapters (12 and 13) on adulthood.

Amidst these historic changes are some universals, evident in the nineteenth-century German proverb "Too soon old, too late smart." The goal—to coordinate body, mind, and culture—is especially elusive in contemporary North American adolescents. That will be apparent in these chapters as we describe teenagers, in all their clumsy, creative, and inspiring selves.

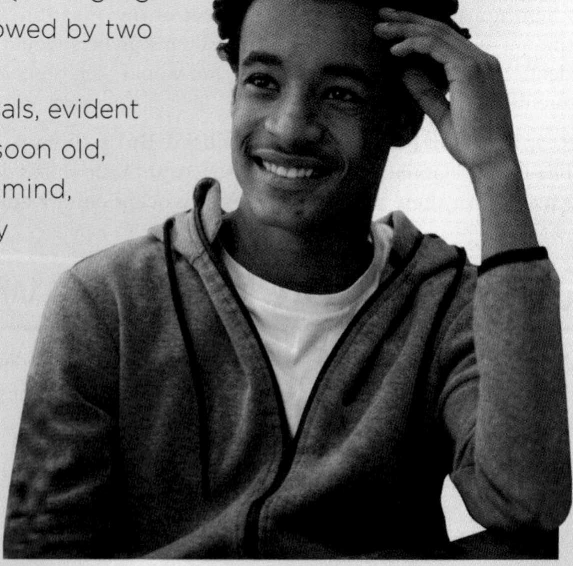

RICHARD BAILEY/CORBIS/GETTY IMAGES

CHAPTER

9

ADOLESCENCE

Body and Mind

what will you know?

- How can you predict when puberty will begin for a particular child?
- What makes teenage sexuality often a problem instead of a joy?
- Why does emotion sometimes overwhelm reason?
- Ideally should everyone to go to college?

Puberty was not easy for me, in body or mind. My family moved two weeks before my 11th birthday. I left a suburban home with a backyard for an urban row house; I left a single-sex primary school and, halfway through the sixth grade, entered a coed middle school.

In retrospect, that move served me well.

- I could no longer take long walks alone in the woods, but I found a public library a block away. I read dozens of self-selected books.
- I learned to talk to boys; later that helped me choose and marry one.
- I made new friends, including three who had been rejected by the popular clique. One was Mormon, one was Jewish, one had just moved from Germany. They introduced me to the larger world; they are still my friends.

But puberty was stressful. Only now, as I write this chapter, do I recognize how hard it was. I reached menarche three weeks after I arrived in the new city; I was afraid of my male classmates and teachers; I was an awkward, pudgy girl who did not know how to sit at my small desk, to style my changing hair, or to dress my new body.

Once I wore my best taffeta dress to school; it was pale blue with black polka dots. A popular girl said, "You must be going somewhere special." "Yes," I lied, suddenly aware that my best dress was not appropriate school attire. Even now, no one would call me a fashionable dresser, but I feel sorry for my young self, who hoped that a fancy dress would bring admiration.

This chapter reviews the physical aspects of puberty, the problems many adolescents have with appearance, peers, and sexuality, and the impact of cognition, which blends egocentrism (that dress) with

PHOTO CREDIT: PIXEL-SHOT/SHUTTERSTOCK.COM

social awareness (my friendships with people unlike me). The teachers at my new school prepared me well for the challenges of college.

I sympathize with every 11-year-old. Changes are difficult at any age, but particularly when the growth spurt and bodily changes occur.

I am grateful for the lessons I learned, and experiences I had. I hope you also sympathize with your adolescent self and appreciate what you learned.

puberty
The time between the first onrush of hormones and full adult physical development. Puberty usually lasts three to five years. Many more years are required to achieve psychosocial maturity.

menarche
A girl's first menstrual period, signaling that she has begun ovulation. Pregnancy is biologically possible, but ovulation and menstruation are often irregular for years after menarche.

spermarche
A boy's first ejaculation of sperm. Erections can occur as early as infancy, but ejaculation signals sperm production. Spermarche may occur during sleep (in a "wet dream") or via direct stimulation.

VIDEO: The Timing of Puberty depicts the usual sequence of physical development for adolescents.

Puberty Begins

Puberty refers to the years of rapid physical growth and sexual maturation that end childhood, producing a person of adult size, shape, and sexuality. It begins with hormones that produce external growth and internal changes, including heightened emotions and sexual desires.

Sequence

For girls, the first observable sign is usually nipple growth. Soon a few pubic hairs are visible, followed by peak growth spurt, widening of the hips, first menstrual period (**menarche**), full pubic-hair pattern, and breast maturation. The average age of menarche in the United States is about 12 years, 4 months (Biro et al., 2013), although nutrition, genes, and stress affect the timing (Brix et al., 2019).

For boys, the usual sequence is growth of the testes, initial pubic-hair growth, growth of the penis, first ejaculation of seminal fluid (**spermarche**), appearance of facial hair, peak growth spurt, deepening of the voice, and final pubic-hair growth (Dorn & Biro, 2011). The typical age of spermarche is 13.0 years, eight months later than menarche.

Unseen Beginnings

The changes just listed are visible, but the entire process begins with an invisible event—a marked increase in hormones.

PIXELCHROME INC/DIGITALVISION/GETTY IMAGES

TIMOTHY ALLEN/PHOTOLIBRARY/GETTY IMAGES

Do They See Beauty? Both young women — the Mexican 15-year-old preparing for her Quinceañara and the Malaysian teen applying a rice facial mask — look wistful, even worried. They are typical of teenage girls everywhere, who do not realize how lovely they are.

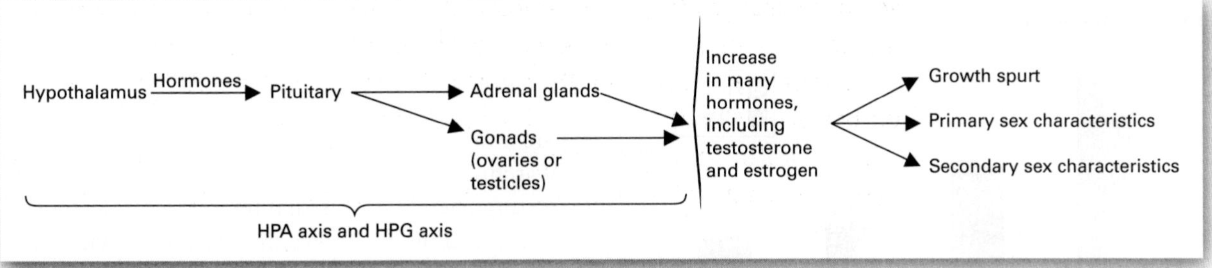

FIGURE 9.1 Biological Sequence of Puberty Puberty begins with a hormonal signal from the hypothalamus to the pituitary gland, both deep within the brain. The pituitary, in turn, sends a hormonal message through the bloodstream to the adrenal glands and the gonads to produce more hormones.

Hormone production is regulated deep within the brain, where biochemical signals from the hypothalamus signal another brain structure, the **pituitary**. The pituitary produces hormones that stimulate the **adrenal glands**, located above the kidneys at either side of the lower back.

The adrenal glands produce more hormones. Many hormones that regulate puberty follow this route, known as the **HPA (hypothalamus–pituitary–adrenal) axis** (see Figure 9.1).

pituitary
A gland in the brain that responds to a signal from the hypothalamus by producing many hormones, including those that regulate growth and sexual maturation.

adrenal glands
Two glands, located above the kidneys, that respond to the pituitary, producing hormones.

HPG (hypothalamus–pituitary–gonad) axis
A sequence of hormone production originating in the hypothalamus and moving to the pituitary and then to the gonads.

gonads
The paired sex glands (ovaries in females, testicles in males). The gonads produce hormones and mature gametes.

HPA (hypothalamus–pituitary–adrenal) axis
A sequence of hormone production originating in the hypothalamus and moving to the pituitary and then to the adrenal glands.

circadian rhythm
A day–night cycle of biological activity that occurs approximately every 24 hours.

SEX HORMONES

Late in childhood, "well before the teens" (Peper & Dahl, 2013, p. 134), the pituitary activates not only the adrenal glands—the HPA axis—but also the **gonads**, or sex glands (ovaries in females; testes, or testicles, in males), following another sequence called the **HPG (hypothalamus–pituitary–gonad) axis**. Throughout adolescence, sex hormones (primarily estrogen in females and testosterone in males) correlate with physiological changes, brain restructuring, emotions, and self-reported development (Goddings et al., 2012; Vijayakumar et al., 2018).

One additional effect of estrogen and testosterone is arousal of sexual thoughts and impulses. Suddenly, children become interested in the other gender (who used to be avoided or disparaged) or attracted to members of the same sex (again often a surprise).

Although emotional surges, nurturant impulses, and lustful urges arise with hormones, remember that body, brain, and behavior always interact. Sexual thoughts themselves can *cause* physiological and neurological processes, not just result from them.

Cortisol rises, making adolescents quick to react with passion, fury, shame, or ecstasy (Goddings et al., 2012; Klein & Romeo, 2013). Then those emotions, in turn, increase various other hormones. Bodies, brains, and behavior all affect one another.

BODY RHYTHMS

Because of hormones, the brain of every living creature responds to environmental changes over the hours, days, and seasons. Many biorhythms are on a 24-hour cycle, called the **circadian rhythm**. (*Circadian* means "about a day.") Puberty affects biorhythms.

For most people, daylight awakens the brain. That's why people experiencing jet lag are urged to take an early-morning walk. But at puberty, night may be more energizing, making some teens wide awake and hungry at midnight but half asleep, with neither appetite nor energy, all morning (Gariépy et al., 2018).

In addition to these circadian changes at puberty, some individuals (especially males) are naturally more alert in the evening than in the morning, a trait called *eveningness.* To some extent, this is genetic: 15 genes differ in people who are natural "early birds" or "night owls" (Hu et al., 2016). Puberty plus eveningness increases risk (drugs, sex, delinquency): Many teenagers are awake when adults are asleep (see Figure 9.2).

Watching late-night TV, working on a computer, or texting friends at 10 P.M. interferes with sleepiness. Any screen time in the evening correlates with later sleep. Social media and web surfing are particularly stimulating of the brain (Hisler et al., 2020).

No wonder many adolescents are unable to sleep when lights are off. The powerful adolescent urge to connect with friends results in sleeping near their smartphones—and then dozing off when they drive a car or sit in class.

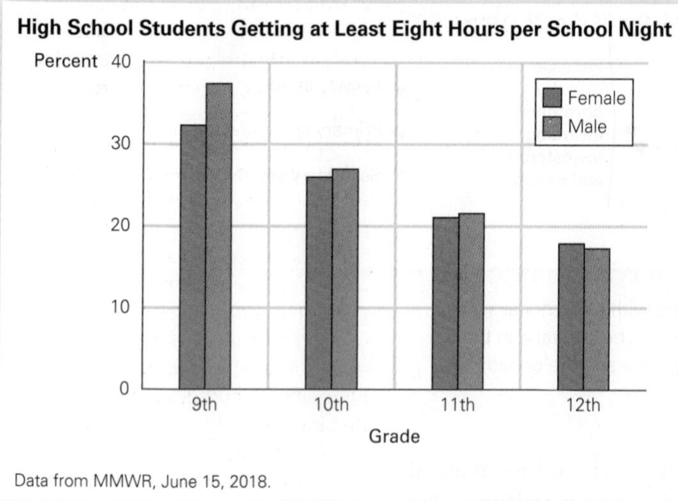

Data from MMWR, June 15, 2018.

FIGURE 9.2 Sleepyheads Three of every four high school seniors are sleep deprived. Even if they go to sleep at midnight, as many do, they must get up before 8 A.M., as almost all do. Then they are tired all day.

◆◆ OBSERVATION QUIZ
As you see, the problems are worse for the girls. Why is that? (see answer, page 307) ↑

CHAPTER APP 9

Sleep Cycle

IOS:
https://tinyurl.com/y36gvtum

ANDROID:
https://tinyurl.com/pgj2jyk

RELEVANT TOPIC:
Circadian rhythms and sleep

This app allows users to track their sleep patterns and get analysis that helps ensure a good night's sleep. Sleep Cycle uses a wake-up phase that ends at the desired alarm time. During this phase, the app monitors body signals to wake users softly, when they are in the lightest possible sleep state.

Many schools remain stuck in schedules set before the hazards of sleep deprivation were known. In August of 2014, the American Academy of Pediatrics concluded that high schools should begin later than 8:30 A.M., because adolescent sleep deprivation causes a cascade of intellectual, behavioral, and health problems. The doctors reported that 43 percent of high schools in the United States start before 8 A.M.

Some schools have heeded the science. One study compared 29 high schools, across seven states, before and after beginning after 8:30 A.M. Graduation rates increased from 79 to 88 percent, and daily attendance rose from 90 to 94 percent (McKeever & Clark, 2017).

Brain Growth

During adolescence, the prefrontal cortex matures gradually. The limbic system, however, is affected more by hormones (the HPG axis) than by time. It grows rapidly at puberty. Thus, the instinctual and emotional areas of the adolescent brain develop ahead of the reflective, analytic areas.

A study compared 886 adolescents (ages 9 to 16) and their parents (average age 44) in Hong Kong and England. All participants were asked questions to assess executive function. The adolescents were less accurate but quicker, indicating that their limbic systems raced ahead while their prefrontal cortex slowly matured (Ellefson et al., 2017).

For everyone, when stress, passion, sensory bombardment, or drugs are extreme, the brain is flooded with hormones that overwhelm the cortex. Adults try to keep their thoughts straight, but adolescents may enjoy such flooding, acting on impulses that adults would curb.

Many teenagers choose to spend a night without sleep, to eat nothing all day, to exercise in pain, to play music at deafening loudness, to drink and do drugs until they black out. They brag about being wasted, smashed, out of their minds—all conditions that most adults try to avoid.

A common example of poor judgment is texting while driving. Teenagers know that this is illegal and dangerous, but the "ping" of a text message evokes emotions that compel immediate attention. In one survey of U.S. high school seniors who had driven a car in the past month, 39 percent had texted while at the wheel (Johns et al., 2020).

When Will Puberty Begin?

Usually, pubertal hormones begin to accelerate sometime between ages 8 and 14, and visible signs of puberty appear between 9 and 15. That six-year range is too great for many people, who want to know exactly when a given child will hit puberty.

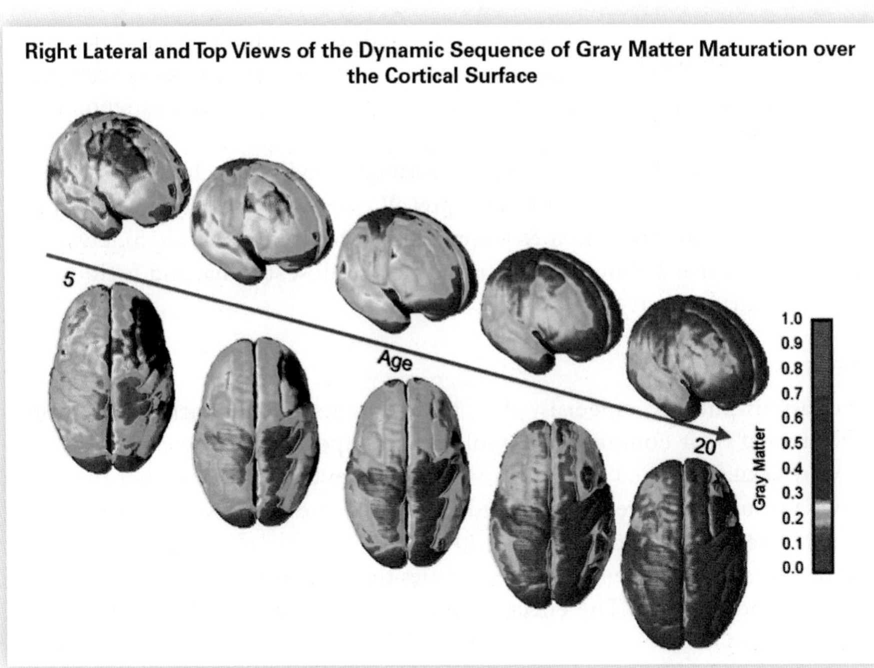

Same People, but Not the Same Brain These brain scans are part of a longitudinal study that repeatedly compared the proportion of gray matter from childhood through adolescence. (Gray matter refers to the cell bodies of neurons, which are less prominent with age as some neurons are unused.) Gray matter is reduced as white matter increases, in part because pruning during the teen years (the last two pairs of images here) allows intellectual connections to build. As the authors of one study that included this chart explained, teenagers may look "like an adult, but cognitively they are not there yet" (Powell, 2006, p. 865).

Fortunately, if genes, gender, body fat, and stress level are known, prediction within a year or two is possible.

GENES AND GENDER

Gender differences in hormones have a marked effect in both onset and sequence. In height, the average pubescent girl is about two years ahead of the average boy. The female height spurt occurs *before* menarche; the male height increase is *after* spermarche (Brix et al., 2019).

Overall, about two-thirds of age variations in onset of puberty is genetic—not only from the XX or XY chromosomes but also from other genes inherited from previous generations. If both parents reached puberty early or late, their child will likely be early or late as well.

BODY FAT AND CHEMICALS

Another influence on the onset of puberty is body fat, which advances puberty for girls but not always for boys. For the boys, obesity may slow down the expression of hormones (Reinehr & Roth, 2019). For all adolescents, chronic hunger delays puberty.

Malnutrition explains why the average young person reaches puberty later in some African nations, while their genetic relatives in North America mature much earlier. Even within the West African nation of Ghana, girls in rural areas—where malnutrition is more common—are behind those in urban areas (Ameade & Garti, 2016).

A more dramatic example arises from sixteenth-century Europe, where puberty may have begun several years later than it does today, because those Europeans were often hungry. Throughout the nineteenth and twentieth centuries, every generation grew taller and reached puberty before the previous one (Brix et al., 2019; Dorn & Biro, 2011).

Now, in most nations, adequate food allows every child to attain their genetic potential. Adolescents no longer look down at their short parents and grandparents, unless the latter were born where hunger was common.

Some scientists suspect that precocious (before age 8) or delayed (after age 14) puberty may be caused by hormones in the food supply. Cattle are fed steroids to

VICKY KASALA/DIGITALVISION/GETTY IMAGES

Fully Grown These 14- to 17-year-old soccer players are in high school, and are probably already at their adult height since girls typically mature before boys. We can be glad that U.S. law (Title IX) mandates equal sports funding for everyone, so all students can also experience the joys of teamwork, competition, and body strength.

◆◆ OBSERVATION QUIZ

What can you surmise about adolescent girls and height by looking at how these four are standing? (see answer, page 307) ↑

THINK CRITICALLY: If a child seems to be unusually short or unusually slow in reaching puberty, would you give the child hormones? Why or why not?

increase bulk and milk production, and hundreds of chemicals and hormones are used to produce the food that children consume. All of these substances *might* affect appetite, body fat, and sex hormones, with effects at puberty (Bourguignon et al., 2016; Lucaccioni et al., 2020).

The data on the effects on humans of hormones and other chemicals, whether natural or artificial, are not easy to interpret. We know that many hormones and chemicals affect puberty (Araki & Jensen, 2020; M. Wolff et al., 2015), but much remains to be learned about the specific effects of dose, timing, and various substances on human puberty.

STRESS

Stress hastens puberty, especially if a child's parents are sick, drug-addicted, or divorced, or if their community is violent and impoverished. One study of girls who were sexually abused found that some began puberty a year earlier than they otherwise would have, a result attributed not only to stress but also to the hormones activated by sexual contact (Noll et al., 2017).

Developmentalists have known for decades that puberty is influenced by genes, hormones, and body fat. The effect of stress is a newer discovery, as A View from Science explains.

A VIEW FROM SCIENCE

Stress and Puberty

Emotional stress precipitates puberty (Ellis & Del Giudice, 2019).

For example, a large longitudinal study in England compared girls whose biological father was absent with girls whose father was present. Father absence was likely to increase mother and daughter stress, especially when the mother had a new partner. In that study, girls with absent fathers were more depressed and reached menarche earlier (Culpin et al., 2015).

Early-childhood stress matters, too, especially for girls. Another study found that some parents demand respect from their young children, often spanking and rarely hugging them. A decade later, their daughters reach puberty early (Belsky et al., 2007).

A follow-up of the same girls at age 15, controlling for genetic differences, found that harsh treatment in early childhood increased sexual problems (more sex partners, pregnancies, sexually transmitted infections) but *not* other risks (drugs, crime) (Belsky et al., 2010). This suggests that stress triggers increased sex hormones but not generalized rebellion.

This seems contrary to evolution, that contends that genetic differences occur to protect society. Logically, stressed teens would benefit from delayed puberty, because their childish appearance would evoke adult protection rather than lust or anger. Protection is needed in conflict-ridden or stressed single-parent homes, yet, paradoxically, such homes produce earlier puberty and less nurturance. Evolutionary theory has an intriguing explanation.

> Maturing quickly and breeding promiscuously would enhance reproductive fitness more than would delaying development, mating cautiously, and investing heavily in parenting. The latter strategy, in contrast, would make biological sense, for virtually the same reproductive-fitness-enhancing reasons, under conditions of contextual support and nurturance.
>
> *[Belsky et al., 2010, p. 121]*

In other words, thousands of years ago, when harsh conditions threatened survival, adolescents needed to reproduce early and often, lest the entire community become extinct.

By contrast, in peaceful times, with plentiful food and loving care, puberty could occur later, allowing children to postpone maturity and enjoy extra years of nurturance. Genes evolved to be adaptive, responding differently to war and peace.

Of course, this no longer applies. Now, early sexual activity is more destructive than protective. However, since the genome has been shaped over millennia, a puberty-starting allele that responds to stress will respond now as it needed to do thousands of years ago. Because of differential susceptibility, not every distressed girl experiences early puberty, but because of ancient genes, stress may speed puberty (Harkness, 2014).

Too Early, Too Late

For a society's health, early puberty is problematic: It increases the rate of emotional and behavioral problems, including serious psychopathology (Dimler & Natsuaki, 2015; Hamlat et al., 2019). Early puberty is also linked to later health problems, including breast cancer, diabetes, and stroke (Day et al., 2015). Delayed puberty may also be a sign of illness, including sickle cell anemia (Alexandre-Heymann et al., 2019).

However, for most adolescents, the link between age of puberty, stress, and health are irrelevant. The only timing that matters: their friends' schedule. No one wants to be too early or too late.

Puberty that is late by world norms, at age 14 or so, is not troubling if one's friends are late as well. However, if students in the same school have diverse ethnic and genetic roots, the fact that some look like children and others like grownups may create tension. Contextual factors interact with biological ones. Peers, cultures, and communities make off-time puberty insignificant or a major problem.

For example, early maturing Swedish girls may encounter problems with sex and drugs. But early maturing Slovak girls do not, presumably because parents and social norms keep them under tight control (Skoog & Stattin, 2014). In the United States, early maturing Mexican American boys may experience trouble (with police and with peers) if their neighborhoods have few Mexican Americans, but not if they live in ethnic enclaves (R. White et al., 2013). The latter are perceived as leaders, not troublemakers. They respond accordingly.

Especially for Parents Worried About Early Puberty
Suppose your cousin's 9-year-old daughter has just had her first period, and your cousin blames hormones in the food supply for this "precocious" puberty. Should you change your young daughter's diet? (see response, page 307)

what have you learned?

1. What are the first visible signs of puberty?
2. What body parts of a teenage boy or girl are the last to reach full growth?
3. How do hormones affect the physical and psychological aspects of puberty?
4. Why do adolescents experience sudden, intense emotions?
5. How does the circadian rhythm affect adolescents?
6. What are the consequences of sleep deprivation?
7. What are the ethnic and cultural differences in the timing of puberty?
8. How does diet affect age of puberty?
9. How does stress affect when a girl is able to become pregnant?

Physical and Sexual Growth

Puberty transforms every body part, with each change affecting all of the others. Here, we discuss biological growth and the nutrition that fuels that growth.

Growing Bigger and Stronger

The first set of changes is called the **growth spurt**—a sudden, uneven jump in size that turns children into adults. Growth proceeds from the extremities to the core (the opposite of earlier proximodistal growth).

Thus, fingers and toes lengthen before hands and feet, hands and feet before arms and legs, arms and legs before the torso. Because the torso is the last to grow, many pubescent children are temporarily big-footed, long-legged, and short-waisted.

growth spurt
The relatively sudden and rapid physical growth that occurs during puberty. Each body part increases in size on a schedule: Weight usually precedes height, and growth of the limbs precedes growth of the torso.

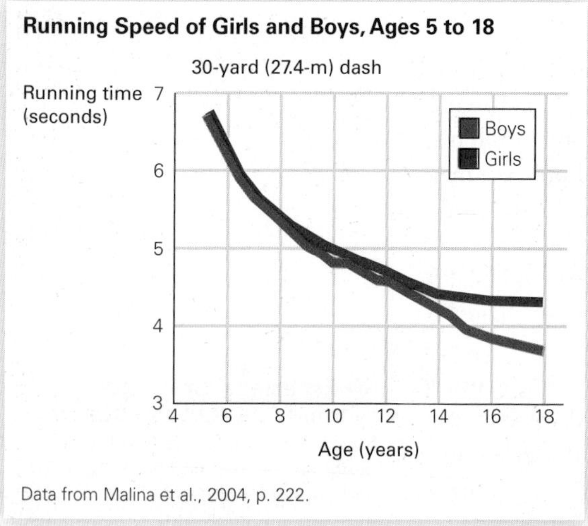

FIGURE 9.3 Little Difference Both girls and boys develop longer and stronger legs during puberty.

If young teenagers complain that their jeans don't fit, they are probably correct—even if those same jeans fit when their parents bought them a month earlier. (Advance warning about rapid body growth occurs when parents first have to buy their children's shoes in the adult section.)

SEQUENCE: WEIGHT, HEIGHT, MUSCLES

When the growth spurt begins, children eat more and gain weight. Exactly when, where, and how much they gain depends on heredity, hormones, diet, exercise, and gender. By age 17, the average girl's body has twice as much body fat as the average boy.

A height spurt follows the weight spurt; a year or two later, a muscle spurt occurs. Thus, the pudginess and clumsiness of early puberty may disappear by late adolescence. Arm muscles develop, particularly in boys, doubling in strength from ages 8 to 18.

Other muscles are gender-neutral. For instance, both sexes run faster each year, with boys not much faster than girls (unless the girls choose to slow down) (see Figure 9.3).

Muscles are heavier than fat, so merely comparing weight and height, as BMI does, may make it seem as if a strong adolescent is overweight—but consider athletic activity. If teenagers are physically active at least an hour every day (as are 31 percent of the boys and 15 percent of the girls), their BMI can be above 25 (technically overweight) but they may be in good physical shape (Johns et al., 2020).

ORGAN GROWTH

Lungs triple in weight; consequently, adolescents breathe more deeply and slowly. The heart (another muscle) doubles in size as the heartbeat slows, decreasing the pulse while increasing blood pressure.

Red blood cells increase, which aids oxygen transport during intense exercise. All these changes allow teenagers to run for miles or dance for hours.

Both weight and height increase *before* muscles and internal organs: To protect immature bodies, athletic training and weightlifting should be tailored to an adolescent's size the previous year. That would reduce sports injuries, which are the most common school accidents (Trentacosta, 2020). The average young athlete is injured every year.

One organ system, the lymphoid system (which includes the tonsils and adenoids), *decreases* in size, so teenagers are less susceptible to colds and asthma. The larynx grows, which also deepens the voice, dramatically so in boys.

The skin becomes oilier, sweatier, smellier, and more prone to acne—which itself is an early sign of puberty (Brix et al., 2019). Hair becomes coarser and darker, with new growth under arms, on faces, on legs, and over genitals (pubic hair, from the same Latin root as *puberty*).

Diet Deficiencies

All of the changes of puberty depend on adequate nourishment. However, many teenagers skip breakfast, binge at midnight, guzzle down unhealthy drinks, and munch on salty, processed snacks. Very few drink three glasses of milk and eat several servings of fruits and vegetables each day, as doctors advise.

In 2019, only about 13 percent of U.S. high school students ate the recommended three or more servings of vegetables a day. That is even less than four years earlier (17 percent). Indeed, some (6 percent of the girls and 9 percent of the boys) ate no vegetables at all in the previous week (Merlo et al., 2020). (Fried potatoes do not count.)

One reason for their eating patterns is that hormones affect the circadian rhythm of their appetites; another reason is that they avoid family dinners if they can. This aspect of independence is counterproductive, since family dinners reduce adolescent stress more than increase it (Armstrong-Carter & Telzer, 2020).

Deficiencies of iron, calcium, zinc, and other minerals are especially frequent during adolescence. Because menstruation depletes iron, anemia is more common among adolescent girls than among any other age or sex group.

Boys everywhere may also be iron-deficient, especially if they engage in physical labor or intensive sports: Muscles need iron for growth and strength. Yet, in developed as well as developing nations, adolescents spurn iron-rich foods in favor of chips, sweets, and fries.

Similarly, although the daily recommended intake of calcium for adolescents is 1,300 milligrams, the average U.S. teen consumes less than 500 milligrams a day. About half of adult bone mass is acquired from ages 10 to 20, which means that many contemporary teenagers will develop osteoporosis (fragile bones), a major cause of disability, injury, and death in late adulthood.

Cultural norms encourage poor nutrition. For example, many high schools allow children to leave school for lunch, and fast-food establishments cluster around high schools, often with extra seating that encourages them to socialize (Walker et al., 2014).

ROBERT ALEXANDER/ARCHIVE PHOTOS/GETTY IMAGES

Next Stop: Masterpieces of the Fifteenth Century These British teens eat chips and soda before they enter the National Gallery in London. Twenty-first century fast food is causing an epidemic of diet deficiencies and disordered eating among youth in every nation.

◆◆ OBSERVATION QUIZ
Conformity among adolescents may be imposed by adults or chosen by teens. One example of each is evident here — what are they? (see answer, page 307) ↑

body image
A person's idea of how their body looks.

Fast-food options proliferate especially if high schools have large populations of low-income students, who are most at risk for obesity and poor health. This problem may be getting worse, not better (Sanchez-Vaznaugh et al., 2019). Price further influences food choices, especially for adolescents: Unhealthy calories are cheaper than healthy ones.

For all these reasons, obesity is increasing. In 2003, only three U.S. states (Kentucky, Mississippi, Tennessee) had high school obesity rates at 15 percent or more. In 2017, 42 states did (MMWR, June 15, 2018).

BODY IMAGE

One reason for poor nutrition among teenagers is that increasing reliance on photos sent via social media increases anxiety about **body image**—that is, the perception of how one's body looks. As one book on body image begins, each person's body "feels, conceives, imagines, represents, evaluates, loves, hates, and manipulates itself" (Cuzzolaro & Fassino, 2018, p. v).

This is true lifelong, but since every part of the body changes dramatically in adolescence, many teenagers have not yet accepted their appearance. Instead, many dwell on how they look, exaggerating and misperceiving. For example, 60 percent of U.S. high school girls are trying to lose weight, yet only one-sixth are overweight (Johns et al., 2020).

One problem is that almost no one's body looks like the pictures in magazines, movies, and media that are marketed to teenagers. Social media, presenting other teens at their most attractive, may lead to depression, body shame, and poor eating habits (Rodgers et al., 2020; Salomon & Brown, 2019).

Eating Disorders

Dissatisfaction with body image can be dangerous, even deadly. Many teenagers, mostly girls, eat erratically or ingest drugs (especially diet pills) to lose weight; others, mostly boys, take steroids to increase muscle mass.

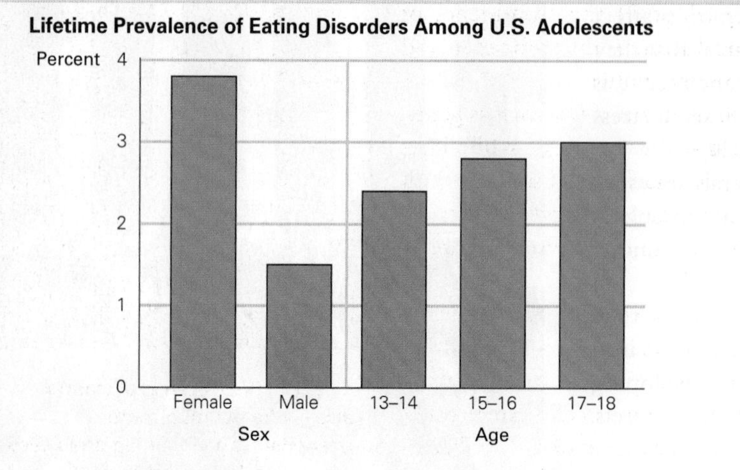

FIGURE 9.4 Have You Ever . . . ? This chart shows lifetime prevalence of eating disorders. Almost all of the adults, and many of the 17- to 18-year-olds, have recovered from an eating disorder. Thus, the 0.2 percent increase from age 15 to 17 suggests that only 1 adolescent in 500 developed a new eating disorder during the final years of high school. That is reassuring, but two facts from this chart are troubling: (1) Almost 1 in 40 young teens (age 13–14) already had an eating disorder, and (2) the prevalence for the oldest teens is higher than for the adults of all ages. That suggests that the rate of eating disorders is increasing.

anorexia nervosa
An eating disorder characterized by self-starvation. Affected individuals voluntarily undereat and often overexercise, depriving their vital organs of nutrition. Anorexia can be fatal.

bulimia nervosa
An eating disorder characterized by binge eating and subsequent purging, usually by induced vomiting and/or use of laxatives.

binge eating disorder
Frequent episodes of uncontrollable overeating to the point that the stomach hurts. Usually the person feels shame and guilt but is unable to stop.

primary sex characteristics
The parts of the body that are directly involved in reproduction, including the vagina, uterus, ovaries, testicles, and penis.

secondary sex characteristics
Physical traits that are not directly involved in reproduction but that indicate sexual maturity, such as a man's beard and a woman's breasts.

Eating disorders are rare in childhood but increase dramatically at puberty, accompanied by distorted body image, food obsession, and depression. Many adolescents switch from obsessive dieting and overexercising to overeating. Although girls are most vulnerable, boys are at risk, too, especially if they aspire to be pop stars or train as wrestlers. (See Figure 9.4.)

When distorted body image and excessive dieting result in severe weight loss, that may be **anorexia nervosa**. Fewer than 1 in 100 girls develop anorexia, but those who do dramatically restrict their calorie intake and have a destructive, distorted body image. Their BMI may fall below 17 in cases of mild anorexia or 15 in extreme cases, but clinicians must be alert to any sudden weight loss or weight that is "less than that minimally expected" (American Psychiatric Association, 2013).

About three times as common as anorexia is **bulimia nervosa**, when a person overeats compulsively, consuming thousands of calories within an hour or two, and then purges through vomiting or laxatives. People with this disorder risk damage to their gastrointestinal system and cardiac arrest from electrolyte imbalance (Mehler, 2018).

A disorder newly recognized in the DSM-5 is **binge eating disorder**. Some adolescents periodically and compulsively overeat, quickly consuming large amounts of ice cream, cake, or snack food until their stomachs hurt. The overeating is typically done in private, at least weekly for several months. The sufferer does not purge (hence this is not bulimia) but feels out of control, distressed, and depressed.

Sexual Maturation

Sexuality is multidimensional, complicated, and variable—not unlike human development overall. Here, we consider biological changes at puberty and some cohort variations. Other aspects of adolescent sexuality and gender identity are discussed in Chapter 10.

SEXUAL CHARACTERISTICS

The body characteristics that are directly involved in conception and pregnancy are called **primary sex characteristics**. During puberty, every primary sex organ (the ovaries, the uterus, the penis, and the testes) increases dramatically in size and matures in function. Reproduction becomes possible after puberty, peak fertility is at about age 17.

While primary sex characteristics mature, **secondary sex characteristics** develop. Those do not directly affect reproduction (hence, *secondary*) but signify masculinity or femininity.

One secondary characteristic is body shape. At puberty males widen at the shoulders and grow about 5 inches taller than females, while girls widen at the hips and develop breasts. Those female curves are often considered signs of womanhood, but neither breasts nor wide hips are required for conception; thus, they are secondary, not primary.

The pattern of hair growth at the scalp line (widow's peak), the prominence of the larynx (Adam's apple), and several other anatomical features differ for men and women; all are secondary sex characteristics that few people notice.

Facial and body hair increases in both sexes, affected by hormones as well as genes. Girls often pluck or wax any facial hair they see and shave their legs, while boys may proudly grow sideburns, soul patches, chinstraps, moustaches, and so on—with specifics dependent on culture and cohort. Hair on the head is cut and styled to be spikey, flat, curled, long, short, or shaved. Hair is far more than a growth characteristic; it is a display of sexuality, a mark of independence.

Secondary sex characteristics are important psychologically, if not biologically. Breasts are an obvious example. Many adolescent girls buy "minimizer," "maximizer," "training," or "shaping" bras in the hope that their breasts will conform to an idealized body image. During the same years, many overweight boys are horrified to notice swelling around their nipples—a temporary result of the erratic hormones of early puberty.

The significance of breasts as a characteristic of men or women is evident in transgender people. They often choose hormones and surgery to make their breasts conform to their gender (Patel et al., 2020).

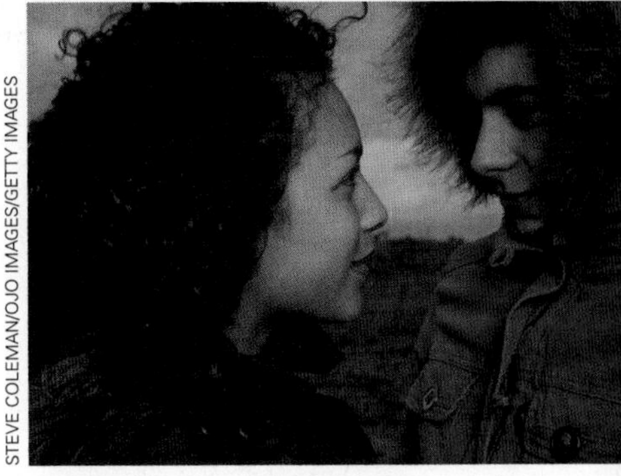

STEVE COLEMAN/OJO IMAGES/GETTY IMAGES

Everywhere Glancing, staring, and—when emotions are overwhelming—averting one's eyes are part of the universal language of love. Although the rate of intercourse among teenagers is lower than it was, passion is expressed in simple words, touches, and, as shown here, the eyes on a cold day.

Sexual Activity

Primary and secondary sex characteristics such as menarche, spermarche, hair, and body shape are not the only evidence of sex hormones. Fantasizing, flirting, hand-holding, staring, standing, sitting, walking, displaying, and touching are all done in particular ways. Cultures shape thoughts and behaviors into enjoyable fantasies, shameful obsessions, frightening impulses, or actual contact (see Figure 9.5).

Emotions regarding sexual experience, like the rest of puberty, are strongly influenced by social norms that indicate what is expected at what age. Recently in the United States, one study found that girls who have sex early in adolescence are likely to be depressed, but those who have sex as older adolescents tend to be quite happy (Golden et al., 2016).

Everyone is influenced by hormones and society, biology and culture. All adolescents have sexual interests that they did not previously have (biology), and this propels teenagers in some nations to do things that teenagers in other nations would never do (culture).

In many nations including the United States, adolescent female rates of sexual activity are now almost even with male rates. For example, among high school seniors, about 56 percent of the girls and 58 percent of the boys have had sexual intercourse, with most of them sexually active in the past three months. A slightly more notable gender difference among high school students is in the number of partners: 7 percent of the girls and 10 percent of the boys have had four or more partners (Johns et al., 2020).

Over the past two decades in the United States, every gender, ethnic, and age group is *less* sexually active than the previous cohort. Between 1993 and 2019, intercourse experience among Hispanic students was down 27 percent (to 42 percent); (Johns et al., 2020) among Black high school students down 42 percent (to 42 percent); among non-Hispanic White students down 18 percent (to 38 percent) (Merlo et al., 2020). Rates among Asian Americans are similar to Whites if their mothers were born in the United States, but much lower if they were born in Asia (Kim et al., 2020).

BARBARA SMALLER/CARTOONSTOCK.COM

"I think I'll be more relaxed once my secondary sex characteristics kick in."

Brain Before Body Hormones affect thoughts, but visible signs reveal maturation.

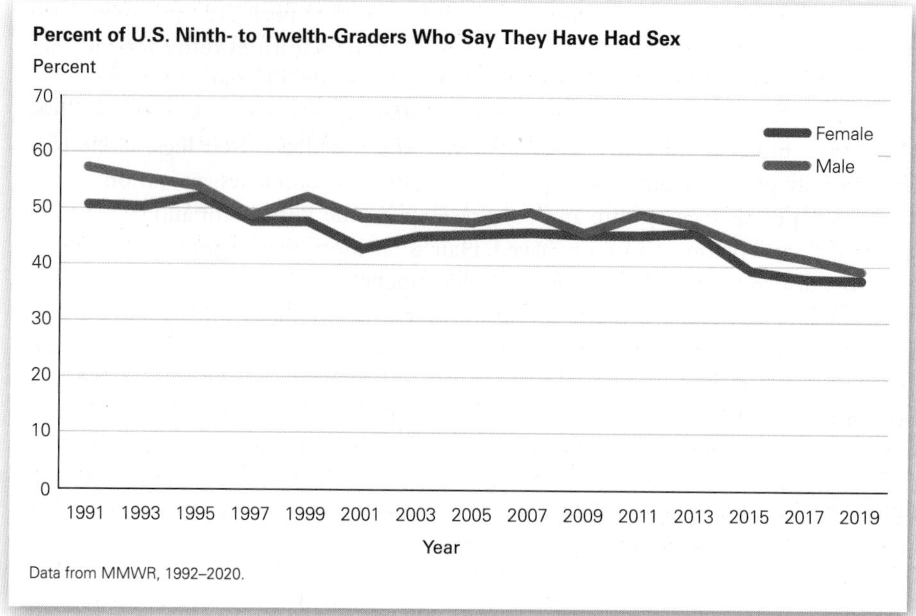

FIGURE 9.5 Boys and Girls Together Boys tend to be somewhat more sexually experienced than girls during the high school years, but since the Youth Risk Behavior Survey began in 1991, the overall trend has been toward equality in rates of sexual activity.

child sexual abuse
Any erotic activity that arouses an adult and excites, shames, or confuses a child, whether or not the victim protests and whether or not genital contact is involved.

sexually transmitted infection (STI)
A disease spread by sexual contact; includes syphilis, gonorrhea, genital herpes, chlamydia, and HIV.

SEXUAL ABUSE

Child sexual abuse is defined as any sexual activity (including fondling and photographing) between a juvenile and an adult. Abuse of younger children gathers headlines, but adolescents are, by far, the most frequent victims. Virtually every adolescent problem, including unwanted pregnancy, drug abuse, bulimia, and suicide, is more frequent if adolescents are sexually abused.

In poor nations, although solid numbers are unknown for obvious reasons, it is apparent that millions of girls in their early teens are forced into marriage or prostitution each year. Some believe they are helping their families by earning money to support them; others are literally sold by their families (Montgomery, 2015).

Trafficking is not the most common form of sexual abuse in the United States. Instead, most adolescent victims know the abuser very well because he (or less often, she) is a parent, stepparent, older sibling, or uncle. Young adolescents who are sexually exploited tend to become adults who fear sex, with higher rates of virtually every developmental problem, including repeated abuse (Pittenger et al., 2018).

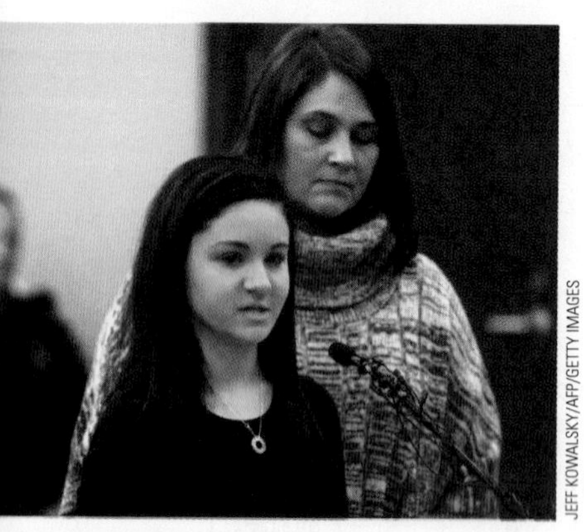
JEFF KOWALSKY/AFP/GETTY IMAGES

You, Too? Millions were shocked to learn that Larry Nassar, a physician for gymnasts training for the Olympics and at Michigan State University, sexually abused more than 150 young women. Among the survivors was Kaylee Lorenz, shown here addressing Nassar in court. Nassar was convicted of multiple counts of sexual assault and sentenced to 40 to 175 years in prison, but his victims wonder why no one stopped him. The president of Michigan State University resigned in disgrace; many others are still in office.

Girls are the most common victims, but boys may also be sexually abused, a direct attack on their fledgling identity. Disclosure of past abuse is particularly difficult for men. Among those whose abuse was verified, girls are more likely to experience problems with their physical health, and boys with their mental health (Daigneault et al., 2017).

After puberty, although sometimes abusers are parents, coaches, religious leaders, or other authorities, often they are other teenagers (Gewirtz-Meydan & Finkelhor, 2020). Many high school girls (13 percent) and boys (4 percent) have been kissed, touched, or forced to have sex within a dating relationship when they did not want to (Johns et al., 2020). Chapter 10 discusses sex education; teenagers have much to learn.

SEXUALLY TRANSMITTED INFECTIONS

Teen pregnancy and sexual abuse are less common in the twenty-first century than earlier (Finkelhor et al., 2014). However, another problem of teenage sex shows no signs of abating.

A **sexually transmitted infection (STI)** (sometimes called a *sexually transmitted disease [STD]*) is any infection transmitted through sexual contact. Worldwide,

sexually active teenagers have higher rates of the most common STIs—*gonorrhea, genital herpes*, and *chlamydia*—than do sexually active people of any other age group.

In the United States, half of all new STIs occur in people ages 15 to 25, even though this age group has less than one-fourth of the sexually active people (Satterwhite et al., 2013). Rates are particularly high among sexually active adolescents, ages 15 to 19.

Biology provides one reason: Pubescent girls are more likely to catch an STI than fully developed women are, probably because adult women have more vaginal secretions that reduce infections. Further, if symptoms appear, teens are less likely to alert their partners or seek treatment unless pain requires it, so STIs spread.

A survey of adolescents in a U.S. pediatric emergency department found that half of the teenagers (average age 15) were sexually active and 20 percent of those had an STI—although that was not why they came for medical help (Miller et al., 2015).

There are hundreds of STIs. Chlamydia is the most frequently reported one; it often begins without symptoms, yet it can cause permanent infertility. Worse is *human papillomavirus (HPV)*, which has no immediate consequences but increases the risk of cancer in adult men and women.

Fortunately, in about 1990, an effective vaccine against HPV was developed that should be given before sexual activity. However, less than half of all U.S. adolescents are fully immunized (Hirth, 2019). Among the reasons: Some state health departments do not promote it, the vaccine was originally recommended only for girls (because HPV was most closely associated with cervical cancer), and full immunization requires three doses (many teens do not see a medical professional regularly).

◆◆ Especially for Health Practitioners
How might you encourage adolescents to seek treatment for STIs? (see response, page 307)

DATA CONNECTIONS: Major Sexually Transmitted Infections: Some Basics offers more information about the causes, symptoms, and rates of various STIs.
Achieve

what have you learned?

1. What is the pattern of growth in adolescent bodies?
2. What complications result from the sequence of growth (weight/height/muscles)?
3. Why are many teenagers deficient in iron and calcium?
4. Why are many adolescents unhappy with their appearance?
5. What are the differences among the three eating disorders explained here?
6. What are the effects of child sexual abuse?
7. Among sexually active people, why do adolescents have more STIs than adults?

Adolescent Cognition

Brain maturation, additional years of schooling, moral challenges, increased independence, and intense conversations all occur between ages 11 and 18. The result is that adolescent cognition differs from childhood cognition in many ways.

Egocentrism

During puberty, young people center on themselves, in part because body changes heighten self-consciousness while social awareness makes them aware of social norms

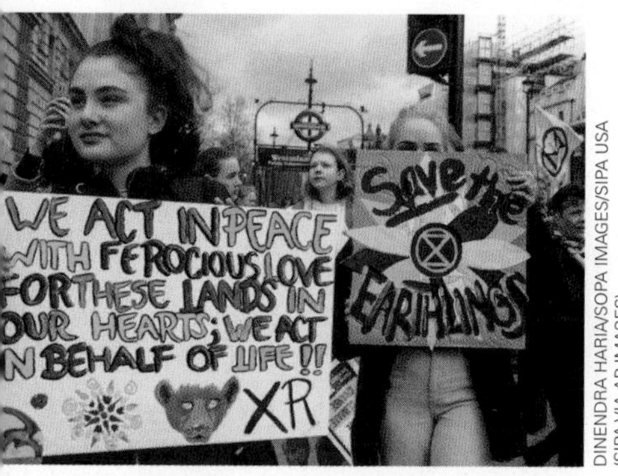

DINENDRA HARIA/SOPA IMAGES/SIPA USA (SIPA VIA AP IMAGES)

Ferocious Earthlings It's hard not to admire the passion of adolescent cognition, not only on climate change, but also on drugs, religion, patriotism, sex, and many other issues. Admiration does not always mean agreement, but that's why adolescents and adults need each other.

OBSERVATION QUIZ
What is the meaning of the four symbols on the bottom of the "ferocious" poster? (see answer, page 307) ↑

adolescent egocentrism
A characteristic of adolescent thinking that leads young people (ages 10 to 13) to focus on themselves to the exclusion of others.

imaginary audience
The other people who, in an adolescent's egocentric belief, are watching and taking note of their appearance, ideas, and behavior. This belief makes many teenagers very self-conscious.

THINK CRITICALLY: How should you judge the validity of the idea of adolescent egocentrism?

(Guzman & Nishina, 2014). Consequently, young adolescents grapple with conflicting feelings about themselves and others, examine details of their own growth, and think about possibilities.

Adolescent egocentrism—when adolescents focus on themselves and on what others think of them—was first described by David Elkind (1967). He found that adolescents regard themselves as much more special, admired, or hated than other people consider them to be. Egocentric adolescents have limited comprehension of others' points of view.

For example, few girls are attracted to boys with pimples and braces, but one boy's eagerness to be seen as growing up kept him from realizing this. According to his older sister:

> Now in the 8th grade, my brother has this idea that all the girls are looking at him in school. He got his first pimple about three months ago. I told him to wash it with my face soap but he refused, saying, "Not until I go to school to show it off." He called the dentist, begging him to approve his braces now instead of waiting for a year. The perfect gifts for him have changed from action figures to a bottle of cologne, a chain, and a fitted baseball hat like the rappers wear.
>
> *[adapted from E., personal communication]*

Egocentrism may lead adolescents to interpret everyone else's behavior as a judgment on them. A stranger's frown or a teacher's critique can make a teenager conclude that "No one likes me," and then deduce that "I am unlovable" or even "I can't leave the house."

More positive casual reactions—a smile from a store clerk or an extra-big hug from a younger brother—could lead to "I am great" or "Everyone loves me." When a famous singer suddenly died, one of my students complained that everyone cared about her but no one would care if he died. "I might be just as wonderful as she was, but nobody knows."

Because adolescents are egocentric, their emotions may not be grounded in reality. A study of 1,310 Dutch and Belgian adolescents found that, for many of them, self-esteem and loneliness were closely tied to their *perception* of how others saw them, not to their actual popularity or acceptance among their peers. Gradually, after about age 15, some realized what others actually thought. Then they became less depressed (Vanhalst et al., 2013).

RUMINATION

Egocentrism is one reason for *rumination*, which is thinking obsessively about self-focused concerns. Some adolescents go over their problems via phone, text, conversation, social media, and private, quiet self-talk (as when they lie in bed, unable to sleep), thinking about each nuance of everything they have done, are doing, might do, and should have done.

Some young adolescents worry so much about what they might say or do that they are fearful of doing anything. Excessive rumination in early adolescence may lead to depression later on (Krause et al., 2018).

Others act impulsively without thinking, blurting out words that they soon regret and taking risks that they later realize were foolish. Then shame and despair can be overwhelming, again out of proportion to the actual event. Prison administrators know that rates of suicide are higher for jailed adolescent boys than for other prisoners (Tartaro, 2019). Impulsive action is one reason for both the crime and the suicide.

THE IMAGINARY AUDIENCE

Egocentrism creates an **imaginary audience** in the minds of many adolescents. They believe that they are at center stage, with all eyes on them, and they imagine how others might react.

One of my students remembered, "If I ran out of hairspray I would refuse to go out because I wouldn't be caught dead outside with flat bangs. . . . I just knew in my mind that everyone would know I ran out of spray and everyone would laugh." Her mother tried to make her leave the house. She sobbed, "Never" (IP, personal reflection).

Another woman recalled:

> When I was 14 and in the 8th grade, I received an award at the end-of-year school assembly. Walking across the stage, I lost my footing and stumbled in front of the entire student body. To be clear, this was not falling flat on one's face, spraining an ankle, or knocking over the school principal—it was a small misstep noticeable only to those in the audience who were paying close attention. As I rushed off the stage, my heart pounded with embarrassment and self-consciousness, and weeks of speculation about the consequence of this missed step were set into motion. There were tears and loss of sleep. Did my friends notice? Would they stop wanting to hang out with me? Would a reputation for clumsiness follow me to high school?
>
> *[Somerville, 2013, p. 121]*

This woman became an expert on adolescent thought. Her research and her personal experience made her aware that "adolescents are hyperaware of others' evaluations and feel they are under constant scrutiny by an imaginary audience" (Somerville, 2013, p. 124).

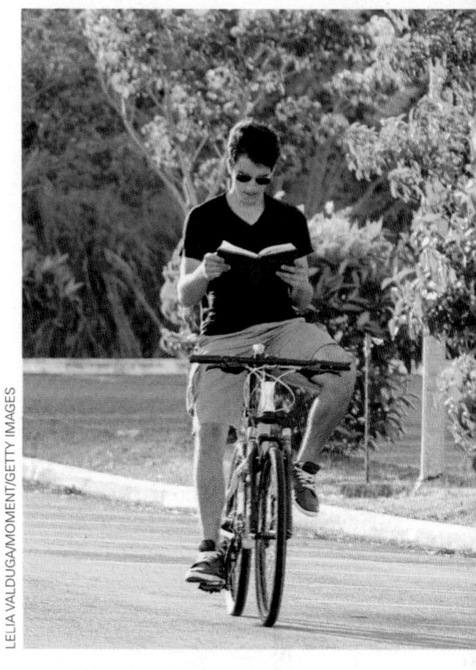

LELIA VALDUGA/MOMENT/GETTY IMAGES

Oblivious? When you see a teenager with purple hair or a nose ring, or riding a bicycle and reading, do you think they do not imagine what others think?

FABLES

Egocentrism also leads to a **personal fable**, the belief that one is unique, destined to have a heroic, fabled, legendary life. Some 12-year-olds plan to be basketball stars, or billionaires.

The personal fable can extend to their entire generation. A worldwide school strike led by high school students in 2019 included thousands who, in both adolescent egocentrism and the personal fable, agreed with one 16-year-old boy in Birmingham who said:

> We are at the point that in 12 to 20 years the effects of climate change are going to be irreversible. The only way to change it is through the younger generation because the older generation don't really care.
>
> *[BBC News, February 15, 2019]*

personal fable
An aspect of adolescent egocentrism characterized by an adolescent's belief that their thoughts, feelings, and experiences are unique or are more wonderful or more awful than anyone else's.

invincibility fable
An adolescent's egocentric conviction that they cannot be overcome or even harmed by anything that might defeat a normal mortal, such as unprotected sex, drug abuse, or high-speed driving.

The personal fable may coexist with the **invincibility fable**, the idea that death will not occur unless it is destined. Some adolescents believe that fast driving, unprotected sex, or addictive drugs will spare them. Believing that one is invincible removes any attempt at self-control, because personal control is neither needed nor possible (Lin, 2016).

The personal fable may include the belief that they might come to a tragic early end. In one study, teens estimated that their chance of dying before age 20 was 1 in 5. In fact, the odds are less than 1 in 1,000.

Even those at highest risk (African American males in center cities) survive to age 20 more than 99 times in 100. Sadly, if teens think that they will die young, they might risk jail, HIV, drug addiction, and so on (Haynie et al., 2014). If they know someone who died, their fatalistic response might be "His number was up," unaware that a self-fulfilling prophecy became a nail in the coffin.

Similarly, teens post comments on Snapchat, Instagram, Facebook, and so on, expecting others to understand, laugh, admire, or sympathize. Their imaginary audience is other teenagers, not parents, teachers, college admission officers, or future employers, all of whom might have another interpretation (boyd, 2014).

Some have piercings, shaved heads, tattoos, and torn jeans, all because they imagine the reactions of others. For the same reason they resist suits and ties, or dresses and pearls.

Formal Operational Thought

The egocentrism of adolescence is sometimes counterbalanced by logic that is detached from personal experience. Piaget described **formal operational thought**, when adolescents can reason abstractly, with "assumptions that have no necessary relation to reality" (Piaget, 1950/2001, p. 163).

formal operational thought
In Piaget's theory, the fourth and final stage of cognitive development, characterized by more systematic logical thinking and by the ability to understand and systematically manipulate abstract concepts.

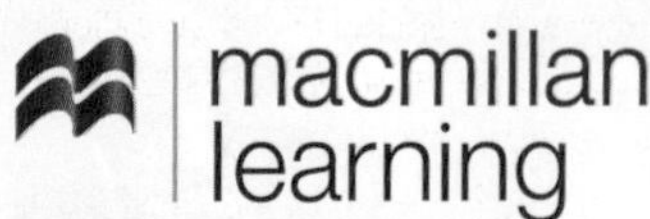

VIDEO: The Balance Scale Task shows children of various ages completing the task and gives you an opportunity to try it as well.

PIAGET'S EXPERIMENTS

Piaget and his colleagues devised many tasks to assess formal operational thought (Inhelder & Piaget, 1958/2013b). They found that "in contrast to concrete operational children, formal operational adolescents imagine all possible determinants . . . [and] systematically vary the factors one by one, observe the results correctly, keep track of the results, and draw the appropriate conclusions" (P. Miller, 2011, p. 57).

One famous experiment (diagrammed in Figure 9.6) required balancing a scale by hooking weights onto the scale's arms. To master this task, a person must recognize the reciprocity of distance and weight.

Balancing was not understood by the 3- to 5-year-olds; when tested, they just played with the weights. By age 7, children understood the concept but balanced the scale only by putting identical weights on each arm: They didn't consider distance from the center.

By age 10, children experimented, using trial and error, not logic. Finally, at about age 13 or 14, some children hypothesized about reciprocity. Formal thought led them to realize that a heavy weight close to the center can be counterbalanced with a light weight far from the center on the other side (Piaget & Inhelder, 1972).

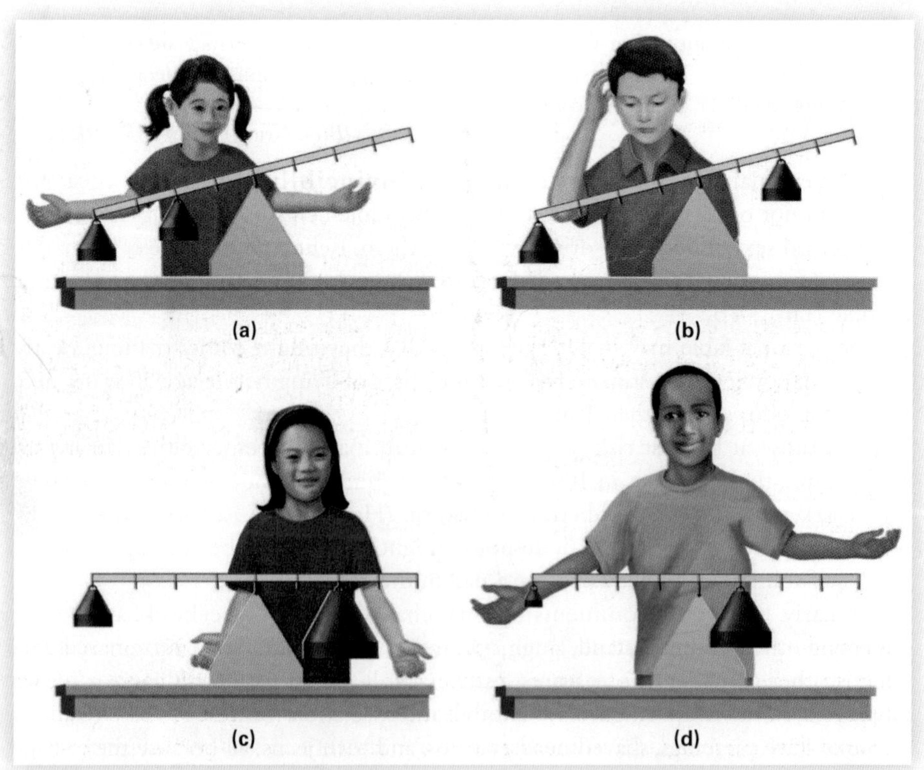

FIGURE 9.6 **How to Balance a Scale** Piaget's balance-scale test of formal reasoning, as it is attempted by (a) a 4-year-old, (b) a 7-year-old, (c) a 10-year-old, and (d) a 14-year-old. The key to balancing the scale is to make weight times distance from the center equal on both sides of the center; the realization of that principle requires formal operational thought.

HYPOTHETICAL-DEDUCTIVE REASONING

One hallmark of formal operational thought is the capacity to think of possibility. "Here and now" is less interesting than "there and then," "long, long ago," "some future day," and "never." As Piaget said:

> The adolescent . . . thinks beyond the present and forms theories about everything, delighting especially in considerations of that which is not.
>
> *[Piaget, 1950/2001, p. 163]*

Adolescents are therefore primed for **hypothetical thought**, reasoning about *if–then* propositions. Consider the following question.

> If all mammals can walk,
> And whales are mammals,
> Can whales walk?

Children answer "No!" They know that whales swim, not walk; the logic escapes them. Some adolescents answer "Yes." They understand the conditional *if*, and therefore they can use logic to interpret the phrase "if all mammals."

> *Possibility* no longer appears merely as an extension of an empirical situation or of action actually performed. Instead, it is *reality* that is now secondary to *possibility*.
>
> *[Inhelder & Piaget, 1958/2013b, p. 251; emphasis in original]*

Hypothetical thought transforms perceptions, not necessarily for the better. Adolescents might criticize everything from their mother's spaghetti (it's not *al dente*) to the Gregorian calendar (it's not the Chinese or Jewish one). They criticize what *is* because they hypothesize what might be. Added to that is a growing awareness of other families and cultures: History, anthropology, and international studies become intriguing.

In developing the capacity to think hypothetically, by age 14 or so adolescents become more capable of **deductive reasoning**, or *top-down reasoning*, which begins with an idea or premise and then uses logic to draw conclusions. In the example above, "if all mammals can walk" is a premise.

By contrast, **inductive reasoning**, or *bottom-up reasoning*, predominates during the concrete operational thought. Children accumulate facts and experiences (the knowledge base) to aid their thinking. Since they know whales cannot walk, knowledge trumps logic.

In essence, a child's reasoning goes like this: "This creature waddles and quacks. Ducks waddle and quack. Therefore, this must be a duck." This is inductive: It progresses from particulars ("waddles" and "quacks") to a general conclusion ("a duck"). By contrast, deduction progresses from general to specific: "If it's a duck, it will waddle and quack."

hypothetical thought
Reasoning that includes propositions and possibilities that may not reflect reality.

deductive reasoning
Reasoning from a general statement, premise, or principle, through logical steps, to figure out (deduce) specifics. (Also called *top-down reasoning*.)

inductive reasoning
Reasoning from one or more specific experiences or facts to reach (induce) a general conclusion. (Also called *bottom-up reasoning*.)

Especially for Natural Scientists
Some ideas that were once universally accepted, such as the belief that the sun moved around Earth, have been disproved. Is it a failure of inductive or deductive reasoning that leads to false conclusions? (see response, page 307)

BAC TOTRONG/DAILY NEWS VIA AP IMAGES

Fire Your Trebuchet! Denis Mujanovic, Anna Dim, Ahmed Kamaludeen, and Ghader Asal are all high school students participating in the Western Kentucky Physics Olympics. Here they compete with their carefully designed trebuchets, a kind of catapult related to the slingshot.

Dual Processing

Remember that Piaget described cognition as a sequence of four stages, from sensorimotor to preoperational to concrete to formal. Others disagree, especially about adolescent cognition. They suggest that adolescent thought does not develop as a shift from one type of thinking (concrete) to another (formal) but splits into two parallel processes.

Dual Processing

System 1	System 2
Intuitive	Analytic
Hot	Cold
Implicit	Explicit
Creative	Factual
Gist	Specific
Experiential	Rational
Qualitative	Quantitative
Contextualized	Decontextualized

FIGURE 9.7 Two Modes Each pair describes two modes of thought. Although researchers who use each pair differ in what they emphasize, all see two contrasting ways to think.

dual processing
The notion that two networks exist within the human brain, one for emotional processing of stimuli and one for analytical reasoning.

intuitive thought
Thought that arises from an emotion or a hunch, beyond rational explanation, and is influenced by past experiences and cultural assumptions.

analytic thought
Thought that results from analysis, such as a systematic ranking of pros and cons, risks and consequences, possibilities and facts. Analytic thought depends on logic and rationality.

Imagine the adolescent as a pianist. The right hand plays the high notes and the left the low notes. An experienced pianist uses both hands together, but in the beginning the right hand plays a melody, unaccompanied by the lower chords. Other times only the loud, low, chords are played. The adolescent is that one-handed piano player.

The idea is that thinking occurs in two ways, called **dual processing** (see Figure 9.7) (Evans, 2018; Powell et al., 2019). Early in this chapter you read about the growth discrepancy between the limbic system and the prefrontal cortex, and you just read about the contrast between egocentrism and formal, abstract logic. Both those suggest two processes of thought. Other terms for this pair are systems one and two, fast and slow, hot and cold, emotional and rational.

Here we use the terms *intuitive* and *analytic*:

- **Intuitive thought** begins with a belief, assumption, or general rule (called a *heuristic*) rather than logic. Intuition is quick and powerful; it feels "right."
- **Analytic thought** is the formal, logical, hypothetical-deductive thinking described by Piaget. It involves rational analysis of many factors whose interactions must be calculated, as in the scale-balancing problem.

To test yourself on intuitive and analytic thinking, answer the following:

1. A bat and a ball cost $1.10 in total. The bat costs $1 more than the ball. How much does the ball cost?
2. If it takes 5 minutes for 5 machines to make 5 widgets, how long would it take 100 machines to make 100 widgets?
3. In a lake, there is a patch of lily pads. Every day the patch doubles in size. If it takes 48 days for the patch to cover the entire lake, how long would it take for the patch to cover half the lake?

[from Gervais & Norenzayan, 2012, p. 494]

Answers are on page 291. As you see, the quick, intuitive responses may be wrong.

One team demonstrated dual processing when they asked participants to report on one half of information and ignore the other half, both presented at the same time (Aïte et al., 2018). They first presented an emotionless task, the *Stroop test*, which asks participants to say the color of words that spell another color. For example, they must say blue when the word RED is written in blue. This is difficult, but children and adolescents become better as they grow older.

After this "cool" (i.e., analytic) Stroop test, the same participants were given a "hot" task: They were supposed to report the emotion they saw on a face, ignoring the written word presented with the emotion. The word *angry* might accompany a smiling face.

On the hot task, adolescents did worse than either children or emerging adults. In other words, dual processing meant that unemotional processing (cool) gradually improved with age, but emotional processing (hot) created confusion and mistakes, more in adolescence than at younger ages (Aïte et al., 2018).

AGE AND TWO PROCESSES

When the two modes of thinking conflict, people of all ages sometimes use one and sometimes the other. To use the piano metaphor, a novice player may uses just one hand. The first impulse of most people is to favor the melody without the chords. That is easier: We are all "predictably irrational" (Ariely, 2010).

Increased myelination reduces reaction time, so adolescents act with lightning speed. They are "fast and furious" intuitive thinkers, unlike their teachers and parents,

who can add slower, analytic thinking. No wonder "people who interact with adolescents often are frustrated by the mercurial quality of their decisions" (Hartley & Somerville, 2015, p. 112).

ANSWERS	Intuitive	Analytic
1.	10 cents	5 cents
2.	100 minutes	5 minutes
3.	24 days	47 days

Interestingly, as adolescents become more aware of structural, social reasons affecting the phenomena they see, they also become more aware of stereotypes and more influenced by them. For some stereotypes, adolescents actually regress, with younger children better able to consider individual variations instead of overgeneralizations.

For example, one stereotype that might regress is *gender intensification*, such as believing that certain jobs are best filled by men and others by women. Adolescents are more likely to endorse this stereotype than children are. According to one study, increased gender stereotyping was temporary, evident in early adolescence until about age 15, and then reduced (Klaczynski et al., 2020).

Many studies have found that neither age nor intelligence necessarily makes an adolescent more logical (Kail, 2013). Having a higher IQ does not advance cognition as much as having more life experience, statistical knowledge, and linguistic proficiency, each of which advances analytic thought. As one team of researchers concludes, the adolescent brain is capable of logic, but sometimes "social variables are better predictors . . . than cognitive abilities" (Klaczynski & Felmban, 2014, pp. 103–104).

PREFERRING EMOTIONS

Why not use formal operational thought? Adolescents learn the scientific method in school, so they know the importance of empirical evidence and deductive reasoning. But they do not always think like scientists. Why?

Dozens of experiments and extensive theorizing have found some answers (Albert & Steinberg, 2011; Blakemore, 2018). Essentially, logic is more difficult than intuition: It requires questioning ideas that are comforting and familiar, and it might lead to conclusions that are rejected by friends and family.

THINK CRITICALLY: When might an emotional response be better than an analytic one?

When people of any age reach an emotional conclusion (sometimes called a "gut feeling"), they resist changing their minds. It is more comfortable to endorse what other people think than to analyze the issue; analysis might lead to an unpopular conclusion.

This is especially apparent when teenagers want to rebel against adults. Adolescents may be quick to flout tradition or suspect authority (Klaczynski, 2011). They may say "it's my body" to justify piercings, shaved heads, tattoos, and torn jeans, for instance. They might react before analysis helps them consider the circumstances (see A Case to Study).

A CASE TO STUDY

Biting the Policeman

Remember from the piano metaphor that experience and practice may be needed before a person can harmonize the chords and melody. Might suspicion of authority lead to impulsive action unless context is taken into account?

In midday, one of my students, herself only 18 years old, was walking in the Bronx with her younger cousin. A police officer stopped them, asking why the cousin was not in school. He patted down the boy and asked him for identification. That cousin was visiting from another state; he did not have an ID.

My student had done well in a college class on U.S. government. When the officer began to "stop and frisk" her cousin, she reacted emotionally, using what she had heard to justify her intuitive reaction. She told the cop he was violating the Constitution.

The officer grabbed her cousin. She bit his hand. He arrested her. After weeks in jail (Rikers Island), she was brought before a judge. Perhaps those weeks, plus a meeting with her public defender, activated her analytic mind. She had prepared a written apology; she read it out loud; the officer did not press charges.

I appeared in court on her behalf; the judge released her to me. She was shivering; the first thing I did was put a warm coat around her.

This was dual processing. In her education, my student had gained a formal understanding of the laws regarding police authority. However, her emotions overwhelmed her logic. She intuitively defended her cousin without analyzing the impact.

It is easy to conclude that more mature thought processes are wiser. The judge thought that my perspective was a needed corrective. Certainly the student should not have bitten the officer. But the entire incident, and the NYPD "stop and frisk" policy in effect at the time, shows that the authorities do not understand the adolescent mind. My student had learned a heuristic in childhood: Protect your family. In the heat of the moment, she reacted emotionally.

She is not alone in that. Do you remember something you did as a teenager that, with the wisdom of time and maturity, you would not do now?

WHAT ARE YOUR PRIORITIES?

A developmental approach to cognition seeks to understand how people think at every age. Adolescents are capable of logic, yet they make foolish choices. Why?

Perhaps adolescents are not illogical; they may have emotional goals that are not the goals of adults. Parents want healthy, long-lived children, so they blame faulty reasoning when adolescents risk their lives. Judges want law-abiding citizens, so they punish those who break the law. Adolescents, however, value the warm glow of friendship and the thrill of rebellion, more than the long lives and legal action.

The problem may be that adolescents act too quickly; they do not "think it over" or "sleep on it" or "count to ten"—all are rubrics that adults use to allow analytic thought. Adolescent hormones and brains are more attuned to immediate admiration from peers than to long-term consequences (Blakemore, 2018).

There is merit in adolescent thought. Our species needs young adults to break away from their original family and find mates of their own. Impulsive thought may help teenagers do so (Hartley & Somerville, 2015).

That may be why some adolescents are thrilled to ride with friends in a speeding car driven by an admired peer, or to take diet pills because having a thin body that others admire is more important than the distant risk of heart disease. Adults need to understand the impulses as well as prevent the dangers.

The systematic, analytic thought that Piaget described is slow and costly, not fast and frugal, wasting precious time when a young person seeks action. Adolescents do not want to weigh alternatives and think of how they will feel in middle age. Some risks are taken impulsively, some reactions are intuitive, and that is not always bad.

It may be that adolescent thinking is "adaptive and rational if one considers that a key developmental goal of this period of life is to mature into an independent adult in the context of a social world that is unstable and changing" (Blakemore, 2018, p. 116).

Societies need some people to question assumptions, and that is exactly what adolescents do. As social circumstances change, traditions need reexamination, lest old customs ossify and societies die. The generational tug between rebellion and tradition is part of human life: Neither generation should be too quick to judge the other, a lesson that pertains to people of every age.

what have you learned?

1. How does adolescent egocentrism differ from early-childhood egocentrism?
2. What perceptions arise from belief in the imaginary audience?
3. Why are the personal fable and the invincibility fable called "fables"?
4. What are the advantages of using inductive rather than deductive reasoning?
5. When might intuition and analysis lead to contrasting conclusions?
6. How might intuitive thinking increase risk-taking?
7. When is intuitive thinking better than analytic thinking?

Secondary Education

secondary education Literally, the period after primary education (elementary or grade school) and before tertiary education (college). It usually occurs from about ages 12 to 18, although there is some variation by school and by nation.

What does our understanding of adolescent cognition imply about school? Educators, developmentalists, political leaders, and parents wonder exactly which curricula and school structures are best. There are dozens of options: academic or vocational, single-sex or coed, competitive or cooperative, large or small, public or private, religious or secular.

To complicate matters, adolescents are far from a homogeneous group. As a result,

> some youth thrive at school—enjoying and benefiting from most of their experiences there; others muddle along and cope as best they can with the stress and demands of the moment; and still others find school an alienating and unpleasant place to be.
>
> [*Eccles & Roeser, 2011, p. 225*]

A further complication arises from the research on cognition just described. Adolescents are egocentric and logical, intuitive and analytic, beset by fables and capable of advanced inductive reasoning. All forms of thought advance as the brain matures, but the connections that allow the entire brain to function as a whole are fragile.

Given all of these variations, no school structure or pedagogy is best for everyone, or even for anyone at every time. Various scientists, nations, schools, and teachers try many strategies, some based on opposite but logical hypotheses.

Adults want to know what works. We have no definite answers. We do have helpful definitions, facts, and ways to measure learning.

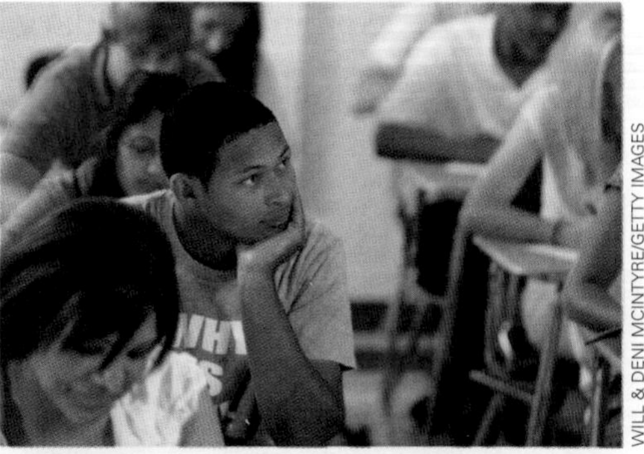

WILL & DENI MCINTYRE/GETTY IMAGES

MELANIE STETSON FREEMAN/THE CHRISTIAN SCIENCE MONITOR/GETTY IMAGES

Same Situation, Far Apart: How to Learn Although developmental psychologists find that adolescents learn best when they are actively engaged with ideas, most teenagers are more compliant when they are taking tests (*top*, Winston-Salem, North Carolina, United States) or reciting scripture (*bottom*, Kabul, Afghanistan).

Definitions and Facts

Secondary education—traditionally grades 7 through 12—denotes the school years after elementary or grade school (known as *primary education*) and before college or university (known as *tertiary education*). Adults are healthier and wealthier if they complete primary education, and then continue on.

Partly because presidents and prime ministers recognize that educated adults advance national wealth and health, every nation is increasing the number of students in secondary schools (see Visualizing Development). Education is compulsory almost everywhere until at least age 12, and new high schools and colleges open daily in developing nations.

HOW MANY ADOLESCENTS ARE IN SCHOOL?

Attendance in secondary school is a psychosocial topic as much as a cognitive one. Whether or not an adolescent is in school reflects every aspect of the social context, including national policies, family support, peer pressures, employment prospects, and other economic concerns. Rates of violence, delinquency, poverty, and births to girls younger than 17 increase as school attendance decreases.

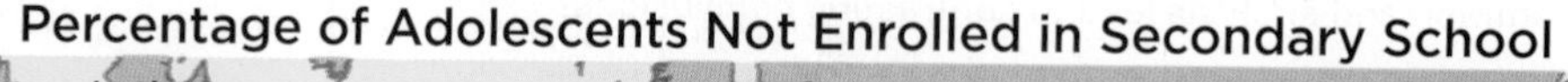

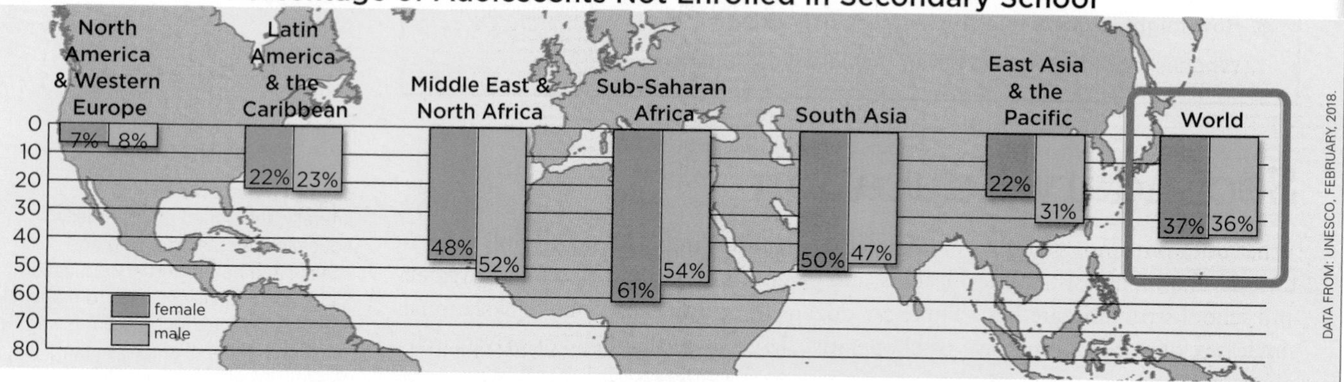

DATA FROM: UNESCO, FEBRUARY, 2018.

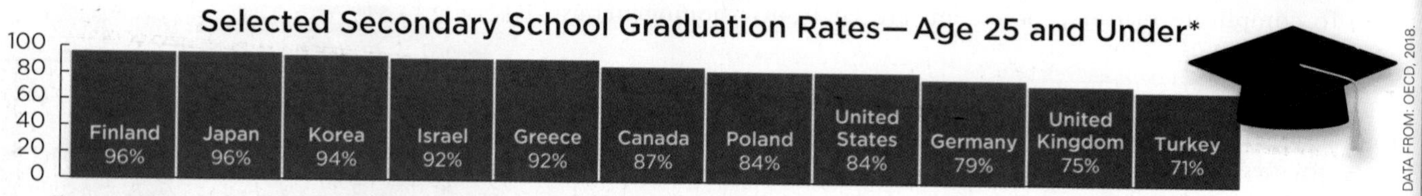

*In some nations, some students do not graduate because they go directly into the job market. For example, Germany has an extensive apprenticeship program.

DATA FROM: OECD, 2018.

U.S. High School Graduation Rate, Class of 2017

Since 2007, the dropout rate among foreign-born youth has declined much faster than for native-born youth, from 27 to 10 percent.

Males are more likely to drop out of high school than their female counterparts, a shift that has occurred since 1980. Before that, more females dropped out, usually because they were pregnant.

INFORMATION FROM CHILD TRENDS DATABANK, 2018.

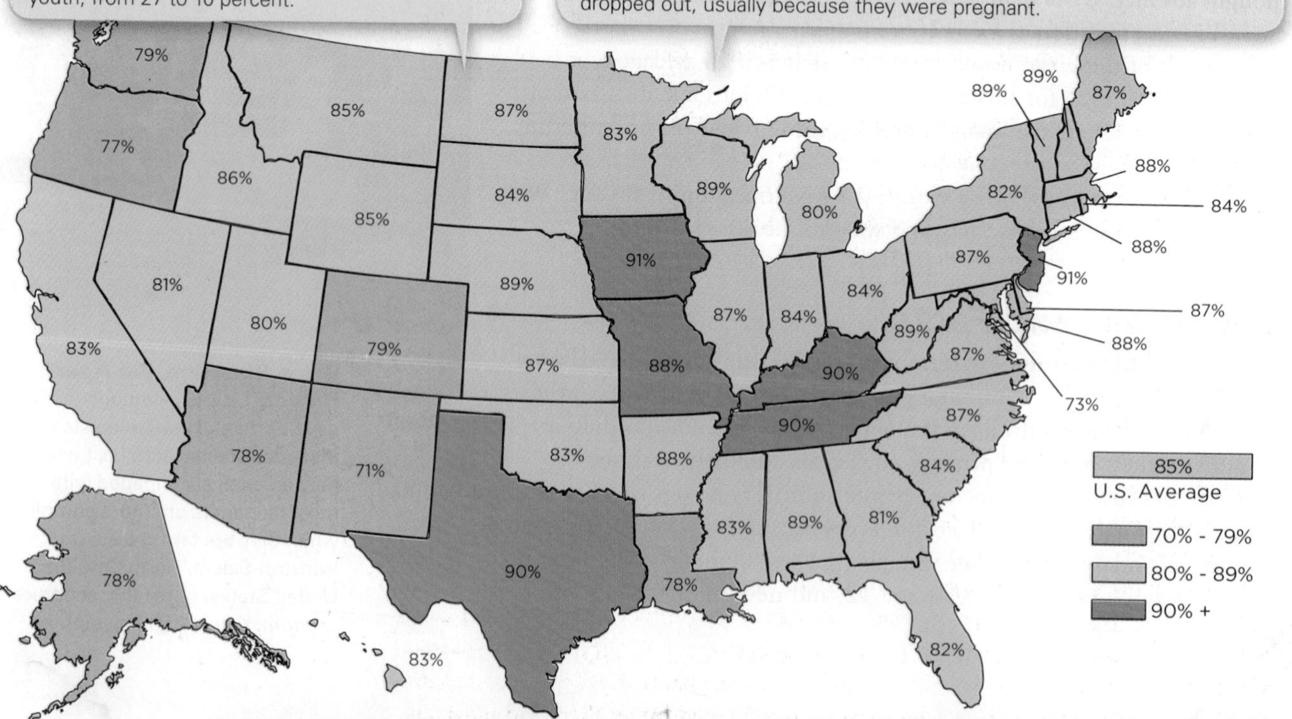

DATA FROM NATIONAL CENTER FOR EDUCATION STATISTICS, MAY, 2019.

Quality matters: Depending on the teacher, a year can propel thinking forward or can have little impact (Hanushek et al., 2019). The most effective teachers advance children a year and a half per year, the least effective only a half.

How can anyone tell if one teacher advances students three times as much as another? The answer usually involves a test of student learning. Three types of tests are often given: national "high-stakes" tests, performance assessments, and international tests.

HIGH STAKES IN THE UNITED STATES

Students in the United States take more tests than they did before 2000. Many of those tests are **high-stakes tests**, so called because of the high cost of failure.

high-stakes test
An evaluation that is critical in determining success or failure. If a single test determines whether a student will graduate or be promoted, it is a high-stakes test.

One example of high-stakes tests are *exit exams*, which determine whether or not a senior earns a diploma. An 18-year-old might have passed every class for the four years of high school, earning all the required credits (such as two years of a second language, three years of math, four years of English) but still not graduate because they fail a high-stakes exit exam.

For high school students, tests not only determine graduation, but also what college they might enter, and what credits they will earn there. Many colleges use scores on the *SAT (Scholastic Achievement Test)* or the *ACT (American College Test)* as a crucial factor in deciding admission. Students earn college credits by scoring well on the *AP (Advanced Placement)* or *IB (International Baccalaureate)* exams.

The increase in testing is evident in the AP exam. About 5 million AP tests were taken in 2018, with many students taking several AP tests. That is seven times as many tests as in 2007, when there were only 10 possible AP tests; now there are 38.

For example, there was one test in physics and relatively few students took it; now there are three AP physics tests. Each AP test is aligned with a rigorous class in high school (Finn & Scanlan, 2019).

The purpose of mandatory exit exams was to standardize and improve instruction, so a diploma earned in one city was equivalent to a diploma in another. But many people complained that tests taught students how to take tests rather than learn how to work with other people, analyze problems, and imagine new solutions. In addition, tests were thought to be unfair to African Americans and to English Language Learners (Acosta et al., 2020; Dworkin & Quiroz, 2019; Koretz, 2017).

Those complaints reached lawmakers. In 2013, Alabama dropped its high-stakes test for graduation. Pennsylvania instituted such a test in that same year, but opponents postponed implementation, and in 2018 the Pennsylvania legislature voted to allow several alternate paths to graduation (including the SAT).

In 2020, Janet Napolitano, president of the University of California, recommended that the entire California college system scrap the SAT and the ACT as admission requirements and use homegrown tests instead (Davis, 2020).

In 2002, more than half of all U.S. states required passing an exit exam before graduation; in 2019, only 13 did (Gewertz, 2019). However, another trend increased testing: More states (25 by 2019) require all students to take the SAT or ACT, in part to encourage them to plan for college. The recent pandemic added new complexity to the controversy about testing, in that the usual grading and testing systems were often suspended (Cairns, 2020).

If graduation tests are not used, how will employers, parents, or colleges know if a graduating student really learned what high school is supposed to teach? Some schools (mostly private ones) use other criteria, such as portfolios or senior papers.

One group of 38 public schools in New York (called the New York Performance Standards Consortium) decided to require students to complete four tasks: an essay that analyzes literature, a research paper in the social sciences, a science project that students design and complete, and an applied demonstration of advanced math. Each of these four includes a written and oral test, judged by teachers and outsiders, according to set rubrics (see Table 9.1).

TABLE 9.1

Performance Indicators	Outstanding	Good	Competent	Needs Revision
Evidence and Sources	• Supporting arguments include specific, relevant, accurate and verifiable, and highly persuasive evidence, drawn from both primary and secondary sources. • Provides specific, relevant, accurate evidence for counter-argument, where appropriate. • Uses quotations and paraphrasing appropriately to sustain an argument.	• Supporting arguments include relevant, accurate and verifiable, and mostly persuasive evidence, drawn from both primary and secondary sources. • Provides relevant, accurate evidence for counter-argument, where appropriate. • Uses quotations and paraphrasing appropriately to sustain an argument.	• Evidence for supporting arguments is accurate and verifiable, mostly specific and relevant, and generally persuasive drawn from secondary sources. • Use of quotations and paraphrasing is mostly evident.	• Supporting arguments may include inaccurate evidence and lack clear, persuasive, or relevant evidence. • Quotations and paraphrasing do not effectively support arguments.

Only One of Eight! The entire set of New York Performance Standards for graduation includes several disciplines (including science and literature), each with several measures. Here is just one of eight measures used for the social studies research paper. The other seven include grammar, organization, and analysis. As you see, several evaluators and five levels of success are rated. The high schools in the Consortium consider these rubrics much more demanding than traditional exit exams.

Those performance criteria led to higher graduation rates and college success (Barlowe & Cook, 2016). But advocates wonder if performance criteria can be used in all the 43,000 secondary schools in the United States. Even students in the Consortium schools are required to take the standardized New York test to demonstrate proficiency in English.

INTERNATIONAL TESTING

Remember from Chapter 7 that the TIMSS and PIRLS measures academic achievement in math, science, and language. The results for secondary students are similar to those for younger students, with East Asian nations scoring high, Middle Eastern and South American children scoring low (with some exceptions), and North American students middling.

The third commonly used international test, the PISA (also mentioned in Chapter 7), is designed to measure 15-year-olds' ability to apply what they have learned. For example, a math question was:

> Chris has just received her car driving license and wants to buy her first car. The table below shows the details of four cars she finds at a local car dealer.
>
> What car's engine capacity is the smallest?
>
> A. Alpha B. Bolte C. Castel D. Dezal

Model	Alpha	Bolte	Castel	Dezal
Year	2003	2000	2001	1999
Advertised price (zeds)	4,800	4,450	4,250	3,990
Distance traveled (kilometers)	105,000	115,000	128,000	109,000
Engine capacity (liters)	1.79	1.796	1.82	1.783

For that and the other PISA questions, the calculations are quite simple—most 10-year-olds can do them; no calculus, calculators, or complex formulas required.

TABLE 9.2 Average PISA Scores of 15-Year-Old Students in 2018—Selected Nations

	Mathematics	Reading	Science
Singapore	564	535	556
Japan	532	516	538
Canada	516	527	528
Netherlands	512	503	509
Germany	506	509	509
Poland	504	506	501
New Zealand	495	509	513
Russian Federation	494	495	487
Australia	494	503	510
United Kingdom	492	498	509
Italy	490	485	481
United States	470	497	496
Chile	423	459	447
Mexico	408	423	416
Lebanon	396	347	386
Indonesia	386	397	403
Brazil	377	407	401
Dominican Republic	328	358	332

However, almost half of the 15-year-olds worldwide got that question wrong. (The answer is D.)

One problem is decimals: Some students do not remember how to interpret them when a practical question, not an academic one, is asked. Another problem is that distance traveled is irrelevant, yet many students are distracted by it.

Overall, U.S. students score lower on the PISA compared to those in many other nations, including Canada, the nation most similar to the United States in ethnicity and location (see Table 9.2). Compared to peers in other nations, the 2018 results rank U.S. 15-year-olds 36th out of 79 countries in math proficiency.

Some 2015 results were not surprising (China, Japan, Korea, and Singapore were all high), but some were unexpected (high scores for Finland, Vietnam, and Estonia). Among the lowest results were Peru, Indonesia, and the Dominican Republic. The results reflect the educational systems more than geography, since low-scoring Indonesia is close to Singapore.

International analysis finds that the following items correlate with high achievement of high school students on the PISA. The standards were first articulated a decade ago, but they continue to apply (OECD, 2010).

- Leaders, parents, and citizens value education overall, with individualized approaches to learning so that all students learn what they need.
- Standards are high and clear, so every student knows what they must do, with a "focus on the acquisition of complex, higher-order thinking skills."
- Teachers and administrators are valued, and they are given "considerable discretion . . . in determining content" and sufficient salary as well as time for collaboration.
- Learning is prioritized "across the entire system," with high-quality teachers assigned to the most challenging schools.

The PISA and other international comparisons of high school students note that students who are immigrants and who are from low-income families do less well. Is this a problem in the students, or in the schools that teach them?

International comparisons of 40 nations also show that students in private schools do better than those in public schools, not only because they are wealthier but also because they take the test seriously and guess or skip questions less often (DeAngelis, 2019).

Middle School

middle school
A school for children in the grades between elementary school and high school. Middle school usually begins with grade 5 or 6 and ends with grade 8.

Many public-school systems provide two levels of secondary education. In the latter half of the twentieth century, because the average age of puberty declined, **middle schools** were created for grades 5 or 6 through 8. Educators recognized that, cognitively and in many other ways, pubescent 11-year-olds are quite different from both 7-year-olds and 17-year-olds. Those 11- to 14-year-olds may belong in middle schools.

However, although it helps primary schools to be free of the pubescent students, young adolescents may not necessarily benefit from being together. Middle school may be the most stressful time in a student's education.

Teachers also may prefer older or younger students. "Teaching is likely to be particularly complex for middle school teachers because it happens amidst a critical period of cognitive, socioemotional, and biological development of students who confront heightened social pressures from peers and gradual decline of parental oversight" (Ladd & Sorensen, 2017).

Thus, middle schools may be "developmentally regressive" (Eccles & Roeser, 2010, p. 13), which means that learning goes backward. For students, the effects of middle school can continue for years (Yeager et al., 2017).

Puberty itself is part of the problem, because those hormones affect the brain, and that reduces openness to education (Goddings et al., 2019). At least for other mammals, especially when they are under stress, learning is reduced at puberty (McCormick et al., 2010). Added to that, the awakening sexual interest causes awkwardness, distractions, and obsessions, which undercut world history, or geometry, or British poetry.

The biological stresses of puberty are not the only reason learning suffers in early adolescence. A crucial factor is emotional: whether the students trust and like their teachers (Binning et al., 2019; Riglin et al., 2013).

OBSERVATION QUIZ
Although the philosophy and strategy of these two schools are quite different, both share one aspect of the hidden curriculum. What is it? (see answer, page 307) ↓

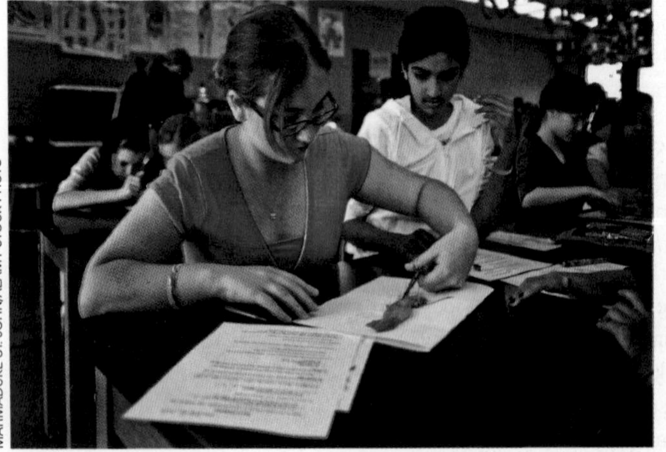

MARMADUKE ST. JOHN/ALAMY STOCK PHOTO

CARLOS OSORIO/TORONTO STAR/GETTY IMAGES

Now Learn This Educators and parents disagree among themselves about how and what middle school children need to learn. Accordingly, some parents send their children to a school where biology is taught via dissecting a squid (*left*), others where uniforms are worn and lining up is routine (*right*).

ENGAGED STUDENTS

How much children learn in school correlates with how engaged they are, as measured by involvement in various groups, by participation in classes, and by feelings about the school (Forster et al., 2020; Wang & Eccles, 2013). Every study finds that student engagement drops between primary and secondary education, with the most precipitous drop in middle school.

The most dramatic data come from a 2016 Gallup Student Poll of almost a million students at 3,000 schools in the United States and Canada. They indicated whether or not they agreed or disagreed with the following statements:

- At this school, I get to do what I do best every day.
- My teachers make me feel my schoolwork is important.
- I feel safe in this school.
- I have fun at school.
- I have a best friend at school.
- In the last seven days, someone has told me I have done good work at school.
- In the last seven days, I have learned something interesting at school.
- The adults at my school care about me.
- I have at least one teacher who makes me excited about the future.

Every year from the fifth to the ninth grade, fewer students agreed with those statements, with a drop from three-fourths engaged to less than half (Calderon & Yu, 2017). High school engagement was also low (about a third), but at least it didn't get much worse each year.

As you remember from Chapter 1, surveys are often inaccurate. For that Gallup poll, schools and students were self-selected, so specific percentages do not reflect middle school students everywhere. However, the general trends are probably correct, since the same design flaws applied in every grade. Smaller, but more valid studies agree: Many students become less disengaged every year of middle school.

Signs of a future high school dropout, among them chronic absenteeism, appear in middle school (Ladd & Sorensen, 2017). Those students most at risk are low-SES boys from minority ethnic groups, yet relatively few middle schools have male guidance counselors or teachers who are African American or Latinx. Given their egocentric and intuitive thinking, adolescents need role models of successful, educated men (Morris & Morris, 2013).

Declines in liking school, trusting teachers, and working hard in class are particularly steep for young adolescents who are African American, Latinx, or Native American, especially when they enter a multiethnic middle school when coming from a neighborhood primary school. Postformal thinking allows them to notice social forces beyond their personal experience; many perceive low expectations and harsh punishment for people of color.

Are they right or biased? One report on 17 middle schools found that for infractions that involved teacher judgment (e.g., disrespect, excessive noise), African Americans were disciplined three times as often as European Americans, but for more objective offenses (cheating, bringing a weapon to school), the rates were more similar (Skiba et al., 2002).

That was decades ago. Has it changed? A more recent report on a large, multiethnic school, found that African American sixth-graders (including those not personally disciplined) expected biased treatment. Incoming Latinx students did not expect bias, but by the eighth grade, they did. Most White students thought the teachers were fair, but they, too, became less trusting of school authorities over time (Yeager et al., 2017).

Even if there were no discrimination in the larger society, students have reasons to dislike middle school. Parents are less involved than in primary school, partly because students want more independence. It is psychologically healthy for adolescents to push their parents away, but the lack of parental support also increases risk. Bullying increases in the first year of middle school (Baly et al., 2014).

A particular concern is *cyberbullying*. Rumors, lies, embarrassing truths, or threats can all be sent from the safe distance of the private computer or smartphone, reaching a large audience just when social acceptance is crucial and empathy for other people is not widespread (Giumetti & Kowalski, 2015; Zych et al., 2019).

Although cyberbullying can occur at any age, three factors converge to make it particularly problematic in middle school.

- With egocentrism and imaginary fables, most young people are extremely self-conscious.
- The prefrontal cortex, which would help young people think of the consequences of their actions, is not fully grown until the mid-20s.
- Many young people have smartphones and computers, in part because parents worry about their safety, and teachers assign homework that requires the internet.

Cyberbullying has captured public attention, fueled by adult fears about the incendiary combination of the three factors above. Are those fears realistic?

Two leading researchers contend that cyberbullying is plagued by "exaggerated claims" and that it is, instead, merely another manifestation of bullying (Olweus & Limber, 2018). Other research finds that adult efforts to halt cyberbullying have some effect, but many efforts are hampered by inadequate understanding of technology and teenagers (Gaffney et al., 2019).

Especially for Teachers You are stumped by a question that one of your students asks. What do you do? (see response, page 307)

Teacher support also decreases in middle school. Unlike in primary school, where each classroom typically has one teacher who knows the families and friends of each student, middle school teachers have hundreds of students. Teachers become impersonal and distant, not the engaging adults that young adolescents need (Meece & Eccles, 2010). Both teachers and students may imagine that the other is hostile toward everyone of their generation, and that imagined hostility harms them both.

CAREER ALERT

The Teacher

Many people who study human development hope to become teachers, for good reason. Teachers can make a huge impact on a child's life. Every adult probably remembers a teacher or two whose interest and insight still affects them.

The need is great, and the demand huge. According to the U.S. Bureau of Labor Statistics' Occupational Outlook Handbook, in 2016 there were 1,500,000 elementary school teachers and 1,008,000 secondary school teachers. But every year, more than 100,000 teachers leave the profession—some retire, some quit, some die. They need to be replaced.

Depending on the local school district, an aspiring teacher can qualify with a bachelor's degree in almost any field. Courses in education can be taken while teaching. Better would be a master's degree in education, which includes on-the-job training with excellent teachers.

Many specialties within the teaching profession are chronically understaffed. In the United States, those trained to teach math, science, a non-English language, or children with special needs will be hired—as long as they are willing to live outside their home community.

Those interested in teaching probably already know that the salary is not that great, but the benefits are adequate, and teaching children can be immensely satisfying as well as challenging. Further, teachers have more vacation days than most professions, and the workday may seem short since most school days end by 3 P.M.

However, good teachers spend as much time preparing and planning as they do in direct teaching. Further, the work is exhausting, physically and emotionally. Teachers become painfully aware that some students have serious problems that teaching cannot solve: abusive or neglectful parents, learning differences, severe poverty, chronic depression.

The greatest openings in the profession are in areas that require special training. Novices may hope to teach high school English or to teach third grade in an affluent suburb. But such jobs are taken by teachers who have seniority; they are unlikely to be filled by new recruits.

Instead, aspiring teachers are most likely to be hired in areas of greatest need: math teachers in cities, teachers who specialize in autism, bilingual teachers, speech teachers who can relate with children and parents of many backgrounds, middle school science teachers.

Some of my students want to be teachers. I encourage them, warning that this profession is more difficult than it may seem. As one leading educator wrote: "Teaching is not rocket science. It is much harder than that" (Sahlberg, 2015, p. 133).

FINDING ACCLAIM

Middle school is a time when children can learn how to cope with challenges, both academic and social. A habit of solving problems rather than blaming oneself—is crucial (Monti et al., 2017). But a habit that worked in primary school may not match the conditions of middle school.

To pinpoint the developmental mismatch between students' needs and the middle school context, note that just when egocentrism leads young people to feelings of shame or fantasies of stardom (the imaginary audience), schools typically require them to change rooms, teachers, and classmates every 40 minutes or so. That context limits friendship and acclaim.

Recognition for academic effort is rare because middle school teachers grade more harshly than their primary school counterparts. Effort without accomplishment is not recognized, and achievement that was previously "outstanding" is now only average. Acclaim for after-school activities is also elusive, because many art, drama, dance, and other programs put adolescents of all ages together, and 11- to 13-year-olds are not as skilled as older adolescents.

Athletic teams become competitive, so those with fragile egos protect themselves by not trying out. If sports require public showers, that is another reason for students in early puberty to avoid them: They do not feel at ease with their changing bodies, and they fear comments from their peers, a fear that is no less powerful if it is a stereotype threat rather than a fact.

As noted in the discussion of the brain, peer acceptance is more cherished at puberty than at any other time. Physical appearance—from eyebrows to foot size—suddenly becomes significant. Status symbols (e.g., trendy sunglasses, a brand-name jacket, the latest smartphone) take on new meaning. Expensive clothes and shoes are coveted.

High School

Many of the patterns and problems just explained continue in high school. However, once the erratic growth and sudden sexual impulses of puberty are less novel, adolescents are better able to cope. Moreover, peers become more encouraging, and teachers and parents allow more autonomy, which encourages more self-motivation.

Added to that is cognitive maturation. If students think abstractly, analytically, hypothetically, and logically (all formal operational thought), they can respond to the usual pedagogy of high school. If a teacher lectures, they can take notes; if someone asks a hypothetical question, they can explore the answer; if a book describes another place and time, they can imagine it.

THE COLLEGE-BOUND

From a developmental perspective, the fact that high schools emphasize formal thinking makes sense, since many older adolescents are capable of abstract logic.

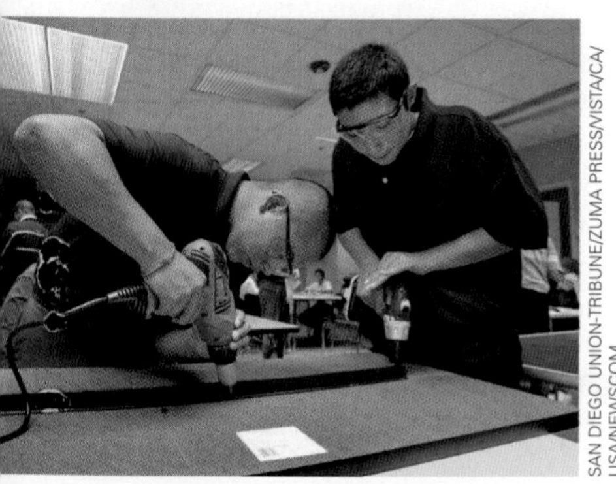

SAN DIEGO UNION-TRIBUNE/ZUMA PRESS/VISTA/CA/USA/NEWSCOM

What Do They Need to Learn? Jesse Olascoaga and José Perez assemble a desk as part of a class in Trade Tech High School in Vista, California. Are they mastering skills that will lead to a good job? Much depends on what else they are learning. It may be collaboration and pride in work well done, in which case this is useful education.

In several nations, attempts are under way to raise standards so that all high school graduates will be ready for college, where analysis is required.

A mantra for some in the United States is "college for all." As already mentioned, many students take difficult classes that are assessed by externally scored exams, either the IB or the AP, hoping for college credit (Finn & Scanlan, 2019).

Other indicators of increasing standards are greater requirements for academic diplomas and more restrictions on vocational or general diplomas. Unlike earlier, most U.S. schools now require two years of math beyond algebra, two years of laboratory science, three years of history, four years of English, and two years of a language other than English.

ALTERNATIVES TO COLLEGE

In 2018, about 31 percent of U.S. high school graduates did not enter college, and many who enrolled did not graduate. To be specific, only 44 percent of new students at four-year colleges and 33 percent at two-year colleges earned a degree. (These data do not include those who transferred to another institution and graduated there, but transferring itself reduces the chance of graduation [Digest of Education Statistics, 2018].)

Instead of encouraging every student to enroll in college, should schools prepare some students for employment after graduation, providing training, social skills, and practical experience? Some nations do that. In Switzerland, students in vocational education have a higher employment rate than students in the academic track, but over a lifetime, their earnings are less (Korber & Oesch, 2019). Which would you rather have at age 40—a steady and secure job or a high salary?

Overall, the data present a dilemma for educators. Suggesting that a student should *not* go to college may be classist, racist, sexist, or worse. On the other hand, since less than half of the students who begin college stay until they graduate, such students may lose time and gain debt when they could have advanced in a vocation. Everyone agrees that adolescents need to be educated for life as well as for employment, but it is difficult to decide what that means.

Students who drop out of high school or fail high-stakes tests might have succeeded if they had been offered courses that lead to employment. Students who believe that colleges will never accept them, or that employers will never hire them, may handicap themselves, an example of stereotype threat.

STEREOTYPE THREAT

It is easy to understand why stereotypes are mistaken, since they do not consider the individuality of each person. Probably every reader of this book knows the sting of being stereotyped and has sometimes too quickly judged someone else, although we are less aware of our own stereotypes than the stereotypes directed at us.

But more insidious than a direct stereotype may be *stereotype threat*, when someone holds a stereotype that someone else holds a stereotype about them. That mistaken idea can boomerang, harming the person who imagined it.

That boomerang begins with a fact that has troubled social scientists for decades: Secondary school achievement varies by ethnicity. This is evident in tests, grades, and, eventually, graduation. For example, in 2018, 42 percent of public high school students were Black or Hispanic, but only 38 percent of graduates were. The reasons seem objective: African Americans do not accumulate high school credits at the same rate as other groups.

One sad outcome is ethnic disparity in *status dropouts*, 16- to 24-year-olds who quit school before graduation. Status dropouts have markedly higher rates of unemployment and early death.

Data from 2017 on men aged 16–25 find that 5 percent of non-Hispanic Whites, 7 percent of non-Hispanic Blacks, and 7.5 percent of Hispanics are status dropouts. (Those ethnic categories are the official ones used by the U.S. government.) For women aged 16–24, status dropout rates are 4.3 percent non-Hispanic White, 4.4 percent non-Hispanic Black, and 7.4 percent Hispanic.

There are many explanations for ethnic differences, including poverty, language, genes, and school quality. Each explanation reflects the perceptions of the person offering it.

But look closely at the gender differences among non-Hispanics. Black girls have the same genes, families, and schools as Black boys, yet their status dropout rates are similar to White girls. Why?

Again, many explanations are proposed, each reflecting perceptions. But a novel explanation was suggested by one African American scholar, Claude Steele. He suggested that Black adolescent boys may think that other people have stereotypes about them. The result may be *stereotype threat*, a "threat in the air," not in reality (Steele, 1997). The mere *possibility* of being negatively stereotyped increases stress, disrupts cognition, and reduces emotional regulation.

Steele suspected that African American males, aware of the stereotypes that they are not smart, become anxious in educational settings. Their anxiety increases stress. Then, heightened cortisol undercuts their achievement test scores, so young men protect their pride by denigrating academics. They avoid the anxiety of writing papers, taking exams, and reading textbooks because they anticipate that teachers will not appreciate their work.

In self-defense, they conclude that school doesn't matter, that people who are "book smart" are not "street smart," that Black classmates who study hard are "acting white." They disengage from school, which results in lower achievement.

Stereotype threat occurs within many other groups and skills. It causes college women to underperform in math, bilingual students to stumble with English, older people to be forgetful, and every member of a stigmatized minority in every nation to handicap themselves because of what they imagine others might think (Baysu & Phalet, 2019; Bouazzaoui et al., 2020; S. Spencer et al., 2016).

Athletic prowess, health habits, and vocational aspiration may be impaired (Aronson et al., 2013). For example, stereotype threat may cause blind people to be underemployed: They hesitate to learn new skills or apply for jobs because they think other people will judge them (Silverman & Cohen, 2014). When star athletes unexpectedly underperform (called *choking*), stereotype threat may be the cause (Smith & Martiny, 2018).

The worst part of stereotype threat is that it is self-imposed. People who are alert to the possibility of prejudice are not only hypersensitive when it occurs, but their minds are hijacked, undercutting potential.

How might this work in secondary school? If students think that teachers expect them to misbehave, anticipating racially biased treatment, that thought will cause them to perceive neutral teacher behavior as disrespectful. That interpretation increases the hormones that, in fact, trigger misbehavior.

Stereotype threat can hobble teachers as well. If they think that students dislike them, in self-defense they might be less personable and more distant, which makes things worse. This becomes a downward spiral, a self-fulfilling prophecy, a sad and hostile teacher.

No one, including Steele, believes that stereotype threat is the only reason for disparities in success and achievement. Further, some adolescents strive to prove the stereotypes wrong.

Nonetheless, adolescence may be a crucial time to reduce stereotype threat and increase school engagement (Binning et al., 2019). Because adolescents are intensely

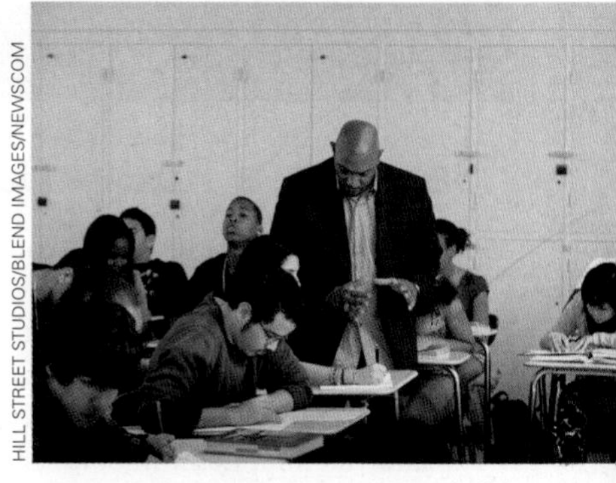

HILL STREET STUDIOS/BLEND IMAGES/NEWSCOM

More Like Him Needed In 2014 in the United States, half of the public-school students were tallied as people of color, and half were male. Meanwhile, only 17 percent of teachers are people of color, and only 24 percent are male. This Gardena, California, high school teacher is a welcome exception in two other ways — he rarely sits behind his desk, and he uses gestures as well as his voice to explain.

THINK CRITICALLY: Is the idea of stereotype a convoluted way of blaming the victim rather than blaming the system, or the teacher, who holds the stereotype?

INSIDE THE BRAIN

Save for a Rainy Day?

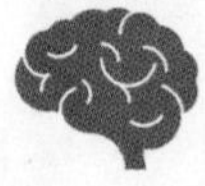

You already know that brain growth is uneven in adolescence, with the limbic system advancing ahead of the prefrontal cortex. This explains dual processing, since intuitions arise from the limbic system while analysis is rooted in the prefrontal cortex. It also explains the impulse in middle school to stop studying, and the impulse in high school to quit before graduation.

One topic in cognitive research is called *delay discounting*, the tendency to discount future rewards and instead seek immediate pleasure. Delay discounting is evident when young children eat one marshmallow rather than waiting for two (as described in Chapter 6), when an addicted person takes the drug in front of them instead of thinking about the next day, when middle-aged adults buy a new car instead of saving for retirement.

Delay discounting is particularly strong in adolescence because of uneven growth in the adolescent brain. One part, the *ventral striatum*, is sensitive to rewards. The striatum grows stronger at puberty, making rewards powerfully attractive (Shulman et al., 2016). As one team expressed it, the "subcortical regions that respond to emotional novelty and reward are more responsive in middle adolescence than in either children or adults" (Harden & Tucker-Drob, 2011, p. 743).

Because the striatum increases the allure of immediate rewards ("don't think about tomorrow"), adolescents are vulnerable to serious problems. Delay discounting is one explanation for impulsive suicide, drug addiction, and eating disorders (Felton et al., 2020).

When delay discounting is added to other aspects of adolescent brain development, with stronger sensations and quicker reactions (sensation-seeking and impulsivity), harm is lifelong. To make it worse, for some adolescents, influences from childhood, such as family chaos and abuse, reduce the brain's ability to wait for future rewards (see Figure 9.8) (Acheson et al., 2019).

Fortunately, sensation-seeking and impulsivity are *not* tightly linked in the brain (Harden & Tucker-Drob, 2011). Both increase, but an adolescent might be drawn to sensory stimulus, but be able to control impulsive reactions. Brains are plastic, and goals need not be long term.

Control of impulses can be taught. Past family stability and nurturance allows better planning, making destructive impulses far from inevitable (Acheson et al., 2019). Sensation-seeking might allow a young person to appreciate the moment, such as an exquisite sunset, a sumptuous meal, or a flowering tree, more than an adult might.

Everyone, of every age, is sometimes discouraged by the daily grind. We can learn from teenagers and appreciate sensations, even as we try to teach them to plan ahead. Stop to smell the roses?

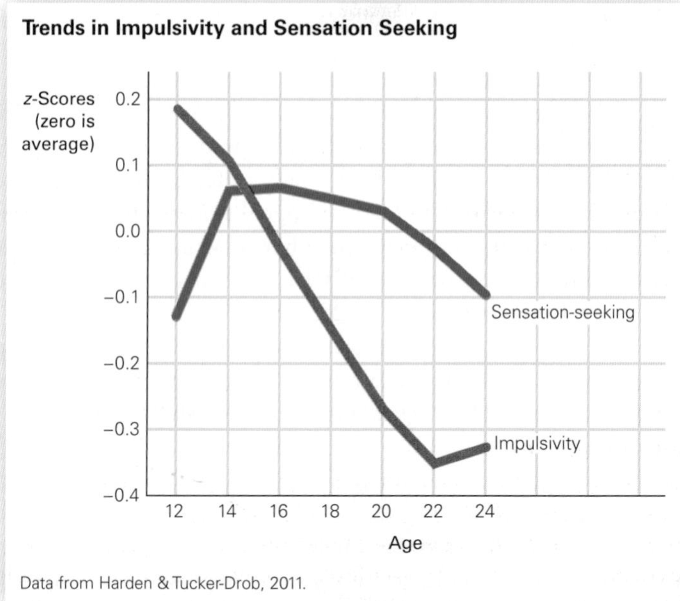

FIGURE 9.8 Look Before You Leap As you can see, adolescents become less impulsive as they mature, but they still enjoy the thrill of a new sensation.

THINK CRITICALLY: Is it more important to prepare high school students for jobs or for college?

self-conscious, with heightened intuition and irrational personal fables, a teacher's praise for work well done, and explicit expression of respect and anticipation for better work, can transform a threat into a promise. The future can be imagined as worth waiting for—if the adolescent brain can allow anticipation (see Inside the Brain).

VARIABILITY

High school students themselves vary: Some are so egocentric that they ruminate obsessively about themselves, some so hypothetical that they think of possibilities

that are actually impossible. Some are intuitive, some analytic; some foolish, some rational; some want to quit school at age 12, some are eager for college; some thrive in school, others will disengage.

In fact, these differences appear not only between adolescents but within them; the same person can be intuitive in the morning and analytic in the afternoon. Every adolescent, however, needs respect, personal encouragement, and intellectual challenge.

That brings us to general conclusions for this chapter. The cognitive skills that boost national economic development and personal happiness are creativity, flexibility, relationship building, and analytic ability. Whether or not an adolescent is college-bound, those skills can develop in adolescence, making a wiser adult.

Every cognitive theorist and researcher believes that adolescents' logical, social, and creative potential is not always realized, but that it can be. The two hands on the piano might play beautiful music together. Does that image end this chapter on a hopeful note?

what have you learned?

1. What are the differences between primary, secondary, and tertiary education?
2. What are the advantages and disadvantages of high-stakes testing?
3. How does the PISA differ from other international tests?
4. What characteristics of middle schools make them more difficult for students than elementary schools?
5. Why does puberty affect a person's ability to learn?
6. How does stereotype threat affect learning in secondary school?
7. Should high schools prepare everyone for college? Why or why not?

SUMMARY

Puberty Begins

1. Puberty refers to the various changes that transform a child's body into an adult one. Even before the teenage years, biochemical signals from the hypothalamus to the pituitary gland to the adrenal glands (the HPA axis) increase production of testosterone, estrogen, and various other hormones that will soon cause rapid growth and reproductive potential.

2. Hormones regulate all of the body rhythms of life, by day, by season, and by year. Changes in these rhythms in adolescence often result in sleep deprivation, partly because the natural circadian rhythm makes teenagers wide awake at night. Sleep deprivation causes numerous health and learning problems.

3. The outward signs of puberty typically begin between ages 9 and 14. The young person's sex, genetic background, body fat, and level of stress all contribute to variation in timing.

Physical and Sexual Growth

4. The growth spurt is an acceleration of growth in every part of the body. Peak weight usually precedes peak height, which is then followed by peak muscle growth, a sequence that makes active adolescents particularly vulnerable to injuries. The lungs and the heart also increase in size and capacity.

5. All of the changes of puberty depend on adequate nourishment, yet adolescents do not always make healthy food choices. Deficiencies of iron, vitamin D, and calcium are common, affecting bone growth and overall development. One reason for poor nutrition is the desire to lose (or, less often, gain) weight because of anxiety about body image.

6. The precursors of eating disorders are evident during puberty. Anorexia involves voluntary starvation, bulimia involves overeating and then purging, and binge eating disorder involves compulsive overeating. All these increase the risk of severe depression and medical complications, including death.

7. The maturation of primary sex characteristics means that by age 13 or so, after experiencing menarche or spermarche, teenagers are capable of conception. Secondary sex characteristics are not directly involved in reproduction but signify that the child is becoming a man or a woman. Body shape, breasts, voice, body hair, and numerous other features differentiate males from females.

8. In the twenty-first century, teenage sexual behavior has changed. Hormones and nutrition cause sexual thoughts and behaviors at younger ages, but teen pregnancy is far less common, condom use has increased, and the average age of first intercourse has risen, as has the use of contraception.

9. However, child sexual abuse is still a major problem that is most likely to occur in early puberty, if the abuser is a family member or familiar adult. Teenage dating relationships also may involve sexual abuse.

10. The other hazard of teenage sexual activity is sexually transmitted infections, which can lead to infertility and even death. Condom use can prevent unwanted pregnancy and AIDS, and immunization to prevent HPV decreases the rates of cancer in adulthood, but many adolescents are not protected.

Adolescent Cognition

11. Cognition in early adolescence may be egocentric, a kind of self-centered thinking. Adolescent egocentrism gives rise to the personal fable, the invincibility fable, and the imaginary audience.

12. Formal operational thought is Piaget's term for the last of his four periods of cognitive development. He realized that adolescents are no longer earthbound and concrete in their thinking; they imagine the possible, the probable, and even the impossible. They develop hypotheses and explore, using deductive reasoning.

13. Many cognitive theories describe two modes of thought, hot and cold, systems one and two, emotional and rational, or, in the terms used here, intuitive and analytic. Both become more forceful during adolescence.

14. Brain development means that intuitive, emotional thinking (the limbic system) matures before analytic, logical thought (the prefrontal cortex). If the priority is adventure, admiration from peers, and independence from parents, adolescents prefer the easier and quicker intuitive thinking.

Secondary Education

15. Education correlates with the health and wealth of individuals and nations. To measure learning, about 100 nations use the TIMSS, the PIRLS, and/or the PISA. The later measures how well 15-year-olds can apply what they have learned. Many schools in the United States use high-stakes test to determine high school graduation and college admission.

16. In middle school, many students struggle both socially and academically. One reason may be that middle schools are not structured to accommodate egocentrism or intuitive thinking. Another reason may be that students become aware of the prejudices of the larger society, sometimes internalizing them in stereotype threat.

17. Education in high school emphasizes formal operational thinking, to prepare students for college. However, many high school students do not go on to college, and only about a third earn a college degree. In other nations, educators pay substantial attention to vocational education, so that students are job-ready when they graduate.

KEY TERMS

puberty (p. 274)
menarche (p. 274)
spermarche (p. 274)
pituitary (p. 275)
adrenal glands (p. 275)
HPA (hypothalamus–pituitary–adrenal) axis (p. 275)
gonads (p. 275)
HPG (hypothalamus–pituitary–gonad) axis (p. 275)
circadian rhythm (p. 275)
growth spurt (p. 279)
body image (p. 281)
anorexia nervosa (p. 282)
bulimia nervosa (p. 282)
binge eating disorder (p. 282)
primary sex characteristics (p. 282)
secondary sex characteristics (p. 282)
child sexual abuse (p. 284)
sexually transmitted infection (STI) (p. 284)
adolescent egocentrism (p. 286)
imaginary audience (p. 286)
personal fable (p. 287)
invincibility fable (p. 287)
formal operational thought (p. 288)
hypothetical thought (p. 289)
deductive reasoning (p. 289)
inductive reasoning (p. 289)
dual processing (p. 290)
intuitive thought (p. 290)
analytic thought (p. 290)
secondary education (p. 293)
high-stakes test (p. 295)
middle school (p. 298)

APPLICATIONS

1. Visit a fifth-, sixth-, or seventh-grade class. Note variations in the size and maturity of the students. Do you see any patterns related to gender, ethnicity, body fat, or self-confidence?

2. Adult reactions to puberty can be reassuring or frightening. Interview two or three people about how adults prepared for, encouraged, or troubled their development. Compare that with your own experience.

3. Talk to a teenager about politics, families, school, religion, or any other topic that might reveal the way they think. Do you hear any adolescent egocentrism? Intuitive thinking? Systematic thought? Flexibility? Cite examples.

4. Describe what happened and what you thought in the first year you attended a middle school or a high school. What made it better or worse than later years in that school?

ESPECIALLY FOR ANSWERS

Response for Parents Worried About Early Puberty (from p. 279): Probably not. If she is overweight, her diet should change, but the hormone hypothesis is speculative. Genes are the main factor; she shares only one-eighth of her genes with her cousin.

Response for Health Practitioners (from p. 285): Many adolescents are intensely concerned about privacy and fearful of adult interference. This means that your first task is to convince the teenagers that you are nonjudgmental and that everything is confidential.

Response for Natural Scientists (from p. 289): Probably both. Our false assumptions are not logically tested because we do not realize that they might need testing.

Response for Teachers (from p. 300): Praise the student by saying, "What a great question!" Egos are fragile, so it's best always to validate the question. Seek student engagement, perhaps asking whether any classmates know the answer or telling the student to discover the answer online or saying you will find out. Whatever you do, don't fake it; if students lose faith in your credibility, you may lose them completely.

OBSERVATION QUIZ ANSWERS

Answer to Observation Quiz (from p. 276): Girls tend to spend more time studying, talking to friends, and getting ready in the morning. Other data show that many girls get less than seven hours of sleep per night.

Answer to Observation Quiz (from p. 277): The tallest girl appears to be trying to look shorter, and the shortest girl is standing as tall as she can. It seems that every girl wants to be about as tall as the others.

Answer to Observation Quiz (from p. 281): Adults often try to control schoolchildren by making them wear uniforms. Do you see that these students all must wear blue shirts and ties—even the girls? And teens tend to buy and eat the same foods: Notice the large paper cups, all from the same store.

Answer to Observation Quiz (from p. 286): The first three you can probably guess: Climate change advocates speak of saving the planet, of scientific evidence, and of animals losing their habitats. Extra credit if you know the fourth: "XR" stands for Extinction Rebellion, a group that started with young people in England and has since spread to other nations.

Answer to Observation Quiz (from p. 298): Both are single-sex. What does that teach these students?

ADOLESCENCE

The Social World

what will you know?

1. Why might a teenager be into sports one year and into books the next?
2. Should parents back off when their teenager disputes every rule, wish, or suggestion they make?
3. Which is more troubling, teen suicide or teen crime?
4. Why are adolescents forbidden to drink and smoke while adults are free to do so?

"You're a terrible mother of a teenager!" yelled an angry adolescent.

"I'm learning on the job," the mother shot back. "I've never been a mother of a teenager before."

I sympathize. Often I needed to listen to my adolescent daughters to figure out how to care for them. One night, Rachel was late coming home. I reassured myself with three truths: We had raised her to be cautious and careful; we knew her friends (they would call us if she was in trouble); we lived in the city (no one was driving, the main cause of teenage death).

Rachel walked in the door before worry overcame reassurance. I was happy to see her; I did not think to punish her.

She asked, "How long am I grounded?"

That alerted me that mothering required more than a hug.

"Two days. Is that fair?"

She nodded.

Parents are not the only ones new to adolescence. Teenagers themselves have never experienced the body transformations or cognitive leaps described in Chapter 9. Their greatest challenges, however, are described in this chapter, on psychosocial development. The social context of current adolescent life has never existed before. Sex, drugs, romance, technology, and delinquency are all quite different for today's youth than for earlier generations. Added to that, the COVID-19 pandemic changed every aspect of their social world.

Parents might remember being an adolescent, but that was before sexting, vaping, social distancing, and much else. Some things have not changed: Adolescents are always more adventurous than their

cautious parents. But even the most understanding parent has never viewed adolescence from an adult perspective before.

This developmental perspective is protective but also limiting. When our children were babies, my husband and I discussed the need to be firm, united, and consistent regarding illicit drugs, unsafe sex, and serious law-breaking. We thought we were ready. Yet none of those issues appeared.

Instead, their clothes, neatness, and homework made us impatient, bewildered, inconsistent. My husband said, "I knew they would become teenagers. I didn't know we would become parents of teenagers."

This chapter on adolescent psychosocial development includes relationships with friends, parents, partners, authorities. It begins with identity and ends with drugs, both of which may seem to be a private choice but are strongly affected by social pressures that change from cohort to cohort.

Moreover, every person is unique. Each of my four daughters presented her own challenges, not only because the times had changed, but also because she was herself, not a younger version of me or of her older sisters.

You will soon read that adults must be alert and supportive, and that they may not know how. Every generation is learning on the job. What did I need to learn? A few years after the incident above, when Rachel was in college, she said to her younger sister, "If ever you think of trying cocaine, talk with me first." I was stunned, quiet. I am still learning.

Identity

identity versus role confusion
Erikson's fifth stage of development, when people wonder "Who am I?" but are confused about which of many possible roles to adopt.

identity achievement
Erikson's term for the attainment of identity, when people know who they are as unique individuals, combining past experiences and future plans.

Psychosocial development during adolescence is often understood as a search for self-understanding. Each young person wants to know, "Who am I?"

According to Erik Erikson, life's fifth psychosocial crisis is **identity versus role confusion**: Working through the complexities of finding oneself is the primary task of adolescence (Erikson, 1968/1994).

Erikson believed that this crisis is resolved with **identity achievement**, when adolescents have reconsidered the goals and values of their parents and culture, accepting some and discarding others, to forge their own identity. That combines emotional separation from childhood with reliance on family and community, a difficult task (Sugimura et al., 2018). Teenagers maintain continuity with the past so that they can move toward the future, establishing their own path, a process that takes years.

Identity achievement is particularly hard for adolescents who are conflicted about the clash between family values and society norms. For example, if their parents are refugees from another nation, they must carry the legacy of their ancestor's homeland, the experience of alienation, and the new identity in their current nation, a combination that can be contradictory and confusing (Johansen & Varvin, 2020).

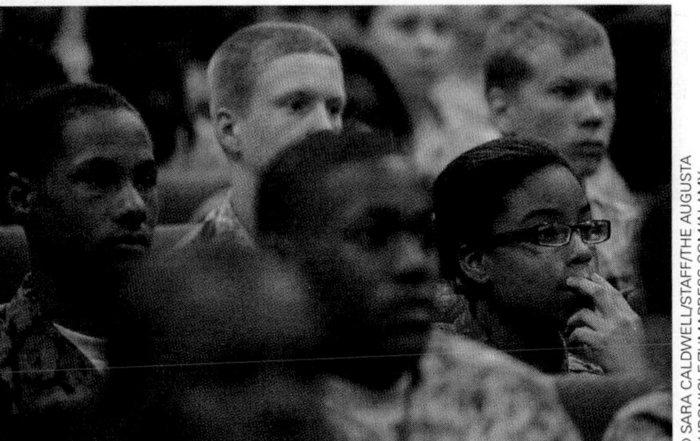

No Role Confusion These are high school students in Junior ROTC training camp. For many youths who cannot afford college, the military offers a temporary identity — complete with haircut, uniform, and comrades.

Not Yet Achieved

Over the past half-century, major psychosocial shifts have complicated identity achievement. It now takes a decade or more, especially in families and nations that can afford to support young people as they struggle to "find themselves"

(Côté & Levine, 2015; Sugimura, 2020). Moments of rage, anxiety, idealism, and fantasy that seem pathological by adult standards may be part of this search (Côté, 2018).

One developmental scholar, James Marcia, described four ways that adolescents and young adults cope with this crisis: (1) role confusion, (2) foreclosure, (3) moratorium, and finally (4) achievement (Kroger & Marcia, 2011; Marcia, 1966).

role confusion
When adolescents have no clear identity, instead fluctuating from one persona to another. (Sometimes called *identity diffusion* or *role diffusion*.)

foreclosure
Erikson's term for premature identity formation, when adolescents adopt their parents' or society's roles and values without questioning or analysis.

Role confusion is the opposite of achievement. Adolescents may lack any commitment to goals or values. Confusion is typical in early adolescence, when the hormones of puberty awaken new sexual impulses while the cognitive advances of hypothetical thought trigger reexamination of traditional values. Old assumptions no longer seem valid.

Foreclosure occurs when, in order to avoid the stress of sorting through all the nuances of identity and beliefs, young people lump traditional roles and values together, to be swallowed whole or rejected totally. Some follow every custom from their parents or culture, never exploring alternatives, taking on traditional values, roles, identities.

Some do the opposite, foreclosing on an oppositional, *negative identity*—rejecting all their elders' values and routines, again without thoughtful questioning. Foreclosure is comfortable but limiting. It is only a temporary shelter (Meeus, 2011). Later the identity search may be paused with a *moratorium*, which is more common after age 18. Accordingly, discussion of moratoria appears in Chapter 11.

VIDEO ACTIVITY: Adolescence Around the World: Rites of Passage presents a comparison of adolescent initiation customs in industrialized and developing societies.

Arenas of Identity Formation

Erikson (1968/1994) highlighted four aspects of identity: religious, political, sexual (now known as gender identity), and vocational. The last of these (vocational) is rarely established before age 25, and thus is discussed in Chapter 11. The others begin in the teen years; they are described here.

RELIGIOUS IDENTITY

Most adolescents question some aspects of their faith, but their *religious identity* is similar to the one they have grown up with. Few reject their religion totally if they have been raised in it, especially if they have a good relationship with their parents (Kim-Spoon et al., 2012).

Although most research has been on Christian youth in Western nations, the search for religious identity may be universal, as a study of youth in eight nations suggests (Benson et al., 2012). Details are reported for Buddhist adolescents in Japan: They also seek to establish their own religious beliefs and practices (Sugimura et al., 2019).

Some teenagers become more devout. A Muslim girl might start to wear a headscarf; a Catholic boy might study for the priesthood; a Baptist teenager might join a Pentecostal youth group. Their parents might be surprised, but none of these changes is a reversal. Adults may convert to a completely different faith; adolescents almost never do.

Although becoming more devout than their parents is possible, as in the examples above, the more common pattern for religious identity is rebellion. Attendance at churches, temples, and mosques decreases when parents no longer enforce it.

With their new cognitive potential, adolescents question "organized religion" because it seems to be a bundle of beliefs and rituals. Particularly if a young person experiments with mind-altering drugs (discussed at the end of this chapter), they may insist they are "spiritual, not religious" (Prosek et al., 2020).

POLITICAL IDENTITY

Parents also influence their children's *political identity*. In the twenty-first century, more U.S. adults identify as nonpartisan (38 percent) than Republican (26 percent), or Democrat (26 percent), or any other party (5 percent) (Pew Research Center, March 14, 2019). Their teenage children reflect their views, some boasting that they

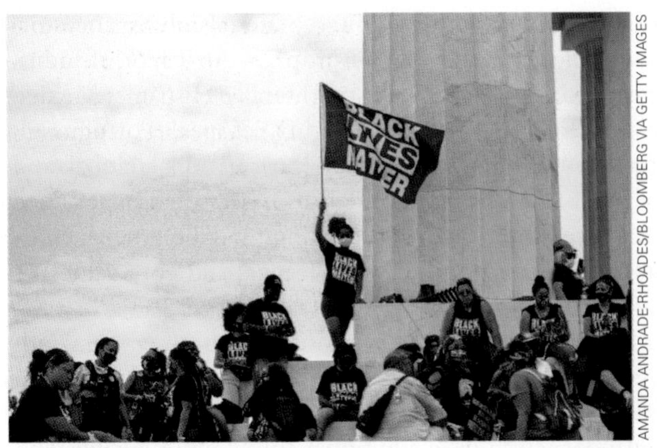

AMANDA ANDRADE-RHOADES/BLOOMBERG VIA GETTY IMAGES

ALEX WONG/GETTY IMAGES

Same Photo, Twice It is easy to see polarities here, between Black Lives Matter and anti-abortion demontrators. Pictured here are primarily older adolescents, separated by less than six months (August 2020 and January 2021) and less than two miles (in Washington, D.C.). Both illustrate the quest for political identity.

support the person, not the party, or that they do not care about politics, echoing their parents without realizing it.

Some proudly vote at age 18, an action that is more likely if the 18-year-old lives with voting parents than if they have already left home. As with other political involvement, voting is a social activity, influenced by family (Hart & van Goethem, 2017). Peers are important, too: Nationwide protests attract many youth too young to vote.

Political identity reflects two influences: parents and current events (Stattin et al., 2017). Adolescents tend to be more liberal, politically, than their elders, especially on social issues (same-sex marriage, reproduction, gun control, the environment). Again, however, major political shifts do not usually occur until later (P. Taylor, 2014).

ETHNIC IDENTITY

Related to political identity is *ethnic identity*, a topic not discussed by Erikson. However, Erikson knew that identity achievement requires interaction between the individual and the historical context, so he would not be surprised that ethnic identity is now essential in many parts of the world.

As one review expressed it, ethnic and racial identity is not "separate from overall identity development, but as basic to it . . . part of each individual's experience. It involves both explicit and implicit processes" (Rogers et al., 2020).

The chronosystem, the macrosystem, and the microsystem all contain implicit racial bias. To counter that, many parents (the microsystem) seek to prepare their adolescents by teaching ethnic pride and ways to cope with prejudice. Such parental socialization becomes a buffer against depression and low achievement (Umaña-Taylor & Hill, 2020).

But no parent knows exactly what teenagers will encounter. Teenagers themselves realize that ethnic identity is "not a matter of one's idiosyncratic self-perception but rather [is] profoundly shaped by one's social context, including one's social role and place in society" (Seaton et al., 2017, p. 683). They must combine parental socialization with current conditions.

THINK CRITICALLY: Since identity is formed lifelong, is your current identity different from what it was five years ago?

In the United States and Canada, about half of all adolescents are of African, Asian, Hispanic, or indigenous heritage. Many also have ancestors of other ethnic groups. The census categories are too broad; teenagers must forge more specific, personal ethnic identities.

For instance, youth officially categorized (as when schools report ethnicity of students) as Hispanic must incorporate their grandparents' birthplaces, often another nation (perhaps Mexico, Dominican Republic, or Cuba) or place (e.g., California, Texas, Puerto Rico, or Florida).

Added to that, many Latinx individuals in the United States also have ancestors from other nations of Central or South America, of Europe or Africa, or of indigenous groups such as the Maya or Navajo. Many are not literally Hispanic: Mexico recognizes 70 national languages; Brazilians identify as Latinx yet speak Portuguese.

Identity challenges also confront Black youth as they learn national, global, and family history. Formal operational thought moves them from personal experience into a wider, troubling narrative. For them, parental teachings may be crucial, especially when parents teach racial pride (noting successful leaders and core values) as well as coping strategies (M.-T. Wang et al., 2020).

Similar factors apply for other youth, with many variations. Asian American youth experience distinct pressures: For them, racial socialization may reduce self-esteem (M.-T. Wang et al., 2020). Research on adolescents in Hawaii also finds that Native Hawaiian and other Pacific Islander youth have additional complexities establishing their own ethnic identity, a source of conflict with their parents (Wills et al., 2019).

European American adolescents also develop ethnic identity. They are less likely to hear parents praise their ethnic ancestry (Loyd & Gaither, 2018), but they may become aware of prejudices that their elders do not recognize. For example, if an adult says, "All lives matter," adolescents may hear that as a trivialization of the Black Lives Matter movement.

Thus, when White children move past concrete operational thought, they must figure out how their heritage and ethnicity affect their identity. Some search back to their roots, talking to grandparents, for instance, or sending a saliva sample to be analyzed for DNA origins.

For every adolescent, of every background, peers and the larger community help sort through stereotypes, resistance, and finally achievement (Santos et al., 2017). Adolescents who are multiracial or adopted by parents of another background must reconcile both influences. Their parents may be less able to help them (Umaña-Taylor & Hill, 2020).

Often biracial and adopted youth identify with their ancestors who are less powerful in U.S. society, and they are depressed if that group does not accept them (Nishina et al., 2018). Problems may be particularly acute for adoptees from Asia, because parents may be unaware of anti-Asian racism (Langrehr et al., 2019). Every adolescent seeks ethnic identity, yet cultural shifts complicate adult efforts to understand adolescent ethnic identity crises.

A CASE TO STUDY

Ancestors and Identity

This case may be your own. How does your personal ancestry affect your perspective? Does your understanding of the second Monday in October (Columbus Day or Indigenous People's Day, a paid holiday in some states but not others) differ from those of other ethnicities? As shown in a study of how adolescents think of slavery, specifics of race, gender, and ethnicity affect interpretations of every historical event (Gross & Wotipka, 2019).

Those who have indigenous ancestors (about 1 percent of the population) often resurrect customs and lineage that outsiders tried to eliminate, and thus refer to a particular group (Diné, Dakota, Lakota, and so on). Other adolescents, whose ancestors fought in the American Revolution, or Civil War, or who were enslaved and brought from Africa, trace their lineage back more than a century, not always to a noble past. Ethnic identity is a social construction, and thus may change from childhood to adolescence to adulthood.

For example, in San Diego, a longitudinal (age 14 to 37) study asked first- and second-generation immigrants, "What do you call yourself?" (Feliciano & Rumbaut, 2019). Few chose pan-ethnic terms (Asian, Hispanic, etc.). Especially in adolescence, many used specific heritage terms (Cambodian, Mexican, and so on), with a trend toward American (hyphenated or not) as time went on.

One adolescent boy said he was Vietnamese. Years later, as an adult, he said he was American, a change facilitated not only by time but also by his surroundings. He said:

> I wouldn't identify myself as Vietnamese. . . . Physically from a phenotype perspective, I don't look typical American . . . most people when they think of Americans they think of just White. But living in San Diego, you see a multicultural group of people.
>
> *[Kim quoted in Feliciano & Rumbaut, 2019, p. 90]*

In the same study, those whose phenotype was White often sought to emphasize their differences from other European Americans. Many Latinx individuals proudly claimed to be a "person of color," even when their parents said they were White. As one said:

> For me it's very important to label me Mexican-American because I wanna show people . . . two sides. I wanna show my parents that, hey, I made it. And I'm proud of being Mexican. . . . I'm an immigrant that came to this country and I succeeded and I don't take advantage of the system.
>
> *[Leo quoted in Feliciano & Rumbaut, 2019, p. 93]*

Ethnic identity is not a private, personal choice but a community one, with differences depending on education (more education leads to more specific ethnic identity), family, and national politics. Those influences affect each person differently. Ethnic identity is "complex and varied" (Feliciano & Rumbaut, 2018, p. 42).

This is evident in my family. My brother increasingly identified with his immigrant roots as he grew older, changing how he pronounced his name. My four adult daughters, each with the same eight great-grandparents, were required by the 2020 U.S. Census to specify their ethnic heritage. After they sent in their forms, they realized that each answered differently.

Back to you, as a case to study. Has your answer to "What is your ethnic identity?" changed as you grow older?

GENDER IDENTITY

Now we come to the most difficult identity of all for adolescents, **gender identity**. As you remember, *sex* refers to certain physical and genetic traits assigned at birth, whereas *gender* refers to cultural and social factors. A half-century ago, psychoanalytic theorists did not make this distinction. They assumed that, with the rush of testosterone or estrogens at puberty, adolescents needed to develop their male or female sexual identity (Erikson, 1968/1994; A. Freud, 1958/2000).

gender identity
A person's acceptance of the roles and behaviors that society associates with a particular gender.

Thus, adolescence was once time for "gender intensification," when hormones compelled children to identify as one or the other of two *opposite* sexes. That reflected the *gender binary*, already explained in Chapter 6.

In contemporary society, the analytic, hypothetical thinking of adolescents makes them question that binary, rejecting traditional ideas of proper dress, hair, and aspirations. People whose gender identity is the same as their birth sex are now called *cisgender*, a term needed because not everyone identifies with the gender they were assigned at birth.

The term illustrates the new recognition of variations in gender identity: It first was used in 1994 and was not added to the Oxford English Dictionary until 2013. Interestingly, more adolescent boys than girls see gender as binary, probably because they experience more pressure to conform (Horn, 2019).

ADAM HESTER/BLEND IMAGES/SUPERSTOCK

The Opposite Sex? Every cohort of adolescents rebels against the conventions of the older generations. Earlier generations of boys grew their hair long. A decade later, some girls shaved their heads. Now many teenagers do not see male and female as opposites, adopting instead a nonbinary approach to gender expression.

Everyone, male or female, cisgender or not, must figure out their gender role and interaction with people of other genders, a task especially difficult for lesbian, gay, bisexual, transgender, or queer/questioning (LGBTQ+) youth.

Earlier, most LGBTQ+ people were "in the closet," unable to tell others (and sometimes themselves) who they were. Then, in about 2000, television aimed at teen audiences began introducing major characters who were gay, and plots portrayed "being out in high school as greatly preferable to being closeted" (Peters, 2016, p. 488). Many people "came out," and the Supreme Court eventually acknowledged

same-sex marriage. However, media depiction is still homophobic (Peters, 2016), and LGBTQ+ youth still experience prejudice and stereotype threat.

Among Western psychiatrists in former decades, people who had "a strong and persistent cross-gender identification" were said to have *gender identity disorder*, a serious diagnosis according to the DSM-IV (1994). However, the DSM-5 (2013) instead describes *gender dysphoria*, when people are distressed to be whatever gender others expect them to be.

This is more than a change in terminology. A "disorder" means something is amiss with the individual, no matter how they feel about it, whereas "dysphoria" means the problem is in the distress, which can be mitigated by social conditions, by cognitive framing, by self-acceptance, or by presenting as another gender. Developing gender identity is not simple for anyone.

Many cisgender adolescents experience dysphoria when they begin dating another sex, because the expected, traditional, and peer standards of how to touch each other, when to agree or disagree, or even how to walk together, varies from one person to another. Every teenager must figure out the nuances of sexual interaction with a particular person, and that may arouse some confusing emotions—that is, dysphoria.

Culture matters as well. Some cultures accept youth who are gender nonbinary. For example, the census in India gives people three choices: male, female, or Hijra (transgender). Other cultures criminalize LGBTQ+ youth (38 of the 53 African nations), even killing them (Uganda). In the latter, almost all adolescents identify as cisgender. Is that because they deny their own biology or because the culture has shaped them?

INTERSECTIONALITY

An added complexity is that each identity overlaps with every other, not just in individuals, but in society. Various identities combine and conflict, as evident in the concept of *intersectionality* (explained in Chapter 1).

Someone who identifies as a religious conservative may be troubled if they also identify as gender nonbinary; someone who identifies as Black may be troubled by assumptions about their politics. One young man became vegan, and then was angry at what others assumed about him. He said, "I am vegan to help animals, not because I am in the vegan club."

Added to the specific aspects of identity, awareness of family social status affects adolescent health, education, and other aspects of their future social status matters much more at age 18 than at age 12. This suggests that it does not predate the identity search but follows from it.

The crucial factor is perception, not objective SES. Thus, an 18-year-old who believes that their family is low in the social hierarchy is much more affected than their twin from the same family who thinks their family has higher status (Rahal et al., 2020; Rivenbark et al., 2020). This research confirms the importance of self-formed, multifaceted identity.

what have you learned?

1. What is Erikson's fifth psychosocial crisis, and how is it resolved?
2. How does foreclosure relate to identity achievement?
3. What role do parents play in adolescent religious and political identity?
4. How does ethnic identity affect self-esteem and achievement?
5. What assumptions about gender identity did most adults hold 50 years ago?
6. Does the term *cisgender* imply a gender binary?
7. Does intersectionality make identity achievement easier or harder?

Close Relationships

The focus on adolescent identity may imply that teenagers are intensely individualistic, seeking their own unique self-definition. However, the opposite is more accurate. Parents, peers, grandparents, siblings, teachers, and cultures shape adolescent lives (Seaton et al., 2017).

It is a myth that adolescents prefer peers and reject parents; usually both are supportive. A longitudinal study of all middle school students in one community (almost 800 of them) found that three-fourths had healthy relationships with their parents *and* their peers. That protected them from serious emotional problems later on (Dishion et al., 2019). If parents are not supportive, trouble with friends is also common.

Family

Family relationships affect identity, expectations, and daily life. As adolescents grow older, parents shift from providing direct guidance to giving advice when asked, but close parent–child relationships continue (E. Chen et al., 2017). Parents may underestimate the role of peers, as I often did (see A Case to Study), but they gradually understand that they must neither insist on parental control nor abandon their role.

Older siblings also become influential, as role models and confidants, as bullies or protectors (Aizpitarte et al., 2019; Gallagher et al., 2018). This is especially important if environment or genes push teens toward negative behavior.

A successful older sibling can be protective. However, the specific influence may not be what parents expect, as "sibling relationships are known as the quintessential love-hate relationship" (Campione-Barr & Killoren, 2019, p. 221).

A CASE TO STUDY

The Naiveté of Your Author

Parents are sometimes unaware of adolescents' desire for respect from their peers. I did not recognize this with my own children:

- Our oldest daughter wore the same pair of jeans in tenth grade, day after day. She washed them each night by hand, and I put them in the dryer early each morning. [Circadian rhythm—I was asleep hours before she was, and awake much earlier.] My husband was bewildered. "Is this some weird female ritual?" he asked. Years later, our daughter explained that if she wore different pants each day, her classmates might think she cared about her clothes, and then they would criticize her choices. To avoid that imaginary audience, she wore only one pair of jeans.
- Our second daughter, at 16, pierced her ears for the third time. I asked if this meant she would do drugs; she laughed at my foolishness. Only later did I notice that many of her friends also had multiple holes in their earlobes.
- At age 15, our third daughter was diagnosed with Hodgkin's disease, a kind of cancer. My husband and I consulted four physicians in four hospitals. Their recommendations differed: We selected the one we thought would minimize the risk of death. Our daughter had other priorities: "I don't care what you choose, as long as I keep my hair." (Now her health is good; her hair grew back.)
- Our youngest, in sixth grade, refused to wear her jacket (it was new; she had chosen it), even in midwinter. Years later she told me why—she wanted her classmates to think she was tough.

In retrospect, I am amazed that I was unaware of the power of peers, a stronger and more immediate influence than self-acceptance, personal choice, long life, or even a warm body.

FAMILY CONFLICT

The fact that families are influential does not mean that family life is peaceful. Disputes are common, because parents seek protective control while biology, cognition, and culture all push for adolescent independence. Consequently, each generation may be angry at the other. Adolescents think parents are overprotective; parents think peers are too loose.

THINK CRITICALLY: When do parents forbid an activity they should approve of, or ignore a behavior that should alarm them?

Both may forget that close relationships include disagreements. Reducing conflict by reducing connection may buy peace at a steep price. Some developmentalists think that disagreement may increase mutual understanding and emotional growth (Branje, 2018).

Thus, experts agree that too much freedom, too early, is a path toward serious trouble (lawbreaking, addiction) (Fosco & LoBraico, 2019). On the other hand, too much control, for too long, fractures connection. One of my college students wrote:

> My parents . . . see me as too independent. I see them as too old-fashioned. . . . My home life is a lie. I pretend to be their good daughter. . . . I used to argue with them all the time when I was in high school but it soon got to the point that screaming and yelling got tiring. Now I just want to get by the couple of hours I'm at home without any problems.
>
> I never confide in my parents. . . . Whenever I need advice I go to my friends. My parents act as if they own my life and that whatever they say goes. It's one of the reasons I wanted to run away at thirteen.
>
> *[E., personal communication]*

Authors of research on mothers and their adolescents suggest that "although too much anger may be harmful . . . some expression of anger may be adaptive" (Hofer et al., 2013, p. 276). In this study, as well as generally, the parent–child relationship usually improved with time as both parties adjust to the adolescent's increasing independence. Clearly, as my student shows, sometimes neither generation adjusts.

Crucial is that caregivers avoid either extreme, strictness or leniency, but instead maintain support while increasing autonomy (Yeager et al., 2018). As a review of dozens of studies expressed it: "parent–adolescent conflict might signal the need for families to adapt and change . . . to accommodate adolescents' increasing needs for independence and egalitarianism" (Weymouth et al., 2016, p. 107).

"So I blame you for everything—whose fault is that?"

Not My Fault Humans always find it easier to blame someone else, but this is particularly true when teenage girls talk to their mothers.

CLOSENESS WITHIN THE FAMILY

Several aspects of parent–child relationships have been studied. Specifically:

1. Communication (Do family members talk openly and honestly?)
2. Support (Do family members rely on each other?)
3. Connectedness (How emotionally close are family members?)
4. Control (Do parents allow independence?)

No social scientist doubts that the first two, communication and support, are crucial. Patterns from childhood continue, ideally buffering the turbulence of adolescence. Regarding the next two, connectedness and control, consequences vary, and observers differ in what they see. How do you react to this example, written by another one of my students?

> I got pregnant when I was sixteen years old, and if it weren't for the support of my parents, I would probably not have my son. And if they hadn't taken care of him, I wouldn't have been able to finish high school or attend college. My parents also helped me overcome the shame that I felt when . . . my aunts, uncles, and especially my grandparents found out that I was pregnant.
>
> *[I., personal communication]*

My student's boyfriend is no longer part of her life. She is grateful that she still lives with her parents, who care for her son. However, did motherhood make her dependent on her parents, preventing her from establishing her own identity? Why didn't her parents monitor her romantic relationship, or at least explain contraception? Were they caring or neglectful? Could they be both?

One issue is **parental monitoring**—that is, parental knowledge about their child's whereabouts, activities, and companions. Many studies have shown that when monitoring arises from a warm, supportive relationship, adolescents usually become confident, well-educated adults, avoiding drugs and risky sex.

However, parents and adolescents do not always agree as to whether or not the parents know what the adolescent does: Sometimes parents believe they know their child's friends and activities, but their adolescents disagree. That bodes ill: Usually, disagreement about parental knowledge correlates with family dysfunction and antisocial (e.g., skipping school, stealing) adolescents (Pouliot & Poulin, 2021).

If parents are cold and punitive, monitoring may lead to deception and rebellion. If mothers are too controlling, depression increases; if fathers are too controlling, drug abuse is more likely (Eun et al., 2018). Thus, a "dynamic interplay between parent and child behaviors," affects monitoring (Abar et al., 2014, p. 2177). Teenagers choose what to reveal. They share details if their parents are supportive; they lie if not (Lushin et al., 2017).

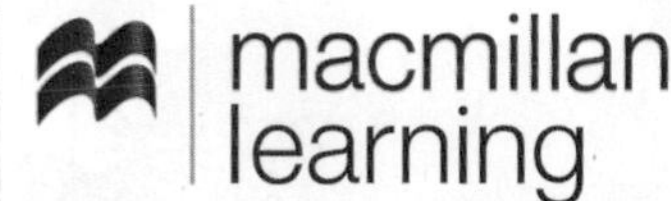

VIDEO: Parenting in Adolescence examines how family structure can help or hinder parent–teen relationships.

parental monitoring
Parents' ongoing knowledge of what their children are doing, where, and with whom.

familism
The belief that family members should support one another, sacrificing individual freedom and success, if necessary, in order to preserve family unity and protect the family.

CULTURAL EXPECTATIONS

Several researchers have noted cultural differences in parent–child relationships. Everywhere, parent–child communication and support (numbers 1 and 2 above) reduce depression and suicide and increase motivation and achievement. However, specifics of connection and control (numbers 3 and 4) vary from one culture to another (Brown & Bakken, 2011; Kapetanovic et al., 2020).

Parent–child conflict is less evident in cultures that stress **familism**, the belief that family members should sacrifice personal freedom and success to care for one another. For example, most refugee youth (Palestinian, Syrian, Iraqi) in Jordan agree that parents have the right to control their children's hairstyles, clothes, and music—contrary to what most U.S. teenagers believe (Smetana et al., 2016).

A developmental shift may occur when adolescents take "active roles in their identity formation . . . [with] increased autonomy in choosing how and with whom to spend their time" (Padilla et al., 2020, p. 1001). If the culture expects teenagers to leave home and forge their own way, then conflict is less problematic.

Personality matters, with differential susceptibility. Some parents listen to whatever opinions their adolescents have; other react with anger. Impulsive, fearful, or adventurous adolescents are more likely to break the law *unless* their family is supportive, in which case they are more law-abiding than the average adolescent (Rioux et al., 2016).

This contrast is evident in school achievement as well. When parents encourage academics, students do better. However, a longitudinal study of intellectually gifted students found that when parents were harsh at puberty, adolescents were less likely to go to college. Gender mattered in what they did instead: Boys were likely to become delinquents; girls to become pregnant (Hentges & Wang, 2018).

Especially for Parents of a Teenager
Your 13-year-old comes home after a sleepover at a friend's house with a new, weird hairstyle—perhaps cut or colored in a bizarre manner. What do you say and do? (see response, page 337)

AN EXAMPLE: MEXICAN AMERICAN FAMILIES

Cultural variations in parent–child interaction are evident not only between nations, but also within U.S. ethnic groups. This is illustrated by in-depth studies of Mexican Americans.

Familism is a strong value in Mexican culture, and teenage independence is a strong value in U.S. culture. Not surprisingly, a recent study found that Mexican

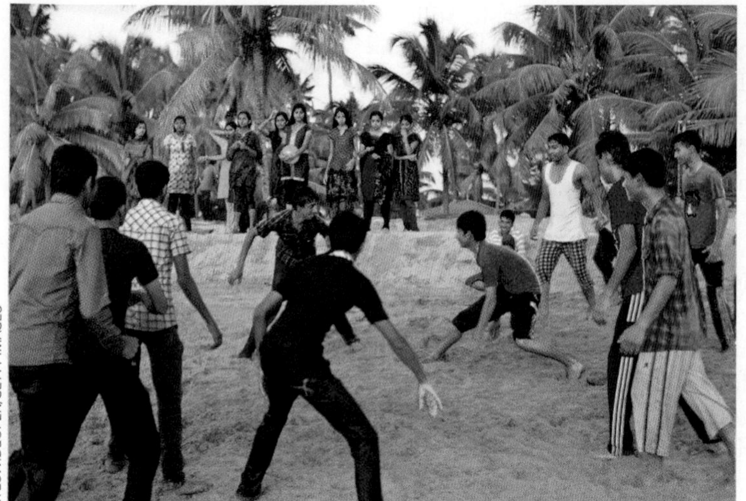
EYESWIDEOPEN/GETTY IMAGES

More Familiar than Foreign? Even in cultures with strong and traditional family influence, teenagers choose to be with peers whenever they can. These boys play at Cherai Beach in India.

◆◆ OBSERVATION QUIZ
What evidence do you see that traditional norms remain in this culture? (see answer, page 337) ↑

American adolescents do not necessarily value familism as their parents do. Fathers, particularly, are likely to endorse familism (e.g., "It is always important to be united as a family"), but older children often do not (Padilla et al., 2020).

Does this mean that conflict is inevitable? No. Among U.S. Latinx families, familism means that parents believe they should ask what their children do and with whom, and children believe they should reply honestly with respect.

That is called a "high-monitoring" family, with everyone sharing information. However, many Latinx parents avoid conflict by not criticizing, especially regarding hair or clothes.

Then, high-monitoring, low-conflict families have happy, helpful, high-performing adolescents. The opposite is true for families who are critical of adolescent choices. High-monitoring, high-conflict families tend to produce low-achieving teens (Roche et al., 2019).

Thus, parental values are sometimes protective. That was one conclusion from a longitudinal study of Mexican American families: Teens who endorsed familism were likely to stay in school and avoid gangs (Wheeler et al., 2017).

Peer Power

Peers can be crucial. They help each other navigate the physical changes of puberty, the social challenges of leaving childhood, and the intellectual challenges of high school. They also share emotions, and by so doing become closer friends (von Salisch, 2018).

MATTHEW STAVER/BLOOMBERG VIA GETTY IMAGES

Everyday Danger After cousins Alex and Arthur, here ages 16 and 20, followed family wishes to shovel snow around their Denver, Colorado, home, they followed their inner risk impulses and jumped from the roof. Not every young man can afford the expense of motocross or hang gliding, but almost every one of them leaps into risks that few 40-year-olds would dare.

CHOOSING FRIENDS

To fully understand the impact of peers, two concepts are helpful: *selection* and *facilitation*. Teenagers *select* friends with similar values and interests, abandoning former friends with other interests. Then, friends *facilitate* destructive or constructive behaviors.

It is easier to do wrong ("Let's all skip school on Friday") or right ("Let's study together for the chem exam") with friends. Peer facilitation helps adolescents do things they are unlikely to do alone. This provides an important clue for adults. Grouping troubled adolescents together (as in special classes in school or residences for young lawbreakers) might make all of them worse, not better (Lochman et al., 2015).

Thus, adolescents select and facilitate, choose and are chosen. Happy, energetic, and successful teens have close friends who themselves are high achievers, with no major emotional problems. A student's grade point average and IQ increase if their friends are highly intelligent (Meldrum et al., 2019).

This works the other way as well. Those who are drug users, sexually active, and alienated from school choose compatible friends. In general, peers provide opportunity, companionship, and encouragement for what young adolescents already might do. Adolescents choose their friends and role models—not always wisely, but never randomly.

PEER PRESSURE

Peer pressure refers to someone being pushed by their friends to do something that they would not do alone. Peer pressure is especially strong in early adolescence, when adults seem clueless about biological and social stresses. Some teenagers are more susceptible to peer pressure than others, with gender one factor. Boys influence other boys more than girls influence other girls (McCoy et al., 2019).

Adults warn children against peer pressure. However, sometimes having friends is beneficial: Peers pressure each other to study, to apply to college, to plan for their future.

This positive take on peer pressure is tempered by another fact: Peers *can* lead one another into trouble. A study of substance misuse and delinquency among twins found that—even controlling for genes and environment—when one twin became a delinquent, the other was more likely to do so (Laursen et al., 2017). Adolescents who are rejected by other peers tend to choose antisocial friends, who then involve them in drugs, aggression, and so on (Kornienko et al., 2020).

Thus, friends choose, teach, and encourage each other. This is shown in **coercive joining**, when two people join together in making derogatory comments about a third person. A pair of teenagers may compete in who can make the most pointed criticisms. Coercive joining at age 12 predicts antisocial violence at age 21 (Dishion et al., 2019).

peer pressure
Encouragement to conform to friends or contemporaries in behavior, dress, and attitude. Adolescents do many things with peers that they would not do alone.

coercive joining
When others strongly encourage someone to join in their activity, usually when the activity is not approved by authorities (e.g., drug use, bullying).

THINK CRITICALLY: Why is peer pressure thought to be much more sinister than it actually is?

A VIEW FROM SCIENCE

The Immediacy of Peers

Given the areas of the brain that are quickest to myelinate and mature in adolescence, it is not surprising that the most influential peers are those nearby at the moment.

This was found in a study in which all eleventh-graders in several public schools in Los Angeles were offered a free online SAT prep course (worth $200) if they signed up on a paper distributed by the organizers (Bursztyn & Jensen, 2015).

In this study, most students had several honors classes and several nonhonors classes, depending on their interests as well as what tests (e.g., AP) they planned to take before college. Students were *not* allowed to talk to each other before deciding whether or not to accept the SAT offer. Consequently, they did not know that, although all of the papers had identical, detailed descriptions of the SAT program, one word differed in who would learn of their decision—either no other students or only the students in that particular class.

The two versions were:

Your decision to sign up for the course will be kept completely private from everyone, except *the other students in the room.*

Your decision to sign up for the course will be kept completely private from everyone, including *the other students in the room.*

It mattered whether students thought their classmates would learn of their decision: The students in an honors class were *more* likely to sign up, and the students in a nonhonors class were *less* likely when they thought their classmates would know what they did.

To make sure this was a peer effect, not just divergent motivation and ability between honors and nonhonors individuals, the researchers compared students who took exactly two honors classes and several nonhonors classes. There were 107 such students, some who happened to be in their honors class when they decided whether or not to sign up for SAT prep and some who happened to be in their nonhonors class.

When the decisions of those two-honors-class students were kept totally private, acceptance rates were similar (72 and 79 percent) no matter where students were at the moment. But if students thought their classmates might know their decision, imagined peer pressure affected them. When in an honors class, 97 percent signed up for the SAT program. Of those in a nonhonors class, only 54 percent signed up (Bursztyn & Jensen, 2015).

Evidence from many other studies finds that peers are especially influential in mid-adolescence. That is reflected in brain activity as well as in behavior (Kim-Spoon et al., 2019). Note that peer influence is not necessarily direct, as when one person tells another what to do. Instead, peer influence is contagious (Reiter et al., 2019).

Just like catching a cold because someone nearby sneezes, adolescents might do what they think nearby peers admire.

HERO IMAGES/GETTY IMAGES

Hang Loose? Are these two dating couples or a group of friends at the basketball court? Notice who has the ball and who appears reluctant to show her face.

OBSERVATION QUIZ
What does the body position of these four suggest? (see answer, page 337) ↑

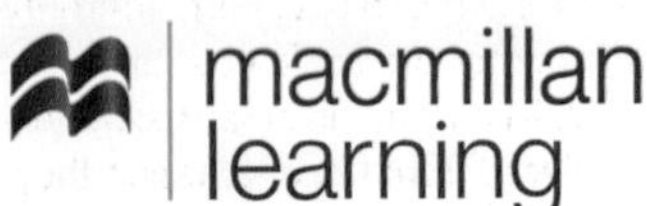

VIDEO: Romantic Relationships in Adolescence explores teens' attitudes and assumptions about romance and sexuality.

sexual orientation
A person's romantic or sexual attraction, which can be to others of the same gender, the other gender, or every gender.

ROMANTIC PARTNERS

Selection is obvious in romance. Adolescents choose and are chosen by romantic partners, and then they influence each other on almost everything—sex, music, work, play, education, food, and so on. Even small things matter: If one gets a new jacket, or tattoo, or sunglasses, the other might, too.

Teens' first romances typically occur in high school, with girls having a steady partner more often than boys. Commitment is the ideal, but the fluidity and rapidity of selection disrupt exclusive relationships. Cheating, flirting, switching, and disloyalty are rife; breakups and unreciprocated crushes are common. Emotions range from exhilaration to despair, leading to impulsive sex, cruel revenge, and deep depression.

Peer support is vital: Friends help adolescents cope with ups and downs. They also influence sexual activity, more by what they say than by what they do (which some keep secret). The friend who brags is more influential than the one who stays quiet.

Most peer relationships are nonsexual: Adolescents have platonic friends of all genders (Kreager et al., 2016a). Norms vary from group to group, school to school, city to city, nation to nation. For instance, twice as many high school students in Cleveland as in Seattle say they have had intercourse (45 percent versus 22 percent) (Johns et al., 2020).

The influence of the social context is undeniable, but sexual impulses are also affected by biology. This is evident in whether or not a romance includes physical activity, and what that physical activity is. Some young people seem driven to risk parental punishment and their own health; others seem content to postpone any sexual activity. Adolescents vary in both the strength of the sexual desire and in their sexual orientation.

Sexual orientation refers to the direction of a person's erotic desires. One meaning of *orient* is "to turn toward"; thus, sexual orientation refers to whether a person is attracted to (turned on by) people of another sex, the same sex, or both. Sexual orientation can be strong, weak, overt, secret, or unconscious.

Every two years, the Youth Risk Behavior Surveillance (YRBS) study asks dozens of questions of high school students from schools throughout the United States. Because this survey was first written two decades ago, the sexual identity options offered are limited. Nonetheless, the data are interesting.

Answers from 344,815 of them between 2005 and 2015 found that 11 percent (14 percent of the girls, 7 percent of the boys) did not choose "heterosexual" as their sexual orientation (Phillips et al., 2019). The number of adolescents who chose something other than heterosexual increased over that decade, and the 2019 data found continued increases (see Figure 10.1).

Particularly interesting is the number of adolescents who choose one sexual orientation at one age and another two years later. Either those teenagers do not know what their sexual interests are, or their interests are shaped by their peers and their culture.

Worldwide, some LGBTQ+ teens date another sex to hide their orientation. Deception puts them at risk for binge drinking, suicidal thoughts, and drug use. Those hazards are less common in cultures where same-sex partnerships are accepted, especially when parents affirm their offspring's sexuality.

At least in the United States, adolescents have similar difficulties and strengths regardless of their gender identity and sexual orientation. Nonsexual friendships with peers of whatever orientation decrease loneliness and increase resilience (Van Harmelen et al., 2017). However, LGBTQ+ youth have a higher risk of depression and anxiety, for reasons relating to every level of Bronfenbrenner's ecological-systems approach (Mustanski et al., 2014).

Gender diversity is increasing, and this is most evident with transgender identity. In 2016, researchers estimated that 1.4 million people in the United States identified as transgender. That is about 0.6 percent, twice the rate a decade earlier (Flores et al., 2018).

The reason for the increase is disputed. Between 2014 and 2016, three times as many U.S. adolescents who had been designated female at birth identified as male (Littman, 2018; Marchiano, 2017).

Some blamed that increase on an encouraging, but mistaken, peer culture. Transgender advocates object to that interpretation, claiming that celebration (not blame) is in order, because more young people can express their identity (Short, 2019; Wadman, 2018).

DATA CONNECTIONS: Sexual Behaviors of U.S. High School Students examines how sexually active teens really are. Achieve

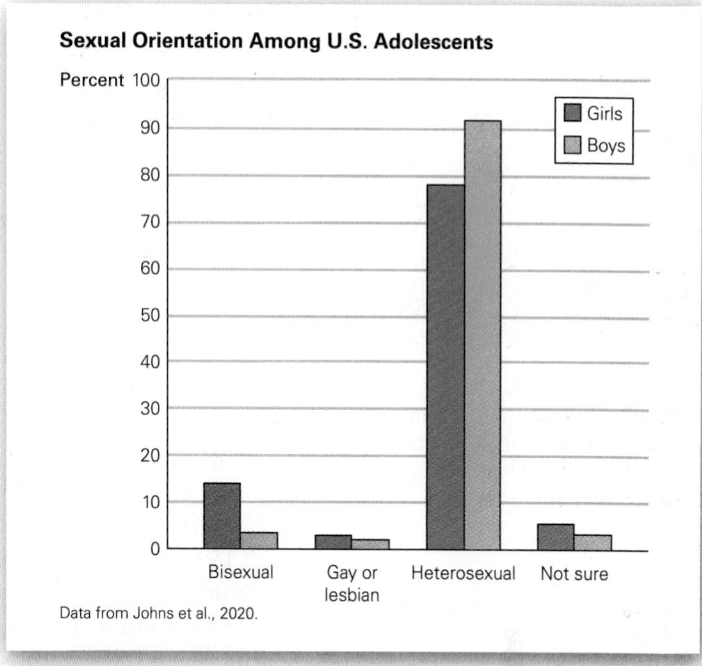

FIGURE 10.1 **Thoughts, Not Actions!** These data come from the answers of high school students throughout the United States, to questions on the Youth Risk Behavior Survey (YRBS). Many had no sexual experiences, and many had sexual experiences that differed from the orientation they indicated for themselves.

Learning About Sex

Some adolescents have strong sexual urges but minimal logic about pregnancy, disease, lust, and love. Millions of teenagers worry that they are oversexed, undersexed, or deviant, unaware that thousands, maybe millions, of others have the same sexual desires.

The most obvious example is with LGBTQ+ youth. When suicide data for these young people became public in about 2010, 50,000 gay and lesbian adults posted "It gets better" videos. They wanted young people to learn that same-sex orientation becomes less burdensome in adulthood (Garrett, 2018).

Indeed, every young person has much to learn. As one observer wrote, adolescents "seem to waffle their way through sexually relevant encounters driven both by the allure of reward and the fear of negative consequences" (Wagner, 2011, p. 193). Where do they learn?

FROM THE MEDIA

Adolescents with intense exposure to sex in music, print, social media, film, and television are more often sexually active, but the direction of this correlation is controversial. The media may reinforce, but not cause, a focus on external appearance, body objectification, and thus sexual activity (Dillman Carpentier & Stevens, 2018; Coyne et al., 2019b).

Not much practical information comes from the media. Television programs that attract teen audiences include sexual content almost seven times per hour (Steinberg & Monahan, 2011). But almost never does a character develop an STI, deal with an unwanted pregnancy, or mention (much less use) a condom.

For questions regarding sexual health, the internet is a common source (Simon & Daneback, 2013). Unfortunately, websites may be frightening (pictures of diseased organs), mesmerizing (pornography), or misleading (false information). A survey of adolescents in England found that they all used the internet for sexual questions, but

they had many criticisms—too much material, too technical, too pornographic, or too simplistic (S. Patterson et al., 2019). As one boy said:

> We're talking about adult issues, you know, with our bodies. We're not here to watch like a Thomas the Tank Engine explain it or anything like that.

FROM PARENTS

It may be that "the most important influences on adolescents' sexual behavior may be closer to home than to Hollywood" (Steinberg & Monahan, 2011, p. 575). As that quote implies, sex education begins at home.

Every study finds that parental communication influences adolescents' behavior. Effective programs of sex education explicitly require parental participation (Silk & Romero, 2014). However, embarrassment and ignorance are common among both generations.

Many parents underestimate their own child's sexual activity while fearing the sexuality of peers and the media (Elliott, 2012). Those fears do not lead to open and honest discussions about sex, love, and life. According to a survey of young women aged 15 to 24 chosen to represent the U.S. population, only 25 percent remembered receiving any sex education from either parent (Vanderberg et al., 2016).

Mothers and daughters more often have detailed conversations than do fathers and sons, but the emphasis is on avoiding pregnancy and diseases, not on pleasure and love. That may be less problematic than it seems.

The strongest influence from parents on sexual relationships was not via conversation about explicit thrills and dangers, but via a strong and supportive parent–child relationship (Cheshire et al., 2019). Religious values also have some influence, but again the impact comes from messages about respect and love rather than from specifics. Almost never does either generation share personal details (Coffelt, 2017).

FROM PEERS

Especially when parents are silent, forbidding, or vague, adolescent sexual behavior is strongly influenced by peers. Boys learn about sex from other boys, girls from other girls. Selection and facilitation are evident again, as adolescents choose friends whose sexual inclinations are similar to their own, and then they talk about it (Trinh et al., 2019).

Partners teach each other. However, their lessons are more about pleasure than consequences: Few U.S. adolescent couples decide together *before* they have sex how they will prevent pregnancy and disease, and what they will do if their efforts fail.

In one study, adolescents were asked with whom they discussed sexual issues. Friends were the most common confidants, then parents, and last of all dating partners. Indeed, only half of them had *ever* discussed specifics of sexual expression with a partner (Widman et al., 2014).

FROM EDUCATORS

Sex education from teachers varies dramatically by school and by nation. The curriculum for middle schools in some Northern European nations includes information about masturbation, same-sex romance, oral and anal sex, and uses and failure rates of methods of contraception. Those subjects are rarely covered in U.S. classes, even in high school.

Rates of teenage pregnancy in Northern European nations are less than half the rates in the United States. Sex education in schools is far from the only reason, but it is one part of it. Indeed, critics explain that most schools in Europe focus more on preventing pregnancy and disease than on the pleasure of an intimate partnership (Bauer et al., 2020; Garzón-Orjuela et al., 2020).

Especially for Sex Educators Suppose adults in your community never talk to their children about sex or puberty. Is that a mistake? (see response, page 337)

Within the United States, the timing and content of sex education vary by state, by community, and by school. Some high schools provide comprehensive education, free condoms, and medical treatment; others provide nothing. Some school systems begin sex education in primary school; others wait until senior year of high school.

A review of official guidelines for sex education in all 50 states found that eight states explicitly condemn same-sex relationships. By contrast, seven states explicitly teach gender diversity of all kinds (Hall et al., 2019). Details about contraception are rarely taught. Instead, some instructors talk privately with individual students who want more information.

Should such private talks be forbidden? One controversy has been whether schools should teach that abstinence is the only acceptable action. Of course, abstaining from sex (including oral and anal sex) prevents STIs and avoids pregnancy, so some adults and most state curricula favor it (Hall et al., 2019).

But longitudinal data comparing students who were taught to avoid all sexual contact until marriage with those who had comprehensive sex education showed similar ages for onset of sexual activity. Indeed, abstinence-only programs increased the rate of teen pregnancy and sexually transmitted infections, since students in those programs never learned about prevention (Fox et al., 2019; Santelli et al., 2017).

THINK CRITICALLY: Why has sex education become a political issue?

Legislative support for abstinence-only education is an example of the problem described in Chapter 1: Opinions may ignore evidence (Hall et al., 2019). It also dismisses medical, psychological, and neurological research. Teen behavior is driven by peer norms and the limbic system, not by textbook facts and the prefrontal cortex. Consequently, sex education must engage students' emotions, not just their minds (Suleiman & Brindis, 2014).

Technology and Human Relationships

Technology has changed the adolescent experience, for better or worse. Today's teenagers are called *digital natives* because they have been networking, texting, and clicking for definitions, directions, and data all their lives. Their smartphones are always within reach; some teens text hundreds of times a day.

In earlier generations, adults thought that the automobile, or the shopping mall, or rock-and-roll music, would lead their children astray. Is digital dependence merely the latest expression of something adults have always feared and teenagers have always sought: connection with peers? Or is it an assault on humanity, alienating students from their families and each other?

The benefits and harms of technology have been brought into focus by the school closings caused by the recent pandemic, which led to many teenagers spending more time online—75 percent of their waking hours, an average of 7 hours per day. However, a nationwide survey found that most adolescents considered social media more helpful than harmful during COVID, a way to feel connected, entertained, and distracted (Harris Insights and Analytics, 2020).

VIDEO: The Impact of Media on Adolescent Development shows how digital technology affects cognition during adolescence.

This was the result of an online poll in May 2020 of 1,516 teenagers from every part of the United States. The sample selection was not random or controlled (a teenager had to have internet access and be willing to answer). However, other data, such as from the American Psychological Association and from the Pew Research Center, point in the same direction.

CYBER ABUSE?

Many parents fear that the internet puts their children at risk for sexual abuse. The facts are reassuring: Although predators lurk online, most teens never encounter them. Sexual abuse is a serious problem, but when the internet first became widespread some adults thought that it allowed perverted older strangers to take sexual advantage of innocent teens. In fact, that was "extremely rare" (Mitchell et al., 2013, p. 1226).

Almost all teen romances begin with a face-to-face attraction to another peer. A survey several years ago found that very few (6 percent) of 13- to 17-year-olds had *ever* had a romance that began online (Lenhart et al., 2015). Teenagers know how to block or unfriend an uncomfortable relationship.

Of course, familiar intimate relationships may also become harmful, not because of technology but because teenagers have much to learn about healthy romances (Liu et al., 2020). Adults need to be more concerned about teens who victimize each other, and less worried about strangers who lurk online.

Earlier in childhood, unpopular children may be bullied, but high school students must contend with a new social dynamic. Popular students maintain their status with online posts that can be both antisocial and prosocial, and thus they often become victims as well as bullies (Ranney & Troop-Gordon, 2020). As with more conventional bullying at earlier ages, parental practices and school climate can mitigate the harm and reduce the prevalence of **cyberbullying** (Zurcher et al., 2018).

cyberbullying
When people try to harm others via electronic means, such as social media, cell phone photos, or texts.

sexting
Sending sexual messages or photographs (usually of one's naked body) via phone or computer.

BENEFITS AND DANGERS

The potential for harm from technology should not prevent us from understanding the benefits. Many teachers and students have found that the vast material available online expands education, allowing students to learn far more than any teacher could be expected to know.

Further, remember the need for peer support during adolescence. Teens who were lonely and isolated a few decades ago, such as those with Down syndrome, or who are deaf, or the only one in their neighborhood with a certain ethnic, religious, or gender identity, can find peers.

The need for peer connection and the benefits of technology are especially obvious with the COVID-19 pandemic (Ellis et al., 2020). To stave off depression, rage, and despair, many adolescents engaged with their friends online, morning, noon, and night. They also searched for accurate information on death and recovery rates, on effective treatments, on testing locations. The virus offered some unexpected benefits, not only cleaner air, but for some, family harmony: The generations could work together to separate facts from scams, partisan politics, and wishful thinking.

THINK CRITICALLY: The older people are, the more likely they are to be critical of social media. Why?

The danger is that adolescents can also connect with people whose views are destructive. The hazards of adolescent egocentrism, and of intuitive rather than analytic cognition, are obvious. Messages are sent in an instant, with no second thoughts. Troubled adolescents can connect with others who share their prejudices and self-destructive compulsions, such as anorexia, gun use, racism, or cutting.

Benefits and harms from technology are evident regarding romance: The internet can provide information that the adolescent's school might not give, and allow romantic interaction with no chance of STI or pregnancy. Texting—hundreds of times a day—is common among adolescent lovers. This can include **sexting**, as sending sexual photographs and videos is called.

However, when a romance ends, it may turn ugly. Of those who have quit a romance, 15 percent report being threatened online (Lenhart et al., 2015). If bullying takes a sexual tone, it can be particularly harmful.

The danger of technology lies not in the equipment but in the mind. As with many adolescent concerns (puberty, sexuality, body image, motivation), cognition and many other factors "shape, mediate, and/or modify effects" of technology (Oakes, 2009, p. 1142). Instead of being *native* users of technology, many teenagers are *naive* users—believing they have privacy settings that they do not have, trusting sites that are markedly biased, believing fake news, not knowing how to find and verify information (boyd, 2014).

ADOLESCENT BULLYING

Bullying is defined as repeated attempts to hurt someone else, physically or socially. It can take many forms. For younger children, it is often physical—hitting, shoving, fighting. That is less common among adolescents, who can hurt each other with words or exclusion. Among teenagers, not being invited to a party can be hurtful and is common—as teenagers develop dominance hierarchies and need peer support. The best protection is to have one or more close friends, and adults who encourage whatever talents the child has.

The Nature of School Bullying

When bullying takes place at school, about two-thirds of it occurs in hallways, schoolyards, bathrooms, cafeterias, or buses. A full one-third occurs in classrooms, while teachers are present. An estimated 30% of school bullying goes unreported.

Features of School Anti-Bullying Programs

- Increased supervision of students
- A school climate that encourages friendship
- Teachers who promote empathy
- School-wide implementation of anti-bullying policies
- Cooperation among school staff, parents, and professionals across disciplines
- Identification of risk factors for bullying

Success varies, with some programs having no effect. But overall, a good program can reduce bullying by 25% or more.

Data from McCallion & Feder, 2013.

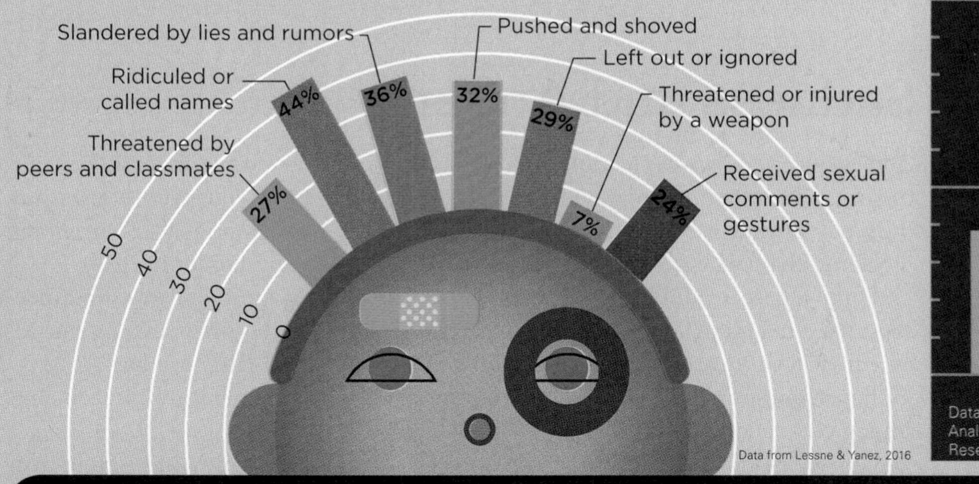

Data from Lessne & Yanez, 2016

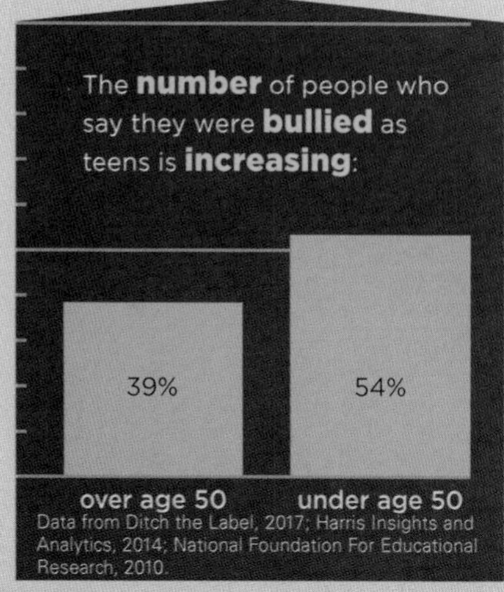

Data from Ditch the Label, 2017; Harris Insights and Analytics, 2014; National Foundation For Educational Research, 2010.

CYBERBULLYING

Cyberbullying takes place via e-mail, text messages, websites and apps, instant messaging, chat rooms, or posted videos or photos. About 60% of boys and girls have been cyberbullied, but girls are more often the targets of online rumor-spreading or nonconsensual explicit messages (Anderson, 2018).

WHY DO TEENS CYBERBULLY?

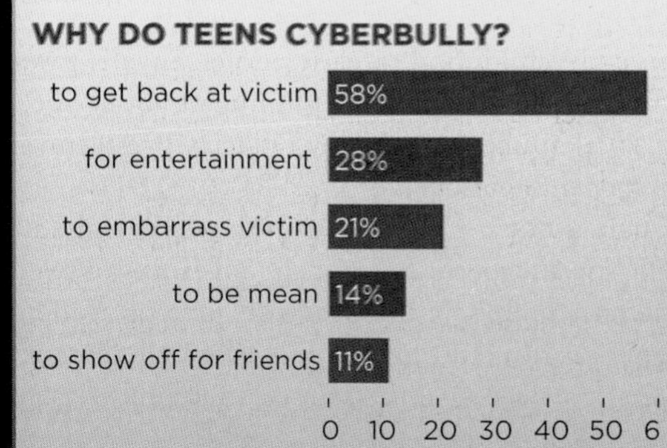

SOCIAL MEDIA AND CYBERBULLYING

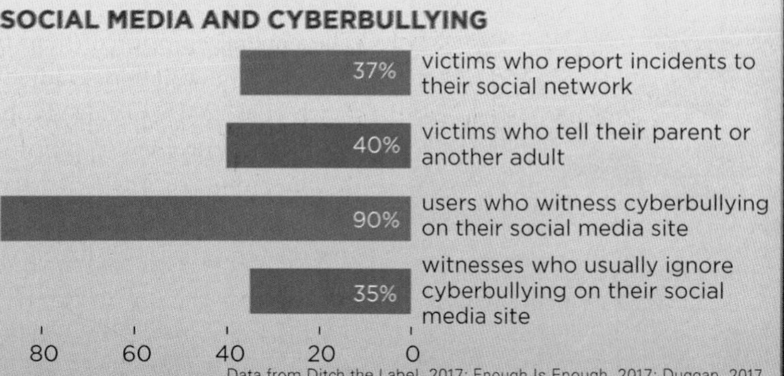

Data from Ditch the Label, 2017; Enough Is Enough, 2017; Duggan, 2017.

Adults can help with all of this—but only if they themselves understand technology and adolescence. Teens are intuitive, impulsive, and egocentric, often unaware of the impact of what they send or the validity of what they see online. Adults should know better.

what have you learned?

1. How do parent–adolescent relationships change over time?
2. When is parental monitoring a sign of a healthy parent–adolescent relationship?
3. How do the influences of peers and parents differ for adolescents?
4. Why do many adults misunderstand the role of peer pressure?
5. How does culture affect sexual orientation?
6. From whom do adolescents usually learn about sex?
7. Why do some schools teach abstinence-only sex education?
8. What are the advantages and disadvantages of technology in adolescence?
9. Why might sexting be a problem?
10. How might the term *digital native* be misleading?

Sadness and Anger

Adolescence can be a wonderful time. Nonetheless, troubles plague about 20 percent of youths. In a national survey, 16 percent of 12- to 17-year-olds said that, within the past year, they had received mental health counseling for emotional or behavioral problems (Substance Abuse and Mental Health Services Administration, 2019).

This 16 percent did not include those whose primary problem was substance abuse. Nor did it include those who experienced severe depression or anxiety caused by efforts to mitigate COVID-19. Solid percentages of the latter are hard to verify, but many sources find that COVID caused additional mental health problems among older adolescents (Guessoum et al., 2020).

Sadness and anger may dissipate, a temporary cloud in a sunny life. Or despair or rage may become intense, chronic, even deadly. Parents and peers can help a sad or angry child regulate emotions, or they can react with extreme emotions of their own, pushing a teenager toward suicide or prison. When does normal moodiness becomes pathological? And what should be done when it does?

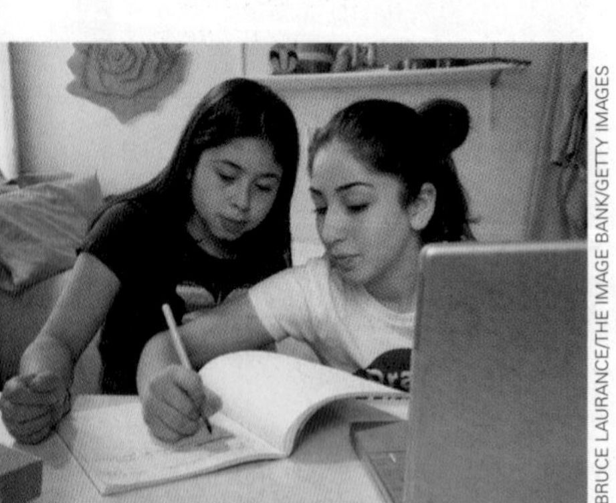
BRUCE LAURANCE/THE IMAGE BANK/GETTY IMAGES

Sibling Rivalry? No! This Latina 15-year-old is a role model for her 11-year-old sister, evident here as she helps with homework.

Depression

The general emotional trend from early childhood to early adolescence is toward less confidence. Then, gradually, self-esteem increases, beginning at about age 15 (Orth et al., 2018; Orth & Robins, 2019). Puberty itself may reduce self-esteem, and so does extensive viewing of social media (Steinsbekk et al., 2021).

The risk of serious self-harm, such as cutting, is greatest in the years right after puberty (Plener et al., 2015). Specific social experiences and circumstances outweigh age-related trends. Positive experiences include a fulfilling romance or academic success; negative ones include peer rejection and prison. For every adolescent of every ethnicity, the immediate social context—in the school, the family, and the community—is crucial.

Most teens cope with stress by talking with friends, but that was more difficult during the COVID-19 pandemic when schools were closed. Sadly, two-thirds of the teens who responded to the aforementioned poll in 2020 said they felt sad or anxious more often than once a week. The same proportion said they tried to keep their feeling to themselves, pretending to be happier in order not to worry anyone (Harris Insights and Analytics, 2020).

MAJOR DEPRESSIVE DISORDER

Some adolescents sink into **major depressive disorder (MDD)**, a deep sadness and hopelessness that disrupts all normal, regular activities. The causes predate adolescence, but puberty—with physical and emotional turbulence—pushes some vulnerable children, especially girls, into despair. The rate of serious depression more than doubles during this time to an estimated 15 percent, affecting about 1 in 5 girls and 1 in 10 boys.

Serious, distressing thoughts about killing oneself (called **suicidal ideation**) are most common at about age 15. Even before COVID, more than a third (41 percent) of U.S. high school girls felt so hopeless that they stopped doing some usual activities for two weeks or more in the previous year (an indication of depression), and more than one-fifth (22 percent) thought seriously about suicide. For boys, the rates were 21 percent and 12 percent (MMWR, June 15, 2018).

Suicidal ideation can lead to **parasuicide**, also called *attempted suicide* or *failed suicide*. Parasuicide includes any deliberate self-harm that could have been lethal. Parasuicide is the preferred term because "failed" suicide implies that to die is to succeed (!). "Attempt" is likewise misleading because, especially in adolescence, the difference between attempt and completion may be luck and treatment, not intent.

As you see in Figure 10.2, parasuicide can be divided according to whether or not medical treatment (surgery, pumped stomach, etc.) was needed, but every parasuicide is a warning. Among U.S. high school students in 2019, 11 percent of the girls and 7 percent of the boys attempted suicide in the previous year (Johns et al., 2020).

COMPLETED SUICIDES

Although suicidal ideation during adolescence is common, completed suicides are not. In the United States in 2016, the rate of completed suicide for White teenagers, aged 15 to 19 (in school or not), was about 5 per 100,000, or 0.005 percent. The rate for teenagers of color was about half that. Suicides are three times as common

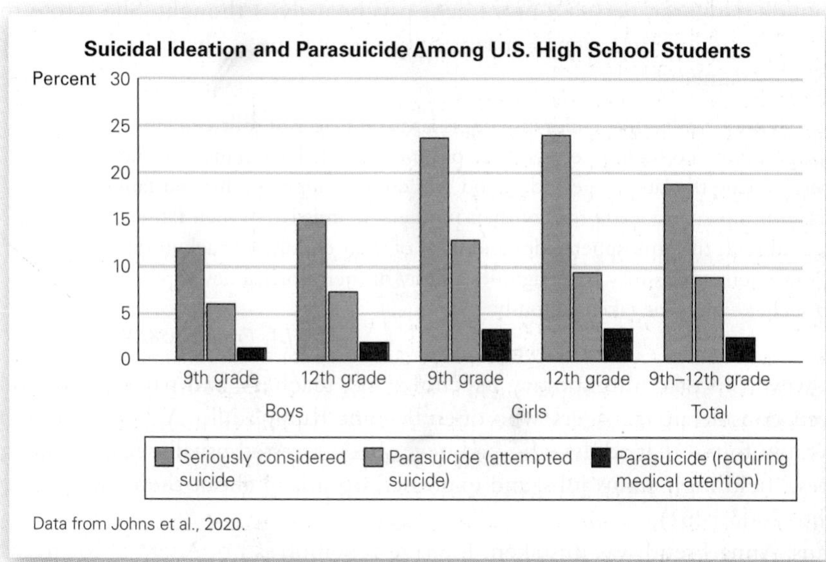

CHAPTER APP 10

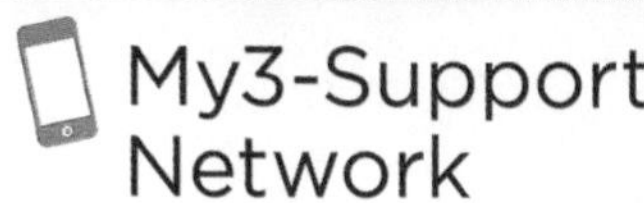

My3-Support Network

iOS:
https://tinyurl.com/yyzlpmqo

ANDROID:
https://tinyurl.com/qgsd6qb

RELEVANT TOPIC:
Suicidal ideation among adolescents

My3-Support Network is a crisis-support app for people who experience suicidal thoughts. Users choose three trusted people from their contacts list to place on the app (911 and the National Suicide Hotline are automatically listed). Users create a safety plan, listing warning signs, coping strategies, distractions, and "reasons to live." The app can link users to organizations that address specific needs, such as suicide attempt survivors, LGBTQ+ youth, and more.

major depressive disorder (MDD)
Feelings of hopelessness, lethargy, and worthlessness that last two weeks or more.

suicidal ideation
Serious thinking about suicide, often including extreme emotions and thoughts.

parasuicide
Any potentially deadly self-harm that does not result in death. (Also called *attempted suicide* or *failed suicide*.)

FIGURE 10.2 **Talk to Me** As you see, about half of the adolescents who think about suicide try it. Often the difference between thought and deed is an empathic listener, who hears the pain and then helps the young person see past it.

OBSERVATION QUIZ
Does thinking seriously about suicide increase or decrease during high school? (see answer, page 337) ←

among adults, with the highest rate of all among White men in their 80s (Stone et al., 2021).

Curiously, although girls have higher rates of parasuicide, boys have higher rates of completed suicide, especially boys who are troubled about their gender identity or sexual orientation. Suicide rates are seven times higher for LGBTQ+ youth than others (Romanelli et al., 2020).

Of course, even one teen suicide is a tragedy, and it is particularly poignant when the media shares the story and a photo of the fresh-faced young person. Those stories can cause teen depression and copycat suicides. Adolescent self-harm (parasuicide, cutting, extreme dieting), and major depression seem to be increasing; extensive media use (TV, social media, the internet) is a correlate (Twenge et al., 2018).

For example, teen suicide rates increased by almost a third after the release of a Netflix program *Thirteen Reasons Why*, which depicted a girl slitting her wrists (Bridge et al., 2019). Netflix's chief executive, Reed Hastings, said "no one has to watch it." Whether he is naive, cynical, or evil is a matter of opinion.

If you or someone you know needs help, call the National Suicide Prevention Lifeline at **1-800-273-8255**. You can also text HOME to **741-741** for free, 24-hour support from the Crisis Text Line.

Because they are more emotional and egocentric than logical and analytical, adolescents are particularly affected when they hear about someone else's suicide. That explains **cluster suicides** (several suicides within a group in the same time period). Although the overall rate is lower in adolescence, a higher proportion are cluster suicides, romantic couple suicides, or suicides by the same means as a recent celebrity suicide (Kral, 2019).

cluster suicides
Several suicides committed by members of a group within a brief period.

Delinquency and Defiance

Like low self-esteem and suicidal ideation, bouts of anger are common in adolescence. In fact, a moody adolescent could be both depressed and angry: Externalizing and internalizing behavior are closely connected during these years. This may explain suicide in jail: Teenagers incarcerated for assault (externalizing) are at greater risk of suicide (internalizing) than adult prisoners (Ruch et al., 2019).

Externalizing actions are hard to ignore. Many adolescents slam doors, curse parents, and tell friends exactly how badly other teenagers (or siblings or teachers) have behaved. Some—particularly boys—"act out" by breaking laws. They steal, damage property, or injure others.

Internalized behavior is less blatant. A teenager might stay in bed all day, or stop eating, or drink alcohol until oblivious.

Is teenage anger necessary for normal development? That is what Anna Freud (Sigmund's daughter, herself a prominent psychoanalyst) thought. She wrote that adolescent resistance to parental authority was "welcome . . . beneficial . . . inevitable." She explained:

> We all know individual children who, as late as the ages of fourteen, fifteen or sixteen, show no such outer evidence of inner unrest. They remain, as they have been during the latency period, "good" children, wrapped up in their family relationships, considerate sons of their mothers, submissive to their fathers, in accord with the atmosphere, idea and ideal of their childhood background. Convenient as this may be, it signifies a delay of their normal development and is, as such, a sign to be taken seriously.
>
> *[A. Freud, 1958/2000, p. 37]*

However, most contemporary psychologists, teachers, and parents like well-behaved, considerate teenagers, who often become happy adults. A 30-year longitudinal study found that adults who had never been arrested usually earned colleges degrees, "held high-status jobs, and expressed optimism about their own futures" (Moffitt, 2003, p. 61).

Thus, Anna Freud was mistaken. Teenage rebellion is not essential for healthy development.

JUSTIN SULLIVAN/GETTY IMAGES

ED JONES/AFP/GETTY IMAGES

In Every Nation Everywhere, older adolescents are most likely to protest against government authority. Adolescents in Alabama *(left)* celebrate the 50-year anniversary of the historic Selma-to-Montgomery march across the Pettus Bridge. In that historic movement, most of those beaten and killed were under age 25. In the fall of 2014, thousands of students in Hong Kong *(right)* led pro-democracy protests, which began peacefully but led, days later, to violent confrontations, show here as they began.

BREAKING THE LAW

Both the *prevalence* (how widespread) and the *incidence* (how frequent) of criminal actions are higher during adolescence than earlier or later. Arrest statistics in every nation reflect this fact, with 30 percent of African American males and 22 percent of European American males being arrested at least once before age 18 (Brame et al., 2014).

Many more broke the law but were not caught, or were caught but not arrested. Self-reports suggest that most adolescents, of every gender, are lawbreakers before age 20. One reason is that many behaviors that are legal for adults—buying cigarettes, having intercourse, skipping school—are illegal for adolescents.

Arrest rates are higher for youth of minority ethnic groups, and boys are three times as likely as girls to be caught, arrested, and convicted. Does this reflect prejudice (Marotta & Voisin, 2017)? Some studies find that female aggression typically targets family and friends. Parents hesitate to call the police to arrest their daughters.

FALSE CONFESSIONS

Determining accurate gender, ethnic, and income differences in actual lawbreaking, not just in arrests, is difficult. Self-reports may be false, with boasting or denial. For instance, researchers in the Netherlands contacted teenagers who were interrogated by the police. (The teens did not know that the researchers knew about the interrogations.) They were asked if they had ever had *any* police contact. One-third said no (van Batenburg-Eddes et al., 2012).

The opposite is also likely. In the United States, about 20 percent of confessions are false, with higher rates among teenagers. Why? Brain immaturity (delay discounting) makes young people ignore long-term consequences. Instead, they may prioritize protecting family members, defending friends, and pleasing adults—including the police (Feld, 2013; Steinberg, 2009).

One dramatic case involved 13-year-old Tyler Edmonds, who confessed to killing his brother-in-law. He was sentenced to life in prison. He then said that he confessed falsely to protect his 26-year-old sister, whom he admired. (She told him to confess, because she said his youth would mean his sentence would be short.) His conviction was overturned—after he spent four years behind bars (Malloy et al., 2014).

The researchers who cited Tyler's case interviewed 194 boys, aged 14 to 17, all convicted of serious crimes. More than one-third (35 percent) said they had confessed falsely to a crime (not necessarily the one for which they were serving time). False confessions were more likely after two hours of intense interrogation: Many adolescents acted on impulse to stop the interrogations, so they lied and said they were guilty (Malloy et al., 2014). And the police believed them.

A CRIMINAL CAREER?

Many researchers distinguish between two kinds of teenage lawbreakers (Levey et al., 2019; Monahan et al., 2013), as first proposed by Terri Moffitt (2001, 2003). Both types are usually arrested for the first time in adolescence and for similar crimes, but their future diverges.

adolescence-limited offender A person who breaks the law as a teenager but whose criminal activity stops by age 20.

life-course-persistent offender A person whose criminal activity begins in adolescence and continues throughout life; a "career" criminal.

- Most are **adolescence-limited offenders**. Their criminal activity stops by age 21. They break the law with their friends, facilitated by their chosen antisocial peers.
- Some are **life-course-persistent offenders**, who become career criminals. Their lawbreaking is often done alone, not with peers. Often they have signs of neurological impairment (either inborn or caused by early experiences), evident in learning disabilities.

During adolescence, the criminal records of both types may be similar. However, if adolescence-limited delinquents are protected from snares (quitting school, incarceration, prejudice, drug addiction), they outgrow their criminal behavior.

CAUSES OF DELINQUENCY

The best way to reduce adolescent crime is to notice early behavior that predicts lawbreaking and to change patterns before puberty. Strong and protective social relationships, emotional regulation, and moral values from childhood keep many teenagers from jail. Since learning disabilities and school failure are precursors to crime, effective remediation at age 6 may reduce delinquency at age 16.

Adolescent crime in the United States and many other nations has decreased in the past 30 years. Only a third as many arrests of people under age 18 occurred in 2018 compared to 2000. There are many possible explanations:

- fewer high school dropouts (more education means less crime);
- wiser judges (more community service than prison);
- better policing (arrests for misdemeanors are up, which may warn parents);
- smaller families (parents attend more to each of 2 children than each of 12);
- better contraception (unwanted children often become delinquents);
- less drug use (binge drinking and crack cocaine use increase crime);
- more immigrants (who are more law-abiding); and
- less lead in the blood (lead poisoning reduces brain functioning).

Nonetheless, adolescents are more likely to break the law than adults, perhaps because of their brains as well as because of the social context. (See Inside the Brain.)

INSIDE THE BRAIN

Impulses, Rewards, and Reflection

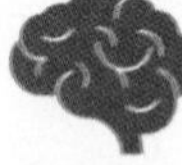

For almost every crime, in almost every nation, the arrest rate for 15- to 17-year-olds is twice that for those over 18 (exceptions are fraud, forgery, and embezzlement).

What is wrong with those teenagers? Irresponsible parents? Poverty? Drug addiction? Maybe none of these. Perhaps the problem is in the brain, not in outside forces.

The limbic system is activated by puberty while the prefrontal cortex is "developmentally constrained," maturing more gradually (Hartley & Somerville, 2015, p. 109). Thus, adolescents are swayed by their intuition instead of by analysis.

Many studies confirm that adolescents show "heightened activity in the striatum, both when anticipating rewards and when receiving rewards" (Crone et al., 2016, p. 360). In choosing between a small but guaranteed reward and a large possible reward, adolescent brains show more activity for the larger reward than do the brains of children or adults.

This means that when teenagers weigh the possible results of a particular action, their brains make them more inclined to imagine success than to fear failure. Whether this makes them brave and bold or foolish and careless is a matter of opinion, but there is no doubt that neurological circuits tip the balance toward action. Nor is there any doubt that the reward circuits in the brain are powerfully activated in adolescence (Cao et al., 2019).

A related aspect of adolescent brains is that peer acclaim or rejection is deeply felt, with activation throughout the limbic system as well as other subcortical areas. This may help explain another aspect of adolescent crime: It often occurs in groups, whereas most adult criminals act alone.

Thus, neurological sensitivity may explain why teens readily follow impulses that promise social approval from friends and shun experiences that might bring social rejection. In experiments in which adults and adolescents, alone or with peers, play video games in which taking risks might lead to crashes or gaining points, adolescents are much more likely than adults are to risk crashing, especially when they are with peers.

When they are with their mothers, not their peers, teenagers are much more cautious in such simulations. However, as the connection between two brain regions (the *anterior insula* and the *ventral striatum*) increases in adolescence, risk-taking when the mother is absent increases, especially if the family relationship is not supportive (Guassi Moreira & Telzer, 2018).

There are other notable differences in brain activity (specifically in the ventral striatum) between adolescents and adults. When with other adults, the adult brain signals caution (inhibition)—opposite to the adolescent brain with peers (Albert et al., 2013) (see Figure 10.3).

This helps explain why teenage drivers like to fill (or overfill) cars with teen passengers who will admire them for speeding, for passing trucks on blind curves, for racing through railroad crossings when the warning lights are flashing, and so on. Fatal accidents are much more likely if the driver and the passengers are adolescents.

The accident rate in adolescence is aided by a third brain change in adolescence. Compared to children, there is a substantial increase in myelination between the emotional and action parts of the brain. This increase in white matter means rapid responses. As a result, adolescents act before slower-thinking adults can stop them (Hartley & Somerville, 2015).

Thus, don't blame teen crashes, juvenile delinquency, or drug use on inexperience; blame it on the brain. Some states now prohibit teen drivers from transporting other teenagers, reducing deaths and banning one source of adolescent excitement. States that allow marijuana always prohibit it before age 18. Some judges hesitate to give life sentences to adolescents.

Teens advocate for some laws, such as those that protect the environment; they do not advocate for laws that restrict drug use, driver's licenses, or gun purchases based on age.

After a mass shooting at a high school in Parkland, Florida, students advocated a ban on rapid-fire guns; the legislature instead banned handgun sales to teenagers.

Does this mean they understood the teen brain or that they understood their voters?

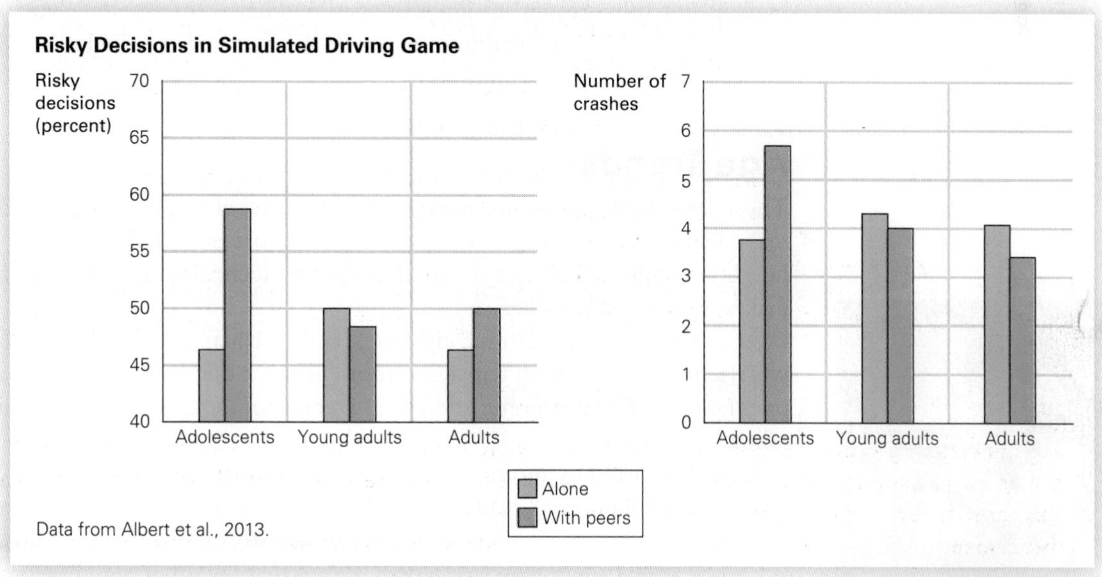

FIGURE 10.3 Losing Is Winning In this game, risk-taking led to more crashes and fewer points. As you see, adolescents were strongly influenced by the presence of peers, so much so that they lost points that they would have kept if they had played alone. In fact, sometimes they laughed when they crashed instead of bemoaning their loss. Note the contrast with emerging adults, who were more likely to take risks when alone.

what have you learned?

1. What is the difference between adolescent sadness and major depression?
2. Why do many adults think adolescent suicide is more common than it is?
3. What are the gender differences in adolescent depression, suicide, and arrest?
4. Why are cluster suicides more common in adolescence than in later life?
5. What are the similarities between life-course-persistent and adolescence-limited offenders?
6. Why would anyone confess to a crime they did not do?

Drug Use and Abuse

Most teenagers try *psychoactive drugs*, that is, drugs that activate the brain. Brain changes in the reward system lead directly to increases in drug abuse, such as binge drinking (Morales et al., 2018). Hormonal surges, the brain's reward centers, and cognitive immaturity make adolescents particularly attracted to the sensations produced by psychoactive drugs. But their immature bodies and brains make drug use especially toxic.

Every psychoactive drug excites the limbic system and interferes with the prefrontal cortex. Because of these neurological reactions, drug users are more emotional (varying from euphoria to terror, from paranoia to rage) and less reflective than they would otherwise be.

That may explain why every hazard—including car crashes, unsafe sex, and suicide—is more common when teens use psychoactive drugs. The same drugs are hazardous in adulthood, but the risk is higher among teenagers because their prefrontal cortex is less able to reign in the limbic system. As you remember, the brain is not fully grown until about age 25. That is one reason that societies try to protect the youth by making the purchase of any drug—including alcohol and tobacco—illegal before adulthood.

Age Trends

Those laws fight against the adolescent urge to rebel and experiment. Those urges make many teenagers eager to try psychoactive drugs, including tobacco and alcohol. Use increases from age 10 to 25 and then decreases, because adult maturation makes drugs less attractive.

Use of legal drugs (alcohol, cigarettes, and marijuana) before age 15 is especially worrisome, because brain damage is more likely at that age. Moreover, early experimentation tends to become addiction. Depression, sexual abuse, and bullying may follow.

JASON LEE/REUTERS

A Man Now? This boy in Tibet is proud to be a smoker—in many Asian nations, smoking is considered manly.

One drug follows another pattern—*inhalants* (fumes from aerosol containers, glue, cleaning fluid, etc.). Sadly, the youngest adolescents are most likely to try inhalants, because they are easiest to get (hardware stores, drug stores, and supermarkets stock them). Cognitive immaturity means that few understand the risks—brain damage and even death (Nguyen et al., 2016).

Cohort differences are evident for every drug, even from one year to the next. Legalization of marijuana, e-cigarettes in many flavors, hundreds of deaths from opioids, dozens of deaths from vaping—these are examples of changes in the adolescent drug scene over the past few years.

Adolescent drug use in the United States has declined since 1976 (see Figure 10.4) with one major exception, vaping. Although adults try to limit adolescent drug use primarily by making drugs less available, perception of risk, not availability, reduces use. Most high school students have always said that they could easily get alcohol, cigarettes, and marijuana (Miech et al., 2016).

Availability is notable for e-cigarettes. Although the United States prohibits adolescent purchase, 13- to 17-year-olds often buy them, in stores and on the internet. When laws are strictly enforced, most young users get their e-cigarettes from other adolescents (Braak et al., 2020; McKeganey et al., 2019).

In 2020, 20 percent of high school students and 5 percent of middle school student in the United States report current e-cigarette use (T. Wang et al., 2020). Availability is widespread. Is that a problem? (See Opposing Perspectives.)

Percent of U.S. High School Seniors Reporting Drug Use in the Past Year

Alcohol
Marijuana
Ritalin
Adderall
Illicit drugs other than marijuana
Any prescription drug*
Amphetamines
Vicodin
Cocaine
OxyContin

**Includes use of amphetamines, sedatives (barbiturates), narcotics other than heroin, or tranquilizers—without a doctor's prescription.*

Data from Miech et al., 2019.

FIGURE 10.4 Rise and Fall By asking the same questions year after year, the Monitoring the Future study shows notable historical effects. It is encouraging that something in society, not in the adolescent, makes drug use increase and decrease and that the most recent data show a continued decline in the drug most commonly abused—alcohol.

Harm from Drugs

Drug use before maturity is particularly likely to harm growth and predict later addiction. However, few adolescents are aware of when they or their friends move past use (experimenting) to abuse (experiencing harm).

OPPOSING PERSPECTIVES

E-Cigarettes: Path to Addiction or Health?

Electronic cigarettes (called e-cigs) are much less damaging to the lungs than conventional cigarettes, because they deliver the drugs by vapor (vaping). Smokers with asthma, heart disease, or lung cancer benefit from vaping if it reduces their smoking of combustible cigarettes (Veldheer et al., 2019).

However, the health risk of e-cigs is not zero. In 2018, over 50 people died of a severe lung disease caused by e-cigs. The youngest death occurred in Texas in 2020. He was 15. The deaths are blamed on a particular ingredient (vitamin E) that most e-cigs do not have. However, all of them produce *benzene*, a known carcinogen (Pankow et al., 2017).

Moreover, many e-cigs contain nicotine, which may be more addictive than heroin. Some contain THC, a compound in marijuana. If the choice is between smoking and vaping, vaping is better. But if the choice is between e-cigs and being free of all cigarettes, vaping is worse.

Developmentalists fear that e-cigarettes will open the door to other drugs. This notion led to a new U.S. law in late 2019 that banned the sale of tobacco products, including e-cigs, to people under age 21. In early 2020, the Food and Drug Administration announced it would crack down on vendors who sold cartridge-based vaping products in kid-friendly flavors.

One company (JUUL) designed e-cigs with a sleek delivery gadget that looks like a USB drive, and advertised on social media. The target consumers were White teenagers (see Figure 10.5). That dramatically increased market share among adolescents, with sales approaching a billion dollars. The executives contend that good business practices and clever advertising, both admired by many adults, have made them successful (Huang et al., 2019).

The arguments from distributors of e-cigarettes are that their products are healthier than cigarettes, that people

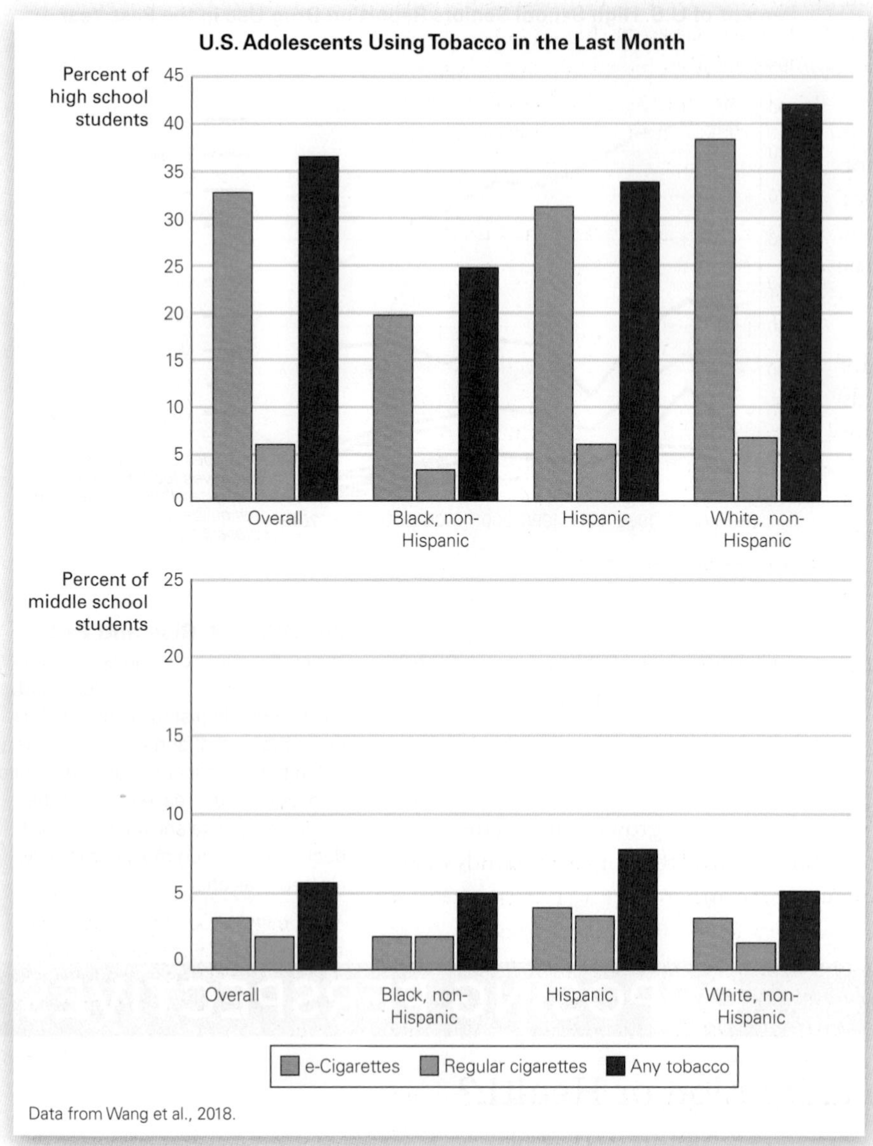

FIGURE 10.5 Getting Better The fact that more than one in five high school students (that's 3 million people) used tobacco—even though purchase of any kind is illegal—in the past month is troubling. This means that more than 3 million students are at risk for addiction and poor health. The surprise (not shown) is that all of these rates are lower than a year earlier. Is that because laws are stricter, or because teenagers are getting wiser?

should make their own choices, and that the fear of adolescent vaping is exaggerated—part of the irrational fear that everything teenagers do is trouble.

Yet most public health doctors advise against e-cigs, and pediatricians worry that fetal and infant lungs suffer if the mother uses them (Carlsen et al., 2018). With rats, vaping decreases birthweight, which increases risks for early death and brain damage (Orzabal et al., 2019).

The evidence says caution, but caution is scarce at adolescence. The media presents mixed messages: Are strict age restrictions protective or puritanical (Morphett et al., 2020)? Opposing perspectives are apparent: Which perspective is yours?

Each drug is harmful in a particular way. *Tobacco* impairs digestion and nutrition, slowing down growth. Since internal organs mature after the height spurt, smoking teenagers who appear to be fully grown may damage their developing hearts, lungs, brains, and reproductive systems.

◆◆ Especially for Parents Who Drink Socially
You have heard that parents should allow their children to drink at home, to teach them to drink responsibly and not get drunk elsewhere. Is that wise? (see response, page 337)

Alcohol is the most frequently abused drug in North America. Heavy drinking impairs memory and self-control by damaging the hippocampus and the prefrontal cortex, perhaps distorting the reward circuits of the brain lifelong (Guerri & Pascual, 2010).

Ironically, many antidrug parents condone adolescent drinking. For instance, a careful longitudinal study in Australia found that parents who provided alcohol to their

teenagers thought they were teaching responsible drinking, but instead they were increasing binge drinking and substance use disorder six years later (Mattick et al., 2018).

Marijuana seems harmless to many people (especially teenagers), partly because users are more relaxed than verbose, and thus do not appear high. Yet adolescents who regularly smoke marijuana are more likely to drop out of school, become teenage parents, be depressed, and later be unemployed. Most of the evidence for this harm comes from years when marijuana was illegal.

In the next few years, we will learn more. Canada legalized marijuana for adults in the summer of 2018. Canadian health researchers hope that, once the brain is mature, benefits outweigh risks (Lake & Kerr, 2017). Marijuana is illegal in Canada for those under 18, although some doctors wish 21 were the cutoff (Rankin, 2017).

Any age restriction encourages younger adolescents to covet drugs used by older youth, which creates a major problem. This was evident when New Zealand lowered the age for legal purchase of alcohol from 20 to 18. Hospital admissions for intoxication, car crashes, and injuries from assault, increased, not only for 18- to 19-year-olds but also for 16- to 17-year-olds (Kypri et al., 2006, 2014).

Preventing Drug Abuse: What Works?

Remember that most adolescents think they are exceptions, sometimes feeling invincible, sometimes fearing social disapproval, but almost never being realistic about potential addiction or about their peers' reaction if they reject a toke, a sip, a line.

Moreover, breaking the law may be thrilling, defying authority may be exciting, and drugs may help them feel smarter, more awake, more fun. They do not see that, over time, stress and depression increase, and achievement decreases (Bagot, 2017; McCabe et al., 2017).

With harmful drugs, as with many other aspects of life, people of each generation prefer to learn things for themselves. A common phenomenon is **generational forgetting**, that each new cohort forgets what the previous cohort learned. New drugs are particularly attractive, because novelty is exciting. That may explain why e-cigarettes have become so popular so quickly. No one used them a decade ago.

generational forgetting
The idea that each new generation forgets what the previous generation learned. As used here, the term refers to knowledge about the harm drugs can do.

Mistrust of the older generation along with a loyalty to one's peers leads not only to generational forgetting but also to a backlash. When adults forbid something, that is a reason to try it, especially if adults exaggerate the dangers. If a friend passes out from drug use, adolescents may be slow to get medical help—a dangerous hesitancy.

Some antidrug curricula and advertisements make drugs seem exciting. Antismoking announcements produced by cigarette companies (such as a clean-cut young person advising viewers to think before they smoke) actually increase use (Strasburger et al., 2009). Yellowed teeth, bad breath, and slowed reaction time are all feared by adolescents more than eventual cancer. Effective ad campaigns target the audience.

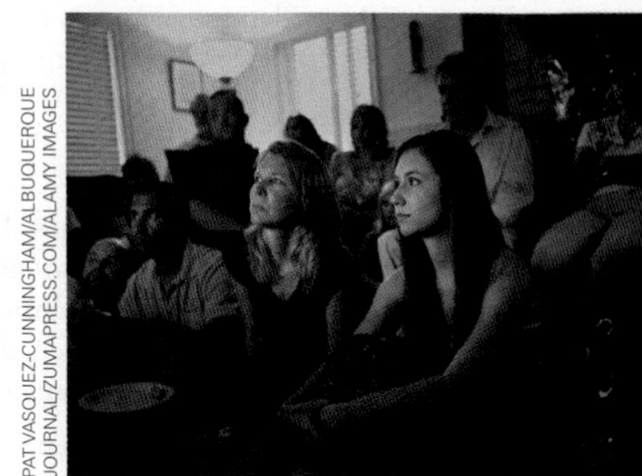

PAT VASQUEZ-CUNNINGHAM/ALBUQUERQUE JOURNAL/ZUMAPRESS.COM/ALAMY IMAGES

Telling Their Story Erika Pohl and her mother, Brenda, reflect on a documentary in which Erika had a leading role — as a teenager addicted to opioids who managed to get clean. Both hope "never again." That is true for about half of teenage addicts; the film was created to improve those odds.

For example, massive ad campaigns by public health advocates in Florida and California cut adolescent smoking almost in half, in part because the publicity appealed to the young. Teenagers respond to graphic images. In one example:

> A young man walks up to a convenience store counter and asks for a pack of cigarettes. He throws some money on the counter, but the cashier says "that's not enough." So the young man pulls out a pair of pliers, wrenches out one of his teeth, and hands it over. . . . A voiceover asks: "What's a pack of smokes cost? Your teeth."
>
> *[Krisberg, 2014]*

Parental example and social norms also make a difference. Throughout the United States, higher prices, targeted warnings, and better law enforcement have led to a marked decline in cigarette smoking among younger adolescents. Looking internationally, laws have an effect.

THINK CRITICALLY: Might the fear of adolescent drug use be foolish, if most adolescents use drugs whether or not they are forbidden?

In Canada, cigarette advertising is outlawed, and cigarette packs have lurid pictures of diseased lungs, rotting teeth, and so on; fewer Canadian 15- to 19-year-olds smoke. What effect Canada's legalization of marijuana will have on teenagers is not yet known.

As explained at the beginning of these two chapters, adolescence starts with puberty; that much is universal. But what happens next depends on parents, peers, schools, communities, and cultures. In other words, the future of adolescents depends, in part, on you.

what have you learned?

1. Why are psychoactive drugs particularly attractive in adolescence?
2. Why are psychoactive drugs particularly destructive in adolescence?
3. What specific harm occurs with tobacco products?
4. How has adolescent drug use changed in the past decade?
5. What methods to reduce adolescent drug use are successful?

SUMMARY

Identity

1. Adolescence is a time for self-discovery. According to Erikson, adolescents seek their own identity, sorting through the traditions and values of their families and cultures.

2. Many young adolescents foreclose on their options without exploring possibilities, and many experience role confusion. Identity achievement takes longer for contemporary adolescents than it did a half-century ago when Erikson first described it.

3. Religious and political identities are strongly influenced by parents. Gender identity has changed markedly as culture has changed. Ethnic identity and pride is part of self-acceptance for contemporary teenagers of all backgrounds.

Close Relationships

4. Parents continue to influence their growing children, despite bickering over minor issues. Ideally, communication and warmth remain high, while parental control decreases and adolescents develop autonomy. Cultures differ in the timing of conflicts and in the benefits of parental monitoring. Too much parental control is harmful, as is neglect.

5. Peers and peer pressure can be beneficial or harmful, depending on who the peers are. Adolescents select their friends, who then facilitate constructive and/or destructive behavior. Peer approval is particularly potent during adolescence.

6. Adolescents experience diverse sexual needs and may be involved in short-term or long-term romances, depending in part on their peer group. Contemporary teenagers are less likely to have intercourse than was true a decade ago.

7. Some youths are attracted to people of the same gender. Social acceptance of same-sex relationships is increasing, but in some communities and nations, gay, lesbian, bisexual, and transgender youth are bullied, rejected, or worse.

8. Many adolescents learn about sexuality from peers and the media—sources that are not comprehensive. Ideally, parents are the best teachers, but many are silent or naive.

9. Some nations provide comprehensive sex education beginning in the early grades, but this is not true in other nations. Marked variation is evident in U.S. schools. Abstinence-only education does not stop adolescent sexual activity, and it may increase STIs.

10. Most adolescents in the United States use technology to connect with their peers. Sexting is also common, and adults see dangers in it that peers do not.

Sadness and Anger

11. Almost all young adolescents become more self-conscious and self-critical than they were as children. A few become chronically sad and depressed. Many adolescents (especially girls) think about suicide, and some attempt it. Few actually kill themselves; most who do so are boys.

12. Many adolescents become more rebellious, independent, and angry as part of growing up, although most still respect their parents. Breaking the law and bursts of anger are common; boys are more likely to be arrested than are girls.

13. Adolescence-limited offenders should be prevented from hurting themselves or others; life-course-persistent offenders may become career criminals. Early intervention—years before the first arrest—is crucial to prevent serious delinquency.

Drug Use and Abuse

14. Most adolescents experiment with drugs, which may temporarily reduce stress and increase peer connections but soon add to stress and social problems. Almost every adolescent tries alcohol, and many use e-cigarettes and marijuana. All are technically illegal for those under 18 but are readily available to teenagers.

15. All psychoactive drugs are particularly harmful in adolescence, as they affect the developing brain and undermine impulse control. Prevention and moderation of adolescent drug use and abuse are possible. Price, perception, and parents have an effect.

KEY TERMS

identity versus role confusion (p. 309)
identity achievement (p. 309)
role confusion (p. 310)
foreclosure (p. 310)
gender identity (p. 313)
parental monitoring (p. 317)
familism (p. 317)
peer pressure (p. 319)
coercive joining (p. 319)
sexual orientation (p. 320)
cyberbullying (p. 324)
sexting (p. 324)
major depressive disorder (MDD) (p. 327)
suicidal ideation (p. 327)
parasuicide (p. 327)
cluster suicides (p. 328)
adolescence-limited offender (p. 330)
life-course-persistent offender (p. 330)
generational forgetting (p. 335)

APPLICATIONS

1. Locate a news article about a teenager who committed suicide. Were there warning signs that were ignored? Does the report inadvertently encourage cluster suicides?

2. Research suggests that most adolescents have broken the law but that few have been arrested or incarcerated. Ask 10 of your fellow students whether they broke the law when they were under 18 and, if so, how often, in what ways, and with what consequences. (Assure them of confidentiality; remind them that drug use, breaking curfew, and skipping school were illegal.) Do you see any evidence of gender or ethnic differences? What additional research needs to be done?

3. Cultures vary in expectations for drug use. Interview three people from different backgrounds (not necessarily from different nations; each SES, generation, or religion has different standards) about their culture's drug use, including reasons for what is allowed and when. (Legal drugs should be included in your study.)

ESPECIALLY FOR ANSWERS

Response for Parents of a Teenager (from p. 317): Remember: Communicate, do not control. Let your child talk about the meaning of the hairstyle. Remind yourself that a hairstyle in itself is harmless. Don't say, "What will people think?" or "Are you on drugs?" or anything that might give your child reason to stop communicating.

Response for Sex Educators (from p. 322): Yes, but forgive them. Ideally, parents should talk to their children about sex, presenting honest information and listening to the child's concerns. However, many parents find it very difficult to do so because they feel embarrassed and ignorant. You might schedule separate sessions for adults over 30, for emerging adults, and for adolescents.

Response for Parents Who Drink Socially (from p. 334): No. Alcohol is particularly harmful for young brains. It is best to drink only when your children are not around. Children who are encouraged to drink with their parents are more likely to drink when no adults are present. It is true that adolescents are rebellious, and they may drink even if you forbid it. But if you condone alcohol, they might rebel with other drugs.

OBSERVATION QUIZ ANSWERS

Answer to Observation Quiz (from p. 318): The girls are only observers, keeping a respectful distance.

Answer to Observation Quiz (from p. 320): Impossible to be sure, but body position suggests dating. The couple on the left seem happy with each other (she leans toward him, his hand is pulling her close), but the couple on the right may be less so.

Answer to Observation Quiz (from p. 327): Both. It increases for boys but decreases for girls.

PART VI

CHAPTER 11 CHAPTER 12 CHAPTER 13

Adulthood

We now begin the sixth part of this text. These three chapters cover 47 years (ages 18 to 65), when bodies mature, minds master new material, and people work productively. No particular year is a logical divider. Adults of many ages marry; raise children; care for aging parents; are hired and fired; grow richer or poorer; experience births, deaths, weddings, divorces, illness, and recovery. Thus, adulthood is punctuated by joys and sorrows, which can occur at any time.

The first years are often preparation for the later ones. As you will soon read, some researchers separated emerging adulthood, roughly age 18–25, from the rest of adulthood. Using 25 as the dividing line is itself somewhat arbitrary: Some people are ready for the responsibilities of adulthood at 20, others not until 30.

However, although events are not programmed by age, they are not random: Adults build on their past — creating their own ecological niche — and prepare for their future. They choose their activities, communities, and habits.

Culture and cohort always have an impact. Some experiences once thought to be universal — midlife crisis, sandwich generation, and empty nest among them — are much less common than assumed. As you will see, adulthood is not what most people think, or thought, or will experience.

TEMPURA/E+/GETTY IMAGES

ADULTHOOD
Emerging Adulthood

what will you know?

- How can risk-taking be considered a good trait?
- When is college education a poor investment?
- Is it best for young adults to be independent from their parents?

I thought I was a pioneer, liberated from the shackles of the past. Unlike my mother, who never went to college and had to quit her job when she married, as a young adult I earned college degrees and began my career. I planned to be a wife, mother, and professional lifelong.

I proudly paid rent on my own studio apartment, had a boyfriend, and taught seventh-grade boys in a public school. I dressed like an adult—with high heels, glasses, and an artificial bun. My goal was to reform American education, so I tutored one student who could not read; gave a clothes voucher (ostensibly from a foundation) to a boy with too-large, torn pants; visited my students' parents to strengthen the home–school connection.

When Martin and I decided to marry, we scheduled our wedding so that our honeymoon would coincide with a school holiday: I wanted to prove that women could be wives, mothers, and professionals simultaneously. The Board of Education did not allow visibly pregnant teachers, so when our first child was conceived, I began graduate school as a full-time student with a federal stipend.

As I reflect on it now, my career, idealism, risk-taking, clothes, hair, marriage, and pregnancy were all traditional. I had more education and independence than my foremothers had, but my expression of those emerging-adult characteristics was quaint by current standards. My life changed because of two government policies that disappeared decades ago: Pregnant women could not teach, but federal grants paid tuition and stipends to students earning a graduate degree.

These memories open Chapter 11 because they illustrate the power of historical circumstances. As described in the next pages, some traits of young adults are universal, but even more than earlier in life, the social context directs adult development.

PHOTO CREDIT: IKO/SHUTTERSTOCK

FRANCK FIFE/AFP/GETTY IMAGES

What a Body Can Do Here at age 27, Tobin Heath leaps to celebrate her goal at the soccer World Cup Final in Vancouver, her most recent of seven years of star performances. All young adults can have moments when their bodies and minds crescendo to new heights.

Development of the Body

The universals of this stage are biological. Early adulthood is prime time for high energy, hard physical labor, and safe reproduction. The rapid and sometimes unsettling changes of adolescence are over, and age-related declines in senses and muscles are not yet apparent.

As has been true for thousands of years, every body system — digestive, respiratory, circulatory, musculoskeletal, and sexual-reproductive — functions optimally. Maximum height is usually reached by age 16 for girls and 18 for boys, with final touches in size and shape complete before age 25. By then, everyone is full grown: Women have adult breasts and hips, and men have full shoulder width and upper-arm strength (Whitbourne & Whitbourne, 2014).

The last body part to mature is the brain. Not until the mid-20s is the prefrontal cortex fully developed, with the entire brain connected and myelinated (Colver & Dovey-Pearce, 2018; Hochberg & Konner, 2020). People can think and act like an adult.

A Universal Stage?

The social context matters. The fact that young adulthood is the best time for carrying rocks, plowing fields, and birthing babies is no longer appreciated. If a young couple quit high school to marry, build a house, till a field, and give birth year after year (as my grandparents did), no one would approve. Contemporary 20-year-olds are physically strong but not ready for adult responsibilities.

A college professor in Missouri, Jeffrey Arnett, recognized that his students were not yet adults: They postponed the usual markers of adulthood (steady jobs, lifelong partners, parenthood) and instead sought more education. He "proposed a new conception of development for the period from the late teens through the twenties, with a focus on ages 18–25," calling that period **emerging adulthood** (Arnett, 2000).

emerging adulthood
The period of life between the ages of 18 and 25. Emerging adulthood is now widely thought of as a distinct developmental stage.

That term is not universally accepted. Some scholars still call these years "late adolescence" or "early adulthood." However, almost everyone agrees that something has changed in the expectations and opportunities of young adults.

The deeper debate is not about the label but about whether this stage is exclusive to a small sector of the world. Might emerging adulthood be a luxury, evident only in *WEIRD (Western, Educated, Industrialized, Rich, Democratic)* nations? Might the experience of young adulthood be quite different in less affluent nations? Might researchers ignore the reality of these years in most nations of the world?

A leading researcher wrote: "The WEIRD group represents maximally 5% of the world's population, but probably more than 90% of the researchers and scientists producing the knowledge that is represented in our textbooks work with participants from that particular context" (Keller, quoted in Armstrong, 2018). Indeed, emerging adulthood is most clearly defined and evident in the fraction of 1 percent who are college students in the United States.

However, the data suggest that emerging adulthood is now everywhere. Between 2015 and 2022, according to Google Scholar, more than 75,000 scholarly articles mentioning "emerging adulthood" have been published by researchers in every continent. The specifics vary by culture — sometimes this stage ends at age 21 or 30 instead of 25 — but everywhere older adolescents postpone full adulthood if they can.

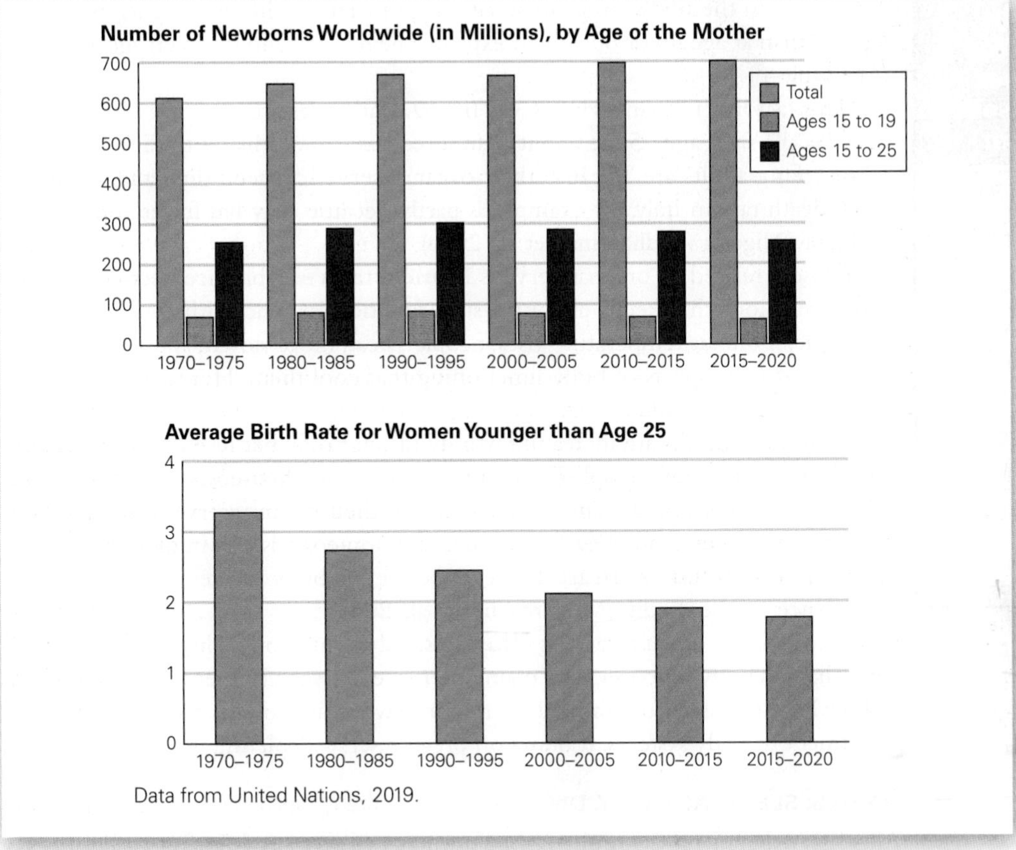

FIGURE 11.1 **In Every Nation** As you see, births continue to increase, because earlier baby booms now result in more adults of childbearing age than ever before. But those adults have far fewer children, especially during emerging adulthood now a worldwide stage.

One statistic illustrates that this stage has swept the globe: In the entire world, young women have half as many children as they did, choosing more education and fewer babies. In many less affluent nations, the average 25-year-old had four or five children in 1970; she has two children now (United Nations, 2019) (see Figure 11.1). In wealthier nations, most young women have no children.

Health and Sickness

In a large U.S. survey, 96.1 percent of 18- to 24-year-olds rated their health as good, very good, or excellent. Only 3.9 percent rated it fair or poor, a significant improvement over the past two decades, and better than older adults (National Center for Health Statistics, 2018).

They may be fooling themselves. A study of biological aging found that some people grow old three times faster than others, with about half of that difference evident by age 26 (Belsky et al., 2015). By the mid-30s, some bodies are like the average 20-year-old, others like 50-year-olds.

CUMULATIVE LOAD

To appreciate this trajectory of adult health, it helps to understand *organ reserve*, *homeostasis*, and *allostatic load*.

Organ reserve is the extra power that each organ employs when needed, allowing many 20-year-olds to stay awake all night, or exercise to exhaustion, or take drugs that disrupt the brain, and still function the next day. Because of organ reserve,

organ reserve
The capacity of organs to allow the body to cope with stress, via extra, unused functioning ability.

TABLE 11.1 U.S. Deaths from the Top Two Causes (Heart Disease and Cancer)

Age Group	Annual Rate per 100,000
15–24	6
25–34	16
35–44	60
45–54	176
55–64	470
65–74	961
75–84	2,119
85+	5,494

Data from National Center for Health Statistics, 2018.

homeostasis
The adjustment of all of the body's systems to keep physiological functions in a state of equilibrium. As the body ages, it takes longer for these homeostatic adjustments to occur, so it becomes harder for older bodies to adapt to stress.

allostasis
A dynamic body adjustment, related to homeostasis, that affects overall physiology over time. The main difference is that homeostasis requires an immediate response whereas allostasis requires longer-term adjustment.

any strain on the body (pregnancy, running a marathon, lifting weights) is easier at age 20 than at age 40 or 80, which explains the relationship between age and death (see Table 11.1).

This factor is relevant when COVID-19 death rates are compared internationally. People over age 75 are about a hundred times more likely to die of the virus than young adults are, because their organ reserve has been depleted. Thus, the high death rate in Italy, for example, is partly because Italy has fewer young adults than, say, Nigeria (Sudharsanan et al., 2020).

Closely related to organ reserve is **homeostasis**—a balance between various body reactions that keeps every physical function in sync with every other. For example, if the air temperature rises, people sweat, move slowly, and thirst for cold drinks—three aspects of body functioning that cool them. Homeostasis is almost immediate in early adulthood.

Heat-wave deaths are increasing worldwide, not only because of climate change but also because more people live to be very old, when homeostasis is slow (Guo et al., 2017). Young bodies can quickly summon their organ reserve to survive temperature extremes. With COVID-19, because homeostasis lags in older people, the immune system may overreact to a fever before the body can restore balance. That imbalance can be deadly (Moderbacher et al., 2020).

Also related to organ reserve is **allostasis**, a dynamic body adjustment that gradually changes body function. The main difference between homeostasis and allostasis is time: Homeostasis is the immediate response whereas allostasis refers to long-term adjustment of body systems. It draws on organ reserve, depleting it over the decades.

HABITS: SLEEP, ACTIVITY, DIET

Allostasis depends on the biological adjustments of every earlier time of life, beginning at conception. Accumulated harm from sleep deprivation, inactivity, unhealthy eating, and so on shortens life by 10 years or more (Y. Li et al., 2020). Given the importance of those health habits, we describe each of them in early adulthood.

One night's short *sleep* makes a person tired the next day—that is homeostasis, the body's way to maintain equilibrium (see Figure 11.2). But if poor sleep is typical every day, then appetite, mood, and activity adjust (more, down, less) to achieve homeostasis. Meanwhile, allostatic load rises and organ reserve declines.

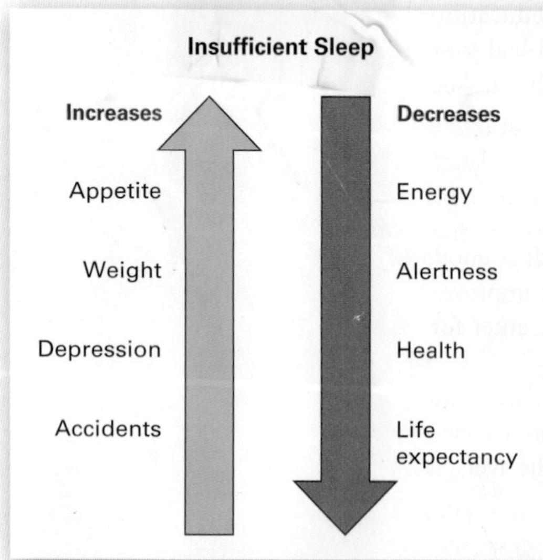

FIGURE 11.2 Don't Set the Alarm? Every emerging adult sometimes sleeps too little and is tired the next day—that is homeostasis. But years of poor sleep habits reduce years of life—a bad bargain. That is allostatic load.

By mid- and late adulthood, years of low-quality sleep decrease overall health (Carroll et al., 2014; McEwen & Karatsoreos, 2015). Sleep quality is determined by many social and psychological factors that are experienced by many emerging adults, including disruptive noise, light, and anxiety.

Like sleep, physical *activity* protects against serious illness lifelong; inactivity takes a toll that begins early on. Exercise reduces blood pressure and strengthens the heart and lungs, reducing depression, osteoporosis, diabetes, arthritis, dementia (now called *major neurocognitive disorder*), and some cancers. Health benefits are substantial for men and women, old and young, former sports stars and those who never joined an athletic team.

Habits are pivotal. If a young adult develops a regular exercise regime, over time, homeostasis adjusts and allows the person to exercise longer and harder. That decreases allostatic load by reducing health risks, evident in blood analysis and body fat.

One longitudinal study, CARDIA (Coronary Artery Risk Development in Young Adults) began with thousands of healthy 18- to 30-year-olds. They were queried about their exercise habits. Blood and body fat markers, as well as strength and endurance, were measured.

Many (3,154) of those young adults were reexamined decades later. Those who were the least fit at the first assessment (more than 400 of them) were four times more likely to have diabetes and high blood pressure in middle age.

Their health problems began, unnoticed (except in blood work), when they were emerging adults. Organ reserve and homeostasis protected them while allostatic load increased (Camhi et al., 2013). By age 65, a disproportionate number died.

Diet is the third example of a healthy habit that sustains life. How much a young adult eats on a given day is affected by dozens of physiological and psychological factors. An empty stomach triggers hormones, stomach pains, low blood sugar, and so on, all signaling hunger.

KEVIN FOY/ALAMY STOCK PHOTO

Fastest Increase Obesity rates are rising faster in China than in any other nation as new American restaurants open every day. McDonald's and Starbucks each have about 5,000 outlets in China, with students particularly likely customers.

If an empty stomach is occasional, the cascade of homeostatic reactions makes a person suddenly realize at 6 P.M. that they haven't eaten since breakfast. The body signals that food is needed. The social context, such as available food, environmental stress, and dinner companions affect quantity.

The social context and food availability explains why many college students find that living away from home increases weight (the "freshman fifteen") (de Vos et al., 2015; Fedewa et al., 2014). Many people put on weight while sheltering in place during the recent pandemic: They were less active, and the kitchen was only a few steps away (Flanagan et al., 2021).

Many mechanisms of the body work to keep people well nourished (Augustine et al., 2018), but stress, extreme dieting, overeating, and drug abuse all affect allostasis. That explains why anorexia, bulimia, and obesity in emerging adults contribute to death in middle age. Even without such extremes, eating habits matter. Young CARDIA adults were not usually overweight, but those whose eating was sometimes out of control were more often obese 25 years later (Yoon et al., 2018).

Obesity increases allostatic load, making people vulnerable to diabetes, heart disease, stroke, and more—all affected by physiological adjustment in early adulthood (Sterling, 2012). At the opposite extreme, allostasis allows people with anorexia to feel energetic, not hungry, but the adjustment of their body eventually kills them.

Overall, the nutritional habits that are established during these years make "emerging adulthood . . . a critical risk period in the development and prevention of disordered eating" (Goldschmidt et al., 2016, p. 480). The lethal consequences come later.

The importance of the psyche for all these health habits suggests long-term harm from childhood poverty, racial discrimination, and maltreatment. This is evident for many Black adults, as well as many others: If a person of any ethnic background experiences frequent social prejudice, then sleep, heart rate, and digestion suffer. That impairs adult health even if the prejudice stopped in childhood (Dustin & Kawachi, 2018; Van Dyke et al., 2020; Widom et al., 2015b).

Fertility, Then and Now

As already mentioned, the sexual-reproductive system is quick and strong during emerging adulthood: Orgasms are frequent, the sex drive is powerful, erotic responses are joyful, fertility is optimal, miscarriage is less common, and serious birth complications are unusual. Historically, most people married before age 20, and had several children before age 25.

For 200,000 years, reproduction is what young-adult bodies did best, maintaining the species. That is why the Bible instructed people to "be fruitful and multiply."

VASYL SHEVCHENKO/AP IMAGES

Ashamed to Use a Condom? This public health effort attempts to remove the stigma, in order to reduce STIs and unwanted babies.

◆◆ OBSERVATION QUIZ
Where is this? (see answer, page 370) ↑

Those ancient genes and hormones, passed down from hundreds of past generations, compel human bonding.

That is why lust and fertility still peak in late adolescence and early adulthood. But now biology and cognition clash: Bodies want sex, but young adults do not want babies. A new problem!

Medical research found a solution: sex without pregnancy. Contraception makes that possible; cultural mores have made that acceptable. Very few adults (4 percent overall) believe that contraception is morally wrong (Mitchell, 2016). This is amazing: Over just a few years, a strong, socially constructed norm (that premarital sex was immoral) collapsed and disappeared (Liu, 2021).

Every cultural shift entails unanticipated problems. When emerging adults have many sex partners without the push to marry, sexually transmitted infections (STIs) become widespread. As we learned with COVID-19, when social connections increase, so does disease transmission.

The second problem is, in some ways, opposite—no partners. Before contraception, social norms meant that everyone sought a lifelong partner. Spinsters were pitied (the old maid was the ugliest card in the deck). But currently, many young adults feel no pressure to marry.

That can lead to social isolation. Marriage rates have fallen, but so has sexual bonding. From 2002 to 2018, the rate of young adults who had no sex in the past year increased from 19 to 31 percent for men and 15 to 19 percent for women, with college women particularly likely to avoid sex (Ueda et al., 2020).

That is good in some ways—fewer abortions, fewer unwanted births, fewer birth control pills, and more time to study. But no sex may also mean no close human connections. Lack of social interaction is as harmful as sleep deprivation, inactivity, and unhealthy eating. Loneliness impairs the immune system (Shields et al., 2020).

Thus, contraception led to two extremes, both harming health for emerging adults. Some had many partners, risking STIs, and some had no partners, risking loneliness.

STUART DUNN/ALAMY STOCK PHOTO

Who and Where? Knowing the attraction to danger of emerging-adult men makes it easy to guess who—a 19-year-old male. But where is harder — that dangerous leap into the ocean could be in many nations. This one is in the Indian Ocean in Sri Lanka.

Taking Risks

Risk-taking is in the DNA of young adults. For millennia, that benefited them and their community. They needed to leave their parents' home, establish families, and find jobs, all of which require some bravery. But now many emerging adults postpone all these, even though their impulses still urge risk-taking. That can be destructive.

For example, sexually transmitted infections, drug abuse, and extreme sports (motocross, hang gliding, drag racing, etc.) begin with foolish risks. Infertility, addiction, and death may follow. Rates of these increase in emerging adulthood, because risky impulses encourage new sexual partners, psychoactive substances, and adventures.

Accidents increase. Although their bodies are strong and their reactions quick, emerging adults have more serious injuries than do people of any older age (see Figure 11.3).

Almost all (estimated 90 percent) deaths of young adults between ages 18–25 can be traced to risk. Motor-vehicle accidents are the most obvious, but other causes of death (HIV/AIDS, homicide, suicide, extreme exercise, drowning, and more) also result from risks taken.

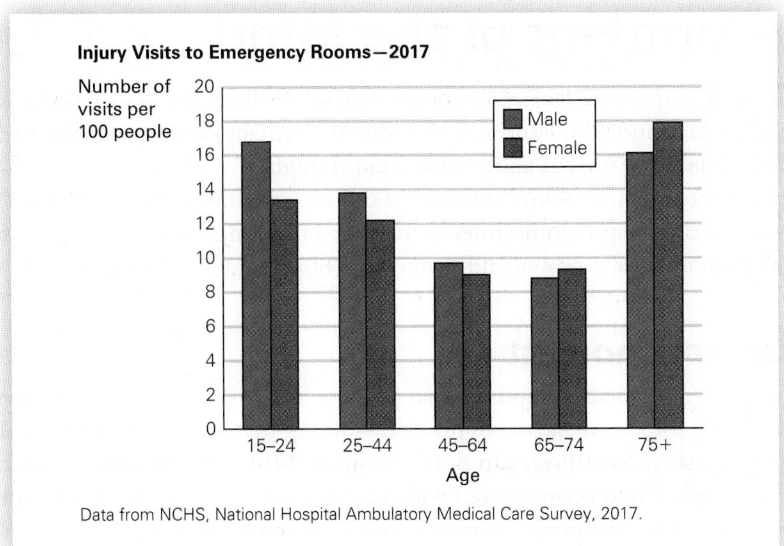

FIGURE 11.3 Safe at Age 70? Two reasons for the major age differences: more risk-taking (young) and impaired balance (old).

Moreover, many actions before age 25 (such as cigarette smoking, unhealthy eating, condomless sex) contribute to illness decades later. For example, only 4 percent of emerging-adult deaths are from untreatable cancer (the main fatal disease during these years), but cancer is the second most common cause of death in adulthood, often because of daily actions when the person was younger.

Especially for Nurses When should you suspect that a patient has an untreated STI? (see response, page 370)

The public health question is "How can young adult risks be reduced?" Laws are enacted to prevent dangerous driving, gun availability, vaccination avoidance, drug overdose. More important may be cognitive maturation: Adults decide to strap on seatbelts, lock up guns, and so on.

The fact that maturation leads to caution is evident in an interesting study. Adolescents and young adults (aged 10 to 30) were asked "how good or bad an idea is it" to do various risky things (such as riding a bicycle down the stairs or taking pills at a party) (Shulman & Cauffman, 2014).

The participants had only two seconds to make a snap judgment on a sliding scale from 0 to 100. For instance, the bicycle riding might be rated at 70 (somewhat bad idea) and the pills at 95 (very bad idea). There also were eight items that were not risky at all, such as eating a sandwich.

Items were rated as less risky (closer to a good idea) every year from ages 10 to 20 and then more risky (closer to a bad idea) every year from ages 20 to 30. This was related to brain maturation, not experience. In fact, the older respondents had done more risky things (the average 15- to 17-year-old had done four of them; the average 20- to 25-year-old had done seven). Maturation, not experience, made people recognize risk.

Indeed, one mother of teenagers told me: "Ideally we could wrap them in thick cotton batting and unwrap them when it was safe."

what have you learned?

1. How and why has emerging adulthood become a distinct stage?
2. How does organ reserve protect against heart attacks?
3. Describe how homeostasis and allostasis are apparent in a basic health habit?
4. What three habits protect health?
5. What are the social benefits of risk-taking?
6. How common are disease deaths in early adulthood?

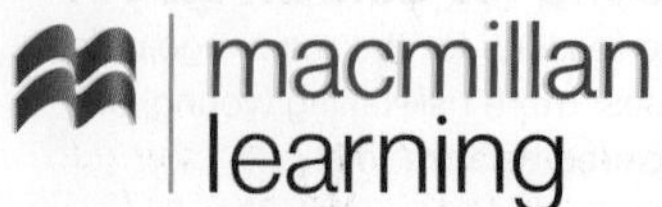

VIDEO ACTIVITY: Brain Development: Emerging Adulthood shows the changes that occur in a person's brain between ages 18 and 25.

Development of the Mind

Although Piaget considered *formal operational thought* the final stage of thinking, evident in adolescence and then continuing in adulthood, many cognitive psychologists find that adult thinking is a cut above adolescent thought.

Adults are more practical and flexible, combining intuition and analysis. This higher stage of thinking is sometimes evident in emerging adulthood, when the brain finally becomes fully grown and connected (Hochberg & Konner, 2020).

Postformal Thought

postformal thought
A proposed adult stage of cognitive development, following Piaget's four stages, that goes beyond adolescent thinking by being more practical, more flexible, and more dialectical (i.e., more capable of combining contradictory elements into a comprehensive whole).

Building on Piaget, some developmentalists propose a fifth stage called **postformal thought**, a "type of logical, adaptive problem-solving that is a step more complex than scientific formal-level Piagetian tasks" (Sinnott, 2014, p. 3). In postformal cognition, "thinking needs to be integrated with emotional and pragmatic aspects, rather than only dealing with the purely abstract" (Labouvie-Vief, 2015, p. 89).

As they integrate emotion and pragmatics, postformal thinkers are flexible, with a "more complex, nuanced, and paradoxical" mode of thinking (Gidley, 2016). They consider all aspects of a situation, anticipating problems and dealing with them rather than denying, avoiding, or procrastinating. Thus, postformal thought is practical and creative (Gidley, 2016; Kallio, 2020).

One developmental scholar wrote:

> we hypothesize that there exists, after the formal thinking stage, a fifth stage of post-formal thinking, as Piaget had already studied its basic forms and would have concluded the same thing, had he the time to do so.
>
> *[Lemieux, 2012, p. 404]*

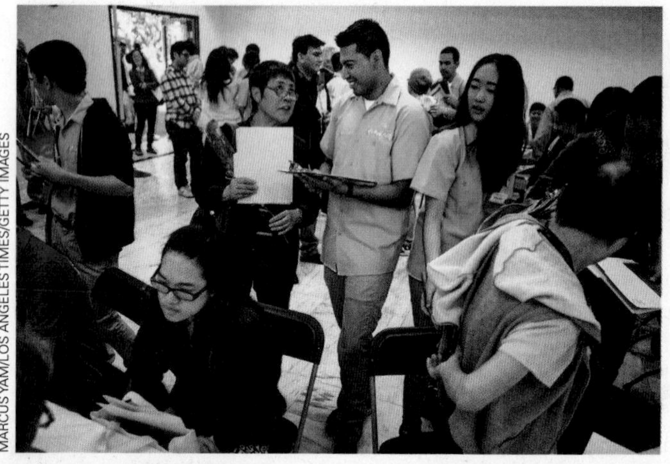

MARCUS YAM/LOS ANGELES TIMES/GETTY IMAGES

Learning About Health Hundreds of health professionals offer free medical care at this Buddhist temple, likely employing postformal thought as they identify problems and risks and recommend strategies for promoting health. One of the professionals is Daniel Garcia, shown here with the clipboard.

OBSERVATION QUIZ
Where is this? (see answer, page 370) ↑

Adult brains are not as quick to activate neurons as adolescent brains are: An adult might lose at a video game that requires fast decisions. However, in adulthood, more regions of the brain react to a single event, and longer fibers connect one area with another (Liu et al., 2018). Adult cognition is "integrative thinking," combining logic and experience (Kallio, 2020).

POSTFORMAL MATE SELECTION

Emerging adults show many signs of that integrative thinking, in their choice of career, in where they live, in how they dress, in what they eat. Their choices do not duplicate what their parents did, but reflect their childhood while moving beyond it.

Similar forces are at work with other decisions: where to go to college, what to study, whether or not to begin living with a partner. A combination of emotion and rationality is often evident, with childhood patterns not usually followed.

The most obvious example is in romance. Emerging adults still experience the same hormonal reactions that youth have always felt, but they do not rush into partnership. When they do cohabit or marry, they consider nuanced compatibility, which may mean crossing ethnic or religious boundaries. Thus, couple by couple, adult thinking is not determined by childhood culture, parental example, or traditional norms.

In 2017, 18 percent of all newlyweds were from different racial or ethnic groups, six times the rate 50 years earlier (U.S. Census Bureau, 2018). Those statistics underestimate the rate of intermarriage, because the census lumps to together all people of

Hispanic, Black, Asian, and non-Hispanic White heritages, ignoring that a marriage between mates whose heritage is Italian and Swedish, or Mexican and Puerto Rican, or Pakistani and Japanese, is an intermarriage.

The people most likely to intermarry have attended college, where they have been encouraged to think for themselves and thus reach postformal cognition. The people least likely to approve of intermarriage are the older, less-educated adults, many of whom married before age 20 (Livingston & Brown, 2017).

Intermarriage is not the only sign of postformal marriage choices. One expert on modern marriages suggests that "every marriage is a cross-cultural experience" (Gottman & Gottman, 2017, p. 19) in that everyone has values that need to be expressed and coordinated with their partner.

Cognitive maturity may be one reason that, between ages 15 and 35, the older newlyweds are, the less likely they are to divorce. Parents may be distressed that their adult children do not marry and may be romantically involved with someone they would not have chosen, but that may be a sign of postformal thinking, not adolescent rebellion.

◆◆ Especially for Someone Who Has to Make an Important Decision
Which is better, to go with your gut feelings or to consider pros and cons as objectively as you can? (see response, page 370)

COMBINING FACTS AND EMOTIONS

A characteristic of postformal thought is moving past dual processing to combine objective and subjective thought. **Objective thought** uses abstract, impersonal logic; **subjective thought** arises from personal experiences and emotions. Preoperational, egocentric thought is subjective; formal operational thought objective; postformal thought includes both (Gidley, 2016; Kallio, 2020).

objective thought
Thinking that is not influenced by the thinker's personal qualities but instead involves facts and numbers that are universally considered true and valid.

subjective thought
Thinking that is strongly influenced by personal qualities of the individual thinker, such as past experiences, cultural assumptions, and goals for the future.

Adult thinkers realize that purely objective, logical thinking is maladaptive when navigating the complexities and commitments of adult life. Instead, emotional sensitivity is needed for productive families, workplaces, and neighborhoods because objective reasoning alone is limited, rigid, and impractical.

Yet adult thinkers know that subjective thinking is also limited. Truly mature thought involves an interaction between abstract, objective forms and expressive, subjective forms of processing.

As an example of such balance, an emerging adult student of mine wrote:

> Unfortunately, alcoholism runs in my family. . . . I have seen it tear apart not only my uncle but my family also. . . . I have gotten sick from drinking, and it was the most horrifying night of my life. I know that I didn't have alcohol poisoning or anything, but I drank too quickly and was getting sick. All of these images flooded my head about how I didn't want to ever end up the way my uncle was. From that point on, whenever I have touched alcohol, it has been with extreme caution. . . . When I am old and gray, the last thing I want to be thinking about is where my next beer will come from or how I'll need a liver transplant.
>
> *[Laura, personal communication]*

Ideal Versus Real One indication of adult cognition is the ability to accept some imperfections in oneself, one's family, and one's nation.

Laura's thinking about alcohol is postformal in that it combines knowledge (e.g., of alcohol poisoning) with emotions (images flooding her head). She is cautious, not abstinent; she has objective awareness of her genetic potential and subjective experience of drinking with her friends.

She combines both to reach a conclusion that works for her. She does not need to wait for searing personal experiences (becoming an uncontrollable drinker and reaching despair). If she had such experiences, postformal thinking might help her recognize her need for subjective, emotional support (perhaps an AA group) to bolster her logical awareness.

Postformal thought regarding alcohol is apparent in most U.S. adults. Those in their early 20s are more likely than those over age 30 to abuse alcohol and other drugs, perhaps with periods of swearing off all harmful substances, only to begin again. Thus, they zigzag from subjective to objective.

With personal experience and learning from others (social norms), cognitive maturity allows occasional, moderate drinking by age 30. Some, for both genetic and social reasons, must stop completely, but most adults can drink a glass or two on occasion. They have moved past the extremes of bingeing and abstinence of their younger selves. Similar moderation is apparent in nutrition. The yo-yo dieter (who gains and loses and gains again) is more often in their 20s (Stevens et al., 2012).

Cognitive Growth and Higher Education

Education improves health and wealth. College graduates are healthier and wealthier than high school graduates, who themselves are ahead of those without a high school diploma (see Figure 11.4).

Each added level of education correlates with everything from happy marriages to strong teeth, from spacious homes to long lives, from healthy children to efficient digestive systems (U.S. Department of Health and Human Services, 2018). On average, when costs and salary over a lifetime are considered, college education returns the initial expense more than five times.

That means if students spend a nickel now, they get a quarter back by age 60, or if a degree costs $200,000, the return is a million. The reason for that ratio is that, by middle age, the average college graduate earns twice as much as the average high school grad (see Figure 11.4).

Some of this is simply continuity from generation to generation, in that wealthy parents are more likely to have college-attending children, but when family income is taken into account, such as in studies of siblings, those who attain college degrees tend to have higher salaries and longer lives than those who do not.

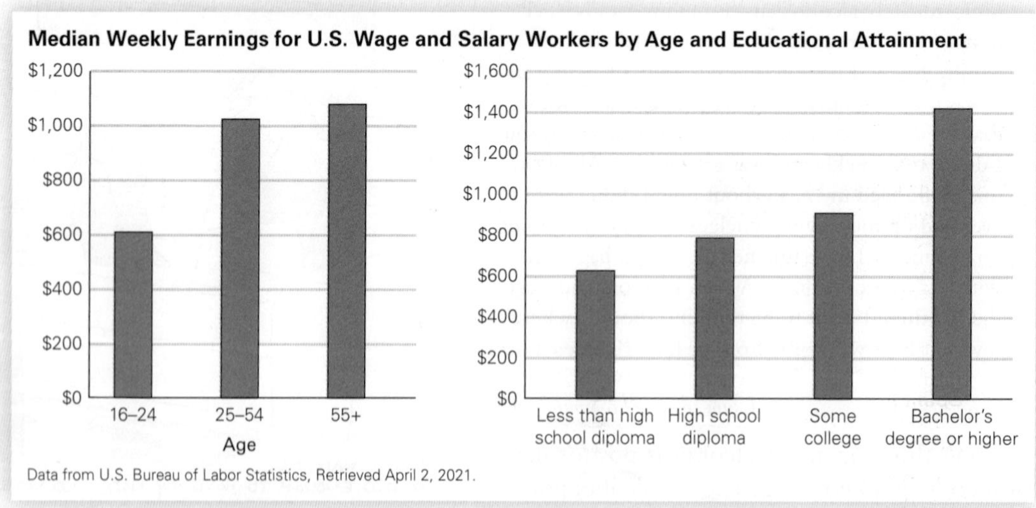

FIGURE 11.4 **Biology Used to be Right** From the dawn of homo sapiens until just a few decades ago, young adults married, had babies, built homes, and began work that would provide a steady income for them and their families. But now, biology is mistaken. A combination of age and education means that the average income of middle-aged adults is more than double that of younger people. No wonder many emerging adults postpone marriage and parenthood and rely on their parents for everything from laundry to rent.

MASSIFICATION

The idea that college might benefit everyone (the masses) has led to the goal of **massification**, that college should be available for all. The United States embraced massification over a century ago, beginning with federal legislation in 1862 that established land grant colleges in every state.

massification
The idea that establishing institutions of higher learning and encouraging college enrollment can benefit everyone (the masses).

Now every state has a publicly supported university and many colleges. California has the most, with 146 public colleges in 2019.

Throughout the twentieth century, the United States led the world in the percentage of adults who were college graduates. Many of those adults are now in their prime earning years. The United States is one of the wealthiest nations, which can be traced to the growth of universities (Brint, 2019).

That international distinction is fading. Twelve other nations now have a higher rate of emerging adults who earn college degrees than the United States does (OECD, 2018), because several developed nations (Canada, Finland, Israel, England) now graduate a higher proportion of emerging adults. Developing nations have not reached that level, but their leaders have created and funded thousands of new colleges and universities (see Figure 11.5).

One recent result is new economic development in nations that once were poor. For example, in 1995, China had about a thousand colleges with six million students. Two decades later, China had about 2,600 colleges (400 of them private) with 30 million students (Normile, 2018). China is no longer a poor nation.

DROPPING OUT

The data just cited on the financial benefits of college reflect only those who graduate. Costs begin with enrollment, but most long-term benefits result from the degree. Thus, for some dropouts, entering college may be a poor investment. Those

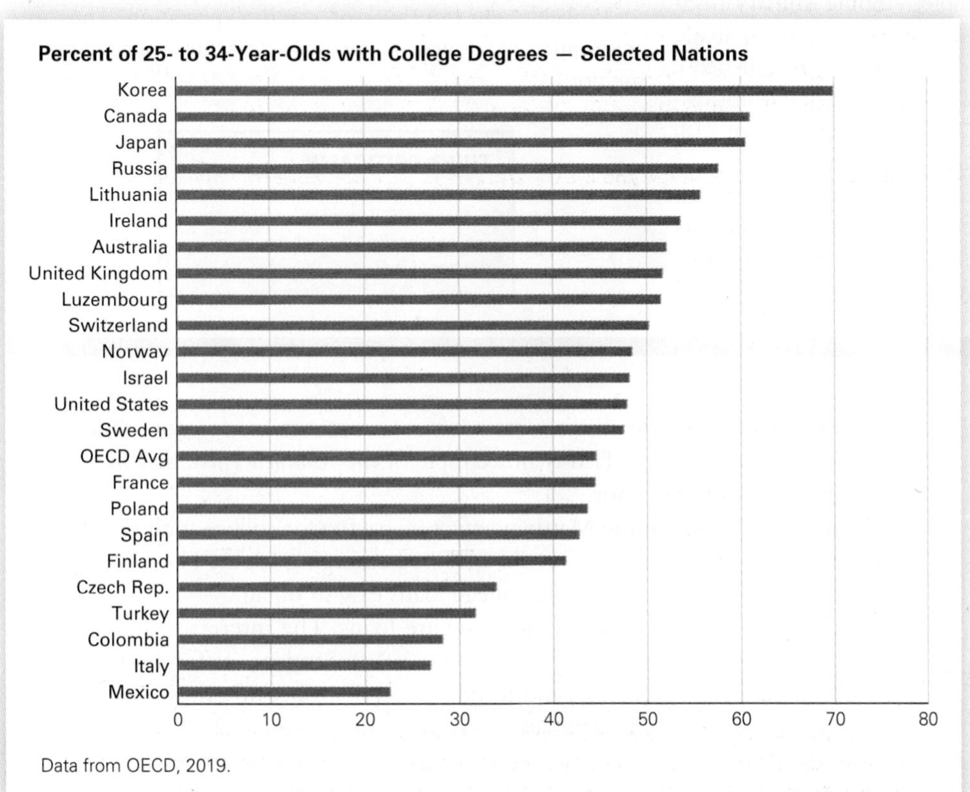

FIGURE 11.5 **Too Many or Not Enough?** Adults in every nation debate whether almost everyone needs to graduate from college. Does your opinion depend on your national origin?

A VIEW FROM SCIENCE

Women and College

As you know from Chapter 1, scientists have many practices to insure valid data. However, interpreting that data is not simple. Alternate explanations are considered as part of the scientific method, but some alternates may not be imagined. Consider data on women in college.

In 1950, college students worldwide were usually men, often educated in exclusively male institutions. In the United States, most of the eight prestigious "Ivy League" colleges (including Harvard, Yale, Brown, Princeton, Columbia) were exclusively male. Some had a smaller college for women associated with them; some did not have even that. By contrast, in 2020 in almost every nation, women outnumbered men in college, and almost every college admits men and women.

Data from the United States reveal the scope of this revolution. Women earned only 24 percent of the bachelor's degrees awarded in 1950. Proportions shifted every year from then on. By 2000 and continuing every year of the twenty-first century thus far, about 57 percent of the bachelor's degrees are earned by women (National Center for Education Statistics, 2020).

Women are now enrolled in virtually every college and discipline, including those once exclusively male (engineering, physics, military). For example, Virginia Military Institute (VMI) is a state-supported military academy that was exclusively male since its founding in 1839. Then, in 1997, the U.S. Supreme Court ruled (7-1) that it could not discriminate based on gender. In 2019, 13 percent (about 218) of the VMI students were female.

These are facts, not disputed, even by those who dispute other facts that scientists consider proven (e.g., climate change). What *is* disputed are the reasons. Why do more women than men earn college degrees?

- It may simply be that women want marriage and motherhood, and they know the path toward that goal has shifted. In 1950, young women became wives and mothers, which made college almost impossible. Now, with contraception, the opposite is true: A college education makes marriage more likely.
- Another interpretation begins with the increasing cost of college, so parental support is more crucial. Since daughters tend to be closer to their parents than sons, perhaps parents are more likely to pay for their daughters' tuition than their sons'.
- A third hypothesis is that something about women's brains makes them better students, so that, when opportunity became equal, women became more likely to want more education.
- A fourth interpretation is that reduced employment discrimination meant that young women realized they could aspire to their chosen profession. They also thought that employers might hire men more readily, so they sought superior credentials in order to compete.
- A fifth explanation is that college itself (perhaps its requirements? dorm living? rules?) discourages males, who want to be more independent than many colleges allow.

Probably you can think of a sixth explanation. Thus, as with much of science, the facts are clear; the interpretations are not.

THINK CRITICALLY: Is it good for society that more young women are planning careers, avoiding motherhood, and refusing domesticity?

who leave without graduating are most often poor, since money, not grades, is the main reason students quit. This is an example of the *Matthew effect*, that the rich get richer but the poor stay poor.

Many nations combat the Matthew effect by paying for college with public funds, thus making higher education free for qualified emerging adults. The United States, instead, relies primarily on making college loans easy to obtain.

Two-thirds of U.S. college students secure loans. The interest is high, as is the default rate—about 10 percent (Friedman, 2019). Students at for-profit colleges are more likely to obtain loans and to default, perhaps because those colleges have the lowest graduation and employment rates (Mohundro et al., 2020).

For many emerging adults, paying back loans is difficult in part because jobs with high salaries are filled by older adults. That is even more true after the COVID-19

pandemic than before, because people with seniority kept their jobs. In November of 2020, 10.7 percent of 20- to 24-year-olds were unemployed, as were 6.1 percent of 25- to 54-year-olds (U.S. Bureau of Labor Statistics, 2021).

Some analysts question whether the burden on students and the cost to taxpayers is worth whatever benefits college might bring. Students who borrow more for college are *less* likely to graduate or earn high incomes later on (Herzog, 2018).

This negative correlation is especially strong for students whose parents never attended college, who are exactly the ones the program is supposed to help. The only clear winners are the lending institutions.

Paying back loans causes anxiety and fear: Some debtors move without a forwarding address, change their name, or even leave the country. One example, hopefully unusual, is a young woman who fled to Berlin, Germany, to escape dunning phone calls about the $50,000 she owes. She says:

> I have this shame on the part of my parents because I really did not want this for them. When I thought about going to college, this is not what I had in mind. I really thought that they were going to be so proud of me. I was the first child in my family . . . to graduate college. But . . . we weren't thinking about the debt when we were signing up for school. And sometimes I think living in New York City and going to a private university maybe wasn't the best idea. I could have gone somewhere else. . . .
>
> I don't have the money to pay for loans. I need to eat and live and not be a slave to this debt. But I'm scared. When I look back, I wonder what I could have done differently.
>
> *[Vanessa quoted in Coggin, 2016]*

CHERISS MAY/NURPHOTO VIA GETTY IMAGES

And Millions More When few U.S. colleges enrolled African Americans, many historically black colleges and universities (HBCUs) educated millions of young adults, benefiting the entire society. This is graduation day at Howard University, chartered by U.S. Congress in 1867.

It is easy to see that her adolescent mind lacked postformal thinking. Her emotional reaction ("I thought they were going to be so proud") overwhelmed practical, future thoughts. Now, as a young adult, she uses postformal thought, too late.

COLLEGE AND COGNITION

For those interested in cognitive development, the crucial question about college is not about wealth, health, or costs. Instead, the question is "does college advance postformal thought?"

Yes, answered many researchers in the late twentieth century. William Perry (1981, 1970/1998) questioned Harvard students every six months. Their thinking advanced with *each year*.

In the first year, students had a simplistic either/or view of knowledge. They believed that questions could be answered either yes or no, that the future led to either success or failure. They wanted their professors to tell them how to distinguish true from false, so they could succeed.

As they moved through college, the students no longer believed in absolutes. Instead, they recognized that many perspectives are possible, multiple factors need to be considered, definitions of success vary, and almost nothing is, totally and forever, right or wrong.

At first that relativism was unsettling, but by their senior year students had become critical thinkers. They could adopt a point of view, yet remain flexible, willing to change course if new challenges, facts, and experiences led to deeper understanding.

◆◆ Especially for Those Considering Studying Abroad Given the effects of college, would it be better for a student to study abroad in the first year or last year of a college education? (see response, page 370)

IMAGINECHINA VIA AP IMAGES/CDSB

Learning from Peers and Computers College students often learn via computer, allowing more education in nations where relatively few older adults are professors. This is true here, in Chengu, China. But note: Computer education works best with other learners nearby.

Perry reported that many aspects of the college experience caused this progression: Peers, professors, books, and class discussion all stimulated new questions and thoughts. In general, years of higher education and varied life experiences led to deeper reflection.

This same conclusion was found by many other scholars. A comprehensive review concluded:

> Compared to freshmen, seniors have better oral and written communication skills, are better abstract reasoners or critical thinkers, are more skilled at using reason and evidence to address ill-structured problems for which there are no verifiably correct answers, have greater intellectual flexibility in that they are better able to understand more than one side of a complex issue, and can develop more sophisticated abstract frameworks to deal with complexity.
>
> *[Pascarella & Terenzini, 1991, p. 155]*

Note that these abilities characterize postformal thinking.

CURRENT CONTEXTS

But wait. You know that historical conditions have a major impact. Does college still advance cognition?

Many recent books criticize college education on exactly those grounds. Notable is a large, longitudinal study of a cross-section of U.S. college students (Arum & Roksa, 2011). Those authors concluded that college produces only half as much critical thinking, analysis, and communication as it did two decades ago. In the first two years of college, the authors report that 45 percent of the students did not advance at all; those who stuck it out to graduate did only a little better.

That study discovered many reasons to explain why current college conditions do not foster critical thinking as much as colleges once did. Compared to decades ago, students study less, professors expect less, and classes that require reading at least 40 pages a week or writing 20 pages a semester are not required; administrators cancel them for low enrollment.

The data find that students avoid English, history, and philosophy, which require writing and critical thinking, choosing instead business (now the most popular major), more socializing, and less studying. Prospective students are more attracted by the quality of the gym than the library.

The researchers of that study traced the students after graduation and found that those who studied less and socialized more were also more likely to have low-paying jobs or no jobs at all. The reason was thought to be their lack of critical thinking, clear communication, or self-discipline (Arum & Roksa, 2014). In other words, college did not teach them what they really needed to learn.

There are other disturbing signs among current college students. One is emotional stress, with a review suggesting "unprecedented levels of distress" and increasing rates of suicide and self-harm (Liu et al., 2018). Compared to a generation ago, today's college students may be more anxious and depressed, not only at high-pressure Ivy League schools, but also in smaller, religious schools.

For example, Franciscan University in Steubenville, Ohio, reported a 231-percent increase over five years in visits to the college counseling center. A survey of the entire student body found that a third of the students were anxious or depressed, with about 10 percent of those severely disturbed. Students in their senior year had the highest rates (Beiter et al., 2015).

Another indicator of trouble is the use of drugs, specifically Adderall, modafinil, and Ritalin, which might enhance cognition and allow all-night studying before an exam. Use of such drugs varies from college to college: less than 1 percent of

students at some institutions and as many as 20 percent at others. Developmentalists worry about such drugs for four reasons:

1. Their use makes it more likely that a student will abuse other drugs, such as cocaine and heroin.
2. The long-term health consequences, especially on the heart and lungs, are unknown.
3. These drugs distort judgment, so students might think that they have become more intelligent or better learners when they actually have not.
4. The drugs are not available to everyone, and that puts users at an unfair advantage.

Every review of the research finds that solid, longitudinal data on such drugs are lacking, but that risk-taking and delay discounting (see Chapter 9) may lead students astray. Some authors are highly suspicious of any such drugs, but others suggest that they might aid cognition and point out that coffee is widely used worldwide for similar reasons (Hall et al., 2021).

One review that considers the possibility that some drugs might bolster cognition concludes that caution is needed:

> Currently available evidence suggests that healthy individuals seeking to preserve or enhance their cognitive capabilities should avoid pharmacological cognitive enhancers and focus instead on a healthy and rewarding lifestyle.
>
> *[Ricci, 2020]*

Those lifestyle habits (sleep, exercise, and diet, as described a few pages ago) benefit the brain over the months and years, but risk-takers want immediate boosts. Since the brain is not fully mature until the mid-20s, if students take a drug that keeps them awake and then study more, they might credit the drug.

Another study of drug use in college found that use of legal and illegal drugs (primarily alcohol and marijuana) increased from enrollment to graduation (the peak was three years after enrollment). Use then slowly declined in the postcollege years (Arria et al., 2017). Thus, college does not necessarily make people wiser.

COLLEGE FOR LOW-INCOME STUDENTS

Many critics of U.S. education wonder if massification is misguided. Might the economic benefits of college occur not from college itself, but from the fact that children from wealthier families are more likely to go to college, graduate, and find good jobs?

That is a plausible hypothesis, because family background compounds the benefits of college. Some of the health and wealth benefits of college are really benefits of family, correlated but not caused by college.

But not entirely. When the relationship between family background and adult success is carefully examined, those from low-SES homes who, against the odds, earn a college degree, benefit even more from that degree than those from wealthier backgrounds (Brand & Xie, 2010; Karlson, 2019).

Especially for High School Teachers
One of your brightest students doesn't want to go to college. They would rather keep waiting tables in a restaurant where they make good money in tips. What do you say? (see response, page 370)

Parents who never went to college may underestimate the advantages of college education for their children. Fifty years ago, the income gap between college graduates and others was much less than it is now (Pew Research Center, February 11, 2014). As a result, many parents and grandparents know people who earned good salaries with only a high school education.

Although most parents hope that their children will go to college, many low-income parents wonder why they should work an extra job in order to pay tuition. Their college child may study obscure subjects with new friends of ethnic backgrounds, political opinions, or moral values unlike their parents. College may encourage their child to criticize the family diet, break family rules, question religious values. Why pay for that?

Ironically, the least expensive colleges (for-profit ones) are less likely to include all the nonclassroom benefits of college education, and thus may appeal to parents and naive students. But they are also less likely to lead to advanced cognition and good jobs, so college credits may not lead to the benefits that once followed the degree.

Many young adults have full-time jobs to pay for college. They attend classes but have less time for study, for making friends, for joining clubs or sports teams (Choi, 2018). Thus, they miss parts of the college experience, which may be essential for learning.

This raises the question of what lasting effects remote classes during the COVID-19 pandemic will have. Many people speculate that virtual instruction is inferior, because the formal and informal interactions among students and instructors are lacking. We will not know until large-scale, longitudinal research comparing in-person and on-screen learning is conducted.

However, there already are reasons to be concerned. College education is more than listening to lectures and writing papers. Remote learning reduces motivation and engagement, especially for students who already are less accustomed to college (Gillis & Krull, 2020).

A CASE TO STUDY

Generation to Generation

One young man said

> People always ask me, why don't you go to college. My dad, he never went. You work, you pay your bills, you help with the rent. My priority right now is to be responsible, to know how adult life works. It might go bad for me, or it might go good. It's going to be hard. . . . I'm scared we'll wake up some day and say "We don't got nothing to eat."
>
> *[Maldonado, quoted in Healy, 2017]*

His thinking is not unusual for young men like him. Students from families with little money are not only unlikely to be able to pay for college, they are unlikely to have role models who went to college, or friends, teachers, and relatives who pave the way for high school seniors.

Giovanni Maldonado's father may be unaware of admission criteria, application deadlines, early admission, scholarship opportunities, and much more. GPA, SAT, ACT, AP, IB, and FAFSA are household acronyms to some, unknown to others. In Giovanni's culture, a good man pays the bills and puts food on the table. His father was a good man; Giovanni wants to be like him.

When Giovanni worries "we don't got nothing to eat," he is reflecting financial stress he learned at home. As mentioned in Chapter 1, food insecurity is a common cause of both shame and fear. Many low-income people live paycheck to paycheck: The term *breadwinner* began because food was basic, whereas college was a luxury for those with "their head in the clouds," or at least high up in an "ivory tower."

No wonder Giovanni is not going to college. Poverty impedes planning, investment, and analysis of the future. If he enrolls, his grammar suggests that he'll need remedial, noncredit courses and thus, more than four years (assuming full-time enrollment) to complete a bachelor's degree (Haushofer & Fehr, 2014).

Perhaps Giovanni will enroll later. Many older adults seek a degree that they did not know they needed, or that their family could not afford. Of the almost 20 million students in tertiary education in 2016, 40 percent of them were over age 24, and 16 percent were over age 35. Most were employed, part-time students, but even among the full-time students, 24 percent were age 25 or older (Digest of Education Statistics, 2019). That age diversity benefits the younger students as well.

DIVERSITY AND LEARNING

Many people meet for the first time a person of another ethnic group, religion, sexual orientation, or life history when they enter college. That can expand their thinking as they listen to experiences and perspectives unlike the ones they knew in childhood.

The most obvious example is racial: More Black students attend historically White colleges, and more White students are at historically Black colleges than was true decades ago. But race is only the beginning.

Religious, economic, national, regional, linguistic, and age differences also matter. Currently in the United States many students have Latinx or Asian classmates. Latinx 18- to 24-year-olds are now as likely to be in college as are Black or non-Hispanic White youth; Asian youth, while a small group overall, have high rates of college attendance (see Figure 11.6).

Diversity can benefit everyone. One catalyst for learning is honest conversations with people from other backgrounds and perspectives. That is what colleges do at their best. A comprehensive study of 48 colleges found that discussions with people of other backgrounds advances thought (Bowman, 2013).

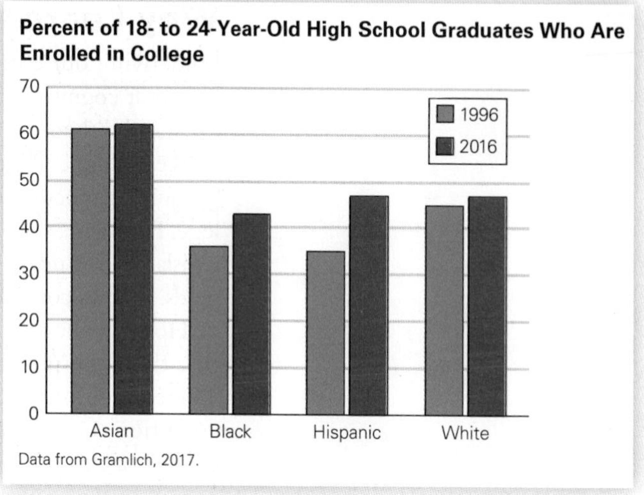

FIGURE 11.6 **More College for Everyone** Most colleges are still quite segregated, but none are as segregated as they were decades ago. Almost every U.S. college student has classmates from other ethnic groups and cultural backgrounds.

OBSERVATION QUIZ
Which group has experienced the largest increase? (see answer, page 370) ↑

Of course, merely sharing a campus does not open up hearts and minds—it may do the opposite. Those particularly likely to be harmed may be those in the minority, if they feel marginalized, or that they are tokens, not equals. Scholars explain that equity demands more than superficial diversity (Puritty et al., 2017).

A study that included many nations as well as many colleges within the United States found that humans may initially respond to someone from another group defensively, confirming stereotypes. However, over time, interaction helped people see the common humanity in everyone (X. Bai et al., 2020).

Beyond ethnic diversity is political diversity. Many people in the United States bewail political polarization. Many people listen to news that presents only one side of various issues, and then they make friends who agree with them.

Fortunately, a basic value of higher education as well as science is to consider alternate views and interpretations. Remember that Piaget stressed that new ideas cause disequilibrium, which leads to deeper thought. That may be why college advances cognitive development.

Sometimes college students are portrayed as political radicals, with extreme left or right views. But most are middling, with only 4 percent of incoming first year students considering themselves "far left" and only 2 percent considering themselves "far right." The most common response to the question "How would you characterize your political views?" was "middle of the road" (41 percent) (Stolzenberg et al., 2019).

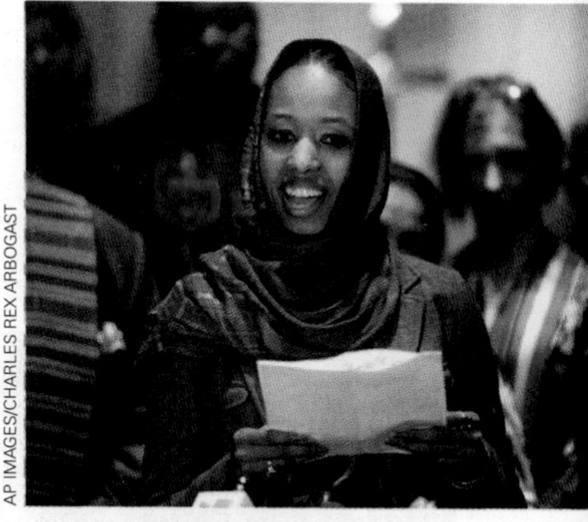

AP IMAGES/CHARLES REX ARBOGAST

Love Thy Neighbor This is Larycia Hawkins, a tenured professor at a Christian college (Wheaton) who in 2017 wore a hijab during Advent to express respect for Muslims, because "we worship the same God." The result: demonstrations of support by many Wheaton students and several bouts of theological questioning by the president of the college, himself a Wheaton graduate (1988). She either was fired or chose to leave (depending on who reports). Nonetheless, every Wheaton student had to think more deeply about the relationship between Christianity and Islam.

Overall, diversity within colleges affects the thinking of emerging adults, who are much more accepting of differences than early generations were. Many studies have found that new ideas *can* lead to intellectual challenge and deeper thought, with benefits lasting for years after graduation (Pascarella et al., 2014).

Colleges that make use of their diversity—via curriculum, assignments, discussions, cooperative education, learning communities, residence halls, and so on—stretch student understanding, not only of other people but also of themselves (Harper & Yeung, 2013; Shim & Perez, 2018). Many colleges require that students take a course in diversity, which usually does, but sometimes does not, expand the students' thinking (Denson et al., 2020).

Given history, and the human tendency to see differences as deficits, simply having classmates from various backgrounds does not necessarily expand a young person's thinking. Appreciation and respect for alternate views needs to be part of the college culture, and discrimination needs to be recognized and stopped (Roksa et al., 2017).

Why Learn?

Underlying our entire discussion of college, indeed our entire discussion of emerging adult cognition, is the assumption that adults benefit from combining the practical and the theoretical, the emotional and the analytic.

Regarding college, adults who have never attended college sometimes believe that "acquiring specific skills and knowledge" is the most important reason to go to college. For some, success is steady employment. That also is the metric used by many legislators. If students hold that perspective, they might seek credentials in expanding fields, such as computer systems, the health professions, or criminal justice.

However, developmentalists, most professors, and many college graduates believe that the main purpose of higher education is "personal and intellectual growth." Therefore, professors hope to foster critical thinking and analysis, as in postformal cognition. Critical thinking, however, requires all of us, textbook authors as well readers of this book, to ask "What is the purpose of higher education?' Is advanced cognition the answer? Does college do that?

what have you learned?

1. Why did scholars choose the term *postformal* to describe the fifth stage of cognition?
2. How does postformal thinking differ from typical adolescent thought?
3. How is combining subjective and objective thought an example of postformal thought?
4. What are the benefits of college education?
5. Why is the United States no longer the world leader in massification?
6. Why might enrolling in college result in less, not more, income later on?
7. What are the benefits and problems in a diverse student body?

Psychosocial Development

As just described, the bodies and minds of young adults grow as they always have, responding to genes and instincts the evolved long ago. What has changed is the manifestation of those long-standing characteristics, with fewer babies and more education.

However, for the final topic of this chapter, psychosocial development, much more dramatic change has occurred. Because of context and culture, contemporary emerging adults are not like those of 50 years ago. This is evident in *identity* and *intimacy* (Erikson's fifth and sixth stages), two foundational psychosocial needs. (See Table 11.2.)

JUNG YEON-JE/AFP/GETTY IMAGES

Grown Up Now? In Korean tradition, age 19 signifies adulthood, when people can drink alcohol and, in modern times, vote. In 2011, administrators invited 100 19-year-olds to a public Coming of Age ceremony, shown here, continuing a tradition that began centuries before. Emerging adults are torn between old and new. For example, in many nations, coming of age ceremonies are exclusive to one gender, but here young men and women participate.

Identity Achievement

Fifty years ago, identity was established by age 18, when older adolescents began their work and started their own families. Their work and chosen family sustained them, emotionally and financially, all their lives. Now identity is

TABLE 11.2 Erikson's Eight Stages of Development

Stage	Virtue/Pathology	Possible in Emerging Adulthood If Not Successfully Resolved
Trust vs. mistrust	Hope/withdrawal	Suspicious of others, making close relationships difficult
Autonomy vs. shame and doubt	Will/compulsion	Obsessively driven, single-minded, not socially responsive
Initiative vs. guilt	Purpose/inhibition	Fearful, regretful (e.g., very homesick in college)
Industry vs. inferiority	Competence/inertia	Self-critical of any endeavor, procrastinating, perfectionistic
Identity vs. role diffusion	Fidelity/repudiation	Uncertain and negative about values, lifestyle, friendships
Intimacy vs. isolation	Love/exclusivity	Anxious about close relationships, jealous, lonely
Generativity vs. stagnation	Care/rejection	[In the future] Fear of failure
Integrity vs. despair	Wisdom/disdain	[In the future] No "mindfulness," no life plan

Information based on Erikson, 1982/1998.

rarely fully achieved by age 18. A new response (*moratorium*) and a new type of identity (*vocational*) are evident after adolescence. Emerging adulthood has become "the period of life that offers the most opportunities for identity exploration" (Luyckx et al., 2013, p. 703).

MORATORIUM

Beyond the foreclosure or confusion that is typical in early adolescence, a **moratorium** is a common way that emerging adults continue their identity quest. A moratorium is a programmed pause, a way to postpone identity achievement by doing something else. Emerging adults may:

moratorium
An adolescent's choice of a socially acceptable way to postpone making identity-achievement decisions. Going to college is a common example.

- take a gap year before college;
- attend college without a specific career goal;
- have an intimate sexual relationship without plans for marriage;
- enlist in the military for two years;
- take a job known to be temporary;
- volunteer for a year of mission work or social justice advocacy;
- intern in a nonprofit for little pay; and/or
- travel around the world.

All these moratoria are socially acceptable ways to postpone commitment, avoiding a definitive answer to the burning question "Who are you?"

Many emerging adults seek more education. That itself may become a moratorium. It is not unusual for students to change majors, colleges, and career goals several times before age 25 (Astorne-Figari & Speer, 2019).

VOCATIONAL IDENTITY

For current youth, vocational identity signifies far more than getting a paycheck.

> Career choices faced by individuals inevitably raise the question of the meaning that they intend to give their lives. To choose their work or sector in which they want to evolve is also to consider the purpose of their existence, the priorities (physical, spiritual, social, aesthetic, etc.) that they want to give, the choices that they wish to operate, the overall style of life that they wish to give themselves.
> *[Bernaud, 2014, p. 36]*

Many emerging adults consult career counselors, who help them explore options, predict future openings, and figure out how their choices affect their "overall style of life." One career that might be considered, especially for students of human development, is career counseling itself (see Career Alert).

The recent pandemic complicated the search for vocational identity, requiring a longer period of exploration. One study found that 40 percent of all college students experienced loss of an internship, job opportunity, or employment because of the virus (Aucejo et al., 2020).

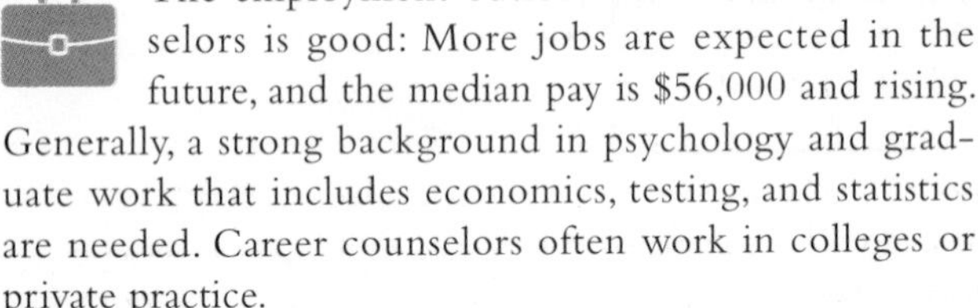

CAREER ALERT

The Career Counselor

The employment outlook for vocational counselors is good: More jobs are expected in the future, and the median pay is $56,000 and rising. Generally, a strong background in psychology and graduate work that includes economics, testing, and statistics are needed. Career counselors often work in colleges or private practice.

Astute career counselors discern answers to three questions before they advise someone.

1. What does the client enjoy? Both genes and culture are relevant. A classic way to explore possibilities is through Holland's six-factor assessment of personality patterns and vocations (see Figure 11.7). Some people like to work with their hands; some hate it. Some like open-ended, creative work; some prefer structure; and so on.
2. What does the client value? Some people want to enjoy their work; others want to help humankind; some want independence; others want to be part of a large organization. Salary and medical benefits are crucial for some, not for others. Again, various measures have been developed to help a person discover their values and interests (Sheldon et al., 2020).
3. What skills and aptitudes does a person have. This is far beyond IQ: Multiple intelligences need to be considered (see Chapter 7).

Added to knowing the job-seeker well, career counselors need to anticipate the job market. Dramatic shifts occur. The historic example is agriculture. Once, 90 percent of U.S. workers were farmers; now less than 1 percent are. Current examples are in health (geriatricians are needed, not pediatricians) and in education (fewer first-grade teachers, but more bilingual, reading, and disability specialists).

Market projections vary not only by industry and occupation but also by location. Career counselors might suggest moving to another community, or might point out the psychic as well as economic costs of commuting. Did you know that North Dakota is experiencing a job boom, or that traveling to and from work is highly stressful for many adults? (Chatterjee et al., 2020)

Career counselors must combine their knowledge of all the systems (micro-, macro-, and exo-, as explained in Chapter 1) with insight into the personality and circumstances of each client. That can lead toward a job that never would have been found without help.

That happened for my daughter, a newspaper reporter, a career she chose when every community had several local papers. The economy shifted: Her paper joined a conglomerate and began firing reporters. She consulted a career coach so she would not be paralyzed if she was let go.

The counselor gave four unexpected suggestions: Quit before she lost her job, recognize interests and skills she did not know she had, think about relocating, and find jobs that were not yet posted. My daughter discovered two openings far from home. Her counselor helped her apply for both, with a resume, references, and follow-up calls.

A newspaper in a smaller, distant city needed a managing editor (not a reporter) and asked my daughter to come for an interview. She almost said no. She told me that to travel many hours for the interview would waste her time, because she probably wouldn't be chosen. And if she were chosen, it would be unfair to the employer, because she would say no; she didn't want to move.

Again, the counselor gave advice. She told my daughter that her task was to apply, not to anticipate. An interview would be good practice. Accordingly, she met with editors and writers; she liked them. She was offered the job, and she took it. Now she loves it. What would have happened if she had not asked for help?

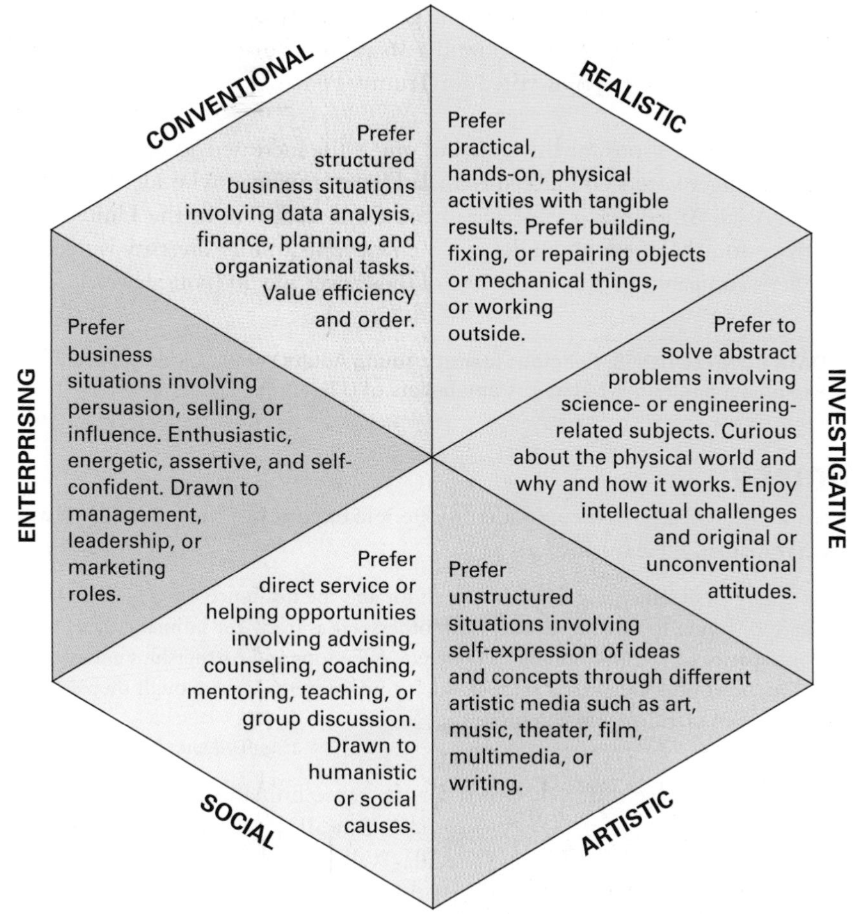

CONVENTIONAL
Prefer structured business situations involving data analysis, finance, planning, and organizational tasks. Value efficiency and order.

REALISTIC
Prefer practical, hands-on, physical activities with tangible results. Prefer building, fixing, or repairing objects or mechanical things, or working outside.

INVESTIGATIVE
Prefer to solve abstract problems involving science- or engineering-related subjects. Curious about the physical world and why and how it works. Enjoy intellectual challenges and original or unconventional attitudes.

ARTISTIC
Prefer unstructured situations involving self-expression of ideas and concepts through different artistic media such as art, music, theater, film, multimedia, or writing.

SOCIAL
Prefer direct service or helping opportunities involving advising, counseling, coaching, mentoring, teaching, or group discussion. Drawn to humanistic or social causes.

ENTERPRISING
Prefer business situations involving persuasion, selling, or influence. Enthusiastic, energetic, assertive, and self-confident. Drawn to management, leadership, or marketing roles.

FIGURE 11.7 Happy at Work John Holland's six-part diagram helps job seekers realize that income and benefits are not the only goals of employment. Workers have healthier hearts and minds if their job fits their personal preferences.

Even before COVID-19, finding one's niche in the world of work often took years. The average U.S. young adult had seven distinct jobs between age 18 and 25, with the college-educated starting and quitting employment even more than the high school graduate (U.S. Bureau of Labor Statistics, August, 2018).

What a contrast to 50 years ago, when many young men followed in their father's footsteps or got jobs at the local factory, while many young women became housewives, helpmates, and mothers. Now young adults may be "sagely avoiding foreclosure and premature commitment in a treacherous job market" (Konstam, 2015, p. 95).

KEVIN WINTER/GETTY IMAGES ENTERTAINMENT/GETTY IMAGES

Who Are You? Many emerging adults refuse to identify as a single ethnicity, sexual orientation, or gender identity. That may be why Halsey, a proudly bisexual singer–songwriter of Irish, Italian, Hungarian, and African American heritage, is a superstar for many of her generation. Among her many record-breaking accomplishments, her album *Badlands* sold 115,000 copies in the first week after its release. She was born in 1994; here she is 24.

OTHER IDENTITIES

As you remember, gender, religious, ethnic, and political identities all develop in adolescence. Further development occurs in emerging adulthood. People express their sexual orientation; people choose their own faith; people delve deep into their ethnic heritage, which allows them to gain respect for others.

Political identity is particularly likely to change. As teenagers, Donald Trump was a Democrat and Hillary Clinton was a Republican. Fifty years ago, emerging adults kept the political identity they had in adolescence, which was the same as their parents, their classmates, their church. In the 2000 presidential contest, only 2 percent of younger voters made a choice that differed from their elders.

In 2008, for the first time in U.S. history, millions of emerging adults elected a candidate (Barack Obama) whom their grandparents did not support. That age divide continues: In 2020, exit polls found a 16-percent age gap: Only one-third (35 percent) of 18- to 29-year-olds voted for Trump/Pence, as did half (51 percent) of voters over age 65.

There are many reasons for this shift, but one is the increased acceptance of diversity. Many younger voters considered Kamala Harris, a woman who identifies as both Black and Asian American, a welcome break from tradition. In the United States, almost three-fourths of people under age 30 believe that more diversity is needed in every sphere, compared to only about half of those over age 50 (Poushter et al., 2019).

 **DATA CONNECTIONS: Religious Identity: Young Adults Versus Older Cohorts** explores the religious behaviors and beliefs of U.S. adults. Achieve

Intimacy

intimacy versus isolation The sixth of Erikson's eight stages of development. Adults seek someone with whom to share their lives in an enduring and self-sacrificing commitment. Without such commitment, they risk profound aloneness and isolation.

In Erikson's theory, after achieving identity, people experience the crisis of **intimacy versus isolation**. He explains:

> The young adult, emerging from the search for and the insistence on identity, is eager and willing to fuse his identity with others. He is ready for intimacy, that is, the capacity to commit himself to concrete affiliations and partnerships and to develop the ethical strength to abide by such commitments, even though they call for significant sacrifices and compromises.
>
> *[Erikson, 1993a, p. 263]*

Other theorists have different words for the same human need: *affiliation, affection, interdependence, communion, belonging, love.* But all developmentalists agree that social connections are pivotal lifelong (Padilla-Walker et al., 2017). Each relationship demands vulnerability and compromise, shattering the isolation caused by too much self-protection.

The social context may be particularly influential when contemporary young adults seek intimacy. Emerging adulthood is called the "frontier" of efforts to prevent emotional problems and foster growth (Schwartz & Petrova, 2019). Young adults strengthen social connections with family and friends in ways unlike in the past.

ROMANTIC PARTNERS

Romance is part of life for many young adults, but, as already pointed out, for contemporary young people, marriage is not. The U.S. Census reports that less than

WAVE/CULTURA IMAGES/MEDIA BAKERY

CHEE GINTAN/E+/GETTY IMAGES

Being Intimate The word *intimacy* was traditionally a euphemism for sexual intercourse, but to developmentalists it is much more than that. Look closely at these two couples, one in Spain *(left)* and one in Malaysia *(right)*. Whether or not they are having sex does not matter: They are intimate in their touching, emotions, and even clothing.

5 percent of 18- to 25-year-olds are married. Many have had steady partners, sometimes breaking up with them after months or years, sometimes marrying eventually (Sassler & Lichter, 2020).

Postponement of marriage does not trouble developmentalists as much as another emerging adult trend, fewer romances. To understand this, it helps to understand the components of romantic love. In a classic analysis, Robert Sternberg (1988) described passion, intimacy, and commitment. The presence or absence of these three gives rise to seven different forms of love (see Table 11.3).

TABLE 11.3 Sternberg's Seven Forms of Love Present in the Relationship?

Form of Love	Passion	Intimacy	Commitment
Liking	No	Yes	No
Infatuation	Yes	No	No
Empty love	No	No	Yes
Romantic love	Yes	Yes	No
Fatuous love	Yes	No	Yes
Companionate love	No	Yes	Yes
Consummate love	Yes	Yes	Yes

Information from Sternberg, 1988.

Early in a relationship, *passion* is evident in falling in love, an intense physical, cognitive, and emotional onslaught characterized by excitement, ecstasy, and euphoria. The entire body and mind, hormones and neurons, are activated; the person is obsessed (Sanz Cruces et al., 2015).

Intimacy is knowing someone well, sharing secrets as well as sex. This aspect of a romance is reciprocal, with each partner gradually revealing more as well as accepting more of the other's revelations. The moonstruck joy of passionate love can become bittersweet as intimacy increases. As one observer explains, "Falling in love is absolutely no way of getting to know someone" (Sullivan, 1999, p. 225).

The research is not clear about the best schedule for passion and intimacy, whether they should progress slowly or quickly, for instance. According to some research, they are not always connected, as lust arises from a different part of the brain than affection (Langeslag et al., 2013; Fisher, 2016a).

For those who follow the current Western pattern of love and marriage, *commitment* is the least common in early adulthood, as it takes time and effort. It grows through decisions to be together, mutual caregiving, shared possessions, and forgiveness (Schoebi et al., 2012). Social forces strengthen or undermine commitment; that's why in-laws are often the topic of jokes and arguments, and why a spouse might be unhappy with their mate's close friends.

Commitment is powerfully influenced by culture. When cultures endorse arranged marriages, commitment occurs early on, before passion or intimacy. A study of husbands and wives in arranged marriages reports that the commitment by both partners to make the marriage work led to love, not vice versa. One husband said:

> Perhaps I could say that love involves commitment or [that] marriage is a commitment to love. From the beginning I was committed to love [my wife]. Sometimes I have been challenged to keep the commitment or just challenged to love her, but I do my best to be a loving husband. Loving her is usually easy but sometimes not.
>
> *[quoted in Epstein et al., 2013, pp. 352–353]*

That husband was of Indian heritage, where arranged marriages are still common. However, especially among middle class emerging adults in southern India, arranged marriages are becoming scarcer. Young adults seek their own life partners (Banerji & Deshpande, 2020; Bhandari, 2020).

Indian parents still want their children to marry within their caste, yet children are much less troubled by intercaste marriage than adults are. The same phenomenon is evident in the United States, with emerging adults more likely to choose partners of other ethnic and religious background than their parents' generation did.

When children are born, passion may fade as financial and emotional stress increase, but commitment increases. This may be one reason why most sexually

JENA CUMBO PHOTOGRAPHY

How to Find Your Soul Mate Tiago and Mariela met on a dating site for people with tattoos, connected on Skype, moved in together, and soon were engaged to marry.

active young adults try to avoid pregnancy unless they believe their partner is a lifelong mate. [**Life-Span Link:** Chapter 13 discusses parenthood and marriage.]

FINDING EACH OTHER AND LIVING TOGETHER

For many young adults, not only in the United States but worldwide, parents no longer are the main matchmakers. Young adults meet each other at colleges, workplaces, or on matchmaking websites that provide dozens of potential partners to meet and evaluate. Often physical attraction is the gateway to a relationship, but intimacy and then commitment require much more.

The large number of possible partners whom young adults find—the thousands of fellow students at most colleges or the hundreds of suggestions that matchmaking sites provide—causes a potential problem, **choice overload**, when too many options are available. Choice overload makes some people unable to choose, and it increases second thoughts after a selection is made (Chernev et al., 2015).

choice overload
When having too many choices is confusing and dizzying. The neurons of the human brain are on/off, approach/avoidance, fire/rest. Too many choices can overwhelm the system, leading to no choice at all.

cohabitation
An arrangement in which a couple lives together in a committed romantic relationship but are not formally married.

Choice overload has been proven with many consumer goods (jams, chocolates, pens, restaurants), but it applies to mate selection as well. Having many complex options that require weighing present and future advantages and disadvantages (trade-offs are inevitable in partner selection) may be overwhelming and lead to poor decisions (Lee & Chiou, 2016).

One solution provided by some internet dating sites is to allow the program to do the filtering, selecting possible mates based on mutual interests and background.

The fact that marriage is often postponed, and that sex sometimes occurs without commitment, does not mean that emerging adults do not hope for a committed romantic partnership. In fact, having a steady partner is still sought. This makes sense for human development: Young adults in romantic relationships tend to be happier and healthier than their lonely peers.

What has changed is the rise of **cohabitation**, living with an unmarried partner. Cohabitation was relatively unusual 50 years ago: Only one in nine marriages in 1970 began with cohabitation. Now cohabitation is the norm (see Figure 11.8). About three of every four couples cohabit before marriage (Rosenfeld & Roesler, 2019).

For many young couples, cohabitation is not just a prelude to marriage but a substitute for it. The benefits of cohabitation may or may not outweigh the problems (higher breakup rates, and, if the couple marries, higher divorce rates later on). One current view is that cohabitation in emerging adulthood is a "smart and savvy" strategy to achieve intimacy without commitment (Manning, 2020).

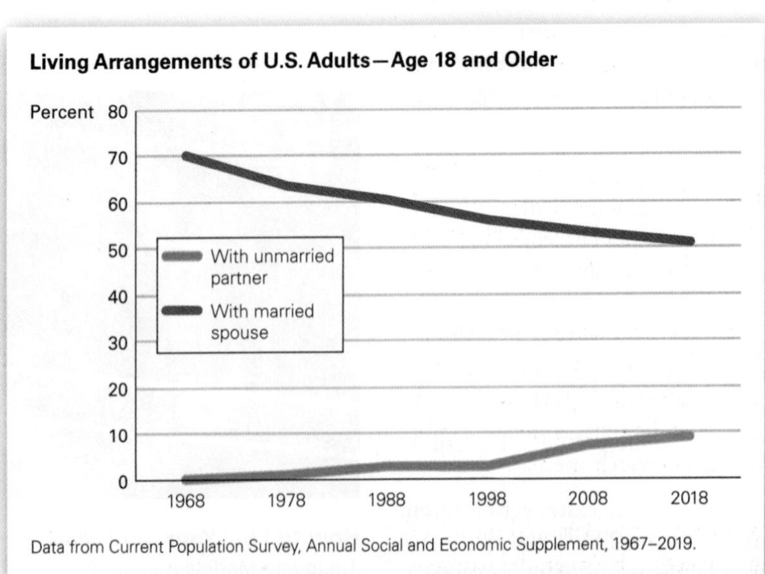

FIGURE 11.8 **Do You See the Problem?** Some people might be troubled by the rise in cohabitation. Since this chart shows adults of every age, it suggests that the ratio of cohabitation to marriage is now about 1 to 5, so a typical adult might spend three years cohabiting and 30 years married. To a developmentalist, there is another change: The number of adults who have no partner at all is increasing.

Cohabitation rates vary from nation to nation. Almost everyone in Canada and Europe cohabits at some point. Many people in Sweden, France, Jamaica, and Puerto Rico live with a partner for decades, sometimes all their lives, never marrying.

Although marriage rates are down and cohabitation is up in every demographic group, education increases the rate of marriage before parenthood. Couples without college degrees are five times more likely to have children without marrying compared to cohabiting couples who are college graduates (Lundberg et al., 2016).

The probable reason is economic. College graduates are more likely to have a steady,

well-paying job, which often is considered a requirement for marriage. Some young women who cannot find a suitable mate decide that they would rather have a child than an unemployable husband.

The meaning and consequences of cohabitation and marriage vary from couple to couple no matter what their education level or sexual orientation. However, one definite advantage and one clear disadvantage have been found in study after study.

The advantage is economic: People save money by living together, so cohabitation is better financially than living alone. This is a reason given by many couples who struggle financially (Sassler & Miller, 2017). The disadvantage occurs if children are born: Cohabiting partners have lower incomes than married partners and are less committed to child rearing. Those two factors may be the underlying reason that their children are less likely to excel in school, graduate, and go to college (Manning, 2015).

Note, however, that income is not the only reason. It is true that low-income parents are less likely to marry, and income matters for a child's education. However, even among parents with the same income level, marriage increases commitment to family life, and that benefits the children.

 **DATA CONNECTIONS: Technology and Romance: Trends for U.S. Adults** examines how emerging adults find romantic partners. Achieve

INTIMATE PARTNER VIOLENCE

Now we turn to a problem that is particularly common among emerging-adult couples: domestic abuse. This problem occurs among dating and married couples, but it is especially common among cohabitating partners (Manning et al., 2018).

A nationwide survey of 14,155 men and women in the United States found that 32 percent of the women and 28 percent of the men had experienced physical violence from an intimate partner, with the most common age at first abuse between ages 18 and 24 (MMWR, September 5, 2014). Most such surveys make the mistake of thinking only about physical harm when considering domestic abuse. Emotional abuse can be worse, if criticism and fear are weaponized.

Why are emerging adults particularly vulnerable? Inexperience, hormones, and freedom from parental supervision all play a part, but two aspects are directly related to emerging adulthood. One of the correlates of intimate partner violence is that one partner is *NEET* (not in education, employment, or training). In that case, abuse is more likely—true for women and for men, married or cohabiting (Alvira-Hammond et al., 2014).

Another factor is substance abuse. As you read, alcohol and drug abuse are more common for people in their early 20s, and that increases the frequency and severity of interpersonal violence. In emerging adulthood, the connection between all forms of abuse (as victim and perpetrator) and drug use may be especially common in women (Ahmadabadi et al., 2019).

In addition, many contemporary young adults have several romantic relationships between age 18 and 25, which increases the odds that at least one of those relationships will include emotional or physical abuse. The risk of abuse is highest when one partner ends a relationship that the other wants to continue. For that, a new weapon is sometimes added, called *revenge porn*, which is posting on social media photos or videos of one's naked partner (Eaton et al., 2020).

Couple abuse can take two forms, each with distinct causes, patterns, and means of prevention. In both cases, it is crucial to understand the interaction between the partners.

Situational couple violence occurs when both partners fight—with words, slaps, and exclusion (leaving home, refusing sex, etc.). The *situation* causes stress, and then the partners attack each other. When coping methods are destructive (such as substance abuse) and external stress is high (such as for many low-income couples), adults may turn on those closest to them.

situational couple violence
Fighting between romantic partners that is brought on more by the situation than by the deep personality problems of the individuals. Both partners are typically victims and abusers.

CHAPTER APP 11

bSafe

IOS:
https://tinyurl.com/y2b4zudq

ANDROID:
https://tinyurl.com/9wbcpjf

RELEVANT TOPIC:
Personal safety

This safety app acts as an SOS system that can be activated by touch or voice, live streaming and recording an emergency situation and sending the user's location to designated "guardians." It also has a timer alarm and a siren.

As best we know, situational abuse increased during the COVID-19 pandemic, because ways to reduce stress (talk a walk, go to work, visit a friend) decreased (Usher et al., 2020).

Same-sex partners are at least as likely to be in an abusive relationship as other-sex couples are, with some research finding that lesbian couples are more likely to be abusive than gay couples (Longobardi & Badenes-Ribera, 2017; Rollè et al., 2018).

The data on lesbian couples confirm what other research has found: Women are as aggressive in situational violence as men. Since men tend to be stronger, with more access to guns, it is true that victims of severe physical abuse are more often women. But remember that verbal and emotional abuse can be as hurtful as physical abuse, and for that, men might be more often victims.

The mistaken male-abuser/female-victim assumption occurred not only because men are physically stronger, and thus cause more injury. In addition, men are reluctant to admit that they are victims, and outsiders are less likely to believe them. Likewise, same-sex couples hesitate to publicly acknowledge conflict, although in most aspects of relationships, they are similar to heterosexual couples (Stults et al., 2019).

Social scientists have identified numerous causes of domestic violence, including youth, poverty, personality (such as poor impulse control), mental illness (such as antisocial personality disorder), and substance use disorder. Developmentalists note that many children who are harshly punished or sexually abused, or who witness domestic assault, grow up to become abusers or victims themselves.

Just as we now know it is mistaken to assume that females are victims and males are perpetrators, it is also mistaken to think that interpersonal violence happens only in established relationships. A study of college students in dating relationships found that about 20 percent had experienced interpersonal violence, with much the same predictors as for those not in college, specifically childhood experiences and current alcohol use (Paat & Markham, 2019).

Often the problem arises from conflicting cultural understandings, not from psychopathology. This explains something that surprised some social workers: Many abused husbands and wives say they love each other and want to stay together. They seek counseling to help their relationship rather than to end it (Visser et al., 2020).

This also explains domestic abuse among Latinx couples. Especially if they live far from other Latinx couples, women are more often perpetrators of partner abuse than men are, in part because boys are taught "never hit a girl." However, if a Latinx couple lives in a neighborhood with many other Latinx people, another cultural value, *familism*, reduces domestic violence toward children and toward mates (Soller & Kuhlemeier, 2019).

The less common but more ominous type of partner abuse is called **intimate terrorism**. Instead of mutual aggression there is a power imbalance, usually with a dominant a male abuser and a passive female victim, although the gender roles can be reversed (Dutton, 2012). (See Figure 11.9.) Terrorism is dangerous to the victim and to anyone who intervenes.

intimate terrorism
A violent and demeaning form of abuse in a romantic relationship, in which the victim (usually female) is frightened to fight back, seek help, or withdraw. In this case, the victim is in danger of physical as well as psychological harm.

With intimate terrorism, the victim needs to be immediately separated from the abuser and relocated to a safe place. Social support is crucial because one strategy used by intimate terrorists is to isolate the victim from other people. That is particularly destructive in emerging adulthood, since almost all the young adults' problems can be mitigated by family and friends. Accordingly, we examine those two sources of support now.

THE FAMILY

Although composed of individuals, a family is much more than the persons who belong to it. In the dynamic synergy of a well-functioning family, children grow, adults find support, and everyone is part of a unit that gives meaning to life. All members of each family have **linked lives**; that is, the experiences and needs of

linked lives
Lives in which the success, health, and well-being of each family member are connected to those of other members.

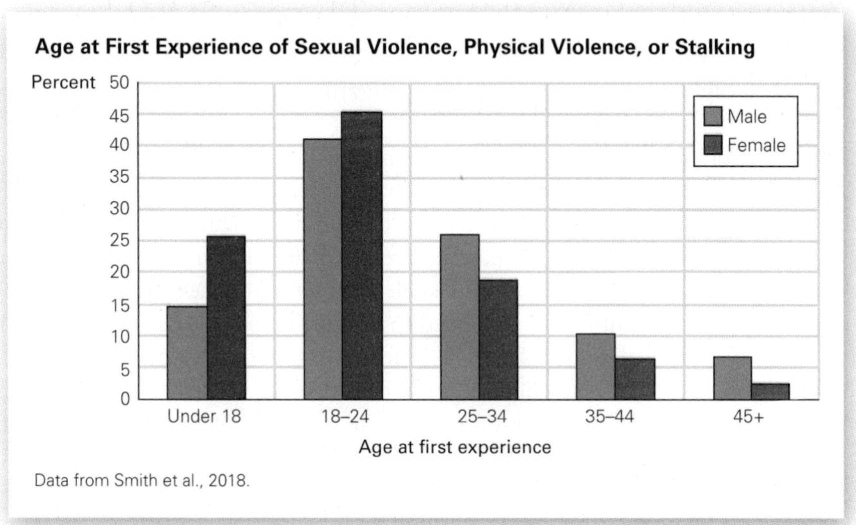

FIGURE 11.9 When Did It Begin? These data are from the U.S. Centers for Disease Control and Prevention, a reputable source. As you see, when victims are asked when the first incident of sexual violence, physical violence, or stalking occurred, emerging adulthood is the most likely time. For a sizable minority, the first incidence occurred before age 18 (especially for females) or after age 25 (especially for males). Almost never does intimate partner violence begin after age 45 (although victimization, once started, often continues). Not shown here are other data from this report, which show that, over their lifetime, about a third of all adults have been victimized in some way (raped, physically abused, threatened, stalked). Rates are similar for both women (36 percent) and men (34 percent), although more women sought medical, legal, or psychological help in recovery than men did (25 percent of all women versus 11 percent of all men).

family members at one stage of life are affected by those at other stages (Elder, 1998; Macmillan & Copher, 2005; Settersten, 2015).

Traditionally, the links to the childhood family weakened at age 18 when young people established their own families. At that age, divorced fathers are no longer required to pay child support, and foster children are considered "emancipated." From 1950 to 2000, more and more emerging adults left their childhood home and lived independently, often with a romantic partner or several young adulthood roommates. Independence was expected and prized.

Now, however, parental support continues to be vital for many emerging adults. As two experts explain, "with delays in marriage, more Americans choosing to remain single, and high divorce rates, a tie to a parent may be the most important bond in a young adult's life" (Fingerman & Furstenberg, 2012).

A longitudinal study of 1,719 individuals, aged 18–27, found that most had parental financial help for years. Those (about one-fourth) without substantial assistance tended to fare worse at age 27 than those with it. The conclusion of this study is that family support is not a barrier to independence but more often the opposite—a helpful launching pad (Bea & Yi, 2019).

Increasingly, parents provide emotional support and material help. In a reversal of earlier trends, an increasing proportion of young adults still live at home. COVID-19 increased that new household composition: In August 2020 in the United States, more than two-thirds (71 percent) of all 18- to 24-year-olds lived with their parents (Fry et al., 2020).

The connections between emerging adults and their parents are reciprocal, with the younger generation being more tech-savvy as well as culturally aware. The attitudes of parents are affected by their young-adult children and vice-versa (Padilla-Walker et al., 2018).

For example, a detailed Dutch study found substantial agreement between parents and their adult children on contentious issues: cohabitation, same-sex partnerships,

Especially for Family Therapists
More emerging-adult children today live with their parents than ever before, yet you have learned that families often function better when young adults live on their own. What would you advise? (see response, page 370)

and divorce. Generational differences appeared, with the young more accepting of social changes than the old; but when parents were compared with their own children (not young adults in general), "intergenerational congruence" was apparent (Bucx et al., 2010, p. 131).

About half of all emerging adults in the United States receive cash from their parents, in addition to tuition, medical care, food, and other material support. Most are also given substantial gifts of time, such as help with laundry, moving, household repairs, and, if the young adult becomes a parent, free child care. Earning a college degree while raising small children is almost impossible without family help (Bea & Yi, 2019).

In the twenty-first century, parents need to provide emotional as well as financial help. This was starkly evident in Sweden, where the government provides housing, college tuition, and food if needed. A study of 65 young adults, aged 18–26, who once were in foster care, found that they had more problems of every kind, including arrest, early parenthood, and mental illness, which the researchers traced to the lack of parental guidance (Höjer & Sjöblom, 2014).

Of course, sometimes parents impede the young adult's need for independence. When parents are overly involved in the lives of their adult children, the parents tend to be depressed, and the children immature (Cui et al., 2019).

Consider the implications of the term *helicopter parent*, when parents hover over the emerging-adult child, ready to swoop down if any problem arises or, worse, *snowplow parent*, who try to clear every obstacle in the adult child's path. This erupted in a major U.S. scandal in 2019, when some parents paid to have college applications distorted to make their children seem more capable and talented than was the case (Coleman, 2019).

Family counselors recommend that each generation find ways to meet their intimacy needs without depending on the other. If a parents' involvement with their emerging adult is a consequence of a dysfunctional, distant marital relationship, that harms the child (Kumar & Mattanah, 2018). On the other hand, mutual care and support is beneficial for the entire family, as the life of each person is linked to the others.

Most emerging adults find a balance: Only about 20 percent of them disclose personal as well as routine information about their lives to their parents. In general, some distance is better, but individuals vary by culture and personality (Son & Padilla-Walker, 2019). Family lives are linked, but specifics of time, place, and family interaction determine if the links become chains.

THINK CRITICALLY: Can a person with many friends also be lonely?

FRIENDSHIP

Friends are another important source of intimacy for emerging adults. They provide *self-expansion* (Aron et al., 2013); they enlarge a person's understanding as friends empathize with each other.

Since fewer emerging adults today are married and have children, their social world can, and usually does, include many peers who provide companionship. Unlike relatives, friends are selected for their ability to be loyal, trustworthy, supportive, and enjoyable—a mutual choice, not an obligatory one.

Thus, friends understand and comfort each other when romance turns sour, and they provide useful information about everything from which college to attend to which socks to wear. For example, many adolescents are depressed about how their bodies appear. Interviews with 26-year-olds found that their negative body image lifted in late adolescence and early adulthood, primarily because friends reassured them about their bodies (Gattario & Frisén, 2019).

People tend to make more friends during emerging adulthood than at any later period. They often use social media to extend and deepen friendships that begin face-to-face, becoming more aware of the day-to-day tribulations and celebrations of their friends.

Friendship patterns change with maturation. Young adults want many friends, and they work to gather them—befriending classmates; attending parties; speaking to

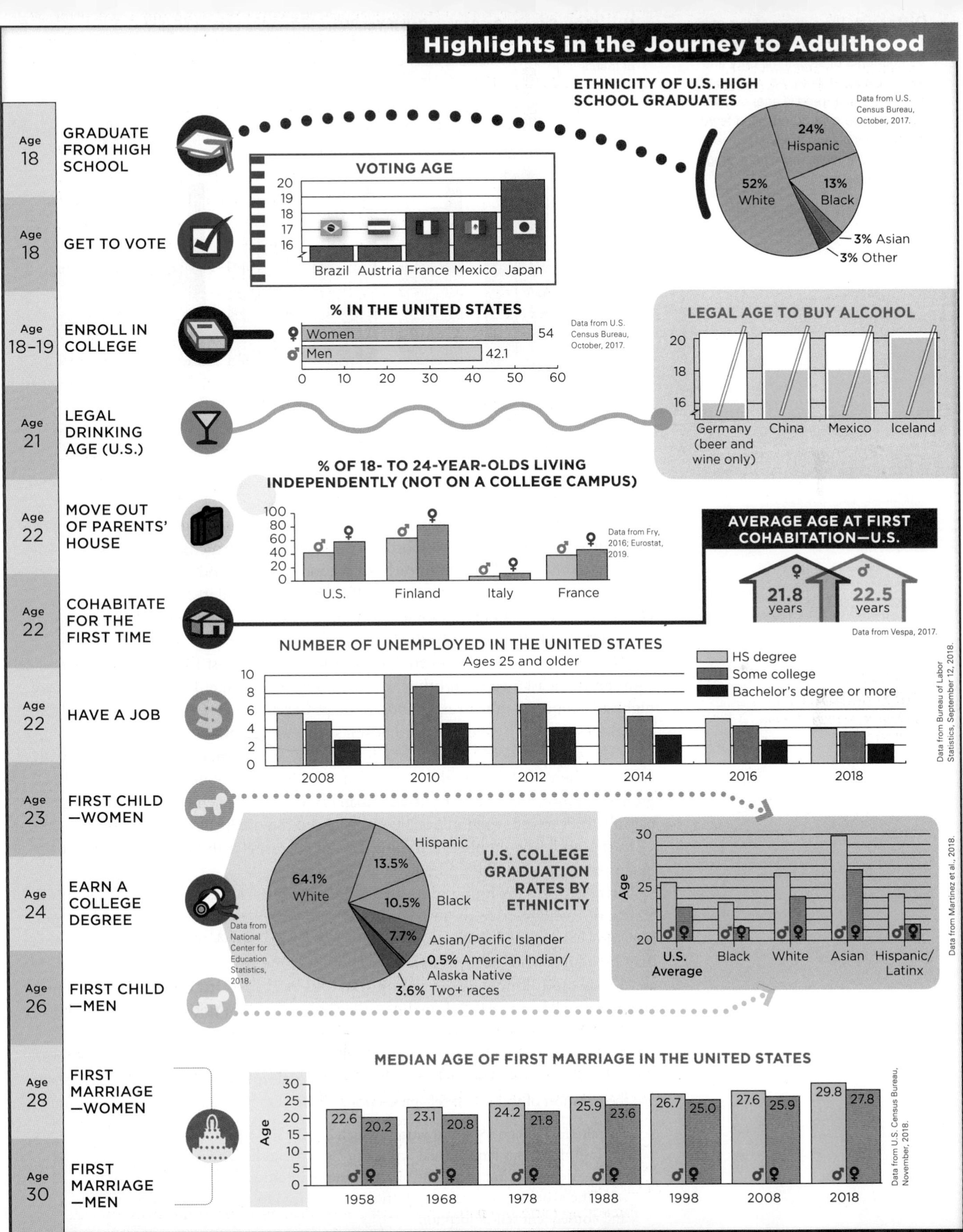

Highlights in the Journey to Adulthood
Age 18 GRADUATE FROM HIGH SCHOOL
Age 18 GET TO VOTE
Age 18–19 ENROLL IN COLLEGE
Age 21 LEGAL DRINKING AGE (U.S.)
Age 22 MOVE OUT OF PARENTS' HOUSE
Age 22 COHABITATE FOR THE FIRST TIME
Age 22 HAVE A JOB
Age 23 FIRST CHILD —WOMEN
Age 24 EARN A COLLEGE DEGREE
Age 26 FIRST CHILD —MEN
Age 28 FIRST MARRIAGE —WOMEN
Age 30 FIRST MARRIAGE —MEN
ETHNICITY OF U.S. HIGH SCHOOL GRADUATES
Data from U.S. Census Bureau, October, 2017.
24% Hispanic
52% White
13% Black
3% Asian
3% Other
VOTING AGE
Brazil Austria France Mexico Japan
% IN THE UNITED STATES
Women 54
Men 42.1
Data from U.S. Census Bureau, October, 2017.
LEGAL AGE TO BUY ALCOHOL
Germany (beer and wine only)
China
Mexico
Iceland
% OF 18- TO 24-YEAR-OLDS LIVING INDEPENDENTLY (NOT ON A COLLEGE CAMPUS)
U.S.
Finland
Italy
France
Data from Fry, 2016; Eurostat, 2019.
AVERAGE AGE AT FIRST COHABITATION—U.S.
21.8 years
22.5 years
Data from Vespa, 2017.
NUMBER OF UNEMPLOYED IN THE UNITED STATES
Ages 25 and older
HS degree
Some college
Bachelor's degree or more
Data from Bureau of Labor Statistics, September 12, 2018.
U.S. COLLEGE GRADUATION RATES BY ETHNICITY
64.1% White
13.5% Hispanic
10.5% Black
7.7% Asian/Pacific Islander
0.5% American Indian/ Alaska Native
3.6% Two+ races
Data from National Center for Education Statistics, 2018.
Age
U.S. Average
Black
White
Asian
Hispanic/ Latinx
Data from Martinez et al., 2018.
MEDIAN AGE OF FIRST MARRIAGE IN THE UNITED STATES
Age
1958 22.6 20.2
1968 23.1 20.8
1978 24.2 21.8
1988 25.9 23.6
1998 26.7 25.0
2008 27.6 25.9
2018 29.8 27.8
Data from U.S. Census Bureau, November, 2018.

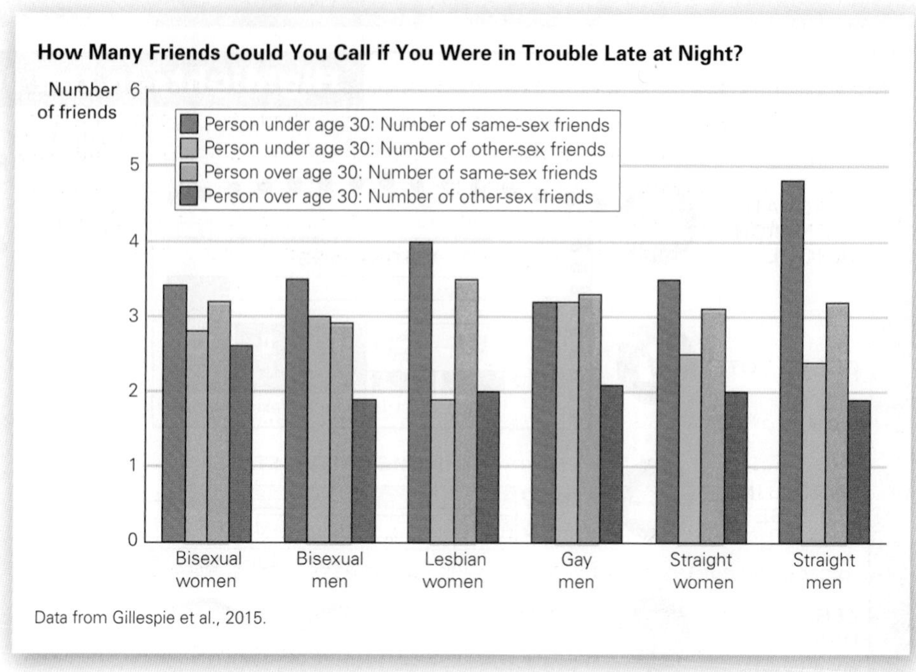

FIGURE 11.10 Same, Yet Different The authors of this study were struck by how similar the friendship patterns of sexual minority and majority people were. As you see, the one noticeable trend is age, not sexuality. People over 30 reported fewer friends overall, and fewer other-sex friends in particular, from an average of 2.6 to an average of 2.1.

strangers at concerts, on elevators, in parks, and so on. At about age 30, a switch begins, when quality becomes more important than quantity (Carmichael et al., 2015). Consequently, some friendships from early adulthood fade away; others deepen.

One study of friendships included 25,185 adults in their 20s and 30s (Gillespie et al., 2015). The number of friends was quite similar among people of every sexual orientation and gender identity.

As earlier research had reported, most people had at least three same-sex friendships and at least two of another sex. Gay men under age 30 tended to have the highest number of other-sex friends, perhaps because such friendships avoided the sexual tension that heterosexual friendships sometimes entail.

In this study, participants were asked how many friends they could discuss sex with, celebrate their birthdays with, or call if in trouble late at night. Not surprisingly, all groups had more birthday party friends than sex-discussing friends. Generally, the number of friends to call when in trouble was between the other two (see Figure 11.10).

In this study, the number of friends did not correlate with life satisfaction, but the quality of friendship did (Gillespie et al., 2015).

There is a paradox found in studies of young-adult friendship. Not only do young adults, on average, have more friends and acquaintances than adults of other ages, they also have more loneliness. The only age group with higher rates of loneliness may be adults who are over age 80, although some research finds that even they are not as often lonely as the young (Barreto et al., 2021; Luhmann & Hawkley, 2016; Yang & Victor, 2011). Loneliness increases the risk of poor mental and physical health, so the loneliness of young adults is a worrisome sign.

This leads us back to Erikson, who notes that each ongoing relationship demands some personal sacrifice, including vulnerability that brings deeper self-understanding and shatters the isolation of too much self-protection. To establish intimacy, the young adult must

> face the fear of ego loss in situations which call for self-abandon: in the solidarity of close affiliations [and] sexual unions, in close friendship and in physical combat, in experiences of inspiration by teachers and of intuition from the recesses of the self. The avoidance of such experiences . . . may lead to a deep sense of isolation and consequent self-absorption.
>
> *[Erikson, 1993a, pp. 163–164]*

Concluding Hopes

Fortunately, most emerging adults, like humans of all ages, have strengths as well as vulnerabilities. Many survive risks, overcome substance abuse, think deeply, combat loneliness, and deal with other problems through further education, maturation, friends, and family. If they postpone marriage, prevent parenthood, and avoid a set career until their identity is firmly established and their education is complete, they are ready for the commitments and responsibilities of adulthood (described in the next chapters).

what have you learned?

1. How does a moratorium differ from identity achievement?
2. How does vocational identity for emerging adults differ compared to for older adults?
3. How have romance and marriage changed for emerging adults?
4. What is the difference between common couple abuse and domestic terrorism?
5. How does the idea of linked lives apply to emerging adults?
6. What kinds of support do parents provide their grown children?
7. What are the advantages and disadvantages of having a "helicopter parent"?
8. What special difficulties occur for emerging adults who were foster children?
9. How are friendships different for young adults and older adults?
10. How does sexual orientation affect friendship?

SUMMARY

Development of the Body

1. The period from age 18 to 25 called emerging adulthood seems to be apparent worldwide. Young adults marry later, have fewer births, and seek more education than they did.

2. Full growth and strength characterize emerging adulthood. Every system—cardiovascular, respiratory, sexual-reproductive, muscular, and so on—functions well.

3. Health habits in emerging adulthood affect later health. The body adjusts to various stresses, which are usually unnoticed at first because of organ reserve and homeostasis.

4. Over time, the insults and adjustments of emerging adulthood may accumulate, causing a heavy allostatic load. All aspects of development adjust and protect the developing body. This is true for sleep, exercise, and diet.

5. The sexual-reproductive system reaches a peak during these years, but most current emerging adults postpone childbearing. Effective contraception allows postponement of parenthood but sexually transmitted infections spread widely.

6. Willingness to take risks is characteristic of emerging adults. This can be positive, but it also increases unprotected sex, drug abuse, and deaths of every kind.

Development of the Mind

7. Postformal thought—more adaptive, practical, and flexible than formal operation thought—is possible in adulthood. Emerging adults become able to combine objective and subjective thinking.

8. College education can be the foundation for health and wealth in adulthood. By middle age, college graduates earn twice as much as noncollege graduates.

9. Increased debt and decreased critical thinking may characterize college students. After graduation, those who did not develop rigorous reading, writing, and analytic skills are handicapped in the job market.

10. Increasing ethnic, gender, and economic diversity characterize recent college students. This may advance cognition, if students of various backgrounds have honest, deep, conversations with each other.

Psychosocial Development

11. As they seek identity achievement, many emerging adults continue to explore aspects of themselves, often with a moratorium. Vocational identity is particularly difficult to form in the current job market.

12. Intimacy needs are sometimes expressed via romantic relationships, which more often include cohabitation than marriage. Many young adults avoid commitment, and some are involved in abusive relationships.

13. Adult children almost always depend on their parents for material and emotional help, often living with them. Family bonds endure lifelong.

14. Young adults have more friends than people of other ages. Paradoxically, they also have high rates of loneliness.

KEY TERMS

emerging adulthood (p. 340)
organ reserve (p. 341)
homeostasis (p. 342)
allostasis (p. 342)
postformal thought (p. 346)
objective thought (p. 347)
subjective thought (p. 347)
massification (p. 349)
moratorium (p. 357)
intimacy versus isolation (p. 360)
choice overload (p. 362)
cohabitation (p. 362)
situational couple violence (p. 363)
intimate terrorism (p. 364)
linked lives (p. 364)

APPLICATIONS

1. Describe an incident during your emerging adulthood when taking a risk could have led to disaster. What were your feelings at the time? What would you do if you knew that a child of yours was about to do the same thing?

2. Read a biography or autobiography that includes information about the person's thinking from adolescence through adulthood. How did personal experiences, education, and maturation affect the person's thinking?

3. Statistics on cohort and culture in students and in colleges are fascinating, but only a few are reported here. Compare your nation, state, or province with another. Analyze the data and discuss causes and implications of differences.

4. Talk to three people you would expect to have contrasting views on love and marriage (differences in age, gender, upbringing, experience, and religion might affect attitudes). Ask each of them the same questions, and then compare their answers.

ESPECIALLY FOR ANSWERS

Response for Nurses (from p. 345): Always. In this context, "suspect" refers to a healthy skepticism, not to prejudice or disapproval. Your attitude should be professional rather than judgmental, but be aware that education, gender, self-confidence, and income do not necessarily mean that a given patient is free of an STI.

Response for Someone Who Has to Make an Important Decision (from p. 347): Both are necessary. Mature thinking requires a combination of emotions and logic. To make sure you use both, take your time (don't act on your first impulse) and talk with people you trust. Ultimately, you will have to live with your decision, so do not ignore either intuitive or logical thought.

Response for Those Considering Studying Abroad (from p. 351): Since one result of college is that students become more open to other perspectives while developing their commitment to their own values, foreign study might be most beneficial after several years of college. If they study abroad too early, some students might be either too narrowly patriotic (they are not yet open) or too quick to reject everything about their national heritage (they have not yet developed their own commitments).

Response for High School Teachers (from p. 353): Even more than ability, motivation is crucial for college success, so don't insist that they attend college immediately. Since your student has money and a steady job (prime goals for today's college-bound youth), they may not realize what they would be missing. Ask them what they hope for, in work and in lifestyle, over the decades ahead.

Response for Family Therapists (from p. 366): The main problem with young adults living with their parents is that both generations have old habits and assumptions that both generations may now resent. As a therapist, you might help them see that that things have changed. New patterns—perhaps about dinner, laundry, independence, privacy, money—need to be discussed and established.

OBSERVATION QUIZ ANSWERS

Answer to Observation Quiz (from p. 344): Kyiv, in Ukraine. As evident in the globalization of emerging adulthood, the same challenges are everywhere.

Answer to Observation Quiz (from p. 346): Los Angeles, California. Garcia is an undergraduate at the University of California at Los Angeles. Clues—ethnic diversity and the temple's architecture.

Answer to Observation Quiz (from p. 355): Hispanic, from 4 percent to 18 percent. If you guessed two or more races, you might be right, but that was not tallied before 2010.

CHAPTER 12

ADULTHOOD
Body and Mind

what will you know?

- When do people start to show their age?
- How can people avoid drug abuse?
- Do people get more or less intelligent as they grow older?
- How do people become experts at what they do?

One of my daughters, herself a professor, was on a committee to select a new college president. Two years later she told me that she is happy with their choice: He is restructuring systems, reforming standards, inspiring students and faculty alike.

"You must be glad they selected the one you wanted," I said.

"He's not the one I wanted. I didn't even want to interview him. Others on the committee outvoted me."

She was unimpressed with his paper résumé. She is a scholar, and he had few publications, none in leading journals. Besides that, she was hoping for a young, energetic visionary who could push forward the changes her institution needed, but he seemed old and deliberate; he had worked for decades outside academia.

Then she listened, rethought her criteria, overcame her assumptions. Ideally that is what all adults do, as you will learn in detail in the second half of this chapter. Experience teaches us.

The first half of this chapter describes how adults protect their health and energy. My daughter might have been happier with a young woman who was eager to lead her college, but fortunately she, and many other adults, recognized the health and energy in this older man.

College teachers need to be strong in analytic intelligence (assessing scholarship), which explains my daughter's initial reaction to this candidate's résumé. But adult cognition led her to listen to her fellow committee members who recognized practical intelligence. This new president, apparently, is an expert at that.

Growing Older

"Aging—we are all doing it," a subway poster proclaims in a public service effort to make younger adults appreciate older ones. Most adults do not realize

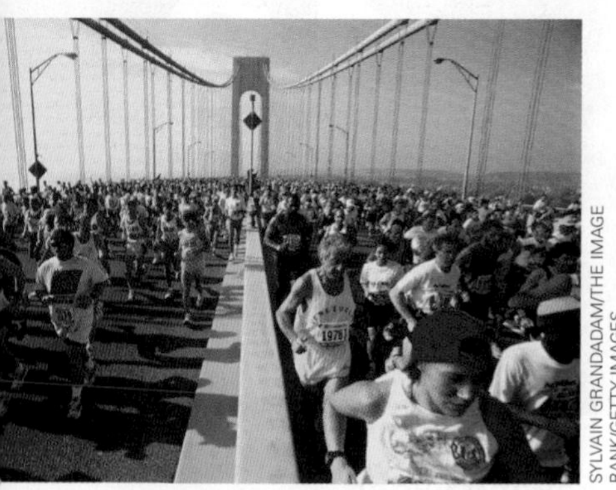
SYLVAIN GRANDADAM/THE IMAGE BANK/GETTY IMAGES

Having Fun? Here are some of the 98,247 aspiring marathoners running on the Verrazano-Narrows Bridge from Staten Island to Brooklyn, New York, as part of a 26-mile race. Everyone should exercise and should figure out how to make that enjoyable to them. Some choose this.

senescence
The process of aging, whereby the body becomes less strong and less efficient.

that they are aging, because organ reserve, homeostasis, and allostasis (described in Chapter 11) render declines unnoticed.

Nonetheless, **senescence**, as the aging process is called, begins as soon as growth stops. It follows a genetic schedule set for every species, affecting skin, hair, the internal organs, and finally life itself. The pace of senescence is affected more by choice and conditions than by genes, but we all grow older every day.

The Aging of the Body

Every organ, every body system, and indeed every cell slows down with age. For that reason, in our culture, aging is often linked to disease and decline, but that link may be broken. Aging—everyone does it; impairment—many avoid it.

THE RESPIRATORY SYSTEM

An easy example of the relationship between senescence and impairment is the respiratory system. Because of homeostasis, the body naturally maintains a certain level of oxygen, so we do not need to think to breathe.

Aging reduces oxygen dispersal in the bloodstream, about 4 percent per decade. Thus, older adults may become winded after running, or they may pause after climbing a long flight of stairs to "catch their breath." That is homeostasis.

However, oxygen is reduced in some people only 2 percent a decade, but an obese, heavy smoker, living in a polluted neighborhood might lose 10 percent. By age 60, they may need an oxygen mask to breathe.

This was tragically evident with COVID-19, which attacked the lungs more than any other organ. Obese smokers had a far higher death rate, even with a ventilator, than others the same age who also caught the virus (Engin et al., 2020).

THE SENSES

Likewise, the senses become less acute over time. Each organ, indeed each part of each organ, is on a particular timetable, but they all weaken with age.

For example, some 30 distinct brain areas as well as at least a dozen aspects of the eye combine to allow sight. Peripheral vision (at the sides) narrows faster than frontal vision; some colors fade more than others. Nearsightedness increases in adolescence, stabilizes, and reverses in midlife, as the shape of the lens changes. Older adults are usually farsighted; they need reading glasses.

C FLANIGAN/GETTY IMAGES

Compensation All of the senses decline with age. Some people accept these losses as inevitable, becoming socially isolated and depressed. Instead, compensation is possible in two ways. One is to increase use of the other senses and abilities. Stevie Wonder illustrates this well – he relies on hearing and touch, which have enabled him to sell over 100 million records and win 25 Grammys. The other way is more direct: Many technological and medical interventions are available for every sensory loss.

Similarly, hearing is most acute at about age 10, with particular frequencies reflecting age-related patterns. High sounds (a small child's voice) are lost earlier than sounds at low frequencies (a man's voice). Although some middle-aged people hear much better than others, everyone's hearing is less acute with age.

All the other senses—touch, smell, taste, balance, pain—also become less acute with age, again with individual variation. As with the respiratory system, sensory loss is affected by the person's actions, and modern technology—when the individual accesses it—can mitigate loss.

The culture can reduce the harm with larger print on medicine bottles and in books, with volume adjustment and microphone sensitivity. Individuals can use glasses and hearing aids, canes and smoke alarms. As you can see, harm from age-related loss depends on both the community and the individual, a theme also apparent later in this chapter when we focus on drugs and obesity.

For the senses as well as every other aspect of aging, attitude is crucial. Modern inventions can mitigate losses, but people need to choose them, and social policies need to support them.

Consider hearing again. Few people use protective headphones unless required to, and few of the one in every five U.S. men aged 45–64 who admits to "trouble hearing" has a hearing aid. The problem is attitudes and priorities (most insurance does not pay for hearing aids).

THINK CRITICALLY: Why are people much more likely to use glasses when sight blurs than hearing aids when sounds soften?

The Sexual-Reproductive System

Like every other body system, the sexual reproductive system slows down with age. Sexual arousal occurs more slowly, orgasm takes longer, fertility disappears. However, this may not be problematic. The sexual-reproductive system changes with age, but each age may have its own benefits, as you will now learn.

SEXUAL PLEASURE

Many people find that sexual activity is maintained, and pleasure may improve with age. For example, a British study of more than 2,000 adults in their 50s found that almost all of them were sexually active (94 percent of the men and 76 percent of the women) with most quite happy with their sexual interactions (D. Lee et al., 2016).

A U.S. study of 38,207 adults who were married or cohabiting found that about half (55 percent of the women and 43 percent of the men) were highly satisfied sexually. About one-third were not. Age was not the determining factor; attitudes and relationships were crucial (Frederick et al., 2017).

What about single adults? They also tend to be sexually satisfied, with age not the determining factor. A U.S. study reported that although men were less active sexually as they grew older, they were not less satisfied with their sex lives in midlife than they were in early adulthood. Women reported more satisfaction with their sex lives as they grew older (Gray et al., 2019).

Women's greater satisfaction may be because of changes in society and in their attitudes, but that is not certain. What *is* certain is that adults vary in sex drive, experience, and pleasure. Some adults of every age are both sexually active and satisfied with their sex lives, and some are troubled or inactive.

SEEKING PREGNANCY

Age matters for fertility. Worldwide, *primary infertility* (not able to conceive naturally) affects about 2 percent of all young couples. By age 40, infertility is about 50 percent. Nonetheless, adults in the United States not only have fewer children than in previous years, but they also have them after the age of peak fertility (see Figure 12.1).

The only women with increasing birth rates are adults over age 39, who bore 129,670 babies in 2019 (Hamilton et al., 2020). Although their rate of birth complications is slightly higher than for younger women, those newborns usually become healthy, well-loved children, benefitting from the emotional (not biological) maturity of their parents.

Long-Lasting Joy In every nation and culture, many couples who have been together for decades continue to delight in their relationship. Talk shows and headline stories tend to focus on bitter divorces, ignoring couples like these who are clearly happy together.

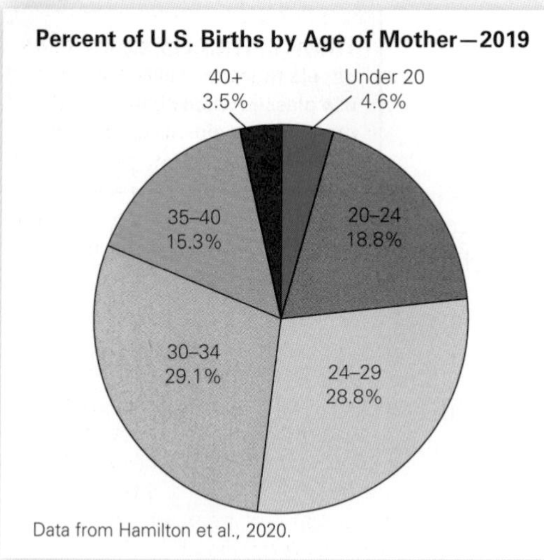

FIGURE 12.1 **When to Have a Baby?** If the only consideration were biology, all newborns would have teenage mothers. However, 77 percent of U.S. births occur after age 24. That bodes well for children, in that parenthood needs cognitive and emotional maturity more than quick conception and easy pregnancy.

As you remember from Chapter 11, most adults under age 25 postpone pregnancy. As with the aging senses, many reproductive problems can now be overcome. Some couples turn to *assisted reproductive technology (ART)* when they want a baby: About 2 percent of all U.S. births involve **in vitro fertilization (IVF)**, ranging from 5 percent in Massachusetts to 0.7 percent in New Mexico (Sunderam et al., 2020).

In IVF, the woman's ova are surgically removed, and one of the man's sperm is inserted into an ovum. If fertilization occurs and the cell multiplies, one cell can be removed and analyzed for genetic defects. If no defects are found, the remaining cells are inserted into the uterus. Those cells may implant and develop just as a natural conception: About one IVF procedure in three results in a baby (Sunderam et al., 2020).

IVF is used not only to avoid genetic problems, but also to avoid infertility caused by blocked fallopian tubes, or a low sperm count, both of which are more common with age. IVF conceptions, if they implant, develop just as other embryos do.

Success is partly age-related. Unfortunately, most women postpone pregnancy, and then try to become pregnant naturally in their 30s. If that fails, some couples try IVF, which is half as likely to succeed at age 40 than at age 20.

Some young adults plan ahead, freezing their ova or sperm for IVF years later. This raises both practical and ethical questions (Polyakov & Rozen, 2021). Should adults in middle age be able to conceive a baby with their own gametes stored years ago? Should gametes of a stranger be used to impregnate someone?

Another ethical question is whether nations should encourage adults to have more or fewer children. In the past decades, the birth rate in more than 50 nations is lower than the replacement rate. The birth rate in the United States has been lower every year since 2000, and for 2020 it was projected that the average young woman would have 1.7 children, much lower than her grandmothers had and substantially below replacement (2.1) (Hamilton et al., 2020).

One argument for increased immigration is that most immigrants are relatively young, which will raise the overall birth rate and lead to more people of working age in the future. The same data are used to oppose immigration, because more children means more need for education.

Another ethical consideration related to fertility occurs with HIV-positive adults. Three decades ago, it seemed that the moral choice would be sterilization or abortion if conception occurred, to reduce the rate of HIV-positive infants destined to be orphaned.

Now, HIV-positive adults can live a long life. Antiviral drugs and cesarean sections allow women who are positive to bear HIV-negative babies, and HIV-positive men to conceive via IVF and special preparation of sperm (Wu & Ho, 2015).

Given that, should HIV-positive adults be encouraged to have children? Such newborns are more often preterm (20 percent, compared to the average of 7 percent weighing under 2,500 grams), but usually they are quite healthy (Piske et al., 2021). This raises the larger question of the effect of parenthood on adult development, a question explored in Chapter 13.

CHIP SOMODEVILLA/GETTY IMAGES NEWS/GETTY IMAGES

Choosing Motherhood In 2018, U.S. Senator Tammy Duckworth, age 50, had her second baby via IVF and won the right to bring her infant daughter to the Senate floor. Next: Will the United States continue to be the only nation (except for New Guinea) without mandated paid maternity leave?

MENOPAUSE

For most women, sometime between ages 42 and 58 (the average age is 51), conception becomes impossible. Ovulation ceases because of a marked drop in estrogen and progesterone. This is **menopause**.

That hormone reduction leads to many physical reactions. Always menstruation and ovulation stop, but other symptoms vary: Vaginal dryness, hot flashes (feeling hot), hot flushes (looking hot), and cold sweats (feeling chilled) may be barely noticeable or deeply disturbing.

The psychological effects of menopause depend on the social context. Some women are regretful and other women are relieved that pregnancy is impossible. Some women are depressed, some moody, and others energetic. Anthropologist Margaret Mead famously said, "There is no more creative force in the world than the menopausal woman with zest."

Evolutionary biologists have wondered why nature causes women to be infertile after age 50 yet live decades after that, unlike human men or primates of any other species. The dominant explanation is the *grandmother hypothesis*, that communities needed older, infertile women to help raise the next generation of children. Worldwide, grandmothers are vital for well-functioning families (Berger, 2019).

in vitro fertilization (IVF)
The union of ova and sperm in a glass dish in a laboratory. This contrasts with "in vivo," or conception in the fallopian tube after a woman's egg is penetrated by a sperm during intercourse. IVF has become a common way for older or unpartnered women or same-sex couples to become pregnant.

menopause
The time in middle age, usually around age 50, when a woman's menstrual periods cease and the production of estrogen, progesterone, and testosterone drops. Strictly speaking, menopause is dated one year after a woman's last menstrual period, although many months before and after that date are menopausal.

A VIEW FROM SCIENCE

Hormone Replacement

The history of **hormone replacement therapy (HRT)** reveals the need for good science. In the final years of the twentieth century, millions of women in every developed nation took estrogen to alleviate symptoms of menopause.

Unanticipated benefits became apparent. Rates of osteoporosis (fragile bones), heart disease, strokes, cancer, and dementia were lower when women took HRT. Doctors prescribed estrogen pills or patches to millions of women, some of them long past menopause, hoping to reduce the diseases of old age.

However, an experiment brought that practice to a sudden halt. In a multiyear study of thousands of women, half (the experimental group) took HRT and half (the control group) did not. The results were shocking: Taking estrogen and progesterone *increased* the risk of heart disease, stroke, and breast cancer (U.S. Preventive Services Task Force, 2002).

The most dramatic difference was an increase in breast cancer, at the rate of 6 per year for 1,000 women taking HRT compared to 4 per 1,000 for women in the control group (Chlebowski et al., 2013). The women had been randomly assigned, which meant that the results were solid. The study was stopped before its planned end date because the researchers feared that the experimental group was at risk.

How could the previous correlation have been wrong? In retrospect, scientists realized that women who took HRT tended to have better medical care and higher SES than women who did not. Their medical care, living conditions, and health habits were why they had lower rates of many diseases, not their HRT.

Current research still finds some benefits from HRT. It relieves the symptoms of menopause, which some women find very troubling. It may decrease osteoporosis, improve hearing, and help the heart, depending on when and what hormones are taken, and on each woman's genes, diet, and exercise (Keck & Taylor, 2018).

This confirms a conclusion from all the science on adult development: Individualized health care is needed. Those background benefits of the earlier HRT women—in medical care, living conditions, and health habits—should be available to all. Beyond that, each person must decide what to do every day, guided by the research but not ruled by it.

hormone replacement therapy (HRT)
Taking hormones (in pills, patches, or injections) to compensate for hormone reduction. HRT is most common in women at menopause or after removal of the ovaries, but it is also used by men as their testosterone decreases. HRT has some medical uses but also carries health risks.

ANDROPAUSE?

A complaint regarding past health research is that many studies included only men, with insurance benefits discriminating against women (Miles & Parker, 1997). Sudden, acute illnesses (e.g., heart attacks) were studied more than chronic ones (e.g., arthritis), because men experience acute illnesses and women, chronic ones.

Some of that has changed in the past decades, as "Race for the Cure" to raise money for breast cancer research now attracts millions of donors. Further, approaches to illness have changed, from an emphasis on immediate surgical cure to an emphasis on social support, more a women's response than a man's (Lehardy & Fowers, 2020).

In a welcome reversal, studies of women and menopause have led to research on male hormones. Do aging men undergo anything like menopause?

Some suggest that the word *andropause* should be used to signify men's age-related lower testosterone level, which reduces sexual desire, erections, and muscle mass (Ali & Parekh, 2020; Samaras et al., 2012). But the term andropause (or *male menopause*) may be misleading because male hormones do not drop precipitously, and men do not suddenly lose reproductive ability: Some 80-year-old men become fathers.

To combat their hormonal decline, some older men take HRT, with their *H* being testosterone, not estrogen. The result seems to be less depression, more sexual desire, and leaner bodies. (Some women also take smaller amounts of testosterone to increase their sexual desire.)

Weighing costs and benefits is essential (Rodrigues dos Santos & Bhasin, 2021). Some of the hoped-for benefits in mobility and cognition seem to reflect SES and thus are as problematic and misleading for men as for women (Kaufman & Lapauw, 2020).

Older men are most likely to seek more testosterone when they are troubled by declining sexual desire and function, but some studies find that added hormones do not necessarily help (Rastrelli et al., 2019). Other benefits, to the heart or brain, do not necessarily occur (Corona et al., 2021; Yeap & Dwivedi, 2020).

The lessons from women's HRT apply to men as well: Individualized medicine is needed. Doctors and patients need to be wary of wishful thinking, a problem for adults of all genders, ages, and ethnic groups.

what have you learned?

1. What three factors determine the rate of senescence?
2. How does vision during midlife compare with vision during adolescence?
3. How does hearing change with age?
4. At what age are people most likely to be sexually satisfied?
5. What causes menopause?
6. What are the positive and negative symptoms of menopause?
7. Why has IVF become more popular in recent decades?
8. Why did women who had HRT have lower rates of heart disease?
9. Why would men take HRT?

Two More Health Hazards

As you read in Chapter 11, three habits influence health lifelong, specifically sleep, exercise, and nutrition. All three are discussed again in Chapter 14.

Here we discuss two other hazards to adult health: drug use and obesity. Like sleep, exercise, and nutrition, these two could be discussed in every chapter. However, they are here because notable effects on the body, for good or ill, occur especially between age 25 and 65.

Drug Use

As apparent in many topics in this text, every substance, every experience, every social context affects not just an isolated aspect of development at one time, but the entire person over the years. That truism was stressed in the discussion of ecological systems in Chapter 1 and echoes throughout.

This is obvious in drug use. Every drug, whether prescribed by a doctor, bought at a nearby store, or obtained from a clandestine drug dealer, is chosen because it might benefit the body or mind. And every drug has effects beyond the ones that led to that choice.

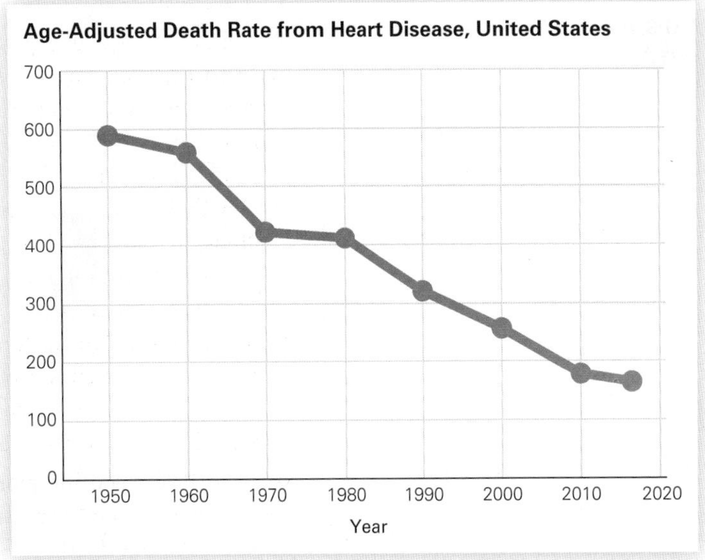

FIGURE 12.2 Prevention Beats Cure Dramatic reduction in heart deaths were caused by many factors, drugs, surgery, and smoking reductions among them. But new drugs are the most important of the three, in that hypertension and cholesterol-lowering drugs became widely used in about 1980. Currently half of all U.S. adults aged 45–65 take pills to prevent heart disease.

ON DOCTOR'S ORDERS

Let us begin with the benefits. Medication has improved health for many people, especially in midlife. In fact, the rate of heart disease (the leading cause of adult death) before late adulthood has been reduced by two-thirds, primarily because of drugs that reduce hypertension and cholesterol (see Figure 12.2).

Cancer deaths are also reduced in adulthood, with chemotherapy (a combination of drugs) the primary reason. Surgery and radiation also stop cancer, but those measures are usually in addition to drugs not instead of them.

Psychological health is also often improved with drugs. One in every eleven adults younger than 45 take antidepressants daily, as does one in five older adults (National Center for Health Statistics, 2019). Antianxiety and antipsychotic drugs are also common.

Thanks to research on insulin, people with diabetes can reach the highest levels of success. U.S. Supreme Court Justice Sonia Sotomayor was diagnosed with childhood diabetes and began injecting insulin when she was 7; now her drugs are precisely calibrated to keep her healthy lifelong (Sotomayor, 2014).

AVOIDING OR SEEKING MEDICINE

Although many adults take at least one prescription drug every day, others do not. This is age-related. According to surveys completed between 2013 and 2014, in the past month, 64 percent of 18- to 44-year-olds and 31 percent of 45- to 64-year-olds took no prescription drugs. Some of them are unusually healthy, and some of them are suspicious of every drug that a doctor recommends.

Virtually every adult, however, uses over-the-counter drugs such as vitamins, analgesics, laxatives, antihistamines, herbal supplements, or some other medication. Obviously they think they benefit, although opinions and practices differ. Many scientists warn of misuse of drugs that can be bought at any grocery or drug store (Chiappini & Schifano, 2020).

Use and concern about readily available drugs vary dramatically from one nation to another: Many drugs that require prescription in the United States are readily available elsewhere. Is the United States too cautious, or are the other nations too careless?

Almost Died Twice As a younger woman, U.S. Supreme Court Justice Sonia Sotomayor twice survived a loss of consciousness from her type 1 diabetes. Fortunately, her friends noticed her crisis. Now she has automatic monitoring and calibrated insulin, and she is expected to interpret the Constitution for 30 more years or so.

OPIOIDS

The harm from one category of prescription drugs has become starkly evident. Doctors prescribe opioids (mostly codeine, Oxycotin, or Vicodin) to reduce pain. These drugs are addictive, and withdrawal is painful. If doctors stop the prescription, some patients turn to heroin or synthetic opioids such as fentanyl. The risk of overdose and suicide increases (Oliva et al., 2020).

To some extent this is economic and cultural. Poor people have less access to prescription drugs, and therefore less addiction to opioids (Wilkerson, 2020).

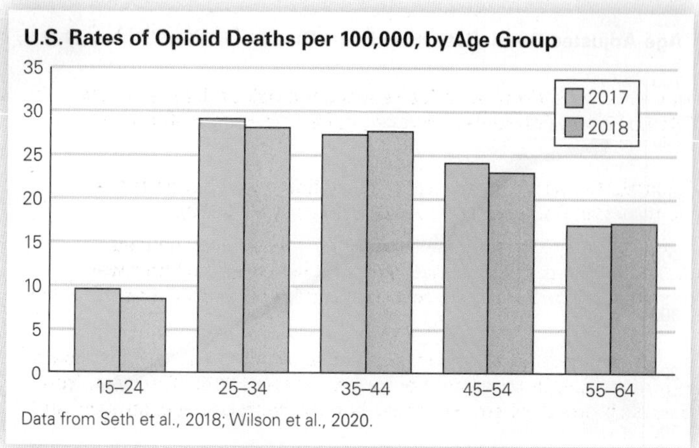

FIGURE 12.3 Two Surprises Experts familiar with drug addiction are surprised at both the rate and age of opioid deaths. First, rates in 2018 are five times higher than two decades earlier. Second, most opioid overdose deaths are after age 30, unlike other drugs that are most deadly before age 25.

A study comparing what doctors prescribed for patients on discharge from hospitals after appendectomy or hernia repair found that 91 percent of the patients in the United States, and only 5 percent of those in other nations, were prescribed opioids (Kaafarani et al., 2020).

Opioid deaths in the United States increased every year from 2000 to 2017, before decreasing slightly in 2018 (see Figure 12.3). Nationwide data reveal fewer overdose deaths in 2018 from prescribed pain medicine, but an increase in deaths from synthetic opioids (Wilson et al., 2020).

Deaths from opioid overdose are highest among 26- to 44-year-olds (Wilson et al., 2020). This is one source of "deaths of despair" (deaths caused by suicide, drug overdose, alcoholism, and obesity), which are particularly likely in middle-aged adults in the United States. (Case & Deaton, 2020).

Several other drugs may relieve pain. Some are chosen illegally by patients; others are bought at drugstores; still others are prescribed by doctors. For example, marijuana may relieve pain, which may reduce opioid use (Meng et al., 2020).

Many psychologists advocate nondrug pain relief. Meditation, hypnosis, and cognitive-behavior therapy all reduce the need for prolonged or intense drug use, and that reduces the risk of overdose (Garland et al., 2019). Deaths of despair are reduced when people are part of well-functioning families and have jobs with good health care (Case & Deaton, 2020).

DRUGS FOR THE MIND, NOT THE BODY

Most adults consume *psychoactive drugs*, or drugs that affect the emotions more than physical functioning. Almost everyone drinks caffeinated soda, tea, or coffee, more than half drink alcohol, about a fourth use tobacco, and a few take illegal drugs. Look at Table 12.1. Each of these drugs has varied effects, with some much worse than others.

JOHN SHEARER/GETTY IMAGES

Pain Killer "Never meant to cause you any pain," sang Prince in his classic song "Purple Rain." But his own pain led to an opioid addiction and then to an accidental overdose of fentanyl, a synthetic opioid that is 50 times more powerful than heroin. His death at age 57 hurt us all.

Obesity

When food is ample, most adults eat as much as they want, so weight increases with age. Metabolism decreases by one-third between ages 20 and 60, and digestion becomes less efficient. To avoid gaining weight, adults must eat less, add more vegetables, and increase physical activity. That does not usually happen.

PREVALENCE OF OBESITY

From ages 25 to 60, adults in the United States steadily gain an average of about 20 pounds, much more than prior generations did. The definitions of overweight and obesity depend on the ratio of height and weight, with a body mass index (BMI) above 25 considered overweight, above 30 considered obese, and above 40 considered severely obese (see Table 12.2). Obesity is a serious health risk.

Whether or not being overweight is a health problem is disputed, with some research finding longer lives in adults who are slightly above 25 BMI, especially if they have strong muscles (Flegal et al., 2013). Muscle weighs more than fat, so people with a BMI of 26 or 27 may be fit, not fat.

The cutoff at 25 was based on White American adults. In the United States, Black adults tend to be heavier and Asian adults lighter than White adults, so the BMI cutoffs may need adjustment. However, for everyone, excess body fat increases the rate of almost every chronic disease.

TABLE 12.1 Psychoactive Drugs Commonly Used in Adulthood

Caffeine	For most of the 85 percent of the world's population who drink it, coffee reduces the risk of depression, type 2 diabetes, and death (Loftfield et al., 2018; Palatini, 2015). For some, however, coffee disrupts nighttime sleep and increases anxiety.
Marijuana	Cannabis is at least partially legal in 44 U.S. states, Canada, and several other nations, which means that research on legal use is now accumulating with mixed findings (Finn, 2020; Graves et al., 2020). Some medical uses seem proven, among them that marijuana improves appetite and reduces nausea in chemotherapy and may be a better pain reliever than opioids. Nonetheless, addiction and withdrawal symptoms — depression, anxiety, aggression, sleep disturbances — occur in about half the regular users (Bahji et al., 2020).
Tobacco	The World Health Organization calls tobacco "the single largest preventable cause of death and chronic disease in the world today," with one billion smoking-related deaths projected between 2010 and 2050. The harm from cigarettes is dose-related: Each puff, each day, each breath of smoke makes cancer, heart disease, strokes, and emphysema more likely. Smoking is an example of the need for an intersectional perspective. How strongly the social context encourages or discourages cigarette smoking depends on gender *and* age *and* nationality *and* income. Each of these affects whether or not a person smokes, but sometimes the influence of one factor depends on another. For example, in 2018, U.S. smoking rates were three times higher for people below the poverty line than for people far above it (23 and 7 percent), a disparity as evident for women as for men. However, the opposite was true a century ago in the United States and still is true internationally, because smoking was a sign of wealth and independence. Currently in the poorest nations, rates of smoking *increase* with income, because people with the lowest income cannot afford cigarettes. This is glaringly evident in Asia, where smoking rates have plateaued in wealthier nations (e.g., Japan, Singapore) but are continuing to increase in China and India (Yang & Dong, 2019).
Alcohol	Unlike for cigarettes, the harm from alcohol does not increase steadily with each increment. In fact, some alcohol may be beneficial: Adults who drink wine, beer, or spirits *in moderation* — never more than two drinks a day — live longer than abstainers (Goel et al., 2018). However, with too much alcohol, harm is widespread. Alcohol destroys brain cells (especially in the cerebellum, which regulates balance), causes liver damage (alcohol use disorder is the main cause of cirrhosis), and contributes to many other diseases, including osteoporosis, infertility, and many cancers. It also increases the rates of suicide, homicide, and accidents — all while wreaking havoc in families. Again, gender, income, and nationality make a difference. In general, low-income nations have more abstainers, more abusers, and fewer moderate drinkers than more affluent nations. One protective factor is Islam: devout Muslims do not drink alcohol, which limits the problem in many nations of the Middle East. However, in other developing nations, prevention and treatment strategies for alcohol use disorder have not been established, regulation is rare, and laws are lax (Bollyky, 2012; Myadze & Rwomire, 2014).

Many people put on weight during the recent pandemic's shelter-in-place (Flanagan et al., 2021). COVID-19 increased poor health in many ways—less exercise, more alcohol, more stress, less preventive care. The result was twice as many non-COVID deaths (called "excess deaths") among adults aged 25–65 in 2020 as in 2019 (Woolf et al., 2021).

COVID-19 targeted people who were obese: Deaths rose among obese adults under age 65 (the oldest adults had higher death rates at every weight) (Anderson et al., 2020).

The consequences are psychological as well. Obese adults experience scorn and prejudice, making them less likely to have partners, employers, friends. Stigma leads them to avoid doctors, eat more, and exercise less—harming health more than weight alone (Puhl et al., 2020).

TABLE 12.2 Body Mass Index (BMI) Categories

Underweight	<18.5
Normal weight	18.5–24.9
Overweight	25–29.9
Obesity	30 or greater

WHAT AND WHEN TO EAT

What can a person do to prevent obesity? The **Mediterranean diet** seems best. Death rates are lower, diabetes less common, and heart health improved (Migliaccio et al., 2020; Romagnolo & Selmin, 2016; Sánchez-Sánchez et al., 2020; Willis et al., 2019). That diet is high in fruits, vegetables, nuts, legumes, fish, whole-grain cereals, and extra virgin olive oil, and low in meat and dairy.

Mediterranean diet
A diet with ample vegetables and very little meat, as well as fish, nuts, whole grains, some dairy, one glass of wine—although specific recommendations vary. This diet's name arose because people in Greece and Italy have less heart disease than people in Northern or Eastern Europe. In many studies worldwide, this diet seems protective of health.

intermittent fasting
A pattern of eating that includes periods of restricted eating interspersed with usual consumption. The most popular pattern is two days per week eating less than 750 calories and five days of normal eating, all while drinking plenty of water.

Those who follow this diet are less likely to become obese. But what if people are already overweight? Does changing to this diet help them lose fat? The answer is yes, sometimes. Thirteen of the 18 studies of weight loss on this diet found significant reduction of obesity, especially in the "central fatness" part of the body, where it is most crucial (Bendall et al., 2018).

Another strategy seems more effective, although not as easy: **intermittent fasting**. There are three common versions of this diet: no food for two of the seven days per week, fasting every other day, or fasting for 14 to 20 hours each day. This lowers blood pressure and improves metabolism, as well as reduces weight, because the digestive system is less active, and other physiological responses protect against temporary starvation (Mani et al., 2018).

ASCENT/PKS MEDIA INC./STONE/GETTY IMAGES

A Deliberate Choice A healthy diet is often contrary to advertising. To increase sales, grocery stores display candy at check out, end-of-aisle displays are never fresh vegetables, cartoon characters help to sell sugary cereals, snack foods are fried and salty. Eating out is particularly hazardous, because people are tempted by foods high in fat, sugar, and salt. But it need not be so: Here, convention attendees in Calgary, Alberta, Canada, fill their plates with vegetables and other nutritious foods. Does this resemble your choices at the most recent event you attended?

One study enrolled about 140 overweight women (Schübel et al., 2018). One group reduced *daily* calories by 20 percent (the classic calorie reduction), one reduced *weekly* calories by 20 percent but were allowed more on some days than others, one group fasted two days a week and then ate without restriction on the other five days, and one group ate as usual.

The result: Weight loss was about the same for all three dieting groups. However, the participants of the two-day fasting version were happiest. This is important, because people find it hard to stick to any diet. Of course, you should never start a diet without first consulting a physician.

Finally, some people in extreme cases opt for surgery. Each year, about 200,000 U.S. residents undergo bariatric surgery, which restructures their digestive system. "Complications are not uncommon" (Schulman & Thompson, 2017, p. 1640), but every year this surgery becomes safer. Less than 1 in a thousand die from the operation, and about 2 in a thousand need additional surgery (Campos et al., 2020).

Such surgery saves lives because it reduces heart diseases, diabetes, and strokes. However, in the decade after bariatric surgery, rates of depression, suicide, and alcohol abuse increase (Maciejewski et al., 2020). This reminds us that the health of our bodies influences the health of our minds, the next topic in this chapter.

◆◆ Especially for Doctors and Nurses
If you had to choose between recommending various screening tests and recommending various lifestyle changes to a 35-year-old, which would you do? (see answer, page 395)

what have you learned?

1. What are the benefits of prescription drugs?
2. Why have drug overdose rates increased 500 percent since 2000?
3. What are called "deaths of despair?"
4. How do the risks of coffee, cigarettes, and alcohol compare?
5. How is drug use affected by income?
6. Why does obesity become a particular risk in adulthood?
7. How did the COVID-19 pandemic affect adult health?
8. What specific elements of diet and exercise seem protective of health in adulthood?
9. What are the benefits and liabilities of bariatric surgery?

ADULT OVERWEIGHT AROUND THE WORLD

A century ago, being overweight was a sign of affluence, as the poor were less likely to enjoy a calorie-rich diet and more likely to be engaged in physical labor. Today, that link is less clear. Overweight—defined as having a body mass index (BMI) over 25—is common across socioeconomic groups and across nations, and obesity (a BMI over 30) is a growing health threat worldwide. In a notable reversal, obesity increases as income falls in wealthier nations.

OVERWEIGHT AND GDP

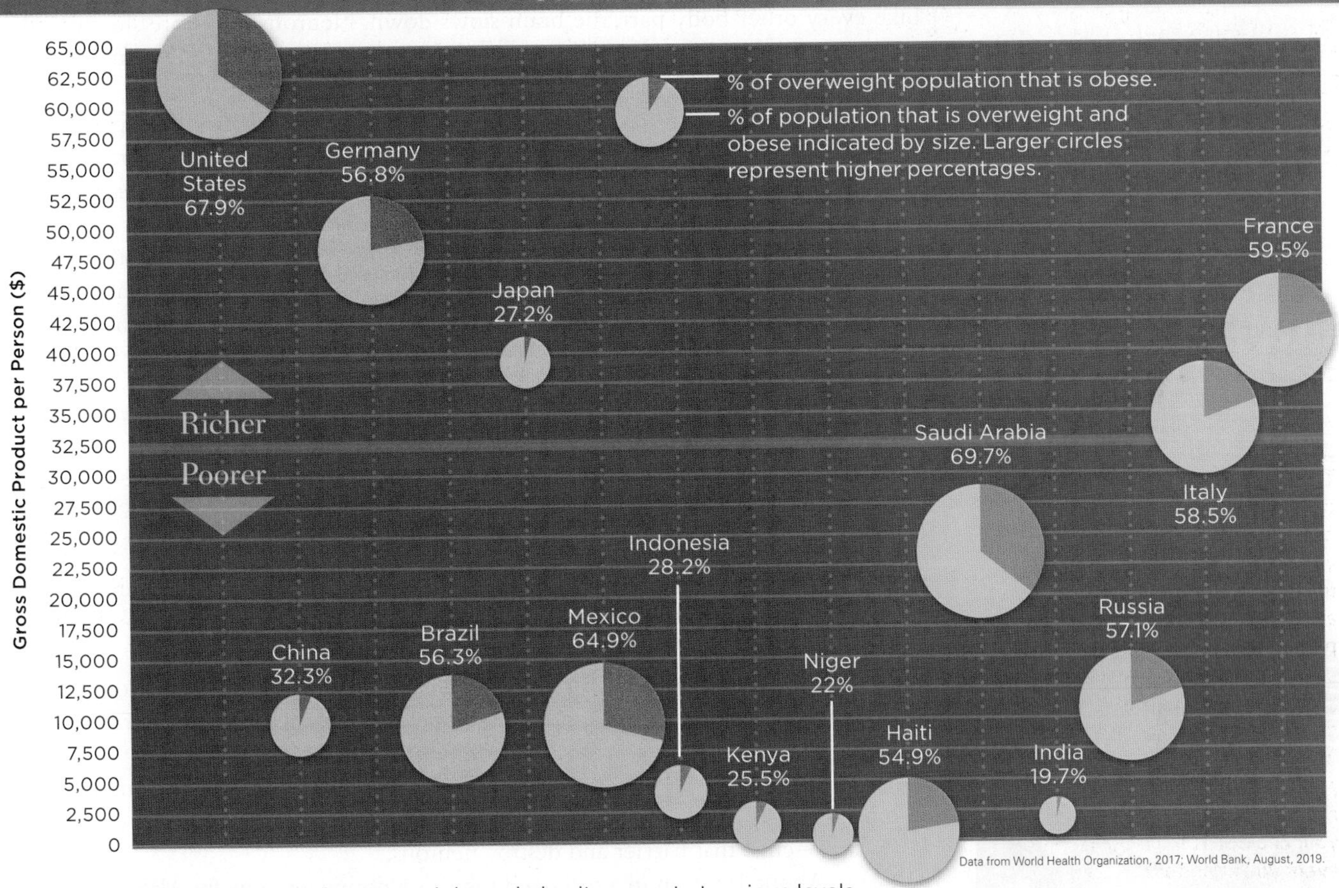

% of overweight population that is obese.
% of population that is overweight and obese indicated by size. Larger circles represent higher percentages.
Gross Domestic Product per Person ($)
65,000
62,500
60,000
57,500
55,000
52,500
50,000
47,500
45,000
42,500
40,000
37,500
35,000
32,500
30,000
27,500
25,000
22,500
20,000
17,500
15,000
12,500
10,000
7,500
5,000
2,500
0
Richer
Poorer
United States 67.9%
Germany 56.8%
Japan 27.2%
France 59.5%
Italy 58.5%
Saudi Arabia 69.7%
Indonesia 28.2%
Russia 57.1%
China 32.3%
Brazil 56.3%
Mexico 64.9%
Niger 22%
Kenya 25.5%
Haiti 54.9%
India 19.7%

Data from World Health Organization, 2017; World Bank, August, 2019.

International cutoff weights for overweight and obesity are set at various levels. These numbers show proportions of adults whose BMI is over 25.

U.S. OBESITY RATES BY INCOME LEVEL AND ETHNICITY

While common wisdom holds that overweight and obesity correlate with income, recent data suggests that culture and gender may play a bigger role.

Income, Ethnicity, and Obesity
Women
Men
Overall
Asian
Black
Hispanic
White
Obese (%)
60
50
40
30
20
10
0
Low
Middle
High
Income Level (based on Federal Poverty Level)

Data from Ogden et al., 2017.

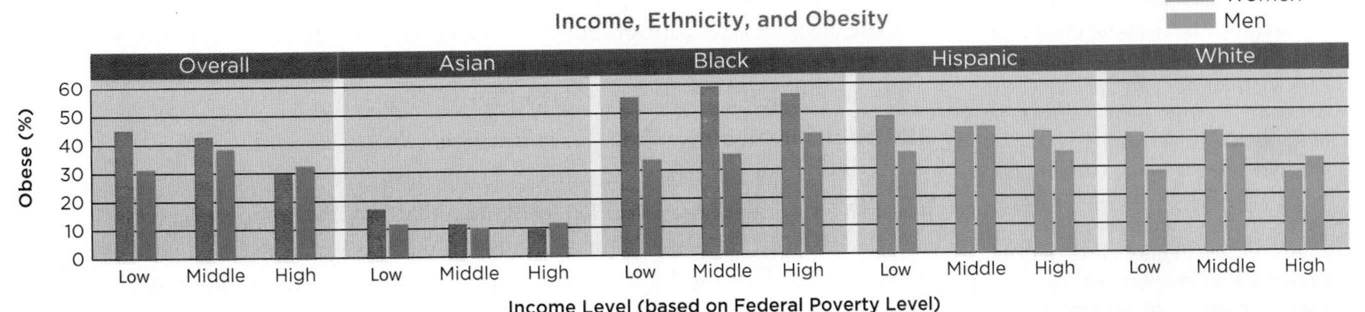

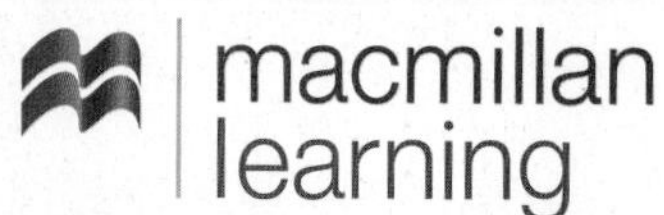

VIDEO: Brain Development Animation: Middle Adulthood offers an animated look at how the brain changes with age.

Development of the Mind

This chapter so far has described body development, from peak strength and health at about age 25 through gradual decline over the adult years. Now we turn to cognition, which follows another pattern. Some losses occur, but gains are evident, too.

The Brain with Age

Like every other body part, the brain slows down. Neurons fire more slowly, and reaction time lengthens because messages from the axon of one neuron are not picked up as quickly by the dendrites of other neurons.

However, research on the brain is quite positive. Remember head-sparing in infancy? That continues. For most adults, cognitive reserve, homeostasis, and allostasis protect the brain, even more than the rest of the body, enabling new learning to occur.

Thus, adults may be slower, losing to a teenager at a video game, but their analysis may be more comprehensive, with the postformal thinking described in Chapter 11. This is one reason why decades of adult experience seem a prerequisite for judges, popes, and world leaders.

CAUSES OF BRAIN LOSS

Evidence-based science requires that we temper this encouraging conclusion. For about 1 percent of all adults, brain loss is significant between ages 25 and 65. There are five main causes.

- *Drug abuse.* Psychoactive drugs can harm the brain. Most common is chronic alcohol abuse, which reduces thiamine (a vitamin) and causes Wernicke-Korsakoff syndrome ("wet brain").
- *Poor circulation.* Everything that impairs blood flow—such as hypertension, extreme obesity, and cigarette smoking—impairs brain circulation. That slows down thought (Sweeney et al., 2018).
- *Viruses.* Various membranes, called the *blood–brain barrier*, protect the brain from most viruses, but a few—including HIV and the prion that causes mad cow disease—cross that barrier and destroy neurons.
- *Genes.* About 1 person in a thousand inherits a dominant gene for Alzheimer's disease. That begins to destroy the brain in middle age. A few other inherited diseases, such as Huntington's chorea, cause severe neurocognitive disorders in midlife (Burlina, 2018).
- *Traumatic brain injury (TBI).* A blow to the skull, an extremely loud noise, or a rapid acceleration of the head can damage the brain. This may occur with a concussion in a contact sport (football, hockey, boxing, and so on), a whiplash in a car crash, a punch in an assault, an explosion in a war. None of these always causes damage, but all can, especially if repeated (Capizzi et al., 2020).

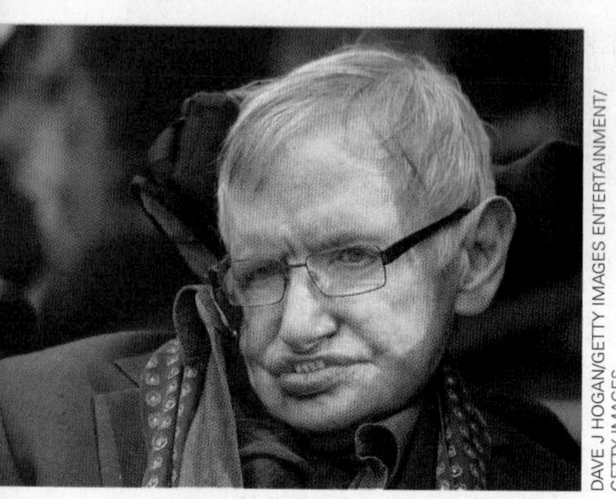

DAVE J HOGAN/GETTY IMAGES ENTERTAINMENT/ GETTY IMAGES

Talk and Think Stephen Hawking (1942–2018) wrote *A Brief History of Time*, which sold more than 10 million copies — an astounding number for a book about theoretical physics and cosmology. He also had ALS, diagnosed at age 21, which did not stop him from marriage (twice), fatherhood (thrice), and becoming a leading international scholar. Toward the end of his life, he could not talk but instead communicated with a muscle in his cheek — striking evidence that intellect cannot always be assessed via speech.

RECOVERY

Brains continue to mature throughout adulthood. Regarding the first and last items above (drug abuse and TBI), the human brain is designed to reestablish broken connections, and to compensate with other brain areas if neurons in one part are destroyed. Time and rest (no more drugs or blows to the head) may allow full recovery.

On the other hand, several causes of brain malfunction may cluster together. An adult with alcohol use disorder who is genetically vulnerable and is repeatedly hit on the head may suffer irreversible brain damage. Time aids recovery, but organ reserve may be reduced, and thus neuronal connections weaken as time goes on (Corps et al., 2015).

Barring these serious problems, age strengthens the connections between various parts of the brain, improving cognition, because better connections enable adults to appreciate how one aspect of life impacts another. This can happen on a global scale—the connection between famine in South Sudan and electricity use in North Dakota—as well as on a more personal level, how a partner's shouted insult connects to a snowstorm outside.

Encouraging evidence comes from stroke victims, whose brains can restructure themselves. Paralysis of one part of the body, or loss of one aspect of language, may not be permanent because the brain can develop other circuits to repair the damage. Plasticity is characteristic of all brains, lifelong (Sampaio-Baptista et al., 2018). One recent example comes from extensive neurological research that confirms that meditation strengthens brain connections (Brandmeyer & Delorme, 2021).

Overall, myelination continues and dendrites grow, depending on experience. An adult who performs a particular action, time and time again, becomes better and quicker at it because of changes in their brain.

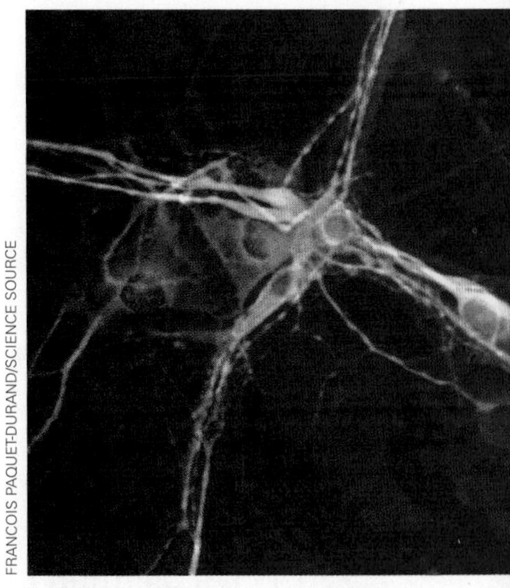

FRANCOIS PAQUET-DURAND/SCIENCE SOURCE

Neurons Growing Even in adulthood, dendrites grow (pale yellow in this picture). Here the cells are in a laboratory and the growth is cancerous, but we now know that healthy neurons develop many new connections in adulthood.

INSIDE THE BRAIN

Brain Growth in Adulthood

It has long been known that brains slow down and shrink with age. Neurons form rapidly during prenatal development, but early pruning eliminates most of them. Based on those facts, neuroscientists thought that human brain growth and *neurogenesis* (the formation of neurons) stopped long before adulthood.

But in the past decades, scientists learned that parts of the brain grow during adulthood. Dendrites form, pathways strengthen, and new neurons may arise, especially in the hippocampus, where memories form.

That neurogenesis "appears to contribute significantly to hippocampal plasticity across the life span" (Kempermann et al., 2015). The specific area of the hippocampus where new neurons settle is the *dentate gyrus*, a region active in forming new memories and exploring new places.

Exercise, particularly, increases circulation, connections, and myelination. The resulting brain changes may reduce depression and other disorders (J-L. Zhao et al., 2020). Thus, shrinkage of some parts of the brain may be counterbalanced by expansion and reorganization. New brain cells facilitate learning and memory (Lepousez et al., 2015).

All neuroscientists now agree that brain plasticity is evident lifelong. But not everyone agrees that a significant number of new neurons are born in adulthood.

One team of 19 scientists reported that the number of new neurons created after age 13 is so low as to be undetectable (Sorrells et al., 2018). That conclusion is contrary to the one found by another team of 12 scientists. They reported that, although the rate of neurogenesis slows down, it does not stop: New neurons form even at age 79 (Boldrini et al., 2018).

The number of scientists (19 and 12) in each of these two studies reveals that this is not a controversy between an optimist and a pessimist; it is a dispute between two teams of careful scientists.

For neuroscientists, this is an exciting dispute because "the role that adult neurogenesis plays within the context of hippocampal function, neuroplasticity, and brain repair brings up many unsolved questions" (Kuhn et al., 2018, p. 10406). Researchers are attracted to new hypotheses and unsolved questions like moths to a flame.

Scientists await more painstaking studies with new techniques to discover exactly how the adult brain develops. Many now believe that neurogenesis can occur (Kempermann et al., 2018; Lucassen et al., 2020). At the moment, they are certain that cognitive reserve, homeostasis, and allostasis protect the brain long after other parts of the body begin to fail.

Intelligence in Adulthood

Is "intelligence" some kind of physical thing, like a lump in the brain that some people have more of than others and that stays about the same size until old age shrinks it? That is what people once thought.

It was assumed that intelligence was born into a person, in the same way as eye color. Genetic instructions were thought to make that inborn intelligence grow until it reached full capacity at about age 18, when the rest of the body was grown.

general intelligence (*g*)
The idea of *g* assumes that intelligence is one basic trait, underlying all cognitive abilities. According to this concept, people have varying levels of this general ability.

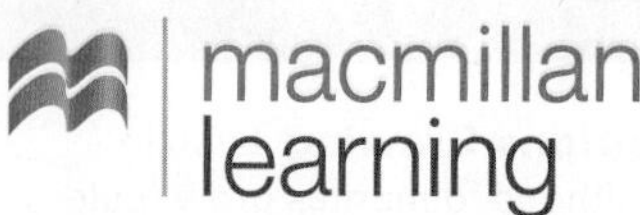

VIDEO ACTIVITY: Research Methods and Cognitive Aging explores how various research methods have been employed to study how intelligence changes with age.

MEASURING INTELLIGENCE

As already mentioned in Chapter 7, that lump could be called **general intelligence** or "*g*." Although *g* cannot be measured directly, Spearman (a leading theorist) thought it could be inferred from various subtests that measured language, memory, math, perception, and knowledge.

By testing various abilities, a person's *g* could be calculated and presented as an IQ score. That belief in *g* continues, as "*g* is one of the most thoroughly studied concepts in the behavioral sciences. Measures of intelligence are predictive of a wide range of educational, occupational, and life outcomes" (Geary, 2018, p. 1028).

Since *g* was thought to be inborn, many researchers searched for the genetic underpinnings of intellectual capacity. One recent effort, contending that "intelligence is highly heritable," examined the entire genome and found 1,016 genes linked to intelligence (Savage et al., 2018, p. 912).

Other researchers looked elsewhere for the origins of *g*—perhaps prenatal brain development, experiences in infancy, or physical health. One leading scholar suggests that how well the mitochondria function is the crucial factor (Geary, 2018). However, no one has succeeded in finding any particular intelligence gene or in proving that a particular biological entity is *g*.

A counter movement from other researchers suggests that no inborn *g* exists. Some criticize the psychometric approach as "neglecting the roles of emotion, motivation, stress, intuition, and creativity in cognitive development" (Zelazo, 2018, p. 44). As one scholar wrote: "Intelligent researchers will likely continue to disagree about *g*" (Gignac, 2016, p. 84).

Nonetheless, no current scholar believes, as Spearman did, that IQ is exclusively inborn. Instead, all agree that IQ overall, as well as specifics such as vocabulary or memory, often change in adulthood.

From about age 20 to age 70, national values, particular experiences, and years of education all affect the size of that lump of intelligence. For decades scientists have known that reflects genes, early education, and other influences before age 20, but it is now also known that adult experiences can cause a major shift in intelligence (Grønkjær et al., 2019).

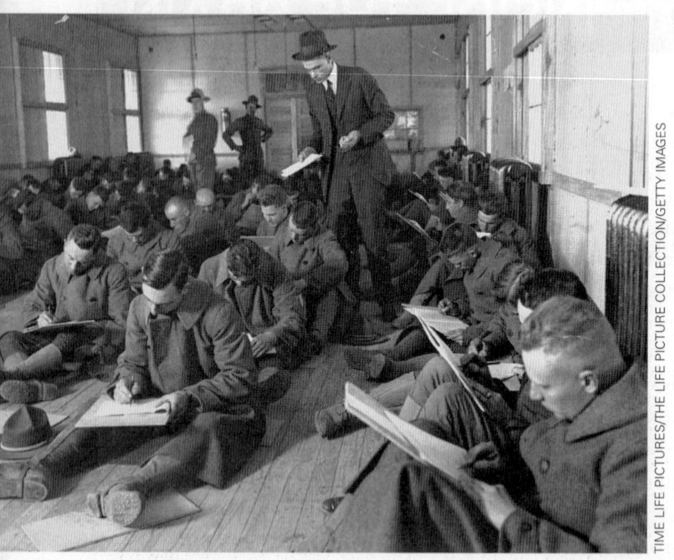

TIME LIFE PICTURES/THE LIFE PICTURE COLLECTION/GETTY IMAGES

Smart Enough for the Trenches? These young men were drafted to fight in World War I. Younger men (about age 17 or 18) did better on the military's intelligence tests than slightly older ones did.

OBSERVATION QUIZ
In addition to intellectual ability, what two aspects of this test situation might affect older men differently than younger men? (see answer, page 395) ↑

When a particular person is assessed longitudinally, researchers find "virtually every possible permutation of individual profiles" (Schaie, 2013, p. 497). Cross-sectional research also finds variability from item to item and age to age (Fagot et al., 2018). The data on adult intelligence illustrate the life-span perspective: Intelligence is multi-directional, multi-cultural, multi-contextual, and plastic.

NEUROSCIENCE AND *G*

Currently, many believe that *g* arises from brain functioning. One scholar notes that the size of one part of the adult midbrain (the *caudate nuclei*) correlates with adult

IQ (Grazioplene et al., 2015). Another neuroscientist, on the contrary, says that no particular part of the brain is crucial, but rather that brain "network flexibility and dynamics are crucial for the diverse range of mental abilities underlying general intelligence" (Barbey, 2018, p. 15).

In other words, the hubs and interconnections of brain parts may be pivotal. An intelligent person has strong and flexible networks, which allows the brain to combine, say, social perception and statistical logic, or verbal proficiency and visual acuity. Details vary from person to person over the life span, but always

> *g* originates from individual differences in the system-wide topology and dynamics of the human brain. . . . the capacity to flexibly transition between network states provides the foundation for individual differences in *g*—supporting the rapid exchange of information across networks and capturing individual differences in cognitive processing at a global level.
>
> *[Barbey, 2018, pp. 16, 18]*

OPPOSING PERSPECTIVES

Age and IQ

You can't teach an old dog new tricks.

Experience is the best teacher.

Which is it? Do people gain or lose intelligence over adulthood?

Most psychometricians throughout the twentieth century assumed that intelligence could be measured and quantified via IQ tests, and before 1950 they were convinced that people gradually lost cognitive ability, starting at about age 20. Then a contrary opinion arose, that adults grew smarter every year.

This dispute was based on conflicting data. Cross-sectional research found that the average younger adult scored higher on IQ tests than the average older person. Massive tests of army recruits—thousands of them from every part of the nation—found that the peak was from ages 18 to 25, followed by a linear loss in IQ with age (Yerkes, 1923). But longitudinal research found that scores increased as people grew older (Bayley & Oden, 1955).

Then in 1956, this dispute was solved because a graduate student at the University of Washington had a brilliant idea. (I mention that detail because some 2022 graduate students may need encouragement to develop new ways to answer developmental questions.)

To earn his Ph.D., K. Warner Schaie tested a cross section of 500 adults, aged 20 to 50, on five standard primary mental abilities that Sternberg considered to be the foundation of *g*: (1) verbal meaning (vocabulary), (2) spatial orientation, (3) inductive reasoning, (4) number ability, and (5) word fluency (rapid verbal associations). The age comparisons showed decline in all five abilities, as other cross-sectional research had found (Schaie, 1958). Schaie wondered if he himself was already on a downward trajectory.

Then he had a brilliant idea—to combine longitudinal and cross-sectional methods. Seven years later, he retested his initial participants and also tested a new group of people who were the same age that his earlier sample had been. Consequently, he could compare people not only to their own previous scores (longitudinal) but also to people currently as old as his original group had been when first tested, and others who were older or younger (cross-sectional).

Schaie did so over his entire career, retesting and adding a new group every seven years. This *cross-sequential* study of adult intelligence confirmed and extended what others had found: Cross-sectional research shows declines, but longitudinal research shows improvement during adulthood (Schaie, 2005/2013). So, *g* varies more than others thought (Figure 12.4).

Predicting the future based on past IQ patterns is suspect, tentative at best and harmful at worst. As one review of recent evidence from many nations concludes:

> Massive IQ gains over time were never written in the sky as something eternal like the law of gravity. They are subject to every twist and turn of social evolution.
>
> *[Flynn & Shayer, 2018]*

The answer to the question at the beginning of this box is that people get smarter *and* dumber with age and experience. Circumstance and maturation matter.

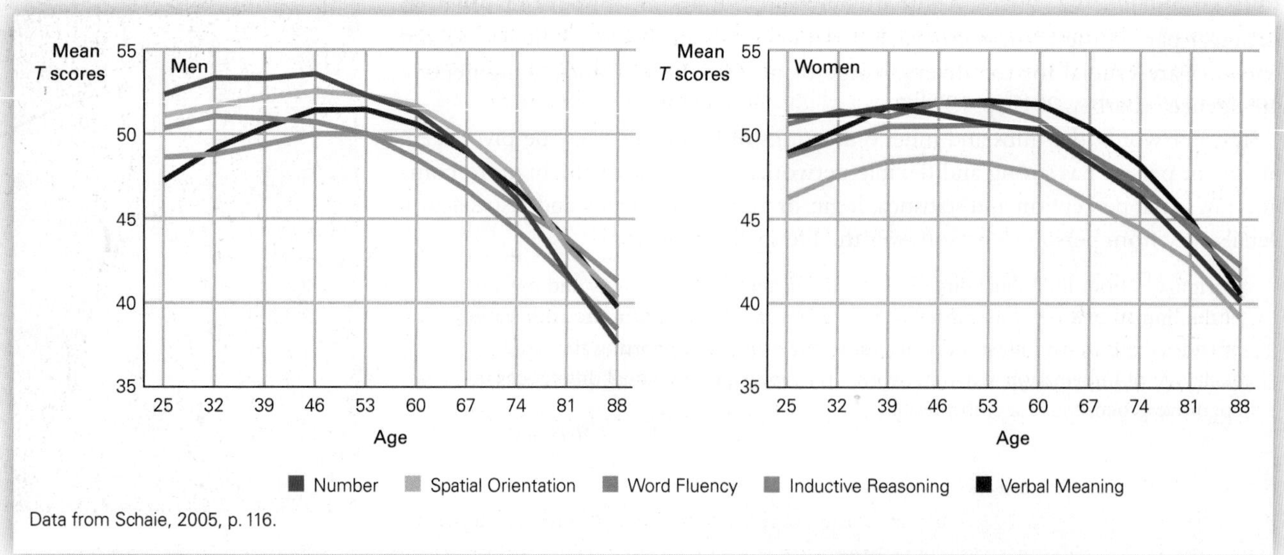

FIGURE 12.4 Age Differences in Intellectual Abilities Cross-sectional data on intellectual abilities at various ages would show much steeper declines. Longitudinal research, in contrast, would show more notable rises. Because Schaie's research is cross-sequential, the trajectories it depicts are more revealing: None of the average scores for the five abilities at any age is above 55 or below 35, which means that the average older person still is able to function intellectually.

OBSERVATION QUIZ
Which ability in which gender shows the steepest decline after age 60? (see answer, page 395) ↑

Components of Intelligence: Many and Varied

Developmentalists seek patterns of cognitive gain and loss. Individuals vary, as does each aspect of intelligence. What are those aspects?

We consider here only two proposals, one that posits two distinct abilities and the other, three. [**Life-Span Link:** There are many more formulations, notably Gardner's theory of nine intelligences, described in Chapter 7.]

TWO CLUSTERS OF INTELLIGENCE

In the 1960s, a leading researcher, Raymond Cattell, teamed up with a promising graduate student, John Horn, to study intelligence tests. They concluded that adult intelligence is best understood by grouping various measures into two categories, which they called *fluid* and *crystallized*.

fluid intelligence
Those types of basic intelligence that make learning of all sorts quick and thorough. Abilities such as short-term memory, abstract thought, and speed of thinking are all usually considered part of fluid intelligence.

As its name implies, **fluid intelligence** is like water, flowing to its own level no matter where it happens to be. Fluid intelligence is quick and flexible, enabling people to learn anything, even things that are unfamiliar and disconnected to what they already know. Curiosity, learning for the joy of it, solving abstract puzzles, and the thrill of discovery are marks of fluid intelligence.

People who are high in fluid abilities draw inferences, grasp relationships between concepts. Working memory is large and flexible. Questions that test fluid intelligence might be:

What comes next in each of these two series?*

4 9 16 25 3

V X Z B D

---

*The correct answers are 6 and F. The clue is to think of multiplication (squares) and the alphabet: Some series are much more difficult to complete.

The accumulation of facts, information, and knowledge is called **crystallized intelligence**. The size of a person's vocabulary, the knowledge of chemical formulas, and long-term memory for dates in history all indicate crystallized intelligence. Tests designed to measure this intelligence might include questions like these:

What is the meaning of the word *eleemosynary*?

Who was Descartes?

Explain the difference between a tangent and a triangle.

Why does the city of Peking no longer exist?

Overall, IQ might be stable over the years of adulthood, but the mix of abilities changes from fluid to crystalized. Other researchers from many nations have found similar trends. IQ scores typically increase, or are at least maintained, in adulthood, because performance on timed items declines but on verbal items increases (Salthouse, 2019).

WALTER MCBRIDE/GETTY IMAGES ENTERTAINMENT/GETTY IMAGES

Intelligence in Action Lin-Manuel Miranda created and starred in *Hamilton: An American Musical,* that has been one of the hottest tickets on Broadway since it opened in 2015. His creative intelligence is obvious, but his analytic and practical intelligence are also part of his success.

THREE FORMS OF INTELLIGENCE

Robert Sternberg (1988, 2015) agrees that a single intelligence score is misleading. He proposed three fundamental forms of intelligence: analytic, creative, and practical (see Table 12.3).

Analytic intelligence includes all of the mental processes that foster academic proficiency by making efficient learning, remembering, and thinking possible. Thus, it draws on abstract planning, strategy selection, focused attention, and information processing, as well as on verbal and logical skills.

Strengths in those areas are valuable in emerging adulthood, particularly in college and in graduate school. Multiple-choice tests and brief essays that call forth remembered information, with only one right answer, indicate analytic intelligence.

Creative intelligence is flexible and innovative, divergent rather than convergent, valuing the unexpected, imaginative, and unusual rather than standard and conventional answers. Sternberg developed tests of creative intelligence that include writing a short story titled "The Octopus's Sneakers" or planning an advertising campaign for a new doorknob. Those with many novel ideas earn high scores.

Practical intelligence is adaptive. This capacity includes an accurate grasp of the expectations and needs of other people and understanding what skills are needed

crystallized intelligence
Those types of intellectual ability that reflect accumulated learning. Vocabulary and general information are examples. Some developmental psychologists think crystallized intelligence increases with age, while fluid intelligence declines.

analytic intelligence
A form of intelligence that involves such mental processes as abstract planning, strategy selection, focused attention, and information processing, as well as verbal and logical skills.

creative intelligence
A form of intelligence that involves the capacity to be intellectually flexible and innovative.

practical intelligence
The intellectual skills used in everyday problem solving. (Sometimes called *tacit intelligence*.)

Table 12.3 Sternberg's Three Forms of Intelligence

	Analytic Intelligence	Creative Intelligence	Practical Intelligence
Mental processes	• Abstract planning • Strategizing • Focused attention • Verbal skills • Logic	• Imagination • Appreciation of the unexpected or unusual • Originality • Vision	• Adaptive actions • Understanding and assessing daily problems • Applied skills and knowledge
Valued for	• Analyzing • Learning and understanding • Remembering • Thinking	• Intellectual flexibility • Originality • Future hopes	• Adaptability • Concrete knowledge • Real-world experience
Indicated by	• Multiple choice tests • Brief essays • Recall of information	• Inventiveness • Innovation • Resourcefulness • Ingenuity	• Performance in real situations • "Street smarts"

Information from Sternberg, 1988, 2003, 2011, 2015.

to meet whatever challenges appear. Then people who are high in practical intelligence can use their social insights and skills to accomplish whatever is needed.

Practical intelligence is sometimes called *tacit intelligence* because it is not obvious on tests (Cianciolo & Sternberg, 2018). Instead, it comes from "the school of hard knocks" and is sometimes called "street smarts," not "book smarts."

Choosing which intelligence to use takes wisdom, which Sternberg considers the fourth ingredient of successful intelligence. He wrote:

> One needs creativity to generate novel ideas, analytical intelligence to ascertain whether they are good ideas, practical intelligence to implement the ideas and persuade others of their value, and wisdom to ensure that the ideas help reach a common good.
>
> *[Sternberg, 2012, p. 21]*

[**Life-Span Link:** Wisdom is discussed in Chapter 14.]

Practical intelligence comes to the fore in adulthood. Few adults need to define obscure words or deduce the next item in a number sequence (analytic intelligence), and few need to compose new music, restructure local government, or invent an innovative gadget (creative intelligence).

Ideally, by adulthood, those few have found people with practical intelligence to implement their analytic or creative ideas. The college professor with their "head in the clouds," or the celebrity entertainer who relies on their manager, are high in analytic or creative intelligence, but they need someone with practical intelligence to get them through the day with their shirt clean and their appointments met.

Practical intelligence helps people maintain a home; advance a career; manage money; sift information (from media, mail, the internet, friends); decide what habits to maintain, stop, or begin; and address the emotional needs of lovers, relatives, neighbors, and colleagues.

what have you learned?

1. What can harm the brain in adulthood?
2. What protects the brain in adulthood?
3. When does TBI in early adulthood affect the brain in later adulthood?
4. Many scientists have searched for *g*; how successful have they been?
5. Which form of intelligence, fluid or crystallized, would you rather have?
6. What might you do to convince your professors that you are smart, and what type of intelligence is that?
7. How might you convince your neighbors to compost their food, and what type of intelligence does that involve?
8. Which intelligence do you think is undervalued in your community?

Selective Gains and Losses

Aging neurons, cultural pressures, historical conditions, and past education all affect adult cognition. None of these can be controlled directly by an individual. Nonetheless, many researchers believe that adults make crucial choices about intellectual development, deciding how to develop their minds.

selective optimization with compensation
The theory, developed by Paul and Margaret Baltes, that people try to maintain a balance in their lives by looking for the best way to compensate for physical and cognitive losses and to become more proficient in activities they can already do well.

Selective Optimization

Paul and Margret Baltes (1990) developed a theory called **selective optimization with compensation** to describe the "general process of systematic functioning" (Baltes, 2003, p. 25), by which people maintain a balance in their lives as they grow older. They believe that people seek to *optimize* their development, *selecting* the best way to *compensate* for physical and cognitive losses, becoming more proficient at activities they want to perform well.

This applies to every aspect of life, ranging from choosing friends to playing baseball. Each adult seeks to maximize gains and minimize losses, practicing some abilities and ignoring others. Choices are critical, because any ability can be enhanced or diminished, depending on how, when, and why a person uses it. It is possible to "teach an old dog new tricks," but learning requires that adults *want* to learn those new tricks.

As Baltes and Baltes (1990) explain, selective optimization means that each adult selects certain aspects of intelligence to optimize and neglects the rest. If those neglected aspects happen to be the ones measured on intelligence tests, then IQ scores will fall, even if the adult's selection improves (optimizes) other aspects of intellect.

The brain is plastic over the entire life span, developing new dendrites and activation sequences, adjusting to whatever the person chooses to learn (Karmiloff-Smith, 2010). Modern life requires continual improvement in vocabulary but less competence in math, as calculators and cash registers replace what once was done by the brain. As you saw in Figure 12.4 on page 386, that is exactly what adult brains do.

BRADFORD VELEY/CARTOONSTOCK

What's the Point? This time, you write the caption! (Use creative intelligence.)

Expert Cognition

Everyone develops *expertise,* becoming a selective expert. Adults are not restrained, as most children and adolescents are, by the demand to do and learn everything: physics and poetry, basketball and baseball, handwriting and texting.

Instead, adults specialize in activities that are personally meaningful—anything from car repair to gourmet cooking, from illness diagnosis to fly fishing. As people develop expertise in some areas, they ignore others.

expert
Someone with specialized skills and knowledge developed around a particular activity or area of specific interest.

DEFINING EXPERTISE

An **expert**, as cognitive scientists define it, is not necessarily someone with rare and outstanding proficiency (Dall'Alba, 2018). Although sometimes the term *expert* connotes an extraordinary genius, to researchers it means more—and less—than that. Expertise is not innate, although it may begin with inherited abilities that are later developed (Hambrick et al., 2016).

Culture and context guide people in this process. A current example is use of technology. Young people are much better at using computers, cell phones, and even smoke alarms than older adults are.

This is glaringly important in texting. In 2014, one teen from Brazil took only 18.19 seconds to text "The razor-toothed piranhas of the genera *Serrasalmus* and *Pygocentrus* are the most ferocious freshwater fish in the world. In reality they seldom attack a human" (Lee, 2014). You may not agree that that young man was an expert (he won a prize), but it is evident that everyone chooses to specialize in some tasks while ignoring others.

Expertise has become increasingly important as societies become more complex: Adults no longer do everything for themselves, unlike thousands of years ago, when families sewed their own clothes, hunted or gathered their own food, and treated their own illnesses.

Currently we find experts to do practically everything for us, with precooked food, medical specialists, technicians who repair just one kind of appliance (and

CHAPTER APP 12

Freedom

IOS:
https://tinyurl.com/y6y6o4u2

ANDROID:
https://tinyurl.com/y58wyjv9

RELEVANT TOPIC:
Multitasking and concentration in adulthood

This app and website blocker helps adults reclaim focus and productivity. Simply select distracting and time-consuming apps from a pre-made blocklist or create your own custom blocklist to temporarily block as many apps as you would like, at a specified time and/or for a certain length of time. Users report gaining an average of 2.5 hours of productive time each day.

sometimes just one brand), and so on. One amusing result of the COVID-19 pandemic was that stores and companies were sold out of flour, because many people suddenly needed and wanted to bake their own bread. My niece tried to order a 25-pound bag online: It was put on back order.

THE FOUR COMPONENTS OF EXPERTISE

Time, education, and effort transform people as they gain knowledge, practice, and experience. They become experts when the quality, not just the quantity, of their cognition advances. Expert thought is (1) intuitive, (2) automatic, (3) strategic, and (4) flexible, as we now describe.

First, *intuition*, which sometimes is portrayed as opposing evidence and therefore inferior. But that is not necessarily true (Wieten, 2018). Expert intuition incorporates past experience, seeming to leap over logic—sometimes with excellent results, sometime not.

Second, the complex action and skill required for many tasks become routine for experts, making it appear that most aspects of the task are performed instinctively. In fact, some *automatic* actions are no longer accessible to the conscious mind. The automatic aspect of expertise is particularly evident in medicine, when experienced specialists diagnose an illness within seconds, unlike the newly minted doctor (Norman et al., 2018).

If you are an experienced driver and try to teach someone else to drive, then you can see both intuition and automaticity in action. Excellent drivers who are inexperienced instructors find it hard to recognize or verbalize their intuitive and automatic responses—such as anticipating the movements of pedestrians and cyclists on the far side of the road, or feeling the gears shift on an incline, or hearing the tires lose traction on a bit of sand. Yet such factors differentiate the expert from the novice.

This may explain why, despite powerful motivation, quicker reactions, and better vision, teenagers have three times the rate of fatal car accidents than adults over age 25 do. Sometimes young drivers deliberately take risks (speeding, running a red light, drinking, and so on), but often they simply do not perceive conditions that a more experienced adult would notice.

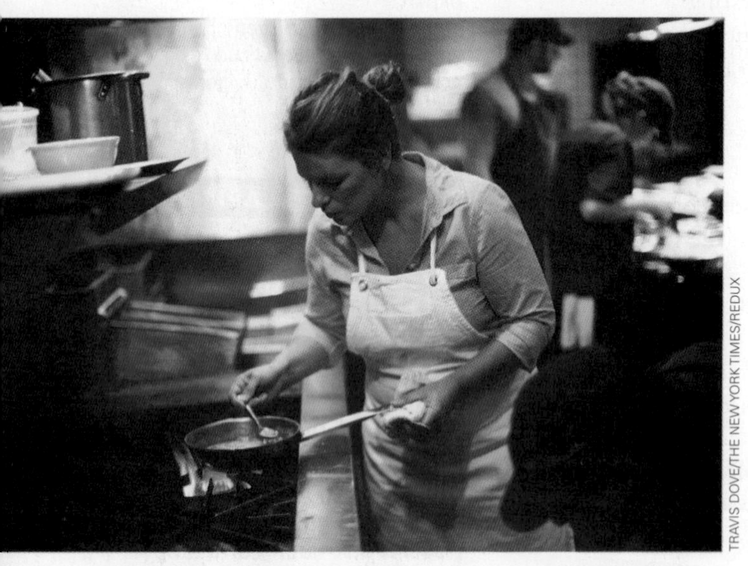

Expertise Illustrated Vivian Howard is chef and creator of Chef and the Farmer, a North Carolina restaurant that gained rave reviews and national attention.

OBSERVATION QUIZ
What do you see that signifies an expert chef? (see answer, page 395) ↑

Experts also are *strategic*, especially when problems are unexpected. Indeed, strategy may be the pivotal difference between a skilled person and an unskilled person. The difference between an expert airplane pilot is not book knowledge but familiarity with contingencies, allowing strategic understanding when unexpected problems occur (Durso et al., 2018). For instance, if the plane must land somewhere other than the runway, an expert pilot can guide the aircraft to safety on a field, or even on the water.

Finally, perhaps because they are intuitive, automatic, and strategic, experts are also *flexible*, which may be the most important aspect of all. The expert artist, musician, chef, or scientist is creative and curious, deliberately experimenting, enjoying the unexpected (Csikszentmihalyi, 2013).

Experts in all walks of life adapt to individual cases and exceptions—much as an expert chef will adjust ingredients, temperature, technique, and timing as a dish develops, tasting to see whether a little more spice is needed, seldom following a recipe exactly. Standards are high: Some cooks throw food in the garbage rather than serve a dish that many people would happily eat. Expert chess players, auto mechanics, and violinists are similarly aware of nuances that might escape the novice.

Human survival may have depended on the brain's plasticity (Winegard et al., 2018). Unlike our primate relatives, who share most genes with us, the "plasticity of evolved cognitive structures" allowed the expertise needed for humans to thrive.

Expertise, Age, and Experience

The relationship between expertise and age is not straightforward (Krampe & Charness, 2018). One essential requirement for expertise is time, both hours of practice and years of maturity.

Each area of expertise has particular practice requirements. For example, in music, violinists need more practice to become proficient than singers do; in medicine, neurosurgeons need more practice than geriatric nurses; among political leaders, presidents need more experience than school board members.

Of course, the latter of each of these pairs also benefit from years of practice, but no one becomes expert without many hours of learning. Circumstances, training, genes, ability, practice, and age all affect expertise, which means that experts in one specific field are often remarkably inexpert in other areas.

◆◆ Especially for Drivers
A number of states have passed laws requiring hands-free technology for people who use cell phones while driving. Do these measures cut down on accidents? (see response, page 395)

For example, humans have adjusted to climate, each group developing the expertise needed for life in the Arctic, the desert, the islands, or the forest. Food, shelter, and child care are radically different in each of these places; each community has experts who teach the young what they need to know.

No other animal lives on every continent. By adulthood people learn to live where we are. This is glaringly evident when someone from the tropics is sent to Canada, or someone in Texas experiences a snowstorm.

One final example of the relationship between age and job effectiveness comes from an occupation familiar to all of us: driving a taxi. This is not an easy job.

In major cities, taxi drivers must find the best route (factoring in traffic, construction, time of day, and many other details) while knowing where new passengers are likely to be found and how to relate to customers, some of whom might want to talk, others not.

Research in England—where taxi drivers "have to learn the layout of 25,000 streets in London and the locations of thousands of places of interest, and pass stringent examinations" (Woollett et al., 2009, p. 1407)—found not only that the drivers became more expert with time but also that their brains adjusted to the need for particular knowledge.

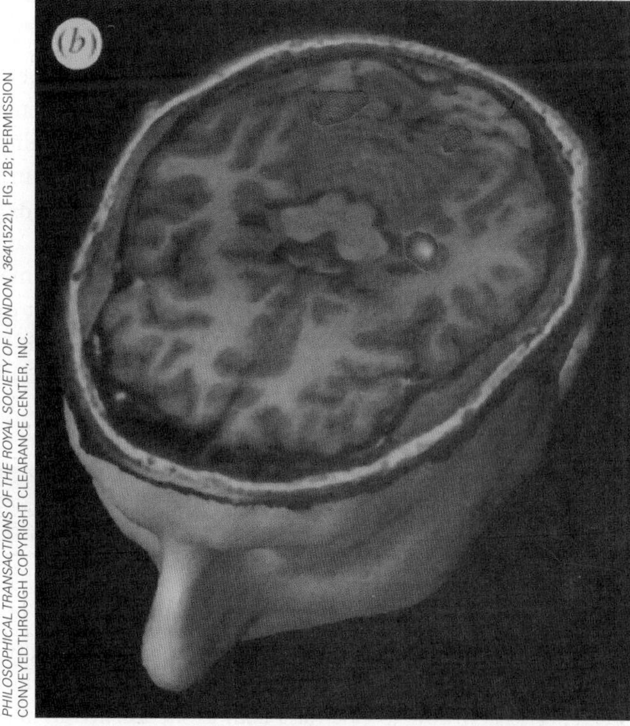

Red Means Go! The red shows the activated brain areas in London taxi drivers as they navigated the busy London streets. Not only were these areas more active than the same areas in the average person's brain, but they also had more dendrites. In addition, the longer a cabby had been driving, the more brain growth was evident. This research confirms plasticity, implying that we all could develop new skills, not only by remembering but also by engaging in activities that change the very structures of our brains.

Some parts of their brains (areas dedicated to spatial representation) were more extensive and active than those of an average person (Woollett et al., 2009). On ordinary IQ tests, the taxi drivers' scores were average, but their expertise was apparent in navigating London.

FAMILY SKILLS

This discussion of expertise has cited occupations (surgeons, musicians, taxi drivers) that once had far more male than female workers. In recent years, three important shifts have occurred that add to this topic.

First, more women are educated than before. As you learned in Chapter 11, in the United States and many other nations, women are more likely to attend college than men are. This has changed entire societies.

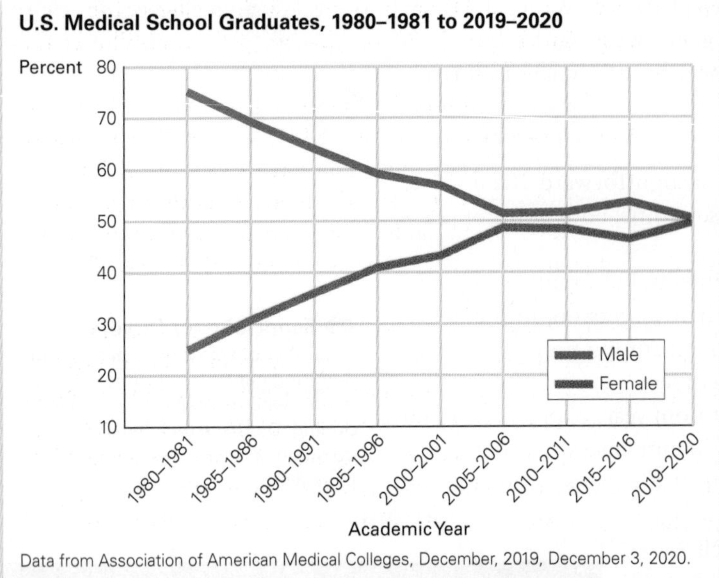

FIGURE 12.5 Expect a Woman Next time you hear "The doctor will see you now," the physician is as likely to be a woman as a man—unless the doctor is over age 50.

Especially for Prospective Parents
In terms of the intellectual challenge, what type of intelligence is most needed for effective parenthood? (see response, page 395)

That allowed the second change: more women working in occupations traditionally reserved for men. Remember from Chapter 2 that Virginia Apgar, when she earned her M.D. in 1933, was told she could not be a surgeon because only men were surgeons. Fortunately for the survival of millions of newborns, she did not quit hospital medicine.

Today that sexist assumption has changed; half of the new M.D.s in the United States are women, including thousands of surgeons (see Figure 12.5). More generally, most college women expect to be professionals, wives, and mothers.

And that led to a third change: What once was called "women's work" has become gender neutral, benefiting men and children. In earlier generations, women sometimes said they were "just a housewife," even though they met the biological, cognitive, and psychosocial needs of several children as well as their husbands, neighbors, and community.

Recently, however, the importance of family work and community is increasingly recognized, and men as well as women do it.

The skill, flexibility, and strategies needed to raise a family are a manifestation of expertise. Here again, age matters. Although fertility and easy births are more common in the late teens, older fathers and mothers tend to be more patient, with lower rates of child abuse as well as more successful offspring.

Of course, the mere passage of time does not make a person a better parent. However, an expert on the science of parenting concludes that, in general, as people gain in maturity and experience, "the more appropriate and optimal their parenting cognitions and practices are likely to be" (Bornstein, 2015, p. 91). (See A Case to Study.)

A CASE TO STUDY

Parenting Expertise

What makes an expert parent? This case to study is about one mother, Magdalene Hurtado, who knew how to care for a baby as she learned in her home community (the United States) and discovered that baby care was not the same in another culture.

She is not the only one who does not always know what is universally true for human development, and what is cultural. You have read several examples: Some infants are fed formula from birth on, some are breast fed for years, some are put to sleep on their stomachs in their own crib from day one, some sleep beside their parents until they are teenagers. When mothers from diverse cultures meet, some are shocked by the routine practices of the others.

However, practices that are well-suited in one cultural context might not be in another. Hurtado is a social scientist who studied the Ache, an indigenous tribe living in the jungle in Paraguay. She had traveled to Paraguay many times, finding the Ache people respectful and deferential. She admired them, and developed close relationships with several of the women.

After each visit, she returned to her work as a professor in the United States, publishing many books and articles that detailed her research. At one point, she married and had a baby.

She returned to Paraguay to do further research, this time with her husband and her infant daughter. She had brought all the things her baby might need, including a baby-basket, designed to be carried easily and yet comfortable, as many other North American mothers have found.

The Ache greeted her in a whole new way. They took her aside and in friendly and intimate but no-nonsense terms told her all the things she was doing wrong as a mother:

> This older woman sat with me and told me I must sleep with my daughter. They were horrified that I had a basket with me for her to sleep in. . . . here was a group of forest hunter-gatherers, people living in what Westerners would call basic conditions, giving instructions to a highly educated woman from a technologically sophisticated culture.
>
> *[Hurtado, quoted in Small, 1998, pp. 213–214]*

The intelligent way to care for an infant in the United States (a basket allows easy transport and protects against SIDS) was not intelligent for the Ache. In that community, babies needed to sleep with their mothers to prevent bites from poisonous snakes or wild dogs, or kidnapping by strangers (that did happen among the Ache).

A team of North American experts have developed a test to measure intelligent parenting, called the *KIDI (Knowledge of Infant Development Inventory)*. In the United States, high scores on the KIDI often correlate with intelligent baby care (e.g., Graybill et al., 2016; Howard, 2010; McMillin et al., 2015).

Thus, it is no surprise that scores on the KIDI predict later high-achievement among U.S.-born children. That is less true for children born elsewhere, because the KIDI does not universally correlate with effective mothering. Happy, successful children can be raised in many ways. Each culture and family adjusts practices to anticipate the needs of adults of that community.

Developmentalists have not yet identified all of the components necessary to become an expert in child rearing, but at least we know that such expertise exists. For example, more experienced and mature parents are more likely to nip problems in the bud and recognize that some behaviors (that hairstyle, that music, that tattoo) are not worth fighting about. Hurtado was wise enough to listen to the Ache experts.

DATA CONNECTIONS: Stress in Adulthood: Balancing Family and Career examines how well parents who are employed balance career and family responsibilities. Achieve

As with all aspects of adult cognition, variation is apparent, and people of every age can be intelligent or ignorant. Remember that how much parents should talk with preverbal infants, whether they should let them cry, what to teach a child about dogs, or strangers, or guns depends on the culture more than on the nature of the child. What one parent thinks is rude, a parent elsewhere might appreciate; what one parent thinks is necessary guidance, another might call abuse. As parents become more experienced within their particular culture, they become expert.

Raising a child teaches adults how to become the intuitive, strategic, and flexible expert parent that children need. For this, the children themselves get some credit. As one of my first two daughters said to the next two, "You should be grateful to me. I broke them [my husband and me] in."

As with all aspects of adult cognition, variation is apparent, and age and gender do not guarantee intelligence of any kind. But experience, on the job or in the family, may help.

what have you learned?

1. At what age should a person begin selective optimization?
2. What selective optimization can you see in your parents?
3. In what domain are you an expert that most people are not?
4. How does automatic processing contribute to expertise?
5. Explain how intuition might help or diminish ability.
6. If you wanted to be strategic about improving your health, what would you do?
7. In what occupations would flexibility be an asset, and why?
8. What do parents learn from experience?

SUMMARY

Growing Older

1. Senescence causes a universal slowdown during adulthood, but aging does not necessarily mean impairment. All the sense organs become less acute, but modern technology (glasses, hearing aids, and more) usually allow the senses to function well over the years.

2. Sexual responsiveness slows down with age, as does speed of recovery after orgasm. However, sexual satisfaction may continue or even improve over adulthood.

3. Fertility problems increase with age. At menopause, ovulation ceases, and levels of estrogen are markedly reduced, making conception impossible. For men, hormones are reduced more gradually. Adults sometimes seek hormone replacement therapy, but this may be unwise.

Two More Health Hazards

4. Drug use is complicated, since both prescription and nonprescription drugs can be harmful. Medication has added health and decades to the average life, but abuse of opioids has led to thousands of midlife deaths.

5. The evidence on nonprescription drugs is also mixed. Coffee usually is beneficial; cigarettes never are.

6. Illegal drugs are usually harmful, which is why most adults avoid them. Alcohol in moderation may reduce heart disease but in excess causes destruction of the brain, body, and family.

7. Obesity is a risk factor for many diseases, including COVID-19. A worldwide "epidemic of obesity" has resulted from more access to abundant food. That is one reason the rates of diabetes are rising.

8. The Mediterranean diet, intermittent fasting, and bariatric surgery are all measures that might curb the problems of poor eating habits in adulthood.

Development of the Mind

9. The brain slows down in adulthood, but unless notable problems occur, several aspects of cognition improve over adulthood.

10. Intelligence is sometimes thought to be general ability, which Spearman called *g*. This idea is disputed by those who think that intelligence is composed of several divergent abilities.

11. As people age, fluid intelligence (which includes working memory and speedy thought) decreases while crystallized intelligence (which is based on accumulated knowledge) increases. Over adulthood, crystallized intelligence increases and fluid intelligence decreases, making overall IQ quite stable.

12. Sternberg proposed three fundamental forms of intelligence: analytic, creative, and practical. Most research finds that although analytic and creative abilities decline with age, practical intelligence may improve. In daily life, practical intelligence may be most important.

Selective Gains and Losses

13. As people grow older, they choose to focus on certain aspects of their lives, optimizing development in those areas and compensating for declines in others. This means that adults specialize in certain aspects of cognition, while the others fade.

14. In addition to being more experienced, experts are better thinkers than novices because they are more intuitive, automatic, strategic, and flexible.

15. Expertise in adulthood is apparent in many professions and family life. Experienced workers may outperform novice workers because they specialize, compensating for losses.

KEY TERMS

senescence (p. 372)
in vitro fertilization (p. 375)
menopause (p. 375)
hormone replacement therapy (HRT) (p. 375)
Mediterranean diet (p. 379)
intermittent fasting (p. 380)
general intelligence (*g*) (p. 384)
fluid intelligence (p. 386)
crystallized intelligence (p. 387)
analytic intelligence (p. 387)
creative intelligence (p. 387)
practical intelligence (p. 387)
selective optimization with compensation (p. 388)
expert (p. 389)

APPLICATIONS

1. Guess the age of five adults you know, ideally of different ages. Then ask them how old they are. Analyze the clues you used for your guesses and the reactions to your question.

2. Find a speaker willing to come to your class who is an expert on weight loss, adult health, smoking, or drinking. Write a one-page proposal explaining why you think this speaker would be good and what topics they should address. Give this proposal to your instructor, with contact information for your speaker. The instructor will call the potential speakers, thank them for their willingness, and decide whether or not to actually invite them to speak.

3. The importance of context and culture is illustrated by the things that people think are basic knowledge. With a partner from the class, write four questions that you think are hard but

fair as measures of general intelligence. Then give your test to your partner, and answer the four questions that your partner has prepared for you. What did you learn from the results?

4. Some people mistakenly assume that almost any high school graduate can become a teacher, since most adults know the basic reading and math skills that elementary children need to learn. Describe aspects of expertise that experienced teachers need to master, with examples from your own experience.

ESPECIALLY FOR ANSWERS

Response for Doctors and Nurses (from p. 380): Obviously, much depends on the specific patient. Overall, however, far more people develop a disease or die because of years of poor health habits than because of various illnesses not spotted early. With some exceptions, age 35 is too early to detect incipient cancers or circulatory problems, but it's prime time for stopping cigarette smoking, curbing alcohol abuse, and improving exercise and diet.

Response for Drivers (from p. 391): No. Car accidents occur when the mind is distracted, not the hands.

Response for Prospective Parents (from p. 392): Because parenthood demands flexibility and patience, Sternberg's practical intelligence is probably most needed. Anything that involves finding a single correct answer, such as analytic intelligence or number ability, would not be much help.

OBSERVATION QUIZ ANSWERS

Answer to Observation Quiz (from p. 384): Older adults might be more stressed by the proctors, and they might find it uncomfortable to sit on the floor while writing.

Answer to Observation Quiz (from p. 386): Spatial ability in men. But note that this ability was also highest overall at age 46. Not until about age 60 were both genders equal.

Answer to Observation Quiz (from p. 390): At least nine things! Full apron, hair in bun (not in eyes), gas flame, tilt of pan, moving pan partly off to adjust heat, long handle on pan, the pan itself (durable, heat-conducting, expensive), constant stirring, and most important of all—intense concentration on the task.

CHAPTER 13

ADULTHOOD

The Social World

what will you know?

- Does personality change from childhood to adulthood?
- Why doesn't everyone get married?
- Is being a parent work or joy?

"Your backpack is open."

I hear that several times a day from strangers on sidewalks, at street corners, in stores. "Thank you. I know," I reply.

My backpack is large, with three deep pockets. I like to zip it up halfway, leaving the top open so that I can see each section. Nothing visible is valuable, and nothing ever falls out when the backpack is strapped to my back, half-open.

Sometimes I sympathize with those strangers; sometimes not. One time, as I was waiting for the subway, next to me sat a young boy, with his father on his other side. The man said,

"Your backpack is open."

"Thank you. I know."

"Do you want me to zip it for you?"

I smiled and shook my head.

"I know you must be tired and busy," he said. "My son could zip it for you."

He seemed upset, and the boy was looking at me, ready to zip. I gave up.

"OK."

The son zipped; the father was happy.

I thanked them both, as if I were grateful.

The merits of open backpacks can be argued either way, but this chapter begins with my backpack because it reveals three characteristics of adult development.

First, this chapter discusses personality: That man and I have quite different attitudes about things being closed. (I keep kitchen cabinets, closet doors, and jackets open, too.) One of the Big Five traits on which people differ is called *openness*; some people are very open (me), and others are troubled when they encounter such openness.

Unless people recognize personality differences, they will misunderstand each other. That father assumed that my backpack was

open because I was tired, not because I liked it that way. That could have led to a disagreement, but I am high on another of the Big Five traits, *agreeableness*.

The second major topic of this chapter is human relationships. All members of this triad were quite social: Father and son were aligned, and I responded to social pressure.

The final topic of this chapter is caregiving. Adults want to care for each other, yet each wants to be independent. I did not want anyone to zip up my backpack, but I recognized the father's need to take care of me. I decided that I would be caring for him by letting him care for me, so I said OK.

Personality Development in Adulthood

You already know that each human is genetically unique, in temperament and inclinations, and that childhood experiences and culture shape personality. Continuity is evident: Few adults develop a personality opposite the one they had at age 8 or 18. But discontinuity can occur, as you will see.

Erikson's Theory

As you remember, Erikson described eight stages of development. His first five stages begin in a particular chronological period. His adult stages are less age-based (see Table 13.1).

TABLE 13.1 Erikson's Stages of Adulthood
Unlike Freud or other early theorists who thought adults simply worked through the legacy of their childhood, four of Erikson's eight psychosocial stages occur after puberty. His most famous book, *Childhood and Society* (1993a), devoted only two pages to each adult stage, but elaborations in later works have led to a much richer depiction (Hoare, 2002).
Identity Versus Role Confusion Although Erikson originally situated the identity crisis during adolescence, he realized that identity concerns could be lifelong. Identity combines values and traditions from childhood with the current social context. Since contexts keep evolving, many adults reassess all four types of identity (sexual/gender, vocational/work, religious/spiritual, and political/ethnic).
Intimacy Versus Isolation Adults seek intimacy — a close, reciprocal connection with another human being. Intimacy is mutual, not self-absorbed, which means that adults need to devote time and energy to one another. This process begins in emerging adulthood and continues lifelong. Isolation is especially likely when divorce or death disrupts established intimate relationships.
Generativity Versus Stagnation Adults need to care for the next generation, either by raising their own children or by mentoring, teaching, and helping others. Erikson's first description of this stage focused on parenthood, but later he included other ways to achieve generativity. Adults extend the legacy of their culture and their generation with ongoing care, creativity, and sacrifice.
Integrity Versus Despair When Erikson himself reached his 70s, he decided that integrity, with the goal of combating prejudice and helping all humanity, was too important to be left to the elderly. He also thought that each person's entire life could be directed toward connecting a personal journey with the historical and cultural purpose of human society, the ultimate achievement of integrity.

The three adult stages—*intimacy versus isolation*, *generativity versus stagnation*, and *integrity versus despair*—do not always appear in chronological sequence; they overlap, with many social and cultural factors influencing all three.

intimacy versus isolation
The sixth of Erikson's eight stages of development. Every adult seeks close relationships with other people in order to live a happy and healthy life.

generativity versus stagnation
The seventh of Erikson's eight stages of development. Adults seek to be productive in a caring way, often as parents. Generativity also occurs through art, caregiving, and employment.

humanism
A theory that stresses the potential of all humans, who have the same basic needs regardless of culture, gender, or background.

Big Five
The five basic clusters of personality traits that remain quite stable throughout adulthood: openness, conscientiousness, extroversion, agreeableness, and neuroticism.

Social influences are most evident in **intimacy versus isolation**. This stage begins in emerging adulthood, as explained in the Chapter 11. It continues throughout adulthood.

According to Erikson, after intimacy comes **generativity versus stagnation**, when adults seek to be productive in a caring way. Erikson wrote that a mature adult "needs to be needed" (1993a, p. 266). Without generativity, adults experience "a pervading sense of stagnation and personal impoverishment" (Erikson, 1993a, p. 267).

Generativity is often expressed by caring for the younger generation, but it occurs in ways other than child rearing. Meaningful employment, important creative production, and caregiving of other adults also are generative ways to avoid stagnation.

The final adult stage, *integrity versus despair*, is described in Chapter 15. However, although the drive to understand the whole of one's life is especially evident in late adulthood, it may come to the fore in midlife as well. Thus, Erikson's three stages of adulthood may be evident for adults aged 25–65.

Maslow's Theory of Personality

Some scientists are convinced that there is something hopeful, unifying, and noble in humans. People seek love and then respect, and finally, if all goes well, people become truly themselves. This is the central idea of **humanism**, a theory developed by Abraham Maslow (1908–1970) and many others.

Maslow believed that all people—no matter what their culture, gender, or background—have the same basic needs. He arranged these needs in a hierarchy, often illustrated as a pyramid (see Figure 13.1):

1. *Physiological*: needing food, water, warmth, and air
2. *Safety*: feeling protected from injury and death
3. *Love and belonging*: having friends, family, and a community (often religious)
4. *Esteem*: being respected by the wider community as well as by oneself
5. *Self-actualization*: becoming truly oneself, fulfilling one's unique potential while appreciating all of life

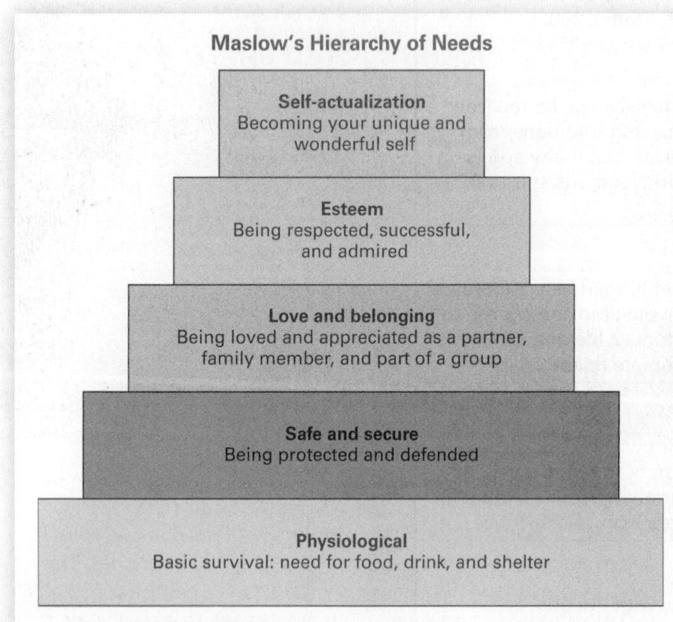

FIGURE 13.1 **Moving Up, Not Looking Back** Maslow's hierarchy is like a ladder: Once a person stands firmly on a higher rung, the lower rungs are no longer needed. Thus, someone who has arrived at step 4 might devalue safety (step 2) and be willing to risk personal safety to gain respect.

This pyramid caught on almost immediately. It was one of the most "contagious ideas in behavioral science," because it seemed insightful about human psychology (Kenrick et al., 2010, p. 292).

Maslow did not believe that the five levels were connected to a particular stage or age, but he thought that lower needs must be met before higher needs. That makes this hierarchy relevant for life-span development. At the highest level, when all four earlier needs have been satisfied, adults can be fully themselves—creative, spiritual, curious, appreciative of nature, respectful of everyone else.

Humanism is prominent among medical professionals because they recognize that illness and pain are connected to the psychological needs of the patient (Felicilda-Reynaldo & Smith, 2018; Jackson et al., 2014b). As a medical team from the famed Mayo

Clinic states, "solely addressing physiological recovery in the ICU, without also placing focus on psychological recovery, is limiting and not sufficient for recovery of the entire patient—both body and mind" (Karnatovskaia et al., 2015, p. 210).

MJ FRYE/CARTOONSTOCK.COM

Maybe Next Year Self-acceptance is a gradual process over the years of adulthood, aided by the appreciation of friends and family. At some point in adulthood, people shift from striving to fulfil their potential to accepting their limitations.

The Big Five

Another theory of personality begins with the idea that people have five distinct clusters of characteristics, expressed in various ways over the decades of the life span. They are called the **Big Five**:

- *Openness*: imaginative, curious, artistic, creative, open to new experiences
- *Conscientiousness*: organized, deliberate, conforming, self-disciplined
- *Extroversion*: outgoing, assertive, active
- *Agreeableness*: kind, helpful, easygoing, generous
- *Neuroticism*: anxious, moody, self-punishing, critical

(To remember the Big Five, the acronym OCEAN is useful.)

Each person is somewhere on a continuum on each of these five. The low end might be described, in the same order as above, with these five adjectives: *closed*, *careless*, *introverted*, *hard to please*, and *placid*.

According to this theory, adults choose vocations, hobbies, health habits, mates, and neighborhoods to reflect their personality. Those high in extroversion might work in sales, those high in openness might be artists, and so on. International research confirms that human personality traits (there are hundreds of them) can be grouped based on these five dimensions.

AGE CHANGES

When adults are followed longitudinally, stability of the Big Five is evident. Change is more likely in emerging adulthood or late adulthood than for 25- to 64-year-olds (Wagner et al., 2019).

The general age trend is positive, as people align with the norms of their community. Adults gradually become less neurotic and more conscientious. Similar trends are found in research on attachment over the life span. Anxious and avoidant attachment become less common, while secure attachment becomes more prominent (Fraley, 2019).

All theories find that people become more accepting of themselves and their community over the decades of adult life. This is a process that develops over adulthood. A longitudinal study found that self-criticism gradually declines from age 23 to 29, which bodes well for later mental health (Michaeli et al., 2019).

Efforts at self-improvement gradually become efforts at self-acceptance. One summary says that people under the age of 30 "actively try to change their environment," moving to new places, finding new friends, seeking new jobs. Later in life, context shapes traits: once adults have their vocation, family, and neighborhoods, they "change the self to fit the environment" (Kandler, 2012, p. 294).

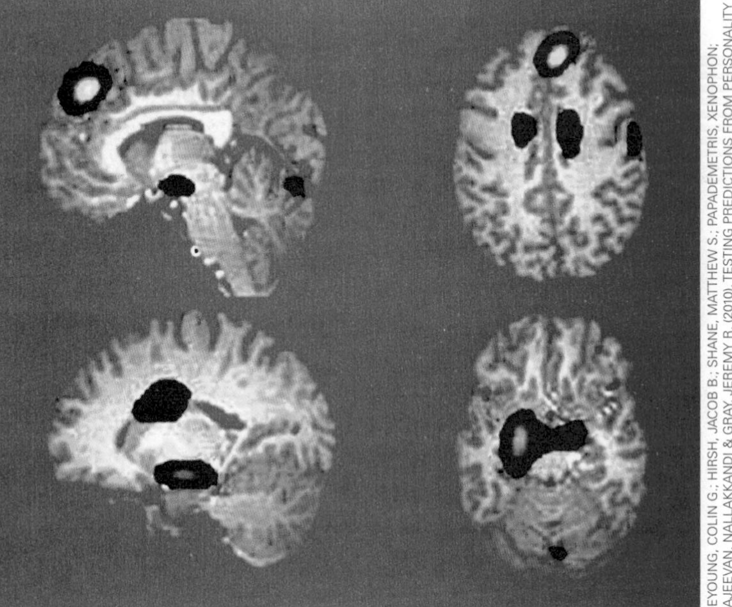

DEYOUNG, COLIN G.; HIRSH, JACOB B.; SHANE, MATTHEW S.; PAPADEMETRIS, XENOPHON; RAJEEVAN, NALLAKKANDI & GRAY, JEREMY R. (2010). TESTING PREDICTIONS FROM PERSONALITY NEUROSCIENCE. *PSYCHOLOGICAL SCIENCE, 21*(6), 820–828. DOI: 10.1177/0956797610370159

Active Brains, Active Personality The hypothesis that individual personality traits originate in the brain was tested by scientists who sought to find correlations between brain activity (shown in red) and personality traits. People who rated themselves high in four of the Big Five (conscientiousness, extroversion, agreeableness, neuroticism — but not openness) also had more activity in brain regions that are known to relate to those traits. Here are two side views *(left)* and a top and bottom view *(right)* of the brains of people high in neuroticism. Their brain regions known to be especially sensitive to stress, depression, threat, and punishment (yellow bullseyes) were more active than the same brain regions in people low in neuroticism (DeYoung et al., 2010).

Same Situation, Far Apart: Scientists at Work Most scientists are open-minded and conscientious (two of the Big Five personality traits), as both of these women are. Culture and social context are crucial, however. If the woman on the left were in Tanzania, would she be a doctor surrounded by patients in the open air, as the woman on the right is? Or is she so accustomed to her North American laboratory, protected by gloves and a screen, that she could not adjust? The answer depends on personality, not knowledge.

CULTURAL INFLUENCES

Over the life span, culture shapes personality. As one team wrote, "personality may acculturate" (Güngör et al., 2013, p. 713).

A study of well-being and self-esteem in 28 nations found that people are happiest if their personality traits match their social context. This has implications for immigrants, who might feel (and be) less appreciated when the personality values of their home culture clash with their new community.

For example, extroversion is valued in Canada and less so in Japan; consequently, Canadians and Japanese have a stronger sense of well-being if their personal ratings on extroversion (high or low) are consistent with their culture (Fulmer et al., 2010).

Many people criticize immigrants for the very traits that are valued in their home cultures. For example, a student who seeks help from others in writing a paper might be accused of cheating in an individualistic culture. A man who tells the police that his brother was among those who stormed the U.S. Capitol on January 6, 2021, may be a patriot or a traitor, depending on cultural values.

◆◆ Especially for Immigrants and Children of Immigrants Poverty and persecution are some of the reasons why some people leave their home for another country, but personality is also influential. Which of the Big Five personality traits do you think is most characteristic of immigrants? (see response, page 425)

THINK CRITICALLY: Would your personality fit better in another culture?

Common Themes

Universal trends are more significant than cultural differences. Regarding the Big Five, adults who are low in neuroticism and high in agreeableness tend to be happier than the opposite. Personal experiences matter, affecting individuals everywhere more than nations anywhere. For example, people who personally experience a happy marriage become less neurotic over time; people in unhappy marriages become more neurotic (O'Meara & South, 2019).

As for universal human needs, every well-known theorist or scholar of adult personality echoes the same themes. Freud did it first: He said that a healthy adult is able to do two things: *lieben und arbeiten* (to love and to work).

Likewise, as you just read, Maslow considered love/belonging and then success/esteem to be steps in his hierarchy. Similarly, extroversion and conscientiousness are two of the Big Five, again suggesting that these are among the basic human attributes.

Other theorists call these two needs *affiliation/achievement*, or *emotional/instrumental*, or *communion/agency*. Every theory recognizes both; all adults seek to love and to work in ways that fit their personality, culture, and gender. In the rest of this chapter, to simplify and organize our discussion, we will use Erikson's terms, *intimacy* and *generativity*, each of which refers to a cluster of adult psychosocial development.

what have you learned?

1. How does personality differ from temperament?
2. What are the three needs of adults, according to Erikson?
3. What do all people strive for, according to Maslow?
4. What are the Big Five traits?
5. How are personality traits affected by age?
6. How does personality interact with culture?

Intimacy: Connecting with Others

Humans are not meant to be loners. Decades of research finds that physical health and psychological well-being flourish if family and friends are supportive.

macmillan learning

VIDEO: Marriage in Adulthood features researcher Ronald Sabatelli and interviews of people discussing the joys and challenges of marriage.

Romantic Partners

We begin with romance. Adults tend to be happiest and healthiest if they have a long-term partner, connected to them with bonds of affection and care.

MARRIAGE

Traditionally, the romantic bond was codified via marriage. Marriage is not what it was only a few decades ago (see Figure 13.2): In every culture and region, marriage is later and less common (prompted more by love than by family approval), is more diverse (as in more same-sex and interracial couples), and is more equal for women (who are no longer "given away" by their fathers). However, despite these variations, most adults hope to marry, believing that society functions better and childrearing is best when couples marry (Sassler & Lichter, 2020).

Most adults seek a partner, and marriage correlates with adult health and longevity everywhere. Humans know this emotionally, although not always logically. For example, people whose marriages have become so intolerable that they divorce have a higher marriage rate than single people of the same age and circumstances.

Further evidence is that, when same-sex marriages became legal in the United States, most same-sex couples chose to marry. This "high take-up rate suggests that marriage is a meaningful marker of a successful personal life" (Cherlin, 2020, p. 75).

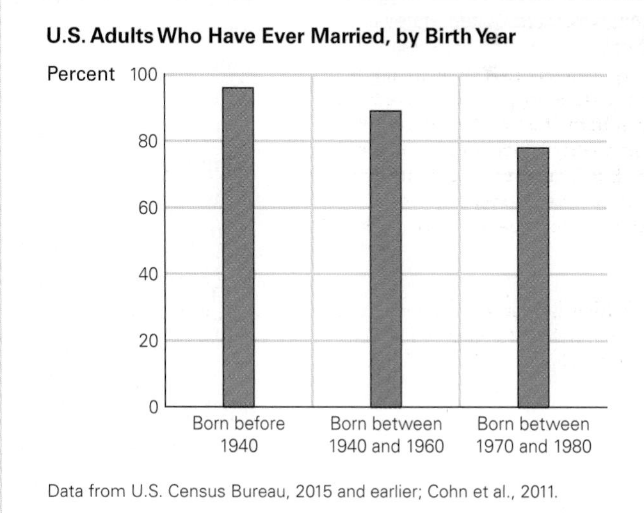

FIGURE 13.2 And Now? Not only are far fewer people marrying, but they also marry later, so it seemed misleading to include a bar for those born between 1980 and 2000. If we had, the rates would be under 50 percent. Most emerging adults are unmarried.

In linked lives, spouses and partners usually adjust to each other's needs, allowing them to function better as a couple than they did as singles. A large survey of married heterosexual couples found that the men's average salary five years after their wedding was notably higher than for men at similar jobs who remained single. Also, their homes were more comfortable, perhaps because their wives made it so (Kuperberg, 2012).

FRANK BARON/CAMERA PRESS/GUARDIAN/REDUX

One Love, Two Homes Their friends and family know that Jonathan and Diana are a couple, happy together day and night, year after year. But one detail distinguishes them from most couples: Each owns a house. They commute 10 miles and are living apart together — LAT.

living apart together (LAT) The term for couples who are committed to each other and spend time together but maintain separate homes. LAT couples are increasingly common in the United States and Europe.

THINK CRITICALLY: Is marriage a failed institution?

That specific detail reflects gender norms, but both spouses should be credited with improvements in each other's lives. As already mention in Chapter 12, currently women are more likely to have jobs and men to be involved in child care, but that does not change the general finding that partners find the roles that make life better for both of them.

NONMARITAL ROMANTIC RELATIONSHIPS

Cohabitation is increasing for adults of all ages. Some couples live together for decades without marrying. That arrangement has a higher rate of dissolution, and less happiness overall, but those effects may be partly socioeconomic, since cohabitation is more often chosen when income is low (Musick & Michelmore, 2018).

To some extent, cohabitation reflects age as well as income. For younger adults, it is chosen as a way to save money and postpone marriage; many older couples decide to cohabit after divorce, avoiding financial entanglements.

By midlife, most cohabiting couples are neither more, nor less, happy than married couples, when income is taken into account. This varies somewhat by gender and national culture. Probably, like marriage, the sheer fact of cohabitation is not a boon or a bust: Specifics of the relationship are crucial (Perelli-Harris et al., 2019).

A sizable number of adults have found a third way (neither marriage nor cohabitation) to meet their intimacy needs with a steady romantic partner. They are **living apart together (LAT)**. They have separate residences, but they function as a couple—sexually faithful, vacationing together, recognized as a couple by other people, and so on.

Some LAT couples must live apart because they have jobs in separate cities, but more often they could share a home but prefer not to. LAT is chosen more often as adults grow older. When a couple under age 30 is living apart, they usually consider their separate residences temporary, expecting to share one home soon. Most LAT couples over age 50, however, prefer to keep separate homes for years (Lewin, 2018).

Financial patterns are a particular issue for LAT couples. Most married couples combine their wealth; many cohabiting couples do not (Hamplová et al., 2014). LAT couples struggle with this aspect of their relationship, with the women particularly wanting to pay their own way (Lyssens-Danneboom & Mortelmans, 2014).

Children often are a strong influence on adult decisions to marry, divorce, cohabit, or LAT. Cohabiters who have had children together are more likely to marry than those who have not, especially when the children start school. Children sometimes are the reason a couple stays together ("for the sake of the children"), and sometimes they keep a couple apart, as when one parent leaves a violent mate in order to protect the children.

Children also keep older couples in LAT relationships. Many older parents maintain separate households because they do not want to upset their grown children (de Jong Gierveld & Merz, 2013).

PARTNERSHIPS OVER THE DECADES

Love is complex. Remember from Chapter 11 that Steinberg described romantic love as having three aspects: *passion*, *intimacy*, and *commitment*. Passion often begins a romance; intimacy occurs when a couple shares secrets, possessions, and a bed; and commitment is expressed in promises—perhaps faithfulness—and then support when trouble (illness, job-loss, a difficult child) happens.

The passage of time makes a difference. In general, establishing a new partnership tends to make both partners happy. For marriages, satisfaction is highest in the

"honeymoon period." Then frustration with a partner increases as conflicts—even those not directly between the couple—arise. On the other hand, over the decades of a committed adult relationship, satisfaction is more likely to improve than not (Bell & Harsin, 2018).

Children tend to decrease happiness in mates, especially when the first child is an infant and again when children reach puberty. The underlying reason may be economic: The cost of children, in both time and money, may be more than the adults budgeted for (Blanchflower & Clark, 2021). There are many exceptions to this generality: Sometimes child rearing increases satisfaction and infertility reduces it.

Divorce rates are higher in the first years of marriage, but long-term marriages sometimes end: "gray divorces" once were rare, but now about one divorce in four occurs when the partners are over age 50.

Remember, however, that averages obscure many differences of age, ethnicity, personality, and circumstances. In the United States, Asian Americans are least likely and African Americans most likely to divorce, according to the American Community Survey, although the rates vary within that community—very low among South Asian couples, higher among Southeast Asian couples. These ethnic differences are partly cultural and partly economic, making any broad effort to promote marriage for everyone doomed to disappoint politicians, social workers, and individuals. Variation in marriage and happiness is evident, as in A Case to Study.

At About This Time: Marital Happiness over the Years

Interval After Wedding	Characterization
First 6 months	Honeymoon period — happiest of all.
6 months to 5 years	Happiness dips; divorce is more common now than later in marriage.
5 to 10 years	Happiness holds steady.
10 to 20 years	Happiness dips as children reach puberty.
20 to 30 years	Happiness rises when children leave the nest.
30 to 50 years	Happiness is high and steady, barring serious health problems.

Not Always These are trends, often masked by more pressing events. For example, some couples stay together because of the children; so for them, unlike most couples, the empty-nest stage becomes a time of conflict or divorce.

A CASE TO STUDY

The Benefits of Marriage

Marriage can be a benefit or a problem, depending on whom you ask. That was one conclusion of a study of long-term cohabiting and married adults in England. Consider two quotations from that study (Soulsby & Bennett, 2017).

Dave, age 45, had been married for seven years when he said:

> Being married is molding the person that I am and who I'm becoming. It's helping me fulfil dreams and ambitions and goals, . . . it's giving me a deeper meaning of love, it's given me a sense of achievement and a sense of encouragement.

Gina, age 50, had been married for 23 years, and she said:

> As a single person you do what you want, you live your life as you like, you do what you want. . . . When you get married, all of a sudden you've got washing to do, you've got to tidy up in case your mess is impinging on someone else, or theirs on you, you've got to think about eating at the same time. You've got someone else that you need to factor in, so your life changes completely.

Which of these two seems more valid to you? Do not get distracted by the gender of the two people, or by how long they have been married, since there are not clear trends favoring gender or age.

It was once thought that men benefited more from marriage than women (Bernard, 1982). However, a meta-analysis in the United States found no marked gender differences in marital happiness (J. B. Jackson et al., 2014). In that study, in the first years of marriage, wives tended to be slightly more satisfied than husbands, but this shifted by about the 15-year mark, with husbands slightly more satisfied.

Age and gender differences in overall averages for marital happiness are small. At the same time, when marriages are considered one-by-one, differences are very large. Some spouses are overjoyed, and some are miserable! (E. Lawrence et al., 2019).

For this Case to Study, the final case is your own. How would you judge your own parents' relationship? If they were married or in a stable cohabiting relationship, did they benefit from this? Did you? If they never lived together, or if they married and divorced, or cohabited and separated,

would they, and you, have been happier if they were legally wed and were still together?

Generally, married adults are happier and healthier than never-married or divorced ones, and usually, bearing and raising children makes people happier with themselves and their partner. But not always. In fact, some research finds the opposite, and one scholar suggests that people want to believe that single people are unhappy and that childless partnerships are troubled, but that is contrary to the evidence (Hansen, 2012).

Consider, as in the quotations above, both perspectives.

Education and religion matter, too: College-educated couples are more likely to marry and less likely to divorce no matter what their ethnic background. Some unhappy couples stay married for religious reasons, and the result may be a long-lasting, troubled relationship, or, instead, a marriage that grows stronger every year.

empty nest
The time in the lives of parents when their children have left the family home. This is often a happy time for everyone.

Contrary to outdated impressions, the **empty nest**—when parents are alone again after the children have left—is usually a time for improved marriages. Simply having time for each other, without crying babies, demanding children, or rebellious teenagers, improves intimacy. Partners can focus on their mates, doing together whatever they both enjoy. Again, as evident in gray divorces, not always.

GAY AND LESBIAN COUPLES

Almost everything just described applies to gay and lesbian partners as well as to heterosexual ones. Some same-sex couples are faithful and supportive of each other; their emotional well-being thrives on their intimacy and commitment, which increases over the decades. Others are conflicted: Problems of finances, communication, and domestic abuse resemble those in different-sex marriages.

The similarity of same-sex and other-sex couples surprised many researchers. For example, one study focused on alcohol abuse in romantic couples, same-sex as well as other-sex. The scientists expected that the stress of being lesbian or gay would increase alcohol abuse. That was *not* what the data revealed. Instead, the crucial variable was whether the couple was married or not. For both same-sex and other-sex couples, excessive drinking was more common among cohabiters than among married couples (Reczek et al., 2014).

An increasing number of families headed by same-sex couples have children, some from a former marriage, some adopted, and some the biological child of one partner, conceived because the couple wanted a child. The well-being of such children depends on the same factors that affect the children of other-sex couples.

Family income may be crucial. On average, same-sex couples have less money than other-sex couples (Cenegy et al., 2018). As you remember from earlier chapters, low SES increases a child's risk of physical, academic, and emotional problems. Economic stress decreases the parents' patience and joy with their children.

JOHN MOORE/GETTY IMAGES

A Dream Come True When Melissa Adams and Meagan Martin first committed to each other, they thought they could never marry, at least in their South Carolina home. On July 11, 2015, they celebrated their union, complete with flower girl, bridesmaids, Reverend Sidden, and all the legal documents.

Another finding also relates to all partnerships: family connections. In a study of married gay couples in Iowa, one man said that he decided to marry because of his mother: "I had a partner that I lived with . . . And I think she, as much as she accepted him, it wasn't anything permanent in her eyes" (Ocobock, 2013, p. 196). In this study, most family members were supportive, but some were not—again eliciting deep emotional reactions.

In marriages of every kind, including interethnic marriages, in-laws usually welcome the new spouse; but when they do not, the partnership may suffer. Family influences are hard to ignore: There may be a premium or a penalty in relationships with in-laws (Danielsbacka et al., 2018).

DIVORCE AND REMARRIAGE

Throughout this text, developmental events that seem isolated, personal, and transitory are shown to be interconnected and socially constructed, with enduring consequences. Family relationships are part of the microsystem, but the macrosystem, mesosystem, and exosystem all have an impact.

Some national norms make divorce impossible. One unhappy spouse was asked if they ever thought of leaving their partner. The answer: "Divorce, never. Death, every day."

Of course, personal factors matter, too. In the United States, separation occurs because at least one partner believes that they would be happier without the other, a conclusion reached in almost half of all marriages. Indeed, fear of divorce is thought to be the reason fewer adults decide to marry. In 1990, the divorce rate was about 50 percent; in 2019, it was below 40 percent.

One reason for the shift is in the age of people who marry. Since people are marrying later, there are fewer marriages at highest risk for divorce. The number of divorces after decades of marriage is increasing, but the rate is still far lower than for younger adults. Maturity encourages couples to work out their disagreements.

Family problems from divorce arise not only with children (usually custodial parents become stricter and noncustodial parents become distant) but also with other relatives. The divorced adults' parents are often supportive financially but not emotionally. Relationships with in-laws typically end when a couple splits, as do many relationships with married friends. No wonder divorce increases loneliness (van Tilburg et al., 2015).

Many divorced people find another partner. Initially, remarriage restores intimacy, health, and financial security. For fathers, bonds with stepchildren who live with them, or with a baby from the new marriage, may replace strained relationships with children who live with their former wives (Noël-Miller, 2013a). That helps the fathers but not their children.

Divorce is never easy, but the negative consequences just explained are not inevitable. If divorce ends an abusive, destructive relationship (as it does about one-third of the time), it usually benefits at least one spouse (Amato, 2010). Such divorces lead to stronger and warmer mother–child and/or father–child relationships after the marital fights are over.

But most divorces occur not because one partner is abusive but because the spouses no longer love each other. Ideally, former lovers are still able to cooperate in child care. This realization has transformed what psychologists recommend to divorcing parents: It is best if parents share physical as well as legal custody, cooperating for the sake of the children, who live with each parent in turn (Braver & Votruba, 2018).

Shared physical custody helps grandparents as well (Jappens, 2018). When mothers had sole custody, the maternal grandparents were often overburdened, and the paternal grandparents rarely saw the children. Joint custody fosters better relationships.

◆◆ Especially for Young Couples Suppose you are one-half of a turbulent relationship in which moments of intimacy alternate with episodes of abuse. Should you break up? (see response, page 425)

Friends and Acquaintances

Each person is part of a **social convoy**. The term *convoy* originally referred to a group of travelers in hostile territory, such as the pioneers in ox-drawn wagons headed for California or soldiers marching across unfamiliar terrain. Individuals were strengthened by the convoy, sharing difficult conditions and defending one another.

social convoy Collectively, the family members, friends, acquaintances, and even strangers who move through the years of life with a person.

LUKE THOMPSON

Fellow Travelers Here that phrase is not a metaphor for life's journey but a literal description of a good friend, Tom, carrying 30-year-old Kevan Chandler, from Fort Wayne, Indiana, as they view the Paris Opera House. Kevan was born with spinal muscular atrophy because both his parents are carriers of the recessive gene. He cannot walk, but three of his friends agreed to take him on a three-week backpacking adventure through Europe. The trip was funded by hundreds of people who read about Kevan's plans online.

As people move through life, their social convoy functions as those earlier convoys did, a group of people who provide "a protective layer of social relations to guide, socialize, and encourage individuals as they move through life" (Antonucci et al., 2001, p. 572).

Sometimes a friend needs care and cannot reciprocate at the time, but it is understood that later the roles may be reversed. Friends provide practical help and useful advice when serious problems—death of a family member, personal illness, job loss—arise. They also offer companionship, information, and laughter in daily life.

Friends are a crucial part of the social convoy; they are chosen for the traits that make them reliable fellow travelers. Mutual loyalty and aid characterize friendship (Rawlins, 2016). An unbalanced friendship (one giving and the other taking) often ends because *both* parties are uncomfortable.

Friendships tend to improve over the decades of adulthood. As adults grow older, they tend to have fewer friends overall, but they keep their close friends and nurture those relationships (English & Carstensen, 2014). One benefit of friendship is that a person has someone to talk with about problems and joys. That itself increases happiness, especially when a friend celebrates accomplishments (Demir et al., 2017).

Although most friendships last for decades, conflicting health habits may end a relationship. For instance, a chain smoker and a friend who quit smoking are likely to part ways. On the other hand, shared health problems can bind a friendship together. For example, overweight people become friends with other overweight people, and together their eating habits reinforce each other as both continue to gain weight (Powell et al., 2015).

Adults who have no close and positive friends suffer in both physical and mental health (Dunbar, 2018; Santini et al., 2015). This seems as true in poor nations as in rich ones: Universally, humans are healthier with social support and sicker when socially isolated.

Social connections come not only from close friends but also from casual contacts, called *consequential strangers*. People are sustained in part by the clerk at the local store, the teammate at the pick-up basketball game, the person standing beside them in line at the local COVID test site.

Indeed, the fact that casual encounters are more difficult with masks and social distancing is thought to be one reason rates of depression rose during the recent pandemic (Rickman, 2021; Iyengar, 2021). Humans need each other—family, friends, and strangers.

Family Bonds

Beyond romance and friendship, family links span generations and endure over time. Childhood history influences people decades after they have left their home; adults of all ages connect with siblings, cousins, grown children and grandchildren, nieces and nephews, parents and grandparents.

THINK CRITICALLY: Does the rising divorce rate indicate stronger or weaker family links?

Past and present family experiences affect adult motivation, fears, and desires. For example, going to museums, reading books, discussing current events, and other family practices during childhood influence adult habits and values.

Adults enjoy discussing current politics, or movies, or sports with their siblings because they were raised to care about those aspects of life. Secure attachment and emotional support begun in early childhood remains strong if a family member is sick, or has a troubled marriage, or a disabled child. The "no visitors" rule enforced by hospitals during the COVID pandemic caused anger and sadness in family members when relatives died alone, even when the dying person was unconscious.

The power of family experiences was documented in data from twins in Denmark. They married less often than single-born Danes, but if they wed, they were less likely to divorce. According to the researchers, the twins may have met

their intimacy needs with each other, but if they married, they knew how to navigate conflict (Petersen et al., 2011).

PARENTS AND THEIR ADULT CHILDREN

A crucial part of family life for many adults is raising children. That work is discussed soon when we describe Erikson's other adult task, generativity. But before we recognize the generativity needed to meet the needs of the younger generation, we need to acknowledge that adults meet their own intimacy needs with their children.

Here we focus not on adults caring for children under age 18, but on adults' relationships to other adults. One source says that "ties between adults and parents are now more common than any other relationship in adulthood" (Fingerman et al., 2020, p. 383). Far from breaking ties with their middle-aged parents, 98 percent of adults aged 25–32 are in regular contact with at least one parent, often calling or texting every day (Hartnett et al., 2018).

STEVE SKJOLD/ALAMY STOCK PHOTO

Picnic in Poland Like families everywhere, these four generations in Zawady (a village in central Poland) enjoy time together, eating, laughing, and supporting each other. At the end of the day, however, each adult generation has their own home if they can afford it. Particularly in emerging adulthood, family bonds are strong, but so is the desire for independence.

Do not confuse intimacy with residence. If income and health allow, adult generations prefer to have separate homes. However, a study of 7,578 adults in seven nations found that physical separation did not weaken family ties. Indeed, intergenerational relationships may be strengthened, not weakened, when adult children and their parents live apart (Treas & Gubernskaya, 2012).

Consider the data on where adults choose to live. When they have the financial means to live wherever they wish, most adults move close to others in their families. One study reports that 75 percent of parents with grown children had at least one child who lived less than 30 miles away (Choi et al., 2020).

Many retirees can afford to sell their homes and move to Florida or Arizona, but many stay instead in Maine, or Iowa, or West Virginia (all states with more elderly residents than the U.S. average). When the older generations move, it is often to be nearer their grandchildren. Family relationships are vital throughout adulthood.

Considerable research has recently focused on *boomerang children*, or adults who live with their parents for a while, making a "swollen nest," not an empty one. In the United States in 1980, only 11 percent of 25- to 34-year-olds lived with their parents for at least a few months. Every year since then, more young adults have lived with older family members, making that the most frequent housing choice (Cohn & Passel, 2018).

Note that this is reciprocal. The fact that more young adults live with their parents mean that more parents live with their adult children. The myth is that older generations live with younger ones because the elders need caregiving. That is not the case: Usually the older generation owns the home, has a job, and is quite independent. Many nonparents think that adults do too much for their grown children (Barroso et al., 2019), but the people in such relationships usually value them.

Indeed, because most women in the twentieth century had their first child at age 20 or so, sometimes three generations of adults live together, a 64-year-old, a 44-year-old, and a 24-year-old, each active, opinionated, and self-sufficient. Conflict increases when adults share kitchens and bathrooms, but opportunities for close friendships increase as well.

FICTIVE KIN

Most adults maintain connections with brothers and sisters, sometimes traveling great distances to attend weddings, funerals, and holidays. The power of this link is apparent when we note that, unlike friends, often family members are on opposite sides of a political or social divide. Even radically different views do not usually keep them apart.

Strangers or Twins? Both. Aysha Lord *(left)* is a "genetic twin" to Peter Milburn *(right)*, a father of four who had a fatal blood cancer. He was saved by stem cells donated by a stranger — Aysha — whose cells were a perfect match.

Sometimes, however, adults avoid their blood relatives because they find them toxic — not because they disagree on politics but because their personal interactions are hostile. Such adults may become **fictive kin** in another family. They are introduced by a family member who says this person is "like a sister" or "my brother" and so on. Over time, the new family accepts them. They are not technically related (hence *fictive*), but they are treated like a family member (hence *kin*).

Fictive kin can be a lifeline for adults who are rejected by their original family (perhaps because of sexual orientation or gender identity) or are unable to visit family (perhaps because of prohibitive immigration policies), or who resist family practices (perhaps by stopping addiction, or by joining a religious group).

Fictive kin can be part of a community strategy to provide personal support. This has been documented among African Americans in the United States. When hostility and prejudice segregated and marginalized them, many African American neighbors became fictive kin. Adults were expected to guide and help each other, allowing survival and success (Glover et al., 2018).

The role of fictive kin reinforces a general theme: Adults benefit from kin, fictive or not.

fictive kin
People who become accepted as part of a family in which they are not genetically or legally members.

what have you learned?

1. What needs do long-term partners meet?
2. Why would people choose to live apart together?
3. How do same-sex marriages compare to heterosexual marriages?
4. What are the consequences of divorce?
5. How does a social convoy aid development?
6. What roles do friends play in a person's life?
7. What is the usual relationship between adult children and their parents?
8. Why do people have fictive kin?

Generativity: The Work of Adulthood

Adults satisfy their need to be generative in many ways, especially through parenthood, caregiving, and employment.

Parenthood

Erikson thought that generativity often became manifest in "establishing and guiding the next generation" (Erikson, 1993a, p. 267). Traditionally, that meant raising one's own biological offspring. Now millions of adults are raising stepchildren, foster children, or adopted (formally or not) children.

Parenthood is never easy, but it is particularly difficult if an adult still struggles with intimacy or identity needs. Marital happiness dips in the first year or two after a birth, because intimacy diminishes. Worse yet is having a baby as part of the search for identity — to prove manhood or womanhood to oneself.

It may be harder than ever to be a good parent. Currently, the culture emphasizes "intensive parenting," which puts the responsibility for a child's health and happiness on the parents, "with joyful, meaningful, and rewarding experiences interwoven with

frustrating, challenges and exhausting workloads of care" (Nomaguchi & Milkie, 2020, p. 201).

One outcome is that parenthood now bumps against gender norms. Many emerging adults believe in gender equality—that men and women are equally suited for employment, housework, and child care. But with birth, breast-feeding, and infant care, they tilt toward believing that women and men differ in their roles and abilities (Endendijk et al., 2018).

That may mean joyous acceptance, or ongoing resentment—for her if she feels stuck with more baby care and housework than she expected, and for him if he feels excluded from the mother–infant bond. Not always, of course, but these emotions arise from the day-to-day needs of an infant, not from cultural sexism.

We know this because the data came from a large study in the Netherlands, where gender equity is a national value. Nonetheless, when Dutch adults become parents, they tend to follow traditional gender roles (Khoudja & Fleischmann, 2018).

This gender division is found despite another fact: Fathers are more involved with child care than they were a few generations ago, and mothers are far more likely to be employed. This does not mean that mothers do less child care. Indeed, the data suggest that mothers are more intensely involved with each child than they were a few generations ago.

The reason for that shift is partly an ideological one. If intensive parenting is required, then both parents need to be more involved with their children than their own parents were. This is possible, despite employment of both parents, because families have fewer children and because appliances, take-out food, and paper diapers mean less housework.

When it comes to child care, however, the gender division of family labor remains (Frejka et al., 2018). Usually, mothers feed infants, schedule pediatric visits, plan birthday parties, arrange play dates, choose schools and after-school activities, and have deeper conversations with teenagers.

What has changed is rigid mother/father boundaries, prompting many to describe a "revolution" in women's roles, with each couple deciding what is best for their family. For example, in 2012, fathers provided primary child care and mothers were the chief wage earners in 8 percent of all U.S. families, almost triple the rate in 2004 (Young & Schieman, 2018).

Employed women not only earn more money, but also have more authority at work. Some are the boss, the doctor, the head of state. Nonetheless, old patterns persist, especially in family life, leading some feminists to say that the push toward gender equity is a "stalled revolution" (Chancer, 2019; Scarborough et al., 2019).

CHAPTER APP 13

Cozi Family Organizer

iOS:
https://tinyurl.com/y5cynkkk

ANDROID:
https://tinyurl.com/y4b4byu8

RELEVANT TOPIC:
Sharing family labor

The Cozi Family Organizer app helps users manage everyday family life with a shared calendar, reminders, to-do lists, and grocery list. This free, easy-to-use app can be used on most mobile devices and computers; a premium ad-free version with additional features is available for a yearly fee.

MOMO PRODUCTIONS/TAXI/GETTY IMAGES

MARKA/UNIVERSAL IMAGES GROUP/GETTY IMAGES

More Dad . . . and Mom
Worldwide, fathers are spending more time playing with their children — daughters as well as sons, as these two photos show. Does that mean that mothers spend less time with their children? No — the data show that mothers are spending more time as well.

OBSERVATION QUIZ
In what ways might these fathers differ from mothers? (see answer, page 425) ←

Men as well as women are affected by traditional patterns. For example, one father was the primary caregiver for his infant and 2-year-old but still wanted to earn a paycheck. He found part-time work (a school bus driver) that allowed his children to be with him. He said:

> In the last generation it's changed so much. . . . it's almost like you're on ice that's breaking up. That's how I felt. Like I was on ice breaking up. You don't really know what or where the father role is. You kind of have to define it for yourself. . . .
> I think that's what I've learned most from staying home with the kids. . . . Does it emasculate me that my wife is making more money?
>
> *[Geoff, quoted in Doucet, 2015, p. 235]*

Another father in the same study opened a day-care business for his own children and several others. Neither of these men felt comfortable being solely caregivers; both felt they should contribute financially.

No matter who does what, parenting is an ongoing challenge. Just when they figure out how to care for their infants, or preschoolers, or schoolchildren, those children grow older, presenting new dilemmas. Will the baby walk, the first-grader read, the adolescent avoid drugs? Each of those requires new actions by the parents: Strategies that work for 4-year-olds are met with rebellion if tried with 14-year-olds.

VIDEO: Interview with Jay Belsky explores how problematic parenting practices are transmitted (or not) from one generation to the next.

Both parents tend to reduce outside work or choose more flexible hours when raising children, but specifics depend on the age of the children and the gender of the parent. Mothers are more likely to scale back during infancy; fathers choose more flexible schedules when the children are in elementary school (Young & Schieman, 2018).

The COVID pandemic added stress to everyone, but especially to parents. One in four parents lost work, many became depressed or anxious, and virtually all experienced disruptions of schedules and routines (Tang et al., 2021).

Nonparents may imagine that the schoolchild's worst problem when the pandemic closed schools was lost instruction, but parents saw emotional stress and social isolation. One said, "bickering has become an everyday ordeal"; another that her child was "afraid to leave the house"; a third that the child "cries a lot" (Lee et al., 2021). Parenting a troubled child, 24/7, with no relief from teachers, friends, and grandparents doubled or tripled the rate of parental stress.

Even without COVID-19, during the child-rearing years, privacy and income rarely seem adequate, and difficulties arise, with shyness or aggression, with talking too much or too little, with reading or math, with being clumsy at sports or having illegible handwriting, and so on.

It is the nature of childhood that challenges come and go, so a second-grader with a problem might, with a different teacher or better friends, have a happy fourth-grade year. It is the nature of generativity that parents care intensely about the well-being of their children. Generativity, then, involves anxiety.

NONBIOLOGICAL PARENTS

The problems just cited arise no matter what the origin of parenthood, but nonbiological parenting adds more challenges. Adoptive parents may experience the best form of alternate parenthood, since their children are theirs for life. Moreover, adoptive children are much wanted, so the parents have chosen to provide the intensive care that children need.

Current adoptions are usually "open," which means that the birth parents decided that someone else would be a better parent, but they still want some connection to their child. The child knows about this arrangement, which makes it easier for everyone than the former "closed" adoption, when children and birth parents felt abandoned (Grotevant, 2020).

Strong parent–child attachments often develop, especially when children are adopted as infants. DSM-5 recognizes *reactive attachment disorder*, when children fail to form secure attachments. That can occur with any child, but the risk increases if a child experienced institutionalization or a series of placements before adoption (Vasquez & Stensland, 2016).

As you remember, adolescence—the time when teenagers seek their own identity—can stress any family. This stage is particularly problematic for adoptive families because normal conflicts in family relationships have an added stress (Neil & Beek, 2020). One college student who felt well loved and cared for by her adoptive parents explains:

> In attempts to upset my parents sometimes I would (foolishly) say that I wish I was given to another family, but I never really meant it. Still when I did meet my birth family, I could definitely tell we were related I fit in with them so well. I guess I have a very similar attitude and make the same faces as my birth mother! It really makes me consider nature to be very strong in personality.
>
> *[A., personal communication]*

TAMPA BAY TIMES/BRENDAN FITTERER/THE IMAGE WORKS

Joy from Generativity Six smiling members of this family from New Port Richey, Florida, are typical in one way and not in another. Unusual is that all four sisters are adopted. Typical is that the parents get great joy from their daughters, as is evident from their wide smiles.

Tensions increase if outsiders hold the mistaken notion that only biological parents are the "real" parents. Of course, no matter what the genetic or ethnic connection between parents and children, the real parents are those who provide generative care. Helping children develop pride in their own history is a challenge for every parent, adoptive or not.

Many adoptive parents who adopt either internationally or interethnically seek multiethnic family friends and teach their children about their heritage. On the other hand, there is no doubt that an adult's ability to adopt is affected by their income, nationality, and ethnicity, and that may be unfair to other adults (Marr et al., 2020).

THINK CRITICALLY: Can parents of one ethnic group teach adopted children of another ethnicity what they need to know?

STEPPARENTS

Generativity is also required for stepparents, who, unlike adoptive parents, did not seek parenthood. Moreover, the average new stepchild is 9 years old, already with habits, morals, and personality traits developed before the stepparent arrived.

New living arrangements are always disruptive for children (Goodnight et al., 2013). The effects are cumulative; emotions erupt in adolescence if not before, especially if the child is coping with a new school, loss of friends, or puberty. Stepchildren may intensify their attachment to their birth parents, which may upset the stepparent.

Added to that, stepchildren make parenting harder. They have higher rates than other children of illness, injury, or, if they are teenagers, pregnancy, addiction, and arrest. Those childish reactions to disruption are understandable; so is the resentment that stepparents feel.

Mothers usually remain attached to their biological children after separation, but fathers, biological or step, are closely connected only if the man earned that relationship when the children were young (van Houdt et al., 2020). This makes generatively more difficult for adult men.

Few adults—biological parents or not—can live up to the generative ideal, day after day. Some stepparents quit trying. Understandable but wrong for both child and parent. Hopefully, the new couple feels happy with each other, and the stepparent is sufficiently mature to react to hostility with patience. But, as one stepmother said:

> The dynamic is too crazy and you're trying as a, you know, as a stepmom I felt like I didn't want to overstep my bounds but yet I didn't want to seem like was aloof either. So it's really hard. It was really hard for me to find my place with the boys.
>
> *[quoted in Perry-Fraser & Fraser, 2018, p. 245]*

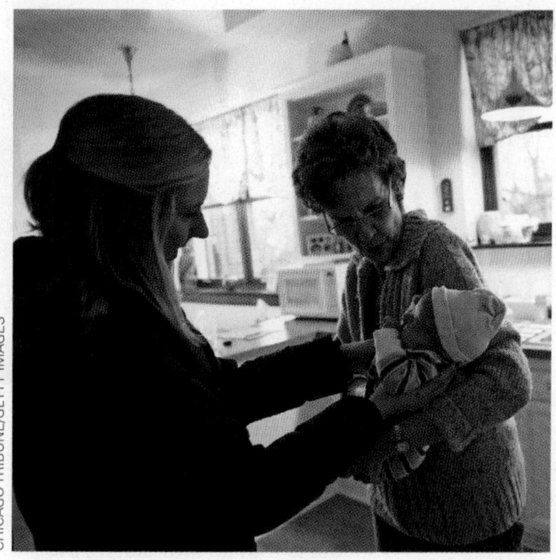
CHICAGO TRIBUNE/GETTY IMAGES

Here's Your Baby But only for a few weeks. More than 70 babies have spent days or weeks with Becky O'Connell until being united with their adoptive parents. As with baby Alex, shown here, the hardest part is giving them up — but, at age 64, Becky is unlikely to become a mother herself.

FOSTER PARENTS

Almost half a million U.S. children were officially in foster care in the United States in 2020, about half of them cared for by adults who were strangers to them, with most of the rest officially under the care of grandparents or other relatives. Many others are unofficially in foster care, because someone other than their biological parent has taken them in.

This is the most difficult form of generativity of all, partly because foster children typically have emotional and behavioral needs that require intense involvement and emotional maturity. The social context makes it worse, as their efforts and commitment are devalued by society and the children themselves.

Contrary to popular prejudice, adults become foster parents more often for psychosocial than financial reasons, part of the adult generativity impulse (Geiger et al., 2013). Official foster parents are paid, but they typically earn far less than a babysitter would, or than they themselves would in a conventional job.

Most children are in foster care for less than a year, as the goal is usually a reunion with the birth parent. Children may be moved back to the original family for reasons unrelated to the wishes, competence, or emotions of the foster parents or the children.

The average child entering the foster-care system is 6 years old (Child Welfare Information Gateway, 2018). Many spent their early years with their birth families and are attached to them. Such human bonding is normally beneficial, not only for the children but also for the adults.

However, if birth parents are so neglectful or abusive that their children are removed, the child's past insecure or disorganized attachment impedes acceptance of the foster parent. Most foster children have experienced long-standing maltreatment and have witnessed violence; they are understandably suspicious of any adult.

Given the realities of life for those half a million U.S. children in official foster care, and the millions more in other nations, it is sad but unsurprising that a review of longitudinal research concludes that many foster children develop serious problems, including less education, more arrests, and earlier death (Gypen et al., 2017). Generative adults needed!

Your knowledge of human development leads to recognition of another problem: Policies make it difficult for foster parents to be generative, because children are removed from their care for reasons that do not reflect the quality of attachment. There is occasional good news: When a child has been with a stable foster family for years, about half the time a healthy, mutual attachment develops (Joseph et al., 2014).

GRANDPARENTS

As already mentioned, the empty-nest stage of a marriage, when children have finally grown up and started independent lives, is often a happy time for parents. Grown children are more often a source of pride than of stress.

A new opportunity for generativity, as well as a new source of stress, occurs if grandchildren appear. Adults traditionally became grandparents at about age 40, but now, in developed nations, grandparenthood begins on average at about age 50. That shifts the grandparent role to later in adulthood, but advances in longevity means that most adults still have decades of active grandparenting (Margolis & Arpino, 2019).

Thus, most adults begin grandparenthood 15 years before the next stage of development, late adulthood, which begins at age 65. Most continue to be grandparents and sometimes great-grandparents for several decades, while they also look after members of the older generation, as discussed in detail in Chapter 15.

Grandparent generativity often has become a new challenge. Specifics depend on policies, customs, gender, past parenting, and income of both adult generations, but for every adult the generative impulse extends to caring for the youngest generation (Price et al., 2018).

Don't make the mistake of thinking that involved grandparents share a residence with their grandchildren. Only about 5 percent of all grandparents do so, and usually the child's mother lives there, too, doing most of the child care. Co-residence may signify poverty, not generativity, and may become problematic for all three generations (Masfety et al., 2019).

Regarding co-residence, one study surprised the researchers. They compared young African American mothers who lived with their mothers and those who did not.

JODI COBB/NATIONAL GEOGRAPHIC/GETTY IMAGES

Everybody Contributes A large four-generation family such as this one helps meet the human need for love and belonging, the middle level of Maslow's hierarchy. When social scientists trace who contributes what to whom, the results show that everyone does their part, but the flow is more down than up: Grandparents give more money and advice to younger generations than vice versa.

The scientists were not surprised that the grandparent generation did not fare as well as grandparents who lived nearby but not with their children. That had already been discovered and replicated. But given "the enthusiasm of policy-makers for three-generation households," the study authors expected that the younger generations would benefit.

Not so. The young women who had their own homes were less often depressed than those who lived with their mothers (Black et al., 2002). Their children also fared better, cognitively and emotionally, when they lived with their mothers but not their grandmothers.

The researchers suggested possible reasons. Perhaps conflicts arose when the mother and grandmother disagreed about child care, or perhaps the grandmothers disrupted mother–child attachment (Black et al., 2002). Income may be a factor: If the family could afford separate homes, then the children may have had advantages that those living with grandmothers did not have. (See A View from Science.)

Other research finds that a grandmother who is employed is more likely to retire early if she has major responsibility for her grandchildren (Timonen, 2018). Typically, the grandfather is also supportive, but marital conflict sometimes erupts because the grandmother seems more concerned about younger generations than about her husband. One grandmother, who said she needed to keep working so she would have a salary, reported:

> When my daughter divorced, they nearly lost the house to foreclosure, so I went on the loan and signed for them. But then again, they nearly foreclosed, so my husband and I bought it. . . . I have to make the payment on my own house and most of the payment on my daughter's house, and that is hard. . . . I am hoping to get that money back from our daughter, to quell my husband's sense that the kids are all just taking, and no one is ever giving back. He sometimes feels used and abused.
>
> *[quoted in Meyer, 2014, pp. 5–6]*

We should not focus only on the intergenerational problems. In every nation, adults who are grandparents usually enjoy helping their children and connecting with grandchildren. Some grandmothers are rhapsodic and spiritual about their experience. As one writes:

> Not until my grandson was born did I realize that babies are actually miniature angels assigned to break through our knee-jerk habits of resistance and to remind us that love is the real reason we're here.
>
> *[Golden, 2010, p. 125]*

A VIEW FROM SCIENCE

The Skipped-Generation Family

Some U.S. households (about 1 percent) are two-generation families because the middle generation is missing. That is a *skipped-generation family*, with all parenting work done by the grandparents.

Skipped-generation families require every ounce of generativity that grandparents can muster, often at the expense of their own health and happiness. This family type sometimes is designated officially to provide kinship care (true for one-third of the foster children), and it may include formal adoption by the grandparents.

In general, skipped-generation families have several strikes against them. Both the grandparents and the grandchildren are sad about the missing middle generation. In addition, difficult grandchildren (such as drug-affected infants and rebellious school-age boys) are more likely to live with grandparents (Hayslip & Smith, 2013). Many grandparents are resilient, but the challenges are real.

But before concluding that grandparents suffer when they are responsible for grandchildren, consider China, where millions of grandparents outside the urban areas become full-time caregivers because members of the middle generation have jobs in the cities and are unable to take children with them. In this way, Chinese culture and policy harms families, but, surprisingly, it does not seem to harm the elders.

The Chinese parents who are employed far from their natal home typically send money and visit once a year, on a national holiday. Studies are contradictory regarding the welfare of the children, but those grandparents seem to have *better* physical and psychological health (Baker & Silverstein, 2012; Chen et al., 2011) than grandparents who are not caregivers.

Better health does not necessarily mean happiness, however. A recent study of skipped-generation families in China found that grandparents under age 70 who live with their grandchildren without the children's parents were less happy overall. Those over age 70 were happier—contrary to the expectation of the researchers (Wen et al., 2019).

This suggests that the social context is crucial: If grandparents are supported and appreciated by their children and the community, a skipped-generation family may benefit the grandparents. Much depends on attitudes, not simply caregiving itself.

Caregiving

Child care is the most common form of generativity for adults, but caregiving can and does occur in many other ways as well. Indeed, "life begins with care and ends with care" (Talley & Montgomery, 2013, p. 3). Some caregiving requires meeting physical needs—feeding, cleaning, and so on—but much of it involves fulfilling psychological needs. Caregiving is part of generative adulthood.

KINKEEPERS

kinkeeper
Someone who becomes the gatherer and communications hub for their family.

sandwich generation
The generation of middle-aged people who are supposedly "squeezed" by the needs of the younger and older members of their families.

A prime example of caregiving is the **kinkeeper**, who gathers all the generations for holidays; spreads the word about illness, relocation, or accomplishments; and reminds family members of one another's birthdays and anniversaries.

Kinkeepers also chronicle the family's history and thereby connect family members, adding to satisfaction and belonging for all family members (Hendry & Ledbetter, 2017). Middle-aged adults allow families and societies "to engage and value the assets found in every generation" (Butts, 2017, p. vi). Mutual caregiving and shared information strengthen family bonds; wise kinkeepers keep those intergenerational channels open; everyone is generative (Hendry & Ledbetter, 2017).

Middle-aged adults have been called the **sandwich generation**, a term that evokes an image of a layer of filling pressed between two slices of bread. This analogy suggests that the middle generation is squeezed because they are expected to support their parents and their growing children. This sandwich metaphor is vivid but misleading (Gonyea, 2013).

Longitudinal data found "relatively few cases where middle aged adults were in a 'sandwich generation' of simultaneously providing care for aging parents and

children younger than 15" (Fingerman et al., 2012d, p. 200). Family members across the generations are especially significant for some adults, but that is more voluntary than obligatory. Moreover, caregiving is mutual, taking many forms.

Far from being squeezed, middle-aged adults who provide some financial and emotional help to their adult children are *less* likely to be depressed than those adults whose children no longer relate to them. The research finds that family members continue to care for each other, less as a matter of obligation but more as a result of valued connections.

Emerging adults, depicted as squeezing their parents, often help their parents understand music, media, fashion, and technology—setting up their smartphones, sending digital photos, fixing computer glitches. They also are more cognizant of nutritional and medical discoveries and guidelines.

Caregiving on the other side of the supposed sandwich, from middle-aged adults to their older parents, is typically much less demanding than the metaphor implies. Most members of the over-60 generation are quite independent.

Financial support is more likely to flow from the older generation to their middle-aged children than vice versa. If full-time elder care is needed, a spouse, another older person, or a paid nurse is the usual caregiver, not an adult child.

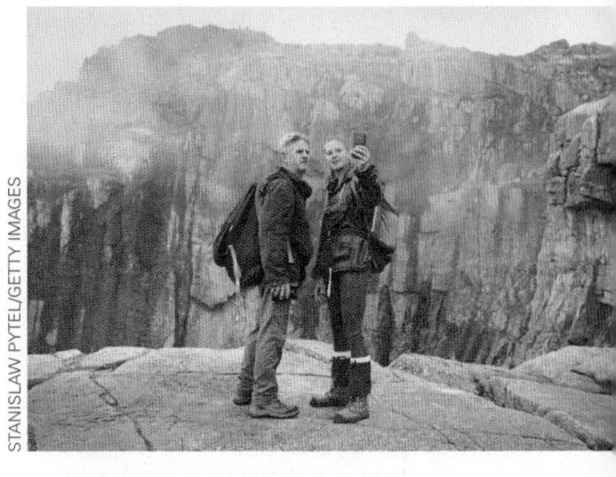

STANISLAW PYTEL/GETTY IMAGES

A Peak Experience For many men, the best part of fatherhood is when their children become old enough to share interest in world events, sports, or, as shown here, climbing a mountain in Norway.

OBSERVATION QUIZ

Father and daughter are each doing something that typifies their care for one another. What is each of them doing? (see answer, page 425) ↑

Employment

Besides parenthood and caregiving, the other major avenue for generativity is employment. Extensive research describes many aspects of employment and economic development. Here we consider only how employment affects human development.

GENERATIVITY AND WORK

As is evident from many terms and phrases (achievement motivation, instrumental needs, Erikson's *generativity*, Maslow's *success* and *esteem*), many developmentalists believe work is central to healthy adulthood. Some work is unpaid, already discussed in the previous pages on parenthood and caregiving. Other work is voluntary, a topic discussed in Chapter 15.

Here we focus on work for pay. Employment allows people to:

- use their personal skills;
- express their creative energy;
- aid and advise coworkers, as mentor or friend;
- support the education and health of their families;
- contribute to the community by providing goods or services; and
- develop pride in themselves.

Psychologists distinguish the **extrinsic rewards of work** (benefits such as salary, health insurance, and pension) from the **intrinsic rewards of work** (personal gratification). Generativity is intrinsic.

extrinsic rewards of work The tangible benefits, usually in salary, insurance, pension, and status, that come with employment.

intrinsic rewards of work The personal gratifications, such as pleasure in a job well done or friendships with coworkers, that accompany employment.

These two types of rewards may be negatively correlated, if employers or labor unions increase pay *instead of* increasing worker satisfaction (Kuvaas et al., 2017). That is a mistake, as intrinsic rewards are crucial for productivity and stability.

Priorities may change over the years of adulthood. Prospective young workers consider salary and hours. As time goes on, the intrinsic rewards of work, especially relationships with coworkers and the culture of the workplace, become more important (Inceoglu et al., 2012).

That may be one reason that older employees are, on average, less often absent or late, and less likely to quit (Rau & Adams, 2014). Seniority makes it more likely that they can satisfy their intrinsic needs, befriending coworkers and mentoring new ones. That gains them status and an outlet for generativity—both intrinsic (Shavit & Carstensen, 2019).

Surprisingly, salary (whether a person earns $40,000 or $100,000 or even $1,000,000 a year) matters less for job satisfaction than how pay compares with others in their profession or neighborhood, or with their own salary years earlier.

This is not to say that income doesn't matter. As often stressed in this book, low SES correlates with poor health, inadequate education, destructive living conditions, and premature death. Health insurance is a driving force in the current U.S. economy. But once basic needs are met (which varies by family circumstances, community characteristics, and government policies), income matters less than people assume.

Instead, resentment about work arises not directly from wages but from perception of fairness. This is not simple: Base salaries, bonuses, and promotions all affect job satisfaction (Trost, 2020).

This explains a puzzle. Most Americans know that corporate heads are paid a hundred times more per year than the lowest employee. However, relatively few consider this a major problem (Brooks & Manza, 2013; Mijs, 2019). Why?

Executives themselves want far more money than they need—they compare themselves with other corporate heads. And people at the bottom believe that social mobility is possible—that they themselves will be able to earn more (Davidai & Gilovich, 2015).

psychological contract
The implicit understanding of the relationship between employer and employee that includes procedures to resolve conflict and expectations for the interaction between supervisors and workers.

A related puzzle is that, compared to men, women earn less but are more satisfied with their jobs. This is called the *paradox of the contented female worker*, first recognized over two decades ago (Clark, 1997; Crosby, 1982).

One explanation is that women value nonmonetary rewards, seeking jobs high in generativity, such as nursing and teaching. They become distressed only if men do the same work as they do for more money (Valet, 2018).

THE PSYCHOLOGICAL CONTRACT

Developmentalists now call attention to the **psychological contract**, which is the implicit understanding of the relationship between employer and the employee. This is beyond the actual contract, which spells out duties, hours, and so on. Just as every family has rules, rituals, and routines, and every school has a hidden agenda, every workplace has a culture. The psychological contract is part of that.

The psychological contract includes procedures to resolve conflict, as well as expectations for the interaction between supervisors and workers (Shen et al., 2019; van Dijke et al., 2018). Some supervisors respect individual differences and needs; others are more rigid regarding, for instance, time, dress, and activity.

This contract develops over time. The first-year experiences of a new employee is crucial, and so is the first year after restructuring, merging, or a new supervisor. One of the biggest problems is implicit understanding of what training is forthcoming and who will provide it (Woodrow & Guest, 2020).

In general, fair promotions, new learning, and relationships with other workers are crucial for the psychological contract. The contract is between the employer and the employee: Sometimes the employee breeches the contract, sometimes the employer does. In both cases, factors beyond the formal agreements matter, and communication is crucial to prevent resentment, lost efficiency, and employees who quit or are fired (DiFonzo et al., 2020).

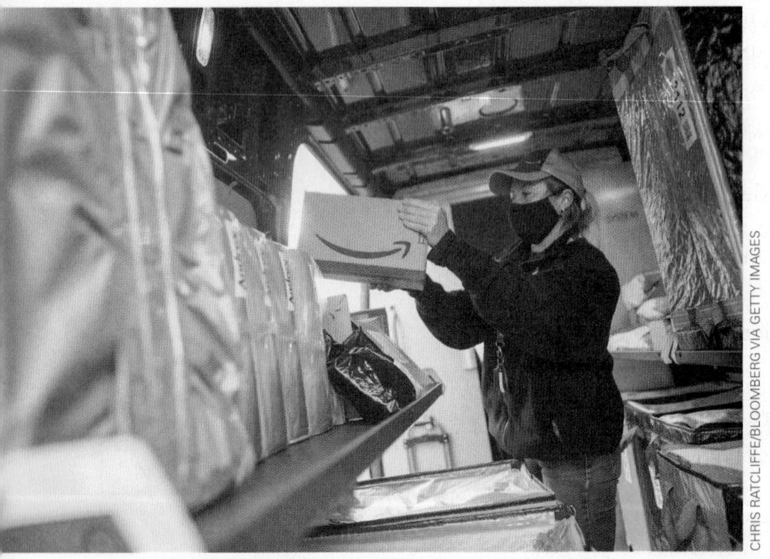
CHRIS RATCLIFFE/BLOOMBERG VIA GETTY IMAGES

What Is Lost? No, not a package. The driver in an Amazon delivery van keeps careful track of where each order should be delivered. Especially with the COVID pandemic (this photo was taken in England in 2020), as more purchases are made online, the human interaction between customer and clerk is lost.

This reiterates a lesson in many aspects of adult psychosocial development. Communication, such as setting parameters when adult children live with their parents, or improving cooperation between romantic partners, or understanding when grandparents should be involved and when they should stay away, is crucial for psychosocial health.

WORK SCHEDULES

Current business practices are often set with profit as the only goal, without regard for the family lives of the employees. We could discuss many of these: factory closings, pension set asides, health benefits, automatization. An objective discussion would highlight costs and benefits, evident in every policy. However here we focus on only one practice, schedule variations, which may affect families in ways that few employers realize.

The standard workweek is 9 A.M. to 5 P.M., Monday through Friday—a schedule that is increasingly unusual. In the United States, about half of all employees have nonstandard schedules. Retail services (online and in-store) are increasingly available 24/7, which requires night and weekend work. Many other parts of the economy (hospitals, police, hotels, restaurants, transportation) need employees before 9 A.M. or after 5 P.M.

In addition, many employees work part time, or seasonally, or hourly, or independently, unlike the 40-hour, 9 to 5, schedule. Even worse for family life may be unpredictability, when schedules change from day to day.

In a study of workers with young children in one California town (Emeryville, near San Francisco), 87 percent experienced an unpredicted schedule change. Sometimes they were told the day before that they were not needed on a particular day; sometimes they were asked to work when they thought they would be home; sometimes they were told not to work when they had already expected to earn money on a particular day (Ananat & Gassman-Pines, 2021).

Varied schedules of any sort upset the body rhythms of adults, making them more vulnerable to physical illness as well as to emotional problems. Hundreds of studies confirm that (Cho, 2018; Schneider & Harknett, 2019). All mammals depend on circadian rhythm. When a person has a nonstandard schedule, or when each family member has nonoverlapping schedules, that undercuts family function and adult social interactions.

Specific data find that, perhaps because of disrupted sleep, shift workers have higher rates of obesity, illness, and death. One detail: Women more often develop breast cancer if their work hours vary (Wegrzyn et al., 2017). Night work itself increases the risk of breast cancer (Cordina-Duverger et al., 2018). Rotating schedules are worse than steady night work, with restful sleep particularly elusive (Kecklund & Axelsson, 2016).

Beyond health, the impact of varying schedules on family life is a major concern for developmentalists (Cho, 2018). Those who are most likely to have mandatory nonstandard schedules are parents of young children, exactly the people who need regular schedules.

THINK CRITICALLY: Is the connection between employment and developmental health cause or correlation?

The focus is often on working mothers, but weekend work, especially with mandatory overtime, is also difficult for father–child relationships, because "normal rhythms of family life are impinged upon by irregular schedules" (Hook, 2012, p. 631). Couples who have less time together are more likely to divorce.

In theory, one solution might be part-time work or self-employment. But reality does not conform to the theory. In many nations, part-time work is underpaid and without benefits. Thus, workers avoid part-time employment if they can, again making a choice that inadvertently undercuts their emotional well-being and family life.

Self-employment often means more work for less money (Lange, 2012; Millán et al., 2013). Remember the paradox of the contented female worker? This holds true for self-employment as well. Women who are their own boss tend to work harder for less money, but be relatively happy doing so (Bender & Roche, 2016). Is that because flexibility of such work is particularly important to women, who more often are family caregivers?

Another scheduling issue that may harm families is the rise of temporary employees, with some companies (including colleges) having more temporary employees than permanent ones. This makes sense for the employers: It provides a buffer against another recession, and it is cheaper to hire workers without full benefits. However, it does not help workers.

Job uncertainty, which underlies many schedule uncertainties, increases job dissatisfaction, which increases family stress (Dawson et al., 2017). Temporary workers themselves have uncertain employment futures, of course, but their presence may affect the permanent workers as well (Akkerman et al., 2020). For this, as well as for other aspects of the work culture, much depends on the hidden elements of the psychological contract.

In this, as in many aspects of scheduling, the needs of employers and employees conflict. Are work teams that include permanent and temporary workers less effective than those that are less blended? The answer, not surprisingly, it that it depends.

What about work groups that include gender, ethnic, and religious diversity? In some teams, a clear understanding of roles and goals makes differences welcomed, because each person's contribution benefits the group (Clinton et al., 2020). This raises a larger issue that has captured the attention of many psychologists: the balance between employee diversity and productivity, especially when teams of people work together. See Opposing Perspectives.

OPPOSING PERSPECTIVES

Teamwork

One dilemma for employers is how to organize employees into groups, or departments, or teams. Should teams be composed of people who are similar in age, gender, ethnicity, background, and personality? Or is diversity best?

A well-functioning team is a matter of life and death in hospitals, or in the military, or in space exploration. To pick an extreme example, NASA is preparing for a mission to Mars that will send four to six people in a small space for three years, with times of intense work followed by no work at all. The team will confront unknown dangers, and sometimes communication from Earth will be impossible (Driskell et al., 2018). Should they seek gender, ethnic, and age diversity? Or would the team function better if they were all White adult men in their 30s?

This question is not hypothetical. The Institute of Medicine (2000) published a report titled *To Err Is Human* that attributed 44,000 U.S. deaths each year to medical errors, many of which could have been avoided if all the medical professionals worked together well. Similarly, studies of airplane crashes often find misunderstandings and misinterpretations among people who needed to work together.

Is diversity an aid or an impediment for a team? Sometimes "racioethnic diversity was related to increased conflict, and decreased trust" (Bell et al., 2018, p. 352). Nonetheless, "the real value of teamwork and collaboration lies in the ability to draw from diverse perspectives and expertise to solve complex problems" (Thayer et al., 2018, p. 363).

Trust is crucial for the three essential parts of a good team: cooperation, coordination, and communication (Salas et al., 2018). Microaggressions may be not be recognized by one person but may be disturbing to another: That reduces cooperation. Effective teams include mutual help, but cultural differences in eye contact, humor, body position, and so on lead to mistrust. For instance, is averted eye contact evidence of dishonesty or respect? Your answer depends on your culture.

Should trust be enhanced by comprising teams of like-minded people, who readily understand each other? That is easiest, but not best. Ideally, each person brings a unique contribution to the group; interdependent team members

may complement each other, making the team greater than the sum of the individuals.

To pick an easy example, doctors want nurses to give prescribed medicine at the proper dose and time. Diversity makes this harder: Picture a young, Black female nurse questioning an older, White, male doctor, and you can see the problem.

Yet nurses need to raise questions, which is more likely when the nurse's perspective is unlike the doctor's. Similar dilemmas can arise with every team. It is crucial that both the nurse and the doctor trust the other: sometimes one is right, sometimes the other is.

The overall conclusion is that diversity may benefit the final product but that simply putting diverse people together does not insure those benefits. How can a work team function well? Psychologists have three suggestions.

1. Help team members get past superficial differences (ethnicity, gender, age) to recognize their common humanity. Team-building might begin with talk about family, pets, or details of daily life, or with stress-free interactions in games, jokes, exercises.
2. Choose team members whose personality traits encourage team functioning. Three of the Big Five (conscientiousness, extraversion, and agreeableness) are needed, yet a team in which everyone is high in these traits is handicapped. Agreeableness, for instance, helps everyone get along, but groups need some disagreement to function best.
3. Have a clear and measurable goal, explained well. When the team sees the team's progress, differences fade.

To help you understand this, consider your college education. Have you learned when teachers or classmates express ideas from a perspective that is unlike yours?

THE PSYCHOLOGICAL COST OF UNEMPLOYMENT

For adults of any age, unemployment—especially if it lasts more than a few weeks—is destructive of mental and physical health. Generative needs are unmet, which increases the rate of domestic abuse, substance use disorder, depression, and many other social and mental health problems (Compton et al., 2014; Wanberg, 2012). Uncertainty about future income and work adds to family stress (Schneider et al., 2017).

Especially for Entrepreneurs Suppose you are starting a business. In what ways would middle-aged adults be helpful to you? (see response, page 425)

A meta-analysis of research on eight stressful events found that losing a job was even worse for mental health than the death of a parent. The stress of unemployment lingered after finding a job (Luhmann et al., 2012). Unemployment is worse for physical health as well, increasing the rate of serious illness, drug addiction, and deaths of despair (Case & Deaton, 2020).

The harm from unemployment depends partly on how old a person is. With the past recession and with COVID-19, jobs were most scarce for emerging adults, especially if they were *NEET (not in education, employment, or training)*. Because attitudes about work are established in early adulthood, lack of a job in early adulthood may harm a cohort lifelong, a "grave concern" (Goldman-Mellor et al., 2016, p. 202).

If young college graduates cannot find a job that matches their education and ambition, they may become depressed, drug addicted (especially to marijuana), and despairing. The gap between hope and reality hits hard.

In the twenty-first century, many young adults have found work in the *gig economy*, which includes all of the temporary, episodic, or independent jobs that do not have an hourly wage or health benefits (see Figure 13.3). They drive cars for hire, tutor children, sell items online, act as social media "influencers," and much more. All of these jobs depend on other people having disposable income, so opportunities disappeared with the COVID pandemic.

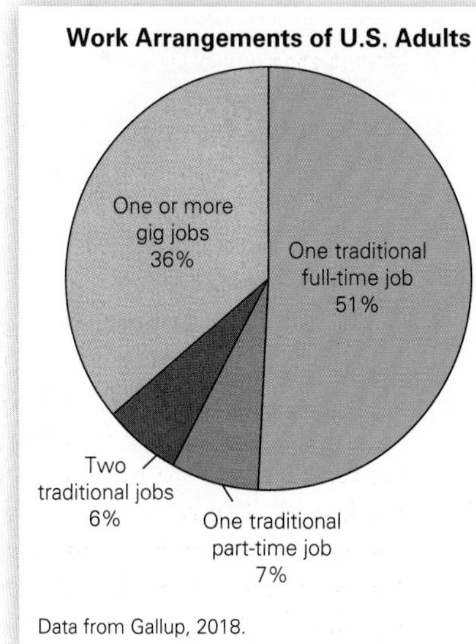

FIGURE 13.3 It Might Be Worse Only half of all U.S. workers have traditional, steady jobs. The other half usually do not have medical or pension benefits, which seems okay at age 25 but disastrous by age 60. How could it be worse? Millions of adults want jobs but are unable to find them.

Another group that may be particularly harmed by job loss are slightly older adults, if they have families of their own, with partners and dependent children. Job loss causes a "cascade" of family stresses, with trouble reverberating within the family (McKee-Ryan & Maitoza, 2018). For developmentalists, the effects on children, and on nonworking adults, are among the unseen costs of one employee losing a job.

For example, sudden loss of work makes parents more stressed. Child-care arrangements change, so children fight more and comply less, and parents punish more. Everyone worries more and sleeps less, so children fall asleep in school and teachers ask parents to come in, which adds parental stress. Family meals become erratic, with less nutrition and less food, causing hunger, obesity, and health problems in everyone, ignored because medical insurance is gone.

Thus, unemployment can turn a happy, supportive family into a sad and destructive one. Relatives and friends are a buffer against the mental health strain of losing a job, but that support is reduced when it is needed most (Crowe & Butterworth, 2016; McKee-Ryan & Maitoza, 2018).

All these difficulties may be magnified for immigrants, who, in 2016, were about 15 percent of the U.S. workforce and 22 percent of the workforce in Canada. They are first to be fired, and they are excluded from many public benefits. They often depend on other immigrants for housing, work, religion, and social connections (thus for their intimacy and generativity needs), but many are from cultures where an extensive extended family buffers against poverty. Often their relatives are unable to join them, and thus cannot provide emotional support.

The last group to consider are middle-aged adults, age 50 or so. Job loss is destructive of their generativity in ways unlike for younger adults for three reasons:

1. Seniority brings higher salaries, more respect, and greater expertise; losing a job is particularly painful, and similar work is impossible to find, not only because of salary but also because new work may require skills that they never learned.
2. Workers believe that age discrimination is widespread. To the extent that is true, finding new work is harder, with stereotype threat adding to the problem. If a job-seeker believes that their age makes new work less likely, that undercuts successful job searching.
3. In some U.S. states (Hawaii, Nevada, California), unemployment is three times that in others (Nebraska, South Dakota). Specifics rates change year by year, but people have a much better chance of finding a job in some places than others. Thus, relocation may improve job prospects. The older a worker is, the harder it is to move.

From a developmental and family perspective, this last factor is crucial. Imagine that you are a 50-year-old who has always lived in Hawaii, and your employer goes out of business. You try to find work, but no one hires you, partly because unemployment in Hawaii in 2019 is highest in the nation. Would you move 2,000 miles to Montana, where the unemployment rate is less than half that of Hawaii?

If you had been unemployed for months, were in deep debt, and your family was hungry, you might apply online and find a job in Butte, where, among the national firms you know, online posts in 2021 said that CVS needed a shift supervisor, FedEx needed a driver, GE Aviation needed a human resources staff person.

But remember that work is more than a paycheck. Leaving friends, community, familiar climate, and local culture is costly, and your new neighbors might look at you with suspicion. If you got a job in Montana, would your family also leave their homes, jobs, schools, places of worship, relatives, and friends to move with you?

If not, you would be deprived of social support. But if they did, their food and housing would be expensive, their schools overcrowded, and their lives lonely. What are the implications of another fact, that the suicide rate in Montana is the highest in the nation?

Do not focus too much here on Hawaii and Montana: State-by-state unemployment and suicide rates change year by year. However, remember the general point, that job openings fluctuate, and job seekers have much better success in some places than others. But a happy and healthy life requires much more than a job.

Work/Family Balance

A major concern for developmentalists is sometimes called *work/life balance*, the idea that employment demands should be limited to protect the rest of life. Here we refer to *work/family balance*, since intimacy and generativity needs are met by both work and family.

A developmental perspective begins with historical changes. A century ago, work/family balance was achieved by men having jobs and women working at home, so that a husband/father could come home from a hard day at work, convinced that his earnings were his contribution to his family. He could relax while the wife/mother, who took care of the house and children all day, got dinner ready.

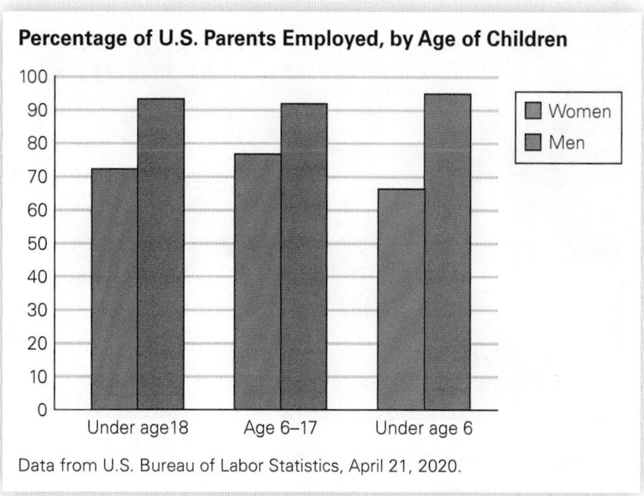

FIGURE 13.4 2019, 2020, 2022? The COVID-19 pandemic meant more children at home, and the number of mothers not employed rose three times as fast as the number of fathers. The question is whether there is a rebound in 2022, or if the numbers show long-term effects. Hypothesize, and then find the data.

Toward the end of the twentieth century, the research as well as the adults themselves realized that that this traditional balance of roles restricted both parents. Many stay-at-home mothers were depressed; many fathers felt excluded from their children.

These problems came to the surface in the divorce wave of the 1980s in the United States, when many wives wanted their independence and many fathers were distressed that their interactions with their children were several restricted, even though they were required to pay alimony child support. The current movement toward joint custody is welcomed by most researchers who saw the problems with the old model. To help adults be generative, mothers usually have jobs (see Figure 13.4), and fathers spend more time providing child care.

No single pattern is best for every family. Instead, each set of parents determines their own work/family balance. This was evident when employed parents were asked what would they do if their child was sick. The traditional mother/caretaker assumption was far from universal; sometimes they said that the father would stay home, sometimes another relative would be called (Cluley & Hecht, 2020).

The same flexibility occurred when the COVID pandemic meant that children had to learn from home. Each family figured out how that should happen. The struggle between obligations of work and parenting were by far the most common problem reported in one study of more than 100 parents (mostly mothers) in Wisconsin (Garbe et al., 2020).

Again, mothers were not automatically in charge. Some of the older children themselves were responsible; sometimes fathers, paid caregivers, neighbors, other relatives were called. At first, many families were themselves thrown back to the traditional gender model. After a month of remote learning, one mother explained:

> The stresses I feel as a wife and mother who works (ordinarily) outside the home. . . . this is absolute hell for me. I wake up every day and dread what awaits me. I can't sleep at night, even though I am desperately tired. I don't know how I'll get through this. I know I must, but I am beyond exhausted.
>
> *[quoted in Garbe et al., 2020, p. 56]*

That mother gathered other resources (family and paid helpers) to restore some balance, acknowledging that she was fortunate that her circumstances allowed that. Other research finds that mothers and fathers with low income found balancing particularly hard. One reason is that, especially among parents who are people of color, the usual helpers—grandparents—were among the most vulnerable to death from COVID-19.

For parents of every ethnicity, throughout the twenty-first century, new compromises, trade-offs, and selective optimization with compensation may be essential to finding an appropriate work/family balance. Policies (such as maternity and paternity leave when a new baby arrives or a child is sick) may help, but no nation prioritizes

FILIPPOBACCI/E+/GETTY IMAGES

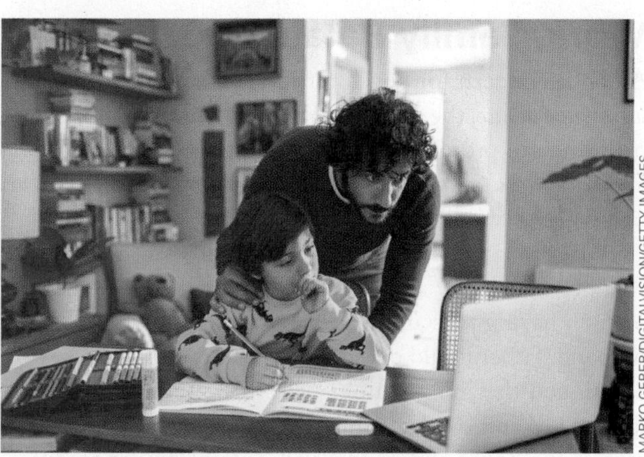
MARKO GEBER/DIGITALVISION/GETTY IMAGES

Remote Learning Even the most devoted parents cannot provide the individualized instruction and social learning of good schools. Specifics depend on the age of the child: The mother in Italy *(left)* needs to monitor her teenager, and the father in Serbia *(right)* needs to guide each step of his 6-year-old. These children are fortunate: Many of the world's children do not have computers, internet, or parents who can provide personal attention.

balancing employment and family life at every age (Ollo-Lopez & Goñi-Legaz, 2017). Usually the task of finding that balance rests with individuals.

DATA CONNECTIONS: Stress in Adulthood: Balancing Family and Career examines how well parents who are employed say they balance their careers with their family responsibilities.  Achieve

Conclusion

As evident in these two chapters, adulthood is filled with opportunities and challenges. Adults choose their mates, their locations, and their lifestyles to express their personality. Extroverts surround themselves with many social activities, and introverts choose a quieter but no less rewarding life.

Adults have many ways to meet their intimacy needs, with partners of the same or other sex, marriage or cohabiting, friends and family, parents or grown children. Ideally, they find some combination of work/family balance that results in solid social support.

Similarly, generativity can focus on raising children, caring for others, or satisfying work, again with more choices and flexibility than in past decades.

In some ways, then, modern life allows adults to "have it all," to combine family and work in such a way that all needs are satisfied at once. However, some very articulate observers suggest that "having it all" is an illusion or, at best, a mistaken ideal achievable only by the very rich and very talented (Slaughter, 2012; Sotomayor, 2014).

Compromises, trade-offs, and selective optimization with compensation may be essential to finding an appropriate work/family balance. Both halves of these two sources of generativity can bring joy, but both can bring stress—and often do. In general, adults—mates, family, and friends—help each other, balancing intimacy and generativity needs.

Because personality is both enduring and variable, opinions about the impact of modern life reflect personality as well as objective research. Some people are optimists—high in extroversion and agreeableness—and they tend to believe that adulthood is better now than it used to be.

Others are pessimists—high in neuroticism and low in openness—and they are likely to conclude that adults were better off before the rise of cohabitation, LAT, divorce, and economic stress. They may laud the time when most people married and stayed married, raising children on the man's steady salary from his 9-to-5 job with one stable employer.

Data could be used to support both perspectives. For instance, in the United States, compared to the 1980s, crime is down, divorce is lower, and teen births are

FAMILY CONNECTIONS

There are many ways to depict family living arrangements, and all of them lead to the same conclusions. Generally, family members remain connected to each other lifelong. Burdensome caregiving is not the norm.

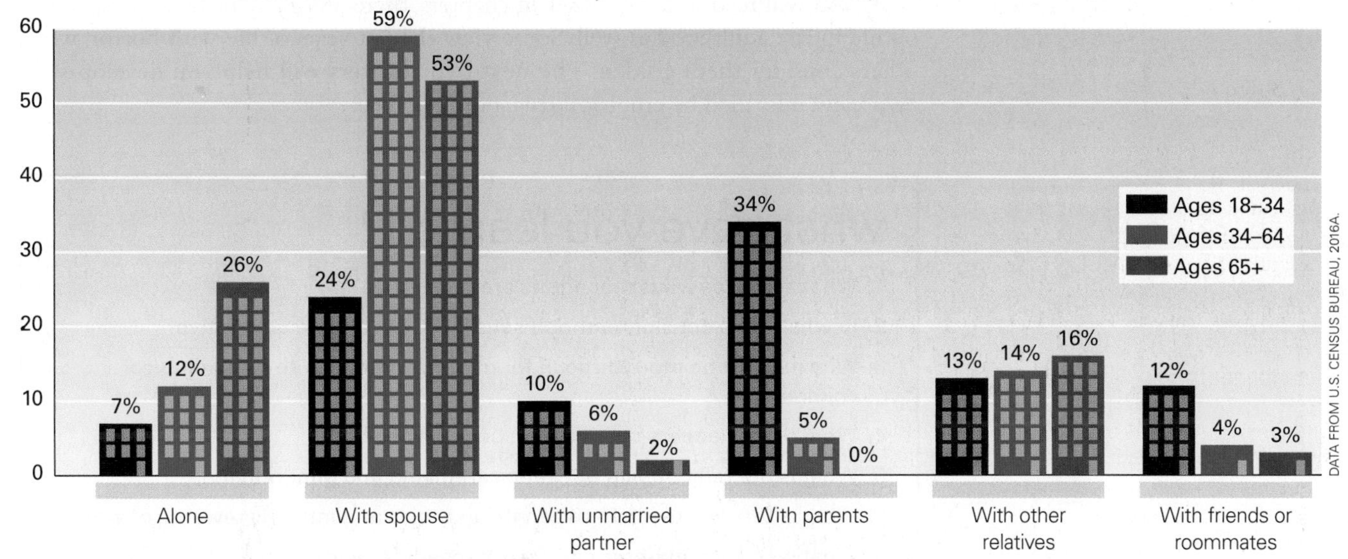

Most families have only one generation of adults, but when two generations are present, parents are more often helping adult children than the reverse.

U.S. FAMILIES WITH ONLY ONE GENERATION OF ADULTS (OVER AGE 18)

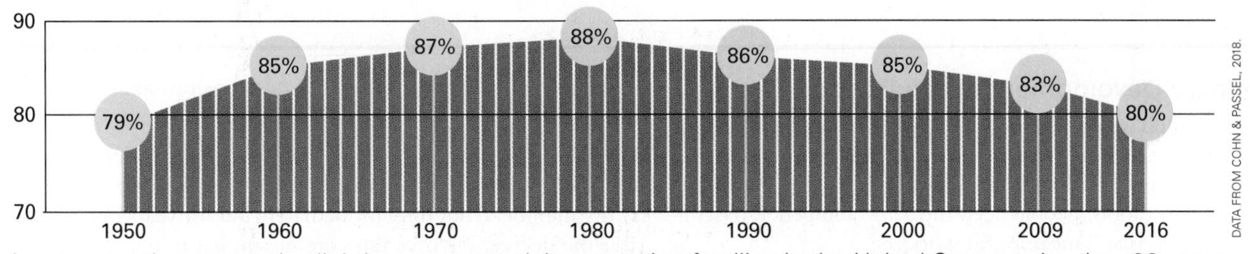

As you see, there are only slightly more two-adult generation families in the United States today than 30 years ago. What *has* changed, however, is that those extra adults are usually adult children, not aged parents. What percentage of adults live with other generations of adults over age 18?

ADULTS LIVING WITH OTHER GENERATIONS

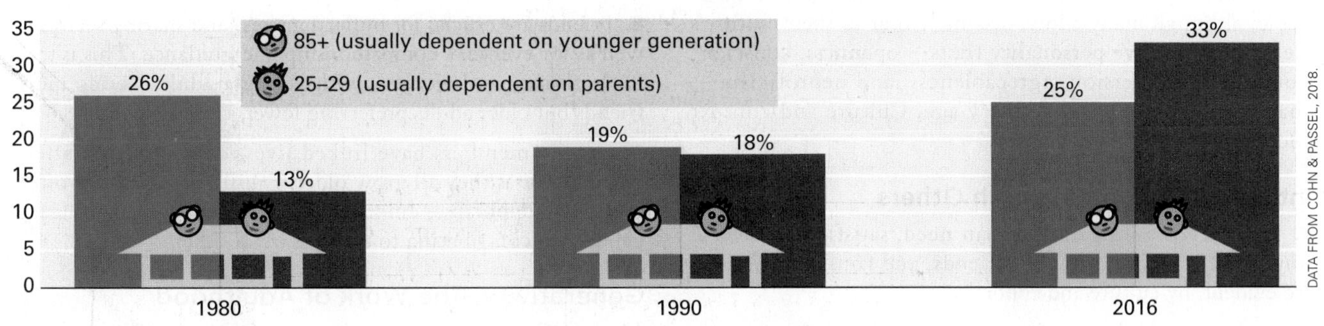

Currently about one-fourth of younger adults and about one-third of the oldest-old are living with the middle generation. Thus, despite the hype of intergenerational living, this is not the norm.

much less frequent (life is better). However, the gap between rich and poor is increasing, as is the frequency of climate-related disasters (life is worse). Fewer people are marrying, and fewer children are born: Is that evidence for improved adulthood or the opposite?

Every adult benefits from friends and family, caregiving responsibilities, and satisfying work. Whether this is easier or more difficult at this historical moment is debatable.

As you will read in the final set of chapters, there are many possible perspectives on life in late adulthood as well. Some view the last years of life with horror, while others consider them golden. The next two chapters will help you develop your own view, informed by empirical data, not prejudice.

what have you learned?

1. What are three ways that adults are generative?
2. In what ways does parenthood satisfy the need to be generative?
3. Why might it be more difficult for parents to bond with nonbiological children?
4. What do kinkeepers do, and who becomes one?
5. What is the relationship between caregiving and generativity?
6. What is the difference between the extrinsic and intrinsic rewards of work?
7. What problems might occur if work schedules vary?
8. Who is most harmed by unemployment?

SUMMARY

Personality Development in Adulthood

1. Erikson emphasized that people at every stage of life are influenced by their social context. The adulthood stages are much less age-based than the childhood stages because throughout adulthood, people need intimacy and generativity (social connections and meaningful work).

2. Maslow and other humanists believe that everyone has the same basic needs, first for survival and safety, and then for love and respect. Finally, people can be truly themselves, becoming self-actualized.

3. Personality traits over the years of adulthood are quite stable, although many adults become closer to their culture's ideal. The Big Five personality traits—openness, conscientiousness, extroversion, agreeableness, and neuroticism—characterize personality at every age. Culture and context affect everyone.

Intimacy: Connecting with Others

4. Intimacy is a universal human need, satisfied in diverse ways with romantic partners, friends, and family. Variations are evident, by culture and cohort.

5. Marriage is no longer the only way to establish a romantic partnership. Although societies benefit if people marry and stay married, many adults prefer cohabitation or living apart together. Same-sex and other-sex relationships are similar in most ways.

6. Divorce sometimes may be the best end for a conflicted relationship, but divorce is difficult for both partners and their family members, not only immediately but for years before and after the decree. Divorce rates are down, because fewer young adults marry.

7. Remarriage is common, especially for men. This solves some of the problems (particularly financial and social) of divorced adults, but the success of second marriages varies. Children add complications.

8. Friends are crucial for buffering stress and sharing secrets as well as for everyday companionship and guidance. This is true for both men and women, with younger adults having more friends but older adults preferring fewer, closer friends.

9. Family members have linked lives, continuing to affect one another as they all grow older. Family members are often mutually supportive, emotionally and financially, with each generation contributing to the welfare of others.

Generativity: The Work of Adulthood

10. Adults seek to be generative, successful, achieving, instrumental—all words used to describe a major psychosocial need that each adult meets in their own ways.

11. Parenthood is a common expression of generativity. Wanted and planned-for biological children pose challenges, and other forms of parenthood may be even harder. Adoptive children, stepchildren, and especially foster children bring additional stresses.

12. Caregiving is more likely to flow from the older generations to the younger ones, so the "sandwich generation" metaphor is misleading. Many families have a kinkeeper, who aids generativity within the family.

13. Employment brings many rewards to adults, including intrinsic benefits such as pride and friendship. Changes in employment patterns—job switches, shift work, and the diversity of fellow workers—affect other aspects of adult development. Unemployment is particularly difficult for self-esteem, and it impacts everyone in the family.

14. Balancing work and family life, personal needs, and social involvement is a major task for adults. This is true for men as well as women, since both now function in both spheres.

15. Combining work demands, caregiving requirements, intimacy, and generativity is not easy; consequences are mixed. Some adults benefit from new patterns within the labor market and in the overall culture; others find that a happy balance is difficult.

KEY TERMS

intimacy versus isolation (p. 398)
generativity versus stagnation (p. 398)
humanism (p. 398)
Big Five (p. 399)
living apart together (LAT) (p. 402)
empty nest (p. 404)
social convoy (p. 405)
fictive kin (p. 408)
kinkeeper (p. 414)
sandwich generation (p. 414)
extrinsic rewards of work (p. 415)
intrinsic rewards of work (p. 415)
psychological contract (p. 416)

APPLICATIONS

1. Describe a relationship that you know of in which a middle-aged person and a younger adult learned from each other.

2. Did your parents' marital and employment status affect you? How would you have fared if they had chosen other marriage or work patterns?

3. Imagine becoming a foster parent or adoptive parent yourself. What do you see as the personal benefits and costs?

4. Ask several people how their personalities have changed in the past decade. The research suggests that changes are usually minor. Is that what you found?

ESPECIALLY FOR ANSWERS

Response for Immigrants and Children of Immigrants (from p. 400): Extroversion and neuroticism, according to one study (Silventoinen et al., 2008). Because these traits decrease over adulthood, fewer older adults migrate.

Response for Young Couples (from p. 405): There is no simple answer, but you should bear in mind that while abuse usually decreases with age, breakups become more difficult with every year, especially if children are involved.

Response for Entrepreneurs (from p. 419): As employees and as customers. Middle-aged workers are steady, with few absences and good "people skills," and they like to work. In addition, household income is likely to be higher at about age 50 than at any other time, so middle-aged adults will probably be able to afford your products or services.

OBSERVATION QUIZ ANSWERS

Answer to Observation Quiz (from p. 409): Mothers could have those facial expressions or use their arms that way—but fathers do it more often.

Answer to Observation Quiz (from p. 415): He carries the pack with supplies for both of them; she memorializes the hike with a selfie.

PART VII

CHAPTER 14 CHAPTER 15

Late Adulthood

What emotions do you expect when you read about late adulthood? Sadness, fear, depression, resignation, sympathy, sorrow? Expect instead surprise and joy. You will learn that most older adults are active, alert, and self-sufficient; that dramatic loss of memory and logic ("senility") is unusual; and that many are independent and happy.

This does not mean that you should anticipate mindless contentment. Earlier personality and social connections continue; the complexities of life are evident; joy is mixed with sorrow. Poverty, loneliness, and chronic illness are difficult. However, most older adults — most of the time — overcome such difficulties.

If you doubt this, you are not alone. Late adulthood, more than any other part of life, is a magnet for misinformation. Ageism may be worse than other *-isms* because everyone experiences it if they live long enough, but almost no one is prepared for it.

MOMO PRODUCTIONS/DIGITALVISION/GETTY IMAGES

CHAPTER 14

LATE ADULTHOOD

Body and Mind

what will you know?

- Does the average 80-year-old have the body of the average 60-year-old?
- Do bodies wear out over time?
- Will we forget everything if we live long enough?
- Are all older people wise?

I took my 1-year-old grandson to the playground. Another woman, watching her son, warned that the sandbox would soon be crowded because children from a nearby day-care center were coming. To my delight, she explained details of the center's curriculum, staffing, scheduling, and tuition as if she assumed I was my grandson's mother.

Soon I realized that she was merely being polite, because a girl glanced at me and asked:

"Is that your grandchild?"

I nodded.

"Where is the mother?" was her next question.

Later came the final blow. As I opened the playground gate for a middle-aged man, he said, "Thank you, young lady." That "young lady" was benevolent ageism: I realized that my pleasure at the first woman's words was my own self-deceptive prejudice.

Now we begin our study of the last phase of life, from age 65 or so until death. This chapter starts by exploring attitudes, evident in all three encounters. We then describe biosocial changes, and ways to mitigate them.

Finally we consider four aspects of cognition: disease, decline, improvement, and wisdom. My playground reactions illustrate two of these four: I forgot the name of the recommended preschool, but I recognized ageism in me.

New Understanding of Old Age

Major changes have occurred in late adulthood for two reasons. First, science: We know more about causes and prevention of senescence. Second, the baby boom: The 1950s babies sparked the youth revolution of the 1960s. They now are creating an elder revolution.

PHOTO CREDIT: MASKOT/GETTY IMAGES

Demography

demographic shift
A shift in the proportions of the populations of various ages.

Demographers are scientists who describe populations. They chronicled a **demographic shift** in the size of the age groups, called "the greatest demographic upheaval in human history" (Bloom, 2011, p. 562).

Two hundred years ago, there were 20 times more children under age 15 than people over age 64. Now there are only three times as many. Worldwide, 9 percent of the population is 65 or older in 2020, a percent that is rising every year.

The demographic shift is much larger in developed nations: Elders are 17 percent in the United States, 18 percent in Canada, 23 percent in Italy (United Nations, Department of Economic and Social Affairs, Population Division, 2019). Projections for Japan are that a third of the population might be over 65 in 2050.

Demographers often depict the age structure of a population as a series of stacked bars, one bar for each age group, with the youngest at the bottom and the oldest at the top. Always, the shape was a *demographic pyramid*. Like a wedding cake, it was wide at the base, with each higher level narrower than the one below it (see Figure 14.1). The pyramid is becoming square, for many reasons (see Table 14.1).

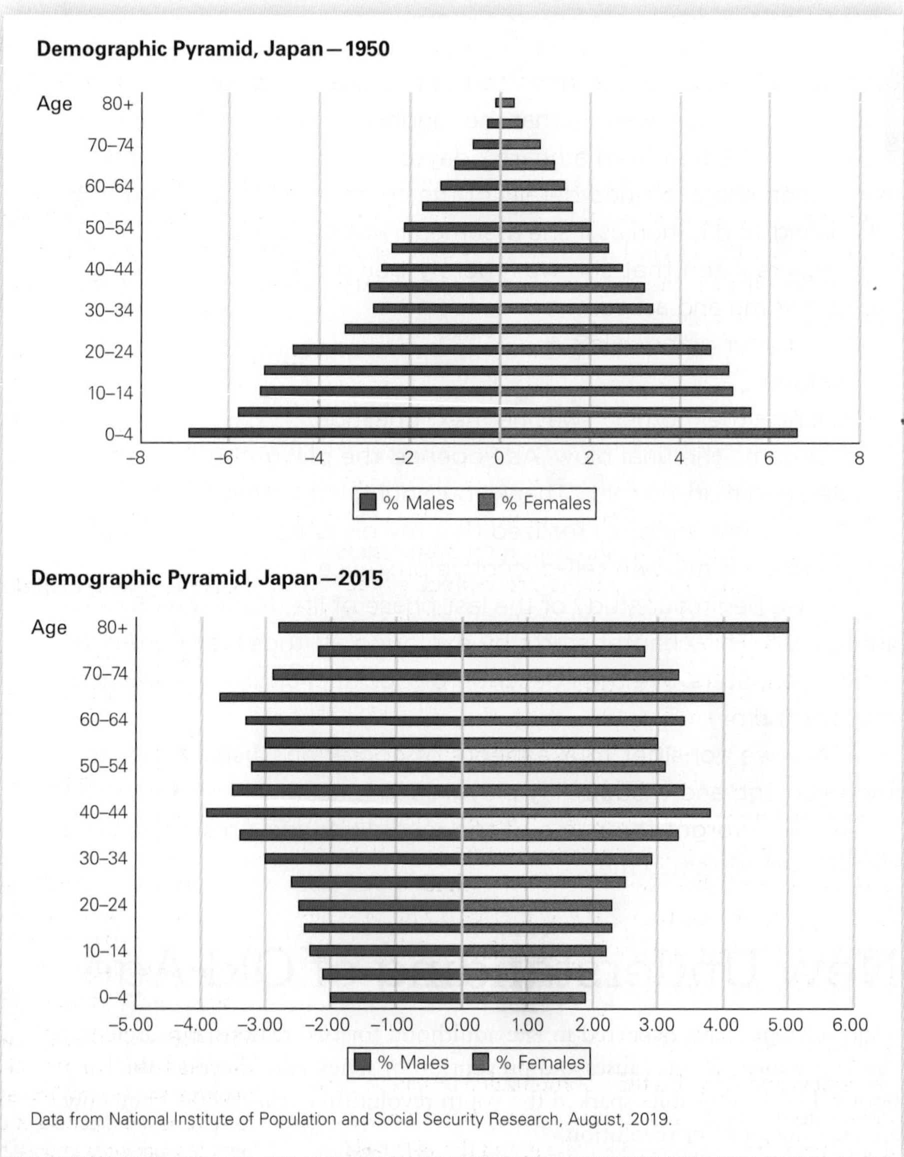

FIGURE 14.1 **Not Yet Square** But certainly not a pyramid. Changes in birth rates worldwide are already making the shape of the population square in some nations, evident in Japan for those under age 25. If trends continue, Japan will be a triangle with the base at the top in 50 years!

Demographers chart the **average life expectancy**, which is how long a typical person will live. Between 1950 and 2020, the average life expectancy in high-income nations became 16 years longer, from 65 to 81. In low-income nations, the average became 28 years longer, from 35 to 63 (United Nations, Department of Economic and Social Affairs, Population Division, 2019).

Why? Less affluent nations added years because of fewer deaths early in life, thanks to clean water, immunization, nutrition, and newborn care. In more affluent nations, mid-life deaths were also reduced, because of lifestyle (less smoking, more exercise) and medical (medication, surgery, early detection) advances. In the most developed nations, the ailments of old age have been pushed back a few years.

Of course, improvement is not inevitable. Indeed, in the United States (not in other nations), beginning in 2014 and continuing for several years, drug overdoses and suicides in middle age slightly reduced average life expectancy (Case & Deaton, 2020).

Then, in 2020 COVID deaths cut life expectancy by about 2 years. This varied by ethnicity, with the average Black American losing three years (see Figure 14.2). Nonetheless, for every ethnic group, the trends remain: U.S. residents who reach age 60 in good health usually live until their early 80s, about five years longer than was true in 1950.

TABLE 14.1 Reasons for the Demographic Pyramid

There were four reasons for the traditional shape, none true today:

1. More babies were born than the replacement rate of one per adult, so each new generation had more children than the previous one. **(NOW FALSE)**
2. Many newborns and young children died, which made each lower bar wider than the next upper one. **(NOW FALSE)**
3. Serious illness was usually fatal, reducing the size of each adult group. **(NOW FALSE)**
4. Depletion of organ reserve and reduced immunity meant that almost no one lived past 80. **(NOW FALSE)**

average life expectancy
The arithmetic mean, calculated by adding up all the ages of death of a group and then dividing by how many people are in that group. If, in a group of five older adults, one dies every decade (60, 70, 80, 90, 100), the average would be 80. Note also that, among the three who reach 80, their average life expectancy would be 90.

STATISTICS THAT FRIGHTEN

Unfortunately, demographic data are sometimes reported in ways designed to alarm, suggesting that the demographic shift is a time bomb that will explode. For instance, some say that the United States had ten times as many people over age 85 in 2020 as in 1950. Or that more and more people have Alzheimer's disease. Both true. Both alarming. Both misleading.

THINK CRITICALLY: Why do many people contemplate aging with sorrow rather than joy?

Consider numbers carefully. Yes, there are more old people alive. But the overall population has also grown. In 2020, only 2 percent of U.S. residents were aged 85 and older, a number that does not overwhelm the other 98 percent. The *proportion* of the population over age 85 is four times, not ten times, higher than it was.

Because age is the main risk factor for Alzheimer's disease, longer lives means more people with that disease. But in Europe and the United States, the *rate* of Alzheimer's is decreasing, because health and education postpone brain disease, and more older people are college graduates (Matthews et al., 2013; Serrano-Pozo & Growdon, 2019; Sullivan et al., 2019).

The leading British medical journal discussed "the time bomb that isn't" (Spijker & MacInnes, 2013). The worst predictions, such as overwhelmed health care systems, are not based on analysis.

One specific statistic makes the point: Older people spend fewer days, on average, in hospitals. That is the primary reason that the United States had about half as many hospital beds in 2018 as in 1980. The rate per thousand was 2.4 compared to 4.5 (National Center for Health Statistics, 2019).

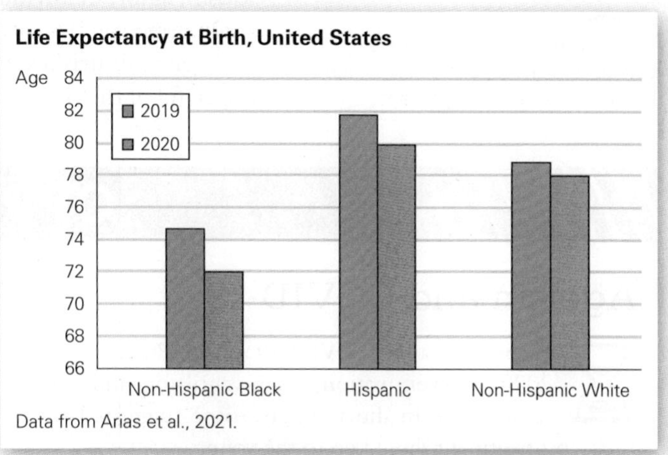

FIGURE 14.2 **Death and Discrimination** The pandemic increased deaths among older adults, not only from COVID but from other causes as well. The ethnic differences are thought to be job-related, as more people of color had jobs where social distancing and remote work were impossible.

WHAT KIND OF OLD?

To understand why this time bomb fizzled despite increasing numbers, the current cohort of baby boomers want to distinguish the *young-old*, the *old-old*, and the *oldest-old*.

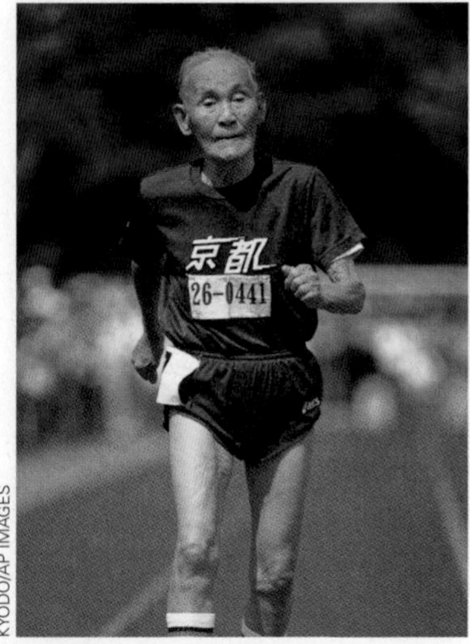

KYODO/AP IMAGES

World's Record for Centenarians Can you sprint 100 meters in less than 30 seconds? Almost until his death in 2019, this man, Hidekichi Miyazaki, could. Maybe you need more practice. Hidekichi had been running for 105 years!

The **young-old** are the largest group (about 74 percent) of over 65s. They are healthy, active, and independent. This group is increasing, in part because serious impairment is decreasing.

Most young-old adults live apart from their younger relatives. If their household is multigenerational, that usually means that their children or grandchildren need their help, not vice versa.

The **old-old** (about 20 percent) suffer losses in body or mind. They need some assistance. Usually, they get help from other people over age 64 (often a spouse).

Only the **oldest-old** (6 percent) are unable to care for themselves. In the United States, about 3 percent of the population over age 64 live in skilled nursing homes or hospitals. Another 3 percent live with family members who provide intensive care.

Sometimes ages are assigned to these categories, with 65–75 young-old, 75–85 old-old, and 85+ oldest-old. However, age is a poor measure of dependency. For example, a detailed study in China of people categorized as oldest-old found that, even at age 100, only half said they were unable to care for themselves (Chen et al., 2020).

Estimates of the prevalence of the oldest-old provides only approximate percentages: Variations in definition make it unclear when the old-old become the oldest-old. Estimates of how many people over age 65 need daily care vary from about 5 to 15 percent. Adults may disagree as to how dependent the oldest generations are.

The overall picture is clear, however. Although many people eventually will depend on others for basic care, most people, most of the time, are competent and independent. For example, if a typical person is young-old from age 65–78, old-old from 78–80, becoming oldest-old at age 80 before dying at 81, only 6 percent of their older years fit the frightening, time-bomb stereotype.

The social environment is crucial. Japanese gerontologists analyzed what would be needed if the typical Japanese person lived to 100 (Akiyama, 2020). To prevent or postpone dependence, they recommended better public transportation, accessible health care, improved social options, and flexible work opportunities. Then people could be young-old for decades.

young-old
Healthy, vigorous, financially secure older adults who are well integrated into the lives of their families and communities.

old-old
Older adults who have physical, mental, or social deficits.

oldest-old
Older adults who are dependent on others for almost everything, requiring supportive services such as nursing homes and hospital stays.

ageism
A prejudice whereby people are categorized and judged solely on the basis of their chronological age.

Ageism

The stereotype that age determines a person is called **ageism**, which, like racism or sexism, ignores individuality. Sometimes ageism seems benevolent, but even so, it is a stereotype.

Ageism flourishes everywhere. This includes nations that outsiders think are respectful of the old, such as in East Asia and sub-Saharan Africa (Chang et al., 2020).

OPPOSING PERSPECTIVES

Ageism and COVID-19

Ageism spread as COVID-19 spread (Previtali et al., 2020). In every nation, when ventilators and medicines were in short supply, some suggested that high-cost treatment should go to the young.

Usually such suggestions were not written, but in the early days of the pandemic in Italy, a published guideline included the following:

> It might be needed to set an age limit for the admission to intensive care . . . to spare resources to those who have . . . the highest chance of survival and . . . more years of life saved.
>
> *[quoted in Cesar & Proietti, 2020]*

Not only in Italy, but also in every nation, elders with COVID-19 were treated differently from the young.

Personal protective equipment was scarce in nursing homes, where deaths were not lamented as much as "super spreader" events among younger adults, such as those who attended a large, maskless wedding of a young couple in Maine. One team of 20 Canadian gerontologists bemoaned the social tendency to be "careless about these lost lives because of ageist attitudes" (Fraser et al., 2020, p. 694).

A year later, vaccine allocation followed an opposite policy. The very old were often first in line, ahead of those with serious health conditions. Was that ageism? Should healthy 75-year-olds be immunized before 50-year-olds with heart conditions?

In one detailed example of mixed attitudes, social scientists analyzed hundreds of comments on Twitter when Texas Lieutenant Governor Dan Patrick opposed COVID-19 restrictions on businesses. He said that people over 70 should be willing to die to save the American dream.

Most Texans expressed an opposing perspective. Of all the tweets regarding Patrick's comments, only 5 percent were approving. The other 95 percent mentioned morals more often than politics. One wrote: "Imagine how morally bankrupt you have to be to be Dan Patrick"; another, "Dan Patrick thinks grandparents would be willing to die to protect the economy. This is morally repugnant" (Barrett et al., 2021, pp. e203, e202).

Many younger people brought groceries to their older relatives and told them what kind of masks to wear. Nationwide, chain stores had special early hours for people over age 65. Such concern for elders is praiseworthy. However, even benevolent ageism is a stereotype.

Consider vaccine allocation again. If it were done by risk category, then people of color should be ahead of White people, and men ahead of women. Would that be racism and sexism? Are age priorities different?

BELIEVING THE STEREOTYPE

Ageism is evident not only among younger people, or in social policies, but also in the aged themselves. It becomes a *self-fulfilling prophecy*, a prediction that comes true because people believe it:

- If younger adults treat older people as if they are frail and confused, that makes older people become more dependent.
- If urban designers consider only the average adult, the needs of elders will be ignored.
- If older adults themselves focus on what they have lost instead of what they have gained, they lose the joy of old age.

Examples of each of these are all around us. For the first, **elderspeak** is the way many people talk to the old. They might address older persons with "honey" or "dear," use a nickname ("Billy," not "Mr. White"), or talk slowly and loudly with simplified vocabulary.

elderspeak
A condescending way of speaking to older adults that resembles baby talk, with simple, short sentences, exaggerated emphasis, repetition, and a slower rate and higher pitch than used in typical speech.

Ironically, elderspeak reduces communication (Kemper, 2015). Higher frequencies are harder to hear, stretching out words makes comprehension worse, shouting causes anxiety, and simplified vocabulary reduces the precision of language. Worse, if people talk to someone as if they are impaired, the person might believe that is the case.

On the second, consider traffic control. Street crossings assume that people can walk quickly. Pedestrian bridges, longer "walk" signals, laws protecting crosswalks are scarce. The result: Older people stay home.

◆◆ Especially for Young Adults
Should you always speak louder and slower when talking to a older people? (see response, page 457)

On the third, many older people undercut other old people, and do not accept their own aging, which makes them shun others their age, maintain poor health habits, and ignore ailments that they should treat.

For example, one study compared 1,877 adults, ages 30 to 95, in Germany, China, and the United States on eight aspects of aging. In every nation and domain, the elders felt that other people were old and impaired, but that their own abilities were more like a younger person (Hess et al., 2017). Consider the logic: If most people say they are younger than average, then "average" is not really average. Instead, it is a sign of ageism.

THINK CRITICALLY: How do you compare to other people your age?

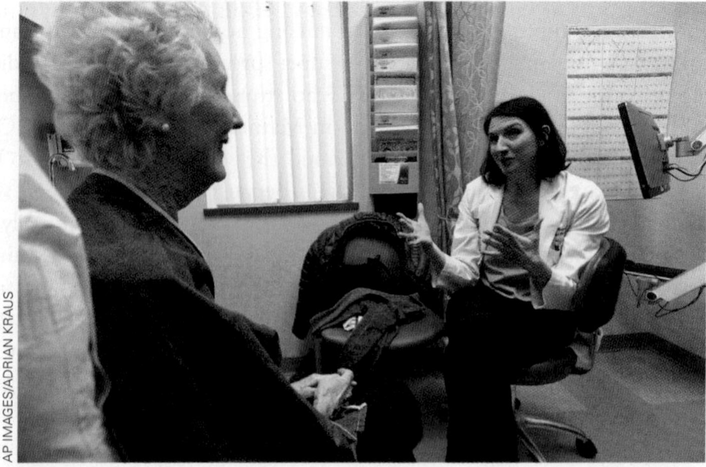

Explaining Her Cancer Dr. Magnuson is a specialist in geriatric oncology, so she knows how to explain treatment options to Nancy Simpson. Older people are quite capable of making informed decisions, as long as their doctors do not oversimplify or use elderspeak.

In another study, 829 women, ages 40 to 75, were asked about how their health compared to the typical person their age. A sizable group said their health was excellent, many said their health was better than average, and very few said worse than average (Holahan et al., 2017). They did not treat health problems that they did not acknowledge.

Most of those women were relatively inactive—despite evidence that activity improves blood pressure, digestion, and almost every other aspect of health. Did ageism undermine health?

The Facts

This is not to deny that illness and disability increase with chronological age. Let us look at two examples—sleep and exercise—to distinguish fact from prejudice.

SLEEP

Sleep changes with age. Restless legs, muscle pain, breathing difficulties, and snoring all make eight solid hours of sleep less common. That can impair physical and mental health (D. Patel et al., 2018).

But wait. Only babies should "sleep like a baby." The circadian rhythm that shifts at adolescence shifts in the other direction in late adulthood, making many elders sleepy in the early evening and up before dawn. That is normal, as is interrupted sleep and napping (Gulia & Kumar, 2018, p. 161).

Insomnia, according to DSM-5, is being distressed with sleep. It is the distress, not the lack of sleep, that is the problem. Distress can lead to self-medication, such as drinking alcohol at bedtime. That increases nighttime falls, disturbs dreams, and causes early waking. In other words, because usual, age-related changes cause distress, that causes insomnia, which causes late-night drinking, which causes real sleep disturbances.

Doctors may make the same mistake. If a patient complains, they might prescribe

> drugs that are commonly used to manage insomnia, such as benzodiazepines and non-benzodiazepines, [which] can lead to several residual side-effects like drug dependence, tolerance, rebound insomnia, muscle relaxation, hallucinations, depression, and amnesia.
>
> *[Gulia & Kumar, 2018]*

LESS EXERCISE OR MORE?

Many people have sought the secret sauce, the fountain of youth, the magic bullet that will slow, stop, or even reverse the effects of senescence. Few realize that it has already been found. Thousands of scientists, studying every disease of aging, have found something that helps every condition—exercise.

Exercise reduces blood pressure, strengthens the heart and lungs, promotes digestion, and makes depression, diabetes, osteoporosis, strokes, arthritis, and several cancers less likely. Yet ageism in everyone works against movement, which explains why older adults exercise much less than younger ones. (See Figure 14.3.)

Blame ageism in the young, who say "Sit down, I will bring your coffee, or sweater, or newspaper to you" (Franco et al., 2015).

Blame ageism in the athletic center, or neighborhood, or community group that sponsors:

- dancing that assumes a balanced sex ratio;
- yoga, aerobics, and so on paced for young adults;
- pickup basketball games that are rough and rapid;
- spandex workout clothes designed for younger bodies; and
- bikes designed for speed, not stability.

Blame the media. Whenever an older person is robbed, raped, or assaulted, sensational headlines appear. In fact, ten times as many young adults as older ones are victims of street crime. To protect them, should we insist that our young adult relatives never leave home alone? That question makes it obvious why telling older adults to stay home is ageist.

And finally blame the elders themselves, who avoid a daily walk, a weekend hike, or, if warranted, shoes designed for stability and equipment that increases safe walking, such as a cane, a walker. They choose to stay home, harming their circulation, digestion, and muscles. Fear overcomes the facts.

FIGURE 14.3 Worse and Worse As people grow older, they should exercise more, because exercise is the best defense against all ailments of age. Unfortunately, the opposite is true: Twice as many of the oldest do not exercise compared to the youngest. These data are from the United States, where the standards for aerobic exercise and weight-bearing exercise are defined by minutes spent per week. Elders could meet the standards even if they walk more slowly, but most of them simply stop.

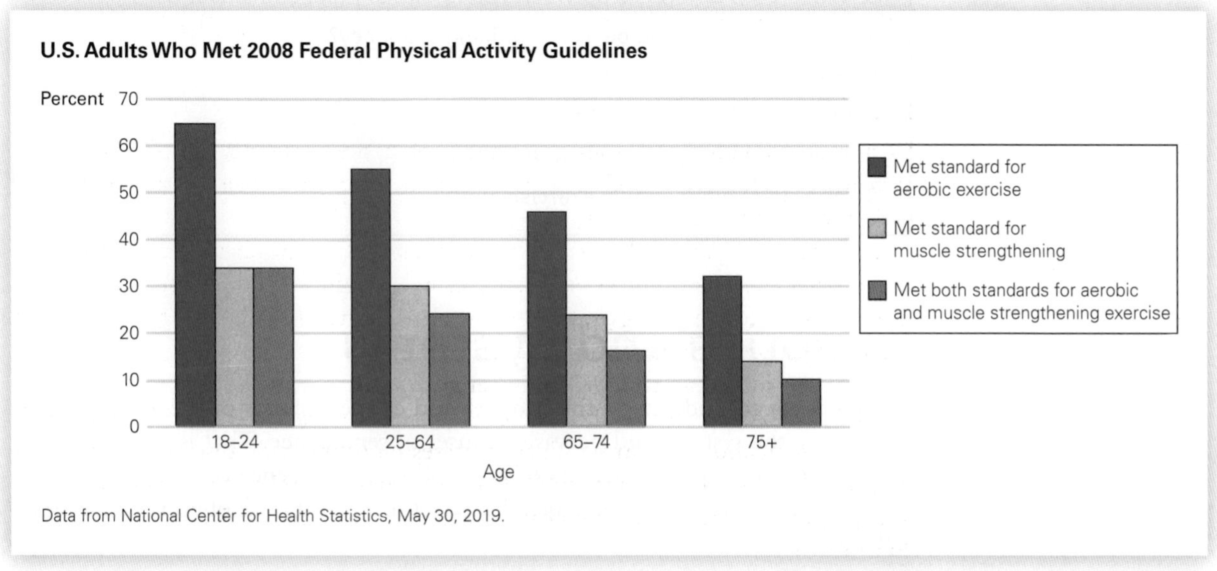

CAREER ALERT

The Physical Therapist

Almost every adult will, at some point, need physical therapy. Bodies age, and with aging comes reduced physical ability. Moreover, dozens of diseases that affect strength and agility—such as diabetes, arthritis, osteoporosis, and heart disease—are increasing, because people are living longer, but fewer exercise as part of their work or normal routine. Cars, riding lawnmowers, and robotic vacuum cleaners have replaced walking, pushing a mower, sweeping the floor.

Thus, for many reasons, physical therapy is among the fastest-growing occupations in the United States today. The U.S. Bureau of Labor Statistics projects a 25-percent increase over the next 10 years in the number of PTs (physical therapists)—and that does not include the closely related, also expanding, profession of occupational therapy.

Salaries are high—in 2016, the median annual salary was $85,400. Education requirements are also high: A physical therapist needs to know how to advise people with every kind of disability.

For instance, I had very minor surgery (one toe kept sticking up, making it hard to wear dress shoes, so the bone needed to be realigned). The surgeon said it would be painful and that I should not walk much for weeks. I was defiant, discarding most of my pain medication and walking two days after the surgery.

I reluctantly followed the surgeon's advice to see a physical therapist. I expected the PT to laugh and tell me that this therapy was for legs, arms, and backs, not for toes. But instead, she put special lotion on her hands, massaged my toes, and taught me six exercises to do every day. When I told her that I was amazed that she knew exercises for a toe, she explained that she was taught what to do for every part of the body and added, "Your toe is connected to the rest of you."

I realized that she knew about my whole body, and everything that might affect my ability to do whatever I wanted to do with it. A worthy profession indeed.

what have you learned?

1. What is the demographic shift and why does it matter?
2. How are the numbers and the rates of Alzheimer's disease changing?
3. What is the difference between young-old, old-old, and oldest-old?
4. How can getting old be a self-fulfilling prophecy?
5. How is ageism similar to racism?
6. What is elderspeak and how is it used?
7. How do sleep patterns change with age?
8. Why don't older people exercise more?

Theories and Systems

Scientists try to understand the broader and deeper aspects of the developmental process, the systems and pervasive causes of senescence. That is the topic now. Accordingly, we consider theories of how and why senescence occurs, and how the various systems identified in Chapter 1 interact to affect the life of every single aging individual.

Theories of Aging

To separate fact from fear, we need to understand why senescence occurs. Theories are clustered into three general groups: one begins with organs, one with genes, and one with cells.

wear-and-tear theory
A view of aging as a process by which the human body wears out because of the passage of time and exposure to environmental stressors.

weathering
The gradual accumulation of wear and tear on the body with age, as with a plank of wood left exposed to the weather over several years.

calorie restriction
The practice of limiting dietary energy intake (while consuming sufficient quantities of vitamins, minerals, and other important nutrients) for the purpose of improving health and slowing down the aging process.

intermittent fasting
A pattern of eating that includes periods of restricted eating interspersed with usual consumption. The most popular pattern is two days per week eating less than 750 calories and five days of normal eating, all while drinking plenty of water.

NO MORE ORGAN RESERVE

The oldest, most general theory of aging is known as **wear-and-tear**, that the body wears out after years of use. Organ reserve is used up, because of time and overuse. Inclement weather, harmful food, pollution, radiation, and social stress wear down the body. Thus, too much sun causes skin cancer, too much animal fat clogs arteries, too much pollution causes cancer, too many blows to the head harms the brain.

Note that social stress is listed here. *Adverse childhood experiences*, described in Chapter 6, can start a cascade of wear that ends with premature death (Asmundson & Afifi, 2020). Thus, wear and tear is not only about biology: This theory recognizes the "structural and cultural conditions" that "accelerate biological decline" (Simons et al., 2020). A lifetime of dealing with discrimination and microaggressions takes a toll on the body, a phenomenon called **weathering** as allostatic load increases.

Weathering may explain ethnic and gender differences in death rates (more people of color, more men). Many COVID deaths were blamed on "preexisting conditions," but those conditions themselves may result from a lifetime of wear, resulting in hypertension and obesity and so on (Wakeel & Njoku, 2021).

Can people reduce wear and tear? One intriguing example is digestion: If people eat 1,800 calories a day instead of the usual 3,000, would that slow all aging processes? That question led to experiments in **calorie restriction**, limiting the quantity of food consumed. That reduces wear and tear, and sometimes doubles the life span in many species, from fruit flies to monkeys (Dorling et al., 2020).

Regarding humans, thousands of members of the Calorie Restriction Society voluntarily undereat. They give up things that others cherish, not just cake and hot dogs but also a strong sex drive and high energy. As a result, they have lower blood pressure, fewer strokes, less cancer, and almost no diabetes. They wear down their bodies much more slowly (Dorling et al., 2020).

Similar results were reported from Cuba. Because the United States led an embargo, Cuba experienced food and gas shortages from 1991 to 1995. People walked more, ate homegrown fruits and vegetables, and lost weight. They had much less heart disease and diabetes, and they lived longer (Franco et al., 2013). But once more food was available, Cubans ate more, gained weight, and died earlier.

Researchers seek the benefits of calorie restriction that most people will accept. There is no particular pill or food that achieves this, but **intermittent fasting** may do so. Millions of people have been able to periodically eat almost nothing, but eat normally most of the time (Fontana & Partridge, 2015; Tinsley & Horne, 2018). (Of course, adults should consult with their doctor before undertaking this or any weight loss method.)

Several versions of intermittent fasting have been tried: Fasting for two of the seven days per week, or every other day, or not eating at all for 14 to 20 hours each day. Intermittent fasting results in lower blood pressure, less obesity, and better metabolism, not only because the digestive system is less active but also because other physiological responses are more active, to protect against temporary starvation (Mani et al., 2018).

That suggests that a simple version of wear and tear is inadequate. Some organs of the body wear down, but others benefit from use. Running improves hearts and

THINK CRITICALLY: Do people want the comforts of daily life — driving and eating — more than longer lives?

DONNA WARD/GETTY IMAGES

Find the Joy Most elders are happier than when they were younger. They appreciate nature, other people, and life itself, and are less often dependent on food, drugs, or possessions.

lungs; tai chi improves balance; weight-training increases muscle mass; sexual activity stimulates the sexual-reproductive system; mental challenge keeps the brain healthy.

A surprising study of 55- to 79-year-olds who bicycled over 100 miles per week (they enjoyed the exercise and the views!) found very little age-based deterioration of the muscles. Indeed, on most measures those older bikers had much stronger legs than the average 30-year-old (Pollock et al., 2018).

IT'S ALL GENETIC

A second cluster of theories focuses on genes, both genes of the entire species and genes that vary from one person to another. You already read about the average life span. In addition, every species has a **maximum life span**, the oldest age that members of that species can attain.

maximum life span
The oldest possible age that members of a species can live under ideal circumstances. For humans, that age is 121 or 122 years.

The maximum life span set by genes: rats, 4 years; rabbits, 13; tigers, 26; house cats, 30; brown bats, 34; brown bears, 37; chimpanzees, 55; Indian elephants, 70; finback whales, 80; humans, 122; lake sturgeon, 150; giant tortoises, 180. Genes affect the entire aging process for every creature, from how long the fetus stays in the womb to when, where, and whether hair on the head grows, greys or disappears.

THINK CRITICALLY: For the benefit of the species as a whole, why would genes promote aging?

Because of the genes of the human species, few people live to 100 and no one has proven to live longer than a French woman named Jeanne Calment, who died in 1997 at the age of 122. Some contend that she was only about 100, because the daughter of the real Jeanne Calment took her identity in middle age to avoid paying some taxes. Most gerontologists accept her claim to 122. Other people have lived to 121, so 122 seems possible (Robine et al., 2019).

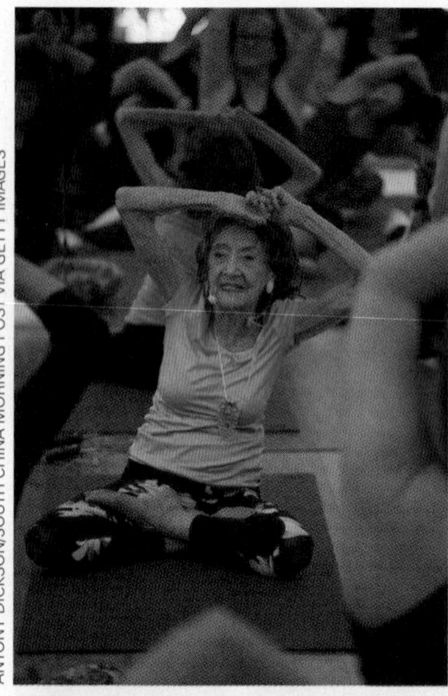

ANTONY DICKSON/SOUTH CHINA MORNING POST VIA GETTY IMAGES

Touch Your Toes? This woman could even put both feet behind her neck. Although everyone loses some flexibility with age, daily practice is crucial. Tao Porchon-Lynch taught yoga for a half-century. At age 99, shown here, she could balance on one leg in tree pose, stretch her hamstrings in downward dog, and then relieve any remaining stress in cobra pose. She died at age 101 in February 2020, peacefully and without pain.

Certainly, Calment lived far longer than most. Her genes included some that are uncommon in the general population but common in centenarians. There are a dozen or more longevity genes, some rare and some more common. If a person happens to inherit many of them, and to have a healthy life, they might live past 100 (Nygaard et al., 2019).

Like wear and tear, this theory explains some aspects of aging, but not all. Children born with the genetic disease called Hutchinson-Gilford syndrome (also called *progeria*) stop growing at about age 5 and begin to look old, with wrinkled skin and balding heads. They die in their teens of genetic conditions more common in people five times their age.

Other genes program a long and healthy life. People who reach age 100 usually have alleles that other people do not (Govindaraju et al., 2015; Nygaard et al., 2019).

Alleles of the ApoE gene prove the importance of genetic variations (Y-W. Huang et al., 2017). Most people have the third allele (ApoE3), which does not seem to affect health. However, about 20 percent of the population have the second allele (ApoE2). In one study, ApoE2 was found in 15 percent of men in their 70s and 29 percent of men from the same population in their 90s. Obviously, Apoe2 is protective (Le Couteur et al., 2020).

Another allele of the same gene, ApoE4, increases the risk of Alzheimer's, especially if a person inherits that gene from both parents. ApoE4 also correlates with heart disease, stroke, and—if a person is HIV-positive—AIDS.

Many other genes (ABCA7, Cr1m, SORL1, TREM2) increase the risk of Alzheimer's. However, no single gene or combination of genes and alleles necessarily results in late onset Alzheimer's. Thus, connecting variations in human senescence directly to one or more genes seems impossible. As you remember, humans have thousands of genes, often with many alleles, and always interacting in hundreds of ways.

A VIEW FROM SCIENCE

Diabetes and Aging

One type of diabetes is called childhood-onset, or type 1, because it begins early in life. That type is heavily influenced by genes, although environmental factors are relevant as well (Redondo & Concannon, 2020).

But most diabetes is adult-onset, type 2. The rate increases with age, such that only 5 percent of U.S. adults aged 20–44 has it, but 29 percent of those over age 65 do (National Center for Health Statistics, 2019). Type 2 is partly related to genes, but not genes alone.

Genome-wide association studies (called *GWAS*), which examine the entire genome, have found more than 100 genes that increase the risk of diabetes, each by a small amount (Visscher et al., 2017). Those genes appear in someone of any ethnicity, but some groups have more of particular ones, and ethnic differences in diabetes include the following.

- In China, Han people have higher rates of diabetes than other Chinese people (Hsu et al., 2015; L. Wang et al., 2017).
- In the United States, African Americans are particularly likely to develop diabetes (Layton et al., 2018).
- Among White residents of the United States, Hispanic people have higher rates than non-Hispanic people, with variations depending on national origin (Baquero & Parra-Medina, 2020).

But these ethnic generalities fall short of understanding the genetics of diabetes. No doubt genetic variants and alleles affect the risk, but ethnicity does not reveal a person's genes. Especially in people whose ancestors lived in Africa, genetic diversity is vast among people who, superficially, seem to be similar (Pennisi, 2021).

To best predict and treat diabetes, genetic variants and combinations, as well as diet and microbiome, need to be considered. This is true for every condition: Precise prescriptions for disease, health, and senescence must be tailored for each individual (Bumpus, 2021).

As a theory of aging, looking at genes makes sense. But research on the genes of diabetes reveals the problems with genetic theories of aging, especially when age is a factor. Focusing on genes may distract us from considering other causes of senescence, disease, and death.

Diabetes is strongly influenced by nongenetic factors. African Americans who live in areas with high residential segregation are more likely to develop diabetes—and the reasons are not genetic (Bancks et al., 2017).

Similarly, the rate for people in the lowest quintile of income is almost double the rate in the highest quintile (19 and 11 percent), a particularly troubling statistic since far more children than older adults live in poverty, so that should skew the statistic in the opposite way. Economic policies and practices, which affect diet and exercise, affect both incidence and treatment of diabetes more than genes.

Genes alone rarely cause the diseases and disabilities of old age until age 90 or so. A few dominant genes make some serious problems almost inevitable (as for progeria and early-onset Alzheimer's), but for most of us, the pace of senescence depends much more on how and where we live our lives than on our genes.

AGING CELLS

The third cluster of theories examines **cellular aging**, focusing on molecules and cells (Khosla et al., 2020; Rattan & Hayflick, 2016). Remember, cells duplicate many times over the life span. Minor errors—repetitions and deletions of triplets—in copying accumulate. Early in life, the immune system repairs such errors, but eventually the immune system itself becomes less adept.

cellular aging
The cumulative effect of stress and toxins, first causing cellular damage and eventually the death of cells.

In general, when the organism can no longer repair cellular errors, senescence occurs. This process is first apparent in the skin, an organ that replaces itself often, particularly if damage occurs (such as peeling skin with sunburn). With senescence, scrapes take a little longer to heal, scarring becomes more obvious. Cellular aging also occurs inside the body; the aging immune system is increasingly unable to control abnormal cells.

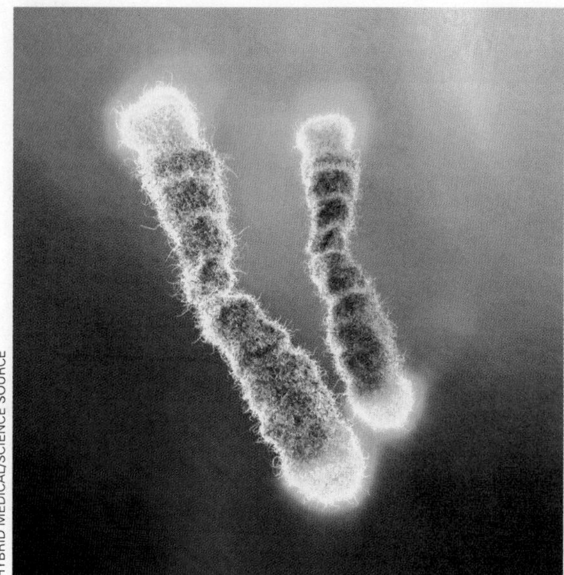
HYBRID MEDICAL/SCIENCE SOURCE

Old Caterpillars? No, these are young chromosomes, stained to show the glowing white telomeres at the ends.

telomeres
The area of the tips of each chromosome that is reduced a tiny amount as time passes. By the end of life, the telomeres are very short.

◆◆ Especially for Biologists
What are some immediate practical uses for research on the causes of aging? (see response, page 457)

Cellular aging, with some cells out of control, is a major cause of all forms of cancer (Beck et al., 2020). Before age 40, biological mechanisms keep cancer cells from reproducing and metastasizing. However, once childbearing years are over, cancer cells duplicate unchecked.

The results are apparent from many statistics. For instance, in the United States in 2017, only 2 percent of those aged 25 to 44 had ever had cancer. Then rates began to increase. By age 74 and older, rates were 23 percent (National Center for Health Statistics, 2019).

There are dozens of cellular changes over time, from the mitochondria to the stem cells (Sameri et al., 2020; Wan & Finkel, 2020). One particular aspect of cell aging focuses on **telomeres**, the material at the end of each chromosome that becomes shorter over time.

Telomeres are longer in children (except those with progeria) and shorter in old adults. Eventually, after many cell divisions over a life span, the telomere is too short, and duplication is impossible. Aging is evident, and, when many cells can no longer replicate, the maximum life span of that person (or mouse, or any other mammal) has been reached and death occurs.

The more stress a person experiences, from childhood on, the shorter their telomeres become. In late adulthood, telomere length predicts death (Yegorov et al., 2020). Not surprising, then, telomere length is about the same in newborns of all genders and ethnic groups, but by late adulthood telomeres are typically longer in women than in men and longer in White people than in Black people.

Cellular-aging theorists believe that weathering chips away at telomeres, and that this is one reason for variations in longevity. Women outlive men, and European Americans outlive African Americans, at least until age 80. Those who live to age 100 or more tend, by temperament, to be less troubled by stress, and that protects their cells.

Systems of Aging

As you have doubtless noticed, these three clusters of theories overlap. Weathering and genes affect cells, and vice versa. However, they share one limitation: All three emphasize details of the *biology* of aging.

We need to look beyond that to consider the systems that sustain human development. Selective optimization with compensation (explained in Chapter 12) involves social contexts and human decisions, which becomes increasingly important on many levels—the biosystem, microsystem, macrosystem, and exosystem.

To illustrate, we now explain the senses, sexual intercourse, driving, and technology, noting how they are part of systems.

BIOSYSTEM COMPENSATION: THE SENSES

As already explained in Chapter 12, every sense becomes slower and less sharp with each passing decade. That continues in late adulthood. For instance, only 10 percent of people of over age 65 see well without glasses, and everyone loses some hearing, especially men. Indeed, 16 percent of U.S. men over age 75 are virtually deaf (National Center for Health Statistics, 2017).

Beyond that, here we emphasize that all the senses are interconnected with each person's body and brain, because each person is a biosystem. Each sense affects all the others, with sensory losses increasing depression and cognitive loss (Hajek & König, 2020).

Suppose hearing is fading. The first defense is visual: People look closely at talkers' lips and facial expressions in order to understand what is said. But, with age, hearing and vision both fade: That multiplies the loss, greater than simply adding the two losses together.

Evidence for this systemic multiplier is substantial. Hearing loss correlates with social isolation and cognitive slowdown (Slade et al., 2020). That means an older person who cannot hear well is likely to have less sensory input of every kind, as well as to experience depression, despair, and disease because of a cascade of losses.

Or consider the propensity to falling, a major problem among older adults. That may seem to involve only one sense, the sense of balance. But it is far more than that: People fall because they cannot see a bump in the sidewalk, or cannot hear a bicycle bell, or cannot touch a fence, a wall, or another person. When specialists seek to help people with balance problems, they often check the person's hearing.

An extreme example of the interconnection among the senses comes from the Netherlands. Unlike in the United States, Dutch law now allows older people who are not terminally ill to request euthanasia because of *multiple geriatric syndrome*. Dozens have done so, choosing death rather than continued life with several sensory losses (van den Berg et al., 2021).

Thus, a combination of sensory losses can become lethal. The solution: Each sense needs to be maintained as well as possible, because each is part of a total biosystem.

MICROSYSTEM COMPENSATION: SEX

As already explained in Chapter 12, physiological sexual responses and activity slow down with age. However, sex does not involve the body of only one person; it is embedded in close relationships, that is, in the microsystem.

That explains the marked variation in sexual activity among the old. For example, a European study of almost 3,000 older adults (age 60 and up, all of whom had a partner) in four nations found that about a fourth had no intercourse in the past month, and another fourth said they had intercourse at least every week (N. Fischer et al., 2018).

In that study, the researchers expected cultural differences between adults in nations with different cultural norms about sex (Norway, Denmark, Belgium, and Portugal). Instead they found similar rates in the various nations but differences from one couple to another.

Health concerns were relevant in every nation, but attitude was even more important. If a person thought sex was important for overall well-being, usually they were sexually active, no matter what their nationality or age (N. Fischer et al., 2018).

Most older people reject the idea that sex means intercourse and orgasm, in part because that indicates individual pleasure, not the microsystem. Relationships are crucial. This was one conclusion from a study of more than 7,000 older adults in England (Tetley et al., 2018). A man in his 80s, when asked about intercourse, replied:

> Now too old but my wife and I sleep in the same bed, and kiss and cuddle each other before settling down to sleep. We enjoy each other's company.

And a woman said:

> The act of sex does not make you "happy" but having a loving partner does.

This explains how older people adapt, sexually, to divorce or widowhood. Since the sex drive varies from person to person, some elders prefer to stay single and

WESTEND61/GETTY IMAGES

What Does a Kiss Mean? Many young adults wonder, but older adults like this couple—she is in her 70s and he in his 80s—know the answer.

alone, some no longer seek intercourse, some cohabit, some begin LAT (living apart together) with a new partner, and some remarry. Each older person selects whether and how to be sexual, by finding the microsystem that works for them.

This was evident in a detailed study of several couples in the United States (see A Case to Study).

A CASE TO STUDY

Should Older Couples Have More Sex?

Sexual needs and interactions vary extremely from one person to another, so no single case illustrates general trends. Further, questionnaires and physiological measures designed for young bodies may be inappropriate for the aged. Accordingly, two researchers studied elders' sexuality using a method called *grounded theory*.

They found 34 people (17 couples, aged 50 to 86, married an average of 34 years), interviewing each privately and extensively. They read and reread all of the transcripts, tallying responses and topics by age and gender (that was the grounded part). Then they analyzed common topics, interpreting trends (that was theory).

They concluded that sexual activity is more a social construction than a biological event (Lodge & Umberson, 2012). All of their cases said that intercourse was less frequent with age, including four couples for whom intercourse stopped completely because of the husband's health. Nonetheless, more respondents said that their sex life had improved than said it deteriorated (44 percent compared to 30 percent).

Surprisingly, those 30 percent were more likely to be middle-aged than older. Some midlife men were troubled by difficulty maintaining an erection, and many women worried that they were not sexy.

One woman said:

> All of a sudden, we didn't have sex after I got skinny. And I couldn't figure that out. I look really good now and we're not having sex. It turns out that he was going through a major physical thing at that point and just had lost his sex drive. . . . I went through years thinking it was my fault.
>
> *[Irene, quoted in Lodge & Umberson, 2012, p. 435]*

The authors theorize that "images of masculine sexuality are premised on high, almost uncontrollable levels of penis-driven sexual desire" (Lodge & Umberson, 2012, p. 430), while the cultural ideals of feminine sexuality emphasize women's passivity and yet "implore women to be both desirable and receptive to men's sexual desires and impulses," deeming "older women and their bodies unattractive" (Lodge & Umberson, 2012, p. 430).

Thus, when middle-aged adults first realize that aging has changed them, they are distressed. By late adulthood they realize that the young idea of good sex (frequent intercourse) is irrelevant. Instead, they *compensate* for physical changes by *optimizing* their relationship in other ways. As one man over age 70 said:

> I think the intimacy is a lot stronger. . . . more often now we do things like holding hands and wanting to be close to each other or touch each other. It's probably more important now than sex is.
>
> *[Jim, quoted in Lodge & Umberson, 2012, p. 438]*

An older woman said her marriage improved because:

> We have more opportunities and more motivation. [Sex] was wonderful. It got thwarted, with . . . the medication he is on. And he hasn't been functional since. The doctors just said that it is going to be this way, so we have learned to accept that. But we have also learned long before that there are more ways than one to share your love.
>
> *[Helen, quoted in Lodge & Umberson, 2012, p. 437]*

The next cohort of older adults may have other attitudes; the male/female and midlife/older differences evident with these 17 couples may not apply. These cases do suggest, however, that selective optimization with compensation is possible.

MACROSYSTEM COMPENSATION: DRIVING

Driving a car becomes more difficult with age: Reading signs takes longer, turning the head is harder, reaction time slows, hearing and vision worsen. Many older people wisely avoid night driving, traffic, and icy roads (Molnar et al., 2018).

However, from a developmental perspective, whether or not to drive should not be decided by an individual but should be part of a macrosystem. Unfortunately, when older adults see teenagers speeding, using cell phones, and driving after drinking, they conclude that they themselves are good drivers, unlike those "young whippersnappers."

That makes many older drivers ignore their own losses. Per mile driven, compared to younger drivers, those over age 80 have more accidents, hit more pedestrians (whom they did not see), and are more likely to be fatally injured themselves in motor vehicle crashes.

The macrosystem needs to set standards, although often it does not. This was evident in 2019 in England, as reported by one physician:

> On 17 January the Duke of Edinburgh was driving his Land Rover when it was in a collision with another car. One of three passengers in the other car was injured, and the duke's car flipped over. The duke, 97, was reportedly left bruised and bewildered. Two days later he was seen driving another Land Rover with no seatbelt and was spoken to by police.
>
> *[Oliver, 2019]*

BEN CAWTHRA/SIPA USA/NEWSCOM

Should She Drive? Queen Elizabeth II was 91 years old when this photo taken. She is the only person in the United Kingdom who is not required to have a driver's license, but her driving is usually limited to her private estates.

But the United States has the same problem: deference for older drivers. Many jurisdictions renew licenses by mail, even for 80-year-old drivers.

Because news accounts rarely emphasize the systems that cause a problem, if an older driver crashes, that person is blamed, not the Department of Motor Vehicles. Instead, the macrosystem could require retesting, via simulation with a computer and video screen. That would allow some older drivers to renew their licenses and some not, with many realizing that they are less capable than they thought.

Moreover, older drivers could be required to attend a driver's education class, as is done for new drivers. For example, they need to learn how to use GPS devices, not rely on memory or paper instructions, which makes accidents more likely (Thomas et al., 2018).

The macrosystem could provide other ways to reduce accidents. Free and efficient public transportation, well-maintained sidewalks, and large print signs would save lives. Ironically, the pedestrians most likely to be killed are under age 10 or over age 70, yet communities rarely design cars, streets, or highways with their safety in mind.

universal design
The creation of settings and equipment that can be used by everyone, whether or not they are able-bodied and sensory-acute.

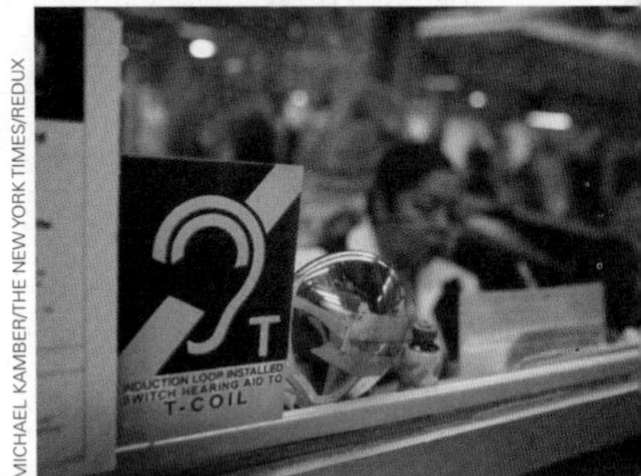

MICHAEL KAMBER/THE NEW YORK TIMES/REDUX

Looped In? This sign indicates that a hearing loop is installed in this New York City subway booth, enabling most people with hearing aids and cochlear implants to receive important messages and to communicate with transit personnel. Frequent riders of public transit, however, complain that the public address system malfunctions, the elevators are often broken, and the signs do not always reflect reality.

EXOSYSTEM: TECHNOLOGY AND NATIONAL POLICY

Every one of the three examples just cited relates to the exosystem in addition to the systems noted for each one. National and cultural norms affect whether old individuals thrive or not.

In sexuality, for instance, many hospitals and nursing homes separate men and women, even if the two are married to each other. On driving, variations in laws and licensing vary markedly state by state, with some considering the needs of older people and some not.

Disability advocates want the exosystem to incorporate **universal design**. The idea is that environments and equipment should be designed to be used by everyone, old or young, able-bodied and sensory-acute or not.

Here we use the example of universal design to accommodate sensory loss, in part because impaired vision, audition, and so on are too easily considered personal problems, not exosystem ones.

ELDERS BEHIND THE WHEEL

Older people often reduce or change their driving habits in order to compensate for their slowing reaction time, avoiding nighttime, bad weather, and long distances. Many states have initiated restrictions, including requiring older drivers to renew their licenses in person, to make sure they stay safe. Consequently, their crash rate is low overall, but not when measured by the rate per miles driven.

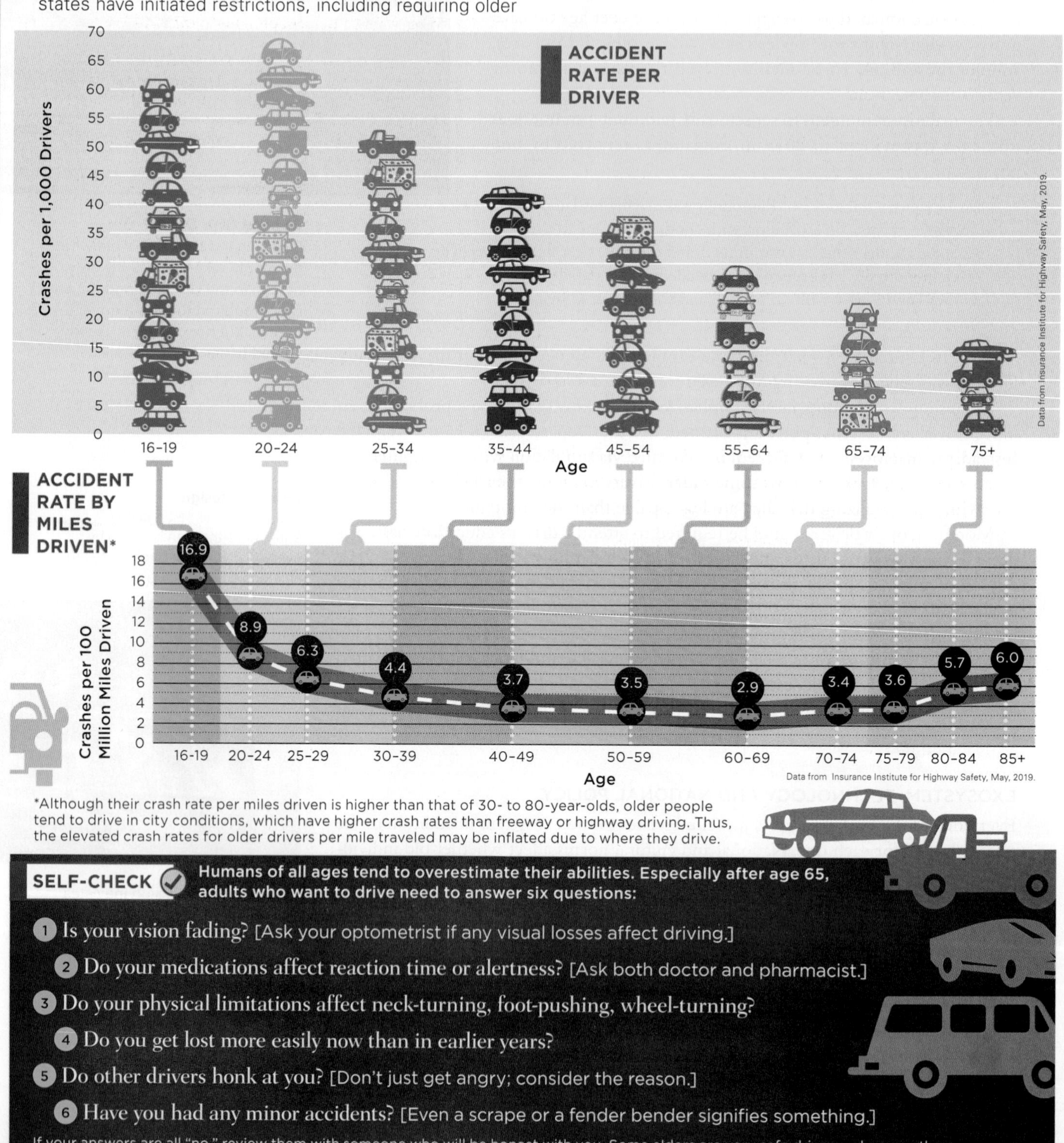

*Although their crash rate per miles driven is higher than that of 30- to 80-year-olds, older people tend to drive in city conditions, which have higher crash rates than freeway or highway driving. Thus, the elevated crash rates for older drivers per mile traveled may be inflated due to where they drive.

SELF-CHECK ✓ **Humans of all ages tend to overestimate their abilities. Especially after age 65, adults who want to drive need to answer six questions:**

1. Is your vision fading? [Ask your optometrist if any visual losses affect driving.]
2. Do your medications affect reaction time or alertness? [Ask both doctor and pharmacist.]
3. Do your physical limitations affect neck-turning, foot-pushing, wheel-turning?
4. Do you get lost more easily now than in earlier years?
5. Do other drivers honk at you? [Don't just get angry; consider the reason.]
6. Have you had any minor accidents? [Even a scrape or a fender bender signifies something.]

If your answers are all "no," review them with someone who will be honest with you. Some elders are very safe drivers, whereas others can be a risk to themselves and to those around them. Before you step on the accelerator, make sure you are one of the safe ones.

Since 1980, many aspects of the exosystem have helped people with sensory limitations. Forty years ago there were no inexpensive eyeglasses at drugstores, no smoke alarms in homes, no volume controls and headphones, no halogen streetlights. All these are now accepted within the culture, making it easier for people to function well despite sensory loss.

However, much more could be done. Quality dental and medical care, canes and service dogs, large-screen computers and much more are free in some nations, but available only to the very rich in others. Several eye diseases (cataracts, glaucoma, and macular degeneration—see Table 14.2) increase with age. If discovered early, blindness can be prevented, yet prevention is not a priority of the U.S. health exosystem. Hearing aids, with the expertise required for individual adjustment, cost thousands of dollars.

Many disabilities would disappear with universal design. Instead, just about everything, from houses to shoes, is fashioned for young adults with no impairments.

TABLE 14.2 Common Vision Impairments Among Older Adults

- *Cataracts.* As early as age 50, about 10 percent of adults have cataracts, a thickening of the lens, causing vision to become cloudy, opaque, and distorted. By age 70, 30 percent do. Cataracts can be removed in outpatient surgery and replaced with an artificial lens.
- *Glaucoma.* About 1 percent of those in their 70s and 10 percent in their 90s have glaucoma, a buildup of fluid within the eye that damages the optic nerve. The early stages have no symptoms, but the later stages cause blindness, which can be prevented if an ophthalmologist or optometrist treats glaucoma before it becomes serious. African Americans and people with diabetes may develop glaucoma as early as age 40.
- *Macular degeneration.* About 4 percent of those in their 60s and about 12 percent over age 80 have a deterioration of the retina, called macular degeneration. An early warning occurs when vision is spotty (e.g., some letters missing when reading). Again, early treatment – in this case, medication – can restore some vision, but without treatment, macular degeneration is progressive, causing blindness about five years after it starts.

what have you learned?

1. How could wear on a child's body affect senescence in later life?
2. When do genes become more influential for health than habits?
3. How is cellular repair related to cancer?
4. How do visual losses affect the other senses?
5. Why does impaired hearing affect the brain?
6. How can falling in late adulthood be a multisensory experience?
7. What determines whether or not an older person has an active sex life?
8. Why is a community to blame if an older adult has a motor-vehicle accident?
9. What are examples of universal design in your community?
10. What advances in technology would be especially helpful in your community?

Neurocognitive Disorders

Although most older people think and remember quite well, nonetheless age is the main risk factor for every **neurocognitive disorder (NCD)**. About 9 percent of the world's population over age 65 (less than 1 percent of the total population) experiences an NCD. Rates are lowest in nations where most people die before age 60.

neurocognitive disorder (NCD) Any of a number of brain diseases that affect a person's ability to remember, analyze, plan, or interact with other people.

In wealthy nations such as the United States, brain diseases are unusual for people in their 60s but become more common with every decade. For example, almost half of the people in Sweden who are age 95 or older have an NCD (Mathillas et al., 2011).

Ageism and Words

Because ageism distorts our perception, we need to use words carefully when referring to neurocognitive disorders. *Senile* simply means "old." Do not use *senility* to mean "severe mental impairment," because that implies that old age brings intellectual failure—an ageist myth.

biomarkers
Indicators (marks) in the body (*bio-*) of some condition, as shown with blood tests that can diagnose diabetes.

Alzheimer's disease (AD)
The most common cause of major NCD, characterized by gradual deterioration of memory and personality and marked by the formation of plaques of beta-amyloid protein and tangles of tau in the brain.

plaques
Clumps of a protein called beta-amyloid, found in brain tissue surrounding the neurons.

tangles
Twisted masses of threads made of a protein called tau within the neurons of the brain.

THINK CRITICALLY: The terms *MCI* and *dementia* are still used. Should they be?

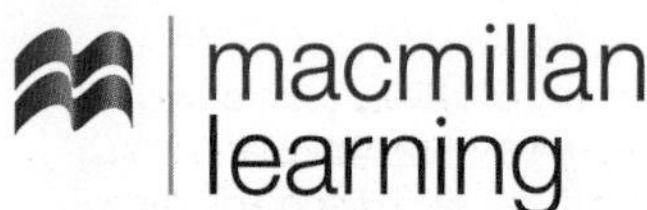

In **VIDEO ACTIVITY: Alzheimer's Disease**, experts and family members discuss the progression of the disease.

Dementia (used in DSM-IV) is a more precise term than *senility* for irreversible, pathological loss of brain functioning. However, the roots of that word include *demon*: People once thought that dementia occurred because a person was possessed.

Accordingly, the DSM-5 has scrapped the word *dementia*. In the fifth diagnostic manual, "neurocognitive disorders" is a major category, subdivided into major (previously called dementia) or mild. *Mild neurocognitive disorder* has replaced the term *mild cognitive impairment (MCI)*, to emphasize that cognitive losses discussed in this section originate in the neurons of the brain, hence *neuro*cognitive.

Diagnosis is complicated. The line between typical age-related changes, mild disorder, and major disorder is not clear. Symptoms and criteria vary from one culture to another, and from one doctor, diagnostician, and impaired individual to another.

Many scientists seek **biomarkers**, which are biological measures (such as in the blood, in cerebrospinal fluid, or in brain scans) to provide diagnosis or guide treatment (Jeromin & Bowser, 2017). None are definitive, however. Combining several biomarkers works better than any single measure, but even that is not always right (Zetterberg & Blennow, 2021).

Both the hope and the problems are summarized thus:

> biomarkers are invaluable [but]. . . . caution must be exercised to ensure appropriate interpretation. . . . there continues to be a grave need for novel biomarkers, improved development of existing tools, standardization, and improved accessibility.
>
> *[Ehrenberg et al., 2020]*

Alzheimer's Disease

In the past century, millions of people in every large nation have been diagnosed with **Alzheimer's disease (AD)** (called *major NCD due to Alzheimer's disease* in DSM-5). Severe and worsening memory loss is the main symptom of AD, which proceeds stage by stage. Definitive diagnosis occurs on autopsy, with extensive plaques and tangles in the cerebral cortex (see Table 14.3).

Plaques are clumps of a protein called *beta-amyloid* in the tissues surrounding the neurons; **tangles** are twisted threads of a protein called *tau* within the neurons.

TABLE 14.3 Stages of Alzheimer's Disease

Stage 1. People in the first stage forget recent events or new information, particularly names and places. For example, they might forget the name of a famous film star or how to get home from a familiar place. This first stage is similar to mild neurocognitive disorder — even experts cannot always tell the difference. In retrospect, it seems clear that President Ronald Reagan had early AD while in office, but no doctor diagnosed it.

Stage 2. Generalized confusion develops, with deficits in concentration and short-term memory. Speech becomes aimless and repetitious, vocabulary is limited, words get mixed up. Personality traits are not curbed by rational thought. For example, suspicious people may decide that others have stolen the things that they themselves have mislaid.

Stage 3. Memory loss becomes dangerous. Although people at stage 3 can care for themselves, they might leave a lit stove or hot iron on or might forget whether they took essential medicine and thus take it twice — or not at all.

Stage 4. At this stage, full-time care is needed. People cannot communicate well. They might not recognize their closest loved ones.

Stage 5. Finally, people with AD become unresponsive. Identity and personality have disappeared. When former president Ronald Reagan was at this stage, a longtime friend who visited him was asked, "Did he recognize you?" The friend answered, "Worse than that — I didn't recognize him." Death comes 10 to 15 years after the first signs appear.

Every brain contains some beta-amyloid and tau, but plaques and tangles proliferate in brains with AD, especially in the hippocampus, where memories are made.

If Alzheimer's develops in middle age, the cause is genetic: Affected people have either trisomy-21 (Down syndrome) or one of three genes: amyloid precursor protein (APP), presenilin 1, or presenilin 2. Early-onset AD progresses quickly, reaching the last phase and death within three to five years.

Most cases of Alzheimer's are late-onset, beginning after age 70. Many genes have some impact, but health habits also matter. People, on average, die 10 years after the first symptoms.

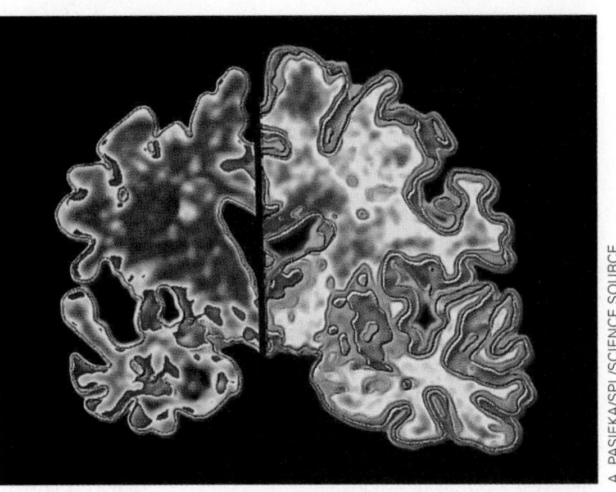

A. PASIEKA/SPL/SCIENCE SOURCE

The Alzheimer's Brain This computer graphic shows a vertical slice through a brain ravaged by Alzheimer's disease *(left)* compared with a similar slice of a typical brain *(right)*. The diseased brain is shrunken because neurons have degenerated. The red indicates plaques and tangles.

Vascular Disease

The second most common cause of neurocognitive disorder is **vascular disease (VD)**, caused by a *stroke* (a temporary obstruction of a blood vessel in the brain) or a series of strokes, called *transient ischemic attacks (TIAs*, or *ministrokes)* (Burhan et al., 2018). The interruption in blood flow reduces oxygen, destroying part of the brain. Symptoms (blurred vision, weak or paralyzed limbs, slurred speech, and mental confusion) suddenly appear.

In a TIA, symptoms may vanish quickly, unnoticed. However, unless recognized and prevented, another TIA is likely, eventually causing *vascular* or *multi-infarct dementia* (Kalaria, 2018). Executive functioning is reduced, which means that poor decisions and uncontrolled impulses are as prevalent as memory problems. Symptoms vary, depending on which part of the brain has been affected.

Vascular disease correlates with the genes and health risks of AD (Vittner et al., 2018), as well as with surgery that requires general anesthesia. It is difficult to know how often surgery is the direct cause, however, since postoperative delirium and dementia may be the manifestation of previously undiagnosed VD (Houghton et al., 2021).

vascular disease
Formerly called *vascular* or *multi-infarct dementia*, vascular disease is characterized by sporadic, and progressive, loss of intellectual functioning caused by repeated infarcts, or temporary obstructions of blood vessels, which prevent sufficient blood from reaching the brain.

Frontotemporal Disorders

Several types of neurocognitive disorders affect the frontal lobes and thus are called **frontotemporal NCDs**, or *frontotemporal lobar degeneration*. This is a diverse collection of disorders: Pick's disease is the most common form (Neumann & Mackenzie, 2019). These disorders cause perhaps 15 percent of all cases of NCDs in the United States.

In frontotemporal NCDs, parts of the brain that regulate emotions and social behavior (especially the amygdala and prefrontal cortex) deteriorate. Emotional and personality changes are the main symptoms.

Frontotemporal NCDs usually occur before age 70, unlike Alzheimer's or vascular disease. The diagnosis is difficult partly because the symptoms appear at younger ages and partly because memory loss is not the primary symptom.

One woman, Ruth French, was furious because her husband

> threw away tax documents, got a ticket for trying to pass an ambulance and bought stock in companies that were obviously in trouble. Once a good cook, he burned every pot in the house. He became withdrawn and silent, and no longer spoke to his wife over dinner. That same failure to communicate got him fired from his job.
>
> *[D. Grady, 2012]*

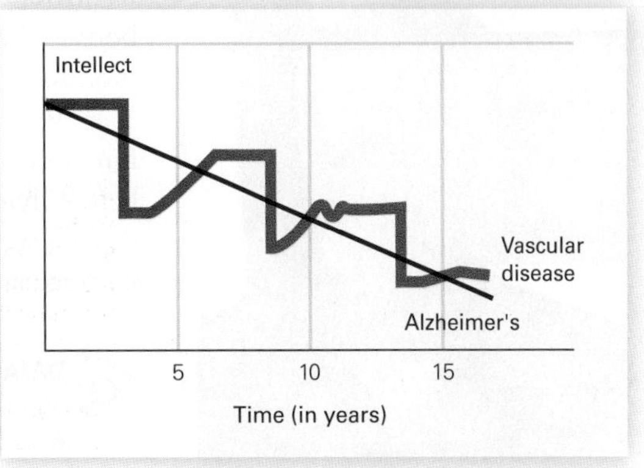

FIGURE 14.4 The Progression of Alzheimer's Disease and Vascular Disease Cognitive decline is apparent in both Alzheimer's disease and vascular disease. However, the pattern of decline for each disease is different. Individuals with Alzheimer's show steady, gradual decline, while those with vascular disease get suddenly much worse, improve somewhat, and then experience another serious loss.

frontotemporal NCDs
Deterioration of the amygdala and frontal lobes that may be the cause of 15 percent of all major neurocognitive disorders. (Also called *frontotemporal lobar degeneration*.)

Parkinson's disease
A chronic, progressive disease that is characterized by muscle tremor and rigidity and sometimes major neurocognitive disorder; caused by reduced dopamine production in the brain.

Lewy body disease
A form of major neurocognitive disorder characterized by an increase in Lewy body cells in the brain. Symptoms include visual hallucinations, momentary loss of attention, falling, and fainting.

terminal decline
For the oldest-old, in the weeks or months before death, all the body functions may decline. This global failure is unlike problems in only one organ.

Finally, he was diagnosed with a frontotemporal NCD. Ruth asked him to forgive her fury. It is not clear that he understood either her anger or her apology.

Other Disorders

Many other brain diseases begin with impaired motor control (shaking when picking up a cup of coffee, falling when trying to walk), not with impaired thinking. The most common of these is **Parkinson's disease**.

Parkinson's starts with rigidity or tremor of the muscles as dopamine-producing neurons degenerate, affecting movement long before cognition (Jankovic, 2018). Middle-aged adults usually have sufficient cognitive reserve to avoid major intellectual loss (Darweesh et al., 2017). When this disorder appears in late adulthood, cognitive problems are soon apparent.

Another 3 percent of people with NCD in the United States suffer from **Lewy body disease**: excessive deposits of a particular kind of protein in their brains. Lewy bodies are also present in Parkinson's disease, but in Lewy body disease they are more numerous and dispersed throughout the brain, interfering with communication between neurons.

The main symptom of Lewy body dementia is loss of inhibition: A person might gamble or become hypersexual. In many ways, symptoms are similar to Parkinson's, but brain impairments are more comprehensive and begin sooner (Walker et al., 2019).

Some other types of NCDs begin in middle age or even earlier, caused by Huntington's disease, multiple sclerosis, a severe head injury, a virus such as ZIKA, or the last stages of syphilis, AIDS, or bovine spongiform encephalopathy (BSE, or mad cow disease). Repeated blows to the head (traumatic brain injury), even without concussions, can cause *chronic traumatic encephalopathy (CTE)*, which causes memory loss and emotional changes.

Differentiating CTE from other neurocognitive disorders is complex, as is distinguishing brain disease from other problems. One "other problem" is **terminal decline**, the drop in function that occurs in the months before death. The entire body—heart, lungs, digestive system, and so on—often slows down in the final months of life; the brain does, too.

A study of 30,064 nursing home residents, already impaired, found that most of them functioned quite well cognitively before experiencing a notable drop in the months before dying (Hülür et al., 2019). The only group who did not experience terminal decline were those who already suffered from a severe neurocognitive disorder. Their intellectual losses continued, but the rate did not accelerate in the final months.

JASON KEMPIN/GETTY IMAGES ENTERTAINMENT/GETTY IMAGES

Why? Many people wonder why actor and comedian Robin Williams died by suicide at age 63. One explanation: He was in the early stages of a serious neurocognitive disorder. Williams was diagnosed with Parkinson's disease a few months before he died, but an autopsy revealed Lewy body disease, whose symptoms include loss of inhibition, severe anxiety, tremors, and difficulty reasoning.

DATA CONNECTIONS: Prevalence of Major NCD among Older Adults explores both age and regional differences in the rates at which older people are diagnosed with a neurocognitive disorder. Achieve

Preventing Impairment

Severe brain damage cannot be reversed. However, education, exercise, and good health not only ameliorate mild losses but may prevent worse ones. According to the World Health Organization

> approximately 40% of dementia cases worldwide could be attributable to 12 modifiable risk factors: low education; midlife hypertension and obesity; diabetes, smoking, excessive alcohol use, physical inactivity, depression, low social contact, hearing loss, traumatic brain injury and air pollution indicating clear prevention potential.
>
> *[Lisko et al., 2021]*

Of these, activity may be most important. Because brain plasticity is lifelong, exercise that improves blood circulation not only prevents cognitive loss but also builds capacity and repairs damage. The benefits of exercise have been repeatedly cited in this text. Now we simply reiterate that physical movement—even more than nutrition and mental exercise—prevents, postpones, and slows cognitive loss of all kinds.

Avoiding specific pathogens is also critical. For example, beef can be tested to ensure that it does not have BSE; condoms can protect against HIV/AIDS; sprays, screens, and bed nets can protect against ZIKA; face masks and vaccines can protect against COVID-19 (see A Case to Study).

JIM WEST/ALAMY

KOSTAS TSIRONIS/BLOOMBERG/GETTY IMAGES

Exercise for Elders In every nation, those who exercise have healthier hearts, lungs, brains, and lives than those who do not. Two contrasting examples are the exercise class in a Michigan Senior Center led by Diane Evans and the stepper machine on a beach in Greece.

OBSERVATION QUIZ

Both are beneficial, but neither is ideal. Why not? (see answer, page 458) ↑

A CASE TO STUDY

COVID-19 and the Brain

Longitudinal data on cognitive impairment caused by COVID-19 are not yet available, but it is already apparent that at least a third of those diagnosed with the virus have neurological symptoms, such as headaches and extreme tiredness (Zangbar et al., 2021). Early in the pandemic, the sick were hospitalized *only* if their fever was above 101 and their blood oxygen was below 70 (these numbers are from one district; other places varied but neurological symptoms were never sufficient).

That ignorance of brain symptoms may have been one reason for the deaths of over half a million people in the United States, because "delayed and misdiagnosed . . . [cases] led to inappropriate management. These patients then become silent contagious sources or 'virus spreaders'" (Jin et al., 2020).

Now we know that high fevers and low oxygen are *not* the main problems when people fall ill and recover. Some people suffer "long-haul COVID" (the name for the condition of those no longer at risk of death but not yet back to normal). Chills and fever may be gone, but neurological symptoms continue.

Consider one case, a 26-year-old teacher who was considered recovered. She was no longer at risk of hospitalization, but

> My chest hurts and head pounds. The body aches and heart races. I can hardly move, it's extreme fatigue. Brain's in a fog, can't remember the name of my dog. Lost my sleep and my appetite. Feet are tingling and ears are ringing. It's the Long-Haul COVID.
>
> *[Nath quoted in Ballard, 2021]*

Few survivors are as impaired as this woman. Scientists have yet to determine how often neurological symptoms occur, how severe they usually are, or how long they will last. But it is evident that the brain is often affected before and after the rest of the body, and that neurocognitive disorders caused by COVID may continue for months.

One doctor predicted:

> We will see the patients with brain fog, intermittent dizziness, and cognitive delay. Most likely, we will have to tell those patients that we don't have the answers—or treatments . . . post-COVID pathology is shaping up to be just as widespread and uncharted as COVID itself.
>
> *[Ballard, 2021]*

Much about the neurological effects of COVID-19 cannot be known until longitudinal studies are published. However, we already know that the effects on the brain may not show up in standard laboratory tests. Some compassion for long haulers, as well as for elders with concerns about their mental capacity, may be forthcoming.

One doctor changed his mind about neurocognitive disorders. His COVID-19 was diagnosed as mild. However, months after the diagnosis the impact on him and his family was "anything but mild." He wrote:

> As an emergency medicine physician, I am trained to develop a hypothesis and to look for objective evidence in support to quickly identify the cause of a patient's suffering. In the absence of objective data—laboratory tests, imaging, examination findings—we are often left to

reassure patients and discharge them with a recommendation for outpatient follow-up, an outcome that too easily can feel dismissive and unsatisfying for the patient and unfulfilling for the physician. My test results were normal: nasopharyngeal swabs for severe acute respiratory syndrome coronavirus 2 (SARS-CoV-2), imaging, laboratory results, oxygen saturation were all fine. But I did not feel fine, and still do not. I have had a rotating constellation of symptoms, different each day and worse each evening: fever, headache, dizziness, palpitations, tachycardia, and others. As a result, I have been reminded of the need to listen to the patient first, even in the absence of conclusive testing. The next time I care for someone with vague abdominal pain, or fatigue, or paresthesia, or any of the myriad conditions that are uncomfortable on the inside but look fine on the outside, I will remember that these symptoms are real and impactful for patients. There is a marked difference between tests being within normal limits and a patient being well.

[Siegelman, 2020, p. 2031]

He wrote that he was "one of the lucky ones" in that he had medical and disability insurance, a fully equipped basement in his home where he quarantined for 40 days, an understanding wife, children, and employer. Even so, he suffered.

YAMAGUCHI HARUYOSHI/CORBIS NEWS/GETTY IMAGES

Comfort and Conversation A cuddly seal robot, PARO, responds to petting with 12 tactile senses, encouraging touch and eye contact. Designed and used in Japan, which has the highest proportion of elders in the world, here PARO is a companion in a nursing home. Critics complain that humans should interact with humans; advocates ask critics whether they also think teddy bears should be removed from children.

Reversible Brain Disease?

Care improves when everyone knows what disease is undermining intellectual capacity. Accurate diagnosis allows targeted treatment and keeps the caregivers from blaming themselves when they are attacked, accused, frustrated, or exhausted. In developing nations, most people with NCD are not diagnosed: They die prematurely with bewildered relatives.

In developed nations, the opposite danger is more likely, a misdiagnosis. Accurate diagnosis is crucial when problems do *not* arise from a neurocognitive disorder. Brain diseases destroy parts of the brain, but some people are thought to be permanently "losing their minds" when the problem is not an incurable disease but, instead, a reversible condition.

EMOTIONAL DISORDERS

The most common reversible condition that is mistaken for NCD is depression. Typically, older people are quite happy. However, for those with ongoing depression or crippling anxiety, treatment is available. Without it, the risk of major NCD increases, in that depression makes people shut out other people and intellectual challenges, both of which keep the brain functioning well.

Ironically, people with untreated anxiety or depression may exaggerate minor memory losses or refuse to talk. Quite the opposite reaction occurs with early Alzheimer's disease, when victims are often surprised that they cannot answer questions, or with Lewy body disease or frontotemporal NCDs, when people talk too much without thinking. Talking, or lack of it, provides an important clue.

Specifics provide other clues. People with neurocognitive loss might forget what they just said, heard, or did because current brain activity is impaired, but they might repeatedly describe details of something that happened long ago. The opposite may be true for emotional disorders, when memory of the past is impaired but short-term memory is not.

MALNUTRITION

Malnutrition and dehydration can also cause symptoms that seem like brain disease. The aging digestive system is less efficient but needs more nutrients and fewer calories. This requires new habits, less fast food, and more grocery money (which some do not have).

Elders may drink less to avoid frequent urination, yet inadequate fluid in the body impedes cell health. Since homeostasis slows with age, older people may not recognize hunger and thirst and thus may inadvertently impair their cognition. Sudden weight loss is a sign of dementia (Shlisky et al., 2017, p. 21).

Beyond the need to drink water, eat vegetables, and strive for a balanced diet (Mediterranean is again recommended) nutritionists find "no consistent evidence exists that nutritional supplements play a protective role" (Shlisky et al., 2017).

Well-controlled longitudinal research on the relationship between particular aspects of the diet and NCD still needs to be done (Coley et al., 2015; Vlachos & Scarmeas, 2019). It is known, however, that people who already have an NCD tend to choose unhealthy foods or forget to eat, hastening their mental deterioration.

POLYPHARMACY

At home as well as in the hospital, most older adults take numerous drugs—not only prescribed medications but also over-the-counter preparations and herbal remedies—a situation known as **polypharmacy**.

polypharmacy
A situation in which older people are prescribed several medications. The various side effects and interactions of those medications can result in dementia symptoms.

Polypharmacy is increasing. For instance, in 1988, among those over 65, 13 percent took five drugs or more. Twenty years later, in 2018, the rate had more than tripled to 42 percent (National Center for Health Statistics, 2020).

Fortunately, older adults smoke, drink alcohol, and overdose on painkillers less often younger adults. However, when they do, the results are worse. Psychoactive drugs, especially alcohol, cause confusion and hallucinations at much lower doses than in the young.

Unfortunately, recommended doses of prescription drugs are determined primarily by clinical trials with younger adults, whose digestive systems eliminate drugs fairly well. With age, homeostasis slows down, and excess lingers.

To make it worse, most safety trials include only healthy people, eliminating those with chronic diseases. This means that drugs are not tested on the older people who are most likely to use them. Moreover, safety trials focus on systemic symptoms, such as shortness of breath, pain, or heart palpitations. Neurological symptoms are not measured.

The average older person in the United States sees a health professional seven times a year (National Center for Health Statistics, 2021). Typically, each of the seven follows *clinical practice guidelines,* which are recommendations for one specific condition. Those recommendations match conditions and treatments, often not taking into account that people of color may respond differently to drugs (Bumpus, 2021).

For everyone, the effectiveness of each medication is affected by diet and other drugs (Fried & Mecca, 2019). Further, people of every age may be confused about when to take which drugs (before, during, or after meals? morning, noon, or night?). Memory loss makes this worse. Thus, for many reasons, elders are more likely to suffer from drug-induced confusion.

The solution seems simple: No drugs. However, that may hasten, not prevent, cognitive decline. For instance, untreated diabetes and hypertension cause cognitive loss. Lack of appropriate medication is one reason why rates of cognitive impairment increase as income falls.

Prevention is less expensive in the long run, but immediate costs may be prohibitive. In one study, physicians referred their patients who might be in the early stages of Alzheimer's for a PET scan. One-third of the patients did not, in fact, have the disease. They simply were aging normally; many had been taking medication that they did not need.

The doctors adjusted their treatment plans based on the results (De Wilde et al., 2018). Searching for biomarkers (as in PET scans) should be routine, but they are expensive and not usually covered by insurance. (In this study, the research grant paid the cost.)

CHAPTER APP 14

IOS:
https://tinyurl.com/y3x7fk75

ANDROID:
https://tinyurl.com/96fvedt

RELEVANT TOPIC:
Polypharmacy

This free app reminds users when it's time to take medication and when they are running low on a prescription. (A "Medifriend" can be designated by the user to receive these reminders as well.) A drug interaction checker notifies users if they have been prescribed medications that aren't supposed to be taken together.

what have you learned?

1. How does changing terminology reflect changing attitudes?
2. How has the prevalence of neurocognitive disorders changed?
3. What are the causes and symptoms of Alzheimer's disease?
4. How does the progression of Alzheimer's differ from that of vascular disease?
5. In what ways are frontotemporal NCDs worse than other types of NCDs?
6. Why is Lewy body disease sometimes mistaken for Parkinson's disease?
7. In addition to brain disease, what other conditions cause NCD?
8. How are depression, anxiety, and neurocognitive disorders connected?
9. How does diet affect the risk of NCD?
10. Why is polypharmacy particularly common among older adults?

Cognition in Late Adulthood

Relatively few adults suffer from major neurocognitive disorders. What about everyone else? Is their thinking the same as it was when they were young? No. It is both better and worse.

VIDEO: Brain Development Animation: Late Adulthood shows gray matter loss in the typical aging brain.

The Structures of the Brain

Brains shrink and slow down over time. By age 80, the average adult brain processes information more slowly than at age 30, or even at age 60. Losses are apparent, not only for speed, but also for memory and logic (Salthouse, 2019).

This is evident in almost every test of intellectual ability and almost every cognitive task. For example, when older adults read out loud, they read more slowly, making more mistakes, such as misreading a word (reading "county" when the word is *country*) or repeating a connecting word (saying "to to" or "in in") (Gollan & Goldrick, 2019).

In general, slower thinking is less proficient. If a person cannot quickly access several ideas at once, that person is less able to think deeply. (See Inside the Brain.)

INSIDE THE BRAIN

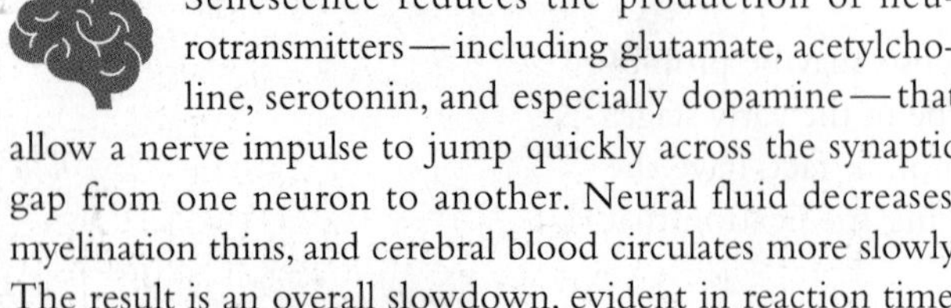

Thinking Slow

Senescence reduces the production of neurotransmitters—including glutamate, acetylcholine, serotonin, and especially dopamine—that allow a nerve impulse to jump quickly across the synaptic gap from one neuron to another. Neural fluid decreases, myelination thins, and cerebral blood circulates more slowly. The result is an overall slowdown, evident in reaction time, movement, speech, and thought.

Speed is crucial for many aspects of cognition. In fact, many experts believe that processing speed underlies all intelligence (Schubert et al., 2020; Tourva & Spanoudis, 2020).

Deterioration of cognition correlates with slower movement and almost every kind of physical disability. For example, gait speed correlates strongly with many measures of intellect (Cosentino et al., 2020). Walks slow? Talks slow? Oh no—thinks slow!

This fear is not baseless. Researchers have studied the connection between walking speed and intellectual sharpness and found that the slower gait predicts cognitive

impairment and brain disease (Montero-Odasso et al., 2017). Remember Jeanne Calment, the woman who lived to 122? Caregivers were astonished that she walked much faster after age 100 than most people in their 80s.

White-matter lesions in the brain accumulate with age and increase the time it takes for a thought to be processed (Rodrigue & Kennedy, 2011). At the same time, overall white matter of the brain decreases, especially with a lifetime of poor health habits, again slowing down thinking (Wassenaar et al., 2019).

Slowed transmission from one neuron to another is not the only problem. With age, transmission of impulses from entire regions of the brain, specifically from parts of the cortex and the cerebellum, is disrupted. Specifics correlate more with cognitive ability than with age.

The crucial question is whether speed is essential for cognition. Language connects the two. A smart person is said to be a *quick* thinker, the opposite of someone who is a *slow* learner. On the other hand, some sayings and stories question those assumptions. We are told to "look before you leap." A fable credited to Aesop, a Greek slave who lived 2,600 years ago, concerns a race between a tortoise and a hare. The rabbit lost: Slow and steady won the race. Which is it?

LESS ACTIVITY

Slow brains may not be bad. Remember that major depression is not caused as much by external events as by neurotransmitters and dendrites that flood, or starve, the brain. Those destructive brain storms happen less often in late adulthood: In 2019, the National Institute of Mental Health reported incidence of major depressive events at various ages: 13 percent for ages 18 to 25; 8 percent for ages 25 to 49; 5 percent for ages 50+.

Those data are from the United States, but elders everywhere are less depressed and anxious than younger people (Jorm, 2000; Machado et al., 2019). Likewise, nationally and internationally, impulsive homicide, assault, and suicide are less common after age 60.

Older women almost never die by suicide; older men (over age 75) have relatively high rates, but not on impulse (Stone et al., 2021). Suicide among aged men is more often a deliberate reaction to months of loneliness, indignity, and loss of power (Canetto, 2015).

Another brain change with age is that older people may use more parts of their brains simultaneously. Both hemispheres of the prefrontal cortex light up on brain scans when older adults solve problems that require only one side of the prefrontal cortex in younger people. Might this be adaptive, and thus not a problem? (See Esteves et al., 2021.)

OBSERVATION QUIZ

Beyond conversation, what do you see that predicts cognition? (see answer, page 458)

MULTITASKING

Multitasking becomes harder with every passing decade because focusing is more difficult when two tasks are done simultaneously. Repeated switches in the brain make multitasking difficult for everyone, but this is particularly true in late adulthood (Lin et al., 2016).

This is why statements such as "I can't do everything at once" and "Don't rush me" are more often spoken by older adults than by teenagers. Adults compensate for slower thinking by selecting one task at a time.

Suppose that a child asks Grandpa a question about dinosaurs while he is reading the newspaper, or asks Grandma which bus to take while she is getting dressed. A wise Grandpa puts down the newspaper and then answers, and Grandma first dresses and then thinks about transportation (avoiding mismatched shoes).

When speed is not an issue, and when older people are able to concentrate on a particular task, they may function, intellectually, as well as younger ones. Indeed, single-minded concentration is sometimes beneficial.

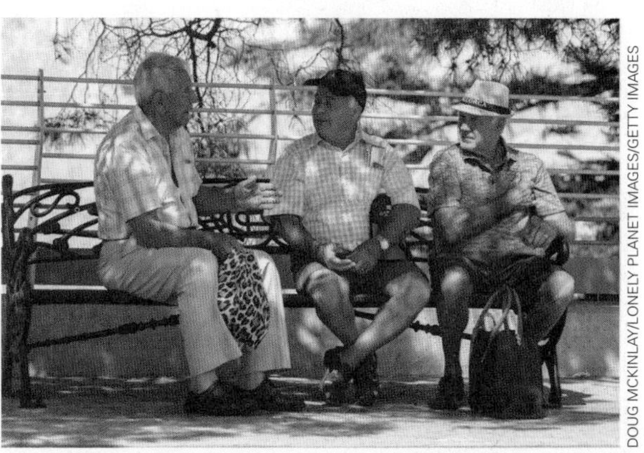

Keeping Alert These three men on a park bench in Malta are doing more than engaging in conversation; they are keeping their minds active through socialization and the discussion of current events and politics.

DOUG MCKINLAY/LONELY PLANET IMAGES/GETTY IMAGES

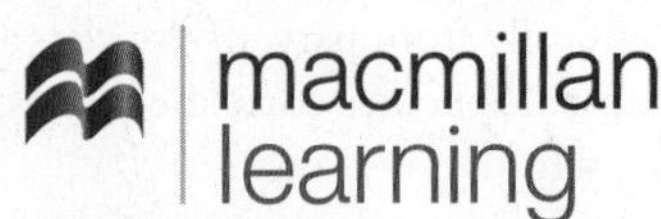

VIDEO: Old Age: Thinking and Moving at the Same Time features a research study demonstrating how older brains are quite adaptable.

In one study, older and younger adults (average age 73 and 24) were asked to judge which of two numbers was higher, "as quickly as possible but try to avoid errors." The older adults were slower but more accurate (Reike & Schwarz, 2019). As a review concludes, changes in brain activation with age can be "adaptive or maladaptive" (Spreng & Turner, 2019, p. 525).

Memory

The aging brain function that causes most concern is memory. As you read in Chapter 9, stereotype threat causes stress that harms cognition; fear may cause forgetfulness. Baring brain disease, age-based stereotypes interfere with memory more than brain deficiencies do (Lamont et al., 2015).

TYPES OF MEMORY

Memory is not one thing but many. The single word *memory* was used before researchers understood the many types of memory—14 of them according to one source, each with distinct traces in distinct parts of the brain (Slotnick, 2017).

In general, *explicit memory* (such as the ability to recall something verbally without clues) fades faster than *implicit memory* (the ability to recognize someone or something as familiar, or to perform a habitual action). Both are affected by age (Fraundorf et al., 2019; Ward et al., 2013).

The distinction between implicit and explicit memory is evident in what the old-old can and cannot do. Old-old people may still swim, bike, and drive even if they cannot name both U.S. senators from their state. Forgetting names is a common and typical memory loss, called the "tip-of-the-tongue" experience (knowing something but not finding the words).

Another common memory deficit with age is *source amnesia*—forgetting the origin of a fact, idea, or snippet of conversation. Source amnesia is particularly problematic currently, with the internet, many channels of television, and many printed sources bombarding the mind.

In practical terms, *source amnesia* means that elders might believe fake news, a rumor, or a political advertisement because they forget that the information came from a biased source. Elders are less likely than younger adults to analyze, or even notice, who said what and why (Devitt & Schacter, 2016).

◆◆ Especially for Students
If you want to remember something that you learn in class for the rest of your life, what should you do? (see response, page 457)

One memory loss might have serious consequences. That is *prospective memory*—remembering to do something in the future (take a pill, meet someone for lunch, buy milk). Prospective memory loss becomes dangerous if, for instance, a cook forgets to turn off the stove, or a driver is in the far lane when the exit appears.

Associative memory, connecting one idea with another, and *episodic memory*, remembering details of a past event, are also likely to be less accurate with age, especially with the stress of stereotype threat (Brubaker & Naveh-Benjamin, 2018).

BETTER WITH AGE

But why focus only on deficiency? Vocabulary is remembered well. Cross-sectional, longitudinal, and cross-sequential studies all show that vocabulary *increases* over most of adulthood. Even at age 90 it is better, on average, than it was from ages 20 to 40 (Salthouse, 2019).

Older people remember words and languages that they learned decades ago. They also continually learn new words and phrases. For example, most elders now know *internet, fax*, and *e-mail*, words that did not exist when they were younger.

Long-term memory may be surprisingly good. Many older people recount in vivid detail events that occurred decades ago. Some tells stories to fascinated

grandchildren about hearing the speeches of Martin Luther King Jr., or participating in the Summer of Love, or life before cell phones, before television, before sliced bread. That is impressive . . . if the memories are accurate. That raises the next question, "What is memory for?"

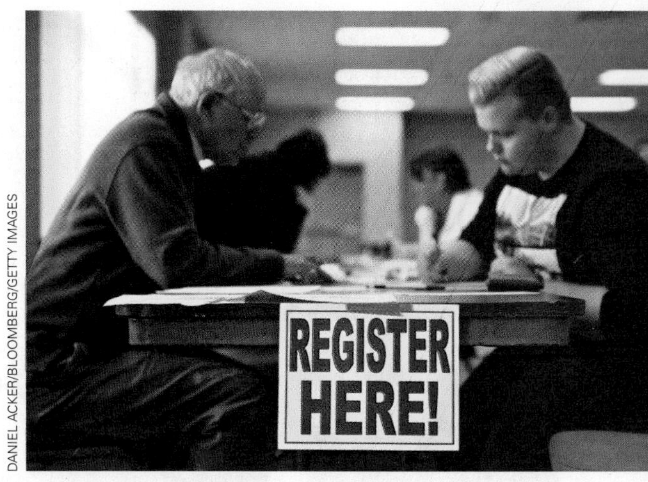

DANIEL ACKER/BLOOMBERG/GETTY IMAGES

Active in the Community One the best ways for older adults to stay mentally active is to be active in their neighborhoods. Registering new voters, as this man is doing, benefits the community while also helping older people to maintain their control processes.

IN DAILY LIFE

Older adults usually think they remember well enough. Fear of memory loss is more typical at age 60 than at age 80, even though actual loss increases with age. Many older adults are conscientious about setting alarms, writing down appointments, and following routines, so they do not forget something important.

When an older person's implicit and prospective memory function well enough for them to be independent and happy, even at age 100, is that memory enough? Those who study memory in late adulthood write about the *prospective memory paradox*: that young adults are better at prospective memory in the laboratory, and older adults are better than the young in daily life (Haines et al., 2020). This raises the question of **ecological validity**.

Ecological validity is measuring memory, or cognition, or anything else as it actually occurs, not as it is indicated in well-controlled, scientific, laboratory experiments. This may be important when measuring cognition in older people, because motivation and attitudes are crucial for cognition in later life (Hess et al., 2019).

Awareness of the need for ecological validity has helped scientists restructure research on memory, trying to avoid tests that are timed and that use abstractions. Restructured studies find fewer deficits than originally thought.

However, any test may misjudge ability. For instance, what is a fair and accurate test of long-term memory? Or is that the wrong question: If an older adult describes life back on the farm to a fascinated grandchild, how important is the accuracy of every detail?

ecological validity
The idea that cognition should be measured in settings that are as realistic as possible and that the abilities measured should be those needed in real life.

self-actualization
The final level of Maslow's hierarchy, when a person becomes (actualizes) their true self. At this stage, people are thought to move past focus on selfish concerns and become more appreciative of nature, of other people, of spiritual concerns.

New Cognitive Development

Remember that the life-span perspective holds that gains as well as losses occur during every period. Are there cognitive gains in late adulthood? Yes, according to many developmentalists.

ERIKSON AND MASLOW

Both Erik Erikson and Abraham Maslow were particularly interested in older adults, interviewing them to understand their thoughts. Erikson's final book, *Vital Involvement in Old Age* (Erikson et al., 1986/1994), written when he was in his 90s, was based on responses from other 90-year-olds who had been studied since they were babies in Berkeley, California.

Erikson found that, over their lives, many older people gained interest in the arts, in children, and in human experience as a whole. He observed that elders are "social witnesses," aware of the interdependence of the generations as well as of all human experience.

Erikson's eighth stage, *integrity versus despair*, marks the time when life comes together in a "re-synthesis of all the resilience and toughness of the basic strengths already developed" (Erikson et al., 1994, p. 40).

Maslow maintained that older adults are more likely than younger people to reach what he originally thought was the highest stage of development, ***self-actualization***.

JGI/JAMIE GRILL/GETTY IMAGES

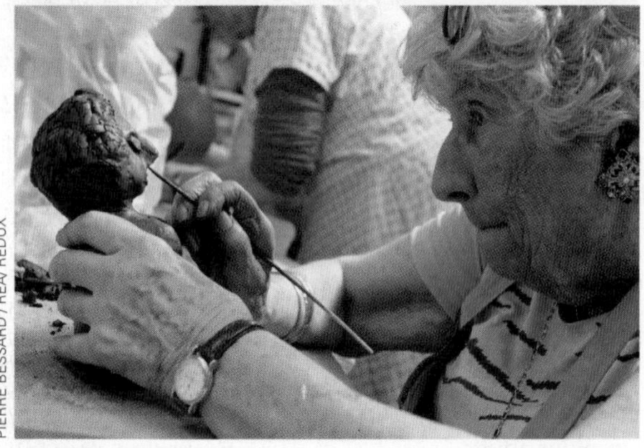

PIERRE BESSARD / REA/ REDUX

Creative Concentration World-famous artists and ordinary people often find that late adulthood allows joyous expression of music, sculpture, and all the arts. That is evident in these two women, one in Jersey City, New Jersey (*top*), and the other in Grenoble, France (*bottom*).

Remember that Maslow rejected an age-based sequence of life, refusing to confine self-actualization to the old. However, Maslow also believed that life experience helps people move forward, so more of the old reach the final stage.

The stage of self-actualization is characterized by aesthetic, creative, philosophical, and spiritual understanding (Maslow, 1954/1997). A self-actualized person might have a deeper spirituality than ever; might be especially appreciative of nature; or might see the humor in many aspects of life, laughing often.

This seems characteristic of many older people. Studies of centenarians find that they often have a deep spiritual grounding and a surprising sense of humor—surprising, that is, to anyone who thinks that a person with limited sight, poor hearing, and an aching body has nothing to laugh about.

AESTHETIC SENSE AND CREATIVITY

Robert Butler was a geriatrician who popularized the study of aging in the United States. He coined the word *ageism* and wrote a book titled *Why Survive: Being Old in America*, first published in 1975. Partly because his grandparents were crucial in his life, Butler understood that elders can contribute to their families and communities.

Butler explained that "old age can be a time of emotional sensory awareness and enjoyment" (Butler et al., 1998, p. 65). Older adults learn new skills and take up new activities. For example, some elders begin gardening, bird-watching, sculpting, painting, or making music, each of which requires new learning.

Many well-known artists continue to work in late adulthood, sometimes producing their best work. Michelangelo painted the awe-inspiring frescoes in the Sistine Chapel at age 75; Verdi composed the opera *Falstaff* when he was 80; Frank Lloyd Wright completed the design of the Guggenheim Museum when he was 91.

In a study of extraordinarily creative people, very few felt that their ability, their goals, or the quality of their work had been much impaired by age. The leader of that study observed, "in their seventies, eighties, and nineties, they may lack the fiery ambition of earlier years, but they are just as focused, efficient, and committed as before . . . perhaps more so" (Csikszentmihalyi, 2013, p. 207).

Music and singing are often used to reduce anxiety in those who suffer from neurocognitive impairment, because the ability to appreciate music is preserved in the brain when other functions fail. The evidence is clear: Music, the visual arts, and creative work of all kinds help the mind, the mood, and overall well-being (Charise & Eginton, 2018).

life review
An examination of one's own role in the history of human life, engaged in by many elders. This can be written or oral.

THE LIFE REVIEW

One particular method to deepen older adults' cognition is the **life review**, in which elders provide an account of their personal lifelong journey by writing or telling their story. They want others to know their history, not only their personal

experiences but also those of their family, cohort, or ethnic group. According to Robert Butler:

> We have been taught that this nostalgia represents living in the past and a preoccupation with self and that it is generally boring, meaningless, and time-consuming. Yet as a natural healing process it represents one of the underlying human capacities on which all psychotherapy depends. The life review should be recognized as a necessary and healthy process in daily life as well as a useful tool in the mental health care of older people.
>
> *[Butler et al., 1998, p. 91]*

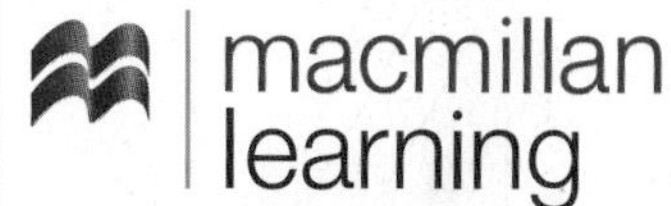

VIDEO: Portrait of Aging: Bill, age 99, shares his secret to longevity.

Hundreds of developmentalists, following Butler's lead, have guided older people in self-review. Sometimes elders write down their thoughts, and sometimes they simply tell their story, responding to questions from the listener.

The result is almost always positive, especially for the person who tells the story. The life review is a potent antidote to depression (Lan et al., 2019).

For instance, half of a group of 202 older people in a study in the Netherlands were randomly assigned to a life-review process. For them, depression and anxiety were markedly reduced compared to the control group (Korte et al., 2012). A study of elders in the United States also found that telling their story helped them see a purpose in life—just what Erikson would hope (Robinson & Murphy-Nugen, 2018).

Wisdom

It is possible that "older adults . . . understand who they are in a newly emerging stage of life, and discovering the wisdom that they have to offer" (Bateson, 2011, p. 9). A massive international survey of 26 nations from every corner of the world found that most people agree that wisdom is a characteristic of elders (Löckenhoff et al., 2009).

Wisdom builds over time. People who are open to new experiences in early adulthood, who cope well with stress in middle age, and who strive for self-actualization in late adulthood, are more likely to be wise. As one study concludes, "a balance between personality adjustment and growth, aided by social support and competence during the formative years, might be required to promote wisdom development throughout life" (Ardelt et al., 2018, p. 1514).

An underlying quandary is that a universal definition of wisdom is elusive: Each culture and each cohort have their own concepts, with fools sometimes seeming wise (as happens in Shakespearean drama) and those who should be wise sometimes acting foolishly (provide your own examples). Older and younger adults differ in how they make decisions; one interpretation of these differences is that the older adults are wiser, but not every younger adult would agree.

Several factors just mentioned, including self-reflective honesty (as in integrity), perspective on past living (the life review), and the ability to put aside one's personal needs (as in self-actualization), are considered part of wisdom.

If this is true, elders may have an advantage in developing wisdom, particularly if they have (1) dedicated their lives to the "understanding of life," (2) learned from their experiences, and (3) become more mature and integrated. That may be why popes and U.S. Supreme Court justices are usually quite old.

As two psychologists explain:

> Wisdom is one domain in which some older individuals excel. . . . [They have] a combination of psychosocial characteristics and life history factors, including openness to experience, generativity, cognitive style, contact with excellent mentors, and some exposure to structured and critical life experiences.
>
> *[Baltes & Smith, 2008, p. 60]*

SEAN CAFFREY/GETTY IMAGES

Long Past Warring Many of the oldest men in Mali, like this imam, are revered. Unfortunately, Mali has experienced violent civil wars and two national coups in recent years, perhaps because 75 percent of the male population are under age 30 and less than 2 percent are over age 70. In 2019, the British newspaper *The Guardian* described Mali as the most dangerous nation in the world.

A review of personality development during adulthood found that some people became wiser but not everyone does (Reitz & Staudinger, 2017). Why not? The next chapter has some answers.

what have you learned?

1. How do the structures of the brain change with age?
2. Which kinds of things are harder to remember with age?
3. What might be benefits from the changing brain in late adulthood?
4. What would be an ecologically valid test of cognition in late adulthood?
5. What do Erikson and Maslow say about cognitive development in late adulthood?
6. What happens with creative ability as people grow older?
7. What is the special role of music in old age?
8. Who benefits from a life review?
9. Why are scientists hesitant to say that wisdom comes from old age?

SUMMARY

New Understanding of Old Age

1. A demographic shift is that fewer children and more older people comprise the population of the world as well as every nation. In the United States, 17 percent of the people are over age 64.

2. As the baby boomers reach these years, our understanding of late adulthood is changing. For example, most people over age 65 are self-sufficient and productive, and the rate of Alzheimer's is decreasing even as the numbers of people with this disease are increasing.

3. A distinction is made between the young-old, the old-old, and the oldest-old. The latter are dependent on others for daily care; they are about 6 percent of the people in the United States over age 65.

4. Ageism is stereotyping people based on their age. Ageism can be dismissive or benevolent, but either way can become a self-fulfilling prophecy, undercutting vital individuality in late adulthood. An example is elderspeak, the way some people talk to people who are old.

5. Sleep patterns change with age, but worries about sleep may, itself, harm well-being. Exercise decreases as people age. Family, community, and elders themselves are to blame for this destructive change.

Theories and Systems

6. Hundreds of theories address the causes of aging. The three most common are wear and tear, genes, and cellular change. All explain some aspects of aging, but none is sufficient.

7. The aging process seems to slow down via calorie restriction. That benefits health and prolongs life in many species, but humans find intermittent fasting easier than calorie restriction.

8. Genes, cellular repair, and telomere length affect aging. This is most evident in late adulthood, although it may originate in childhood.

9. One concern is that the focus of most theories of senescence is on the biology of aging, but personal and policy choices are most influential for most people.

10. The senses, sexuality, and driving a car all are affected by age. For all of these, a systems approach seems most helpful, because each loss is affected by other losses, other people, and the culture.

Neurocognitive Disorders

11. Major neurocognitive disorders (formerly called dementia) are characterized by diseases that reduce brain functioning. This may begin with mild neurocognitive disorders. Diagnosis is difficult, and no foolproof biomarkers are yet available.

12. The most common cause of major NCD in the United States is Alzheimer's disease, an incurable ailment that becomes more prevalent with age and worsens over time. The main symptom is extreme memory loss.

13. Also common is vascular disease (also called vascular or multi-infarct dementia), which results from a series of ministrokes that occur when impairment of blood circulation destroys portions of brain tissue.

14. Other NCDs, including frontotemporal NCD and Lewy body disease, also become more common with age. Some cognitive disorders can occur at any age of adulthood. One is Parkinson's disease, which begins with loss of muscle control and eventually causes significant cognitive decline.

15. Major NCDs are sometimes mistakenly diagnosed when individuals are suffering from a reversible problem, such as anxiety, depression, or polypharmacy. Older adults take many drugs, sometimes with uncertain side effects.

Cognition in Late Adulthood

16. Speed of processing slows down, parts of the brain shrink, and more areas of the brain are activated in older people.

17. Memory is affected by aging, but specifics vary. Some types of memory fade, but other types—notably vocabulary—increase. Ecological validity suggests that memory should be measured as it actually functions in daily life.

18. Many people become more interested and adept in creative endeavors, as well as more philosophical, as they grow older. The life review helps many older people remember earlier experiences, allowing them to gain perspective and achieve integrity and self-actualization.

19. Wisdom does not necessarily increase as a result of age, but some elders are unusually wise or insightful.

KEY TERMS

demographic shift (p. 428)
average life expectancy (p. 429)
young-old (p. 430)
old-old (p. 430)
oldest-old (p. 430)
ageism (p. 430)
elderspeak (p. 431)
wear-and-tear theory (p. 435)
weathering (p. 435)
calorie restriction (p. 435)
intermittent fasting (p. 435)
maximum life span (p. 436)
cellular aging (p. 437)
telomeres (p. 438)
universal design (p. 441)
neurocognitive disorder (NCD) (p. 443)
biomarkers (p. 444)
Alzheimer's disease (AD) (p. 444)
plaques (p. 444)
tangles (p. 444)
vascular disease (p. 445)
frontotemporal NCDs (p. 445)
Parkinson's disease (p. 446)
Lewy body disease (p. 446)
terminal decline (p. 446)
polypharmacy (p. 449)
ecological validity (p. 453)
self-actualization (p. 453)
life review (p. 454)

APPLICATIONS

1. Write down the degree of independence of all your relatives over age 65, such as grandparents and great-grandparents, great aunts and great uncles, and so on. What percent are in nursing homes? How and why is that percent higher or lower than the national average?

2. Compensating for sensory losses is difficult because it involves learning new habits. To better understand the experience, reduce your hearing or vision for a day by wearing earplugs or dark glasses that let in only bright lights. (Use caution and common sense: Don't drive a car while wearing earplugs or cross streets while wearing dark glasses.) Report on your emotions, the responses of others, and your conclusions.

3. Ask five people of various ages whether they want to live to age 100 and record their responses. Would they be willing to eat half as much, exercise much more, experience weekly dialysis, or undergo other procedures in order to extend life? Analyze the responses.

4. Many factors affect intellectual sharpness. Think of an occasion when you felt inept and an occasion when you felt smart. How did the contexts of the two experiences differ? How might those differences affect the performance of elders and young adults who go to a university laboratory for testing?

ESPECIALLY FOR ANSWERS

Response for Young Adults (from p. 431): No. Some older people hear well, and they would resent it.

Response for Biologists (from p. 438): Although ageism and ambivalence limit the funding of research on the causes of aging, the applications include prevention of AIDS, cancer, neurocognitive disorders, and physical damage from pollution—all urgent social priorities.

Response for Students (from p. 452): Review it several times over the next days and weeks, and you will probably remember it in 50 years, with a little review.

OBSERVATION QUIZ ANSWERS

Answer to Observation Quiz (from p. 447): Neither photo depicts exercise that is likely to become an enjoyable routine. The teacher is not facing the class, so she may not know when someone cannot follow her pose, and the beach exerciser is unlikely to return every day, because exercise machines are often symbols of good intentions that do not last longer than a few days.

Answer to Observation Quiz (from p. 451): Friendship is protective at every age. In addition, being outside in daylight, wearing appropriate clothing (note the hats and shoes), and simply experiencing fresh air and greenery are all correlates of a healthy mind and body.

LATE ADULTHOOD
The Social World

what will you know?

- Do older people withdraw from the activity of their former lives?
- Do elders want to move to a distant, warm place?
- Is home care better than nursing-home care?

Almost every week I walk through Washington Square Park with my friend Doris, a 92-year-old widow. Many people greet her by name, including men playing cards on a park table and a woman who owns a nearby hotel. Doris is an icon for street performers, including Colin, who plays his piano (on wheels) for dozens of onlookers on sunny days, and Tic and Tac, who are middle-aged twins who do astonishing tumbling tricks with audience participation. The police watch the card players because they suspect drug-dealing. Colin was ticketed for unlawful noise.

Doris organized a protest. She got Community Board 2 (she has been reappointed by the City Council every two years since 1964) to pass a resolution supporting entertainment in the park. The city withdrew the ticket, and the Parks Department revised their policy.

We walk slowly because Doris greets babies, birds, and animals. Squirrels scamper up to grab peanuts from her hand, and sometimes pigeons perch on her arm. Tourists photograph her; the local press admires her (Google "Doris Diether").

Doris dresses well, appropriate for each season. But one hot August day she wore a long-sleeved blouse. She proudly told me why: Her arm was scratched because two pigeons fought over the same spot. She tells me about her grandmother from Finland, her two marriages, her journalist days as a dance critic, her efforts to style her very white hair.

We often stop at a mailbox to drop in a timely greeting card: I have become one of hundreds on her list. Colorful envelopes arrive in my box—green for St. Patrick's Day, orange for Halloween, gray for Thanksgiving, red for July 4th, and multicolored for my birthday. She sends 426 Christmas cards; she orders stamps from a Post Office catalog.

IRA BERGER / ALAMY STOCK PHOTO

Not a Puppet One park regular is a puppeteer, Ricky Syers, who entertains hundreds of tourists with an array of puppets. He recently made a puppet of Doris, one more bit of evidence that the real Doris is beloved by many—and not controlled by anyone.

Usually friends have much in common, but Doris is not like me. I have four children; she has none. I never send cards, feed squirrels, or protect pianists (although Doris did get me to help Colin). We belong to opposing political parties. Often, she is the lone "nay" vote on Community Board resolutions.

How did we become friends? Fifteen years ago, Doris had knee surgery. She asked for volunteers to push her wheelchair to her many meetings, appointments, and social engagements. Many people did: I escorted her once a week.

Soon she could walk, but she wanted me to keep coming. I bring her the Sunday paper (she pays me back, with cash and a wrapped piece of chocolate), I watch for cars when we cross the street; I lift her walker down the two stairs from her front door. I have grown to enjoy her anecdotes, her memories, her attitudes.

Eight years ago, Doris had surgery for a broken hip. The hospital soon put her in a private room because her younger roommate complained that Doris had too many visitors. Among them were street people from the park, our state senator, and a man who credits her for his victory over his landlord. He avoided eviction: Doris is an expert on zoning and rent laws.

A month ago, another fall put her in our local nursing home, temporarily. COVID-19 kept us from visiting, but on her birthday, a neighbor arranged a party on the street. Three dozen people gathered with balloons, bubbles, and noisemakers outside a large window, where the staff had wheeled Doris so she could hear us sing.

Doris defies stereotyping, which makes her an illustration of the theme of this chapter. Each older person is unique, not just one of millions. Some are frail, lonely, and vulnerable. But even the very old, with several disabilities, may be like Doris—active, involved, and beloved. I hope to be like her someday.

Theories of Late Adulthood

Some older people run marathons and lead nations; others no longer walk or talk. Social scientists theorize about this diversity.

Self Theories

self theories
Theories of late adulthood that emphasize the core self, or the search to maintain one's integrity and identity.

Certain theories of late adulthood can be called **self theories**; they focus on individuals, especially each person's self-concept and self-expression. One study found that, with age, people feel closer to their "authentic self" (Seto & Schlegel, 2018). Many older people think that, if anything, they continue being who they are, or more so (Cook, 2018).

Indeed, one theory of late adulthood is called *continuity theory*, which holds that people continue to be themselves as their bodies age (Atchley, 1989). That theory was illustrated in a study of centenarians in Oklahoma. One said, "I have books I've read, some of them two times, some of them three times . . . I get them out and reread them and put them back on the shelf" (Heinz et al., 2017).

Another study, this one of retired men who had been professors, found that they maintained their scholarly interests. One said, "I never really left the university" (Rowson & Phillipson, 2020).

More generally, many studies find that the sense of self is crucial, not only for happiness but also for survival. Centenarians who keep their personal beliefs, including

that they can still do things themselves, are likely to stay healthy. Part of that is having other people recognize them as individuals, a "self" not one of the "old ones" (Yorgason et al., 2018).

At every age, adults who feel that they have personal control of their lives are happier. One impressive study followed over a thousand people ages 40 to 85 for 15 years. Reduced sense of control predicted later illness, loneliness, and dependence (Drewelies et al., 2017).

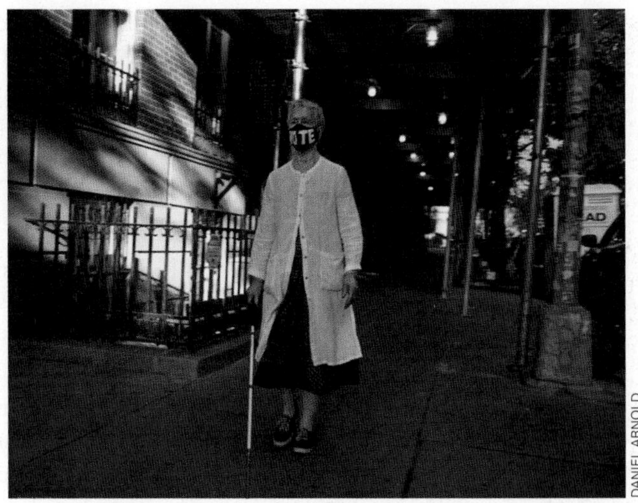

Still Active Diana is in her 80s, legally blind, still working, with Pilates instruction two days a week. She walks alone on her city block, protected by strangers and her own determination.

DANIEL ARNOLD

OBSERVATION QUIZ
What five things in this photo indicate Diana's personal choices to remain active? (see answer, page 490) ↑

THE SELF AND CARING FOR OTHERS

A series of studies focused on one particular aspect of the self, called *prosociality* ("contribution to the welfare and well-being of other people") or *altruism* ("motivation to help others, even when doing so is costly") (Shane et al., 2021, p. 24; Sparrow et al., 2021, p. 49). That personality trait shows continuity over the years: A caring, sharing, middle-aged adult is likely to be a caring and sharing older adult.

Expression of that trait may be constrained in late adulthood, if a person has diminished control of their time and wealth. Physical ailments may require more personal care; reduced income means reduced donations. However, the general finding is that altruism is increased, or at least maintained, throughout life.

Many people become more, rather than less, themselves with age. That is what Anna Quindlen found:

> It's odd when I think of the arc of my life from child to young woman to aging adult. First I was who I was, then I didn't know who I was, then I invented someone and became her, then I began to like what I'd invented, and finally I was what I was again. It turned out I wasn't alone in that particular progression.
>
> *[Quindlen, 2012, p. ix]*

Overall, research on personality over the life-span finds that most fluctuation occurs before age 25. Then stability is notable over the decades of middle and late adulthood (Briley & Tucker-Drob, 2017). Even when a neurocognitive disorder erases memory and health, the self is usually preserved (Lim & Song, 2020; Tippett et al., 2018).

Outsiders have sometimes been awed at the dedication of relatives who care for an elder who is entirely bedbound or who is in the last stages of Alzheimer's. Self theory provides an explanation: Relationships continue, in part because the care receiver is still, in many ways, themselves (Lang & Fowers, 2019). So is the caregiver, who usually is also an older person.

People in the final stages of Alzheimer's may appreciate flowers, or ice cream, or music as they always did. As you learned in Chapter 14, some neurocognitive disorders attack the personality, but that is not the norm. Most people "was what I was" again.

This also explains why caring for someone with a frontotemporal neurocognitive disorder (NCD) is much harder, although less physical care is needed than for other conditions (Nowaskie et al., 2019). When the prefrontal cortex is destroyed, personality traits that defined the person may disappear. A loving mother might reject her children, or a formerly astute businessman might invest in a hare-brained scheme.

REMEMBERING THE PAST

Older adults have lived through historic decades. The current cohort can remember "whites only" signs on public restrooms, or the space shuttle Challenger exploding in 1986. Personal memories may be more salient than ones for public events. Many elders recount why they did, or did not, attend college, or the details of their first job,

of the birth of their children, or the early death of a friend. Those memories may be formative for the self.

My aged mother recounted, that, when she was 9 years old, her older sisters (she had five of them) threw away sketches she drew. That explained why she had only two children, and why she kept many of my childhood papers.

Memories echo. One team of psychologists begins their discussion of "witnessing, remembering, and testifying" with the following words:

> For human beings, the past is special. We think of the past as defining almost all aspects of our lives: where we belong, who our friends are, what our social status is, what kind of person we are.
>
> *[Mahr & Csibra, 2020, p. 428]*

As people remember and learn from their personal life history, they develop values, strategies, and opinions that endure in old age, as touchstones of who they have been and will continue to be. In other words, integrity is achieved. This can explain what may strike younger listeners as odd: Many older people repeat aspects of their personal history that younger people think should be forgotten.

integrity versus despair
The final stage of Erik Erikson's developmental sequence, in which older adults seek to integrate their unique experiences with their vision of community.

You may have heard an older person boasting about skipping school, taking drugs, escaping arrest, or being severely punished. A racial insult is repeatedly retold to the grandchildren, sexual harassment at employment 50 years ago is not forgotten. Elders might describe details of appearance and actions of one horrible third-grade teacher, or the unexpected praise from a wonderful fourth-grade teacher.

Some past experiences cannot be glorified. Even then, self-theory explains why some elders claim them as part of who they are. For example, one man said:

> Well, I had a hard life, I can say that, but I'm glad that I lived the way that I lived it. It taught you a lot about life. There was parts of it I wish I never had to go through, but . . . I've always felt that's part of what we was here for.
>
> *[quoted in Heinz et al., 2017]*

Feeling pride at surviving past problems may explain an interesting finding: Several studies report that depression is more common in middle age than in late adulthood. A sense of mastery is protective of the self (Blanchflower & Oswald, 2017; Nicolaisen et al., 2017).

This may be particularly true for the current cohort of U.S. women aged 65 and older. In 2019, older women died by suicide less than half as often as women aged 45–54 (4.3 compared to 10.4 per 100,000) (Stone et al., 2021). Rates are far higher for older men than older women (over 12 times higher after age 84), perhaps because age may strip older men of their status; they lose what made them themselves.

This stark gender difference in suicide among older adults is less apparent in other nations. In China, women traditionally died by suicide more often than men. In the past two decades, the Chinese rate of suicide has decreased dramatically, although older women are still at higher risk than in other nations (J. Zhang, 2019). Does self theory offer an explanation?

Always Himself Leading nonviolent protest was a sign of lifelong integrity for John Lewis. In his early 20s, he was beaten and arrested dozens of times as he sought civil rights for African Americans. At age 23, he spoke at the 1963 March on Washington, when Martin Luther King Jr. proclaimed "I have a dream." In this photo, at age 73, Lewis was at the unveiling of a stamp commemorating that march 50 years earlier. Lewis was elected to represent Georgia in the U.S. Congress in 1986 and was reelected 15 times. At age 76, he led a sit-in on the Congressional floor, asking the leadership to allow discussion and a vote on a bill to require background checks for gun ownership. He died in 2020 at age 80, a national hero.

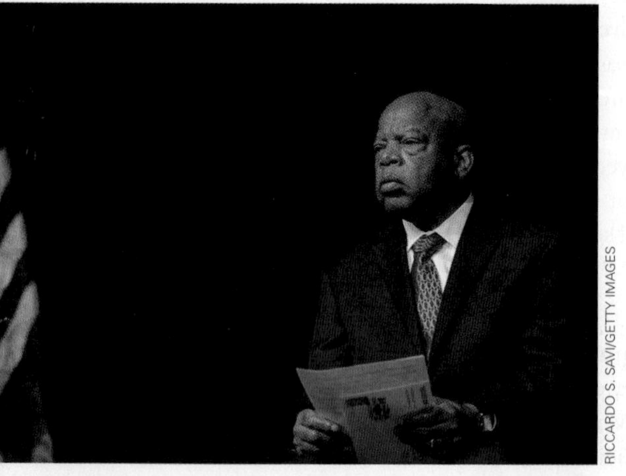
RICCARDO S. SAVI/GETTY IMAGES

INTEGRITY

The most comprehensive self theory came from Erik Erikson. His eighth and final stage of development, **integrity versus despair**, requires adults to integrate their unique experiences with their community concerns (Erikson et al., 1986/1994). The word *integrity* may mean honesty, but it also means a feeling of being whole, not scattered, comfortable with oneself.

Self-glorifying memories and self-acceptance counteract despair, because "time is now short, too short for the attempt to start another life" (Erikson, 1993a, p. 269). For every stage, the tension between the two opposing aspects (here integrity versus despair) propels growth.

The need for continuity and integrity may explain why many older people strive to maintain childhood cultural practices. For instance, grandparents may teach a grandchild a language that is rarely spoken, or repeat clichés from their youth, or encourage younger generations to follow traditional rituals. In cultures that emphasize newness, elders worry that they themselves will disappear if tradition is lost.

As Erikson wrote, the older person

> knows that an individual life is the accidental coincidence of but one life cycle with but one segment of history and that for him all human integrity stands or falls with the one style of integrity of which he partakes. . . . In such a final consolation, death loses its sting.
>
> *[Erikson, 1993a, p. 268]*

JIM WILKES/ZUMA PRESS/TORONTO/NEWSCOM

Trash or Treasure? Tryphona Flood, threatened with eviction, admitted she's a hoarder and got help from Megan Tolen, shown here discussing what in this four-room apartment can be discarded. Flood sits on the only spot of her bed that is not covered with stuff. This photo was taken midway through a three-year effort to clean out the apartment — the clutter was worse a year earlier.

HOLDING ON TO THE SELF

Most older people consider their personalities and attitudes quite stable over their life span, even as they acknowledge physical changes and mental lapses (Klein, 2012). One 103-year-old woman, wrinkled, shrunken, and severely crippled by arthritis, displayed a photo of herself as a beautiful young woman. She said, "My core has stayed the same. Everything else has changed" (quoted in Troll & Skaff, 1997, p. 166).

Many older people resist moving from drafty and dangerous dwellings into safer apartments, because leaving old places means abandoning personal history. They keep objects and papers that a younger person would throw away. This difficulty discarding objects is the prime symptom of a disorder called **compulsive hoarding**, which can become so extreme that it impedes health and safety.

compulsive hoarding
The urge to accumulate and hold on to familiar objects and possessions, sometimes to the point of their becoming health and/or safety hazards. This impulse tends to increase with age.

Hoarding actually begins in adolescence, when young people save things that others would discard. However it becomes most severe and most prevalent in late adulthood (about 6 percent of those over age 65) (Cath et al., 2017).

Hoarding may arise from the desire to maintain the self (see A Case to Study). Likewise, elders may refuse surgery, chemotherapy, or medicine because they fear it might distort their minds: They want to be themselves, even if it shortens their life.

A CASE TO STUDY

Saving Old Newspapers

My friend Doris (in the opening anecdote) keeps old newspaper clippings, phonograph records, and many other things. She has accumulated these possessions over the 60 years she has lived in the same small, rent-controlled apartment, with almost every surface covered.

To her, all of her saved items are meaningful; she sometimes offers them to libraries and other institutions. Not only does she send hundreds of cards; she also receives hundreds, displayed around her small space, taken down when each holiday is over. Is that a problem?

Doris grew up in the Great Depression, becoming an entertainer for the troops during World War II. Saving, rationing, and reusing meant survival and patriotism, and homes typically had attics or basements with space for old magazines, clothes, toys, knickknacks. Sayings like "a penny saved is a penny earned" and "waste not, want not" were passed down as wisdom from one generation to the next.

Times have changed. Unlike the DSM I, II, III, and IV, DSM-5 classifies hoarding as a psychological disorder (American Psychiatric Association, 2013, pp. 247–251). Saving is no longer admired; pennies on the street are rarely

picked up; expiration dates are stamped on food and drugs; electronics, from computers to televisions, are designed to become quickly obsolete. More than a third of the food in the United States is thrown away, not eaten.

Perhaps elders are expressing values formed decades ago. As an expression of the self, hoarding may bring emotional satisfaction (Frost et al., 2015), the same joy a younger person might get from buying the latest smartphone. Older people seek to maintain childhood mores, lifelong habits, and past history. Faded photographs and chipped china may do that, a buffer when memories of long-dead people cause anxiety (David et al., 2021).

Currently hoarding correlates with social isolation and physical and psychological problems (Roane et al., 2017). In today's smaller dwellings, there is no space for extra possessions. A hoarder may limit current visitors, to forestall criticism. (At least Doris lets me in; she asks me to change her cats' water.)

Because stacks of old papers and junk can attract dirt, mold, and insects, not to mention pose a fire hazard, I thought of offering to help Doris get rid of her stuff. But then I realized that would be too painful for both of us.

I understand the general conclusions from the research: Hoarding may signify pathology, including social isolation that worsens over time. But I justify Doris's stacks of papers as her way to maintain her sense of self.

I wonder about my justification. I know that people tend to ignore pathology in people they care about. Scientists should not do that.

KEEPING OLD FRIENDS

Another self theory is *socio-emotional selectivity theory* (Carstensen, 1993), that older people select familiar social contacts who reinforce their generativity, pride, and joy. As socio-emotional theory would predict, when people understand that their future time is limited, their appreciation of family, old friends, and nature increases, thus furthering their happiness.

positivity effect
The tendency for older people to perceive, prefer, and remember positive images and experiences more than negative ones.

An outgrowth of socio-emotional selectivity is known as the **positivity effect**. Elders perceive, prefer, and remember positive experiences more than negative ones, the good in people more than the bad (Carstensen & DeLiema, 2018; Reed et al., 2014). Unpleasant images are ignored, forgotten, or reinterpreted.

By contrast, younger adults often have a "negativity bias." An easy example is where the gaze lingers when people see a photo of a snake and a rose. Younger people stare more at the snake, older people at the rose.

THINK CRITICALLY: Does the positivity effect avoid reality?

That example is hypothetical, but a longitudinal study of a traumatic event confirmed the positivity effect and the negativity bias (Ford et al., 2018). In 2013, during the Boston Marathon, two pressure cooker bombs exploded, killing three immediately, injuring 264, followed by a manhunt that killed two more. Thousands helped the injured and searched for the killers.

In a longitudinal study that began days after the disaster, 147 Bostonians, aged 19–85, rated the following statements from 1 to 7, where 1 indicated extreme disagreement and 7 indicated extreme agreement:

- When I think of the marathon bombing, I think about the negative aspects—the hurt and devastation caused.
- When I think of the marathon bombing, I think about the positive aspects—the heroism and the way the city has come together.

In the first days after the event, almost everyone strongly agreed (6) with both statements. Six months later, however, responses had shifted: The older adults were thinking more about the positive aspects and the younger ones, the negative (see Figure 15.1).

This focus on the best, not the worst, is also evident when long-married people talk about their spouse, or when older parents brag about their grown children or grandchildren. For example, one grandmother (Donne Davis) created a popular group for grandmothers called GaGa Sisterhood, where grandmas "bond, brag, and benefit."

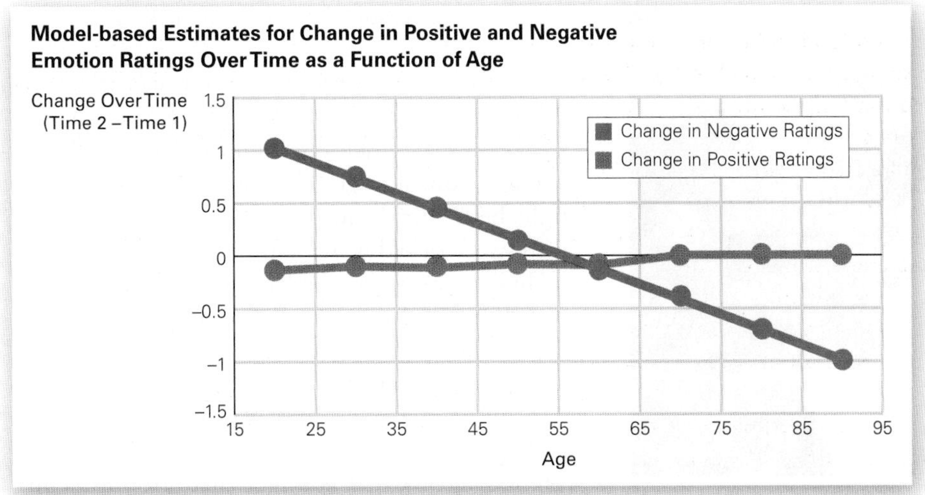

FIGURE 15.1 Forget the Deaths Memory is always selective, but six months after the bombing at the Boston Marathon, younger people were more likely to remember the dead but older adults the heroes. You can confirm the positivity effect by asking older adults about World War II— they remember victories more than losses.

Stratification Theories

As just explained, self theories focus on individuals, specifically on unique, personal, and positive perceptions. That contrasts with another set of theories, called **stratification theories**, which emphasize social forces that place each person in a social stratum or level. That positioning creates disadvantages for some and advantages for others, affecting old age because of strictures that set them on a trajectory decades before.

stratification theories
Theories emphasizing that social forces, particularly those related to a person's social stratum or social category, limit individual choices and affect a person's ability to function in late adulthood because past stratification continues to limit life.

Stratification begins in the womb, because "individuals are born into a society that is already stratified—that is, differentiated—along key dimensions, including sex, race, and SES" (Lynch & Brown, 2011, p. 107). As a result, "major health and disease conditions in adulthood and later life often have early developmental origins, stemming even from the prenatal period" (Settersten et al., 2020).

An easy example is the diet of pregnant women, which is influenced by the stratification of culture and SES. If a woman is undernourished, her baby is more likely to be low birthweight, which stratifies that newborn, increasing the likelihood of obesity, diabetes, and heart disease in late adulthood (de Mendonça et al., 2020). Indeed, whether or not a fetus will become a college graduate, a wealthy adult, and a mentally healthy elder depends partly on whether that fetus was born too early, which correlates with low SES (Bilgin et al., 2018).

GENDER STRATIFICATION

Older women are typically financially disadvantaged because of past stratification as unpaid caregivers or low-wage workers. That accumulates: In late adulthood, more women than men live in poverty (see Figure 15.2).

In a practical example, adult children urge their widowed mothers more often than their widowered fathers to live with them. The reason is cultural, not logical, since men are more at risk of a sudden health crisis: Living alone is more dangerous for them.

Gender stratification may harm males, too, however. Boys are taught to be stoic, repressing emotions and avoiding doctors, thus shortening their lives (Hamm et al., 2017). In 2016 in the United States, about twice as many men as women never saw a health professional (19 versus 10 percent) (Ashman et al., 2019).

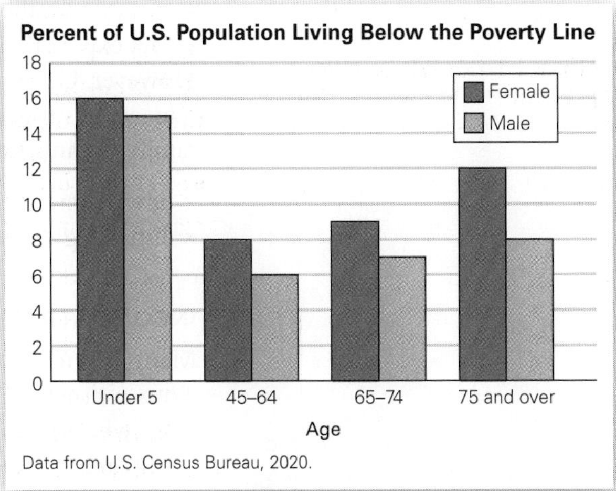

FIGURE 15.2 **Systems, Not Individuals** Stratification theories stress social systems more than personal choices. No one decided to discriminate against children or older women, yet sexism and ageism are evident here.

AP IMAGES/WANG ZHIDE - IMAGINECHINA

Twice Fortunate Ageism takes many forms. Some cultures are youth-oriented and devalue older people, while others are the opposite. These twin sisters are lucky to be alive: They were born in rural China in 1905, a period when most female twins died. When this photo was taken, they were age 103, and fortunate again, venerated because they have lived so long.

Is that one reason that men die at younger ages than women?

In another example of gender stratification, women are the recipients of benevolent sexism (the "weaker sex"), which continues in late adulthood. An older woman might be a "sweet old lady," a man might be a "dirty old man." Why aren't old men called sweet, or old women dirty?

Thus, everyone may be harmed by gender stratification. One final example: A few decades ago, wives relied on husbands to manage money and men relied on wives to prepare food, a gender divide maintained by many couples who married decades ago. Most were influenced by another gender divide—brides were expected to be younger than grooms. Thus, because of past gender stratification, men die too soon, and women are poor and lonely for too long.

ETHNIC STRATIFICATION

Ethnic differences overlap with racial differences, harming many people over the life span. Past discrimination reduced quality of education, health of neighborhoods, wages earned. All of this affects older people who experienced systemic racism decades earlier.

Consider one detailed example: home ownership. Sixty years ago, stratification prevented many people of color from buying homes. Forty years ago, new laws reduced housing discrimination.

At that point in U.S. economic history, interest rates were high, but mortgages were easy to obtain. Thus, the foreclosure crisis that began in 2007 fell particularly hard on those who bought homes in about 2000, disproportionately Black Americans, who found themselves with homes that were "under water"—more money owed than the houses were worth. Home ownership became a new example of an old story: past stratification causing poverty in old age (Forrest, 2021; Saegert et al., 2011).

Ethnic stratification may fall doubly hard on immigrants. Many Asian and African elders expect their descendants to care for them, as was true in their home cultures. However, U.S. houses are built for parents and their young children, not for three generations together. That sets up a cultural clash leading to one of two harmful family dynamics:

- unwelcome closeness in crowded, multigenerational homes, or
- distressing distance between resentful elders and their descendants.

INCOME STRATIFICATION

Many of the poorest older adults never had employers who paid Social Security. Thus, a crucial income stream for middle-class older Americans is absent for the poor, who never could save for late adulthood (Haushofer & Fehr, 2014).

Income stratification weighs most heavily on the oldest-old, who did not expect to live so long (Lu et al., 2021). Moreover, the current age demographics of poverty bode ill for future generations. In a shift that began in 1975, more children than older people lived in poverty. By 2017, poverty rates for those under 18 were twice that for those over 65 (18 to 9 percent).

That shift may be good news for current elders, but a stratification perspective predicts problems. Since childhood poverty reduces education and employment later on, the cohorts born after 1975 may see increasing rates of aged poor.

DATA CONNECTIONS: The Link Between Education and Longevity shows how, for everyone, more education often means longer, healthier lives. Achieve

AGE STRATIFICATION

Ageism and age segregation affect people of every income stratum. Even those who had good jobs and benefits find that income and status drop after retirement.

At the same time, health costs increase. Some young adults think Medicare pays all medical expenses of citizens older than age 65, but that is far from true. Medical crises are the most common cause of bankruptcy, especially among older adults who thought they had sound investments. Further, the drugs and devices that have led to longer lives for the old are least likely to be covered by medical plans that were developed a few decades ago.

For example, Medicare payments for radiology, including bone density scans and MRIs, have been reduced. Since these are less likely to be paid completely by Medicare, they are less likely to be used for preventive care (Kumar et al., 2020). Dental care, hearing aids, and foot care are not covered by Medicare, except in special circumstances. Again, stratification hurts the old.

The most controversial version of age stratification is **disengagement theory** (Cumming & Henry, 1961), which holds that four significant changes occur as people age: (1) traditional roles become unavailable; (2) the social circle shrinks; (3) coworkers disengage; and (4) adult children attend to their own children.

disengagement theory
The view that aging makes a person's social sphere increasingly narrow, resulting in role relinquishment, withdrawal, and passivity.

activity theory
The view that older people want and need to remain active in a variety of social spheres—with relatives, friends, and community groups—and become withdrawn only unwillingly, as a result of ageism.

Meanwhile, older people become less mobile and less able to engage in social interaction. According to this theory, disengagement is mutual, chosen by both adult generations. As younger adults disengage from the old, the latter withdraw.

Disengagement theory provoked a storm of protest. Many gerontologists insisted that if age stratification occurs, it harms older people, who need and want new involvements. Experts proposed an opposing theory, **activity theory**. They said that if elders disengage, they do so unwillingly and suffer because of it (Kelly, 1993; Rosow, 1985).

Over the past decades, thousands of social scientists have investigated both theories. Activity theory seems more accurate: Disengagement correlates with illness and depression and occurs when culture or poverty pushes elders down.

For example, five scientists interviewed people over age 100 in Oklahoma. Each of the centenarians spoke at length (usually more than an hour) (Heinz et al., 2017). Whenever they mentioned something that seemed to affirm a theory of late adulthood, that snippet was noted. By far, activity theory had the most mentions, 62 of them. For example:

> Do all you can for as long as you can. I think positive. I think what you think is who you are. As a man thinketh, so he is. I'm not lazy, and I like to be busy.

The actual tasks that kept the elders active varied. One was still employed full time, one drove his car, one had a trainer twice a week who gave her a "good workout." Many centenarians mentioned gardening. For example, one said:

> Well, the main thing is, you can't be lazy and have a garden like that . . . You've got something that needs to be done, get your tail out there and do it.

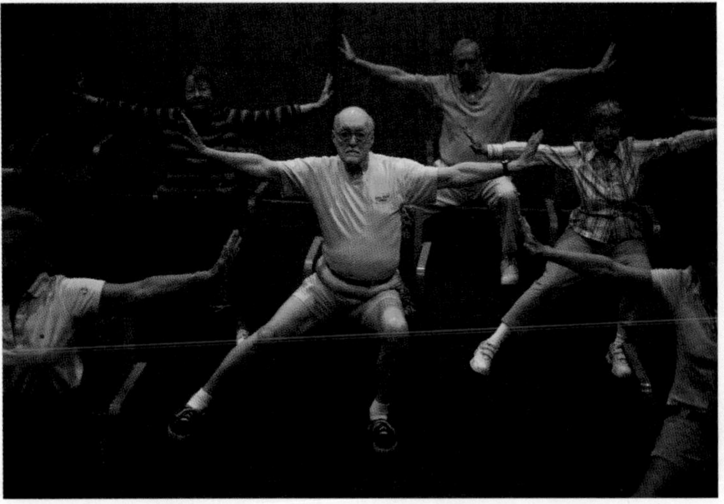

MELANIE STETSON FREEMAN/THE CHRISTIAN SCIENCE MONITOR/ GETTY IMAGES

Reach Wide for Wellness One of the impediments to life and health is the notion that people who exercise must look young and attractive. This man is wise and brave, as well as admirably balanced.

OBSERVATION QUIZ
He has help with balance. What is it? (see answer, page 490) ↑

Disengagement was suggested far less often, 27 times, and seemed chosen and only after physical disabilities or social rejection (Heinz et al., 2017). One said:

> Well, when you get to be 100, you learn you don't give advice because people don't want it, and you might as well not waste your breath.

◆◆ Especially for Social Scientists
The various social science disciplines tend to favor different theories of aging. Can you tell which theories would be more acceptable to psychologists and which to sociologists? (see response, page 490)

Another spoke of her inability to fully engage with her descendants (also over 65) because she couldn't hear very well:

> The only thing right now that bothers me is the fact that I'm losing my hearing. That bothers me because I know I'm missing a lot with my children. They get around here, the bunch of them, and they yak yak yak yak and I can't understand what they're talking about.

It may be that "both theories can be valid, and the validity of each of them could be linked to unique sets of socio-economic and demographic factors" (Asiamah, 2017). For example, if a community lacks paved and protected roads, elders are forced to disengage rather than remain active (Asiamah et al., 2021). Thus, both the social context and individual motivation matter for stratification of the old, which is exactly what gerontologists have found.

MULTIPLE JEOPARDY

Every form of stereotyping makes it difficult for people to break free from social institutions that assign them to a particular stratum. The results of stratification are cumulative, over the entire life span. That is *intersectionality*, explained in Chapter 1.

For example, one group used an intersectional approach to examine the relationship between neighborhood conditions, race, income, gender, and immigration. All were interrelated, affecting cognition in late adulthood. Specifics depended on the particular intersections. For example, unfavorable neighborhoods affected older Black men more than older Black women (Thierry et al., 2021).

This raises a question. Could some aspects of past stratification be protective, not harmful, in late adulthood? One scholar suggests that the mental health of older Black women benefits from the intersection of age, race, and gender. He does not think that "stratification systems such as gender, race, and class" always result in high risk for older adults. Instead, "multiple minority statuses affect mental health in paradoxical ways . . . that refute triple jeopardy approaches" (Rosenfield, 2012, p. 1791).

In another paradox, immigrant elders are often happier than nonimmigrants the same age, a phenomenon called the *happiness paradox* (Calvo et al., 2019). How could that be? Might those who experienced negative stratification in adulthood develop coping strategies, such as laughter, religion, and strong social bonds, that buffer ageism?

Of course, such findings do not discount the harm from stereotypes. But they do suggest that many factors interact in every life, catapulting an older person toward joy or misery.

what have you learned?

1. How does Erikson's use of the word *integrity* differ from its usual meaning?
2. How does hoarding relate to self theory?
3. Is there any harm in older people striving to become themselves?
4. Which type of stratification is most burdensome: economic, ethnic, or gender?
5. How can disengagement be mutual?
6. If activity theory is correct, what does that suggest older adults should do?
7. What is the evidence for, and against, stratification theory?

Activities in Late Adulthood

As you read, most elders are active and independent. That might surprise emerging adults, who see few gray hairs at sports events, political rallies, job sites, or midnight concerts. But do not let ageism conjure up images of older people sitting quietly at home. Not so, especially for the young-old. Large-scale research finds that, if anything, elders are more socially engaged than younger generations (Ang, 2019).

Friends and Relatives

Companions are particularly important during old age. As socio-emotional theory predicts, the size of the social circle shrinks, but close relationships are crucial. Bonds formed over the years allow people to share triumphs and tragedies with others who understand and appreciate them. Siblings, old friends, and spouses are ideal convoy members.

The specifics depend on particulars, with some elders relying more on partners, some on adult children, some on friends. In every case, however, active social connections (visiting, chatting, eating together) are important. Lonely elders have higher rates of mental and physical problems, including clinical depression, heart disease, fibromyalgia, dementia, insomnia, stroke.

LONG-TERM PARTNERSHIPS

For most of the current cohort of elders, their spouse is the central convoy member, a buffer against the problems of old age. Even more than other social contacts, a spouse is protective of health and well-being (Wong & Waite, 2015).

Mutual interaction is crucial: Each healthy and happy partner improves the other's well-being (Ruthig et al., 2012). A lifetime of shared experiences—living together, raising children, and dealing with financial and emotional crises—brings partners closer.

Older couples have learned how to disagree, considering conflicts to be discussions, not fights. I know one example personally. Irma and Bill are proud parents of two adults, are devoted grandparents, and are knowledgeable about current events. They seem happily married, and they cooperate admirably when caring for their grandchildren.

However, they vote for opposing candidates, an oddity in today's politically polarized climate. Irma explained: "We sit together on the fence, seeing both perspectives, and then, when it's time to vote, Bill and I fall on opposite sides." I can always predict

A Lover's Kiss Ralph Young awakens Ruth *(left)* with a kiss each day, as he has for most of the 78 years of their marriage. Here they are both 99, sharing a room in their Indiana residence, "more in love than ever." Half a world away, in Ukraine *(right)*, more kisses occur, with 70 newly married couples and one couple celebrating their golden anniversary. Developmental data suggest that now, several years after these photos, the two old couples (if both partners are still alive) are more likely to be happily married than the 70 young ones.

AP IMAGES/BLOOMINGTON HERALD-TIMES, CHRIS HOWELL

VIKTOR DRACHEV/AFP/GETTY IMAGES

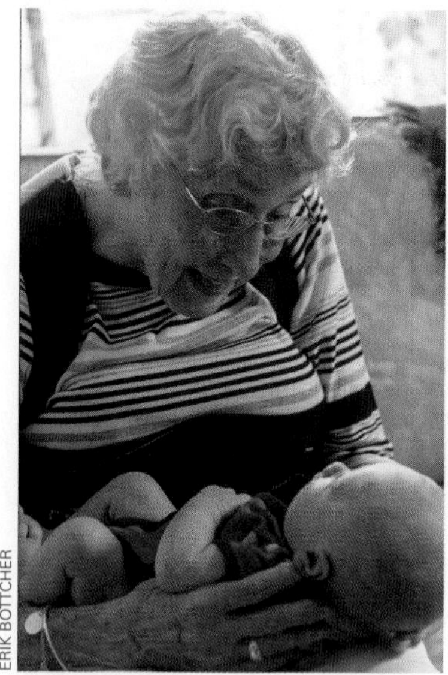

Close or Distant? More than a century separated Irene Harriet Brimlow and her great-grandson, one of her 27 living descendants shown here. Family closeness characterizes them all: I know well, because she died a year before another descendant, Erik Bottcher, was campaigning to become my City Councilman.

who will fall on which side, but for them, the discussion is productive. Their long-term affection avoids polarization.

As with Irma and Bill, older couples often find patterns of interaction that work for them. One study found that older husbands were generally satisfied with their marriages because their wives took good care of them, and wives were satisfied because they were able to take care of their husbands (Carr et al., 2014). Younger people may see this as sexist, but both partners may be content.

A couple together can achieve selective optimization with compensation. For example, I know another couple in their early 90s. His memory is fading; her legs are so weak that she cannot walk alone. The husband helps the wife move, and she keeps track of what needs to be done: Together they need only minimal outside help.

That is a common pattern. When one spouse's memory is fading, typically the other one keeps track of what needs to be remembered (Han et al., 2021). That is one of many way couples tend to keep each other healthy.

This does not work with every health habit. One study found that whether or not an old man or woman smoked cigarettes had little to do with the quality of their marriage (most had stopped smoking decades earlier). However, the same study reported that exercise habits were influenced by the activity of the spouse and the strength of the relationship. Particularly for husbands, a good marriage tended to increase physical activity (Curl et al., 2020).

Another study examined the influence of education and literacy. If an older person was unable to read and write (true for about 14 percent in a study of 8,000 elder Mexican adults), having a literate spouse aided cognition and health. Presumably the literate spouse discussed what was read with their partner (Saenz, 2020).

INTERGENERATIONAL RELATIONSHIPS

Since the average couple now has fewer children, the *beanpole family*, with multiple generations but few members at each level, is becoming common (see Figure 15.3). Some children have no cousins, brothers, or sisters but have a dozen older relatives. The result is "a primacy of intergenerational ties over other relationships" (Fingerman et al., 2020, p. 383).

filial responsibility
The obligation of adult children to care for their aging parents.

As you remember, *familism* prompts family caregiving. One norm is **filial responsibility**, the obligation of adult children to care for their aging parents. This is a strong cultural ideal among many ethnic groups, even when the young adults have emigrated to another nations (Albertini & Mantovani, 2021; Cheung et al., 2020).

However, filial responsibility is controversial. Some argue that it is a way to absolve governments from providing care for older people, and to burden women unfairly: Typically, daughters and daughters-in-law are expected to provide care, while sons are not.

A twenty-first century crossover has occurred with regard to governments and family life. More public support (e.g., housing, meals, education, medical care) *increases* intergenerational involvement overall but decreases the intensity of involvement. This is particularly evident in whether grandmothers do child care, or middle-aged children care for their older parents.

If a nation provides early education, most grandmothers babysit on evenings or when the children are sick. By contrast, when the government does not educate children until age 5 or so, fewer grandmothers provide care, but those who do are often more involved, caring for grandchildren over 20 hours a week (Price et al., 2018).

Do not confuse living arrangements with intergenerational closeness. When several generations live together, that more often is a sign of poverty or illness, in either the older generations or the younger ones. Family links are often stronger when families live apart (Berger, 2019; Timonen, 2019).

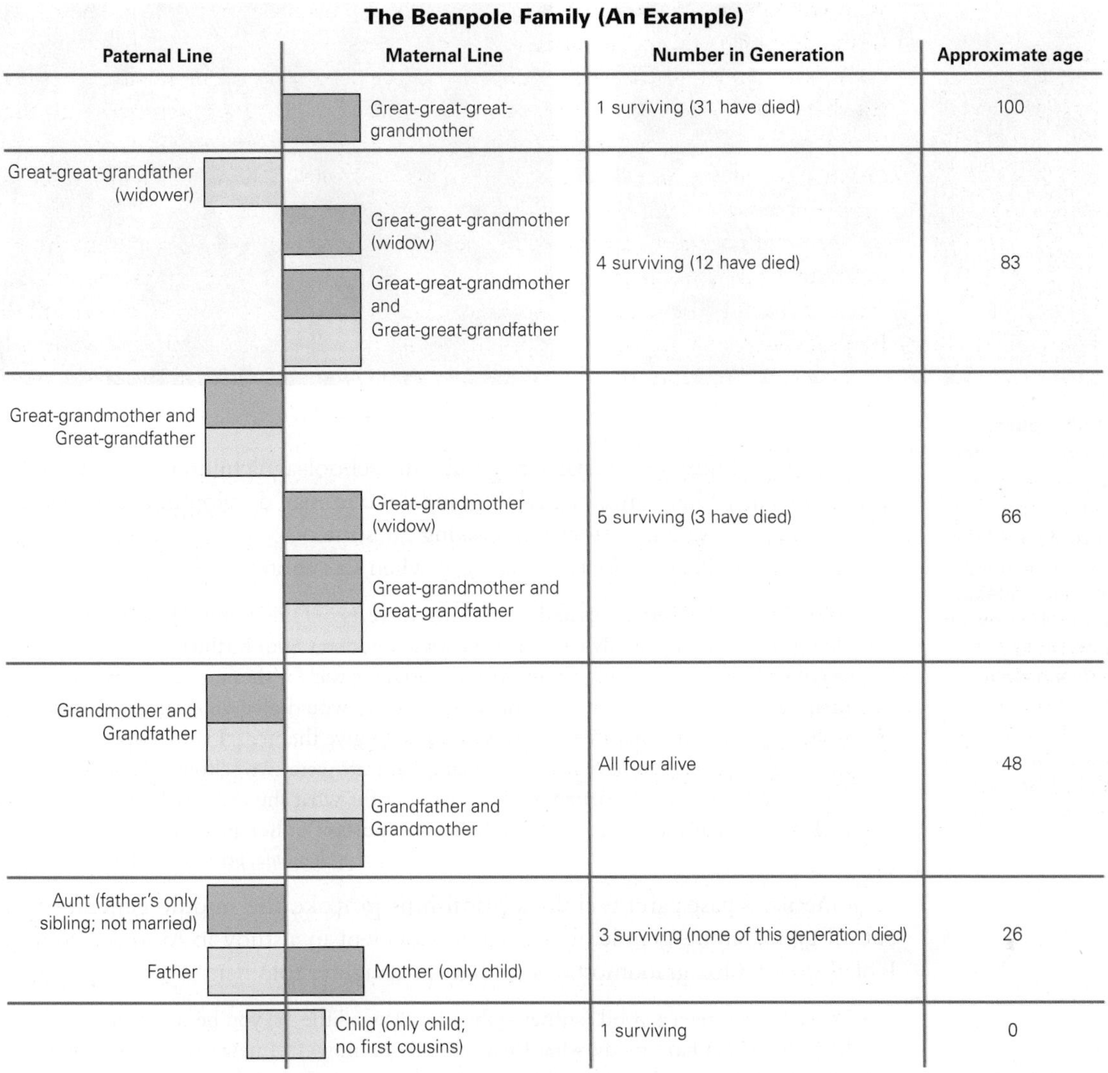

The Beanpole Family (An Example)

Paternal Line	Maternal Line	Number in Generation	Approximate age
	Great-great-great-grandmother	1 surviving (31 have died)	100
Great-great-grandfather (widower)	Great-great-grandmother (widow) Great-great-grandmother and Great-great-grandfather	4 surviving (12 have died)	83
Great-grandmother and Great-grandfather	Great-grandmother (widow) Great-grandmother and Great-grandfather	5 surviving (3 have died)	66
Grandmother and Grandfather	Grandfather and Grandmother	All four alive	48
Aunt (father's only sibling; not married) Father	Mother (only child)	3 surviving (none of this generation died)	26
	Child (only child; no first cousins)	1 surviving	0

FIGURE 15.3 Many Households, Few Members The traditional nuclear family consists of two parents and their children living together. Today, as couples have fewer children, the beanpole family is becoming more common. This kind of family has many generations, each typically living in its own household, with only a few members in each generation. In this example, the child has zero relatives in his generation, but 17 elder relatives!

One indicator is financial: Sometimes the middle generation pays for care of the older ones, but more often money flows in the other direction, with older generations paying for expenses, especially education, of the younger ones. Typically, a strong value among the oldest generation is that they not "be a burden," which means they try to be as independent of their children as they can. If that is no longer possible, they feel diminished (Kitayama et al., 2020).

GRANDPARENTS AND GREAT-GRANDPARENTS

Eighty-five percent of U.S. elders today are grandparents. (The rate was lower in previous cohorts because of a low birth rate during the 1930s, and it is expected to be lower again.) Almost all grandparents provide some caregiving and gifts, unless the middle generation does not allow it (Berger, 2019).

As with parents and children, specifics of the grandparent–grandchild relationship depend on culture, personality, and age. Grandparents typically provide active care of

FLORESCO PRODUCTIONS/FUSE/CORBIS

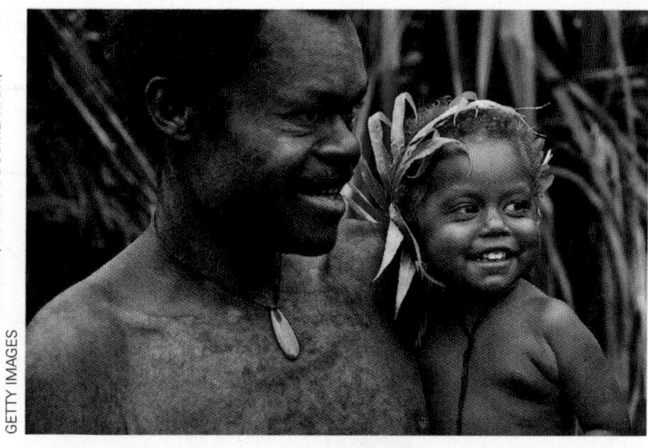
ATLANTIDE PHOTOTRAVEL/CORBIS DOCUMENTARY/GETTY IMAGES

Same Situation, Far Apart: Happy Grandfathers No matter where they are, grandparents and grandchildren often enjoy each other partly because conflict is less likely, as grandparents are usually not as strict as parents are. Indeed, Sam Levinson quipped, "The reason grandparents and grandchild get along so well is that they have a common enemy."

the youngest children, material support for the school-age children, and advice for the adolescents. Then emerging adult grandchildren may develop new appreciation of their elders, listening to stories and asking questions.

One of my college students realized this when she wrote:

> Brian and Brianna are twins and are turning 13 years old this coming June. Over the spring break my family celebrated my grandmother's 80th birthday and I overheard the twins' talking about how important it was for them to still have grandma around because she was the only one who would give them money if they really wanted something their mom wasn't able to give them. . . . I lashed out . . . how lucky we were to have her around and that they were two selfish little brats. . . . Now that I am older, I learned to appreciate her for what she really is. She's the rock of the family and "the bank" is the least important of her attributes now.
>
> *[Giovanna, personal communication]*

Sometimes past parent–child relationships provoke the middle generation to cut off grandparent–grandchild interaction, evident in a study in Australia (Sims & Rofail, 2014). One grandmother said that her daughter told her:

> You've never been a good mother, only when I was little . . . you be quiet and listen to what I have to say, what I have to tell you now . . . I never want to see or hear from you the rest of your life.

How did the grandmother respond? She was angry and defensive, saying:

> Now that is ridiculous and you know that is ridiculous . . . I have fought hard. I have provided for both of your children. I've done all that I can to help you and [son-in-law].

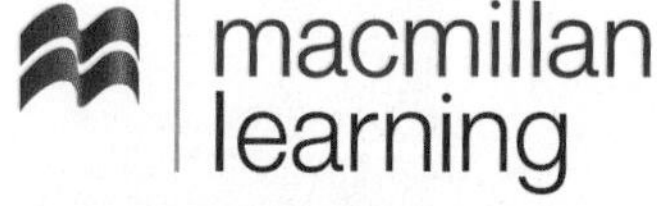

In **VIDEO: Grandparenting**, several individuals discuss their close, positive attachments to their grandchildren.

Anger provokes anger. When the grandmother said "ridiculous," she shut down discussion. "Provided for both of your children" might be heard as criticism, that somehow the daughter and her husband were deficient in caring for their children. Implications, accusations, and misperceptions across generations cause the middle generation to keep grandparents away.

Broken ties are destructive for every generation. Developmental research finds:

1. Adults change over time, even in late adulthood. A grandparent can become less, or more, strict, following parental rules that differ from the elders' past practices. As with every human relationship, mutual compromise and explicit communication are essential.
2. Intergenerational relationships affect the emotional and physical well-being of everyone, especially the older generation. Heart problems, high blood pressure, sleepless nights, and even life itself are affected by family interaction, sometimes reducing problems, sometimes increasing them.

3. Family bonds continue to be strong among every generation, more important than personal safety, status, or anything else, according to data from 27 nations (Ko et al., 2020). Fears that adult children are abandoning their care for their elders are unfounded.

FRIENDSHIP

For older people, "friend relationships are as important as family ties in predicting psychological well-being in adulthood and old age" (Blieszner et al., 2019). Spouses often say that their mate is their best friend, but when a partner dies, friends may be more crucial than other relatives.

The friendship circle shrinks every decade of adult life. Elders are healthiest if some family friends (a favorite cousin, for instance) are among their close friends, yet having at least one or two nonfamily friends correlates with better health (Shiovitz-Ezra & Litwin, 2015). Older adults prefer keeping longtime friends over finding new ones (Wrzus & Neyer, 2016).

One study found that friends were particularly likely to be both the cause and the result of good health in late adulthood (Shane et al., 2020). Another study considered the well-being of older adults who lived alone during the social isolation imposed by COVID-19 restrictions. Social contact relieved some of the psychological stress, particularly if the social contact was with friends (Fingerman et al., 2021).

However, solitude is not necessarily harmful: It sometimes is a way to avoid negative social interactions (Birditt et al., 2019). The goal is to be selective: Negative interactions more often occur with relatives than friends, in part because, at every age, friends are chosen.

Working

Every adult is happiest and healthiest when they are productive, but with age, variation in the specifics of work—such as paid or unpaid—is more apparent than for younger adults.

PAID WORK

A significant proportion of older adults keep whatever job they have, because that provides income, social support, and status. The employment rate for older adults, especially for women, has risen since 2005 (see Figure 15.4). This is particularly striking for women in their 70s, who almost never were salaried fifty years ago.

A major reason for continued work is financial. Pensions—federal as well as private—begin later and are less secure than they once were. Health-care expenses are high and often unexpected, especially in the United States. Adequate income is a crucial predictor of health and happiness in late adulthood, so many elders postpone retirement.

The effects of COVID-19 on employment illustrate age differences. Unemployment increased for people of every age, but for both personal and systemic reasons, older workers were far more likely to keep their jobs than younger workers (Moen et al., 2020).

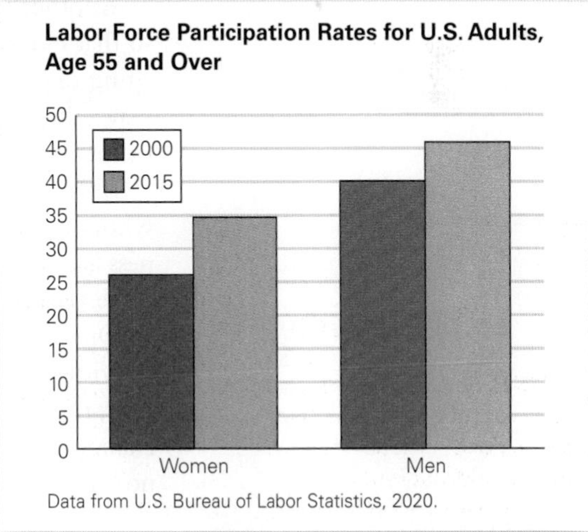

FIGURE 15.4 **When and Why Retire?** In some professions (police, pilots, construction workers), retirement begins at age 55 but the average retirement age in the United States in 2020 is 65 for men and 63 for women. Many 80-year-olds are still in the labor force, and those who are not are still working at caregiving, home repair, gardening, and so on.

RETIREMENT

The United States no longer allows mandated retirement at a certain age (except in some occupations, such as firefighters and airplane pilots). Many older adults continue working until they believe that their retirement income is adequate, or unless poor health requires it.

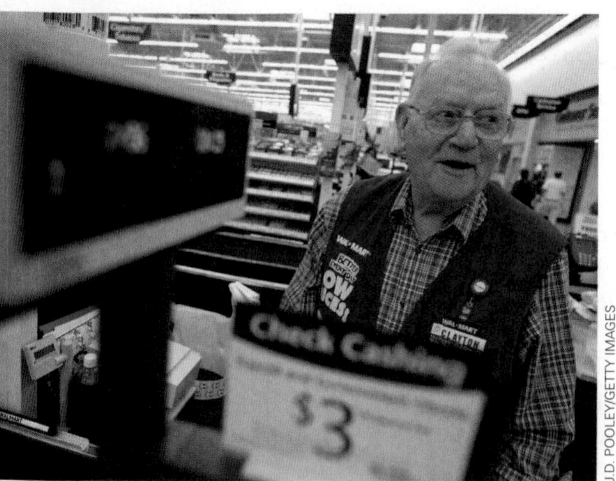

J.D. POOLEY/GETTY IMAGES

The Best New Hire Clayton Fackler, age 72, is shown here at his new job, a cashier at a Wal-Mart in Bowling Green, Ohio. He is among thousands of older adults hired by that corporation, in part because retired people are reliable workers. They are also more willing than younger adults to work for minimum wage at part-time hours — a boon for employers but not for young adults.

Family needs matter. Generally, fathers tend to work a little longer than other men, perhaps because they want to support their adult children. Mothers, on average, tend to retire a little earlier, perhaps because they want or need to become caregivers (Hank & Korbmacher, 2013).

For many women, being a caregiving grandmother is a reason for earlier retirement, although for others it is a reason to keep a paying job (Meyer & Abdul-Malak, 2020; Meyer, 2014). Of course, caregiving is work, as discussed soon.

Many retirees work part time or become self-employed, with small businesses or consulting work. Some employers provide *bridge* jobs, enabling older workers to transition from full employment. Crafting an employment bridge, or consulting work, is an option more available to educated, long-term employees; thus, SES continues to stratify older people (Calvo et al., 2018).

A longitudinal study of older adults in the Netherlands before and after retirement found that self-esteem decreased in the five years *before* retirement (Bleidorn & Schwaba, 2018). Then, for many, self-esteem rose again because they no longer experienced work–family conflicts: Apparently many older workers found it hard to be a good worker, spouse, and grandparent simultaneously, and they were happy to stop their paid job.

Thus, retirement was a relief for many—but not everyone. Some followed the opposite trajectory—decreasing in self-esteem—presumably because the socialization and status of employment was lost. Is it significant that this study was of Dutch workers, where public support for retirees is relatively good?

The social context (particularly culture, pensions, and health care) makes a difference in how older adults feel about retirement. One study found that retirement is more likely to increase self-esteem in Europe and North America, but decrease it in Asia (Mukku et al., 2018).

Another study found the opposite, that Western cultures value activity and work, so that elders who retire try to stay active, and feel happy if they do so. However, if aging makes that difficult, they may become depressed. By contrast, Asian cultures may value elders who are not as active, and therefore older Asians who are less active maintain dignity (Kitayama et al., 2020).

Beyond that, as self-theory would predict, personality makes a difference. Those who are high in the Big Five traits of Extraversion, Agreeableness, and Consciousness are likely to appreciate retirement; those who are high in Neuroticism are likely to be anxious and depressed (Hansson et al., 2020).

One reason extraverts retire early is that they have many friends and community activities, so they do not depend on the workplace for social interactions. By contrast, those high in neuroticism are anxious about the future, so they try to avoid change. All of this reinforces the general theme of this chapter: older individuals are not all the same.

VOLUNTEER WORK

Volunteering provides some of the benefits of paid employment (generativity, social connections). Longitudinal as well as cross-sectional research find a strong link between volunteering, health, and well-being, especially for older adults (Kahana et al., 2013; Russell et al., 2019; Tabassum et al., 2016). A *regular* volunteer commitment to a social-service organization, religious institution, or community group is best.

> **THINK CRITICALLY**: Can you think of another definition of volunteering that would increase the rate for older adults?

Overall, people are more likely to volunteer if they are married, employed, and young-old. About half of all volunteers do so because someone in the organization

asked them—which should alert everyone as to how to help both elders and organizations.

One meta-analysis found that volunteering cuts the death rate in half. Even when various confounds (such as marital status and health before volunteering) were taken into account, being a volunteer correlated with a longer and healthier life (Okun et al., 2013).

In one project, older people interested in "active retirement" attended a two-hour session that explained the benefits of volunteering, the importance of planning and initiative, and various ways to find an activity that suited one's values and preferences. They were given a list of nearby volunteer opportunities (Warner et al., 2014).

Six weeks later, the rate of volunteering among the attendees doubled. Some began volunteering for the first time. Many who already were volunteers increased their commitment.

Finding opportunities is good; forcing is not. Efforts to *require* elders to volunteer may backfire, reducing rather than increasing well-being. It seems that those who want to help various organizations should be offered the chance, but at every age, people are most satisfied if they have some personal choice (Bjalkebring et al., 2021). (See Figure 15.5.)

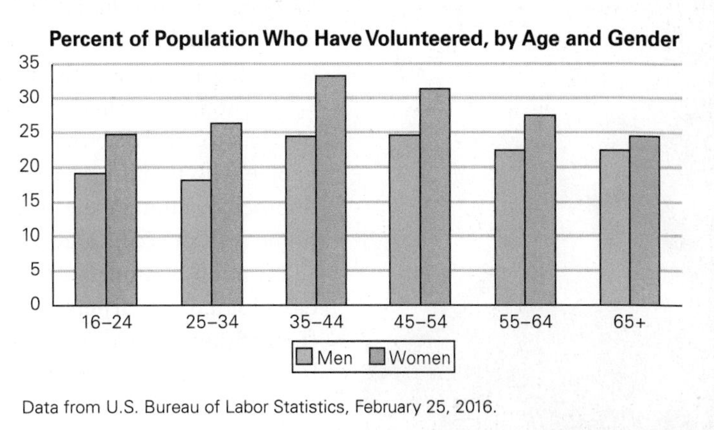

FIGURE 15.5 Official Volunteers As you can see, older adults volunteer less often than do middle-aged adults, according to official statistics. However, this counts people who volunteer for organizations—schools, churches, social service groups, and so on. Not counted is help given to friends, family members, neighbors, and even strangers. If that were counted, would elders have higher rates than everyone else?

OBSERVATION QUIZ
When is the gender gap least evident? (see answer, page 490)

Home Sweet Home

One of the favorite activities of many retirees is caring for their own homes and personal needs. Typically, people do more housework and meal preparation (less fast food, more fresh ingredients) after retirement (Luengo-Prado & Sevilla, 2012). They go to fewer restaurants, stores, and parties; they like to stay home.

Older adults garden, redecorate, build shelves, hang pictures, rearrange furniture. One study found that husbands did much more housework and yard work when they retired, yet wives did not reduce their housework when husbands became more helpful. Apparently, everyone finds more to do when they have time to do it (Leopold & Skopek, 2015a).

As already mentioned, gardening is particularly popular: More than half of older adults in the United States do it (see Figure 15.6). Growing flowers, herbs, and vegetables is productive because it involves creativity, exercise, and social interaction (E. Miller et al., 2018; Schupp & Sharp, 2012).

age in place
To remain in the same home and community in later life, adjusting but not leaving when health fades.

AGING IN PLACE

In keeping up with household tasks and maintaining property, almost all older people prefer to **age in place** rather than move. That means they like to stay where they are.

The preference for aging in place is evident in state statistics. Of the 50 states, Florida has the largest percentage of people over age 65, many of whom moved there not only for the climate but also because they already had friends there. Then the next three states highest in proportion of population over age 65 are Maine, West Virginia, and Pennsylvania, where elders age in place when younger adults leave.

Fortunately, gerontologists now recognize that elders want to stay put, and they have made that easier to accomplish. One project sent a team (a nurse, occupational

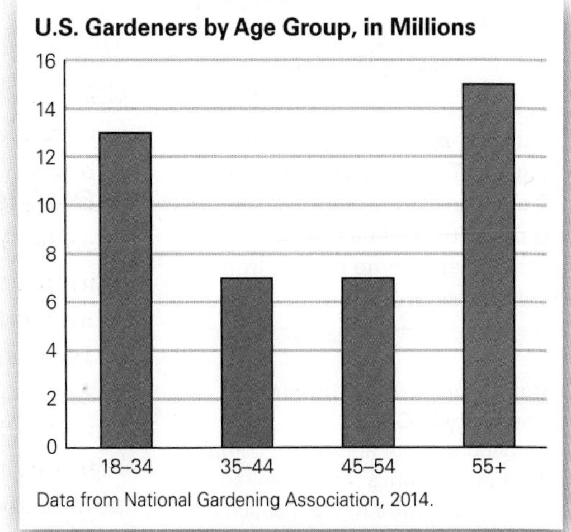

FIGURE 15.6 Farmers by Choice Gardening is only one of the activities that attracts millions of older adults. The number of knitters, puzzlers, bakers, hikers, golfers and much else also increases with age.

SUSANHSMITH/GETTY IMAGES

Lifting Body and Soul This 93-year-old can age in place because she can move in place. Over a million North Americans are able to stay in their own homes, because blindness, deafness, immobility and so on have become problems to overcome, not reasons to leave.

therapist, and handyman) to vulnerable older adults. The professionals taught exercises, checked medical care, fixed floors, and added railings. The elders then became better at self-care, avoiding nursing homes and hospitals (Szanton et al., 2015).

About 4,000 consultants are now certified by the National Association of Homebuilders to advise about *universal design*, which includes making a home livable for people who find it hard to reach the top shelves, to climb the stairs, to respond to the doorbell. Planning experts have many auditing measures to assess how age-friendly a home is (Kan et al., 2020)

Nondesign aspects of housing also allow aging in place; bright lights without dangling cords, carpets affixed to the floor, and seats and grab bars in the shower. [**Life-Span Link**: *Universal design* is described in Chapter 14.] Neighborhoods can be age-friendly, with walkable sidewalks, nearby stores, and benches.

Public policy matters. For older people in many jurisdictions, laws reduce rents; transportation is provided; aides, therapists, and meal services come to homes. Doris (opening anecdote) tells me that none of this works as well in practice as in pronouncements. Nonetheless, she—and many others—could not age in place without them.

NORCs

Some homes have become part of a **naturally occurring retirement community (NORC)**. A NORC develops when young adults move into a new suburb or large building and then stay for decades. People in NORCs may live alone, after children leave and partners die. They enjoy home repair, housework, and gardening, partly because their lifelong neighbors notice the newly painted door, the mopped floor, the blooming rosebush.

If a NORC develops within a high-crime neighborhood, neighbors sometimes form a protective social network. NORCs can be granted public money to change community centers, replacing after-school karate with senior exercise, or piano teachers with visiting nurses (Greenfield et al., 2012; Vladeck & Altman, 2015).

Recognition of NORCs helped with distribution of COVID-19 vaccines, since high-risk older adults often find traveling difficult and computerized scheduling confusing. The city of Toronto located 489 NORCS, where 30,346 Canadians over age 80 lived, and sent mobile vaccination vans to them. Authorities anticipated saving 168 lives that would have been lost if the prioritization strategy had been based on age alone (Huynh et al., 2021).

Many of the older adults in **VIDEO: Active and Healthy Aging: The Importance of Community** frequent senior centers for continual social contact, and some benefit from volunteering.

naturally occurring retirement community (NORC)
A neighborhood or apartment complex whose population is mostly retired people who moved to the location as younger adults and never left.

Religious Activity

Worldwide, religiosity increases with age (Pew Research Center, June 13, 2018). This may not be obvious, because the old-old find it more difficult to attend religious services than they did when they were younger.

Nonetheless, faith and praying increase over the life span. For example, two-thirds of Americans over age 65 pray every day, as do only about one-third of those in their 20s (Pew Research Center, November 3, 2015). Many elders study religious texts, repeat prayers, and believe in an afterlife. Churches and temples are often the location for social gatherings and volunteering, both of which correlate with long life.

The psychological construct of *attachment* has been applied to late-life religious activity. Remember that attachment was described Chapter 4: Some babies are securely attached to their caregivers and some are not. In late adulthood, attachment can describe a person's relationship with God (Granqvist & Kirkpatrick, 2013).

One study found that elders who feel attached to God (e.g., "When I talk to God, I know he listens to me") are more likely to be optimistic, accepting their faults but

also feeling good about themselves (Kent et al., 2018). Another study found that prayer itself does not promote a sense of well-being, but if prayer is part of a personal connection to the divine, it benefits the old (Bradshaw & Kent, 2018).

Many studies find that religious faith and activity correlate with physical and emotional health in late adulthood. Developmentalists have several explanations:

1. Religious prohibitions encourage good habits (e.g., less drug use).
2. Faith communities promote caring social relationships.
3. Beliefs include that life and death have a purpose, thus reducing stress.

Religious identity and institutions are especially important for older members of minority groups, who often identify more strongly with their religious heritage than with their national or ethnic background. A nearby house of worship, with familiar words, music, and rituals, is one reason that elders prefer to age in place.

Immigrants bring their religion with them. In the United States, about a third of all Catholics are immigrants or children of immigrants, as are most Hindus and Buddhists and many Muslims (Pew Research Center, November 3, 2015). Although the average adherent of these groups is younger than the average member of traditional congregations, in every faith the older members tend to be most devout.

RICHARD ELLIS/ALAMY STOCK PHOTO

Resisting Jeopardy These men and women in Beijing, China, are gathering at dawn for a prayer meeting. As it is for many older adults who identify with a particular ethnic group, their community is a powerful antidote to the harm of stratification.

◆◆ Especially for Religious Leaders
Why might older people have strong faith but poor church attendance? (see response, page 490)

Political Activity

Many government policies affect elders, especially those regarding housing, pensions, prescription drugs, and medical costs. However, people older than 65 do not necessarily vote their own economic interests or vote as a bloc. Instead, they are divided among themselves on the same issues that divide younger voters, including global warming, international wars, and immigration.

The difference is not in what they advocate, but in how they advocate it. Fewer older people attend rallies, and only about 2 percent do the leafletting, petitioning, phone-banking, texting, and door-knocking that are essential for political campaigns. By other measures, however, elders are very political. More than any other age group, they write letters to their representatives, identify with a political party (independents are more often young), and vote (see Figure 15.7).

Older people are also more likely to keep up with news about national politics. The Pew Research Center periodically asks a cross section of U.S. residents

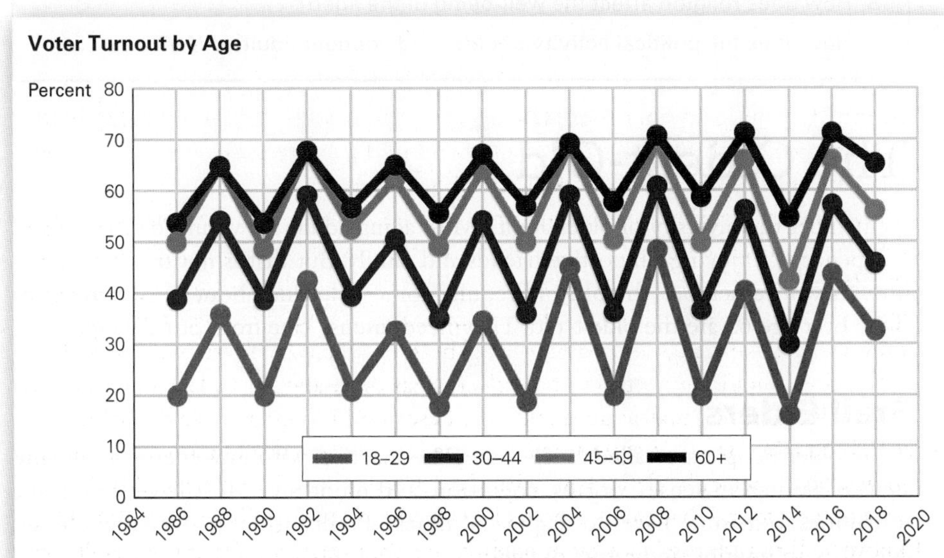

FIGURE 15.7 More and More Data on voting and age are never completely accurate, since some people say they voted because they are ashamed to admit that they did not. However, no matter how age and voting is measured, or what cohort is assessed, voting rates increase with age.

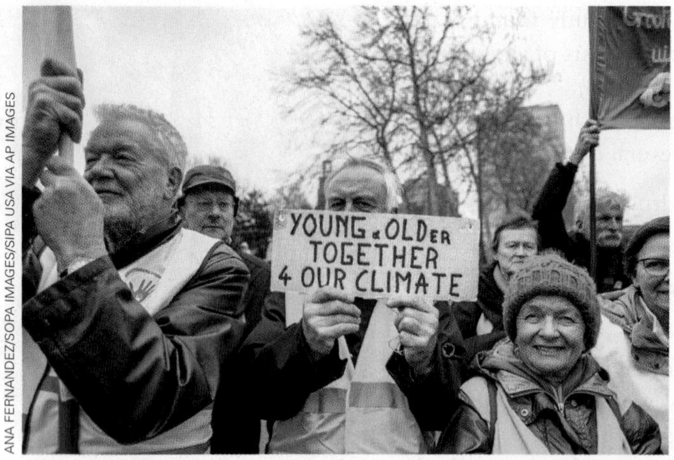

Legacy and Politics Older adults are sometimes stereotyped as caring only for their own political issues, such as Social Security. In fact, many care about the future world, as evident here. These elders organized their protest on the same day in 2019 that thousands of teenagers marched for the climate.

questions about current events and civic understanding. Older adults usually best younger adults.

For example, in 2017, 73 percent of elders (65 and older) but only half as many (38 percent) of young adults (ages 18–29) knew that the vice president casts the deciding vote if the U.S. Senate is split 50/50 (as it was in 2017 for Secretary of Education Betsy DeVos's confirmation and it was for emergency funds for pandemic relief in 2021) (Pew Research Center, April 26, 2018).

Unfortunately, greater knowledge does not protect against being misled. Older adults seem more likely to believe lies told by political leaders (Brashier & Schacter, 2020).

Why would older voters be more vulnerable to fake news? The reasons include their overall trusting nature, their deficiency in source memory, and their unfamiliarity with social media algorithms and distortions. This highlights again the need for ongoing education.

One effort has been to establish an educational network called Universities of the Third Age, specifically designed for older people. Such programs are more common in Europe and Asia than in the United States. History and politics are common topics; community engagement is a goal (Formosa, 2014; Rynkowska, 2020).

what have you learned?

1. What is the usual relationship between older adults who have been partners for decades?
2. Who benefits most from intergenerational family relationships?
3. Why do older people tend to have fewer friends as they age?
4. Why would a person want to keep their job in late adulthood?
5. How does retirement affect the health and happiness?
6. Who is more likely to volunteer and why?
7. What are the benefits and liabilities for elders who want to age in place?
8. How does religion affect the well-being of the aged?
9. How does the political activity of older and younger adults differ?

The Oldest-Old

Remember the diversity of older adults. Most aging adults are young-old, active and independent, enjoying supportive friends and family. But that is not true for everyone. As you remember, the old-old require some help, and about 6–10 percent of those over age 65 are the oldest-old. They need intense care from other people.

Frail Elders

frail
The term for people over age 65, and often over age 85, who are physically infirm, very ill, or cognitively disabled.

Some older people are called **frail**—they are inactive, with low energy and many signs of failing, in senses, organs, cognition, and emotions. Most have significant infirmities, but some have no diagnosed illness. Frailty is defined by low energy overall, with multiple indicators of failing.

LIVING INDEPENDENTLY AFTER AGE 65

Most people who reach age 65 not only survive a decade or more, but also live independently.

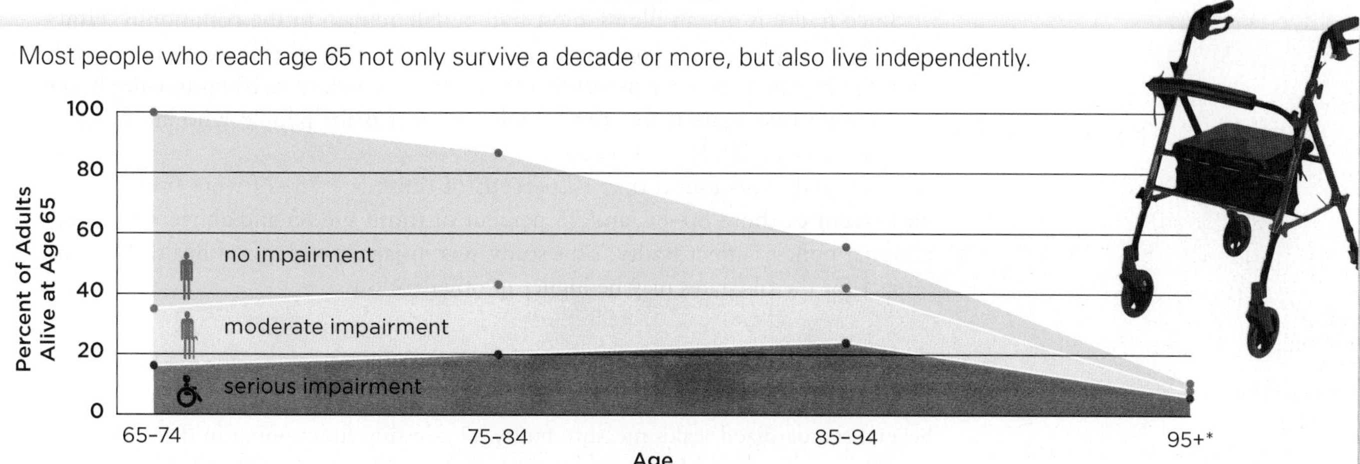

*With each year after 95, some survivors are still self-sufficient!

AGE 65
Of 100 people, in the next decade: Most will care for all their basic needs. But, 35 will become unable to take care of at least one instrumental activity of daily living (IADL) like household chores or taking care of finances, or one activity of daily living (ADL) like bathing, dressing, or getting in and out of bed. And 16 are so impaired that they need extensive care. 87 will survive another decade.

AGE 75
Of the 87 people who survived, in the next decade: About half will not need help caring for their basic needs. But 43 will become unable to take care of at least one IADL or ADL. And half of these 43 become so impaired that they require extensive care. 56 will survive another decade.

AGE 85
Of the 56 people who survived, in the next decade: Most need help. 42 will be unable to take care of at least one IADL or ADL. And 24 of them become so impaired that they require extensive care. Only 11 will survive another decade.

AGE 95
Of the 11 people who survived, in the next decade: Those who reach 95 live for about four more years, on average. Most need some help, and about half require extensive care.

Data from Arias et al., 2017.

With whom? Where?

As you see, there are many ways to depict life after 65, but the overall conclusion is the same: Most older people function well, especially if they are in a relationship with a partner who provides emotional and practical support, in the community where they have always lived. It is also true that over age 85, most people need some help.

LIVING ARRANGEMENTS OF PERSONS 65+

Age
65–74
75–84
85+
0 10 20 30 40 50 60 70 80

In group quarters*
Alone
With spouse or partner
With nonfamily

*Include nursing homes, assisted living, and other health care facilities

Data from Roberts et al., 2018.

PERSONS 65+ AS A PERCENTAGE OF TOTAL POPULATION

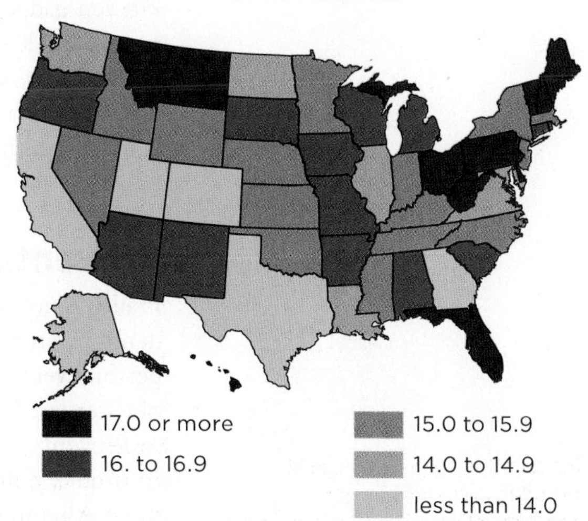

Data from U.S. Census Bureau, October 30, 2018.

One symptom of frailty is weight loss (especially in men); another is extreme fatigue (especially in women). For everyone, feeling depressed, forgetting the date, and difficulty walking are among the signs of frailty.

Since frailty is not an illness, most frail people remain in the community. However, they are likely to become seriously impaired. To be specific, one careful study found that, when an older person becomes frail, the risk of needing nursing home care within two years is five times higher than it is for people who are not frail (Makizako et al., 2015).

That study also found that 10 percent of those age 75–79 were frail, as were 20 percent of those 80–84, and 35 percent of those age 85 and above. Of course, national policies affect frailty: This study was in Japan, with good health care and respect for the old; rates may be higher in other nations.

Activities of Daily Life

Several standardized scales measure frailty, all assessing functioning in daily life. Self-care is a significant marker for medical insurance and public health experts.

activities of daily life (ADLs) Typically identified as five tasks of self-care that are important to independent living: eating, bathing, toileting, dressing, and transferring from a bed to a chair. The inability to perform any of these tasks is a sign of frailty.

instrumental activities of daily life (IADLs) Actions (e.g., paying bills and car maintenance) that are important to independent living and that require some intellectual competence and forethought. The ability to perform these tasks may be even more critical to self-sufficiency than ADL ability.

Gerontologists often note five physical **activities of daily life (ADLs)**: putting on clothes, feeding oneself, moving (transferring) from a bed to a chair, using the toilet, bathing. In part because mortality increases if a person cannot perform ADLs, a mnemonic is DEATH [dressing, eating, ambulating (moving), toileting, hygiene (bathing)]. Sometimes additional ADLs are included, such as brushing teeth and walking 50 feet.

Many people have temporary problems with their ADLs, such as when severely ill or after surgery. With COVID-19, the worst physical symptom was in breathing, but the worst long-term symptom was impaired ADL. To foster recovery, nurses make hospitalized patients walk, eat, and so on (Ciol et al., 2014).

Physical and occupational therapists speed recovery by teaching someone to don shoes without needing to reach way down, or to get out of bed without risking a fall. They know the equipment, exercises, and moves that make ADLs possible.

More crucial than ADLs are **instrumental activities of daily life (IADLs)**, which require intellectual competence and forethought. IADLs vary by context.

In developed nations, IADLs may include interpreting the labels on medicine bottles, preparing nutritious meals, filling out tax forms, keeping track of investments and expenses, scheduling doctor appointments, or using a computer, a cell phone, a kitchen gadget (see Table 15.1). Elsewhere, feeding the animals, following religious rituals, and keeping the home clean, warm, and dry are IADLs.

Difficulty with IADLs often precede problems with ADLs since planning and problem-solving help elders maintain self-care. When self-care falters, frailty begins. If frailty continues for too long, more intense care may soon be needed.

Preventing Frailty

Frailty is not inevitable: A person could be healthy and self-sufficient and then suddenly severely ill and dying, with no frailty in between. Instead, almost every older person eventually has difficulty with ADLs or IADLs. Before death, about one-third of elders are frail for a year or more.

Prevention or reversal of frailty depends on the individual, the family, and the community, all of whom need to remember that disability at any age is dynamic, not static. A temporary failing need not become a long-term problem. We focus on two examples: first, an ADL (immobility) and then, an IADL (disorientation).

MUSCLE WEAKNESS

The preeminent symptom of frailty is weakness. To some extent, that is universal. Muscles weaken with age, a condition called *sarcopenia*. In fact, muscle mass at age 90 is only half of what it was at age 30. Most of that loss occurs after age 60 (McLean & Kiel, 2015). Grip strength (measured by opening the lid of a jar) is a prime indicator of senescence (Halaweh, 2020).

Bones and balance are impaired as well. Thus, older people are more likely to fall than younger people, and to break a bone when doing so. As already mentioned, osteoporosis (weak bones) is a common problem in old age, and broken bones—particularly the hip bone—can cause immobility, morbidity, and eventual death.

Unfortunately, well-intentioned caregivers may increase frailty. For instance, someone might think they are helping an older adult if they bring meals and buy a remote control for a large bedroom TV. City planners may prioritize regulations for nursing home care and ignore the need for affordable, senior housing near stores, bus stops with benches, and well-maintained sidewalks. The TV news may highlight violent crime, making elders fearful.

Instead, to prevent frailty, everyone needs to encourage older people to move. For example, the community could provide pathways that are safe and pleasant, and visitors could walk instead of sitting to talk. A physical therapist—paid by the individual, the family, or the government—could individualize exercise and recommend appropriate equipment (a walker? a cane? special shoes?). Homes could be redesigned for an active life.

Even for the oldest-old, some movement is better than none. Indeed, a remarkable study in Australia found that an exercise program improved health for people with major neurocognitive disorders, living in long-term care facilities (Traynor et al., 2018).

TABLE 15.1 Instrumental Activities of Daily Life

Domain	Exemplar Task
Managing medical care	Keeping current on checkups, including teeth, ears, and eyes
	Assessing supplements as good, worthless, or harmful
Food preparation	Evaluating nutritional information on food labels
	Preparing and storing food to prevent spoilage
Transportation	Comparing costs of car, taxi, bus, and train
	Determining quick and safe walking routes
Communication	Knowing when, whether, and how to use landline, cell, texting, mail, e-mail
	Programming speed dial for friends, emergencies
Maintaining household	Following instructions for operating an appliance
	Keeping safety devices (fire extinguishers, CO_2 alarms) active
Managing one's finances	Budgeting future expenses (housing, utilities, etc.)
	Completing timely income tax returns
	Avoiding costly scams, cancelling unread subscriptions

Cognitive Failure

Consider this example.

> A 70-year-old Hispanic man came to his family doctor following a visit to his family in Colombia, where he had appeared to be disoriented (he said he believed he was in the United States, and he did not recognize places that were known to be familiar to him) and he was very agitated, especially at night. An interview with the patient and a family member revealed a history that had progressed over the past six years, at least, of gradual worsening cognitive deficit, which that family had interpreted as part of normal aging. Recently his symptoms had included difficulty operating simple appliances, misplacement of items, and difficulty finding words, with the latter attributed to his having learned English in his late 20s. . . . [His] family had been very protective and increasingly had compensated for his cognitive problems.
>
> . . . He had a lapse of more than five years without proper control of his medical problems [hypertension and diabetes] because of difficulty gaining access to medical care. . . .

> Based on the medical history, a cognitive exam . . . and a magnetic resonance imaging of the brain . . . the diagnosis of moderate Alzheimer's disease was made. Treatment with ChEI [cholinesterase inhibitors] was started. . . . His family noted that his apathy improved and that he was feeling more connected with the environment.
>
> *[Griffith & Lopez, 2009, p. 39]*

Both the community (those five years without treatment for hypertension and diabetes) and the family (making excuses, protecting him) contributed to major neurocognitive disorder that could have been delayed, if not prevented altogether.

No one, not the relatives nor the man himself, recognized the need for preventative care. Instead, the family arranged his trip to Colombia, thinking that would be a gift for him. If, instead, they had consulted a professional, they would have learned travel, especially to an unfamiliar place, increases anxiety and confusion.

A professional could also help with the night agitation, a common problem. The family could accommodate his sleep patterns by having headphones and a playlist, a sandwich in the refrigerator, a chair near a lamp, and magazines. Depression and apathy are characteristics of frailty: A loss of joy may occur when someone is told they must sleep at a certain time, eat particular foods, never leave the house alone.

A VIEW FROM SCIENCE

Frail No More?

It is not hard to appreciate that young people after surgery need to recover ADLs, again becoming *robust*, a word that means being strong and vital. But it might seem that reversal of age-related frailty after age 75 is unrealistic, even delusional, since senescence is inexorable.

That hard fact troubles many demographers and legislators, since the numbers of frail people are increasing as more people live to 90 or 100. For this statistic, Japan has the dubious distinction of being the leader, with 28 percent of their residents estimated to be age 65 or older in 2020. Fortunately, Japan is also a leader of gerontological science, discovering how to maintain independence among the old-old.

A survey in one Japanese city (Ikoma) assessed everyone over age 74 living in the community, not certified as needing long-term care. Over 12,000 people were asked to fill out a standardized frailty measure, specifically a checklist of 25 questions that measured ADLs, IADLs, social interactions, and mood. About half of the people asked to fill out the survey did so.

If the score was 0–3, that was "robust", 4–7 was "prefrail," and 8 or more was frail. Two years later, 5,050 who were still in the community and not certified as now needing full-term care were asked to answer the 25 questions again (Takatori & Matsumoto, 2021). Their answers were compared to what they themselves had written two years earlier.

It was not surprising that, with two more years, the percent who were frail inched up, from 19.7 to 21.7, with many of the pre-frail people becoming frail. But almost a third who were initially frail were frail no longer. Many improved from frailty to pre-frail (26 percent, $N = 245$) but some from frail to robust (5.8 percent, $N = 55$).

What correlated with the improvement? Prior work had considered biological measures—diet, better health care—that had nudged people toward better health. This study focused instead on social factors. Three of them, "trust in community, interaction with neighbors, and social participation," were even more significant than biological factors.

In practical terms, this means that older people need to play games with friends, take walks with relatives, join campaigns for political office, attend worship services, work for clean water, or whatever. Yes, senescence is inevitable. No, frailty is not.

When People Need Care

Prevention is best but not always sufficient. Some problems, such as major neurocognitive disorder or severe heart failure, can be postponed or slowed but not eliminated. Caregivers themselves are usually older people, and they often have poor health, limited strength, and failing immune systems. Thus, an aging parent who

cares for the other parent is especially likely to need help, and their children need to recognize this.

Caregiving is especially burdensome if IADLs are failing. If a neurocognitive disorder causes not only memory loss but also agitation, confusion, and aggression, the burden on the caregiver may be crushing. Such caregivers are often stressed and depressed, vulnerable to cognitive loss and physical illness themselves.

This needs to be emphasized, because other relatives and outsiders may not recognize the impact on the caregiver of a spouse with an NCD. Consider the problem: If people have trouble with an ADL, they know that they cannot walk, for instance, and other relatives can see that the caregiver needs help as well as sympathy.

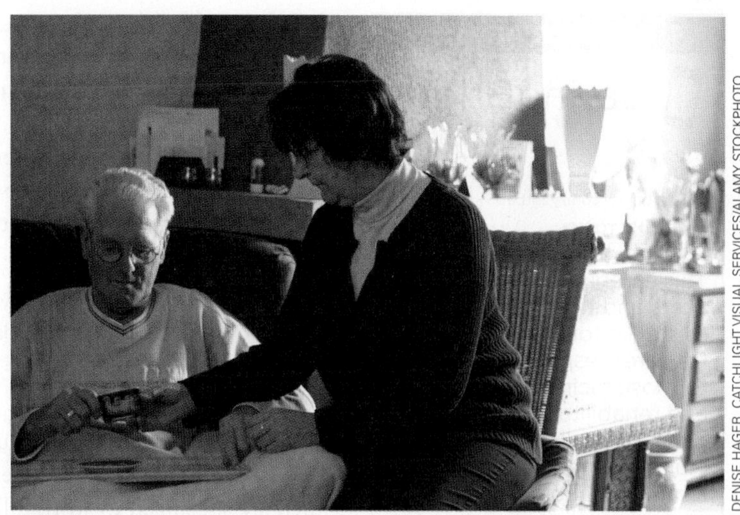

DENISE HAGER, CATCHLIGHT VISUAL SERVICES/ALAMY STOCKPHOTO

A Fortunate Man Henk Huisman gets care from his wife, Ria, who is happy to provide it. One reason is that this couple has three daughters, all of whom also help. Another reason may be that they live in the Netherlands, which provides extensive public assistance for everyone over age 65.

But if a person has trouble with an IADL, they might appear healthy and insist on their competence. They file taxes, go to the doctor, make dinner, and blame someone else if the Internal Revenue Service fines them, if the doctor charges for a missed appointment, if the dinner burns. They may complain to visitors, who may agree to blame the caregiver.

FILIAL RESPONSIBILITY?

Moreover, relatives may disagree about proper care, and nations, cultures, and ethnic groups vary as well. In most nations of Northern Europe, elder care is provided via a public safety net of day-care centers, senior homes, and skilled nurses; in most nations of Africa, families are responsible for their elders. In many Asian nations, daughters and daughters-in-law are expected to care for their aging parents.

In the United States, the diversity of income and ethnicity results in diverse norms: Paid caregivers are often sought, sons are sometimes thought to be as responsible as daughters, grandchildren may be pressed into service. The multi-cultural perspective outlined in Chapter 1 is particularly relevant: No one should assume that their personal perspective is best.

Everyone tends to think others should do it: Governments blame relatives, who blame the government, and family members blame each other. Demography has changed faster than cultures have.

The clash between numbers and ideology is evident when people romanticize elder care, believing that frail older adults should live with their devoted children. That assumption worked when the demographic pyramid meant that most people died by age 70, and each surviving elder had many descendants. Currently, however, a marriage between two "only" children may result in one middle-aged couple having four grandparents and eight great-grandparents, while their teenager or emerging adult still lives at home.

Fortunately, most older relatives can care for themselves. Elders who believe that they are in control of their lives and are not dependent on their children, are less likely to become frail (Elliot et al., 2018). But "not wanting to be a burden" can result in "not accepting needed care".

When an older person needs more care, the specifics are always complex, with each solution entailing costs and benefits. Some older men, particularly, are fiercely independent, refusing help from family, doctors, and technology (such as walkers and hearing aids). That shortens their lives (Hamm et al., 2017).

Currently in the United States, the usual caregiver is the spouse (the wife twice as often as the husband), who often has no prior experience caring for a frail elder.

CHAPTER APP 15

CaringBridge

iOS:
https://tinyurl.com/y2ntba95

RELEVANT TOPIC:
Caring for frail elders

This caregiver app enables users and their loved ones to stay in touch and arrange for care—especially useful to those facing procedures and rehabilitation and to older adults living alone. Multiple caregivers and family members can share updates and encouragement, including via a guest book with room for journal entries, medical updates, photos, stories, and tributes.

Not only does the culture assume that it is her job, she herself assumes that she must provide care, an assumption that may make her chronically ill and depressed. Although "spousal caregiving may be a labor of love, it also is a chronic stressor" (Glauber & Day, 2018, p. 538).

Most of the younger generation assumes that aging couples will care for each other. An older couple may become impaired and homebound, isolated from their friends and family—who visit less often and help even less. As one review explains:

> Spousal caregivers report more emotional, physical, and financial burden when compared with other caregivers, such as those who care for their elderly parents. They experience greater isolation and less help.
>
> *[Glauber & Day, 2018, p. 537]*

What if an older caregiver also has a part-time job? If she is the wife, that relieves some of the depression, because coworkers provide sympathy and comfort. But if he is the husband, part-time employment increases depression, presumably because men are socialized to work full time or to enjoy retirement—and he can do neither (Glauber & Day, 2018).

Adult siblings may fight. In general, men expect women to provide care for dependent elders, which can result in resentful sisters, wives, and daughters. Family members disagree with each other and with professionals about nutrition, medicine, surgery, and independence.

It is not uncommon for one family member to insist that an older person *never* enter a nursing home, another to feel overwhelmed with caregiving, and a third may believe a doctor who contends that surgery is urgent, contrary to the opinion of a fourth.

THE ROLE OF PROFESSIONALS

integrated care
Care of frail elders that combines the caregiving strengths of everyone—family, medical professionals, social workers, and the elders themselves.

The ideal is **integrated care**, in which professionals and family members cooperate to provide individualized care, whether at a long-term care facility, at the elder's home, or at someone else's home (Lopez-Hartmann et al., 2012). Just as a physical therapist knows which specific exercises and movements improve mobility, a professional can evaluate an impaired elder and figure out which tasks are best done by a relative, which by the frail person themselves, and which by a medical professional.

Multidisciplinary teams are needed, because frail elders need medical, social, and financial care (Pollina et al., 2017). Integrated care does not erase the burden of caregiving, but it helps. Much of the burden is emotional, and simply having someone else to explain what needs to be done, and what does not, is helpful.

In one study, a year after a professional helped plan and coordinate care, family caregivers improved in their overall attitude and quality of life. Total time relatives spent on caregiving did not change, but the tasks did. Family spent more time on household tasks (e.g., meal preparation and cleanup) and less on direct care (Janse et al., 2014).

Professionals also can tell caregivers what devices promote independence. For example, a pill container can be locked until an alarm signals time to take the medicine. That avoids over and under medication and encourages independence.

Similarly, a large-screen video connection can allow aging in place when the caregiver lives elsewhere. This is a step beyond Zoom, Skype, or Facetime: Elder and caregiver can talk face-to-face day and night, whenever either wishes. Telehealth during COVID-19 has taught doctors and patients to avoid many in-person contacts; similar measures can keep frail elders connected to their families. Visits can focus on emotional support, not medical tasks.

In the United States, public agencies rarely intervene unless a crisis arises. This troubles developmentalists, who study "change over time." From a life-span perspective, caregiver exhaustion and elder abuse are predictable and preventable.

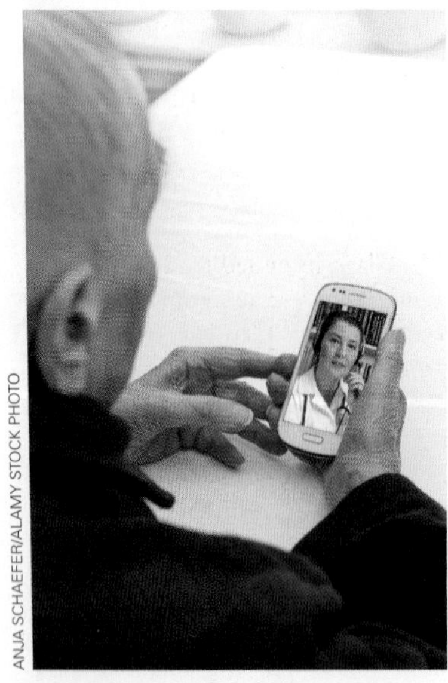

ANJA SCHAEFER/ALAMY STOCK PHOTO

Always There This older man can simply push one button to speak with his doctor.

ELDER ABUSE

When caregiving results in resentment and social isolation, the risk of depression, sickness, and abuse (of either the frail person or the caregiver) escalates. Abuse is likely if:

- the *caregiver* suffers from emotional problems or substance abuse;
- the *care receiver* is frail, confused, and demanding; or
- the *care location* is isolated, where visitors are few.

Each of these factors increases the risk, and each of them is apparent before abuse begins (Chen & Dong, 2017). Ironically, although professionals have extensive training in coping with resistant patients, relatives with no training or experience often provide round-the-clock care. Those who are most often abused are older women who live with their caregivers and who suffer from neurocognitive problems as well as medical ones (Lachs & Pillemer, 2015).

Ideally, when one person is a caregiver, other family members provide respite care. However, many avoid visiting. If they suspect abuse, they may accuse the abuser, but they often keep "family secrets," avoiding outsiders. Everyone suffers.

Often professionals are not alert to early signs of abuse. For example, doctors are taught to respond to a medical crisis (a fall, heart attack, and so on) not to a social one, bankers follow privacy norms which keep them from recognizing financial abuse, legal authorities intervene only after repeated and blatant abuse.

Some caregivers overmedicate, lock doors, and use physical restraints, all of which may be abusive. They may resort to inadequate feeding, medical neglect, or rough treatment. Obvious abuse is less likely in nursing homes and hospitals, not only because laws forbid it but also because workers are not alone, nor expected to work 24/7.

Some people may question that home is more often the site of abuse than nursing homes, because the press highlights nursing home maltreatment. However, most victims at home are never reported.

International research finds that elder abuse occurs in every nation: A meta-analysis estimated the prevalence at 16 percent (Yon et al., 2017). That number may be too high or too low because accurate incidence data and intervention are complicated by definitions. If an elder feels abused but a caregiver disagrees, who is right (see A Case to Study)?

A CASE TO STUDY

Is That Abuse?

Most elder abuse is not physical. If a frail older person loses weight, or is usually quiet, or has bruises that are unexplained, that may or may not signify abuse. Of course, those signs suggest that the caregiver needs help. However, if elder abuse is financial, bankers, lawyers, and investment advisors, may not recognize that help is needed until it reaches a crisis.

Consider this example.

> A sister [Mrs. Watson] made large withdrawals from her elderly brother's bank account. The victim, Mr. Clark, was admitted to hospital after a serious fall. He had cognitive impairment and subsequently his mental capacity deteriorated. His sister began to look after his finances. Mrs. Watson claimed that Mr. Clark intended for her to have the money which she withdrew, describing it as her 'slush fund'. The Judge noted that Mr. Clark was suffering from dementia and therefore was vulnerable, he trusted his sister but she had betrayed his trust, and she did not show remorse or appreciate that her actions were wrong, but acted out of greed rather than need. Mrs. Watson was sentenced to ten months under house arrest followed by one year of probation. The Judge took into account that she had no prior criminal record, was unlikely to reoffend, and had provided personal care to her brother before he was admitted to hospital.
>
> *[Matthews, 2018, p. 75]*

Greed or need? Is a courtroom the place to decide such a case? Probably not. Developmental psychologists might distinguish frailty or confusion from neglect or abuse. But they also are not clear. Many current researchers are working to define elder abuse (S. Han et al., 2019).

A recent review by the U.S. Preventive Services Task Force reported "no valid, reliable screening tools in the primary care setting to identify abuse of older or vulnerable adults without recognized signs and symptoms of abuse" (U.S. Preventive Services Task Force, 2018, p. 1681).

In other words, although financial and emotional abuse is far more common among elders than bruises and broken limbs, there is no good method to decide if abuse is the problem. This is a challenge for future scientists, include some who are reading this book! Do you side with the sister, the brother, or the judge?

Long-Term Care

Although most people over age 65 are independent, many will someday need intensive care. Most enter a nursing home or rehabilitation center for a few weeks after a few days in a hospital. However, some elders need specialized care for more than a year, and a very few—the oldest and least capable—live in a long-term care setting for 10 years or more. Variations in such care are vast.

NURSING HOMES

The trend in the United States and elsewhere is away from institutions and toward aging in place. Currently, residents of nursing homes tend to be the oldest-old—at least age 85—with significant cognitive decline and several medical problems (Moore et al., 2012). They are usually women, often widows. (Husbands usually die before their wives, and if both partners are alive and one needs constant care, women are more likely than men to provide home care for years.)

The skill of the staff, especially of the aides who provide personal care, is crucial: Simple tasks, such as helping a frail person out of bed, can be done either clumsily or skillfully, quickly or patiently.

Quality care is much more labor-intensive and expensive than most people realize: A good facility has many well-paid and well-trained staff. According to John Hancock Life & Health Insurance Company in 2015, the cost of a year in a private room at a nursing home was $200,750 in Alaska and $56,575 in Louisiana. (Most people think that Medicare, Medicaid, or long-term insurance covers the entire cost—a gross misconception.)

Same Situation, Far Apart: Diversity Continues No matter where they live, elders thrive with individualized care and social interaction, as is apparent here. Lenore Walker *(left)* celebrates her 100th birthday in a Florida nursing home with her younger sister nearby, and an older chess player in a senior residence in Kosovo *(right)* contemplates protecting his king. Both photos show, in details such as the women's earrings and the men's head coverings, that these elders maintain their individuality.

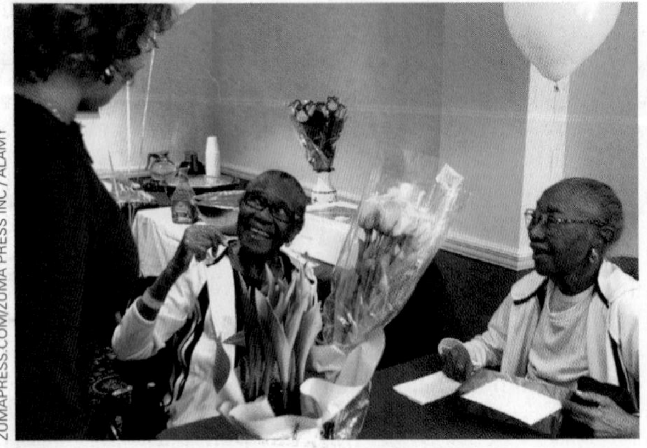

TAYLOR JONES ©THE PALM BEACH POST/ZUMAPRESS.COM/ZUMA PRESS INC / ALAMY

VALDRIN XHEMAJ/NEWSCOM/EUROPEAN PRESSPHOTO AGENCY/PRISTINA/KOSOVO/SERBIA

Currently in the United States, many aides in nursing homes are immigrants, some with limited understanding of the language or background of the residents. Some of the best come from African or Asian nations, with a tradition of respect for the aged but frustration with the low pay and lack of mobility for immigrants in the United States.

They hope for better jobs soon, an understandable goal but not ideal for them or their patients (Covington-Ward, 2017). The highest death rate, by far, from COVID-19 was in nursing homes, of both patients and staff, a statistic that highlights the problem.

In North America, good nursing-home care is available for those who can afford it and know what to look for. Some nursing homes provide individualized, humane care, allowing residents to decide what to eat, where to walk, whether to have a pet. Some excellent nonprofit homes are subsidized by religious organizations.

Good care encourages independence, individual choice, and privacy. This is called "person-centered care," the goal of most nursing homes (Simmons & Rahman, 2014). As with early-childhood education, continuity of care matters: High staff turnover is a bad sign.

◆◆ Especially for Those Uncertain About Future Careers Would you like to work in a nursing home? (see response, page 490)

ALTERNATIVE CARE

An ageist stereotype is that older people are either completely capable of self-care or completely dependent on others. In actuality, everyone is on a continuum, capable of some self-care and yet needing some help.

Once that is understood, a range of options can be envisioned. Most people with ADL problems can be helped by caregivers at home, or in assisted living with special equipment that makes bathing or walking possible.

Those who need IADL care are increasingly likely to enter nursing homes. For example, in 1991 in England, 56 percent of the residents were cognitively impaired; 20 years later, 65 percent were (Matthews et al., 2013).

In the United States and many other nations, the number of assisted-living facilities has increased as the number of nursing homes have decreased. Typically, assisted-living residences provide private apartments for each person and allow pets and furnishings as in a traditional home.

The "assisted" aspects vary, but they often include one daily communal meal, special transportation and activities, household cleaning, and medical assistance, such as supervision of pill-taking, blood pressure or diabetes monitoring, with a nurse, doctor, and ambulance if needed. Oversight and regulations have not caught up with the demand, so quality and services vary a great deal (Han et al., 2017).

Assisted-living facilities range from group homes for three or four people to townhouse developments for hundreds. Almost every state, province, or nation has its own standards for assisted-living facilities, but many such places are unlicensed. Some regions of the world (e.g., northern Europe) have many assisted-living options, while others (e.g., sub-Saharan Africa) have almost none.

The first step in figuring out the best care—a step that should be taken long before intensive care is required—is professional assessment of current and future needs of an older adult. As one advocate of personalized care wrote:

> In the home, nurses sit around all kinds of kitchen tables, on rickety wooden chairs and sleek bar stools, experiencing firsthand the diverse ways people live, care and connect. Interactions with family, friends and neighbours are generally frequent—and in some cases, noticeably absent.
>
> *[Sharkey & Lefebre, 2017, p. 11]*

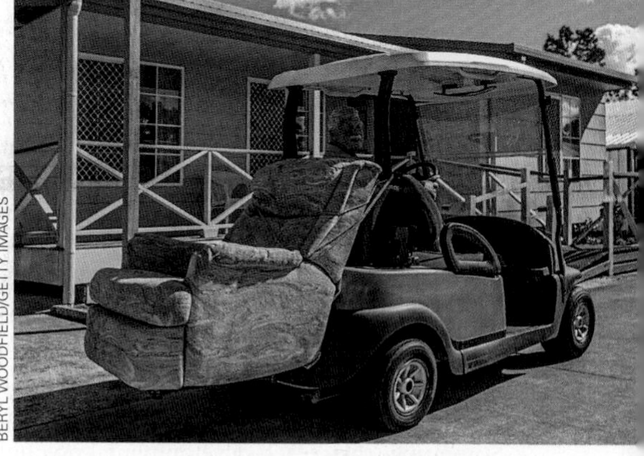

BERYL WOODFIELD/GETTY IMAGES

Many Possibilities Older adults like this man, seen here helping a friend move furniture in a retirement village in Queensland, Australia, ideally have a range of choices when it comes to living arrangements. When that is true, almost no one needs nursing-home care.

As with many other aspects of aging, selective optimization with compensation is crucial for living arrangements. Elders need settings that allow them to be safe, social, and respected, as independent as possible. Housing solutions vary depending not only on ADLs and IADLs but also on the elder's personality and social network of family and friends.

We close with a wonderful example of family care and nursing-home care at their best. A young adult named Rob related that his 98-year-old great-grandmother "began to fail. We . . . thought, well, maybe she is growing old" (quoted in Adler, 1995, p. 242). All three younger generations decided that she should move to a nearby nursing home, leaving the place she had lived for decades. She reluctantly agreed.

Fortunately, this nursing home did not assume that decline is always a sign of "final failing" (Rob's phrase). The doctors discovered that her pacemaker was not working properly. Rob tells what happened next:

> We were very concerned to have her undergo surgery at her age, but we finally agreed. . . . Soon she was back to being herself, a strong, spirited, energetic, independent woman. It was the pacemaker that was wearing out, not Great-grandmother.
>
> *[quoted in Adler, 1995, p. 242]*

This story contains a lesson repeated throughout this book. Whenever a toddler does not talk, a preschooler grabs a toy, a teenager gets drunk, an emerging adult takes risks, an adult avoids marriage, or an older person becomes frail, it is easy to conclude that these problems are typical at that age.

Indeed, they are. But that does not mean they should simply be accepted. Each should alert others to encourage talking, sharing, moderation, caution, connection, or self-care. The life-span perspective holds that, at every age, people can be "strong, spirited, and energetic."

CAREER ALERT

The Developmental Scientist

The need for developmental scientists is apparent: Much more must be learned about "how and why people—all kinds of people—change over time." Would-be researchers must become scholars who know what has already been studied—earning at least a master's degree. Leaders in developmental science almost always need a Ph.D. as well.

Often young scholars study after earning a Ph.D. as "post-docs," researching and writing under the direction of a leading scientist at a major university. Sometimes they work in government offices such as the Centers for Disease Control and Prevention (CDC) or the Bureau of Labor Statistics. Sometimes they teach developmental psychology at colleges, universities, or community centers.

The difference between a professional who is familiar with human development and one who is a developmental scientist is that the latter continues to ask new questions and seek answers using the scientific method. The general principles explained in Chapter 1 are a beginning, but scientists do much more. They analyze hundreds of published studies, consult dozens of colleagues, and debate every aspect of the work.

Expertise in statistics, in research design, in multicultural sensitivity is needed. For example, to learn about other cultures, many scientists live in another place for years, seeking alternate perspectives. If they decide to use a standard questionnaire, they might have it translated by a bilingual native speaker and then back-translated by someone else.

Before beginning a project, it might be preregistered, with calculations about how many participants are needed to find valid results. Many other measures have been developed to assure accurate conclusions, and developmental scientists understand and use them.

For example, often study participants are deliberately kept ignorant about the goal of the research: They are said to be *blind* to the experimenter's goal. This deception prevents conscious or unconscious efforts to validate, or undermine, the study. An ethical mandate is that any deception must be explained to the participants after their involvement.

Scientists may need to be "blind," as well: They do not directly interact with the participants of the study so that they cannot inadvertently clue responses. The entire endeavor requires many people to design, implement, and

interpret the research, which is why senior researchers need graduate students and post docs.

All of this is expensive: One task of the principal leader of a research project is to convince other people (foundations, government, private philanthropists) to support a particular study. Good communication skills are essential.

Once a study is completed and analyzed and its conclusions are drawn, but before it is published, the written report is subject to peer review. This means that other scientists (peers) who are not involved in the study read the unpublished report, make suggestions, and, finally, determine whether it is sufficiently well-designed, honest, and clear for publication.

As with every Career Alert in this text, some readers of this book might consider this career. If they hope to earn a Ph.D., they must undertake innovative research and write the results, usually in a thesis that is at least 100 pages long—more often double or triple that. Every step of the way, and in the final product, other scholars will criticize and evaluate, which means the student must not only be diligent but must learn how to respond to criticism.

Some of the work of developmental scientists is tedious, some requirements seem irrelevant, and some results of the research are discouraging. Developmentalists are aware of the "file drawer" problem, which is research completed but never published, relegated to sit in a desk drawer instead.

However, for those who choose this career, the joy of new discovery seems well worth the effort, and the potential reward—a better life for thousands of people who benefit from the research—makes all the work worthwhile.

what have you learned?

1. What factors make an older person frail?
2. What are the basic differences between ADLs and IADLs?
3. Why might IADLs be more important than ADLs in deciding whether a person needs care?
4. How is cognitive decline related to prevention of frailty?
5. What three factors increase the likelihood of elder abuse?
6. What are the advantages and disadvantages of assisted living for older people?
7. When is a nursing home a good solution for frail elders?
8. What factors distinguish a good nursing home from a bad one?

SUMMARY

Theories of Late Adulthood

1. Self theories hold that adults make personal choices in ways that allow them to become fully themselves. One such theory arises from Erikson's last stage, integrity versus despair, in which individuals seek integrity that connects them to the human community.

2. Compulsive hoarding can be understood as an effort to hold onto the self, keeping objects from the past that others might consider worthless.

3. Stratification theories maintain that social forces—such as ageism, racism, and sexism—limit personal choices throughout the life span, keeping people on a particular level or stratum of society. Intersectionality confirms that multiple stereotypes often combine to impair development.

4. Age stratification can be blamed for the disengagement of older adults. Activity theory counters disengagement theory, stressing that older people need to be active.

Activities in Late Adulthood

5. Older adults in long-standing partnerships tend to be satisfied with their relationships and to safeguard each other's health. As a result, married elders tend to live longer, happier, and healthier lives than unmarried ones.

6. Friends and other relatives are important for health and happiness. The social circle shrinks, but it may become more intense.

7. Relationships with adult children and grandchildren are usually mutually supportive, although conflicts arise as well. Financial support usually flows down the generational ladder.

8. At every age, employment can provide social and personal satisfaction as well as needed income. Retirement may be welcomed because it enables other activities.

9. Some older people perform volunteer work and are active politically—writing letters, voting, staying informed. Many also value religious beliefs and practices.

10. Most elders want to age in place, in part because their friends, familiar stores, and religious or community groups are nearby. Many engage in home improvement.

The Oldest-Old

11. Most older people are self-sufficient, but some eventually become frail. They need help, either with physical tasks (ADLs such as eating and bathing) or with instrumental ones (IADLs such as completing income taxes).

12. Care of frail elders is usually undertaken by adult children or spouses, who are often older adults themselves. Most families have a strong sense of filial responsibility, but in practice, adult children may resent each other and may not provide needed care.

13. Elder abuse is a problem worldwide. It occurs because of a combination of the characteristics of the caregiver and care receiver, in a social context that makes getting help difficult. Abuse can be financial, physical, or emotional.

14. Nursing homes, assisted living, and professional home care are of varying quality and availability. Good care for frail elders is personalized, combining professional and family support, recognizing diversity in needs and personality.

KEY TERMS

self theories (p. 460)
integrity versus despair (p. 462)
compulsive hoarding (p. 463)
positivity effect (p. 464)
stratification theories (p. 465)
disengagement theory (p. 467)
activity theory (p. 467)
filial responsibility (p. 470)
age in place (p. 475)
naturally occurring retirement community (NORC) (p. 476)
frail (p. 478)
activities of daily life (ADLs) (p. 480)
instrumental activities of daily life (IADLs) (p. 480)
integrated care (p. 484)

APPLICATIONS

1. Political attitudes vary by family and by generation. Interview several generations within the same family about issues of national and local importance, such as education, immigration, climate, or LGBTQ+ acceptance. How do you explain the similarities and differences between the generations? What is more influential: experience, SES, heritage, or age?

2. People of different ages, cultures, and experiences vary in their values regarding family caregiving, including the need for safety, privacy, independence, and professional help. Find four people whose backgrounds (age, ethnicity, SES) differ. Ask their opinions and analyze the results.

3. A major expense for many older people is health care, both routine and catastrophic. Government payment for health care expenses (hospitals, drugs, and preventive care) varies widely from nation to nation. Compare two nations, your own and one other, on specifics of the health of older adults (rates of longevity, diseases, caregiving etc.).

4. Visit a nursing home or assisted-living residence in your community. Record details about the physical setting, the social interactions of the residents, and the activities of the staff. Would you like to work or live in this place? Why or why not?

ESPECIALLY FOR ANSWERS

Response for Social Scientists (from p. 468): In general, psychologists favor self theories, and sociologists favor stratification theories. Of course, each discipline respects the other, but each believes that its perspective is more honest and accurate.

Response for Religious Leaders (from p. 477): There are many possible answers, including the specifics of getting to church (transportation, stairs), physical comfort in church (acoustics, temperature), and content (unfamiliar hymns and language).

Response for Those Uncertain About Future Careers (from p. 487): Why not? The demand for good workers will obviously increase as the population ages, and the working conditions are likely to improve. An important problem is that the quality of nursing homes varies, so you need to make sure you work in one whose policies incorporate the view that older adults can be quite capable, social, and independent.

OBSERVATION QUIZ ANSWERS

Answer to Observation Quiz (from p. 461): To enable walking, Diana has flat, rubber soled shoes and taps with her cane, and to prevent COVID-19 she wears gloves and a mask. The fifth thing is indicated by her mask, which says "VOTE."

Answer to Observation Quiz (from p. 467): A chair.

Answer to Observation Quiz (from p. 475): Late adulthood. The hard question is why that is the case.

EPILOGUE

Death and Dying

what will you know?

- Why is death a topic of hope, not despair?
- What is the difference between a good death and a bad one?
- How does mourning help with grief?

"When is Pappy going to die?" asked a 4-year-old when he was in the car with his grandfather (Pappy), his grandmother, and his parents. Pappy was quiet, but the other three adults answered, "A lot of years"; "Not for a long, long time"; "We hope he never does" (Sekeres, 2013).

That quieted the boy for the moment. His birthday had been the week before, so he was acutely aware that he was no longer 3. He was happy that he had "a new number, 4." That evening he asked his parents, "What is Pappy's last number?" And then, "What is my last number?"

The answer came after a pause. "We don't know."

This chapter explores what we know and do not know about death. We know that everyone will have a "last number" and that Pappy's number is likely to come sooner than his grandson's. We also know that humans, everywhere and for hundreds of thousands of years, have experienced grief and developed beliefs and rituals to deal with dying and death.

Much is known about cultural variations, enduring traditions, and new ethical dilemmas, such as how to make a good death more likely. There is *hope* in death, *choices* in dying, and *affirmation* in mourning, as each of the three sections of this Epilogue describe. But when it comes to individuals like Pappy, or me, or you, much is still unknown.

Death and Hope

A multi-cultural life-span perspective reveals that reactions to death are filtered through many cultural prisms, affected by historical changes, regional variations, and the age of both the dying and the bereaved.

One emotion is constant, however: hope. It appears in many ways: hope for life after death, hope that the world is better because someone lived, hope that death occurred for a reason, hope that survivors will dedicate themselves to whatever is meaningful in life. Immortality of some kind is the hope of everyone who thinks about death (Robben, 2018).

Conversation Who is talking here? Unless you are an Egyptologist, you would not guess that this depicts a dead man conversing with the gods of the Underworld. Note that the deceased is relatively young and does not seem afraid – both typical for people in ancient Egypt.

Cultures, Epochs, and Death

Few people in affluent nations have witnessed someone their age die. This was not always the case (see Table EP.1). If someone reached age 50 in 1900 in the United States and had had 20 high school classmates, at least six of those fellow students would have already died. The survivors had probably visited their dying friends at home, perhaps promising to see them in heaven.

People in other cultures may not have believed in heaven, but they still reassured contemporaries and family members who were dying. In earlier centuries, almost every family experienced the death of a young child, a sad but not unexpected event. We begin by describing traditional responses to death to help us understand what is universal for humankind, and what has changed.

ANCIENT TIMES

Paleontologists have evidence from 120,000 years ago that the Neanderthals buried their dead with tools, bowls, or jewelry, signifying belief in an afterlife (Stiner, 2017). The date is controversial: Burial with objects could have begun earlier, but for millennia death was an occasion for hope, mourning, and remembrance.

Two ancient Western civilizations with written records—Egypt and Greece—had elaborate death rituals. Egyptians built magnificent pyramids, refined mummification, and scripted instructions (called the *Book of the Dead*) to help the soul (*ka*), personality (*ba*), and shadow (*akh*) reunite, so that the dead could protect the living (Taylor, 2010).

Another set of beliefs came from the ancient Greeks. Again, continuity between life and death was evident, with hope for this world and the next. The fate of a dead person depended on that person's actions when alive. A few would have a blissful afterlife, a few were condemned to torture in Hades, and most would enter a shadow world until they were reborn.

TABLE EP.1 How Death Has Changed in the Past 100 Years

Death occurs later. A century ago, the average life span worldwide was less than 40 years (47 in the rapidly industrializing United States). Half of the world's babies died before age 5. Now newborns are expected to live to age 72 (79 in the United States); in many nations, centenarians are the fastest-growing age group.

Dying takes longer. In the early 1900s, death was usually fast and unstoppable; once the brain, the heart, or any other vital organ failed, the rest of the body quickly followed. Now death can often be postponed through medical technology: Hearts can beat for years after the brain stops functioning, respirators can replace lungs, and dialysis does the work of failing kidneys.

Death often occurs in hospitals. For most of our ancestors, death occurred at home, with family nearby. Now most deaths occur in hospitals or other institutions, with the dying surrounded by medical personnel and machines.

The causes of death have changed. People of all ages once usually died of infectious diseases (tuberculosis, typhoid, smallpox), or, for many women and most infants, in childbirth. Now disease deaths before age 50 are rare, and in developed nations most newborns (99%) and their mothers (99.99%) live.

And after death . . . People once knew about life after death. Some believed in heaven and hell; others, in reincarnation; others, in the spirit world. Prayers were repeated – some on behalf of the souls of the deceased, some for remembrance, some to the dead asking for protection. Believers were certain that their prayers were heard. People now are aware of cultural and religious diversity; many raise doubts that never occurred to their ancestors.

Ancient Chinese, Mayan, Indian, and African cultures also had rituals about death, venerating ancestors as connected to the living in some way (Hill & Hageman, 2016). People in West Africa connected death with birth: Death was interwoven with hope for the future, reverence for the past of the community with ongoing life (Parker, 2021).

In every region of the world:

- Actions during life were thought to affect destiny after death.
- An afterlife was assumed.
- Mourners said prayers and made offerings to prevent the spirit of the dead from haunting and hurting them, and to gain blessing and strength from the ancestors.

CONTEMPORARY BELIEFS

Now consider contemporary beliefs. Diversity of customs and beliefs is apparent, yet common themes are evident. Connections between the living and the dead are recognized; people and communities memorialize the dead to help the survivors live on (Klass & Steffen, 2017).

Belief in an afterlife continues. An international study of 1,595 people (890 people from four Asian cultures and 695 North Americans) found that most (including 295 who said they were not religious) believed in life after death (Nichols et al., 2018).

For many people, death increases their religious actions, as they light candles, say prayers, and perform rituals. Currently, an increasing number of people are not religious. They nonetheless develop ideas and practices about death, repeating the names of those who died and using memories as inspiration (MacMurray & Fazzino, 2017). As one nonbeliever said:

> Death makes life worth living. . . . death should be the inspiration to get out there and live your life.
>
> *[Joe, quoted in MacMurray & Fazzino, 2017, p. 288]*

THINK CRITICALLY: Is your own belief about life after death more influenced by your religion or your culture?

OBSERVATION QUIZ
Beyond the coffin, do you see any other signs of ritual? (see answer, page 514) ↓

Understanding Death Throughout the Life Span

Thoughts about death (and about everything else) are influenced by each person's age, cognitive maturation, culture, and past experiences. Here are some of the specifics.

CHILDREN'S UNDERSTANDING OF DEATH

Some adults think children are oblivious to death; others believe children should participate in funerals and other rituals, just as adults do. You know from your study of childhood cognition that neither view is completely correct.

Children are affected by the attitudes of others. They may be upset if they see grown-ups cry or if parents keep them away from death rituals for someone they loved. Thus, adults should neither ignore a child's emotions nor expect mature reactions. Since the limbic system matures before the prefrontal cortex, a bereaved child may be happy one day and despondent the next.

Young children become aware of death by age 4, but they do not necessarily understand that everyone dies, or that the dead cannot come back to life (Panagiotaki et al., 2018). When children understand the biology of death (sometime between ages 6 and 10), that does not contradict their psychological, spiritual understanding of death.

Sorrow All Around When a 5-day-old baby died in Santa Rosa, Guatemala, the entire neighborhood mourned. Symbols and a procession help with grief: The coffin is white to indicate that the infant was without sin and will therefore be in heaven.

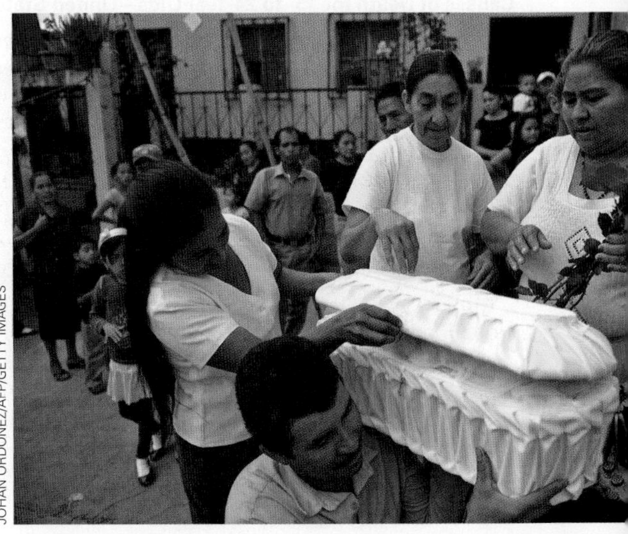

JOHAN ORDOÑEZ/AFP/GETTY IMAGES

For example, a 6-year-old might know that a dead grandparent is not coming back to life, but may believe that the grandparent still cares about what they do (Menendez et al., 2020). Hope comes naturally to children.

A child's cognitive maturation and personal experience has less impact than what their parents and their culture has told them. Parents sometimes convey messages they themselves do not believe, such as saying "your granny can still see you now that she is in the sky" even when a parent does not believe in life after death (Panagiotaki et al., 2018).

The general advice from psychologists is that adults need to listen to children, avoiding lies or platitudes (Stevenson, 2017). Children who lose a friend, a relative, or a pet might, or might not, seem sad, lonely, or angry. If a child is told that Grandma is sleeping, that God wanted a sibling in heaven, or that Grandpa went on a trip, that risks two problems:

1. If children believe the explanation, they may insist on waking up Grandma, complaining to God, or phoning Grandpa to say, "Come home."
2. If children realize that adults lie, they may conclude that adults are terrified about death, and cannot talk honestly about it.

As children become concrete operational thinkers, they seek facts. They want to know why and how a person died and where they are now. The cause of death is important to older children.

For children as well as for adults, actions of remembrance aid acceptance. They want to bring flowers, repeat a prayer, write a letter, visit a grave. As they become better able to understand that death is a biological end, children also are more likely to believe a religious/spiritual understanding. They see no contradiction in that (Harris, 2018; Panagiotaki et al., 2018).

terror management theory
The idea that people adopt cultural values and moral principles in order to cope with their fear of death. This system of beliefs protects individuals from anxiety about their mortality and bolsters their self-esteem.

DEATH IN ADOLESCENCE AND EMERGING ADULTHOOD

Remember that adolescent emotions are powerful and erratic, changing quickly. Adolescents confronting death may be self-absorbed, philosophical, analytic, or distraught—or all four at different moments. [**Life-Span Link:** Adolescent dual processing is discussed in Chapter 9.] Death does not stop the search for identity. Some adolescents use social media to write to the dead person or to vent their grief—an effective way to express their personal identity concerns (Balk & Varga, 2017).

"Live fast, die young, and leave a good-looking corpse" is advice often attributed to actor James Dean, who died in a car crash at age 24. At what stage would a person be most likely to agree? Emerging adulthood, of course (see Figure EP.1).

FIGURE EP.1 **Tuberculosis Versus Driving into a Tree**
Medical science has become better at curing cancer, preventing heart disease, controlling HIV, and treating gunshot wounds. But more adults drive dangerously or despair of living. Better psychological science needed!

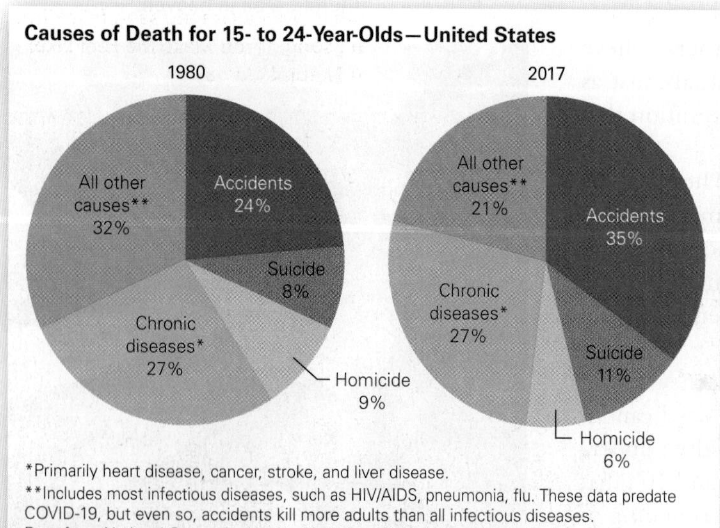

Terror management theory explains some young adult responses to death. The idea is that people who fear death become more defensive of their own culture, more ageist, and more likely to take risks. They manage their terror by defying death. Terror management is particularly evident among college students and fades with maturity (Maxfield et al., 2017).

Terror management may explain an illogical action by some adolescents in Florida who have asthma. Compared to high school students without asthma, they are *more* likely to use tobacco products (28 percent versus 24 percent). That includes higher rates of smoking cigarettes and cigars, which they know are harmful for their lungs (Reid et al., 2018).

DEATH IN ADULTHOOD

When adults become responsible for work and family, attitudes shift. Death is not romanticized. Many adults quit addictive drugs, start wearing seat belts, and adopt other death-avoiding behaviors when they reach age 30 or so.

Dying adults may be less concerned about themselves than about the people they will leave, especially if they have children. Some write a letter to their children to be opened years later, to express their ongoing love and care.

Many adults seek comfort in religion. That helps many but not everyone. Research finds that religious beliefs sometimes increase death anxiety, although they usually decrease it (Bassett & Bussard, 2021; Jong et al., 2018). Variation occurs partly because religions differ in whether God is primarily loving or punishing, whether death is an end or a transition.

To defend against their own fears, adults may not accept the death of others. When Dylan Thomas was about age 30, he wrote to his dying father: "Do not go gentle into that good night/Rage, rage against the dying of the light" (Thomas, 2003). Nor do adults accept their own death. A woman diagnosed at age 42 with a rare and almost always fatal cancer (a sarcoma) wrote:

> I hate stories about people dying of cancer, no matter how graceful, noble, or beautiful. . . . I refuse to accept I am dying; I prefer denial, anger, even desperation.
>
> *[Robson, 2010, pp. 19, 27]*

Adult reactions to the death of others depend partly on the age of the deceased. Millions of people mourned James Dean, Whitney Houston, Kobe Bryant (ages 24, 48, and 41, respectively). Equally talented celebrities who die at age 80 or 90 are less mourned. When someone in late adulthood dies, younger adults may say it was time for them to die—a statement that is seen as ageist by some older people.

THINK CRITICALLY: What other examples of irrational behavior are evident in how adults responded to COVID?

Logically, adults should work to change social factors that increase the risk of mortality—such as air pollution, junk food, and unsafe cars. Instead, many react more strongly to rare causes of death, such as anthrax and avalanches. They particularly fear deaths beyond their control.

One telling example: People fear travel by plane more than by car. In fact, flying is safer: In 2020, in the entire world, only 299 people were killed in commercial airplane accidents, but in the United States alone, 42,060 were killed by motor vehicles.

The 2020 numbers were affected by COVID-19, which led more people to drive instead of fly. But the disparity has been evident for decades: In 2017, there were 399 plane deaths worldwide and 41,000 U.S. motor-vehicle deaths.

ROSS D. FRANKLIN/GETTY IMAGES

SCOTT OLSON/GETTY IMAGES

Both on August 31, 2018
Every culture mourns the dead, but variations are vast. Two famous Americans died at the end of August 2018. Senator John McCain lay in state at the U.S. Capitol in Washington, D.C., with his widow kissing his flag-draped casket. The Queen of Soul, Aretha Franklin, lay in a flower-covered casket in a Detroit church, as thousands cried while Ariana Grande sang Franklin's hit song, "(You Make Me Feel Like) A Natural Woman."

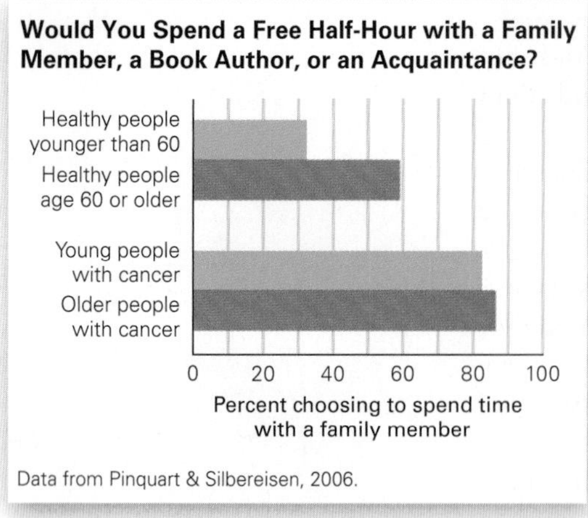

FIGURE EP.2 Turning to Family as Death Approaches Both young and old people diagnosed with cancer (one-fourth of whom died within five years) more often preferred to spend a free half-hour with a family member rather than with an interesting person whom they did not know well.

DEATH IN LATE ADULTHOOD

In late adulthood, attitudes shift again. Anxiety decreases; hope rises (De Raedt et al., 2013).

Some older people remain happy when they are terminally ill. Many developmentalists believe that one sign of mental health among older adults is acceptance of mortality, which increases concern for others. Some elders engage in *legacy work*, trying to leave something meaningful for later generations (Lattanzi-Licht, 2013).

As evidence of this attitude change, older people seek to reconcile with estranged family members and tie up loose ends. Do not be troubled when elders allocate heirlooms, discuss end-of-life wishes, or buy a burial plot: All of those actions are developmentally appropriate.

Acceptance of death does not mean that older people give up on living; rather, their priorities shift. In an intriguing series of studies (Carstensen, 2011), people were presented with the following scenario:

> Imagine that in carrying out the activities of everyday life, you find that you have half an hour of free time, with no pressing commitments. You have decided that you'd like to spend this time with another person. Assuming that the following three persons are available to you, whom would you want to spend that time with?
>
> - A member of your immediate family
> - The author of a book you have just read
> - An acquaintance with whom you seem to have much in common

Older adults, more than younger ones, choose the family member (see Figure EP.2). The researchers explain that family becomes more important when death seems near.

Near-Death Experiences

At every age, coming close to death may be an occasion for hope. This is most obvious in what is called a *near-death experience*, in which a person almost dies. Survivors sometimes report having left the body and moved toward a bright light while feeling peace and joy. The following classic report is typical:

> I was in a coma for approximately a week. . . . I felt as though I were lifted right up, just as though I didn't have a physical body at all. A brilliant white light appeared. . . . The most wonderful feelings came over me—feelings of peace, tranquility, a vanishing of all worries.
>
> *[quoted in Moody, 1975, p. 56]*

Near-death experiences often include religious elements (angels seen, celestial music heard). Survivors often become more spiritual, less materialistic.

THINK CRITICALLY: When a person is almost dead, might thoughts occur that are not limited by the neuronal connections in the brain?

A reviewer of near-death experiences was struck by their endorsement of religious beliefs. In every culture, "all varieties of the dying experience" moved people toward the same realizations: (1) the limitations of social status, (2) the insignificance of material possessions, and (3) the narrowness of self-centeredness (Greyson, 2009).

In fact, people who have merely heard about near-death experiences from other people tend to feel more spiritual and less materialistic (Tassell-Matamua et al., 2017). Similarly, hospice volunteers who witness death say that some dying people hear voices, see visions, and so on, which strengthens the religious beliefs of the witnesses (Claxton-Oldfield et al., 2020).

That brings us back to a general theme. Observing and thinking about death can make people more hopeful about the future—their own and that of others.

what have you learned?

1. In ancient cultures, how did people deal with death?
2. What are the common themes in religious understanding about death?
3. How do children respond to death?
4. Why might fear of death lead to more risk-taking?
5. How does being closer to one's own death affect a person's attitudes?
6. In what ways do people change after a near-death experience?

Choices in Dying

Do you recoil at the heading "Choices in Dying"? If so, you may be living in the wrong century. Every twenty-first-century death involves choices, beginning with risks taken or avoided, habits sustained, and specific measures to postpone or hasten death.

A Good Death

People everywhere hope for a good death, one that is:

- at the end of a long life;
- peaceful;
- quick;
- at home;
- with family and friends; and
- without pain, confusion, or discomfort.

Many would add that *control over circumstances* and *acceptance of the outcome* are also characteristic of a good death, but cultures and individuals differ on those two. Some willingly cede control; others fight every sign that death is near.

A review finds that family, medical personnel, and the dying person emphasize different aspects of "a good death" (Meier et al., 2016). One issue is psychological and spiritual well-being, which is important for many patients but less so for physicians.

OBSERVATION QUIZ
One of the five senses is particularly important for the dying, even when sight and hearing are fading. What is it? (see answer, page 514)

Same Situation, Far Apart: As It Should Be Dying individuals and their families benefit from physical touch and suffer from medical practices (gowns, tubes, isolation) that restrict movement and prevent contact. A good death is likely for these two patients — a husband with his wife in their renovated hotel/hospital room in North Carolina *(left)*, and a man with his family in a Catholic hospice in Andhra Pradesh, India *(right)*.

JERRY WOLFORD/POLARIS/NEWSCOM

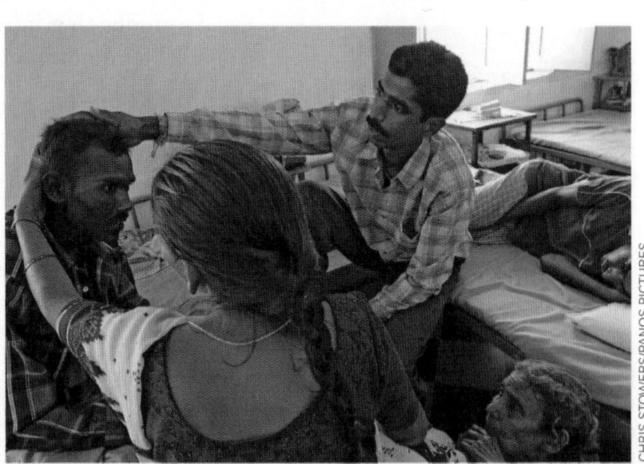

CHRIS STOWERS/PANOS PICTURES

VIDEO: End of Life: Interview with Laura Rothenberg features a young woman with a terminal illness discussing her feelings about death.

MEDICAL CARE

In some ways, modern medicine makes a good death more likely. The first item on the list has become the norm: Death usually occurs at the end of a long life. Younger people still get sick, but surgery, drugs, radiation, and rehabilitation typically mean that the seriously ill may enter a hospital and then return home. If young people die, their death is typically quick (a fatal accident or suicide) and without pain, although painful for their loved ones.

In other ways, however, the medical profession "rewards cure more than care" (Butler, 2019), which makes a bad death more likely. When cure is impossible, physical and emotional care deteriorate. Among the specific problems common in hospitals:

- Nurses are slower to respond to a bell.
- Doctors explain less.
- Hospital protocols promote medical measures that increase pain.
- Visitors may be excluded. [This was almost universal during the COVID-19 pandemic.]
- Treatment may make the patient delirious or comatose, so last words are never spoken.

This list makes it apparent why people want to die at home. However, in developed nations most deaths occur in hospitals or nursing institutions. Even in England, where one published goal of public medicine is a good death, half of the deaths occur in hospitals, one-fourth in *care homes* (called *nursing homes* in the United States), and only one-fourth at home (Bone et al., 2018).

The underlying problem may be medical care itself, which is so focused on lifesaving that dying is resisted (Lee, 2019). Medical staff members are taught about drugs, surgeries, and other actions that treat the body; they may ignore the emotions.

Students in their final years of medical school were asked about deaths they had witnessed while interning in hospitals. They were troubled that they did not remain detached and professional: Emotional responses to some patients were distressful (Jedlicska et al., 2021). From a psychological perspective, detachment is not the goal. In fact, distress in not a problem; lack of distress may be.

STAGES OF DYING

In about 1960, Elisabeth Kübler-Ross decided to speak with people who were dying. She asked the administrator of a large hospital for permission and names. He told her that no one was dying! Eventually, she found terminally ill patients who were eager to talk.

From ongoing interviews, Kübler-Ross identified reactions of dying people. She divided their emotions into five sequential stages.

1. Denial ("I am not really dying.")
2. Anger ("I blame my doctors, or my family, or my God.")
3. Bargaining ("I will be good from now on if I can live.")
4. Depression ("I don't care; nothing matters anymore.")
5. Acceptance ("I accept my death as part of life.")

(Kübler-Ross, 1975, 1997)

◆◆ Especially for Relatives of a Person Who Is Dying Why would a healthy person want the attention of hospice caregivers? (see response, page 514)

These five stages are no longer considered the best way to describe responses to death. However, contemporary social scientists are grateful to Kübler-Ross: She pioneered the study of human reactions to death (Corr, 2019; Kuczewski, 2019).

Another set of stages of dying is based on Maslow's hierarchy (Zalenski & Raspa, 2006):

1. Physiological needs (freedom from pain)
2. Safety (no abandonment)
3. Love and acceptance (from close family and friends)
4. Respect (from caregivers)
5. Self-actualization (appreciating one's unique past and present)

Other researchers have *not* found stages of dying. Remember the woman dying of a sarcoma, cited earlier? She said that she would never *accept* death and that Kübler-Ross should have included desperation as a stage. Kübler-Ross said that her stages have been misunderstood, that "our grief is as individual as our lives" (Kübler-Ross & Kessler, 2005, p. 7).

Nevertheless, both lists remind caregivers that each dying person has strong emotions that may be unlike that same person's emotions a few days or weeks earlier. Those emotions are not identical to those of doctors, friends or relatives, who themselves have varied and changing emotions. A good death recognizes those dynamic reactions.

TELLING THE TRUTH

Many wise contemporary physicians advocate honest conversations regarding the body's responses to death (Gawande, 2014; Kalanithi, 2016). Knowing the truth allows the dying to choose appropriate care, including addictive painkillers, music or prayers that are personal to the individual, favorite foods, visits from distant relatives, and so on.

Providing care for a dying person is difficult, because patients misunderstand, symptoms change, priorities shift. Some dying people do *not* want the whole truth, some do *not* want medical intervention, some do *not* want visitors, some do *not* want to hear music. Others are the opposite. Ideally, heartfelt talk among all is ongoing, over many weeks (Cripe & Frankel, 2017).

DATA CONNECTIONS: How Death Has Changed in the Last 100 Years presents several graphs that show increases in life expectancy over the past century while also prompting reflection on the importance of a "good death." Achieve

Better Ways to Die

Several practices have become more prevalent since the contrast between a good death and the usual hospital death has become clear. Hospice and palliative care are examples. Both try to relieve symptoms rather than provide a cure, perhaps using aromatherapy, meditation, and massage, as well as salves and drugs that provide comfort (Zeng et al., 2018).

HOSPICE

In London in the 1950s, Cecily Saunders started the first modern **hospice**, where terminally ill people could spend their last days. Since then, thousands of hospices have opened in many nations. In addition, hundreds of thousands of caregivers bring hospice care to people at home.

hospice
An institution or program in which terminally ill patients receive palliative care to reduce suffering; family and friends of the dying are helped as well.

Two principles characterize hospice care:

1. Each patient's autonomy is respected. For example, pain medication is readily available on request, neither pushed nor denied, not on a schedule or set dosage.

2. Family members and friends are counseled before the death, taught to provide care, and guided in mourning. Death is thought to happen to a family, not just to an individual.

Even when hospice care is in an institution, measures are allowed that many hospitals forbid: acupuncture, special foods, flexible schedules, visitors at midnight, excursions outside, massage, aromatic oils, religious rituals, and so on (Doka, 2013). Comfort takes precedence over cure, and that itself reduces stress and extends life. Family care helps everyone, including the patient.

Originally, hospice did not include treatment that might cure the disease, but now curative measures (radiation, drugs) are allowed, although insurance payment for them may be complex. Some (about 21 percent) U.S. hospice patients are discharged alive. Some of these people live several more years, but most are sent to hospitals where they soon die, not a good death (Russell et al., 2017).

Another large group (about 30 percent) die within a few days of entering hospice care, too late for them and their families to have care attuned to their individual needs. One reason for this late care is that it is difficult to know a month in advance that death is soon, especially when the problem is heart disease or neurocognitive loss.

Even when death is predictable, hospice care may not be available (see Table EP.2). Hospice is more common in England than in mainland Europe, more common in the western part of the United States than in the Southeast, and rare in less affluent nations.

FIGURE EP.3 Not with Family Almost everyone prefers to die at home, yet most people die in an institution, surrounded by medical personnel and high-tech equipment, not by the soft voices and gentle touch of loved ones. The "other" category is even worse, as it includes most lethal accidents or homicides. But don't be too saddened by this chart—improvement is possible. Twenty years ago, the proportion of home deaths was notably lower.

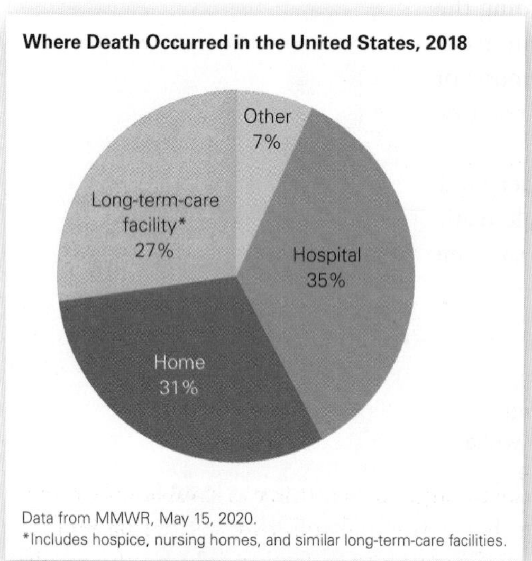

This is changing: The number of hospice deaths in the United States doubled between 2000 and 2010, with about half the deaths in 2020 including some hospice care (Aldridge et al., 2015). (See Figure EP.3.) In that year, hospice care was most common for people dying of cancer, less common for people dying of heart disease, and rare for COVID deaths (the third most common cause of death in the United States in 2020, when 3,358,814 died) (Ahmad et al., 2021).

Economic, ethnic, and cultural differences are apparent. For example, in the United States, affluent people are more likely to receive hospice care than people with lower income, and people of color receive hospice care much less often than White people (Harris-Kojetin et al., 2019).

If given a choice, people of color are more likely to die at home with no medical care, or to seek aggressive hospital care—which, ironically, means more pain and distress. One team suggests that African American churches should explain the spiritual benefits of hospice: Clergy are typically involved in hospice care and are much less involved in hospital care (Townsend et al., 2017).

TABLE EP.2 Barriers to Entering Hospice Care

- Hospice patients must be terminally ill, with death anticipated within six months, but predictions are difficult. For example, in one study of noncancer patients, physician predictions were 90% accurate for those who died within a week but only 13% accurate when death was predicted in three to six weeks (usually the patients died sooner) (Brandt et al., 2006). Other research confirms that "death is highly unpredictable" (Einav et al., 2018, p. 1462).
- Patients and caregivers must accept death. Traditionally, entering a hospice meant the end of curative treatment (chemotherapy, dialysis, etc.). This is no longer true. Now treatment can continue. Many hospice patients survive for months, and some are discharged alive (Salpeter et al., 2012).
- Hospice care is costly. Skilled workers – doctors, nurses, psychologists, social workers, clergy, music therapists, and so on – provide individualized care day and night.
- Availability varies. Hospice care is more common in England than in mainland Europe and is a luxury in poor nations. In the United States, western states have more hospices than midwestern states do. Even in one region (northern California) and among clients of one insurance company (Kaiser), the likelihood that people with terminal cancer will enter hospice depends on exactly where they live (Keating et al., 2006).

PALLIATIVE CARE

In 2006, the American Medical Association approved a new specialty, **palliative care**, which focuses on relieving pain and suffering. Palliative measures are not only for the dying; every patient may benefit. Palliative-care doctors prescribe powerful drugs and procedures to treat nonlethal symptoms, such as rashes, muscle soreness, and nausea, with salves, foods, exercise, and meditation.

The need for skilled palliative care is obvious when one considers pain relief. Doctors have become very cautious in prescribing addictive opioids, yet high doses may be needed if someone has progressive cancer or another painful condition. Morphine and other opiates have a **double effect**: They relieve pain (a positive effect), but slow down respiration (a negative effect). Painkillers that reduce both pain and breathing are allowed by law, ethics, and medical practice.

Indeed, almost any medical measure has multiple effects on brain and body. Surgery removes or repairs something harmful, but causes pain, infection, and sometimes death; every drug or radiation affects the person in many ways.

One controversial example is heavy sedation that alleviates pain, but that delays death more than extends life. If an unconscious patient cannot think or feel, with no chance of recovery, is that worse than death?

palliative care
Medical treatment designed primarily to provide physical and emotional comfort to the dying patient and guidance to their loved ones.

double effect
When an action (such as administering opiates) has both a positive effect (relieving a terminally ill person's pain) and a negative effect (hastening death by suppressing respiration).

Ethical Issues

As you see, medical success creates moral dilemmas. Dying is no longer the natural outcome of age and disease; when and how death occurs involves human choices. (See A Case to Study.)

DECIDING WHEN DEATH OCCURS

A related ethical issue is deciding when a person is dead. When death occurs, organs can be donated to others who would die without them, and funerals can be scheduled. Otherwise, not.

A CASE TO STUDY

What Is Your Intention?

The law focuses on intent: If a drug or surgery is intended to relieve suffering, then a resulting death is morally and legally justifiable. Otherwise, not (Sulmasy, 2018).

However, people disagree as to whether a drug, or surgery, or any other medical measure is, on balance, more positive than negative. About half of all palliative-care physicians have been accused of killing a patient. The accusation usually comes from a grief-stricken loved one, and then medical facts exonerate the doctors. Sometimes the accusation comes from another medical person. Then judgment becomes more complicated.

Consider a court case. A man with terminal cancer was terrified of future pain and loss of control, so his doctor gave him a drug he could take if he could not bear living. That man told another doctor, who accused the first doctor of breaking the law as well as defying medical ethics.

The first doctor argued that this was double effect: He was relieving the "existential suffering" of the patient (a positive effect), knowing that death might be the result (the negative effect). A court found him guilty of breaking the law. He appealed and was exonerated.

Both the conviction and the appeal troubled many others. One wrote:

> The offer to provide the drug was described as a palliative treatment in that it gave reassurance and comfort to the patient. Double effect reasoning was extended in this instance to encompass potentially facilitating a patient's death. This extension further muddies the murky double effect reasoning waters.
>
> *[Duckett, 2018, p. 33]*

Deciding when death occurred used to be simple: The heart stopped beating and the lungs no longer took in air, and those organ failures caused death. Now stopped hearts are restarted, breathing continues with respirators, stomach tubes provide calories, drugs fight pneumonia. At what point, if ever, should those interventions stop?

Almost every life-threatening condition leads to treatments started, stopped, or avoided, with death postponed, prevented, or welcomed. This has fostered impassioned moral arguments, between nations (evidenced by radically different laws) and within them.

THINK CRITICALLY: At what point, if ever, should intervention stop to allow death?

Religious advisers, doctors, and lawyers disagree with colleagues within their respective professions; family members have opposite opinions; and people within every other group diverge. For example, outsiders might imagine that all Roman Catholic priests share the same views, but that is far from the truth (Bedford et al., 2017).

EVIDENCE OF DEATH

Historically, death was determined by listening to a person's chest: No heartbeat meant death. To make sure, a feather was put to the person's nose to indicate respiration—a person who had no heartbeat and did not exhale was pronounced dead. Very rarely, but widely publicized when it happened, death was declared when the person was still alive.

Modern medicine has changed that: Hearts and lungs need not function on their own. Many life-support measures and medical interventions circumvent the organ failures that once were tantamount to death. Checking breathing with feathers, thankfully, is never used today.

But the issue remains. When is someone in a *permanent* vegetative state (and thus will never be able to think), and when are they merely in a temporary coma? Is a person with an unresponsive brain, unable to ever breathe again without a respirator, dead? Does "ever" mean 10 or 20 years hence?

Few laypeople understand all of the tests that determine brain death, and even doctors using brain scans struggle with the ethical and practical problems of deciding when a person is brain dead and when they are merely "locked in" and might someday become able to respond to life (Fins & Bernat, 2018; Underwood, 2014).

In 2020, an international panel of neuroscientists delineated many specific measures of brain function, include reactions of eyes, throat, and limbs. No response at all, to any one of these tests, meant death (Greer et al., 2020). (See Table EP.3.)

Family members may cling to hope long after medical experts determine that recovery is impossible. This raises moral issues for many reasons: cost, psychic distress, and organs that cannot be donated if too much time elapses between brain death and donation.

TABLE EP.3 Dead or Not? Yes, No, and Maybe

Brain death: Prolonged cessation of all brain activity with complete absence of voluntary movements; no spontaneous breathing; no response to pain, noise, and other stimuli. Brain waves have ceased; the electroencephalogram is flat; *the person is dead.*

Locked-in syndrome: The person cannot move, except for the eyes, but normal brain waves are still apparent; *the person is not dead.*

Coma: A state of deep unconsciousness from which the person cannot be aroused. Some people awaken spontaneously from a coma; others enter a vegetative state; *the person is not yet dead.*

Vegetative state: A state of deep unconsciousness in which all cognitive functions are absent, although eyes may open, sounds may be emitted, and breathing may continue; *the person is not yet dead.* The vegetative state can be *transient, persistent,* or *permanent.* No one has ever recovered after two years; most who recover (about 15%) improve within three weeks (Preston & Kelly, 2006). After sufficient time has elapsed, the person may, effectively, be dead.

EUTHANASIA

Ethical dilemmas also arise with an opposite issue, *euthanasia* (sometimes called *mercy-killing*), letting someone die who could live longer. There are two kinds of euthanasia.

In **passive euthanasia**, a person near death is allowed to die. The person's medical chart may include a **DNR (do not resuscitate) order**, instructing medical staff not to restore breathing or restart the heart if pulsating stops. A more detailed version is **POLST (physician-ordered life-sustaining treatment)**, which describes when antibiotics, feeding tubes, and so on should not be used.

Passive euthanasia is legal everywhere. Every doctor decides, at some point, that intervention is futile. However, POLSTs are not always followed, because many emergency personnel automatically start artificial respiration and stimulate hearts (Moore et al., 2016). Passive euthanasia may be contrary to patient wishes, but more often the opposite occurs: Patients want to die in peace, but medical measures prolong painful life.

Active euthanasia is deliberate action to cause death, such as taking a lethal drug. Some physicians accept active euthanasia when three conditions occur: (1) Suffering cannot be relieved, (2) illness is incurable, and (3) patients want to die. Active euthanasia is legal in the Netherlands, Belgium, Luxembourg, Colombia, Western Australia, Spain, and Canada (each nation has different requirements) and illegal (but rarely prosecuted) elsewhere.

In every nation, some physicians would *never* perform active euthanasia (even in nations in which it is legal); but others have done so (even in nations where it is illegal). Acceptance of active euthanasia is increasing among physicians. For example, in 1999 and again in 2015, hundreds of doctors in Finland were given the following situation:

> A 60-year-old male patient is suffering from prostatic cancer with metastases. Metastases in the thoracic spine led to total paraparesis [paralysis of the legs] 1 month earlier. There is no hope for a cure. The patient is well aware of the situation. He has totally lost his will to live. When you are together with him alone, he asks for a sufficient dose of morphine to "get away." You have denied the overdose, explaining that it is against your ethical principles. During the following days, you notice that the patient asks you to double his morphine dose because of unbearable pain. You suppose that increasing the dose in such a way would lead to the patient's death.

The doctors were asked, anonymously, what they would do. Most declined to give the deadly dose, but the percentage of those who would double the morphine increased over the 16 years, from 25 percent to 34 percent. Interestingly, rates were higher among older men than younger women (Piili et al., 2018). Is that because they could imagine themselves being that man?

passive euthanasia
When a seriously ill person is allowed to die naturally, without active attempts to prolong life.

DNR (do not resuscitate) order
A written order from a physician (sometimes initiated by a patient's advance directive or by a health care proxy's request) that no attempt should be made to revive a patient if they suffer cardiac or respiratory arrest.

POLST (physician-ordered life-sustaining treatment)
This is an order from a doctor regarding end-of-life care. It advises nurses and other medical staff which treatments (e.g., feeding, antibiotics, respirators) should be used and which not. It is similar to a living will, but it is written for medical professionals and thus is more specific.

active euthanasia
When someone does something that hastens another person's death, with the intention of ending that person's suffering.

physician-assisted suicide
A form of active euthanasia in which a doctor provides the means for someone to end their own life, usually by prescribing lethal drugs.

PHYSICIAN HELP WITH DEATH

Between passive and active euthanasia is another option: A doctor may provide the means for patients to end their own lives in **physician-assisted suicide**, typically by prescribing lethal medication that patients can take when they are ready to die.

Oregon was the first U.S. state to legalize this practice, asserting that such deaths are "death with dignity," not suicide. As of 2021, physician-assisted suicide is legal in California, Colorado, the District of Columbia, Hawaii, Maine, Montana, New Jersey, New Mexico (one county), Oregon, Vermont, and Washington.

The original law in Oregon required the following:

- The dying person must be an Oregon resident, over age 17.
- The dying person must request the drugs three times, twice spoken and once in writing.

Too Late for Her When Brittany Maynard was diagnosed with progressive brain cancer that would render her unable to function before killing her, she moved from her native California to establish residence in Oregon so that she could die with dignity. A year later, the California Senate Health Committee debated a similar law, with Brittany's photo on a desk. They approved the law, 5–2.

AP IMAGES/RICH PEDRONCELLI

TABLE EP.4 Oregon Residents' Reasons for Requesting "Deaths with Dignity"

Percent of Patients Giving Reason (most had several reasons)	
Less able to enjoy life	91
Loss of autonomy	92
Loss of dignity	67
Burden on others	54
Loss of control over body	37
Pain	26
Financial implications of treatment	5

Data from Oregon Public Health Division, 2019, p. 6.

- Fifteen days must elapse between the first request and the prescription.
- Two physicians must confirm that the person is terminally ill, has less than six months to live, and is competent (i.e., not cognitively impaired or depressed).

Even if all of this occurs, approval is not automatic. Only about one-third of the initial requests are granted.

Opposite opinions are deeply held. Everywhere, some people die by suicide for the honor of their nation, their family, or themselves. Buddhist monks publicly burned themselves to death to advocate Tibetan independence from China; one individual's suicide set off the Arab Spring.

The most publicized U.S. example was Brittany Maynard, who was suffering an incurable and debilitating progressive brain disease. She pleaded to die with dignity in her native California, but the law forbade it. She moved to Oregon, and died as she wished. California then changed the law.

Personality and religion affect acceptance of physician-assisted suicide. The practice is anathema in Islamic nations; in North America, people who are devout Christians often are strongly opposed (Bulmer et al., 2017). Other Christians, as well as people of other faiths or no faith, believe that humans have a God-given right to die (Frandsen, 2020).

PAIN: PHYSICAL AND PSYCHOLOGICAL

The Netherlands has permitted active euthanasia since 1980, updating the law in 2002. The Dutch now allow euthanasia not only when a person is soon to die, but also when a person is chronically ill and in pain.

Physicians are now allowed to relieve "unbearable suffering," which can include "fatigue, pain, decline, negative feelings, loss of self, fear of future suffering, dependency, loss of autonomy, being worn out, being a burden, loneliness, loss of all that makes life worth living, hopelessness, pointlessness and being tired of living" (Dees et al., 2011, p. 727). Before any doctor ends a life, they must consult another physician and register the death with the authorities.

That raises additional ethical questions, as Opposing Perspectives explains. Is psychological pain as hurtful as physical pain? Or even worse?

Advance Directives

advance directives
Any description of what a person wants to happen as they die and after death. This can include medical measures, visitors, funeral arrangements, cremation, and so on.

Recognizing that people differ, many professionals recommend **advance directives**. That allows each individual to specify desired medical treatment, where and how death occurs, what should happen to the body (cremation or burial, with coffin or merely cloth), and details of the funeral or memorial.

The legality of such directives varies by jurisdiction: Sometimes a lawyer must ensure that documents are legal; sometimes a written request, signed and witnessed, is adequate. Every reader of this book needs to explore the requirements in their home jurisdiction.

Many people approve of personal choice and advance directives in theory, but they are uncertain about specifics, which vary because of other circumstances. For example, restarting the heart may extend life for decades in a young, healthy adult but may cause a major neurocognitive disorder in an older person with no cognitive reserve.

Given all the individual differences in the body, it is hard to know when artificial feeding, breathing, or heart stimulation results only in a temporary respite, or when

OPPOSING PERSPECTIVES

The "Right to Die"?

Some legal scholars believe that people have a right to choose their death, but others believe that the right to life forbids the right to die (Wicks, 2012). Might legalizing euthanasia or physician-assisted suicide create a *slippery slope*, a slide toward ending life for people with disabilities, low income, or minority status?

The data refute that concern. In Oregon and elsewhere, the oldest-old, less affluent people, and people of color are *less* likely to use fatal prescriptions. In Oregon, almost everyone who chose "death with dignity" was White (96 percent), had health insurance, was educated (73 percent had some college), and had lived a long life (see Figure EP.4). Most died at home, with friends or family.

Thus, laws allowing euthanasia do not seem unfair to people who already experience discrimination. However, those laws may encourage everyone to consider death a choice, contrary to the ethics of some people. On this, the data are less clear.

In the Netherlands, the number of people choosing euthanasia is increasing. Some form of euthanasia accounted for about 1 in 50 deaths when the law was first in place but 1 in 30 deaths in 2014. Some might interpret these data as evidence of a slippery slope; others see it as proof that the law is useful, allowing both the 3.3 percent and the 96.6 percent to die as they wish.

Addressing the slippery-slope argument, a cancer specialist wrote:

> To be forced to continue living a life that one deems intolerable when there are doctors who are willing either to end one's life or to assist one in ending one's own life, is an unspeakable violation of an individual's freedom to live—and to die—as he or she sees fit. Those who would deny patients a legal right to euthanasia or assisted suicide typically appeal to two arguments: a "slippery slope" argument, and an argument about the dangers of abuse. Both are scare tactics, the rhetorical force of which exceeds their logical strength.
>
> *[Benatar, 2011, p. 206]*

Not everyone agrees with that doctor. Might deciding to die be a sign of depression? Should physicians consult with a psychiatrist rather than prescribe lethal drugs (Finlay & George, 2011)? Declining ability to enjoy life was cited by 91 percent of Oregonians who requested physician-assisted suicide in 2018 (see Table EP.4). Is that sanity or depression?

Might acceptance of death be mentally healthy in the old but not in the young? If only those over age 64 were allowed the right to die, that would exclude 22 percent of Oregonians who opted to die with dignity. Might they consider age-based restrictions an example of ageism, that assumes that the young are not capable of choice, or that life matters less for the old?

In 2018, 240 Oregonians obtained lethal prescriptions, and 158 of them legally used those drugs to die. Most of the others died naturally, but some were alive in January 2019, keeping the drugs for possible future use (in the past, about 10 percent used their prescriptions the year after obtaining them). These numbers have increased every year: Only 16 died with physician assistance in 1998.

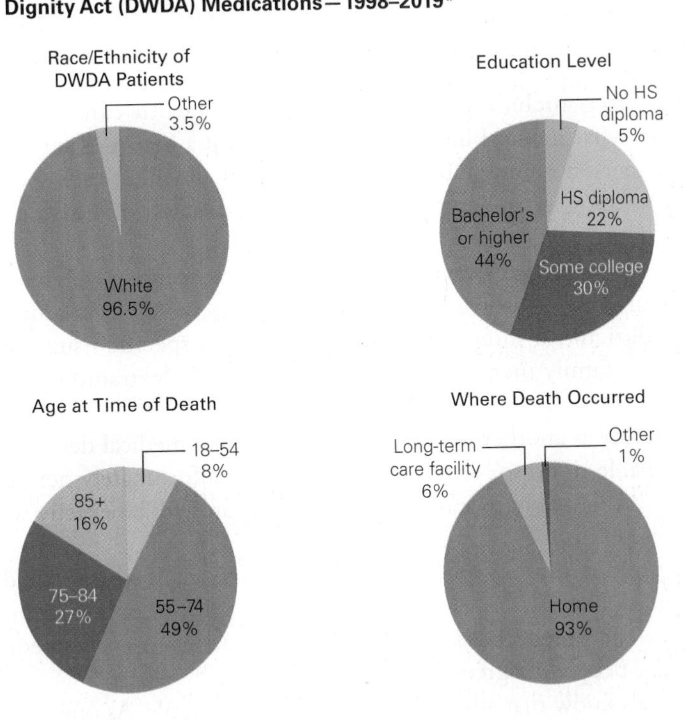

FIGURE EP.4 Death with Dignity? The data do not suggest that people of low SES are unfairly pushed to die. Quite the opposite—people who choose physician-assisted suicide tend to be among the better-educated, more affluent citizens.

There are two other arguments against physician-assisted-suicide. One is that it distracts from care for the dying. In the words of one doctor:

> We still need to deal with the problem that confronts most dying patients: how to get optimal symptom relief, and how to avoid the hospital and [instead] stay at home in the final weeks. Legalizing euthanasia and PAS is really a sideshow in end-of-life care—championed by the few for the few, extensively covered by the media, but not targeted to improve the care for most dying patients who still suffer.
>
> *[Emanuel, 2017]* .

Could a law designed to allow death with dignity actually undercut death with dignity?

The second argument is the opposite of the fear explained in the first paragraph of this Opposing Perspectives. Instead of making it too easy for low-income people to die, it might discriminate against their right to die with dignity. The Oregon requirements—repeated requests, certified by two physicians—are easier for those high in SES. Is that fair?

A position statement from the International Association of Hospice and Palliative Care says:

> no country or state should consider the legalization of euthanasia or PAS until it ensures universal access to palliative care services and to appropriate medications, including opioids for pain and dyspnea.
>
> *[De Lima et al., 2017, p. 8]*

Since no state or nation has "universal access to palliative care," by that standard, no nation is ready to offer physician-assisted suicide. A contrary opinion is evident in Canada, where its Supreme Court unanimously approved physician-assisted suicide after the Canadian Medical Association withdrew their objection to it (Attaran, 2015).

Most jurisdictions recognize the dilemma: Doctors are almost never prosecuted for helping with death as long as it is done privately and quietly. Opposing perspectives, and opposite choices, are evident.

THINK CRITICALLY: Why would someone take all of the steps to obtain a lethal prescription and then not use it?

antibiotics or pain medication causes coma or hallucinations. Even if this is known, people make opposite choices.

living will
A document that indicates what medical intervention an individual prefers if they are not conscious when a decision is to be expressed. For example, some do not want mechanical breathing.

health care proxy
A person chosen to make medical decisions if a patient is unable to do so, as when in a coma.

WILLS AND PROXIES

Advance directives often include a living will and/or a health care proxy. A **living will** indicates what medical intervention is desired if a person is unable to communicate. (If the person is conscious, hospital personnel ask about each specific procedure, often requiring written consent. Patients who are lucid can override any instructions of their living will.)

Why would anyone override their own earlier wishes? Because living wills include phrases such as "incurable," "reasonable chance of recovery," and "extraordinary measures," and it is difficult to interpret such phrases until a specific issue arises. Even then, doctors and family members disagree about what is "extraordinary" or "reasonable."

A **health care proxy** is another person delegated to make medical decisions if someone becomes unable to do so. That seems logical, but unfortunately neither a living will nor a health care proxy guarantees that medical care will be exactly what a person would choose.

◆◆ Especially for People Without Advance Directives Why do very few young adults have advance directives? (see response, page 514)

For one thing, proxies often find it difficult to allow a loved one to die, unless the living will demands it. A larger problem is that few people—experts included—anticipate the precise risks, benefits, and alternatives to every medical procedure. No wonder people disagree.

Medical professionals know that advance directives are not simple. As one couple wrote:

> Working within the reality of mortality, coming to death is then an inevitable part of life, an event to be lived rather than a problem to be solved. Ideally, we would live the end of our life from the same values that have given meaning to the story of our life up to that time. But in a medical crisis, there is little time, language, or ritual to guide patients and families in conceptualizing or expressing their values and goals.
>
> *[Farber & Farber, 2014, p. 109]*

what have you learned?

1. What is a good death?
2. What are Kübler-Ross's five stages of dying, and why doesn't everyone agree with them?
3. What determines whether or not a person will receive hospice care?
4. Why is the double effect legal, even though it speeds death?
5. How is it determined that death has occurred?
6. What is the difference between passive and active euthanasia?
7. What are the four prerequisites of "death with dignity" in Oregon?
8. Why would a person who has a living will also need a health care proxy?

Affirmation of Life

Human relationships are life sustaining, but all adults eventually lose someone they love. Grief and mourning are part of living.

Grief

Grief is the powerful sorrow felt after a profound loss, especially when a loved one dies. Grief is deep and personal, an anguish that can overwhelm daily life.

grief
The deep sorrow that people feel at the death of another. Grief is personal and unpredictable.

UNIVERSAL GRIEF

Grief is normal, even when it includes odd actions and thoughts. The specifics vary from person to person, but uncontrollable sobbing, sleeplessness, and irrational and delusional thoughts are common (Doka, 2016).

Sheryl Sandberg described her grief a year after her husband died:

> I was swallowed in the deep fog of grief—what I think of as the void. An emptiness that fill your heart and your lungs, constricts your ability to think, or even to breathe.
>
> *[Sandberg & UC Berkeley, 2016, 05:07–05:19]*

Joan Didion remembers her reaction after her husband's sudden death. She refused the offers of her friends to come stay with her:

> Grief has no distance. Grief comes in waves, paroxysms, sudden apprehensions that weaken the knees and blind the eyes and obliterate the dailiness of life. . . . I see now that my insistence on spending that first night alone was more complicated than it seemed, a primitive instinct. . . . There was a level on which I believed that what had happened remained reversible. . . . I needed to be alone so that he could come back.
>
> *[Didion, 2005, pp. 27, 32, 33]*

When a loved one dies, loneliness, denial, anger, and sorrow come in sudden torrents. Many people want time alone, yet the bereaved also need other people. Grief typically hits hardest in the first week, but unexpected rushes can occur months or years later.

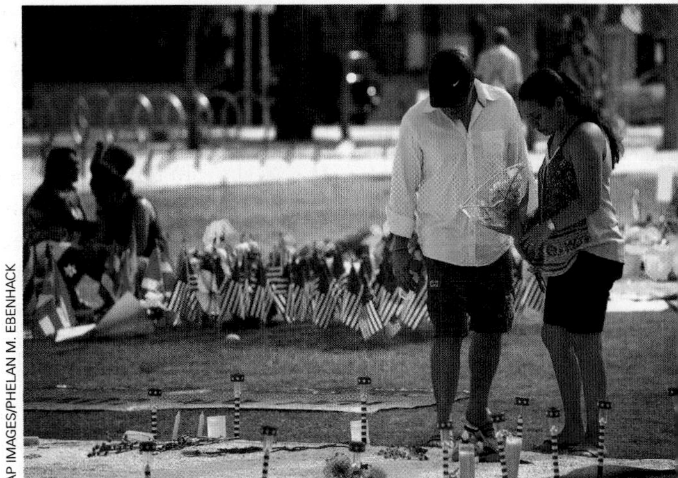

AP IMAGES/PHELAN M. EBENHACK

Why Flags? This couple expresses their grief after a mass shooting at the Pulse nightclub by bringing flowers to a memorial at the Phillips Center for Performing Arts in Orlando, Florida. Some mourners bring candles and flags, and others join marches and protests. Grief is expressed in many ways — some simple, some complicated.

COMPLICATED GRIEF

complicated grief
A type of grief that impedes a person's future life, usually because the person clings to sorrow or is buffeted by contradictory emotions.

absent grief
When mourners do not grieve, either because other people do not allow expressions of grief or because the mourners do not allow themselves to feel sadness.

disenfranchised grief
A situation in which certain people, although they are bereaved, are prevented from mourning publicly by cultural customs or social restrictions.

incomplete grief
When circumstances, such as a police investigation or an autopsy, interfere with the process of grieving.

Sometimes grief festers, becoming what is called **complicated grief**, impeding life over a long period. The DSM-IV had a "bereavement exclusion," stating that major depression could not be diagnosed within two months of a death, but DSM-5 changed that. Major depression can begin soon after someone dies (LeBlanc et al., 2019).

Depression may begin with **absent grief**, when a bereaved person does not seem to grieve. This is a common first reaction, but ongoing unexpressed grief can trigger physical or psychological symptoms, such as trouble breathing, panic attacks, or crippling sorrow.

Another kind of complicated grief is **disenfranchised grief**, "not merely unnoticed, forgotten, or hidden; it is socially disallowed and unsupported" (Corr & Corr, 2013b, p. 135). Some people experience deep grief but are forbidden by social norms to express it.

For instance, often only a current spouse or close blood relative is legally allowed to decide on funeral arrangements, disposal of the body, and other matters. This made sense when all family members were in frequent contact within the same cultural community, but it may now result in "gagged grief and beleaguered bereavement" (Green & Grant, 2008, p. 275).

Sometimes a long-time but unmarried partner is excluded, especially when that partner is of the same sex (Curtin & Garrison, 2018). Relatives, especially those who live far away, may not know the deceased person's friends. Thus, some mourners are not informed about the funeral. They are bereft, not only of someone they loved, but also of the comfort of fellow mourners.

INCOMPLETE GRIEF

Grief is a process, usually intense at first, diminishing over time, and eventually reaching closure. Customs such as viewing the dead, or throwing dirt on the grave, or scattering ashes, all allow expression and then closure. However, circumstances can interfere, creating **incomplete grief**.

Traumatic death is always unexpected, and then denial, anger, and depression undercut the emotions of grief (Kauffman, 2013). Murders and suicides often trigger police, judges, and the press, so mourners who need private time to grieve instead must answer questions, with answers sometimes printed in newspapers. An autopsy may prevent grief, especially if someone believes that the body will rise or that the soul remains in the body.

Inability to recover a body, as with soldiers who are missing in action or with victims of a major flood or fire, may prevent grief from being expressed and thereby hinder completion. That explains why, after the 9/11 destruction of the World Trade Center, when DNA identified a fragment of bone, families often had a funeral and burial of that tiny piece, to allow grieving.

In natural or human-caused disasters such as hurricanes and wars, incomplete grief is common, because survival—food, shelter, medical care—takes precedence. In the days and weeks after disasters, some people die of causes not directly attributable to the trauma, because other people are distracted, and survivors do not care for themselves as they normally would.

In the coronavirus pandemic, whether or not a person died of COVID-19 became a political issue, which interfered with grief. Some denied that the virus killed someone they knew, and others wanted to tell everyone about a COVID death and also about other "excess deaths" that indirectly were caused by the pandemic. Many hospitals banned all visitors, which compounded grief.

One particular developmental concern is the effect of COVID deaths on children and grandchildren. Adolescents may be particularly likely to experience a "grief

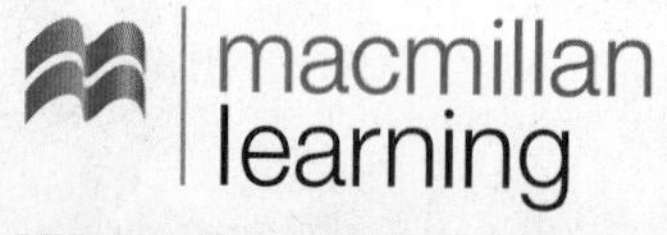

VIDEO: Bereavement: Grief in Early and Late Adulthood presents the views of a young-adult daughter and middle-aged mother on the death of the mother's brother, to whom they were both close.

pandemic" of complicated or incomplete grief, with increased risk years later of accidental death, substance abuse, or major depression (Weinstock et al., 2021).

The reality that grief is a process suggests that other people should not try to cut it short or prescribe its course. No one should tell parents who lost a baby that "You never knew that baby; you can have another," or pet owners that "It was only a cat," or those with aged relatives that "It was time." Such phrases may bring comfort to some mourners but not all. Grief has its own expressions and boundaries; others should not decide what is appropriate (Doka, 2016).

People who live and work where no one knows their personal lives may lack customs to help them grieve. The laws of some nations — China, Chile, and Spain, for example — mandate paid bereavement leave, but this is not true in the United States (Meagher, 2013).

MICHAEL DANTAS/AFP VIA GETTY IMAGES

Rest in Peace? The COVID-19 pandemic not only disrupted life for everyone, it also disrupted death. Here, Brazilians are about to be buried in a mass grave after dying alone. Many of the living are as troubled by their exclusion from the bedside and the grave as they are by the loss of a loved one.

Indeed, for workers at large corporations or students in universities, grief may become "an unwelcome intrusion (or violent intercession) into the normal efficient running of everyday life" (Anderson, 2001, p. 141). Many college professors (me included) wish students would not miss classes or delay assignments because of a death.

I may be wrong. My rationale is that people should move past intense grief. Maintaining the obligations of usual life is one way to survive a loss. But incomplete grief impedes recovery.

Mourning

Grief splinters people into jumbled pieces, making them vulnerable. Mourning reassembles them, making them whole again and able to rejoin the larger community. To be more specific, **mourning** is the public and ritualistic expression of bereavement, the ceremonies and behaviors that a religion or culture prescribes to honor the dead and allow recovery in the living.

mourning
The ceremonies and behaviors that a religion or culture prescribes for people to express their grief after a death.

HOW MOURNING HELPS

Mourning customs are a buffer between normal and complicated grief. That buffer is needed because the grief-stricken are vulnerable to irrational thoughts and self-destructive acts. Some eat too little or drink too much; some forget caution as they drive or even as they walk across the street. Physical and mental health dips in the recently bereaved; the rate of suicide increases.

Sometimes death continues to affect people years later. The death of a child is particularly hard on the parents. They need each other but, in the irrationality of grief, one may blame the other. Years after the loss of a child, illness and death rates of parents rise (Brooten et al., 2018).

A large study in Sweden found that adults whose brother or sister died years ago had higher death rates in adulthood. This was true no matter how the sibling died, but if suicide was the cause, adult survivors were themselves three times more likely to die by suicide than were other Swedes of the same age and background (Rostila et al., 2013).

Similarly, after the suicide of a celebrity, rates rise for ordinary people. This alerts us that shared mourning is especially important when suicide occurs. Survivors tend to blame themselves, feel angry at the deceased, or consider following the example of the dead person.

After an adult's suicide, the friends of the immediate family may stay away because they do not know what to say. All of this adds difficulty to expressions of grief and rituals of mourning, yet both are especially crucial.

Honor Your Father Worldwide, children mourn their deceased parents by performing rituals developed by their community, as these four young men do while they spread ashes in the sea. Some secular adults, born and raised in Western Europe or North America, fly thousands of miles back to India with their Hindu fathers' ashes, comforted by thus respecting their heritage.

DBIMAGES/ALAMY STOCK PHOTO

Fortunately, humans have developed many customs to help people move from grief toward reaffirmation. For example, eulogies emphasize the dead person's good qualities; people who did not personally know the deceased attend wakes, funerals, or memorial services to comfort the survivors.

Public expression channels and contains private grief. Examples include the Jewish custom of sitting shiva at home for a week and then walking around the block to signify a return to life, or the three days of active sorrow among some Muslim groups, or the 10 days of ceremonies beginning at the next full moon following a Hindu death.

In many cultures, the continuity of life is symbolized by flowers, or ashes, or long-lasting candle flames, or a baby named after a dead person. Naming a child for a dead person or a religious leader is expected in some cultures, not in others.

Mohammed, Moses, and Jesus are common names in devout Muslim, Jewish, or Latin American families. However, one Tennessee judge "ordered that a 7-month-old boy's name be changed from Messiah to Martin," because she thought that name belonged only to Jesus (Steinmetz, 2013). Her order was declared illegal, in part because religious freedom recognizes that people differ in their reactions to death and life.

Many cultures set a day aside each year to honor the dead. The Latin American holiday Day of the Dead is an obvious example. It may be less obvious that Halloween originated as All Hallows Eve, the day before All Saints' Day, when memories of the dead were extolled. This is why costumes of witches and ghosts are common.

One example of cultural differences compares individualistic cultures (e.g., the United States and Western Europe) and collectivist cultures (e.g., many Asian and African nations). In an individualistic culture, the person is memorialized, and mourners take action—with gravestones, black armbands, and so on to remember that particular person. A photo is framed and placed where everyone can see it.

By contrast, many Asian people see human beings as interdependent. Therefore, mourning is a family and group event, when a dead person joins the ancestors, reflecting continuity over the generations (Valentine, 2017). A family area is designated for all the ancestors, whose portraits may be on the wall in some cultures. Note that in other cultures, that portrait may be a religious afront, evident when Muslims are outraged when a cartoon depicts Mohammed.

Likewise, building a memorial, dedicating a plaque, or naming a location for a dead person is expected in some cultures, antithetical in others. Indeed, some people believe that the deceased should be allowed to rest in peace, and thus all possessions, signs, and other evidence of a particular dead person are removed after proper prayers.

This created a cultural clash when terrorist bombs in Bali killed 38 Indonesians and 164 foreigners (mostly Australian and British). The Indonesians prayed intensely and then destroyed all reminders; the Australians raised money to build a memorial (de Jonge, 2011). Indonesian officials posed many obstacles to prevent construction; the Australians were frustrated; the memorial was never built. Neither group understood the deep emotions of the other.

The Human Touch Benetha Coleman fights Ebola in this treatment center by taking temperatures, washing bodies, and drawing blood, but she also comforts those with symptoms. Why would anyone risk working here? Benetha has recovered from Ebola, and, like many survivors of a disaster, she wants to help others who suffer.

JOHN MOORE/GETTY IMAGES

GROWTH AFTER DEATH

In recent decades, many people everywhere have become less religiously devout, and mourning practices are less ritualized. Has death become a source of despair, not hope? Maybe not. Many people worldwide become more spiritual when confronted with death (Lattanzi-Licht, 2013).

Religion was important in determining how people coped with COVID deaths. Many people who had some religious background increased their faith, praying, and attendance at religious services (Molteni et al., 2021).

Another example of growth after death occurs when the dead person was a public figure. Thousands, even millions, express their sorrow, stare at photos, and play the music or repeat the words of the dead person. They then affirm the best actions and values of the deceased. Old critiques are forgotten.

Some observers suggest that mourning can lead people to *post-traumatic growth* (the opposite of *post-traumatic stress disorder*, or *PTSD*) (Tedeschi et al., 2017). As you remember, Kübler-Ross found that reactions to death might eventually lead to acceptance. Finding meaning may be crucial to the reaffirmation that follows grief. In some cases, this search starts with preserving memories: Displaying photographs and personal effects and telling anecdotes about the deceased person are central to many memorial services in the United States.

Organizations that are devoted to combating a particular problem (such as breast cancer or HIV/AIDS) find their most dedicated donors, demonstrators, and advocates among people who have lost a loved one to that specific danger. That also explains why, when someone dies, survivors often designate a charity that is connected to the deceased. Then mourners contribute, hoping the death has led to good.

Placing Blame and Seeking Meaning

A common impulse after death is for the survivors to assess blame—for medical measures not taken, for laws not enforced, for unhealthy habits not changed. The bereaved sometimes blame the deceased person, sometimes themselves, and sometimes others.

THINK CRITICALLY: Are current wars fueled by a misguided impulse to assign blame?

The medical establishment is often blamed. In November 2011, Michael Jackson's personal doctor, Conrad Murray, was found guilty and jailed for prescribing the drugs that led to the singer's death. Many fans and family members cheered at the verdict; Murray was one of the few who blamed Jackson, not himself.

In 2018, the doctor who prescribed painkillers to Prince was fined $30,000, but he was not prosecuted because he was not the source of the illegal drugs that killed Prince. Many of Prince's friends knew about his addiction: They blamed themselves and each other.

For public tragedies, nations accuse one another. Blame is not rational or proportional to guilt. For instance, outrage at the assassination of Archduke Francis Ferdinand of Austria by a Serbian terrorist in 1914 provoked a conflict between Austria and Serbia—soon joined by a dozen other nations—that led to the four years and 16 million deaths of World War I.

When death occurs from a major disaster, survivors often seek a meaning that honors the loss. Many people believe that Israel would not have been created without the Holocaust, or that same-sex marriage would not have been be legalized if the HIV/AIDS epidemic had not occurred, or that laws allowing police immunity from prosecution would not have been questioned without the death of George Floyd.

Mourners often resolve to bring those responsible to justice. Blame can land on many people. After 17 people died in a gun massacre at a high school in Parkland, Florida, surviving students accused adults of not curbing the National Rifle Association (NRA), and they successfully persuaded major companies to discontinue discounts for NRA members. Florida enacted a law to raise the age for gun purchase to 21 and to require a wait period before a person can buy a gun (the NRA opposed that law); school districts nationwide considered arming teachers.

The search for blame in Parkland included:

- the security guard (a sworn law enforcement officer) who stayed outside;
- the mental health workers who did not hospitalize the gunman months earlier;

A Childish Response to Death? The survivors of the high school shooting in Parkland, Florida, sparked a nationwide protest against the National Rifle Association and the lawmakers and corporations who support it. Are these protestors in Washington, D.C., naive? People on both sides of the gun control debate believe so.

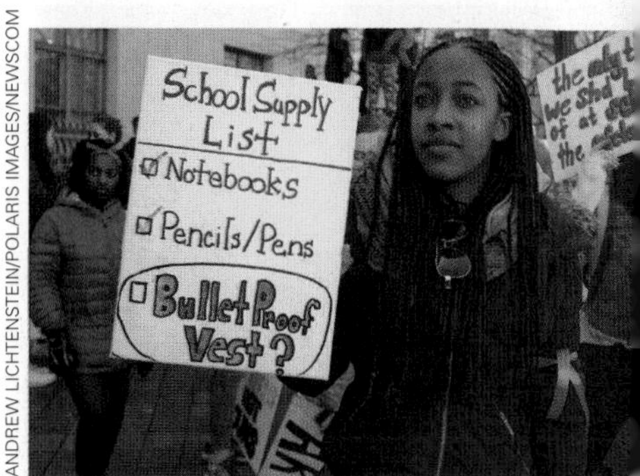

ANDREW LICHTENSTEIN/POLARIS IMAGES/NEWSCOM

- the design of the school classrooms that made killing easier;
- the specifics of gun manufacture (e.g., assault weapons, bump stocks);
- the sheriff;
- the FBI;
- the school superintendent (who almost was fired);
- the Republican president (Trump) at the time; and
- the former Democratic president (Obama).

As evident in this example, humans seek to blame someone—and the response may not be logical. The students who became spokespeople for gun laws were both lauded and derided.

Ideally, counselors, politicians, and clergy can steer grief-stricken survivors toward beneficial ends. That may have happened in 2015, when a gunman killed nine people in a prayer group at Emanuel African Methodist Episcopal Church in Charleston, South Carolina. Some people noted that the killer identified with the Confederate soldiers who fought in the U.S. Civil War. Within a month, the state Senate voted to remove the Confederate flag from the center of Charleston, and major retailers stopped selling that flag. The church members chose forgiveness.

Those church members may have had the right idea. When homicides occur, some family members want revenge, and others forgive. More generally, some people forgive the dead for past misdeeds rather than blaming them, a practice more likely to lead to psychological well-being (Gassin, 2017).

In **VIDEO: Bereavement and Grief: Late Adulthood**, people discuss their experiences with the loss of beloved family members and friends—and all agree that these losses have been very difficult experiences.

Diversity of Reactions

The specifics of bereavement and blame vary. No particular reaction is necessarily best. Culture affects the costs and benefits of any practice. For example, mourners who keep the dead person's possessions, talk to the deceased, and frequently review memories are notably *less* well adjusted than other mourners 18 months after death if they live in the United States, but they are *better* adjusted if they live in China (Lalande & Bonanno, 2006).

Past experiences affect bereavement. Children who lost their parents might be more distraught decades later when someone else dies. Past attachment also matters (Kosminsky, 2017). Older adults who were securely attached as children are likely to experience normal grief; those whose attachment was insecure-avoidant are likely to have absent grief; and those who were insecure-resistant may become stuck, focusing on complicated blame, unable to reaffirm their own lives.

continuing bonds The ongoing attachment and connection that the living have with the dead. Currently, continuing bonds are considered common and often beneficial.

CONTINUING BONDS

Reaffirmation does not mean forgetting; **continuing bonds** are evident years after death (Klass & Steffen, 2017; M. Stroebe et al., 2012). Such bonds are memories and connections that link the living and the dead. They may help or hinder ongoing life, depending on past relationships and on the circumstances of death. Often survivors write letters or talk to the deceased person, or consider events—a sunrise, a butterfly, a rainstorm—a messages of comfort.

Bereavement theory once held an "unquestioned assumption" that mourners should grieve and then move on, accepting that the dead person is gone forever (Neimeyer, 2017). It was thought that if this progression did not take place, pathological grief could result, with the bereaved either not grieving enough (absent grief) or grieving too long (incomplete grief).

But now a much wider variety of reactions is recognized. Continuing bonds are not only normal but, as one researcher notes, the "centrality of relations between the living and the dead" is helpful to the mourner and to everyone else (Neimeyer, 2017).

She Didn't Forget Eleven years after planes crashed into the World Trade Center, the field in Pennsylvania, and the Pentagon, killing 2,977 innocent people, several memorial ceremonies were held. Alice Watkins attended one of them to remember a friend who died. Are continuing bonds an expression of our connection to heritage and history, or a sign that some people are stuck in the past?

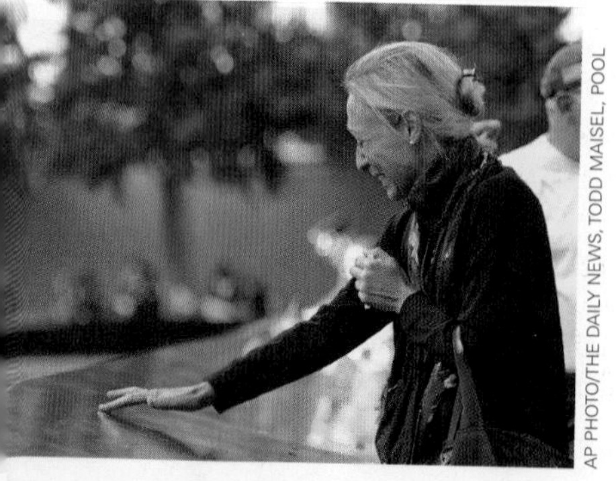
AP PHOTO/THE DAILY NEWS, TODD MAISEL, POOL

A bereaved person *might or might not* want to visit the grave, light a candle, cherish a memento, pray, or sob. Mourners may need time alone or may need company. Those who have been taught to bear grief stoically may be distressed if they are told to cry. Conversely, those whose cultures expect loud wailing may resent being told to hush.

DON'T ASSUME

Assumptions arising from one culture or religion might be inaccurate; people's reactions about death and hope vary for many reasons. One example came from a 13-year-old girl who refused to leave home after her 17-year-old brother was shot dead on his way to school. A therapist was supposed to get her to go to school again.

> It would have been easy to assume that she was afraid of dying on the street, and to arrange for a friend to accompany her on her way to school. But careful listening revealed the real reason she stayed home: She worried that her depressed mother might kill herself if she were left alone.
>
> *[Crenshaw, 2013]*

To help the daughter, the mother had to be helped.

No matter what fears arise, what rituals are followed, or what grief entails, mourning gives the living a deeper appreciation of themselves and others. In fact, a theme frequently sounded by those who work with the dying and the bereaved is that death leads to a greater appreciation of life, especially of the value of intimate, caring relationships.

It is fitting to end this Epilogue, and this book, with a reminder of the creative work of living. As first described in Chapter 1, the study of human development is a science, with topics to be researched, understood, and explained.

But the process of living is an art as well as a science, with strands of love and sorrow woven into each person's unique tapestry. Death, when it leads to hope; dying, when it is accepted; and grief, when it fosters affirmation—all add meaning to birth, growth, development, and love.

what have you learned?

1. What is grief, and what are some of its signs?
2. What are some of the complications of grief?
3. What are the differences among grief, mourning, and bereavement?
4. If a person still feels a loss six months after a death, is that pathological?
5. How can other people help someone who is grieving?

SUMMARY

Death and Hope

1. In ancient times, death connected the living, the dead, and the spirit world. People respected the dead and tried to live their lives so that their own death and afterlife would be good.

2. Every modern religion includes rituals and beliefs about death. These vary a great deal, but all bring hope to the living and strengthen the community. Those without religious beliefs also are inspired by death.

3. Death has various meanings, depending partly on the age of the person involved. For example, young children want companionship; older children want to know specifics of death.

4. Terror management theory finds that some emerging adults cope with death anxiety by defiantly doing whatever is risky. In adulthood, people tend to worry about leaving something undone or abandoning family members; older adults are more accepting of death.

Choices in Dying

5. A death that is painless and that comes at the end of a long life may be more possible currently than a century ago. However, other aspects of a good death—quick, at home, surrounded by loved ones—are less likely than in earlier times.

6. The emotions of people who are dying change over time. Some may move from denial to acceptance, although stages of dying are much more variable than originally proposed. Honest conversation helps many, but not all, dying persons.

7. Hospice caregivers meet the biological and psychological needs of terminally ill people and their families. Comfort is prioritized over cure, especially when attempts to cure prolong suffering and keep families away.

8. Palliative care relieves pain and suffering. This is now an important part of care in most hospitals and every hospice.

9. Drugs that reduce pain may decrease breathing, producing a double effect. That is legal everywhere. However, euthanasia and physician-assisted suicide are controversial. Several nations and U.S. states allow some forms of these; most do not.

10. Since 1980, death has been defined as occurring when brain waves stop; however, many measures now prolong life when no conscious thinking occurs.

11. Advance directives, such as a living will and a health care proxy, are recommended for everyone. However, no one can anticipate the specifics of possible interventions. Family members as well as professionals and nations often disagree.

Affirmation of Life

12. Grief is overwhelming sorrow. It may be irrational and complicated, absent, disenfranchised, or incomplete.

13. Mourning rituals channel human grief, helping people move to affirm life. Specifics vary by culture and cohort. Everywhere, bereavement is a community experience, not borne by the individual alone.

14. Continuing bonds with the deceased are no longer thought to be pathological. Past attachment history affects how a person responds to death.

KEY TERMS

- terror management theory (p. 494)
- hospice (p. 499)
- palliative care (p. 501)
- double effect (p. 501)
- passive euthanasia (p. 503)
- DNR (do not resuscitate) order (p. 503)
- POLST (physician-ordered life-sustaining treatment) (p. 503)
- active euthanasia (p. 503)
- physician-assisted suicide (p. 503)
- advance directives (p. 504)
- living will (p. 506)
- health care proxy (p. 506)
- grief (p. 507)
- complicated grief (p. 508)
- absent grief (p. 508)
- disenfranchised grief (p. 508)
- incomplete grief (p. 508)
- mourning (p. 509)
- continuing bonds (p. 512)

APPLICATIONS

1. The text recommends that everyone should have a health care proxy and a living will. Ask 10 people if they have these, and why or why not. Analyze the reasons—including your own.

2. Find quotes about death in *Bartlett's Familiar Quotations* or a similar collection that includes many centuries and cultures. Do you see any historical or cultural patterns of acceptance, denial, or fear?

3. People of varying ages have different attitudes toward death. Ask someone younger than 20, someone between 20 and 60, and someone over 60 what thoughts they have about their own death. What differences do you find?

ESPECIALLY FOR ANSWERS

Response for Relatives of a Person Who Is Dying (from p. 498): Death affects the entire family, including children and grandchildren. I learned this myself when my mother was dying. A hospice nurse not only administered my mother's pain medication (which made it easier for me to be with her) but also counseled me. At the nurse's suggestion, I asked for forgiveness. My mother indicated that there was nothing to forgive. We both felt a peace that would have eluded us without hospice care.

Response for People Without Advance Directives (from p. 506): Young adults tend to avoid thinking realistically about their own deaths. This attitude is emotional, not rational. The actual task of preparing the documents is easy (the forms can be downloaded; no lawyer is needed). Young adults find it much easier to do other future-oriented things, such as enrolling in a pension plan or signing a mortgage. Why is an advanced directive so hard?

OBSERVATION QUIZ ANSWERS

r to Observation Quiz (from p. 493): The chief mourners ing white (unlike the others), and the grandmother has red luxury often reserved for weddings and funerals.

Answer to Observation Quiz (from p. 497): Touch. That is why the exclusion of family when a patient had COVID-19 was so devastating for the dying and the family.

Appendix
More About Research Methods

This appendix explains how to learn about any topic. One of the most important lessons from the recent pandemic is that we need accurate information, reported honestly and analyzed carefully, to protect our mental and physical health. Science is essential to keep speculation and wishful thinking from destroying us.

Remember that almost no conclusion is entirely certain, now and forever. That is why the scientific method requires testing every hypothesis, basing conclusions on evidence, and reporting methods and statistics so that others can confirm, dispute, and replicate.

One of the most important aspects is in the selection of the participants in a study. Ideally, they are diverse in gender, ethnicity, race, and economic background, but if not, the biases and limitations of a restricted sample must be acknowledged.

Beyond that, when doing research connected with your own study in learning about human development, here are several suggestions.

Make It Personal

Think about your life, observe your behavior, and watch the people around you. Pay careful attention to details of expression, emotion, and behavior. The more you see, the more fascinated, curious, and reflective you will become. Ask questions and listen carefully and respectfully to what other people say regarding development.

Whenever you ask specific questions as part of an assignment, remember that observing ethical standards (see Chapter 1) comes first. *Before* you interview anyone, inform the person of your purpose and assure them of confidentiality. Promise not to identify the person in your report (use a pseudonym), and do not repeat any personal details that emerge in the interview to anyone (friends or strangers). Your instructor will provide further ethical guidance. If you might publish what you've learned, get in touch with your college's Institutional Review Board (IRB).

Read the Research

No matter how deeply you think about your own experiences, and no matter how intently you listen to others whose background is unlike yours, you also need to read scholarly published work in order to fully understand any topic that interests you. Be skeptical about magazine or newspaper reports; some are bound to be simplified, exaggerated, or biased.

Professional Journals and Books

Part of the process of science is that conclusions are not considered solid until they are corroborated in many studies, which means that you should consult several sources on any topic. Seven journals in human development are:

- *Developmental Psychology* (published by the American Psychological Association)
- *Child Development* (Society for Research in Child Development)
- *Developmental Review* (Elsevier)
- *Human Development* (Karger)
- *Developmental Science* (Wiley)
- *Psychology and Aging* (American Psychological Association)
- *Journal of Marriage and Family* (National Council of Family Relations)

These journals differ in the types of articles and studies they publish, but all are well respected and peer-reviewed, which means that other scholars review each article submitted and recommend that it be accepted, rejected, or revised. Every article includes references to other recent work.

Also look at journals that specialize in longer reviews from the perspective of a researcher:

- *Child Development Perspectives* (from Society for Research in Child Development)
- *Perspectives on Psychological Science* (This is published by the Association for Psychological Science. APS publishes several excellent journals, none specifically on development but every issue has at least one article that is directly relevant.)

Beyond these are literally thousands of other professional journals, each with a particular perspective or topic, including many in sociology, family studies, economics, medicine, demography, education, and more. To judge them, look for journals that are peer-reviewed.

Also consider the following background of the author (research funded by corporations tends to favor their products); nature of the publisher (professional organizations, as in several journals above, protect their reputations); and how long the journal has been published (the volume number tells you that). Some interesting work is misleading, so be careful before believing what you read.

Many *books* cover some aspect of development. Single-author books are likely to present only one viewpoint. That view may be insightful, but it is limited. You might consult a *handbook*, which is a book that includes many authors and many topics. However, handbook editors are selective, which may limit what is included.

The Internet

The *internet* is a mixed blessing, useful to every novice and experienced researcher but dangerous as well. Every library worldwide and most homes in North America, Western Europe, and East Asia have computers that provide access to journals and other information. If you're doing research in a library, ask for help from the librarians; many of them can guide you in the most effective ways to conduct online searches. In addition, other students, friends, and even strangers can be helpful.

Virtually everything is on the internet, not only massive national and international statistics but also accounts of very personal experiences. Photos, charts, quizzes, ongoing experiments, newspapers from around the world, videos, and much more are available at a click. Every journal has a website, with tables of contents, abstracts, and sometimes full texts. (An abstract gives the key findings; for the full text, most colleges and universities have access. Again, ask librarians for help.)

Unfortunately, you can spend many frustrating hours sifting through information that is useless, tangential, or trash. *Directories* (which list general topics or areas and then move you step by step in the direction you choose) and *search engines* (which give you all the sites that use a particular word or words) can help you select appropriate information.

Each directory or search engine provides somewhat different lists; none provides only the most comprehensive and accurate sites. Sometimes organizations pay, or find other ways, to make their links appear first, even though they are biased. With experience and help, you will find quality on the internet, but you will also encounter some junk no matter how experienced you are.

Anybody can put anything online, regardless of its truth or fairness, so you need a very critical eye. Make sure you have several divergent sources for every "fact" you find; consider who provided the information and why. Every controversial issue has sites that forcefully advocate opposite viewpoints, sometimes with biased statistics and narrow perspectives.

Here are four internet sites that are quite reliable:

- *childtrends.org* A leading U.S. research organization focusing on improving children's lives. Its site contains a wealth of data and evidence-based research.
- *childdevelopmentinfo.com* Child Development Institute. A useful site, with links and articles on child development and information on common childhood psychological disorders.
- *eric.ed.gov* Education Resources Information Center (ERIC). Provides links to many education-related sites and includes brief descriptions of each.
- *www.cdc.gov/nchs/hus.htm* The National Center for Health Statistics issues an annual report on health trends, called *Health, United States.*

Every source—you, your interviewees, journals, books, and the internet—is helpful. Do not depend on any particular one. Avoid plagiarism and prejudice by citing every source and noting objectivity, validity, and credibility. Your own analysis, opinions, words, and conclusions are crucial, backed up by science.

Additional Terms and Concepts

As emphasized throughout the text, the study of development is a science. Social scientists spend years in graduate school, studying methods and statistics. Chapter 1 touches on some of these matters (observation and experiments; correlation and causation; independent and dependent variables; experimental and control groups; cross-sectional, longitudinal, and cross-sequential research), but there is much more. A few additional aspects of research are presented here to help you evaluate research wherever you find it.

Who Participates?

The entire group of people about whom a scientist wants to learn is called a **population**. Generally, a research population is quite large—not usually the world's entire population of more than 7 billion, but, for statistics on birthweight or unwed mothers, all of the 3,788,235 babies born in the United States in 2019.

The particular individuals who are studied in a specific research project are called the **participants**. They are usually a **sample** of the population. Ideally, the participants are a **representative sample**, that is, a sample that reflects the population. Every peer-reviewed, published study reports details on the sample.

population
The entire group of individuals who are of particular concern in a scientific study, such as all the children of the world or all newborns who weigh less than 3 pounds.

participants
The people who are studied in a research project. *Participants* is the term now used in psychology; other disciplines still call these people *subjects*.

sample
A group of individuals drawn from a specified population. A sample might be the low-birthweight babies born in four particular hospitals that are representative of all hospitals.

representative sample
A group of research participants who reflect the relevant characteristics of the larger population whose attributes are under study.

Selection of the sample is crucial. People who volunteer, or people who have telephones, or people who have some particular condition are not a *random sample*; in a random sample, everyone in a particular population is equally likely to be selected. To avoid *selection bias*, some studies are *prospective*, beginning with an entire cluster of people (for instance, every baby born on a particular day) and then tracing the development of some particular characteristic. Ideally, the sample is diverse in gender, ethnicity, and other ways: If it is not, the bias must be explained.

For example, prospective studies find the antecedents of heart disease, or child abuse, or high school dropout rates—all of which are much harder to find if the study is *retrospective,* beginning with those who had heart attacks, experienced abuse, or left school.

For example, although retrospective research finds that most high school dropouts say they disliked school, prospective research finds that some who like school decide to drop out. Later they say they hated school. Others dislike school but stay to graduate. Prospective research discovers how many students are in these last two categories; retrospective research on people who have already dropped out does not.

Research Design

Every researcher begins not only by formulating a hypothesis but also by learning what other scientists have discovered about the topic in question and what methods might be useful and ethical in designing research. Often they include measures to prevent inadvertently finding only the results they expect.

For example, the people who actually gather the data may not know the purpose of the research. Scientists say that these data gatherers are **blind** to the hypothesized outcome. Participants are sometimes "blind" as well, because otherwise they might, for instance, respond the way they think they should.

blind
The condition of data gatherers (and sometimes participants, as well) who are deliberately kept ignorant of the purpose of the research so that they cannot unintentionally bias the results.

operational definition
A description of the specific, observable behavior that will constitute the variable that is to be studied, so that any reader will know whether that behavior occurred or not. Operational definitions may be arbitrary (e.g., an IQ score at or above 130 is operationally defined as "gifted"), but they must be precise.

Another crucial aspect of research design is to define exactly what is to be studied. Researchers establish an **operational definition** of whatever phenomenon they will be examining, defining each variable by describing specific, observable behavior. This is essential in quantitative research, but it is also useful in qualitative research.

For example, if a researcher wants to know when babies begin to walk, does walking include steps taken while holding on? Is one unsteady step enough? Some parents say yes, but the usual operational definition of *walking* is "takes at least three steps without holding on." This operational definition allows comparisons worldwide, making it possible to discover, for example, that well-fed African babies tend to walk earlier than well-fed European babies.

When emotions or personality traits are studied, operational definitions are difficult to formulate but crucial for interpretation of results. How should *aggression* or *sharing* or *shyness* be defined? Lack of an operational definition leads to contradictory results. For instance, critics report that infant day care makes children more aggressive, but advocates report that it makes them more assertive and outgoing.

In this case, both may be seeing the same behavior but defining it differently. For any scientist, operational definitions are crucial, and studies usually include descriptions of how they measured attitudes or behavior.

Reporting Results

You already know that results should be reported in sufficient detail so that another scientist can analyze the conclusions and replicate the research. Various methods, populations, and research designs may produce divergent conclusions. For that reason, handbooks, some journals, and some articles are called *reviews*: They summarize past research. Often, when studies are similar in operational definitions and methods, the review is a **meta-analysis**, which combines the findings of many studies to present an overall conclusion.

meta-analysis
A technique of combining results of many studies to come to an overall conclusion. Meta-analysis is powerful, in that small samples can be added together to lead to significant conclusions, although variations from study to study sometimes make combining them impossible.

effect size
A way of indicating statistically how much of an impact the independent variable in an experiment had on the dependent variable.

Table App.1 describes some statistical measures. One of them is *statistical significance*, which indicates whether or not a particular result could have occurred by chance.

A crucial statistic is **effect size**, a way of measuring how much impact one variable has on another. Effect size ranges from 0 (no effect) to 1 (total transformation, never found in actual studies). Effect size may be particularly important when the sample size is large, because a large sample often leads to highly "significant" results (results that are unlikely to have occurred by chance) that have only a tiny effect on the variable of interest.

Hundreds of statistical measures are used by developmentalists. Often the same data can be presented in many ways: Some scientists examine statistical analysis intently before they accept conclusions as valid. A specific example involved methods to improve students' writing ability between grades 4 and 12. A meta-analysis found that many methods of writing instruction have a significant impact, but effect size is much larger for some methods (teaching strategies and summarizing) than

TABLE APP.1 Statistical Measures Often Used to Analyze Search Results

Measure	Use
Effect size	There are many kinds, but the most useful in reporting studies of development is called *Cohen's d*, which can indicate the power of an intervention. An effect size of 0.2 is called small, 0.5 moderate, and 0.8 large.
Significance	Indicates whether the results might have occurred by chance. If chance would produce the results only 5 times in 100, that is significant at the 0.05 level; once in 100 times is 0.01; once in 1,000 is 0.001.
Cost-benefit analysis	Calculates how much a particular independent variable costs versus how much it saves. This is useful for analyzing public spending, such as finding that preschool education programs or preventative health measures save money.
Odds ratio	Indicates how a particular variable compares to a standard, set at 1. For example, one study found that although less than 1% of all child homicides occurred at school, the odds were similar for public and private schools. The odds of it in high schools, however, were 18.47 times that of elementary or middle schools (set at 1.0) (MMWR, January 18, 2008).
Factor analysis	Hundreds of variables could affect any given behavior. In addition, many variables (such as family income and parental education) overlap. To take this into account, analysis reveals variables that can be clustered together to form a factor, which is a composite of many variables. For example, SES might become one factor, child personality another.
Meta-analysis	A "study of studies." Researchers use statistical tools to synthesize the results of previous, separate studies. Then they analyze the accumulated results, using criteria that weigh each study fairly. This approach improves data analysis by combining studies that were too small, or too narrow, to lead to solid conclusions.

for others (prewriting exercises and studying models). For teachers, this statistic is crucial, for they want to know what has a big effect, not merely what is better than chance (significant).

Numerous articles published in the past decade are meta-analyses that combine similar studies to search for general trends. Often effect sizes are also reported, which is especially helpful for meta-analyses since standard calculations almost always find some significance if the number of participants is in the thousands.

An added problem is the *file drawer problem*—that studies without significant results tend to be filed away rather than published. Thus, an accurate effect size may be much smaller than the published meta-analysis finds, or may be nonexistent. For this reason, replication is an important step.

Overall, then, designing and conducting valid research is complex yet crucial. Remember that with your own opinions: As this appendix advises, it is good to "make it personal," but do not stop there.

Glossary

A

absent grief When mourners do not grieve, either because other people do not allow expressions of grief or because the mourners do not allow themselves to feel sadness.

active euthanasia When someone does something that hastens another person's death, with the intention of ending that person's suffering.

activities of daily life (ADLs) Typically identified as five tasks of self-care that are important to independent living: eating, bathing, toileting, dressing, and transferring from a bed to a chair. The inability to perform any of these tasks is a sign of frailty.

activity theory The view that older people want and need to remain active in a variety of social spheres—with relatives, friends, and community groups—and become withdrawn only unwillingly, as a result of ageism.

adolescence-limited offender A person who breaks the law as a teenager but whose criminal activity stops by age 20.

adolescent egocentrism A characteristic of adolescent thinking that leads young people (ages 10 to 13) to focus on themselves to the exclusion of others.

adrenal glands Two glands, located above the kidneys, that respond to the pituitary, producing hormones.

advance directives Any description of what a person wants to happen as they die and after death. This can include medical measures, visitors, funeral arrangements, cremation, and so on.

adverse childhood experiences (ACEs) A range of potentially traumatic childhood stresses, including abuse, neglect, family disruption and dysfunction, and parental incarceration, that can have lasting, negative effects on health and well-being.

age in place To remain in the same home and community in later life, adjusting but not leaving when health fades.

age of viability The age (about 22 weeks after conception) at which a fetus might survive outside the mother's uterus if specialized medical care is available.

ageism A prejudice whereby people are categorized and judged solely on the basis of their chronological age.

aggressive-rejected A type of childhood rejection, when other children do not want to be friends with a child because of that child's antagonistic, confrontational behavior.

allele A variation that makes a gene different in some way from other genes for the same characteristics. Many genes never vary; others have several possible alleles.

allocare Literally, "other-care"; the care of children by people other than the biological parents.

allostasis A dynamic body adjustment, related to homeostasis, that affects overall physiology over time. The main difference is that homeostasis requires an immediate response whereas allostasis requires longer-term adjustment.

Alzheimer's disease (AD) The most common cause of major NCD, characterized by gradual deterioration of memory and personality and marked by the formation of plaques of beta-amyloid protein and tangles of tau in the brain.

amygdala A tiny brain structure that registers emotions, particularly fear and anxiety.

analytic intelligence A form of intelligence that involves such mental processes as abstract planning, strategy selection, focused attention, and information processing, as well as verbal and logical skills.

analytic thought Thought that results from analysis, such as a systematic ranking of pros and cons, risks and consequences, possibilities and facts. Analytic thought depends on logic and rationality.

animism The belief that natural objects and phenomena are alive, moving around, and having sensations and abilities that are humanlike.

anorexia nervosa An eating disorder characterized by self-starvation. Affected individuals voluntarily undereat and often overexercise, depriving their vital organs of nutrition. Anorexia can be fatal.

antipathy Feelings of dislike or even hatred for another person.

Apgar scale A quick assessment of a newborn's health, from 0 to 10. Below 5 is an emergency—a neonatal pediatrician is summoned immediately. Most babies are at 7, 8, or 9—almost never a perfect 10.

asthma A chronic disease of the respiratory system in which inflammation narrows the airways from the nose and mouth to the lungs, causing difficulty in breathing. Signs and symptoms include wheezing, shortness of breath, chest tightness, and coughing.

attachment According to Ainsworth, "an affectional tie" that an infant forms with a caregiver—a tie that binds them together in space and endures over time.

attention-deficit/hyperactivity disorder (ADHD) A condition characterized by a persistent pattern of inattention and/or by hyperactive or impulsive behaviors; ADHD interferes with a person's functioning or development.

authoritarian parenting An approach to child rearing that is characterized by high behavioral standards, strict punishment of misconduct, and little communication from child to parent.

authoritative parenting An approach to child rearing in which the parents set limits and enforce rules but are flexible and listen to their children.

autism spectrum disorder (ASD) A developmental disorder marked by difficulty with social communication and interaction—including difficulty seeing things from another person's point of view—and restricted, repetitive patterns of behavior, interests, or activities.

autonomy versus shame and doubt Erikson's second crisis of psychosocial development. Toddlers either succeed or fail in gaining a sense of self-rule over their actions and their bodies.

average life expectancy The arithmetic mean, calculated by adding up all the ages of death of a group and then dividing by how many people are in that group. If, in a group of five older adults, one dies every decade (60, 70, 80, 90, 100), the average would be 80. Note also that, among the three who reach 80, their average life expectancy would be 90.

axon A fiber that extends from a neuron and transmits electrochemical impulses from that neuron to the dendrites of other neurons.

B

babbling An infant's repetition of certain syllables, such as *ba-ba-ba*, that begins when babies are between 6 and 9 months old.

bed-sharing When two or more people sleep in the same bed.

behaviorism A theory of human development that studies observable actions. Behaviorism is also called *learning theory* because it describes how people learn to do what they do.

Big Five The five basic clusters of personality traits that remain quite stable throughout adulthood: openness, conscientiousness, extroversion, agreeableness, and neuroticism.

bilingual education A strategy in which school subjects are taught in both the learner's original language and the second (majority) language.

binge eating disorder Frequent episodes of uncontrollable overeating to the point that the stomach hurts. Usually the person feels shame and guilt but is unable to stop.

binocular vision The ability to focus the two eyes in a coordinated manner in order to see one image.

biomarkers Indicators (marks) in the body (bio-) of some condition, as shown with blood tests that can diagnose diabetes.

body image A person's idea of how their body looks.

Brazelton Neonatal Behavioral Assessment Scale (NBAS) A test that is often administered to newborns, which measures responsiveness and records 46 behaviors, including 20 reflexes.

bulimia nervosa An eating disorder characterized by binge eating and subsequent purging, usually by induced vomiting and/or use of laxatives.

bullying aggression Unprovoked, repeated physical or verbal attack, especially on victims who are unlikely to defend themselves.

bullying Repeated, systematic efforts to inflict harm on other people through physical, verbal, or social attack on a weaker person.

bully-victim Someone who attacks others and who is attacked as well. (Also called *provocative victims* because they do things that elicit bullying.)

C

calorie restriction The practice of limiting dietary energy intake (while consuming sufficient quantities of vitamins, minerals, and other important nutrients) for the purpose of improving health and slowing down the aging process.

carrier A person whose genotype includes a gene that is not expressed in the phenotype. The carried gene occurs in half of the carrier's gametes and thus is passed on to half of the carrier's children. If such a gene is inherited from both parents, the characteristic appears in the phenotype.

cellular aging The cumulative effect of stress and toxins, first causing cellular damage and eventually the death of cells.

centration A characteristic of preoperational thought in which a young child focuses (centers) on one idea, excluding all others.

cesarean section (c-section) A surgical birth in which incisions through the mother's abdomen and uterus allow the fetus to be removed quickly instead of being delivered through the vagina.

child culture The idea that each group of children has games, sayings, clothing styles, and superstitions that are not common among adults, just as every culture has distinct values, behaviors, and beliefs.

child maltreatment Intentional harm to or avoidable endangerment of anyone under 18 years of age.

child sexual abuse Any erotic activity that arouses an adult and excites, shames, or confuses a child, whether or not the victim protests and whether or not genital contact is involved.

childhood obesity In a child, having a BMI above the 95th percentile, according to the U.S. Centers for Disease Control and Prevention's 1980 standards for children of a given age.

choice overload When having too many choices is confusing and dizzying. The neurons of the human brain are on/off, approach/avoidance, fire/rest. Too many choices can overwhelm the system, leading to no choice at all.

circadian rhythm A day–night cycle of biological activity that occurs approximately every 24 hours.

classification The logical principle that things can be organized into groups (or categories or classes) according to some characteristic that they have in common.

cluster suicides Several suicides committed by members of a group within a brief period.

coercive joining When others strongly encourage someone to join in their activity, usually when the activity is not approved by authorities (e.g., drug use, bullying).

cognitive theory A theory of human development that focuses on how people think. According to this theory, our thoughts shape our attitudes, beliefs, and behaviors.

cohabitation An arrangement in which a couple lives together in a committed romantic relationship but are not formally married.

cohort People born within the same historical period who therefore move through life together, experiencing the same events, new technologies, and cultural shifts at the same ages.

comorbid Refers to the presence of two or more unrelated disease conditions at the same time in the same person.

complicated grief A type of grief that impedes a person's future life, usually because the person clings to sorrow or is buffeted by contradictory emotions.

compulsive hoarding The urge to accumulate and hold on to familiar objects and possessions, sometimes to the point of their becoming health and/or safety hazards. This impulse tends to increase with age.

concrete operational thought Piaget's term for the ability to reason logically about direct experiences and perceptions.

conservation The principle that the amount of a substance remains the same (i.e., is conserved) even when its appearance changes.

continuing bonds The ongoing attachment and connection that the living have with the dead. Currently, continuing bonds are considered common and often beneficial.

conventional moral reasoning Kohlberg's second level of moral reasoning, emphasizing social rules.

corporal punishment Discipline techniques that hurt the body (*corpus*) of someone, from spanking to serious harm, including death.

corpus callosum A long, thick band of nerve fibers that connects the left and right hemispheres of the brain and allows communication between them.

correlation Usually a number between +1.0 and −1.0 that indicates whether and how much two variables are related. Correlation indicates whether an increase in one variable will increase or decrease another variable. Correlation indicates only that two variables are somehow related, not that one variable causes the other to increase or decrease.

cortex The outer layers of the brain in humans and other mammals. Most thinking, feeling, and sensing involves the cortex.

cortisol The primary stress hormone; fluctuations in the body's cortisol level affect human emotions.

co-sleeping A custom in which parents and their children (usually infants) sleep together in the same room.

couvade Symptoms of pregnancy and birth experienced by fathers.

creative intelligence A form of intelligence that involves the capacity to be intellectually flexible and innovative.

critical period Time when a particular development must occur. If it does not, as when something toxic prevents that growth, then it cannot develop later.

cross-sectional research A research design that compares people who differ in age but not in other important characteristics.

cross-sequential research A hybrid research design that includes cross-sectional and longitudinal research. (Also called *cohort-sequential research* or *time-sequential research*.)

crystallized intelligence Those types of intellectual ability that reflect accumulated learning. Vocabulary and general information are examples. Some developmental psychologists think crystallized intelligence increases with age, while fluid intelligence declines.

culture A system of shared beliefs, norms, behaviors, and expectations that persist over time and prescribe social behavior and assumptions.

cyberbullying When people try to harm others via electronic means, such as social media, cell phone photos, or texts.

D

deductive reasoning Reasoning from a general statement, premise, or principle, through logical steps, to figure out (deduce) specifics. (Also called *top-down reasoning*.)

demographic shift A shift in the proportions of the populations of various ages.

dendrite A fiber that extends from a neuron and receives electrochemical impulses transmitted from other neurons via their axons.

dependent variable In an experiment, the variable that may change as a result of the independent variable (whatever new condition the experimenter adds). In other words, the dependent variable depends on the independent variable.

developmental theory A group of ideas, assumptions, and generalizations about human growth. A developmental theory provides a framework to interpret growth and change.

difference-equals-deficit error The mistaken belief that a deviation from some norm is necessarily inferior.

differential susceptibility The idea that people vary in how sensitive (for better or worse) they are to particular experiences, either because of their genes or because of their past experiences. (Also called *differential sensitivity*.)

disenfranchised grief A situation in which certain people, although they are bereaved, are prevented from mourning publicly by cultural customs or social restrictions.

disengagement theory The view that aging makes a person's social sphere increasingly narrow, resulting in role relinquishment, withdrawal, and passivity.

disorganized attachment A type of attachment that is marked by an infant's inconsistent reactions to the caregiver's departure and return.

distal parenting Caregiving practices that involve remaining distant from the baby, providing toys, food, and face-to-face communication with minimal holding and touching.

dizygotic (DZ) twins Twins who are formed when two separate ova are fertilized by two separate sperm at roughly the same time. (Also called *fraternal twins*.)

DNR (do not resuscitate) order A written order from a physician (sometimes initiated by a patient's advance directive or by a health care proxy's request) that no attempt should be made to revive a patient if they suffer cardiac or respiratory arrest.

double effect When an action (such as administering opiates) has both a positive effect (relieving a terminally ill person's pain) and a negative effect (hastening death by suppressing respiration).

doula A woman who helps with the birth process. In Latin America, traditionally a doula was the only professional who attended childbirth. Now doulas are likely to arrive at the woman's home during early labor and later work alongside a hospital's staff.

Down syndrome A condition in which a person has 47 chromosomes instead of the usual 46, with 3 rather than 2 chromosomes at the 21st site. People with Down syndrome typically have distinctive characteristics, including unusual facial features, heart abnormalities, and language difficulties. (Also called *trisomy-21.*)

dual processing The notion that two networks exist within the human brain, one for emotional processing of stimuli and one for analytical reasoning.

dynamic-systems approach A view of human development as an ongoing, ever-changing interaction between the physical, cognitive, and psychosocial influences.

dyscalculia Unusual difficulty with math, probably originating from a distinct part of the brain.

dyslexia Unusual difficulty with reading; thought to be the result of some neurological underdevelopment.

E

ecological validity The idea that cognition should be measured in settings that are as realistic as possible and that the abilities measured should be those needed in real life.

ecological-systems approach A perspective on human development that considers all of the influences from the various contexts of development. (Later renamed *bioecological theory.*)

egocentrism Piaget's term for children's tendency to think about the world entirely from their own personal perspective.

elderspeak A condescending way of speaking to older adults that resembles baby talk, with simple and short sentences, exaggerated emphasis, repetition, and a slower rate and a higher pitch than used in typical speech.

embryo The name for a developing human organism from about the third week through the eighth week after conception.

embryonic period The stage of prenatal development from approximately the third week through the eighth week after conception, during which the basic forms of all body structures, including internal organs, develop.

emerging adulthood The period of life between the ages of 18 and 25. Emerging adulthood is now widely thought of as a distinct developmental stage.

emotional regulation The ability to control when and how emotions are expressed.

empathy The ability to understand the emotions and concerns of another person, especially when they differ from one's own.

empty nest The time in the lives of parents when their children have left the family home. This is often a happy time for everyone.

English Language Learners (ELLs) Children in the United States whose proficiency in English is low—usually below a cutoff score on an oral or written test. Many children who speak a non-English language at home are also capable in English; they are *not* ELLs.

epigenetics The study of how environmental factors affect genes and genetic expression—enhancing, halting, shaping, or altering the expression of genes.

ESL (English as a Second Language) A U.S. approach to teaching English that gathers all of the non-English speakers together and provides intense instruction in English. Students' first languages are never used; the goal is to prepare them for regular classes in English.

ethnic group People whose ancestors were born in the same region. Usually they share a language, culture, and/or religion.

evolutionary theory When used in human development, the idea that many current human emotions and impulses are a legacy from thousands of years ago.

executive function The cognitive ability to organize and prioritize the many thoughts that arise from the various parts of the brain, allowing the person to anticipate, strategize, and plan behavior.

experience-dependent Brain functions that depend on particular, variable experiences and therefore may or may not develop in a particular infant.

experience-expectant Brain functions that require certain basic common experiences (which an infant can be expected to have) in order to develop normally.

experiment A research method in which the researcher adds one variable (called the independent variable) and then observes the effect on another variable (called the dependent variable) in order to learn if the independent variable causes change in the dependent variable.

expert Someone with specialized skills and knowledge developed around a particular activity or area of specific interest.

explicit memory Memory that can be recalled in the conscious mind, usually factual memories that are expressed with words.

extended family A family of relatives in addition to the nuclear family, usually three or more generations living in one household.

extremely low birthweight (ELBW) A body weight at birth of less than 1,000 grams (2 pounds, 3 ounces).

extrinsic motivation A drive, or reason to pursue a goal, that arises from the wish to have external rewards, perhaps by earning money or praise.

extrinsic rewards of work The tangible benefits, usually in salary, insurance, pension, and status, that come with employment.

F

familism The belief that family members should support one another, sacrificing individual freedom and success, if necessary, in order to preserve family unity and protect the family.

family function The way a family works to meet the needs of its members. Children need families to provide basic material necessities, to encourage learning, to help them develop self-respect, to nurture friendships, and to foster harmony and stability.

family structure The legal and genetic relationships among relatives living in the same home. Possible structures include nuclear family, extended family, stepfamily, single-parent family, and many others.

fast-mapping The speedy and sometimes imprecise way in which children learn new words by tentatively placing them in mental categories according to their perceived meaning.

fetal alcohol syndrome (FAS) A cluster of birth defects, including abnormal facial characteristics, slow physical growth, and reduced intellectual ability, that may occur in the fetus of a woman who drinks alcohol while pregnant.

fetal period The stage of prenatal development from the ninth week after conception until birth, during which the fetus gains about 7 pounds (more than 3,000 grams) and organs become more mature, gradually able to function on their own.

fetus The name for a developing human organism from the start of the ninth week after conception until birth.

fictive kin People who become accepted as part of a family in which they are not genetically or legally members.

filial responsibility The obligation of adult children to care for their aging parents.

fine motor skills Physical abilities involving small body movements, especially of the hands and fingers, such as drawing and picking up a coin. (The word *fine* here means "small.")

fluid intelligence Those types of basic intelligence that make learning of all sorts quick and thorough. Abilities such as short-term memory, abstract thought, and speed of thinking are all usually considered part of fluid intelligence.

focus on appearance A characteristic of preoperational thought in which a young child ignores all attributes that are not apparent.

foreclosure Erikson's term for premature identity formation, when adolescents adopt their parents' or society's roles and values without questioning or analysis.

formal operational thought In Piaget's theory, the fourth and final stage of cognitive development, characterized by more systematic logical thinking and by the ability to understand and systematically manipulate abstract concepts.

foster care When a person (usually a child) is cared for by someone other than the parents.

fragile X syndrome A genetic disorder in which part of the X chromosome seems to be attached to the rest of it by a very thin string of molecules. The cause is a single gene that has more than 200 repetitions of one triplet.

frail The term for people over age 65, and often over age 85, who are physically infirm, very ill, or cognitively disabled.

frontotemporal NCDs Deterioration of the amygdala and frontal lobes that may be the cause of 15 percent of all major neurocognitive disorders. (Also called *frontotemporal lobar degeneration*.)

G

gamete A reproductive cell. In humans it is a sperm or an ovum.

gender binary The idea that gender comes in two—and only two—forms, male and female.

gender differences Differences in male and female roles, behaviors, clothes, and so on that arise from society, not physiology.

gender identity A person's acceptance (or not) of the roles and behaviors that society associates with a particular gender.

general intelligence (*g*) The idea of *g* assumes that intelligence is one basic trait, underlying all cognitive abilities. According to this concept, people have varying levels of this general ability.

generational forgetting The idea that each new generation forgets what the previous generation learned. As used here, the term refers to knowledge about the harm drugs can do.

generativity versus stagnation The seventh of Erikson's eight stages of development. Adults seek to be productive in a caring way, often as parents. Generativity also occurs through art, caregiving, and employment.

genome The full set of genes that are the instructions to make an individual member of a certain species.

genotype An organism's entire genetic inheritance, or genetic potential.

germinal period The first two weeks of prenatal development after conception, characterized by rapid cell division and the beginning of cell differentiation.

gonads The paired sex glands (ovaries in females, testicles in males). The gonads produce hormones and mature gametes.

grammar All of the methods—word order, verb forms, and so on—that languages use to communicate meaning, apart from the words themselves.

grief The deep sorrow that people feel at the death of another. Grief is personal and unpredictable.

gross motor skills Physical abilities involving large body movements, such as walking and jumping. (The word *gross* here means "big.")

growth spurt The relatively sudden and rapid physical growth that occurs during puberty. Each body part increases in size on a schedule: Weight usually precedes height, and growth of the limbs precedes growth of the torso.

H

harm reduction/injury control Reducing the potential negative consequences of behavior, such as safety surfaces replacing cement at a playground.

Head Start A federally funded early-childhood intervention program for low-income children of preschool age.

head-sparing A biological mechanism that protects the brain when malnutrition disrupts body growth. The brain is the last part of the body to be damaged by malnutrition.

health care proxy A person chosen to make medical decisions if a patient is unable to do so, as when in a coma.

hidden curriculum The unofficial, unstated, or implicit patterns within a school that influence what children learn. For instance, teacher background, organization of the play space, and tracking are all part of the hidden curriculum—not formally prescribed, but instructive to the children.

high-stakes test An evaluation that is critical in determining success or failure. If a single test determines whether a student will graduate or be promoted, it is a high-stakes test.

hippocampus A brain structure that is a central processor of memory, especially memory for locations.

holophrase A single word that is used to express a complete, meaningful thought.

homeostasis The adjustment of all of the body's systems to keep physiological functions in a state of equilibrium. As the body ages, it takes longer for these homeostatic adjustments to occur, so it becomes harder for older bodies to adapt to stress.

hormone replacement therapy (HRT) Taking hormones (in pills, patches, or injections) to compensate for hormone reduction. HRT is most common in women at menopause or after removal of the ovaries, but it is also used by men as their testosterone decreases. HRT has some medical uses but also carries health risks.

hospice An institution or program in which terminally ill patients receive palliative care to reduce suffering; family and friends of the dying are helped as well.

HPA (hypothalamus–pituitary–adrenal) axis A sequence of hormone production originating in the hypothalamus and moving to the pituitary and then to the adrenal glands.

HPG (hypothalamus–pituitary–gonad) axis A sequence of hormone production originating in the hypothalamus and moving to the pituitary and then to the gonads.

humanism A theory that stresses the potential of all humans, who have the same basic needs regardless of culture, gender, or background.

hypothalamus A brain area that responds to the amygdala and the hippocampus to produce hormones that activate other parts of the brain and body.

hypothesis A specific prediction that can be tested, and proven or disproved.

hypothetical thought Reasoning that includes propositions and possibilities that may not reflect reality.

I

identity achievement Erikson's term for the attainment of identity, when people know who they are as unique individuals, combining past experiences and future plans.

identity versus role confusion Erikson's fifth stage of development, when people wonder "Who am I?" but are confused about which of many possible roles to adopt.

imaginary audience The other people who, in an adolescent's egocentric belief, are watching and taking note of their appearance, ideas, and behavior. This belief makes many teenagers very self-conscious.

immersion A strategy in which instruction in all school subjects occurs in the second (usually the majority) language that a child is learning.

immigrant paradox The surprising, paradoxical fact that low-SES immigrant women tend to have fewer birth complications than native-born peers with higher incomes.

immunization A process that stimulates the body's immune system by causing production of antibodies to defend against attack by a particular contagious disease. Creation of antibodies may be accomplished either naturally (by having the disease), by injection, by drops that are swallowed, or by a nasal spray.

implicit memory Memory that is not verbal, often unconscious. Many motor and emotional memories are implicit.

in vitro fertilization (IVF) The union of ova and sperm in a glass dish in a laboratory. This contrasts with "in vivo," or conception in the fallopian tube after a woman's egg is penetrated by a sperm during intercourse. IVF has become a common way for older or unpartnered women or same-sex couples to become pregnant.

incomplete grief When circumstances, such as a police investigation or an autopsy, interfere with the process of grieving.

independent variable In an experiment, the variable that is added by the researcher to see if it affects the dependent variable.

individual education plan (IEP) A document that specifies educational goals and plans for a child with special needs.

induction A disciplinary technique in which the parent tries to get the child to understand why a certain behavior was wrong. Listening, not lecturing, is crucial.

inductive reasoning Reasoning from one or more specific experiences or facts to reach (induce) a general conclusion. (Also called *bottom-up reasoning*.)

industry versus inferiority The fourth of Erikson's eight psychosocial crises, during which children attempt to master many skills, developing a sense of themselves as either industrious or inferior, competent or incompetent.

initiative versus guilt Erikson's third psychosocial crisis, in which young children undertake new skills and activities and feel guilty when they do not succeed at them.

insecure-avoidant attachment A pattern of attachment in which an infant avoids connection with the caregiver, as when the infant seems not to care about the caregiver's presence, departure, or return.

insecure-resistant/ambivalent attachment A pattern of attachment in which an infant's anxiety and uncertainty are evident, as when the infant becomes very upset at separation from the caregiver and both resists and seeks contact on reunion.

instrumental activities of daily life (IADLs) Actions (for example, paying bills and car maintenance) that are important to independent living and that require some intellectual competence and forethought. The ability to perform these tasks may be even more critical to self-sufficiency than ADL ability.

instrumental aggression Hurtful behavior that is intended to get something that another person has.

integrated care Care of frail elders that combines the caregiving strengths of everyone—family, medical professionals, social workers, and the elders themselves.

integrity versus despair The final stage of Erik Erikson's developmental sequence, in which older adults seek to integrate their unique experiences with their vision of community.

intermittent fasting A pattern of eating that includes periods of restricted eating interspersed with usual consumption. The most popular pattern is two days per week eating less than 750 calories and five days of normal eating, all while drinking plenty of water.

intersectionality The idea that the various identities need to be combined. This is especially important in determining modes of privilege and discrimination.

intimacy versus isolation The sixth of Erikson's eight stages of development. Adults seek someone with whom to share their lives in an enduring and self-sacrificing commitment. Without such commitment, they risk profound aloneness and isolation.

intimate terrorism A violent and demeaning form of abuse in a romantic relationship, in which the victim (usually female) is frightened to fight back, seek help, or withdraw. In this case, the victim is in danger of physical as well as psychological harm.

intrinsic motivation A drive, or reason to pursue a goal, that comes from inside a person, such as the joy of reading a good book.

intrinsic rewards of work The personal gratifications, such as pleasure in a job well done or friendships with coworkers, that accompany employment.

intuitive thought Thought that arises from an emotion or a hunch, beyond rational explanation, and is influenced by past experiences and cultural assumptions.

invincibility fable An adolescent's egocentric conviction that they cannot be overcome or even harmed by anything that might defeat a normal mortal, such as unprotected sex, drug abuse, or high-speed driving.

irreversibility A characteristic of preoperational thought in which a young child thinks that nothing can be undone. A thing cannot be restored to the way it was before a change occurred.

K

kangaroo care A form of newborn care in which mothers (and sometimes fathers) rest their babies on their naked chests, like kangaroo mothers that carry their immature newborns in a pouch on their abdomen.

kinkeeper Someone who becomes the gatherer and communications hub for their family.

kinship care A form of foster care in which a relative, usually a grandmother, becomes the approved caregiver.

knowledge base A body of knowledge in a particular area that makes it easier to master new information in that area.

L

language acquisition device (LAD) Chomsky's term for a hypothesized mental structure that enables humans to learn language, including the basic aspects of grammar, vocabulary, and intonation.

lateralization Literally, "sidedness," referring to the specialization in certain functions by each side of the brain, with one side dominant for each activity. The left side of the brain controls the right side of the body, and vice versa.

least restrictive environment (LRE) A legal requirement that children with special needs be assigned to the most general educational context in which they can be expected to learn.

Lewy body disease A form of major neurocognitive disorder characterized by an increase in Lewy body cells in the brain. Symptoms include visual hallucinations, momentary loss of attention, falling, and fainting.

life review An examination of one's own role in the history of human life, engaged in by many elders. This can be written or oral.

life-course-persistent offender A person whose criminal activity begins in adolescence and continues throughout life; a "career" criminal.

life-span perspective An approach to the study of human development that includes all phases, from birth to death.

limbic system The parts of the brain that interact to produce emotions, including the amygdala, the hypothalamus, and the hippocampus. Many other parts of the brain also are involved with emotions.

linked lives Lives in which the success, health, and well-being of each family member are connected to those of other members.

little scientist Piaget's term for toddlers' insatiable curiosity and active experimentation as they engage in various actions to understand their world.

living apart together (LAT) The term for couples who are committed to each other and spend time together but maintain separate homes. LAT couples are increasingly common in the United States and Europe.

living will A document that indicates what medical intervention an individual prefers if they are not conscious when a decision is to be expressed. For example, some do not want mechanical breathing.

longitudinal research A research design that follows the same individuals over time.

low birthweight (LBW) A body weight at birth of less than 2,500 grams (5½ pounds).

M

major depressive disorder (MDD) Feelings of hopelessness, lethargy, and worthlessness that last two weeks or more.

massification The idea that establishing institutions of higher learning and encouraging college enrollment can benefit everyone (the masses).

maximum life span The oldest possible age that members of a species can live under ideal circumstances. For humans, that age is approximately 122 years.

mean length of utterance (MLU) The average number of words in a typical sentence (called utterance because children may not talk in complete sentences). MLU is often used to measure language development.

Mediterranean diet A diet with ample vegetables and very little meat, as well as fish, nuts, whole grains, some dairy, one glass of wine—although specific recommendations vary. This diet's name arose because people in Greece and Italy have less heart disease than people in Northern or Eastern Europe. In many studies worldwide, this diet seems protective of health.

menarche A girl's first menstrual period, signaling that she has begun ovulation. Pregnancy is biologically possible, but ovulation and menstruation are often irregular for years after menarche.

menopause The time in middle age, usually around age 50, when a woman's menstrual periods cease and the production of estrogen, progesterone, and testosterone drops. Strictly speaking, menopause is dated one year after a woman's last menstrual period, although many months before and after that date are menopausal.

mentor Someone who teaches a person. Mentors teach by example and encouragement, as well as directly. Anyone can be a mentor: peers, relatives, neighbors, strangers, or teachers.

microbiome All the microbes (bacteria, viruses, and so on) with all their genes in a community; here the millions of microbes of the human body.

middle school A school for children in the grades between elementary school and high school. Middle school usually begins with grade 5 or 6 and ends with grade 8.

monozygotic (MZ) twins Twins who originate from one zygote that splits apart very early in development. (Also called *identical twins.*) Other monozygotic multiple births (such as triplets and quadruplets) can occur as well.

Montessori schools Schools that offer early-childhood education based on the philosophy of Maria Montessori, which emphasizes careful work and tasks that each young child can do.

moratorium An adolescent's choice of a socially acceptable way to postpone making identity-achievement decisions. Going to college is a common example.

motor skill The learned abilities to move some part of the body, in actions ranging from a large leap to a flicker of the eyelid. (The word *motor* here refers to movement of muscles.)

mourning The ceremonies and behaviors that a religion or culture prescribes for people to express their grief after a death.

myelin The fatty substance coating axons that speeds the transmission of nerve impulses from neuron to neuron.

N

naming explosion A sudden increase in an infant's vocabulary, especially in the number of nouns, that begins at about 18 months of age.

National Assessment of Educational Progress (NAEP) An ongoing and nationally representative measure of U.S. children's achievement in reading, mathematics, and other subjects over time; nicknamed "the Nation's Report Card."

naturally occurring retirement community (NORC) A neighborhood or apartment complex whose population is mostly retired people who moved to the location as younger adults and never left.

nature In development, nature refers to genes. Thus, traits, capacities, and limitations inherited at conception are nature.

neglectful/uninvolved parenting An approach to child rearing in which the parents seem indifferent toward their children, not knowing or caring about their children's lives.

neurocognitive disorder (NCD) Any of a number of brain diseases that affect a person's ability to remember, analyze, plan, or interact with other people.

neurodiversity The idea that each person has neurological strengths and weaknesses that should be appreciated, in much the same way diverse cultures and ethnicities are welcomed. Neurodiversity seems particularly relevant for children with disorders on the autism spectrum.

neuron One of billions of nerve cells in the central nervous system, especially in the brain.

neurotransmitter A brain chemical that carries information from the axon of a sending neuron to the dendrites of a receiving neuron.

norm An average, or standard, calculated from many individuals within a specific group or population.

nurture In development, nurture includes all environmental influences that occur after conception, from the mother's nutrition while pregnant to the culture of the nation.

O

object permanence The realization that objects (including people) still exist when they can no longer be seen, touched, or heard.

objective thought Thinking that is not influenced by the thinker's personal qualities but instead involves facts and numbers that are universally considered true and valid.

oldest-old Older adults (generally, those over age 85) who are dependent on others for almost everything, requiring supportive services such as nursing homes and hospital stays.

old-old Older adults (generally, those over age 75) who suffer from physical, mental, or social deficits.

operant conditioning The learning process that reinforces or punishes behavior. (Also called *instrumental conditioning.*)

organ reserve The capacity of organs to allow the body to cope with stress, via extra, unused functioning ability.

overimitation When a person imitates an action that is not a relevant part of the behavior to be learned. Overimitation is common among 2- to 6-year-olds when they imitate adult actions that are irrelevant and inefficient.

overregularization The application of rules of grammar even when exceptions occur, making the language seem more "regular" than it actually is.

P

palliative care Medical treatment designed primarily to provide physical and emotional comfort to the dying patient and guidance to their loved ones.

parasuicide Any potentially deadly self-harm that does not result in death. (Also called *attempted suicide* or *failed suicide.*)

parental monitoring Parents' ongoing knowledge of what their children are doing, where, and with whom.

parentification When a child acts more like a parent than a child. Parentification may occur if the actual parents do not act as caregivers, making a child feel responsible for the family.

Parkinson's disease A chronic, progressive disease that is characterized by muscle tremor and rigidity and sometimes major neurocognitive disorder; caused by reduced dopamine production in the brain.

passive euthanasia When a seriously ill person is allowed to die naturally, without active attempts to prolong life.

peer pressure Encouragement to conform to friends or contemporaries in behavior, dress, and attitude. Adolescents do many things with peers that they would not do alone.

percentile A point on a ranking scale of 0 to 100. The 50th percentile is the midpoint; half of the people in the population being studied rank higher and half rank lower.

permanency planning An effort by child-welfare authorities to find a long-term living situation that will provide stability and support for a maltreated child. A goal is to avoid repeated caregiver or school changes, which are particularly harmful.

permissive parenting An approach to child rearing that is characterized by high nurturance and communication but little discipline, guidance, or control.

personal fable An aspect of adolescent egocentrism characterized by an adolescent's belief that their thoughts, feelings, and experiences are unique or are more wonderful or more awful than anyone else's.

phenotype The observable characteristics of a person, including appearance, personality, intelligence, and all other traits.

physician-assisted suicide A form of active euthanasia in which a doctor provides the means for someone to end their own life, usually by prescribing lethal drugs.

pituitary A gland in the brain that responds to a signal from the hypothalamus by producing many hormones, including those that regulate growth and that control other glands, among them the adrenal and sex glands.

plaques Clumps of a protein called *beta-amyloid*, found in brain tissue surrounding the neurons.

plasticity The idea that abilities, personality, and other human characteristics are moldable, and thus can change.

POLST (physician-ordered lifesustaining treatment) This is an order from a doctor regarding end-of-life care. It advises nurses and other medical staff which treatments (e.g., feeding, antibiotics, respirators) should be used and which not. It is similar to a living will, but it is written for medical professionals and thus is more specific.

polypharmacy A situation in which older people are prescribed several medications. The various side effects and interactions of those medications can result in dementia symptoms.

positivity effect The tendency for older people to perceive, prefer, and remember positive images and experiences more than negative ones.

postconventional moral reasoning Kohlberg's third level of moral reasoning, emphasizing moral principles.

postformal thought A proposed adult stage of cognitive development, following Piaget's four stages, that goes beyond adolescent thinking by being more practical, more flexible, and more dialectical (i.e., more capable of combining contradictory elements into a comprehensive whole).

postpartum depression A new mother's feelings of inadequacy and sadness in the days and weeks after giving birth.

practical intelligence The intellectual skills used in everyday problem solving. (Sometimes called *tacit intelligence.*)

pragmatics The practical use of language that includes the ability to adjust language communication according to audience and context.

preconventional moral reasoning Kohlberg's first level of moral reasoning, emphasizing rewards and punishments.

prefrontal cortex The area of the cortex at the very front of the brain that specializes in anticipation, planning, and impulse control.

preoperational intelligence Piaget's term for cognitive development between the ages of about 2 and 6; it includes language and imagination (which involve symbolic thought), but logical, operational thinking is not yet possible at this stage.

preterm A birth that occurs two or more weeks before the full 38 weeks of the typical pregnancy—that is, at 36 or fewer weeks after conception.

primary circular reaction The first of three types of feedback loops in sensorimotor intelligence, this one involving the infant's own body. The infant senses motion, sucking, noise, and other stimuli and tries to understand them.

primary prevention Actions that change overall background conditions to prevent some unwanted event or circumstance.

primary sex characteristics The parts of the body that are directly involved in reproduction, including the vagina, uterus, ovaries, testicles, and penis.

private speech The internal dialogue that occurs when people talk to themselves (either silently or out loud).

Programme for International Student Assessment (PISA) An international test taken by 15-year-olds in 50 nations that is designed to measure problem solving and cognition in daily life.

Progress in International Reading Literacy Study (PIRLS) Inaugurated in 2001, a planned five-year cycle of international trend studies in the reading ability of fourth-graders.

prosocial behavior Actions that are helpful and kind but that are of no obvious benefit to the person doing them.

protein-calorie malnutrition A condition in which a person does not consume sufficient food of any kind. This deprivation can result in several illnesses, severe weight loss, and even death.

proximal parenting Caregiving practices that involve being physically close to the baby, with frequent holding and touching.

psychoanalytic theory A theory of human development that contends that irrational, unconscious drives and motives underlie human behavior.

psychological contract The implicit understanding of the relationship between employer and employee that includes procedures to resolve conflict and expectations for the interaction between supervisors and workers.

psychological control A disciplinary technique that involves threatening to withdraw love and support, using a child's feelings of guilt and gratitude to the parents.

puberty The time between the first onrush of hormones and full adult physical development. Puberty usually lasts three to five years. Many more years are required to achieve psychosocial maturity.

Q

qualitative research Research that considers individual qualities instead of quantities (numbers).

quantitative research Research that provides data expressed with numbers, such as ranks or scales.

R

race The concept that some people are distinct from others because of physical appearance, typically skin color. Social scientists think race is a misleading idea, although race can be a powerful sociological idea, not based in biology.

reactive aggression An impulsive retaliation for another person's intentional or accidental hurtful action.

Reggio Emilia A program of early-childhood education that originated in the town of Reggio Emilia, Italy, and that encourages each child's creativity in a carefully designed setting.

reinforcement In behaviorism, the positive experience that follows a behavior, making it likely that the behavior will occur again.

relational aggression Nonphysical acts, such as insults or social rejection, aimed at harming the social connection between the victim and other people.

replication Repeating a study, usually using different participants, perhaps of another age, SES, or culture.

reported maltreatment Harm or endangerment about which someone has notified the authorities.

resilience The capacity to adapt well to significant adversity and to overcome serious stress.

response to intervention (RTI) An educational strategy intended to help children who demonstrate below-average achievement in early grades, using special intervention.

role confusion When adolescents have no clear identity, instead fluctuating from one persona to another. (Sometimes called *identity diffusion* or *role diffusion*.)

rough-and-tumble play Play that seems to be rough, as in play wrestling or chasing, but in which there is no intent to harm.

S

sandwich generation The generation of middle-aged people who are supposedly "squeezed" by the needs of the younger and older members of their families.

scaffolding Temporary support that is tailored to a learner's needs and abilities and aimed at helping the learner master the next task in a given learning process.

science of human development The science that seeks to understand how and why people of all ages and circumstances change or remain the same over time.

scientific method A way to answer questions using empirical research and data-based conclusions.

scientific observation Watching and recording participants' behavior in a systematic and objective manner—in a natural setting, in a laboratory, or in searches of archival data.

secondary circular reaction The first of three types of feedback loops in sensorimotor intelligence, involving the infant and an object or another person, as with shaking a rattle or playing peek-a-boo.

secondary education Literally, the period after primary education (elementary or grade school) and before tertiary education (college). It usually occurs from about ages 12 to 18, although there is some variation by school and by nation.

secondary prevention Actions that avert harm in a high-risk situation, such as using seat belts in cars.

secondary sex characteristics Physical traits that are not directly involved in reproduction but that indicate sexual maturity, such as a man's beard and a woman's breasts.

secure attachment A relationship in which an infant obtains both comfort and confidence from the presence of his or her caregiver.

selective optimization with compensation The theory, developed by Paul and Margaret Baltes, that people try to maintain a balance in their lives by looking for the best way to compensate for physical and cognitive losses and to become more proficient in activities they can already do well.

self theories Theories of late adulthood that emphasize the core self, or the search to maintain one's integrity and identity.

self-actualization The final level of Maslow's hierarchy, when a person becomes (actualizes) their true self. At this stage, people are thought to move past focus on selfish concerns and become more appreciative of nature, of other people, of spiritual concerns.

self-awareness A person's realization that he or she is a distinct individual whose body, mind, and actions are separate from those of other people.

senescence The process of aging, whereby the body becomes less strong and less efficient.

sensitive period A time when a particular developmental growth is most likely to occur, although it may still happen later.

sensorimotor intelligence Piaget's term for the way infants think—by using their senses and motor skills—during the first period of cognitive development.

separation anxiety An infant's distress when a familiar caregiver leaves; most obvious between 9 and 14 months.

seriation The concept that things can be arranged in a logical series, such as the number sequence or the alphabet.

sex differences Physical differences between males and females, in organs, hormones, and body shape.

sexting Sending sexual messages or photographs (usually of one's naked body) via phone or computer.

sexual orientation A person's romantic or sexual attraction, which can be to others of the same gender, the other gender, or every gender.

sexually transmitted infection (STI) A disease spread by sexual contact; includes syphilis, gonorrhea, genital herpes, chlamydia, and HIV.

shaken baby syndrome A life-threatening injury that occurs when an infant is forcefully shaken back and forth, a motion that ruptures blood vessels in the brain and breaks neural connections.

situational couple violence Fighting between romantic partners that is brought on more by the situation than by the deep personality problems of the individuals. Both partners are typically victims and abusers.

small for gestational age (SGA) A term for a baby whose birthweight is significantly lower than expected, given the time since conception. For example, a 5-pound (2,265-gram) newborn is considered SGA if born on time but not SGA if born two months early. (Also called *small-for-dates.*)

social comparison The tendency to assess one's abilities, achievements, social status, and other attributes by measuring them against those of other people, especially one's peers.

social construction An idea that is built on shared perceptions, not on objective reality.

social convoy Collectively, the family members, friends, acquaintances, and even strangers who move through the years of life with a person.

social learning theory A theory that emphasizes the influence of other people. Even without reinforcement, people learn via role models. (Also called *observational learning.*)

social mediation Human interaction that expands and advances understanding, often through words that one person uses to explain something to another.

social referencing Seeking information about how to react to an unfamiliar or ambiguous object or event by observing someone else's expressions and reactions. That other person becomes a social reference.

social smile A smile evoked by a human face, normally first evident in infants about 6 weeks after birth.

sociodramatic play Pretend play in which children act out various roles and themes in plots or roles that they create.

socioeconomic status (SES) A person's position in society as determined by income, occupation, education, and place of residence. (Sometimes called *social class.*)

specific learning disorder A marked deficit in a particular area of learning that is not caused by an apparent physical disability, by an intellectual disability, or by an unusually stressful home environment.

spermarche A boy's first ejaculation of sperm. Erections can occur as early as infancy, but ejaculation signals sperm production. Spermarche may occur during sleep (in a "wet dream") or via direct stimulation.

Standard North American Family (SNAF) A family with a mother and a father and their biological children, which is no longer the norm in the United States.

static reasoning A characteristic of preoperational thought in which a young child thinks that nothing changes. Whatever is now has always been and always will be.

still-face technique An experimental practice in which an adult keeps his or her face unmoving and expressionless in face-to-face interaction with an infant.

Strange Situation A laboratory procedure for measuring attachment by evoking infants' reactions to the stress of various adults' comings and goings in an unfamiliar playroom.

stranger wariness An infant's expression of concern—a quiet stare while clinging to a familiar person, or a look of fear—when a stranger appears.

stratification theories Theories emphasizing that social forces, particularly those related to a person's social stratum or social category, limit individual choices and affect a person's ability to function in late adulthood because past stratification continues to limit life in various ways.

stunting The failure of children to grow to a normal height for their age due to severe and chronic malnutrition.

subjective thought Thinking that is strongly influenced by personal qualities of the individual thinker, such as past experiences, cultural assumptions, and goals for the future.

substantiated maltreatment Harm or endangerment that has been reported, investigated, and verified.

sudden infant death syndrome (SIDS) A situation in which a seemingly healthy infant, usually between 2 and 6 months old, suddenly stops breathing and dies unexpectedly while asleep.

suicidal ideation Serious thinking about suicide, often including extreme emotions and thoughts.

survey A research method in which information is collected from a large number of people by interviews, written questionnaires, or some other means.

symbolic thought A major accomplishment of preoperational intelligence that allows a child to think symbolically, including understanding that words can refer to things not seen and that an item, such as a flag, can symbolize something else (in this case, a country).

synapse The intersection between the axon of one neuron and the dendrites of other neurons.

synchrony A coordinated, rapid, and smooth exchange of responses between a caregiver and an infant.

T

tangles Twisted masses of threads made of a protein called tau within the neurons of the brain.

telomeres The area of the tips of each chromosome that is reduced a tiny amount as time passes. By the end of life, the telomeres are very short.

temperament Inborn differences between one person and another in emotions, activity, and self-regulation. It is measured by the person's typical responses to the environment.

teratogen An agent or condition, including viruses, drugs, and chemicals, that can impair prenatal development and result in birth defects or even death.

terminal decline For the oldest-old, in the weeks or months before death, all the body functions may decline. This global failure is unlike problems in only one organ.

terror management theory The idea that people adopt cultural values and moral principles in order to cope with their fear of death. This system of beliefs protects individuals from anxiety about their mortality and bolsters their self-esteem.

tertiary circular reaction Piaget's description of the cognitive processes of the 1-year-old, who gathers information from experiences with the wider world and then acts on it. The response to those actions leads to further understanding, which makes this circular.

tertiary prevention Actions, such as immediate and effective medical treatment, after an adverse event (such as illness or injury).

theory of mind A person's theory of what other people might be thinking. In order to have a theory of mind, children must realize that other people are not necessarily thinking the same thoughts that they themselves are. That realization seldom occurs before age 4.

time-out A disciplinary technique in which a person is separated from other people and activities for a specified time.

transgender A broad term for people whose gender identity and/or gender expression differ from what is typically expected of the sex they were assigned at birth. Some (but not all) transgender people take hormones or undergo surgery to make their bodies align with their gender identity.

transient exuberance The great but temporary increase in the number of dendrites that develop in an infant's brain during the first two years of life.

Trends in Math and Science Study (TIMSS) An international assessment of the math and science skills of fourth- and eighth-graders. Although the TIMSS is very useful, different countries' scores are not always comparable because sample selection, test administration, and content validity are hard to keep uniform.

trust versus mistrust Erikson's first crisis of psychosocial development. Infants learn basic trust if the world is a secure place where their basic needs (for food, comfort, attention, and so on) are met.

U

universal design The creation of settings and equipment that can be used by everyone, whether or not they are able-bodied and sensory-acute.

V

vascular disease Formerly called *vascular* or *multi-infarct dementia*, vascular disease is characterized by sporadic, and progressive, loss of intellectual functioning caused by repeated infarcts, or temporary obstructions of blood vessels, which prevent sufficient blood from reaching the brain.

very low birthweight (VLBW) A body weight at birth of less than 1,500 grams (3 pounds, 5 ounces).

W

Waldorf An early-childhood education program than emphasizes creativity, social understanding, and emotional growth. It originated in Germany with Rudolf Steiner, and now is used in thousands of schools throughout the world.

wasting The tendency for children to be severely underweight for their age as a result of malnutrition.

wear-and-tear theory A view of aging as a process by which the human body wears out because of the passage of time and exposure to environmental stressors.

weathering The gradual accumulation of wear and tear on the body with age, as with a plank of wood left exposed to the weather over several years.

withdrawn-rejected A type of childhood rejection, when other children do not want to be friends with a child because of their timid, withdrawn, and anxious behavior.

working memory Memory that is active at any given moment.

working model In cognitive theory, a set of assumptions that the individual uses to organize perceptions and experiences. For example, a person might assume that other people are trustworthy and be surprised by an incident in which this working model of human behavior is erroneous.

X

X-linked A gene carried on the X chromosome. If a male inherits an X-linked recessive trait from his mother, he expresses that trait because the Y from his father has no counteracting gene. Females are more likely to be carriers of X-linked traits but are less likely to express them.

Y

young-old Healthy, vigorous, financially secure older adults (generally, those aged 65 to 75) who are well integrated into the lives of their families and communities.

Z

zone of proximal development (ZPD) Vygotsky's term for the skills—cognitive as well as physical—that a person can exercise only with assistance, not yet independently.

zygote The single cell formed from the union of two gametes, a sperm and an ovum.

References

Abar, Caitlin C.; Jackson, Kristina M. & Wood, Mark. (2014). Reciprocal relations between perceived parental knowledge and adolescent substance use and delinquency: The moderating role of parent–teen relationship quality. *Developmental Psychology, 50*(9), 2176–2187.

Abraham, Eyal & Feldman, Ruth. (2018). The neurobiology of human allomaternal care; implications for fathering, coparenting, and children's social development. *Physiology & Behavior, 193*, 25–34.

Abramovitch, Amitai; Anholt, Gideon; Raveh-Gottfried, Sagi; Hamo, Naama & Abramowitz, Jonathan. (2018). Meta-analysis of intelligence quotient (IQ) in obsessive-compulsive disorder. *Neuropsychology Review, 28*(1), 111–120.

Acharya, Kartikey; Leuthner, Stephen; Clark, Reese; Nghiem-Rao, Tuyet-Hang; Spitzer, Alan & Lagatta, Joanne. (2017). Major anomalies and birth-weight influence NICU interventions and mortality in infants with trisomy 13 or 18. *Journal of Perinatology, 37*(4), 420–426.

Acheson, Ashley; Vincent, Andrea S.; Cohoon, Andrew & Lovallo, William R. (2019). Early life adversity and increased delay discounting: Findings from the Family Health Patterns project. *Experimental and Clinical Psychopharmacology, 27*(2), 153–159.

Acosta, Sandra; Garza, Tiberio; Hsu, Hsien-Yuan; Goodson, Patricia; Padrón, Yolanda; Goltz, Heather H. & Johnston, Anna. (2020). The accountability culture: A systematic review of high-stakes testing and English learners in the United States during no Child Left Behind. *Educational Psychology Review, 32*(2), 327–352.

Adamson, Lauren B. & Bakeman, Roger. (2006). Development of displaced speech in early mother-child conversations. *Child Development, 77*(1), 186–200.

Adeyeye, Temilayo E.; Yeung, Edwina H.; McLain, Alexander C.; Lin, Shao; Lawrence, David A. & Bell, Erin M. (2019). Wheeze and food allergies in children born via cesarean delivery: The Upstate KIDS Study. *American Journal of Epidemiology, 188*(2), 355–362.

Adler, Lynn Peters. (1995). *Centenarians: The bonus years.* Health Press.

Adolph, Karen E.; Cole, Whitney G.; Komati, Meghana; Garciaguirre, Jessie S.; Badaly, Daryaneh; Lingeman, Jesse M.; . . . Sotsky, Rachel B. (2012). How do you learn to walk? Thousands of steps and dozens of falls per day. *Psychological Science, 23*(11), 1387–1394.

Adolph, Karen E. & Franchak, John M. (2017). The development of motor behavior. *WIREs, 8*(1/2), e1430.

Adolph, Karen E. & Robinson, Scott. (2013). The road to walking: What learning to walk tells us about development. In Zelazo, Philip D. (Ed.), *The Oxford handbook of developmental psychology* (Vol. 1, pp. 402–447). Oxford University Press.

Afdal, Hilde Wågsås. (2019). The promises and limitations of international comparative research on teacher education. *European Journal of Teacher Education, 42*(2).

Aggarwal, Bharat B. & Yost, Debora. (2011). *Healing spices: How to use 50 everyday and exotic spices to boost health and beat disease.* Sterling.

Ahmad, Farida B.; Cisewski, Jodi A.; Miniño, Arialdi & Anderson, Robert N. (2021, April 9). *Provisional mortality data — United States, 2020. 70*(14), 519–522. Atlanta, GA: Morbidity and Mortality Weekly Report.

Ahmadabadi, Zohre; Najman, Jackob M.; Williams, Gail M.; Clavarino, Alexandra M.; d'Abbs, Peter & Smirnov, Andrew. (2019). Intimate partner violence in emerging adulthood and subsequent substance use disorders: Findings from a longitudinal study. *Addiction, 114*(7), 1264–1273.

Ainsworth, Mary D. Salter. (1967). *Infancy in Uganda: Infant care and the growth of love.* Johns Hopkins Press.

Ainsworth, Mary D. Salter. (1973). The development of infant-mother attachment. In Caldwell, Bettye M. & Ricciuti, Henry N. (Eds.), *Child development and social policy* (pp. 1–94). University of Chicago Press.

Ainsworth, Mary D. Salter. (1982). *Attachment: Retrospect and prospect.* Basic.

Aïte, Ania; Cassotti, Mathieu; Linzarini, Adriano; Osmont, Anaïs; Houdé, Olivier & Borst, Grégoire. (2018). Adolescents' inhibitory control: Keep it cool or lose control. *Developmental Science, 21*(1), e12491.

Aitken, Jess; Ruffman, Ted & Taumoepeau, Mele. (2020). Toddlers' self-recognition and progression from goal- to emotion-based helping: A longitudinal study. *Child Development, 91*(4), 1219–1236.

Aizpitarte, Alazne; Atherton, Olivia E.; Zheng, Lucy R.; Alonso-Arbiol, Itziar & Robins, Richard W. (2019). Developmental precursors of relational aggression from late childhood through adolescence. *Child Development, 90*(1), 117–126.

Akhtar, Nameera & Jaswal, Vikram K. (2013). Deficit or difference? Interpreting diverse developmental paths: An introduction to the special section. *Developmental Psychology, 49*(1), 1–3.

Akiyama, Hiroko. (2020). Aging well: An update. *Nutrition Reviews, 78*(Suppl. 3), 3–9.

Akkerman, Agnes; Sluiter, Roderick & Jansen, Giedo. (2020). Temporary work and deviant behavior the role of workplace cohesion. *The Sociological Quarterly, 61*(4), 678–702.

Akombi, Blessing J.; Agho, Kingsley E.; Hall, John J.; Wali, Nidhi; Renzaho, Andre M. N. & Merom, Dafna. (2017). Stunting, wasting and underweight in sub-Saharan Africa: A systematic review. *International Journal of Environmental Research and Public Health, 14*(8).

Aksglaede, Lise; Link, Katarina; Giwercman, Aleksander; Jørgensen, Niels; Skakkebæk, Niels E. & Juul, Anders. (2013). 47,XXY Klinefelter syndrome: Clinical characteristics and age-specific recommendations for medical management. *American Journal of Medical Genetics Part C: Seminars in Medical Genetics, 163*(1), 55–63.

Aktar, Evin; Mandell, Dorothy J.; de Vente, Wieke; Majdandžić, Mirjana; Oort, Frans J.; van Renswoude, Daan R.; . . . Bögels, Susan M. (2018). Parental negative emotions are related to behavioral and pupillary correlates of infants' attention to facial expressions of emotion. *Infant Behavior and Development, 53*, 101–111.

Aldridge, Melissa D.; Canavan, Maureen; Cherlin, Emily & Bradley, Elizabeth H. (2015). Has hospice use changed? 2000–2010 utilization patterns. *Medical Care, 53*(1), 95–101.

Al Otaiba, Stephanie; Wanzek, Jeanne & Yovanoff, Paul. (2015). Response to intervention. *European Scientific Journal, 1*, 260–264.

Albataineh, Samah R.; Badran, Eman F. & Tayyem, Reema F. (2019). Overweight and obesity in childhood: Dietary, biochemical, inflammatory and lifestyle risk factors. *Obesity Medicine, 15*(100112).

Albert, Dustin; Chein, Jason & Steinberg, Laurence. (2013). The teenage brain: Peer influences on adolescent decision making. *Current Directions in Psychological Science, 22*(2), 114–120.

Albert, Dustin & Steinberg, Laurence. (2011). Judgment and decision making in adolescence. *Journal of Research on Adolescence, 21*(1), 211–224.

Albertini, Marco & Mantovani, Debora. (2021). Older parents and filial support obligations: A comparison of family solidarity norms between native and immigrant populations in Italy. *Ageing & Society*, (In Press).

Alberts, Bruce. (2017). Science for life. *Science, 355*(6332), 1353.

Alexander, Karl L.; Entwisle, Doris R. & Olson, Linda Steffel. (2014). *The long shadow: Family background, disadvantaged urban youth, and the transition to adulthood.* Russell Sage Foundation.

Alexandre-Heymann, Laure; Dubert, Marie; Diallo, Dapa A.; Diop, Saliou; Tolo, Aissata; Belinga, Suzanne; . . . Ranque, Brigitte. (2019). Prevalence and correlates of growth failure in young African patients with sickle cell disease. *British Journal of Haematology, 184*(2), 253–262.

Alfano, Candice A.; Laua, Simon; Balderas, Jessica; Bunnell, Brian E. & Beidel, Deborah C. (2016). The impact of military deployment on children: Placing developmental risk in context. *Clinical Psychology Review, 43*, 17–29.

Ali, Marwan & Parekh, Neel. (2020). Male age and andropause: Contemporary clinical approaches, andrology, ART and antioxidants. In Parekattil, Sijo J.; Esteves, Sandro C. & Agarwal, Ashok (Eds.), *Male infertility* (pp. 469–477). Springer.

Alvira-Hammond, Marta; Longmore, Monica A.; Manning, Wendy D. & Giordano, Peggy C. (2014). Gainful activity and intimate partner aggression in emerging adulthood. *Emerging Adulthood, 2*(2), 116–127.

Amato, Michael S.; Magzamen, Sheryl; Imm, Pamela; Havlena, Jeffrey A.; Anderson, Henry A.; Kanarek, Marty S. & Moore, Colleen F. (2013). Early lead exposure (<3 years old) prospectively predicts fourth grade school suspension in Milwaukee, Wisconsin (USA). *Environmental Research, 126*, 60–65.

Amato, Paul R. (2010). Research on divorce: Continuing trends and new developments. *Journal of Marriage and Family, 72*(3), 650–666.

Ameade, Evans Paul Kwame & Garti, Helene Akpene. (2016). Age at menarche and factors that influence it: A study among female university students in Tamale, northern Ghana. *PLoS ONE, 11*(5), e0155310.

American Academy of Pediatrics. (2016). Media and young minds. *Pediatrics, 138*(5).

American Academy of Pediatrics. (2018, May 1). Children and media tips from the American Academy of Pediatrics [Press release]. American Academy of Pediatrics.

American Psychiatric Association. (2013). *Diagnostic and statistical manual of mental disorders: DSM-5* (5th ed.). American Psychiatric Association.

Ananat, Elizabeth O. & Gassman-Pines, Anna. (2021). Work schedule unpredictability: Daily occurrence and effects on working parents' well-being. *Journal of Marriage and Family, 83*(1), 10–26.

Andere, Eduardo. (2020). *The future of schools and teacher education: How far ahead is Finland?* Oxford University Press.

Anderson, Daniel R. & Hanson, Katherine G. (2016). Screen media and parent–child interactions. In Barr, Rachel & Linebarger, Deborah Nichols (Eds.), *Media exposure during infancy and early childhood: The effects of content and context on learning and development* (pp. 173–194). Springer.

Anderson, Michael. (2001). 'You have to get inside the person' or making grief private: Image and metaphor in the therapeutic reconstruction of bereavement. In Hockey, Jenny; Katz, Jeanne & Small, Neil (Eds.), *Grief, mourning, and death ritual* (pp. 135–143). Open University Press.

Anderson, Michaela R.; Geleris, Joshua; Anderson, David R.; Zucker, Jason; Nobel, Yael R.; Freedberg, Daniel; . . . Baldwin, Matthew R. (2020). Body mass index and risk for intubation or death in SARS-CoV-2 infection: A retrospective cohort study. *Annals of Internal Medicine, 73*(10), 782–790.

Anderson, Monica. (2018, September 27). A majority of teens have experienced some form of cyberbullying. Washington, DC: Pew Research Center.

Andreas, Nicholas J.; Kampmann, Beate & Le-Doare, Kirsty Mehring. (2015). Human breast milk: A review on its composition and bioactivity. *Early Human Development, 91*(11), 629–635.

Ang, Shannon. (2019). Life course social connectedness: Age-cohort trends in social participation. *Advances in Life Course Research, 39*, 13–22.

Ansado, Jennyfer; Collins, Louis; Fonov, Vladimir; Garon, Mathieu; Alexandrov, Lubomir; Karama, Sherif; . . . Beauchamp, Miriam H. (2015). A new template to study callosal growth shows specific growth in anterior and posterior regions of the corpus callosum in early childhood. *European Journal of Neuroscience, 42*(1), 1675–1684.

Antonucci, Toni C.; Akiyama, Hiroko & Merline, Alicia. (2001). Dynamics of social relationships in midlife. In Lachman, Margie E. (Ed.), *Handbook of midlife development* (pp. 571–598). Wiley.

Araki, Atsuko & Jensen, Tina Kold. (2020). Endocrine-distributing chemicals and reproductive function. In Kishi, Reiko & Grandjean, Philippe (Eds.), *Health impacts of developmental exposure to environmental chemicals* (pp. 101–129). Springer.

Ardelt, Monika; Gerlach, Kathryn R. & Vaillant, George E. (2018). Early and midlife predictors of wisdom and subjective well-being in old age. *The Journals of Gerontology Series B: Psychological Sciences and Social Sciences, 73*(8), 1514–1525.

Areba, Eunice M.; Eisenberg, Marla E. & McMorris, Barbara J. (2018). Relationships between family structure, adolescent health status and substance use: Does ethnicity matter? *Journal of Community Psychology, 46*(1), 44–57.

Arias, Elizabeth; Tejada-Vera, Betzaida & Ahmad, Farida B. (2021, February). *Provisional life expectancy estimates for January through June, 2020. Vital Statistics Rapid Release.* Hyattsville, MD: National Center for Health Statistics. 10.

Ariely, Dan. (2010). *Predictably irrational: The hidden forces that shape our decisions* (Revised and Expanded ed.). Harper Perennial.

Armstrong, Kim. (2018). The WEIRD science of culture, values, and behavior. *Observer.* Association for Psychological Science.

Armstrong-Carter, Emma & Telzer, Eva H. (2020). Family meals buffer the daily emotional risk associated with family conflict. *Developmental Psychology, 56*(11), 2110–2120.

Arnett, Jeffrey Jensen. (2000). Emerging adulthood: A theory of development from the late teens through the twenties. *American Psychologist, 55*(5), 469–480.

Arnott, Lorna. (2016). An ecological exploration of young children's digital play: Framing children's social experiences with technologies in early childhood. *Early Years, 36*(3), 271–288.

Aron, Arthur; Lewandowski, Gary W.; Mashek, Debra & Aron, Elaine N. (2013). The self-expansion model of motivation and cognition in close relationships. In Simpson, Jeffry A. & Campbell, Lorne (Eds.), *The Oxford handbook of close relationships* (pp. 90–115). Oxford University Press.

Aronson, Joshua; Burgess, Diana; Phelan, Sean M. & Juarez, Lindsay. (2013). Unhealthy interactions: The role of stereotype threat in health disparities. *American Journal of Public Health, 103*(1), 50–56.

Arria, Amelia M.; Caldeira, Kimberly M.; Allen, Hannah K.; Bugbee, Brittany A.; Vincent, Kathryn B. & O'Grady, Kevin E. (2017). Prevalence and incidence of drug use among college students: An 8-year longitudinal analysis. *American Journal of Drug and Alcohol Abuse, 43*(6).

Arum, Richard & Roksa, Josipa. (2011). *Academically adrift: Limited learning on college campuses.* University of Chicago Press.

Arum, Richard & Roksa, Josipa. (2014). *Aspiring adults adrift: Tentative transitions of college graduates.* University of Chicago Press.

Ash, Tayla; Davison, Kirsten K.; Haneuse, Sebastien; Horan, Christine; Kitos, Nicole; Redline, Susan & Taveras, Elsie M. (2019). Emergence of racial/ethnic differences in infant sleep duration in the first six months of life. *Sleep Medicine: X, 1*, 100003.

Ashman, Jill J.; Rui, Pinyao & Okeyode, Titilayo. (2019). *Centers for Disease Control and Prevention National Center for Health Statistics Characteristics of office-based physician visits, 2016. 331.* Hyattsville, MD: U.S. Department of Health And Human Services.

Ashraf, Quamrul & Galor, Oded. (2013). The 'Out of Africa' hypothesis, human genetic diversity, and comparative economic development. *American Economic Review, 103*(1), 1–46.

Ashwin, Sarah & Isupova, Olga. (2014). "Behind every great man . . . ": The male marriage wage premium examined qualitatively. *Journal of Marriage and Family, 76*(1), 37–55.

Asiamah, Nestor. (2017). Social engagement and physical activity: Commentary on why the activity and disengagement theories of ageing may both be valid. *Cogent Medicine, 4*(1).

Asiamah, Nestor; Petersen, Carl; Kouveliotis, Kyriakos & Eduafo, Richard. (2021). The built environment and socio-demographic correlates of partial and absolute sedentary behaviours in community-dwelling older adults in Accra, Ghana. *Journal of Cross-Cultural Gerontology, 36*, 21–42.

Aslin, Richard N. (2012). Language development: Revisiting Eimas et al.'s /ba/ and /pa/ study. In Slater, Alan M. & Quinn, Paul C. (Eds.), *Developmental psychology: Revisiting the classic studies* (pp. 191–203). Sage.

Asmundson, Gordon J. G. & Afifi, Tracie O. (Eds.). (2020). *Adverse childhood experiences: Using evidence to advance research, practice, policy, and prevention.* Academic Press.

Association of American Medical Colleges. (2020). *Table B–2.2: Total graduates by U.S. medical school and sex, 2015–2016 through 2019–2020.* Washington, DC: Association of American Medical Colleges.

Association of American Medical Colleges. (2020, December). *2020 Fall applicant, matriculant, and enrollment data tables.* Washington, DC: Association of American Medical Colleges.

Astorne-Figari, Carmen & Speer, Jamin D. (2019). Are changes of major major changes? The roles of grades, gender, and preferences in college major switching. *Economics of Education Review, 70*, 75–93.

Atchley, Rachel M. (1989). A continuity theory of normal aging. *Gerontologist, 29*(2), 183–190.

Attaran, Amir. (2015). Unanimity on death with dignity — Legalizing physician-assisted dying in Canada. *New England Journal of Medicine, 372*, 2080–2082.

Atzaba-Poria, Naama; Deater-Deckard, Kirby & Bell, Martha Ann. (2017). Mother-child interaction: Links between mother and child frontal electroencephalograph asymmetry and negative behavior. *Child Development, 88*(2), 544–554.

Aucejo, Esteban M.; French, Jacob; Araya, Maria Paola Ugalde & Zafar, Basit. (2020). The impact of COVID-19 on student experiences and expectations: Evidence from a survey. *Journal of Public Economics, 191*(104271).

Augustine, Vineet; Gokce, Sertan Kutal & Oka, Yuki. (2018). Peripheral and central nutrient sensing underlying appetite regulation. *Trends in Neurosciences, 41*(8), 526–539.

Babchishin, Lyzon K.; Weegar, Kelly & Romano, Elisa. (2013). Early child care effects on later behavioral outcomes using a Canadian nation-wide sample. *Journal of Educational and Developmental Psychology, 3*(2), 15–29.

Baddock, Sally A.; Purnell, Melissa T.; Blair, Peter S.; Pease, Anna S.; Elder, Dawn E. & Galland, Barbara C. (2019). The influence of bed-sharing on infant physiology, breastfeeding and behaviour: A systematic review. *Sleep Medicine Reviews, 43,* 106–117.

Bagchi, Debasis (Ed.) (2019). *Global perspectives on childhood obesity: Current status, consequences and prevention* (2nd ed.). Academic Press.

Bagot, Kara. (2017). Making the grade: Adolescent prescription stimulant use. *Journal of the American Academy of Child & Adolescent Psychiatry, 56*(3), 189–190.

Bagwell, Catherine L. & Schmidt, Michelle E. (2011). *Friendships in childhood and adolescence.* Guilford Press.

Bahji, Anees; Stephenson, Callum; Tyo, Richard; Hawken, Emily R. & Seitz, Dallas P. (2020). Prevalence of cannabis withdrawal symptoms among people with regular or dependent use of cannabinoids a systematic review and meta-analysis. *JAMA Network Open, 3*(4), e202370.

Bai, Xuechunzi; Ramos, Miguel R. & Fiske, Susan T. (2020). As diversity increases, people paradoxically perceive social groups as more similar. *PNAS, 117*(23), 12741–12749.

Baillargeon, Renée & DeVos, Julie. (1991). Object permanence in young infants: Further evidence. *Child Development, 62*(6), 1227–1246.

Baker, Lindsey A. & Silverstein, Merril. (2012). The wellbeing of grandparents caring for grandchildren in rural China and the United States. In Arber, Sara & Timonen, Virpi (Eds.), *Contemporary grandparenting: Changing family relationships in global contexts* (pp. 51–70). Policy Press.

Balk, David & Varga, Mary Alice. (2017). Continuing bonds and social media in the lives of bereaved college students. In Klass, Dennis & Steffen, Edith Maria (Eds.), *Continuing bonds in bereavement: New directions for research and practice.* Routledge.

Ball, Helen L. & Volpe, Lane E. (2013). Sudden infant death syndrome (SIDS) risk reduction and infant sleep location—Moving the discussion forward. *Social Science & Medicine, 79*(1), 84–91.

Ballard, Dustin. (2021, February 23). Long-haul COVID: A contested illness is born. *Emergency Medical News.*

Baltes, Paul B. (2003). On the incomplete architecture of human ontogeny: Selection, optimization and compensation as foundation of developmental theory. In Staudinger, Ursula M. & Lindenberger, Ulman (Eds.), *Understanding human development: Dialogues with lifespan psychology* (pp. 17–43). Kluwer Academic Publishers.

Baltes, Paul B. & Baltes, Margret M. (1990). Psychological perspectives on successful aging: The model of selective optimization with compensation. In Baltes, Paul B. & Baltes, Margret M. (Eds.), *Successful aging: Perspectives from the behavioral sciences* (pp. 1–34). Cambridge University Press.

Baltes, Paul B.; Lindenberger, Ulman & Staudinger, Ursula M. (2006). Life span theory in developmental psychology. In Damon, William & Lerner, Richard M. (Eds.), *Handbook of child psychology* (6th ed., Vol. 1, pp. 569–664). Wiley.

Baltes, Paul B. & Smith, Jacqui. (2008). The fascination of wisdom: Its nature, ontogeny, and function. *Perspectives on Psychological Science, 3*(1), 56–64.

Baly, Michael W.; Cornell, Dewey G. & Lovegrove, Peter. (2014). A longitudinal investigation of self- and peer reports of bullying victimization across middle school. *Psychology in the Schools, 51*(3), 217–240.

Bancks, Michael P.; Kershaw, Kiarri; Carson, April P.; Gordon-Larsen, Penny; Schreiner, Pamela J. & Carnethon, Mercedes R. (2017). Association of modifiable risk factors in young adulthood with racial disparity in incident type 2 diabetes during middle adulthood. *JAMA, 318*(24), 2457–2465.

Bandura, Albert. (1986). *Social foundations of thought and action: A social cognitive theory.* Prentice-Hall.

Bandura, Albert. (1997). The anatomy of stages of change. *American Journal of Health Promotion, 12*(1), 8–10.

Banerji, Manjistha & Deshpande, Ashwini S. (2020). Does 'love' make a difference? Marriage choice and post-marriage decision-making power in India. *Asian Population Studies,* (In Press).

Banks, James R. & Andrews, Timothy. (2015). Outcomes of childhood asthma to the age of 50 years. *Pediatrics, 136*(Suppl. 3).

Baquero, Barbara & Parra-Medina, Deborah M. (2020). Chronic disease and the Latinx population: Threats, challenges, and opportunities. In Martínez, Airín D. & Rhodes, Scott D. (Eds.), *New and emerging issues in Latinx health* (pp. 19–44). Springer.

Baranowski, Tom & Taveras, Elsie M. (2018). Childhood obesity prevention: Changing the focus. *Childhood Obesity, 14*(1), 1–3.

Barber, Brian K. (Ed.) (2002). *Intrusive parenting: How psychological control affects children and adolescents.* American Psychological Association.

Barbey, Aron K. (2018). Network neuroscience theory of human intelligence. *Trends in Cognitive Sciences, 22*(1), 8–20.

Barlow, Jane; Herath, Nadeeja; Torrance, Christine B.; Bennett, Cathy & Wei, Yinghui. (2018). The Neonatal Behavioral Assessment Scale (NBAS) and Newborn Behavioral Observations (NBO) system for supporting caregivers and improving outcomes in caregivers and their infants. *Cochrane Database of Systematic Reviews.*

Barlowe, Avram & Cook, Ann. (2016). Putting the focus on student engagement: The benefits of performance-based assessment. *American Educator, 40*(1).

Barr, Rachel. (2013). Memory constraints on infant learning from picture books, television, and touchscreens. *Child Development Perspectives,* 7(4), 205–210.

Barreto, Manuela; Victor, Christina; Hammond, Claudia; Eccles, Alice; Richins, Matt T. & Qualter, Pamela. (2021). Loneliness around the world: Age, gender, and cultural differences in loneliness. *Personality and Individual Differences, 169*(110066).

Barrett, Anne E.; Michael, Cherish & Padavic, Irene. (2021). Calculated ageism: Generational sacrifice as a response to the COVID-19 pandemic. *The Journals of Gerontology: Series B, 76*(4), e201–e205.

Barroso, Amanda; Parker, Kim & Fry, Richard. (2019, October 23). *Majority of Americans say parents are doing too much for their young adult children: Young men are taking longer to reach financial independence, as young women have gained ground. Social & Demographic Trends.* Washington, DC: Pew Research Center.

Bassett, Jonathan F. & Bussard, Mel L. (2021). Examining the complex relation among religion, morality, and death anxiety: Religion can be a source of comfort and concern regarding fears of death. *OMEGA, 82*(3), 467–487.

Bassok, Daphna; Latham, Scott & Rorem, Anna. (2016). Is kindergarten the new first grade? *AERA Open, 2*(1).

Bateson, Mary Catherine. (2011). *Composing a further life: The age of active wisdom*. Vintage Books.

Bateson, Patrick & Martin, Paul. (2013). *Play, playfulness, creativity and innovation*. Cambridge University Press.

Battal, Ceren; Occelli, Valeria; Bertonati, Giorgia; Falagiarda, Federica & Collignon, Olivier. (2020). General enhancement of spatial hearing in congenitally blind people. *Psychological Science, 31*(9), 1129–1139.

Baude, Amandine; Pearson, Jessica & Drapeau, Sylvie. (2016). Child adjustment in joint physical custody versus sole custody: A meta-analytic review. *Journal of Divorce & Remarriage, 57*(5), 338–360.

Bauer, Max; Hämmerli, Silvan & Leeners, Brigitte. (2020). Unmet needs in sex education—What adolescents aim to understand about sexuality of the other sex. *Journal of Adolescent Health, 67*(2), 245–252.

Baumrind, Diana. (1967). Child care practices anteceding three patterns of preschool behavior. *Genetic Psychology Monographs, 75*(1), 43–88.

Baumrind, Diana. (1971). Current patterns of parental authority. *Developmental Psychology, 4*(1, Pt. 2), 1–103.

Bayley, Nancy & Oden, Melita H. (1955). The maintenance of intellectual ability in gifted adults. *The Journal of Gerontology Series B: Psychological Sciences and Social Sciences, 10*(1), 91–107.

Baysu, Gülseli & Phalet, Karen. (2019). The up- and downside of dual identity: Stereotype threat and minority performance. *Journal of Social Issues, 75*(2), 568–591.

BBC News. (2019, February 15). Schools' climate strike: 'Why we skipped school to protest'. BBC.

Bea, Megan Doherty & Yi, Youngmin. (2019). Leaving the financial nest: Connecting young adults' financial independence to financial security. *Journal of Marriage and Family, 81*(2), 397–414.

Beal, Susan. (1988). Sleeping position and sudden infant death syndrome. *The Medical Journal of Australia, 149*(10), 562.

Beauregard, Jennifer L.; Drews-Botsch, Carolyn; Sales, Jessica M.; Flanders, W. Dana & Kramer, Michael R. (2018). Does socioeconomic status modify the association between preterm birth and children's early cognitive ability and kindergarten academic achievement in the United States? *American Journal of Epidemiology, 187*(8), 1704–1713.

Beck, Jessica; Turnquist, Casmir; Horikawa, Izumi & Harris, Curtis. (2020). Targeting cellular senescence in cancer and aging: Roles of p53 and its isoforms. *Carcinogenesis, 41*(8), 1017–1029.

Beck, Melinda. (2009, May 26). How's your baby? Recalling the Apgar score's namesake. *Wall Street Journal.*

Bedford, Elliott Louis; Blaire, Stephen; Carney, John G.; Hamel, Ron; Mindling, J. Daniel & Sullivan, M. C. (2017). Advance care planning, palliative care, and end-of-life care. *The National Catholic Bioethics Quarterly, 17*(3), 489–501.

Beilin, Lawrence & Huang, Rae-Chi. (2008). Childhood obesity, hypertension, the metabolic syndrome and adult cardiovascular disease. *Clinical and Experimental Pharmacology and Physiology, 35*(4), 409–411.

Beiter, R.; Nash, R.; McCrady, M.; Rhoades, D.; Linscomb, M.; Clarahan, M. & Sammut, S. (2015). The prevalence and correlates of depression, anxiety, and stress in a sample of college students. *Journal of Affective Disorders, 173*, 90–96.

Bell, Georgie; Hiscock, Harriet; Tobin, Sherryn; Cook, Fallon & Sung, Valerie. (2018). Behavioral outcomes of infant colic in toddlerhood: A longitudinal study. *The Journal of Pediatrics, 201*, 154–159.

Bell, Linda G. & Harsin, Amanda. (2018). A prospective longitudinal study of marriage from midlife to later life. *Couple and Family Psychology, 7*(1), 12–21.

Bell, Martha Ann. (2020). Mother-child behavioral and physiological synchrony. In Benson, Janette B. (Ed.), *Advances in child development and behavior* (pp. 163–188). Academic Press.

Bell, Suzanne T.; Brown, Shanique G.; Colaneri, Anthony & Outland, Neal. (2018). Team composition and the ABCs of teamwork. *American Psychologist, 73*(4), 349–362.

Bellinger, David C. (2016). Lead contamination in Flint—An abject failure to protect public health. *New England Journal of Medicine, 374*(12), 1101–1103.

Belsky, Daniel W.; Caspi, Avshalom; Houts, Renate; Cohen, Harvey J.; Corcoran, David L.; Danese, Andrea; . . . Moffitt, Terrie E. (2015). Quantification of biological aging in young adults. *Proceedings of the National Academy of Sciences of the United States of America, 112*(30), e4104–e4110.

Belsky, Jay; Bakermans-Kranenburg, Marian J. & van IJzendoorn, Marinus H. (2007). For better and for worse: Differential susceptibility to environmental influences. *Current Directions in Psychological Science, 16*(6), 300–304.

Belsky, Jay; Steinberg, Laurence; Houts, Renate M. & Halpern-Felsher, Bonnie L. (2010). The development of reproductive strategy in females: Early maternal harshness → earlier menarche → increased sexual risk taking. *Developmental Psychology, 46*(1), 120–128.

Benatar, David. (2011). A legal right to die: Responding to slippery slope and abuse arguments. *Current Oncology, 18*(5), 206–207.

Bendall, C. L.; Mayr, H. L.; Opie, R. S.; Bes-Rastrollo, M.; Itsiopoulos, C. & Thomas, C. J. (2018). Central obesity and the Mediterranean diet: A systematic review of intervention trials. *Critical Reviews in Food Science and Nutrition, 58*(18), 3070–3084.

Bender, Heather L.; Allen, Joseph P.; McElhaney, Kathleen Boykin; Antonishak, Jill; Moore, Cynthia M.; Kelly, Heather O'Beirne & Davis, Steven M. (2007). Use of harsh physical discipline and developmental outcomes in adolescence. *Development and Psychopathology, 19*(1), 227–242.

Bender, Keith A. & Roche, Kristen. (2016). Self-employment and the paradox of the contented female worker. *Small Business Economics, 47*(2), 421–435.

Benn, Peter. (2016). Prenatal diagnosis of chromosomal abnormalities through chorionic villus sampling and amniocentesis. In Milunsky, Aubrey & Milunsky, Jeff M. (Eds.), *Genetic disorders and the fetus: Diagnosis, prevention, and treatment* (7th ed., pp. 178–266). Wiley-Blackwell.

Benson, Peter L.; Scales, Peter C.; Syvertsen, Amy K. & Roehlkepartain, Eugene C. (2012). Is youth spiritual development a universal developmental process? An international exploration. *The Journal of Positive Psychology, 7*(6), 453–470.

Berger, Kathleen S. (1980). *The developing person* (1st ed.). Worth.

Berger, Kathleen S. (2019). *Grandmothering: Building strong ties with every generation*. Rowman & Littlefield.

Berko, Jean. (1958). The child's learning of English morphology. *Word, 14*, 150–177.

Berlin, Lisa J.; Martoccio, Tiffany L. & Jones Harden, Brenda. (2018). Improving early Head Start's impacts on parenting through attachment-based intervention: A randomized controlled trial. *Developmental Psychology, 54*(12), 2316–2327.

Berman, Jonathan M. (2020). *Anti-vaxxers: How to challenge a misinformed movement*. MIT Press.

Bermudez, Patrick; Lerch, Jason P.; Evans, Alan C. & Zatorre, Robert J. (2009). Neuroanatomical correlates of musicianship as revealed by cortical thickness and voxel-based morphometry. *Cerebral Cortex, 19*(7), 1583–1596.

Bernard, Jessie S. (1982). *The future of marriage* (Revised ed.). Yale University Press.

Bernard, Kristin; Hostinar, Camelia E. & Dozier, Mary. (2019). Longitudinal associations between attachment quality in infancy, C-reactive protein in early childhood, and BMI in middle childhood: Preliminary evidence from a CPS-referred sample. *Attachment & Human Development, 21*(1), 5–22.

Bernard, Kristin; Lind, Teresa & Dozier, Mary. (2014). Neurobiological consequences of neglect and abuse. In Korbin, Jill E. & Krugman, Richard D. (Eds.), *Handbook of child maltreatment* (pp. 205–223). Springer.

Bernaud, Jean-Luc. (2014). Career counseling and life meaning: A new perspective of life designing for research and applications. In Di, Fabio A. & Bernaud, J- L. (Eds.), *The construction of the identity in 21st century: A Festschrift for Jean Guichard* (pp. 29–40). Nova Science.

Berwick, Robert C. & Chomsky, Noam. (2016). *Why only us: Language and evolution*. MIT Press.

Betancourt, Theresa S.; McBain, Ryan; Newnham, Elizabeth A. & Brennan, Robert T. (2013). Trajectories of internalizing problems in war-affected Sierra Leonean youth: Examining conflict and postconflict factors. *Child Development, 84*(2), 455–470.

Bettelheim, Bruno. (1975). *The empty fortress: Infantile autism and the birth of the self.* Free Press.

Bhandari, Parul. (2020). *Matchmaking in middle class India: Beyond arranged and love marriage*. Springer.

Bi, Shuang & Keller, Peggy S. (2019). Parental empathy, aggressive parenting, and child adjustment in a noncustodial high-risk sample. *Journal of Interpersonal Violence*, (In Press).

Bick, Johanna & Nelson, Charles A. (2016). Early adverse experiences and the developing brain. *Neuropsychopharmacology, 41*, 177–196.

Bick, Johanna; Palmwood, Erin N.; Zajac, Lindsay; Simons, Robert & Dozier, Mary. (2019). Early parenting intervention and adverse family environments affect neural function in middle childhood. *Biological Psychiatry, 85*(4), 326–335.

Biemiller, Andrew. (2009). Parent/caregiver narrative: Vocabulary development (0–60 Months). In Phillips, Linda M. (Ed.), *Handbook of language and literacy development: A roadmap from 0–60* (Online ed.). Canadian Language and Literacy Research Network.

Biesecker, Barbara B.; Peters, Kathryn F. & Resta, Robert. (2019). *Advanced genetic counseling: Theory and practice*. Oxford University Press.

Bilgin, Ayten; Mendonca, Marina & Wolke, Dieter. (2018). Preterm birth/low birth weight and markers reflective of wealth in adulthood: A meta-analysis. *Pediatrics, 142*(1), e20173625.

Binning, Kevin R.; Cook, Jonathan E.; Purdie-Greenaway, Valerie; Garcia, Julio; Chen, Susie; Apfel, Nancy; . . . Cohen, Geoffrey L. (2019). Bolstering trust and reducing discipline incidents at a diverse middle school: How self-affirmation affects behavioral conduct during the transition to adolescence. *Journal of School Psychology, 75*, 74–88.

Birditt, Kira S.; Manalel, Jasmine A.; Sommers, Heidi; Luong, Gloria & Fingerman, Karen L. (2019). Better off alone: Daily solitude is associated with lower negative affect in more conflictual social networks. *Gerontologist, 59*(6), 1152–1161.

Birdsong, David. (2006). Age and second language acquisition and processing: A selective overview. *Language Learning, 56*(Suppl. 1), 9–49.

Biro, Frank M.; Greenspan, Louise C.; Galvez, Maida P.; Pinney, Susan M.; Teitelbaum, Susan; Windham, Gayle C.; . . . Wolff, Mary S. (2013). Onset of breast development in a longitudinal cohort. *Pediatrics, 132*(6), 1019–1027.

Bjorklund, David F. & Ellis, Bruce J. (2014). Children, childhood, and development in evolutionary perspective. *Developmental Review, 34*(3), 225–264.

Black, Maureen M.; Papas, Mia A.; Hussey, Jon M.; Hunter, Wanda; Dubowitz, Howard; Kotch, Jonathan B.; . . . Schneider, Mary. (2002). Behavior and development of preschool children born to adolescent mothers: Risk and 3-generation households. *Pediatrics, 109*(4), 573–580.

Blakemore, Sarah-Jayne. (2018). Avoiding social risk in adolescence. *Current Directions in Psychological Science, 27*(2), 116–122.

Blanchflower, David G. & Clark, Andrew E. (2021). Children, unhappiness and family finances. *Journal of Population Economics, 34*(2), 625–653.

Blanchflower, David G. & Oswald, Andrew. (2017). *Do humans suffer a psychological low in midlife? Two approaches (with and without controls) in seven data sets. NBER Working Paper.* Cambridge, MA: National Bureau of Economic Research. Working Paper No. 23724.

Bleich, Sara N.; Segal, Jodi; Wu, Yang; Wilson, Renee & Wang, Youfa. (2013). Systematic review of community-based childhood obesity prevention studies. *Pediatrics, 132*(1), e201–e210.

Bleidorn, Wiebke & Schwaba, Ted. (2018). Retirement is associated with change in self-esteem. *Psychology and Aging, 33*(4), 586–594.

Blencowe, Hannah; Krasevec, Julia; de Onis, Mercedes; Black, Robert E.; An, Xiaoyi; Stevens, Gretchen A.; . . . Cousens, Simon. (2019). National, regional, and worldwide estimates of low birthweight in 2015, with trends from 2000: A systematic analysis. *The Lancet Global Health, 7*(7), e849–e860.

Blieszner, Rosemary. (2014). The worth of friendship: Can friends keep us happy and healthy? *Generations, 38*(1), 24–30.

Blieszner, Rosemary; Ogletree, Aaron M. & Adams, Rebecca G. (2019). Friendship in later life: A research agenda. *Innovation in Aging, 3*(1), igz005.

Bloom, David E. (2011). 7 billion and counting. *Science, 333*(6042), 562–569.

Blossfeld, Hans-Peter; Kulic, Nevena; Skopek, Jan & Triventi, Moris (Eds.). (2017). *Childcare, early education and social inequality: An international perspective.* Edward Elgar.

Blurton-Jones, Nicholas G. (1976). Rough-and-tumble play among nursery school children. In Bruner, Jerome S.; Jolly, Alison & Sylva, Kathy (Eds.), *Play: Its role in development and evolution* (pp. 352–363). Basic.

Bodner-Adler, Barbara; Kimberger, Oliver; Griebaum, Julia; Husslein, Peter & Bodner, Klaus. (2017). A ten-year study of midwife-led care at an Austrian tertiary care center: A retrospective analysis with special consideration of perineal trauma. *BMC Pregnancy and Childbirth, 17,* 357–371.

Bodrova, Elena & Leong, Deborah J. (2018). Tools of the Mind: The Vygotskian-based early childhood program. *Journal of Cognitive Education and Psychology, 17*(3).

Bøe, Tormod; Serlachius, Anna; Sivertsen, Børge; Petrie, Keith & Hysing, Mari. (2018). Cumulative effects of negative life events and family stress on children's mental health: The Bergen Child Study. *Social Psychiatry and Psychiatric Epidemiology, 53*(1), 1–9.

Boerma, Ties; Ronsmans, Carine; Melesse, Dessalegn Y.; Barros, Aluisio J. D.; Barros, Fernando C.; Juan, Liang; . . . Temmerman, Marleen. (2018). Global epidemiology of use of and disparities in caesarean sections. *The Lancet, 392*(10155), 1341–1348.

Boertien, Diederik & Bernardi, Fabrizio. (2019). Same-sex parents and children's school progress: An association that disappeared over time. *Demography, 56,* 477–501.

Bohn, Manuel & Köymen, Bahar. (2018). Common ground and development. *Child Development Perspectives, 12*(2), 104–108.

Boldrini, Maura; Fulmore, Camille A.; Tartt, Alexandria N.; Simeon, Laika R.; Pavlova, Ina; Poposka, Verica; . . . Mann, John. (2018). Human hippocampal neurogenesis persists throughout aging. *Cell Stem Cell, 22*(4), 589–599.e5.

Bollyky, Thomas J. (2012). Developing symptoms: Noncommunicable diseases go global. *Foreign Affairs, 91*(3), 134–144.

Bone, Anna E.; Gomes, Barbara; Etkind, Simon N.; Verne, Julia; Murtagh, Fliss Em; Evans, Catherine J. & Higginson, Irene J. (2018). What is the impact of population ageing on the future provision of end-of-life care? Population-based projections of place of death. *Palliative Medicine, 32*(2), 329–336.

Booth, Alan & Dunn, Judy (Eds.). (2014). *Stepfamilies: Who benefits? Who does not?* Routledge.

Booth-LaForce, Cathryn & Roisman, Glenn I. (2014). The adult attachment interview: Psychometrics, stability and change from infancy, and developmental origins. *Monographs of the Society for Research in Child Development, 79*(3).

Boren, James H. (1972). *When in doubt, mumble: A bureaucrat's handbook.* Van Nostrand Reinhold.

Bornstein, Marc H. (2015). Children's parents. In Lerner, Richard M. (Ed.), *Handbook of child psychology and developmental science* (7th ed., Vol. 4, pp. 55–132). Wiley.

Bornstein, Marc H. (2017). The specificity principle in acculturation science. *Perspectives on Psychological Science, 12*(1), 3–45.

Bornstein, Marc H.; Mortimer, Jeylan T.; Lutfey, Karen & Bradley, Robert. (2011). Theories and processes in life-span socialization. In Fingerman, Karen L.; Berg, Cynthia; Smith, Jacqui & Antonucci, Toni (Eds.), *Handbook of life-span development* (pp. 27–56). Springer.

Bornstein, Marc H.; Putnick, Diane L.; Bradley, Robert H.; Deater-Deckard, Kirby & Lansford, Jennifer E. (2016). Gender in low- and middle-income countries: Introduction. *Monographs of the Society for Research in Child Development, 81*(1), 7–23.

Bouazzaoui, B.; Fay, S.; Guerrero-Sastoque, L; Semaine, M.; Isingrini, M. & Taconnat, L. (2020). Memory age-based stereotype threat: Role of locus of control and anxiety. *Experimental Aging Research, 46*(1), 39–51.

Bouchard, Thomas J.; Lykken, David T.; McGue, Matthew; Segal, Nancy L. & Tellegen, Auke. (1990). Sources of human psychological differences: The Minnesota Study of Twins Reared Apart. *Science, 250*(4978), 223–228.

Boundy, Ellen O.; Dastjerdi, Roya; Spiegelman, Donna; Fawzi, Wafaie W.; Missmer, Stacey A.; Lieberman, Ellice; . . . Chan, Grace J. (2016). Kangaroo mother care and neonatal outcomes: A meta-analysis. *Pediatrics, 137*(1), e20152238.

Bourguignon, Jean-Pierre; Juul, Anders; Franssen, Delphine; Fudvoye, Julie; Pinson, Anneline & Parent, Anne-Simone. (2016). Contribution of the endocrine perspective in the evaluation of endocrine disrupting chemical effects: The case study of pubertal timing. *Hormone Research in Paediatrics, 86*(4), 221–232.

Bowlby, John. (1982). *Loss: Sadness and depression.* Basic.

Bowleg, Lisa. (2020). We're not all in this together: On COVID-19, intersectionality, and structural inequality. *American Journal of Public Health, 110*(7), 917.

Bowman, Nicholas A. (2013). How much diversity is enough? The curvilinear relationship between college diversity interactions and first-year student outcomes. *Research in Higher Education, 54*(8), 874–894.

boyd, danah. (2014). *It's complicated: The social lives of networked teens.* Yale University Press.

Braak, David; Michael Cummings, K.; Nahhas, Georges J.; Reid, Jessica L. & Hammond, David. (2020). How are adolescents getting their vaping products? Findings from the international tobacco control (ITC) youth tobacco and vaping survey. *Addictive Behaviors, 105,* 106345.

Brabeck, Kalina M. & Sibley, Erin. (2016). Immigrant parent legal status, parent–child relationships, and child social emotional wellbeing: A middle childhood perspective. *Journal of Child and Family Studies, 25*(4), 1155–1167.

Bradshaw, Matt & Kent, Blake Victor. (2018). Prayer, attachment to God, and changes in psychological well-being in later life. *Journal of Aging and Health, 30*(5), 667–691.

Brame, Robert; Bushway, Shawn D.; Paternoster, Ray & Turner, Michael G. (2014). Demographic patterns of cumulative arrest prevalence by ages 18 and 23. *Crime & Delinquency, 60*(3), 471–486.

Brand, Jennie E. & Xie, Yu. (2010). Who benefits most from college?: Evidence for negative selection in heterogeneous economic returns to higher education. *American Sociological Review, 75*(2), 273–302.

Brandmeyer, Tracy & Delorme, Arnaud. (2021). Meditation and the wandering mind: A theoretical framework of underlying neurocognitive mechanisms. *Perspectives on Psychological Science, 16*(1), 39–66.

Brandt, Hella E.; Ooms, Marcel E.; Ribbe, Miel W.; van der Wal, Gerrit & Deliens, Luc. (2006). Predicted survival vs. actual survival in terminally ill noncancer patients in Dutch nursing homes. *Journal of Pain and Symptom Management, 32*(6), 560–566.

Branje, Susan. (2018). Development of parent–adolescent relationships: Conflict interactions as a mechanism of change. *Child Development Perspectives, 12*(3), 171–176.

Brashier, Nadia M. & Schacter, Daniel L. (2020). Aging in an era of fake news. *Current Directions in Psychological Science, 29*(3), 316–323.

Braver, Sanford L. & Votruba, Ashley M. (2018). Does joint physical custody "cause" children's better outcomes? *Journal of Divorce & Remarriage, 59*(5), 452–468.

Brennan, Arthur. (2010). *Couvade syndrome in Australian men: A national survey. Our national couvade survey—Full report article.* Kingston University, St. George's & University of London, London.

Brenneman, Kimberly; Lange, Alissa & Nayfeld, Irena. (2019). Integrating STEM into preschool education: Designing a professional development model in diverse settings. *Early Childhood Education Journal, 47*, 15–28.

Bridge, Jeffrey A.; Greenhouse, Joel B.; Ruch, Donna; Stevens, Jack; Ackerman, John; Sheftall, Arielle H.; . . . Campo, John V. (2019). Association between the release of Netflix's *13 Reasons Why* and suicide rates in the United States: An interrupted times series analysis. *Journal of the American Academy of Child & Adolescent Psychiatry.*

Bridgett, David J.; Burt, Nicole M.; Edwards, Erin S. & Deater-Deckard, Kirby. (2015). Intergenerational transmission of self-regulation: A multidisciplinary review and integrative conceptual framework. *Psychological Bulletin, 141*(3), 602–654.

Briley, Daniel A. & Tucker-Drob, Elliot M. (2017). Comparing the developmental genetics of cognition and personality over the life span. *Journal of Personality, 85*(1), 51–64.

Brint, Steven. (2019). *Two cheers for higher education why American universities are stronger than ever—and how to meet the challenges they face.* Princeton University Press.

Brix, Nis; Ernst, Andreas; Lauridsen, Lea Lykke Braskhoj; Parner, Erik; Stovring, Henrik; Olsen, Jorn; . . . Ramlau-Hansen, Cecilia Høst. (2019). Timing of puberty in boys and girls: A population-based study. *Paediatric and Perinatal Epidemiology, 33*(1), 70–78.

Brodsky, Michael C. (2016). *Pediatric neuro-ophthalmology* (3rd ed.). Springer.

Broekhuizen, Martine L.; Aken, Marcel A. G.; Dubas, Judith S. & Leseman, Paul P. M. (2018). Child care quality and Dutch 2- and 3-year-olds' socio-emotional outcomes: Does the amount of care matter? *Infant and Child Development, 27*(1), e2043.

Bronfenbrenner, Urie & Morris, Pamela A. (2006). The bioecological model of human development. In Damon, William & Lerner, Richard M. (Eds.), *Handbook of child psychology* (6th ed., Vol. 1, pp. 793–828). Wiley.

Brooks, Rechele; Singleton, Jenny L. & Meltzoff, Andrew N. (2019). Enhanced gaze-following behavior in Deaf infants of Deaf parents. *Developmental Science*, e12900.

Brooksa, Clem & Manza, Jeff. (2013). A broken public? Americans' responses to the great recession. *American Sociological Review, 78*(5), 727–748.

Brooten, Dorothy; Youngblut, Joanne M.; Caicedo, Carmen; Del Moral, Teresa; Cantwell, G. Patricia & Totapally, Balagangadhar. (2018). Parents' acute illnesses, hospitalizations, and medication changes during the difficult first year after infant or child NICU/PICU death. *American Journal of Hospice and Palliative Medicine, 35*(1), 75–82.

Brown, B. Bradford & Bakken, Jeremy P. (2011). Parenting and peer relationships: Reinvigorating research on family–peer linkages in adolescence. *Journal of Research on Adolescence, 21*(1), 153–165.

Brown, Christia Spears & Tam, Michelle. (2019). Ethnic discrimination predicting academic attitudes for Latinx students in middle childhood. *Journal of Applied Developmental Psychology, 65*(101061).

Brown, Peter C.; Roediger, Henry L. & McDaniel, Mark A. (2014). *Make it stick: The science of successful learning.* Belknap Press of Harvard University Press.

Brubaker, Matthew S. & Naveh-Benjamin, Moshe. (2018). The effects of stereotype threat on the associative memory deficit of older adults. *Psychology and Aging, 33*(1), 17–29.

Brummelman, Eddie; Nelemans, Stefanie A.; Thomaes, Sander & Orobio De Castro, Bram. (2017). When parents' praise inflates, children's self-esteem deflates. *Child Development, 88*(6), 1799–1809.

Bucx, Freek; Raaijmakers, Quinten & van Wel, Frits. (2010). Life course stage in young adulthood and intergenerational congruence in family attitudes. *Journal of Marriage and Family, 72*(1), 117–134.

Buehler, Cheryl. (2020). Family processes and children's and adolescents' well-being. *Journal of Marriage and Family, 82*(1), 145–174.

Bulmer, Maria; Böhnke, Jan R. & Lewis, Gary J. (2017). Predicting moral sentiment towards physician-assisted suicide: The role of religion, conservatism, authoritarianism, and Big Five personality. *Personality and Individual Differences, 105*, 244–251.

Bumpus, Namandjé N. (2021). For better drugs, diversify clinical trials. *Science, 371*(6529), 570–571.

Burchinal, Margaret R.; Lowe Vandell, Deborah & Belsky, Jay. (2014). Is the prediction of adolescent outcomes from early child care moderated by later maternal sensitivity? Results from the NICHD study of early child care and youth development. *Developmental Psychology, 50*(2), 542–553.

Burhan, Amer M.; Anazodo, Udunna C. & Soucy, Jean-Paul. (2018). Neuroimaging in clinical geriatric psychiatry. In Hategan, Ana; Bourgeois, James A.; Hirsch, Calvin H. & Giroux, Caroline (Eds.), *Geriatric psychiatry: A case-based textbook* (pp. 47–89). Springer.

Burlina, Alessandro P. (Ed.) (2018). *Neurometabolic hereditary diseases of adults*. Springer.

Bursztyn, Leonardo & Jensen, Robert. (2015). How does peer pressure affect educational investments? *Quarterly Journal of Economics, 130*(3), 1329–1367.

Butler, Katy. (2019). *The art of dying well: A practical guide to a good end of life*. Scribner.

Butler, Robert N.; Lewis, Myrna I. & Sunderland, Trey. (1998). *Aging and mental health: Positive psychosocial and biomedical approaches* (5th ed.). Allyn & Bacon.

Butterworth, Brian & Kovas, Yulia. (2013). Understanding neurocognitive developmental disorders can improve education for all. *Science, 340*(6130), 300–305.

Butterworth, Brian; Varma, Sashank & Laurillard, Diana. (2011). Dyscalculia: From brain to education. *Science, 332*(6033), 1049–1053.

Butts, Donna. (2017). Foreword. In Kaplan, Matthew; Sanchez, Mariano & Hoffman, Jaco (Eds.), *Intergenerational pathways to a sustainable society* (pp. v–vii). Springer.

Byard, Roger W. (2014). "Shaken baby syndrome" and forensic pathology: An uneasy interface. *Forensic Science, Medicine, and Pathology, 10*(2), 239–241.

Cacioppo, Stephanie; Capitanio, John P. & Cacioppo, John T. (2014). Toward a neurology of loneliness. *Psychological Bulletin, 140*(6), 1464–1504.

Cairns, Rebecca. (2020). Exams tested by Covid-19: An opportunity to rethink standardized senior secondary examinations. *Prospects*.

Calderon, Valerie J. & Yu, Daniela. (2017, June 1). *Student enthusiasm falls as high school graduation nears*. Washington, DC: Gallup.

Calvo, Esteban; Madero-Cabib, Ignacio & Staudinger, Ursula M. (2018). Retirement sequences of older Americans: Moderately destandardized and highly stratified across gender, class, and race. *The Gerontologist, 58*(6), 1166–1176.

Calvo, Rocío; Carr, Dawn C. & Matz-Costa, Christina. (2019). Expanding the happiness paradox: Ethnoracial disparities in life satisfaction among older immigrants in the United States. *Journal of Aging and Health, 31*(2), 231–255.

Camhi, Sarah M.; Katzmarzyk, Peter T.; Broyles, Stephanie; Church, Timothy S.; Hankinson, Arlene L.; Carnethon, Mercedes R.; . . . Lewis, Cora E. (2013). Association of metabolic risk with longitudinal physical activity and fitness: Coronary Artery Risk Development in Young Adults (CARDIA). *Metabolic Syndrome and Related Disorders, 11*(3), 195–204.

Campbell, Frances; Conti, Gabriella; Heckman, James J.; Moon, Seong H.; Pinto, Rodrigo; Pungello, Elizabeth & Pan, Yi. (2014). Early childhood investments substantially boost adult health. *Science, 343*(6178), 1478–1485.

Campbell, Frances A.; Pungello, Elizabeth P.; Miller-Johnson, Shari; Burchinal, Margaret & Ramey, Craig T. (2001). The development of cognitive and academic abilities: Growth curves from an early childhood educational experiment. *Developmental Psychology, 37*(2), 231–242.

Campione-Barr, Nicole & Killoren, Sarah E. (2019). Love them and hate them: The developmental appropriateness of ambivalence in the adolescent sibling relationship. *Child Development Perspectives, 13*(4), 221–226.

Campos, Guilherme M.; Khoraki, Jad; Browning, Matthew G.; Pessoa, Bernardo M.; Mazzini, Guilherme S. & Wolfe, Luke. (2020). Changes in utilization of bariatric surgery in the United States from 1993 to 2016. *Annals of Surgery, 271*(2), 201–209.

Canetto, Silvia Sara. (2015). Suicide: Why are older men so vulnerable? *Science, 20*(1), 49–70.

Cantillon, Bea; Chzhen, Yekaterina; Handa, Sudhanshu & Nolan, Brian (Eds.). (2017). *Children of austerity: Impact of the Great Recession on child poverty in rich countries*. Oxford University Press.

Cao, Zhipeng; Bennett, Marc; Orr, Catherine; Icke, Ilknur; Banaschewski, Tobias; Barker, Gareth J.; . . . Whelan, Robert. (2019). Mapping adolescent reward anticipation, receipt, and prediction error during the monetary incentive delay task. *Human Brain Mapping, 40*(1), 262–283.

Capizzi, Allison; Woo, Jean & Verduzco-Gutierrez, Monica. (2020). Traumatic brain injury: An overview of epidemiology, pathophysiology, and medical management. *Medical Clinics of North America, 104*(2), 213–238.

Cardenas, Victor; Fischbach, Lori & Chowdhury, Parimal. (2019). The use of electronic nicotine delivery systems during pregnancy and the reproductive outcomes: A systematic review of the literature. *Tobacco Induced Diseases, 17*, 52.

Cargnelutti, Elisa; Tomasino, Barbara & Fabbro, Franco. (2019). Language brain representation in bilinguals with different age of appropriation and proficiency of the second language: A meta-analysis of functional imaging studies. *Frontiers in Human Neuroscience, 13*(154).

Carlsen, Karin C. Lødrup; Skjerven, Håvard O. & Carlsen, Kai-Håkon. (2018). The toxicity of e-cigarettes and children's respiratory health. *Paediatric Respiratory Reviews, 28*, 63–67.

Carlson, Stephanie M.; Koenig, Melissa A. & Harms, Madeline B. (2013). Theory of mind. *Wiley Interdisciplinary Reviews: Cognitive Science, 4*(4), 391–402.

Carmichael, Cheryl L.; Reis, Harry T. & Duberstein, Paul R. (2015). In your 20s it's quantity, in your 30s it's quality: The prognostic value of social activity across 30 years of adulthood. *Psychology and Aging, 30*(1), 95–105.

Carr, Deborah; Freedman, Vicki A.; Cornman, Jennifer C. & Schwarz, Norbert. (2014). Happy marriage, happy life? Marital quality and subjective well-being in later life. *Journal of Marriage and Family, 76*(5), 930–948.

Carra, Cecilia; Lavelli, Manuela; Keller, Heidi & Kärtner, Joscha. (2013). Parenting infants: Socialization goals and behaviors of Italian mothers and immigrant mothers from West Africa. *Journal of Cross-Cultural Psychology, 44*(8), 1304–1320.

Carroll, Linda J.; Cassidy, David; Cancelliere, Carol; Côté, Pierre; Hincapié, Cesar A.; Kristman, Vicki L.; . . . Hartvigsen, Jan. (2014). Systematic review of the prognosis after mild traumatic brain injury in adults: Cognitive, psychiatric, and mortality outcomes: Results of the international collaboration on mild traumatic brain injury prognosis. *Archives of Physical Medicine and Rehabilitation, 95*(3, Suppl.), S152–S173.

Carstensen, Laura L. (1993). Motivation for social contact across the life span. In Jacobs, Janis E. (Ed.), *Developmental perspectives on motivation: Nebraska Symposium on Motivation (1992)* (pp. 209–254). University of Nebraska.

Carstensen, Laura L. (2011). *A long bright future: Happiness, health, and financial security in an age of increased longevity.* PublicAffairs.

Carstensen, Laura L. & DeLiema, Marguerite. (2018). The positivity effect: A negativity bias in youth fades with age. *Current Opinion in Behavioral Sciences, 19,* 7–12.

Carwile, Jenny L.; Willett, Walter C.; Spiegelman, Donna; Hertzmark, Ellen; Rich-Edwards, Janet W.; Frazier, A. Lindsay & Michels, Karin B. (2015). Sugar-sweetened beverage consumption and age at menarche in a prospective study of US girls. *Human Reproduction, 30*(3), 675–683.

Case, Anne & Deaton, Angus. (2020). *Deaths of despair and the future of capitalism.* Princeton University Press.

Caspi, Avshalom; Moffitt, Terrie E.; Morgan, Julia; Rutter, Michael; Taylor, Alan; Arseneault, Louise; . . . Polo-Tomas, Monica. (2004). Maternal expressed emotion predicts children's antisocial behavior problems: Using monozygotic-twin differences to identify environmental effects on behavioral development. *Developmental Psychology, 40*(2), 149–161.

Catron, Mandy Len. (2019). What you lose when you gain a spouse. *The Atlantic.*

Cavanagh, Shannon E. & Fomby, Paula. (2019). Family instability in the lives of American children. *Annual Review of Sociology, 45,* 493–513.

Cavas, Bulent & Cavas, Pinar. (2020). Multiple intelligences theory—Howard Gardner. In Akpan, Ben & Kennedy, Teresa J. (Eds.), *Science education in theory and practice: An introductory guide to learning theory* (pp. 405–418). Springer.

Cebolla-Boado, Héctor; Radl, Jonas & Salazar, Leire. (2017). Preschool education as the great equalizer? A cross-country study into the sources of inequality in reading competence. *Acta Sociologica, 60*(1), 41–60.

Cenegy, Laura Freeman; Denney, Justin T. & Kimbro, Rachel Tolbert. (2018). Family diversity and child health: Where do same-sex couple families fit. *Journal of Marriage and Family, 80*(1), 198–218.

Centers for Disease Control and Prevention. (2015, May 15). *Epidemiology and prevention of vaccine-preventable diseases* (Hamborsky, Jennifer; Kroger, Andrew & Wolfe, Charles Eds. 13th ed.). Public Health Foundation.

Centers for Disease Control and Prevention. (2018, June 29). *Blood lead levels (µg/dl) among U.S. children < 72 months of age, by state, year, and blood lead level (bll) group. CDC's National Surveillance Data (2012–2016).* Atlanta, GA: U.S. Department of Health and Human Services.

Centers for Disease Control and Prevention. (2019). Breastfeeding rates: Breastfeeding among U.S. children born 2009–2016, CDC National Immunization Survey. U.S. Department of Health & Human Services.

Centers for Disease Control and Prevention. (2019, June 17). Measles cases and outbreaks. Centers for Disease Control and Prevention.

Centers for Disease Control and Prevention. (2020, February 20). WISQARS: Fatal injury reports, national, regional and state, 1981–2018. U.S. Department of Health & Human Services.

Centers for Disease Control and Prevention, National Center for Health Statistics. (2018, July 3). *Underlying cause of death, 1999–2017 on CDC WONDER Online Database* [Data set]. CDC WONDER.

Cesana-Arlotti, Nicoló; Martín, Ana; Téglás, Ernő; Vorobyova, Liza; Cetnarski, Ryszard & Bonatti, Luca L. (2018). Precursors of logical reasoning in preverbal human infants. *Science, 359*(6381), 1263–1266.

Cesari, Matteo & Proietti, Marco. (2020). COVID-19 in Italy: Ageism and decision making in a pandemic. *JAMDA, 21*(5), 576–577.

Chancer, Lynn S. (2019). *After the rise and stall of American feminism: Taking back a revolution.* Stanford University Press.

Chang, E-Shien; Kannoth, Sneha; Levy, Samantha; Wang, Shi-Yi; Lee, John E. & Levy, Becca R. (2020). Global reach of ageism on older persons' health: A systematic review. *PLoS ONE, 15*(1), e0220857.

Charise, Andrea & Eginton, Margaret L. (2018). Humanistic perspectives: Arts and the aging mind. In Rizzo, Matthew; Anderson, Steven & Fritzsch, Bernd (Eds.), *The Wiley handbook on the aging mind and brain.* Wiley.

Chatterjee, Kiron; Chng, Samuel; Clark, Ben; Davis, Adrian; De Vos, Jonas; Ettema, Dick; . . . Reardon, Louise. (2020). Commuting and wellbeing: A critical overview of the literature with implications for policy and future research. *Transport Reviews, 40*(1), 5–34.

Chen, C.; Liu, G. G.; Shi, Q. L.; Sun, Y.; Zhang, H.; Wang, M. J.; . . . Yao, Yao. (2020). Health-related quality of life and associated factors among oldest-old in China. *The Journal of Nutrition, Health & Aging, 24,* 330–338.

Chen, Edith; Brody, Gene H. & Miller, Gregory E. (2017). Childhood close family relationships and health. *American Psychologist, 72*(6), 555–566.

Chen, Mu-Hong; Lan, Wen-Hsuan; Bai, Ya-Mei; Huang, Kai-Lin; Su, Tung-Ping; Tsai, Shih-Jen; . . . Hsu, Ju-Wei. (2016). Influence of relative age on diagnosis and treatment of Attention-deficit hyperactivity disorder in Taiwanese children. *The Journal of Pediatrics, 172,* 162–167.e1.

Chen, Ruijia & Dong, XinQi. (2017). Risk factors of elder abuse. In Dong, XinQi (Ed.), *Elder abuse: Research, practice and policy* (pp. 93–107). Springer.

Chen, Xinyin. (2011). Culture and children's socioemotional functioning: A contextual-developmental perspective. In Chen, Xinyin & Rubin, Kenneth H. (Eds.), *Socioemotional development in cultural context* (pp. 29–52). Guilford Press.

Chen, Xinyin. (2019). Culture and shyness in childhood and adolescence. *New Ideas in Psychology, 53,* 58–66.

Chen, Xinyin; Cen, Guozhen; Li, Dan & He, Yunfeng. (2005). Social functioning and adjustment in Chinese children: The imprint of historical time. *Child Development, 76*(1), 182–195.

Chen, Xinyin; Fu, Rui; Li, Dan & Liu, Junsheng. (2019). Developmental trajectories of shyness-sensitivity from middle childhood to early adolescence in China: Contributions of peer preference and mutual friendship. *Journal of Abnormal Child Psychology, 47*(7), 1197–1209.

Chen, Xinyin; Rubin, Kenneth H. & Sun, Yuerong. (1992). Social reputation and peer relationships in Chinese and Canadian children: A cross-cultural study. *Child Development, 63*(6), 1336–1343.

Chen, Xinyin; Yang, Fan & Wang, Li. (2013). Relations between shyness-sensitivity and internalizing problems in Chinese children: Moderating effects of academic achievement. *Journal of Abnormal Child Psychology, 41*(5), 825–836.

Chen, Yuncai & Baram, Tallie Z. (2016). Toward understanding how early-life stress reprograms cognitive and emotional brain networks. *Neuropsychopharmacology, 41*, 197–206.

Cherlin, Andrew J. (2009). *The marriage-go-round: The state of marriage and the family in America today.* Knopf.

Cherlin, Andrew J. (2020). Degrees of change: An assessment of the deinstitutionalization of marriage thesis. *Journal of Marriage and Family, 82*(1), 62–80.

Chernev, Alexander; Böckenholt, Ulf & Goodman, Joseph. (2015). Choice overload: A conceptual review and meta-analysis. *Journal of Consumer Psychology, 25*(2), 333–358.

Cheshire, Emily; Kaestle, Christine E. & Miyazaki, Yasuo. (2019). The influence of parent and parent–adolescent relationship characteristics on sexual trajectories into adulthood. *Archives of Sexual Behavior, 48*(3), 893–910.

Cheung, Sie-Long; Barf, Hans; Cummings, Sarah; Hobbelen, Hans & Chui, Ernest Wing-Tak. (2020). Changing shapes of care: Expressions of filial piety among second-generation Chinese in the Netherlands. *Journal of Family Issues, 41*(12), 2400–2422.

Chiappini, Stefania & Schifano, Fabrizio. (2020). What about "pharming"? Issues regarding the misuse of prescription and over-the-counter drugs. *Brain Sciences, 10*(10), 736.

Child Trends. (2019, March 7). Dual language learners. Child Trends.

Child Trends Databank. (2015, March). *Lead poisoning: Indicators on children and youth.* Bethesda, MD: Child Trends.

Child Trends Databank. (2018). High school dropout rates. Child Trends.

Child Welfare Information Gateway. (2018). *Foster care statistics, 2016.* Washington, DC: U.S. Department of Health and Human Services, Children's Bureau.

Chlebowski, Rowan T.; Manson, JoAnn E.; Anderson, Garnet L.; Cauley, Jane A.; Aragaki, Aaron K.; Stefanick, Marcia L.; . . . Prentice, Ross L. (2013). Estrogen plus progestin and breast cancer incidence and mortality in the Women's Health Initiative observational study. *Journal of the National Cancer Institute, 105*(8), 526–535.

Cho, Youngmin. (2018). The effects of nonstandard work schedules on workers' health: A mediating role of work-to-family conflict. *International Journal of Social Welfare, 27*(1), 74–87.

Choe, Daniel E.; Lane, Jonathan D.; Grabell, Adam S. & Olson, Sheryl L. (2013a). Developmental precursors of young school-age children's hostile attribution bias. *Developmental Psychology, 49*(12), 2245–2256.

Choe, Daniel E.; Olson, Sheryl L. & Sameroff, Arnold J. (2013b). The interplay of externalizing problems and physical and inductive discipline during childhood. *Developmental Psychology, 49*(11), 2029–2039.

Choi, HwaJung; Schoeni, Robert F.; Wiemers, Emily E.; Hotz, V. Joseph & Seltzer, Judith A. (2020). Spatial distance between parents and adult children in the United States. *Journal of Marriage and Family, 82*(2), 822–840.

Choi, Jayoung. (2019). A child's trilingual language practices in Korean, Farsi, and English: From a sustainable translanguaging perspective. *International Journal of Multilingualism, 16*(4), 534–548.

Choi, Yool. (2018). Student employment and persistence: Evidence of effect heterogeneity of student employment on college dropout. *Research in Higher Education, 59*(1), 88–107.

Chomsky, Noam. (1968). *Language and mind.* Harcourt Brace & World.

Chomsky, Noam. (1980). *Rules and representations.* Columbia University Press.

Chong, Jessica X.; Buckingham, Kati J.; Jhangiani, Shalini N.; Boehm, Corinne; Sobreira, Nara; Smith, Joshua D.; . . . Bamshad, Michael J. (2015). The genetic basis of Mendelian phenotypes: Discoveries, challenges, and opportunities. *American Journal of Human Genetics, 97*(2), 199–215.

Choudhury, Ananyo; Aron, Shaun; Sengupta, Dhriti; Hazelhurst, Scott & Ramsay, Michèle. (2018). African genetic diversity provides novel insights into evolutionary history and local adaptations. *Human Molecular Genetics, 27*(R2), R209–R218.

Christakis, Erika. (2016). *The importance of being little: What preschoolers really need from grownups.* Viking.

Christian, Cindy W. & Block, Robert. (2009). Abusive head trauma in infants and children. *Pediatrics, 123*(5), 1409–1411.

Chu, Shuyuan; Chen, Qian; Chen, Yan; Bao, Yixiao; Wu, Min & Zhang, Jun. (2017). Cesarean section without medical indication and risk of childhood asthma, and attenuation by breastfeeding. *PLoS ONE, 12*(9), e0184920.

Cianciolo, Anna T. & Sternberg, Robert J. (2018). Practical intelligence and tacit knowledge: An ecological view of expertise. In Ericsson, K. Anders; Hoffman, Robert R.; Kozbelt, Aaron & Williams, A. Mark (Eds.), *The Cambridge handbook of expertise and expert performance* (pp. 770–792). Cambridge University Press.

Cicchetti, Dante. (2013a). Annual research review: Resilient functioning in maltreated children—past, present, and future perspectives. *Journal of Child Psychology and Psychiatry, 54*(4), 402–422.

Cicchetti, Dante. (2013b). An overview of developmental psychopathology. In Zelazo, Philip D. (Ed.), *The Oxford handbook of developmental psychology* (Vol. 2, pp. 455–480). Oxford University Press.

Cicchetti, Dante. (2016). Socioemotional, personality, and biological development: Illustrations from a multilevel developmental psychopathology perspective on child maltreatment. *Annual Review of Psychology, 67*, 187–211.

Cierpka, Manfred & Cierpka, Astrid. (2016). Developmentally appropriate vs. persistent defiant and aggressive behavior. In Cierpka, Manfred (Ed.), *Regulatory disorders in infants.* Springer.

Cillessen, Antonius H. N. & Marks, Peter E. L. (2011). Conceptualizing and measuring popularity. In Cillessen, Antonius H. N.; Schwartz, David & Mayeux, Lara (Eds.), *Popularity in the peer system* (pp. 25–56). Guilford Press.

Cillessen, Antonius H. N. & Mayeux, Lara. (2004). From censure to reinforcement: Developmental changes in the association between aggression and social status. *Child Development, 75*(1), 147–163.

Ciol, Marcia A.; Rasch, Elizabeth K.; Hoffman, Jeanne M.; Huynh, Minh & Chan, Leighton. (2014). Transitions in mobility, ADLs, and IADLs among working-age Medicare beneficiaries. *Disability and Health Journal,* 7(2), 206–215.

cjcsoon2bnp. (2017, February 13). Becoming dad: A humbling birth experience of a new father and nurse. *cjcsoon2bnp's Nursing log.* Allnurses.

Claessen, Jacques. (2017). *Forgiveness in criminal law through incorporating restorative mediation.* Wolf Legal Publishers.

Clark, Andrew E. (1997). Job satisfaction and gender: Why are women so happy at work? *Labour Economics, 4*(4), 341–372.

Clark, Lee Anna; Cuthbert, Bruce; Lewis-Fernández, Roberto; Narrow, William E. & Reed, Geoffrey M. (2017). Three approaches to understanding and classifying mental disorder: ICD-11, *DSM-5*, and the National Institute of Mental Health's Research Domain Criteria (RDoC). *Psychological Science in the Public Interest, 18*(2), 72–145.

Claxton-Oldfield, Stephen; Gallant, Megan & Claxton-Oldfield, Jane. (2020). The impact of unusual end-of-life phenomena on hospice palliative care volunteers and their perceived needs for training to respond to them. *OMEGA, 81*(4), 577–591.

Clayborne, Zahra M.; Giesbrecht, Gerald F.; Bell, Rhonda C. & Tomfohr-Madsen, Lianne M. (2017). Relations between neighbourhood socioeconomic status and birth outcomes are mediated by maternal weight. *Social Science & Medicine, 175*, 143–151.

Clift, Kristin; Macklin, Sarah; Halverson, Colin; McCormick, Jennifer B.; Abu Dabrh, Abd Moain & Hines, Stephanie. (2020). Patients' views on variants of uncertain significance across indications. *Journal of Community Genetics, 11*, 139–145.

Clinton, Michael E.; Pratista, Nathia & Sturges, Jane. (2020). Do temporary workers always lower workgroup effectiveness? The moderating effect of job similarity in blended workgroups. *Applied Psychology*, (In Press).

Cluley, Heather & Hecht, Tracy D. (2020). Micro work-family decision-making of dual-income couples with young children: What does a couple like us do in a situation like this? *Journal of Occupational and Organizational Psychology, 93*(1), 45–72.

Coe, Jesse L.; Davies, Patrick T. & Sturge-Apple, Melissa L. (2018). Family instability and young children's school adjustment: Callousness and negative internal representations as mediators. *Child Development, 89*(4), 1193–1208.

Coffelt, Tina A. (2017). Deciding to reveal sexual information and sexuality education in mother-daughter relationships. *Sex Education, 17*(5), 571–587.

Coggin, Alexander. (2016, January 17). Debt dodgers: Meet the Americans who moved to Europe and went AWOL on their student loans. *Vice.*

Cohen, Jon. (2014). Saving lives without new drugs. *Science, 346*(6212), 911.

Cohn, D'Vera & Passel, Jeffrey S. (2018, April 5). *A record 64 million Americans live in multigenerational households. Fact Tank.* Washington, DC: Pew Research Center.

Coleman, Patrick A. (2019, March 22). Snowplow parenting isn't just morally repulsive, it's bad for kids. *Fatherly.*

Coleman-Jensen, Alisha; Rabbitt, Matthew P.; Gregory, Christian & Singh, Anita. (2015). *Household food security in the United States in 2014.* Washington, DC: U.S. Department of Agriculture, Economic Research Service. ERR–194.

Coles, Robert. (1997). *The moral intelligence of children: How to raise a moral child.* Random House.

Coley, Nicola; Vaurs, Charlotte & Andrieu, Sandrine. (2015). Nutrition and cognition in aging adults. *Clinics in Geriatric Medicine, 31*(3), 453–464.

Colver, Allan & Dovey-Pearce, Gail. (2018). The anatomical, hormonal and neurochemical changes that occur during brain development in adolescents and young adults. In Hergenroeder, Albert C. & Wiemann, Constance M. (Eds.), *Health care transition* (pp. 15–19). Springer.

Common Sense Media. (2017). *The common sense census: Media use by kids age zero to eight, 2017.* San Francisco, CA: Common Sense Media.

Common Sense Media. (2020). *The common sense census: Media use by kids age zero to eight, 2020.* San Francisco, CA: Common Sense Media.

Compton, Wilson M.; Gfroerer, Joe; Conway, Kevin P. & Finger, Matthew S. (2014). Unemployment and substance outcomes in the United States 2002–2010. *Drug & Alcohol Dependence, 142*, 350–353.

Cook, Peta S. (2018). Continuity, change and possibility in older age: Identity and ageing-as-discovery. *Journal of Sociology, 54*(2), 178–190.

Coovadia, Hoosen M. & Wittenberg, Dankwart F. (Eds.). (2004). *Paediatrics and child health: A manual for health professionals in developing countries* (5th ed.). Oxford University Press.

Coplan, Robert J. & Weeks, Murray. (2009). Shy and soft-spoken: Shyness, pragmatic language, and socio-emotional adjustment in early childhood. *Infant and Child Development, 18*(3), 238–254.

Cordina-Duverger, Emilie; Menegaux, Florence; Popa, Alexandru; Rabstein, Sylvia; Harth, Volker; Pesch, Beate; . . . Guénel, Pascal. (2018). Night shift work and breast cancer: A pooled analysis of population-based case–control studies with complete work history. *European Journal of Epidemiology, 33*(4), 369–379.

Corenblum, Barry. (2014). Relationships between racial–ethnic identity, self-esteem and in-group attitudes among First Nation children. *Journal of Youth and Adolescence, 43*(3), 387–404.

Corona, Giovanni; Guaraldi, Federica; Rastrelli, Giulia; Sforza, Alessandra & Maggi, Mario. (2021). Testosterone deficiency and risk of cognitive disorders in aging males. *World Journal of Men's Health, 39*(1), 9–18.

Corps, Kara N.; Roth, Theodore L. & McGavern, Dorian B. (2015). Inflammation and neuroprotection in traumatic brain injury. *JAMA Neurology, 72*(3), 355–362.

Corr, Charles A. (2019). Should we incorporate the work of Elisabeth Kübler-Ross in our current teaching and practice and, if so, how? *OMEGA*.

Corr, Charles A. & Corr, Donna M. (2013a). Culture, socialization, and dying. In Meagher, David K. & Balk, David E. (Eds.), *Handbook of thanatology: The essential body of knowledge for the study of death, dying, and bereavement* (2nd ed., pp. 3–8). Routledge.

Corr, Charles A. & Corr, Donna M. (2013b). Historical and contemporary perspectives on loss, grief, and mourning. In Meagher, David & Balk, David E. (Eds.), *Handbook of thanatology: The essential body of knowledge for the study of death, dying, and bereavement* (2nd ed., pp. 135–148). Routledge.

Cosentino, Elena; Palmer, Katie; Della Pietà, Camilla; Mitolo, Micaela; Meneghello, Francesca; Levedianos, Giorgio; . . . Venneri, Annalena. (2020). Association between gait, cognition, and gray matter volumes in mild cognitive impairment and healthy controls. *Alzheimer Disease & Associated Disorders, 34*(3), 231–237.

Costa, Albert & Sebastián-Gallés, Núria. (2014). How does the bilingual experience sculpt the brain? *Nature Reviews Neuroscience, 15*(5), 336–345.

Costa, Albert; Vives, Marc-Lluís & Corey, Joanna D. (2017). On language processing shaping decision making. *Current Directions in Psychological Science, 26*(2), 146–151.

Côté, James E. (2018). The enduring usefulness of Erikson's concept of the identity crisis in the 21st century: An analysis of student mental health concerns. *Identity, 18*(4), 251–263.

Côté, James E. & Levine, Charles. (2015). *Identity formation, youth, and development: A simplified approach.* Psychology Press.

Covington-Ward, Yolanda. (2017). African immigrants in low-wage direct health care: Motivations, job satisfaction, and occupational mobility. *Journal of Immigrant and Minority Health, 19*(3), 709–715.

Cowan, Nelson. (2014). Working memory underpins cognitive development, learning, and education. *Educational Psychology Review, 26*(2), 197–223.

Cowell, Jason M.; Lee, Kang; Malcolm-Smith, Susan; Selcuk, Bilge; Zhou, Xinyue & Decety, Jean. (2017). The development of generosity and moral cognition across five cultures. *Developmental Science, 20*(4), e12403.

Coyne, Sarah M.; Stockdale, Laura & Summers, Kjersti. (2019a). Problematic cell phone use, depression, anxiety, and self-regulation: Evidence from a three year longitudinal study from adolescence to emerging adulthood. *Computers in Human Behavior, 96*, 78–84.

Coyne, Sarah M.; Ward, L. Monique; Kroff, Savannah L.; Davis, Emilie J.; Holmgren, Hailey G.; Jensen, Alexander C.; . . . Essig, Lee W. (2019b). Contributions of mainstream sexual media exposure to sexual attitudes, perceived peer norms, and sexual behavior: A meta-analysis. *Journal of Adolescent Health, 64*(4), 430–436.

Crain, William C. (2011). *Theories of development: Concepts and applications* (6th ed.). Prentice-Hall.

Crenshaw, David A. (2013). The family, larger systems, and traumatic death. In Meagher, David K. & Balk, David E. (Eds.), *Handbook of thanatology: The essential body of knowledge for the study of death, dying, and bereavement* (2nd ed., pp. 305–309). Routledge.

Crenshaw, Kimberle. (1989). Demarginalizing the intersection of race and sex: A Black feminist critique of antidiscrimination doctrine, feminist theory and antiracist politics. *University of Chicago Legal Forum*, 139–167.

Cripe, Larry D. & Frankel, Richard M. (2017). Dying from cancer: Communication, empathy, and the clinical imagination. *Journal of Patient Experience, 4*(2), 69–73.

Crivello, Cristina & Poulin-Dubois, Diane. (2019). Infants' ability to detect emotional incongruency: Deep or shallow? *Infancy, 24*(4), 480–500.

Crnic, Keith A.; Neece, Cameron L.; McIntyre, Laura Lee; Blacher, Jan & Baker, Bruce L. (2017). Intellectual disability and developmental risk: Promoting intervention to improve child and family well-being. *Child Development, 88*(2), 436–445.

Crone, Eveline A.; van Duijvenvoorde, Anna C. K. & Peper, Jiska S. (2016). Annual research review: Neural contributions to risk-taking in adolescence—developmental changes and individual differences. *Journal of Child Psychology and Psychiatry, 57*(3), 353–368.

Crosby, Faye J. (1982). *Relative deprivation and working women.* Oxford University Press.

Crosnoe, Robert; Purtell, Kelly M.; Davis-Kean, Pamela; Ansari, Arya & Benner, Aprile D. (2016). The selection of children from low-income families into preschool. *Developmental Psychology, 52*(4), 599–612.

Crowe, Laura & Butterworth, Peter. (2016). The role of financial hardship, mastery and social support in the association between employment status and depression: Results from an Australian longitudinal cohort study. *BMJ Open, 6*, e009834.

Csikszentmihalyi, Mihaly. (2013). *Creativity: Flow and the psychology of discovery and invention.* Harper Perennial.

Cui, Ming; Darling, Carol A.; Coccia, Catherine; Fincham, Frank D. & May, Ross W. (2019). Indulgent parenting, helicopter parenting, and well-being of parents and emerging adults. *Journal of Child and Family Studies, 28*, 860–871.

Culpin, Iryna; Heron, Jon; Araya, Ricardo & Joinson, Carol. (2015). Early childhood father absence and depressive symptoms in adolescent girls from a UK cohort: The mediating role of early menarche. *Journal of Abnormal Child Psychology, 43*(5), 921–931.

Cumming, Elaine & Henry, William Earl. (1961). *Growing old: The process of disengagement.* Basic.

Cunningham, F. Gary; Leveno, Kenneth; Bloom, Steven; Spong, Catherine Y.; Dashe, Jodi; Hoffman, Barbara; . . . Sheffield, Jeanne S. (2014). *Williams obstetrics* (24th ed.). McGraw-Hill Education.

Curl, Angela; Bulanda, Jennifer & Roberts, Amy Restorick. (2020). Older couples' marital quality and health behaviors. *Innovation in Aging, 4*(Suppl. 1), 348.

Currie, Janet & Widom, Cathy S. (2010). Long-term consequences of child abuse and neglect on adult economic well-being. *Child Maltreatment, 15*(2), 111–120.

Curtin, Nancy & Garrison, Mary. (2018). "She was more than a friend": Clinical intervention strategies for effectively addressing disenfranchised grief issues for same-sex couples. *Journal of Gay & Lesbian Social Services, 30*(3), 261–281.

Curtis, Alexa C. (2015). Defining adolescence. *Journal of Adolescent and Family Health, 7*(2).

Cutuli, J. J.; Ahumada, Sandra M.; Herbers, Janette E.; Lafavor, Theresa L.; Masten, Ann S. & Oberg, Charles N. (2017). Adversity and children experiencing family homelessness: Implications for health. *Journal of Children and Poverty, 23*(1), 41–55.

Cuzzolaro, Massimo & Fassino, Secondo (Eds.). (2018). *Body image, eating, and weight: A guide to assessment, treatment, and prevention.* Springer.

Dadds, Mark R. & Tully, Lucy A. (2019). What is it to discipline a child: What should it be? A reanalysis of time-out from the perspective of child mental health, attachment, and trauma. *American Psychologist, 74*(7), 794–808.

Daigneault, Isabelle; Vézina-Gagnon, Pascale; Bourgeois, Catherine; Esposito, Tonino & Hébert, Martine. (2017). Physical and mental health of children with substantiated sexual abuse: Gender comparisons from a matched-control cohort study. *Child Abuse & Neglect, 66*, 155–165.

Daley, Dave; Jones, Karen; Hutchings, Judy & Thompson, Margaret. (2009). Attention deficit hyperactivity disorder in pre-school children: Current findings, recommended interventions and future directions. *Child, 35*(6), 754–766.

Dall'Alba, Gloria. (2018). Reframing expertise and its development: A lifeworld perspective. In Ericsson, K. Anders; Hoffman, Robert R.; Kozbelt, Aaron & Williams, A. Mark (Eds.), *The Cambridge handbook of expertise and expert performance* (pp. 33–39). Cambridge University Press.

Dalrymple, Rebecca Amy. (2019). Earlier introduction of solid food is associated with improved sleep in infants. *Archives of Disease in Childhood—Education and Practice.*

Dalsager, Louise; Fage-Larsen, Bettina; Bilenberg, Niels; Jensen, Tina Kold; Nielsen, Flemming; Kyhl, Henriette Boye; . . . Andersen, Helle Raun. (2019). Maternal urinary concentrations of pyrethroid and chlorpyrifos metabolites and attention deficit hyperactivity disorder (ADHD) symptoms in 2-4-year-old children from the Odense Child Cohort. *Environmental Research, 176*, 108533.

Daneri, M. Paula; Blair, Clancy & Kuhn, Laura J. (2019). Maternal language and child vocabulary mediate relations between socioeconomic status and executive function during early childhood. *Child Development, 90*(6), 2001–2018.

Daniels, Harry (Ed.) (2017). *Introduction to Vygotsky* (3rd ed.). Routledge.

Danielsbacka, Mirkka; Tanskanen, Antti & Rotkirch, Anna. (2018). The "kinship penalty": Parenthood and in-law conflict in contemporary Finland. *Evolutionary Psychological Science, 4*(1), 71–82.

Dantchev, Slava; Zammit, Stanley & Wolke, Dieter. (2018). Sibling bullying in middle childhood and psychotic disorder at 18 years: A prospective cohort study. *Psychological Medicine, 48*(14), 2321–2328.

Darweesh, Sirwan K. L.; Wolters, Frank J.; Postuma, Ronald B.; Stricker, Bruno H.; Hofman, Albert; Koudstaal, Peter J.; . . . Ikram, M. Arfan. (2017). Association between poor cognitive functioning and risk of incident Parkinsonism: The Rotterdam study. *JAMA Neurology, 74*(12), 1431–1438.

Darwin, Charles. (1859). *On the origin of species by means of natural selection.* J. Murray.

Darwin, Zoe; Galdas, Paul; Hinchliff, Sharron; Littlewood, Elizabeth; McMillan, Dean; McGowan, Linda & Gilbody, Simon. (2017). Fathers' views and experiences of their own mental health during pregnancy and the first postnatal year: A qualitative interview study of men participating in the UK Born and Bred in Yorkshire (BaBY) cohort. *BMC Pregnancy and Childbirth, 17*(45).

Dashraath, Pradip; Jing Lin Jeslyn, Wong; Mei Xian Karen, Lim; Li Min, Lim; Sarah, Li; Biswas, Arijit; . . . Lin, Su Lin. (2020). Coronavirus disease 2019 (COVID-19) pandemic and pregnancy. *American Journal of Obstetrics and Gynecology, 222*(6), P521–531.

Daum, Moritz M.; Ulber, Julia & Gredebäck, Gustaf. (2013). The development of pointing perception in infancy: Effects of communicative signals on covert shifts of attention. *Developmental Psychology, 49*(10), 1898–1908.

David, Jonathan; Aluh, Deborah O.; Blonner, Marika & Norberg, Melissa M. (2021). Excessive object attachment in hoarding disorder: Examining the role of interpersonal functioning. *Behavior Therapy*, (In Press).

Davidai, Shai & Gilovich, Thomas. (2015). Building a more mobile America: One income quintile at a time. *Perspectives on Psychological Science, 10*(1), 60–71.

Davis, Charles. (2020, May 12). University of California president recommends suspending SAT or ACT test requirement until 2025. Business Insider: India.

Davis, Corey S.; Green, Traci C.; Hernandez-Delgado, Hector & Lieberman, Amy Judd. (2018). Status of US state laws mandating timely reporting of nonfatal overdose. *American Journal of Public Health, 108*(9), 1159–1161.

Davis, Jac T. M. & Hines, Melissa. (2020). How large are gender differences in toy preferences? A systematic review and meta-analysis of toy preference research. *Archives of Sexual Behavior, 49*, 373–394.

Davis, Linell. (1999). *Doing culture: Cross-cultural communication in action.* Foreign Language Teaching & Research Press.

Dawson, Chris; Veliziotis, Michail & Hopkins, Benjamin. (2017). Temporary employment, job satisfaction and subjective well-being. *Economic and Industrial Democracy, 38*(1), 69–98.

Day, Felix R.; Elks, Cathy E.; Murray, Anna; Ong, Ken K. & Perry, John R. B. (2015). Puberty timing associated with diabetes, cardiovascular disease and also diverse health outcomes in men and women: The UK Biobank study. *Scientific Reports, 5*(11208).

Dayanim, Shoshana & Namy, Laura L. (2015). Infants learn baby signs from video. *Child Development, 86*(3), 800–811.

de Haan, Irene & Connolly, Marie. (2019). More nuanced universal services for new parents: Avoiding assumptions of homogeneity. *Journal of Social Service Research, 45*(5), 727–738.

de Jong Gierveld, Jenny & Merz, Eva-Maria. (2013). Parents' partnership decision making after divorce or widowhood: The role of (step)children. *Journal of Marriage and Family, 75*(5), 1098–1113.

de Mendonça, Elaine Luiza Santos Soares; de Lima Macêna, Mateus; Bueno, Nassib Bezerra; de Oliveira, Alane Cabral Menezes & Mello, Carolina Santos. (2020). Premature birth, low birth weight, small for gestational age and chronic non-communicable diseases in adult life: A systematic review with meta-analysis. *Early Human Development, 149*(105154).

de Vos, Paul; Hanck, Christoph; Neisingh, Marjolein; Prak, Dennis; Groen, Henk & Faas, Marijke M. (2015). Weight gain in freshman college students and perceived health. *Preventive Medicine Reports, 2*, 229–234.

de Vrieze, Jop. (2018). The metawars. *Science, 361*(6408), 1184–1188.

De Wilde, Arno; Van Der Flier, Wiesje M.; Pelkmans, Wiesje; Bouwman, Femke; Verwer, Jurre; Groot, Colin; . . . Scheltens, Philip. (2018). Association of amyloid positron emission tomography with changes in diagnosis and patient treatment in an unselected memory clinic cohort: The abide project. *JAMA Neurology, 75*(9), 1062–1070.

DeAngelis, Corey A. (2019). Does private schooling affect noncognitive skills? International evidence based on test and survey effort on PISA. *Social Science Quarterly, 11*(6), 2256–2276.

Dearing, Eric; Walsh, Mary E.; Sibley, Erin; Lee St. John, Terry; Foley, Claire & Raczek, Anastacia E. (2016). Can community and school-based supports improve the achievement of first-generation immigrant children attending high-poverty schools? *Child Development, 87*(3), 883–897.

Dearing, Eric & Zachrisson, Henrik D. (2017). Concern over internal, external, and incidence validity in studies of child-care quantity and externalizing behavior problems. *Child Development Perspectives, 11*(2), 133–138.

Deater-Deckard, Kirby & Lansford, Jennifer E. (2016). Daughters' and sons' exposure to childrearing discipline and violence in low- and middle-income countries. *Monographs of the Society for Research in Child Development, 81*(1), 78–103.

Dees, Marianne K.; Vernooij-Dassen, Myrra J.; Dekkers, Wim J.; Vissers, Kris C. & van Weel, Chris. (2011). 'Unbearable suffering': A qualitative study on the perspectives of patients who request assistance in dying. *Journal of Medical Ethics, 37*(12), 727–734.

Dehaene-Lambertz, Ghislaine. (2017). The human infant brain: A neural architecture able to learn language. *Psychonomic Bulletin & Review, 24*(1), 48–55.

Deighton, Jessica; Humphrey, Neil; Belsky, Jay; Boehnke, Jan; Vostanis, Panos & Patalay, Praveetha. (2018). Longitudinal pathways between mental health difficulties and academic performance during middle childhood and early adolescence. *British Journal of Developmental Psychology, 36*(1), 110–126.

de Jonge, Huub. (2011). Purification and remembrance: Eastern and Western ways to deal with the Bali bombing. In Margry, Peter Jan & Sánchez-Carretero, Cristina (Eds.), *Grassroots memorials: The politics of memorializing traumatic death* (pp. 262–284). Berghahn Books.

Delaunay-El Allam, Maryse; Soussignan, Robert; Patris, Bruno; Marlier, Luc & Schaal, Benoist. (2010). Long-lasting memory for an odor acquired at the mother's breast. *Developmental Science, 13*(6), 849–863.

De Lima, Liliana; Woodruff, Roger; Pettus, Katherine; Downing, Julia; Buitrago, Rosa; Munyoro, Esther; . . . Radbruch, Lukas. (2017). International Association for Hospice and Palliative Care position statement: Euthanasia and physician-assisted suicide. *Journal of Palliative Medicine, 20*(1), 8–14.

Demers, Lauren A.; Handley, Elizabeth D.; Hunt, Ruskin H.; Rogosch, Fred A.; Toth, Sheree L.; Thomas, Kathleen M. & Cicchetti, Dante. (2019). Childhood maltreatment disrupts brain-mediated pathways between adolescent maternal relationship quality and positive adult outcomes. *Child Maltreatment, 24*(4).

Demir, Meliksah; Haynes, Andrew & Potts, Shannon K. (2017). My friends are my estate: Friendship experiences mediate the relationship between perceived responses to capitalization attempts and happiness. *Journal of Happiness Studies, 18*(4), 1161–1190.

Denson, Nida; Bowman, Nicholas A.; Ovenden, Georgia; Culver, K. C. & Holmes, Joshua M. (2020). Do diversity courses improve college student outcomes? A meta-analysis. *Journal of Diversity in Higher Education*, (In Press).

De Raedt, Rudi; Koster, Ernst H. W. & Ryckewaert, Ruben. (2013). Aging and attentional bias for death related and general threat-related information: Less avoidance in older as compared with middle-aged adults. *The Journals of Gerontology Series B: Psychological Sciences and Social Sciences, 68*(1), 41–48.

DeSantiago-Cardenas, Lilliana; Rivkina, Victoria; Whyte, Stephanie A.; Harvey-Gintoft, Blair C.; Bunning, Bryan J. & Gupta, Ruchi S. (2015). Emergency epinephrine use for food allergy reactions in Chicago public schools. *American Journal of Preventive Medicine, 48*(2), 170–173.

DeStefano, Frank; Bodenstab, Heather Monk & Offit, Paul A. (2019). Principal controversies in vaccine safety in the United States. *Clinical Infectious Diseases, 69*(4), 726–731.

Devine, Rory T. & Hughes, Claire. (2014). Relations between false belief understanding and executive function in early childhood: A meta-analysis. *Child Development, 85*(5), 1777–1794.

Devitt, Aleea L. & Schacter, Daniel L. (2016). False memories with age: Neural and cognitive underpinnings. *Neuropsychologia, 91*, 346–359.

DeYoung, Colin G.; Hirsh, Jacob B.; Shane, Matthew S.; Papademetris, Xenophon; Rajeevan, Nallakkandi & Gray, Jeremy R. (2010). Testing predictions from personality neuroscience. *Psychological Science, 21*(6), 820–828.

Diamond, Adele. (2016). Why improving and assessing executive functions early in life is critical. In Griffin, James Alan; McCardle, Peggy D. & Freund, Lisa (Eds.), *Executive function in preschool-age children: Integrating measurement, neurodevelopment, and translational research* (pp. 11–43). American Psychological Association.

Diamond, Marian C. (1988). *Enriching heredity: The impact of the environment on the anatomy of the brain.* Free Press.

Didion, Joan. (2005). *The year of magical thinking.* Knopf.

DiFonzo, Nicholas; Alongi, Anthony & Wiele, Paul. (2020). Apology, restitution, and forgiveness after psychological contract breach. *Journal of Business Ethics, 161*(1), 53–69.

Digest of Education Statistics. (2018). *Table 326.50: Number and percentage distribution of first-time postsecondary students starting at 2- and 4-year institutions during the 2011-12 academic year, by attainment and enrollment status and selected characteristics: Spring 2014.* Washington, DC: National Center for Education Statistics.

Dillman Carpentier, Francesca & Stevens, Elise. (2018). Sex in the media, sex on the mind: Linking television use, sexual permissiveness, and sexual concept accessibility in memory. *Sexuality & Culture, 22*(1), 22–38.

Dimler, Laura M. & Natsuaki, Misaki N. (2015). The effects of pubertal timing on externalizing behaviors in adolescence and early adulthood: A meta-analytic review. *Journal of Adolescence, 45*, 160–170.

Dishion, Thomas J.; Mun, Chung; Ha, Thao & Tein, Jenn-Yun. (2019). Observed family and friendship dynamics in adolescence: A latent profile approach to identifying "mesosystem" adaptation for intervention tailoring. *Prevention Science, 20*(1), 41–55.

Ditch the Label. (2017). *The annual bullying survey 2017.* Los Angeles, CA: Ditch the Label.

Dix, Theodore & Yan, Ni. (2014). Mothers' depressive symptoms and infant negative emotionality in the prediction of child adjustment at age 3: Testing the maternal reactivity and child vulnerability hypotheses. *Development and Psychopathology, 26*(1), 111–124.

Doebel, Sabine. (2020). Rethinking executive function and its development. *Perspectives on Psychological Science, 15*(4), 942–956.

Doka, Kenneth J. (2013). Historical and contemporary perspectives on dying. In Meagher, David K. & Balk, David E. (Eds.), *Handbook of thanatology: The essential body of knowledge for the study of death, dying, and bereavement* (2nd ed., pp. 17–23). Routledge.

Doka, Kenneth J. (2016). *Grief is a journey: Finding your path through loss.* Atria.

Dominguez-Bello, Maria Gloria; Godoy-Vitorino, Filipa; Knight, Rob & Blaser, Martin J. (2019). Role of the microbiome in human development. *Gut, 68*(6), 1108–1114.

Dorling, James L.; Martin, Corby K. & Redman, Leanne M. (2020). Calorie restriction for enhanced longevity: The role of novel dietary strategies in the present obesogenic environment. *Ageing Research Reviews, 64*, 101038.

Dorn, Lorah D. & Biro, Frank M. (2011). Puberty and its measurement: A decade in review. *Journal of Research on Adolescence, 21*(1), 180–195.

Doucet, Andrea. (2015). Parental responsibilities: Dilemmas of measurement and gender equality. *Journal of Marriage and Family, 77*(1), 224–242.

Dowd, Will. (2008). The myth of the Mozart Effect. *Skeptic, 13*(4).

Downing, Katherine L.; Hinkley, Trina; Salmon, Jo; Hnatiuk, Jill A. & Hesketh, Kylie D. (2017). Do the correlates of screen time and sedentary time differ in preschool children? *BMC Public Health, 17*(285).

Drake, Patrick; Driscoll, Anne K. & Mathews, T. J. (2018). *Cigarette smoking during pregnancy: United States, 2016.* Hyattsville, MD: National Center for Health Statistics. NCHS Data Brief No. 305.

Drake, Stacy A.; Wolf, Dwayne A.; Yang, Yijiong; Harper, Sherhonda; Ross, Jennifer; Reynolds, Thomas & Giardino, Eileen R. (2019). A descriptive and geospatial analysis of environmental factors attributing to sudden unexpected infant death. *American Journal of Forensic Medicine and Pathology, 40*(2), 108–116.

Drewelies, Johanna; Wagner, Jenny; Tesch-Römer, Clemens; Heckhausen, Jutta & Gerstorf, Denis. (2017). Perceived control across the second half of life: The role of physical health and social integration. *Psychology and Aging, 32*(1), 76–92.

Driskell, James E.; Salas, Eduardo & Driskell, Tripp. (2018). Foundations of teamwork and collaboration. *American Psychologist, 73*(4), 334–348.

Duckett, Stephen. (2018). Knowing, anticipating, even facilitating but still not intending: Another challenge to double effect reasoning. *Journal of Bioethical Inquiry, 15*(1), 33–37.

Dugas, Lara R.; Fuller, Miles; Gilbert, Jack & Layden, Brian T. (2016). The obese gut microbiome across the epidemiologic transition. *Emerging Themes in Epidemiology, 13*(1).

Duggan, Maeve. (2017, July 11). *Online harassment 2017. Internet & Technology.* Washington, DC: Pew Research Center.

Dumas, A.; Simmat-Durand, L. & Lejeune, C. (2014). Pregnancy and substance use in France: A literature review. *Journal de Gynécologie Obstétrique et Biologie de la Reproduction, 43*(9), 649–656.

Dunbar, R. I. M. (2018). The anatomy of friendship. *Trends in Cognitive Sciences, 22*(1), 32–51.

Duncan, Dustin T. & Kawachi, Ichiro (Eds.). (2018). *Neighborhoods and health* (2nd ed.). Oxford University Press.

Duncan, Greg J. & Magnuson, Katherine. (2013). Investing in preschool programs. *Journal of Economic Perspectives, 27*(2), 109–132.

Dunn, Kirsty & Bremner, J. Gavin. (2017). Investigating looking and social looking measures as an index of infant violation of expectation. *Developmental Science, 20*(6), e12452.

Dunn, Kirsty & Bremner, James Gavin. (2019). Investigating the social environment of the A-not-B search task. *Developmental Science*, e12921.

Duran, Chelsea A. K.; Cottone, Elizabeth; Ruzek, Erik A.; Mashburn, Andrew J. & Grissmer, David W. (2019). Family stress processes and children's self-regulation. *Child Development, 91*(2), 577–595.

Durso, Francis T.; Dattel, Andrew R. & Pop, Vlad L. (2018). Expertise and transportation. In Ericsson, K. Anders; Hoffman, Robert R.; Kozbelt, Aaron & Williams, A. Mark (Eds.), *The Cambridge handbook of expertise and expert performance* (2nd ed., pp. 356–371). Cambridge University Press.

Dutton, Donald G. (2012). The case against the role of gender in intimate partner violence. *Aggression and Violent Behavior, 17*(1), 99–104.

Dweck, Carol S. (2013). Social development. In Zelazo, Philip D. (Ed.), *The Oxford handbook of developmental psychology* (Vol. 2, pp. 167–190). Oxford University Press.

Dweck, Carol S. (2016). *Mindset: The new psychology of success.* Random House.

Dworkin, A. Gary & Quiroz, Pamela Anne. (2019). The United States of America: Accountability, high-stakes testing, and the demography of educational inequality. In Stevens, Peter A. J. & Dworkin, A. Gary (Eds.), *The Palgrave handbook of race and* *ethnic inequalities in education* (2nd ed., pp. 1097–1181). Palgrave Macmillan.

Dyer, Ashley A.; Rivkina, Victoria; Perumal, Dhivya; Smeltzer, Brandon M.; Smith, Bridget M. & Gupta, Ruchi S. (2015). Epidemiology of childhood peanut allergy. *Allergy and Asthma Proceedings, 36*(1), 58–64.

Eagly, Alice H. & Wood, Wendy. (2013). The nature–nurture debates: 25 years of challenges in understanding the psychology of gender. *Perspectives on Psychological Science, 8*(3), 340–357.

Eaton, Asia A.; Noori, Sofia; Bonomi, Amy; Stephens, Dionne P. & Gillum, Tameka L. (2020). Nonconsensual porn as a form of intimate partner violence: Using the power and control wheel to understand nonconsensual porn perpetration in intimate relationships. *Trauma, Violence, & Abuse*, (In Press).

Eccles, Jacquelynne S. & Roeser, Robert W. (2010). An ecological view of schools and development. In Meece, Judith L. & Eccles, Jacquelynne S. (Eds.), *Handbook of research on schools, schooling, and human development* (pp. 6–22). Routledge.

Eccles, Jacquelynne S. & Roeser, Robert W. (2011). Schools as developmental contexts during adolescence. *Journal of Research on Adolescence, 21*(1), 225–241.

Ehrenberg, Alexander J.; Khatun, Ayesha; Coomans, Emma; Betts, Matthew J.; Capraro, Federica; Thijssen, Elisabeth H.; . . . Paterson, Ross W. (2020). Relevance of biomarkers across different neurodegenerative diseases. *Alzheimer's Research & Therapy, 12*(56).

Einav, Liran; Finkelstein, Amy; Mullainathan, Sendhil & Obermeyer, Ziad. (2018). Predictive modeling of U.S. health care spending in late life. *Science, 360*(6396), 1462–1465.

El-Sheikh, Mona & Kelly, Ryan J. (2017). Family functioning and children's sleep. *Child Development Perspectives, 11*(4), 264–269.

Elder, Glen H. (1998). The life course as developmental theory. *Child Development, 69*(1), 1–12.

Elicker, James & Ruprecht, Karen M. (2019). Child care quality rating and improvement systems (QRIS): National experiment for improving early childhood education quality. In Brown, Christopher P.; McMullen, Mary Benson & File, Nancy (Eds.), *The Wiley handbook of early childhood care and education* (pp. 515–536). Wiley.

Elkind, David. (1967). Egocentrism in adolescence. *Child Development, 38*(4), 1025–1034.

Ellefson, Michelle R.; Ng, Florrie Fei-Yin; Wang, Qian & Hughes, Claire. (2017). Efficiency of executive function: A two-generation cross-cultural comparison of samples from Hong Kong and the United Kingdom. *Psychological Science, 28*(5), 555–566.

Ellemers, Naomi. (2018). Gender stereotypes. *Annual Review of Psychology, 69*, 275–298.

Elliot, Ari J.; Mooney, Christopher J.; Infurna, Frank J. & Chapman, Benjamin P. (2018). Perceived control and frailty: The role of affect and perceived health. *Psychology and Aging, 33*(3), 473–481.

Elliott, Sinikka. (2012). *Not my kid: What parents believe about the sex lives of their teenagers.* New York University Press.

Ellis, Bruce J. & Boyce, W. Thomas. (2008). Biological sensitivity to context. *Current Directions in Psychological Science, 17*(3), 183–187.

Ellis, Bruce J.; Boyce, W. Thomas; Belsky, Jay; Bakermans-Kranenburg, Marian J. & Van Ijzendoorn, Marinus H. (2011a). Differential susceptibility to the environment: An evolutionary–neurodevelopmental theory. *Development and Psychopathology, 23*(1), 7–28.

Ellis, Bruce J. & Del Giudice, Marco. (2019). Developmental adaptation to stress: An evolutionary perspective. *Annual Review of Psychology, 70*(1), 111–139.

Ellis, Bruce J.; Shirtcliff, Elizabeth A.; Boyce, W. Thomas; Deardorff, Julianna & Essex, Marilyn J. (2011b). Quality of early family relationships and the timing and tempo of puberty: Effects depend on biological sensitivity to context. *Development and Psychopathology, 23*(1), 85–99.

Ellis, Wendy E.; Dumas, Tara M. & Forbes, Lindsey M. (2020). Physically isolated but socially connected: Psychological adjustment and stress among adolescents during the initial COVID-19 crisis. *Canadian Psychological Association, 52*(3), 177–187.

Ellison, Christopher G.; Musick, Marc A. & Holden, George W. (2011). Does conservative Protestantism moderate the association between corporal punishment and child outcomes? *Journal of Marriage and Family, 73*(5), 946–961.

Emanuel, Ezekiel J. (2017). Euthanasia and physician-assisted suicide: Focus on the data. *Medical Journal of Australia, 206*(8), 1–2e1.

Endendijk, Joyce J.; Derks, Belle & Mesman, Judi. (2018). Does parenthood change implicit gender-role stereotypes and behaviors? *Journal of Marriage and Family, 80*(1), 61–79.

Enever, Janet & Lindgren, Eva (Eds.). (2017). *Early language learning: Complexity and mixed methods.* Multilingual Matters /Channel View.

Engelberts, Adèle C. & de Jonge, Guustaaf Adolf. (1990). Choice of sleeping position for infants: Possible association with cot death. *Archives of Disease in Childhood, 65*(4), 462–467.

Engin, Ayse Basak; Engin, Evren Doruk & Engin, Atilla. (2020). Two important controversial risk factors in SARS-CoV-2 infection: Obesity and smoking. *Environmental Toxicology and Pharmacology, 78*(103411).

English, Tammy & Carstensen, Laura L. (2014). Selective narrowing of social networks across adulthood is associated with improved emotional experience in daily life. *International Journal of Behavioral Development, 38*(2), 195–202.

Ennis, Linda Rose. (2015). *Intensive mothering: The cultural contradictions of modern motherhood.* Demeter Press.

Enough Is Enough. (2017). *Cyberbullying statistics.* Great Falls, VA: Enough Is Enough.

Epstein, Robert; Pandit, Mayuri & Thakar, Mansi. (2013). How love emerges in arranged marriages: Two cross-cultural studies. *Journal of Comparative Family Studies, 44*(3), 341–360.

Erikson, Erik H. (1968). *Identity: Youth and crisis.* Norton.

Erikson, Erik H. (1982). *The life cycle completed: A review.* Norton.

Erikson, Erik H. (1993a). *Childhood and society* (2nd ed.). Norton.

Erikson, Erik H. (1993b). *Gandhi's truth: On the origins of militant nonviolence.* Norton.

Erikson, Erik H. (1994). *Identity and the life cycle.* Norton.

Erikson, Erik H. (1998). *The life cycle completed.* Norton.

Erikson, Erik H.; Erikson, Joan M. & Kivnick, Helen Q. (1986). *Vital involvement in old age.* Norton.

Erikson, Erik H.; Erikson, Joan M. & Kivnick, Helen Q. (1994). *Vital involvement in old age.* Norton.

Ernst, Monique. (2016). A tribute to the adolescent brain. *Neuroscience & Biobehavioral Reviews, 70,* 334–338.

Ernst, Michelle M.; Liao, Lih-Mei; Baratz, Arlene B. & Sandberg, David E. (2018). Disorders of sex development/intersex: Gaps in psychosocial care for children. *Pediatrics, 142*(2), e20174045.

Espy, Kimberly Andrews. (2016). *Monographs of the society for research in child development: The changing nature of executive control in preschool, 81*(4), 1–179.

Esteves, Inês; Nan, Wenya; Alves, Cristiana; Calapez, Alexandre; Melício, Fernando & Rosa, Agostinho. (2021). An exploratory study of training intensity in EEG neurofeedback. *Neural Plasticity*(8881059).

Eun, John; Paksarian, Diana; He, Jian-Ping & Merikangas, Kathleen R. (2018). Parenting style and mental disorders in a nationally representative sample of US adolescents. *Social Psychiatry and Psychiatric Epidemiology, 53*(1), 11–20.

Evans, Angela D.; Xu, Fen & Lee, Kang. (2011). When all signs point to you: Lies told in the face of evidence. *Developmental Psychology, 47*(1), 39–49.

Evans, Gary W. & Kim, Pilyoung. (2013). Childhood poverty, chronic stress, self-regulation, and coping. *Child Development Perspectives,* 7(1), 43–48.

Evans, Jonathan. (2018). Dual process theory: Perspectives and problems. In De Neys, Wim (Ed.), *Dual process theory 2.0.* Routledge.

Eyer, Diane E. (1992). *Mother-infant bonding: A scientific fiction.* Yale University Press.

Fabrigar, Leandre R.; Wegener, Duane T. & Petty, Richard E. (2020). A validity-based framework for understanding replication in psychology. *Personality and Social Psychology Review, 24*(4), 316–344.

Fagan, Jay & Palkovitz, Rob. (2018). Longitudinal associations between mothers' perceptions of nonresidential fathers' investment of resources and influence in decision-making. *Journal of Family Psychology, 32*(1), 103–113.

Fagnani, Jeanne. (2013). Equal access to quality care: Lessons from France on providing high quality and affordable early childhood education and care. In *Equal access to childcare: Providing quality early childhood education and care to disadvantaged families* (pp. 77–99). Policy Press.

Fagot, Delphine; Mella, Nathalie; Borella, Erika; Ghisletta, Paolo; Lecerf, Thierry & De Ribaupierre, Anik. (2018). Intra-individual variability from a lifespan perspective: A comparison of latency and accuracy measures. *Journal of Intelligence, 6*(1).

Fairbank, John; Briggs, Ernestine; Lee, Robert; Corry, Nida; Pflieger, Jacqueline; Gerrity, Ellen; . . . Murphy, Robert. (2018). Mental health of children of deployed and nondeployed US military service members: The millennium cohort family study. *Journal of Developmental & Behavioral Pediatrics, 39*(9), 683–692.

Faircloth, Charlotte. (2020). 'Utterly heart-breaking and devastating': Couple relationships and intensive parenting culture in a time of 'cold intimacies'. In Carter, Julia & Arocha, Lorena (Eds.), *Romantic relationships in a time of 'cold intimacies'.* Palgrave Macmillan.

Fairhurst, Merle T.; Löken, Line & Grossmann, Tobias. (2014). Physiological and behavioral responses reveal 9-month-old infants' sensitivity to pleasant touch. *Psychological Science, 25*(5), 1124–1131.

Farber, Stu & Farber, Annalu. (2014). It ain't easy: Making life and death decisions before the crisis. In Rogne, Leah & McCune, Susana Lauraine (Eds.), *Advance care planning: Communicating about matters of life and death* (pp. 109–122). Springer.

Fareed, Mohd; Anwar, Malik Azeem & Afzal, Mohammad. (2015). Prevalence and gene frequency of color vision impairments among children of six populations from North Indian region. *Genes & Diseases, 2*(2), 211–218.

Fast, Anne A. & Olson, Kristina R. (2018). Gender development in transgender preschool children. *Child Development, 89*(2), 620–637.

Fearon, R. M. Pasco & Roisman, Glenn I. (2017). Attachment theory: Progress and future directions. *Current Opinion in Psychology, 15,* 131–136.

Fedewa, Michael V.; Das, Bhibha M.; Evans, Ellen M. & Dishman, Rod K. (2014). Change in weight and adiposity in college students: A systematic review and meta-analysis: A systematic review and meta-analysis. *American Journal of Preventive Medicine, 47*(5), 641–652.

Feld, Barry C. (2013). *Kids, cops, and confessions: Inside the interrogation room.* New York University Press.

Feldman, Heidi M. (2019). How young children learn language and speech. *Pediatrics in Review, 40*(8), 398–411.

Feldman, Ruth. (2012a). Oxytocin and social affiliation in humans. *Hormones and Behavior, 61*(3), 380–391.

Feldman, Ruth. (2012b). Parent-infant synchrony: A biobehavioral model of mutual influences in the formation of affiliative bonds. *Monographs of the Society for Research in Child Development,* 77(2), 42–51.

Feliciano, Cynthia & Rumbaut, Rubén G. (2018). Varieties of ethnic self-identities: Children of immigrants in middle adulthood. *RSF: The Russell Sage Foundation Journal of the Social Sciences, 4*(5), 26–46.

Feliciano, Cynthia & Rumbaut, Rubén G. (2019). The evolution of ethnic identity from adolescence to middle adulthood: The case of the immigrant second generation. *Emerging Adulthood,* 7(2), 85–96.

Felicilda-Reynaldo, Rhea & Smith, Lucretia. (2018). Needs based frameworks. In Utley, Rose; Henry, Kristina & Smith, Lucretia (Eds.), *Frameworks for advanced nursing practice and research: Philosophies, theories, models, and taxonomies* (pp. 157–172). Springer.

Felton, Julia W.; Collado, Anahí; Ingram, Katherine; Lejuez, Carl W. & Yi, Richard. (2020). Changes in delay discounting, substance use, and weight status across adolescence. *Health Psychology, 39*(5), 413–420.

Feola, Brandee; Dougherty, Lea R.; Riggins, Tracy & Bolger, Donald J. (2020). Prefrontal cortical thickness mediates the association between cortisol reactivity and executive function in childhood. *Neuropsychologia, 148*(107636).

Ferguson, Christopher J. (2013). Spanking, corporal punishment and negative long-term outcomes: A meta-analytic review of longitudinal studies. *Clinical Psychology Review, 33*(1), 196–208.

Fewtrell, Mary; Wilson, David C.; Booth, Ian & Lucas, Alan. (2011). Six months of exclusive breast feeding: How good is the evidence? *BMJ, 342*, c5955.

Fields, R. Douglas. (2014). Myelin—More than insulation. *Science, 344*(6181), 264–266.

Filipovic, Jill. (2020). *OK boomer, let's talk: How my generation got left behind.* Atria Books.

Fine, Cordelia. (2014). His brain, her brain? *Science, 346*(6212), 915–916.

Finer, Lawrence B. & Zolna, Mia R. (2016). Declines in unintended pregnancy in the United States, 2008–2011. *New England Journal of Medicine, 374*, 843–852.

Fingerman, Karen L.; Berg, Cynthia; Smith, Jacqui & Antonucci, Toni C. (2011). *Handbook of lifespan development.* Springer.

Fingerman, Karen L.; Cheng, Yen-Pi; Birditt, Kira & Zarit, Steven. (2012a). Only as happy as the least happy child: Multiple grown children's problems and successes and middle-aged parents' well-being. *The Journals of Gerontology Series B: Psychological Sciences and Social Sciences, 67B*(2), 184–193.

Fingerman, Karen L.; Cheng, Yen-Pi; Tighe, Lauren; Birditt, Kira S. & Zarit, Steve. (2012b). Relationships between young adults and their parents. In Booth, Alan; Brown, Susan L.; Landale, Nancy S.; Manning, Wendy D. & McHale, Susan M. (Eds.), *Early adulthood in family context* (pp. 59–85). Springer.

Fingerman, Karen L.; Cheng, Yen-Pi; Wesselmann, Eric D.; Zarit, Steven; Furstenberg, Frank & Birditt, Kira S. (2012c). Helicopter parents and landing pad kids: Intense parental support of grown children. *Journal of Marriage and Family, 74*(4), 880–896.

Fingerman, Karen L. & Furstenberg, Frank F. (2012, May 30). You can go home again. *New York Times.*

Fingerman, Karen L.; Huo, Meng & Birditt, Kira S. (2020). A decade of research on intergenerational ties: Technological, economic, political, and demographic changes. *Journal of Marriage and Family, 82*(1), 383–403.

Fingerman, Karen L.; Ng, Yee To; Zhang, Shiyang; Britt, Katherine; Colera, Gianna; Birditt, Kira S. & Charles, Susan T. (2021). Living alone during COVID-19: Social contact and emotional well-being among older adults. *The Journals of Gerontology: Series B, 76*(3), e116–e121.

Fingerman, Karen L.; Pillemer, Karl A.; Silverstein, Merril & Suitor, J. Jill. (2012d). The baby boomers' intergenerational relationships. *The Gerontologist, 52*(2), 199–209.

Finkelhor, David; Shattuck, Anne; Turner, Heather A. & Hamby, Sherry L. (2014). The lifetime prevalence of child sexual abuse and sexual assault assessed in late adolescence. *Journal of Adolescent Health, 55*(3), 329–333.

Finlay, Ilora G. & George, R. (2011). Legal physician-assisted suicide in Oregon and the Netherlands: Evidence concerning the impact on patients in vulnerable groups—Another perspective on Oregon's data. *Journal of Medical Ethics, 37*(3), 171–174.

Finn, Chester E. & Scanlan, Andrew E. (2019). *Learning in the fast lane: The past, present, and future of advanced placement.* Princeton University Press.

Finn, Kenneth (Ed.) (2020). *Cannabis in medicine: An evidence-based approach.* Springer Nature.

Fins, Joseph J. & Bernat, James L. (2018). Ethical, palliative, and policy considerations in disorders of consciousness. *Archives of Physical Medicine and Rehabilitation, 99*(9), 1927–1931.

Fischer, Nantje; Træen, Bente & Hald, Gert Martin. (2018). Predicting partnered sexual activity among older adults in four European countries: The role of attitudes, health, and relationship factors. *Sexual and Relationship Therapy.*

Fisher, Dorothy Canfield. (1922). *What grandmother did not know.* Pilgrim Press.

Fisher, Helen E. (2016a). *Anatomy of love: A natural history of mating, marriage, and why we stray.* Norton.

Fisher, Helen E. (2016b). Broken hearts: The nature and risks of romantic rejection. In Booth, Alan; Crouter, Ann C. & Snyder, Anastasia (Eds.), *Romance and sex in adolescence and emerging adulthood* (pp. 3–28). Routledge.

Flanagan, Emily W.; Beyl, Robbie A.; Fearnbach, S. Nicole; Altazan, Abby D.; Martin, Corby K. & Redman, Leanne M. (2021). The Impact of COVID-19 stay-at-home orders on health behaviors in adults. *Obesity, 29*(2), 438–445.

Flegal, Katherine M.; Kit, Brian K.; Orpana, Heather & Graubard, Barry I. (2013). Association of all-cause mortality with overweight and obesity using standard body mass index categories: A systematic review and meta-analysis. *JAMA, 309*(1), 71–82.

Fletcher, Richard; St. George, Jennifer & Freeman, Emily. (2013). Rough and tumble play quality: Theoretical foundations for a new measure of father–child interaction. *Early Child Development and Care, 183*(6), 746–759.

Fleuriet, Jill & Sunil, Thankam (2018). The Latina birth weight paradox: The role of subjective social status. *Journal of Racial and Ethnic Health Disparities, 5*, 747–757.

Flores, Andrew R.; Haider-Markel, Donald P.; Lewis, Daniel C.; Miller, Patrick R.; Tadlock, Barry L. & Taylor, Jami K. (2018). Transgender prejudice reduction and opinions on transgender rights: Results from a mediation analysis on experimental data. *Research & Politics, 5*(1).

Flynn, James & Shayer, Michael. (2018). IQ decline and Piaget: Does the rot start at the top? *Intelligence, 66*(112–121).

Fontana, Luigi & Partridge, Linda. (2015). Promoting health and longevity through diet: From model organisms to humans. *Cell, 161*(1), 106–118.

Foo, Koong Hean. (2019). *Intercultural parenting: How Eastern and Western parenting styles affect child development.* Routledge.

Ford, Jaclyn H.; DiBiase, Haley D.; Ryu, Ehri & Kensinger, Elizabeth A. (2018). It gets better with time: Enhancement of age-related positivity effect in the six months following a highly negative public event. *Psychology and Aging, 33*(3), 419–424.

Forestell, Catherine A. & Mennella, Julie A. (2017). The relationship between infant facial expressions and food acceptance. *Current Nutrition Reports, 6*(2), 141–147.

Formosa, Marvin. (2014). Four decades of Universities of the Third Age: Past, present, future. *Ageing & Society, 34*(1).

Forrest, Ray. (2021). Housing wealth, social structures and changing narratives. *International Journal of Urban Sciences, 25*(1), 1–15.

Forster, Myriam; Gower, Amy L.; Gloppen, Kari; Sieving, Renee; Oliphant, Jennifer; Plowman, Shari; . . . McMorris, Barbara J. (2020). Associations between dimensions of school engagement and bullying victimization and perpetration among middle school students. *School Mental Health, 12*, 296–307.

Fortin, Andrée; Doucet, Martin & Damant, Dominique. (2011). Children's appraisals as mediators of the relationship between domestic violence and child adjustment. *Violence and Victims, 26*(3), 377–392.

Fosco, Gregory M. & LoBraico, Emily J. (2019). Elaborating on premature adolescent autonomy: Linking variation in daily family processes to developmental risk. *Development and Psychopathology, 31*(5), 1741–1755.

Fox, Ashley; Himmelstein, Georgia; Khalid, Hina & Howell, Elizabeth A. (2019). Funding for abstinence-only education and adolescent pregnancy prevention: Does state ideology affect outcomes? *American Journal of Public Health*, e1–e8.

Fox, Molly; Thayer, Zaneta M.; Ramos, Isabel F.; Meskal, Sarah J. & Wadhwa, Pathik D. (2018). Prenatal and postnatal mother-to-child transmission of acculturation's health effects in Hispanic Americans. *Journal of Women's Health, 27*(8), 154–1063.

Fox, Nathan A.; Henderson, Heather A.; Marshall, Peter J.; Nichols, Kate E. & Ghera, Melissa M. (2005). Behavioral inhibition: Linking biology and behavior within a developmental framework. *Annual Review of Psychology, 56*, 235–262.

Fox, Nathan A.; Henderson, Heather A.; Rubin, Kenneth H.; Calkins, Susan D. & Schmidt, Louis A. (2001). Continuity and discontinuity of behavioral inhibition and exuberance: Psychophysiological and behavioral influences across the first four years of life. *Child Development, 72*(1), 1–21.

Fox, Nathan A.; Reeb-Sutherland, Bethany C. & Degnan, Kathryn A. (2013). Personality and emotional development. In Zelazo, Philip D. (Ed.), *The Oxford handbook of developmental psychology* (Vol. 2, pp. 15–44). Oxford University Press.

Fraley, R. Chris. (2019). Attachment in adulthood: Recent developments, emerging debates, and future directions. *Annual Review of Psychology, 70*, 401–422.

Franco, Manuel; Bilal, Usama; Orduñez, Pedro; Benet, Mikhail; Alain, Morejón; Benjamín, Caballero; . . . Cooper, Richard S. (2013). Population-wide weight loss and regain in relation to diabetes burden and cardiovascular mortality in Cuba 1980–2010: Repeated cross sectional surveys and ecological comparison of secular trends. *BMJ, 346*(7903), f1515.

Franco, Marcia R.; Tong, Allison; Howard, Kirsten; Sherrington, Catherine; Ferreira, Paulo H.; Pinto, Rafael Z. & Ferreira, Manuela L. (2015). Older people's perspectives on participation in physical activity: A systematic review and thematic synthesis of qualitative literature. *British Journal of Sports Medicine, 49*, 1268–1276.

Frandsen, Barbara. (2020). *Dignity in death: Accepting, assisting, and preparing for the end of life.* Atlantic.

Frankenburg, William K.; Dodds, Josiah; Archer, Philip; Shapiro, Howard & Bresnick, Beverly. (1992). The Denver II: A major revision and restandardization of the Denver Developmental Screening Test. *Pediatrics, 89*(1), 91–97.

Fraser, Sarah; Lagacé, Martine; Bongué, Bienvenu; Ndeye, Ndatté; Guyot, Jessica; Bechard, Lauren; . . . Tougas, Francine. (2020). Ageism and COVID-19: What does our society's response say about us? *Age and Ageing, 49*(5), 692–695.

Fraundorf, Scott H.; Hourihan, Kathleen L.; Peters, Rachel A. & Benjamin, Aaron S. (2019). Aging and recognition memory: A meta-analysis. *Psychological Bulletin, 145*(4), 339–371.

Frederick, David A.; Lever, Janet; Gillespie, Brian Joseph & Garcia, Justin R. (2017). What keeps passion alive? Sexual satisfaction is associated with sexual communication, mood setting, sexual variety, oral sex, orgasm, and sex frequency in a national U.S. study. *The Journal of Sex Research, 54*(2), 186–201.

Freeman, Joan. (2010). *Gifted lives: What happens when gifted children grow up?* Routledge.

Frejka, Tomas; Goldscheider, Frances & Lappegård, Trude. (2018). The two-part gender revolution, women's second shift and changing cohort fertility. *Comparative Population Studies, 43*, 99–130.

Frémondière, Pierre; Marchal, François; Thollon, Lionel & Saliba-serre, Bérangère. (2019). Change in head shape of newborn infants in the week following birth: Contributing factors. *Journal of Pediatric Neurology, 17*(5), 168–175.

Freud, Anna. (1958). Adolescence. *Psychoanalytic Study of the Child, 13*, 255–278.

Freud, Anna. (2000). Adolescence. In McCarthy, James B. (Ed.), *Adolescent development and psychopathology* (pp. 29–52). University Press of America.

Freud, Anna & Burlingham, Dorothy T. (1943). *War and children.* Medical War Books.

Freud, Sigmund. (1935). *A general introduction to psychoanalysis.* Liveright.

Freud, Sigmund. (1989). *Introductory lectures on psycho-analysis.* Liveright.

Freud, Sigmund. (2001). An outline of psycho-analysis. In *The standard edition of the complete psychological works of Sigmund Freud* (Vol. 23). Vintage.

Fried, Terri R. & Mecca, Marcia C. (2019). Medication appropriateness in vulnerable older adults: Healthy skepticism of appropriate polypharmacy. *Journal of the American Geriatrics Society, 67*(6), 1123–1127.

Friedman, Zack. (2019). Student loan debt statistics in 2019: A $1.5 trillion crisis. *Forbes.*

Friedman-Krauss, Allison H.; Barnett, W. Steven; Garver, Karin A.; Hodges, Katherine S.; Weisenfeld, G. G. & DiCrecchio, Nicole. (2019). *The state of preschool 2018: State preschool yearbook*. New Brunswick, NJ: National Institute for Early Education Research.

Friend, Stephen H. & Schadt, Eric E. (2014). Clues from the resilient. *Science, 344*(6187), 970–972.

Frost, Randy O.; Steketee, Gail; Tolin, David F.; Sinopoli, Nicole & Ruby, Dylan. (2015). Motives for acquiring and saving in hoarding disorder, OCD, and community controls. *Journal of Obsessive-Compulsive and Related Disorders, 4*, 54–59.

Fry, Douglas P. (2014). Environment of evolutionary adaptedness, rough-and-tumble play, and the selection of restraint in human aggression. In Narvaez, Darcia; Valentino, Kristin; Fuentes, Agustin; McKenna, James J. & Gray, Peter (Eds.), *Ancestral landscapes in human evolution: Culture, childrearing and social wellbeing* (pp. 169–188). Oxford University Press.

Fry, Richard. (2016, May 24). *For first time in modern era, living with parents edges out other living arrangements for 18- to 34-year-olds*. Washington, DC: Pew Research Center.

Fry, Richard; Passel, Jeffrey S. & Cohn, D'Vera. (2020, September 4). *A majority of young adults in the U.S. live with their parents for the first time since the Great Depression. Fact Tank*. Washington, DC: Pew Research Center.

Frydenberg, Erica. (2017). *Coping and the challenge of resilience*. Palgrave.

Fuentes-Afflick, Elena; Odouli, Roxana; Escobar, Gabriel J.; Stewart, Anita L. & Hessol, Nancy A. (2014). Maternal acculturation and the prenatal care experience. *Journal of Women's Health, 23*(8), 688–706.

Fulmer, C. Ashley; Gelfand, Micheke J.; Kruglanski, Arie W.; Kim-Prieto, Chu; Diener, Ed; Pierro, Antonio & Higgins, E. Tory. (2010). On "feeling right" in cultural contexts: How person-culture match affects self-esteem and subjective well-being. *Psychological Science, 21*(11), 1563–1569.

Gad, Rasha F.; Dowling, Donna A.; Abusaad, Fawzia E.; Bassiouny, Mohamed R. & Abd El Aziz, Magda A. (2019). Oral sucrose versus breastfeeding in managing infants' immunization-related pain: A randomized controlled trial. *MCN, 44*(2), 108–114.

Gaffney, Hannah; Farrington, David P.; Espelage, Dorothy L. & Ttofi, Maria M. (2019). Are cyberbullying intervention and prevention programs effective? A systematic and meta-analytical review. *Aggression and Violent Behavior, 45*, 134–153.

Galak, Jeff; Givi, Julian & Williams, Elanor F. (2016). Why certain gifts are great to give but not to get: A framework for understanding errors in gift giving. *Current Directions in Psychological Science, 25*(6), 380–385.

Galasso, Vincenzo; Profeta, Paola; Pronzato, Chiara & Billari, Francesco. (2017). Information and women's intentions: Experimental evidence about child care. *European Journal of Population, 33*(1), 109–128.

Gallagher, Annabella; Updegraff, Kimberly; Padilla, Jenny & McHale, Susan M. (2018). Longitudinal associations between sibling relational aggression and adolescent adjustment. *Journal of Youth and Adolescence, 47*(10), 2100–2113.

Gallup. (2017, August). *Time to play: A study on children's free time—how it is spent, prioritized and valued*. Washington, DC: Gallup.

Gallup. (2018). *The gig economy and alternative work arrangements*. Washington, DC: Gallup.

Gambaro, Ludovica; Stewart, Kitty & Waldfogel, Jane (Eds.). (2014). *An equal start?: Providing quality early education and care for disadvantaged children*. Policy Press.

Ganapathy, Thilagavathy. (2014). Couvade syndrome among 1st time expectant fathers. *Muller Journal of Medical Science Research, 5*(1), 43–47.

Gao, Wei; Lin, Weili; Grewen, Karen & Gilmore, John H. (2017). Functional connectivity of the infant human brain: Plastic and modifiable. *Neuroscientist, 23*(2), 169–184.

Garbe, Amber; Ogurlu, Uzeyir; Logan, Nikki & Cook, Perry. (2020). COVID-19 and remote learning: Experiences of parents with children during the pandemic. *American Journal of Qualitative Research, 4*(3), 45–65.

Gardner, Howard. (1983). *Frames of mind: The theory of multiple intelligences*. Basic.

Gardner, Howard. (1999). Are there additional intelligences? The case for naturalist, spiritual, and existential intelligences. In Kane, Jeffrey (Ed.), *Education, information, and transformation: Essays on learning and thinking* (pp. 111–131). Merrill.

Gardner, Howard. (2006). *Multiple intelligences: New horizons in theory and practice*. Basic.

Gardner, Howard. (2011). *Frames of mind: The theory of multiple intelligences*. Basic.

Gariépy, Geneviève; Riehm, Kira E.; Whitehead, Ross D.; Doré, Isabelle & Elgar, Frank J. (2018). Teenage night owls or early birds? Chronotype and the mental health of adolescents. *Journal of Sleep Research*, e12723.

Garland, Eric L.; Atchley, Rachel M.; Hanley, Adam W.; Zubieta, Jon-Kar & Froeliger, Brett. (2019). Mindfulness-Oriented Recovery Enhancement remediates hedonic dysregulation in opioid users: Neural and affective evidence of target engagement. *Science Advances, 5*(10), eaax1569.

Garrett, Mallory. (2018). "It Gets Better" media campaign and gay youth suicide. In Stewart, Chuck (Ed.), *Lesbian, gay, bisexual, and transgender Americans at risk: Problems and solutions* (pp. 119–128). Praeger.

Gartstein, Maria A. & Skinner, Michael K. (2018). Prenatal influences on temperament development: The role of environmental epigenetics. *Development and Psychopathology, 30*(4), 1269–1303.

Garvis, Susanne; Harju-Luukkainen, Heidi; Sheridan, Sonja & Williams, Pia (Eds.). (2019). *Nordic families, children and early childhood education*. Palgrave Macmillan.

Garzón-Orjuela, Nathaly; Samacá-Samacá, Daniel; Moreno-Chaparro, Jaime; Ballesteros-Cabrera, Magnolia Del Pilar & Eslava-Schmalbach, Javier. (2020). Effectiveness of sex education interventions in adolescents: An overview. *Comprehensive Child and Adolescent Nursing*.

Gassin, Elizabeth A. (2017). Forgiveness and continuing bonds. In Klass, Dennis & Steffen, Edith Maria (Eds.), *Continuing bonds in bereavement: New directions for research and practice*. Routledge.

Gattario, Kristina Holmqvist & Frisén, Ann. (2019). From negative to positive body image: Men's and women's journeys from early adolescence to emerging adulthood. *Body Image, 28*, 53–65.

Gawande, Atul. (2014). *Being mortal: Medicine and what matters in the end.* Metropolitan Books.

Geary, David C. (2018). Efficiency of mitochondrial functioning as the fundamental biological mechanism of general intelligence (g). *Psychological Review, 125*(6), 1028–1050.

Geiger, Jennifer Mullins; Hayes, Megan J. & Lietz, Cynthia A. (2013). Should I stay or should I go? A mixed methods study examining the factors influencing foster parents' decisions to continue or discontinue providing foster care. *Children and Youth Services Review, 35*(9), 1356–1365.

Gelfand, Amy. (2018). Episodic syndromes of childhood associated with migraine. *Current Opinion in Neurology, 31*(3), 281–285.

Gellert, Anna S. & Elbro, Carsten. (2017). Does a dynamic test of phonological awareness predict early reading difficulties? A longitudinal study from kindergarten through grade 1. *Journal of Learning Disabilities, 50*(3), 227–237.

Gershoff, Elizabeth; Sattler, Kierra M. P & Holden, George W. (2019). School corporal punishment and its associations with achievement and adjustment. *Journal of Applied Developmental Psychology, 63*, 1–8.

Gervais, Will M. & Norenzayan, Ara. (2012). Analytic thinking promotes religious disbelief. *Science, 336*(6080), 493–496.

Gewertz, Catherine. (2019, April 9). Which states require an exam to graduate?: An interactive breakdown of states' 2016–17 testing plans. Education Week.

Gewirtz-Meydan, Ateret & Finkelhor, David. (2020). Sexual abuse and assault in a large national sample of children and adolescents. *Child Maltreatment, 25*(2), 203–214.

Gibbs, John C. (2019). *Moral development and reality: Beyond the theories of Kohlberg, Hoffman, and Haidt.* Oxford University Press.

Gibson-Davis, Christina & Rackin, Heather. (2014). Marriage or carriage? Trends in union context and birth type by education. *Journal of Marriage and Family, 76*(3), 506–519.

Gidley, Jennifer M. (2016). *Postformal education: A philosophy for complex futures.* Springer.

Gignac, Gilles E. (2016). On the evaluation of competing theories: A reply to van der Maas and Kan. *Intelligence, 57*, 84–86.

Gillespie, Brian Joseph; Frederick, David; Harari, Lexi & Grov, Christian. (2015). Homophily, close friendship, and life satisfaction among gay, lesbian, heterosexual, and bisexual men and women. *PLoS ONE, 10*(6), e0128900.

Gilligan, Carol. (1982). *In a different voice: Psychological theory and women's development.* Harvard University Press.

Gillis, Alanna & Krull, Laura M. (2020). COVID-19 remote learning transition in spring 2020: Class structures, student perceptions, and inequality in college courses. *Teaching Sociology, 48*(4), 283–299.

Gillon, Raanan. (2015). Defending the four principles approach as a good basis for good medical practice and therefore for good medical ethics. *Journal of Medical Ethics, 41*(1), 111–116.

Gilmour, Heather; Ramage-Morin, Pamela L. & Wong, Suzy L. (2019). Infant bed sharing in Canada. *Health Reports, 30*(7), 13–19.

Gingrich, Jeremy; Ticiani, Elvis & Veiga-Lopez, Almudena. (2020). Placenta disrupted: Endocrine disrupting chemicals and pregnancy. *Trends in Endocrinology and Metabolism, 31*(7), P508–524.

Giubilini, Alberto & Savulescu, Julian. (2019). Vaccination, risks, and freedom: The seat belt analogy. *Public Health Ethics, 12*(3), 237–249.

Giumetti, Gary W. & Kowalski, Robin M. (2015). Cyberbullying matters: Examining the incremental impact of cyberbullying on outcomes over and above traditional bullying in North America. In Navarro, Raúl; Yubero, Santiago & Larrañaga, Elisa (Eds.), *Cyberbullying across the globe: Gender, family, and mental health* (pp. 117–130). Springer.

Glauber, Rebecca & Day, Melissa D. (2018). Gender, spousal caregiving, and depression: Does paid work matter? *Journal of Marriage and Family, 80*(2), 537–554.

Glenn, Dana E.; Demir-Lira, Özlem Ece; Gibson, Dominic J.; Congdon, Eliza L. & Levine, Susan C. (2018). Resilience in mathematics after early brain injury: The roles of parental input and early plasticity. *Developmental Cognitive Neuroscience, 30*, 304–313.

Glock, Sabine & Kleen, Hannah. (2019). Attitudes toward students from ethnic minority groups: The roles of preservice teachers' own ethnic backgrounds and teacher efficacy activation. *Studies in Educational Evaluation, 62*, 82–91.

Glover, Crystal Polite; Jenkins, Toby S. & Troutman, Stephanie. (2018). *Culture, community, and educational success: Reimagining the invisible knapsack.* Lexington.

Goddings, Anne-Lise; Heyes, Stephanie Burnett; Bird, Geoffrey; Viner, Russell M. & Blakemore, Sarah-Jayne. (2012). The relationship between puberty and social emotion processing. *Developmental Science, 15*(6), 801–811.

Goddings, Anne Lise; Beltz, Adriene; Peper, Jiska S.; Crone, Eveline A. & Braams, Barbara R. (2019). Understanding the role of puberty in structural and functional development of the adolescent brain. *Journal of Research on Adolescence, 29*(1), 32–53.

Godinet, Meripa T.; Li, Fenfang & Berg, Teresa. (2014). Early childhood maltreatment and trajectories of behavioral problems: Exploring gender and racial differences. *Child Abuse & Neglect, 38*(3), 544–556.

Goel, Sunny; Sharma, Abhishek & Garg, Aakash. (2018). Effect of alcohol consumption on cardiovascular health. *Current Cardiology Reports, 20*(4).

Golden, Marita. (2010). Angel baby. In Graham, Barbara (Ed.), *Eye of my heart: 27 writers reveal the hidden pleasures and perils of being a grandmother* (pp. 125–133). HarperCollins.

Golden, Rachel Lynn; Furman, Wyndol & Collibee, Charlene. (2016). The risks and rewards of sexual debut. *Developmental Psychology, 52*(11), 1913–1925.

Goldin-Meadow, Susan. (2015). From action to abstraction: Gesture as a mechanism of change. *Developmental Review, 38*, 167–184.

Goldin-Meadow, Susan & Alibali, Martha W. (2013). Gesture's role in speaking, learning, and creating language. *Annual Review of Psychology, 64*, 257–283.

Goldman-Mellor, Sidra; Caspi, Avshalom; Arseneault, Louise; Ajala, Nifemi; Ambler, Antony; Danese, Andrea; . . .

Moffitt, Terrie E. (2016). Committed to work but vulnerable: Self-perceptions and mental health in NEET 18-year-olds from a contemporary British cohort. *Journal of Child Psychology and Psychiatry, 57*(2), 196–203.

Goldschmidt, Andrea B.; Wall, Melanie M.; Zhang, Jun; Loth, Katie A. & Neumark-Sztainer, Dianne. (2016). Overeating and binge eating in emerging adulthood: 10-year stability and risk factors. *Developmental Psychology, 52*(3), 475–483.

Goldstein, Thalia R. & Lerner, Matthew D. (2018). Dramatic pretend play games uniquely improve emotional control in young children. *Developmental Science, 21*(4), e12603.

Golinkoff, Roberta M. & Hirsh-Pasek, Kathy. (2016). *Becoming brilliant: What science tells us about raising successful children.* American Psychological Association.

Gollan, Tamar H. & Goldrick, Matthew. (2019). Aging deficits in naturalistic speech production and monitoring revealed through reading aloud. *Psychology and Aging, 34*(1), 25–42.

Golm, Dennis; Maughan, Barbara; Barker, Edward D.; Hill, Jonathan; Kennedy, Mark; Knights, Nicky; . . . Sonuga-Barke, Edmund J. S. (2020). Why does early childhood deprivation increase the risk for depression and anxiety in adulthood? A developmental cascade model. *Journal of Child Psychology and Psychiatry, 61*(9), 1043–1053.

Gonyea, Judith G. (2013). Midlife, multigenerational bonds, and caregiving. In Talley, Ronda C. & Montgomery, Rhonda J.V. (Eds.), *Caregiving across the lifespan: Research, practice, policy* (pp. 105–130). Springer.

González, Roberto; Lickel, Brian; Gupta, Manisha; Tropp, Linda R.; Luengo Kanacri, Bernadette P.; Mora, Eduardo; . . . Bernardino, Michelle. (2017). Ethnic identity development and acculturation preferences among minority and majority youth: Norms and contact. *Child Development, 88*(3), 743–760.

Goodlad, James K.; Marcus, David K. & Fulton, Jessica J. (2013). Lead and Attention-deficit/hyperactivity disorder (ADHD) symptoms: A meta-analysis. *Clinical Psychology Review, 33*(3), 417–425.

Goodnight, Jackson A.; D'Onofrio, Brian M.; Cherlin, Andrew J.; Emery, Robert E.; Van Hulle, Carol A. & Lahey, Benjamin B. (2013). Effects of multiple maternal relationship transitions on offspring antisocial behavior in childhood and adolescence: A cousin-comparison analysis. *Journal of Abnormal Child Psychology, 41*(2), 185–198.

Gopnik, Alison. (2009). *The philosophical baby: What children's minds tell us about truth, love, and the meaning of life.* Farrar, Straus and Giroux.

Gopnik, Alison. (2016). *The gardener and the carpenter: What the new science of child development tells us about the relationship between parents and children.* Farrar, Strauss and Giroux.

Gopnik, Alison; Meltzoff, Andrew N. & Kuhl, Patricia K. (1999). *The scientist in the crib: Minds, brains, and how children learn.* William Morrow.

Gordon, Linda. (2017). *The second coming of the KKK: The Ku Klux Klan of the 1920s and the American political tradition.* Liveright.

Gordon-Hollingsworth, Arlene T.; Becker, Emily M.; Ginsburg, Golda S.; Keeton, Courtney; Compton, Scott N.; Birmaher, Boris B.; . . . March, John S. (2015). Anxiety disorders in Caucasian and African American children: A comparison of clinical characteristics, treatment process variables, and treatment outcomes. *Child Psychiatry & Human Development, 46*(5), 643–655.

Gostin, Lawrence; Phelan, Alexandra; Coutinho, Alex Godwin; Eccleston-Turner, Mark; Erondu, Ngozi; Filani, Oyebanji; . . . Kavanagh, Matthew. (2019). Ebola in the Democratic Republic of the Congo: Time to sound a global alert? *The Lancet, 393*(10172), 617–620.

Gottman, John & Gottman, Julie. (2017). The natural principles of love. *Journal of Family Theory & Review, 9*(1), 7–26.

Gough, Ethan K.; Moodie, Erica E. M.; Prendergast, Andrew J.; Johnson, Sarasa M. A.; Humphrey, Jean H.; Stoltzfus, Rebecca J.; . . . Manges, Amee R. (2014). The impact of antibiotics on growth in children in low and middle income countries: Systematic review and meta-analysis of randomised controlled trials. *BMJ, 348*, g2267.

Govindaraju, Diddahally; Atzmon, Gil & Barzilai, Nir. (2015). Genetics, lifestyle and longevity: Lessons from centenarians. *Applied & Translational Genomics, 4*(Suppl. 1), 23–32.

Grady, Denise. (2012, May 5). When illness makes a spouse a stranger. *New York Times.*

Grady, Sarah. (2017, September 26). A fresh look at homeschooling in the U.S. *NCES Blog.* Institute of Education Sciences.

Graf, Nikki. (2019, November 6). *Key findings on marriage and cohabitation in the U.S. Fact Tank.* Washington, DC: Pew Research Center.

Granqvist, Pehr & Kirkpatrick, Lee A. (2013). Religion, spirituality, and attachment. In Pargament, Kenneth I. (Ed.), *APA handbook of psychology, religion, and spirituality* (Vol. 1). American Psychological Association.

Grassetti, Stevie N.; Hubbard, Julie A.; Smith, Marissa A.; Bookhout, Megan K.; Swift, Lauren E. & Gawrysiak, Michael J. (2018). Caregivers' advice and children's bystander behaviors during bullying incidents. *Journal of Clinical Child & Adolescent Psychology, 47*(Suppl. 1), S329–S340.

Graves, Brian M.; Johnson, Tyler J.; Nishida, Robert T.; Dias, Ryan P.; Savareear, Benjamin; Harynuk, James J.; . . . Boies, Adam M. (2020). Comprehensive characterization of mainstream marijuana and tobacco smoke. *Scientific Reports, 10*(7160).

Gray, Peter B.; Garcia, Justin R. & Gesselman, Amanda N. (2019). Age-related patterns in sexual behaviors and attitudes among single U.S. Adults: An evolutionary approach. *Evolutionary Behavioral Sciences, 13*(2), 111–126.

Graybill, Emily; Self-Brown, Shannon; Lai, Betty; Vinoski, Erin; McGill, Tia & Crimmins, Daniel. (2016). Addressing disparities in parent education: Examining the effects of learn the signs/act early parent education materials on parent outcomes. *Early Childhood Education Journal, 44*(1), 31–38.

Grazioplene, Rachael G.; Ryman, Sephira G.; Gray, Jeremy R.; Rustichini, Aldo; Jung, Rex E. & DeYoung, Colin G. (2015). Subcortical intelligence: Caudate volume predicts IQ in healthy adults. *Human Brain Mapping, 36*(4), 1407–1416.

Gredebäck, Gustaf; Astor, Kim & Fawcett, Christine. (2018). Gaze following is not dependent on ostensive cues: A critical test of natural pedagogy. *Child Development, 89*(6), 2091–2098.

Green, James A.; Whitney, Pamela G. & Potegal, Michael. (2011). Screaming, yelling, whining, and crying: Categorical and intensity differences in vocal expressions of anger and sadness in children's tantrums. *Emotion, 11*(5), 1124–1133.

Green, Lorraine & Grant, Victoria. (2008). "Gagged grief and beleaguered bereavements?" An analysis of multidisciplinary theory and research relating to same sex partnership bereavement. *Sexualities, 11*(3), 275–300.

Greenfield, Emily A.; Scharlach, Andrew; Lehning, Amanda J. & Davitt, Joan K. (2012). A conceptual framework for examining the promise of the NORC program and Village models to promote aging in place. *Journal of Aging Studies, 26*(3), 273–284.

Greenough, William T.; Black, James E. & Wallace, Christopher S. (1987). Experience and brain development. *Child Development, 58*(3), 539–559.

Greenough, William T. & Volkmar, Fred R. (1973). Pattern of dendritic branching in occipital cortex of rats reared in complex environments. *Experimental Neurology, 40*(2), 491–504.

Greer, David M.; Shemie, Sam D.; Lewis, Ariane; Torrance, Sylvia; Varelas, Panayiotis; Goldenberg, Fernando D.; . . . Sung, Gene. (2020). Determination of brain death/death by neurologic criteria: The world brain death project. *JAMA, 324*(11), 1078–1097.

Gregory, Robert. (1993). *Diz: The story of Dizzy Dean and baseball during the Great Depression*. Penguin.

Greyson, Bruce. (2009). Near-death experiences and deathbed visions. In Kellehear, Allan (Ed.), *The study of dying: From autonomy to transformation* (pp. 253–275). Cambridge University Press.

Griffith, Patrick & Lopez, Oscar. (2009). Disparities in the diagnosis and treatment of Alzheimer's disease in African American and Hispanic patients: A call to action. *Generations, 33*(1), 37–46.

Griffiths, Nadine; Spence, Kaye; Loughran-Fowlds, Alison & Westrup, Bjorn. (2019). Individualised developmental care for babies and parents in the NICU: Evidence-based best practice guideline recommendations. *Early Human Development, 139*, 104840.

Grobman, Kevin H. (2008). Learning & teaching developmental psychology: Attachment theory, infancy, & infant memory development. DevPsy.

Grogan-Kaylor, Andrew; Ma, Julie & Graham-Bermann, Sandra A. (2018). The case against physical punishment. *Current Opinion in Psychology, 19*, 22–27.

Groh, Ashley M.; Narayan, Angela J.; Bakermans-Kranenburg, Marian J.; Roisman, Glenn I.; Vaughn, Brian E.; Fearon, R. M. Pasco & van IJzendoorn, Marinus H. (2017). Attachment and temperament in the early life course: A meta-analytic review. *Child Development, 88*(3), 770–795.

Groh, Ashley M.; Roisman, Glenn I.; van IJzendoorn, Marinus H.; Bakermans-Kranenburg, Marian J. & Fearon, R. Pasco. (2012). The significance of insecure and disorganized attachment for children's internalizing symptoms: A meta-analytic study. *Child Development, 83*(2), 591–610.

Grønkjær, Marie; Osler, Merete; Flensborg-Madsen, Trine; Sørensen, Holger J. & Mortensen, Erik L. (2019). Associations between education and age-related cognitive changes from early adulthood to late midlife. *Psychology and Aging, 34*(2), 177–186.

Grönqvist, Hans; Nilsson, J. Peter & Robling, Per Olof. (2014). *Childhood lead exposure and criminal behavior: Lessons from the Swedish phase-out of leaded gasoline*. Stockholm: Swedish Institute for Social Research. Working Paper 9/2014.

Gross, Magdalena H. & Wotipka, Christine Min. (2019). Students' understanding of the history of enslavement in America: Differences by race, ethnicity, and gender. *The Social Studies, 110*(5), 220–236.

Grossman, Arnold H.; Park, Jung Yeon; Frank, John A. & Russell, Stephen T. (2019). Parental responses to transgender and gender nonconforming youth: Associations with parent support, parental abuse, and youths' psychological adjustment. *Journal of Homosexuality*.

Grotevant, Harold D. (2020). Open adoption. In Wrobel, Gretchen Miller; Helder, Emily & Marr, Elisha (Eds.), *The Routledge handbook of adoption*. Routledge.

Grotevant, Harold D. & McDermott, Jennifer M. (2014). Adoption: Biological and social processes linked to adaptation. *Annual Review of Psychology, 65*, 235–265.

Grünebaum, Amos; McCullough, Laurence B.; Orosz, Brooke & Chervenak, Frank A. (2020). Neonatal mortality in the United States is related to location of birth (hospital versus home) rather than the type of birth attendant. *American Journal of Obstetrics and Gynecology, 223*(2), 254.e1–254.e8.

Grusec, Joan E.; Danyliuk, Tanya; Kil, Hali & O'Neill, David. (2017). Perspectives on parent discipline and child outcomes. *International Journal of Behavioral Development, 41*(4), 465–471.

Guassi Moreira, João F. & Telzer, Eva H. (2018). Family conflict is associated with longitudinal changes in insular-striatal functional connectivity during adolescent risk taking under maternal influence. *Developmental Science, 21*(5), e12632.

Guerra, Nancy G.; Williams, Kirk R. & Sadek, Shelly. (2011). Understanding bullying and victimization during childhood and adolescence: A mixed methods study. *Child Development, 82*(1), 295–310.

Guerri, Consuelo & Pascual, María. (2010). Mechanisms involved in the neurotoxic, cognitive, and neurobehavioral effects of alcohol consumption during adolescence. *Alcohol, 44*(1), 15–26.

Guessoum, Sélim Benjamin; Lachal, Jonathan; Radjack, Rahmeth; Carretier, Emilie; Minassian, Sevan; Benoit, Laelia & Moro, Marie Rose. (2020). Adolescent psychiatric disorders during the COVID-19 pandemic and lockdown. *Psychiatry Research, 291*(113264).

Gulia, Kamalesh K. & Kumar, Velayudhan Mohan. (2018). Sleep disorders in the elderly: A growing challenge: Sleep in elderly. *Psychogeriatrics, 18*(3), 155–165.

Güngör, Derya; Bornstein, Marc H.; De Leersnyder, Jozefien; Cote, Linda; Ceulemans, Eva & Mesquita, Batja. (2013). Acculturation of personality: A three-culture study of Japanese, Japanese Americans, and European Americans. *Journal of Cross-Cultural Psychology, 44*(5), 701–718.

Guo, Yuming; Gasparrini, Antonio; Armstrong, Ben G.; Tawatsupa, Benjawan; Tobias, Aurelio; Lavigne, Eric; . . . Tong, Shilu. (2017). Heat wave and mortality: A multicountry, multicommunity study. *Environmental Health Perspectives 125*(8).

Gutierrez-Galve, Leticia; Stein, Alan; Hanington, Lucy; Heron, Jon & Ramchandani, Paul. (2015). Paternal depression in the postnatal period and child development: Mediators and moderators. *Pediatrics, 135*(2), e339–e347.

Guyer, Amanda E.; Pérez-Edgar, Koraly & Crone, Eveline A. (2018). Opportunities for neurodevelopmental plasticity from infancy through early adulthood. *Child Development, 89*(3), 687–697.

Guyon-Harris, Katherine L.; Humphreys, Kathryn L.; Fox, Nathan A.; Nelson, Charles A. & Zeanah, Charles H. (2018). Course of disinhibited social engagement disorder from early childhood to early adolescence. *Journal of the American Academy of Child & Adolescent Psychiatry, 57*(5), 329–335.e2.

Guzman, Natalie S. de & Nishina, Adrienne. (2014). A longitudinal study of body dissatisfaction and pubertal timing in an ethnically diverse adolescent sample. *Body Image, 11*(1), 68–71.

Gypen, Laura; Vanderfaeillie, Johan; De Maeyer, Skrallan; Belenger, Laurence & Van Holen, Frank. (2017). Outcomes of children who grew up in foster care: Systematic-review. *Children and Youth Services Review, 76*, 74–83.

Habibi, Assal; Damasio, Antonio; Ilari, Beatriz; Sachs, Matthew Elliott & Damasio, Hanna. (2018a). Music training and child development: A review of recent findings from a longitudinal study. *Annals of the New York Academy of Sciences, 1423*(1), 73–81.

Habibi, Assal; Damasio, Antonio; Ilari, Beatriz; Veiga, Ryan; Joshi, Anand A.; Leahy, Richard M.; . . . Damasio, Hanna. (2018b). Childhood music training induces change in micro and macroscopic brain structure: Results from a longitudinal study. *Cerebral Cortex, 28*(12), 4336–4347.

Hagerman, Margaret A. (2020). Racial ideology and white youth: From middle childhood to adolescence. *Sociology of Race and Ethnicity, 6*(3), 319–332.

Haidt, Jonathan. (2013). *The righteous mind: Why good people are divided by politics and religion.* Vintage Books.

Haines, Simon J.; Randall, Susan E.; Terrett, Gill; Busija, Lucy; Tatangelo, Gemma; McLennan, Skye N.; . . . Rendell, Peter G. (2020). Differences in time-based task characteristics help to explain the age-prospective memory paradox. *Cognition, 202*(104305).

Hajal, Nastassia J. & Paley, Blair. (2020). Parental emotion and emotion regulation: A critical target of study for research and intervention to promote child emotion socialization. *Developmental Psychology, 56*(3), 403–417.

Hajek, André & König, Hans-Helmut. (2020). Dual sensory impairment and psychosocial factors: Findings based on a nationally representative sample. *Archives of Gerontology and Geriatrics, 91*(104234).

Halaweh, Hadeel. (2020). Correlation between health-related quality of life and hand grip strength among older adults. *Experimental Aging Research, 46*(2), 178–191.

Halberda, Justin. (2018). Logic in babies. *Science, 359*(6381), 1214–1215.

Hales, Craig M.; Carroll, Margaret D.; Fryar, Cheryl D. & Ogden, Cynthia L. (2017, October). *Prevalence of obesity among adults and youth: United States, 2015–2016.* Atlanta, GA: Centers for Disease Control and Prevention, National Center for Health Statistics.

Hall, Matthew; Forshaw, Mark & Montgomery, Catharine (Eds.). (2021). *Chemically modified minds: Substance use for cognitive enhancement.* Palgrave Macmillan.

Hall, Matthew L.; Eigsti, Inge-Marie; Bortfeld, Heather & Lillo-Martin, Diane. (2017). Auditory deprivation does not impair executive function, but language deprivation might: Evidence from a parent-report measure in deaf native signing children. *Journal of Deaf Studies and Deaf Education, 22*(1), 9–21.

Hall, William J.; Jones, Benjamin L. H.; Witkemper, Kristen D.; Collins, Tora L. & Rodgers, Grayson K. (2019). State policy on school-based sex education: A content analysis focused on sexual behaviors, relationships, and identities. *American Journal of Health Behavior, 43*(3), 506–519.

Halperin, Jeffrey M. & Healey, Dione M. (2011). The influences of environmental enrichment, cognitive enhancement, and physical exercise on brain development: Can we alter the developmental trajectory of ADHD? *Neuroscience & Biobehavioral Reviews, 35*(3), 621–634.

Hamada, Hirotaka & Matthews, Stephen G. (2019). Prenatal programming of stress responsiveness and behaviours: Progress and perspectives. *Journal of Neuroendocrinology, 31*(3), e12674.

Hambrick, David Z.; Burgoyne, Alexander P.; Macnamara, Brooke N. & Ullén, Fredrik. (2018). Toward a multifactorial model of expertise: Beyond born versus made. *Annals of the New York Academy of Sciences, 14231*(1), 284–295.

Hambrick, David Z.; Macnamara, Brooke N.; Campitelli, Guillermo; Ullén, Fredrik & Mosing, Miriam A. (2016). Beyond born versus made: A new look at expertise. *Psychology of Learning and Motivation, 64*, 1–55.

Hamerton, John L. & Evans, Jane A. (2005). Sex chromosome anomalies. In Butler, Merlin G. & Meaney, F. John (Eds.), *Genetics of developmental disabilities* (pp. 585–650). Taylor & Francis.

Hamilton, Alice. (1914). Lead poisoning in the United States. *American Journal of Public Health, 4*(6), 477–480.

Hamilton, Brady E.; Martin, Joyce A.; Osterman, Michelle J. K. & Division of Vital Statistics National Center for Health Statistics. (2020, May). *Births: Provisional data for 2019. Vital Statistics Rapid Release Report.* Hyattsville, MD: National Center for Health Statistics. 8.

Hamlat, Elissa J.; Snyder, Hannah R.; Young, Jami F. & Hankin, Benjamin L. (2019). Pubertal timing as a transdiagnostic risk for psychopathology in youth. *Clinical Psychological Science, 7*(3), 411–429.

Hamlett, Eric D.; Ledreux, Aurélie; Potter, Huntington; Chial, Heidi J.; Patterson, David; Espinosa, Joaquin M.; . . . Granholm, Ann-Charlotte. (2018). Exosomal biomarkers in Down syndrome and Alzheimer's disease. *Free Radical Biology and Medicine, 114*, 110–121.

Hamm, Jeremy M.; Chipperfield, Judith G.; Perry, Raymond P.; Parker, Patti C. & Heckhausen, Jutta. (2017). Tenacious self-reliance in health maintenance may jeopardize late life survival. *Psychology and Aging, 32*(7), 628–635.

Hamplová, Dana; Le Bourdais, Céline & Lapierre-Adamcyk, Évelyne. (2014). Is the cohabitation–marriage gap in money pooling universal? *Journal of Marriage and Family, 76*(5), 983–997.

Han, Kihye; Trinkoff, Alison M.; Storr, Carla L.; Lerner, Nancy & Yang, Bo Kyum. (2017). Variation across U.S. assisted living facilities: Admissions, resident care needs, and staffing. *Journal of Nursing Scholarship, 49*(1), 24–32.

Han, S. Duke; Olsen, Bonnie J. & Mosqueda, Laura A. (2019). Elder abuse identification and intervention. In Ravdin, Lisa D. & Katzen, Heather L. (Eds.), *Handbook on the neuropsychology of aging and dementia* (pp. 197–203). Springer.

Han, Sae Hwang; Kim, Kyungmin & Burr, Jeffrey A. (2021). Activity limitations and depressive symptoms among older couples: The moderating role of spousal care. *The Journals of Gerontology: Series B, 76*(2), 360–369.

Han, Wen-Jui. (2012). Bilingualism and academic achievement. *Child Development, 83*(1), 300–321.

Hank, Karsten & Korbmacher, Julie M. (2013). Parenthood and retirement: Gender, cohort, and welfare regime differences. *European Societies, 15*(3), 446–461.

Hanna-Attisha, Mona; LaChance, Jenny; Sadler, Richard Casey & Schnepp, Allison Champney. (2016). Elevated blood lead levels in children associated with the Flint drinking water crisis: A spatial analysis of risk and public health response. *American Journal of Public Health, 106*(2), 283–290.

Hannon, Erin E.; Schachner, Adena & Nave-Blodgett, Jessica E. (2017). Babies know bad dancing when they see it: Older but not younger infants discriminate between synchronous and asynchronous audiovisual musical displays. *Journal of Experimental Child Psychology, 159*, 159–174.

Hansen, Thomas. (2012). Parenthood and happiness: A review of folk theories versus empirical evidence. *Social Indicators Research, 108*(1), 29–64.

Hansson, Isabelle; Henning, Georg; Buratti, Sandra; Lindwall, Magnus; Kivi, Marie; Johansson, Boo & Berg, Anne Ingeborg. (2020). The role of personality in retirement adjustment: Longitudinal evidence for the effects on life satisfaction. *Journal of Personality, 88*(4), 642–658.

Hanushek, Eric A.; Piopiunik, Marc & Wiederhold, Simon. (2019). Do smarter teachers make smarter students? International evidence on teacher cognitive skills and student performance. *Education Next, 19*(2).

Hanushek, Eric A. & Woessmann, Ludger. (2015). *The knowledge capital of nations: Education and the economics of growth.* MIT Press.

Harden, K. Paige & Tucker-Drob, Elliot M. (2011). Individual differences in the development of sensation seeking and impulsivity during adolescence: Further evidence for a dual systems model. *Developmental Psychology, 47*(3), 739–746.

Hardy, Ben. (2019). Steroid hormones in social science research. In Foster, Gigi (Ed.), *Biophysical measurement in experimental social science research: Theory and practice* (pp. 105–148). Academic Press.

Hari, Riitta. (2017). From brain–environment connections to temporal dynamics and social interaction: Principles of human brain function. *Neuron, 94*(5), 1033–1039.

Harkness, Sara. (2014). Is biology destiny for the whole family? Contributions of evolutionary life history and behavior genetics to family theories. *Journal of Family Theory & Review, 6*(1), 31–34.

Harkness, Sara; Super, Charles M. & Mavridis, Caroline J. (2011). Parental ethnotheories about children's socioemotional development. In Chen, Xinyin & Rubin, Kenneth H. (Eds.), *Socioemotional development in cultural context* (pp. 73–98). Guilford Press.

Harper, Casandra E. & Yeung, Fanny. (2013). Perceptions of institutional commitment to diversity as a predictor of college students' openness to diverse perspectives. *The Review of Higher Education, 37*(1), 25–44.

Harrington, Ellie M.; Trevino, Shaina D.; Lopez, Sheila & Giuliani, Nicole R. (2020). Emotion regulation in early childhood: Implications for socioemotional and academic components of school readiness. *Emotion, 20*(1), 48–53.

Harris Insights and Analytics. (2014, February 19). *6 in 10 Americans say they or someone they know have been bullied.* New York, NY: Harris Interactive.

Harris Insights and Analytics. (2020, June). *Teen mental health.* New York, NY: Harris Interactive.

Harris, Judith R. (1998). *The nurture assumption: Why children turn out the way they do.* Free Press.

Harris, Judith R. (2002). Beyond the nurture assumption: Testing hypotheses about the child's environment. In Borkowski, John G.; Ramey, Sharon Landesman & Bristol-Power, Marie (Eds.), *Parenting and the child's world: Influences on academic, intellectual, and social-emotional development* (pp. 3–20). Erlbaum.

Harrison, Kristen; Bost, Kelly K.; McBride, Brent A.; Donovan, Sharon M.; Grigsby-Toussaint, Diana S.; Kim, Juhee; . . . Jacobsohn, Gwen Costa. (2011). Toward a developmental conceptualization of contributors to overweight and obesity in childhood: The Six-Cs model. *Child Development Perspectives, 5*(1), 50–58.

Harrison, Linda J.; Elwick, Sheena; Vallotton, Claire D. & Kappler, Gregor. (2014). Spending time with others: A time-use diary for infant-toddler child care. In Harrison, Linda J. & Sumsion, Jennifer (Eds.), *Lived spaces of infant-toddler education and care: Exploring diverse perspectives on theory, research and practice* (pp. 59–74). Springer.

Harris, Paul L. (2018). Children's understanding of death: From biology to religion. *Philosophical Transactions of the Royal Society B: Biological Sciences, 373*(1754).

Harris-Kojetin, Lauren; Sengupta, Manisha; Lendon, Jessica; Rome, Vincent; Valverde, Roberto & Caffrey, Christine. (2019). *Long-term care providers and services users in the United States, 2015–2016. National Center for Health Statistics. Vital and Health Statistics, 3*(43). Hyattsville, MD: National Center for Health Statistics.

Hart, Betty & Risley, Todd R. (1995). *Meaningful differences in the everyday experience of young American children.* P. H. Brookes.

Hart, Daniel & Van Goethem, Anne. (2017). The role of civic and political participation in successful early adulthood. In Padilla-Walker, Laura M. & Nelson, Larry J. (Eds.), *Flourishing in emerging adulthood: Positive development during the third decade of life* (pp. 139–166). Oxford University Press.

Hart, Sybil L. (2018). Jealousy and attachment: Adaptations to threat posed by the birth of a sibling. *Evolutionary Behavioral Sciences, 12*(4), 263–275.

Harter, Susan. (2012). *The construction of the self: Developmental and sociocultural foundations* (2nd ed.). Guilford Press.

Hartley, Catherine A. & Somerville, Leah H. (2015). The neuroscience of adolescent decision-making. *Current Opinion in Behavioral Sciences, 5*, 108–115.

Hartnett, Caroline Sten; Fingerman, Karen L. & Birditt, Kira S. (2018). Without the ties that bind: U.S. young adults who lack active parental relationships. *Advances in Life Course Research, 35*, 103–113.

Hassevoort, Kelsey M.; Khan, Naiman A.; Hillman, Charles H.; Kramer, Arthur F. & Cohen, Neal J. (2018). Relational memory is associated with academic achievement in preadolescent children. *Trends in Neuroscience and Education, 13*, 8–16.

Hasson, Ramzi & Fine, Jodene Goldenring. (2012). Gender differences among children with ADHD on continuous performance tests: A meta-analytic review. *Journal of Attention Disorders, 16*(3), 190–198.

Hatch, J. Amos. (2012). From theory to curriculum: Developmental theory and its relationship to curriculum and instruction in early childhood education. In File, Nancy; Mueller, Jennifer J. & Wisneski, Debora B. (Eds.), *Curriculum in early childhood education: Re-examined, rediscovered, renewed*. Routledge.

Haushofer, Johannes & Fehr, Ernst. (2014). On the psychology of poverty. *Science, 344*(6186), 862–867.

Hayden, Ceara; Bowler, Jennifer O.; Chambers, Stephanie; Freeman, Ruth; Humphris, Gerald; Richards, Derek & Cecil, Joanne E. (2013). Obesity and dental caries in children: A systematic review and meta-analysis. *Community Dentistry and Oral Epidemiology, 41*(4), 289–308.

Hayne, Harlene; Scarf, Damian & Imuta, Kana. (2015). Childhood memories. In Wright, James D. (Ed.), *International encyclopedia of the social & behavioral sciences* (2nd ed., pp. 465–470). Elsevier.

Haynie, Dana L.; Soller, Brian & Williams, Kristi. (2014). Anticipating early fatality: Friends', schoolmates' and individual perceptions of fatality on adolescent risk behaviors. *Journal of Youth and Adolescence, 43*(2), 175–192.

Hayslip, Bert & Smith, Gregory C. (Eds.). (2013). *Resilient grandparent caregivers: A strengths-based perspective*. Routledge.

Healy, Jack. (2017, June 23). Out of high school, into real life. *New York Times*.

Hein, Sascha; Tan, Mei; Aljughaiman, Abdullah & Grigorenko, Elena L. (2014). Characteristics of the home context for the nurturing of gifted children in Saudi Arabia. *High Ability Studies, 25*(1), 23–33.

Heinz, Melinda; Cone, Nicholas; Da Rosa, Grace; Bishop, Alex J. & Finchum, Tanya. (2017). Examining supportive evidence for psychosocial theories of aging within the oral history narratives of centenarians. *Societies*, 7(2).

Heitzer, Andrew M.; Piercy, Jamie C.; Peters, Brittany N.; Mattes, Allyssa M.; Klarr, Judith M.; Batton, Beau; . . . Raz, Sarah. (2020). Cumulative antenatal risk and kindergarten readiness in preterm-born preschoolers. *Journal of Abnormal Child Psychology, 48*(1), 1–12.

Hemingway, Susan J. Astley; M. Bledsoe, Julia; K. Davies, Julian; Brooks, Allison; Jirikowic, Tracy; M. Olson, Erin & C. Thorne, John. (2019). Twin study confirms virtually identical prenatal alcohol exposures can lead to markedly different fetal alcohol spectrum disorder outcomes-fetal genetics influences fetal vulnerability. *Advances in Pediatric Research, 5*(23).

Hendry, Mandy P. & Ledbetter, Andrew M. (2017). Narrating the past, enhancing the present: The associations among genealogical communication, family communication patterns, and family satisfaction. *Journal of Family Communication, 17*(2), 117–136.

Hentges, Rochelle F. & Wang, Ming-Te. (2018). Gender differences in the developmental cascade from harsh parenting to educational attainment: An evolutionary perspective. *Child Development, 89*(2), 397–413.

Herholz, Sibylle C. & Zatorre, Robert J. (2012). Musical training as a framework for brain plasticity: Behavior, function, and structure. *Neuron, 76*(3), 486–502.

Hernández, Maciel M.; Robins, Richard W.; Widaman, Keith F. & Conger, Rand D. (2017). Ethnic pride, self-esteem, and school belonging: A reciprocal analysis over time. *Developmental Psychology, 53*(12), 2384–2396.

Herschensohn, Julia R. (2007). *Language development and age*. Cambridge University Press.

Herzog, Serge. (2018). Financial aid and college persistence: Do student loans help or hurt? *Research in Higher Education, 59*(3), 273–301.

Hess, Thomas M.; Growney, Claire M. & Lothary, Allura F. (2019). Motivation moderates the impact of aging stereotypes on effort expenditure. *Psychology and Aging, 34*(1), 56–67.

Heyer, Djai B. & Meredith, Rhiannon M. (2017). Environmental toxicology: Sensitive periods of development and neurodevelopmental disorders. *NeuroToxicology, 58*, 23–41.

Hidalgo, Marco A. & Chen, Diane. (2019). Experiences of gender minority stress in cisgender parents of transgender/gender-expansive prepubertal children: A qualitative study. *Journal of Family Issues, 40*(7), 865–886.

Hill, Erica & Hageman, Jon B. (Eds.). (2016). *The archaeology of ancestors: Death, memory, and veneration*. University Press of Florida.

Hill, Holly A.; Yankey, David; Elam-Evans, Laurie D.; Singleton, James A.; Pingali, S. Cassandra & Santibanez, Tammy A. (2020, October 23). *Vaccination coverage by age 24 months among children born in 2016 and 2017—National immunization survey-child, United States, 2017–2019. Morbidity and Mortality Weekly Report, 69*(42), 1505–1511. Atlanta, GA: Centers for Disease Control and Prevention.

Hill, Sarah E.; Prokosch, Marjorie L.; DelPriore, Danielle J.; Griskevicius, Vladas & Kramer, Andrew. (2016). Low childhood socioeconomic status promotes eating in the absence of energy need. *Psychological Science, 27*(3), 354–364.

Hillman, Charles H. (2014). An introduction to the relation of physical activity to cognitive and brain health, and scholastic achievement. *Monographs of the Society for Research in Child Development, 79*(4), 1–6.

Hindman, Annemarie H.; Wasik, Barbara A. & Bradley, Donald E. (2019). How classroom conversations unfold: Exploring teacher-child exchanges during shared book reading. *Early Education and Development, 30*(4), 478–495.

Hirai, Masahiro; Muramatsu, Yukako & Nakamura, Miho. (2020). Role of the embodied cognition process in perspective-taking ability during childhood. *Child Development, 91*(1), 214–235.

Hirsh-Pasek, Kathy & Golinkoff, Roberta M. (2016, March 11). The preschool paradox: It's time to rethink our approach to early education [Review of the book *The importance of being little: What preschoolers really need from grownups*, by Erika Christakis]. *Science, 351*(6278), 1158.

Hirth, Jacqueline. (2019). Disparities in HPV vaccination rates and HPV prevalence in the United States: A review of the literature. *Human Vaccines & Immunotherapeutics, 15*(1), 146–155.

Hisler, Garrett; Twenge, Jean M. & Krizan, Zlatan. (2020). Associations between screen time and short sleep duration among adolescents varies by media type: Evidence from a cohort study. *Sleep Medicine, 66*, 92–102.

Hoare, Carol Hren. (2002). *Erikson on development in adulthood: New insights from the unpublished papers.* Oxford University Press.

Hochberg, Ze'ev & Konner, Melvin. (2020). Emerging adulthood, a pre-adult life-history stage. *Frontiers in Endocrinology, 10*(918).

Hoehl, Stefanie; Keupp, Stefanie; Schleihauf, Hanna; Mcguigan, Nicola; Buttelmann, David & Whiten, Andrew. (2019). 'Over-imitation': A review and appraisal of a decade of research. *Developmental Review, 51*, 90–108.

Hofer, Claire; Eisenberg, Nancy; Spinrad, Tracy L.; Morris, Amanda S.; Gershoff, Elizabeth; Valiente, Carlos; . . . Eggum, Natalie D. (2013). Mother-adolescent conflict: Stability, change, and relations with externalizing and internalizing behavior problems. *Social Development, 22*(2), 259–279.

Hoff, Erika. (2013). Interpreting the early language trajectories of children from low-SES and language minority homes: Implications for closing achievement gaps. *Developmental Psychology, 49*(1), 4–14.

Hoff, Erika. (2018). Bilingual development in children of immigrant families. *Child Development Perspectives, 12*(2), 80–86.

Hoffman, Jessica L.; Teale, William H. & Paciga, Kathleen A. (2014). Assessing vocabulary learning in early childhood. *Journal of Early Childhood Literacy, 14*(4), 459–481.

Hoffmann, Florian; Lee, David S. & Lemieux, Thomas. (2020). Growing income inequality in the United States and other advanced economies. *Journal of Economic Perspectives, 34*(4), 52–78.

Hogan, Andrew J. (2019). Moving away from the "medical model": The development and revision of the World Health Organization's classification of disability. *Bulletin of the History of Medicine, 93*(2), 241–269.

Höjer, Ingrid & Sjöblom, Yvonne. (2014). Voices of 65 young people leaving care in Sweden: "There is so much I need to know!". *Australian Social Work, 67*(1), 71–87.

Holahan, Carole K.; Holahan, Charles J.; Li, Xiaoyin & Chen, Yen T. (2017). Association of health-related behaviors, attitudes, and appraisals to leisure-time physical activity in middle-aged and older women. *Women & Health, 57*(2), 121–136.

Holzer, Jessica; Canavan, Maureen & Bradley, Elizabeth. (2014). County-level correlation between adult obesity rates and prevalence of dentists. *JADA, 145*(9), 932–939.

Hong, David S. & Reiss, Allan L. (2014). Cognitive and neurological aspects of sex chromosome aneuploidies. *The Lancet Neurology, 13*(3), 306–318.

Hook, Jennifer L. (2012). Working on the weekend: Fathers' time with family in the United Kingdom. *Journal of Marriage and Family, 74*(4), 631–642.

Horn, Stacey S. (2019). Sexual orientation and gender identity-based prejudice. *Child Development Perspectives, 13*(1), 21–27.

Horton, Megan K.; Kahn, Linda G.; Perera, Frederica; Barr, Dana B. & Rauh, Virginia. (2012). Does the home environment and the sex of the child modify the adverse effects of prenatal exposure to chlorpyrifos on child working memory? *Neurotoxicology and Teratology, 34*(5), 534–541.

Hostinar, Camelia E.; Nusslock, Robin & Miller, Gregory E. (2018). Future directions in the study of early-life stress and physical and emotional health: Implications of the neuroimmune network hypothesis. *Journal of Clinical Child & Adolescent Psychology, 47*(1), 142–156.

Hou, Xiao-Hui; Gong, Zhu-Qing; Wang, Liu-Ji; Zhou, Yuan & Su, Yanjie. (2020). A reciprocal and dynamic development model for the effects of siblings on children's theory of mind. *Frontiers in Psychology, 11*(554023).

Houghton, John S. M.; Nickinson, Andrew T. O.; Bridgwood, Bernadeta; Nduwayo, Sarah; Pepper, Coral J.; Rayt, Harjeet S.; . . . Sayers, Rob D. (2021). Prevalence of cognitive impairment in individuals with vascular surgical pathology: A systematic review and meta-analysis. *European Journal of Vascular & Endovascular Surgery, 61*(4), 664–674.

Howard, Kimberly S. (2010). Paternal attachment, parenting beliefs and children's attachment. *Early Child Development and Care, 180*(1/2), 157–171.

Hoyme, H. Eugene; Kalberg, Wendy O.; Elliott, Amy J.; Blankenship, Jason; Buckley, David; Marais, Anna-Susan; . . . May, Philip A. (2016). Updated clinical guidelines for diagnosing fetal alcohol spectrum disorders. *Pediatrics, 138*(2), e20154256.

Hoyne, Clara & Egan, Suzanne M. (2019). Shared book reading in early childhood: A review of influential factors and developmental benefits. *An Leanbh Og, 12*(1), 77–92.

Hrdy, Sarah B. (2009). *Mothers and others: The evolutionary origins of mutual understanding.* Harvard University Press.

Hsu, William C.; Araneta, Maria Rosario G.; Kanaya, Alka M.; Chiang, Jane L. & Fujimoto, Wilfred. (2015). BMI cut points to identify at-risk Asian Americans for type 2 diabetes screening. *Diabetes Care, 38*(1), 150–158.

Hu, Youna; Shmygelska, Alena; Tran, David; Eriksson, Nicholas; Tung, Joyce Y. & Hinds, David A. (2016). GWAS of 89,283 individuals identifies genetic variants associated with self-reporting of being a morning person. *Nature Communications, 7*(10448).

Huang, Jidong; Duan, Zongshuan; Kwok, Julian; Binns, Steven; Vera, Lisa E.; Kim, Yoonsang; . . . Emery, Sherry L. (2019). Vaping versus JUULing: How the extraordinary growth and marketing of JUUL transformed the US retail e-cigarette market. *Tobacco Control, 28*(2), 146.

Huang, Yu-Wen Alvin; Zhou, Bo; Wernig, Marius & Südhof, Thomas C. (2017). ApoE2, ApoE3, and ApoE4 differentially stimulate APP transcription and Aβ secretion. *Cell, 168*(3), 427–441.e21.

Hughes, Karen; Bellis, Mark A.; Hardcastle, Katherine A.; Sethi, Dinesh; Butchart, Alexander; Mikton, Christopher; . . . Dunne, Michael P. (2017). The effect of multiple adverse childhood experiences on health: A systematic review and meta-analysis. *The Lancet Public Health, 2*(8), e356–e366.

Huguley, James P.; Wang, Ming-Te; Vasquez, Ariana C. & Guo, Jiesi. (2019). Parental ethnic–racial socialization practices and the construction of children of color's ethnic–racial identity: A research synthesis and meta-analysis. *Psychological Bulletin, 145*(5), 437–458.

Hülür, Gizem; Wolf, Henrike; Riese, Florian & Theill, Nathan. (2019). Cognitive change at the end of life in nursing home residents: Differential trajectories of terminal decline. *Gerontology, 65*(1), 57–67.

Hurwitz, Lisa B. & Schmitt, Kelly L. (2020). Raising readers with Ready to Learn: A six-year follow-up to an early educational computer game intervention. *Computers in Human Behavior, 104*(106176).

Hussar, Bill; Zhang, Jijun; Hein, Sarah; Wang, Ke; Roberts, Ashley; Cui, Jiashan; . . . Dilig, Rita. (2020). *The Condition of Education 2020.* Washington, DC: National Center for Education Statistics. NCES 2020-144.

Huynh, Tai; Sava, Nathalie; Hahn-Goldberg, Shoshana; Recknagel, Jen; Bogoch, Isaac I.; Brown, Kevin A.; . . . Brown, Adalsteinn D. (2021). *Mobile on-site COVID-19 vaccination of naturally occurring retirement communities by neighbourhood risk in Toronto. Science briefs of the Ontario COVID-19 science advisory table, 2*(14). Ontario COVID-19 Science Advisory Table.

Hviid, Anders; Hansen, Jørgen Vinsløv; Frisch, Morten & Melbye, Mads. (2019). Measles, mumps, rubella vaccination and autism: A nationwide cohort study. *Annals of Internal Medicine, 170*(8), 513–520.

Hyde, Janet S. (2016). Sex and cognition: Gender and cognitive functions. *Current Opinion in Neurobiology, 38*, 53–56.

Hyde, Janet Shibley; Bigler, Rebecca S.; Joel, Daphna; Tate, Charlotte Chucky & van Anders, Sari M. (2019). The future of sex and gender in psychology: Five challenges to the gender binary. *American Psychologist, 74*(2), 171–193.

Hyson, Marilou & Douglass, Anne L. (2019). More than academics: Supporting the whole child. In Brown, Christopher P.; McMullen, Mary Benson & File, Nancy (Eds.), *The Wiley handbook of early childhood care and education* (pp. 279–300). Wiley.

Inceoglu, Ilke; Segers, Jesse & Bartram, Dave. (2012). Age-related differences in work motivation. *Journal of Occupational and Organizational Psychology, 75*(2), 300–329.

India State-Level Disease Burden Initiative Malnutrition Collaborators. (2019). The burden of child and maternal malnutrition and trends in its indicators in the states of India: The Global Burden of Disease Study 1990–2017. *The Lancet Child & Adolescent Health, 3*(12), 855–870.

Inhelder, Bärbel & Piaget, Jean. (1958). *The growth of logical thinking from childhood to adolescence: An essay on the construction of formal operational structures.* Basic.

Inhelder, Bärbel & Piaget, Jean. (2013a). *The early growth of logic in the child: Classification and seriation.* Routledge.

Inhelder, Bärbel & Piaget, Jean. (2013b). *The growth of logical thinking from childhood to adolescence: An essay on the construction of formal operational structures.* Routledge.

Insel, Thomas R. (2014). Mental disorders in childhood: Shifting the focus from behavioral symptoms to neurodevelopmental trajectories. *JAMA, 311*(17), 1727–1728.

Institute of Medicine. (2000). *To err is human: Building a safer health system.* The National Academies Press.

Iorio, Marilena V. & Palmieri, Dario. (2019). Editorial: From "junk DNA" to clinically relevant tools for cancer diagnosis, staging, and tailored therapies: The incredible case of non-coding RNAs. *Frontiers in Oncology, 9*(389).

Iotti, Nathalie Ophelia; Thornberg, Robert; Longobardi, Claudio & Jungert, Tomas. (2020). Early adolescents' emotional and behavioral difficulties, student-teacher relationships, and motivation to defend in bullying incidents. *Child & Youth Care Forum, 49*(1), 59–75.

Iyengar, Shanto. (2021). *Fear and loathing in American politics.* John S. and James L. Knight Foundation.

Jackson, Jeffrey B.; Miller, Richard B.; Oka, Megan & Henry, Ryan G. (2014). Gender differences in marital satisfaction: A meta-analysis. *Journal of Marriage and Family, 76*(1), 105–129.

Jackson, James C.; Pandharipande, Pratik P.; Girard, Timothy D.; Brummel, Nathan E.; Thompson, Jennifer L.; Hughes, Christopher G.; . . . Ely, E. Wesley. (2014a). Depression, post-traumatic stress disorder, and functional disability in survivors of critical illness in the BRAIN-ICU study: A longitudinal cohort study. *The Lancet Respiratory Medicine, 2*(5), 369–379.

Jackson, James C.; Santoro, Michael J.; Ely, Taylor M.; Boehm, Leanne; Kiehl, Amy L.; Anderson, Lindsay S. & Ely, E. Wesley. (2014b). Improving patient care through the prism of psychology: Application of Maslow's hierarchy to sedation, delirium, and early mobility in the intensive care unit. *Journal of Critical Care, 29*(3), 438–444.

Jambon, Marc; Madigan, Sheri; Plamondon, André; Daniel, Ella & Jenkins, Jennifer M. (2019a). The development of empathic concern in siblings: A reciprocal influence model. *Child Development, 90*(5), 1598–1613.

Jambon, Marc; Madigan, Sheri; Plamondon, André & Jenkins, Jennifer. (2019b). Developmental trajectories of physical aggression and prosocial behavior in early childhood: Family antecedents and psychological correlates. *Developmental Psychology, 55*(6), 1211–1225.

Jambon, Marc & Smetana, Judith G. (2014). Moral complexity in middle childhood: Children's evaluations of necessary harm. *Developmental Psychology, 50*(1), 22–33.

Jankovic, Joseph. (2018). Parkinson's disease tremors and serotonin. *Brain, 141*(3), 624–626.

Janse, Benjamin; Huijsman, Robbert; de Kuyper, Ruben Dennis Maurice & Fabbricotti, Isabelle Natalina. (2014). The effects of an integrated care intervention for the frail elderly on informal caregivers: A quasi-experimental study. *BMC Geriatrics, 14*(1).

Jappens, Maaike. (2018). Children's relationships with grandparents in married and in shared and sole physical custody families. *Journal of Divorce & Remarriage, 59*(5), 359–371.

Jarcho, Johanna M.; Fox, Nathan A.; Pine, Daniel S.; Etkin, Amit; Leibenluft, Ellen; Shechner, Tomer & Ernst, Monique. (2013). The neural correlates of emotion-based cognitive control in adults with early childhood behavioral inhibition. *Biological Psychology, 92*(2), 306–314.

Jaschke, Artur C.; Honing, Henkjan & Scherder, Erik J. A. (2018). Longitudinal analysis of music education on executive functions in primary school children. *Frontiers in Neuroscience, 12*(103).

Jedlicska, Nana; Srnová, Dagmara; Scheide, Laura; Wijnen-Meijer, Marjo; Gartmeier, Martin & Berberat, Pascal O. (2021). Medical trainees' experiences with dying and death. *OMEGA, 83*(1), 64–83.

Jennings, Sue & Holmwood, Clive (Eds.). (2020). *Routledge international handbook of play, therapeutic play and play therapy.* Routledge.

Jeromin, Andreas & Bowser, Robert. (2017). Biomarkers in neurodegenerative diseases. In Beart, Philip; Robinson, Michael; Rattray, Marcus & Maragakis, Nicholas J. (Eds.), *Neurodegenerative diseases: Pathology, mechanisms, and potential therapeutic targets* (pp. 491–528). Springer.

Jimerson, Shane R.; Burns, Matthew K. & VanDerHeyden, Amanda M. (Eds.). (2016). *Handbook of response to intervention: The science and practice of multi-tiered systems of support.* Springer.

Jin, Huijuan; Hong, Candong; Chen, Shengcai; Zhou, Yifan; Wang, Yong; Mao, Ling; . . . Hu, Bo. (2020). Consensus for prevention and management of coronavirus disease 2019 (COVID-19) for neurologists. *Stroke and Vascular Neurology, 5*(2).

Joel, Daphna; Berman, Zohar; Tavor, Ido; Wexler, Nadav; Gaber, Olga; Stein, Yaniv; . . . Assaf, Yaniv. (2015). Sex beyond the genitalia: The human brain mosaic. *Proceedings of the National Academy of Sciences, 112*(50), 15468–15473.

Johansen, Jennifer Drummond & Varvin, Sverre. (2020). Negotiating identity at the intersection of family legacy and present time life conditions: A qualitative exploration of central issues connected to identity and belonging in the lives of children of refugees. *Journal of Adolescence, 80*, 1–9.

Johns, Michelle M.; Lowry, Richard; Haderxhanaj, Laura T.; Rasberry, Catherine N.; Robin, Leah; Scales, Lamont; . . . Suarez, Nicolas A. (2020, August 21). *Trends in violence victimization and suicide risk by sexual identity among high school students—Youth risk behavior survey, United States, 2015–2019. Morbidity and Mortality Weekly Report, 69*(Suppl. 1), 19–27. Atlanta, GA: Centers for Disease Control and Prevention.

Johnson, James E. & Wu, Viana Mei-Hsuan. (2019). Perspectives on play in early childhood care and education. In Brown, Christopher P.; McMullen, Mary Benson & File, Nancy (Eds.), *The Wiley handbook of early childhood care and education* (pp. 79–98). Wiley.

Johnson, Katharine; Caskey, Melinda; Rand, Katherine; Tucker, Richard & Vohr, Betty. (2014). Gender differences in adult-infant communication in the first months of life. *Pediatrics, 134*(6), e1603–e1610.

Johnson, Mark H. & de Haan, Michelle. (2015). *Developmental cognitive neuroscience: An introduction* (4th ed.). Wiley.

Jones, Christopher M.; Merrick, Melissa T. & Houry, Debra E. (2020). Identifying and preventing adverse childhood experiences: Implications for clinical practice. *JAMA, 323*(1), 25–26.

Jones, Catherine R. G.; Simonoff, Emily; Baird, Gillian; Pickles, Andrew; Marsden, Anita J. S.; Tregay, Jenifer; . . . Charman, Tony. (2018). The association between theory of mind, executive function, and the symptoms of autism spectrum disorder. *Autism Research, 11*(1), 95–109.

Jong, Jonathan; Ross, Robert; Philip, Tristan; Chang, Si-Hua; Simons, Naomi & Halberstadt, Jamin. (2018). The religious correlates of death anxiety: A systematic review and meta-analysis. *Religion, Brain & Behavior, 8*(1), 4–20.

Jorm, Anthony F. (2000). Does old age reduce the risk of anxiety and depression? A review of epidemiological studies across the adult life span. *Psychological Medicine, 30*(1), 11–22.

Joseph, Michelle A.; O'Connor, Thomas G.; Briskman, Jacqueline A.; Maughan, Barbara & Scott, Stephen. (2014). The formation of secure new attachments by children who were maltreated: An observational study of adolescents in foster care. *Development and Psychopathology, 26*(1), 67–80.

Julian, Megan M. (2013). Age at adoption from institutional care as a window into the lasting effects of early experiences. *Clinical Child and Family Psychology Review, 16*(2), 101–145.

Jung, Courtney. (2015). *Lactivism: How feminists and fundamentalists, hippies and yuppies, and physicians and politicians made breastfeeding big business and bad policy.* Basic.

Juster, Robert-Paul; Russell, Jennifer J.; Almeida, Daniel & Picard, Martin. (2016). Allostatic load and comorbidities: A mitochondrial, epigenetic, and evolutionary perspective. *Development and Psychopathology, 28*(4), 1117–1146.

Juvonen, Jaana & Graham, Sandra. (2014). Bullying in schools: The power of bullies and the plight of victims. *Annual Review of Psychology, 65*, 159–185.

Kaafarani, Haytham M. A.; Han, Kelsey; El Moheb, Mohamad; Kongkaewpaisan, Napaporn; Jia, Zhenyi; El Hechi, Majed W.; . . . Lillemoe, Keith. (2020). Opioids after surgery in the United States versus the rest of the world: The International Patterns of Opioid Prescribing (IPOP) multicenter study. *Annals of Surgery, 272*(6), 879–886.

Kahana, Eva; Bhatta, Tirth; Lovegreen, Loren D.; Kahana, Boaz & Midlarsky, Elizabeth. (2013). Altruism, helping, and volunteering: Pathways to well-being in late life. *Journal of Aging and Health, 25*(1), 159–187.

Kail, Robert V. (2013). Influences of credibility of testimony and strength of statistical evidence on children's and adolescents' reasoning. *Journal of Experimental Child Psychology, 116*(3), 747–754.

Kalanithi, Paul. (2016). *When breath becomes air.* Random House.

Kalaria, Raj N. (2018). The pathology and pathophysiology of vascular dementia. *Neuropharmacology, 134,* 226–239.

Kallio, Eeva K. (2020). From multiperspective to contextual integrative thinking in adulthood. In Kallio, Eeva K. (Ed.), *Development of adult thinking: Interdisciplinary perspectives on cognitive development and adult learning.* Routledge.

Kan, Har Ye; Forsyth, Ann & Molinsky, Jennifer. (2020). Measuring the built environment for aging in place: A review of neighborhood audit tools. *Journal of Planning Literature, 35*(2), 180–194.

Kandler, Christian. (2012). Nature and nurture in personality development: The case of neuroticism and extraversion. *Current Directions in Psychological Science, 21*(5), 290–296.

Kang, Hye-Kyung. (2014). Influence of culture and community perceptions on birth and perinatal care of immigrant women: Doulas' perspective. *The Journal of Perinatal Education, 23*(1), 25–32.

Kapetanovic, Sabina; Rothenberg, W. Andrew; Lansford, Jennifer E.; Bornstein, Marc H.; Chang, Lei; Deater-Deckard, Kirby; . . . Bacchini, Dario. (2020). Cross-cultural examination of links between parent–adolescent communication and adolescent psychological problems in 12 cultural groups. *Journal of Youth and Adolescence, 49,* 1225–1244.

Karlson, Kristian Bernt. (2019). College as equalizer? Testing the selectivity hypothesis. *Social Science Research, 80,* 216–229.

Karlsson, Omar; De Neve, Jan-Walter & Subramanian, S.V. (2019). Weakening association of parental education: Analysis of child health outcomes in 43 low- and middle-income countries. *International Journal of Epidemiology, 48*(1), 83–97.

Karmiloff-Smith, Annette. (2010). A developmental perspective on modularity. In Glatzeder, Britt; Goel, Vinod & Müller, Albrecht (Eds.), *Towards a theory of thinking* (pp. 179–187). Springer.

Karnatovskaia, Lioudmila V.; Gajic, Ognjen; Bienvenu, O. Joseph; Stevenson, Jennifer E. & Needham, Dale M. (2015). A holistic approach to the critically ill and Maslow's hierarchy. *Journal of Critical Care, 30*(1), 210–211.

Kärtner, Joscha; Keller, Heidi & Yovsi, Relindis D. (2010). Mother–infant interaction during the first 3 months: The emergence of culture-specific contingency patterns. *Child Development, 81*(2), 540–554.

Kauffman, James M.; Anastasiou, Dimitris & Maag, John W. (2017). Special education at the crossroad: An identity crisis and the need for a scientific reconstruction. *Exceptionality, 25*(2), 139–155.

Kaufman, Jean-Marc & Lapauw, Bruno. (2020). Role of testosterone in cognition and mobility of aging men. *Andrology, 8*(6), 1567–1579.

Kauffman, Jeffery. (2013). Culture, socialization, and traumatic death. In Meagher, David K. & Balk, David E. (Eds.), *Handbook of thanatology: The essential body of knowledge for the study of death, dying, and bereavement* (2nd ed.). Routledge.

Kaur, Arshdeep. (2019). My child transformed me: Reflections of involved fathers. In Sriram, Rajalakshmi (Ed.), *Fathering in India* (pp. 141–152). Springer.

Kavanaugh, Robert D. (2011). Origins and consequences of social pretend play. In Pellegrini, Anthony D. (Ed.), *The Oxford handbook of the development of play* (pp. 296–307). Oxford University Press.

Kealy, David & Ogrodniczuk, John S. (Eds.). (2019). *Contemporary psychodynamic psychotherapy: Evolving clinical practice.* Academic Press.

Kearney, Christopher A.; Sanmartín, Ricardo & Gonzálvez, Carolina. (2020). The School Climate and Academic Mindset Inventory (SCAMI): Confirmatory factor analysis and invariance across demographic groups. *Frontiers in Psychology, 11*(2061).

Keating, Nancy L.; Herrinton, Lisa J.; Zaslavsky, Alan M.; Liu, Liyan & Ayanian, John Z. (2006). Variations in hospice use among cancer patients. *Journal of the National Cancer Institute, 98*(15), 1053–1059.

Keck, Carson & Taylor, Marian. (2018). Emerging research on the implications of hormone replacement therapy on coronary heart disease. *Current Atherosclerosis Reports, 20*(12).

Kecklund, Göran & Axelsson, John. (2016). Health consequences of shift work and insufficient sleep. *BMJ, 355.*

Keers, Robert & Pluess, Michael. (2017). Childhood quality influences genetic sensitivity to environmental influences across adulthood: A life-course Gene × Environment interaction study. *Development And Psychopathology, 29*(5), 1921–1933.

Keller, Heidi; Borke, Jörn; Chaudhary, Nandita; Lamm, Bettina & Kleis, Astrid. (2010). Continuity in parenting strategies: A cross-cultural comparison. *Journal of Cross-Cultural Psychology, 41*(3), 391–409.

Kelly, John. (2005). *The great mortality: An intimate history of the Black Death, the most devastating plague of all time.* HarperCollins.

Kelly, John R. (1993). *Activity and aging: Staying involved in later life.* Sage.

Kempe, Ruth S. & Kempe, C. Henry. (1978). *Child abuse.* Harvard University Press.

Kemper, Susan. (2015). Language production in late life. In Gerstenberg, Annette & Voeste, Anja (Eds.), *Language development: The lifespan perspective* (pp. 59–75). John Benjamins.

Kempermann, Gerd; Gage, Fred H.; Aigner, Ludwig; Song, Hongjun; Curtis, Maurice A.; Thuret, Sandrine; . . . Frisén, Jonas. (2018). Human adult neurogenesis: Evidence and remaining questions. *Cell Stem Cell, 23*(1), 25–30.

Kempermann, Gerd; Song, Hongjun & Gage, Fred H. (2015). Neurogenesis in the adult hippocampus. *Cold Spring Harbor Perspectives in Biology, 7,* a018812.

Kendall-Taylor, Nathaniel; Lindland, Eric; O'Neil, Moira & Stanley, Kate. (2014). Beyond prevalence: An explanatory approach to reframing child maltreatment in the United Kingdom. *Child Abuse & Neglect, 38*(5), 810–821.

Kenrick, Douglas T.; Griskevicius, Vladas; Neuberg, Steven L. & Schaller, Mark. (2010). Renovating the pyramid of needs: Contemporary extensions built upon ancient foundations. *Perspectives on Psychological Science, 5*(3), 292–314.

Kern, Ben D.; Graber, Kim C.; Shen, Sa; Hillman, Charles H. & McLoughlin, Gabriella. (2018). Association of school-based physical activity opportunities, socioeconomic status, and third-grade reading. *Journal of School Health, 88*(1), 34–43.

Kersken, Verena; Zuberbühler, Klaus & Gomez, Juan-Carlos. (2017). Listeners can extract meaning from non-linguistic infant vocalisations cross-culturally. *Scientific Reports, 7.*

Khosla, Sundeep; Farr, Joshua N.; Tchkonia, Tamara & Kirkland, James L. (2020). The role of cellular senescence in ageing and endocrine disease. *Nature Reviews Endocrinology, 16*(5), 263–275.

Kidd, Celeste; Palmeri, Holly & Aslin, Richard N. (2013). Rational snacking: Young children's decision-making on the marshmallow task is moderated by beliefs about environmental reliability. *Cognition, 126*(1), 109–114.

Killen, Melanie & Smetana, Judith G. (Eds.). (2014). *Handbook of moral development* (2nd ed.). Psychology Press.

Kim, BoRam; Cai, Yurun & Aronowitz, Teri. (2020). How do acculturation, maternal connectedness, and mother-daughter sexual communication affect Asian American daughters' sexual initiation. *Pacific Island Nursing Journal, 5*(1).

Kim, Hojin I. & Johnson, Scott P. (2013). Do young infants prefer an infant-directed face or a happy face? *International Journal of Behavioral Development, 37*(2), 125–130.

Kim, Su-Mi & Kim, Jong-Soo. (2017). A review of mechanisms of implantation. *Development & Reproduction, 21*(4), 351–359.

Kim-Spoon, Jungmeen; Deater-Deckard, Kirby; Brieant, Alexis; Lauharatanahirun, Nina; Lee, Jacob & King-Casas, Brooks. (2019). Brains of a feather flocking together? Peer and individual neurobehavioral risks for substance use across adolescence. *Development and Psychopathology, 31*(5), 1661–1674.

Kim-Spoon, Jungmeen; Longo, Gregory S. & McCullough, Michael E. (2012). Parent-adolescent relationship quality as a moderator for the influences of parents' religiousness on adolescents' religiousness and adjustment. *Journal of Youth and Adolescence, 41*(12), 1576–1587.

King, Christian. (2018). Food insecurity and child behavior problems in fragile families. *Economics and Human Biology, 28*, 14–22.

Kinney, Hannah C. & Thach, Bradley T. (2009). The sudden infant death syndrome. *New England Journal of Medicine, 361*, 795–805.

Kirk, Elizabeth; Howlett, Neil; Pine, Karen J. & Fletcher, Ben. (2013). To sign or not to sign? The impact of encouraging infants to gesture on infant language and maternal mind-mindedness. *Child Development, 84*(2), 574–590.

Kirkham, Julie Ann & Kidd, Evan. (2017). The effect of Steiner, Montessori, and National Curriculum Education upon children's pretence and creativity. *Journal of Creative Behavior, 51*(1), 20–34.

Kitayama, Shinobu; Berg, Martha K. & Chopik, William J. (2020). Culture and well-being in late adulthood: Theory and evidence. *American Psychologist, 75*(4), 567–576.

Klaczynski, Paul A. (2011). Age differences in understanding precedent-setting decisions and authorities' responses to violations of deontic rules. *Journal of Experimental Child Psychology, 109*(1), 1–24.

Klaczynski, Paul A. & Felmban, Wejdan S. (2014). Heuristics and biases during adolescence: Developmental reversals and individual differences. In Markovits, Henry (Ed.), *The developmental psychology of reasoning and decision-making* (pp. 84–111). Psychology Press.

Klaczynski, Paul A.; Felmban, Wejdan S. & Kole, James. (2020). Gender intensification and gender generalization biases in pre-adolescents, adolescents, and emerging adults. *British Journal of Developmental Psychology, 38*(3), 415–433.

Klass, Dennis & Steffen, Edith Maria (Eds.). (2017). *Continuing bonds in bereavement: New directions for research and practice.* Routledge.

Klaus, Marshall H. & Kennell, John H. (1976). *Maternal-infant bonding: The impact of early separation or loss on family development.* Mosby.

Klein, Denise; Mok, Kelvin; Chen, Jen-Kai & Watkins, Kate E. (2014). Age of language learning shapes brain structure: A cortical thickness study of bilingual and monolingual individuals. *Brain and Language, 131*, 20–24.

Klein, Stanley B. (2012). The two selves: The self of conscious experience and its brain. In Leary, Mark R. & Tangney, June Price (Eds.), *Handbook of self and identity* (pp. 617–637). Guilford Press.

Klein, Zoe A. & Romeo, Russell D. (2013). Changes in hypothalamic–pituitary–adrenal stress responsiveness before and after puberty in rats. *Hormones and Behavior, 64*(2), 357–363.

Klinger, Laura G.; Dawson, Geraldine; Burner, Karen & Crisler, Megan. (2014). Autism spectrum disorder. In Mash, Eric J. & Barkley, Russell A. (Eds.), *Child psychopathology* (3rd ed., pp. 531–572). Guilford Press.

Ko, Ahra; Pick, Cari M.; Kwon, Jung Yul; Pick, Cari M.; Kwon, Jung Yul; Barlev, Michael; . . . Kenrick, Douglas T. (2020). Family matters: Rethinking the psychology of human social motivation. *Perspectives on Psychological Science, 15*(1), 173–201.

Kochanek, Kenneth D.; Murphy, Sherry L.; Xu, Jiaquan & Arias, Elizabeth. (2019, June 24). *Deaths: Final data for 2017. National Vital Statistics Reports, 68*(9). Hyattsville, MD: National Center for Health Statistics.

Kochel, Karen P.; Ladd, Gary W.; Bagwell, Catherine L. & Yabko, Brandon A. (2015). Bully/victim profiles' differential risk for worsening peer acceptance: The role of friendship. *Journal of applied developmental psychology, 41*, 38–45.

Kohlberg, Lawrence. (1963). The development of children's orientations toward a moral order: I. Sequence in the development of moral thought. *Vita Humana, 6*(1/2), 11–33.

Kolb, Bryan; Harker, Allonna & Gibb, Robbin. (2017). Principles of plasticity in the developing brain. *Developmental Medicine & Child Neurology, 59*(12), 1218–1223.

Kolb, Bryan; Whishaw, Ian Q. & Teskey, G. Campbell. (2019). *An introduction to brain and behavior* (6th ed.). Worth.

Komisar, Erica. (2017). *Being there: Why prioritizing motherhood in the first three years matters.* TarcherPerigee.

Konner, Melvin. (2010). *The evolution of childhood: Relationships, emotion, mind.* Harvard University Press.

Konner, Melvin. (2016). Hunter gatherer infancy and childhood in the context of human evolution. In Crittenden, Alyssa N. & Meehan, Courtney L. (Eds.), *Childhood: Origins, evolution, and implications.* University of New Mexico Press.

Konner, Melvin. (2018). Nonmaternal care: A half-century of research. *Physiology & Behavior, 193*(Part A), 179–186.

Kono, Yumi; Yonemoto, Naohiro; Nakanishi, Hidehiko; Kusuda, Satoshi & Fujimura, Masanori. (2018). Changes in survival and neurodevelopmental outcomes of infants born at <25 weeks' gestation: A retrospective observational study in tertiary centres in Japan. *BMJ Paediatrics Open, 2*(1), e000211.

Konstam, Varda. (2015). *Emerging and young adulthood: Multiple perspectives, diverse narratives*. Springer.

Korber, Maïlys & Oesch, Daniel. (2019). Vocational versus general education: Employment and earnings over the life course in Switzerland. *Advances in Life Course Research, 40*, 1–13.

Kordas, Katarzyna; Burganowski, Rachael; Roy, Aditi; Peregalli, Fabiana; Baccino, Valentina; Barcia, Elizabeth; . . . Queirolo, Elena I. (2018). Nutritional status and diet as predictors of children's lead concentrations in blood and urine. *Environment International, 111*, 43–51.

Koress, Cody M.; Jones, Mark R. & Kaye, Alan David. (2019). Development of pain behavior in the fetus and newborn. In Abd-Elsayed, Alaa (Ed.), *Pain* (pp. 53–55). Springer.

Koretz, Daniel. (2017). *The testing charade: Pretending to make schools better.* University of Chicago Press.

Kornienko, Olga; Ha, Thao & Dishion, Thomas J. (2020). Dynamic pathways between rejection and antisocial behavior in peer networks: Update and test of confluence model. *Development and Psychopathology, 32*(1), 175–188.

Korte, J.; Bohlmeijer, E. T.; Cappeliez, P.; Smit, F. & Westerhof, G. J. (2012). Life review therapy for older adults with moderate depressive symptomatology: A pragmatic randomized controlled trial. *Psychological Medicine, 42*(6), 1163–1173.

Kosminsky, Phyllis. (2017). Working with continuing bonds from an attachment theoretical perspective. In Klass, Dennis & Steffen, Edith Maria (Eds.), *Continuing bonds in bereavement: New directions for research and practice*. Routledge.

Koster-Hale, Jorie & Saxe, Rebecca. (2013). Functional neuroimaging of theory of mind. In Baron-Cohen, Simon; Tager-Flusberg, Helen & Lombardo, Michael (Eds.), *Understanding other minds: Perspectives from developmental social neuroscience* (3rd ed., pp. 132–163). Oxford University Press.

Kostović, I.; Sedmak, G. & Judaš, M. (2019). Neural histology and neurogenesis of the human fetal and infant brain. *NeuroImage, 188*, 743–773.

Kozhimannil, Katy B. & Kim, Helen. (2014). Maternal mental illness. *Science, 345*(6198), 755.

Kral, Michael J. (2019). *The idea of suicide: Contagion, imitation, and cultural diffusion*. Routledge.

Kramer, Stephanie. (2020, December 7). *Polygamy is rare around the world and mostly confined to a few regions. Fact Tank.* Washington, DC: Pew Research Center.

Krampe, Ralf T. & Charness, Neil. (2018). Aging and expertise. In Ericsson, K. Anders; Hoffman, Robert R.; Kozbelt, Aaron & Williams, A. Mark (Eds.), *The Cambridge handbook of expertise and expert performance* (pp. 835–856). Cambridge University Press.

Kraus, Nina & White-Schwoch, Travis. (2020). Listening in on the listening brain. *The Hearing Journal, 73*(7), 46.

Krause, Elizabeth D.; Vélez, Clorinda E.; Woo, Rebecca; Hoffmann, Brittany; Freres, Derek R.; Abenavoli, Rachel M. & Gillham, Jane E. (2018). Rumination, depression, and gender in early adolescence: A longitudinal study of a bidirectional model. *Journal of Early Adolescence, 38*(7), 923–946.

Kreager, Derek A.; Molloy, Lauren E.; Moody, James & Feinberg, Mark E. (2016a). Friends first? The peer network origins of adolescent dating. *Journal of Research on Adolescence, 26*(2), 257–269.

Kreager, Derek A.; Staff, Jeremy; Gauthier, Robin; Lefkowitz, Eva S. & Feinberg, Mark E. (2016b). The double standard at sexual debut: Gender, sexual behavior and adolescent peer acceptance. *Sex Roles, 75*, 377–392.

Krisberg, Kim. (2014). Public health messaging: How it is said can influence behaviors: Beyond the facts. *The Nation's Health, 44*(6), 1, 20.

Kroger, Jane & Marcia, James E. (2011). The identity statuses: Origins, meanings, and interpretations. In Schwartz, Seth J.; Luyckx, Koen & Vignoles, Vivian L. (Eds.), *Handbook of identity theory and research* (pp. 31–53). Springer.

Krueger, Robert F. & Eaton, Nicholas R. (2015). Transdiagnostic factors of mental disorders. *World Psychiatry, 14*(1), 27–29.

Krzych-Fałta, Edyta; Furmańczyk, Konrad; Piekarska, Barbara; Raciborski, Filip; Tomaszewska, Aneta; Walkiewicz, Artur; . . . Samoliński, Bolesław Krzysztof. (2018). Extent of protective or allergy-inducing effects in cats and dogs. *Annals of Agricultural and Environmental Medicine, 25*(2), 268–273.

Kubin, Laura. (2019). Is there a resurgence of vaccine preventable diseases in the U.S.? *Journal of Pediatric Nursing, 44*, 115–118.

Kübler-Ross, Elisabeth. (1975). *Death: The final stage of growth*. Prentice-Hall.

Kübler-Ross, Elisabeth. (1997). *On death and dying*. Scribner.

Kübler-Ross, Elisabeth & Kessler, David. (2005). *On grief and grieving: Finding the meaning of grief through the five stages of loss*. Scribner.

Kuczewski, Mark G. (2019). Everything I really needed to know to be a clinical ethicist, I learned from Elisabeth Kübler-Ross. *The American Journal of Bioethics, 19*(12), 13–18.

Kuete, Victor (Ed.) (2017). *Medicinal spices and vegetables from Africa: Therapeutic potential against metabolic, inflammatory, infectious and systemic diseases*. Academic Press.

Kuhn, H. Georg; Toda, Tomohisa & Gage, Fred H. (2018). Adult hippocampal neurogenesis: A coming-of-age story. *Journal of Neuroscience, 38*(49), 10401–10410.

Kumar, Soryan; Khurana, Aditya; Haglin, Jack M.; Hidlay, Douglas T.; Neville, Kevin; Daniels, Alan H. & Eltorai, Adam E. M. (2020). Trends in diagnostic imaging Medicare reimbursements: 2007 to 2019. *Journal of the American College of Radiology, 17*(12), 1584–1590.

Kumar, Shaina A. & Mattanah, Jonathan F. (2018). Interparental conflict, parental intrusiveness, and interpersonal functioning in emerging adulthood. *Personal Relationships, 25*(1), 120–133.

Kuperberg, Arielle. (2012). Reassessing differences in work and income in cohabitation and marriage. *Journal of Marriage and Family, 74*(4), 688–707.

Kurt, Didem; Inman, J. Jeffrey & Gino, Francesca. (2018). Religious shoppers spend less money. *Journal of Experimental Social Psychology, 78*, 116–124.

Kuvaas, Bård; Buch, Robert; Weibel, Antoinette; Dysvik, Anders & Nerstad, Christina G. L. (2017). Do intrinsic and extrinsic motivation relate differently to employee outcomes? *Journal of Economic Psychology, 61*, 244–258.

Kypri, Kypros; Davie, Gabrielle; McElduff, Patrick; Connor, Jennie & Langley, John. (2014). Effects of lowering the minimum alcohol purchasing age on weekend assaults resulting in hospitalization in New Zealand. *American Journal of Public Health, 104*(8), 1396–1401.

Kypri, Kypros; Voas, Robert B.; Langley, John D.; Stephenson, Shaun C. R.; Begg, Dorothy J.; Tippetts, A. Scott & Davie, Gabrielle S. (2006). Minimum purchasing age for alcohol and traffic crash injuries among 15- to 19-year-olds in New Zealand. *American Journal of Public Health, 96*(1), 126–131.

Labouvie-Vief, Gisela. (2015). *Integrating emotions and cognition throughout the lifespan*. Springer.

Lachs, Mark S. & Pillemer, Karl A. (2015, November 12). Elder abuse. *New England Journal of Medicine, 373*(20), 1947–1956.

Ladd, Helen F. & Sorensen, Lucy C. (2017). Returns to teacher experience: Student achievement and motivation in middle school. *Education Finance and Policy, 12*(2), 241–279.

Lagattuta, Kristin H. (2014). Linking past, present, and future: Children's ability to connect mental states and emotions across time. *Child Development Perspectives, 8*(2), 90–95.

Lake, Gillian & Evangelou, Maria. (2019). Let's talk! An interactive intervention to support children's language development. *European Early Childhood Education Research Journal, 27*(2), 221–240.

Lake, Stephanie & Kerr, Thomas. (2017). The challenges of projecting the public health impacts of marijuana legalization in Canada. *International Journal of Health Policy Management, 6*(5), 285–287.

Lalande, Kathleen M. & Bonanno, George A. (2006). Culture and continuing bonds: A prospective comparison of bereavement in the United States and the People's Republic of China. *Death Studies, 30*(4), 303–324.

Lam, Chun Bun; McHale, Susan M. & Crouter, Ann C. (2012). Parent–child shared time from middle childhood to late adolescence: Developmental course and adjustment correlates. *Child Development, 83*(2), 2089–2103.

Lamb, Michael E. (1982). Maternal employment and child development: A review. In Lamb, Michael E. (Ed.), *Nontraditional families: Parenting and child development* (pp. 45–69). Erlbaum.

Lamichhane, Dirga Kumar; Lee, So-Yeon; Ahn, Kangmo; Kim, Kyung Won; Shin, Youn Ho; Suh, Dong In; . . . Kim, Hwan-Cheol. (2020). Quantile regression analysis of the socioeconomic inequalities in air pollution and birth weight. *Environment International, 142*, 105875.

Lamm, Bettina; Keller, Heidi; Teiser, Johanna; Gudi, Helene; Yovsi, Relindis D.; Freitag, Claudia; . . . Lohaus, Arnold. (2018). Waiting for the second treat: Developing culture-specific modes of self-regulation. *Child Development, 89*(3), e261–e277.

Lamont, Ruth A.; Swift, Hannah J. & Abrams, Dominic. (2015). A review and meta-analysis of age-based stereotype threat: Negative stereotypes, not facts, do the damage. *Psychology and Aging, 30*(1), 180–193.

Lan, Xiaoyu; Wang, Wenchao & Radin, Rendy. (2019). Depressive symptoms in emerging adults with early left-behind experiences in rural China. *Journal of Loss and Trauma, 24*(4), 339–355.

Landgren, Kajsa; Lundqvist, Anita & Hallström, Inger. (2012). Remembering the chaos—But life went on and the wound healed: A four year follow up with parents having had a baby with infantile colic. *The Open Nursing Journal, 6*, 53–61.

Lane, Jonathan D. & Harris, Paul L. (2014). Confronting, representing, and believing counterintuitive concepts: Navigating the natural and the supernatural. *Perspectives on Psychological Science, 9*(2), 144–160.

Lane, Karen & Garrod, Jayne. (2016). The return of the traditional birth attendant. *Journal of Global Health, 6*(2).

Lang, Frieder R.; Rohr, Margund K. & Williger, Bettina. (2011). Modeling success in life-span psychology: The principles of selection, optimization, and compensation. In Fingerman, Karen L.; Berg, Cynthia; Smith, Jacqui & Antonucci, Toni C. (Eds.), *Handbook of lifespan development* (pp. 57–86). Springer.

Lang, Samantha F. & Fowers, Blaine J. (2019). An expanded theory of Alzheimer's caregiving. *American Psychologist, 74*(2), 194–206.

Lange, Thomas. (2012). Job satisfaction and self-employment: Autonomy or personality? *Small Business Economics, 38*(2), 165–177.

Langeslag, Sandra J. E.; Muris, Peter & Franken, Ingmar H. A. (2013). Measuring romantic love: Psychometric properties of the infatuation and attachment scales. *The Journal of Sex Research, 50*(8), 739–747.

Langrehr, Kimberly J.; Morgan, Sydney K.; Ross, Jessica; Oh, Monica & Chong, Wen Wen. (2019). Racist experiences, openness to discussing racism, and attitudes toward ethnic heritage activities: Adoptee–parent discrepancies. *Asian American Journal of Psychology, 10*(2), 91–102.

Laninga-Wijnen, Lydia; Gremmen, Mariola C.; Dijkstra, Jan Kornelis; Veenstra, René; Vollebergh, Wilma A. M. & Harakeh, Zeena. (2019). The role of academic status norms in friendship selection and influence processes related to academic achievement. *Developmental Psychology, 55*(2), 337–350.

Lansford, Jennifer E.; Sharma, Chinmayi; Malone, Patrick S.; Woodlief, Darren; Dodge, Kenneth A.; Oburu, Paul; . . . Di Giunta, Laura. (2014). Corporal punishment, maternal warmth, and child adjustment: A longitudinal study in eight countries. *Journal of Clinical Child & Adolescent Psychology, 43*(4), 670–685.

Lansford, Jennifer E.; Zietz, Susannah; Putnick, Diane L.; Deater-Deckard, Kirby; Bradley, Robert H.; Costa, Megan; . . . Bornstein, Marc H. (2020). Men's and women's views on acceptability of husband-to-wife violence and use of corporal punishment with children in 21 low- and middle-income countries. *Child Abuse & Neglect, 108*(104692).

Lapan, Candace & Boseovski, Janet J. (2017). When peer performance matters: Effects of expertise and traits on children's self-evaluations after social comparison. *Child Development, 88*(6), 1860–1872.

Lara-Cinisomo, Sandraluz; Fuligni, Allison Sidle & Karoly, Lynn A. (2011). Preparing preschoolers for kindergarten. In Laverick, DeAnna M. & Jalongo, Mary Renck (Eds.), *Transitions to early care and education* (Vol. 4, pp. 93–105). Springer.

Larsen, Peter A. (2018). Transposable elements and the multidimensional genome. *Chromosome Research, 26*(1/2), 1–3.

Larzelere, Robert E. & Cox, Ronald B. (2013). Making valid causal inferences about corrective actions by parents from longitudinal data. *Journal of Family Theory & Review, 5*(4), 282–299.

Larzelere, Robert E.; Gunnoe, Marjorie Lindner; Roberts, Mark W. & Ferguson, Christopher J. (2017). Children and parents deserve better parental discipline research: Critiquing the evidence for exclusively "positive" parenting. *Marriage & Family Review, 53*(1), 24–35.

Lattanzi-Licht, Marcia. (2013). Religion, spirituality, and dying. In Meagher, David K. & Balk, David E. (Eds.), *Handbook of thanatology: The essential body of knowledge for the study of death, dying, and bereavement* (2nd ed., pp. 9–16). Routledge.

Laurent, Heidemarie K. (2014). Clarifying the contours of emotion regulation: Insights from parent–child stress research. *Child Development Perspectives, 8*(1), 30–35.

Laursen, Brett; Hartl, Amy C.; Vitaro, Frank; Brendgen, Mara; Dionne, Ginette & Boivin, Michel. (2017). The spread of substance use and delinquency between adolescent twins. *Developmental Psychology, 53*(2), 329–339.

Lawrence, Elizabeth M.; Rogers, Richard G.; Zajacova, Anna & Wadsworth, Tim. (2019). Marital happiness, marital status, health, and longevity. *Journal of Happiness Studies, 20*, 1539–1561.

Layton, Jill; Li, Xiaochen; Shen, Changyu; de Groot, Mary; Lange, Leslie; Correa, Adolfo & Wessel, Jennifer. (2018). Type 2 diabetes genetic risk scores are associated with increased type 2 diabetes risk among African Americans by cardiometabolic status. *Clinical Medicine Insights: Endocrinology and Diabetes, 11*.

Lazzara, Alexandra; Daymont, Carrie; Ladda, Roger; Lull, Jordan; Ficicioglu, Can; Cohen, Jennifer & Aprile, Justen. (2019). Failure to thrive: An expanded differential diagnosis. *Journal of Pediatric Genetics, 8*(1), 27–32.

LeBlanc, Nicole J.; Simon, Naomi M.; Reynolds, Charles F.; Shear, M. Katherine; Skritskaya, Natalia & Zisook, Sidney. (2019). Relationship between complicated grief and depression: Relevance, etiological mechanisms, and implications. In Quevedo, João; Carvalho, André F. & Zarate, Carlos A. (Eds.), *Neurobiology of depression: Road to novel therapeutics* (pp. 231–239). Academic Press.

Le Couteur, David G.; Stanaway, Fiona; Waite, Louise M.; Cullen, John; Lindley, Richard I.; Blyth, Fiona M.; . . . Handelsman, David J. (2020). Apolipoprotein E and health in older men: The Concord Health and Ageing in Men Project. *The Journals of Gerontology: Series A, 75*(10), 1858–1862.

Le Duc, James W. & Yuan, Zhiming. (2018). Network for safe and secure labs. *Science, 362*(6412), 267.

Leach, Penelope. (2011). The EYFS and the real foundations of children's early years. In House, Richard (Ed.), *Too much, too soon?: Early learning and the erosion of childhood*. Hawthorn.

Leavitt, Judith W. (2009). *Make room for daddy: The journey from waiting room to birthing room*. University of North Carolina Press.

Lecheile, Bridget M.; Spinrad, Tracy L.; Xu, Xiaoye; Lopez, Jamie & Eisenberg, Nancy. (2020). Longitudinal relations among household chaos, SES, and effortful control in the prediction of language skills in early childhood. *Developmental Psychobiology, 6*(4), 727–738.

Lee, Barbara Coombs. (2019). *Finish strong: Putting your priorities first at life's end*. Compassion & Choices.

Lee, Chun-Chia & Chiou, Wen-Bin. (2016). More eagerness, more suffering from search bias: Accuracy incentives and need for cognition exacerbate the detrimental effects of excessive searching in finding romantic partners online. *Journal of Behavioral Decision Making, 29*(1), 3–11.

Lee, Dohoon; Brooks-Gunn, Jeanne; McLanahan, Sara S.; Notterman, Daniel & Garfinkel, Irwin. (2013). The Great Recession, genetic sensitivity, and maternal harsh parenting. *Proceedings of the National Academy of Sciences, 110*(34), 13780–13784.

Lee, David M.; Nazroo, James; O'Connor, Daryl B.; Blake, Margaret & Pendleton, Neil. (2016). Sexual health and well-being among older men and women in England: Findings from the English longitudinal study of ageing. *Archives of Sexual Behavior, 45*(1), 133–144.

Lee, Jolie. (2014, May 16). Teen breaks Guinness record for fastest texter. USA Today Network.

Lee, Jihyun & Porretta, David L. (2013). Enhancing the motor skills of children with autism spectrum disorders: A pool-based approach. *JOPERD, 84*(1), 41–45.

Lee, Shawna J. & Altschul, Inna. (2015). Spanking of young children: Do immigrant and U.S.-born Hispanic parents differ? *Journal of Interpersonal Violence, 30*(3), 475–498.

Lee, Shawna J.; Altschul, Inna & Gershoff, Elizabeth T. (2015). Wait until your father gets home? Mother's and fathers' spanking and development of child aggression. *Children and Youth Services Review, 52*, 158–166.

Lee, Shawna J.; Ward, Kaitlin P.; Chang, Olivia D. & Downing, Kasey M. (2021). Parenting activities and the transition to home-based education during the COVID-19 pandemic. *Children and Youth Services Review, 122*(105585).

Lehardy, Emaan N. & Fowers, Blaine J. (2020). Ultimate (evolutionary) explanations for the attraction and benefits of chronic illness support groups: Attachment, belonging, and collective identity. *Current Psychology, 39*(4), 1405–1415.

Leiter, Valerie & Herman, Sarah. (2015). Guinea pig kids: Myths or modern Tuskegees? *Sociological Spectrum, 35*(1), 26–45.

Leman, Patrick J. & Björnberg, Marina. (2010). Conversation, development, and gender: A study of changes in children's concepts of punishment. *Child Development, 81*(3), 958–971.

Lemieux, André. (2012). Post-formal thought in gerontagogy or beyond Piaget. *Journal of Behavioral and Brain Science, 2*(3), 399–406.

Lemish, Daphna & Kolucki, Barbara. (2013). Media and early childhood development. In Britto, Pia Rebello; Engle, Patrice L. & Super, Charles M. (Eds.), *Handbook of early childhood development research and its impact on global policy*. Oxford University Press.

Lengua, Liliana J.; Garstein, Maria A. & Prinzie, Peter. (2019). Temperament and personality trait development in the family: Interactions and transactions with parenting from infancy through adolescence. In McAdams, Dan P.; Shiner, Rebecca L. & Tackett, Jennifer L. (Eds.), *Handbook of personality development* (pp. 201–220). Guilford.

Lenhart, Amanda; Anderson, Monica & Smith, Aaron. (2015, October 1). *Teens, technology and romantic relationships. Pew Research Center: Internet, Science & Tech.* Washington, DC: Pew Research Center.

Leonard, Hayley C. & Hill, Elisabeth L. (2014). Review: The impact of motor development on typical and atypical social cognition and language: A systematic review. *Child and Adolescent Mental Health, 19*(3), 163–170.

Leonard, Julia A.; Lee, Yuna & Schulz, Laura E. (2017). Infants make more attempts to achieve a goal when they see adults persist. *Science, 357*(6357), 1290–1294.

Leopold, Thomas & Skopek, Jan. (2015a). The delay of grandparenthood: A cohort comparison in East and West Germany. *Journal of Marriage and Family*, 77(2), 441–460.

Leopold, Thomas & Skopek, Jan. (2015b). The demography of grandparenthood: An international profile. *Social Forces, 94*(2), 801–832.

Lepousez, Gabriel; Nissant, Antoine & Lledo, Pierre-Marie. (2015). Adult neurogenesis and the future of the rejuvenating brain circuits. *Neuron, 86*(2), 387–401.

Leshner, Alan I. & Dzau, Victor J. (2018). Good gun policy needs research. *Science, 359*(6381), 1195.

Leslie, Mitch. (2012). Gut microbes keep rare immune cells in line. *Science, 335*(6075), 1428.

Lessne, Deborah & Yanez, Christina. (2016, December 20). *Student reports of bullying: Results from the 2015 School Crime Supplement to the National Crime Victimization Survey.* Washington, DC: National Center for Education Statistics.

Lesthaeghe, Ron J. (2020). The second demographic transition: Cohabitation. In Halford, W. Kim & van de Vijver, Fons (Eds.), *Cross-cultural family research and practice* (pp. 103–141). Academic Press.

Leventhal, Bennett L. (2013). Complementary and alternative medicine: Not many compliments but lots of alternatives. *Journal of Child and Adolescent Psychopharmacology, 23*(1), 54–56.

Levey, Emma K. V.; Garandeau, Claire F.; Meeus, Wim & Branje, Susan. (2019). The longitudinal role of self-concept clarity and best friend delinquency in adolescent delinquent behavior. *Journal of Youth and Adolescence, 48*(6), 1068–1081.

Levy, Jonathan; Goldstein, Abraham & Feldman, Ruth. (2019). The neural development of empathy is sensitive to caregiving and early trauma. *Nature Communications, 10*(1).

Lewandowski, Lawrence J. & Lovett, Benjamin J. (2014). Learning disabilities. In Mash, Eric J. & Barkley, Russell A. (Eds.), *Child psychopathology* (3rd ed., pp. 625–669). Guilford Press.

Lewin, Alisa. (2018). Intentions to live together among couples living apart: Differences by age and gender. *European Journal of Population, 34*(5), 721–743.

Lewin, Kurt. (1945). The Research Center for Group Dynamics at Massachusetts Institute of Technology. *Sociometry, 8*(2), 126–136.

Lewis, John D.; Theilmann, Rebecca J.; Townsend, Jeanne & Evans, Alan C. (2013). Network efficiency in autism spectrum disorder and its relation to brain overgrowth. *Frontiers in Human Neuroscience*, 7, 845.

Lewis, Lawrence B.; Antone, Carol & Johnson, Jacqueline S. (1999). Effects of prosodic stress and serial position on syllable omission in first words. *Developmental Psychology, 35*(1), 45–59.

Lewis, Michael. (2010). The emergence of human emotions. In Lewis, Michael; Haviland-Jones, Jeannette M. & Barrett, Lisa Feldman (Eds.), *Handbook of emotions* (3rd ed.). Guilford Press.

Lewis, Michael & Brooks, Jeanne. (1978). Self-knowledge and emotional development. In Lewis, Michael & Rosenblum, L. A. (Eds.), *Genesis of behavior* (Vol. 1, pp. 205–226). Plenum Press.

Lewis, Michael & Kestler, Lisa (Eds.). (2012). *Gender differences in prenatal substance exposure.* American Psychological Association.

Li, Bai; Adab, Peymané & Cheng, Kar Keung. (2015). The role of grandparents in childhood obesity in China—Evidence from a mixed methods study. *International Journal of Behavioral Nutrition and Physical Activity, 12*, 91.

Li, Pin; Becker, Jill B.; Heitzeg, Mary M.; Mcclellan, Michele L.; Reed, Beth Glover & Zucker, Robert A. (2017). Gender differences in the transmission of risk for antisocial behavior problems across generations. *PLoS ONE, 12*(5), e0177288.

Li, Wei; Woudstra, Mi-lan J.; Branger, Marjolein C. E.; Wang, Lamei; Alink, Lenneke R. A.; Mesman, Judi & Emmen, Rosanneke A. G. (2019). The effect of the still-face paradigm on infant behavior: A cross-cultural comparison between mothers and fathers. *Infancy, 24*(6), 893–910.

Li, Yanping; Schoufour, Josje; Wang, Dong D.; Dhana, Klodian; Pan, An; Liu, Xiaoran; . . . Hu, Frank B. (2020). Healthy lifestyle and life expectancy free of cancer, cardiovascular disease, and type 2 diabetes: Prospective cohort study. *BMJ, 368*(l6669).

Licari, Amelia; Manti, Sara; Marseglia, Alessia; Brambilla, Ilaria; Votto, Martina; Castagnoli, Riccardo; . . . Marseglia, Gian Luigi. (2019). Food allergies: Current and future treatments. *Medicina, 55*(5), 120.

Lillard, Angeline S. (2013). Playful learning and Montessori education. *American Journal of Play, 5*(2), 157–186.

Lillard, Angeline S. & Taggart, Jessica. (2019). Pretend play and fantasy: What if Montessori was right? *Child Development Perspectives, 13*(2), 85–90.

Lim, Cher Ping; Zhao, Yong; Tondeur, Jo; Chai, Ching Sing & Tsai, Chin-Chung. (2013). Bridging the gap:

Technology trends and use of technology in schools. *Educational Technology & Society, 16*(2), 59–68.

Lim, S. & Song, J. A. (2020). Strategies to improve continuity maintenance for people with dementia: A rapid realist review. *Public Health, 181*(46–52).

Lin, Lin; Cockerham, Deborah; Chang, Zhengsi & Natividad, Gloria. (2016). Task speed and accuracy decrease when multitasking. *Technology, Knowledge and Learning, 21*(3), 307–323.

Lin, Nan. (2017). Building a network theory of social capital: Theory and research. In Lin, Nan; Cook, Karen & Burt, Ronald S. (Eds.), *Social capital: Theory and research.* Taylor & Francis.

Lin, Phoebe. (2016). Risky behaviors: Integrating adolescent egocentrism with the theory of planned behavior. *Review of General Psychology, 20*(4), 392–398.

Linsell, Louise; Johnson, Samantha; Wolke, Dieter; O'Reilly, Helen; Morris, Joan K.; Kurinczuk, Jennifer J. & Marlow, Neil. (2018). Cognitive trajectories from infancy to early adulthood following birth before 26 weeks of gestation: A prospective, population-based cohort study. *Archives of Disease in Childhood, 103*, 363–370.

Lionetti, Francesca; Aron, Arthur; Aron, Elaine N.; Burns, G. Leonard; Jagiellowicz, Jadzia & Pluess, Michael. (2018). Dandelions, tulips and orchids: evidence for the existence of low-sensitive, medium-sensitive and high-sensitive individuals. *Translational Psychiatry, 8*(24).

Lisko, I.; Kulmala, J.; Annetorp, M.; Ngandu, T.; Mangialasche, F. & Kivipelto, M. (2020). How can dementia and disability be prevented in older adults: Where are we today and where are we going? *Journal of Internal Medicine.*

Littman, Lisa. (2018). Parent reports of adolescents and young adults perceived to show signs of a rapid onset of gender dysphoria. *PloS One, 13*(8), e0202330.

Liu, Andrew H. (2015). Revisiting the hygiene hypothesis for allergy and asthma. *The Journal of Allergy and Clinical Immunology, 136*(4), 860–865.

Liu, Chien. (2021). A theory of sexual revolution: Explaining the collapse of the norm of premarital abstinence. *Mind & Society, 20*, 41–58.

Liu, Junsheng; Chen, Xinyin; Coplan, Robert J.; Ding, Xuechen; Zarbatany, Lynne & Ellis, Wendy. (2015). Shyness and unsociability and their relations with adjustment in Chinese and Canadian children. *Journal of Cross-Cultural Psychology, 46*(3), 371–386.

Liu, Weiwei; Taylor, Bruce G. & Mumford, Elizabeth A. (2020). Profiles of adolescent relationship abuse and sexual harassment: A latent class analysis. *Prevention Science, 21*(3), 377–387.

Liu, Xiaojing; Gao, Xiaodong; Zhang, Li; Yuan, Zilong; Zhang, Chen; Lu, Weizhao; . . . Xie, Jindong. (2018). Age-related changes in fiber tracts in healthy adult brains: A generalized q-sampling and connectometry study. *Journal of Magnetic Resonance Imaging, 48*(2), 369–381.

Livingston, Gretchen & Brown, Anna. (2017, May 18). *Intermarriage in the U.S. 50 years after Loving v. Virginia. Social & Demographic Trends.* Washington, DC: Pew Research Center.

Livingston, Gretchen & Parker, Kim. (2019, June 12). *8 facts about American dads. Fact Tank.* Washington, DC: Pew Research Center.

Livingston, Lucy Anne & Happé, Francesca. (2017). Conceptualising compensation in neurodevelopmental disorders: Reflections from autism spectrum disorder. *Neuroscience and Biobehavioral Reviews, 80*, 729–742.

LoBue, Vanessa & Adolph, Karen E. (2019). Fear in infancy: Lessons from snakes, spiders, heights, and strangers. *Developmental Psychology, 55*(9), 1889–1907.

Locey, Matthew L. (2020). The evolution of behavior analysis: Toward a replication crisis? *Perspectives on Behavior Science, 43*(4), 655–675.

Lochman, John E.; Dishion, Thomas J.; Powell, Nicole P.; Boxmeyer, Caroline L.; Qu, Lixin & Sallee, Meghann. (2015). Evidence-based preventive intervention for preadolescent aggressive children: One-year outcomes following randomization to group versus individual delivery. *Journal of Consulting and Clinical Psychology, 83*(4), 728–735.

Löckenhoff, Corinna E.; De Fruyt, Filip; Terracciano, Antonio; McCrae, Robert R.; De Bolle, Marleen; Costa, Paul T.; . . . Yik, Michelle. (2009). Perceptions of aging across 26 cultures and their culture-level associates. *Psychology and Aging, 24*(4), 941–954.

Lockhart, Kristi L.; Goddu, Mariel K. & Keil, Frank C. (2018). When saying "I'm best" is benign: Developmental shifts in perceptions of boasting. *Developmental Psychology, 54*(3), 521–535.

Lodge, Amy C. & Umberson, Debra. (2012). All shook up: Sexuality of mid- to later life married couples. *Journal of Marriage and Family, 74*(3), 428–443.

Loftfield, Erikka; Cornelis, Marilyn C.; Caporaso, Neil; Yu, Kai; Sinha, Rashmi & Freedman, Neal. (2018). Association of coffee drinking with mortality by genetic variation in caffeine metabolismfindings from the UK biobank. *JAMA Internal Medicine, 178*(8), 1086–1097.

Longobardi, Claudio & Badenes-Ribera, Laura. (2017). Stressors: A systematic review of the past 10 years. *Journal of Child and Family Studies, 26*(8), 2039–2049.

Lopez-Hartmann, Maja; Wens, Johan; Verhoeven, Veronique & Remmen, Roy. (2012). The effect of caregiver support interventions for informal caregivers of community-dwelling frail elderly: A systematic review. *International Journal of Integrated Care, 12*, 1–16.

Lordier, Lara; Meskaldji, Djalel-Eddine; Grouiller, Frédéric; Pittet, Marie P.; Vollenweider, Andreas; Vasung, Lana; . . . Hüppi, Petra S. (2019). Music in premature infants enhances high-level cognitive brain networks. *PNAS, 116*(24), 12103–12108.

Lorthe, Elsa; Torchin, Héloïse; Delorme, Pierre; Ancel, Pierre-Yves; Marchand-Martin, Laetitia; Foix-L'Hélias, Laurence; . . . Kayem, Gilles. (2018). Preterm premature rupture of membranes at 22–25 weeks' gestation: Perinatal and 2-year outcomes within a national population-based study (EPIPAGE-2). *American Journal of Obstetrics and Gynecology, 219*(3), 298.e1–298.e14.

Loyd, Aerika Brittian & Gaither, Sarah E. (2018). Racial/ethnic socialization for white youth: What we know and future directions. *Journal of Applied Developmental Psychology, 59*, 54–64.

Lu, Peiyi; Shelley, Mack & Liu, Yi-Long. (2021). Reexamining the poverty cycle in middle and late adulthood: Evidence from the Health and Retirement Study 2002–2014. *International Journal of Social Welfare, 30*(2), 140–151.

Lubke, Gitta H.; Mcartor, Daniel B.; Boomsma, Dorret I. & Bartels, Meike. (2018). Genetic and environmental contributions to the development of childhood aggression. *Developmental Psychology, 54*(1), 39–50.

Luby, Joan L.; Tillman, Rebecca & Barch, Deanna M. (2019). Association of timing of adverse childhood experiences and caregiver support with regionally specific brain development in adolescents. *JAMA Network Open, 2*(9), e1911426.

Lucaccioni, Laura; Trevisani, Viola; Marrozzini, Lucia; Bertoncelli, Natascia; Predieri, Barbara; Lugli, Licia; . . . Iughetti, Lorenzo. (2020). Endocrine-disrupting chemicals and their effects during female puberty: A review of current evidence. *International Journal of Molecular Sciences, 21*(6).

Lucassen, Paul J.; Toni, Nicolas; Kempermann, Gerd; Frisen, Jonas; Gage, Fred H. & Swaab, Dick F. (2020). Limits to human neurogenesis—really? *Molecular Psychiatry, 25*, 2207–2209.

Lucca, Kelsey & Wilbourn, Makeba Parramore. (2018). Communicating to learn: Infants' pointing gestures result in optimal learning. *Child Development, 89*(3), 941–960.

Luecken, Linda J.; Lin, Betty; Coburn, Shayna S.; MacKinnon, David P.; Gonzales, Nancy A. & Crnic, Keith A. (2013). Prenatal stress, partner support, and infant cortisol reactivity in low-income Mexican American families. *Psychoneuroendocrinology, 38*(12), 3092–3101.

Luengo-Prado, María J. & Sevilla, Almudena. (2012). Time to cook: Expenditure at retirement in Spain. *The Economic Journal, 123*(569), 764–789.

Luhmann, Maike & Hawkley, Louise C. (2016). Age differences in loneliness from late adolescence to oldest old age. *Developmental Psychology, 52*(6), 943–959.

Luhmann, Maike; Hofmann, Wilhelm; Eid, Michael & Lucas, Richard E. (2012). Subjective well-being and adaptation to life events: A meta-analysis. *Journal of Personality and Social Psychology, 102*(3), 592–615.

Lundberg, Shelly; Pollak, Robert A. & Stearns, Jenna. (2016). Family inequality: Diverging patterns in marriage, cohabitation, and childbearing. *Journal of Economic Perspectives, 30*(2), 79–102.

Lushin, Viktor; Jaccard, James & Kaploun, Victor. (2017). Parental monitoring, adolescent dishonesty and underage drinking: A nationally representative study. *Journal of Adolescence, 57*, 99–107.

Luthar, Suniya S. (2015). Resilience in development: A synthesis of research across five decades. In Cicchetti, Dante & Cohen, Donald J. (Eds.), *Developmental psychopathology* (2nd ed., Vol. 3). Wiley.

Luthar, Suniya S.; Cicchetti, Dante & Becker, Bronwyn. (2000). The construct of resilience: A critical evaluation and guidelines for future work. *Child Development, 71*(3), 543–562.

Luthar, Suniya S.; Small, Phillip J. & Ciciolla, Lucia. (2018). Adolescents from upper middle class communities: Substance misuse and addiction across early adulthood. *Development and Psychopathology, 30*(1), 315–335.

Luyckx, Koen; Klimstra, Theo A.; Duriez, Bart; Van Petegem, Stijn & Beyers, Wim. (2013). Personal identity processes from adolescence through the late 20s: Age trends, functionality, and depressive symptoms. *Social Development, 22*(4), 701–721.

Lynch, Scott M. & Brown, J. Scott. (2011). Stratification and inequality over the life course. In Binstock, Robert H. & George, Linda K. (Eds.), *Handbook of aging and the social sciences* (7th ed., pp. 105–117). Academic Press.

Lyssens-Danneboom, Vicky & Mortelmans, Dimitri. (2014). Living apart together and money: New partnerships, traditional gender roles. *Journal of Marriage and Family, 76*(5), 949–966.

MacCann, Carolyn; Jiang, Yixin; Brown, Luke E. R.; Double, Kit S.; Bucich, Micaela & Minbashian, Amirali. (2020). Emotional intelligence predicts academic performance: A meta-analysis. *Psychological Bulletin, 146*(2), 150–186.

MacDorman, Marian F. & Declercq, Eugene. (2019). Trends and state variations in out-of-hospital births in the United States, 2004–2017. *Birth: Issues in Perinatal Care, 46*(2), 279–288.

Machado, Liana; Thompson, Laura M. & Brett, Christopher H. R. (2019). Visual analogue mood scale scores in healthy young versus older adults. *International Psychogeriatrics, 31*(3), 417–424.

Maciejewski, Matthew L.; Smith, Valerie A.; Berkowitz, Theodore S. Z.; Arterburn, David E.; Mitchell, James E.; Olsen, Maren K.; . . . Bradley, Katharine A. (2020). Association of bariatric surgical procedures with changes in unhealthy alcohol use among US veterans. *JAMA Network Open, 3*(12), e2028117.

Mackenzie, Karen J.; Anderton, Stephen M. & Schwarze, Jürgen. (2014). Viral respiratory tract infections and asthma in early life: Cause and effect? *Clinical & Experimental Allergy, 44*(1), 9–19.

MacKenzie, Michael J.; Nicklas, Eric; Brooks-Gunn, Jeanne & Waldfogel, Jane. (2011). Who spanks infants and toddlers? Evidence from the fragile families and child well-being study. *Children and Youth Services Review, 33*(8), 1364–1373.

Macmillan, Ross & Copher, Ronda. (2005). Families in the life course: Interdependency of roles, role configurations, and pathways. *Journal of Marriage and Family, 67*(4), 858–879.

MacMurray, Nicholas J. & Fazzino, Lori L. (2017). Doing death without deity: Constructing nonreligious tools at the end of life. In Cragun, Ryan T.; Manning, Christel & Fazzino, Lori L. (Eds.), *Organized secularism in the United States* (pp. 279–300). Gruyter.

MacWhinney, Brian. (2015). Language development. In Lerner, Richard M. (Ed.), *Handbook of child psychology and developmental science* (7th ed., Vol. 2, pp. 296–338). Wiley.

Madigan, Sheri; Browne, Dillon; Racine, Nicole; Mori, Camille & Tough, Suzanne. (2019). Association between screen time and children's performance on a developmental screening test. *JAMA Pediatrics, 173*(3), 244–250.

Maenner, Matthew J.; Shaw, Kelly A.; Baio, Jon; Washington, Anita; Patrick, Mary; DiRienzo, Monica; . . . Dietz, Patricia M. (2020, March 27). *Prevalence of autism spectrum disorder among children aged 8 years — Autism and* *developmental disabilities monitoring network, 11 sites, United States, 2016. Morbidity and Mortality Weekly Report: Surveillance Summaries, 69*(4), 1–12. Atlanta, GA: Centers for Disease Control and Prevention.

Mahr, Johannes B. & Csibra, Gergely. (2020). Witnessing, remembering, and testifying: Why the past is special for human beings. *Perspectives on Psychological Science, 15*(2), 428–443.

Main, Mary & Solomon, Judith. (1990). Procedures for identifying infants as disorganized/disoriented during the Ainsworth strange situation. In Greenberg, Mark T.; Cicchetti, Dante & Cummings, E. Mark (Eds.), *Attachment in the preschool years: Theory, research, and intervention.* University of Chicago Press.

Makizako, Hyuma; Shimada, Hiroyuki; Doi, Takehiko; Tsutsumimoto, Kota & Suzuki, Takao. (2015). Impact of physical frailty on disability in community-dwelling older adults: A prospective cohort study. *BMJ Open, 5*(e008462).

Malina, Robert M.; Bouchard, Claude & Bar-Or, Oded. (2004). *Growth, maturation, and physical activity* (2nd ed.). Human Kinetics.

Malloy, Lindsay C.; Shulman, Elizabeth P. & Cauffman, Elizabeth. (2014). Interrogations, confessions, and guilty pleas among serious adolescent offenders. *Law and Human Behavior, 38*(2), 181–193.

Malpas, Jean. (2011). Between pink and blue: A multi-dimensional family approach to gender nonconforming children and their families. *Family Process, 50*(4), 453–470.

Maltby, Lauren E.; Callahan, Kelly L.; Friedlander, Scott & Shetgiri, Rashmi. (2019). Infant temperament and behavioral problems: Analysis of high-risk infants in child welfare. *Journal of Public Child Welfare, 13*(5), 512–528.

Mani, Kartik; Javaheri, Ali & Diwan, Abhinav. (2018). Lysosomes mediate benefits of intermittent fasting in cardiometabolic disease: The janitor is the undercover boss. *Comprehensive Physiology, 8*(4), 1639–1667.

Manning, Wendy D. (2015). Cohabitation and child wellbeing. *Marriage and Child Wellbeing Revisited, 25*(2), 51–66.

Manning, Wendy D. (2020). Young adulthood relationships in an era of uncertainty: A case for cohabitation. *Demography, 57*(3), 799–819.

Manning, Wendy D.; Longmore, Monica A. & Giordano, Peggy C. (2018). Cohabitation and intimate partner violence during emerging adulthood: High constraints and low commitment. *Journal of Family Issues, 39*(4), 1030–1055.

Marazita, John M. & Merriman, William E. (2010). Verifying one's knowledge of a name without retrieving it: A U-shaped relation to vocabulary size in early childhood. *Language Learning and Development*, 7(1), 40–54.

Marchiano, Lisa. (2017). Outbreak: On transgender teens and psychic epidemics. *Psychological Perspectives: Gender Diversity, 60*(3), 345–366.

Marcia, James E. (1966). Development and validation of ego-identity status. *Journal of Personality and Social Psychology, 3*(5), 551–558.

Marcus, Gary F. & Rabagliati, Hugh. (2009). Language acquisition, domain specificity, and descent with modification. In Colombo, John; McCardle, Peggy & Freund, Lisa (Eds.), *Infant pathways to language: Methods, models, and research disorders* (pp. 267–285). Psychology Press.

Margolis, Rachel & Arpino, Bruno. (2019). The demography of grandparenthood in 16 European countries and two North American countries. In Timonen, Virpi (Ed.), *Grandparenting practices around the world.* Policy Press.

Markova, Gabriela. (2018). The games infants play: Social games during early mother–infant interactions and their relationship with oxytocin. *Frontiers in Psychology, 9*(1041).

Marks, Amy K.; Ejesi, Kida & García Coll, Cynthia. (2014). Understanding the U.S. immigrant paradox in childhood and adolescence. *Child Development Perspectives, 8*(2), 59–64.

Marotta, Phillip L. & Voisin, Dexter R. (2017). Testing three pathways to substance use and delinquency among low-income African American adolescents. *Children and Youth Services Review, 75*, 7–14.

Marouli, Eirini; Graff, Mariaelisa; Medina-Gomez, Carolina; Lo, Ken Sin; Wood, Andrew R.; Kjaer, Troels R.; . . . Perola, Markus. (2017). Rare and low-frequency coding variants alter human adult height. *Nature, 542*, 186–190.

Marr, Elisha; Helder, Emily & Wrobel, Gretchen Miller. (2020). Historical and contemporary contexts of US adoption: An overview. In Marr, Elisha; Helder, Emily & Wrobel, Gretchen Miller (Eds.), *The Routledge handbook of adoption.* Routledge.

Marshall, Eliot. (2014). An experiment in zero parenting. *Science, 345*(6198), 752–754.

Martin, Carmel. (2014). *Common Core implementation best practices. New York State Office of the Governor Common Core Implementation Panel.* Washington, DC: Center for American Progress.

Martin, Joyce A.; Hamilton, Brady E.; Osterman, Michelle J. K. & Driscoll, Anne K. (2019, November 27). *Births: Final data for 2018. National Vital Statistics Reports, 68*(13). Hyattsville, MD: National Center for Health Statistics.

Martinson, Melissa L. & Reichman, Nancy E. (2016). Socioeconomic inequalities in low birth weight in the United States, the United Kingdom, Canada, and Australia. *American Journal of Public Health, 106*(4), 748–754.

Masarik, April S. & Conger, Rand D. (2017). Stress and child development: A review of the Family Stress Model. *Current Opinion in Psychology, 13*, 85–90.

Mascarelli, Amanda. (2013). Growing up with pesticides. *Science, 341*(6147), 740–741.

Masfety, Viviane; Aarnink, Carlijn; Otten, Roy; Bitfoi, Adina; Mihova, Zlatka; Lesinskiene, Sigita; . . . Husky, Mathilde. (2019). Three-generation households and child mental health in European countries. *Social Psychiatry and Psychiatric Epidemiology, 54*(4), 427–436.

Maslow, Abraham H. (1954). *Motivation and personality* (1st ed.). Harper & Row.

Maslow, Abraham H. (1997). *Motivation and personality* (3rd ed.). Pearson.

Masonbrink, Abbey R. & Hurley, Emily. (2020). Advocating for children during the COVID-19 school closures. *Pediatrics, 146*(3), e20201440.

Masten, Ann S. (2014). *Ordinary magic: Resilience in development.* Guilford Press.

Mathillas, Johan; Lövheim, Hugo & Gustafson, Yngve Gunnar. (2011). Increasing prevalence of dementia among very old people. *Age and Ageing, 40*(2), 243–249.

Matthews, Fiona E.; Arthur, Antony; Barnes, Linda E.; Bond, John; Jagger, Carol; Robinson, Louise & Brayne, Carol. (2013). A two-decade comparison of prevalence of dementia in individuals aged 65 years and older from three geographical areas of England: Results of the Cognitive Function and Ageing Study I and II. *The Lancet, 382*(9902), 1405–1412.

Matthews, Timothy C. (2018). Perspectives on financial abuse of elders in Canada. *Trusts & Trustees, 24*(1), 73–78.

Mattick, Richard P.; Clare, Philip J.; Aiken, Alexandra; Wadolowski, Monika; Hutchinson, Delyse; Najman, Jackob; . . . Degenhardt, Louisa. (2018). Association of parental supply of alcohol with adolescent drinking, alcohol-related harms, and alcohol use disorder symptoms: A prospective cohort study. *The Lancet Public Health, 3*(2), e64–e71.

Maxfield, Molly; Pyszczynski, Tom; Greenberg, Jeff & Bultmann, Michael N. (2017). Age differences in the effects of mortality salience on the correspondence bias. *The International Journal of Aging and Human Development, 84*(4), 329–342.

Maxwell, Lynne G.; Fraga, María V. & Malavolta, Carrie P. (2019). Assessment of pain in the newborn. *Clinics in Perinatology, 46*(4), 693–707.

Mayberry, Rachel I. & Kluender, Robert. (2018). Rethinking the critical period for language: New insights into an old question from American Sign Language. *Bilingualism: Language and Cognition, 21*(5), 938–944.

Mazza, Julia Rachel; Pingault, Jean-Baptiste; Booij, Linda; Boivin, Michel; Tremblay, Richard; Lambert, Jean; . . . Côté, Sylvana. (2017). Poverty and behavior problems during early childhood: The mediating role of maternal depression symptoms and parenting. *International Journal of Behavioral Development, 41*(6), 670–680.

McAlister, Anna R. & Peterson, Candida C. (2013). Siblings, theory of mind, and executive functioning in children aged 3–6 years: New longitudinal evidence. *Child Development, 84*(4), 1442–1458.

McCabe, Sean Esteban; Veliz, Philip; Wilens, Timothy E. & Schulenberg, John E. (2017). Adolescents' prescription stimulant use and adult functional outcomes: A national prospective study. *Journal of the American Academy of Child and Adolescent Psychiatry, 56*(3), 226–233.e4.

McCallion, Gail & Feder, Jody. (2013, October 18). *Student bullying: Overview of research, federal initiatives, and legal issues.* Washington, DC: Congressional Research Service. R43254.

McCarthy, Neil & Eberhart, Johann K. (2014). Gene–ethanol interactions underlying fetal alcohol spectrum disorders. *Cellular and Molecular Life Sciences, 71*(14), 2699–2706.

McCormick, Cheryl M.; Mathews, Iva Z.; Thomas, Catherine & Waters, Patti. (2010). Investigations of HPA function and the enduring consequences of stressors in adolescence in animal models. *Brain and Cognition, 72*(1), 73–85.

McCoy, Shelly; Dimler, Laura; Samuels, Danielle & Natsuaki, Misaki N. (2019). Adolescent susceptibility to deviant peer pressure: Does gender matter? *Adolescent Research Review, 4*(1), 59–71.

McEwen, Bruce S. & Karatsoreos, Ilia N. (2015). Sleep deprivation and circadian disruption: Stress, allostasis, and allostatic load. *Sleep Medicine Clinics, 10*(1), 1–10.

McEwen, Craig A. & Gregerson, Scout F. (2019). A critical assessment of the adverse childhood experiences study at 20 years. *American Journal of Preventive Medicine, 56*(6), 790–794.

McEwen, Craig A. & McEwen, Bruce S. (2017). Social structure, adversity, toxic stress, and intergenerational poverty: An early childhood model. *Annual Review of Sociology, 43*, 445–472.

McFarland, David H.; Fortin, Annie Joëlle & Polka, Linda. (2020). Physiological measures of mother–infant interactional synchrony. *Developmental Psychobiology, 62*(1), 50–61.

McFarland, Joel; Hussar, Bill; Zhang, Jijun; Wang, Xiaolei; Wang, Ke; Hein, Sarah; . . . Barmer, Amy. (2019). *The condition of education 2019.* Washington, DC: National Center for Education Statistics. NCES 2019–144.

McFarlane, Alexander C. & Van Hooff, Miranda. (2009). Impact of childhood exposure to a natural disaster on adult mental health: 20-year longitudinal follow-up study. *The British Journal of Psychiatry, 195*(2), 142–148.

McGillion, Michelle; Herbert, Jane S.; Pine, Julian; Vihman, Marilyn; dePaolis, Rory; Keren-Portnoy, Tamar & Matthews, Danielle. (2017). What paves the way to conventional language? The predictive value of babble, pointing, and socioeconomic status. *Child Development, 88*(1), 156–166.

McKee-Ryan, Frances & Maitoza, Robyn. (2018). Job loss, unemployment, and families. In Klehe, Ute-Christine & van Hooft, Edwin (Eds.), *The Oxford handbook of job loss and job search.* Oxford University Press.

McKeever, Pamela M. & Clark, Linda. (2017). Delayed high school start times later than 8:30 a.m. and impact on graduation rates and attendance rates. *Sleep Health, 3*(2), 119–125.

McKeganey, Neil; Russell, Christopher; Katsampouris, Evangelos & Haseen, Farhana. (2019). Sources of youth access to JUUL vaping products in the United States. *Addictive Behaviors Reports, 10*, 100232.

McLean, Robert R. & Kiel, Douglas P. (2015). Developing consensus criteria for sarcopenia: An update. *Journal of Bone and Mineral Research, 30*(4), 588–592.

McLeod, Bryce D.; Wood, Jeffrey J. & Weisz, John R. (2007). Examining the association between parenting and childhood anxiety: A meta-analysis. *Clinical Psychology Review, 27*(2), 155–172.

McMillin, Stephen Edward; Hall, Lacey; Bultas, Margaret W.; Grafeman, Sarah E.; Wilmott, Jennifer; Maxim, Rolanda & Zand, Debra H. (2015). Knowledge of child development as a predictor of mother-child play interactions. *Clinical Pediatrics, 54*(11), 1117–1119.

McNally, Shelley A. & Slutsky, Ruslan. (2017). Key elements of the Reggio Emilia approach and how they are interconnected to create the highly regarded system of early childhood education. *Early Child Development and Care, 187*(12), 1925–1937.

McRae, Kateri & Gross, James J. (2020). Emotion regulation. *Emotion, 20*(1), 1–9.

Meagher, David K. (2013). Ethical and legal issues and loss, grief, and mourning. In Meagher, David K. & Balk, David E. (Eds.), *Handbook of thanatology: The essential body of knowledge for the study of death, dying, and bereavement* (2nd ed.). Routledge.

Meece, Judith L. & Eccles, Jacquelynne S. (Eds.). (2010). *Handbook of research on schools, schooling, and human development.* Routledge.

Meeus, Wim. (2011). The study of adolescent identity formation 2000–2010: A review of longitudinal research. *Journal of Research on Adolescence, 21*(1), 75–94.

Mehler, Philip S. (2018). Medical complications of anorexia nervosa and bulimia nervosa. In Agras, W. Stewart & Robinson, Athena (Eds.), *The Oxford handbook of eating disorders* (2nd ed.). Oxford University Press.

Meier, Emily A.; Gallegos, Jarred V.; Thomas, Lori P. Montross; Depp, Colin A.; Irwin, Scott A. & Jeste, Dilip V. (2016). Defining a good death (successful dying): Literature review and a call for research and public dialogue. *The American Journal of Geriatric Psychiatry, 24*(4), 261–271.

Meldrum, Ryan; Kavish, Nicholas & Boutwell, Brian. (2018). On the longitudinal association between peer and adolescent intelligence: Can our friends make us smarter? *PsyArXiv*, (In Press).

Meldrum, Ryan Charles; Young, Jacob T. N.; Kavish, Nicholas & Boutwell, Brian B. (2019). Could peers influence intelligence during adolescence? An exploratory study. *Intelligence, 72*, 28–34.

Mellerson, Jenelle L.; Maxwell, Choppell B.; Knighton, Cynthia L.; Kriss, Jennifer L.; Seither, Ranee & Black, Carla L. (2018, October 12). *Vaccination coverage for selected vaccines and exemption rates among children in kindergarten—United States, 2017–18 school year. Morbidity and Mortality Weekly Report, 67*(40), 1115–1122. Atlanta, GA: Centers for Disease Control and Prevention.

Meltzoff, Andrew N. & Gopnik, Alison. (2013). Learning about the mind from evidence: Children's development of intuitive theories of perception and personality. In Baron-Cohen, Simon; Tager-Flusberg, Helen & Lombardo, Michael (Eds.), *Understanding other minds: Perspectives from developmental social neuroscience* (3rd ed., pp. 19–34). Oxford University Press.

Mendonça, Marina; Bilgin, Ayten & Wolke, Dieter. (2019). Association of preterm birth and low birth weight with romantic partnership, sexual intercourse, and parenthood in adulthood: A systematic review and meta-analysis. *JAMA Network Open, 2*(7), e196961.

Menendez, David; Hernandez, Iseli G. & Rosengren, Karl S. (2020). *Children's emerging understanding of death. Child Development Perspectives, 14*(1), 55–60.

Meng, Howard; Dai, Tianyang; Hanlon, John G.; Downar, James; Alibhai, Shabbir & Clarke, Hance. (2020). Cannabis and cannabinoids in cancer pain management. *Current Opinion in Supportive and Palliative Care, 14*(2), 87–93.

Merewether, Jane. (2018). Listening with young children: Enchanted animism of trees, rocks, clouds (and other things). *Pedagogy, Culture & Society*, 233–250.

Merikangas, Kathleen R.; He, Jian-ping; Rapoport, Judith; Vitiello, Benedetto & Olfson, Mark. (2013). Medication use in US youth with mental disorders. *JAMA Pediatrics, 167*(2), 141–148.

Merlo, Caitlin L.; Jones, Sherry Everett; Michael, Shannon L.; Chen, Tiffany J.; Sliwa, Sarah A.; Lee, Seung Hee; . . . Park, Sohyun. (August 21, 2020). *Dietary and physical activity behaviors among high school students—Youth risk behavior survey, United States, 2019. Morbidity and Mortality Weekly Report, 69*(Suppl. 1), 64–76. Atlanta, GA: U.S. Department of Health and Human Services, Centers for Disease Control and Prevention.

Mermelshtine, Roni. (2017). Parent–child learning interactions: A review of the literature on scaffolding. *British Journal of Educational Psychology, 87*(2), 241–254.

Merriam, Sharan B. (2009). *Qualitative research: A guide to design and implementation.* Jossey-Bass.

Merrick, Melissa T.; Ford, Derek C.; Ports, Katie A.; Guinn, Angie S.; Chen, Jieru; Klevens, Joanne; . . . Mercy, James A. (2019, November 8). *Vital signs: Estimated proportion of adult health problems attributable to adverse childhood experiences and implications for prevention—25 states, 2015–2017. Morbidity and Mortality Weekly Report, 68*(44), 999–1005. Atlanta, GA: Department of Health and Human Services, Centers for Disease Control and Prevention.

Meyer, Madonna Harrington. (2014). *Grandmothers at work: Juggling families and jobs.* New York University Press.

Meyer, Madonna Harrington & Abdul-Malak, Ynesse. (2020). Rethinking work and retirement. In *Grandparenting children with disabilities* (pp. 227–239). Springer.

Michaeli, Yossi; Kalfon Hakhmigari, Maor; Dickson, Daniel J.; Scharf, Miri & Shulman, Shmuel. (2019). The role of change in self-criticism across young adulthood in explaining developmental outcomes and psychological wellbeing. *Journal of Personality, 87*(4), 785–798.

Mie, Axel; Rudén, Christina & Grandjean, Philippe. (2018). Safety of safety evaluation of pesticides: Developmental neurotoxicity of chlorpyrifos and chlorpyrifos-methyl. *Environmental Health, 17*(77).

Miech, Richard A.; Johnston, Lloyd D.; O'Malley, Patrick M.; Bachman, Jerald G. & Schulenberg, John E. (2016). *Monitoring the future, national survey results on drug use, 1975–2015: Volume I, secondary school students.* Ann Arbor, MI: Institute for Social Research, The University of Michigan.

Miech, Richard A.; Johnston, Lloyd D.; O'Malley, Patrick M.; Bachman, Jerald G.; Schulenberg, John E. & Patrick, Megan E. (2019). *Monitoring the future, national survey results on drug use, 1975–2018: Volume I, secondary school students.* Ann Arbor, MI: Institute for Social Research, The University of Michigan.

Migliaccio, Silvia; Brasacchio, Caterina; Pivari, Francesca; Salzano, Ciro; Barrea, Luigi; Muscogiuri, Giovanna; . . . Colao, Annamaria. (2020). What is the best diet for cardiovascular wellness? A comparison of different nutritional models. *International Journal of Obesity Supplements, 10*, 50–61.

Mijs, Jonathan J. B. (2019). The paradox of inequality: Income inequality and belief in meritocracy go hand in hand. *Socio-Economic Review*, (mwy051).

Miles, Steven & Parker, Kara. (1997). Men, women, and health insurance. *New England Journal of Medicine, 336*, 218–221.

Millán, José María; Hessels, Jolanda; Thurik, Roy & Aguado, Rafael. (2013). Determinants of job satisfaction: A European comparison of self-employed and paid employees. *Small Business Economics, 40*(3), 651–670.

Miller, Evonne; Donoghue, Geraldine; Sullivan, Debra & Buys, Laurie. (2018). Later life gardening in a retirement community: Sites of identity, resilience and creativity. In Davenport, David; Newman, Andrew & Goulding, Anna (Eds.), *Resilience and ageing: Creativity, culture and community*. Policy Press.

Miller, Melissa K.; Dowd, M. Denise; Harrison, Christopher J.; Mollen, Cynthia J.; Selvarangan, Rangaraj & Humiston, Sharon. (2015). Prevalence of 3 sexually transmitted infections in a pediatric emergency department. *Pediatric Emergency Care, 31*(2), 107–112.

Miller, Patricia H. (2011). *Theories of developmental psychology* (5th ed.). Worth.

Milunsky, Aubrey & Milunsky, Jeff M. (2016). *Genetic disorders and the fetus: Diagnosis, prevention, and treatment* (7th ed.). Wiley-Blackwell.

Mindell, Jodi A.; Sadeh, Avi; Wiegand, Benjamin; How, Ti Hwei & Goh, Daniel Y. T. (2010). Cross-cultural differences in infant and toddler sleep. *Sleep Medicine, 11*(3), 274–280.

Miranda, Alfonso & Zhu, Yu. (2013). English deficiency and the native–immigrant wage gap. *Economics Letters, 118*(1), 38–41.

Mischel, Walter. (2014). *The marshmallow test: Mastering self-control*. Little, Brown.

Mischel, Walter; Ebbesen, Ebbe B. & Raskoff Zeiss, Antonette. (1972). Cognitive and attentional mechanisms in delay of gratification. *Journal of Personality and Social Psychology, 21*(2), 204–218.

Missana, Manuela; Rajhans, Purva; Atkinson, Anthony P. & Grossmann, Tobias. (2014). Discrimination of fearful and happy body postures in 8-month-old infants: An event-related potential study. *Frontiers in Human Neuroscience, 8*, 531.

Mitchell, Edwin A. (2009). SIDS: Past, present and future. *Acta Paediatrica, 98*(11), 1712–1719.

Mitchell, Kimberly J.; Jones, Lisa M.; Finkelhor, David & Wolak, Janis. (2013). Understanding the decline in unwanted online sexual solicitations for U.S. youth 2000–2010: Findings from three Youth Internet Safety Surveys. *Child Abuse & Neglect, 37*(12), 1225–1236.

Mitchell, Travis. (2016, September 28). *Where the public stands on religious liberty vs. nondiscrimination. Religion & Public Life.* Washington, DC: Pew Research Center.

Miyake, A.; Friedman, N. P.; Emerson, M. J.; Witzki, A. H.; Howerter, A. & Wager, T. D. (2000). The unity and diversity of executive functions and their contributions to complex "Frontal Lobe" tasks: A latent variable analysis. *Cognitive Psychology, 41*(1), 49–100.

Mize, Krystal D. & Jones, Nancy Aaron. (2012). Infant physiological and behavioral responses to loss of maternal attention to a social-rival. *International Journal of Psychophysiology, 83*(1), 16–23.

Mize, Krystal D.; Pineda, Melannie; Blau, Alexis K.; Marsh, Kathryn & Jones, Nancy A. (2014). Infant physiological and behavioral responses to a jealousy provoking condition. *Infancy, 19*(3), 338–348.

MMWR. (2008, January 18). *School-associated student homicides — United States, 1992–2006. Morbidity and Mortality Weekly Report, 57*(2), 33–36. Atlanta, GA: U.S. Department of Health and Human Services, Centers for Disease Control and Prevention.

MMWR. (2013, April 5). *Blood lead levels in children aged 1–5 Years — United States, 1999–2010. Morbidity and Mortality Weekly Report, 62*(13), 245–248. Atlanta, GA: U.S. Department of Health and Human Services, Centers for Disease Control and Prevention.

MMWR. (2014, March 28). *Prevalence of autism spectrum disorder among children aged 8 years — Autism and Developmental Disabilities Monitoring Network, 11 sites, United States, 2010. Morbidity and Mortality Weekly Report, 63*(2). Atlanta, GA: U.S. Department of Health and Human Services, Centers for Disease Control and Prevention.

MMWR. (2014, September 5). *Prevalence of smokefree home rules — United States, 1992–1993 and 2010–2011. Morbidity and Mortality Weekly Report, 63*(35), 765–769. Atlanta, GA: Department of Health and Human Services, Centers for Disease Control and Prevention.

MMWR. (2018, June 15). *Youth risk behavior surveillance — United States, 2017. Morbidity and Mortality Weekly Report, 67*(8). Atlanta, GA: U.S. Department of Health and Human Services, Centers for Disease Control and Prevention.

Moderbacher, Carolyn Rydyznski; Ramirez, Sydney I.; Dan, Jennifer M.; Smith, Davey M.; Sette, Alessandro & Crotty, Shane. (2020). Antigen-specific adaptive immunity to SARS-CoV-2 in acute COVID-19 and associations with age and disease severity. *Cell, 183*(4), 996-1012.e19.

Moen, Phyllis; Pedtke, Joseph H. & Flood, Sarah. (2020). Disparate disruptions: Intersectional COVID-19 employment effects by age, gender, education, and race/ethnicity. *Work, Aging and Retirement, 6*(4), 207–228.

Moffitt, Terrie E. (2003). Life-course-persistent and adolescence-limited antisocial behavior: A 10-year research review and a research agenda. In Lahey, Benjamin B.; Moffitt, Terrie E. & Caspi, Avshalom (Eds.), *Causes of conduct disorder and juvenile delinquency* (pp. 49–75). Guilford Press.

Moffitt, Terrie E.; Caspi, Avshalom; Rutter, Michael & Silva, Phil A. (2001). *Sex differences in antisocial behaviour: Conduct disorder, delinquency, and violence in the Dunedin Longitudinal Study*. Cambridge University Press.

Moheghi, Mohammadanwar; Ghorbanzadeh, Mohammad & Abedi, Jalil. (2020). The investigation and criticism moral development ideas of Kohlberg, Piaget and Gilligan. *International Journal of Multicultural and Multireligious Understanding*, 7(2).

Mohundro, J. D.; Joanis, Steve & Burnley, James. (2020). Geographic region, student loans, and college graduation rates. *International Journal of Education Economics and Development, 11*(3).

Mojdehi, Atiyeh Shohoudi; Shohoudi, Azadeh & Talwar, Victoria. (2020). Children's moral evaluations of different types of lies and parenting practices and across cultural contexts. *Current Psychology*, (In Press).

Mokrova, Irina L.; O'Brien, Marion; Calkins, Susan D.; Leerkes, Esther M. & Marcovitch, Stuart. (2013). The role of persistence at preschool age in academic skills at kindergarten. *European Journal of Psychology of Education, 28*(4), 1495–1503.

Moldavsky, Maria & Sayal, Kapil. (2013). Knowledge and attitudes about Attention-deficit/hyperactivity disorder (ADHD) and its treatment: The views of children, adolescents, parents, teachers and healthcare professionals. *Current Psychiatry Reports, 15,* 377.

Moles, Laura; Manzano, Susana; Fernández, Leonides; Montilla, Antonia; Corzo, Nieves; Ares, Susana; . . . Espinosa-Martos, Irene. (2015). Bacteriological, biochemical, and immunological properties of colostrum and mature milk from mothers of extremely preterm infants. *Journal of Pediatric Gastroenterology & Nutrition, 60*(1), 120–126.

Molnar, Lisa J.; Eby, David W.; Bogard, Scott E.; LeBlanc, David J. & Zakrajsek, Jennifer S. (2018). Using naturalistic driving data to better understand the driving exposure and patterns of older drivers. *Traffic Injury Prevention, 19*(Suppl. 1), S83–S88.

Molteni, Francesco; Ladini, Riccardo; Biolcati, Ferruccio; Chiesi, Antonio M.; Dotti Sani, Giulia Maria; Guglielmi, Simona; . . . Vezzoni, Cristiano. (2021). Searching for comfort in religion: Insecurity and religious behaviour during the COVID-19 pandemic in Italy. *European Societies, 23*(Suppl. 1), S704–S720.

Monahan, Kathryn C.; Steinberg, Laurence; Cauffman, Elizabeth & Mulvey, Edward P. (2013). Psychosocial (im) maturity from adolescence to early adulthood: Distinguishing between adolescence-limited and persisting antisocial behavior. *Development and Psychopathology, 25*(4), 1093–1105.

Montero-Odasso, Manuel M.; Sarquis-Adamson, Yanina; Speechley, Mark; Borrie, Michael J.; Hachinski, Vladimir C.; Wells, Jennie; . . . Muir-Hunter, Susan. (2017). Association of dual-task gait with incident dementia in mild cognitive impairment: Results from the gait and brain study. *JAMA Neurology, 74*(7), 857–865.

Montgomery, Heather. (2015). Understanding child prostitution in Thailand in the 1990s. *Child Development Perspectives, 9*(3), 154–157.

Monthly Vital Statistics Report. (1980). *Final mortality statistics, 1978: Advance report. Monthly Vital Statistics Report, 29*(6, Suppl. 2). Hyattsville, MD: National Center for Health Statistics.

Monti, Jennifer D.; Rudolph, Karen D. & Miernicki, Michelle E. (2017). Rumination about social stress mediates the association between peer victimization and depressive symptoms during middle childhood. *Journal of Applied Developmental Psychology, 48,* 25–32.

Montirosso, Rosario; Casini, Erica; Provenzi, Livio; Putnam, Samuel P.; Morandi, Francesco; Fedeli, Claudia & Borgatti, Renato. (2015). A categorical approach to infants' individual differences during the Still-Face paradigm. *Infant Behavior and Development, 38,* 67–76.

Moody, Raymond A. (1975). *Life after life: The investigation of a phenomenon—Survival of bodily death.* Mockingbird Books.

Moore, Kelly L.; Boscardin, W. John; Steinman, Michael A. & Schwartz, Janice B. (2012). Age and sex variation in prevalence of chronic medical conditions in older residents of U.S. nursing homes. *Journal of the American Geriatrics Society, 60*(4), 756–764.

Moore, Keith L. & Persaud, T. V. N. (2007). *The developing human: Clinically oriented embryology* (8th ed.). Saunders/Elsevier.

Moore, Kendra A.; Rubin, Emily B. & Halpern, Scott D. (2016). The problems with physician orders for life-sustaining treatment. *JAMA, 315*(3), 259–260.

Moore, Sarah A.; Faulkner, Guy; Rhodes, Ryan E.; Brussoni, Mariana; Chulak-Bozzer, Tala; Ferguson, Leah J.; . . . Tremblay, Mark S. (2020). Impact of the COVID-19 virus outbreak on movement and play behaviours of Canadian children and youth: A national survey. *International Journal of Behavioral Nutrition & Physical Activity, 17*(1).

Morales, Angelica; Jones, Scott; Ehlers, Alissa; Lavine, Jessye & Nagel, Bonnie. (2018). Ventral striatal response during decision making involving risk and reward is associated with future binge drinking in adolescents. *Neuropsychopharmacology, 43*(9), 1884–1890.

Morales-Muñoz, Isabel; Nolvi, Saara; Virta, Minna; Karlsson, Hasse; Paavonen, Juulia & Karlsson, Linnea. (2020). The longitudinal associations between temperament and sleep during the first year of life. *Infant Behavior and Development, 61*(101485).

Moran, Lyndsey R.; Lengua, Liliana J. & Zalewski, Maureen. (2013). The interaction between negative emotionality and effortful control in early social-emotional development. *Social Development, 22*(2), 340–362.

Morawska, Alina & Sanders, Matthew. (2011). Parental use of time out revisited: A useful or harmful parenting strategy? *Journal of Child and Family Studies, 20*(1), 1–8.

Moreno, Sylvain; Lee, Yunjo; Janus, Monika & Bialystok, Ellen. (2015). Short-term second language and music training induces lasting functional brain changes in early childhood. *Child Development, 86*(2), 394–406.

Morgan, David L. (2018). Living within blurry boundaries: The value of distinguishing between qualitative and quantitative research. *Journal of Mixed Methods Research, 12*(3), 268–279.

Morgan, Hani. (2019). Does high-quality preschool benefit children? What the research shows. *Education Sciences, 9*(1).

Morphett, Kylie; Herron, Lisa & Gartner, Coral. (2020). Protectors or puritans? Responses to media articles about the health effects of e-cigarettes. *Addiction Research & Theory, 28*(2), 95–102.

Morris, Amanda Sheffield; Wakschlag, Lauren; Krogh-Jespersen, Sheila; Fox, Nathan; Planalp, Beth; Perlman, Susan B.; . . . Johnson, Scott P. (2020). Principles for guiding the selection of early childhood neurodevelopmental risk and resilience measures: HEALthy brain and child development study as an exemplar. *Adversity and Resilience Science, 1,* 247–267.

Morris, Vivian G. & Morris, Curtis L. (2013). A call for African American male teachers: The supermen expected to solve the problems of low-performing schools. In Lewis, Chance W. & Toldson, Ivory A. (Eds.), *Black male teachers: Diversifying the United States' teacher workforce* (pp. 151–165). Emerald Group.

Morrongiello, Barbara A. (2018). Preventing unintentional injuries to young children in the home: Understanding and influencing parents' safety practices. *Child Development Perspectives, 12*(4), 217–222.

Moultrie, Fiona; Goksan, Sezgi; Poorun, Ravi & Slater, Rebeccah. (2016). Pain in neonates and infants. In Battaglia, Anna A. (Ed.), *An introduction to pain and its relation to nervous system disorders* (pp. 283–293). Wiley.

Mrayan, Lina; Abujilban, Sanaa; Abuidhail, Jamila; Bani Yassein, Muneer & Al-Modallal, Hanan. (2019). Couvade syndrome among Jordanian expectant fathers. *American Journal of Men's Health, 13*(1).

Mueller, Isabelle & Tronick, Ed. (2019). Early life exposure to violence: Developmental consequences on brain and behavior. *Frontiers in Behavioral Neuroscience, 13*(156).

Mueller, Noel T.; Mao, G.; Bennett, Wendy L.; Hourigan, Suchi K.; Dominguez-Bello, Maria G.; Appel, Lawrence J. & Wang, Xiaobin. (2017). Does vaginal delivery mitigate or strengthen the intergenerational association of overweight and obesity? Findings from the Boston Birth Cohort. *International Journal of Obesity, 41*, 497–501.

Mukku, Shiva Shanker Reddy; Harbishettar, Vijaykumar & Sivakumar, P. T. (2018). Psychological morbidity after job retirement: A review. *Asian Journal of Psychiatry, 37*, 58–63.

Muller, Jerry Z. (2018). *The tyranny of metrics*. Princeton University Press.

Mullis, Ina V. S.; Martin, Michael O.; Foy, Pierre & Arora, A. (2012a). *TIMSS 2011 international results in mathematics*. Chestnut Hill, MA: TIMSS & PIRLS International Study Center, Boston College.

Mullis, Ina V. S.; Martin, Michael O.; Foy, Pierre & Drucker, Kathleen T. (2012b). *PIRLS 2011 international results in reading*. Chestnut Hill, MA: TIMSS & PIRLS International Study Center, Boston College.

Mullis, Ina V. S.; Martin, Michael O.; Foy, Pierre & Hooper, Martin. (2016). *TIMSS 2015 international results in mathematics*. Chestnut Hill, MA: TIMSS & PIRLS International Study Center, Boston College.

Mullis, Ina V. S.; Martin, Michael O.; Foy, Pierre & Hooper, Martin. (2017a). *International results in reading PIRLS 2016*. Chestnut Hill, MA: TIMSS & PIRLS International Study Center, Boston College.

Mullis, Ina V. S.; Martin, Michael O.; Foy, Pierre; Kelly, Dana L. & Fishbein, Bethany. (2020). *TIMSS 2019 international results in mathematics and science*. Boston, MA: Boston College, TIMSS & PIRLS International Study Center.

Mullis, Ina V. S.; Martin, Michael O.; Kennedy, Ann M. & Foy, Pierre. (2007b). International student achievement in reading. In *IEA's progress in international reading literacy study in primary school in 40 countries* (pp. 35–64). TIMSS & PIRLS International Study Center, Boston College.

Muñoz, Carmen & Singleton, David. (2011). A critical review of age-related research on L2 ultimate attainment. *Language Teaching, 44*(1), 1–35.

Muris, Peter & Meesters, Cor. (2014). Small or big in the eyes of the other: On the developmental psychopathology of self-conscious emotions as shame, guilt, and pride. *Clinical Child and Family Psychology Review, 17*(1), 19–40.

Murphy, Colleen; Gardoni, Paolo & McKim, Robert (Eds.). (2018). *Climate change and its impacts: Risks and inequalities*. Springer.

Murphy, Tia Panfile; McCurdy, Kelsey; Jehl, Brianna; Rowan, Megan & Larrimore, Kelsey. (2020). Jealousy behaviors in early childhood: Associations with attachment and temperament. *International Journal of Behavioral Development, 44*(3), 266–272.

Musick, Kelly & Michelmore, Katherine. (2018). Cross-national comparisons of union stability in cohabiting and married families with children. *Demography, 55*(4), 1389–1421.

Mustanski, Brian; Birkett, Michelle; Greene, George J.; Hatzenbuehler, Mark L. & Newcomb, Michael E. (2014). Envisioning an America without sexual orientation inequities in adolescent health. *American Journal of Public Health, 104*(2), 218–225.

Mwene-Batu, Pacifique; Bisimwa, Ghislain; Ngaboyeka, Gaylord; Dramaix, Michelle; Macq, Jean; Lemogoum, Daniel & Donnen, Philippe. (2020). Follow-up of a historic cohort of children treated for severe acute malnutrition between 1988 and 2007 in Eastern Democratic Republic of Congo. *PLoS ONE, 15*(3), e0229675.

Myadze, Theresa I. & Rwomire, Apollo. (2014). Alcoholism in Africa during the late twentieth century: A socio-cultural perspective. *International Journal of Business and Social Science, 5*(2).

Næss, Kari-Anne B. (2016). Development of phonological awareness in Down syndrome: A meta-analysis and empirical study. *Developmental Psychology, 52*(2), 177–190.

NAEYC. (2014). *NAEYC Early Childhood Program standards and accreditation criteria & guidance for assessment*. Washington, DC: National Association for the Education of Young Children.

Nanji, Ayaz. (2005, February 8). World's smallest baby goes home. *CBS News*. AP.

Natarajan, Mangai (Ed.) (2017). *Drugs of abuse*. Routledge.

National Academies of Sciences, Engineering, and Medicine (Ed.) (2016). *Preventing bullying through science, policy, and practice*. National Academies Press.

National Center for Education Statistics. (2018). *The nation's report card*. Washington, DC: Institute of Education Sciences, U.S. Department of Education.

National Center for Education Statistics. (2019, May). Public high school graduation rates. The Condition of Education. National Center for Education Statistics.

National Center for Education Statistics. (2020). College enrollment rates. Institute of Education Sciences.

National Center for Education Statistics. (2020, May). Students with disabilities. The Condition of Education. National Center for Education Statistics, Institute of Education Sciences.

National Center for Health Statistics. (2016). *National ambulatory medical care survey*. Hyattsville, MD: U.S. Department of Health and Human Services, Centers for Disease Control and Prevention.

National Center for Health Statistics. (2017). *Health, United States, 2016: With chartbook on long-term trends in health*. Hyattsville, MD: U.S. Department of Health and Human Services.

National Center for Health Statistics. (2018). *Health, United States, 2017: With a special feature on mortality*. Hyattsville, MD: U.S. Department of Health and Human Services.

National Center for Health Statistics. (2019). *Health, United States, 2018*. Hyattsville, MD: U.S. Department of Health and Human Services.

National Center for Health Statistics. (2019). Table 39: Prescription drug use in the past 30 days, by sex, race and Hispanic origin, and age: United States, selected years 1988–1994 through 2015–2018. U.S. Department of Health and Human Services.

National Center for Health Statistics. (2019, October). Table 25: Participation in leisure-time aerobic and muscle-strengthening activities that meet the federal 2008 *Physical Activity Guidelines for Americans* among adults aged 18 and over, by selected characteristics: United States, selected years 1998–2017. Health, United States, 2018—Data Finder. U.S. Department of Health & Human Services.

National Center for Health Statistics. (2021). Percentage of having a doctor visit for any reason in the past 12 months for adults aged 18 and over, United States, 2019. National Health Interview Survey.

National Center for Statistics and Analysis. (2019, June). *Early estimate of motor vehicle traffic fatalities for 2018. Crash•Stats Brief Statistical Summary*. Washington, DC: National Highway Traffic Safety Administration.

National Foundation for Educational Research. (2010). *Tellus4 national report*. Berkshire, UK: National Foundation for Educational Research. DCSF Research Report 218.

Neary, Marianne T. & Breckenridge, Ross A. (2013). Hypoxia at the heart of sudden infant death syndrome? *Pediatric Research, 74*(4), 375–379.

Needleman, Herbert L. & Gatsonis, Constantine A. (1990). Low-level lead exposure and the IQ of children: A meta-analysis of modern studies. *JAMA, 263*(5), 673–678.

Needleman, Herbert L.; Schell, Alan; Bellinger, David; Leviton, Alan & Allred, Elizabeth N. (1990). The long-term effects of exposure to low doses of lead in childhood. *New England Journal of Medicine, 322*(2), 83–88.

Neggers, Yasmin & Crowe, Kristi. (2013). Low birth weight outcomes: Why better in Cuba than Alabama? *Journal of the American Board of Family Medicine, 26*(2), 187–195.

Neil, Elsbeth & Beek, Mary. (2020). Respecting children's relationships and identities in adoption. In Wrobel, Gretchen Miller; Helder, Emily & Marr, Elisha (Eds.), *The Routledge handbook of adoption*. Routledge.

Neimeyer, Robert A. (2017). Series foreword. In Klass, Dennis & Steffen, Edith Maria (Eds.), *Continuing bonds in bereavement: New directions for research and practice*. Routledge.

Nelson, Charles A.; Fox, Nathan A. & Zeanah, Charles H. (2014). *Romania's abandoned children: Deprivation, brain development, and the struggle for recovery*. Harvard University Press.

Nelson, Helen; Kendall, Garth; Burns, Sharyn; Schonert-Reichl, Kimberly & Kane, Robert. (2019). Development of the student experience of teacher support scale: Measuring the experience of children who report aggression and bullying. *International Journal of Bullying Prevention, 1*(2), 99–110.

Nerren, Jannah. (2020). An educated nation: Governmental policy and early childhood education in America. In Donovan, Jenny; Trimmer, Karen & Flegg, Nick (Eds.), *Curriculum, schooling and applied research: Challenges and tensions for researchers* (pp. 77–102). Palgrave.

Nesdale, Drew; Zimmer-Gembeck, Melanie J. & Roxburgh, Natalie. (2014). Peer group rejection in childhood: Effects of rejection ambiguity, rejection sensitivity, and social acumen. *Journal of Social Issues, 70*(1), 12–28.

Neumann, Manuela & Mackenzie, Ian R. A. (2019). Review: Neuropathology of non-tau frontotemporal lobar degeneration. *Neuropathology and Applied Neurobiology, 45*(1), 19–40.

Ngo, Chi T.; Newcombe, Nora S. & Olson, Ingrid R. (2018). The ontogeny of relational memory and pattern separation. *Developmental Science, 21*(2), e12556.

Nguyen, Jacqueline; O'Brien, Casey & Schapp, Salena. (2016). Adolescent inhalant use prevention, assessment, and treatment: A literature synthesis. *Drug Policy, 31*, 15–24.

Nichols, Shaun; Strohminger, Nina; Rai, Arun & Garfield, Jay. (2018). Death and the self. *Cognitive Science, 42*(Supp. 1), 314–332.

Niclasen, Janni; Andersen, Anne-Marie N.; Strandberg-Larsen, Katrine & Teasdale, Thomas W. (2014). Is alcohol binge drinking in early and late pregnancy associated with behavioural and emotional development at age 7 years? *European Child & Adolescent Psychiatry, 23*(12), 1175–1180.

Nicolaisen, Magnhild; Moum, Torbjørn & Thorsen, Kirsten. (2017). Mastery and depressive symptoms: How does mastery influence the impact of stressors from midlife to old age? *Journal of Aging and Health.*

Nielsen, Mark; Tomaselli, Keyan; Mushin, Ilana & Whiten, Andrew. (2014). Exploring tool innovation: A comparison of Western and Bushman children. *Journal of Experimental Child Psychology, 126*, 384–394.

Nieto, Marta; Romero, Dulce; Ros, Laura; Zabala, Carmen; Martínez, Manuela; Ricarte, Jorge J.; . . . Latorre, Jose M. (2019). Differences in coping strategies between young and older adults: The role of executive functions. *The International Journal of Aging and Human Development.*

Nieto, Sonia. (2000). *Affirming diversity: The sociopolitical context of multicultural education* (3rd ed.). Longman.

Nigg, Joel T. & Barkley, Russell A. (2014). Attention-deficit /hyperactivity disorder. In Mash, Eric J. & Barkley, Russell A. (Eds.), *Child psychopathology* (3rd ed., pp. 75–144). Guilford Press.

Nilsson, Kristine Kahr & de López, Kristine Jensen. (2016). Theory of mind in children with specific language impairment: A systematic review and meta-analysis. *Child Development, 87*(1), 143–153.

Nishina, Adrienne; Bellmore, Amy; Witkow, Melissa R.; Nylund-Gibson, Karen & Graham, Sandra. (2018). Mismatches in self-reported and meta-perceived ethnic identification across the high school years. *Journal of Youth and Adolescence, 47*(1), 51–63.

Nishizato, Minaho; Fujisawa, Takashi; Kosaka, Hirotaka & Tomoda, Akemi. (2017). Developmental changes in social attention and oxytocin levels in infants and children. *Scientific Reports, 7*(1), 2540–2540.

Nkomo, Palesa; Naicker, Nisha; Mathee, Angela; Galpin, Jacky; Richter, Linda M. & Norris, Shane A. (2018). The association between environmental lead exposure with aggressive behavior, and dimensionality of direct and indirect aggression during mid-adolescence: Birth to Twenty Plus cohort. *Science of the Total Environment, 612*, 472–479.

Nocentini, Annalaura; Fiorentini, Giada; Di Paola, Ludovica & Menesini, Ersilia. (2019). Parents, family characteristics and bullying behavior: A systematic review. *Aggression and Violent Behavior, 45*, 41–50.

Noël-Miller, Claire M. (2013a). Repartnering following divorce: Implications for older fathers' relations with their adult children. *Journal of Marriage and Family, 75*(3), 697–712.

Noël-Miller, Claire M. (2013b). Former stepparents' contact with their stepchildren after midlife. *The Journals of Gerontology Series B: Psychological Sciences and Social Sciences, 68*(3), 409–419.

Noll, Jennie G.; Trickett, Penelope K.; Long, Jeffrey D.; Negriff, Sonya; Susman, Elizabeth J.; Shalev, Idan; . . . Putnam, Frank W. (2017). Childhood sexual abuse and early timing of puberty. *Journal of Adolescent Health, 60*(1), 65–71.

Nomaguchi, Kei & Milkie, Melissa A. (2020). Parenthood and well-being: A decade in review. *Journal of Marriage and Family, 82*(1), 198–223.

Norman, Geoffrey R.; Grierson, Lawrence E. M.; Sherbino, Jonathan; Hamstra, Stanley J.; Schmidt, Henk G. & Mamede, Silvia. (2018). Expertise in medicine and surgery. In Ericsson, K. Anders; Hoffman, Robert R.; Kozbelt, Aaron & Williams, A. Mark (Eds.), *The Cambridge handbook of expertise and expert performance* (2nd ed., pp. 331–355). Cambridge University Press.

Normile, Dennis. (2018). Biologist unveils China's first private research university. *Science, 359*(6378).

Nowaskie, Dusitn; Austrom, Mary & Morhardt, Darby. (2019). Understanding the challenges, needs, and qualities of frontotemporal dementia family caregivers. *The American Journal of Geriatric Psychiatry, 27*(3, Suppl.), S98–S99.

Nxumalo, Fikile & Adair, Jennifer Keys. (2019). Social justice and equity in early childhood education. In Brown, Christopher P.; McMullen, Mary Benson & File, Nancy (Eds.), *The Wiley handbook of early childhood care and education* (pp. 661–682). Wiley.

Nygaard, Haakon B.; Erson-Omay, E. Zeynep; Wu, Xiujuan; Kent, Brianne A.; Bernales, Cecily Q.; Evans, Daniel M.; . . . Strittmatter, Stephen M. (2019). Whole-exome sequencing of an exceptional longevity cohort. *The Journals of Gerontology: Series A, 74*(9), 1386–1390.

O'Dougherty, Maureen. (2013). Becoming a mother through postpartum depression: Narratives from Brazil. In Faircloth, Charlotte; Hoffman, Diane M. & Layne, Linda L. (Eds.), *Parenting in global perspective: Negotiating ideologies of kinship, self and politics* (pp. 184–199). Routledge.

O'Hara, Michael W. & McCabe, Jennifer E. (2013). Postpartum depression: Current status and future directions. *Annual Review of Clinical Psychology, 9*, 379–407.

O'Meara, Madison S. & South, Susan C. (2019). Big Five personality domains and relationship satisfaction: Direct effects and correlated change over time. *Journal of Personality, 87*(6), 1206–1220.

O'Neal, Colleen R. (2018). The impact of stress on later literacy achievement via grit and engagement among dual language elementary school students. *School Psychology International, 39*(2), 138–155.

Oakes, J. Michael. (2009). The effect of media on children: A methodological assessment from a social epidemiologist. *American Behavioral Scientist, 52*(8), 1136–1151.

Ocobock, Abigail. (2013). The power and limits of marriage: Married gay men's family relationships. *Journal of Marriage and Family, 75*(1), 191–205.

OECD. (2010). *PISA 2009 results: Learning to learn: Student engagement, strategies and practices* (Vol. 3). PISA, OECD Publishing.

OECD. (2011). *Education at a glance 2011: OECD indicators.* Paris, France: Organisation for Economic Cooperation and Development.

OECD. (2018). *Adult education level (indicator). OECDiLibrary.* [Data set].

OECD. (2019). *Secondary graduation rate: Upper secondary, men/upper secondary, women, percentage, 2016. OECDiLibrary* [Data set].

OECD Family Database. (2019, August). PF2.1. Parental leave systems.

Oesterdiekhoff, Georg W. (2014). The role of developmental psychology to understanding history, culture and social change. *Journal of Social Sciences, 10*(4), 185–195.

Ogden, Cynthia L.; Fakhouri, Tala H.; Carroll, Margaret D.; Hales, Craig M.; Fryar, Cheryl D.; Li, Xianfen & Freedman, David S. (2017, December 22). *Prevalence of obesity among adults, by household income and education—United States, 2011–2014. Morbidity and Mortality Weekly Report, 66*(50), 1369–1373. Atlanta, GA: Centers for Disease Control and Prevention.

Ogren, Marissa; Burling, Joseph M. & Johnson, Scott P. (2018). Family expressiveness relates to happy emotion matching among 9-month-old infants. *Journal of Experimental Child Psychology, 174*, 29–40.

Okun, Morris A.; Yeung, Ellen WanHeung & Brown, Stephanie. (2013). Volunteering by older adults and risk of mortality: A meta-analysis. *Psychology and Aging, 28*(2), 564–577.

Olfson, Mark; Crystal, Stephen; Huang, Cecilia & Gerhard, Tobias. (2010). Trends in antipsychotic drug use by very young, privately insured children. *Journal of the American Academy of Child and Adolescent Psychiatry, 49*(1), 13–23.

Oliva, Elizabeth M.; Bowe, Thomas; Manhapra, Ajay; Kertesz, Stefan; Hah, Jennifer M.; Henderson, Patricia; . . . Trafton, Jodie A. (2020). Associations between stopping prescriptions for opioids, length of opioid treatment, and overdose or suicide deaths in US veterans: Observational evaluation. *BMJ, 368*(m283).

Oliver, David. (2019). When is it time for older drivers to stop? *BMJ, 364*(l403).

Ollo-López, Andrea & Goñi-Legaz, Salomé. (2017). Differences in work–family conflict: Which individual and national factors explain them? *The International Journal of Human Resource Management, 28*(3), 499–525.

Olson, Kristina R. & Dweck, Carol S. (2009). Social cognitive development: A new look. *Child Development Perspectives, 3*(1), 60–65.

Olson, Sheryl L.; Lopez-Duran, Nestor; Lunkenheimer, Erika S.; Chang, Hyein & Sameroff, Arnold J. (2011). Individual differences in the development of early peer aggression: Integrating contributions of self-regulation, theory of mind, and parenting. *Development and Psychopathology, 23*(1), 253–266.

Olweus, Dan. (1999). Sweden. In Smith, Peter K.; Morita, Yohji; Junger-Tas, Josine; Olweus, Dan; Catalano, Richard F. & Slee, Phillip T. (Eds.), *The nature of school bullying: A cross-national perspective* (pp. 7–27). Routledge.

Olweus, Dan & Limber, Susan P. (2018). Some problems with cyberbullying research. *Current Opinion in Psychology, 19,* 139–143.

Oregon Public Health Division. (2019, February 15). *Oregon Death with Dignity Act: 2018 data summary.* Portland, OR: Oregon Health Authority, Public Health Division.

Oregon Public Health Division. (2020, March 6). *Oregon Death with Dignity Act: 2019 data summary.* Portland, OR: Oregon Health Authority, Public Health Division.

Orth, Ulrich; Erol, Ruth Yasemin & Luciano, Eva C. (2018). Development of self-esteem from age 4 to 94 years: A meta-analysis of longitudinal studies. *Psychological Bulletin, 144*(10), 1045–1080.

Orth, Ulrich & Robins, Richard W. (2019). Development of self-esteem across the lifespan. In Shiner, Rebecca L.; Tackett, Jennifer L. & McAdams, Dan P. (Eds.), *Handbook of personality development* (pp. 328–344). Guilford.

Orzabal, Marcus R.; Lunde-Young, Emilie R.; Ramirez, Josue I.; Howe, Selene Y. F.; Naik, Vishal D.; Lee, Jehoon; . . . Ramadoss, Jayanth. (2019). Chronic exposure to e-cig aerosols during early development causes vascular dysfunction and offspring growth deficits. *Translational Research, 207,* 70–82.

Ostfeld, Barbara M.; Esposito, Linda; Perl, Harold & Hegyi, Thomas. (2010). Concurrent risks in sudden infant death syndrome. *Pediatrics, 125*(3), 447–453.

Ostrov, Jamie M.; Kamper, Kimberly E.; Hart, Emily J.; Godleski, Stephanie A. & Blakely-McClure, Sarah J. (2014). A gender-balanced approach to the study of peer victimization and aggression subtypes in early childhood. *Development and Psychopathology, 26*(3), 575–587.

Ozernov-Palchik, Ola; Norton, Elizabeth S.; Sideridis, Georgios; Beach, Sara D.; Wolf, Maryanne; Gabrieli, John D. E. & Gaab, Nadine. (2017). Longitudinal stability of pre-reading skill profiles of kindergarten children: Implications for early screening and theories of reading. *Developmental Science, 20*(5), e12471.

Paarlberg, Robert; Mozaffarian, Dariush; Micha, Renata & Chelius, Carolyn. (2018). Keeping soda in SNAP: Understanding the other iron triangle. *Society, 55*(4), 308–317.

Paat, Yok-Fong & Markham, Christine. (2019). The roles of family factors and relationship dynamics on dating violence victimization and perpetration among college men and women in emerging adulthood. *Journal of Interpersonal Violence, 34*(1), 81–114.

Pace, Amy; Luo, Rufan; Hirsh-Pasek, Kathy & Golinkoff, Roberta Michnick. (2017). Identifying pathways between socioeconomic status and language development. *Annual Review of Linguistics, 3,* 285–308.

Padilla, Jenny; Jager, Justin; Updegraff, Kimberly A.; McHale, Susan M. & Umaña-Taylor, Adriana J. (2020). Mexican-origin family members' unique and shared family perspectives of familism values and their links with parent-youth relationship quality. *Developmental Psychology, 56*(5), 993–1008.

Padilla-Walker, Laura; Memmott-Elison, Madison & Nelson, Larry. (2017). Positive relationships as an indicator of flourishing during emerging adulthood. In Padilla-Walker, Laura M. & Nelson, Larry J. (Eds.), *Flourishing in emerging adulthood: Positive development during the third decade of life* (pp. 212–235). Oxford University Press.

Padilla-Walker, Laura; Nelson, Larry; Fu, Xinyuan & Barry, Carolyn. (2018). Bidirectional relations between parenting and prosocial behavior for Asian and European-American emerging adults. *Journal of Adult Development, 25*(2), 107–120.

Padilla-Walker, Laura M. & Carlo, Gustavo. (2014). The study of prosocial behavior. In Padilla-Walker, Laura M. & Carlo, Gustavo (Eds.), *Prosocial development: A multidimensional approach.* Oxford University Press.

Pal, Tuya; Agnese, Doreen; Daly, Mary; La Spada, Albert; Litton, Jennifer; Wick, Myra; . . . Jarvik, Gail P. (2020). Points to consider: Is there evidence to support BRCA1/2 and other inherited breast cancer genetic testing for all breast cancer patients? A statement of the American College of Medical Genetics and Genomics (ACMG). *Genetics in Medicine, 22,* 681–685.

Pala, F. Cansu & Lewis, Charlie. (2020). Do preschoolers grasp the importance of regulating emotional expression? *European Journal of Developmental Psychology.*

Palatini, Paolo. (2015). Coffee consumption and risk of type 2 diabetes. *Diabetologia, 58*(1), 199–200.

Palmer, Sally B. & Abbott, Nicola. (2018). Bystander responses to bias-based bullying in schools: A developmental intergroup approach. *Child Development Perspectives, 12*(1), 39–44.

Paltiel, A. David; Zheng, Amy & Schwartz, Jason L. (2021). Speed versus efficacy: Quantifying potential tradeoffs in COVID-19 vaccine deployment. *Annals of Internal Medicine.*

Panagiotaki, Georgia; Hopkins, Michelle; Nobes, Gavin; Ward, Emma & Griffiths, Debra. (2018). Children's and adults' understanding of death: Cognitive, parental, and experiential influences. *Journal of Experimental Child Psychology, 166,* 96–115.

Pankow, James F.; Kim, Kilsun; McWhirter, Kevin J.; Luo, Wentai; Escobedo, Jorge O.; Strongin, Robert M.; . . . Peyton, David H. (2017). Benzene formation in electronic cigarettes. *PLoS ONE, 12*(3), e0173055.

Parade, Stephanie H.; Armstrong, Laura M.; Dickstein, Susan & Seifer, Ronald. (2018). Family context moderates the association of maternal postpartum depression and stability of infant temperament. *Child Development, 89*(6), 2118–2135.

Park, Hyun; Bothe, Denise; Holsinger, Eva; Kirchner, H. Lester; Olness, Karen & Mandalakas, Anna. (2011). The impact of nutritional status and longitudinal recovery of motor and cognitive milestones in internationally adopted children. *International Journal of Environmental Research and Public Health, 8*(1), 105–116.

Parke, Ross D. (2013). Gender differences and similarities in parental behavior. In Wilcox, Bradford & Kline, Kathleen K. (Eds.), *Gender and parenthood: Biological and social scientific perspectives* (pp. 120–163). Columbia University Press.

Parker, John. (2021). *In my time of dying: A history of death and the dead in West Africa.* Princeton University Press.

Parker, Kim; Horowitz, Juliana Menasce & Stepler, Renee. (2017, December 5). *On gender differences, no consensus on nature vs. nurture: Americans say society places a higher premium on masculinity than on femininity. Social & Demographic Trends.* Washington, DC: Pew Research Center.

Parker, Samantha E.; Mai, Cara T.; Canfield, Mark A.; Rickard, Russel; Wang, Ying; Meyer, Robert E.; . . . Correa, Adolfo. (2010). Updated national birth prevalence estimates for selected birth defects in the United States, 2004–2006. *Birth Defects Research Part A: Clinical and Molecular Teratology, 88*(12), 1008–1016.

Pascal, Aurelie; Govaert, Paul; Oostra, Ann; Naulaers, Gunnar; Ortibus, Els & Van den Broeck, Christine. (2018). Neurodevelopmental outcome in very preterm and very-low-birthweight infants born over the past decade: A meta-analytic review. *Developmental Medicine and Child Neurology, 60*(4), 342–355.

Pascarella, Ernest T.; Martin, Georgianna L.; Hanson, Jana M.; Trolian, Teniell L.; Gillig, Benjamin & Blaich, Charles. (2014). Effects of diversity experiences on critical thinking skills over 4 years of college. *Journal of College Student Development, 55*(1), 86–92.

Pascarella, Ernest T. & Terenzini, Patrick T. (1991). *How college affects students: Findings and insights from twenty years of research.* Jossey-Bass.

Pate, Matthew & Gould, Laurie A. (2012). *Corporal punishment around the world.* Praeger.

Patel, Dhaval; Steinberg, Joel & Patel, Pragnesh. (2018). Insomnia in the elderly: A review. *Journal of Clinical Sleep Medicine, 14*(6), 1017–1024.

Patel, Harsh; Arruarana, Victor; Yao, Lucille; Cui, Xiaojiang & Ray, Edward. (2020). Effects of hormones and hormone therapy on breast tissue in transgender patients: A concise review. *Endocrine, 68*(1), 6–15.

Patel, Manisha; Lee, Adria D.; Clemmons, Nakia S.; Redd, Susan B.; Poser, Sarah; Blog, Debra; . . . Gastañaduy, Paul A. (2019, October 11). *National update on measles cases and outbreaks— United States, January 1–October 1, 2019. Morbidity and Mortality Weekly Report.* Atlanta, GA: U.S. Department of Health and Human Services.

Patil, Rakesh N.; Nagaonkar, Shashikant N.; Shah, Nilesh B. & Bhat, Tushar S. (2013). A cross-sectional study of common psychiatric morbidity in children aged 5 to 14 years in an urban slum. *Journal of Family Medicine and Primary Care, 2*(2), 164–168.

Patterson, Susan Patricia; Hilton, Shona; Flowers, Paul & McDaid, Lisa M. (2019). What are the barriers and challenges faced by adolescents when searching for sexual health information on the internet? Implications for policy and practice from a qualitative study. *Sexually Transmitted Infections, 95*(6), 462–467.

Pattnaik, Aryamav; Sahoo, Bikash R. & Pattnaik, Asit K. (2020). Current status of Zika virus vaccines: Successes and challenges. *Vaccines, 8*(2), 266.

Patton, Mary H.; Blundon, Jay A. & Zakharenko, Stanislav S. (2019). Rejuvenation of plasticity in the brain: Opening the critical period. *Current Opinion in Neurobiology, 54,* 83–89.

Pellegrini, Anthony D. (2011). Introduction. In Pellegrini, Anthony D. (Ed.), *The Oxford handbook of the development of play* (pp. 3–6). Oxford University Press.

Pellegrini, Anthony D. (2013). Play. In Zelazo, Philip D. (Ed.), *The Oxford handbook of developmental psychology* (Vol. 2, pp. 276–299). Oxford University Press.

Pellegrini, Anthony D.; Roseth, Cary J.; Van Ryzin, Mark J. & Solberg, David W. (2011). Popularity as a form of social dominance: An evolutionary perspective. In Cillessen, Antonius H. N.; Schwartz, David & Mayeux, Lara (Eds.), *Popularity in the peer system* (pp. 123–139). Guilford Press.

Pellis, Sergio M.; Himmler, Brett T.; Himmler, Stephanie M. & Pellis, Vivien C. (2018). Rough-and-tumble play and the development of the social brain: What do we know, how do we know it, and what do we need to know? In Gibb, Robbin & Kolb, Bryan (Eds.), *The neurobiology of brain and behavioral development* (pp. 315–337). Academic Press.

Pennisi, Elizabeth. (2021). Genomes arising. *Science, 371*(6529), 556–559.

Peper, Jiska S. & Dahl, Ronald E. (2013). The teenage brain: Surging hormones Brain-behavior interactions during puberty. *Current Directions in Psychological Science, 22*(2), 134–139.

Perelli-Harris, Brienna; Hoherz, Stefanie; Lappegård, Trude & Evans, Ann. (2019). Mind the "happiness" gap: The relationship between cohabitation, marriage, and subjective well-being in the United Kingdom, Australia, Germany, and Norway. *Demography, 56*(4), 1219–1246.

Perlovsky, Leonid; Cabanac, Arnaud; Bonniot-Cabanac, Marie-Claude & Cabanac, Michel. (2013). Mozart Effect, cognitive dissonance, and the pleasure of music. *Behavioural Brain Research, 244,* 9–14.

Perner, Josef. (2000). Communication and representation: Why mentalistic reasoning is a lifelong endeavour. In Mitchell, Peter & Riggs, Kevin John (Eds.), *Children's reasoning and the mind* (pp. 367–401). Psychology Press.

Perreira, Krista M. & Pedroza, Juan M. (2019). Policies of exclusion: Implications for the health of immigrants and their children. *Annual Review of Public Health, 40,* 7.1–7.20.

Perrin, Robin; Miller-Perrin, Cindy & Song, Jeongbin. (2017). Changing attitudes about spanking using alternative biblical interpretations. *International Journal of Behavioral Development, 41*(4), 514–522.

Perry, Sylvia P.; Skinner, Allison L. & Abaied, Jamie L. (2019). Bias awareness predicts color conscious racial socialization methods among white parents. *Journal of Social Issues, 75*(4), 1035–1056.

Perry, William G. (1970). *Forms of intellectual and ethical development in the college years: A scheme.* Holt, Rinehart and Winston.

Perry, William G. (1981). Cognitive and ethical growth: The making of meaning. In Chickering, Arthur (Ed.), *The modern American college: Responding to the new realities of diverse students and a changing society* (pp. 76–116). Jossey-Bass.

Perry, William G. (1998). *Forms of intellectual and ethical development in the college years: A scheme.* Jossey-Bass.

Perry-Fraser, Charity & Fraser, Rick. (2018). A qualitative analysis of the stepparent role on transition days in blended families. *Open Journal of Social Sciences, 6*(8), 240–251.

Perszyk, Danielle R. & Waxman, Sandra R. (2018). Linking language and cognition in infancy. *Annual Review of Psychology, 69,* 231–250.

Peters, Wendy. (2016). Bullies and blackmail: Finding homophobia in the closet on teen TV. *Sexuality & Culture, 20*(3), 486–503.

Petersen, Inge; Martinussen, Torben; McGue, Matthew; Bingley, Paul & Christensen, Kaare. (2011). Lower marriage and divorce rates among twins than among singletons in Danish birth cohorts 1940–1964. *Twin Research and Human Genetics, 14*(2), 150–157.

Pew Research Center. (2014, February 11). *The rising cost of not going to college. Social & Demographic Trends.* Washington, DC: Pew Research Center.

Pew Research Center. (2015, December 17). *Parenting in America: Outlook, worries, aspirations are strongly linked to financial situation. Social & Demographic Trends.* Washington, DC: Pew Research Center.

Pew Research Center. (2015, November 3). *U.S. public becoming less religious: Modest drop in overall rates of belief and practice, but religiously affiliated Americans are as observant as before. Religion & Public Life.* Washington, DC: Pew Research Center.

Pew Research Center. (2018, April 26). *The public, the political system and American democracy.* Washington, DC: Pew Research Center.

Pew Research Center. (2018, June 13). *The age gap in religion around the world. Religion & Public Life.* Washington, DC: Pew Research Center.

Pew Research Center. (2019, March 14). *Political independents: Who they are, what they think. U.S. Politics and Policy.* Washington, DC: Pew Research Center.

Phillips, Gregory; Beach, Lauren B.; Turner, Blair; Feinstein, Brian A.; Marro, Rachel; Philbin, Morgan M.; . . . Birkett, Michelle. (2019). Sexual identity and behavior among U.S. high school students, 2005–2015. *Archives of Sexual Behavior, 48*(5), 1463–1479.

Piaget, Jean. (1932). *The moral judgment of the child.* K. Paul, Trench, Trubner & Co.

Piaget, Jean. (1950). *The psychology of intelligence.* Routledge & Paul.

Piaget, Jean. (1952). *The origins of intelligence in children.* International Universities Press.

Piaget, Jean. (1954). *The construction of reality in the child.* Basic.

Piaget, Jean. (2001). *The psychology of intelligence.* Routledge.

Piaget, Jean. (2011). *The origins of intelligence in children.* Routledge.

Piaget, Jean. (2013a). *The construction of reality in the child.* Routledge.

Piaget, Jean. (2013b). *The moral judgment of the child.* Routledge.

Piaget, Jean. (2013c). *Play, dreams and imitation in childhood.* Routledge.

Piaget, Jean & Inhelder, Bärbel. (1972). *The psychology of the child.* Basic.

Piechowski-Jozwiak, Bartlomiej & Bogousslavsky, Julien. (2018). Couvade syndrome—Custom, behavior or disease? *Frontiers of Neurology and Neuroscience, 42,* 51–58.

Pierce, Hayley & Heaton, Tim B. (2019). Cohabitation or marriage? How relationship status and community context influence the well-being of children in developing nations. *Population Research and Policy Review, 39,* 719–737.

Piili, Reetta P.; Metsänoja, Riina; Hinkka, Heikki; Kellokumpu-Lehtinen, Pirkko-Liisa I. & Lehto, Juho T. (2018). Changes in attitudes towards hastened death among Finnish physicians over the past sixteen years. *BMC Medical Ethics, 19*(1).

Pilkauskas, Natasha. (2014). Breastfeeding initiation and duration in coresident grandparent, mother and infant households. *Maternal and Child Health Journal, 18*(8), 1955–1963.

Pinker, Steven. (1999). *Words and rules: The ingredients of language.* Basic.

Pinker, Steven. (2018). *Enlightenment now: The case for reason, science, humanism, and progress.* Viking.

Pinquart, Martin & Kauser, Rubina. (2018). Do the associations of parenting styles with behavior problems and academic achievement vary by culture? Results from a meta-analysis. *Cultural Diversity and Ethnic Minority Psychology, 24*(1), 75–100.

Pinquart, Martin & Silbereisen, Rainer K. (2006). Socioemotional selectivity in cancer patients. *Psychology and Aging, 21*(2), 419–423.

Piotrowski, Jessica Taylor & Valkenburg, Patti M. (2015). Finding orchids in a field of dandelions: Understanding children's differential susceptibility to media effects. *American Behavioral Scientist, 59*(14), 1776–1789.

Piske, Micah; Qiu, Annie Q.; Maan, Evelyn J.; Sauvé, Laura J.; Forbes, John C.; Alimenti, Ariane; . . . Côté, Hélène C. F. (2021). Preterm birth and antiretroviral exposure in infants HIV-exposed uninfected. *The Pediatric Infectious Disease Journal, 40*(3), 245–250.

Pittenger, Samantha L.; Huit, Terrence Z. & Hansen, David J. (2016). Applying ecological systems theory to sexual revictimization of youth: A review with implications for research and practice. *Aggression and Violent Behavior, 26,* 35–45.

Pittenger, Samantha L.; Pogue, Jessica K. & Hansen, David J. (2018). Predicting sexual revictimization in childhood and adolescence: A longitudinal examination using ecological systems theory. *Child Maltreatment, 23*(2), 137–146.

Planalp, Elizabeth M. & Goldsmith, H. Hill. (2020). Observed profiles of infant temperament: Stability, heritability, and associations with parenting. *Child Development, 91*(3), e563–e580.

Plener, Paul L.; Schumacher, Teresa S.; Munz, Lara M. & Groschwitz, Rebecca C. (2015). The longitudinal course of non-suicidal self-injury and deliberate self-harm: A systematic review of the literature. *Borderline Personality Disorder and Emotion Dysregulation, 2*(1).

Plomin, Robert; DeFries, John C.; Knopik, Valerie S. & Neiderhiser, Jenae M. (2013). *Behavioral genetics.* Worth.

Pluess, Michael. (2015). Individual differences in environmental sensitivity. *Child Development Perspectives, 9*(3), 138–143.

Poelker, Katelyn E. & Gibbons, Judith L. (2019). Sharing and caring: Prosocial behavior in young children around the world. In Tulviste, Tiia; Best, Deborah L. & Gibbons, Judith L. (Eds.), *Children's social worlds in cultural context* (pp. 89–102). Springer.

Pogrebin, Abigail. (2010). *One and the same: My life as an identical twin and what I've learned about everyone's struggle to be singular.* Anchor.

Polanczyk, Guilherme V.; Willcutt, Erik G.; Salum, Giovanni A.; Kieling, Christian & Rohde, Luis A. (2014). ADHD prevalence estimates across three decades: An updated systematic review and meta-regression analysis. *International Journal of Epidemiology, 43*(2), 434–442.

Pollina, Laura Di; Guessous, Idris; Petoud, Véronique; Combescure, Christophe; Buchs, Bertrand; Schaller, Philippe; . . . Gaspoz, Jean-Michel. (2017). Integrated care at home reduces unnecessary hospitalizations of community-dwelling frail older adults: A prospective controlled trial. *BMC Geriatrics, 17*(53).

Pollock, Ross D.; O'Brien, Katie A.; Daniels, Lorna J.; Nielsen, Kathrine B.; Rowlerson, Anthea; Duggal, Niharika A.; . . . Harridge, Stephen D. R. (2018). Properties of the vastus lateralis muscle in relation to age and physiological function in master cyclists aged 55–79 years. *Aging Cell, 17*(2), e12735.

Polyakov, Alex & Rozen, Genia. (2021). Social egg freezing and donation: Waste not, want not. *Journal of Medical Ethics,* (In Press).

Pons, Ferran & Lewkowicz, David J. (2014). Infant perception of audio-visual speech synchrony in familiar and unfamiliar fluent speech. *Acta Psychologica, 149,* 142–147.

Poon, Kean. (2018). Hot and cool executive functions in adolescence: Development and contributions to important developmental outcomes. *Frontiers in Psychology, 8*(2311).

Posada, Germán E. & Waters, Harriet Salatas. (2018). The mother-child attachment partnership in early childhood: Secure base behavioral and representational processes. *Monographs of the Society for Research in Child Development, 83*(4).

Pouliot, Marie-Agnès Tremblay & Poulin, François. (2021). Congruence and incongruence in father, mother, and adolescent reports of parental monitoring: Examining the links with antisocial behaviors. *Journal of Early Adolescence, 41*(2), 225–252.

Poushter, Jacob; Fetterolf, Janell & Tamir, Christine. (2019, April 22). *A changing world: Global views on diversity, gender equality, family life and the importance of religion.* Washington, DC: Pew Research Center.

Pouwels, J. Loes; Lansu, Tessa A. M. & Cillessen, Antonius H. N. (2016). Participant roles of bullying in adolescence: Status characteristics, social behavior, and assignment criteria. *Aggressive Behavior, 42*(3), 239–253.

Pouwels, J. Loes; Salmivalli, Christina; Saarento, Silja; Van Den Berg, Yvonne H. M.; Lansu, Tessa A. M. & Cillessen, Antonius H. N. (2017). Predicting adolescents' bullying participation from developmental trajectories of social status and behavior. *Child Development.*

Powell, Cynthia M. (2013). Sex chromosomes, sex chromosome disorders, and disorders of sex development. In Gersen, Steven L. & Keagle, Martha B. (Eds.), *The principles of clinical cytogenetics* (pp. 175–211). Springer.

Powell, Kendall. (2006). Neurodevelopment: How does the teenage brain work? *Nature, 442*(7105), 865–867.

Powell, Katie; Wilcox, John; Clonan, Angie; Bissell, Paul; Preston, Louise; Peacock, Marian & Holdsworth, Michelle. (2015). The role of social networks in the development of overweight and obesity among adults: A scoping review. *BMC Public Health, 15*(996).

Powell, Kevin M.; Rahm-Knigge, Ryan L. & Conner, Bradley T. (2020). Resilience Protective Factors Checklist (RPFC): Buffering childhood adversity and promoting positive outcomes. *Psychological Reports,* (In Press).

Powell, Shaun; Langlands, Stephanie & Dodd, Chris. (2011). Feeding children's desires? Child and parental perceptions of food promotion to the "under 8s". *Young Consumers: Insight and Ideas for Responsible Marketers, 12*(2), 96–109.

Powell, Thomas E.; Boomgaarden, Hajo G.; De Swert, Knut & de Vreese, Claes H. (2019). Framing fast and slow: A dual processing account of multimodal framing effects. *Media Psychology, 22*(4), 572–600.

Pozzoli, Tiziana & Gini, Gianluca. (2013). Why do bystanders of bullying help or not? A multidimensional model. *Journal of Early Adolescence, 33*(3), 315–340.

Prasad, Sahdeo; Gupta, Subash C. & Aggarwal, Bharat B. (2012). Micronutrients and cancer: Add spice to your life. In Shankar, Sharmila & Srivastava, Rakesh K. (Eds.), *Nutrition, Diet and Cancer* (pp. 23–48).

Preckel, Katrin; Kanske, Philipp & Singer, Tania. (2018). On the interaction of social affect and cognition: Empathy, compassion and theory of mind. *Current Opinion in Behavioral Sciences, 19,* 1–6.

Preston, Tom & Kelly, Michael. (2006). A medical ethics assessment of the case of Terri Schiavo. *Death Studies, 30*(2), 121–133.

Previtali, Federica; Allen, Laura D. & Varlamova, Maria. (2020). Not only virus spread: The diffusion of ageism during the outbreak of COVID-19. *Journal of Aging & Social Policy, 32*(4/5), 506–514.

Price, Debora; Ribe, Eloi; Di Gessa, Giorgio & Glaser, Karen. (2018). Grandparental childcare: A reconceptualisation of family policy regimes. In Timonen, Virpi (Ed.), *Grandparenting practices around the world* (pp. 43–64). Policy Press.

Proctor, Laura J. & Dubowitz, Howard. (2014). Child neglect: Challenges and controversies. In Korbin, Jill E. & Krugman, Richard D. (Eds.), *Handbook of child maltreatment* (pp. 27–61). Springer.

Prosek, Elizabeth A.; Giordano, Amanda L.; Woehler, Elliott S.; Loseu, Sahar; Stamman, Julia; Lollar, Shannon; . . . Stroh, Lauren. (2020). The experience of religion and spirituality among college students who use illicit substances. *Counseling and Values, 65*(2), 189–205.

Prothero, Arianna. (2016, April 20). Charters help alums stick with college. *Education Week, 35*(28), 1, 13.

Provenzi, Livio; Fumagalli, Monica; Scotto di Minico, Giunia; Giorda, Roberto; Morandi, Francesco; Sirgiovanni, Ida; . . . Montirosso, Rosario. (2020). Pain-related increase in serotonin transporter gene methylation associates with emotional regulation in 4.5-year-old preterm-born children. *Acta Paediatrica, 109*(6), 1166–1174.

Provenzi, Livio; Guida, Elena & Montirosso, Rosario. (2018). Preterm behavioral epigenetics: A systematic review. *Neuroscience & Biobehavioral Reviews, 84*, 262–271.

Puhl, Rebecca M.; Himmelstein, Mary S. & Pearl, Rebecca L. (2020). Weight stigma as a psychosocial contributor to obesity. *American Psychologist, 75*(2), 274–289.

Pulvermüller, Friedemann. (2018). Neural reuse of action perception circuits for language, concepts and communication. *Progress in Neurobiology, 160*, 1–44.

Puritty, Chandler; Strickland, Lynette R.; Alia, Eanas; Blonder, Benjamin; Klein, Emily; Kohl, Michel T.; . . . Gerber, Leah R. (2017). Without inclusion, diversity initiatives may not be enough. *Science, 357*(6356), 1101–1102.

Qiao, Jia; Dai, Li-Jing; Zhang, Qing & Ouyang, Yan-Qiong. (2020). A meta-analysis of the association between breastfeeding and early childhood obesity. *Journal of Pediatric Nursing, 53*, 57–66.

Qin, Desiree B. & Chang, Tzu-Fen. (2013). Asian fathers. In Cabrera, Natasha J. & Tamis-LeMonda, Catherine S. (Eds.), *Handbook of father involvement: Multidisciplinary perspectives* (2nd ed., pp. 261–281). Routledge.

Quindlen, Anna. (2012). *Lots of candles, plenty of cake.* Random House.

Raeburn, Paul. (2014). *Do fathers matter?: What science is telling us about the parent we've overlooked.* Farrar, Straus and Giroux.

Rahal, Danny; Huynh, Virginia; Cole, Steve; Seeman, Teresa & Fuligni, Andrew. (2020). Subjective social status and health during high school and young adulthood. *Developmental Psychology, 56*(6), 1220–1232.

Rahilly, Elizabeth P. (2015). The gender binary meets the gender-variant child: Parents' negotiations with childhood gender variance. *Gender & Society, 29*(3), 338–361.

Raipuria, Harinder Dosanjh; Lovett, Briana; Lucas, Laura & Hughes, Victoria. (2018). A literature review of midwifery-led care in reducing labor and birth interventions. *Nursing for Women's Health, 22*(5), 387–400.

Rakic, Snezana; Jankovic Raznatovic, Svetlana; Jurisic, Aleksandar; Anicic, Radomir & Zecevic, Nebojsa. (2016). Fetal neurosonography and fetal behaviour: Genesis of fetal movements and motor reflexes. *Ultrasound in Obstetrics and Gynecology, 48*(Suppl. 1), 196.

Raley, R. Kelly & Sweeney, Megan M. (2020). Divorce, repartnering, and stepfamilies: A decade in review. *Journal of Marriage and Family, 82*(1), 81–99.

Ramírez, Naja Ferjan; Ramírez, Rey R.; Clarke, Maggie; Taulu, Samu & Kuhl, Patricia K. (2017). Speech discrimination in 11-month-old bilingual and monolingual infants: A magnetoencephalography study. *Developmental Science, 20*(1), e12427.

Ramírez-Esparza, Nairán; García-Sierra, Adrián & Kuhl, Patricia K. (2017). The impact of early social interactions on later language development in Spanish–English bilingual infants. *Child Development, 88*(4), 1216–1234.

Ramscar, Michael & Dye, Melody. (2011). Learning language from the input: Why innate constraints can't explain noun compounding. *Cognitive Psychology, 62*(1), 1–40.

Rand, David G. & Nowak, Martin A. (2016). Cooperation among humans. In Messner, Dirk & Weinlich, Silke (Eds.), *Global cooperation and the human factor in international relations* (pp. 113–138). Routledge.

Rankin, Jay. (2017). Physicians disagree on legal age for cannabis. *CMAJ, 189*(4), E174–E175.

Ranney, John D. & Troop-Gordon, Wendy. (2020). The role of popularity and digital self-monitoring in adolescents' cyberbehaviors and cybervictimization. *Computers in Human Behavior, 102*, 293–302.

Rasmussen, Line Jee Hartmann; Moffitt, Terrie E.; Arseneault, Louise; Danese, Andrea; Eugen-Olsen, Jesper; Fisher, Helen L.; . . . Caspi, Avshalom. (2020). Association of adverse experiences and exposure to violence in childhood and adolescence with inflammatory burden in young people. *JAMA Pediatrics, 174*(1), 38–47.

Rastrelli, Giulia; Guaraldi, Federica; Reismann, Yacov; Sforza, Alessandra; Isidori, Andrea M.; Maggi, Mario & Corona, Giovanni. (2019). Testosterone replacement therapy for sexual symptoms. *Sexual Medicine Reviews, 7*(3), 464–475.

Rattan, Suresh I. S. & Hayflick, Leonard (Eds.). (2016). *Cellular ageing and replicative senescence.* Springer.

Rau, Barbara L. & Adams, Gary A. (2014). Recruiting older workers: Realities and needs of the future workforce. In Cable, Daniel M.; Yang, Kang & Yu, Trevor (Eds.), *The Oxford handbook of recruitment* (pp. 88–109). Oxford University Press.

Rauscher, Frances H.; Shaw, Gordon L. & Ky, Catherine N. (1993). Music and spatial task performance. *Nature, 365*(6447), 611.

Rawlins, William K. (2016). Foreword. In Hojjat, Mahzad & Moyer, Anne (Eds.), *The psychology of friendship.* Oxford University Press.

Ray, Brian D. (2013). Homeschooling rising into the twenty-first century: Editor's introduction. *Peabody Journal of Education, 88*(3), 261–264.

Raymond, Jaime & Brown, Mary Jean. (2017, January 20). *Childhood blood lead levels in children aged <5 Years — United States, 2009–2014. Morbidity and Mortality Weekly Report, 66*(3), 1–10. Atlanta, GA: Centers for Disease Control and Prevention.

Raz, Naftali & Lindenberger, Ulman. (2013). Life-span plasticity of the brain and cognition: From questions to evidence and back. *Neuroscience & Biobehavioral Reviews, 37*(9), 2195–2200.

Reczek, Corinne; Liu, Hui & Spiker, Russell. (2014). A population-based study of alcohol use in same-sex and different-sex unions. *Journal of Marriage and Family, 76*(3), 557–572.

Redondo, Maria J. & Concannon, Patrick. (2020). Genetics of type 1 diabetes comes of age. *Diabetes Care, 43*(1), 16–18.

Reed, Andrew E.; Chan, Larry & Mikels, Joseph A. (2014). Meta-analysis of the age-related positivity effect: Age differences in preferences for positive over negative information. *Psychology and Aging, 29*(1), 1–15.

Reid, Keshia M.; Forrest, Jamie R. & Porter, Lauren. (2018, June 1). *Tobacco product use among youths with and without lifetime asthma—Florida, 2016. Morbidity and Mortality Weekly Report, 67*(21), 599–601. Atlanta, GA: Centers for Disease Control and Prevention.

Reike, Dennis & Schwarz, Wolf. (2019). Aging effects on symbolic number comparison: No deceleration of numerical information retrieval but more conservative decision-making. *Psychology and Aging, 34*(1), 4–16.

Reimann, Zakary; Miller, Jacob R.; Dahle, Kaitana M.; Hooper, Audrey P.; Young, Ashley M.; Goates, Michael C.; . . . Crandall, AliceAnn. (2018). Executive functions and health behaviors associated with the leading causes of death in the United States: A systematic review. *Journal of Health Psychology.*

Reinehr, Thomas & Roth, Christian Ludwig. (2019). Is there a causal relationship between obesity and puberty? *The Lancet Child & Adolescent Health, 3*(1), 44–54.

Reiter, Andrea M. F.; Suzuki, Shinsuke; O'Doherty, John P.; Li, Shu-Chen & Eppinger, Ben. (2019). Risk contagion by peers affects learning and decision-making in adolescents. *Journal of Experimental Psychology, 148*(9), 1494–1504.

Reitz, Anne K. & Staudinger, Ursula M. (2017). Getting older, getting better? Toward understanding positive personality development across adulthood. In Specht, Jule (Ed.), *Personality Development Across the Lifespan* (pp. 219–241). Academic Press.

Renfrew, Mary J.; McFadden, Alison; Bastos, Maria Helena; Campbell, James; Channon, Andrew Amos; Cheung, Ngai Fen; . . . Declercq, Eugene. (2014). Midwifery and quality care: Findings from a new evidence-informed framework for maternal and newborn care. *The Lancet, 384*(9948), 1129–1145.

Reuben, Aaron; Schaefer, Jonathan D.; Moffitt, Terrie E.; Broadbent, Jonathan; Harrington, Honalee; Houts, Renate M.; . . . Caspi, Avshalom (2019). Association of childhood lead exposure with adult personality traits and lifelong mental health. *JAMA Psychiatry, 76*(4), 418–425.

Reynolds, Arthur J. (2000). *Success in early intervention: The Chicago Child-Parent Centers.* University of Nebraska Press.

Reynolds, Arthur J. & Ou, Suh-Ruu. (2011). Paths of effects from preschool to adult well-being: A confirmatory analysis of the Child-Parent Center Program. *Child Development, 82*(2), 555–582.

Reynolds, Jamila E. & Gonzales-Backen, Melinda A. (2017). Ethnic-racial socialization and the mental health of African Americans: A critical review. *Journal of Family Theory & Review, 9*(12), 182–200.

Ricci, Giovanna. (2020). Pharmacological human enhancement: An overview of the looming bioethical and regulatory challenges. *Frontiers in Psychiatry, 11*(53).

Richards, Jennifer S.; Hartman, Catharina A.; Franke, Barbara; Hoekstra, Pieter J.; Heslenfeld, Dirk J.; Oosterlaan, Jaap; . . . Buitelaar, Jan K. (2014). Differential susceptibility to maternal expressed emotion in children with ADHD and their siblings? Investigating plasticity genes, prosocial and antisocial behaviour. *European Child & Adolescent Psychiatry, 24*(2), 209–217.

Richards, Morgan K.; Flanagan, Meghan R.; Littman, Alyson J.; Burke, Alson K. & Callegari, Lisa S. (2016). Primary cesarean section and adverse delivery outcomes among women of very advanced maternal age. *Journal of Perinatology, 36*, 272–277.

Rickman, Cheryl. (2021). *Navigating loneliness how to connect with yourself and others: A mental health handbook.* Welbeck.

Riglin, Lucy; Frederickson, Norah; Shelton, Katherine H. & Rice, Frances. (2013). A longitudinal study of psychological functioning and academic attainment at the transition to secondary school. *Journal of Adolescence, 36*(3), 507–517.

Rijken, A. J. & Liefbroer, A. C. (2016). Differences in family norms for men and women across Europe. *Journal of Marriage and Family, 78*(4), 1097–1113.

Riordan, Jan & Wambach, Karen (Eds.). (2009). *Breastfeeding and human lactation* (4th ed.). Jones and Bartlett.

Rioux, Charlie; Castellanos-Ryan, Natalie; Parent, Sophie & Séguin, Jean R. (2016). The interaction between temperament and the family environment in adolescent substance use and externalizing behaviors: Support for diathesis–stress or differential susceptibility? *Developmental Review, 40*(10), 117–150.

Rissanen, Inkeri; Kuusisto, Elina; Tuominen, Moona & Tirri, Kirsi. (2019). In search of a growth mindset pedagogy: A case study of one teacher's classroom practices in a Finnish elementary school. *Teaching and Teacher Education, 77*, 204–213.

Ristori, Jiska; Cocchetti, Carlotta; Romani, Alessia; Mazzoli, Francesca; Vignozzi, Linda; Maggi, Mario & Fisher, Alessandra Daphne. (2020). Brain sex differences related to gender identity development: Genes or hormones? *International Journal of Molecular Sciences, 21*(6), 2123.

Rivenbark, Joshua; Arseneault, Louise; Caspi, Avshalom; Danese, Andrea; Fisher, Helen L.; Moffitt, Terrie E.; . . . Odgers, Candice L. (2020). Adolescents' perceptions of family social status correlate with health and life chances: A twin difference longitudinal cohort study. *PNAS, 117*(38), 23323–23328.

Rizzo, Michael T. & Killen, Melanie. (2016). Children's understanding of equity in the context of inequality. *British Journal of Developmental Psychology, 34*(4), 569–581.

Rizzo, Michael T.; Li, Leon; Burkholder, Amanda R. & Killen, Melanie. (2019). Lying, negligence, or lack of knowledge? Children's intention-based moral reasoning about resource claims. *Developmental Psychology, 55*(2), 274–285.

Roane, David M.; Landers, Alyssa; Sherratt, Jackson & Wilson, Gillian S. (2017). Hoarding in the elderly: A critical review of the recent literature. *International Psychogeriatrics, 29*(7), 1077–1084.

Robben, Antonius C. G. M. (2018). Death and anthropology: An introduction. In Robben, Antonius C. G. M. (Ed.), *Death, mourning, and burial: A cross-cultural reader* (2nd ed., pp. 1–16). Wiley-Blackwell.

Roberts, Leslie. (2020). Global polio eradication falters in the final stretch. *Science, 367*(6473), 14–15.

Robertson, Cassandra & O'Brien, Rourke. (2018). Health endowment at birth and variation in intergenerational economic mobility: Evidence from U.S. county birth cohorts. *Demography, 55*(1), 249–269.

Robine, Jean-Marie; Allard, Michel; Herrmann, François R. & Jeune, Bernard. (2019). The real facts supporting Jeanne Calment as the oldest ever human. *The Journals of Gerontology: Series A, 74*(Suppl. 1), S13–S20.

Robinson, Julia T. & Murphy-Nugen, Amy B. (2018). It makes you keep trying: Life review writing for older adults. *Journal of Gerontological Social Work, 61*(2), 171–192.

Robson, Ruthann. (2010). Notes on my dying. In Maglin, Nan Bauer & Perry, Donna Marie (Eds.), *Final acts: Death, dying, and the choices we make* (pp. 19–28). Rutgers University Press.

Rochat, Philippe. (2013). Self-conceptualizing in development. In Zelazo, Philip D. (Ed.), *The Oxford handbook of developmental psychology* (Vol. 2, pp. 378–397). Oxford University Press.

Roche, Kathleen M.; Lambert, Sharon F.; White, Rebecca M. B.; Calzada, Esther J.; Little, Todd D.; Kuperminc, Gabriel P. & Schulenberg, John E. (2019). Autonomy-related parenting processes and adolescent adjustment in Latinx immigrant families. *Journal of Youth and Adolescence, 48*, 1161–1174.

Rodgers, Rachel F.; Slater, Amy; Gordon, Chloe S.; Mclean, Siân A.; Jarman, Hannah K. & Paxton, Susan J. (2020). A biopsychosocial model of social media use and body image concerns, disordered eating, and muscle-building behaviors among adolescent girls and boys. *Journal of Youth and Adolescence, 49*(2), 399–409.

Rodrigue, Karen M. & Kennedy, Kristen M. (2011). The cognitive consequences of structural changes to the aging brain. In Schaie, K. Warner & Willis, Sherry L. (Eds.), *Handbook of the psychology of aging* (7th ed., pp. 73–91). Academic Press.

Rodrigues dos Santos, Marcelo & Bhasin, Shalender. (2021). Benefits and risks of testosterone treatment in men with age-related decline in testosterone. *Annual Review of Medicine, 72*, 75–91.

Rodriguez, Christina M.; Silvia, Paul J. & Gaskin, Regan E. (2019). Predicting maternal and paternal parent-child aggression risk: Longitudinal multimethod investigation using social information processing theory. *Psychology of Violence, 9*(3), 370–382.

Rogers, Leoandra Onnie; Kiang, Lisa; White, Lauren; Calzada, Esther J.; Umaña-Taylor, Adriana J.; Byrd, Christy; . . . Whitesell, Nancy. (2020). Persistent concerns: Questions for research on ethnic-racial identity development. *Research in Human Development.*

Rogoff, Barbara. (2016). Culture and participation: A paradigm shift. *Current Opinion in Psychology, 8*, 182–189.

Roksa, Josipa; Trolian, Teniell L.; Pascarella, Ernest T.; Kilgo, Cindy A.; Blaich, Charles & Wise, Kathleen S. (2017). Racial inequality in critical thinking skills: The role of academic and diversity experiences. *Research in Higher Education, 58*, 119–140.

Rollè, Luca; Giardina, Giulia; Caldarera, Angela M.; Gerino, Eva & Brustia, Piera. (2018). When intimate partner violence meets same sex couples: A review of same sex intimate partner violence. *Frontiers in Psychology, 9*(1506).

Romagnolo, Donato F. & Selmin, Ornella I. (Eds.). (2016). *Mediterranean diet: Dietary guidelines and impact on health and disease.* Springer.

Romanelli, Meghan; Xiao, Yunyu & Lindsey, Michael A. (2020). Sexual identity-behavior profiles and suicide outcomes among heterosexual, lesbian, and gay sexually active adolescents: Sexual identity-behavior profiles and suicide. *Suicide and Life-Threatening Behavior, 50*(4), 921–933.

Ronkainen, Rina; Kuusisto, Elina & Tirri, Kirsi. (2019). Growth mindset in teaching: A case study of a Finnish elementary school teacher. *International Journal of Learning, Teaching and Educational Research, 18*(8), 141–154.

Rook, Graham A. W.; Lowry, Christopher A. & Raison, Charles L. (2014). Hygiene and other early childhood influences on the subsequent function of the immune system. *Brain Research*, (Corrected Proof).

Roopnarine, Jaipaul L. & Hossain, Ziarat. (2013). African American and African Caribbean fathers. In Cabrera, Natasha J. & Tamis-LeMonda, Catherine S. (Eds.), *Handbook of father involvement: Multidisciplinary perspectives* (2nd ed., pp. 223–243). Routledge.

Rose, Amanda J. & Asher, Steven R. (2017). The social tasks of friendship: Do boys and girls excel in different tasks? *Child Development Perspectives, 11*(1), 3–8.

Rose, Dawn; Jones Bartoli, Alice & Heaton, Pamela C. (2019). Measuring the impact of musical learning on cognitive, behavioural and socio-emotional wellbeing development in children. *Psychology of Music, 47*(2), 284–303.

Rose, Katherine K.; Johnson, Amy; Muro, Joel & Buckley, Rhonda R. (2018). Decision making about nonparental child care by fathers: What is important to fathers in a nonparental child care program. *Journal of Family Issues, 39*(2), 299–327.

Rose, Steven. (2008). Drugging unruly children is a method of social control. *Nature, 451*(7178), 521.

Roseberry, Lynn & Roos, Johan. (2016). *Bridging the gender gap: Seven principles for achieving gender balance.* Oxford University Press.

Rosenfeld, Michael J. & Roesler, Katharina. (2019). Cohabitation experience and cohabitation's association with marital dissolution: The short-term benefits of cohabitation. *Journal of Marriage and Family, 81*(1), 42–58.

Rosenfield, Sarah. (2012). Triple jeopardy? Mental health at the intersection of gender, race, and class. *Social Science & Medicine, 74*(11), 1791–1801.

Rosow, Irving. (1985). Status and role change through the life cycle. In Binstock, Robert H. & Shanas, Ethel (Eds.), *Handbook of aging and the social sciences* (2nd ed., pp. 62–93). Van Nostrand Reinhold.

Ross, Gail S.; Rescorla, Leslie A. & Perlman, Jeffrey M. (2020). Patterns and prediction of behavior problems during the toddler and preschool periods in preterm children. *International Journal of Behavioral Development, 44*(5), 404–411.

Ross, Josephine; Yilmaz, Mandy; Dale, Rachel; Cassidy, Rose; Yildirim, Iraz & Zeedyk, M. Suzanne. (2017). Cultural differences in self-recognition: The early development of autonomous and related selves? *Developmental Science, 20*(3), e12387.

Rossignol, Michel; Chaillet, Nils; Boughrassa, Faiza & Moutquin, Jean-Marie. (2014). Interrelations between four antepartum obstetric interventions and cesarean delivery in women at low risk: A systematic review and modeling of the cascade of interventions. *Birth, 41*(1), 70–78.

Rostila, Mikael; Saarela, Jan & Kawachi, Ichiro. (2013). Suicide following the death of a sibling: A nationwide follow-up study from Sweden. *BMJ Open, 3*(4), e002618.

Roth, Benjamin J.; Crea, Thomas M.; Jani, Jayshree; Underwood, Dawnya; Hasson, Robert G.; Evans, Kerri & Zuch, Michael. (2018). Detached and afraid: U.S. immigration policy and the practice of forcibly separating parents and young children at the border. *Children Welfare, 96*(5), 29–49.

Rothbart, M. K. & Derryberry, D. (1981). Development of individual differences in temperament. In Lamb, Michael E. & Brown, Ann L. (Eds.), *Advances in developmental psychology* (pp. 37–86). Lawrence Erlbaum Associates.

Rothstein, Mark A. (2015). The moral challenge of Ebola. *American Journal of Public Health, 105*(1), 6–8.

Roubinov, Danielle S. & Boyce, William Thomas. (2017). Parenting and SES: Relative values or enduring principles? *Current Opinion in Psychology, 15*, 162–167.

Rovee-Collier, Carolyn. (1987). Learning and memory in infancy. In Osofsky, Joy Doniger (Ed.), *Handbook of infant development* (2nd ed., pp. 98–148). Wiley.

Rovee-Collier, Carolyn. (1990). The "memory system" of prelinguistic infants. *Annals of the New York Academy of Sciences, 608*, 517–542.

Rowe, Meredith L.; Denmark, Nicole; Harden, Brenda Jones & Stapleton, Laura M. (2016). The role of parent education and parenting knowledge in children's language and literacy skills among white, Black, and Latino families. *Infant and Child Development, 25*(2), 198–220.

Rowson, Tatiana S. & Phillipson, Christopher. (2020). 'I never really left the university:' Continuity amongst male academics in the transition from work to retirement. *Journal of Aging Studies, 53*(100853).

Rubin, Kenneth H.; Bowker, Julie C.; McDonald, Kristina L. & Menzer, Melissa. (2013). Peer relationships in childhood. In Zelazo, Philip D. (Ed.), *The Oxford handbook of developmental psychology* (Vol. 2, pp. 242–275). Oxford University Press.

Ruch, Donna A.; Sheftall, Arielle H.; Schlagbaum, Paige; Fontanella, Cynthia A.; Campo, John V. & Bridge, Jeffrey A. (2019). Characteristics and precipitating circumstances of suicide among incarcerated youth. *Journal of the American Academy of Child & Adolescent Psychiatry, 58*(5), 514–524.e1.

Rudaz, Myriam; Ledermann, Thomas; Margraf, Jürgen; Becker, Eni S. & Craske, Michelle G. (2017). The moderating role of avoidance behavior on anxiety over time: Is there a difference between social anxiety disorder and specific phobia? *PLoS ONE, 12*(7), e0180298.

Runions, Kevin C. & Shaw, Thérèse. (2013). Teacher–child relationship, child withdrawal and aggression in the development of peer victimization. *Journal of Applied Developmental Psychology, 34*(6), 319–327.

Russell, Allison; Nyame-Mensah, Ama; Wit, Arjen & Handy, Femida. (2019). Volunteering and wellbeing among ageing adults: A longitudinal analysis. *VOLUNTAS, 30*(1), 115–128.

Russell, Charlotte K.; Robinson, Lyn & Ball, Helen L. (2013). Infant sleep development: Location, feeding and expectations in the postnatal period. *The Open Sleep Journal, 6*(Suppl. 1: M9), 68–76.

Russell, David; Diamond, Eli L.; Lauder, Bonnie; Dignam, Ritchell R.; Dowding, Dawn W.; Peng, Timothy R.; . . . Bowles, Kathryn H. (2017). Frequency and risk factors for live discharge from hospice. *Journal of the American Geriatrics Society, 65*(8), 1726–1732.

Ruthig, Joelle C.; Trisko, Jenna & Stewart, Tara L. (2012). The impact of spouse's health and well-being on own well-being: A dyadic study of older married couples. *Journal of Social and Clinical Psychology, 31*(5), 508–529.

Rutter, Michael. (2012). Resilience as a dynamic concept. *Development and Psychopathology, 24*(2), 335–344.

Rynkowska, Dorota. (2020). Universities of the Third Age and their role in education and preventive gerontology. *European Journal of Sustainable Development, 9*(3).

Sabates, Ricardo & Di Cesare, Mariachiara. (2019). Can maternal education sustain or enhance the benefits of early life interventions? Evidence from the Young Lives Longitudinal Study. *Compare: A Journal of Comparative and International Education*, (In Press).

Sabeti, Pardis & Salahi, Lara. (2018). *Outbreak culture: The Ebola crisis and the next epidemic.* Harvard University Press.

Sadeh, Avi; Mindell, Jodi A.; Luedtke, Kathryn & Wiegand, Benjamin. (2009). Sleep and sleep ecology in the first 3 years: A web-based study. *Journal of Sleep Research, 18*(1), 60–73.

Sadler, Thomas W. (2015). *Langman's medical embryology* (13th ed.). Lippincott Williams & Wilkins.

Saegert, Susan; Fields, Desiree & Libman, Kimberly. (2011). Mortgage foreclosure and health disparities: Serial displacement as asset extraction in African American populations. *Journal of Urban Health, 88*(3), 390–402.

Saenz, Joseph. (2020). Literacy and cognitive function in the context of marriage: A study of older Mexican couples. *Innovation in Aging, 4*(Suppl. 1), 859.

Saey, Tina Hesman. (2016). Neandertal DNA poses health risks. *Science News, 189*(5), 18–19.

Saffran, Jenny R. & Kirkham, Natasha Z. (2018). Infant statistical learning. *Annual Review of Psychology, 69*, 181–203.

Sahlberg, Pasi. (2011). *Finnish lessons: What can the world learn from educational change in Finland?* Teachers College Press.

Sahlberg, Pasi. (2015). *Finnish lessons 2.0: What can the world learn from educational change in Finland?* (2nd. ed.). Teachers College Press.

Sahlberg, Pasi. (2021). *Finnish lessons 3.0: What can the world learn from educational change in Finland?* Teachers College Press.

Sahoo, Krushnapriya; Sahoo, Bishnupriya; Choudhury, Ashok Kumar; Sofi, Nighat Yasin; Kumar, Raman & Bhadoria, Ajeet Singh. (2015). Childhood obesity: Causes and consequences. *Journal of Family Medicine and Primary Care, 4*(2), 187–192.

Saitou, Marie & Gokcumen, Omer. (2020). An evolutionary perspective on the impact of genomic copy number variation on human health. *Journal of Molecular Evolution, 88*(1), 104–119.

Sakai, Jill. (2020). How synaptic pruning shapes neural wiring during development and, possibly, in disease. *Proceedings of the National Academy of Sciences of the United States of America, 117*(28), 16096–16099.

Salas, Gabriela Barrón; Lagos, María Eugenia Ciofalo & Perez, Manuel González. (2018). Analysis of emotional intelligence as a competition for effective productivity. *International Journal of Advanced Engineering, Management and Science, 4*(8), 615–621.

Salkind, Neil J. (2004). *An introduction to theories of human development.* Sage.

Salomon, Ilyssa & Brown, Christia Spears. (2019). The selfie generation: Examining the relationship between social media use and early adolescent body image. *Journal of Early Adolescence, 39*(4), 539–560.

Salpeter, Shelley R.; Luo, Esther J.; Malter, Dawn S. & Stuart, Brad. (2012). Systematic review of noncancer presentations with a median survival of 6 months or less. *The American Journal of Medicine, 125*(5), 512.e1–512.e16.

Salthouse, Timothy A. (2019). Trajectories of normal cognitive aging. *Psychology and Aging, 34*(1), 17–24.

Samaras, Nikolass; Frangos, Emilia; Forster, Alexandre; Lang, P. O. & Samaras, Dimitrios. (2012). Andropause: A review of the definition and treatment. *European Geriatric Medicine, 3*(6), 368–373.

Sameri, Saba; Samadi, Pouria; Dehghan, Razieh; Salem, Elham; Fayazi, Nashmin & Amini, Razieh. (2020). Stem cell aging in lifespan and disease: A state-of-the-art review. *Current Stem Cell Research & Therapy, 15*(4), 362–378.

Sammler, Daniela & Elmer, Stefan. (2020). Advances in the neurocognition of music and language. *Brain Sciences, 10*(8), 509.

Sampaio, Waneli Cristine Morais; Ribeiro, Mara Cláudia; Costa, Larice Feitosa; Souza, Wânia Cristina de; Castilho, Goiara Mendonça de; Assis, Melissa Sousa de; . . . Ferreira, Vania Moraes. (2017). Effect of music therapy on the developing central nervous system of rats. *Psychology & Neuroscience, 10*(2), 176–188.

Sampaio-Baptista, Cassandra; Sanders, Zeena-Britt & Johansen-Berg, Heidi. (2018). Structural plasticity in adulthood with motor learning and stroke rehabilitation. *Annual Review of Neuroscience, 41*, 25–40.

Sanchez, Gabriel R. & Vargas, Edward D. (2016). Taking a closer look at group identity: The link between theory and measurement of group consciousness and linked fate. *Political Research Quarterly, 69*(1), 160–174.

Sánchez-Mira, Núria & Saura, Dafne Muntanyola. (2020). Attachment parenting among middle-class couples in Spain: Gendered principles and labor divisions. *Journal of Family Studies*, (In Press).

Sánchez-Sánchez, María Luz; García-Vigara, Alicia; Hidalgo-Mora, Juan José; García-Pérez, Miguel-Ángel; Tarín, Juan & Cano, Antonio. (2020). Mediterranean diet and health: A systematic review of epidemiological studies and intervention trials. *Maturitas, 136*, 25–37.

Sanchez-Vaznaugh, Emma V.; Weverka, Aiko; Matsuzaki, Mika & Sánchez, Brisa N. (2019). Changes in fast food outlet availability near schools: Unequal patterns by income, race/ethnicity, and urbanicity. *American Journal of Preventive Medicine, 57*(3), 338–345.

Sandberg, Sheryl & UC Berkeley (Producer). (2016). *Sheryl Sandberg gives UC Berkeley Commencement keynote speech.* [Video]. YouTube.

Sanner, Caroline; Ganong, Lawrence & Coleman, Marilyn. (2020). Shared children in stepfamilies: Experiences living in a hybrid family structure. *Journal of Marriage and Family, 82*(2), 605–621.

Santelli, John S.; Kantor, Leslie M.; Grilo, Stephanie A.; Speizer, Ilene S.; Lindberg, Laura D.; Heitel, Jennifer; . . . Ott, Mary A. (2017). Abstinence-only-until-marriage: An updated review of U.S. policies and programs and their impact. *Journal of Adolescent Health, 61*(3), 273–280.

Santini, Ziggi Ivan; Koyanagi, Ai; Tyrovolas, Stefanos; Mason, Catherine & Haro, Josep Maria. (2015). The association between social relationships and depression: A systematic review. *Journal of Affective Disorders, 175*, 53–65.

Santos, Carlos E.; Kornienko, Olga & Rivas-Drake, Deborah. (2017). Peer influence on ethnic-racial identity development: A multi-site investigation. *Child Development, 88*(3), 725–742.

Sanz Cruces, José Manuel; Hawrylak, María Fernández & Delegido, Ana Benito. (2015). Interpersonal variability of the experience of falling in love. *International Journal of Psychology and Psychological Therapy, 15*(1), 87–100.

Saracho, Olivia N. (2016). *Contemporary perspectives on research on bullying and victimization in early childhood education.* Information Age.

Sasser, Tyler R.; Bierman, Karen L.; Heinrichs, Brenda & Nix, Robert L. (2017). Preschool intervention can promote sustained growth in the executive-function skills of children exhibiting early deficits. *Psychological Science, 28*(12), 1719–1730.

Sassler, Sharon & Lichter, Daniel T. (2020). Cohabitation and marriage: Complexity and diversity in union-formation patterns. *Journal of Marriage and Family, 82*(1), 35–61.

Sassler, Sharon & Miller, Amanda Jayne. (2017). *Cohabitation nation: Gender, class, and the remaking of relationships.* University of California Press.

Satterwhite, Catherine Lindsey; Torrone, Elizabeth; Meites, Elissa; Dunne, Eileen F.; Mahajan, Reena; Ocfemia, M. Cheryl Bañez; . . . Weinstock, Hillard. (2013). Sexually transmitted infections among US women and men: Prevalence and incidence estimates, 2008. *Sexually Transmitted Diseases, 40*(3), 187–193.

Savage, Jeanne E.; Jansen, Philip R.; Stringer, Sven; Watanabe, Kyoko; Bryois, Julien; de Leeuw, Christiaan A.; . . . Posthuma, Danielle. (2018). Genome-wide association meta-analysis in 269,867 individuals identifies new genetic and functional links to intelligence. *Nature Genetics, 50*(7), 912–919.

Saxbe, Darby E. (2017). Birth of a new perspective? A call for biopsychosocial research on childbirth. *Current Directions in Psychological Science, 26*(1), 81–86.

Scarborough, William J.; Sin, Ray & Risman, Barbara. (2019). Attitudes and the stalled gender revolution: Egalitarianism, traditionalism, and ambivalence from 1977 through 2016. *Gender & Society, 33*(2), 173–200.

Scarr, Sandra. (1985). Constructing psychology: Making facts and fables for our times. *American Psychologist, 40*(5), 499–512.

Scelzo, Anna; Di Somma, Salvatore; Antonini, Paola; Montross, Lori; Schork, Nicholas; Brenner, David & Jeste, Dilip V. (2018). Mixed-methods quantitative-qualitative study of 29 nonagenarians and centenarians in rural Southern Italy: Focus on positive psychological traits. *International Psychogeriatrics, 30*(1), 31–38.

Schacter, Hannah L. & Juvonen, Jaana. (2019). Dynamic changes in peer victimization and adjustment across middle school: Does friends' victimization alleviate distress? *Child development, 90*(5), 1738–1753.

Schafer, Markus H.; Morton, Patricia M. & Ferraro, Kenneth F. (2014). Child maltreatment and adult health in a national sample: Heterogeneous relational contexts, divergent effects? *Child Abuse & Neglect, 38*(3), 395–406.

Schaie, K. Warner. (1958). Rigidity-flexibility and intelligence: A cross-sectional study of the adult life span from 20 to 70 years. *Psychological Monographs, 72*(9), 1–26.

Schaie, K. Warner. (2005). *Developmental influences on adult intelligence: The Seattle Longitudinal Study.* Oxford University Press.

Schaie, K. Warner. (2013). *Developmental influences on adult intelligence: The Seattle Longitudinal Study* (2nd ed.). Oxford University Press.

Schanler, Richard. J. (2011). Outcomes of human milk-fed premature infants. *Seminars in Perinatology, 35*(1), 29–33.

Schapira, Rotem; Anger Elfenbein, Hillary; Amichay-Setter, Meirav; Zahn-Waxler, Carolyn & Knafo-Noam, Ariel. (2019). Shared environment effects on children's emotion recognition. *Frontiers in Psychiatry, 10*(215).

Scharf, Miri. (2014). Parenting in Israel: Together hand in hand, you are mine and I am yours. In Selin, Helaine (Ed.), *Parenting across cultures: Childrearing, motherhood and fatherhood in non-Western cultures* (pp. 193–206). Springer.

Scharf, Miri & Goldner, Limor. (2018). "If you really love me, you will do/be . . . ": Parental psychological control and its implications for children's adjustment. *Developmental Review, 49*, 16–30.

Schermerhorn, Alice C.; D'Onofrio, Brian M.; Turkheimer, Eric; Ganiban, Jody M.; Spotts, Erica L.; Lichtenstein, Paul; . . . Neiderhiser, Jenae M. (2011). A genetically informed study of associations between family functioning and child psychosocial adjustment. *Developmental Psychology, 47*(3), 707–725.

Schmid, Monika S.; Gilbers, Steven & Nota, Amber. (2014). Ultimate attainment in late second language acquisition: Phonetic and grammatical challenges in advanced Dutch–English bilingualism. *Second Language Research, 30*(2), 129–157.

Schneider, Daniel & Harknett, Kristen. (2019). Consequences of routine work-schedule instability for worker health and well-being. *American Sociological Review, 84*(1), 82–114.

Schneider, William; Waldfogel, Jane & Brooks-Gunn, Jeanne. (2017). The Great Recession and risk for child abuse and neglect. *Children and Youth Services Review, 72*, 71–81.

Schoebi, Dominik; Karney, Benjamin R. & Bradbury, Thomas N. (2012). Stability and change in the first 10 years of marriage: Does commitment confer benefits beyond the effects of satisfaction? *Journal of Personality and Social Psychology, 102*(4), 729–742.

Schroeder, Philip H.; Napoli, Nicholas J.; Barnhardt, William F.; Barnes, Laura E. & Young, Jeffrey S. (2019). Relative mortality analysis of the "golden hour": A comprehensive acuity stratification approach to address disagreement in current literature. *Prehospital Emergency Care, 23*(2), 254–262.

Schübel, Ruth; Nattenmüller, Johanna; Sookthai, Disorn; Nonnenmacher, Tobias; Graf, Mirja E.; Riedl, Lena; . . . Kühn, Tilman. (2018). Effects of intermittent and continuous calorie restriction on body weight and metabolism over 50 wk: A randomized controlled trial. *American Journal of Clinical Nutrition, 108*(5), 933–945.

Schubert, Anna-Lena; Hagemann, Dirk; Löffler, Christoph & Frischkorn, Gidon T. (2020). Disentangling the effects of processing speed on the association between age differences and fluid intelligence. *Journal of Intelligence, 8*(1).

Schulman, Allison R. & Thompson, Christopher C. (2017). Complications of bariatric surgery: What you can expect to see in your GI practice. *American Journal of Gastroenterology, 112*(11), 1640–1655.

Schupp, Justin & Sharp, Jeff. (2012). Exploring the social bases of home gardening. *Agriculture and Human Values, 29*(1), 93–105.

Schwartz, Seth & Petrova, Mariya. (2019). Prevention science in emerging adulthood: A field coming of age. *Prevention Science, 20*(3), 305–309.

Schwartz, Shalom H. (2015). Basic individual values: Sources and consequences. In Brosch, Tobias & Sander, David (Eds.), *Handbook of value: Perspectives from economics, neuroscience, philosophy, psychology and sociology.* Oxford University Press.

Schweinhart, Lawrence J.; Montie, Jeanne; Xiang, Zongping; Barnett, W. Steven; Belfield, Clive R. & Nores, Milagros. (2005). *Lifetime effects: The High/Scope Perry Preschool Study through age 40.* High/Scope Press.

Schweinhart, Lawrence J. & Weikart, David P. (1997). *Lasting differences: The High/Scope Preschool curriculum comparison study through age 23.* High/Scope Educational Research Foundation.

Scott, Diane L.; Lee, Chang-Bae; Harrell, Susan W. & Smith-West, Mary B. (2013). Permanency for children in foster care: Issues and barriers for adoption. *Child & Youth Services, 34*(3), 290–307.

Sears, William & Sears, Martha. (2001). *The attachment parenting book: A commonsense guide to understanding and nurturing your baby.* Little Brown.

Seaton, Eleanor K. (2020). A luta continua: Next steps for racism research among Black American youth. *Child Development Perspectives, 14*(4), 244–250.

Seaton, Eleanor K.; Quintana, Stephen; Verkuyten, Maykel & Gee, Gilbert C. (2017). Peers, policies, and place: The relation between context and ethnic/racial identity. *Child Development, 88*(3), 683–692.

Sedlak, Andrea J. & Ellis, Raquel T. (2014). Trends in child abuse reporting. In Korbin, Jill E. & Krugman, Richard D. (Eds.), *Handbook of child maltreatment* (pp. 3–26). Springer.

Seemiller, Eric S.; Cumming, Bruce G. & Candy, T. Rowan. (2018). Human infants can generate vergence responses to retinal disparity by 5 to 10 weeks of age. *Journal of Vision, 18*(6).

Sekeres, Mikkael A. (2013, January 31). A doctor's struggle with numbers. *New York Times.*

Senese, Vincenzo Paolo; Azhari, Atiqah; Shinohara, Kazuyuki; Doi, Hirokazu; Venuti, Paola; Bornstein, Marc H. & Esposito, Gianluca. (2019). Implicit associations to infant cry: Genetics and early care experiences influence caregiving propensities. *Hormones and Behavior, 108*, 1–9.

Serrano-Pozo, Alberto & Growdon, John H. (2019). Is Alzheimer's disease risk modifiable? *Journal of Alzheimer's Disease, 67*(3), 795–819.

Seth, Puja; Scholl, Lawrence; Rudd, Rose A. & Bacon, Sarah. (2018). *Overdose deaths involving opioids, cocaine, and psychostimulants — United States, 2015–2016. Morbidity and Mortality Weekly Report, 67*(12), 349–358. Atlanta, GA: Centers for Disease Control and Prevention.

Seto, Elizabeth & Schlegel, Rebecca J. (2018). Becoming your true self: Perceptions of authenticity across the lifespan. *Self and Identity, 17*(3), 310–326.

Settersten, Richard A. (2015). Relationships in time and the life course: The significance of linked lives. *Research in Human Development, 12*(3/4), 217–223.

Settersten, Richard A.; Bernardi, Laura; Härkönen, Juho; Antonucci, Toni C.; Dykstra, Pearl A.; Heckhausen, Jutta; . . . Thomson, Elizabeth. (2020). Understanding the effects of Covid-19 through a life course lens. *Advances in Life Course Research, 45*(100360).

Sewell, Andrew. (2016). *English pronunciation models in a globalized world: Accent, acceptability and Hong Kong English.* Rutledge.

Shanahan, Timothy & Lonigan, Christopher J. (2010). The National Early Literacy Panel: A summary of the process and the report. *Educational Researcher, 39*(4), 279–285.

Shane, Jacob; Luerssen, Anna & Carmichael, Cheryl L. (2020). Friends, family, and romantic partners: Three critical relationships in older women's lives. *Journal of Women & Aging*, (In Press).

Shane, Jacob; Niwa, Erika Y. & Heckhausen, Jutta. (2021). Prosociality across adulthood: A developmental and motivational perspective. *Psychology and Aging, 36*(1), 22–35.

Sharkey, Shirlee & Lefebre, Nancy. (2017). Leadership perspective: Bringing nursing back to the future through people-powered care. *Nursing Leadership, 30*(1), 11–22.

Sharot, Tali. (2017). *The influential mind: What the brain reveals about our power to change others.* Henry Holt.

Shavit, Yochai Z. & Carstensen, Laura L. (2019). Age and occupational time perspective are associated with preference for helping others at work. *Innovation in Aging, 3*(Suppl. 1), S127–S128.

Shearera, C. Branton & Karanian, Jessica M. (2017). The neuroscience of intelligence: Empirical support for the theory of multiple intelligences? *Trends in Neuroscience and Education, 6*, 211–223.

Shechner, Tomer; Fox, Nathan A.; Mash, Jamie A.; Jarcho, Johanna M.; Chen, Gang; Leibenluft, Ellen; . . . Britton, Jennifer C. (2018). Differences in neural response to extinction recall in young adults with or without history of behavioral inhibition. *Development and Psychopathology, 30*(1), 179–189.

Sheldon, Kennon M.; Holliday, Greyson; Titova, Liudmila & Benson, Craig. (2020). Comparing holland and self-determination theory measures of career preference as predictors of career choice. *Journal of Career Assessment, 28*(1), 28–42.

Shen, Yimo; Schaubroeck, John M.; Zhao, Lei & Wu, Lei. (2019). Work group climate and behavioral responses to psychological contract breach. *Frontiers in Psychology, 10*(67).

Sheridan, Margaret A.; Mclaughlin, Katie A.; Winter, Warren; Fox, Nathan; Zeanah, Charles & Nelson, Charles A. (2018). Early deprivation disruption of associative learning is a developmental pathway to depression and social problems. *Nature Communications, 9*(1), 2216.

Sherlock, James M. & Zietsch, Brendan P. (2018). Longitudinal relationships between parents' and children's behavior need not implicate the influence of parental behavior and may reflect genetics: Comment on Waldinger and Schulz (2016). *Psychological Science, 29*(1), 154–157.

Shi, Bing & Xie, Hongling. (2012). Popular and nonpopular subtypes of physically aggressive preadolescents: Continuity of aggression and peer mechanisms during the transition to middle school. *Merrill-Palmer Quarterly, 58*(4), 530–553.

Shi, Rushen. (2014). Functional morphemes and early language acquisition. *Child Development Perspectives, 8*(1), 6–11.

Shields, Grant S.; Spahr, Chandler M. & Slavich, George M. (2020). Psychosocial interventions and immune system function: A systematic review and meta-analysis of randomized clinical trials. *JAMA Psychiatry*, 77(10), 1031–1043.

Shim, Woo-Jeong & Perez, Rosemary Jane. (2018). A multi-level examination of first-year students' openness to diversity and challenge. *Journal of Higher Education, 89*(4), 453–477.

Shiovitz-Ezra, Sharon & Litwin, Howard. (2015). Social network type and health among older Americans. In Nyqvist, Fredrica & Forsman, Anna K. (Eds.), *Social capital as a health resource in later life: The relevance of context* (pp. 15–31). Springer.

Shlisky, Julie; Bloom, David E.; Beaudreault, Amy R.; Tucker, Katherine L.; Keller, Heather H.; Freund-Levi, Yvonne; . . . Meydani, Simin N. (2017). Nutritional considerations for healthy aging and reduction in age-related chronic disease. *Advances in Nutrition, 8*(1), 17–26.

Shoda, Yuichi; Mischel, Walter & Peake, Philip K. (1990). Predicting adolescent cognitive and self-regulatory competencies from preschool delay of gratification: Identifying diagnostic conditions. *Developmental Psychology, 26*(6), 978–986.

Short, Clara Schaertl. (2019). Comment on "Outbreak: On transgender teens and psychic epidemics". *Psychological Perspectives, 62*(2/3), 285–289.

Shpancer, Noam & Schweitzer, Stefanie N. (2018). A history of non-parental care in childhood predicts more positive adult attitudes towards non-parental care and maternal employment. *Early Child Development and Care, 188*(3), 375–386.

Shulman, Cory. (2016). *Research and practice in infant and early childhood mental health.* Springer.

Shulman, Elizabeth P. & Cauffman, Elizabeth. (2014). Deciding in the dark: Age differences in intuitive risk judgment. *Developmental Psychology, 50*(1), 167–177.

Shwalb, David W.; Shwalb, Barbara J. & Lamb, Michael E. (Eds.). (2013). *Fathers in cultural context.* Psychology Press.

Siegal, Michael & Surian, Luca (Eds.). (2012). *Access to language and cognitive development.* Oxford University Press.

Siegelman, Jeffrey N. (2020). Reflections of a COVID-19 long hauler. *JAMA, 324*(20), 2031–2032.

Silk, Jessica & Romero, Diana. (2014). The role of parents and families in teen pregnancy prevention: An analysis of programs and policies. *Journal of Family Issues, 35*(10), 1339–1362.

Silva, Meghan R.; Collier-Meek, Melissa A.; Codding, Robin S.; Kleinert, Whitney L. & Feinberg, Adam. (2020). Data collection and analysis in response-to-intervention: A survey of school psychologists. *Contemporary School Psychology,* (In Press).

Silventoinen, Karri; Hammar, Niklas; Hedlund, Ebba; Koskenvuo, Markku; Ronnemaa, Tapani & Kaprio, Jaakko. (2008). Selective international migration by social position, health behaviour and personality. *European Journal of Public Health, 18*(2), 150–155.

Silverman, Arielle M. & Cohen, Geoffrey L. (2014). Stereotypes as stumbling-blocks: How coping with stereotype threat affects life outcomes for people with physical disabilities. *Personality and Social Psychology Bulletin, 40*(10), 1330–1340.

Sim, Zi L. & Xu, Fei. (2017). Learning higher-order generalizations through free play: Evidence from 2- and 3-year-old children. *Developmental Psychology, 53*(4), 642–651.

Simmons, Joseph P.; Nelson, Leif D. & Simonsohn, Uri. (2011). False-positive psychology: Undisclosed flexibility in data collection and analysis allows presenting anything as significant. *Psychological Science, 22*(11), 1359–1366.

Simmons, Sandra F. & Rahman, Anna N. (2014). Next steps for achieving person-centered care in nursing homes. *JAMDA, 15*(9), 615–619.

Simon, Laura & Daneback, Kristian. (2013). Adolescents' use of the internet for sex education: A thematic and critical review of the literature. *International Journal of Sexual Health, 25*(4), 305–319.

Simons, Ronald L.; Lei, Man-Kit; Klopack, Eric; Beach, Steven R. H.; Gibbons, Frederick X. & Philibert, Robert A. (2020). The effects of social adversity, discrimination, and health risk behaviors on the accelerated aging of African Americans: Further support for the weathering hypothesis. *Social Science & Medicine,* (In Press), 113169.

Singanayagam, Aran; Ritchie, Andrew I. & Johnston, Sebastian L. (2017). Role of microbiome in the pathophysiology and disease course of asthma. *Current Opinion in Pulmonary Medicine, 23*(1), 41–47.

Singer, Judith D. & Braun, Henry I. (2018). Testing international education assessments. *Science, 360*(6384), 38–40.

Singh, Amika; Uijtdewilligen, Léonie; Twisk, Jos W. R.; van Mechelen, Willem & Chinapaw, Mai J. M. (2012). Physical activity and performance at school: A systematic review of the literature including a methodological quality assessment. *Archives of Pediatrics & Adolescent Medicine, 166*(1), 49–55.

Singh, Krittika; Parveen, Sheeba; Sharma, Ginni & Joshi, Gunjan. (2020). Impact of COVID-19 and lockdown on mental health of children and adolescents: A narrative review with recommendations. *Psychiatry Research, 293*(113429).

Sinnott, Jan D. (2014). *Adult development: Cognitive aspects of thriving close relationships.* Oxford University Press.

Sisson, Susan B.; Krampe, Megan; Anundson, Katherine & Castle, Sherri. (2016). Obesity prevention and obesogenic behavior interventions in child care: A systematic review. *Preventive Medicine, 87,* 57–69.

Skiba, Russell J.; Michael, Robert S.; Nardo, Abra Carroll & Peterson, Reece L. (2002). The color of discipline: Sources of racial and gender disproportionality in school punishment. *The Urban Review, 34*(4), 317–342.

Skinner, B. F. (1953). *Science and human behavior.* Macmillan.

Skinner, B. F. (1957). *Verbal behavior.* Appleton-Century-Crofts.

Skoog, Therése & Stattin, Håkan. (2014). Why and under what contextual conditions do early-maturing girls develop problem behaviors? *Child Development Perspectives, 8*(3), 158–162.

Slade, Kate; Plack, Christopher J. & Nuttall, Helen E. (2020). The effects of age-related hearing loss on the brain and cognitive function. *Trends in Neurosciences, 43*(10), 810–821.

Slagt, Meike; Dubas, Judith Semon; Deković, Maja & van Aken, Marcel A. G. (2016). Differences in sensitivity to parenting depending on child temperament: A meta-analysis. *Psychological Bulletin, 142*(10), 1068–1110.

Slaughter, Anne-Marie. (2012). Why women still can't have it all. *The Atlantic, 310*(1), 84–102.

Slotnick, Scott D. (2017). *Cognitive neuroscience of memory.* Cambridge University Press.

Small, Meredith F. (1998). *Our babies, ourselves: How biology and culture shape the way we parent.* Anchor Books.

Smetana, Judith G.; Ahmad, Ikhlas & Wray-Lake, Laura. (2016). Beliefs about parental authority legitimacy among refugee youth in Jordan: Between- and within-person variations. *Developmental Psychology, 52*(3), 484–495.

Smith, Dorothy E. (1993). The standard North American family: SNAF as an ideological code. *Journal of Family Issues, 14*(1), 50–65.

Smith, Daniel M. & Martiny, Sarah E. (2018). Stereotype threat in sport: Recommendations for applied practice and research. *The Sport Psychologist, 32*(4), 311–320.

Smith, Hannah E.; Ryan, Kelsey N.; Stephenson, Kevin B.; Westcott, Claire; Thakwalakwa, Chrissie; Maleta, Ken; . . . Manary, Mark J. (2014). Multiple micronutrient supplementation transiently ameliorates environmental enteropathy in Malawian children aged 12–35 months in a randomized controlled clinical trial. *Journal of Nutrition, 144*(12), 2059–2065.

Smith, Justin D.; Fu, Emily & Kobayashi, Marissa A. (2020). Prevention and management of childhood obesity and its psychological and health comorbidities. *Annual Review of Clinical Psychology, 16*, 351–378.

Smith, Michelle I.; Yatsunenko, Tanya; Manary, Mark J.; Trehan, Indi; Mkakosya, Rajhab; Cheng, Jiye; . . . Gordon, Jeffrey I. (2013). Gut microbiomes of Malawian twin pairs discordant for kwashiorkor. *Science, 339*(6119), 548–554.

Smith, Sharon G.; Zhang, Xinjian; Basile, Kathleen C.; Merrick, Melissa T.; Wang, Jing; Kresnow, Marcie-jo & Chen, Jieru. (2018). *The national intimate partner and sexual violence survey: 2015 data brief—Updated release.* Atlanta, GA: National Center for Injury Prevention and Control, Centers for Disease Control and Prevention.

Smithells, R. W.; Sheppard, S.; Schorah, C. J.; Seller, M. J.; Nevin, N. C.; Harris, R.; . . . Fielding, D. W. (2011). Apparent prevention of neural tube defects by periconceptional vitamin supplementation. *International Journal of Epidemiology, 40*(5), 1146–1154.

Smits, Jeroen & Monden, Christiaan. (2011). Twinning across the developing world. *PLoS ONE, 6*(9), e25239.

Snyder, Thomas D. & Dillow, Sally A. (2013). *Digest of education statistics, 2012.* Washington, DC: National Center for Education Statistics, Institute of Education Sciences, U.S. Department of Education.

Society for Developmental and Behavioral Pediatrics. (2018, July 18). SDBP statement related to the separation of children from families at the border [Press release]. Society for Developmental and Behavioral Pediatrics.

Solheim, Elisabet; Wichstrøm, Lars; Belsky, Jay & Berg-Nielsen, Turid Suzanne. (2013). Do time in child care and peer group exposure predict poor socioemotional adjustment in Norway? *Child Development, 84*(5), 1701–1715.

Soller, Brian & Kuhlemeier, Alena. (2019). Gender and intimate partner violence in Latino immigrant neighborhoods. *Journal of Quantitative Criminology, 35*(1), 61–88.

Somerville, Leah H. (2013). The teenage brain: Sensitivity to social evaluation. *Current Directions in Psychological Science, 22*(2), 121–127.

Son, Daye & Padilla-Walker, Laura M. (2019). Whereabouts and secrets: A person-centered approach to emerging adults' routine and self-disclosure to parents. *Emerging Adulthood*, 145–157.

Sontag, Marci K.; Yusuf, Careema; Grosse, Scott D.; Edelman, Sari; Miller, Joshua I.; McKasson, Sarah; . . . Shapira, Stuart K. (2020, September 11). *Infants with congenital disorders identified through newborn screening—United States, 2015–2017. Morbidity and Mortality Weekly Report, 69*(36), 1265–1268. Atlanta, GA: Centers for Disease Control and Prevention.

Sonuga-Barke, Edmund J. S.; Kennedy, Mark; Kumsta, Robert; Knights, Nicky; Golm, Dennis; Rutter, Michael; . . . Kreppner, Jana. (2017). Child-to-adult neurodevelopmental and mental health trajectories after early life deprivation: The young adult follow-up of the longitudinal English and Romanian Adoptees study. *The Lancet, 389*(10078), 1539–1548.

Sorrells, Shawn F.; Paredes, Mercedes F.; Cebrian-Silla, Arantxa; Sandoval, Kadellyn; Qi, Dashi; Kelley, Kevin W.; . . . Alvarez-Buylla, Arturo. (2018). Human hippocampal neurogenesis drops sharply in children to undetectable levels in adults. *Nature, 555*, 377–381.

Sotomayor, Sonia. (2014). *My beloved world.* Vintage Books.

Soulsby, Laura K. & Bennett, Kate M. (2017). When two become one: Exploring identity in marriage and cohabitation. *Journal of Family Issues, 38*(3), 358–380.

Sparks, Sarah D. (2016, July 20). Dose of empathy found to cut suspension rates. *Education Week, 35*(36), 1, 20.

Sparrow, Erika P.; Swirsky, Liyana T.; Kudus, Farrah & Spaniol, Julia. (2021). Aging and altruism: A meta-analysis. *Psychology and Aging, 36*(1), 49–56.

Spelke, Elizabeth S. (1993). Object perception. In Goldman, Alvin I. (Ed.), *Readings in philosophy and cognitive science* (pp. 447–460). MIT Press.

Spencer, Steven J.; Logel, Christine & Davies, Paul G. (2016). Stereotype threat. *Annual Review of Psychology, 67*, 415–437.

Spijker, Jeroen & MacInnes, John. (2013). Population ageing: The timebomb that isn't? *BMJ, 347*, f6598.

Spolaore, Enrico & Wacziarg, Romain. (2018). Ancestry and development: New evidence. *Journal of Applied Econometrics, 33*(5), 748–762.

Spreng, R. Nathan & Turner, Gary R. (2019). The shifting architecture of cognition and brain function in older adulthood. *Perspectives on Psychological Science, 14*(4), 523–542.

Springsteen, Bruce. (2017). *Born to run.* Simon & Schuster.

Sriram, Rajalakshmi. (2019). A global perspective on fathering. In Sriram, Rajalakshmi (Ed.), *Fathering in India* (pp. 19–34). Springer.

Staddon, John. (2014). *The new behaviorism* (2nd ed.). Psychology Press.

Stålnacke, Sofia Ryytty; Tessma, Mesfin; Böhm, Birgitta & Herlenius, Eric. (2019). Cognitive development trajectories in preterm children with very low birth weight longitudinally followed until 11 years of age. *Frontiers in Physiology, 10*, 307.

Standing, E. M. (1998). *Maria Montessori: Her life and work.* Plume.

Statistics Norway. (2018). Facts about education in Norway 2018. Statistics Norway's Information Centre.

Stattin, Håkan; Hussein, Oula; Özdemir, Metin & Russo, Silvia. (2017). Why do some adolescents encounter everyday events that increase their civic interest whereas others do not? *Developmental Psychology, 53*(2), 306–318.

Steele, Claude M. (1997). A threat in the air: How stereotypes shape intellectual identity and performance. *American Psychologist, 52*(6), 613–629.

Stefansen, Kari; Smette, Ingrid & Strandbu, Åse. (2018). Understanding the increase in parents' involvement in organized youth sports. *Sport, Education and Society, 23*(2), 162–172.

Steinberg, Laurence. (2009). Should the science of adolescent brain development inform public policy? *American Psychologist, 64*(8), 739–750.

Steinberg, Laurence & Monahan, Kathryn C. (2011). Adolescents' exposure to sexy media does not hasten the initiation of sexual intercourse. *Developmental Psychology, 47*(2), 562–576.

Steinmetz, Katy. (2013, August 12). From Messiah to Hitler, what you can and cannot name your child. *Time*.

Steinsbekk, Silje; Bjørklund, Oda; Llewelly, Clare & Wichstrøm, Lars. (2020). Temperament as a predictor of eating behavior in middle childhood—A fixed effects approach. *Appetite, 150*(104640).

Steinsbekk, Silje; Wichstrøm, Lars; Stenseng, Frode; Nesi, Jacqueline; Hygen, Beate Wold & Skalická, Věra. (2021). The impact of social media use on appearance self-esteem from childhood to adolescence—A 3-wave community study. *Computers in Human Behavior, 114*(106528).

Stenseng, Frode; Belsky, Jay; Skalicka, Vera & Wichstrøm, Lars. (2015). Social exclusion predicts impaired self-regulation: A 2-year longitudinal panel study including the transition from preschool to school. *Journal of Personality, 83*(2), 212–220.

Stepler, Renee. (2017, March 9). *Led by baby boomers, divorce rates climb for America's 50+ population. Fact Tank*. Washington, DC: Pew Research Center.

Sterling, Peter. (2012). Allostasis: A model of predictive regulation. *Physiology & Behavior, 106*(1), 5–15.

Stern, Gavin. (2015). For kids with special learning needs, roadblocks remain. *Science, 349*(6255), 1465–1466.

Stern, Jessica A.; Botdorf, Morgan; Cassidy, Jude & Riggins, Tracy. (2019). Empathic responding and hippocampal volume in young children. *Developmental Psychology, 55*(9), 1908–1920.

Stern, Mark; Clonan, Sheila; Jaffee, Laura & Lee, Anna. (2015). The normative limits of choice: Charter schools, disability studies, and questions of inclusion. *Educational Policy, 29*(3), 448–477.

Sternberg, Robert J. (1988). Triangulating love. In Sternberg, Robert J. & Barnes, Michael L. (Eds.), *The psychology of love* (pp. 119–138). Yale University Press.

Sternberg, Robert J. (2003). *Wisdom, intelligence, and creativity synthesized*. Cambridge University Press.

Sternberg, Robert J. (2011). The theory of successful intelligence. In Sternberg, Robert J. & Kaufman, Scott Barry (Eds.), *The Cambridge handbook of intelligence* (pp. 504–526). Cambridge University Press.

Sternberg, Robert J. (2012). Why I became an administrator ... and why you might become one too: Applying the science of psychology to the life of a university. *Observer, 25*(2), 21–22.

Sternberg, Robert J. (2015). Multiple intelligences in the new age of thinking. In Goldstein, Sam; Princiotta, Dana & Naglieri, Jack A. (Eds.), *Handbook of intelligence* (pp. 229–241). Springer.

Stevens, Victoria L.; Jacobs, Eric J.; Sun, Juzhong; Patel, Alpa V.; McCullough, Marjorie L.; Teras, Lauren R. & M., Gapstur Susan. (2012). Weight cycling and mortality in a large prospective US study. *American Journal of Epidemiology, 175*(8), 785–792.

Stevenson, Robert G. (2017). Children and death: What do they know and when do they learn it? In Stevenson, Robert G. & Cox, Gerry R. (Eds.), *Children, adolescents, and death: Questions and answers*. Routledge.

Stiles, Joan & Jernigan, Terry. (2010). The basics of brain development. *Neuropsychology Review, 20*(4), 327–348.

Stiner, Mary C. (2017). Love and death in the stone age: What constitutes first evidence of mortuary treatment of the human body? *Biological Theory, 12*(4), 248–261.

Stives, Kristen L.; May, David C.; Pilkinton, Melinda; Bethel, Cindy L. & Eakin, Deborah K. (2019). Strategies to combat bullying: Parental responses to bullies, bystanders, and victims. *Youth & Society, 51*(3), 358–376.

Stochholm, Kirstine; Bojesen, Anders; Jensen, Anne Skakkebæk; Juul, Svend & Gravholt, Claus Højbjerg. (2012). Criminality in men with Klinefelter's syndrome and XYY syndrome: A cohort study. *BMJ Open, 2*(1), e000650.

Stolzenberg, Ellen Bara; Eagan, Kevin; Aragon, Melissa C.; Cesar-Davis, Natacha M.; Jacobo, Sidronio; Couch, Victoria & Rios-Aguilar, Cecilia. (2019). *The American freshman: National norms fall 2017*. Los Angeles, CA: Higher Education Research Institute, UCLA.

Stone, Adam & Bosworth, Rain G. (2019). Exploring infant sensitivity to visual language using eye tracking and the preferential looking paradigm. *Journal of Visualized Experiments*(147), e59581.

Stone, Deborah M.; Jones, Christopher M. & Mack, Karin A. (2021, February 26). *Changes in suicide rates—United States, 2018–2019. Morbidity and Mortality Weekly Report, 70*(8). Atlanta, GA: Centers for Disease Control and Prevention.

Stone, Jeff; Harrison, C. Keith & Mottley, JaVonte. (2012). "Don't call me a student-athlete": The effect of identity priming on stereotype threat for academically engaged African American college athletes. *Basic and Applied Social Psychology, 34*(2), 99–106.

Strasburger, Victor C.; Wilson, Barbara J. & Jordan, Amy B. (2009). *Children, adolescents, and the media* (2nd ed.). Sage.

Stroebe, Margaret S.; Abakoumkin, Georgios; Stroebe, Wolfgang & Schut, Henk. (2012). Continuing bonds in adjustment to bereavement: Impact of abrupt versus gradual separation. *Personal Relationships, 19*(2), 255–266.

Strouse, Gabrielle A. & Ganea, Patricia A. (2017). Toddlers' word learning and transfer from electronic and print books. *Journal of Experimental Child Psychology, 156*, 129–142.

Stults, Christopher B.; Javdani, Shabnam; Kapadia, Farzana & Halkitis, Perry N. (2019). Determinants of intimate partner violence among young men who have sex with men: The P18 cohort study. *Journal of Interpersonal Violence*, (In Press).

Substance Abuse and Mental Health Services Administration. (2019). *Key substance use and mental health indicators in the United States: Results from the 2018 National Survey on Drug Use and Health.* Rockville, MD: Center for Behavioral Health Statistics and Quality, Substance Abuse and Mental Health Services Administration. HHS Publication No. PEP19-5068, NSDUH Series H-54.

Sudharsanan, Nikkil; Didzun, Oliver; Bärnighausen, Till & Geldsetzer, Pascal. (2020). The contribution of the age distribution of cases to COVID-19 case fatality across countries: A nine-country demographic study. *Annals of Internal Medicine, 173*(9), 714–720.

Sugimura, Kazumi. (2020). Adolescent identity development in Japan. *Child Development Perspectives, 14*(2), 71–77.

Sugimura, Kazumi; Crocetti, Elisabetta; Hatano, Kai; Kaniušonytė, Goda; Hihara, Shogo & Žukauskienė, Rita. (2018). A cross-cultural perspective on the relationships between emotional separation, parental trust, and identity in adolescents. *Journal of Youth and Adolescence, 47*(4), 749–759.

Sugimura, Kazumi; Matsushima, Kobo; Hihara, Shogo; Takahashi, Masami & Crocetti, Elisabetta. (2019). A culturally sensitive approach to the relationships between identity formation and religious beliefs in youth. *Journal of Youth and Adolescence, 48*(4), 668–679.

Suleiman, Ahna B. & Brindis, Claire D. (2014). Adolescent school-based sex education: Using developmental neuroscience to guide new directions for policy and practice. *Sexuality Research and Social Policy, 11*(2), 137–152.

Sullivan, Kevin J.; Dodge, Hiroko H.; Hughes, Tiffany F.; Chang, Chung-Chou H.; Zhu, Xinmei; Liu, Anran & Ganguli, Mary. (2019). Declining incident dementia rates across four population-based birth cohorts. *The Journals of Gerontology: Series A, 74*(9), 1439–1445.

Sullivan, Sheila. (1999). *Falling in love: A history of torment and enchantment.* Macmillan.

Sulmasy, Daniel. (2018). The last low whispers of our dead: When is it ethically justifiable to render a patient unconscious until death? *Theoretical Medicine and Bioethics, 39*(3), 233–263.

Sunderam, Saswati; Kissin, Dmitry M.; Zhang, Yujia; Jewett, Amy; Boulet, Sheree L.; Warner, Lee; . . . Barfield, Wanda D. (2020, December 18). *Assisted reproductive technology surveillance— United States, 2017. Morbidity and Mortality Weekly Report, 69*(9), 1–20.

Sundqvist, Christel; Björk-Åman, Camilla & Ström, Kristina. (2019). The three-tiered support system and the special education teachers' role in Swedish-speaking schools in Finland. *European Journal of Special Needs Education, 34*(5), 601–616.

Suomi, Steven J. (2002). Parents, peers, and the process of socialization in primates. In Borkowski, John G.; Ramey, Sharon L. & Bristol-Power, Marie (Eds.), *Parenting and the child's world: Influences on academic, intellectual, and social-emotional development* (pp. 265–279). Erlbaum.

Suurland, Jill; van der Heijden, Kristiaan B.; Huijbregts, Stephan C. J.; Smaling, Hanneke J. A.; de Sonneville, Leo M. J.; Van Goozen, Stephanie H. M. & Swaab, Hanna. (2016). Parental perceptions of aggressive behavior in preschoolers: Inhibitory control moderates the association with negative emotionality. *Child Development, 87*(1), 256–269.

Suzumori, Nobuhiro; Kumagai, Kyoko; Goto, Shinobu; Nakamura, Akira & Sugiura-Ogasawara, Mayumi. (2015). Parental decisions following prenatal diagnosis of chromosomal abnormalities: Implications for genetic counseling practice in Japan. *Journal of Genetic Counseling, 24*(1), 117–121.

Sweeney, Melanie D.; Kisler, Kassandra; Montagne, Axel; Toga, Arthur W. & Zlokovic, Berislav V. (2018). The role of brain vasculature in neurodegenerative disorders. *Nature Neuroscience, 21*(10), 1318–1331.

Swit, Cara & McMaugh, Anne. (2012). Relational aggression and prosocial behaviours in Australian preschool children. *Australasian Journal of Early Childhood, 37*(3), 30–34.

Szanton, Sarah L.; Wolff, Jennifer L.; Leff, Bruce; Roberts, Laken; Thorpe, Roland J.; Tanner, Elizabeth K.; . . . Gitlin, Laura N. (2015). Preliminary data from Community Aging in Place, advancing better living for elders, a patient-directed, team-based intervention to improve physical function and decrease nursing home utilization: The first 100 individuals to complete a Centers for Medicare and Medicaid Services innovation project. *Journal of the American Geriatrics Society, 63*(2), 371–374.

Tabassum, Faiza; Mohan, John & Smith, Peter. (2016). Association of volunteering with mental well-being: A lifecourse analysis of a national population-based longitudinal study in the UK. *BMJ Open, 6*(8), e011327.

Taillieu, Tamara L.; Afifi, Tracie O.; Mota, Natalie; Keyes, Katherine M. & Sareen, Jitender. (2014). Age, sex, and racial differences in harsh physical punishment: Results from a nationally representative United States sample. *Child Abuse & Neglect, 38*(12), 1885–1894.

Takala, Marjatta; Nordmark, Marie & Allard, Karin. (2019). University curriculum in special teacher education in Finland and Sweden. *Nordic Journal of Comparative and International Education, 3*(2), 20–36.

Takatori, Katsuhiko & Matsumoto, Daisuke. (2021). Social factors associated with reversing frailty progression in community-dwelling late-stage elderly people: An observational study. *PLoS ONE, 16*(3), e0247296.

Talley, Ronda C. & Montgomery, Rhonda J. V. (2013). Caregiving: A developmental lifelong perspective. In Talley, Ronda C. & Montgomery, Rhonda J. V. (Eds.), *Caregiving across the lifespan: Research, practice, policy* (pp. 3–10). Springer.

Talwar, Victoria; Lavoie, Jennifer; Gomez-Garibello, Carlos & Crossman, Angela M. (2017). Influence of social factors on the relation between lie-telling and children's cognitive abilities. *Journal of Experimental Child Psychology, 159*, 185–198.

Tamis-LeMonda, Catherine S.; Bornstein, Marc H. & Baumwell, Lisa. (2001). Maternal responsiveness and children's achievement of language milestones. *Child Development, 72*(3), 748–767.

Tamura, Naomi; Hanaoka, Tomoyuki; Ito, Kumiko; Araki, Atsuko; Miyashita, Chihiro; Ito, Sachiko; . . . Kishi, Reiko. (2018). Different risk factors for very low birth weight, term-small-for-gestational-age, or preterm birth in Japan. *International Journal of Environmental Research and Public Health, 15*(2), 369.

Tan, Patricia Z.; Armstrong, Laura M. & Cole, Pamela M. (2013). Relations between temperament and anger regulation over early childhood. *Social Development, 22*(4), 755–772.

Tang, Hua & Barsh, Gregory S. (2017). Skin color variation in Africa. *Science, 358*(6365), 867–868.

Tang, Suqin; Xiang, Mi; Cheung, Teris & Xiang, Yu-Tao. (2021). Mental health and its correlates among children and adolescents during COVID-19 school closure: The importance of parent-child discussion. *Journal of Affective Disorders, 279*, 353–360.

Tartaro, Christine. (2019). *Suicide and self-harm in prisons and jails* (2nd ed.). Lexington.

Tassell-Matamua, Natasha; Lindsay, Nicole; Bennett, Simon; Valentine, Hukarere & Pahina, John. (2017). Does learning about near-death experiences promote psycho-spiritual benefits in those who have not had a near-death experience? *Journal of Spirituality in Mental Health, 19*(2), 95–115.

Taylor, John H. (Ed.) (2010). *Journey through the afterlife: Ancient Egyptian Book of the Dead*. Harvard University Press.

Taylor, Marjorie; Mottweiler, Candice M.; Aguiar, Naomi R.; Naylor, Emilee R. & Levernier, Jacob G. (2020). Paracosms: The imaginary worlds of middle childhood. *Child Development, 91*(1), e164–e178.

Taylor, Paul. (2014). *The next America: Boomers, millennials, and the looming generational showdown*. PublicAffairs.

Taylor, Zoe E.; Eisenberg, Nancy; Spinrad, Tracy L.; Eggum, Natalie D. & Sulik, Michael J. (2013). The relations of ego-resiliency and emotion socialization to the development of empathy and prosocial behavior across early childhood. *Emotion, 13*(5), 822–831.

Tedeschi, Richard; Orejuela-Davila, Ana & Lewis, Paisley. (2017). Posttraumatic growth and continuing bonds. In Klass, Dennis & Steffen, Edith Maria (Eds.), *Continuing bonds in bereavement: New directions for research and practice*. Routledge.

Telles, Edward. (2018). Latinos, race, and the U.S. census. *The ANNALS of the American Academy of Political and Social Science, 677*(1), 153–164.

Teoh, Yee San & Lamb, Michael E. (2013). Interviewer demeanor in forensic interviews of children. *Psychology, Crime & Law, 19*(2), 145–159.

Tetley, Josie; Lee, David M.; Nazroo, James & Hinchliff, Sharron. (2018). Let's talk about sex—What do older men and women say about their sexual relations and sexual activities? A qualitative analysis of ELSA Wave 6 data. *Ageing & Society, 38*(3), 497–521.

Thayer, Amanda L.; Petruzzelli, Alexandra & McClurg, Caitlin E. (2018). Addressing the paradox of the team innovation process: A review and practical considerations. *American Psychologist, 73*(4), 363–375.

Thiam, Melinda A.; Flake, Eric M. & Dickman, Michael M. (2017). Infant and child mental health and perinatal illness. In Thiam, Melinda A. (Ed.), *Perinatal mental health and the military family: Identifying and treating mood and anxiety disorders*. Routledge.

Thibodeaux, Jordan; Bock, Allison; Hutchison, Lindsey A. & Winsler, Adam. (2019). Singing to the self: Children's private speech, private song, and executive functioning. *Cognitive Development, 50*, 130–141.

Thierry, Amy D.; Sherman-Wilkins, Kyler; Armendariz, Marina; Sullivan, Allison & Farmer, Heather R. (2021). Perceived neighborhood characteristics and cognitive functioning among diverse older adults: An intersectional approach. *International Journal of Environmental Research and Public Health, 18*(5), 2661.

Thomaes, Sander; Brummelman, Eddie & Sedikides, Constantine. (2017). Why most children think well of themselves. *Child Development, 88*(6), 1873–1884.

Thomas, Dennis; Dickerson, Anne E.; Blomberg, Richard D.; Graham, Lindsey A.; Wright, Timothy J.; Finstad, Kraig A. & Romoser, Matthew E. (2018). *Older drivers and navigation devices*. Washington, DC: National Highway Traffic Safety Administration. DOT HS 812 587.

Thomas, Dylan. (2003). *The poems of Dylan Thomas* (Rev. ed.). New Directions.

Thomas, Michael S. C.; Mareschal, Denis & Dumontheil, Iroise (Eds.). (2020). *Educational neuroscience: Development across the life span*. Routledge.

Thomas, Michael S. C.; Van Duuren, Mike; Purser, Harry R. M.; Mareschal, Denis; Ansari, Daniel & Karmiloff-Smith, Annette. (2010). The development of metaphorical language comprehension in typical development and in Williams syndrome. *Journal of Experimental Child Psychology, 106*(2/3), 99–114.

Thompson, Brittany N. & Goldstein, Thalia R. (2019). Children learn from both embodied and passive pretense: A replication and extension. *Child Development, 91*(4), 1364–1374.

Thompson, Richard; Kaczor, Kim; Lorenz, Douglas J.; Bennett, Berkeley L.; Meyers, Gabriel & Pierce, Mary Clyde. (2017). Is the use of physical discipline associated with aggressive behaviors in young children? *Academic Pediatrics, 17*(1), 34–44.

Thornton, Jacqui. (2020). In the aftermath: The legacy of measles in Samoa. *The Lancet, 395*(10236), 1535–1536.

Timonen, Virpi (Ed.) (2018). *Grandparenting practices around the world*. Policy Press.

Tinsley, Grant M. & Horne, Benjamin D. (2018). Intermittent fasting and cardiovascular disease: Current evidence and unresolved questions. *Future Cardiology, 14*(1), 47–54.

Tippett, Lynette J.; Prebble, Sally C. & Addis, Donna Rose. (2018). The persistence of the self over time in mild cognitive impairment and Alzheimer's disease. *Frontiers in Psychology, 9*(94).

Todes, Daniel P. (2014). *Ivan Pavlov: A Russian life in science*. Oxford University Press.

Tomasello, Michael. (2016a). The ontogeny of cultural learning. *Current Opinion in Psychology, 8*, 1–4.

Tomasello, Michael. (2016b). Cultural learning redux. *Child Development, 87*(3), 643–653.

Tomasello, Michael. (2017). What did we learn from the ape language studies? In Hare, Brian & Yamamoto, Shinya (Eds.), *Bonobos: Unique in mind, brain, and behavior* (pp. 95–104). Oxford University Press.

Toth, Sheree L. & Manly, Jody T. (2019). Developmental consequences of child abuse and neglect: Implications for intervention. *Child Development Perspectives, 13*(1), 59–65.

Tourva, Anna & Spanoudis, George. (2020). Speed of processing, control of processing, working memory and crystallized and fluid intelligence: Evidence for a developmental cascade. *Intelligence, 83*(101503).

Townsend, Apollo; March, Alice L. & Kimball, Jan. (2017). Can faith and hospice coexist: Is the African American church the key to increased hospice utilization for African Americans? *Journal of Transcultural Nursing, 28*(1), 32–39.

Trawick-Smith, Jeffrey. (2019). Not all children grow up the same: Child development, diversity, and early care and education. In Brown, Christopher P.; McMullen, Mary Benson & File, Nancy (Eds.), *The Wiley handbook of early childhood care and education* (pp. 29–58). Wiley.

Traynor, Victoria; Veerhui, Nadine & Gopalan, Shiva. (2018). Evaluating the effects of a physical activity program on agitation and wandering experienced by individuals living with a dementia in care homes. *Australian Nursing & Midwifery Journal, 25*(7), 44.

Treas, Judith & Gubernskaya, Zoya. (2012). Farewell to moms? Maternal contact for seven countries in 1986 and 2001. *Journal of Marriage and Family, 74*(2), 297–311.

Treffers-Daller, Jeanine & Milton, J. (2013). Vocabulary size revisited: The link between vocabulary size and academic achievement. *Applied Linguistics Review, 4*(1), 151–172.

Trentacosta, Natasha. (2020). Pediatric sports injuries. *Pediatric Clinics, 67*(1), 205–225.

Trinh, Sarah L.; Lee, Jaemin; Halpern, Carolyn T. & Moody, James. (2019). Our buddies, ourselves: The role of sexual homophily in adolescent friendship networks. *Child Development, 90*(1), e132–e147.

Troll, Lillian E. & Skaff, Marilyn McKean. (1997). Perceived continuity of self in very old age. *Psychology and Aging, 12*(1), 162–169.

Tronick, Edward. (1989). Emotions and emotional communication in infants. *American Psychologist, 44*(2), 112–119.

Tronick, Edward & Weinberg, M. Katherine. (1997). Depressed mothers and infants: Failure to form dyadic states of consciousness. In Murray, Lynne & Cooper, Peter J. (Eds.), *Postpartum depression and child development* (pp. 54–81). Guilford Press.

Trost, Armin. (2020). *Human resources strategies: Balancing stability and agility in times of digitization*. Springer.

Trusz, Slawomir. (2017). The teacher's pet phenomenon 25 years on. *Social Psychology of Education, 20*(4), 707–730.

Tsang, Christine; Falk, Simone & Hessel, Alexandria. (2017). Infants prefer infant-directed song over speech. *Child Development, 88*(4), 1207–1215.

Turner, Heather A.; Finkelhor, David; Ormrod, Richard; Hamby, Sherry; Leeb, Rebecca T.; Mercy, James A. & Holt, Melissa. (2012). Family context, victimization, and child trauma symptoms: Variations in safe, stable, and nurturing relationships during early and middle childhood. *American Journal of Orthopsychiatry, 82*(2), 209–219.

Tuulari, Jetro J.; Scheinin, Noora M.; Lehtola, Satu; Merisaari, Harri; Saunavaara, Jani; Parkkola, Riitta; . . . Björnsdotter, Malin. (2019). Neural correlates of gentle skin stroking in early infancy. *Developmental Cognitive Neuroscience, 35*, 36–41.

Twenge, Jean M.; Joiner, Thomas E.; Rogers, Megan L. & Martin, Gabrielle N. (2018). Increases in depressive symptoms, suicide-related outcomes, and suicide rates among U.S. adolescents after 2010 and links to increased new media screen time. *Clinical Psychological Science, 6*(1), 3–17.

Twito, Louise & Knafo-Noam, Ariel. (2020). Beyond culture and the family: Evidence from twin studies on the genetic and environmental contribution to values. *Neuroscience & Biobehavioral Reviews, 112*, 135–143.

U.S. Bureau of Labor Statistics. (2018, August). *Labor force characteristics by race and ethnicity, 2017. BLS Reports.* Washington, DC: U.S. Bureau of Labor Statistics.

U.S. Bureau of Labor Statistics. (2020, April 21). *Employment characteristics of families summary.* Washington, DC: U.S. Bureau of Labor Statistics.

U.S. Census Bureau. (2011). *America's families and living arrangements: 2011.* Washington, DC: U.S. Department of Commerce, Economics and Statistics Administration, U.S. Census Bureau.

U.S. Census Bureau. (2015). Current population reports: Estimates and projections.

U.S. Census Bureau. (2016a). *Selected population profile in the United States: 2014 American community survey 1-year estimates. American FactFinder.* Washington, DC: U.S. Department of Commerce.

U.S. Census Bureau. (2016b). *Selected population profile in the United States: 2009 American community survey 1-year estimates. American FactFinder.* Washington, DC: U.S. Department of Commerce.

U.S. Census Bureau. (2018). *American community survey.* Washington, DC: U.S. Census Bureau.

U.S. Census Bureau. (2018, November). *Historical living arrangements of children: Living arrangements of children under 18 years old: 1960 to present.* U.S. Census Bureau.

U.S. Census Bureau. (2020). *Current population survey* [Data set].

U.S. Department of Agriculture. (2018, September 5). *Key statistics & graphics: Food insecurity in the U.S.* Washington, DC: U.S. Department of Agriculture.

U.S. Department of Health and Human Services. (2000, December 31). *Child maltreatment 2000.* Washington, DC: Administration on Children, Youth and Families, Children's Bureau.

U.S. Department of Health and Human Services. (2010). *Head Start impact study: Final report.* Washington, DC: Administration for Children and Families.

U.S. Department of Health and Human Services. (2011). *The Surgeon General's call to action to support breastfeeding.* Washington, DC: U.S. Department of Health and Human Services, Office of the Surgeon General.

U.S. Department of Health and Human Services. (2018, February 1). *Child maltreatment 2016.* Washington, DC: Administration for Children and Families, Administration on Children, Youth and Families, Children's Bureau.

U.S. Department of Health and Human Services. (2019, January 28). *Child maltreatment 2017.* Washington, DC: Administration for Children and Families, Administration on Children, Youth and Families, Children's Bureau.

U.S. Department of Health and Human Services. (2020, January 15). *Child maltreatment 2018.* Washington, DC: Administration for Children and Families, Administration on Children, Youth and Families, Children's Bureau.

U.S. Department of Health and Human Services, National Institute of Mental Health. (2017). Mental illness. Health and Human Services.

U.S. Department of State. (2019). Adoption statistics—Adoptions by year. Travel.State.gov.

U.S. Preventive Services Task Force. (2002). Postmenopausal hormone replacement therapy for primary prevention of chronic conditions: Recommendations and rationale. *Annals of Internal Medicine, 137*(10), 834–839.

U.S. Preventive Services Task Force. (2018). Screening for intimate partner violence, elder abuse, and abuse of vulnerable adults US Preventive Services Task Force final recommendation statement. *JAMA, 320*(16), 1678–1687.

U.S. Social Security Administration. (2019). Popular names by birth year. U.S. Social Security Administration.

Ueda, Peter; Mercer, Catherine H.; Ghaznavi, Cyrus & Herbenick, Debby. (2020). Trends in frequency of sexual activity and number of sexual partners among adults aged 18 to 44 years in the US, 2000–2018. *JAMA Network Open, 3*(6), e203833.

Umaña-Taylor, Adriana J. & Hill, Nancy E. (2020). Ethnic–racial socialization in the family: A decade's advance on precursors and outcomes. *Journal of Marriage and Family, 82*(1), 244–271.

Underwood, Emily. (2013). Why do so many neurons commit suicide during brain development? *Science, 340*(6137), 1157–1158.

Underwood, Emily. (2014, October 31). An easy consciousness test? *Science, 346*(6209), 531–532.

UNESCO. (2018, February). *One in five children, adolescents and youth is out of school. Fact Sheet No. 48.* Montreal, Canada: UNESCO. UIS/FS/2018/ED/48.

UNESCO. (2019, September). *New methodology shows that 258 million children, adolescents and youth are out of school. Fact sheet no. 56.* Montreal, Canada: UNESCO. UIS/2019/ED/FS/56.

UNICEF. (2019, April). *Malnutrition* [Data set]. UNICEF Data.

United Nations. (2020). World population prospects 2019: Data query.

United Nations, Department of Economic and Social Affairs, Population Division. (2019). *World population prospects 2019.* New York, NY: (Volumes 1 & 2: ST/ESA/SER.A/426 & ST/ESA/SER.A/427).

Usher, Kim; Bhullar, Navjot; Durkin, Joanne; Gyamfi, Naomi & Jackson, Debra. (2020). Family violence and COVID-19: Increased vulnerability and reduced options for support. *International Journal of Mental Health Nursing, 29*(4), 549–552.

Valente, Dannyelle; Theurel, Anne & Gentaz, Edouard. (2018). The role of visual experience in the production of emotional facial expressions by blind people: A review. *Psychonomic Bulletin & Review, 25*, 483–497.

Valentine, Christine. (2017). Identity and continuing bonds in cross-cultural perspective: Britain and Japan. In Klass, Dennis & Steffen, Edith Maria (Eds.), *Continuing bonds in bereavement: New directions for research and practice.* Routledge.

Valet, Peter. (2018). Social structure and the paradox of the contented female worker: How occupational gender segregation biases justice perceptions of wages. *Work and Occupations, 45*(2), 168–193.

Valtorta, Nicole K.; Kanaan, Mona; Gilbody, Simon; Ronzi, Sara & Hanratty, Barbara. (2016). Loneliness and social isolation as risk factors for coronary heart disease and stroke: Systematic review and meta-analysis of longitudinal observational studies. *Heart, 102*, 1009–1016.

van Batenburg-Eddes, Tamara; Butte, Dick & van de Looij-Jansen, Petra. (2012). Measuring juvenile delinquency: How do self-reports compare with official police statistics? *European Journal of Criminology, 9*(1), 23–37.

Van de Vondervoort, Julia W. & Hamlin, J. Kiley. (2016). Evidence for intuitive morality: Preverbal infants make sociomoral evaluations. *Child Development Perspectives, 10*(3), 143–148.

van den Berg, Vera; van Thiel, Ghislaine; Zomers, Margot; Hartog, Iris; Leget, Carlo; Sachs, Alfred; . . . van Wijngaarden, Els. (2021). Euthanasia and physician-assisted suicide in patients with multiple geriatric syndromes. *JAMA Internal Medicine, 181*(2), 245–250.

van den Bunt, M. R.; Groen, M. A.; van Der Kleij, S. W.; Noordenbos, M. W.; Segers, E.; Pugh, K. R. & Verhoeven, L. (2018). Deficient response to altered auditory feedback in dyslexia. *Developmental Neuropsychology, 43*(7), 622–641.

van Dijke, Marius; De Cremer, David; Langendijk, Gerben & Anderson, Cameron. (2018). Ranking low, feeling high: How hierarchical position and experienced power promote prosocial behavior in response to procedural justice. *Journal of Applied Psychology, 103*(2), 164–181.

Van Dyke, Miriam E.; Baumhofer, Nicole Kau'i; Slopen, Natalie; Mujahid, Mahasin S.; Clark, Cheryl R.; Williams, David R. & Lewis, Tené T. (2020). Pervasive discrimination and allostatic load in African American and white adults. *Psychosomatic Medicine, 82*(3), 316–323.

van Goozen, Stephanie H. M. (2015). The role of early emotion impairments in the development of persistent antisocial behavior. *Child Development Perspectives, 9*(4), 206–210.

Van Harmelen, A-L.; Kievit, R. A.; Ioannidis, K.; Neufeld, S.; Jones, P. B.; Bullmore, E.; . . . Goodyer, I. (2017). Adolescent friendships predict later resilient functioning across psychosocial domains in a healthy community cohort. *Psychological Medicine, 47*(13), 2312–2322.

van Houdt, Kirsten; Kalmijn, Matthijs & Ivanova, Katya. (2020). Stepparental support to adult children: The diverging roles of stepmothers and stepfathers. *Journal of Marriage and Family, 82*(2), 639–656.

van Tilburg, Theo G.; Aartsen, Marja J. & van der Pas, Suzan. (2015). Loneliness after divorce: A cohort comparison among Dutch young-old adults. *European Sociological Review, 31*(3), 243–252.

Vanderberg, Rachel H.; Farkas, Amy H.; Miller, Elizabeth; Sucato, Gina S.; Akers, Aletha Y. & Borrero, Sonya B. (2016). Racial and/or ethnic differences in formal sex education and sex education by parents among young women in the United States. *Journal of Pediatric and Adolescent Gynecology, 29*(1), 69–73.

Vanderloo, Leigh M.; Carsley, Sarah; Aglipay, Mary; Cost, Katherine T.; Maguire, Jonathon & Birken, Catherine S. (2020). Applying harm reduction principles to address screen time in young children amidst the COVID-19 pandemic. *Journal of Developmental & Behavioral Pediatrics, 41*(5), 335–336.

Vanhalst, Janne; Luyckx, Koen; Scholte, Ron H. J.; Engels, Rutger C. M. E. & Goossens, Luc. (2013). Low self-esteem as a risk factor for loneliness in adolescence: Perceived—but not actual—social acceptance as an underlying mechanism. *Journal of Abnormal Child Psychology, 41*(7), 1067–1081.

Vannucci, Robert C. & Vannucci, Susan J. (2019). Brain growth in modern humans using multiple developmental databases. *American Journal of Physical Anthropology, 168*(2), 247–261.

Vasquez, Matthew & Stensland, Meredith. (2016). Adopted children with reactive attachment disorder: A qualitative study on family processes. *Clinical Social Work Journal, 44*(3), 319–332.

Vedantam, Shankar. (2011, December 5). *What's behind a temper tantrum? Scientists deconstruct the screams. Hidden Brain.* Washington DC: National Public Radio.

Veldheer, Susan; Yingst, Jessica; Midya, Vishal; Hummer, Breianna; Lester, Courtney; Krebs, Nicolle; . . . Foulds, Jonathan. (2019). Pulmonary and other health effects of electronic cigarette use among adult smokers participating in a randomized controlled smoking reduction trial. *Addictive Behaviors, 91*, 95–101.

Vendetti, Corrie; Kamawar, Deepthi & Andrews, Katherine E. (2019). Theory of mind and preschoolers' understanding of misdeed and politeness lies. *Developmental Psychology, 55*(4), 823–834.

Verdine, Brian N.; Golinkoff, Roberta Michnick; Hirsh-Pasek, Kathy & Newcombe, Nora S. (2017). Spatial skills, their development, and their links to mathematics. *Monographs of the Society for Research in Child Development: Links between spatial and mathematical skills across the preschool, 82*(1), 7–30.

Vernon-Feagans, Lynne; Bratsch-Hines, Mary; Reynolds, Elizabeth & Willoughby, Michael T. (2020). How early maternal language input varies by race and education and predicts later child language. *Child Development, 91*(4), 1098–1115.

Verona, Sergiu. (2003). Romanian policy regarding adoptions. In Littel, Victor (Ed.), *Adoption update* (pp. 5–10). Nova Science.

Verrusio, Walter; Ettorre, Evaristo; Vicenzini, Edoardo; Vanacore, Nicola; Cacciafesta, Mauro & Mecarelli, Oriano. (2015). The Mozart Effect: A quantitative EEG study. *Consciousness and Cognition, 35*, 150–155.

Verschueren, Karine. (2020). Attachment, self-esteem, and socio-emotional adjustment: There is more than just the mother. *Attachment & Human Development, 22*(1), 105–109.

Vickery, Brian P.; Berglund, Jelena P.; Burk, Caitlin M.; Fine, Jason P.; Kim, Edwin H.; Kim, Jung In; . . . Burks, A. Wesley. (2017). Early oral immunotherapy in peanut-allergic preschool children is safe and highly effective. *Journal of Allergy and Clinical Immunology, 139*(1), 173–181.e8.

Vijayakumar, Nandita; Op de Macks, Zdena; Shirtcliff, Elizabeth A. & Pfeifer, Jennifer H. (2018). Puberty and the human brain: Insights into adolescent development. *Neuroscience and Biobehavioral Reviews, 92*, 417–436.

Vikram, Kriti & Vanneman, Reeve. (2020). Maternal education and the multidimensionality of child health outcomes in India. *Journal of Biosocial Science, 52*(1), 57–77.

Viljaranta, Jaana; Aunola, Kaisa; Mullola, Sari; Virkkala, Johanna; Hirvonen, Riikka; Pakarinen, Eija & Nurmi, Jari-Erik. (2015). Children's temperament and academic skill development during first grade: Teachers' interaction styles as mediators. *Child Development, 86*(4), 1191–1209.

Villar, Feliciano. (2012). Successful ageing and development: The contribution of generativity in older age. *Ageing and Society, 32*(7), 1087–1105.

Visscher, Peter M.; Wray, Naomi R.; Zhang, Qian; Sklar, Pamela; McCarthy, Mark I.; Brown, Matthew A. & Yang, Jian. (2017). 10 years of GWAs discovery: Biology, function, and translation. *AJHG, 101*(1), 5–22.

Visser, Margreet; Van Lawick, Justine; Stith, Sandra M. & Spencer, Chelsea M. (2020). Violence in families: Systemic practice and research. In Ochs, Matthias; Borcsa, Maria & Schweitzer, Jochen (Eds.), *Systemic research in individual, couple, and family therapy and counseling* (pp. 299–315). Springer.

Vittner, Dorothy; Mcgrath, Jacqueline; Robinson, Joann; Lawhon, Gretchen; Cusson, Regina; Eisenfeld, Leonard; . . . Cong, Xiaomei. (2018). Increase in oxytocin from skin-to-skin contact enhances development of parent–infant relationship. *Biological Research for Nursing, 20*(1), 54–62.

Vlachos, George S. & Scarmeas, Nikolaos. (2019). Dietary interventions in mild cognitive impairment and dementia. *Dialogues in Clinical Neuroscience, 21*(1), 69–82.

Vladeck, Fredda & Altman, Anita. (2015). The future of the NORC-supportive service program model. *Public Policy Aging Report, 25*(1), 20–22.

Voelcker-Rehage, Claudia; Niemann, Claudia & Hübner, Lena. (2018). Structural and functional brain changes related to acute and chronic exercise effects in children, adolescents and young adults. In Meeusen, Romain; Schaefer, Sabine; Tomporowski, Phillip & Bailey, Richard (Eds.), *Physical activity and educational achievement: Insights from exercise neuroscience* (pp. 143–163). Routledge.

Vöhringer, Isabel A.; Kolling, Thorsten; Graf, Frauke; Poloczek, Sonja; Fassbender, Iina; Freitag, Claudia; . . . Knopf, Monika. (2018). The development of implicit memory from infancy to childhood: On average performance levels and interindividual differences. *Child Development, 89*(2), 370–382.

von Salisch, Maria. (2018). Emotional competence and friendship involvement: Spiral effects in adolescence. *European Journal of Developmental Psychology, 15*(6), 678–693.

Votruba-Drzal, Elizabeth & Dearing, Eric (Eds.). (2017). *Handbook of early childhood development programs, practices, and policies.* Wiley.

Vygotsky, Lev S. (1980). *Mind in society: The development of higher psychological processes.* Harvard University Press.

Vygotsky, Lev S. (1987). Thinking and speech. In Rieber, Robert W. & Carton, Aaron S. (Eds.), *The collected works of L. S. Vygotsky* (Vol. 1, pp. 39–285). Springer.

Vygotsky, Lev S. (1994a). The development of academic concepts in school aged children. In van der Veer, René & Valsiner, Jaan (Eds.), *The Vygotsky reader* (pp. 355–370). Blackwell.

Vygotsky, Lev S. (1994b). Principles of social education for deaf and dumb children in Russia. In van der Veer, Rene & Valsiner, Jaan (Eds.), *The Vygotsky reader* (pp. 19–26). Blackwell.

Vygotsky, Lev S. (2012). *Thought and language.* MIT Press.

Wade, Mark; Prime, Heather; Jenkins, Jennifer; Yeates, Keith; Williams, Tricia & Lee, Kang. (2018). On the relation between theory of mind and executive functioning: A developmental cognitive neuroscience perspective. *Psychonomic Bulletin & Review, 25*(6), 2119–2140.

Wadman, Meredith. (2018). 'Rapid onset' of transgender identity ignites storm. *Science, 361*(6406), 958–959.

Wagner, Jenny; Lüdtke, Oliver & Robitzsch, Alexander. (2019). Does personality become more stable with age? Disentangling state and trait effects for the Big Five across the life span using local structural equation modeling. *Journal of Personality and Social Psychology, 116*(4), 666–680.

Wagner, Katie; Dobkins, Karen & Barner, David. (2013). Slow mapping: Color word learning as a gradual inductive process. *Cognition, 127*(3), 307–317.

Wagner, Paul A. (2011). Socio-sexual education: A practical study in formal thinking and teachable moments. *Sex Education: Sexuality, Society and Learning, 11*(2), 193–211.

Wakeel, Fathima & Njoku, Anuli. (2021). Application of the weathering framework: Intersection of racism, stigma, and COVID-19 as a stressful life event among African Americans. *Healthcare, 9*(2), 145.

Walker, James Johnston. (2017). Planned home birth. *Best Practice & Research Clinical Obstetrics & Gynaecology, 43*, 76–86.

Walker, Lauren; Stefanis, Leonidas & Attems, Johannes. (2019). Clinical and neuropathological differences between Parkinson's disease, Parkinson's disease dementia and dementia with Lewy bodies—Current issues and future directions. *Journal of Neurochemistry, 150*(5), 467–474.

Walker, Renee; Block, Jason & Kawachi, Ichiro. (2014). The spatial accessibility of fast food restaurants and convenience stores in relation to neighborhood schools. *Applied Spatial Analysis and Policy*, 7(2), 169–182.

Walle, Eric A. & Campos, Joseph J. (2014). Infant language development is related to the acquisition of walking. *Developmental Psychology, 50*(2), 336–348.

Wallerstein, Judith S. & Blakeslee, Sandra. (2006). *The good marriage: How and why love lasts.* Grand Central.

Wallis, Claudia. (2014). Gut reactions: Intestinal bacteria may help determine whether we are lean or obese. *Scientific American, 310*(6), 30–33.

Walter, Melissa Clucas & Lippard, Christine N. (2017). Head Start teachers across a decade: Beliefs, characteristics, and time spent on academics. *Early Childhood Education Journal, 45*(5), 693–702.

Wambach, Karen & Spencer, Becky. (2019). *Breastfeeding and human lactation* (6th ed.). Jones & Bartlett.

Wan, Yong & Finkel, Toren. (2020). The mitochondria regulation of stem cell aging. *Mechanisms of Ageing and Development, 191*(111334).

Wanberg, Connie R. (2012). The individual experience of unemployment. *Annual Review of Psychology, 63*, 369–396.

Wang, Chen; Horby, Peter W.; Hayden, Frederick G. & Gao, George F. (2020). A novel coronavirus outbreak of global health concern. *The Lancet, 395*(10223), 470–473.

Wang, Ke; Rathbun, Amy & Musu, Lauren. (2019). *School choice in the United States: 2019.* Washington, DC: U.S. Department of Education, National Center for Education Statistics. NCES 2019–106.

Wang, Limin; Gao, Pei; Zhang, Mei; Huang, Zhengjing; Zhang, Dudan; Deng, Qian; . . . Wang, Linhong. (2017). Prevalence and ethnic pattern of diabetes and prediabetes in China in 2013. *JAMA, 317*(24), 2515–2523.

Wang, Meifang & Liu, Li. (2018). Reciprocal relations between harsh discipline and children's externalizing behavior in China: A 5-year longitudinal study. *Child Development, 89*(1), 174–187.

Wang, Ming-Te & Degol, Jessica L. (2016). School climate: A review of the construct, measurement, and impact on student outcomes. *Educational Psychology Review, 28*, 315–352.

Wang, Ming-Te & Eccles, Jacquelynne S. (2013). School context, achievement motivation, and academic engagement: A longitudinal study of school engagement using a multidimensional perspective. *Learning and Instruction, 28*, 12–23.

Wang, Ming-Te; Henry, Daphne A.; Smith, Leann V.; Huguley, James P. & Guo, Jiesi. (2020). Parental ethnic-racial socialization practices and children of color's psychosocial and behavioral adjustment: A systematic review and meta-analysis. *American Psychologist, 75*(1), 1–22.

Wang, Teresa W.; Gentzke, Andrea; Sharapova, Saida; Cullen, Karen A.; Ambrose, Bridget K. & Jamal, Ahmed. (2018, June 8). *Tobacco product use among middle and high school students—United States, 2011–2017. Morbidity and Mortality Weekly Report, 67*(22), 629–633. Atlanta, GA: Centers for Disease Control and Prevention.

Wang, Teresa W.; Neff, Linda J.; Park-Lee, Eunice; Ren, Chunfeng; Cullen, Karen A. & King, Brian A. (2020, September 18). *E-cigarette use among middle and high school students—United States, 2020. Morbidity and Mortality Weekly Report, 69*(37), 1310–1312. Atlanta, GA: Centers for Disease Control and Prevention.

Ward, Emma V.; Berry, Christopher J. & Shanks, David R. (2013). Age effects on explicit and implicit memory. *Frontiers in Psychology, 4*(639).

Warner, Lisa M.; Wolff, Julia K.; Ziegelmann, Jochen P. & Wurm, Susanne. (2014). A randomized controlled trial to promote volunteering in older adults. *Psychology and Aging, 29*(4), 757–763.

Wassenaar, Thomas M.; Yaffe, Kristine; van der Werf, Ysbrand D. & Sexton, Claire E. (2019). Associations between modifiable risk factors and white matter of the aging brain: Insights from diffusion tensor imaging studies. *Neurobiology of Aging, 80,* 56–70.

Watson, John B. (1928). *Psychological care of infant and child.* Norton.

Watson, John B. (1972). *Psychological care of infant and child.* Arno Press.

Watson, Mark & McMahon, Mary (Eds.). (2017). *Career exploration and development in childhood: Perspectives from theory, practice and research.* Routledge.

Watts, Nicolas; Amann, Markus; Ayeb-Karlsson, Sonja; Belesova, Kristine; Bouley, Timothy; Boykoff, Maxwell; . . . Costello, Anthony. (2018). The *Lancet* Countdown on health and climate change: From 25 years of inaction to a global transformation for public health. *The Lancet, 391*(10120), 581–630.

Watts, Tyler W.; Duncan, Greg J. & Quan, Haonan. (2018). Revisiting the marshmallow test: A conceptual replication investigating links between early delay of gratification and later outcomes. *Psychological Science, 29*(7), 1159–1177.

Webb, Alexandra R.; Heller, Howard T.; Benson, Carol B. & Lahav, Amir. (2015). Mother's voice and heartbeat sounds elicit auditory plasticity in the human brain before full gestation. *Proceedings of the National Academy of Sciences, 112*(10), 3152–3157.

Weber, Ann; Fernald, Anne & Diop, Yatma. (2017). When cultural norms discourage talking to babies: Effectiveness of a parenting program in rural Senegal. *Child Development, 88*(5), 1513–1526.

Webster, Collin A. & Suzuki, Naoki. (2014). Land of the rising pulse: A social ecological perspective of physical activity opportunities for schoolchildren in Japan. *Journal of Teaching in Physical Education, 33*(3), 304–325.

Wegrzyn, Lani R.; Tamimi, Rulla M.; Rosner, Bernard A.; Brown, Susan B.; Stevens, Richard G.; Eliassen, A. Heather; . . . Schernhammer, Eva S. (2017). Rotating night-shift work and the risk of breast cancer in the nurses' health studies. *American Journal of Epidemiology, 186*(5), 532–540.

Weinstein, Netta & DeHaan, Cody. (2014). On the mutuality of human motivation and relationships. In Weinstein, Netta (Ed.), *Human motivation and interpersonal relationships: Theory, research, and applications* (pp. 3–25). Springer.

Weinstock, Louis; Dunda, Dunja; Harrington, Hannah & Nelson, Hannah. (2021). It's complicated—Adolescent grief in the time of Covid-19. *Frontiers in Psychiatry, 12*(638940).

Weiss, Noel S. & Koepsell, Thomas D. (2014). *Epidemiologic methods: Studying the occurrence of illness* (2nd ed.). Oxford University Press.

Weissberg, Roger P.; Durlak, Joseph A.; Domitrovich, Celene E. & Gullotta, Thomas P. (2016). Social and emotional learning: Past, present, and future. In Durlak, Joseph A.; Domitrovich, Celene E.; Weissberg, Roger P. & Gullotta, Thomas P. (Eds.), *Handbook of social and emotional learning: Research and practice* (pp. 3–19). Guilford Press.

Weisskirch, Robert S. (2017a). A developmental perspective on language brokering. In Weisskirch, Robert S. (Ed.), *Language brokering in immigrant families: Theories and contexts.* Routledge.

Weisskirch, Robert S. (2017b). *Language brokering in immigrant families: Theories and contexts.* Routledge.

Wellman, Henry M.; Fang, Fuxi & Peterson, Candida C. (2011). Sequential progressions in a theory-of-mind scale: Longitudinal perspectives. *Child Development, 82*(3), 780–792.

Wen, Ming; Ren, Qiang; Korinek, Kim & Trinh, Ha N. (2019). Living in skipped generation households and happiness among middle-aged and older grandparents in China. *Social Science Research, 80,* 145–155.

Westover, Tara. (2018). *Educated: A memoir.* Random House.

Weymouth, Bridget B.; Buehler, Cheryl; Zhou, Nan & Henson, Robert A. (2016). A meta-analysis of parent–adolescent conflict: Disagreement, hostility, and youth maladjustment. *Journal of Family Theory & Review, 8*(1), 95–112.

Wheeler, Lorey A.; Zeiders, Katharine H.; Updegraff, Kimberly A.; Umaña-Taylor, Adriana J.; Rodríguez de Jesús, Sue A. & Perez-Brena, Norma J. (2017). Mexican-origin youth's risk behavior from adolescence to young adulthood: The role of familism values. *Developmental Psychology, 53*(1), 126–137.

Whitbourne, Susan K. & Whitbourne, Stacey B. (2014). *Adult development and aging: Biopsychosocial perspectives* (5th ed.). Wiley.

White, Rebecca M. B.; Deardorff, Julianna; Liu, Yu & Gonzales, Nancy A. (2013). Contextual amplification or attenuation of the impact of pubertal timing on Mexican-origin boys' mental health symptoms. *Journal of Adolescent Health, 53*(6), 692–698.

White, Sue; Gibson, Matthew & Wastell, David. (2019). Child protection and disorganized attachment: A critical commentary. *Children and Youth Services Review, 105*(104415).

White-Traut, Rosemary C.; Rankin, Kristin M.; Yoder, Joe; Zawacki, Laura; Campbell, Suzann; Kavanaugh, Karen; . . . Norr, Kathleen F. (2018). Relationship between mother-infant mutual dyadic responsiveness and premature infant development as measured by the Bayley III at 6 weeks corrected age. *Early Human Development, 121,* 21–26.

Wicks, Elizabeth. (2012). The meaning of 'life': Dignity and the right to life in international human rights treaties. *Human Rights Law Review, 12*(2), 199–219.

Widman, Laura; Choukas-Bradley, Sophia; Helms, Sarah W.; Golin, Carol E. & Prinstein, Mitchell J. (2014). Sexual communication between early adolescents and their dating partners, parents, and best friends. *The Journal of Sex Research, 51*(7), 731–741.

Widom, Cathy Spatz; Czaja, Sally J. & DuMont, Kimberly A. (2015a). Intergenerational transmission of child abuse and neglect: Real or detection bias? *Science, 347*(6229), 1480–1485.

Widom, Cathy Spatz; Horan, Jacqueline & Brzustowicz, Linda. (2015b). Childhood maltreatment predicts allostatic load in adulthood. *Child Abuse & Neglect, 47,* 59–69.

Wieten, Sarah. (2018). Expertise in evidence-based medicine: A tale of three models. *Philosophy, Ethics, and Humanities in Medicine, 13*(1).

Wigger, J. Bradley. (2018). Invisible friends across four countries: Kenya, Malawi, Nepal and the Dominican Republic. *International Journal of Psychology, 53*(Suppl. 1), 46–52.

Wilcox, W. Bradford (Ed.) (2011). *The sustainable demographic dividend: What do marriage and fertility have to do with the economy?* Social Trends Institute.

Wilkerson, Isabel. (2020). *Caste: The origins of our discontents.* Random House.

Willer, David & Emanuelson, Pamela. (2020). Theory and the replication problem. *Sociological Methodology.*

Williams, Anne M.; Chantry, Caroline; Geubbels, Eveline L.; Ramaiya, Astha K.; Shemdoe, Aloisia I.; Tancredi, Daniel J. & Young, Sera L. (2016). Breastfeeding and complementary feeding practices among HIV-exposed infants in coastal Tanzania. *Journal of Human Lactation, 32*(1), 112–122.

Williams, Lela Rankin; Fox, Nathan A.; Lejuez, C. W.; Reynolds, Elizabeth K.; Henderson, Heather A.; Perez-Edgar, Koraly E.; . . . Pine, Daniel S. (2010). Early temperament, propensity for risk-taking and adolescent substance-related problems: A prospective multi-method investigation. *Addictive Behaviors, 35*(2), 1148–1151.

Williamson, Victoria; Stevelink, Sharon A. M.; Da Silva, Eve & Fear, Nicola T. (2018). A systematic review of wellbeing in children: A comparison of military and civilian families. *Child and Adolescent Psychiatry and Mental Health, 12*(46).

Willis, Amy; Greene, Michael & Braxton-Lloyd, Kimberly. (2019). An experimental study of a Mediterranean-style diet supplemented with nuts and extra-virgin olive oil for cardiovascular disease risk reduction: The healthy hearts program. *Current Developments in Nutrition, 3*(Suppl. 1).

Willoughby, Michael T.; Mills-Koonce, W. Roger; Gottfredson, Nisha C. & Wagner, Nicholas J. (2014). Measuring callous unemotional behaviors in early childhood: Factor structure and the prediction of stable aggression in middle childhood. *Journal of Psychopathology and Behavioral Assessment, 36*(1), 30–42.

Wills, Thomas A.; Okamoto, Scott K.; Knight, Rebecca & Pagano, Ian. (2019). Parental support, parent-adolescent conflict, and substance use of native Hawaiian and other Pacific Islander youth: Ethnic differences in stress-buffering and vulnerability effects. *Asian American Journal of Psychology, 10*(3), 218–226.

Wilmshurst, Linda. (2011). *Child and adolescent psychopathology: A casebook* (2nd ed.). Sage.

Wilson, Nana; Kariisa, Mbabazi; Seth, Puja; Smith, Herschel & Davis, Nicole L. (2020). *Drug and opioid-involved overdose deaths—United States, 2017–2018. Morbidity and Mortality Weekly Report, 69*(11), 290–297. Atlanta, GA: U.S. Department of Health and Human Services, Centers for Disease Control and Prevention.

Winegard, Bo; Winegard, Benjamin & Geary, David C. (2018). The evolution of expertise. In Ericsson, K. Anders; Hoffman, Robert R.; Kozbelt, Aaron & Williams, A. Mark (Eds.), *The Cambridge handbook of expertise and expert performance* (pp. 40–48). Cambridge University Press.

Winn, Phoebe; Acharya, Krishna; Peterson, Erika & Leuthner, Steven R. (2018). Prenatal counseling and parental decision-making following a fetal diagnosis of trisomy 13 or 18. *Journal of Perinatology, 38*(7), 788–796.

Wolff, Mary S.; Teitelbaum, Susan L.; McGovern, Kathleen; Pinney, Susan M.; Windham, Gayle C.; Galvez, Maida; . . . Biro, Frank M. (2015). Environmental phenols and pubertal development in girls. *Environment International, 84,* 174–180.

Womack, Lindsay S.; Rossen, Lauren M. & Martin, Joyce A. (2018). *Singleton low birthweight rates, by race and Hispanic origin: United States, 2006–2016. NCHS Data Briefs.* Hyattsville, MD: National Center for Health Statistics.

Wong, Jaclyn S. & Waite, Linda J. (2015). Marriage, social networks, and health at older ages. *Journal of Population Ageing, 8*(1/2), 7–25.

Woodrow, Chris & Guest, David E. (2020). Pathways through organizational socialization: A longitudinal qualitative study based on the psychological contract. *Journal of Occupational and Organizational Psychology, 93*(1), 110–133.

Woodward, Amanda L. & Markman, Ellen M. (1998). Early word learning. In Kuhn, Deanna & Siegler, Robert S. (Eds.), *Handbook of child psychology* (5th ed., Vol. 2, pp. 371–420). Wiley.

Woolf, Steven H.; Chapman, Derek A. & Lee, Jong Hyung. (2021). COVID-19 as the leading cause of death in the United States. *JAMA, 325*(2), 123–124.

Woollett, Katherine; Spiers, Hugo J. & Maguire, Eleanor A. (2009). Talent in the taxi: A model system for exploring expertise. *Philosophical Transactions of the Royal Society of London, 364*(1522), 1407–1416.

Woolley, Jacqueline D. & Ghossainy, Maliki E. (2013). Revisiting the fantasy–reality distinction: Children as naïve skeptics. *Child Development, 84*(5), 1496–1510.

World Bank. (2018). *World development indicators: Mortality rate, infant (per 1,000 live births)* [Data set].

World Bank. (2019). World Bank open data. World Bank.

World Bank. (2019, August). *GDP per capita (current US$)* [Data set].

World Health Organization. (2006). WHO Motor Development Study: Windows of achievement for six gross motor development milestones. *Acta Paediatrica, 95*(Suppl. 450), 86–95.

World Health Organization. (2017, April 28). Measles vaccines: WHO position paper—April 2017. *Weekly Epidemiological Record, 17*(92), 205–228.

World Health Organization. (2017, September 29). Global Health Observatory data repository: Prevalence of obesity among children and adolescents, BMI>+2 standard deviation above the median, crude estimates by country, among children aged 5–19 years. World Health Organization.

World Health Organization. (2019, May 29). *WHO vaccine-preventable diseases: Monitoring system—2019 global summary: Global and regional immunization profile* [Data set].

World Health Organization. (2020, March 13). *Immunization, vaccines and biologicals: Measles and rubella surveillance data* [Data set].

Wrzus, Cornelia & Neyer, Franz J. (2016). Co-development of personality and friendships across the lifespan: An empirical review on selection and socialization. *European Psychologist, 21*(4), 254–273.

Wu, Ming-Yih & Ho, Hong-Nerng. (2015). Cost and safety of assisted reproductive technologies for human immunodeficiency virus-1 discordant couples. *World Journal of Virology, 4*(2), 142–146.

Wubbena, Zane C. (2013). Mathematical fluency as a function of conservation ability in young children. *Learning and Individual Differences, 26*, 153–155.

Xiong, Xiang-Dong; Xiong, Wei-Dong; Xiong, Shang-Shen & Chen, Gui-Hai. (2018). Age- and gender-based differences in nest-building behavior and learning and memory performance measured using a radial six-armed water maze in C57BL/6 mice. *Behavioural Neurology, 2018*(8728415).

Xu, Fei. (2013). The object concept in human infants: Commentary on Fields. *Human Development, 56*(3), 167–170.

Xu, Guifeng; Strathearn, Lane; Liu, Buyun; O'Brien, Matthew; Kopelman, Todd G.; Zhu, Jing; . . . Bao, Wei. (2019). Prevalence and treatment patterns of autism spectrum disorder in the United States, 2016. *JAMA Pediatrics, 173*(2), 153–159.

Xu, Guifeng; Strathearn, Lane; Liu, Buyun; Yang, Binrang & Bao, Wei. (2018). Twenty-year trends in diagnosed Attention-deficit/hyperactivity disorder among US children and adolescents, 1997–2016. *JAMA Network Open, 1*(4), e181471.

Xu, Jiaquan; Murphy, Sherry L.; Kochanek, Kenneth D. & Arias, Elizabeth. (2020, January). *Mortality in the United States, 2018. NCHS Data Brief.* U.S. Department of Health and Human Services, Centers for Disease Control and Prevention, National Center for Health Statistics. 355.

Xu, Yaoying. (2010). Children's social play sequence: Parten's classic theory revisited. *Early Child Development and Care, 180*(4), 489–498.

Xu, Yin; Norton, Sam & Rahman, Qazi. (2020). A longitudinal birth cohort study of early life conditions, psychosocial factors, and emerging adolescent sexual orientation. *Developmental Psychobiology, 62*(1), 5–20.

Yackobovitch-Gavan, Michal; Wolf Linhard, D.; Nagelberg, Nessia; Poraz, Irit; Shalitin, Shlomit; Phillip, Moshe & Meyerovitch, Joseph. (2018). Intervention for childhood obesity based on parents only or parents and child compared with follow-up alone. *Pediatric Obesity, 13*(11), 647–655.

Yan, J.; Han, Z. R.; Tang, Y. & Zhang, X. (2017). Parental support for autonomy and child depressive symptoms in middle childhood: The mediating role of parent–child attachment. *Journal of Child and Family Studies, 26*(7), 1970–1978.

Yang, Bo-Yi & Dong, Guang-Hui. (2019, March 29). Tobacco smoking in Asia—A public health threat. *JAMA Network Open, 2*(3), e191471.

Yang, Keming & Victor, Christina R. (2011). Age and loneliness in 25 European nations. *Ageing & Society, 31*(8), 1368–1388.

Yang, Rongwang; Zhang, Suhan; Li, Rong & Zhao, Zhengyan. (2013). Parents' attitudes toward stimulants use in China. *Journal of Developmental & Behavioral Pediatrics, 34*(3), 225.

Yeager, David S.; Dahl, Ronald E. & Dweck, Carol S. (2018). Why interventions to influence adolescent behavior often fail but could succeed. *Perspectives on Psychological Science, 13*(1), 101–122.

Yeager, David S.; Purdie-Vaughns, Valerie; Hooper, Sophia Yang & Cohen, Geoffrey L. (2017). Loss of institutional trust among racial and ethnic minority adolescents: A consequence of procedural injustice and a cause of life-span outcomes. *Child Development, 88*(2), 658–676.

Yeap, Bu B. & Dwivedi, Girish. (2020). Androgens and heart failure: New observations illuminating an aging conundrum. *The Journal of Clinical Endocrinology & Metabolism*, (dgaa676).

Yegorov, Yegor E.; Poznyak, Anastasia V.; Nikiforov, Nikita G.; Sobenin, Igor A. & Orekhov, Alexander N. (2020). The link between chronic stress and accelerated aging. *Biomedicines, 8*(7), 198.

Yerkes, Robert Mearns. (1923). Testing the human mind. *Atlantic Monthly, 131*, 358–370.

Yon, Yongjie; Mikton, Christopher R.; Gassoumis, Zachary D. & Wilber, Kathleen H. (2017). Elder abuse prevalence in community settings: A systematic review and meta-analysis. *The Lancet Global Health, 5*(2), e147–e156.

Yong, Jose C. & Li, Norman P. (2018). The adaptive functions of jealousy. In Lench, Heather C. (Ed.), *The function of emotions: When and why emotions help us* (pp. 121–140). Springer.

Yoon, Cynthia; Jacobs, David R.; Duprez, Daniel A.; Dutton, Gareth; Lewis, Cora E.; Neumark-Sztainer, Dianne; . . . Mason, Susan M. (2018). Questionnaire-based problematic relationship to eating and food is associated with 25 year body mass index trajectories during midlife: The Coronary Artery Risk Development In Young Adults (CARDIA) study. *International Journal of Eating Disorders, 51*(1), 10–17.

Yorgason, Jeremy B.; Draper, Thomas W.; Bronson, Haley; Nielson, Makayla; Babcock, Kate; Jones, Karolina; . . . Howard, Myranda. (2018). Biological, psychological, and social predictors of longevity among Utah centenarians. *International Journal of Aging and Human Development, 87*(3), 225–243.

Young, Marisa & Schieman, Scott. (2018). Scaling back and finding flexibility: Gender differences in parents' strategies to manage work–family conflict. *Journal of Marriage and Family, 80*(1), 99–118.

Yu, Qijing; McCall, Dana M.; Homayouni, Roya; Tang, Lingfei; Chen, Zhijian; Schoff, Daniel; . . . Ofen, Noa. (2018). Age-associated increase in mnemonic strategy use is linked to prefrontal cortex development. *NeuroImage, 181*(1), 162–169.

Yudell, Michael; Roberts, Dorothy; DeSalle, Rob & Tishkoff, Sarah. (2016). Taking race out of human genetics. *Science, 351*(6273), 564–565.

Zahran, Hatice S.; Bailey, Cathy M.; Damon, Scott A.; Garbe, Paul L. & Breysse, Patrick N. (2018). *Vital signs: Asthma in children—United States, 2001–2016. Morbidity and Mortality Weekly Report, 67*(5), 149–155. Atlanta, GA: Centers for Disease Control and Prevention.

Zalenski, Robert J. & Raspa, Richard. (2006). Maslow's hierarchy of needs: A framework for achieving human potential in hospice. *Journal of Palliative Medicine, 9*(5), 1120–1127.

Zametkin, Alan J. & Solanto, Mary V. (2017). A Review of *ADHD nation* [Review of the book *ADHD nation: Children, doctors, big pharma, and the making of an American epidemic*, by Alan Schwarz]. *The ADHD Report, 25*(2), 6–10.

Zangbar, Hamid Soltani; Gorji, Ali & Ghadiri, Tahereh. (2021). A review on the neurological manifestations of COVID-19 infection: A mechanistic view. *Molecular Neurobiology, 58*, 536–549.

Zehnhoff-Dinnesen, Antoinette am; Bolz, Hanno J.; Carr, Gwen; Gross, Manfred; Parfitt, Ross; Poisson-Markova, Simona; . . . Tigges, Monika. (2020). Prevention of disorders of hearing development. In Zehnhoff-Dinnesen, Antoinette am; Wiskirska-Woznica, Bozena; Neumann, Katrin & Nawkam, Tadeus (Eds.), *Phoniatrics I: European manual of medicine* (pp. 963–981). Springer.

Zeifman, Debra M. (2013). Built to bond: Coevolution, coregulation, and plasticity in parent-infant bonds. In Hazan, Cindy & Campa, Mary I. (Eds.), *Human bonding: The science of affectional ties* (pp. 41–73). Guilford Press.

Zeitlin, Marian. (2011). *New information on West African traditional education and approaches to its modernization.* Tostan.

Zelazo, Philip David. (2018). Abstracting and aligning essential features of cognitive development. *Human Development, 61*(1), 43–48.

Zelazo, Philip David. (2020). Executive function and psychopathology: A neurodevelopmental perspective. *Annual Review of Clinical Psychology, 16*, 431–454.

Zeng, Yvette S.; Wang, Connie; Ward, Kristina E. & Hume, Anne L. (2018). Complementary and alternative medicine in hospice and palliative care: A systematic review. *Journal of Pain and Symptom Management, 56*(5), 781–794.

Zetterberg, Henrik & Blennow, Kaj. (2021). Moving fluid biomarkers for Alzheimer's disease from research tools to routine clinical diagnostics. *Molecular Neurodegeneration, 16*(10).

Zhang, Jie. (2019). Suicide reduction in China. *American Journal of Public Health, 109*(11), 1533–1534.

Zhang, Linlin & Eggum-Wilkens, Natalie D. (2018). Correlates of shyness and unsociability during early adolescence in urban and rural China. *Journal of Early Adolescence, 38*(3), 408–421.

Zhang, Ming; Dilliott, Allison A.; Khallaf, Roaa; Robinson, John F.; Hegele, Robert A.; Comishen, Michael; . . . Rogaeva, Ekaterina. (2019). Genetic and epigenetic study of an Alzheimer's disease family with monozygotic triplets. *Brain, 142*(11), 3375–3381.

Zhang, Qian. (2019). Enlightenment of Kohlberg's theory of moral development in the context of moral education in mainland China. *Open Access Library Journal, 6*, 1–8.

Zhao, Fei; Franco, Heather L.; Rodriguez, Karina F.; Brown, Paula R.; Tsai, Ming-Jer; Tsai, Sophia Y. & Yao, Humphrey H-C. (2017). Elimination of the male reproductive tract in the female embryo is promoted by COUP-TFII in mice. *Science, 357*(6352), 717–720.

Zhao, Jin-Lei; Jiang, Wan-Ting; Wang, Xing; Cai, Zhi-Dong; Liu, Zu-Hong & Liu, Guo-Rong. (2020). Exercise, brain plasticity, and depression. *CNS Neuroscience & Therapeutics, 26*(9), 885–895.

Zuo, Xi-Nian; He, Ye; Betzel, Richard F.; Colcombe, Stan; Sporns, Olaf & Milham, Michael P. (2017). Human connectomics across the life span. *Trends in Cognitive Sciences, 21*(1), 32–45.

Zurcher, Jessica D.; Holmgren, Hailey G.; Coyne, Sarah M.; Barlett, Christopher P. & Yang, Chongming. (2018). Parenting and cyberbullying across adolescence. *Cyberpsychology, Behavior, and Social Networking, 21*(5), 294–303.

Zych, Izabela; Baldry, Anna C.; Farrington, David P. & Llorent, Vicente J. (2019). Are children involved in cyberbullying low on empathy? A systematic review and meta-analysis of research on empathy versus different cyberbullying roles. *Aggression and Violent Behavior, 45*, 83–97.

Zych, Izabela; Farrington, David P.; Llorent, Vicente J. & Ttofi, Maria M. (Eds.). (2017). *Protecting children against bullying and its consequences.* Springer.

Name Index

Note: In page references, "p" indicates a photo, "f" indicates a figure, and "t" indicates a table.

Subject Index

Note: Page numbers followed by f, p, or t indicate figures, pictures, or tables, respectively. Boldface page numbers indicate key terms.